GATEWAYS TO ART

Debra J. DeWitte • Ralph M. Larmann • M. Kathryn Shields

GATEWAYS
TO ART

Understanding the Visual Arts

SECOND EDITION

With 1706 illustrations, 1478 in color

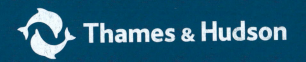

Thames & Hudson

First published in 2012 in paperback in the United States of America as *Gateways to Art* by
Thames & Hudson Inc., 500 Fifth Avenue, New York, New York 10110

thamesandhudsonusa.com

This second edition 2015

Reprinted 2016

Library of Congress Catalog Card Number 2015932504

ISBN 978-0-500-29203-7

Printed and bound in Malaysia by Times Offset (M) Sdn. Bhd.

FRONT COVER

Frida Kahlo, *The Two Fridas*, 1939. Photo Gianni Dagli Orti/Museum of Modern Art, Mexico/The Art Archive. © 2015
Banco de México Diego Rivera Frida Kahlo Museums Trust, Mexico, D.F./DACS

BACK COVER

Left to right:

Katsushika Hokusai, "The Great Wave off Shore at Kanagawa," (detail) from *Thirty-Six Views of Mount Fuji*,
1826–33 (printed later). Library of Congress, Washington, D.C.

Artemisia Gentileschi, *Judith Decapitating Holofernes*, c. 1620 (detail). Uffizi Gallery, Florence

Raphael, *The School of Athens*, 1510–11 (detail). Stanza della Segnatura, Vatican City

Dorothea Lange, *Migrant Mother, Nipomo, California*, 1936 (detail). Library of Congress, Washington, D.C.

The Taj Mahal, Agra, India. © Dietmar Temps/Dreamstime.com

Francisco De Goya, *The Third of May, 1808*, 1814 (detail). Museo Nacional del Prado, Madrid

Colossal Head, Olmec, Basalt, 1500–1300 BCE. Museo de Antropología, Veracruz, Mexico.
Photo Irmgard Groth-Kimball © Thames & Hudson Ltd, London

Contents

How to Use *Gateways to Art: Understanding the Visual Arts*

Gateways to Art is an introduction to the visual arts, divided into four parts: Fundamentals, the essential elements and principles of art that constitute the "language" of artworks; Media, the many materials and processes that artists use to make art; History, the forces and influences that have shaped art throughout the course of human history; and Themes, the major cultural and historical themes that have motivated artists to create. Each of these parts is color coded to help you move easily from one section to the next.

Gateways to Art gives you complete flexibility in finding your own pathway to understanding and appreciating art. Once you have read the Introduction, which outlines the core knowledge and skills you will need to analyse and understand art, you can read the chapters of our book in any order. Each chapter is entirely modular, giving you just the information you need when you need it. Concepts are clearly explained and definitions of terminology in the margins ensure that you are never at a loss to understand a term.

This means that you can learn about art in the order that works best for you. You can, of course, read the chapters in the order that they are printed in the book. This will tell you all you need to know to appreciate art. But you can also choose your own path. For example, the Introduction discusses how we define art and what it contributes to our lives. Next you might read chapter 2.6, "The Tradition of Craft," which deals with media that artists have used for centuries to create artworks, but which our Western culture sometimes considers less important than "fine art." Then the discussion of Japanese art in chapter 3.3, "Art of India, China, Japan, and Southeast Asia," reveals how an expertly made kimono (an item of traditional clothing) is appreciated as much as a painting that in our culture is usually considered more prestigious.

In *Gateways to Art* you will discover the pleasure of looking at great artworks many times and always finding something new because there are many ways of seeing and analysing art. That is why our book takes its title from its unique feature, the "Gateways to Art." Through eight iconic works of world art (introduced on pp. 17–25), we invite you to come back to these Gateways to discover something new: about the design characteristics of the work; the materials used to make it; how history and culture influenced its creation; or how the work expressed something personal. Sometimes we compare the Gateway image with another artwork, or consider what it tells us about the great mysteries of our existence, such as spirituality or life and death. We hope to encourage you to revisit not only our Gateways, but also other works, as sources of enjoyment for years to come.

Our Gateways to Art boxes are just one of numerous features we provide to help you in your studies. In many chapters you will find Perspectives on Art boxes, in which artists, art historians, critics, and others involved in the world of art explain how diverse people involved in art think and work. Other boxes will, for example, help you to focus in depth on a single artwork, or alternately to compare and contrast artworks that deal with a similar subject or theme.

Resources for Instructors

- The authors of *Gateways to Art* have written an Instructors' Manual that is available in print and digital form. In addition, they have created a test bank that is available in print, on disk with free software, and also as a download from our instructors' website.
- Images from the book are available as Jpegs and PowerPoint slides. Contact your W. W. Norton representative for details.
- With the first edition of *Gateways to Art* we provided 50 multimedia animations to demonstrate the elements and principles of art; 15 in-the-studio videos demonstrating

how art is made; and 20 video presentations of key works of world art. For the second edition we have added quizzes to the videos to provide another valuable means of assessment.

New to the second edition

An exclusive arrangement with the Museum of Modern Art, New York, offers you 20 additional videos in which MoMA curators discuss works in the collection. For example:

- In our *Starry Night* (Van Gogh, 1853–1890) video, the camera zooms in on the canvas, bringing students face to face with the artist's distinctive use of thick layers of oil paint to create vivid landscape scenes.
- An audio recording of Marcel Duchamp (1887–1968) himself in our *Bicycle Wheel* video introduces students to Duchamp's wit and the inspiration behind his series of ready-mades.

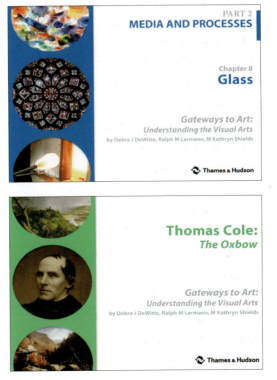

1 Fifteen media and process videos made by art educators at Bowling Green State University demonstrate how art is made.

2 Twenty videos examine individual artworks in depth or set a work in a broader context.

- An examination of Barnett Newman's (1905–1970) *Vir Heroicus Sublimis* gives students a greater understanding of the meanings implicit in abstract art and the difficulties inherent in the process of artistic creation.

For full details of all instructors' resources go to thamesandhudsonusa.com/college.

Resources for Students

Our student website offers a wide range of review materials designed to improve your understanding and your grades: self-test quizzes; flash cards; chapter summaries; a glossary; multimedia demonstrations of key concepts; and videos that explain how art is made. Other content-rich resources for students include an audio glossary of foreign-language terms and artists' names.

For full details of our student resources go to http://wwnorton.com/studyspace/gateways-to-art.

The Authors

Debra J. DeWitte
is ABD at the University of Texas at Dallas and has an MA from Southern Methodist University. She has devised an award-winning online art appreciation course at the University of Texas at Arlington.

Ralph M. Larmann
has a BFA from the University of Cincinnati and an MFA from James Madison University. He currently teaches at the University of Evansville and is a past President of Foundations in Art: Theory and Education.

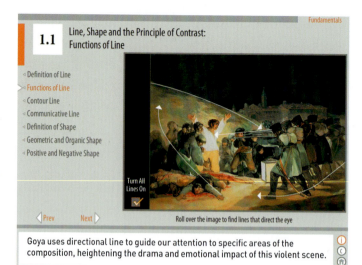

Goya uses directional line to guide our attention to specific areas of the composition, heightening the drama and emotional impact of this violent scene.

3 Fifty-one Interactive Exercises help students to understand the elements and principles of art.

4 A free and open student website presents an array of review opportunities, using the analytical framework of the text throughout

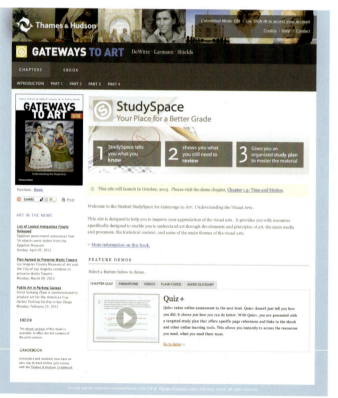

M. Kathryn Shields
has a PhD in art history from Virginia Commonwealth University. She is Associate Professor of Art History at Guilford College, where she also serves as Chair of the Art Department.

Gateway Features
for *Gateways to Art*

One of the important lessons you will learn from this book is that every time you look at a great work of art, it will have something new to say to you. If you consider, for example, the way an artist designed the work, you may notice something about the use of color or contrast that had not struck you before. When you study the medium the artist chose (such as the particular choice of paint selected), you will appreciate how it contributed to the impact of the work.

Another approach that we can take to an artwork is to look at it from a historical point of view: how does this work reflect the circumstances and the society in which it was created? Does it express the values of those who held political and economic power, or could it tell us something about the status of women at the time? Alternately, you could ask yourself whether the work addresses issues that have absorbed the attention of artists ever since humans began to paint, draw, and make sculpture. Does it touch on very big questions, such as the nature of the universe, or life and death? Or is it engaged with more personal concerns, such as gender, sexuality, race, and our own identities?

You can appreciate a work of art by examining it closely from one or more of these perspectives. You can also learn more about one work by studying another and comparing the two. For example, consider how an artist might depict a famous event, such as a battle, or render the dramatic plight of sailors whose boat is caught in a terrible storm, or the poignancy of a family ruined by an economic disaster. The artist might choose a large-scale work that shows the enormous impact of events on a large number of people. But an alternative would be to create a work on a much more intimate scale, showing how such events affect a single person or a family, or even portraying that family in a moment of rest and quiet before the enormity of events becomes apparent.

There are many approaches to art, and to help you develop the important skills of looking at, analysing, and interpreting works of art, we have selected eight iconic works—the "Gateways to Art"—which you will encounter repeatedly as you read this book. Each time you see one, you will learn something new about art and how to appreciate it. Let's begin by taking our first look at the Gateways in the pages that follow.

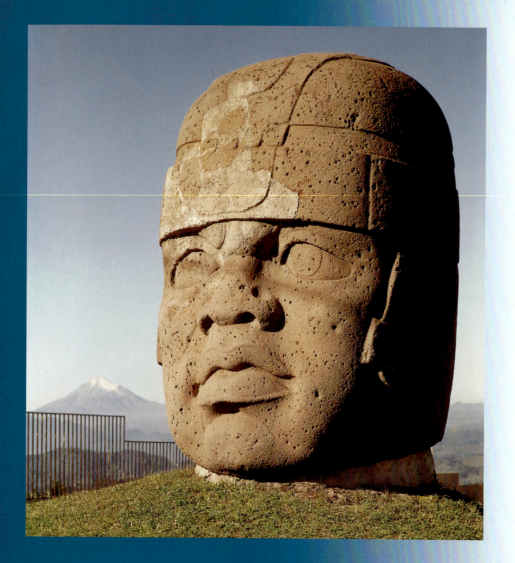

The Colossal Olmec Heads

The Olmecs, a people who lived on the Gulf Coast of eastern Mexico from about 2500 BCE to 400 CE, were great sculptors of stone. Probably sometime around 900 BCE they made colossal heads like the one shown here. These are amongst the most impressive sculptures of ancient Mexico. Seventeen such heads have been discovered at four sites. They range in size from 5 to 12 ft. tall and weigh approximately 6 to 25 tons each. All portray mature males with flat noses, large cheeks, and slightly crossed eyes. Many scholars believe that the heads depict individual Olmec rulers.

FUNDAMENTALS

1.2 (p. 75) See how Olmec artists used the sheer mass of colossal heads to create a sense of power.

MEDIA AND PROCESSES

2.4 (p. 251) Compare the colossal heads with an Olmec ceramic sculpture.

HISTORY AND CONTEXT

3.4 (p. 439) Experience the discovery and excavation of four colossal heads found buried at La Venta, Mexico.

THEMES

4.6 (p. 628) Examine how the evidence suggests that the colossal heads were portraits of Olmec rulers.

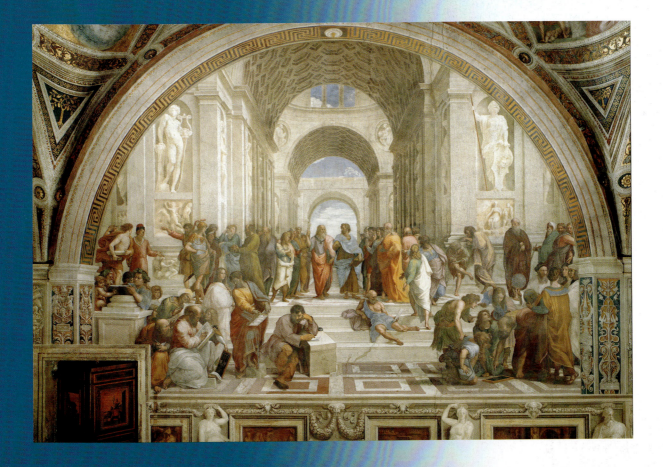

Raphael,
The School of Athens

In 1510–11 the Italian artist Raphael (1483–1520) painted one of the great works of the Italian Renaissance, *The School of Athens*. This was one of four wall paintings commissioned by Pope Julius II to decorate the Stanza della Segnatura (his private library) in the Vatican Palace in Rome, Italy. *The School of Athens* measures 16 ft. 8 in. high by 25 ft. wide.

   The School of Athens derives its name from the reputation of Athens, Greece, as the great center of Classical learning, and from the painting's subject matter: the work depicts an imaginary gathering of the great scholars of ancient Greece and Rome.

FUNDAMENTALS

1.3 (p. 96) Understand how the illusion of three-dimensional depth is created on a flat surface.

1.7 (p. 151) Discern how the artist used scale and proportion in the work and drew the attention of the viewer to the figures in the center of the painting.

MEDIA AND PROCESSES

2.1 (p. 200) Study how Raphael used drawings to plan and design this large wall painting.

HISTORY AND CONTEXT

3.6 (p. 472) See how Raphael used famous artists of his time as models for portraits of great thinkers from ancient Greece and Rome.

THEMES

4.5 (p. 612) Visualize how the other paintings in Pope Julius's library work in harmony with *The School of Athens* to create the illusion of an architecturally compelling space.

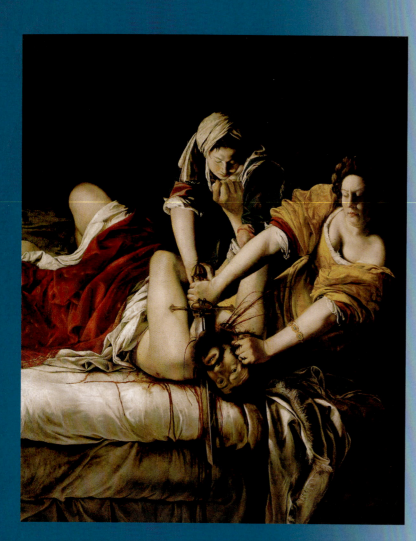

Artemisia Gentileschi, *Judith Decapitating Holofernes*

Around 1620, the Italian artist Artemisia Gentileschi (1593–*c*. 1656) made a dramatic painting of the story from the Old Testament of the Israelite heroine Judith killing the Assyrian general Holofernes, who had been sent by his king to punish the Israelites for not supporting his reign. Gentileschi's dramatic work, executed in oil paint on canvas, and measuring 6 ft. 6 in. by 5 ft. 4 in., addressed a subject that was popular amongst painters of the Baroque era. The artist is remarkable, however, as a woman who was determined to succeed in the male-dominated art world of her time.

FUNDAMENTALS

1.8 (p. 163) Observe how the artist directs the viewer's eye toward the decapitated head.

MEDIA AND PROCESSES

2.2 (p. 224) Examine Gentileschi's paintings as personal statements.

HISTORY AND CONTEXT

3.6 (p. 485) Compare Gentileschi's style with that of a leading male painter of her time.

3.8 (p. 523) See how Gentileschi's depiction of the scene differs from that of Gustav Klimt, painted nearly 300 years later.

THEMES

4.10 (p. 680) Interpret this painting as a response to Gentileschi's experience as a victim of rape.

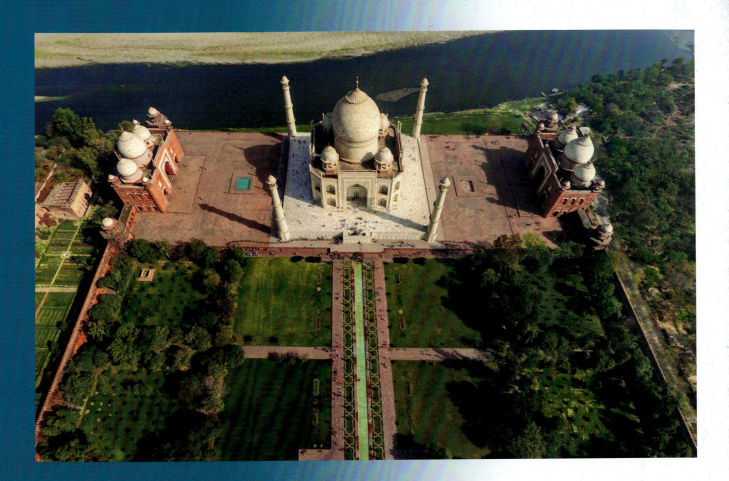

The Taj Mahal

The Taj Mahal is a great tomb built by Shah Jahan (1592–1666) for his wife, Mumtaz Mahal (1593–1631). Shah Jahan created this monument to her after she died giving birth to their fourteenth child.

The Taj Mahal is covered in white marble inlaid with semiprecious stones; it glistens beautifully in the sun. The eye-catching and awe-inspiring central dome is 213 ft. tall and 58 ft. in diameter. Carefully designed around it are four further chambers, and identical towers, known as minarets, stand at each corner of the structure, creating a perfectly symmetrical and balanced site. Shah Jahan and his architects deliberately emphasized this formal balance in their design, in order not only to create an outstandingly beautiful memorial but also to evoke a sense of harmony, order, and stability. The Taj Mahal is part of a larger complex including a mosque, smaller tombs, enormous gardens, and a reflecting pool.

FUNDAMENTALS

1.6 (pp. 142–43) Understand how the symmetrical balance of the Taj Mahal was designed to symbolize Shah Jahan's love for his wife.

MEDIA AND PROCESSES

2.5 (p. 278–79) Learn about the design of the Taj Mahal and the importance of the site of the colossal mausoleum.

HISTORY AND CONTEXT

3.3 (pp. 418–19) Examine the importance of gardens as symbols of paradise in the art of Shah Jahan and other Islamic rulers.

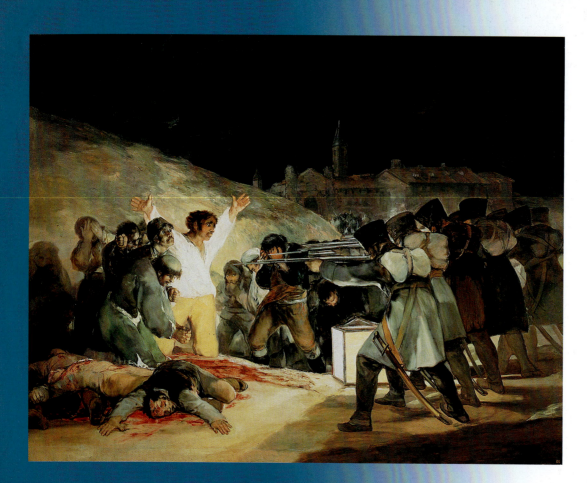

Francisco Goya, *The Third of May, 1808*

In 1814 the Spanish artist Francisco Goya (1746–1828) painted a dramatic depiction of war, *The Third of May, 1808*. Goya's work shows Spanish patriots being executed by invading French troops. This large oil painting (it measures around 8 ft. 4 in. by 11 ft . 4 in.) was commissioned by King Ferdinand of Spain, who had recently returned to the throne after the defeat of the French. Goya's work is generally considered one of the finest portrayals of the horrors of war.

FUNDAMENTALS

1.1 (p. 56) Analyse Goya's use of line to guide the viewer's eye through his painting.

1.9 (p. 174) Understand how Goya uses visual rhythm to direct our attention to the victims of the French troops, and see how he uses rhythm in another of his works.

MEDIA AND PROCESSES

2.3 (p. 239) Study the connection between Goya's famous print series *Disasters of War* and his painting.

HISTORY AND CONTEXT

3.7 (p. 503) Examine Goya's relationship with Spain's royal family through his paintings.

THEMES

4.7 (p. 637) Consider how Goya's painting of Spanish resistance to the French invaders might add to your views of the war depicted in *The Third of May, 1808*.

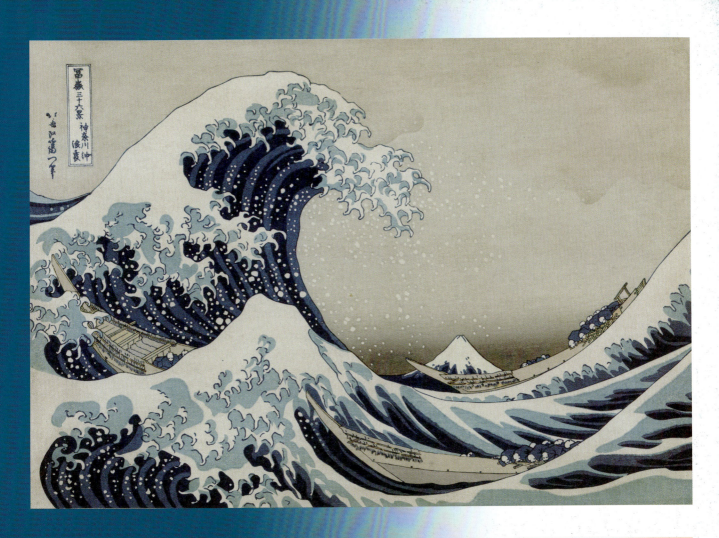

Katsushika Hokusai, "The Great Wave off Shore at Kanagawa"

Katsushika Hokusai (1760–1849) is regarded as one of the greatest Japanese printmakers. In 1831 he published a series of woodblock prints titled *Thirty-Six Views of Mount Fuji*: the prints were so successful that in fact he made 46 of them. All feature a view of Japan's sacred mountain, Fuji. One of the prints, "The Great Wave off Shore at Kanagawa," measuring around 9 in. by 14 in., portrays a dramatic scene of fishermen caught in a storm at sea. Interestingly, Hokusai's work became popular in Europe before it did in Japan.

FUNDAMENTALS

1.6 (p. 132) Study how Hokusai arranges the elements of his composition to create a harmonious design.

MEDIA AND PROCESSES

2.3 (p. 235) Investigate the process Hokusai used to make this woodblock print.

HISTORY AND CONTEXT

3.3 (p. 423) Learn about the importance of Mount Fuji in Japanese culture.

THEMES

4.8 (p. 653) See how a contemporary artist has been inspired by Hokusai to make a work that highlights environmental concerns.

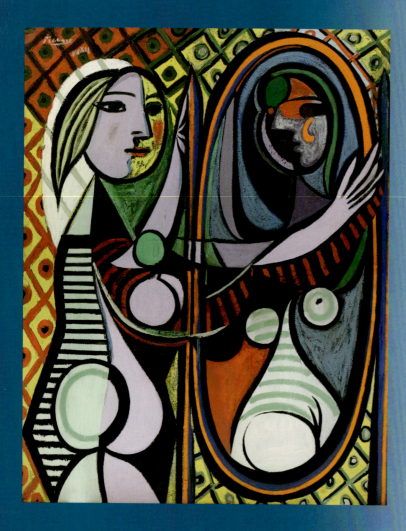

Pablo Picasso,
Girl before a Mirror

The Spaniard Pablo Picasso (1881–1973) is recognized as one of the most important artists of the twentieth century. In a prodigiously prolific and versatile career, he explored a wide range of media including painting, sculpture, drawing, printmaking, ceramics, and stage design.

Girl before a Mirror, painted in 1932, is a portrait of Picasso's mistress Marie-Thérèse Walter, whom he never married but with whom he had one daughter, named Maya. The painting, which measures 5 ft. 4 in. by just over 4 ft. 3 in., shows his mistress studying her own reflection in a mirror, which suggests multiple sides to or facets of her personality.

FUNDAMENTALS

1.1 (p. 59) See how Picasso used contour line to describe the figures in some of his images.

HISTORY AND CONTEXT

3.8 (p. 528) Explore Picasso's portrayal of women through this painting and his famous work *Les Demoiselles d'Avignon*.

THEMES

4.3 (p. 593) Understand how Picasso used symbols of vanity and mortality in this artwork.
4.4 (p. 605) Learn how an x-ray of the painting taught scholars more about Picasso's creative process.

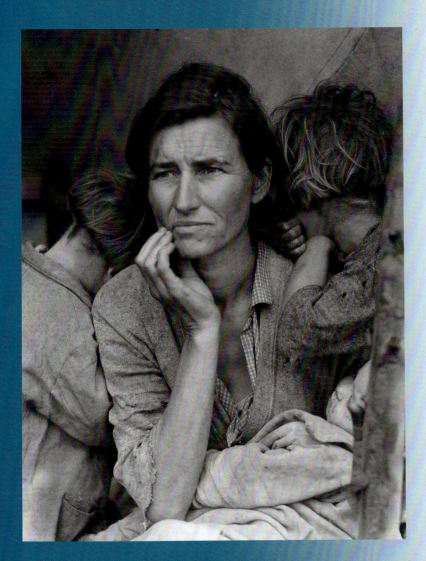

Dorothea Lange,
Migrant Mother

The black-and-white photograph of a homeless and hungry family, *Migrant Mother*, is widely recognized as an iconic image of the hardships of the Great Depression of the 1930s in America. The documentary photographer Dorothea Lange (1895–1965) took the picture in 1936. She had been hired by a government agency, the Farm Security Administration, to record social and economic conditions in California. Since then, *Migrant Mother* has been frequently reproduced as a record of American social history.

FUNDAMENTALS

1.5 (p. 127) Study the sequence of images taken by Lange to see how time and motion are captured even in a still photograph.

MEDIA AND PROCESSES

2.8 (p. 324) Read Dorothea Lange's own account of how and why she took photos of this family.

THEMES

4.8 (p. 651) Understand how the image became a symbol of society's responsibility toward the poor, and how the work and its reception affected the family it portrayed.

Introduction

What Is Art?

The Japanese artist Katsushika Hokusai (1760–1849) is said to have created a painting, titled *Maple Leaves on a River*, by dipping the feet of a chicken in red paint and letting the bird run freely on a sheet of paper he had just covered in blue paint. Although we know that Hokusai was an unconventional character, we cannot be certain that the story is true, because *Maple Leaves on a River* no longer exists. If we think

about this curious story for a while, however, we can begin to understand the most basic question addressed in this book: What is art? This question is not an easy one to answer, because people define art in many ways. In Hokusai's case, he captured the peaceful sensations of a fall day by a river, without showing what an actual river and real leaves look like. In this instance, art communicates a sensation to its audience.

In nineteenth-century Japan, art could be a means to encourage the quiet contemplation of nature, but to an Egyptian artist almost 3,000 years earlier, art would have meant something very different. The Egyptian who in the tenth century BCE decorated the wooden coffin of Nespawershefi with a painting of the sun god Re had a quite different idea of rivers in mind from the one Hokusai conceived. For ancient Egyptians, rivers were important for survival, because they depended on the flooding of the River Nile to grow their crops. Rivers also had religious significance. Egyptians believed that during the daytime Re sailed across a great celestial ocean in his day boat. By night, the sun god traveled in his evening boat along a river in the underworld, but before he could rise again he had to defeat his enemy, the serpent Apophis, which in **0.0.1** can be seen swimming in the river. Here the river is again suggested rather than being realistically portrayed. It is a place of

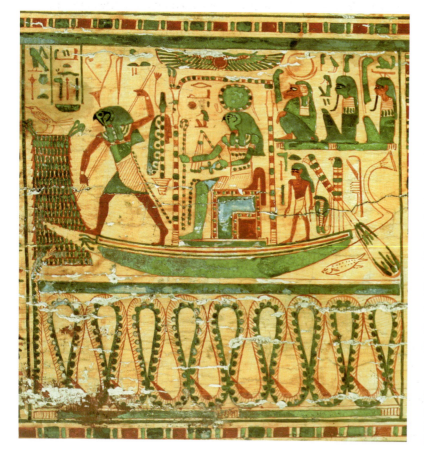

0.0.1 *The Journey of the Sun God Re*, detail from the inner coffin of Nespawershefi, Third Intermediate Period, 990–969 BCE. Plastered and painted wood. Fitzwilliam Museum, Cambridge, England

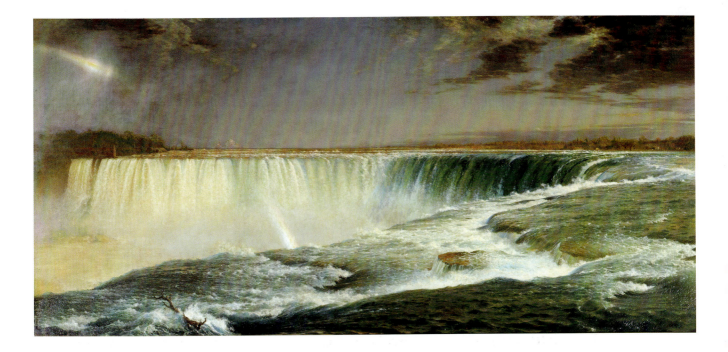

0.0.2 Frederic Edwin Church, *Niagara*, 1857. Oil on canvas, 3′6¼″ × 7′6½″. Corcoran Gallery of Art, Washington, D.C.

danger, not of contemplation, and if Re does not emerge victorious, the world will be deprived of the life-giving light of the sun. Re, who in the image is seated, is protected by another god carrying a spear. He travels with several attendants, including a baboon. The choice of this subject was appropriate for a coffin: no doubt Nespawershefi hoped to emerge from the underworld to live a happy afterlife, just as Re rose again every morning. For the painter of this coffin, art was a way to express profound religious ideas and to invoke beliefs in a happy life after death.

Frederic Edwin Church (1826–1900), a famous American landscape artist, created a very dramatic painting of a river (or, to be more precise, a waterfall) for a very different purpose than that of the Egyptian artist who decorated the coffin. Church used **oil paint** (a **medium** not available in ancient Egypt) on canvas for several views of the Niagara River and Falls, intended for exhibition to a public eager to learn about the landscape of the still-young American Republic. Niagara was a popular subject for artists in the second half of the nineteenth century, both because of its grandeur and because it symbolized America's territorial expansion and ambitions: it marks the northern border of the United States. Church's *Niagara* of 1857 (**0.0.2**) is more than 7 ft. wide. It positions the viewer as if on the very edge of, or even in, the falls. The miraculous vantage point inspired one critic to remark, "This is Niagara, with the roar left out!" Landscape painters in Church's time also used the beauty and power of the landscape to symbolize the presence of God in nature, and this painting came to represent America, and, for many, God's support for the country. It is a magnificent statement of religion, an expression of national pride, and a spectacular form of public education and entertainment.

Finally, consider a work by Louise Nevelson (1899–1988) that also features a waterfall (**0.0.3**, see p. 28). Nevelson constructed twenty-five painted rectangular and square wooden sections inside an overall rectangular frame, measuring 18 × 9 ft. Inside some of the rectangles we can see undulating curved forms that suggest a cascading waterfall or the froth of white water. Other forms in the upper right of the square resemble squirming fish. Clearly, Nevelson's purpose in this artwork is not to show to us an instantly recognizable likeness of a waterfall full of fish. Instead we are invited to examine her carefully constructed work closely and to feel the sensations of watching water cascade and fish swimming.

If we go back to our original question, what is art?, can our consideration of these four very

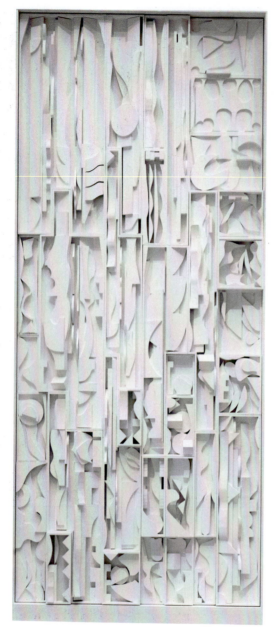

being by a river, but in her case with a meticulously constructed **geometric** suggestion of one.

Perhaps the works do have some things in common, however. For example, Louise Nevelson's sculpture does not simply consist of wood and white paint. The artist carefully cut and arranged each piece to create the work she intended. Similarly, the Egyptian coffin is made of plaster, wood, and paint, but we consider it to be a work of art because the artist carefully organized the painted scene. These two artists arranged their materials so that they communicate ideas and emotions (religious feelings, or the sensation of watching fish swim down a waterfall, for example). Art communicates ideas by visual means that can help us see the world in new and exciting ways and strengthen our understanding. In other words, art is a form of language.

Fine Art and Graphic Art

The terms we choose to label things often tell us more about our own attitudes and stereotypes than about the object under consideration. For example, art from cultures outside the Western tradition (such as the traditional arts of Africa or the Pacific Islands) was once termed "Primitive Art," implying that it was of lesser quality than the "fine" or "high" arts of Europe. But while—as in this case—such labels can be misused, they can none the less reflect cultural judgments and sometimes lead to ways of identifying, categorizing, and understanding art.

For example, fine art usually refers to a work of art (traditionally a painting, drawing, carved sculpture, and sometimes a print) made with skill and creative imagination to be pleasing or beautiful to look at. When the Italian artist Agnolo Bronzino (1503–1572) painted a portrait of *Eleonora di Toledo and Her Son Giovanni* (**0.0.4**), he was clearly determined to demonstrate great skill in his lavish portrait of this wife of the powerful Duke of Florence, Cosimo de' Medici, who was a great **patron** of the arts. Eleonora's dress, which was so

different works help us to find a quick and simple definition that will tell us whether we are looking at something called art? The four works certainly do not have much in common in terms of their appearance. The definition also cannot include a common range of materials (in fact, art can be made from almost anything). Nor do these works have a common purpose. The Egyptian coffin painting has a clear religious message. Church's oil painting portrays a dramatic landscape but also carries a powerful message of nationalism and patriotic pride. Hokusai's painting uses very simple means to convey restful sensations. Nevelson's work also focuses on communicating the sensations of

Geometric: predictable and mathematical
Patron: an organization or individual who sponsors the creation of works of art

sumptuous that it would have cost more than the painting itself, is depicted with such great care that one can almost feel the texture of the embroidery. Eleonora, her complexion perfect and her beauty flawless, is composed and icily aloof, her hand resting on the shoulder of her young son to draw our attention to him. The young boy, destined to become a powerful duke like his father, is equally serious and composed, as befits a person of high status. Looking at this painting we can see that Bronzino intended us to marvel at his skill in producing a supreme example of fine art that conveys a vivid sense of wealth and power.

Historically, the graphic arts (those made by a method that enables reproduction of many copies of the same image) have been considered less important, and perhaps less accomplished, than the fine arts. While Bronzino's portrait is unique, made for a single, powerful patron, and probably to be viewed by a select audience, works of graphic art are made to be available to many people and are in that sense much more democratic, which is considered an advantage by many artists and viewers. Graphic art includes a wide range of media: books, magazines, posters, advertising, signage, television, computer screens, and social media.

The essence of graphic design is communication. The simplicity of a logo created in 1994 to identify the global brand of the logistics company FedEx (**0.0.5**) contrasts with the elaborate luxury of Bronzino's *Eleonora*. The designer, Lindon Leader, discovered that the company's name at the time, Federal Express, gave customers the impression that it operated only in the United States, rather than internationally. In addition, everybody called the company simply FedEx. Leader's task was to design a logo that could be used on package labels, advertisements, trucks, and planes to identify FedEx as a dynamic, global organization. The solution was a design that retained the colors (slightly modified) of the existing logo, but shortened the company name to FedEx. The type was arranged so that the white space between the E and x formed a white arrow that suggested speed and precision.

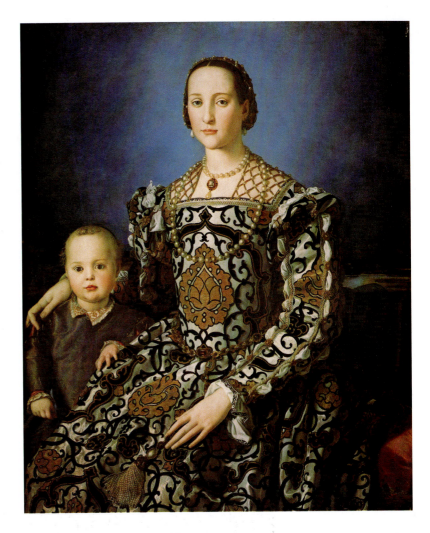

The design is very simple but we should be careful not to assume that it required much less skill and effort than Bronzino's portrait. The logo did not involve the same kind of technical finesse as the detailed realism of the oil painting, or Bronzino's ability to communicate the human character. But Leader and his colleagues held focus groups to research the public's impressions of the company and developed about 200 design concepts before they settled on their chosen design. Then they made protoypes of planes, vans, and trucks to test it. Leader's logo has won more than forty design awards. There is one crucial difference between the two works,

0.0.4 Agnolo Bronzino, *Portrait of Eleonora of Toledo with Her Son Giovanni de' Medici*, 1544–55. Oil on panel, 45¼ × 37¾″. Uffizi Gallery, Florence, Italy

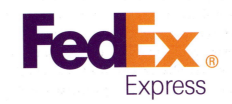

0.0.5 FedEx Express logo

however. The purpose of the logo is to identify a company and sell its services. Bronzino's portrait was made to please an individual patron, while the FedEx logo is intended to communicate with a worldwide audience.

The Visual World

When we look at an artwork made by a single artist, we often assume that it was created entirely from the artist's own ideas and inspirations. But art historians now recognize that art is part of a wider **context** of things we experience: the visual culture in which we live, which includes all of the images that we encounter in our lives. Think about how many images you saw on your way to class today. They will have included traffic signs, roadside billboards, and the logos of businesses along the highway. Once you arrived on campus, you will have seen posters informing you of an upcoming event, the logo of the coffee shop, and maps directing you to where your class takes place. Then a glance at your smartphone or e-mail revealed more ads, all clamoring for your attention. We live in, and respond to, a world of images, and so have artists, whether in ancient Egypt, sixteenth-century Italy, or twenty-first-century America. In other words, art reflects the visual culture in which it was created, not just the creative achievement of its maker.

The contemporary artist El Anatsui (b. 1944) makes artworks that reference the colonial history of Africa and the impact of modern consumerism on cultural values. *Old Man's Cloth* (**0.0.6**) is made from discarded liquor-bottle tops. El Anatsui chose bottle tops as his material because European traders bartered alcohol for African goods. Slaves were shipped from Ghana to the sugar plantations of the Caribbean; then in turn, rum was shipped from there back to Africa. El Anatsui's bottle tops thus remind us of the slave trade, as well as highlighting the way in which modern consumerism discards waste. At the same time, the artist's use of traditional designs suggests both the enduring power and the fragility of Ghanaian culture.

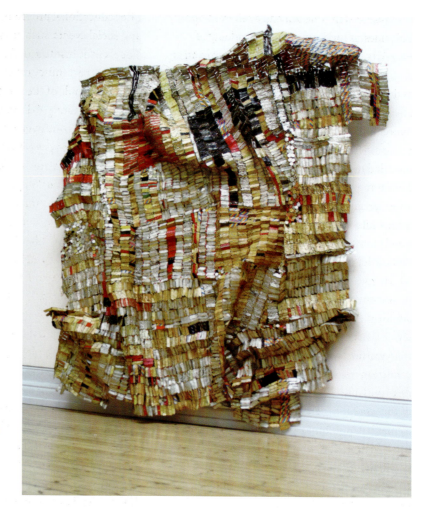

0.0.6 El Anatsui, *Old Man's Cloth*, 2002. Aluminum and copper wire, 15'9" x 17'3¾"

Where Is Art?

You have probably figured out by now that art can be found in many places: in a coffin, in a book, in any number of contemporary media, and, of course, in an art museum.

Our word "museum" comes from the ancient Greek *mouseion*, meaning a temple dedicated to the arts and sciences. The mouseion of Alexandria in Egypt, founded about 2,400 years ago, collected and preserved important objects, still a key function of museums today. Many of the great European art museums began as private collections. The famous Louvre Museum in Paris, France, was originally a fortress and then a royal palace where the king kept his personal art collection. When King Louis XIV moved to his new palace at Versailles, the Louvre became a residence for the artists he employed. After the French Revolution (1789–99), the king's collection was opened to the public in the Louvre.

Context: Circumstances surrounding the creation of a work of art, including historical events, social conditions, biographical facts about the artist, and his or her intentions

Museums in America had a different history. The oldest is the Pennsylvania Academy of Fine Arts, founded in 1805 as a museum and an art school. It continues to serve both functions, as do many other American museums. During the nineteenth century, prominent business figures amassed large private collections of European art. These collectors founded museums modeled on those of Europe. The Brooklyn Museum was founded in 1823 and in the 1870s alone, great museums opened in Boston, New York, Philadelphia (**0.0.7**), and Chicago. Many public buildings, including museums, in the United States were built in the Neoclassical style, which involves symmetrical forms that represent democratic ideals derived from ancient Greece and Rome, where the Classical architectural style was first developed.

Most art museums hold permanent collections of artworks that are regularly displayed, although some can show only a portion of the works in their large collections. Museums also organize exhibitions of works on loan from other institutions. They often have conservation departments to care for and restore the artworks.

Museums also play an important part in the cultural life of their communities. They offer educational programs and other cultural and social events, such as music concerts. The Detroit Institute of Arts, one of the most significant art museums in the United States, is a good example of the importance of a museum to the community. Administrators caused considerable controversy by proposing to sell the collection to pay off Detroit's $18 billion of debt, but the state of Michigan opposed the sale. In 2014 a court approved an agreement to enable the museum to keep its collection in return for a commitment to contribute $100 million to Detroit's bankruptcy fund. By August of that year the museum had raised more than $80 million—but most importantly a great art collection had been saved for the city's residents and visitors.

If we consider only works that are displayed in museums and galleries, however, we will ignore many works that are certainly art. In fact, a great deal of art exists outside such institutions.

You almost certainly have some art in your home: perhaps a painting in the living room, a poster in your bedroom, or a beautifully made flower vase; and there are sculptures and memorials in parks or other public spaces in most cities. For example, from 1921 to 1954

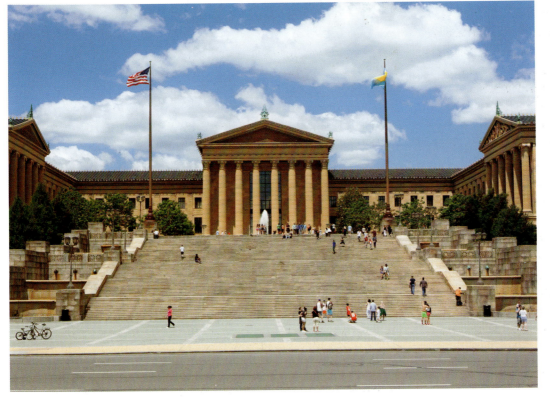

0.0.7 Philadelphia Museum of Art, Pennsylvania

Simon Rodia (1879–1965) built seventeen interconnected structures on a residential lot in a neighborhood of Los Angeles (**0.0.8**). Rodia's work is now known as the Watts Towers, although he named it *Nuestro Pueblo* (Spanish for "our town"). Rodia, a construction worker, made his structures out of materials he found or that local people brought to him. The towers are made of steel rods and pipes, wire mesh, and mortar, and decorated with bits of broken glass and pottery. Rodia's neighbors and the City of Los Angeles did not approve of his work, and unsuccessful efforts were made to destroy it, but the tide eventually turned in his favor. In 1990 Watts Towers was named a National Historic Landmark, and today it is recognized internationally as an important work of public art.

Art and Creativity

Simon Rodia's work demonstrates that art can be found in one's own neighborhood, and that many—perhaps most—people possess the creative impulse to make art, and express it in numerous, and often surprising, ways. Rodia devoted many years of his life to creating a single artwork. He had never trained to be an artist but he shared with professional artists a creative impulse that dominated his life. If we consider the role of creativity in our own lives, we see that images are ever present in our world: we make our own photos and videos, and share them through social-networking services or using our cell phones. These activities, so common now, show how people naturally respond to images and seek to express themselves visually—just as they did 3,000 years ago in ancient Egypt. In other words, most of us instinctively relate to human creativity.

If you are still not convinced that you can be as creative as an artist, think about other things you may have done in your life that are creative: for example, the way you decorate your room. In the first two parts of this book you will also find many creative exercises you can try: these will help you to understand how people who are recognized as artists achieve what they do, and

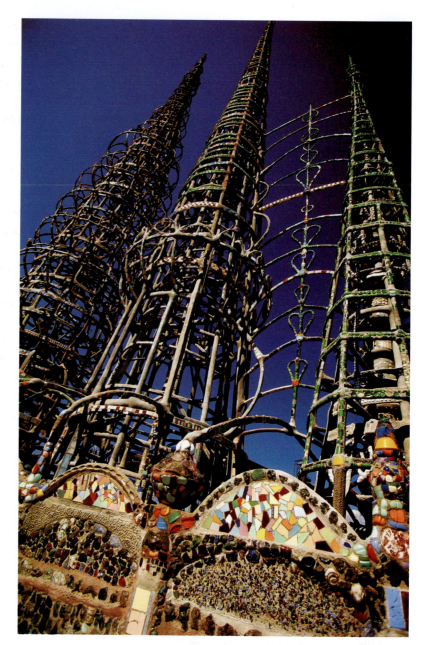

how to discover and apply your own creativity to making art.

Who Makes Art?

Who decides what an artwork looks like? The simple answer might seem to be the artist who makes it. We know that art has been made for thousands of years: at least since humans first painted images on the walls of caves, and probably long before then. Much artwork made in the past has not survived, however, so we do not know what it looked like. Even when art did survive, we often have no idea who made it, or

0.0.8 Simon Rodia, Watts Towers, 1921–54. Seventeen mortar-covered steel sculptures with mosaic, 99½' high at tallest point. 1761–1765 East 107th Street, Los Angeles, California

if it was made by and for the community that existed at the time it originated. In general, art from earlier cultures was a communal effort in which spirituality and notions of the cycle of life were common themes. As time progressed, artists addressed social issues (war and social conscience) and created more individual expressions of their identity (gender and race).

The great temples of ancient Egypt, Greece, and Rome were certainly not the work of one person, and in some cases, we cannot tell if their overall design was the idea of a single individual. Archaeologists have discovered near the Valley of the Kings in Egypt an entire village, Deir el-Medina, which was occupied by artisans who made the tombs that we admire today. The cathedrals of **medieval** Europe were the result of the skills of many different artists and artisans: stone carvers, the makers of stained-glass windows, and carpenters who made the furniture. These skilled workers remain mostly anonymous, except for a very few whose names have been found in manuscripts or carved on works of art—for example, the sculptor Gislebertus carved his name on sculptures that adorn the cathedral of Autun, France. But though we may never identify most of these early artists, it is clear that humans have always wanted to create art. This urge is part of our nature, just like our need to eat and sleep.

Due to the efforts of **Renaissance** artists to elevate their profession as a liberal art, the Western world has popularized the idea of a lone individual creating his or her own art to express something very personal. In the nineteenth and twentieth centuries it became more common for artists to determine individually the appearance and content of their own work, and, in their search for new forms of self-expression, to make art that was often very controversial. This remains true today. But for many centuries before this, very few artists worked alone. Even Renaissance artists who promoted the idea of creative genius operated workshops staffed by artist assistants who carried out most of the work involved in turning their master's design into a work of art. In nineteenth-century Japan, the eccentric Katsushika Hokusai was famous around the world for his prints, but he could

not have made them alone. A wood carver cut his designs into blocks from which a printer manufactured copies. Even today, some famous artists, such as Jeff Koons, employ other artists to realize their ideas (**0.0.9**).

In other words, there is no simple definition to enable us to tell who is an artist and who is not. If we take a global view, we certainly cannot define an artist by what he or she made. In Western culture during some eras of history, particularly since the Renaissance, painting and sculpture have been considered to be the most important categories of art ("high art"), while others, such as **ceramics** and furniture, were once considered less important. The term craft was usually applied to such works, and their makers were considered less skilled or of lower status than painters and sculptors. This distinction arose partly because the cost of producing a fine painting or a beautifully carved marble statue was high. Therefore, those became status symbols of the rich and powerful.

Medieval: relating to the Middle Ages; roughly, between the fall of the Roman empire and the Renaissance

Renaissance: a period of cultural and artistic change in Europe from the fourteenth to the seventeenth century

Ceramic: fire-hardened clay, often painted, and normally sealed with shiny protective coating

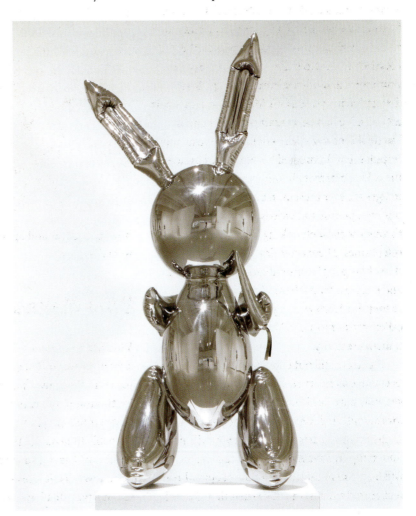

0.0.9 Jeff Koons, *Rabbit*, 1986. Stainless steel, 41 × 19 × 12". Edition of 3 and artist's proof

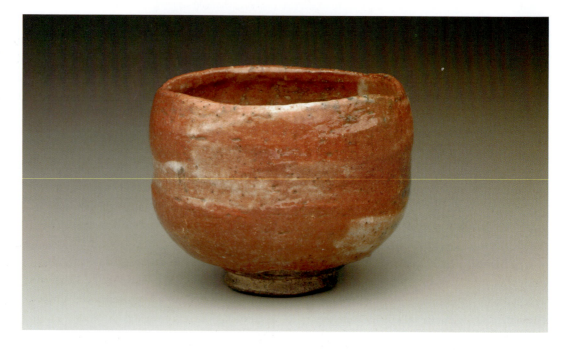

0.0.10 Tea bowl, 16th century. Stoneware with red glaze (Karatsu ware), 3⅞ × 5". Indianapolis Museum of Art

In other cultures, the relative importance of various forms of art was quite different. The people of ancient Peru seem to have placed special value on wool, and those who made fine woolen textiles were likely considered as skillful as a painter would be in our society. In China the art of **calligraphy** (elegantly painted lettering) was considered one of the highest forms of art. A Chinese encyclopedia of 624 CE included calligraphy and painting in "Skills and arts," alongside, for example, archery and chess.

For centuries, in Japan, such ceramic objects as tea bowls have been highly esteemed for their beauty. The bowl seen in **0.0.10** would have been prized for its subtle variations of color, the pleasant tactile sensations of its slightly irregular surface, and its shape. It was designed to be appreciated slowly as the user sipped tea. The artist who made this bowl worked at roughly the same time as the Italian Renaissance artist Leonardo da Vinci (1452–1519), but the two had different ideas of what it meant to be an artist. The Japanese maker of the tea bowl worked in a society that valued tradition. Japanese artists followed with supreme skill the established methods of working and making. Leonardo, however, became famous in an era in Europe that valued individual ingenuity. He was a supremely talented artist whose visionary interests and inventions extended far beyond the visual arts, to engineering and science. Between 1503 and 1506 he created a portrait that is now probably the most famous painting in the world, although in his own time the work was virtually unknown because it was not commissioned by an important patron. Leonardo was not content to create a likeness of the **subject** (Lisa Gherardini, wife of a silk merchant in Florence). The *Mona Lisa* smiles and looks out at the viewer, inviting us to seek in her face, her pose, and the surrounding landscape a meditation on the human soul (**0.0.11**). Both the tea cup and the portrait are great works of art, but they display very different ideas of what it means to be an artist.

We must also consider that artworks are not only the result of the work of those who made them, but are also influenced by the input of others: the patrons who employ an artist to make a work; the collectors who buy it; and the dealers and gallery owners who sell it. In contemporary times, both the publicist who presents artworks and the critic who reviews them in a newspaper, on TV, or on the Internet help to make an artist's work well known and desirable. All of these people, not just the artist, help to determine what art we see, and to some extent they can influence what we consider to be art. By controlling access to those who buy art, the places where art is displayed, and the media

Calligraphy: the art of emotive or carefully descriptive hand lettering or handwriting
Subject: the person, object, or space depicted in a work of art
Manuscripts: handwritten texts

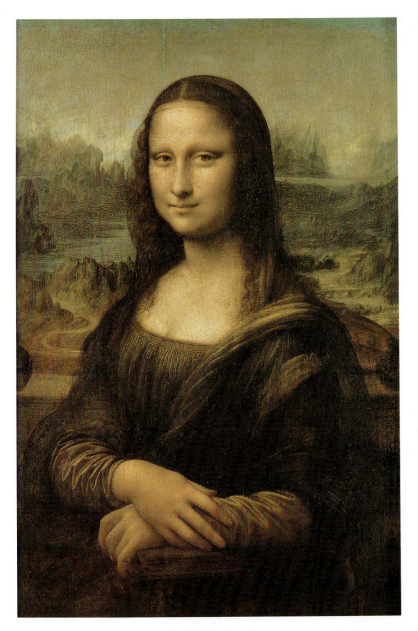

Marchesa presents her as a formidable woman who enjoys the finer things in life (**0.0.12**). This elegant woman wears a turban she designed, fine embroidered clothes, and a white ermine stole (a sign of wealth and refinement) over her shoulder. Although the Marchesa was in her sixties when she commissioned this painting, Titian portrays her as a youthful beauty.

Fame and success do not always come in an artist's lifetime. Perhaps the most famous example of this is the Dutch painter Vincent van Gogh (1853–1890). In his ten years as an active artist, Van Gogh produced about 1,000 drawings, sketches and watercolors, as well as around 1,250 other paintings. Very few people saw his work in his lifetime, however; he received only one favorable notice in a newspaper; his work was shown in only one exhibition; and he sold only one painting. Yet today his work is extraordinarily famous, it sells for millions of dollars, and in his native Netherlands an entire museum is devoted to his work.

0.0.12 Titian, *Isabella d'Este*, 1536. Oil on canvas, 40¼ × 25¼". Kunsthistorisches Museum, Vienna, Austria

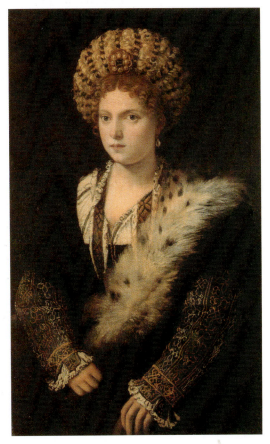

0.0.11 Leonardo da Vinci, *Mona Lisa, c.* 1503–6. Oil on wood, 30⅜ × 20⅞". Musée du Louvre, Paris, France

that inform the public about art and artists, they also often influence what kind of art an artist actually produces.

One individual who greatly impacted the production and presentation of art was Isabella d'Este (1474–1539), Marchesa of the city of Mantua, Italy, and the wife of the ruler of the city, which she governed in her husband's absence. As an influential patron of the arts, Isabella funded a variety of artists to create luxurious objects for her collections, including such items as gems, musical instruments, **manuscripts**, and ceramics. Her money and tastes therefore played an important part in determining what art was produced in Mantua. Titian's (*c.* 1485/90–1576) portrait of the

The training of artists also helps to determine who makes art and what art is shown in galleries and museums. For example, traditional training for painters in China focused on the passing of artistic skill from a master to his students, who learned by copying his works and those of other famous artists. Only scholars and government officials could become professional painters. Other painters were considered to be just craftspeople whose work was of lower status. Similarly, in medieval Europe, only those trained in associations of craftsmen called **guilds** were allowed to make works of art. For example, there were guilds of carpenters, glassmakers, and goldsmiths. The system in Europe changed in the sixteenth century. Schools called **academies** were organized (first in Italy) to train artists in a very strict curriculum devised by specialized teachers. It was very difficult to succeed as an artist without being trained in an Academy. In modern Europe and North America, most practicing artists are trained in art schools, which are sometimes independent schools, but often part of a university or college that teaches many different subjects. It would be a mistake, however, to assume that artists must be formally trained: as we have seen in the case of Simon Rodia, non-professional, self-taught artists (often referred to as "naïve" or "outsider" artists) have always produced art. Today their work is often avidly collected.

The Power and Value of Art

On November 8, 2006 a sale at Christie's auction house in New York City broke records by selling 491 million dollars' worth of artworks. The most expensive item for sale that evening was a portrait, *Adele Bloch-Bauer II* (**0.0.13**), painted in 1912 by the Austrian artist Gustav Klimt (1862–1918). It sold for $87.9 million. Klimt made a comfortable living from painting portraits of the wives and sisters of wealthy Austrian businessmen, but in his own lifetime he was certainly never paid anything like the enormous sum for which his portrait of

Mrs. Bloch-Bauer sold in 2006. One reason for the painting's increase in price was its controversial history. In 1938 it had been looted by the Nazis, who had occupied Austria, and the work later became the subject of a lawsuit by the heirs of the Bloch-Bauer family.

When we read that some works of art sell for large amounts of money while others do not, we quite reasonably ask ourselves why such a high financial value is placed on a single work. Works of art by famous artists of the past tend to be valued at a high price, especially if they are very rarely available.

In our modern society art is often valued by its sale price, but there are many other ways of valuing it. When we visit art museums and see artworks displayed inside glass cases or at a distance from the viewer, who must not touch, the care to preserve them in perfect condition is an indication that these works are highly valued. Sometimes a work is valued because it is very old or rare, or indeed unique.

In many societies, however, artworks were not made to be sold or displayed where they cannot be touched. As we have seen, the Japanese

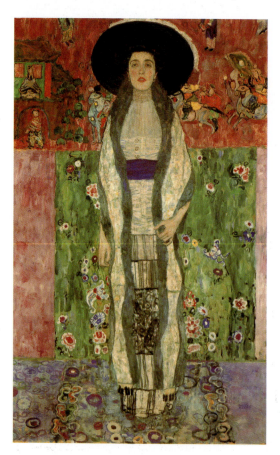

0.0.13 Gustav Klimt, *Adele Bloch-Bauer II*, 1912. Oil on canvas, 6'2⅞" × 3'11¼". Private collection

Perspectives on Art: Robert Wittman
What Is the Value of an Artwork?

A work of art will usually attract a high price if works by the artist who made it are rarely available for sale. Some artists' works are so rare that thieves will go to great trouble to steal them. Special Agent Robert Wittman is a former FBI investigative expert for stolen artworks. Here he explains how criminals valued a self-portrait by Dutch artist Rembrandt Harmenszoon van Rijn (1606–1669).

Value can be defined as the price that a willing buyer will pay to a willing seller. But that value changes as a result of the circumstances surrounding an artwork. One needs only to look at auction records to determine the value of a painting. These prices are records of what

a willing buyer paid to a willing seller to obtain a work of art that had a good **provenance** and title that could be transferred on the market.

These are the legitimate prices in the art world, but there are other prices that have no basis in legitimacy. These others are the prices that are paid when an artwork is stolen and sold on the black market. Even criminals need a basis to place a value on their ill-gotten gains and that is usually about 10 percent of the legitimate market value of the stolen artwork; but even that sum is usually not paid.

For example, in December 2000 a Rembrandt self-portrait (**0.0.14**) was stolen from the Swedish National Museum in Stockholm. Three men entered the museum wielding machine guns. After placing the guards, visitors, and guides on the floor, two of the men raced around the museum and stole three paintings: two by Auguste Renoir, and the Rembrandt. The self-portrait was painted in 1630 and is very rare: it is the only known portrait by the Dutch master that is painted on copper. Its market value is $35 million. The men had set two car bombs off in the city to snarl traffic and prevent the police from responding. They made their escape in a motorboat moored to a pier near the entrance of the museum.

It was not until nearly five years later, in September 2005, that the Rembrandt self-portrait was recovered in a multi-national police undercover operation in Copenhagen, Denmark. The thieves attempted to sell it to me when I posed as an art expert working for the Mafia. The price was $250,000, or less than one percent of the market value of the artwork. Stolen art has no real value: the lack of good title, improper provenance, and inability of a buyer to sell the painting in the future all decrease the value of an artwork. As most thieves eventually learn, the true art in an art theft is in the selling, not the stealing.

0.0.14 Rembrandt van Rijn, *Self-Portrait*, 1630. Oil on copper, 6⅛ × 4¾". Nationalmuseum, Stockholm, Sweden

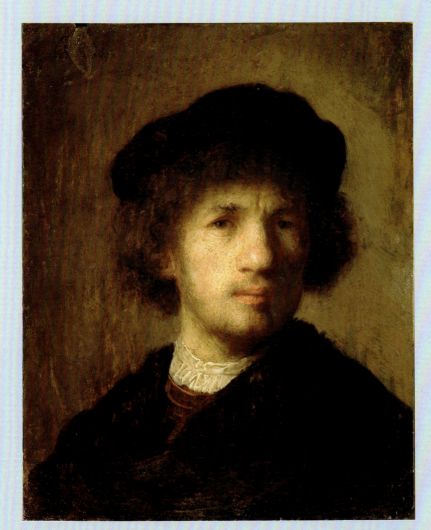

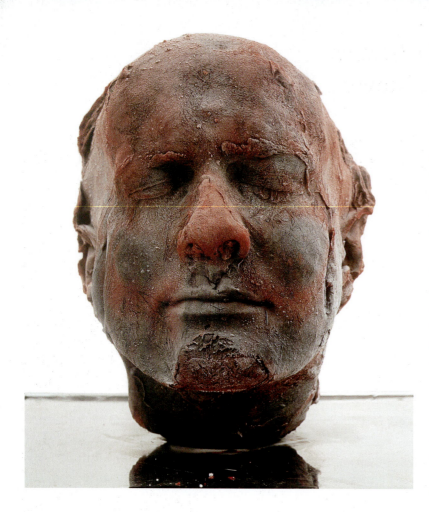

0.0.15 Marc Quinn, *Self*, 1991. Blood (artist's), stainless steel, Perspex, and refrigeration equipment, 81⅞ × 24 × 24¾". Private collection

Form: an object that can be defined in three dimensions (height, width, and depth)
Cast: a sculpture or artwork made by pouring a liquid (for example molten metal or plaster) into a mold
Monumental: having massive or impressive scale

made fine tea bowls. These bowls were to be used as part of a ceremony, involving other fine objects, good conversation, and, of course, excellent tea. The tea bowl was valued because it formed part of a ritual that had social and spiritual significance. Similarly, in the African art section of many museums we can see masks displayed that were originally made to form part of a costume that, in turn, was used in a ceremony involving other costumed figures, music, and dancing. In other words, the mask often had some kind of spiritual or magic significance for its original creators: but they would have regarded it as holding this value only when used as intended, not when displayed in isolation in a museum.

An essential reason why we value art is because it has the power to tell us something important about ourselves, to confront us with ideas and feelings about the human condition that we recognize as true, but may otherwise struggle to understand fully. Art is a powerful means of self-expression because it enables us

to give physical shape or **form** to thoughts and sensations and to see them for what they are. Marc Quinn (b. 1964) is a British artist whose art often not only focuses on the body but also deliberately uses his actual body as a basis for making the work. Since 1991, Quinn has been making a life-size self-portrait of his head every five years, each time using between eight and ten pints of his blood, **cast** and then frozen by means of a refrigerating device. These works have an immediate impact, partly because they are made of blood, a substance we recognize as viscerally related to the life force and that we all depend on for survival: looking at *Self*, we naturally contemplate our own mortality and our fear of it. The effect is underscored by our knowledge that if the refrigerator should fail, the sculpture would dissolve.

Self is powerful too because when we look at such a raw portrait we instinctively compare its effect on us with how we appear to other people, which makes us think about self-image: who we really are, physically, and who we think ourselves to be. The use of the head and face, which are so intimately connected to our sense of identity, also make the image dramatically arresting, in a way that is similar to sculptures from ancient cultures, such as Africa and Oceania, where people have created carved heads, often on a **monumental** scale, that still resonate with compelling power. Despite its title, which could be interpreted as if it were only a portrait of the artist, this is a work that strikes a universal human chord as we view and recognize in it our own physical vulnerability.

So we see that price is, of course, not the only, or the most important, measure of the value of an artwork. We might place a high value on a work because it is aesthetically pleasing or because its creation involved great skill. This can be true even if there is no possibility of our owning it. Many museums organize large exhibitions of the work of famous artists because they know that great numbers of people will pay to see the work. Enthusiasts will travel long distances, even to other continents, to visit such exhibitions. In 2012, for example, 758,000 people visited an exhibition of the work of various Old Master artists, including

Perspectives on Art: Tracy Chevalier
Art Inspires a Novel and a Movie

Art can have value as a source of inspiration. Tracy Chevalier is the author of the bestselling novel Girl with a Pearl Earring *(1999), which in turn inspired a movie (2003) starring Scarlett Johansson and Colin Firth. Tracy tells how her novel was inspired by a poster of the famous painting by the Dutch painter Johannes Vermeer.*

I first saw the painting *Girl with a Pearl Earring* (**0.0.16**) when I was nineteen and visiting my sister in Boston for spring break. She'd hung a poster of it in her apartment. I was so struck by it—the color! the light! the girl's look!—that the next day I bought a poster of it myself. That same poster has accompanied me for twenty-nine years, hanging in my bedroom or—as it does now—in my study.

Over the years I've hung many other paintings on my walls. But most art, even great art, loses its punch after a while. It becomes part of the space designated for it; it becomes decorative rather than challenging. It turns into wallpaper. Occasionally someone will ask a question about one of the paintings in my house, or I'll notice one's crooked and straighten it, and I'll look at it again and think, "Oh yeah, nice painting. I forgot about you."

Girl with a Pearl Earring is not like that. She has never become wallpaper. I have never grown tired or bored of her. I notice her all the time, even after twenty-nine years. Indeed, you'd think I'd have nothing left to say about the painting. But even after writing a whole novel about her, I still can't answer the most basic question about the girl: Is she happy or sad?

That is the painting's power. *Girl with a Pearl Earring* is unresolved, like a piece of music that stops on the penultimate chord. Vermeer draws us in with his technique—his remarkable handling of light and color—but he holds us with her. He has somehow managed the impossible, capturing a flickering moment in a permanent medium. You would think that, with the paint static, the girl would be too. But no, her mood is always changing, for we ourselves are different each time we look at her. She reflects us, and life, in all its variations. Few paintings do that so well, which is why *Girl with a Pearl Earring* is a rare masterpiece.

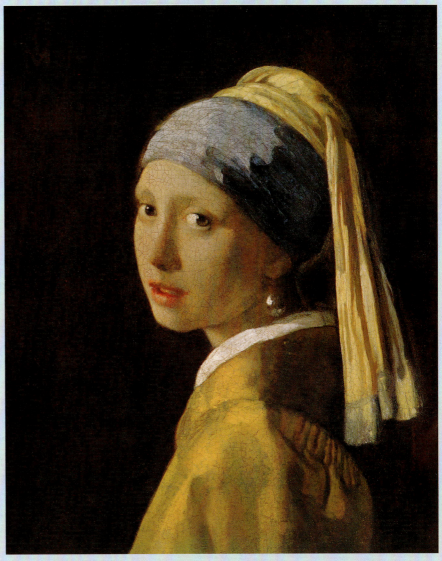

0.0.16 Johannes Vermeer, *Girl with a Pearl Earring, c.* 1665. Oil on canvas, 17½ × 15⅜". Mauritshuis, The Hague, The Netherlands

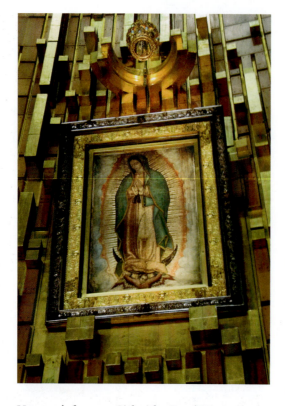

Vermeer's famous *Girl with a Pearl Earring* (see Perspectives on Art: Art Inspires a Novel and a Movie, p. 39), as well as paintings by Rembrandt, Frans Hals, and Anthony Van Dyck at the Tokyo National Museum, Japan.

Artworks can also acquire great religious, cultural, or political significance. Perhaps the most enduring example of such a work is the painting of the Virgin of Guadalupe (**0.0.17**). According to Catholic tradition, in December 1531 the Virgin appeared several times, first on Tepeyac hill, then outside Mexico City, to an indigenous peasant, Juan Diego, and miraculously imprinted her own image on his cloak made of cactus fiber. Historical evidence, however, suggests that the Virgin was painted in **tempera** on linen, probably by an indigenous artist. Whichever account of the painting's origin one accepts, the Virgin is seen, in the words of the Bible (Revelation 12:1) "clothed with the sun, with the moon under her feet," but she has the dark skin of an indigenous woman, emphasizing the Virgin's role as the protector of her "Indian" kingdom in Mexico.

The Virgin became the symbol of the Mexican nation, not just for Mexicans of Indian descent but also for all the citizens of the country—and not only for devout Catholics.

She now appears in countless paintings and in churches throughout the country. When the Father of Mexican Independence, Miguel Hidalgo y Costilla, called for freedom from Spain, he declared "long live our most holy mother of Guadalupe."

Today, the original painting of the Virgin is housed in the National Basilica of St. Mary of Guadalupe at the base of Tepeyac hill, which receives hundreds of thousands of pilgrims annually. Catholics demonstrate their devotion to the Virgin by keeping an image of her in their home or their vehicle, by wearing jewelry bearing her image, and in many other ways. Her image is also seen outside Mexico: there are churches and shrines devoted to her in Dallas, Texas, La Crosse, Wisconsin, and Des Plaines, Illinois.

Censorship of Art

Art can be a form of expression and communication so powerful that those who are challenged or offended by it wish to censor it. If we examine the history of the censorship of art, we see that people have found many reasons to attack, destroy, or prevent the display of artworks. Art may be censored because it challenges the politically or economically powerful; because some consider it pornographic; because it offends religious beliefs; or because it represents values that somebody considers offensive or improper.

Probably the most famous contemporary artist who has suffered for his work and his opinions is Chinese artist Ai Weiwei (b. 1957). Ai's father was a revered Chinese poet and a member of the ruling Communist Party, and Ai was involved in the design of the stadium for the Beijing Olympics in 2008. He was therefore, in some ways, an establishment figure in China. But 2008 was also the year of a devastating earthquake during which several schools collapsed, killing many children. Their parents complained that poor construction, because of official corruption, was responsible for their children's deaths. Ai made a memorial to the dead out of children's backpacks and exhibited it in Munich, Germany. In January 2011 Chinese government officials ordered the demolition of his studio and in April Ai was arrested for "economic crimes."

Ai used his imprisonment as inspiration for an artwork. Ai told a reporter that for the eighty-one days of his imprisonment "I memorized every crack in the ceiling, every mark on the wall. I'm an artist and architect, so I have a good memory for these things." After his release Ai had six iron boxes, roughly half-scale models of his cell, installed in a disused **Baroque** church in Venice, Italy, at the Biennale exhibition (**0.0.18a**). He named each box (*S upper, A ccusers, C leansing, R itual, E ntropy, D oubt*) and titled the work *S.A.C.R.E.D,* from the initial letters of the box titles. Viewers could step onto a block to look through a small slit in the wall to view a scene from Ai's captivity as if they were themselves guards checking on him. In *E ntropy* (**0.0.18b**), viewers see detailed figures of Ai asleep and two guards who stand by his bed.

Other scenes show him eating, being interrogated, taking a shower, walking the length of his cell, and using the toilet, all under guard in extremely cramped quarters. Ai is considered by many people around the world to be a hero, yet his artwork is highly skeptical, even irreverent. At the same time it is informed by Chinese history and of great integrity. In addition to sculptures, photographs, and videos, he has also made a music video and inspired a play. The power of art pervades Ai's work and he willingly uses it to share his personal message, even though his work cannot be shown in China and he is forbidden from leaving the country.

Studying Art

Why take a course that teaches you how to look at art? Surely we all have eyes and we all see the same thing when we look at a work of art, so we can decide what we like or dislike about it. In fact, it is not quite that simple. Our interpretations of works of art may differ from other people's according to our perceptions, beliefs, and ideas. Art is also a form of language;

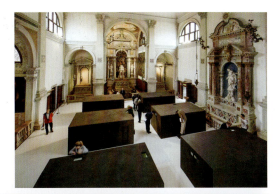

0.0.18a (right) Ai Weiwei, *S.A.C.R.E.D.*, a six-part work composed of (i) *S upper*, (ii) *A ccusers*, (iii) *C leansing*, (iv) *R itual*, (v) *E ntropy*, (vi) *D oubt*, 2011–13. Six dioramas in fiberglass and iron, 148½ × 77½ × 58½". Installed in Church of Sant' Antonin, Venice, Italy for the Venice Biennale 2013

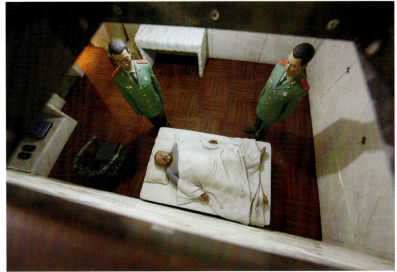

0.0.18b (above) Ai Weiwei, *E ntropy* (detail), from *S.A.C.R.E.D.*, 2011–13

one that can communicate with us even more powerfully than written language. Art communicates so directly with our senses (of sight, touch, even smell and sound) that it helps us to understand our own experiences. By learning to see, we experience new sensations and ideas that expand our horizons beyond our daily lives.

Content

Art, as we have already seen, is a form of communication using visual language. All communication has a purpose, a message—in other words, content. In art, content may be thought of as consisting of three types, all of them important for understanding a work: the subject matter; its underlying meanings (perhaps the ideas or feelings that the work communicates, the beliefs it affirms); and the work's arrangement of the visual elements of which it is composed. These are important concepts, so it is worth examining them in some detail.

Tempera: fast-drying painting medium made from pigment mixed with water-soluble binder, such as egg yolk

Baroque: European artistic and architectural style of the late sixteenth to early eighteenth century, characterized by extravagance and emotional intensity

Subject Matter

In many cases the subject matter of an artwork will be a clear indication of its content. Subject matter may be visually apparent (for example, a painting of a Boston terrier is clearly about a dog); or the title given to the work by the artist (see for example *Self*, p. 38), or later by critics and scholars, may tell us the subject (for example, works depicting the Virgin Mary and the baby Jesus are traditionally titled "Madonna and Child").

Of course, there are many artworks in which the subject matter is not clear, and many have no title (indeed, there are artworks that the artist specifically designates as "Untitled") — but such artworks still have content. This point will be clearer if we understand the concepts of representation, non-objectivity, and abstraction.

Works of art may be **representational** (depicting objects or people so that we can recognize them) or **non-objective** (depicting subject matter that is unrecognizable). These concepts help us to analyse what the artist had in mind or wished to communicate to us when creating the work.

For example, the statue of the Roman emperor Marcus Aurelius in **0.0.19** shows him seated on a horse, gesturing in a very lifelike way. This is a representational artwork, because anyone looking at it would agree that the sculpture is of a man on a horse. The proportions of the figures, the sense of movement, and the details in the emperor's face were all made by the artist to represent reality as closely as possible. Non-objective works of art are deliberately not recognizable as something

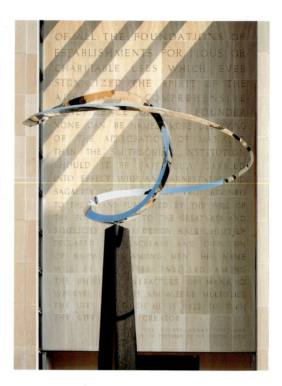

0.0.20 José de Rivera, *Infinity*, 1967. Stainless steel sculpture in front of National Museum of American History, Smithsonian Institution, Washington, D.C., 13½ × 8 × 16'

we might see in the world around us. José de Rivera's *Infinity* is an example of a non-objective work (**0.0.20**). As it rotates one full cycle every six minutes, the ribbon-like form continually changes. Made of polished steel, the sculpture literally reflects aspects of the world around it, such as the sunlight and the buildings. Non-objective art is also, by definition, subjective: we each determine our own interpretations of what the artwork means or communicates—or whether it means anything at all. In this case, of course, the title does give us a clue as to the subject matter of the sculpture but does not explain it outright. It invites us to think about what the idea of infinity means to us. It goes further, though, because just as the loop is endless, the reflections are also, and our experience also may not have bounds.

We also need to ask ourselves when we study an artwork to what extent the artist has used **abstraction** to communicate visually with us. "To abstract" means to extract something or to emphasize it. Abstraction in art refers to the ways artists can emphasize, distort, simplify, or arrange the formal (visual) elements of an

0.0.19 Equestrian statue of Marcus Aurelius, *c.* 175 CE. Bronze, 11'6" high. Musei Capitolini, Rome, Italy

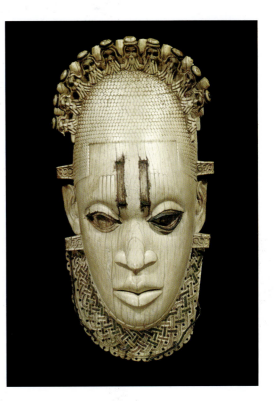

artwork. An artwork may be representational or non-objective, or something in between; this can be described as its degree of abstraction.

Allan Houser's *Reverie* is representational because we can recognize two faces, one larger and one smaller (**0.0.21**). We also interpret the swoop of the form downward from the larger face to be a back, and that the smaller face probably represents a baby being held in its mother's arms. The mother's entire body (her back, arms, and knees) is, however, abstracted to be one smooth form in which to cradle the baby. The baby's body is just a bump on the lap of the mother, as if it is swaddled tightly. We can interpret the subject and form of the sculpture because the detailed representation of the figures' faces enables us to see a mother holding her baby. *Reverie* is a representational work with a considerable degree of abstraction.

0.0.21 Allan Houser, *Reverie*, 1981. Bronze, 25 × 23 × 13", edition of 10. Allan Houser Archives

Context

Next, in our discussion of content, we will consider how we can interpret the underlying meanings of an artwork. If we know what questions to ask about a work of art, we can learn more about it than we probably expected when we first saw it. How can we interpret a work that is several centuries old and comes from a completely different culture than our own? For example, if we look closely enough at the face in **0.0.22**, we might conclude that its perfect and pleasing oval shape and the beauty of its eyes, nose, mouth, and ears suggest that this is the face of a woman. We will probably think it strange, however, that she wears a headdress decorated with odd-looking human heads. Some research will help us to learn more about this artwork by understanding its context. Context includes, for example, information about the society in which it was created: how was the society organized, who ruled it, and

how? Context also includes information about the economics and religion of the people who created it; specific details about the person who ordered it made; and the status of the artist who carved it.

In this case we can find out that the face was made in Benin, West Africa, in the mid-sixteenth century. The artist chose as materials **ivory**, iron, and bronze, rare items in Benin, so presumably the pendant was made for someone wealthy. Although we now see this work in a glass case in a museum, this was not how it was used in Benin. Research into its history tells us that this was a decoration worn by a king. Therefore, it formed part of the presumably impressive royal finery: the artist did not design it to be seen alone in a display case. We know that the king maintained groups of specialist artists (including ivory-carvers) and paid them in food, slaves, and wives. Anybody who made ivory objects without the king's permission was severely punished. Therefore, we can tell that this was an object of great luxury intended to show the wealth and power of a ruler. Finally, the face also tells us something about the history of Africa and the religion of Benin. Those odd-looking heads around the top of the headdress represent the faces of men from Portugal, which

0.0.22 (right) Carved ivory mask-shaped pendant, mid-16th century. Ivory inlaid with iron and bronze, 9⅝ × 5 × 2⅜". British Museum, London, England

was then a powerful European trading nation that had conquered some parts of Africa. The Portuguese were important in Benin because they had worked with the king, whose power had grown as a result. This pendant from Benin means much more to us if we take the time and effort to understand and analyse it. Part 3 of this book gives you a survey of the history of art from prehistoric times right through to the present day.

Formal Analysis

Finally, since art communicates with the viewer through vision, we should introduce briefly how examining the arrangement of the visual elements of an artwork helps us to analyse its content. This process is known as formal (also visual) analysis, and will be discussed in greater detail in Part 1 of this book.

The word formal derives from the noun "form" and relates to the way the formal elements are used in the work of art. For example, the formal elements might include color, shape, the surface **texture** (perhaps rough or smooth), and so on. It is worth pointing out that form has another meaning in art: it describes an artwork that can be defined in three dimensions (height, width, and depth). We will examine form in that sense in chapter 1.2. For the purposes of understanding formal analysis, however, we are concerned here with form in the sense of understanding the use of the formal elements in an artwork.

Artists traditionally discuss the formal qualities of an artwork in terms of the elements and principles of art. When we communicate in writing or speech, our communication consists of a vocabulary of individual words that are structured by rules of grammar that enable us to determine meaning. Similarly, in art, the elements (like vocabulary) are organized by the principles (the visual equivalent of grammar). In Part 1 of this book we will examine in depth the elements and principles of art: color; form; line; mass; shape; space; texture; time and motion; value; volume.

In addition, we will discuss the principles: balance; contrast; emphasis; focal point; pattern; proportion; rhythm; scale; unity; variety.

Artists can utilize the elements and principles in many ways to communicate visually ideas, emotions, beliefs, social or political convictions, sensations: in fact there is almost no limit to what an artist can achieve by combining creative imagination with the elements and principles of art.

A brief formal analysis of a painting by British artist David Hockney (b. 1937) will show us how he used the visual language of the elements and principles to create an apparently simple artwork that in fact reflects on and expresses important events and complex emotions that were unresolved in his life at the time **(0.0.23)**.

Hockney had visited Los Angeles for the first time in 1964, where he lived in the Hollywood Hills. He was fascinated by the colors, the sun, and the landscape of the city, so different from his native Yorkshire in the North of England. Color plays an important part in this painting, as it did in all of Hockney's Los Angeles works. The light, sunny gold of the tiles around the pool **contrasts** both with the dazzling bright blue of the part of the pool in the **middle ground** and with the lush greens and sparkling aquamarine of the hills immediately behind. The hills furthest from us are painted in lighter, hazier colors, using **atmospheric perspective** to convey a sense of distance. Together with the white, wavy lines suggesting the motion of rippling water, in which we can sense the movement of the swimmer below, the artist thus creates what appears initially to be a calm and beautiful scene, a kind of untroubled paradise.

The portrait also conveys a sense of **space**. The pool and the standing figure on the right occupy more than half the surface, overlapping the hills, behind. The light **value** of the tiles around the pool contrasts with the much darker greens of the nearby hills, emphasizing how close the viewer is to the pool. Hockney intensifies this sense of being on the edge through his use of shape. The sharp, geometric angles and shapes formed by the pool contrast with the softer, **organic** shapes of the hills. The further the hills stretch away toward the horizon, the more they lack contrast, detail, and definition. Even on the **two-dimensional** surface of the canvas, this

Texture: the surface quality of a work, for example fine/coarse, detailed/lacking in detail

Contrast: a drastic difference between such elements as color or value (lightness/darkness)

Middle ground: the part of a work between the foreground and the background

Atmospheric perspective: use of shades of color and clarity to create the illusion of depth. Closer objects have warmer tones and clear outlines, while objects set further away are cooler and become hazy

Space: the distance between identifiable points or planes

Value: the lightness or darkness of a plane or area

Organic: having forms and shapes derived from living organisms

Two-dimensional: having height and width

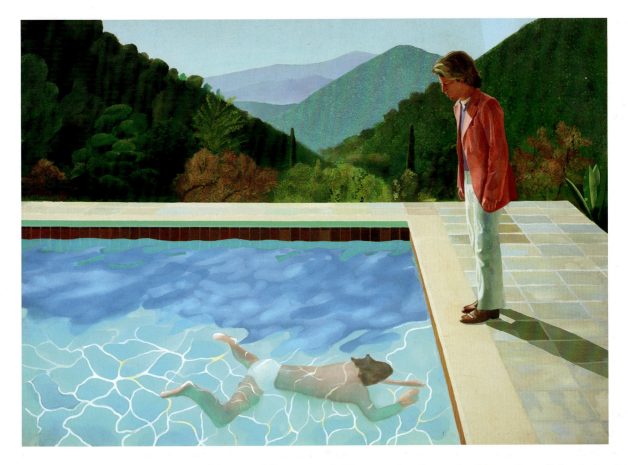

0.0.23 David Hockney, *Portrait of an Artist (Pool with two figures)*, 1972. Acrylic on canvas, 7' × 10'. Art Gallery of New South Wales, Sydney, Australia

Emphasis: the principle of drawing attention to a particular content within a work
Foreground: the part of a work depicted as nearest to the viewer
Background: the part of a work depicted furthest from the viewer's space, often behind the main subject matter
Scale: the size of an object or an artwork relative to another object or artwork, or to a system of measurement
Focal point: the center of interest or activity in a work of art, often drawing the viewer's attention to the most important element
Implied line: a line not actually drawn but suggested by elements in the work

gives us a powerful sense of distance: and this, as we look more closely at the work, is a clue to the emotional predicament it seeks to express.

The first figure in the painting that the artist **emphasizes** is the man on the right, in reality the artist's ex-lover, Peter Schlesinger. Our eyes are drawn to him by the red of his jacket and also because he is the largest figure in the work. Because he is in the **foreground**, Peter appears to be taller than the hills in the **background**: the artist uses **scale** to focus our attention on him and to bring him close to the viewer. Line also plays a part in making him the **focal point** of the painting: the lines of the far edge of the pool seem to point to Peter's figure, as do those of the tiles he stands on. In turn, Peter's gaze toward the water forms a kind of invisible line (artists call this an **implied line**) down to the swimmer in the pool, John St. Clair, a friend of Hockney, whose face is concealed underwater, and who forms the second area of emphasis in the painting.

The artist was not just concerned with the formal aspects of his painting for their own sake, however. In fact, in this work, painted in

the aftermath of the ending of his relationship with Peter Schlesinger, Hockney was painting a portrait of a lost love. Peter stands still and reserved by the edge of the pool in the bright sun, gazing down at the swimmer. As we perceive him from the same viewpoint as the artist, his figure conveys a certain detachment, an absence or loss of emotion, which suggests the end of their connection. At the same time, the fractured surface of the pool, in its watery dissolve, communicates a sense of things breaking up, and of deep sadness and loss beneath the brightly colored surface of this deceptively tranquil scene. Finally, the pale, enigmatic figure of the swimmer, heading toward Peter, who looks at him rather than at us, intimates that he may already have his eyes on the future—from which the artist is excluded.

As such examples show, if we learn how to look at art, and appreciate the skill involved in its making, we will discover how fascinating and even exciting it can be. This book aims to help you not just to get a good grade in your course, but also to begin a lifetime of enjoying and being inspired by art.

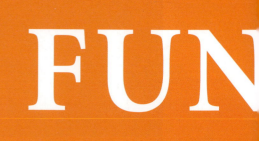

FUN

Art is a form of visual language, and much as we use vocabulary and grammar to communicate verbally, artists use a visual vocabulary (the elements of art) and rules similar to grammar (the principles of art). When we study an artwork, we can use the same elements and principles to analyse the work: a process called visual analysis. In this part you will learn about the elements and principles and will be shown how to apply them in a visual analysis. You will also learn how to use two other concepts when you analyse a work of art: style and content.

PART 1

DAMENTALS

The ten elements of art are: The ten principles of art are:

Color	1 Balance
Form	2 Contrast
Line	3 Emphasis
Mass	4 Focal Point
Shape	5 Pattern
Space	6 Proportion
Texture	7 Rhythm
Time and Motion	8 Scale
Value	9 Unity
Volume	10 Variety

C
F
4
M
S
S
T
T
V
V

for

Poor

starving

veterans

Frank, sold line to very valuable
simple minded tuskeegee Children

every, saturday carl bring us
raspberry pie for poor villager

1.1

Line, Shape, and the Principle of Contrast

Elements: the basic vocabulary of art—line, form, shape, volume, mass, color, texture, space, time and motion, and value (lightness/darkness)

Principles: the ways the elements of art are constructed in a work of art—contrast, balance, unity, variety, rhythm, emphasis, pattern, scale, proportion, and focal point

Line: a mark, or implied mark, between two endpoints

Shape: a two-dimensional area the boundaries of which are defined by lines or suggested by changes in color or value

Two-dimensional: having height and width

Three-dimensional: having height, width, and depth

Contrast: a drastic difference between such elements as color or value when they are presented together

Engraving: a printmaking technique where the artist gouges or scratches the image into the surface of the printing plate

Just as we use the principles of grammar to turn vocabulary into sentences, so the language of art consists of **elements** (the basic vocabulary of art) and **principles** (the grammar that artists apply to turn the elements into art). The principles of design are a set of rules that explain how the elements of a work of art are organized.

In this chapter we will look at **line** and **shape**, basic elements of any kind of artwork, and we will principally consider how they function in examples of **two-dimensional** art. (In chapter 1.2, we will focus more on **three-dimensional** art.) We will then see how to apply them to the understanding of works of art by using the principle of **contrast**.

Two-dimensional art is a remarkably elegant way to express ideas and share our mental pictures of the world. A two-dimensional object, such as a drawing of a triangle, is flat. It has height and width, but not depth. It can be made very simply, for example with a pencil on paper. The first plans for the grandest of designs can be drawn up on a napkin with a few squiggles of a pen. As well as drawing and painting, two-dimensional arts include the graphic arts: printmaking, graphic design, and photography.

Line

Lines are the most fundamental element artists use. They are there in almost every work of art or design. Lines organize the visible world. Without line, an artist hardly knows where to begin.

The ancient designs known as the Nazca Lines, on the high desert plains of Peru, include some of the most unusual drawings in the world. They show us much about line and shape.

In the spider "drawing," lines define the shape onto the landscape at such an enormous scale that it can be seen only from the sky (**1.1.1**). (In fact, the Nazca Lines were first discovered in modern times by overflying commercial aircraft.) Unlike most drawings, the Nazca Lines cannot be rolled up in a tube or carried off in a portfolio. First of all, they are too huge: the spider shown here is 150 ft. long; side by side, two such spiders would nearly fill up a football field. Second, they are hardly "drawings" at all. Instead, they were made by scraping off the layer of dark gravel that covers the flat Nazca plain, to expose the white gypsum that lies just beneath the surface. In this sense, they are a sort of incision or **engraving**.

The lines are mysterious. Why would such huge designs, so huge they can hardly be understood at ground level, be made? What was their purpose? The designs resemble symbolic decorations found on local pottery made at least 1,300 years ago. We do not know what they were used for, but their size suggests they played an important part in the lives of the people who made them. How were they made? There are postholes found at intervals along their edges—perhaps strings from post to post formed guidelines for the scraping of the pathway. Notably, the Nazca Lines do not cross over themselves—in the photograph, the parallel tracks intersecting with the spider were made by

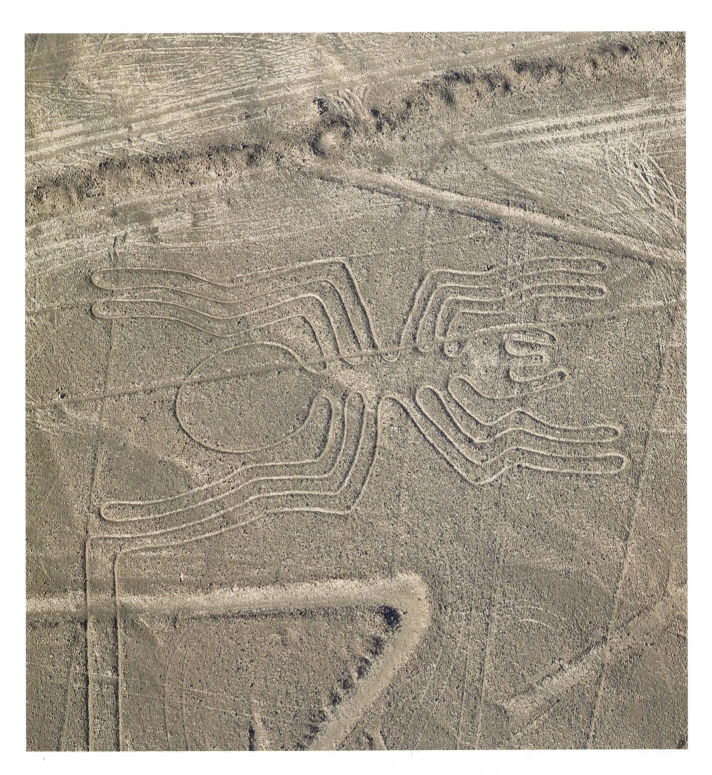

1.1.1 Spider, *c.* 500 BCE–500 CE. 150' long. Nazca, Peru

off-road vehicles. The lines define the **outline** of the shape.

Definition and Functions of Line

A line can be a mark that connects two points, like the strings that must have run from post to post at Nazca. Artists can use lines to define the boundaries between **planes** in a two-

dimensional work of art: notice how the lines at Nazca divide one area of the gravel surface of the land from another. In two-dimensional art, line can also define shapes (in this case, the shape of a giant spider). A line may direct our eyes to look at something the artist particularly wants us to notice. Finally, line can convey a sense of movement and energy, even the movement of a giant spider. We can see many of these uses

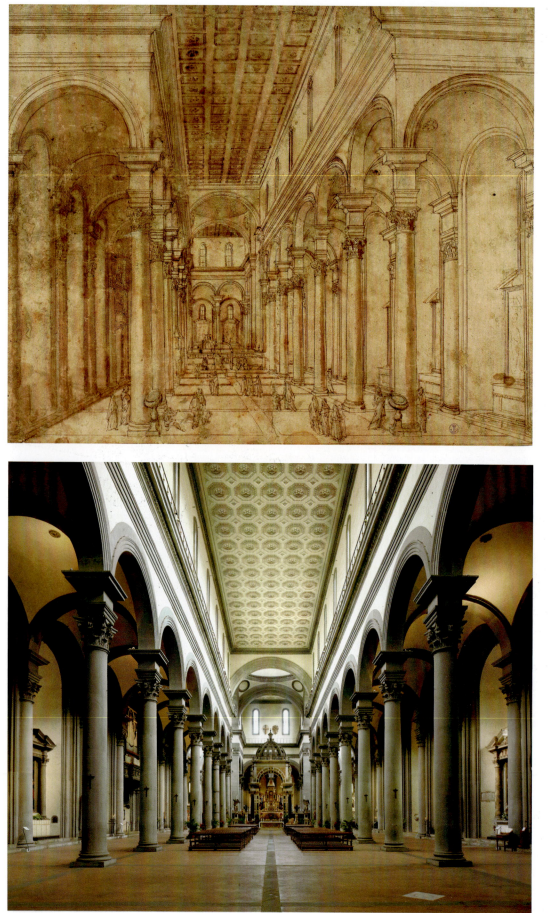

1.1.2a Giovanni Antonio
Dosio, *Church of Santo
Spirito at Florence*,
(n. 6746 Ar), *c.* 1576–90.
Pen and watercolor on
yellowish paper, traces
of black chalk, 14⅜ × 18".
Department of Prints and
Drawings, Uffizi Gallery,
Florence, Italy

1.1.2b Filippo
Brunelleschi, Santo
Spirito, 1436–82, inside
view toward the apse.
Florence, Italy

of line in two very different artworks, one from fifteenth-century Italy and the other from modern Japan.

In Figures **1.1.2a** and **1.1.2b** we see a **perspective** drawing, the *Church of Santo Spirito at Florence*, and a modern photograph of the Church of Santo Spirito in Florence, Italy. The drawing is by the architect and antiquarian Giovanni Antonio Dosio (1533–1609) and shows a church designed by the Italian artist and architect Filippo Brunelleschi (1377–1446). In the drawing, Dosio uses line to differentiate one part of the building from another and to give an illusory sense of depth. Although line is two-dimensional, by using it the artist points out where one plane meets another, and creates an illusion of three dimensions. Line is thus a tool for describing, in a simple way and in two dimensions, the boundaries and edges of three-dimensional surfaces. For example, Dosio's drawing uses line (rather than lightness, darkness, and **texture**) to define where the flat ceiling at the top of the building ends and the walls begin. The artist was thus creating a visual record so that others interested in historic buildings could see in detail how the church was designed.

In the photo of the church, we see the dividing line between the ceiling and the vertical walls because of the changes in lightness, darkness, and texture. The lines in the drawing therefore represent the places where, in the real building, the different planes meet.

Some of Dosio's lines also create a sense of surface and depth. The artist accentuates the patterned surface of the ceiling using lines that increase in frequency to define and differentiate the ceiling from the walls. Dosio also uses converging lines to help the viewer visualize the architectural **space**. If you compare the drawing with the photo, you can see how accurately the artist was able to communicate, with line, how the building actually looks.

Besides demarcating boundaries, indicating depth, and noting surface changes, line can also communicate direction and movement. The page from the manga (Japanese comic/cartoon book) *Tsubasa RESERVoir CHRoNiCLE* (**1.1.3**) is divided into two major sections. A close-up

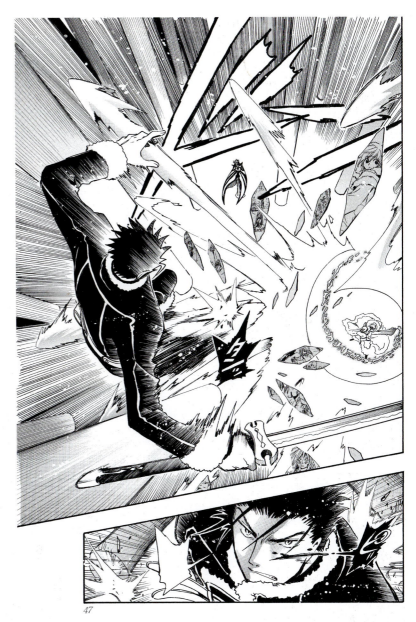

47

view of a character is compressed into the bottom, and a larger action scene occupies the upper two-thirds of the page. In this section, directional lines converge on a light area in the upper right of the page, then our attention is redirected to the left, where a figure is being blasted away by an explosion. The mangaka (group of manga artists) CLAMP has cleverly used the strong diagonals to add an intense feeling of movement to the page.

Lines to Regulate and Control

The variety of different types of line is virtually infinite. Whether straight or curved, a line can be regular and carefully measured. Regular lines

1.1.3 CLAMP, page from the *Tsubasa RESERVoir CHRoNiCLE*, volume 21, page 47, 2007

Perspective: the creation of the illusion of depth in a two-dimensional image by using mathematical principles

Texture: the surface quality of a work, for example fine/coarse, detailed/lacking in detail

Space: the distance between identifiable points or planes

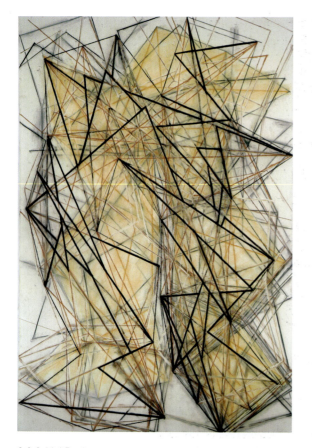

express control and planning, and impart a sense of cool-headed deliberation and accuracy. Such lines are effective for communicating ideas that must be shared objectively by groups of people, such as the plans an architect provides to guide builders.

American **conceptual artist** Mel Bochner (b. 1940) uses ruled line in his work *Vertigo* (**1.1.4**). By using a regular line drawn with the aid of a straightedge, Bochner speaks in the language of mechanical planning. He seems to contradict the use of regular line to convey a sense of control, however. The repetitious diagonal movement and hectic crossing and overlapping of his lines impart a sense of motion in disarray, as if his machine has somehow gone out of whack.

The British sculptor Barbara Hepworth (1903–1975) utilized regulated line in the preliminary drawings she made for her sculptures. The lines she uses are crisp and clear. They combine to represent feelings or sensations that Hepworth wants to make visible in her sculpture. Hepworth said, "I rarely draw what I see. I draw what I feel in my body."

1.1.4 Mel Bochner, *Vertigo*, 1982. Charcoal, Conté crayon, and pastel on canvas, 9' × 6'2". Albright-Knox Art Gallery, Buffalo, New York

1.1.5 Barbara Hepworth, *Drawing for Sculpture (with color)*, 1941. Pencil and gouache on paper mounted on board, 14 × 16". Private collection

Conceptual art: a work in which the communication of an idea or group of ideas are most important to the work
Automatic: suppressing conscious control to access subconscious sources of creativity and truth
Style: a characteristic way in which an artist or group of artists uses visual language to give a work an identifiable form of visual expression

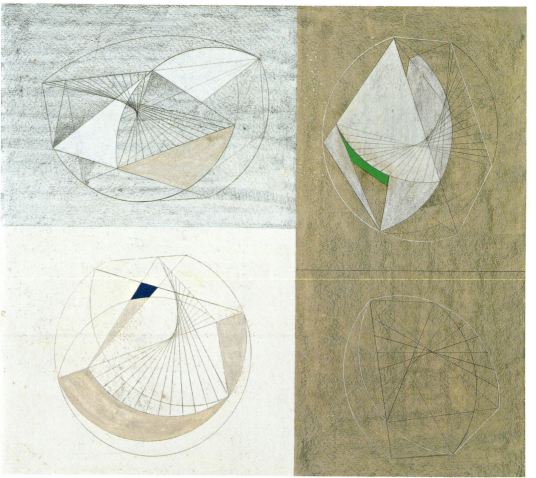

In **1.1.5**, the artist has projected four views of a future sculpture. As she rotates this imaginary work in her mind's eye, the precision of her line helps her comprehend the complexity of her sensations. Like a dancer who responds to the rhythm of music, Hepworth has revealed the kind of lines that she feels, rather than sees, and has translated them into a visual "dance." Like an architect preparing the blueprints of a real building, Hepworth uses regulated line to translate her feelings into drawing and then, finally, into a real sculpture.

Lines to Express Freedom and Passion

Lines can also be irregular, reflecting the wildness of nature, chaos, and accident. Such lines—free and unrestrained—seem passionate and full of feelings otherwise hard to express. Some artists decide to use irregular lines to reflect their drawing and thinking process. French artist André Masson (1899–1987) wanted to create images that expressed the depths of his subconscious. Sometimes he would go for days without food or sleep in an attempt to force himself to explore deeper-rooted sources of creativity and truth. His **automatic** drawings look spontaneous and free, and also perhaps unstructured and rambling (**1.1.6**).

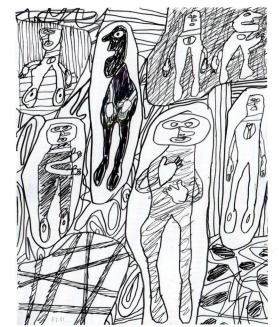

The drawings of French artist Jean Dubuffet (1901–1985) are uninhibited in **style**. Their lines appear irregular and loose. At first sight, his *Suite avec 7 Personnages* (*Suite with 7 Characters*) may seem chaotic and unpredictable, even scribbled, but the overall composition is controlled and orderly (**1.1.7**).

Regular and Irregular Lines

Although line can be either regular or irregular, most art exhibits a combination of both. American artist George Bellows (1882–1925) uses both varieties of line in his work *Woodstock Road, Woodstock, New York, 1924* (**1.1.8**). He

1.1.8 George Bellows, *Woodstock Road, Woodstock, New York, 1924*, 1924. Black crayon on wove paper, image 6⅛ × 8⅞", sheet 9¼ × 12⅜". Collection of Mr. and Mrs. Paul Mellon, National Gallery of Art, Washington, D.C.

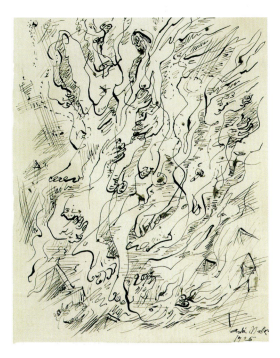

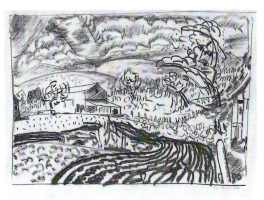

1.1.6 (left) André Masson, *Automatic Drawing*, 1925–26. Ink on paper, 12 × 9½". Musée National d'Art Moderne, Centre Georges Pompidou, Paris, France

contrasts the natural and organic lines of landscape and sky with the restrained and regular line of the man-made and architectural features. It seems that Bellows made this drawing as a preliminary sketch for another work. In the center at the bottom is the inscription, "all lights as high as possible/get color out of shadows." He wrote this to remind himself later of ideas he had while sketching the scene.

Implied Line

The lines we have discussed so far can be clearly seen as continuous marks. We can call these lines **actual lines**. But line can also be implied by series of marks. An **implied line** gives us the impression we are seeing a line where there is no continuous mark (**1.1.9**).

Implied line is important in the Jewish art of micrography, the creation of designs using very small writing.

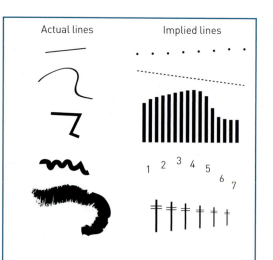

1.1.9 Actual and implied lines

1.1.10 Franco-German hand, *Pentateuch with Prophetical Readings and the Five Scrolls*, 13th–14th century. Illustrated manuscript. British Library, London, England

1.1.11 Detail of *Pentateuch with Prophetical Readings and the Five Scrolls*

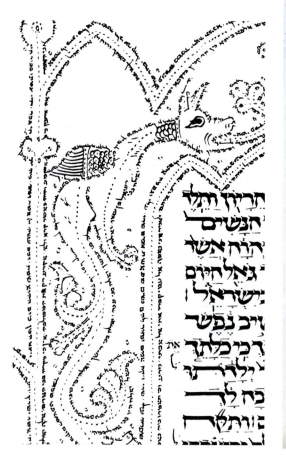

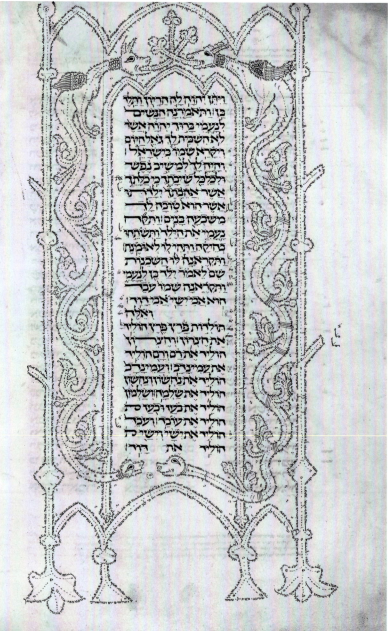

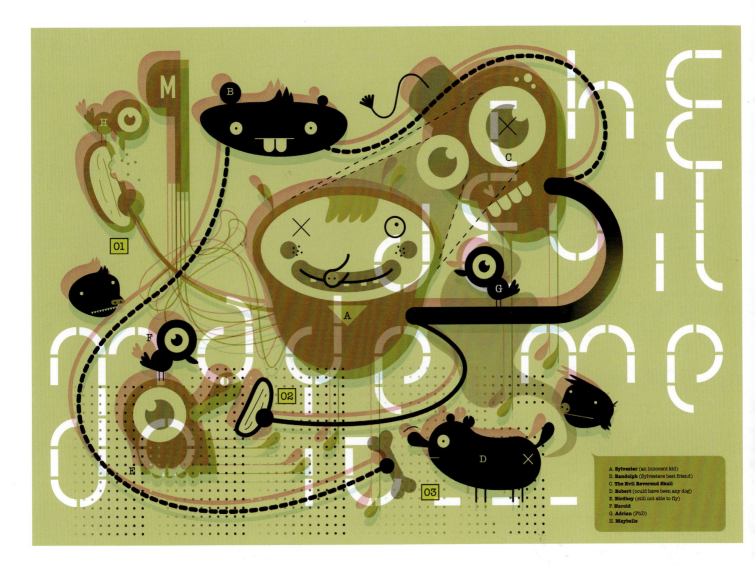

1.1.12 Sauerkids, *The Devil Made Me Do It*, 2006. Digital image, 16½ × 8¼"

A. **Sylvester** (an innocent kid)
B. **Randolph** (Sylvester's best friend)
C. **The Evil Reverend Skull**
D. **Robert** (could have been any dog)
E. **Birdboy** (still not able to fly)
F. **Harold**
G. **Adrian** (PhD)
H. **Maybelle**

Actual line: a continuous, uninterrupted line
Implied line: a line not actually drawn but suggested by elements in the work
Rhythm: the regular or ordered repetition of elements in the work
Etching: a printmaking process that uses acid to bite (or etch) the engraved design into the printing surface

At first glance, the text border in **1.1.10** appears to be an ornate line drawing that has been used to help embellish the text. In fact, the ornate frame is made from tiny Hebrew letters and words. If we look at the detail in **1.1.11**, it becomes more obvious there is no line at all, but an implied line created by the skillful arrangement of the lettering. The "microscopic" text has been added as a guide (called a *masorah*) that provides advice about pronunciation and intonation.

Implied line is used in a more freeform way in the work by Sauerkids, the Dutch graphic designers Mark Moget (b. 1970) and Taco Sipma (b. 1966). *The Devil Made Me Do It* uses implied line to influence visual **rhythms** that add to the excitement of the design (**1.1.12**).

The many dashes and the grid of dots at the bottom of the work imply vertical and horizontal lines. Even the title of the work is spelled out using implied line.

Directional Line

An artist can use line to direct our attention to something he or she wants us to notice (see Gateway Box: Goya, **1.1.13**, p. 56). An example of directional line occurs in the American artist James Allen's (1894–1964) **etching** of Depression-era construction workers (see p. 57). They are depicted working in New York City on the Empire State Building, which was to become the tallest building in the world at the time.

In *The Connectors*, the steel girders are closer together at the bottom of the picture than at the

Gateway to Art: Goya, *The Third of May, 1808*
Using Line to Guide the Viewer's Eye

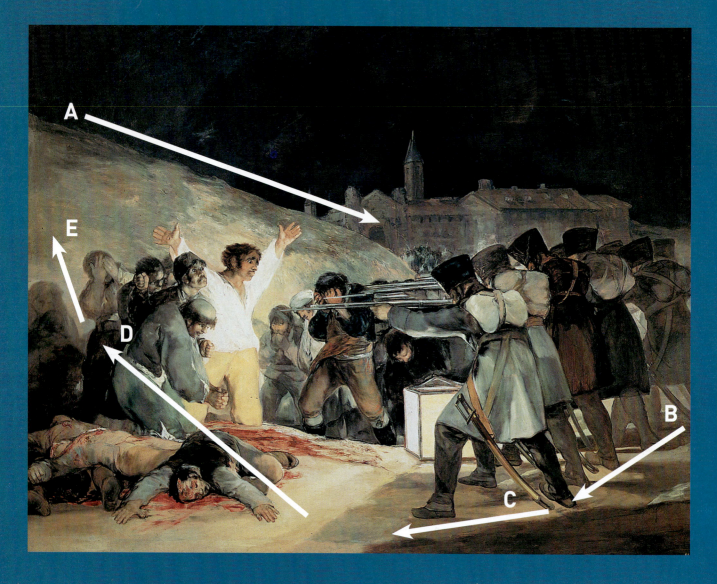

1.1.13 Francisco Goya, *The Third of May, 1808*, 1814. Oil on canvas, 8'4⅝" × 11'3⅞". Museo Nacional del Prado, Madrid, Spain

Directional lines can be either actual or implied. Painters often use implied line to guide a viewer's eye as it scans the canvas. In Francisco Goya's *The Third of May, 1808*, the artist portrays the execution of Spaniards who had resisted the occupation of their country by the French army of Emperor Napoleon (**1.1.13**). Goya uses contrast to draw our attention to a particular line (A)—created in the place where the dark background sky meets and contrasts with the lighted hillside—that separates the two areas of **value**. Our attention is drawn downward and to the right toward an area where there is more visual activity. Goya

holds our attention by using other directional lines; (B), for example, follows the line implied by the feet of the soldiers. Then a shadowed area (C) at the bottom of the page directs our eye to the left, where other lines, such as (D) and (E), draw our gaze up toward the area of high contrast (A). Goya is keen to keep our attention on the atrocities committed by the army of Napoleon. The strong horizontal of the rifles is so distinct that our eye is pulled toward the group of victims: we identify not with the line of executioners, but with the victims.

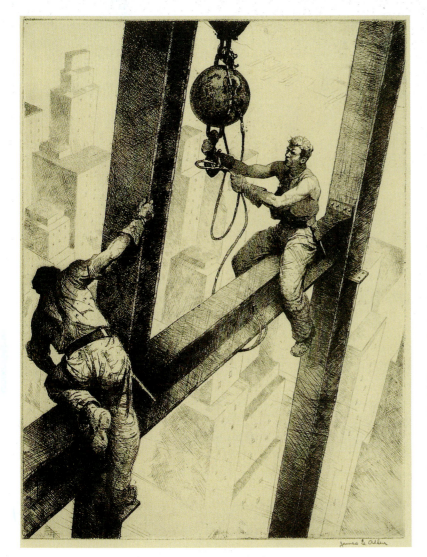

top; they direct the viewer's eye downward in order to accentuate great height (**1.1.14**). The narrowing lines showing the buildings in the **background** of the print help reinforce the same effect.

Communicative Line

The directions of lines (whether they go up, across, or diagonally) both guide our attention and suggest particular feelings. Vertical lines tend to communicate strength and energy; horizontal lines can suggest calmness and passivity; diagonal lines are associated with action, motion, and change.

Graphic designers use the communicative qualities of directional line when creating logos (**1.1.15**). To convey the strength of government or the stability of a financial institution, they may choose verticals. **Logos** for vacation resorts often have horizontal lines to communicate peaceful repose. Diagonals can express the excitement and energy of athletic activity. For example, Carolyn Davidson's (b. *c.* 1943) distinctive Nike "swoosh" conveys action with a shape comprising a stylized, diagonal line (**1.1.16**).

1.1.14 James Allen, *The Connectors*, 1934. Etching, 12⅞ × 9⅞". British Museum, London, England

Vertical lines communicate strength, stability, and authority

Horizontal lines communicate calm, peace, and passiveness

Diagonal lines communicate movement, action, and drama

1.1.15 Communicative qualities of line

Background: the part of a work depicted furthest from the viewer's space, often behind the main subject matter
Logo: a graphic image used to identify an idea or entity
Value: the lightness or darkness of a plane or area

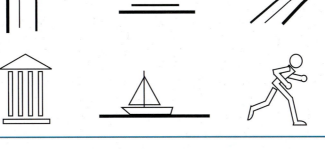

1.1.16 Carolyn Davidson, Nike Company logo, 1971

Color: the optical effect caused when reflected white light of the spectrum is divided into separate wavelengths

Volume: the space filled or enclosed by a three-dimensional figure or object

Draftsman: a person who draws

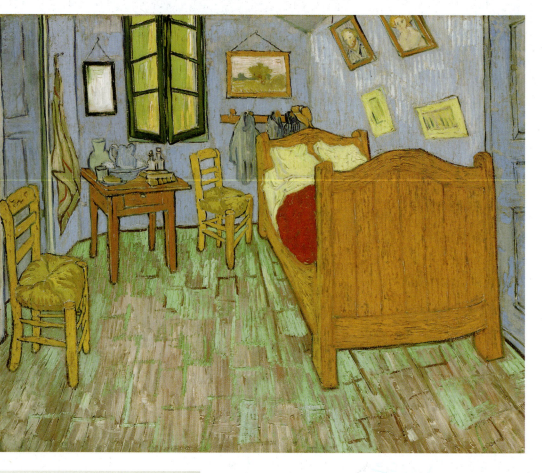

1.1.17 Vincent van Gogh, *The Bedroom*, 1889. Oil on canvas, 28¾ × 36¼". Art Institute of Chicago

1.1.18 Henri Matisse, *Themes and Variations*, series P, *Woman Seated in an Armchair*, pl. 2, 1942. Pen and ink, 19¾ × 15¾". Musée des Beaux-Arts, Lyons, France

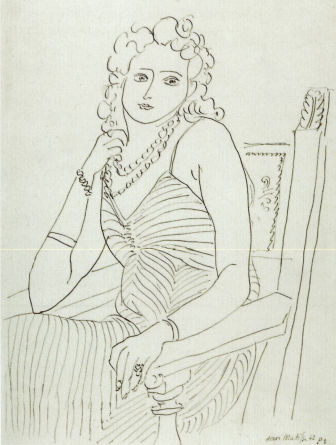

Line gives an unsettling energy to a painting of the bedroom (**1.1.17**) of the Dutch artist Vincent van Gogh (1853–1890). Most of the lines that make up the room are strong verticals. This suggests that Van Gogh's bedroom was not a calm place of rest, as horizontal lines might imply. The floor also nervously changes **color** and value. The varying width of the vertical lines communicates the anxiety Van Gogh may have felt in the months leading up to his suicide in 1890.

The strength of the verticals combined with the agitation of the emphatic diagonals makes for a powerful sense of unease. Yet Van Gogh may also have been trying to ground himself in the here and now by painting the simple room in which he slept.

Contour Line

A contour is the outer edge or profile of an object. Contour lines can suggest a **volume** in space by giving us clues about the changing character of a surface.

Woman Seated in an Armchair by the French artist Henri Matisse (1869–1954) is drawn almost entirely using contour lines (**1.1.18**). The confident outline that sets the boundary between the figure and the background

Gateway to Art: Picasso, *Girl before a Mirror*
Describing a Surface Using Contour Line

Pablo Picasso (1881–1973) was one of the great **draftsmen** of the twentieth century. His unparalleled ability was most likely developed with the help of his father, José Ruiz Blasco, an art instructor who would have known the value of drawing. Drawing is the most fundamental skill in art, and line is the basic element that every artist employs when creating a drawing.

Contour drawing is a process that requires an artist's focused attention on the outer edge of a shape. Imagine focusing your stare on a single point, perhaps on the top of a forehead in profile, then moving your eye painstakingly slowly around the tip of the nose and on along the roundness of the lips and around the chin until it meets the neckline. If you carefully follow that edge and move your pencil along a sheet of paper, recording your progress across the page in a long continuous line, then you are engaging in contour drawing. This type of drawing helps to develop eye–hand coordination and reveal subtle changes in a subject.

Pablo Picasso also used contour line to describe some of his figures. In his line drawing *Blonde Woman in Profile*, the artist uses a continuous line that follows the contours of the profile (**1.1.19**). The drawing also wraps around the perimeter (or outer edge) of the subject, a woman's head, describing the undulating texture of the hair. By giving the viewer clues resembling the kind of curves found in real life, these contour lines communicate shape and indicate some depth using just directional changes.

Picasso also exploited line to describe contours in his painting *Girl before a Mirror* (**1.1.20**). If you look at the reflected image on the right of the painting, the torso of the woman features some curved blue-green strokes that imply the roundness of her body. Picasso has applied the lines as a way of describing the surface of the body in a simple, direct way. The artist probably chose this simplicity of line so that the viewer might see more immediately the comparison between the images of youth and age.

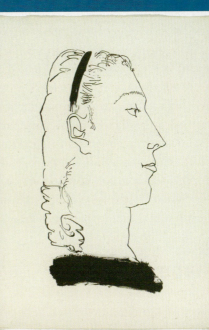

1.1.19 Pablo Picasso, *Blonde Woman in Profile*, plate, folio 16 from the illustrated book *Vingt poëmes*, 1947. Lift ground aquatint, 11⅞ × 6½". MoMA, New York

1.1.20 (below) Pablo Picasso, *Girl before a Mirror*, Boisgeloup, March 1932. Oil on canvas, 64 × 51¼". MoMA, New York

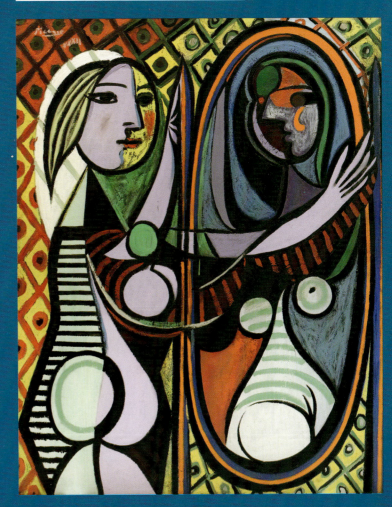

represents one kind of contour line, marking the edge of the figure's overall shape. Although contour drawing is a methodical and measured process (see Gateway Box: Picasso, **1.1.19** and **1.1.20**, p. 59), here Matisse manages to create an impression of spontaneity that gives the work a fresh, relaxed feeling. He has none the less paid close attention to the lines that define the woman's face. Contour lines are also used in her dress to describe its surface as it falls across her figure. Matisse, a master of artistic simplicity and directness, uses solid continuous lines to reveal complex three-dimensional shapes and surfaces. He loved bold, simple lines and shapes and used them deliberately to put the viewer at ease, as if he or she, too, like the subject of this drawing, were sitting in a comfortable armchair.

Shape

A shape is a two-dimensional area the boundaries of which are defined by lines or suggested by changes in color or value. In **1.1.21** we can see the central circular shape because its edges are defined by the sudden transition from white to medium gray. Two-dimensional figures can be defined only by their height and width: they have no depth. As a result, they can function as a simple concept (for example, circles, squares, triangles) that can be used to organize what we see. So a three-dimensional object, such as a sphere, can be drawn using a circle shape, then an artistic device, such as shading, can be used to suggest depth. In art, shape is a basic, two-dimensional element that can be used to define space.

1.1.21 Two-dimensional circular shapes

1.1.22 Geometric and organic shapes

Geometric and Organic Shapes

Shapes can be classified into two types: geometric and organic. Geometric shapes are composed of regular lines and curves. Organic shapes, however, as the examples in the right-hand part of **1.1.22** show, are made up of unpredictable, irregular lines that suggest the natural world. Organic shapes may seem unrestrained and sometimes chaotic, reflecting the never-ending change characteristic of living things.

Geometry is a branch of mathematics dating back more than 2,000 years. It is concerned with space, area, and size. Traditionally defined, a geometric shape is mathematically regular and precise. The simple shapes we know—circle, square, triangle—are all examples of geometric shapes. These can be created by plotting a series of points and connecting them with lines, or simply enclosing a space using regulated and controlled line. Although artists can draw by hand something similar to a geometric shape, they often use tools to control and regulate the precision of the line. For example, an artist may use a ruler to create perfectly straight lines, or alternatively, a computer graphics application can be used to generate a clean, sharp edge. In both cases the artist adds a layer of control that gives the shape greater predictability.

While line may be the most fundamental element of art, often shape is the element we see most clearly. The **collage** by Canadian-born feminist artist Miriam Schapiro (b. 1923) illustrates differences between geometric and organic shapes (**1.1.23**). In *Baby Blocks*—also the name of a traditional quilting pattern—images of flowers and children's clothes overlap a tiling of orange, blue, and black diamond shapes. The work's title suggests a **pattern** of diamond shapes creating an illusion of cubes. The organic shapes of the flowers are clearly distinct from the hard geometric shapes of the "blocks" and the red frame; they overflow the boundaries of both.

The stylized floral designs, derived from old-fashioned wallpaper and upholstery patterns, are simplified representations of real flowers. Even so, the shapes have an irregularity that reflects the kind of shapes we find in living things. By contrast, the interlocked blue and yellow blocks

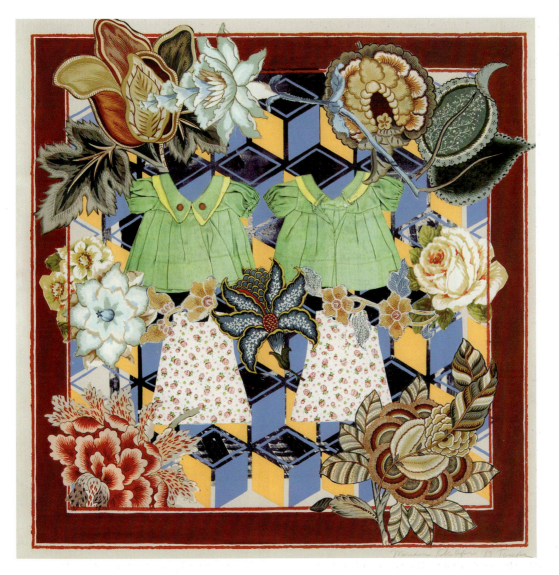

1.1.23 Miriam Schapiro, *Baby Blocks*, 1983. Collage on paper, 29⅞ × 30". University of South Florida Collection, Tampa

are so predictable and regular that we can even envision the pattern where it disappears behind the flowers. This geometric regularity acts as a foil to the organic shapes casually arranged "on" it.

By incorporating doll clothes, home decorations, and sewing materials into her "femmages" (homages to the work of women), Schapiro opens our eyes both to the remarkable artistry of much traditional "women's work," and to the cultural forces that undervalue it.

Implied Shape

Most shapes are defined by a visible boundary, but we can also see a shape where no continuous boundary exists. Just as line can be implied, so too can shape (**1.1.24**).

The AT&T logo, created in the 1980s by American graphic designer Saul Bass (1920–

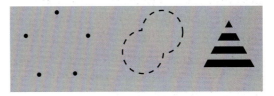

1.1.24 Implied shapes

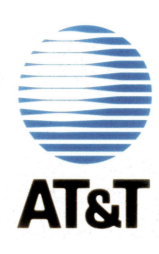

1.1.25 Saul Bass, Bass & Yager, AT&T logo, 1984

1.1.26a and **1.1.26b**
Shepard Fairey, *Obey*, 1996. Campaign poster and a view of the posters as they were installed in public

1996), uses horizontal lines to imply a sphere or globe (**1.1.25**, p. 61). Twelve horizontal lines are trimmed to form a circle. By constricting the width of nine of these lines, a **highlight** appears on the circular shape, implying the swell of a globe. This logo communicates the idea of an expansive telecommunication network operating all over the globe. The image is simple, creating an appropriately meaningful and readily recognizable symbol for a global company.

Contrast

When an artist uses two noticeably different states of an element, he or she is applying the principle of contrast. For example, lines can be both regular and irregular, or shapes can be both geometric and organic. Strong differences in the state of an element can be a very useful effect for an artist to use; it is especially effective to use opposites.

Positive and Negative Shapes

In everyday life, positive and negative are opposites: one needs the other for contrast and comparison. Without positives, negatives would not exist, and vice versa. When we speak of positive and negative in visual form, they are most often represented by black and white. The words on this page, for example, are **positive shapes** of printed black ink that we can see on the **negative space** of the white paper. The space, which is the ground area where such shapes are present, supports the solidity of the placement of the words or shapes. Although black and white are common examples of positive and negative, any color combination can work the same way. Sometimes, too, the lighter color becomes the positive shape.

We can see the interlock of positive and negative shape in the work of American Shepard Fairey (b. 1970). The black features and the blank white space contrast with and complement each other, intensifying the design of this poster (**1.1.26a** and **1.1.26b**). Fairey wants a strong impact because, as a street artist, he needs to catch his audience's attention quickly

as they pass by. In this case, the image is of the professional wrestler Andre the Giant (Fessick in the movie *The Princess Bride*), captioned with the word "Obey." Without seeking prior permission, Fairey posts these images in public places as an expression of guerrilla marketing and street theater. The tension between

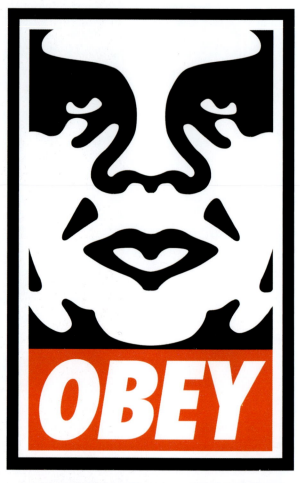

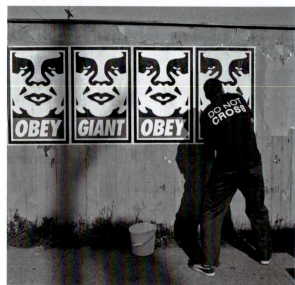

Highlight: an area of lightest value in a work
Positive shape: a shape defined by its surrounding empty space
Negative space: an empty space given shape by its surround, for example the right-pointing arrow between the E and x in **FedEx** (see p. 29)

1.1.27 Georgia O'Keeffe, *Music—Pink and Blue II*, 1919. Oil on canvas, 35 × 29⅛". Whitney Museum of American Art, New York

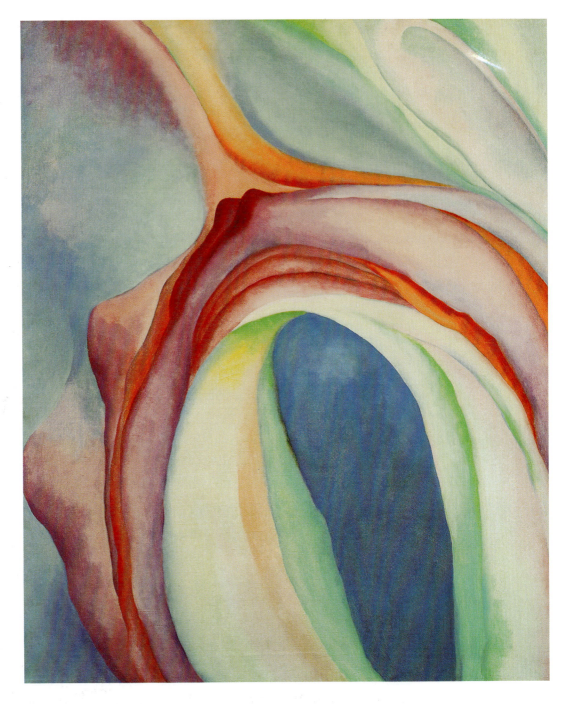

contrasting positive and negative shapes draws our attention, while the cryptic slogan makes us wonder what it is all about.

The works of the American artist Georgia O'Keeffe (1887–1986) often play upon the relationship between positive and negative shape. Her **abstract** shapes derive from a close observation of organic objects. In the painting *Music—Pink and Blue II*, O'Keeffe puts emphasis on the negative blue shape in the bottom right of the picture (**1.1.27**). That negative shape initially draws our attention into a deep interior, so that the positive shape of the pink arc above it carries us back to the surface through a maze of tender folds. O'Keeffe's paintings use landscape and flower shapes to make associations to the female body. The interplay of positive and negative space becomes symbolic of the erotic and life-giving nature of womanhood.

Sometimes illustrators use negative shape to convey information subtly. For example, the Israel-born illustrator and designer Noma Bar (b. 1973) cleverly combined complementary symbols to superimpose two connected ideas.

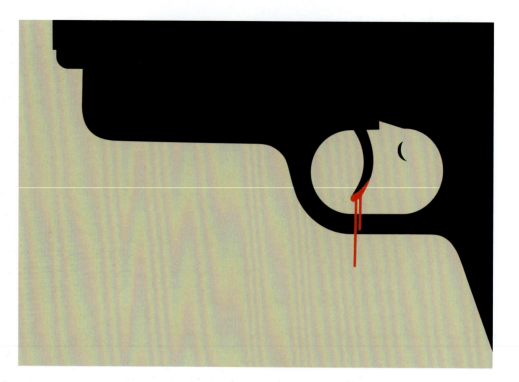

1.1.28 Noma Bar, *Gun Crime*, 2009. Digital, dimensions variable

1.1.29 M. C. Escher, *Sky and Water I*, 1938. Woodcut, 17⅛ × 17⅜". The M. C. Escher Company, The Netherlands

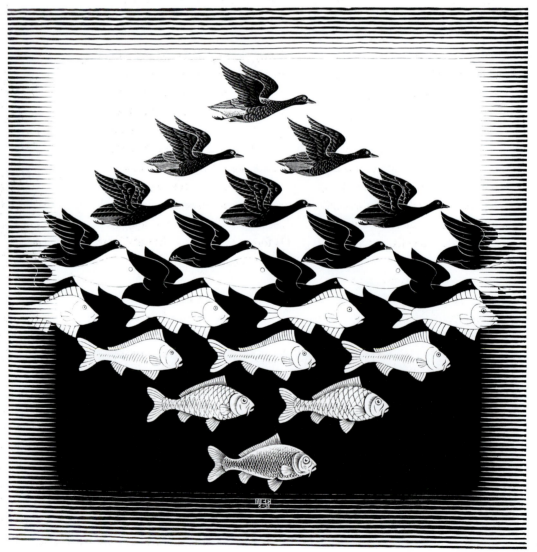

Silhouette: a portrait or figure represented in outline and solidly colored in

Woodcut: a print created from an incised piece of wood

Figure–ground reversal: the reversal of the relationship between one shape (the figure) and its background (the ground), so that the figure becomes background and the ground becomes the figure

In his illustration *Gun Crime* (**1.1.28**), Bar uses a **silhouette** of a handgun to create the positive, or black, shape on the lighter tan background. But in the area where the trigger has been drawn, we see a small crescent shape and a vertical swatch of red. When we consider the image by looking at the negative tan space in this area, we see a simple image of a head with blood running from its mouth. The alternation of positive and negative shape communicates the act of gun crime and the terrible result in a single image.

In the **woodcut** *Sky and Water I*, the Dutch artist M. C. Escher (1898–1972) applies many of the concepts we have been exploring in this chapter (**1.1.29**). The negative shape changes from white in the upper part of the picture to black in the lower. The most refined version of each animal occurs at the top and bottom extremes of the image. As we follow each transition upward or downward, each animal becomes more simplified until it forms part of the background negative shape. Strong geometric patterns change into the organic shapes of animals. The woodcut, where removed material prints white and preserved material prints black, is conducive to exploring **figure–ground reversal**, which is the very essence of Escher's technique here.

Active Learning Exercises

To understand better the role line and shape play in the creation of a work of art or design, it is a good idea to seek out examples actively and examine how they function. Line can be found everywhere, but it is not always used the same way. The following are suggestions for how to analyse line and shape.

1. Take a photo, or find an image of, a building. Print this image on a piece of paper and, using colored markers or highlighters, pick out the vertical, horizontal, diagonal, curved, and organic lines. You will often find vertical lines in the sides of doors, windows, columns, tree trunks, and the sides of a building. Horizontal lines are often found at the foundation of the building, above and below doors and windows, and in the horizon. Any straight line that is not vertical or horizontal will be diagonal. Curved lines appear in circular and rounded areas. Organic lines appear in natural objects, such as the landscape, people, animals, and treetops. After you have defined the lines and where they are in the picture, look at which kind of line is most common. Why do you think the architect used that particular line orientation so often?

2. Using a pencil or pen, place a series of five dots on a page, pass it to another person and ask him or her to add five more, then return the paper to you. Look carefully at the collection of dots nearest to the top of the page. Using a pencil, connect each dot without crossing over any line that you have drawn. Did you see the resulting lines and shapes before you connected the dots? Why, or why not?

3. Take black and white paper (construction paper is fine) and fold each sheet in half. Trace one-half of a leaf on each one, aligning the center of the leaf with the edge of the paper. Using a pair of scissors, cut out the half-leaf shape from the black paper and another from the white. Place each cutout on the opposite-value paper (in other words, place the white cutout on black paper, and the black cutout on white paper). Abut the two halves

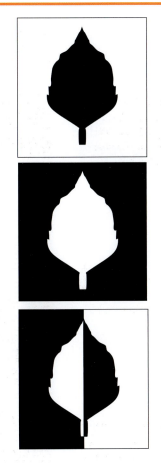

of the leaf (one should be a white half-leaf on a black background, and one a black half-leaf on a white background). As you look at the image, which half-leaf is a positive shape and which is negative? Can a white half-leaf be a positive shape? Or negative? Why, or why not?

Images Related to 1.1:
Line, Shape, and the Principle of Contrast

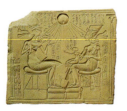

4.6.7 Relief of Akhenaten, Egypt, c. 1353–1335 BCE, p. 630

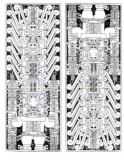

3.4.2b and **c** Drawings of Raimondi Stela, Peru, 460–300 BCE, p. 434

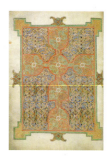

3.2.11a Cross-carpet page, Lindisfarne Gospels, 710–721 CE, p. 399

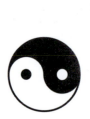

3.3.15 Yin and yang symbol, p. 423

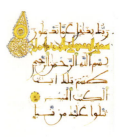

3.2.10 Page from Koran, probably late 12th century, p. 398

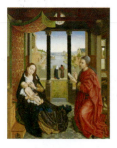

3.6.12 Rogier Van der Weyden, *Saint Luke Drawing the Virgin*, c. 1435–40, p. 476

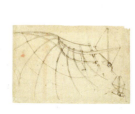

2.1.1. Leonardo da Vinci, *Drawing for a wing of a flying machine*, p.198

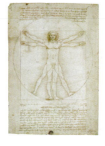

4.4.1 Leonardo da Vinci, *Vitruvian Man*, c. 1490, p. 599

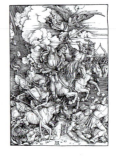

2.3.2 Albrecht Dürer, *Four Horsemen of the Apocalypse*, c. 1497–98, p. 233

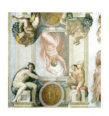

2.4.8 Michelangelo, *Separation of Light and Darkness*, 1508–10, p. 252

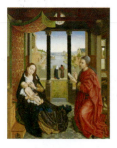

1.3.8 Michelangelo, *Head of a Satyr*, c. 1520–30, p. 86

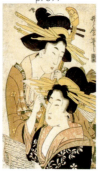

2.8.1 Stefano Della Bella, *Camera Obscura with view of Florence*, 1540s, p.320

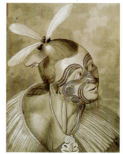

3.3.22 Kitagawa Utamaro, *Two Courtesans*, 2nd half of 18th century, p. 428

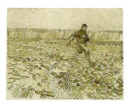

3.5.11 Sydney Parkinson, Drawing of a Maori tattoo, 1784, p. 457

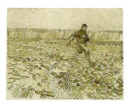

2.1.19 Vincent van Gogh, *Sower with Setting Sun*, 1888, p. 210

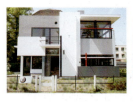

3.9.15 Gerrit Rietveld, Schröder House, 1924–25, p. 551

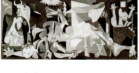

4.7.5 Pablo Picasso, *Guernica*, 1937, p. 638

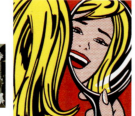

3.9.5 Roy Lichtenstein, *Girl in Mirror*, 1964, p. 545

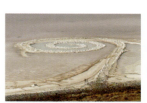

2.4.15 Robert Smithson, *Spiral Jetty*, 1969–70, p. 257

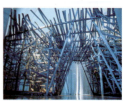

1.2.12 Carol Mickett and Robert Stackhouse, *In the Blue (Crest)*, 2008, p. 74

1.2

Form, Volume, Mass, and Texture

In 1802 a French artist and archaeologist described his impression of the great pyramids of Egypt:

> On approaching these colossal monuments, their angular and inclined form diminishes the appearance of their height and deceives the eye . . . but as soon as I begin to measure . . . these gigantic productions of art, they recover all their immensity . . .
>
> (Vivant Denon, *Travels in Upper and Lower Egypt*)

The massive structures that so impressed Denon have three dimensions, like every object in our world, which can be expressed as their height, width, and depth (**1.2.1**). Because the pyramids can be measured in these three dimensions they are classified as **three-dimensional** works of art, and like all the art discussed in this chapter they possess four of the visual **elements**: form, volume, mass, and texture. We need to understand these terms in sequence so that we can analyse and understand three-dimensional art.

1.2.1 Three dimensions: height, width, and depth

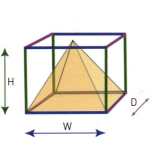

Three-dimensional: having height, width, and depth
Elements: the basic vocabulary of art—line, form, shape, volume, mass, color, texture, space, time and motion, and value (lightness/darkness)
Two-dimensional: having height and width
Shape: a two-dimensional area, the boundaries of which are defined by lines or suggested by changes in color or value
Form: an object that can be defined in three dimensions (height, width, and depth)
Scale: the size of an object or artwork relative to another object or artwork, or to a system of measurement
Volume: the space filled or enclosed by a three-dimensional figure or object
Mass: a volume that has, or gives the illusion of having, weight, density, and bulk
Space: the distance between identifiable points or planes
Texture: the surface quality of a work, for example fine/coarse, detailed/lacking in detail

Form

A **two-dimensional** object, such as a drawing of a triangle, is called a **shape**. Shapes are flat and do not have mass or volume. A three-dimensional object, such as a pyramid, is called a **form**. A form occupies three-dimensional space and exists in a real and solid way. Forms are tactile; we can feel them with our hands. Some forms are so tiny they cannot be seen with the naked eye, while others are as large as a galaxy. When artists and designers create forms, they consider how we will experience them in three dimensions. Architects usually make buildings that accord with our physical size, in proportions that are convenient and easy to live in, but sometimes they might build to a larger **scale** in order to leave us in awe. A jeweler makes objects at a small scale that few people can experience at once: we are drawn closer to examine the work more intimately.

Forms have two fundamental attributes: **volume** and **mass**. Volume is the amount of **space** a form occupies. Mass is the expression that a volume is solid and occupies space, whether it is enormous, such as a pyramid, or relatively small, such as a piece of jewelry.

The surface of a form can be cool and slick, rough and jagged, soft and warm. Such sensations arise from the **texture** of the form. Texture can be experienced directly, but we can also imagine how the surface of a form may feel simply by looking at it. Some hand-made objects, such as ceramics or basketry, attract our touch naturally. They were touched by the hands that formed them, and they fit in our hands just as they used to fit in the hands of the artist. Some machine-made forms reflect the crisp precision of mechanical perfection; their smooth, shiny forms seduce our senses. Artists and designers create forms with full knowledge that they can evoke our memories of other three-dimensional objects in the world and allow us to experience our own world in a richer way.

The forms created by artists in the ancient world reflected the everyday experiences of people of that time. For example, stone was a common material in ancient Egypt, easily accessible and so durable that artists must have thought it would last for a very long time—a correct assumption, as we can still see.

The Great Sphinx guards the tombs of the Egyptian kings at Giza, near Cairo (**1.2.2**). It is the largest carving in the world made from a single stone. The sculpture stands as a symbol of the power to change our surroundings. The Egyptians who created this work changed the

very earth by sculpting the living rock. We do not know what the Egyptians called this half-man, half-lion, but we now call it a "sphinx" after the creature from Greek mythology with the body of a lion, the wings of an eagle, and the head of a man. The Great Sphinx is believed to be a likeness of the Egyptian king Khafre.

There are two types of form: geometric and organic.

Geometric Form

Geometric forms are regular and are readily expressible in words or mathematics: cubes, spheres, cylinders, cones, and pyramids are simple examples. The Pyramid of Khafre, which is guarded by the Great Sphinx of Giza in **1.2.2**, is a stunning example of geometric form in architectural design because of the straight, controlled **planes** that articulate the four sides. The crisp regularity of the pyramids derives from the attention to detail. For example, the

1.2.2 Great Sphinx of Giza (front), *c.* 2500 BCE, and Pyramid of Khafre, *c.* 2500 BCE, Giza, Egypt

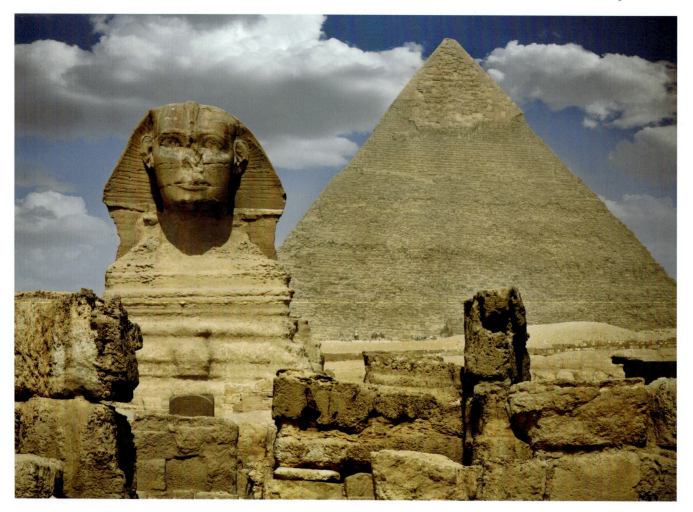

base of another of the pyramids, Khufu's, is level to within less than an inch, and the greatest difference in the length of its sides is 1¾ in. The emphasis on precise mathematical proportion reflects an ordered culture in which artists were governed by a canon, or set of rules, that imposed strict controls on how an artist worked and the images that he or she created.

The American sculptor David Smith (1906–1965) also relied on geometric forms to create his compositions. In *Cubi XIX*, made of stainless steel, Smith uses cubes, cuboids, and a thick disk (**1.2.3**). Smith learned welding in an automobile factory and became expert while fabricating tanks of thick armor plate during World War II. The late works of his *Cubi* series combine geometric forms in angular relationships. The diagonal angles imply movement, giving these basic geometric forms a visual energy. Smith burnished their surfaces to create a counterpoint between industrial and natural form.

1.2.3 David Smith, *Cubi XIX*, 1964. Stainless steel, 113¼ × 21⅝ × 20⅝". Tate Gallery, London, England

Organic Form

The form of most things in the natural world is organic: it is irregular and unpredictable. Living things, such as plants and animals, change constantly, and their forms change too. Artists accentuate the irregular character of **organic form** for expressive effect.

The human figure gives an artist a subject that can communicate the rich experience of humanity and organic form in a way we can all understand. The human body, like other organic forms, constantly changes in concert with its surroundings. Forms representing the human figure can provide the artist with a subject conveying symmetry and balance. But by visually contradicting such order, an artist can make a work seem uncomfortable or uneasy to look at. The unknown artist who carved the *Roettgen Pietà* in the fourteenth century expresses the agony of death and grief by making the bodies of Jesus and Mary irregular, awkward, and distorted (**1.2.4**). The suffering of torture

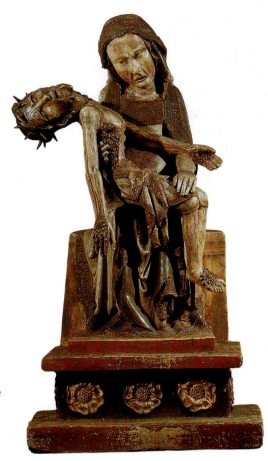

1.2.4 *Roettgen Pietà* (*Vesperbild*), Middle Rhine region, *c.* 1330. Wood, 34½" high. Rheinisches Landesmuseum, Bonn, Germany

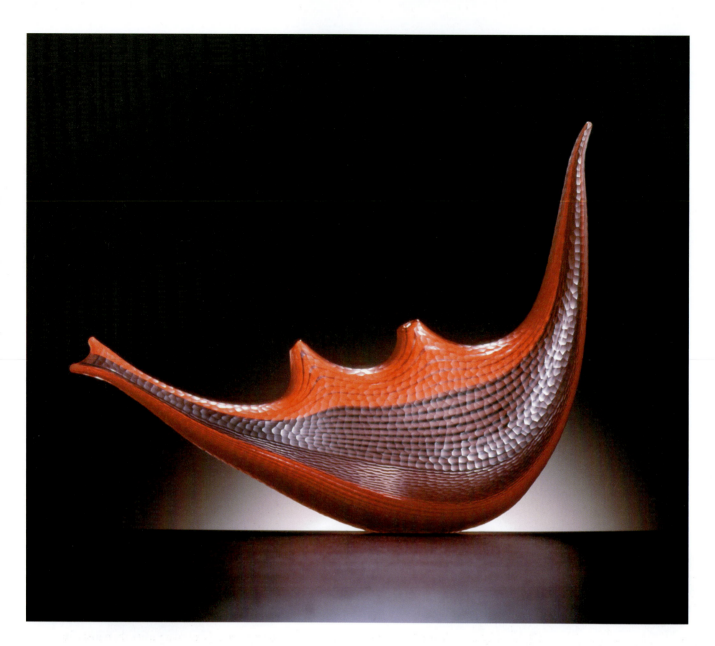

is made shocking by the disjointedness of the lifeless Jesus. Stiffly angular, he is stretched across the lap of his mother Mary. Prickly thorns, gushing wounds, and crumpled drapery give texture to pain and anguish. The disproportionate size of Mary's twisted face makes her unbearable sorrow all the more inescapable.

The expression of vigor and uplift in Italian glass artist Lino Tagliapietra's *Batman* (**1.2.5**) contrasts with the expression of death and despair in the *Roettgen Pietà*. Tagliapietra (b. 1934) wanted to convey the idea of "a creature who emerges from his dark cave to share goodness and light." He has enhanced the positive emotion of this **abstract** image by

using bright **color** and stretching the extreme edges upward as if this were a growing, living object. Rather than having hard, angular distortions, the artist uses a form that is lively and organic. The natural energy of light is captured in the glowing transparency of the glass. Tagliapietra, a master of glassblowing technique, wants the form to allude, without making a literal reference, to the idea behind the character Batman. Thus we are free to revel in the life, energy, and power of the superhero through an expressive form, rather than a carefully depicted, lifelike representation. Tagliapietra says of the work, "I imaged pieces that allow the viewer to see both the reality and fantasy of Batman's world."

1.2.5 Lino Tagliapietra, *Batman*, 1998. Glass, 11½ × 15½ × 3½"

Abstract: art imagery that departs from recognizable images from the natural world
Color: the optical effect caused when reflected white light of the spectrum is divided into separate wavelengths
Relief: a raised form on a largely flat background. For example, the design on a coin is "in relief"

1.2.6 Imperial Procession from the Ara Pacis Augustae, 13 BCE. Marble altar, Museo dell'Ara Pacis, Rome, Italy

1.2.7 Stela with supernatural scene, Mexico or Guatemala, 761 CE. Limestone, 92 × 42 × 3". Fine Arts Museums of San Francisco

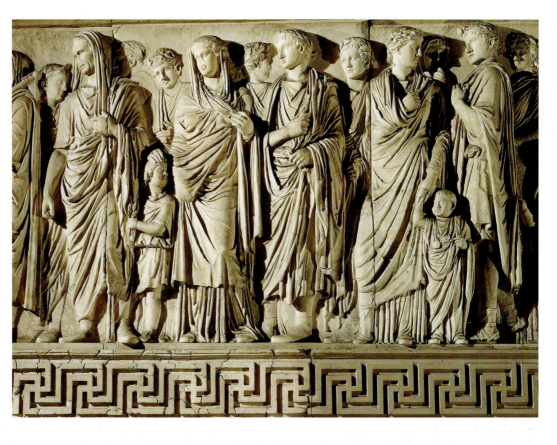

Form in Relief and in the Round

An artist who works with three-dimensional form can choose to create a work in **relief** or **in the round**. A relief is a work in which forms project from a flat surface. It is designed to be viewed from one side only. A form in the round can be seen from all sides.

Forms in relief combine aspects of two-dimensional and three-dimensional works of art. Like a two-dimensional work, a relief can be mounted on a wall or other surface. Although relief may appear to limit the work's potential visual impact, in fact the sculptor can create the illusion of a three-dimensional space, with dramatic results.

In the relief sculptures on the south **facade** of the Ara Pacis Augustae (Latin for Altar of Peace of Augustus) in Rome, Italy, a sculptor chose to fit many figures into a limited space (**1.2.6**). The unknown artist uses the depth of the carvings to suggest that some areas of the composition are further away from us than others. The figures in the **foreground** are deeply carved (in **high relief**) so that the folds in their togas are strongly delineated by shadows. But the artist wanted to imply a large crowd rather than just a line of people. The figures behind those in the foreground are also carved in relief, but not quite so deeply. They appear to be further away because there is less shadow defining their shape. The artist suggests even greater depth by using a third group of figures who are carved in shallow relief, so that there is no shadow at all to make them stand out. This effect is clear in the upper left-hand corner, where the carving overlaps and diminishes in height.

The Maya artist who carved **1.2.7** in **bas-relief** worked in a tradition quite different from that of the Roman sculptor of the Ara Pacis, with its deeply incised figures. On the Maya **stela** all the carving is carefully arranged on the same plane. The sculptor has created a large figure of a Maya ruler, shown wearing a highly detailed and elaborate costume. The Maya writing to the left of the figure seems to be of equal visual weight; the sculptor intended the viewer to read every element of the **composition**.

A sculpture is no longer a relief when the work can be viewed from all sides: this kind of form is known as in the round. Such **freestanding** works of art occupy space in the same way that other real-life objects do. When an artist composes a work that is designed in the round, he or she considers how the viewer will interact with the work. In the ancient Roman statue *Naked Aphrodite Crouching at Her Bath*, also known as *Lely's Venus*, the artist rewards the viewer who walks around the work, by constantly changing the elements of the design. You can see that the figure's face is turned away from a forward-looking position, and the body is slightly twisted. So, if a viewer

moves from one side to another, there will be new surface changes and interesting angles from which to look, which make the experience interesting and hold the viewer's attention. Each time he or she moves, the design of the work reveals a different aspect, and the viewer's perception of it changes. From the view in **1.2.8a**, for example, you are encouraged to move to the opposite side to view Aphrodite's face (**1.2.8b**). The artist has effectively designed the work so that you feel compelled to look further and experience the work more fully, while the sculpture's form remains satisfying from every viewpoint. This is one important attribute of good three-dimensional design.

1.2.8a and **1.2.8b** *Aphrodite Crouching at Her Bath* (*"Lely's Venus"*). Marble, Roman, 2nd century CE; copy of lost Greek original of the late 3rd/2nd century BCE, 44 1/8" high. British Museum, London, England (on loan from Her Majesty the Queen)

Stela (plural **stelae**): upright stone slab decorated with inscriptions or pictorial relief carvings
Composition: the overall design or organization of a work
Freestanding: any sculpture that stands separate from walls or other surfaces so that it can be viewed from a 360-degree range
Focal point: the center of interest or activity in a work of art, often drawing the viewer's attention to the most important element
Axis: an imaginary line showing the center of a shape, volume, or composition

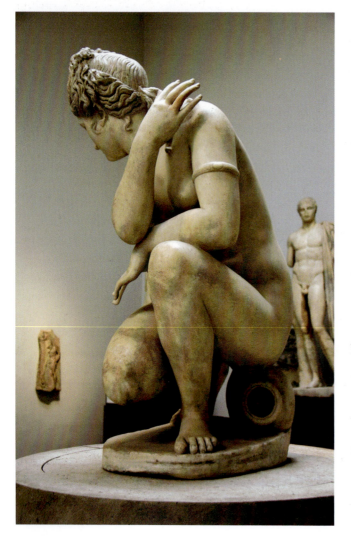

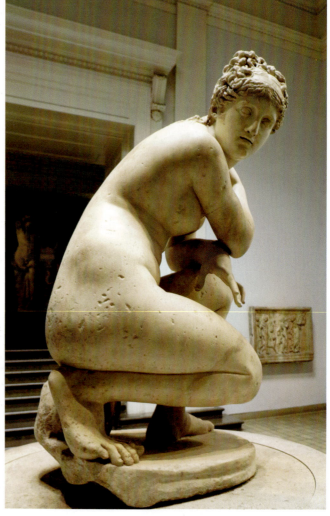

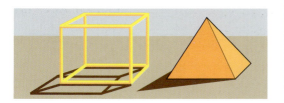

1.2.9 Volume (left) and mass (right)

Volume

Three-dimensional objects necessarily have volume. Volume is the amount of space occupied by an object. Solid objects have volume; so do objects that enclose an empty space. Mass, by contrast, suggests that something is solid and occupies space (**1.2.9**). Architectural forms usually enclose a volume of interior space to be used for living or working. For example, some hotel interiors feature a large, open atrium that becomes the **focal point** of the lobby. Some sculptures accentuate weight and solidity rather than openness. Such works have very few open spaces that we can see. The presence of mass suggests weight, gravity, and a connection to the earth. The absence of mass suggests lightness, airiness, flight. Asymmetrical masses—or masses that cannot be equally divided on a central **axis**—can suggest dynamism, movement, change.

Open Volume

When artists enclose a space with materials that are not completely solid, they create an open volume. In *Ghostwriter*, Ralph Helmick (b. 1952) and Stuart Schechter (b. 1958) use carefully suspended pieces of metal to make an open volume that, when looked at as a whole, creates the image of a large human head (**1.2.10a** and **1.2.10b**). The small metal pieces, which represent letters of the alphabet, little heads, and other objects, are organized so that they delineate the shape of the head but do not enclose the space. In the stairwell where the piece hangs, the empty space and the "head" are not distinct or separate, but the shape is nonetheless implied.

The Russian artist Vladimir Tatlin's (1885–1953) *Monument to the Third International* was intended to be a huge tower with rooms

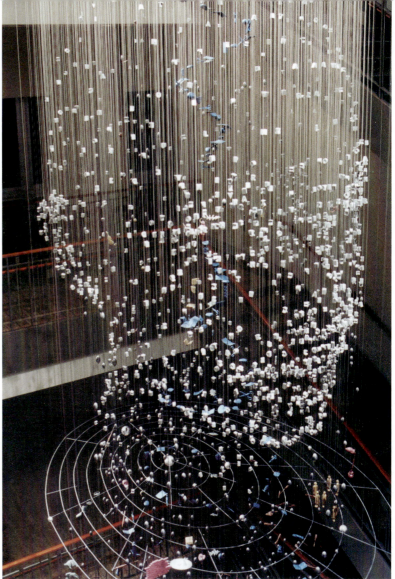

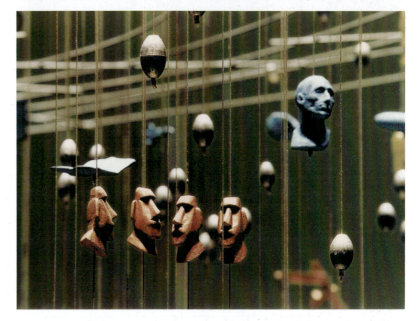

1.2.10a (top) Ralph Helmick and Stuart Schechter, *Ghostwriter*, 1994. Cast metal/stainless cable, 36 × 8 × 10'. Evanston Public Library, Illinois

1.2.10b (above) Detail of *Ghostwriter*

housing the offices and chamber of delegates of the Communist International. It was going to commemorate the triumph of Russia's Bolshevik Revolution. Never built, it would have been much higher than the Eiffel Tower in Paris, France. In its form as we see it in **1.2.11**, the spiraling open volume of the interior, and its proposed novel use of such materials as steel and glass, symbolize the modernism and dynamism of Communism. Tatlin believed that art should support and reflect the new social and political order.

Open volume can make a work feel light. *In the Blue (Crest)*, a collaborative work by American sculptors Carol Mickett (b. 1952) and Robert Stackhouse (b. 1942), was created to imply the presence of water (**1.2.12**). By creating **negative space** (the openings between the wooden slats) with crowds of horizontal members, the artists make the work seem to float. Mickett and Stackhouse also curve the pieces and place them at irregular intervals to create many subtle changes in direction. This arrangement gives a feeling of motion, like the gentle ripples of flowing water. The artists

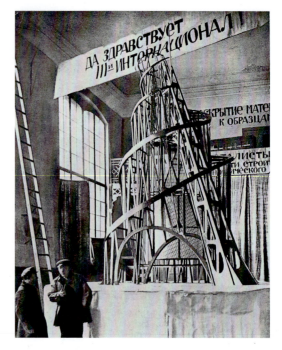

1.2.11 Vladimir Tatlin, Model for *Monument to the Third International*, 1919

hope that viewers will experience a sensation of being surrounded by water as they walk through the passage.

1.2.12 Carol Mickett and Robert Stackhouse, *In the Blue (Crest)*, 2008. Painted cypress, 24 × 108 × 11'. Installation at St. Petersburg Art Center, Florida

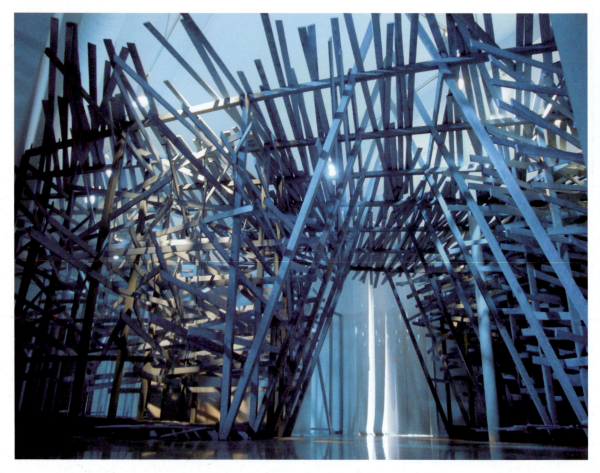

Negative space: an empty space given shape by its surround, for example the right-pointing arrow between the E and x in FedEx (see p. 29)

Mass

Mass suggests that a volume is solid and occupies space. Every substance has mass. Our perception of mass influences how we react to and what we feel about that substance (see Gateway Box: Colossal Olmec Heads, **1.2.13**). We can feel the weight of a pebble in the palm of our hand, or the heaviness of a chair as we pull it away from a table. Our perception of mass in large objects is derived from our imagination, our previous experience with smaller objects, and our understanding of the forces of nature. Artists tap into these various intuitions when they create a work of art.

Mass can suggest weight in a three-dimensional object. Some artists imply mass (without it necessarily being there) to give us the impression that the object we are looking at is very heavy. In movies, special-effect artists play on the use of illusion to create the impression of great weight; for instance, boulders that look

Gateway to Art: Colossal Olmec Heads
Mass and Power

The monumental quality of some artworks is directly related to their mass. This 8-foot-high Olmec sculpture of a colossal head has an imposing physical presence (**1.2.13**). The sheer size of the work was almost certainly intended to impress and overwhelm. At La Venta, in Mexico, three heads were positioned in a "processional arrangement" requiring the viewer to walk from one head to another, which must have increased their visual impact. Some of the colossal Olmec heads are flat at the back because they have been carved out of earlier monuments known as "altars," although they may in fact have been thrones. The flat back to the head was the base of the altar. While a similar head could be carved on a pebble that would fit the palm of the hand, the massive scale of this head makes an imposing statement. Its intimidating size suggests the power of a mighty ruler or an important ancestor. The full lips and nose amplify the head's massive scale.

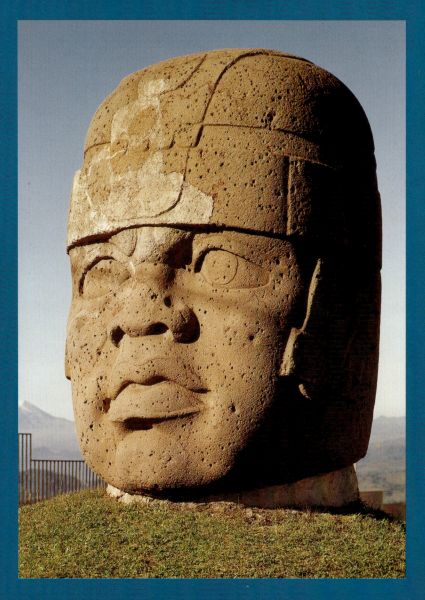

1.2.13 Colossal Head, Olmec, 1500–1300 BCE. Basalt. Museo de Antropología, Veracruz, Mexico

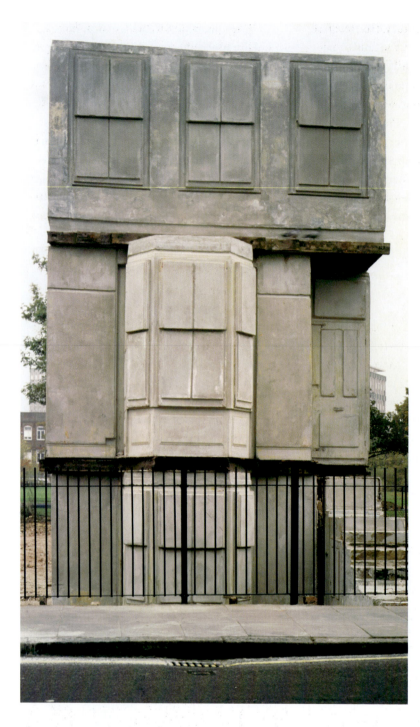

commemoration of its former self. Whiteread has taken the volume of this building's interior and transformed it into a lasting memorial of the lives of the people who used to live in it, and in other houses just like it. We comprehend not only the weight of the concrete, but also the related associations of life and death, memory and change.

The sculpture of Father Damien by the American artist Marisol (b. Maria Sol Escobar, 1930) stands as an immovable object against an irresistible force (**1.2.15**). It depicts the courage of a humanitarian hero. Father Damien was a Catholic missionary who supervised a leper colony on the Hawaiian island of Molokai

1.2.15 Marisol (Escobar), *Father Damien*, 1969. Bronze, 7′. State Capitol Building, Honolulu, Hawaii

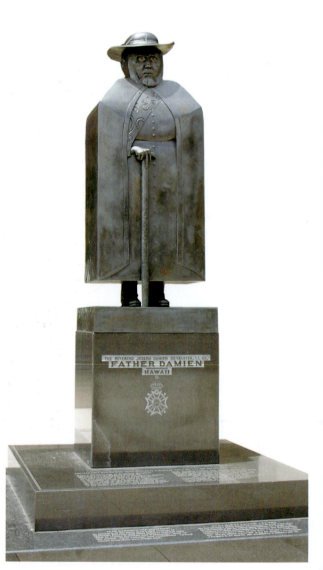

1.2.14 Rachel Whiteread, *House*, 1993. Concrete. Bow, London, England (demolished 1994)

crushingly *heavy* (and real) are actually made of foam. Mass does not necessarily imply heaviness, only that a volume is solid and occupies space.

The mass of British sculptor Rachel Whiteread's *House* suggests great weight and solidity (**1.2.14**). To create this work, Whiteread (b. 1963) filled the interior space of a house with tons of concrete before demolishing the exterior walls and windows. The empty volume that was once filled with the happy and sad moments of ordinary domestic life has been turned into a

during the nineteenth century. His steadfast compassion is suggested by the four-square mass of Marisol's work, while his upright correctness is reflected in its vertical lines—in the cane, in the cape, and in the straight row of buttons. The stout form communicates stability and determination. Father Damien, who himself died of leprosy while serving its victims, exemplified such heroism that the Hawaiian legislature voted to place this memorial to him in front of the State Capitol Building in Honolulu.

Texture

Any three-dimensional object that can be touched and felt has actual texture, the tactile sensation we experience when we physically encounter a three-dimensional form (two-dimensional images have *implied* texture, which means the artist creates an effect that reminds us of our tactile memory of an actual texture). Textures vary, from the slick, cold surface of a finely finished metal object, to the rough-hewn splintery character of a broken branch, to the pebbly surface of a rocky beach.

When you hold this book in your hands, you feel its weight and the surface of its pages. We mostly rely on the impressions we receive from our hands when we think of texture, and these tactile experiences influence the way we look at art.

Even if we do not touch three-dimensional works of art, we can still think of them as having actual texture. This is an association we can make based on our previous experience of touching objects that have similar surfaces. We know what polished stone feels like (cool and smooth), so when we look at a highly polished marble sculpture we can imagine how its texture feels, based on our past experience. Our experience of texture will be different, though, if we look at a picture of it in a book or if we stand next to it in the same room.

Viewers of Indian-born British artist Anish Kapoor's (b. 1954) sculpture *Cloud Gate* experience actual texture when they see and touch the work (**1.2.16**). We understand the tactile sensation of touching a smooth, slick, stainless-steel surface. Kapoor presents us with a highly polished, organic (bean-like) form that literally reflects the city of Chicago

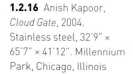

1.2.16 Anish Kapoor, *Cloud Gate*, 2004. Stainless steel, 32'9" × 65'7" × 41'12". Millennium Park, Chicago, Illinois

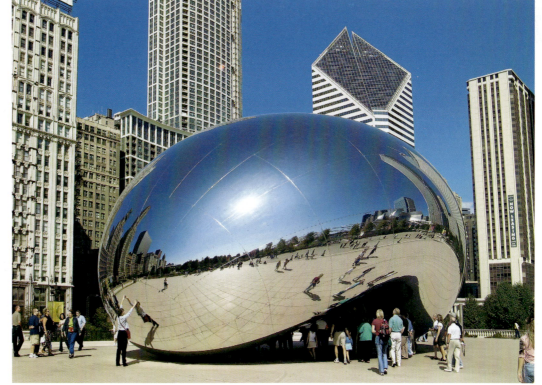

and the surrounding activity as it takes place. By providing such an invitingly slick surface, he wants the viewer to interact with the sculpture in visual and tactile ways. A viewer feels welcome to touch the work, knowing that it will feel cool and slippery: the invitation would not be as clear, or as appealing, if a rougher surface had been presented. The sleek actual texture of this work influences the actions of those viewers who encounter it.

The Guggenheim Museum, Bilbao

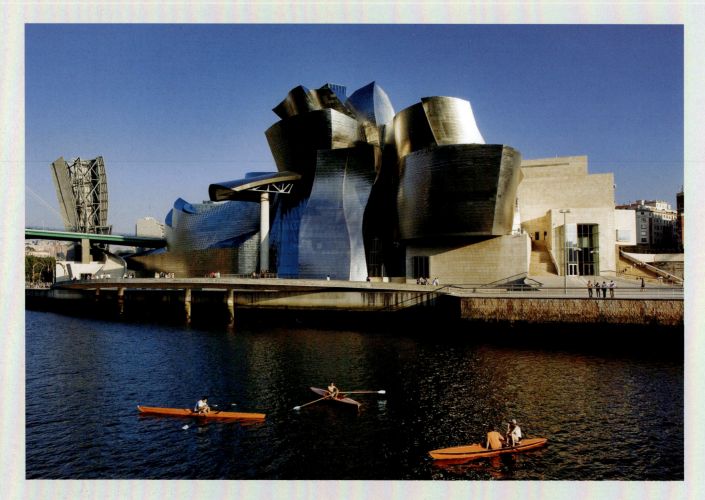

1.2.17 Frank Gehry, Guggenheim Museum, 1997, Bilbao, Spain

The American architect Frank Gehry (b. 1929) designed the Guggenheim Museum, located between a river and a motorway, in Bilbao, Spain; it was completed in 1997 (**1.2.17**). Bilbao was once a center for shipbuilding, and the undulating surfaces of Gehry's creation suggest ships and ship construction. Gehry's design uses contrasts in geometric and organic form. Historically, architectural design has relied on geometric form. Organic forms, by comparison, are more difficult to visualize and plan in advance; curved and irregular structures are difficult to survey, measure, plumb, and level. But Gehry used computer programs originally invented for aerospace design to plan buildings that contradict our preconceived ideas about architecture as geometric form. Most of the walls of the Guggenheim Museum consist of irregular, curving, organic forms that rise and fall unpredictably. The undulating surfaces give a sense of movement and life to the structure. This could make some visitors feel disoriented, but Gehry counters this at critical junctures by using strongly geometric form. At the entrance, for instance, the reassurance

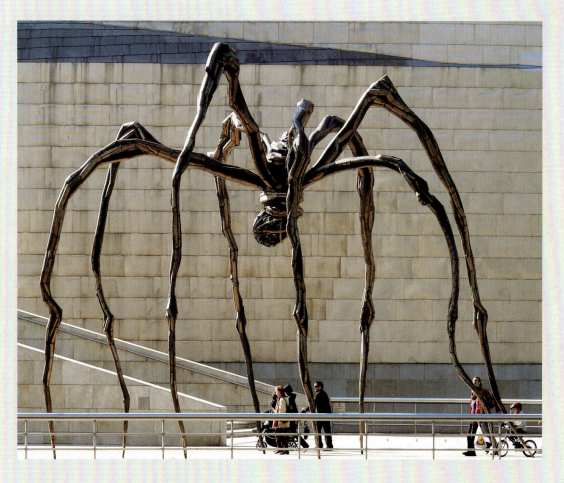

of geometric form encourages even the most apprehensive visitor to enter the building.

Gehry employs both sculptural relief and in-the-round forms. The surfaces of the organic portion of the building are covered with titanium tiles. The subtle changes to the surfaces of this material resemble an abstract bas-relief. But the entire building is also like a sculpture in the round that the viewer can stroll around to appreciate its unexpected juts and curves.

Gehry's museum has reshaped its location. The interior space, designed to meet the changing needs of art and artists in the future, can also be extended or reduced, creating interesting exhibition opportunities. The complex shapes of the building extend out into space like a huge boat, emphasizing its relationship to the nearby River Nervión. When it was first constructed, the building stood in stark contrast to the surrounding urban landscape. It was designed to offer an optimistic vision in what was at that time a deteriorating industrial district, and has done

so in the most extraordinary way: inspired by Gehry's creation, this part of the city has been transformed into the vibrant cultural and commercial area it is today.

The shimmering titanium tiles of Gehry's building are complemented by a sculpture that stands beside the museum, *Maman* (**1.2.18**; meaning "Momma" in French), by French artist Louise Bourgeois (1911–2010). The Guggenheim's apparently solid mass is contrasted with the spindly form and open volume of *Maman*. The negative space surrounding its legs and body imparts lightness. The subtle variations of angle in the legs imply movement. The wobbly vulnerability of the spider contrasts with the massive solidity of the building. Even though this spider is made of bronze, the effect is one of lightness. And by suspending below the central body a container of marble spheres like an egg sac, Bourgeois wants to suggest both the tenderness and fierce protectiveness of motherhood.

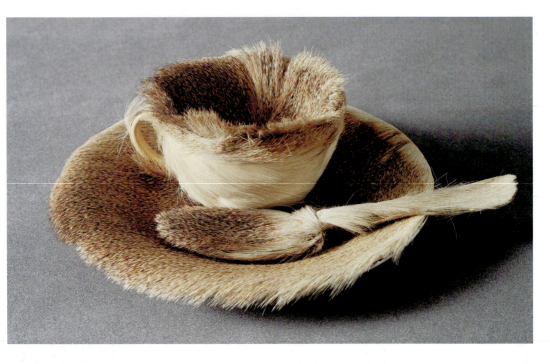

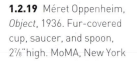
1.2.19 Méret Oppenheim, *Object*, 1936. Fur-covered cup, saucer, and spoon, 2⅞" high. MoMA, New York

Subversive Texture

A subversive texture contradicts our previous tactile experience. Some types of cactus appear to have a soft, furry covering, but touching them will be painful. Artists and designers use the contradictions and contrasts of subversive texture to invite viewers to reconsider their preconceptions about the world around them.

In the early twentieth century, artists calling themselves **Surrealists** created work that drew on ideas and images from dreams and the unconscious mind. The Swiss Surrealist

Méret Oppenheim (1913–1985) used texture to contradict the conscious logical experiences of viewers. In her sculpture *Object*, Oppenheim takes a cup, saucer, and spoon, normally hard and cool to the touch, and instead makes them soft and furry (**1.2.19**). The idea of sipping tea from this object conjures up an unexpected sensation of fur tickling our lips. The artist is counting on our tactile memory to conflict with the actual experience of sipping tea from a shiny teacup. In this case, the form is recognizable, but the associated experience is not.

Active Learning Exercises

1. Like the water in a glass, the area that is occupied by a real object is its volume. In the glass of water we see the liquid in a cylindrical shape. If the glass were frozen, the ice would also describe its volume. An empty glass describes the cylindrical shape of the air inside. What shape did the architect create when designing the room you are in? How does that affect the people who use this space?

2. In filmmaking, implied mass makes it possible for the director to create illusions of great weight in objects that are relatively light. If you were creating your own movie about building the Great Pyramid, what strategies or materials could you use to imply heavy stones?

3. Actual texture is texture that can be experienced firsthand. Some artists, historians, and artists translate actual texture into implied texture by doing rubbings. To do a rubbing you place a piece of paper over a textured surface and rub a wax crayon, charcoal, graphite, or other drawing material over the paper surface, producing on the paper an impression of the texture below. Do your own rubbing of an actual texture. Compared to the actual texture, what qualities does the paper image lack?

Images Related to 1.2:
Form, Volume, Mass, and Texture

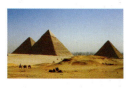

3.1.14 Pyramids at Giza, Egypt, c. 2500 BCE, p. 374

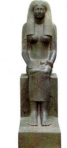

2.4.1 *Sculpture of Lady Sennuwy*, Egypt, 1971–1926 BCE, p. 249

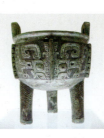

1.6.13 *Liu Ding* (ritual container), China, 1600–1100 BCE, p. 140

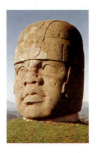

1.2.13 Colossal Olmec Head, 1500–1300 BCE, p. 75

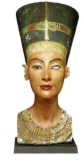

1.10.1a Bust of Queen Nefertiti, Egypt, c. 1340 BCE, p. 179

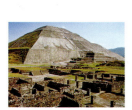

3.4.11 Pyramid of the Sun, Teotihuacan, c. 225 CE, p. 440

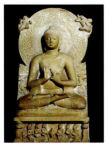

3.3.4 Seated Buddha, Gupta period, India, 320–550, p. 415

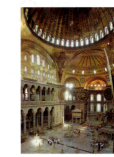

2.5.5 Maya Temple, Tikal, Guatemala, c. 300–900, p. 269

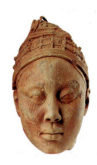

2.5.19 Hagia Sophia, Istanbul, Turkey, 532–35, p. 276

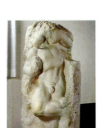

4.9.6 Ife culture, Head of king (?), 12th–14th century, p. 663

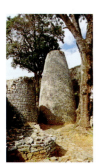

3.5.8 Conical tower, Great Zimbabwe, c. 1350–1450, p. 456

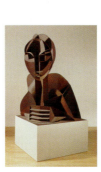

2.4.8 Michelangelo, *Awakening Slave*, 1519–20, p. 252

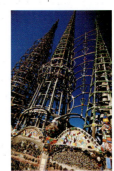

2.4.16 Naum Gabo, *Constructed Head No. 2*, 1916, p. 258

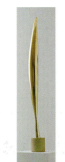

0.0.8 Simon Rodia, Watts Towers, 1921–54, p. 32

3.8.39 Constantin Brancusi, *Bird in Space*, c. 1928, p. 538

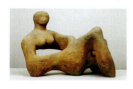

4.9.15 Henry Moore, *Recumbent Figure*, 1938, p. 670

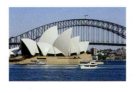

2.5.34 Jørn Utzon, Sydney Opera House, Australia, 1973, p. 286

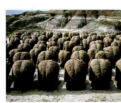

1.10.7 Magdalena Abakanowicz, *80 Backs*, 1976–80, p. 186

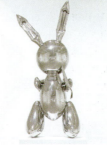

0.0.9 Jeff Koons, *Rabbit*, 1986, p. 33

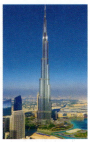

2.5.31 Adrian Smith and Bill Baker, Burj Khalifa, Dubai, 2010, p. 283

1.3

Implied Depth:
Value and Space

Three-dimensional: having height, width, and depth
Two-dimensional: having height and width
Value: the lightness or darkness of a plane or area
Space: the distance between identifiable points or planes
Perspective: the creation of the illusion of depth in a two-dimensional image by using mathematical principles

1.3.1 René Magritte, *The Treachery of Images ("This Is not a Pipe"),* 1929. Oil on canvas, 23¾ × 32". LACMA

Reality is merely an illusion, albeit a very persistent one.

(Albert Einstein, physicist and Nobel Prize winner)

When Albert Einstein suggested that not everything we see is real, he probably did not have art in mind. But artists readily understand his remark, because when they create a picture of real space on a flat surface they know they are creating an illusion. When we watch a magician perform a trick, we instinctively wonder how the magic was achieved. In this chapter we will reveal some of the secrets that artists rely upon to create the appearance of **three-dimensional** depth in a **two-dimensional** work of art.

The techniques artists use to imply depth—**value**, **space**, and **perspective**—evoke our past visual experiences and the way we see. Value, the lightness or darkness of a surface, emulates the effects of light and shadow, and can be used to suggest solidity. Artists have a variety of techniques based on the optics of vision that enable them to create the illusion of pictorial space. One of these is called atmospheric perspective, a method that mimics our visual perceptions of color, clarity, and form at a distance (see p. 89). Linear and isometric perspective (also explained on p. 89) are drawing methods that can express the idea of three-dimensional space on a two-dimensional surface. In this chapter we will introduce these methods of creating the illusion of space and discuss why some artists choose to use them.

In *The Treachery of Images*, Belgian **Surrealist** artist René Magritte (1898–1967) uses value and perspective to imply depth (**1.3.1**). The pipe is painted in varying values (light and dark tones), which creates the appearance of shadows that suggest depth. The top of the pipe bowl is composed of two concentric ellipses, which is how circles appear in perspective. We know what a real pipe looks like in real space, and Magritte understands our habits of visual perception. He paints a picture of a pipe that "feels" solid, but then playfully invites us to re-examine our habits of mind.

In this painting, Magritte tells us that painting is a visual trick. By writing "Ceci n'est pas une pipe" ("This is not a pipe"), Magritte wants us to recognize that what appears to be a pipe is not really a pipe: it is an illusion, nothing more than paint on a flat surface. Magritte

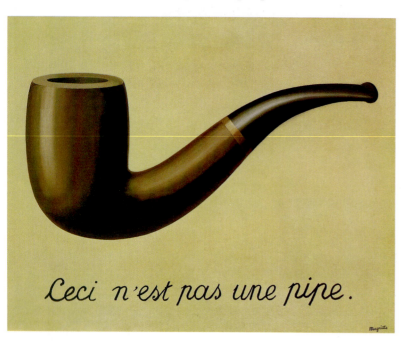

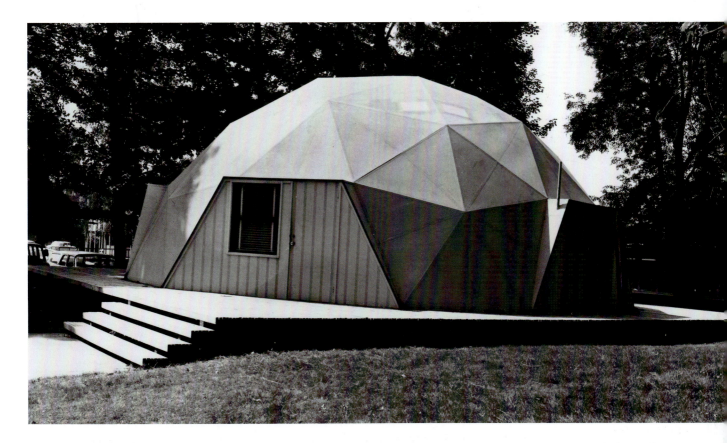

confirmed this when someone asked him about the painting once. He replied that it obviously was not a real pipe, as anyone who tried to fill it with tobacco would discover.

Value

Value refers to lightness and darkness. An artist's use of value can produce a sense of solidity and influence our mood. For example, detective movies of the 1940s were filmed in such dark tones that they had their own **style** called *film noir*, French for "black film." The serious mood of these mysteries was enhanced by the filmmaker's choice of dark values. Artists use dark and light values as tools for creating depth.

Artists learn to mimic the appearance of things by observing the effects of light as it illuminates a surface. The Art Dome, formerly used as a sculpture studio at Reed College in Portland, Oregon, demonstrates the effect of light on **planes** in varying locations (**1.3.2**). Many triangular flat planes make up this surface. Each of these planes has a different value, the relative degree of lightness or darkness of the plane

depending upon the amount of light shining on it. The light source (high and to the left of the dome here) hits some of the triangular planes of the Art Dome more directly than others. The planes that have a lighter value are facing the light source; the darker ones are facing away.

Value changes often occur gradually. If you look at the Art Dome, you will notice that the relative dark values increase as the planes get

1.3.2 Buckminster Fuller, Geodesic Dome (Art Dome), 1963–79, Reed College, Portland, Oregon

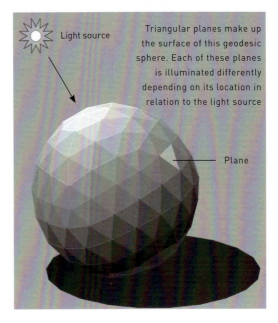

Light source

Triangular planes make up the surface of this geodesic sphere. Each of these planes is illuminated differently depending on its location in relation to the light source

Plane

1.3.3 Values and planes of a geodesic sphere

Surrealism, Surrealist: an artistic movement in the 1920s and later; its works were inspired by dreams and the subconscious
Style: a characteristic way in which an artist or group of artists uses visual language to give a work an identifiable form of visual expression
Plane: a flat surface, often implied in the composition

further away and face away from the light (see also **1.3.3**, p. 83). These changes occur on any object. There are subtle value changes even in a white object.

A value range refers to a series of different values. In the image of the geodesic sphere (see p. 83) there is a value range of black, white, and eight values of gray. Black and white are the values at the extreme ends of this value range.

Chiaroscuro

Chiaroscuro (Italian for "light-dark") is a method of applying value to a two-dimensional piece of artwork to create the illusion of a three-dimensional solid form (**1.3.4**). The illusion of solidity and depth in two dimensions can be achieved by using an approach devised by artists of the Italian **Renaissance**. Using a sphere as their model, Renaissance artists identified five distinct areas of light and shadow. A **highlight** marks the point where the object is most directly lit. This is most often depicted as bright white. From the highlight, moving toward the shadow, progressively less light is cast on the object until the point is reached where the surface faces away from the light. Here there is a more sudden transition to darker values, or core shadow. At the bottom of the sphere a lighter value is

1.3.4 Diagram of chiaroscuro

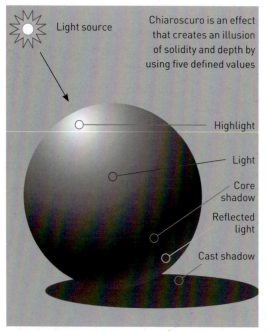

Chiaroscuro is an effect that creates an illusion of solidity and depth by using five defined values

Light source

Highlight

Light

Core shadow

Reflected light

Cast shadow

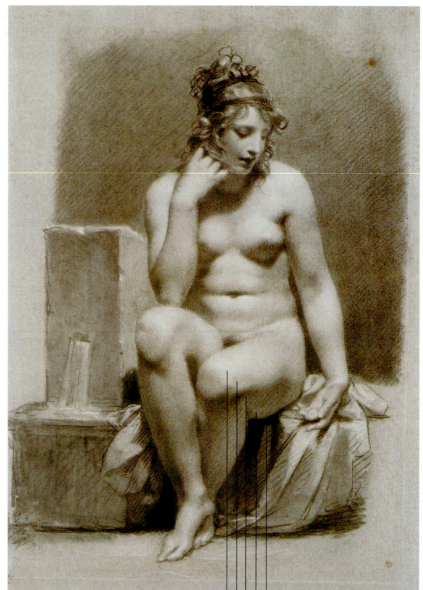

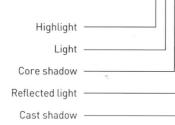

Highlight —————

Light —————

Core shadow —————

Reflected light —————

Cast shadow —————

1.3.5 Chiaroscuro graphic applied to Pierre-Paul Prud'hon, *Study for La Source*, c. 1801. Black and white chalk on blue paper, 21¾ × 15¼". Sterling and Francine Clark Art Institute, Williamstown, Massachusetts

produced by shadow mixed with light reflected from the surrounding environment. This lighter value defines the bottom edge of the sphere. In contrast, the sphere casts a shadow away from the direction of the light source. Near the edge of the cast shadow, as light from the surrounding environment increases, the shadow becomes lighter.

Renaissance: a period of cultural and artistic change in Europe from the fourteenth to the seventeenth century
Highlight: an area of lightest value in a work

In *Study for La Source*, the French artist Pierre-Paul Prud'hon (1758–1823) uses chiaroscuro to draw a female figure (**1.3.5**). If you look carefully at the figure's upper left leg (the leg on the viewer's right), you can see that the chiaroscuro is used just as it is in **1.3.4**. There is an area of highlight on the knee transitioning to the lighted thigh. Under the knee and thigh there is a strong core shadow: reflected light can be seen on the calf and the underside of the thigh. This light is accentuated by the dark cast shadow behind the calf. Prud'hon's use of black and white chalk on a gray paper allows him to accentuate the lightest and darkest areas, the chiaroscuro.

Dramatic and beautiful effects can be achieved through the use of chiaroscuro, especially if it is exaggerated. *The Calling of St. Matthew* by the Italian artist Caravaggio (1571–1610) uses strongly contrasting values to convert a quiet gathering into a pivotal and powerful event (**1.3.6**). The intense difference between lights and darks places extra **emphasis** on Christ's hand as he singles out Matthew, who points to himself in response. The light also frames Matthew and highlights the surprised looks of the others in the room as he is called to become one of Christ's disciples.

Emphasis: the principle of drawing attention to particular content in a work

1.3.6 Caravaggio, *The Calling of St. Matthew*, c. 1599–1600. Oil on canvas, 11'1" × 11'5". Contarelli Chapel, San Luigi dei Francesi, Rome, Italy

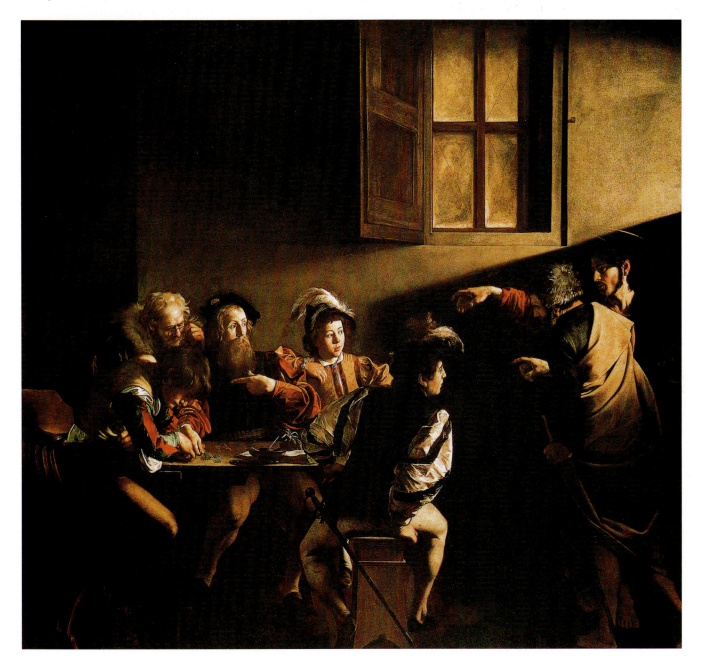

Hatching: the use of non-overlapping parallel lines to convey darkness or lightness

Medium (plural media): the material on or from which an artist chooses to make a work of art, for example canvas and oil paint, marble, engraving, video, or architecture

Cross-hatching: the use of overlapping parallel lines to convey darkness or lightness

Shape: a two-dimensional area, the boundaries of which are defined by lines or suggested by changes in color or value

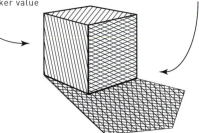

Increasing frequency of hatch lines implies darker value

Overlapping lines, or cross-hatching, intensifies the darkness of the value

1.3.7 Creating value using hatching and cross-hatching

1.3.8 Michelangelo, *Head of a Satyr, c.* 1520–30. Pen and ink on paper, 10⅝ × 7⅞". Musée du Louvre, Paris, France

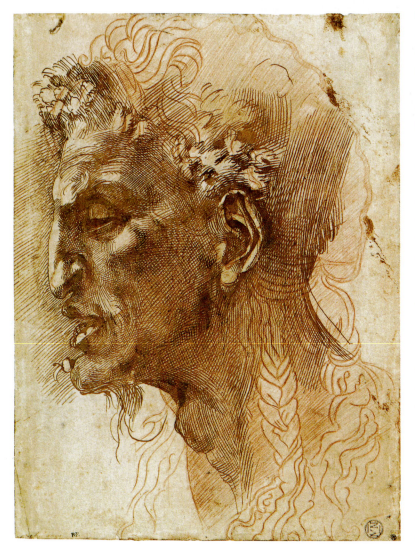

Hatching and Cross-Hatching

Artists also use a method called **hatching** to express value (**1.3.7**). Hatching consists of a series of lines, close to and parallel to each other. **Media** that demand a thin line, for example engraving or pen-and-ink drawing, do not allow much variation in the width of the line. Here an artist may choose hatching or **cross-hatching** (a variant of hatching in which the lines overlap) to suggest values that create a greater sense of form and depth.

The Italian artist Michelangelo (1475–1564) uses cross-hatching in his pen and ink drawing *Head of a Satyr* (**1.3.8**). Cross-hatching gives the face of the satyr solidity and depth. By building up layers of brown ink, Michelangelo overcomes the restrictions created by the thin line of the pen. For example, if we look carefully at the cheekbone of the satyr it appears to be jutting out toward us. This effect is created by hatching and cross-hatching. The bright white highlight uses no lines; the surrounding hatch lines define the transition from bright light to a darker value.

As we move our gaze downward and to the right of the highlight, we notice that a second layer of overlapping hatching lines intersects the diagonals bordering the highlight. Then, as we continue to scan downward and to the right, we see more layers of hatching lines crossing over the previous ones. As the hatching lines cross over and over, the value appears to get darker. Michelangelo communicates three-dimensional depth by using narrow and two-dimensional lines.

Space

Value is just one of a variety of techniques artists use to create a sense of depth and the illusion of space in a work of art. We will now explain some other methods.

Size, Overlapping, and Position

In a work of art, the size of one **shape** compared to another often suggests that the larger object is closer to us. Another way to create the illusion of depth is to overlap shapes. If one shape appears

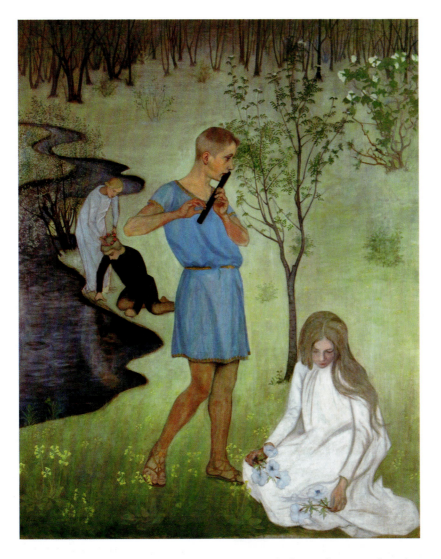

1.3.9 Beda Stjernschantz, *Pastoral (Primavera)*, 1897. Oil on canvas, 49⅝" × 41¾". K. H. Renlund Museum, Kokkola, Finland

to overlap another, the shape in front seems closer than the shape that is partially covered. Position in the **picture plane** is also an effective device for implying depth. A shape lower in the picture plane appears to be closer.

The Finnish artist Beda Stjernschantz (1865–1910) uses all of these devices—relative size, overlapping, and strategic positioning of shapes in the picture plane—to create an illusion of depth in her work *Pastoral (Primavera)* (**1.3.9**). The passive, idyllic scene draws us into a landscape that does not exist, but we feel a sense of depth because the artist makes it possible for us to be imaginatively transported there. In the painting there are two pairs of figures; one is larger than the other, which influences the viewer's understanding of space. The two figures in the center left of the image, who are positioned near a river, are notably smaller than those that dominate the lower right corner of the work.

We see the larger figures as closer because of this difference in size between the figural pairs.

Stjernschantz also implies depth by positioning the larger figure with the flute in a way that conceals the foot of one of the smaller figures. Similarly, we interpret the woman in the white dress as being closest to us because she partly obscures the left foot of the flute player. The artist further enhances the illusion of depth by placing the figure in white against the bottom of the work and setting the smaller pair of figures higher in the composition.

In using such **relative placement**, the artist invites us to saunter visually from the **foreground** (where the two largest figures are placed) to the middle ground (where the smaller group of figures is set), and continue on our visual journey along the softly curving river and into the beckoning woods in the **background** (the uppermost area of the work).

Picture plane: the surface of a painting or drawing
Relative placement: the arrangement of shapes or lines to form a visual relationship to each other in a design
Foreground: the part of a work depicted as nearest to the viewer
Background: the part of a work depicted furthest from the viewer's space, often behind the main subject matter

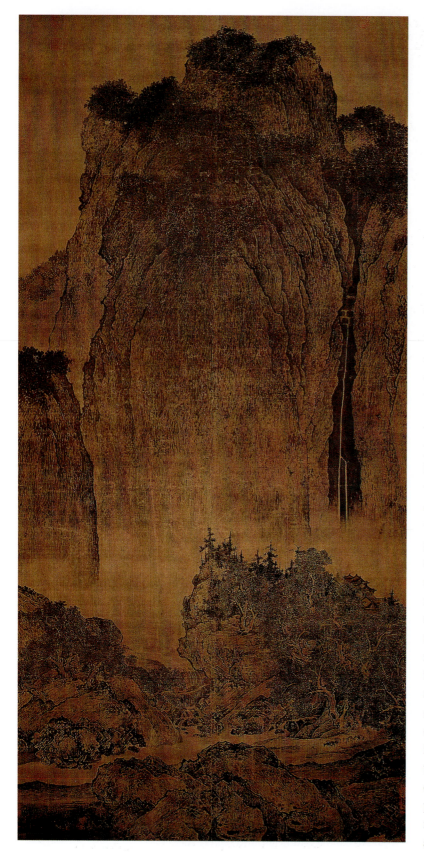

1.3.10 Fan Kuan, *Travelers among Mountains and Streams*, Northern Song Dynasty, 11th century. Hanging scroll, ink and colors on silk, 81¼ × 40⅝". National Palace Museum, Taipei, Taiwan

Even though there are no noticeable value differences between the groups, Stjernschantz uses enough placement strategy and size change to imply depth to a viewer.

Beda Stjernschantz was one of a group of artists known as the Finnish Symbolists, who were influential at the turn of the twentieth century. They were especially interested in landscape and the relationship between the arts, including music and what is known as synesthesia, where one of the body's senses experiences something that triggers an experience in another sense—hence the inclusion of the flute player in this painting.

Alternating Value and Texture

The illusion of depth in two dimensions is often influenced by the arrangement of value and texture. Artists intersperse value and visual texture to create a sense of **rhythm**. Look at *Travelers among Mountains and Streams* (**1.3.10**), by Chinese painter Fan Kuan (*c.* 990–1020). From the bottom up, we first confront a large boulder, followed by a light opening (a road with travelers), and then some trees and foliage clinging to a rocky landscape. After this section there is another light area, after which the values gradually darken as our view climbs the face of a mountain. Finally, the sky is lighter, although somewhat darkened, completing the alternating rhythm from bottom to top. Each area of light and dark occupies different amounts of space, making the design more interesting. We can also note the change in visual texture from bottom to top. The texture appears to be extremely rough and detailed near the bottom, with craggy rocks dominating the foreground, and the ripples on the stream close behind. From this point it progressively becomes less precise as the travelers (just discernible near the lower right corner) and twisted trees create a transition point into the mists at the foot of the towering mountain. As Fan Kuan's landscape rises, it also appears to recede behind the soft mist, then reappear with great vertical strength. The trees at the top of the scroll have lost the gnarled texture and now look soft and fuzzy as they crown the mountain crest. These visual layers create a sense

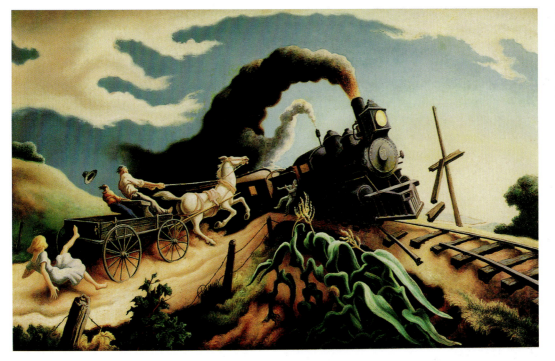

1.3.11 Thomas Hart Benton, *The Wreck of the Ole '97*, 1943. Egg tempera on gessoed masonite, 28½ × 44½". Hunter Museum of Art, Chattanooga, Tennessee

of depth as they accentuate differences in both value and texture.

Brightness and Color

Brightness and color can both be used to suggest depth in a work of art. Lighter areas seem to be closer as dark areas appear to recede. This is especially true of color. For example, we are more likely to think that a green that is very pure and intense is closer to us than a darker green. American painter Thomas Hart Benton (1889–1975) used brightness and color to create and manipulate our sense of distance in his painting *The Wreck of the Ole '97* (**1.3.11**). Benton wanted the viewer to be a witness to one of the most notorious train disasters in American history, in which several people died. In the green areas we see the bright pure greens come forward as the darker, less intense greens fall away. The greens in the lower central portion of the work are more intense than the greens on the far left. Because we perceive color that is more intense as being closer, this difference in color **intensity** helps us to feel that we are *just* at enough distance to witness the terrible train wreck without becoming another of its casualties. Yet by painting the engine steaming ahead, at an angle that suggests it is about to hit the broken rail in the foreground and head

straight out of the picture, hurtling inevitably toward us, Benton simultaneously manages to convey a fearful sense of danger.

Perspective

Artists, architects, and designers who wish to suggest the illusion of depth on a two-dimensional surface use perspective. They have the choice of several ways to do this, of which three are the most common. **Atmospheric perspective** modifies value, color, and texture to create the sense that some parts of an image are situated further away than others. **Isometric perspective** uses diagonal parallels to communicate depth, while **linear perspective** relies on a system where lines appear to converge at points in space. All these forms of perspective tap into some of the ways we see the world and think about space.

Atmospheric Perspective

Some artists use atmospheric perspective to create the illusion of depth. Distant objects lack contrast, detail, and sharpness of focus because the air that surrounds us is not completely transparent. The effect makes objects with strong color take on a blue-gray middle value as they get further away: the atmosphere progressively veils a scene as the distance increases. Contemporary

Rhythm: the regular or ordered repetition of elements in the work

Intensity: the relative clarity of color in its purest raw form, demonstrated through luminous or muted variations

Atmospheric perspective: use of shades of color and clarity to create the illusion of depth. Closer objects have warmer tones and clear outlines, while objects set further away are cooler and become hazy

Isometric perspective: a system using diagonal parallel lines to communicate depth

Linear perspective: a system using converging imaginary sight lines to create the illusion of depth

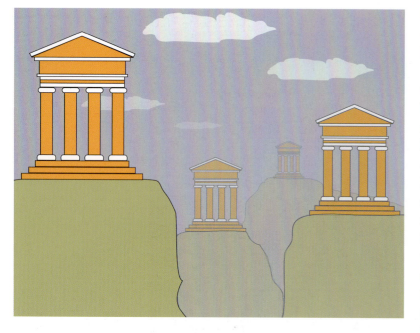

1.3.12 The effects of atmospheric perspective

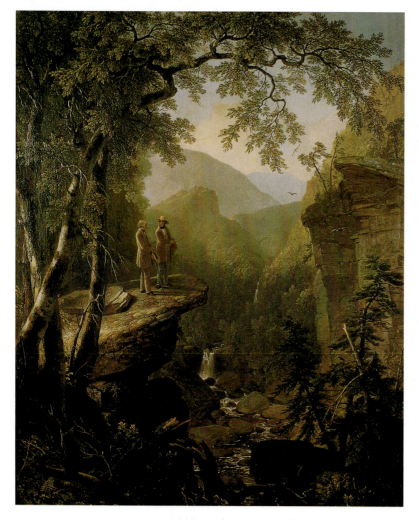

1.3.13 Asher Brown Durand, *Kindred Spirits*, 1849. Oil on canvas, 44 × 36″. Crystal Bridges Museum of American Art, Bentonville, Arkansas

filmmakers use this atmospheric effect to give the illusion of great depth, just as traditional artists have always done.

In **1.3.12** the Greek temple to the left appears to be closer to the viewer than the other temples because its colors are brighter and its shape is more sharply defined. The smallest temple lacks detail and is tinged blue-gray, making it seem the furthest away. American Asher Brown Durand (1796–1886) used comparable effects in his painting *Kindred Spirits* (**1.3.13**). The trees in the foreground are detailed and bright green, but as the trees recede into the landscape behind the two figures, they become a lighter gray and increasingly out of focus. Lines and shapes also become less distinct as the illusion of distance increases. By using atmospheric perspective, Durand conveys an impression of the vastness of the American landscape.

Isometric Perspective

Isometric perspective arranges parallel lines diagonally in a work to give a sense of depth. The word isometric derives from the Greek meaning "equal measure." The system has been used by artists in China for more than a thousand years. It was particularly suitable for painting on scrolls, which can be examined only in sections. Since Chinese landscape painters were never really interested in portraying space from a single viewing point—they preferred to convey multiple viewpoints simultaneously—isometric perspective was their chosen technique to convey the illusion of space in the structural lines of architecture and other rectilinear objects.

A section from the painting *The Qianlong Emperor's Southern Inspection Tour, Scroll Six: Entering Suzhou and the Grand Canal* by Xu Yang shows this system in action (**1.3.14**). The parallel diagonal lines that define the small L-shaped building in the center right of the work suggest a three-dimensional object (**1.3.15**). Xu Yang, a Chinese artist working in the 1770s, uses this method to give the architecture along the Grand Canal the illusion of depth. This method of implying depth is not "realistic" according to the Western tradition, but the artist makes use of other spatial devices to help us understand how the space is structured. For example, the

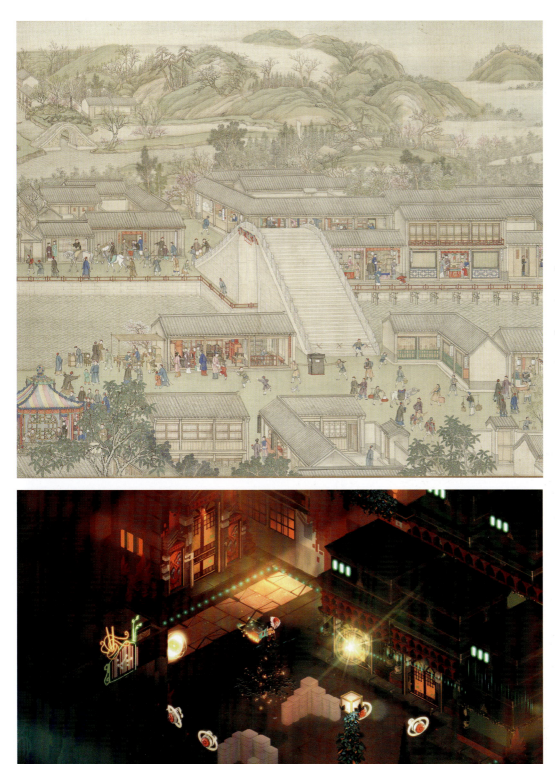

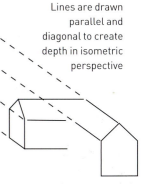

1.3.14 Xu Yang, *The Qianlong Emperor's Southern Inspection Tour, Scroll Six: Entering Suzhou and the Grand Canal*, Qing Dynasty, 1770 (detail). Hand scroll, ink and color on silk, 2'3⅛" × 65'4½". Metropolitan Museum of Art, New York

Lines are drawn parallel and diagonal to create depth in isometric perspective

1.3.15 Graphic detailing isometric perspective in scroll image

1.3.16 Supergiant Games, screenshot from *Transistor*, 2014. Art Director, Jen Zee

diminishing size of the trees as they recede into the distance reinforces the sense of depth.

Isometric perspective is now common in contemporary computer graphics as well. The computer and video console game *Transistor* (**1.3.16**) is designed to express depth using a perspective method similar to the one Xu Yang used in 1770. The designers have created the architecture of the game with parallel diagonal lines so that the playing area consists of small rectangular graphic images that are known as tiles. The tiles allow uniform objects to remain the same size, yet as the objects are moved around the game environment they still imply depth. The game designers' choice of isometric perspective allows players to move from level to level and space to space without distortion because the individual tiles remain the same size.

Linear Perspective

Linear perspective is a mathematical system that uses lines to create the illusion of depth in a two-dimensional artwork. (The "lines" can be **actual lines**, for example of buildings, or **implied lines** of figures or shapes.) The linear perspective systems used by artists are based on observation of space in the world we see around us: the two sides of a straight railway line or road appear to converge as they recede into the distance, even though in reality they are parallel.

Origins and History

Like many ideas in human history, linear perspective was developed with knowledge acquired over centuries. Mozi, a Chinese philosopher working in the fifth century BCE; Alhazen, an Arab mathematician from around the year 1000; and Leon Battista Alberti (1404–1472), an Italian Renaissance architect, each contributed ideas that helped artists to understand light and its properties more fully. Knowledge of light's properties led other Renaissance artists to use a projection device called a camera obscura (Latin for "dark room") to explore the possibilities of naturalistic illusion and the re-creation of reality. The device consisted of a small dark box, which by means of a little pinhole would conduct sunlight through the hole and allow a real, full-color, upside-down image of the objects outside the device to be

1.3.17a The Baptistery, Florence, Italy

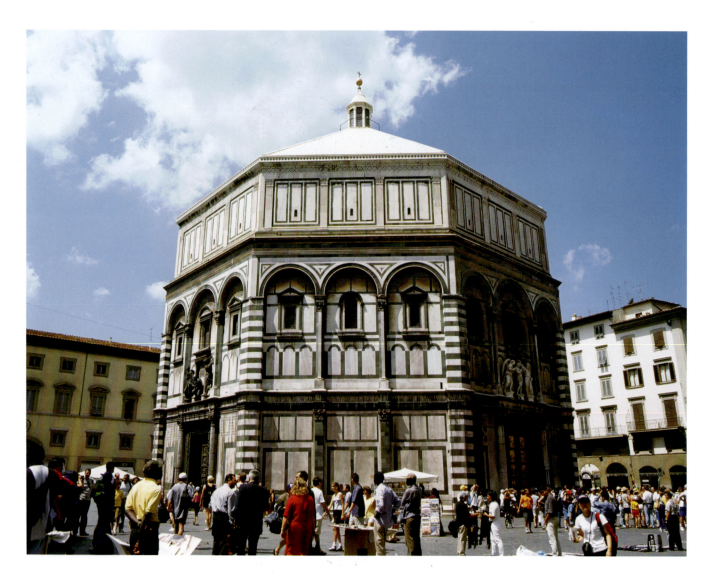

projected with light onto a surface. The artist could then draw the projected image, or trace it directly onto paper or canvas. Images created using this device revealed recurring ways in which lines could be arranged that influenced the artist Filippo Brunelleschi (1377–1446) to create a practical way of expressing the theories of depth using linear perspective.

Because Brunelleschi, as an architect, was interested in the realistic representation of buildings, he began to work with ideas about perspective and the idea that light enters the eye. He combined this with use of the camera obscura to prove that reality could be re-created in art using a system of lines. It had been demonstrated that an image projected onto a surface in a camera obscura could be traced to produce a convincing illusion of depth, but this did not explain exactly how the illusion of depth was created. Brunelleschi took this discovery one step further by formulating rules of linear perspective to allow an artist to depict realistically something observed without the aid of a camera obscura. To prove his point, Brunelleschi painted an image of the Florence Baptistery (**1.3.17a**), applying his rules, on a polished piece of silver. He then drilled a small hole in the silver plate so that a viewer could look through the back of it and, holding a mirror up in front of it, could see the painted image of the Baptistery reflected in the mirror (**1.3.17b**). The viewer could then compare the degree of realism of the painting with the real Baptistery itself to confirm that Brunelleschi's rules worked. Although many artists had effectively approximated linear perspective, Brunelleschi was the first to define it formally as a practical system.

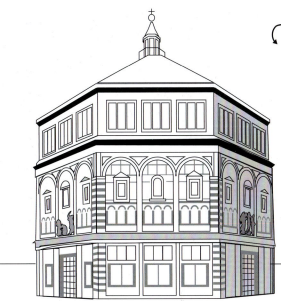

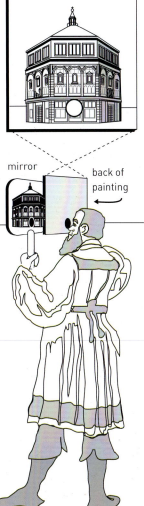

front of painting

mirror

back of painting

1.3.17b Brunelleschi's proof of the accuracy of linear perspective

Brunelleschi's Proof:
A viewer would look through a hole in the back of his painting of the Baptistery while holding a mirror in front to reflect it. When the mirror was removed, and the viewer could see the building, it revealed how accurately the architecture could be rendered using the system.

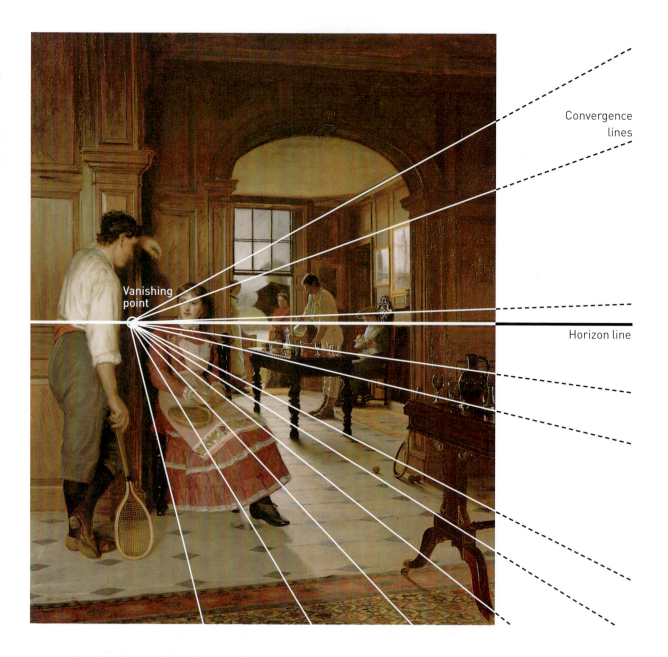

Convergence
lines

Vanishing
point

Horizon line

1.3.18 The effect of convergences: Edith Hayllar, *A Summer Shower*, 1883. Oil on panel, 21 × 17⅜". Private collection

Brunelleschi's discovery became for hundreds of years a standard systematic process for creating an impression of realistic depth. The British artist Edith Hayllar (1860–1948) exhibited many works at the Royal Academy (a rare honor for a woman artist at the time) between 1882 and 1897. The enhanced photograph of her painting *A Summer Shower* shows the basis for linear perspective (**1.3.18**). The converging lines represent planes that are parallel to each other in reality. Notice how, if we were to draw lines from the right side of the image and continue them until they intersect, these parallel lines would appear to converge on one single point in front of the male tennis

player on the left of the painting. This is the **vanishing point**. These converging parallel lines are also known as **orthogonals**; the artist uses them here to create a composition that reflects the orderly life of upper-middle-class Victorian England.

There are a number of variations of linear perspective—one-point, two-point, and multiple-point—depending on the effect the artist wants to achieve. These formal approaches to conveying a sense of depth are important tools, so we will now look at each one in some detail to see how they function and the different kinds of effects they produce.

1.3.19 Applying one-point perspective technique

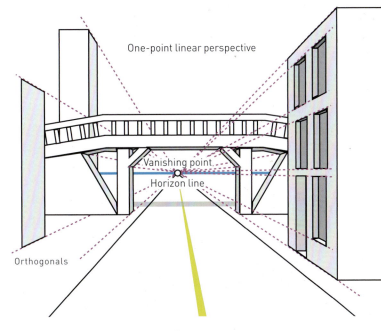

One-point linear perspective

Vanishing point

Horizon line

Orthogonals

Vanishing point: the point in a work of art at which imaginary sight lines appear to converge, suggesting depth

Orthogonals: in perspective systems, imaginary sightlines extending from forms to the vanishing point

One-point perspective: a perspective system with a single vanishing point on the horizon

Fresco: a technique where the artist paints onto freshly applied plaster. From the Italian *fresco*, "fresh"

1.3.20 Use of one-point perspective: Masaccio, *Trinity, c.* 1425–26. Fresco, 21'10½" × 10'4⅞". Santa Maria Novella, Florence, Italy

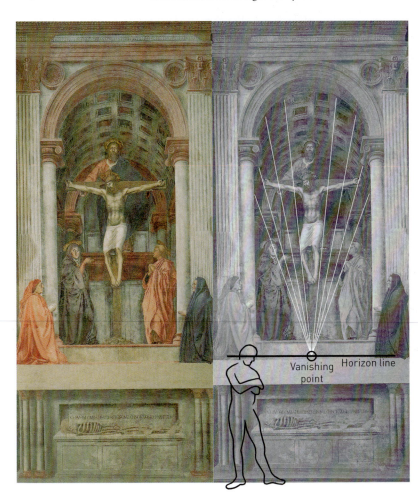

Vanishing point

Horizon line

One-Point Perspective

Brunelleschi created his painting of the Florence Baptistery using one-point perspective, but the **one-point perspective** system has some limitations. Although the system makes it possible to represent "real" space, certain rules have to be followed. Since one-point perspective relies on a single vanishing point, the scene must be directly in front of the artist and receding. The effect is something like standing on an empty highway facing an underpass (**1.3.19**). The sides of the road and the inside of the underpass appear to follow converging paths to a single point on the horizon. But if you redirect your gaze to the right or left of the underpass, the edges of the roadway and underpass are out of direct sight and it is not as easy to see the recession of space.

One of the first artists to use one-point perspective was the Italian Masaccio (1401–1428). In his **fresco** of the *Trinity*, Masaccio places the horizon line, an imaginary line that mimics the horizon, at the viewer's eye level (note the figure) and centers the vanishing point in the middle of that line (**1.3.20**). The horizon line represents our eye level and is the basis for the setting-out of a perspective drawing. The orthogonals create an illusion that the background is an architectural setting. The end result is an effective illusion of depth on a two-dimensional surface that must have amazed visitors at the church of Santa Maria Novella in Florence, Italy. Masaccio's work was innovative for its time and influenced other significant artists of the Renaissance, including Michelangelo.

Gateway to Art: Raphael, *The School of Athens*
Perspective and the Illusion of Depth

In *The School of Athens* Raphael combines one-point perspective and two-point perspective in one composition (**1.3.21a** and **1.3.21b**). The figure in the foreground is leaning against an object set at an angle that is not perpendicular and parallel to the rest of the architectural setting. Consequently, it cannot depend on the central vanishing point that has been determined following the rules of one-point perspective, or it will be distorted. Raphael deals with this situation by introducing two additional vanishing points. Notice that both of these fall on the horizon line, following the established rules of perspective (vanishing points must fall on the horizon line). One vanishing point is positioned to the left of the central vanishing point that anchors the architecture, and the right vanishing point is outside of the picture. The block in the center is the only object in the composition that uses these two vanishing points, because the viewer is not perpendicular or parallel to it. Since it is turned at an angle, Raphael had to integrate another level of perspective into the work. All of the objects and architectural spaces depicted in this painting rely on one of these two perspective points.

1.3.21a Raphael, *The School of Athens*, 1510–11. Fresco, 16'8" × 25'. Stanza della Segnatura, Vatican City, Italy

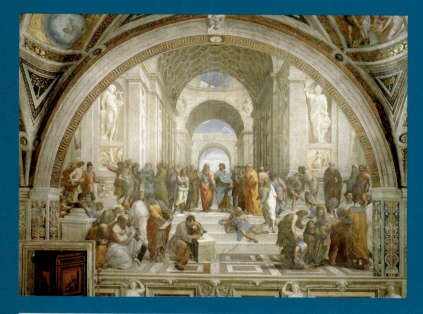

1.3.21b Applying two-point perspective: detail from Raphael, *The School of Athens*

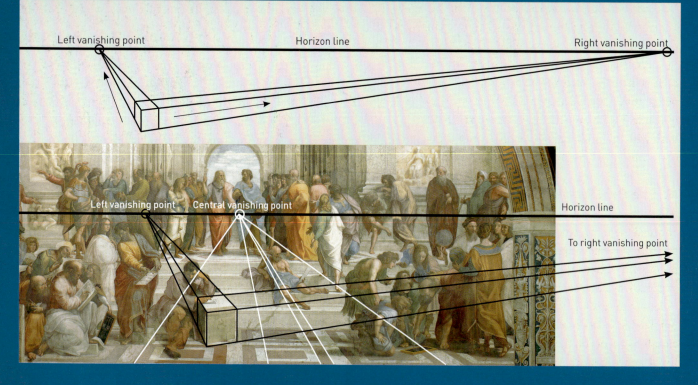

Vanishing point ← Horizon line Vanishing point

1.3.22 Cone of vision

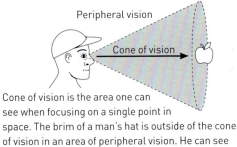

Peripheral vision

Cone of vision

Cone of vision is the area one can
see when focusing on a single point in
space. The brim of a man's hat is outside of the cone
of vision in an area of peripheral vision. He can see
things in this area only if he moves his eyes.

1.3.23 Three-point
perspective, bird's-eye
view: M. C. Escher,
Ascending and Descending,
March 1960. Woodcut,
14 × 11¼". The M. C.
Escher Company, The
Netherlands

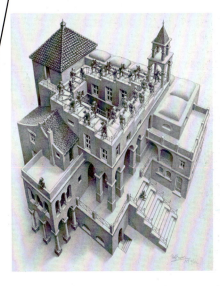

Vanishing point

Two-Point Perspective

The one-point perspective system worked for
Masaccio because his composition relied on the
viewer standing directly in front of the vanishing
point. But if the vanishing point is not directly
(or near directly) in front of a viewer, or if the
objects in the work are not all parallel, one-point
perspective does not create a believable illusion
of depth. The Italian artist Raphael (1483–1520)
dealt with this problem in his famous painting
The School of Athens (**1.3.21a** and **1.3.21b**).

Multiple-Point Perspective

As artists discovered that linear perspective
afforded them many new possibilities for
creating illusions of space, they began to expand
on the idea of multiple-point perspective
systems. Any object that exists in our cone of
vision—the area we can see without moving
our head or eyes—can usually be depicted using
vanishing points on the horizon line (**1.3.22**).
But if we are looking at an object from a position

other than ground level, then we will need points
away from the horizon line and other variations
on perspective.

Objects and spaces that have right angles
make it easy to work out where vanishing points
should be: we can use one-point perspective.
Unfortunately, many objects are made up of
multiple angles that need even more vanishing

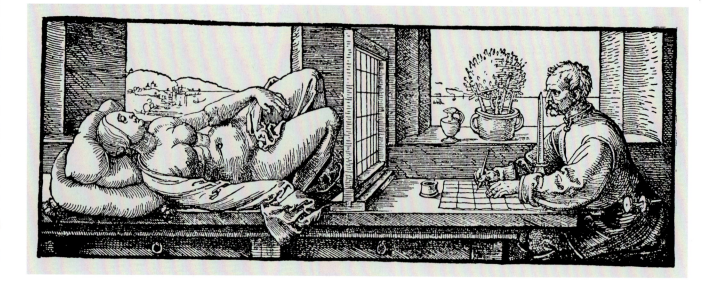

1.3.24 Albrecht Dürer, *Draftsman Drawing a Recumbent Woman*, 1525. Woodcut, 3 × 8¾". Graphische Sammlung Albertina, Vienna, Austria

1.3.25 Wonder Woman, Superman and Batman, pages from *Trinity*: Volume 1. ™ and © DC Comics

points. As more of these are incorporated into a design, the artist can more readily reflect the complexities of the real world.

The most common multiple-point perspective system is **three-point perspective**: here a vanishing point is placed above or below the horizon line to accommodate a high or low angle of observation. Whether this third vanishing point is above or below the horizon depends on whether the viewer has a worm's-eye (looking up) or bird's-eye (looking down) view. Dutch graphic artist M. C. Escher (1898–1972) uses a third vanishing point in *Ascending and Descending*; we can see three distinct vanishing

points (**1.3.23**, see p. 97). Two of the vanishing points are placed on the horizon line, but one is well below it. This gives us a bird's-eye view of the structure that allows us to see its sides while looking down on it as if from above.

Foreshortening

Foreshortening results when the rules of perspective are applied to represent unusual points of view. The German artist Albrecht Dürer (1471–1528), in his **woodcut** *Draftsman Drawing a Recumbent Woman*, portrays an artist at work drawing a figure (**1.3.24**). At this

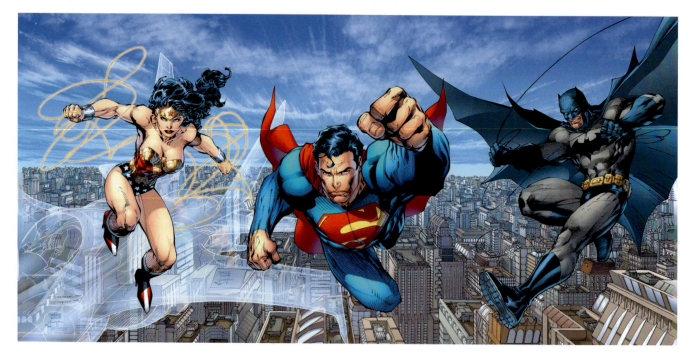

oblique angle, the usual proportions of different parts of the body do not apply. The artist has a fixed lens or aperture in front of him to make sure he always views from the same point. As he looks through the gridded window, he can see the coordinates, in relation to the grid, of the different parts of the model's body. He can then transfer those coordinates onto the similar grid marked on the piece of paper in front of him. The gridded screen in the illustration helps the artist to translate a three-dimensional form into a foreshortened two-dimensional composition.

An illustration of Superman for DC Comics also illustrates foreshortening (**1.3.25**). The figure of Superman is oriented so that his fist is placed in the extreme foreground, with the rest of the body receding away from the reader back into space. The artist makes the fist on the right side larger than Superman's head, exaggerating the depth. The entire figure is vertically shortened, compared to a frontal standing position, because of the oblique angle from which we are viewing the character. Like the linear perspective in the city below, foreshortening has the effect of grabbing our interest. In this work we feel as though Superman is blasting toward us through the air over downtown Metropolis, on his way to save the day.

Active Learning Exercises

1. Value is the relative lightness or darkness of a plane and is used to distinguish one area of an image from another. By carefully allocating light and dark values so that they imitate the light and shadow that we see in real space, artists create the illusion of depth in two dimensions. Photographers who work in black and white also have to try to anticipate how light and shadow will combine for optimum results. Using a black-and-white photograph as your source, pick out five different values of gray (not including pure white and pure black) and create a value scale. The scale should have five 1-in. × 1-in. squares that you will fill, each with a different gray value. You can achieve this either by cutting out different gray values from pieces of gray paper of varying shades; completely filling in each of the squares with a pencil; or by using cross-hatching with a pen. Arrange the scale vertically, with the lightest value at the top, and gradually get darker as you go down. What does this exercise reveal about the photograph? Are there more than five gray values?

2. When two or more shapes are placed in a design, depth can be implied by changing the relative size of each shape, overlapping them, or placing them higher or lower in the space. Using black paper, cut out a series of simple geometric shapes: circles, squares, triangles, etc. There should be at least two of each shape, and some of different sizes. Arrange these shapes on your page and describe which is closest and which is furthest away. What makes the closest object seem closest? Furthest? Can you think of a way to make the objects all seem the same distance from the viewer?

3. Architectural drawings using linear perspective have a great deal in common with architectural photography. During the Renaissance, the use of a camera obscura helped lead to the development of linear perspective by means of a single pinhole that allowed light into the box of the device. The images that artists created from this process revealed single points, called vanishing points, where parallel lines (orthogonals) appeared to converge. You can see the same effect in architectural photography because, like the pinhole in the camera obscura, the modern camera relies on a single lens. Either shoot your own picture of a building or find an existing photograph and print it on regular printer paper. Using a marker or highlighter, draw directly on the printed page and illustrate where the vanishing point(s) and orthogonals are. Since orthogonals appear to converge at a vanishing point, you should be able to draw a series of lines over the diagonal lines in the photograph until you find a point where they all appear to converge. How many vanishing points did you find? Since most vanishing points are on the horizon line, is this line obvious? Compare your findings with others.

Images Related to 1.3:
Implied Depth: Value and Space

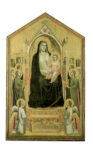

3.2.27 Giotto, *Virgin and Child Enthroned*, c. 1310, p. 410

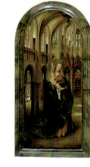

1.7.4 Jan van Eyck, *Madonna in a Church*, 1437–38, p.148

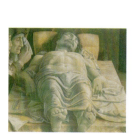

4.3.3 Andrea Mantegna, *Dead Christ*, c. 1480, p. 590

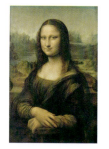

0.0.11 Leonardo da Vinci, *Mona Lisa*, 1503–6, p. 35

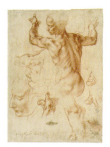

2.1.13 Michelangelo, *Studies for the Libyan Sibyl*, 1510–11, p. 206

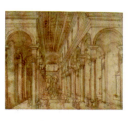

1.1.2a Giovanni Dosio, *Church of Santo Spirito at Florence*, c. 1576–90, p. 50

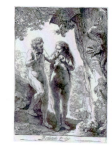

2.3.10 Rembrandt van Rijn, *Adam and Eve*, 1638, p. 237

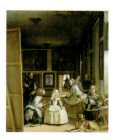

1.10.11 Diego de Silva y Velázquez, *Las Meninas*, c. 1656, p. 190

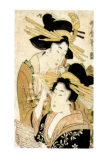

3.3.22 Kitagawa Utamaro, *Two Courtesans*, 2nd half of 18th century, p. 428

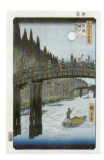

1.8.10 Ando Hiroshige, "Riverside Bamboo Market, Kyōbashi", 1857, p. 164

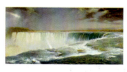

0.0.2 Frederic Edwin Church, *Niagara*, 1857, p. 27

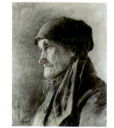

2.1.11 Léon Augustin Lhermitte, *An Elderly Peasant Woman*, c. 1878, p. 205

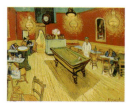

1.4.26 Vincent van Gogh, *The Night Café*, 1888, p. 114

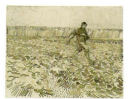

2.1.19 Vincent van Gogh, *Sower with Setting Sun*, 1888, p. 210

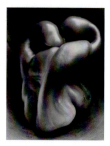

2.8.12 Edward Weston, *Pepper No. 30*, 1930, p. 326

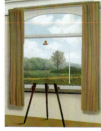

4.5.12 René Magritte, *The Human Condition*, 1933, p. 619

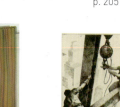

1.1.14 James Allen, *The Connectors*, 1934, p. 57

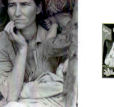

1.5.13f Dorothea Lange, *Migrant Mother*, 1936, p. 127

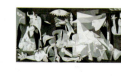

4.7.5 Pablo Picasso, *Guernica*, 1937, p. 638

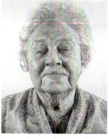

4.5.14 Chuck Close, *Fanny/Fingerpainting*, 1985, p. 621

1.4

Color

The first colors that made a strong impression on me were bright, juicy green, white, carmine red, black and yellow ochre. These memories go back to the third year of my life. I saw these colors on various objects which are no longer as clear in my mind as the colors themselves.

(Vasily Kandinsky, Russian painter)

Color is the most vivid element of art and design. By its very essence, color attracts our attention and excites our emotion. Just as personality and mood vary from one person to the next, our perceptions of color are personal and subjective. Few other phenomena touch our innermost feelings as deeply and directly.

Color and Light

Scientists understand a great deal about how we perceive color, although, because it is a complicated element, there are dimensions of color that are not yet fully explained. But the science of color is the best place to begin to understand the role of color in art.

Science tells us that we cannot perceive color without light. Light consists of energy that travels in waves, much as water forms waves. The distance between the peak of each wave of this energy is its **wavelength**. If white or normal daylight passes through a **prism** we see that it is composed of constituent colors of light, which have different wavelengths (**1.4.1**). Therefore, the colors of light make up the spectrum of potential visible colors. But if we need light in order to perceive color, and daylight is white, how is it that we can see individual colors (blue, red, and so on) when we look at particular objects? Our perception of the color of objects is the result of the interaction between light and something in the surface of an object that we call **pigment**. Light is necessary to activate the color of an object, but light alone does not determine the color that we perceive. This depends on light and pigment.

Color and Pigment

We see a blue sweater as blue only when light strikes. If light consists of all the colors of the spectrum, not just blue, how is it that we perceive only the blue portion of the spectrum when we look at the sweater? This occurs because the colors we see in objects are those portions of the light spectrum that a surface fails to absorb, and reflects instead. So, if the surface of the sweater contains blue pigment, when white light reaches that surface, all the other colors in the spectrum are absorbed by the pigment, and only the blue is reflected back. Physiologists explain that our visual perception of reflected colors begins when

1.4.1 White light can be separated into the visible spectrum using a prism

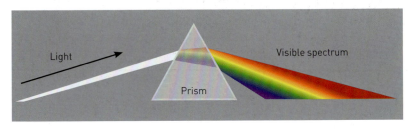

Light

Visible spectrum

Prism

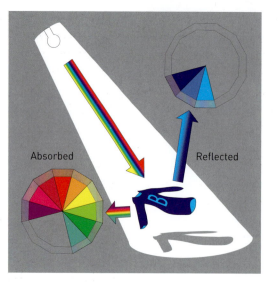

1.4.2 White light reaches a blue object and blue light is reflected

Additive color: the colors produced from light
Binder: a substance that makes pigments adhere to a surface
Subtractive color: the colors produced from pigment
Hue: general classification of a color; the distinctive characteristics of a color as seen in the visible spectrum, such as green or red

the reflected color excites the nerve cells that line the back of our eyes. These nerve signals are processed and interpreted as color in the brain. Thus, when we see someone wearing a blue sweater, the blue we see is the portion of the spectrum that is reflected back to our eyes; the rest of the light is absorbed by the sweater (**1.4.2**).

Subtractive Color

Although light and pigment are both essential for the perception of color, when colors of light are mixed together, the result is not the same as when we mix colors of pigment. Imagine that we take two flashlights with different colored lenses. If we shine the two colored beams of light onto a white surface, the resulting color tends to be lighter than the original two. Because the lightness of the color created by combining two colors of light increases, this mixing of colors of light is termed **additive** (and adding more and more color will eventually lead to white light).

Although our perception of the colors of pigment depends on the reflection of the colors of light to our eyes, when we mix pigments together, they do not behave in the same way as when we mix colors of light. Since paint is made of pigment mixed with a **binder**, if two different-colored paints, containing different-coloured pigments, are mixed, the result is not lighter but tends to be darker. This is called

subtractive color because in such a pigment mixture, more of the spectrum is absorbed (or subtracted) from the light that hits the pigmented surface.

Color Wheels

Because when we mix colors of light—such as the light mixtures used by designers in televisions and computer monitors, or two beams of differently colored light from flashlights—the results are different from when we mix colors of pigment (such as paint), artists are faced with many ways of mixing color to achieve different effects. In addition, our eyes can perceive a total of 360 colors. These two factors, taken together, mean that predicting and managing the effects of color mixing is often an important aspect of an artist's work. For several centuries, artists have been able to rely on a useful tool known as a color wheel to help them control the complexity of color.

A color wheel displays important information about **hue** relationships. It is a kind of color "map" that allows us to assess the attributes of hues as they relate to each other. There are many color wheels that chart color combinations, but three basic wheels are most commonly used. The first two that we will study show the fundamental hues of pigment-based color, that is, the color that we associate with colored objects. These two wheels are maps or models of subtractive color combinations. The third color wheel maps out the ways that colors of light combine with one another.

There are different color wheels for the hues of light and the hues of pigment because the two types of hues react and are perceived independently of each other. As we have seen, when pigments are mixed, the result is referred to as subtractive color, as the blended hues tend to be less intense than in their original, unmixed state. When colored light is blended, the resulting hues tend to be lighter, and this is referred to as additive color. We will start by discussing color wheels used to manage the mixing of hues of pigment as they occur in white light (see p. 103). In this text we

1.4.3 Traditional twelve-step color wheel using "artist's colors"

1.4.4 Vasily Kandinsky, *Yellow-Red-Blue*, 1925. Oil on canvas, 50⅜ × 79¼". Musée National d'Art Moderne, Centre Georges Pompidou, Paris, France

describe subtractive color only as it behaves in white light.

Since the eighteenth century, scientists and color theorists have produced color wheels that artists have used (and continue to use today) to manage the mixing of paint and any other pigment-based **medium**. The hues of this color wheel are the building blocks of most color combinations (**1.4.3**). "Artist's colors" are the traditional **primary colors**—red, yellow, blue. They are called primary because they cannot

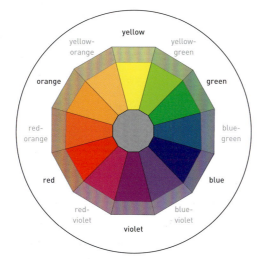

be created by mixing any other two colors. The **secondary colors** can be produced by mixing two primary colors. They are the hues orange (that can be created by blending red and yellow), green (a blend of yellow and blue), and violet (a blend of red and blue). In this color wheel, the secondary colors are located between the primary ones because they naturally fall between them in the visible spectrum. The remaining hues in the wheel are called **tertiary colors** and can be created by blending a primary and a secondary color: for example, red-violet is (as its name suggests) a blend of red and violet.

One work that uses the traditional combination of primary red, yellow, and blue is a painting by the Russian artist Vasily Kandinsky (1866–1944) (**1.4.4**). Appropriately titled *Yellow-Red-Blue*, this work utilizes the basic colors of the traditional color wheel, along with black and white. Kandinsky advocated the use of these fundamental elements to simplify and celebrate art and design in their purest sense. Since no primary can be mixed from any other two colors in this wheel, the three he chose exemplified the purest and simplest color available.

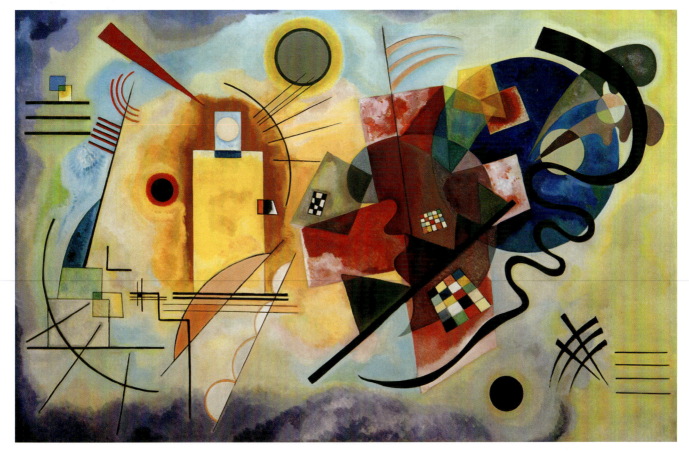

If you look again at the color wheel in figure **1.4.3** (p. 103), you will notice the gray in the center. In theory, a perfect subtractive mix of the primary colors of red, yellow, and blue should result in a perfect black, which absorbs all the colors of the spectrum. In practice, however, if an artist mixes the primaries as they are arranged on this color wheel, the result is not black but a brownish gray. This is not a problem for artists who are accustomed to working with this color wheel; their past experience with color and their knowledge of their own personal preferences enable them to create the colors they need. But for graphic designers working on materials that need to be printed using layers of transparent printing inks in a very exact way, it is necessary to be able to create more accurate color mixtures that conform to universal rules. Modern research has therefore provided a new set of primary colors that are better suited to producing specific blended colors when these are printed.

Although the colors red, yellow, and blue have traditionally been accepted as the basic hues of pigment, scientific discoveries in physics have provided a new set of primaries that can be combined into a subtractive mix that enables designers to produce a real ("true") black for printing purposes. If we mix these primaries—cyan (a slightly greenish light blue), magenta (a pinkish light violet), and yellow—their color combination results in black (**1.4.5**). The entire spectrum of white light is absorbed (subtracted) in the combination of cyan, magenta, and yellow pigments, so not a single segment of the spectrum is reflected.

Like Kandinsky, the contemporary Argentine-born artist Analia Saban (b. 1980) also works with primary colors to distill art and design to their purest state. But in her 2008 work *Layer Painting (CMY): Flowers* (**1.4.7**), Saban wants to "debunk the mysteries of contemporary art." To do this she has adopted the scientifically proven primary combination of cyan, magenta, and yellow to paint a still life of flowers. In so doing, Saban challenges traditional beliefs about color. Red, considered a primary color since the eighteenth century, can now be mixed from the two colors magenta and yellow. Although Saban is questioning ideas about color in painting, the

CMY primaries are already the accepted colors used in most visual communication design and commercial printing (**1.4.6**).

These two subtractive color wheels are used to manage the mixing of pigments and to help artists predict the results (**1.4.5** and **1.4.6**). They

1.4.5 Cyan, Magenta, Yellow (CMY) pigment twelve-color wheel with black center

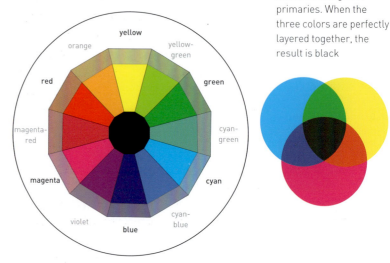

1.4.6 Subtractive color mixtures using CMY primaries. When the three colors are perfectly layered together, the result is black

1.4.7 Analia Saban, *Layer Painting (CMY): Flowers*, 2008. Acrylic and screen printing ink on canvas, 36 × 36 × 1½". Thomas Solomon Gallery

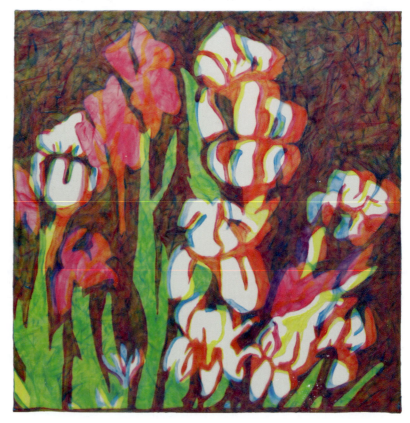

Matrix: an origination point, such as a woodblock, from which a print is derived
Complementary colors: colors opposite one another on the color wheel

are useful for painters who mix paints, graphic designers who design for the mixing of printing inks, and for anyone making color combinations of any pigment-based medium. But subtractive color wheels are not useful for artists who work with the colors of light. For this, an additive color wheel is required.

Additive color is not generated from pigment, like the traditional or subtractive hue combinations, but from light. For example, an artist who creates an installation consisting of different colored lights in a room painted white needs to understand how the colors of the different lights combine. Digital artists use the color combinations of red, green, and blue that make up the **matrix** for color in computer monitors. Although white light contains the entire spectrum, it is useful to divide light into individual colors so that we can manage combinations of the colors of light as simply as possible (**1.4.8**). The primary hues of light are red, green, and blue. When colors of light are mixed, they react differently than those in pigment. We call the mixture of colors in light additive color, because each time a color of light is added to a mixture it gets lighter, until eventually it results in white (**1.4.8**). The

secondary colors in light are cyan, yellow, and magenta and are created by mixing two primary colors. As in the pigment color wheels, tertiary colors in light are derived from combinations of a primary and a secondary color (**1.4.9**).

Dynamics of Color

Color wheels place hues in a visual arrangement that can be a guide to the many attributes of color and how to use them. We will now consider two other important aspects of color that can be clearly understood by looking at color wheels.

Complementary Color

Complementary colors can be found on opposite sides of a color wheel. For example, in the CMY subtractive color wheel (**1.4.5**), magenta is the complement of green. For an artist or designer, understanding the juxtaposition of these two colors on the color wheel can be very helpful.

When complementary colors are mixed, they produce gray (or black); they tend to dull one another. But when two complementary colors are painted side by side, these "opposite" colors create visual anomalies: they intensify one another. This happens because complementary colors have markedly different wavelengths, creating an illusion (in the photoreceptors of the eye) of vibrating movement where their edges meet (**1.4.10**). When the eye tries to compensate for the different wavelengths of two complementary colors, we tend to see each

1.4.8 Red, green, blue (RGB) light twelve-color wheel with white center (primary mixture)

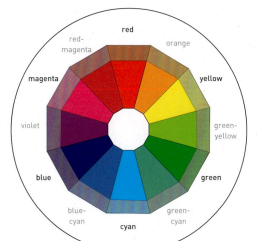

1.4.9 Additive color mixtures using red, green, and blue (RGB) primaries

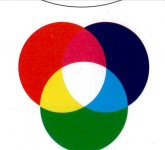

1.4.10 Color combinations and color complements in pigment

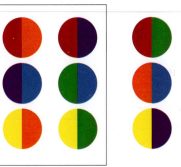

primary/secondary analogous combinations

primary/secondary, and tertiary complements

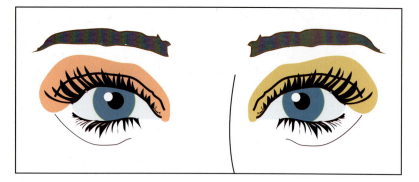

Color complements for blue eyes

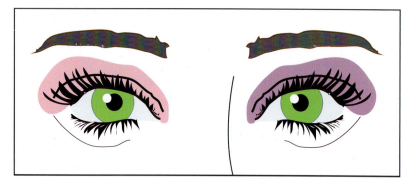

Color complements for green eyes

Brown eyes, a natural tone, can be enhanced using any color eye shadow

color more intensely than when we see them separately. So when red is present, greens tend to appear more vibrantly green.

Practical applications of complementary colors mimic the system that is observed on the color wheel. For example, makeup artists, whose work involves making their clients' eyes show to maximum effect, will apply an eyeshadow with red undertones to green eyes (**1.4.11**). Even though the combination is not exactly the same as that of the strong hues of the color wheel, it uses the same principle.

More traditionally, American landscape painter Frederic Edwin Church (1826–1900) used complementary colors for dramatic effect. In *Twilight in the Wilderness*, the intense red-orange clouds complement swathes of the blue-

1.4.11 Makeup artists' guide to complementary colors

1.4.12 Frederic Edwin Church, *Twilight in the Wilderness*, 1860. Oil on canvas, 40 × 64". Cleveland Museum of Art, Ohio

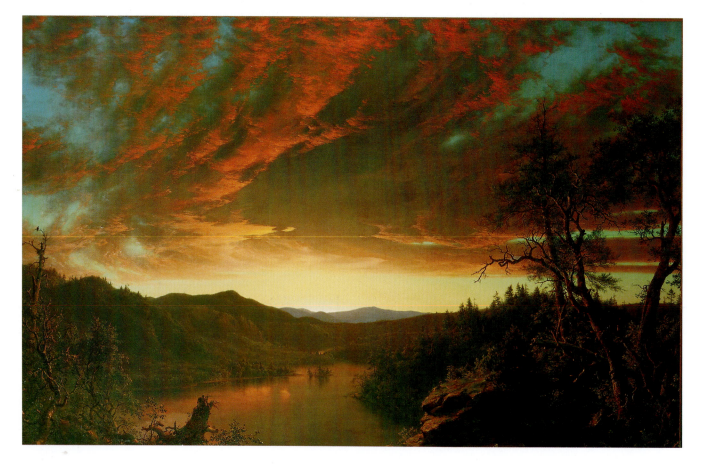

green evening sky, giving magnificence to a quiet landscape (**1.4.12**). The powerful color of the sky and its reflection in the water below reveal Church's awe and respect for the American landscape.

Analogous Color

Analogous colors fall adjacent to each other on a color wheel and are similar in wavelength, so they do not create optical illusions or visual vibrations the way complementary colors do. Painters use analogous color to create color unity and harmonies that steer viewers toward a particular attitude or emotion. By keeping the color within a similar range, artists avoid jarring, contrasting combinations of colors and moods.

In *The Boating Party* by Mary Cassatt (1844–1926), her color palette creates a harmonious effect (**1.4.13**). This is the result of using analogous colors that are next to one another on the color wheel. In this painting, yellows, greens, and blues predominate. These colors have relatively similar wavelengths and do not intensify each other when placed in close proximity. Cassatt's color seems relaxed, reinforcing her theme. Cassatt was one of the few female members of the **Impressionists**, a group of artists who shared an interest in the effects of light and color on the natural world, which they depicted in their paintings of everyday life.

We will now examine some other important aspects of color.

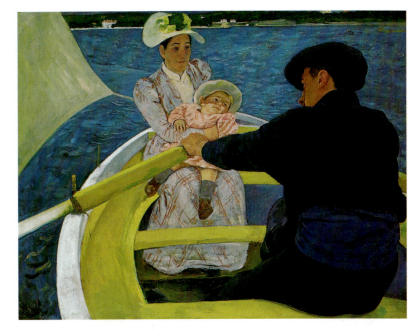

1.4.13 Mary Cassatt, *The Boating Party*, 1893–94. Oil on canvas, 35⅜ × 46⅛". National Gallery of Art, Washington, D.C.

associated with the psychological and social aspects of our lives.

In fact, the interpretation of color is very personal and subjective. When we interpret color we not only see it; we also associate such tangible feelings as warmth and coolness with it. Such feelings are influenced by and associated with the culture we inhabit, as well as personal preference, past experience, physiological differences in our visual perception, and many other variables. For example, brides in some Asian countries wear red on their wedding day, since in their culture white, the traditional bridal color of choice for Western women, is associated with mourning. Each color can carry a multitude of complex associations that will change from one individual to the next. We will explore and discuss some of these complexities a little later in this chapter.

Subjective Perceptions of Color

Although science explains how light can be separated or refracted so that we can experience it, color is also experienced in ways that are non-objective—that is, dependent on our individual character, background and nature—as well. Ancient Greek philosophers speculated that color might be a state of mind and that the color we see is a unique experience for every person, because our interpretations of color are deeply

Key Characteristics of Color

Because of the wide range of attributes associated with color, artists and designers use specific terms to be more descriptive. We will now identify these terms as we examine the main properties of color.

Analogous colors: colors adjacent to each other on the color wheel
Impressionist, Impressionism: a late nineteenth-century painting style conveying the impression of the effects of light; Impressionists were artists working in this style

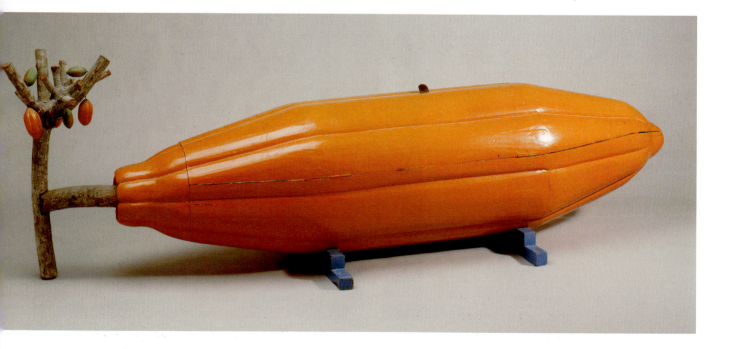

Properties of Color

All colors have four basic properties: hue, value, chroma, and tone. By manipulating these four properties, artists and designers can achieve an endless range of visual effects.

Hue

When many of us refer to "the color orange", we are really referring to the hue orange. Hues represent the individual color ranges of the spectrum, that is, red, yellow, blue, green, orange, and violet. Orange is therefore a hue that describes a broad color range, while cocoa-pod orange (**1.4.14**) refers to a specific single point in the spectrum of that overall hue family.

For the sake of reference, we associate a hue with an ideal version of a given color. For example, the hue orange is usually associated with a bright, warm, intense orange color of the kind we might see in sports jerseys and industrial surfaces, such as farm equipment. So, when we use the term "hue," we most often are making associations to a brilliant color, or at least one as strong as it can be.

Color is such an important aspect of a coffin created by the African sculptor Kane Kwei (1922–1992) that the work is sometimes nicknamed *Coffin Orange* (**1.4.14**). Kwei's coffin is painted with a brilliant mid-hue orange color,

that of a half-ripened cocoa pod. Although ripening cocoa pods generally turn some sort of orange hue, the specific color chosen by the artist for this coffin is intentionally bright and exaggerated.

In Ghana, Kwei's native country, funerals are celebratory, loud affairs where bright color adds to the festive mood. Ghanaians believe that having lots of happy people at a funeral gives solace to the family of the deceased, reminding them that they still have many friends. Kwei got started in his career when his dying uncle asked Kwei to build him a boat-shaped coffin. It was such a hit in the community that others began to ask for coffins made in interesting shapes. *Coffin in the Shape of a Cocoa Pod* was commissioned by a cocoa farmer who wanted to tell everybody about his lifelong passion at his last party on Earth.

Value

Each hue has a **value**, meaning its relative lightness or darkness compared to another hue. For example, a pure yellow has a light value, and a pure blue has a dark value. Similarly, different colors of the same hue vary in terms of their value: there are light reds and dark reds. **Tints** are colors that are lighter than their basic hue, implying that they have been mixed with white; **shades** are colors that are darker and imply that

1.4.14 Kane Kwei, *Coffin in the Shape of a Cocoa Pod (Coffin Orange)*, c. 1970. Polychrome wood, 2'10" × 8'6" × 2'5". Fine Arts Museums of San Francisco

Value: the lightness or darkness of a plane or area
Tint: a color lighter in value than its purest state
Shade: a color darker in value than its purest state
Neutral: colors (such as blacks, whites, grays, and dull gray-browns) made by mixing complementary hues
Monochromatic: having one or more values of one color

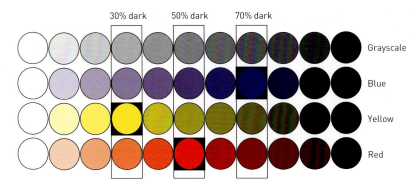

30% dark   50% dark   70% dark

Grayscale

Blue

Yellow

Red

1.4.15 Color–value relationships

they have been mixed with black. Figure **1.4.15** shows relative values of red, blue, and yellow. The purest values, compared with those visible in the spectrum, are indicated by the black outline. Figure **1.4.15** also shows the grayscale values; these are described as **neutral**, meaning there is an absence of color.

A work that uses only one hue is called **monochromatic**. An artist can give variety to such a work by using a range of values. Creating dramatic differences in the values of a color allows for ordered transitions from one value to another. Many of American Mark Tansey's (b. 1949) large paintings are monochromatic. In *Picasso and Braque*, Tansey depicts two figures,

whom he calls "Orville and Wilbur," a reference to aviators the Wright Brothers (**1.4.16**). He is also referring wryly to Pablo Picasso's (1881–1973) and Georges Braque's (1882–1963) habit of calling each other Orville and Wilbur during the pioneering days of **Cubism**. The two figures here have created a flying machine that resembles an early Cubist **collage**. The monochromatic **palette** is reminiscent of the black-and-white photos of the Wright Brothers' experiments with flight, and the blue tone refers to an early **style** of Picasso's known as his Blue Period. Tansey uses humor to comment on historic discoveries in art and flight within a single monochromatic composition.

Chroma

When we think of the color yellow, we often imagine something strong, bright, and intense. Many shades of yellow exist, but we tend to associate a color with its purest state, or its highest level of **chroma**. The color mustard yellow, which has a brownish tone, has a weaker chroma, because the intensity of the color is less than the purest hue. Chroma is sometimes described as **saturation**, chromaticness, or

Cubism, Cubist: a twentieth-century art movement that favored a new perspective emphasizing geometric forms; the Cubists were artists who formed part of the movement. "Cubist" is also used to describe the painting style they used
Collage: a work of art assembled by gluing materials, often paper, onto a surface. From the French *coller*, to glue
Palette: the range of colors used by an artist
Style: a characteristic way in which an artist or group of artists uses visual language to give a work an identifiable form of visual expression
Chroma: the degree of purity of a color

1.4.16 Mark Tansey, *Picasso and Braque*, 1992. Oil on canvas, 5'4" × 7'

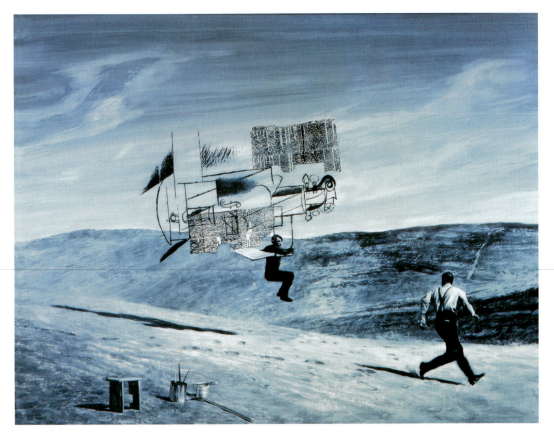

1.4.17 Barnett Newman, *Vir Heroicus Sublimis,* 1950–51. Oil on canvas, 7'11⅜" × 17'8¼". MoMA, New York

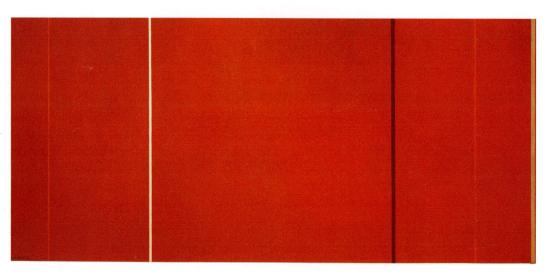

intensity, but these terms all generally refer to the strength of color.

Such works as *Vir Heroicus Sublimis* (Latin for "heroic sublime man") by the American painter Barnett Newman (1905–1970) rely, for their visual impact, on value and strong chroma (**1.4.17**). The differing colors of the vertical lines (which Newman calls "zips") break up a broad red **plane**. The white zip makes a gap, while the maroon zip seems to meld into the red field. Subtle variations in the red hues create the sensation that parts of the work are separately lit.

Newman wants viewers to stand close to the canvas, engulfed by color, meeting the

artwork as one might another person. The square area in the center of this painting suggests Newman's idealistic vision of the perfectibility of humankind.

The French painter André Derain (1880–1954) was a great advocate of strong chroma. In his work *The Turning Road, L'Estaque,* his use of vivid, bright color makes the entire scene glow with energy and vitality (**1.4.18**). Derain was a member of an artistic movement known as the **Fauves** (French for "wild beasts"). The Fauves delighted in using the new and brighter-colored pigments made available by advances in industrial manufacturing. They used colors

1.4.18 André Derain, *The Turning Road, L'Estaque,* 1906. Oil on canvas, 4'3" × 6'4¾". Museum of Fine Arts, Houston, Texas

Saturation (also known as Chroma): the degree of purity of a color
Plane: a flat surface, often implied in the composition
Fauves: a group of early twentieth-century French artists whose paintings used vivid colors. From the French *fauve,* "wild beast"

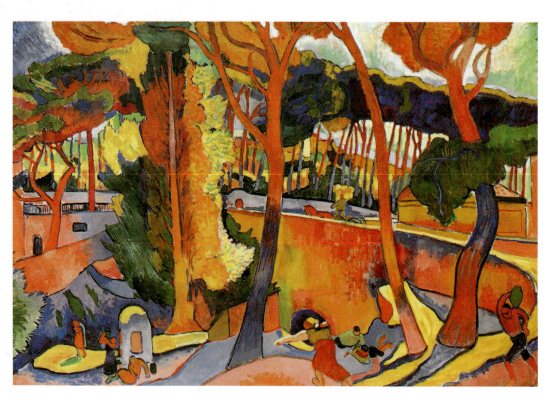

Tone: a color that is weaker than its brightest, or most pure, state

in their purest and strongest states as an act of defiance against the Academy, a state-sponsored school of art that set rigid rules for acceptable standards for art and artists at the turn of the twentieth century. Although today, it might seem as though the Fauves' subjects and colors are tame by comparison with those of contemporary artists, in their day they were perceived as revolutionary and fierce, challenging the Academy and Western artistic conventions generally and earning the artists their nickname. Derain's painting is energized by high chroma and color complements that intensify adjacent colors when seen close together.

Tone

Chroma is a term that also describes the purity of a hue derived from the spectrum of pure white light. A red at its highest chroma is closest to its pure state in the spectrum of light (**1.4.19**), and when a color is in its strongest chromatic state, it has no tints or shades. Yet red, for example, can also be a very muted hue. The weaker chromatic states of any hue are known as **tones**. A hue that is almost gray is a tone

because it has been dulled from its most intense chromatic state, even though it may be similar in *value* to the hue at its highest chroma. Therefore a muted tone, whatever its hue, is less intense as it gets further from the purity of its spectral origin. A pastel-red tone and a dark-red tone would each have a restricted value of red, but a grayed-red hue that is just as dark as the original red would also have a low chroma.

Many artists have used the tonal qualities of color and associated them with sound. In the painting *Ancient Sound* (**1.4.20**) by the Swiss artist Paul Klee (1879–1940), varying tones of green and orange are organized so that a viewer might make associations to sounds, for example seeing the yellows as similar to bright, high-pitched noises, and the darks as similar to deep, low sounds. Klee, who excelled as both artist and accomplished violinist, organized a grid full of colors that varied from an extremely light tone of yellow-orange to greens and browns that nearly become black in value. The tones are carefully darkened and lightened to take full advantage of the adjacent colors to increase

1.4.19 A sampling of chroma, tone, shades, and tints in red hue

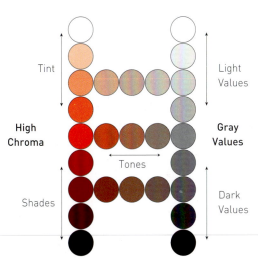

Tint

Light Values

High Chroma

Gray Values

Tones

Shades

Dark Values

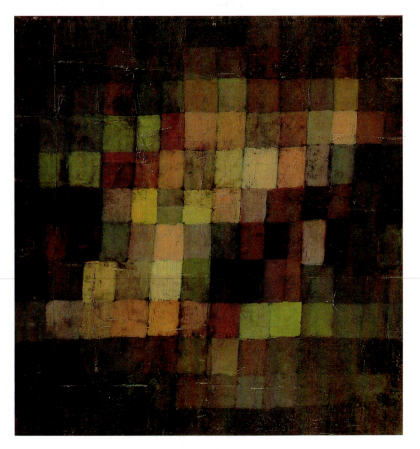

1.4.20 Paul Klee, *Ancient Sound*, 1925. Oil on cardboard, 15 × 15″. Kunstmuseum Basel, Switzerland

or decrease the **contrast**. Like the changing notes in a piece of music, the chroma of these colors rises and falls as if they are notes that have been unleashed through a voice or musical instrument.

The Sensation of Color

Our sensations of color are both evocative and physical. Some colors are associated with emotional states: if we say we are feeling "blue," we are describing a psychological state of mind. Blue is also associated with cold, and red with hot: an association that can be referred to as color **temperature**. Color temperature is relative to other surrounding colors, and interpretation is highly subjective.

Color can also affect the way we see. Because of the difference in color wavelengths, our eyes cannot fully comprehend all the colors at the same time, so our brain translates (or distorts) the incoming information. This is the basis of an illusion known as optical color. Our interpretation of color can also be completely inaccurate because of the limitations of our optical senses.

Color Temperature

We associate color with temperature because of our previous experiences. We may have been burned by something red-hot, or chilled by cool blue water. Our perception of the temperature of a color can be altered if it is placed next to an analogous, or similar, color. For example, green, a color we might associate with coolness, can be warm if we see it next to a cooler color, such as blue. A yellow-green would be warmer than a blue-green. Color temperature is relative to the other colors nearby. Artists use such associations to communicate physical and emotional states.

The colors chosen for the underglaze-painted lamp from the Islamic shrine the Dome of the Rock, in Jerusalem, are blue and green, on a white **ground** for contrast (**1.4.21**). They reflect the kind of color influence valued in the meditative atmosphere of a holy place. The choice of colors is cool and peaceful. Many people associate green and blue with water, plant life, or a clear sky. Our life experiences with blue and green things can easily be associated with passive environments. The color green has positive associations in Islamic art and supports the peacefulness of prayer.

Optical Color

Sometimes our brains receive so much information that they simplify it. Optical colors are colors our minds create based on the information we can perceive. In **1.4.22**, the square on the left contains so many red and blue dots that our brain interprets them as a violet color. In the square on the right, red and yellow dots are interpreted as an orange tone.

The French painter Georges Seurat (1859–1891) used the optical qualities of color to create a new style of painting, called **pointillism** because it relied on small dots (or points) of color. In *The Circus* Seurat paints a scene of lively entertainment, imbued with bright color and texture through the use of small dots (**1.4.23a** and **b**). Because these dots are so close together, the colors we see are different from the actual colors of the dots.

This optical mixing makes the colors more intense because they have retained their individual intensity, whereas if they were mixed on the palette they would appear more subdued. *The Circus*'s jewel-like diffusion of light and the

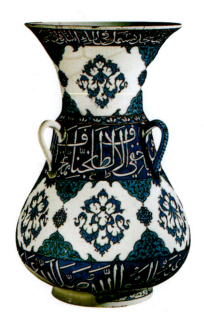

1.4.21 Mosque lamp from the Dome of the Rock in Jerusalem, 1549. Iznik pottery, 15" high. British Museum, London, England

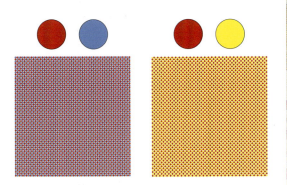

1.4.22 Two squares, one filled with red and blue dots and the other with red and yellow dots to create optical color mixing effect

illusion of visual vibrations between the colors make it visually exciting.

Color Deception

We can be deceived by a color because of the influences of color next, or adjacent, to it. As we see from optical color mixtures that can imply colors that are not actually present, color can trick our perception. The color theorist Josef Albers described some of these color deceptions in his experiments. In Figures **1.4.24 a and b** Albers, a teacher of color theory and design at the Bauhaus in Germany, Black Mountain College, and Yale, has created an illustration of how one color can look like two. If you look at state A, the brown squares on either side of the horizontal center stripes look distinctly different, but when the blue and yellow center stripes are

1.4.24a Josef Albers, *Two Colors Look Like One, State A*. From *Interaction of Color*, Ch. IV, plate 1

1.4.24b Josef Albers, *Two Colors Look Like One, State B*. From *Interaction of Color*, Ch. IV, plate 2

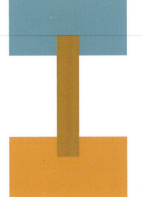

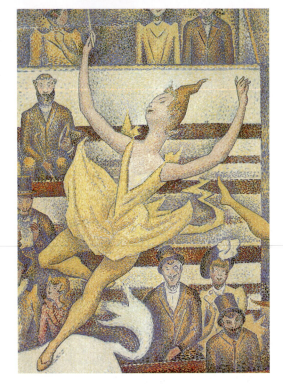

1.4.23a Georges Seurat, *The Circus*, 1890–91. Oil on canvas, 6′7⅞″ × 4′11⅞″. Musée d'Orsay, Paris, France

1.4.23b Detail of Georges Seurat, *The Circus*

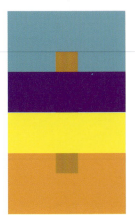

removed, we see that the different browns are actually exactly the same. Albers realized that color is relative to its surroundings and that by changing the adjacent colors, he could change how a color is perceived.

Buddha wore yellow or gold; Jews and Christians associate the color blue with God (the Virgin Mary is most frequently depicted wearing blue). Our cultural beliefs about color also affect the way we think and feel.

Interpreting Color

Color can affect how we think and feel. Studies by Faber Birren (1900–1988), a color psychologist, indicate that when people are constantly exposed to red light they can often become loud, grow argumentative, and eat voraciously: it appears that red can influence aggression in our behavior. We also make associations between colors and language—we might call a severe depression a "black" mood, or, when we don't want to upset someone, tell "white" lies—that can make our meaning clearer to others in the same culture and affect how we feel about those colors.

Colors also have traditional symbolic values. As we have seen, green, traditionally, has positive associations for Muslims; Confucius and

The Psychology of Color

Color affects us because it can alter the way we feel and react. In Western cultures, we associate love with red and sadness with blue. The potential impact of color on our sense of well-being is such that some ancient cultures, such as the Egyptians and Chinese, used colors for healing. The ancient Persian philosopher Avicenna created a chart that associated color with medical symptoms and their treatment. For example, it was believed that a bleeding open wound would be aggravated by the presence of red, but if the patient was exposed to blue (by simply looking at it) the effect would be beneficial.

Artists understand that color affects the way we think and react to the world. Some of these

1.4.25 Vincent van Gogh, *The Night Café*, 1888. Oil on canvas, 28½ × 36¼". Yale University Art Gallery, New Haven, Connecticut

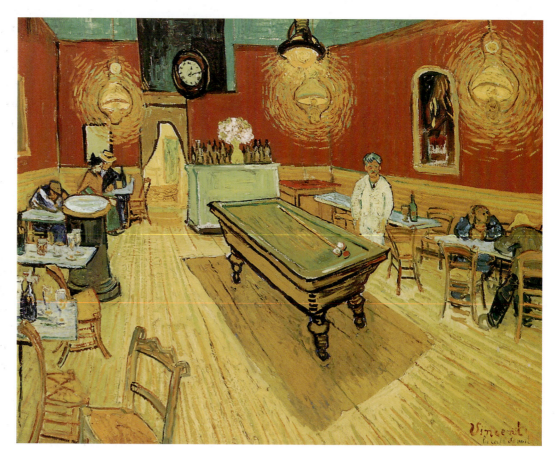

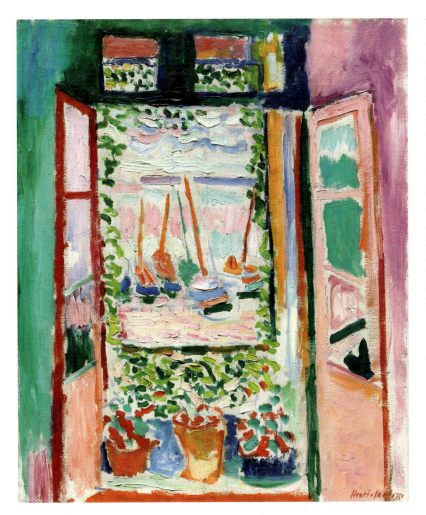

1.4.26 Henri Matisse, *Open Window, Collioure*, 1905. Oil on canvas, 21¾″ × 18⅛″. National Gallery of Art, Washington, D.C.

Van Gogh interpreted the color of the Café de la Gare (as it was called) as he painted it, in order to express something more about the place. The color intensifies the psychological implications of the scene, in a seedy nightspot in Arles, France, as we wander visually into this menacing place as outsiders. By choosing fierce and oppressive red, a feverish yellow, and the rather bilious or sickly green, Van Gogh expresses his sense that this nightspot had a detrimental psychological influence on its patrons. The almost lurid hues convey a strong feeling of unease and sorrow, and the strange, lurching perspective in the room opens up irregular spaces that intensify the painting's lonely atmosphere.

Expressive Aspects of Color

Such artists as Van Gogh wanted viewers to "feel" artworks, rather than merely to understand them. Color in particular can express a wide range of emotions. Artists and designers know that the bright yellow of a happy-face symbol attracts our attention and lifts our spirits. They can use color to engage the viewer, whether it is the use of blue around the image of a political candidate to suggest traditional values, or green as an identifier of environmental awareness.

Henri Matisse (1869–1954) was a French artist who was a great and influential practitioner of the expressive use of color. He and the artists of the Fauve movement focused especially on using color as intensely as they could to reveal the rich character of painting. For example, in Matisse's *The Open Window, Collioure* (**1.4.26**), the artist uses pairs of complementary colors to enhance the painting. In this scene we see such combinations as the orange and blue boats, through the window, and the red-pink wall on the right paired with the greenish-blue one on the left. Since complementary colors influence each other, the resulting experience is a brilliant expression of vibrant color.

The French painter Paul Gauguin (1848–1903) used yellow for its uplifting associations when he painted *The Yellow Christ* (**1.4.27**, p. 116). Gauguin painted this scene—a deliberately populist portrayal of folk spirituality—while

reactions are culturally biased: in the United States blue is paired with masculinity, but in China it is associated with the feminine. As we have seen, red (which we can easily associate with blood) can arouse feelings not only of anxiety, aggression, and anger, but also of passion, eroticism, and vitality. Green, a color we associate with growing plant life, encourages restfulness, but it also suggests decay and illness.

The Dutch painter Vincent van Gogh (1853–1890) was enormously affected by color, and studied its psychological effects. Van Gogh was plagued by periods of deep depression and was hospitalized on many occasions; through his treatment he learned a great deal about psychology. The colors in his painting *The Night Café* are not taken from life, but were carefully chosen to elicit emotional responses from viewers (**1.4.25**). In a letter to his brother Theo, Van Gogh writes about the work, "I have tried to express with red and green the terrible passions of human nature." Like any good artist,

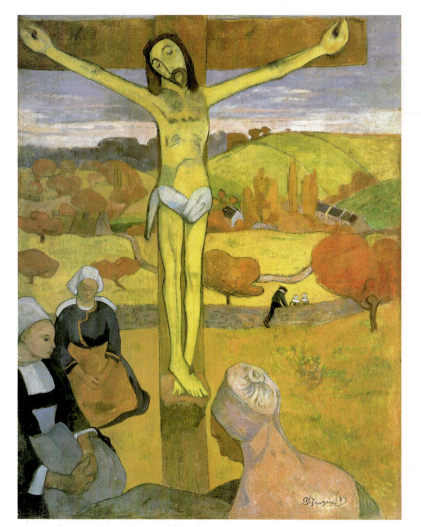

and personal, are also to some extent shared within the culture or society we grew up in. The color red is especially potent because it can be associated with blood, fire, and other powerful forces of conflict and danger. The artist Cecilia Beaux (1855–1942) may have used color to emphasize the great pain she was experiencing as she painted her final self-portrait (**1.4.28**). Beaux was one of the great portrait painters of her time and was selected for the honor of creating a self-portrait for the famous and prestigious Uffizi Gallery in Florence, Italy. This was her first major painting since she had suffered a painful life-changing injury to her hip, an incident that limited her movement. The strong red used in the work reflects not only the searing pain she endured while painting it, but also the strength and resolve she exhibited in mustering the sheer will to complete it. Beaux may not have intended to show her personal pain, but it seems evident when one sees the color and knows the circumstances of the artist's life at the time the portrait was created.

Color has always been used expressively by artists and designers, sometimes to change

1.4.27 Paul Gauguin, *The Yellow Christ*, 1889. Oil on canvas, 36¼ × 27⅞". Albright-Knox Art Gallery, Buffalo, New York

in Brittany, France. In it, three women in traditional Breton dress appear to attend the crucifixion. Although Gauguin is known to have been inspired by a woodcarving in a local chapel, his choice of color is primarily symbolic. Through color he connects the crucifixion of Christ to the seasons of Earth and the cycle of life. Here, yellows and browns correspond to the colors of the surrounding autumnal countryside, harvested fields, and turning leaves. Gauguin's color palette relates the background natural world to the body on the cross, so that our gaze too is drawn in and upward. By using bright color, Gauguin creates a simple and direct emotional connection with the viewer. While depicting death, Gauguin chose colors that yet express the optimism of rebirth.

Color can express deep personal experiences. Our associations to it, although often subjective

1.4.28 Cecilia Beaux, *Self-Portrait*, 1925. Oil on canvas, 43 × 28½". Uffizi Gallery, Florence, Italy

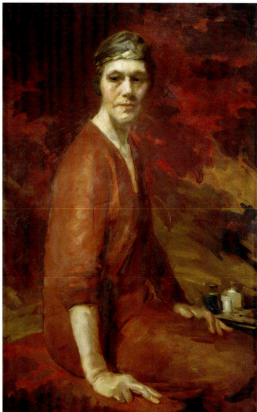

the way that a viewer feels about his or her surroundings. Take for example a project by the Polish-born New York artist Adrian Kondratowicz (b. 1984), where the artist has asked his Harlem neighbors to look at trash a bit differently (**1.4.29**). Adrian, as he is known locally, distributed bright pink, rodent-repellent, biodegradable trash bags to his community. When these pink polka-dotted bags were used, they subverted the standard black and elicited a positive emotion from the community.

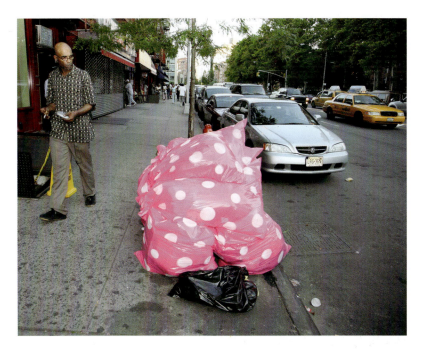

1.4.29 Adrian Kondratowicz, *TRASH maximalism NYC (Harlem), TRASH project*, 2008–

Active Learning Exercises

1. One important property of color is value. The hue blue can have many dark or light variations of color. Search and find pieces of colored paper from magazines, brochures, product packaging, construction paper, color printed images, etc. From this collection of colors, clip out only the sections that are blue. Take all your blue color clippings and glue as many of them as you can into a 6-in. × 6-in. square that you have made on a white sheet of paper. Feel free to modify their shape and size for more variety. Does your collection have both light blues and dark blues? Do some of the blues look slightly red and others a little green? Why do you think that you might be seeing reddish or greenish tones?

2. The way that we perceive color is sometimes complex because we interpret its effects. This is what happens in optical color mixing, when two colors look like a completely new color that is not present in the surface being viewed. Using some colored paper, such as construction paper, a glue stick, a ruler with a metal edge, and a utility knife with a sharp blade, cut a 2-in. strip of colored paper into 8 pieces each measuring ⅛ in. × 2 in. Then do the same with another piece of colored paper so that you have 16 strips each measuring ⅛ in. × 2 in. In a 2-in. × 2-in. square, glue the strips down side by side, alternating the color with each new strip added. A striped pattern should emerge and fill the 2-in. square. After you have completed this process, stand away and consider the color. Do you perceive a new color, different from the originals? What results do you think would you get with other color combinations?

3. Color can be deceptive because our interpretation of it changes depending on the other adjacent colors. Using colored paper and glue, re-create Joseph Albers's experiment *Two Colors Look Like One* from **1.4.24**. Based on the process of isolating color in such fields, could you make a blue look more like green? How?

Images Related to 1.4: Color

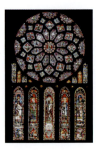

2.6.11 Rose window and lancets, Chartres Cathedral, France, 13th century, p. 298

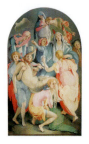

3.6.11a Jan van Eyck, *The Arnolfini Portrait*, 1434, p. 474

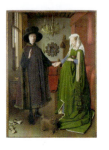

3.6.19 Jacopo da Pontormo, *Deposition*, 1525–28, p. 482

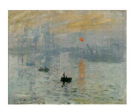

3.8.4 Claude Monet, *Impression, Sunrise*, 1872, p. 516

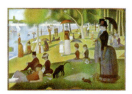

4.4.14 Georges Seurat, *Sunday on La Grande Jatte*, 1884–86, p. 607

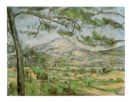

3.8.10 Paul Cézanne, *Mont Sainte-Victoire*, c. 1886–88, p. 521

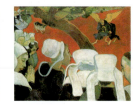

3.8.11 Paul Gauguin, *The Vision after the Sermon*, 1888, p. 521

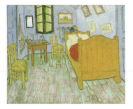

1.1.17 Vincent van Gogh, *The Bedroom*, 1889, p. 58

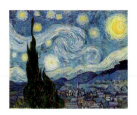

3.8.12 Vincent van Gogh, *Starry Night*, 1889, p. 522

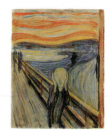

1.10.10 Edvard Munch, *The Scream*, 1893, p. 188

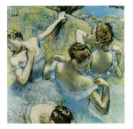

3.8.9 Edgar Degas, *The Blue Dancers*, 1897, p. 520

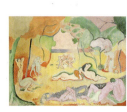

3.8.18 Henri Matisse, *Joy of Life*, 1905–6, p. 525

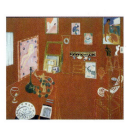

3.8.19 Henri Matisse, *The Red Studio*, 1911, p. 526

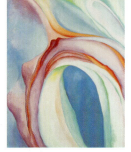

1.1.27 Georgia O'Keeffe, *Music—Pink and Blue II*, 1919, p. 63

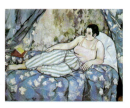

1.9.2 Suzanne Valadon, *The Blue Room*, 1923, p. 168

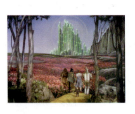

2.9.6 Victor Fleming, *The Wizard of Oz* (scene), 1939, p. 341

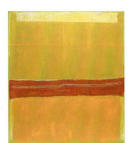

3.9.3 Mark Rothko, Untitled, *No. 5/No. 22*, 1950 (dated 1949 on reverse), p. 543

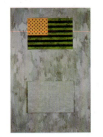

4.4.15 Jasper Johns, *Flag*, 1965, p. 607

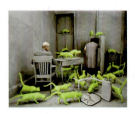

2.8.25 Sandy Skoglund, *Radioactive Cats*, 1980, p. 335

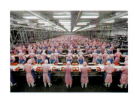

2.8.26 Edward Burtynsky, "Manufacturing #17," 2005, p. 336

1.5

Time and Motion

Moving images are part of our daily experience of life in the twenty-first century. We see them on our TV and computer screens, on displays in stores, and on the street. In an age where we can see hugely sophisticated and dynamic movies in 3-D, and we know that what we are seeing are brilliant illusions and special effects created through technological wizardry, it is difficult to imagine how astonished, even afraid, audiences were when they first watched footage of objects hurtling through space. But such reactions are understandable. If we could travel back in time little more than a century, our visual experience would be quite different: all art images were still.

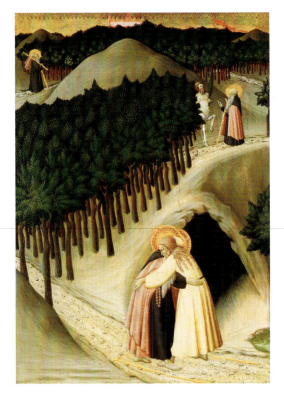

1.5.1 Workshop of the Master of Osservanza (Sano di Pietro?), *The Meeting of St. Anthony and St. Paul*, c. 1430–35. Tempera on panel, 18½ × 13¼". National Gallery of Art, Washington, D.C.

Time and **motion** are closely linked elements in art. Most of the traditional art **media** are inherently motionless and timeless. Paintings, for example, are static, holding a moment so that it can be experienced through the ages. But artists who work in static media have found imaginative ways to indicate the passage of time and the appearance of motion. And film and video have overturned the conventions of traditional art, as new technology and media allow artists to capture time and motion.

Time

Since events necessarily take place over time, any artwork that deals with events must show how time goes by. Writers use chapters and other tools to give us a sense of how stories unfold. Artists also find ways to communicate the passage of time and to remind us of its influence on our lives.

The Passage of Time

In **1.5.1**, *The Meeting of St. Anthony and St. Paul*, painters in the workshop of the fifteenth-century artist known as the Master of Osservanza solved the problem of how to tell a story in a single painting by merging a series of episodes into one picture. The story begins in the upper left-hand corner, where St. Anthony sets out across the desert to seek the hermit St. Paul. In the upper right, St. Anthony encounters a mythical

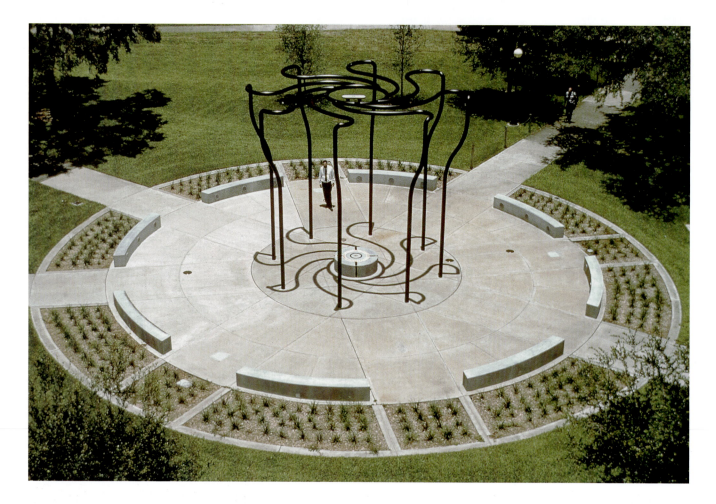

1.5.2 Nancy Holt, *Solar Rotary*, 1995. Aluminum, concrete, and meteorite, approx. height 20', approx. diameter 24'. University of South Florida

creature called a centaur: half-man, half-horse, it was associated with the Greek god of wine, Bacchus. This symbol of earthly temptation does not deter St. Anthony. He continues on his lone journey through thick forest until he finally meets and embraces St. Paul: their meeting is the culminating incident in the foreground. The entire painting signifies a pilgrimage on the long and winding road of time, rather than merely a single moment. This linear method is still used by artists, comic-book writers, and designers as a story-telling device and a way of expressing the passing of time.

The American artist Nancy Holt (1938–2014) examines cycles of time in her works. Many of Holt's sculptures intertwine the passage of time with the motion of the sun. Her *Solar Rotary*, at the University of South Florida, Tampa, is designed to express meaning from shadows cast by the sun throughout the year (**1.5.2**). The work features an aluminum sculptural "shadow caster" perched on eight poles high above the center of a circular concrete plaza. The shadow caster—a

ring with eight serpentine arms—is oriented so that shadows cast by its central ring encircle notable dates set into the surrounding concrete. The different angles of the sun at different times of the year make shadows at different locations in the sculpture. For example, on March 27 a circle shadow surrounds a marker that recounts the day in 1513 when the Spanish explorer Juan Ponce de León first sighted Florida. In the center, a concrete circular bench, into which a meteorite has been set, is encircled by the shadow at noon on the summer solstice, the longest day of the year (in the northern hemisphere), when the sun reaches its northernmost point. The meteorite symbolizes the connection between our world and the larger universe.

The Attributes of Time

Time-based arts, such as film, embody six basic attributes of time: duration, tempo, intensity, scope, setting, and chronology. All these attributes exist in one of the first American

1.5.3 Thomas Edison and W. K. Dickson, *Fred Ott's Sneeze*, 1894. Still frames from kinetoscope film. Library of Congress, Washington, D.C.

movies, *Fred Ott's Sneeze*, made by Thomas Edison and W. K. Dickson in 1894 (**1.5.3**). The duration, or length, of this film is 5 seconds. The tempo, or speed, is 16 frames per second. The intensity, or level of energy, is high because the activity is sudden and strong. This film has a limited scope, or range of action, because it is confined to a simple activity. The setting, or context, is Thomas Edison's studio. The chronology, or order of events, can be seen in the still frames as Fred Ott appears to be placing some snuff in his nose, recoiling, then jerking forward as he sneezes.

By the end of the nineteenth century, many visual artists had created their own techniques that made time part of the language of visual art.

Motion

The aim of every artist is to arrest motion, which is life, by artificial means and hold it fixed so that a hundred years later, when a stranger looks at it, it moves again since it is life.

(William Faulkner, American novelist)

Faulkner tells us that an artist can make even a still image move and come to life. Motion occurs when an object changes location or position. Because this process occurs as time passes, motion is directly linked to time. To communicate motion without actually making anything move, artists can choose to imply time or, alternatively, create the illusion of it.

Implied Motion

When artists imply motion, they give us clues that a static work of art portrays a scene in which motion is occurring or has just occurred. In the case of implied motion, we do not actually see the motion happening, but visual clues tell us that it is a key aspect of the work.

The seventeenth-century Italian sculptor Gianlorenzo Bernini (1598–1680) emphasizes implied motion in many of his marble sculptures. *Apollo and Daphne* illustrates a story from ancient Greek mythology in which the sun god Apollo falls madly in love with the wood nymph Daphne (**1.5.4**). Terrified, she runs from him and begs her father, the river god Peneius, to save her. As Apollo reaches Daphne, Peneius transforms his daughter into a bay laurel tree. To convey the action, Bernini uses diagonal lines in the flowing drapery, limbs, and hair. Daphne's fingers sprout leaves as bark encases her legs. At the pivotal moment in the story, the scene is suddenly frozen in time. Thereafter, since she could not be Apollo's wife, Daphne became his

1.5.4 Gianlorenzo Bernini, *Apollo and Daphne*, 1622–24. Carrara marble, 8' high, Galleria Borghese, Rome, Italy

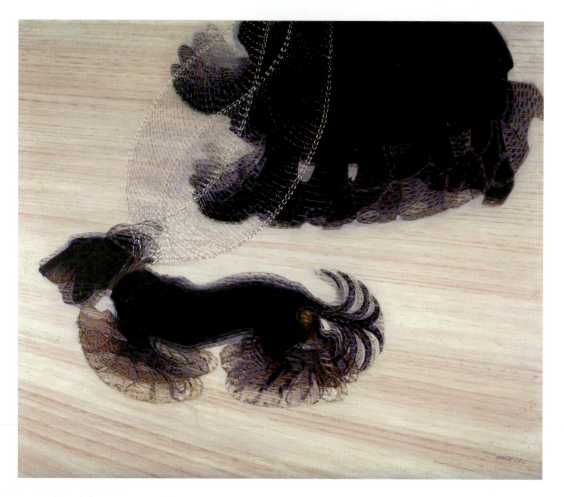

1.5.5 Giacomo Balla,
*Dynamism of a Dog on
a Leash*, 1912. Oil on
canvas, 35⅜ × 43¼".
Albright-Knox Art Gallery,
Buffalo, New York

tree, and Apollo made the laurel wreath
his crown.

The Italian **Futurist** Giacomo Balla (1871–
1958) uses a different method of implying
motion in his painting *Dynamism of a Dog on
a Leash* (**1.5.5**). Balla paints a series of repeating
marks to give the impression that we are seeing
motion as it happens, as if we are viewing
several separate moments at once. He paints
the dog's tail in eight or nine different positions
to communicate movement. Its feet are merely
indicated by a series of strokes that give a sense
of very rapid motion. The leash, a white **implied
line**, is also repeated in four different positions.
The **composition** gives viewers a sense of
ongoing forward motion even though the paint
on the canvas is perfectly still.

The Illusion of Motion

In the works by Bernini and Balla, the artists
imply motion: we do not actually see it
occurring, but visual clues tell us that the works,
although static, portray motion. Artists can also
communicate the idea of motion by creating an
illusion of it. Artists create this illusion through
visual tricks that deceive our eyes into believing
there is motion as time passes, even though no
actual motion occurs.

The American artist Jenny Holzer (b. 1950)
uses the illusion of motion to enhance her
text-based presentations. Her untitled 1989
installation (in the Guggenheim Museum,
New York, which was designed by Frank Lloyd
Wright) displays messages as text (**1.5.6**).
Although the text does not actually move, it
appears to spiral up the ramped circular atrium
of the museum as the tiny light-emitting diodes
(LEDs) are illuminated and then switched off in
an automated sequence. Thus the impression is
created that the text is moving as time elapses.
The intermittent flashing of lights creates a
scrolling series of letters and words, like the
flashing lights of the casinos on the Las Vegas
Strip. Holzer uses this illusion to invigorate her
messages and critiques of society.

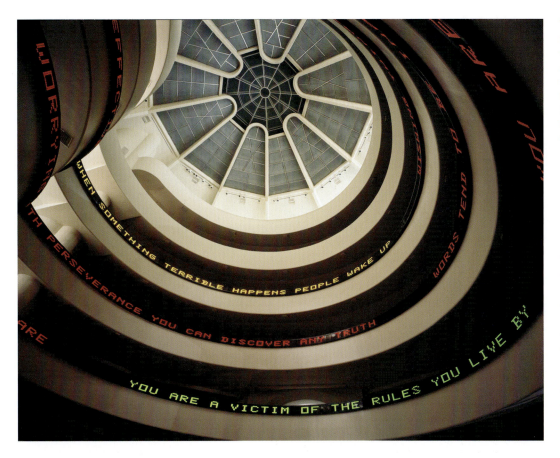

1.5.6 Jenny Holzer, *Untitled (Selections from Truisms, Inflammatory Essays, The Living Series, The Survival Series, Under a Rock, Laments, and Child Text)*, 1989. Extended helical tricolor LED, electronic display signboard, site-specific dimensions. Solomon R. Guggenheim Museum, New York

1.5.7 Bridget Riley, *Cataract 3*, 1967. PVA on canvas, 7'3¾" × 7'3¾". British Council Collection

Another illusion of motion that deceives the eye forms the basis for **Op art** (short for Optical art). During the 1960s, painters in this **style** experimented with discordant **positive–negative** relationships. There is a noticeable sense of movement when we look at *Cataract 3* (**1.5.7**), by British artist Bridget Riley (b. 1931). If we focus on a single point in the center of the work, it appears there is an overall vibrating motion. This optical illusion grows out of the natural physiological movement of the human eye; we can see it because the artist uses sharp contrast and hard-edged graphics set close enough together that the eye cannot compensate for its own movement. Riley understands that the natural oscillation of the eye combined with the passage of time makes us feel a sense of motion.

Stroboscopic Motion

When we see two or more repeated images in quick succession, they tend visually to fuse together. Many early attempts to show moving images were based on this effect, known as

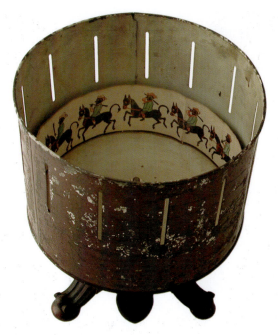

1.5.8 Zoetrope, 19th century. Bill Douglas Centre for the History of Film and Popular Culture, University of Exeter, England

1.5.9 Walt Disney Pictures, frame from *Finding Nemo*, 2003.

stroboscopic motion. One was the zoetrope, in which a series of drawings was placed in a slotted cylinder (**1.5.8**). A viewer who looked through the slots as the cylinder was spun could see an image appearing to move and repeat, even though the drawings that made up the series were, of course, static. Such inventions as the zoetrope were early forms of animation.

Cartoon animation grew out of these early stroboscopic experiments, and today's computer animation follows the same principle. Disney's *Finding Nemo* is compiled from individual frames that were computer-generated using 3-D modeling software (**1.5.9**). The animator can make changes to the images and then produce all the individual frames in a sequence that the computer plays in rapid succession. This succession of images is combined with other scenes and eventually committed to film—or, increasingly, digital media—for distribution to movie theaters.

"Movie" is an abbreviation of "moving picture," and movies became the dominant mode of artistic expression in motion during the twentieth century. Film relies on individual frames played in quick succession. Similar advanced forms of stroboscopic motion have been developed to stream digital video for the Web. Files with a series of multiple images (and sound files) are electronically transferred to a computer where they are played in rapid succession, much like a film movie. Internet users experience this when they view Flash animations posted on YouTube.

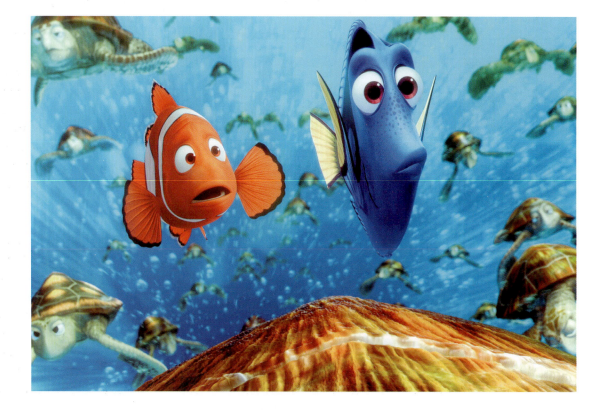

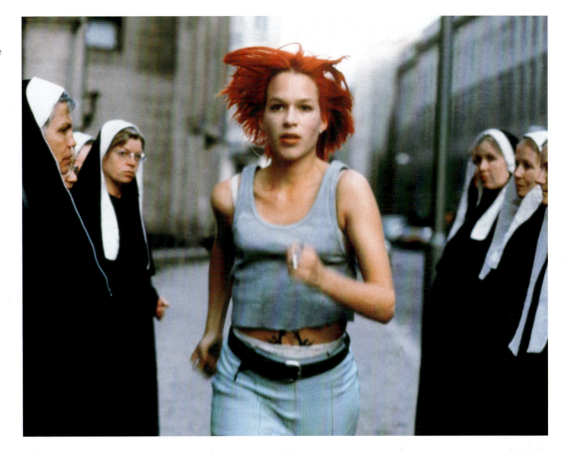

Such films as Tom Tykwer's (b. 1965) *Run Lola Run* (**1.5.10**) experiment with the notion of story and time. Set in Berlin, the story revolves around a young woman, Lola, who receives a panicked call from her boyfriend, Manni. If she does not get him 100,000 Deutschmarks (approximately $70,000) within 20 minutes, he will be forced to rob a grocery store in order to escape being killed by the mobster who is threatening him. Lola, desperate to save his life, does everything in her power to obtain the money, but only gets shot herself.

We discover, however, that the scope of the storyline extends beyond the everyday passage of time. Lola refuses to die, and so the story reboots and begins again, this time with a new set of circumstances, some of which Lola is now prepared for from the first version of events. In all, she does three runs: in each, the time allowed for the run is the same, but the action takes a different course.

The film's reinterpretation of time engages the viewer and helps to explore the characters in greater depth with each reset. The director thus uses stroboscopic motion as a tool to question the nature of time, and to demonstrate the impact that a few seconds' difference can make.

Actual Motion

We perceive actual motion when something really changes over time. We see it in **performance art** and in **kinetic art,** when objects physically move and change in real **space** and time. Performance art is theatrical; the artist's intention is to create not an art object, but an experience that can exist only in one place and time in history. Kinetic art plays out the passage of time through an art object, usually a sculpture, that moves.

Performance art emerged as a specific form of visual art during the twentieth century when such artists as the German Joseph Beuys (1921–1986) began performing his works, which he called actions. Following his traumatic experiences in the German Air Force in World War II, Beuys incorporated everyday objects—such as animals, fat, machinery, and sticks—into his actions, a series of self-performed situations in which the artist would interact with these

Performance art: a work involving the human body, usually including the artist, in front of an audience
Kinetic art: art, usually three-dimensional, with moving parts, impelled by wind, personal interaction, or motors
Space: the distance between identifiable points or planes

things in a defined space and time. By putting common items in new situations, Beuys conjured up different ways of thinking about our world so that we might question past practices. For example, Beuys once played a piano filled with animal fat that changed the sound and mechanics.

Performance artists need not focus on a social or political issue. For example, from the 1980s the Blue Man Group performed in ways that integrated humor and music for passersby on the streets of New York (**1.5.11**). They used sound and **mime**, relying on bodily movements to communicate ideas without speech.

Kinetic sculpture has evolved during the twentieth century and is a notable example of art that moves. The earliest kinetic artwork is credited to French artist Marcel Duchamp (1887–1968), who mounted a bicycle wheel on a barstool so that the wheel could be spun. Later, the American sculptor Alexander Calder (1898– 1976) invented the **mobile**, taking the name from a suggestion by Duchamp. The mobile relies on air currents to power its movement, and Calder's kinetic sculptures were so finely balanced that even the smallest breeze would set

them in motion. His final sculpture is the huge aluminum-and-steel mobile suspended in the National Gallery of Art in Washington, D.C. (**1.5.12**). It resembles its predecessors in being made up of counterbalanced **abstract** elements that move independently of each other. The result is a constantly changing visual **form**.

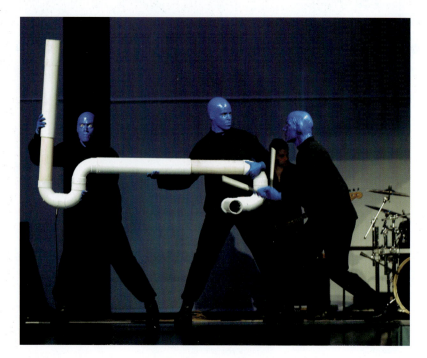

1.5.11 Blue Man Group perform at the Venetian Hotel, Las Vegas, Nevada, September 17, 2005

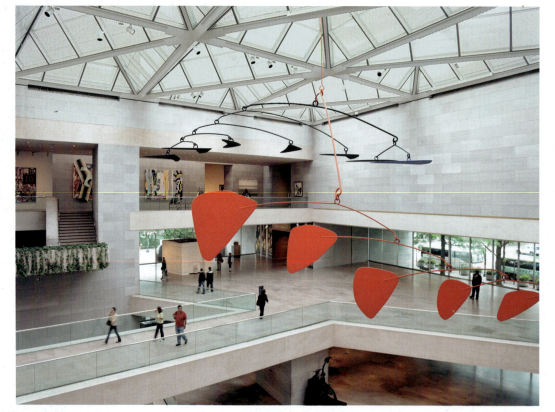

1.5.12 Alexander Calder, *Untitled*, 1976. Aluminum and steel, 29'10⅜" × 75'11¾". National Gallery of Art, Washington, D.C.

Mime: a silent performance work; actors use only body movements and facial expressions
Kinetic sculpture: three-dimensional art that moves, impelled by air currents, motors, or people
Mobile: suspended moving sculptures, usually impelled by natural air currents
Abstract: art imagery that departs from recognizable images from the natural world
Form: an object that can be defined in three dimensions (height, width, and depth)

Gateway to Art: Lange, *Migrant Mother*
Time and Motion in Photography

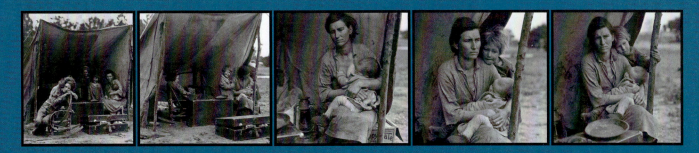

Although photography is a still medium, the work of a photographer is deeply concerned with motion and time. Photographers move around their subject, choosing the right focus for the shot and putting the camera in the best position to obtain the image they seek. We can get a sense of how a still photographer captures a moment in time in the sequence of photographs Dorothea Lange (1895–1965) took of Florence Thompson and her children (**1.5.13a–f**). In the span of a few minutes, Lange went from showing the family in the environment in which they lived—a tent—to an intimate portrayal of an individual. The first frame Lange photographed includes the barren landscape of the farm and the lean-to in which the family lived. In the second shot, Lange has moved her camera closer to the tent, but the image does not give us much information about the people. In the third through the sixth shots, Lange zooms in on the woman and the children around her.

Still photographers must make decisions about the images they create. If we look at this series, the process of selection becomes clear. Lange chose specific moments to photograph, and from those moments she further selected the one she felt most effectively communicated what she wanted to capture about the situation (**1.5.13f**). Lange's careful composition of her image of the family did not end with taking her photographs. Further changes were made to the negative in the dark room. Lange's original shot included the mother's hand holding onto the tent pole; Lange retouched the negative to crop out the

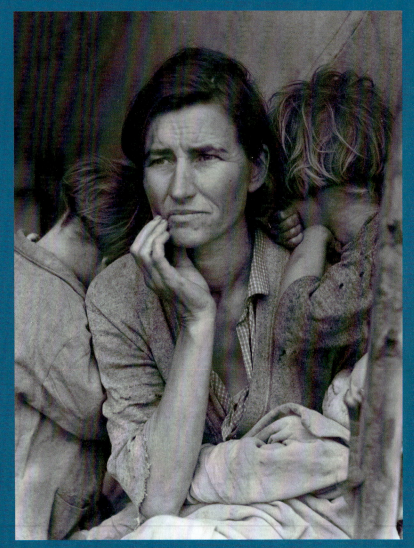

1.5.13f Dorothea Lange, *Migrant Mother*, 1936. Library of Congress, Washington, D.C.

hand. Because this photograph was meant to be an objective portrayal, the change was kept secret at the time, and has since been considered controversial.

1.5.13a–e (top of page) Dorothea Lange, *Destitute Pea-Pickers in California, Mother of Seven Children. Age Thirty-two. Nipomo, California*, 1936. Images a, c–e: Library of Congress, Washington, D.C. Image b: Oakland Museum of California

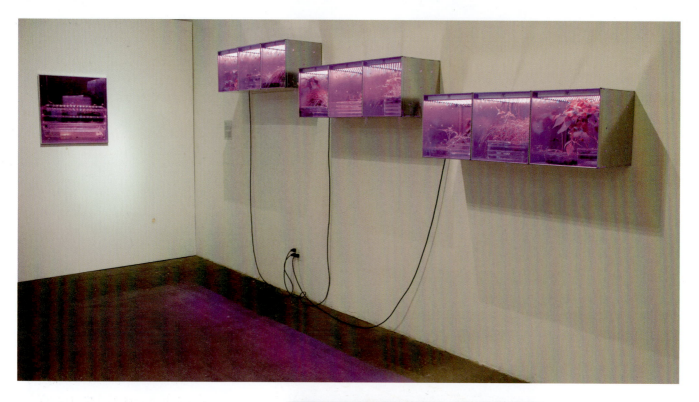

Natural Processes and the Passage of Time

Motion is not the only indicator of the passage of time in art. Some artists use biology and organic materials to create their artwork. **Bioart** is art that reflects the passage of time through the natural processes of growth and decay that organic materials undergo. Thus, work by "bioartists" is always changing. In her work *Astroculture (Shelf Life)* (**1.5.14**), the American bioartist Suzanne Anker (b. 1946) has created a piece of bioart that experiments with how plants might react in such artificial conditions as those necessary to sustain life in outer space. In this case, the artist has used red and blue LED lights to provide the equivalent of the nourishing rays of sunlight, reducing the amount of light and energy required. Even though the leaves would appear green if under normal light, in this environment they appear to be a strong magenta color. The artificial conditions eliminate the need for insecticide and result in lower carbon emissions, and are therefore a better option for such rarefied environments as outer space. Anker's work blurs the lines between science

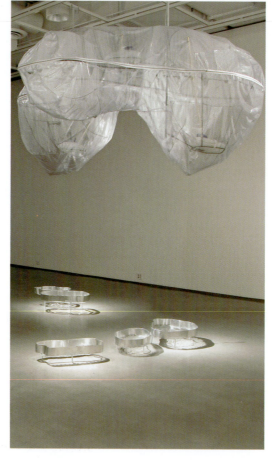

1.5.14 (above) Suzanne Anker, *Astroculture (Shelf Life)*, 2009. Aluminum, plastic, red and blue LED lights, plants, water, soil, and no pesticides. Dimensions variable. Vegetable-producing plants grown from seed using LED lights. Installation view at Corpus Extremus (LIFE+), Exit Art, New York

1.5.15 Ron Lambert, *Sublimate (Cloud Cover)*, 2004. Water, vinyl, humidifiers, steel, aluminum, and acrylic, dimensions variable

and art, contributing to our understanding of the universe while delivering interesting and colorful visual forms.

Natural processes also dominate the work of American sculptor Ron Lambert (b. 1975), for whom the water cycle illustrates the passage of time. For *Sublimate (Cloud Cover)* he created a large transparent plastic environment in which water endlessly evaporates and condenses (**1.5.15**). Lambert draws attention to our immediate environment as he shows how the rhythms of nature become a measure of natural time that we gauge by how long we have to wait for the next rain.

Active Learning Exercises

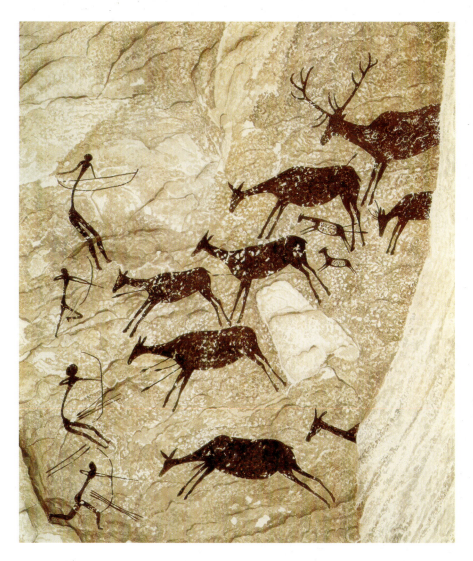

1.5.16 *Hunting Scene*, painting from Cova dels Cavalls (Horses' Cave), Mesolithic period. Valltorta, Valencia, Spain

1. Depicting time in art is not a concept that exists only in the modern world. The most ancient pieces of art that we know, cave paintings, show the passage of time. Cave paintings at Valltorta Gorge, Spain, show, variously, bow hunters as the bow is aimed; the arrows in flight; and arrows piercing deer (**1.5.16**). On notebook paper, draw in cave-art style an activity in which you often engage. How does your drawing communicate the passage of time? Can you think of other, still images in the media that communicate time?

2. Scoreboards at professional sporting events often feature active imagery that helps to energize the crowd and replay important moments. A spectator could easily be convinced that there are moving parts in the scoreboard, but it is based on a panel of flickering lights, which can be coordinated to create an illusion of motion. What illusions of motion have you noticed in scoreboards and lighted active billboards?

3. Cameras and smartphones now offer video modes that almost anyone can use. This is a fairly recent development. Most users don't think about the design of the video: they are simply recording from their normal vantage point. Good videographers consider other ways of approaching the subject by changing lighting, setting, and camera angle. Take two short videos with a smartphone or camera, but shoot them from the point of view of someone tiny and then someone gigantic. How does each angle change the message of the video? Why?

Images Related to 1.5:
Time and Motion

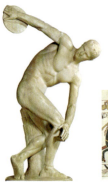

4.9.4 Myron, *Discus Thrower*, c. 450 BCE, p. 662

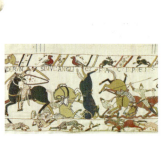

4.7.7 Detail of the Battle of Hastings, *Bayeux Tapestry*, c. 1066–82 CE, p. 640

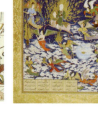

3.2.13 *The Ascent of the Prophet Muhammad*, from Nizami's *Khamsa*, 1539–43, p. 400

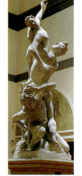

2.4.2a Giambologna, *Rape of a Sabine*, 1583, p. 249

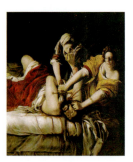

1.8.9 Artemisia Gentileschi, *Judith Decapitating Holofernes*, c. 1620, p. 163

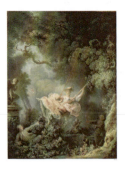

3.7.4 Jean-Honoré Fragonard, *The Swing*, 1766, p. 493

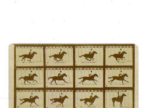
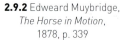

2.9.2 Edweard Muybridge, *The Horse in Motion*, 1878, p. 339

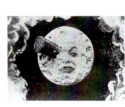

2.9.3 Georges Méliès, *A Trip to the Moon* (scene), 1902, p. 340

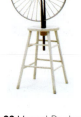

3.8.30 Marcel Duchamp, *Bicycle Wheel*, original version 1913, 3rd version 1951, p. 533

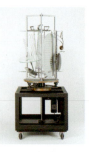

2.4.21 László Moholy-Nagy, *Light Prop for an Electric Stage*, 1929–30, p. 261

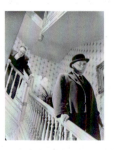

2.9.5 Orson Welles, *Citizen Kane* (scene), 1941, p. 341

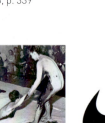

4.9.11a Yves Klein, *Anthropométries de l'époque bleue*, 1960, p. 666

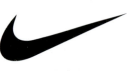

1.1.16 Carolyn Davidson, Nike Company logo, 1971, p. 57

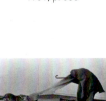
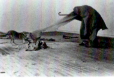

2.10.7 Joseph Beuys, *Coyote, I Like America and America Likes Me*, 1974, p. 357

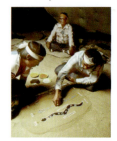

4.2.5 Navajo medicine man in healing ceremony, photo 20th century, p. 578

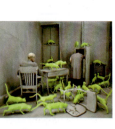

2.8.25 Sandy Skoglund, *Radioactive Cats*, 1980, p. 335

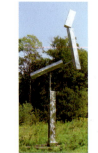

2.4.20 George Rickey, *Breaking Column*, 1986 (completed 2009), p. 260

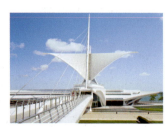

2.5.36 Santiago Calatrava, Quadracci Pavilion, Milwaukee Art Museum, 2001, p. 287

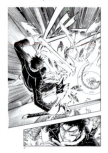

1.1.3 *CLAMP*, page from the Tsubasa RESERVoir CHRoNiCLE, 2007, p. 51

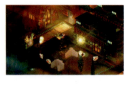

1.3.16 Screenshot from *Transistor* game, 2014, p. 91

1.6

Unity, Variety, and Balance

Unity: the imposition of order and harmony on a design

Elements: the basic vocabulary of art—line, form, shape, volume, mass, color, texture, space, time and motion, and value (lightness/darkness)

Principles: the "grammar" applied to the elements of art—contrast, balance, unity, variety, rhythm, emphasis, pattern, scale, proportion, and focal point

Composition: the overall design or organization of a work

Variety: the diversity of different ideas, media, and elements in a work

Medium (plural **media**): the material on or from which an artist chooses to make a work of art, for example canvas and oil paint, marble, engraving, video, or architecture

Grid: a network of horizontal and vertical lines; in an artwork's composition, the lines are implied

Gestalt: complete order and indivisible unity of all aspects of an artwork's design

Unity, variety, and balance are central principles that artists use to create visual impact. **Unity**—creating order or wholeness, the opposite of disorder—is central in the creation of a work of art or design. Unity refers to the imposition of order and harmony on a design. It is the sense of visual harmony that separates the work of art from the relative chaos of the surrounding world. Unity refers to the "oneness" or organization of similarities between **elements** that make up a work of art. Artists use the **principle** of unity to make choices that link visual elements to each other in a **composition**.

By comparison, **variety** is a kind of visual diversity that brings many different ideas, **media**, and elements together in one composition. It is expressed in contrast and difference, which create visual interest and excitement. Sometimes artists will use the discordance of variety to create uneasy relationships between visual elements. Sometimes, too, this lack of similarity between elements can actively create a sense of unity when an artist imposes on the work a **grid** or other visual structure.

Balance refers to the distribution of elements, whether unified or varied, within a work. The number and distribution of different elements

influence the composition. Balance in visual art is much like the balance we experience in real life. If we carry a large heavy bucket in one hand it pulls us to one side and we orient our body to offset its weight. In art, the visual elements in one half of a work are offset by the elements on the opposite side. By making sure that the elements are distributed in an organized way, artists create balance.

Unity

Unity provides an artwork with its cohesiveness and helps to communicate the visual idea it embodies. Artists face a communication challenge: to find a structure within the chaos of nature and to select and organize materials into a harmonious composition. An artist will identify specific elements in a scene and use them to create unity (see Gateway Box: Hokusai, p. 132). Artists are concerned with three kinds of unity: compositional, conceptual, and **gestalt**.

Compositional Unity

An artist creates compositional unity by organizing all the visual aspects of a work. This kind of harmony is not easy to achieve. The three similar diagrams in **1.6.1** illustrate the idea of compositional unity. Although A is unified, it lacks the visual interest of B. While C is a unified work, its visual variety feels incoherent and chaotic. These diagrams show how too much similarity of shape, color, line, or any single

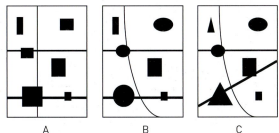

1.6.1 Three diagrams of compositional unity

A   B   C

Gateway to Art: Hokusai, "The Great Wave off Shore at Kanagawa"
A Masterpiece of Unity and Harmony

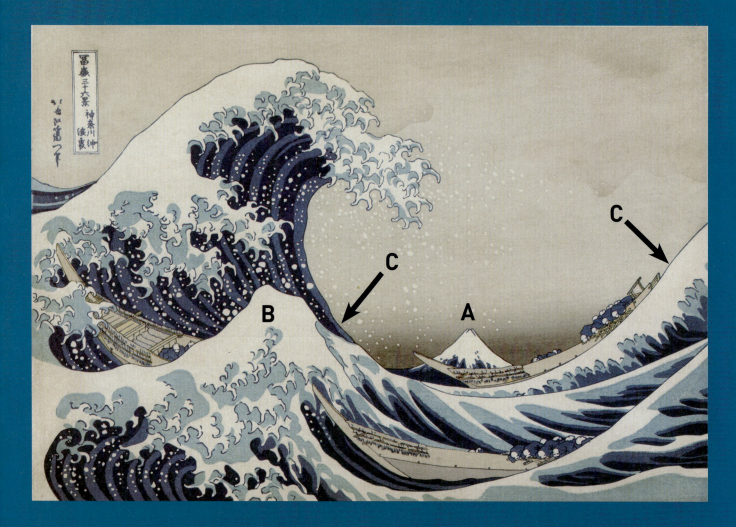

1.6.2 Katsushika Hokusai, "The Great Wave off Shore at Kanagawa," from *Thirty-Six Views of Mount Fuji*, 1826–33 (printed later). Print, color woodcut. Library of Congress, Washington, D.C.

In his print "The Great Wave off Shore at Kanagawa," Japanese artist Katsushika Hokusai (1760–1849) created a unified composition by organizing repetitions of shapes, colors, textures, and patterns to create a visual harmony even though the scene is chaotic (1.6.2). These repetitions visually link different parts of the picture. Even Mount Fuji (A), in the middle of the bottom third of the work, almost blends into the ocean: because whitecaps on the waves (B) mimic the snow atop Mount Fuji, the mountain's presence is felt and reiterated throughout the composition. The shape and placement of the boats also create a pattern amongst the waves. Because the great wave on the left is not repeated, it has a singular strength

that dominates the scene. Hokusai has also carefully selected the solids and voids in his composition to create opposing but balancing areas of interest. As the solid shape of the great wave curves around the deep trough below it (C), the two areas compete for attention, neither one possible without the other.

The words unity and harmony suggest peaceful positive coexistence in a chaotic world. A skillful artist can depict unity and harmony even in a work portraying a scene that in reality would be chaotic and threatening. Here, Hokusai has organized a group of visual elements into a structure that makes sense because it has been simplified and ordered.

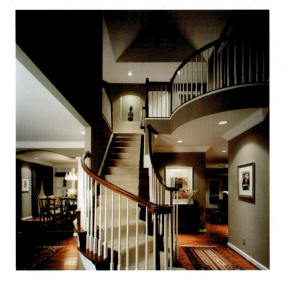

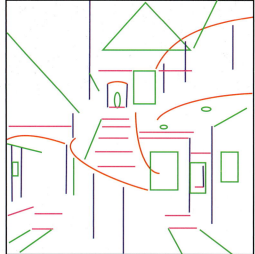

element or principle of art can be monotonous and make us lose interest. Too much variety can lead to a lack of structure and the absence of a central idea. Experienced artists learn to restrict the range of elements: working within limitations can be liberating.

The interior designed by I. Michael Winegrad (**1.6.3**) closely reflects the design in **1.6.4**. The interior has a balance of curved and straight lines that complement each other. The linear patterns of curved lines repeat (red), as do the other directional lines. Shapes are distributed throughout the scene (green). The composition appears harmonious without being boring.

In the work of Russian artist Marie Marevna (1892–1984), the unifying features are the angular lines and flat areas of color or pattern (**1.6.5**). Marevna was one of the first female

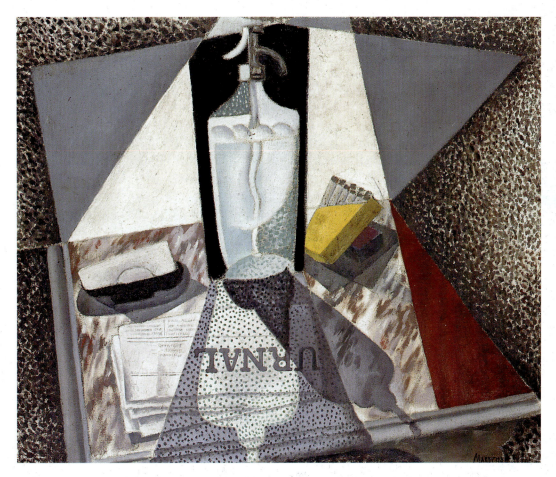

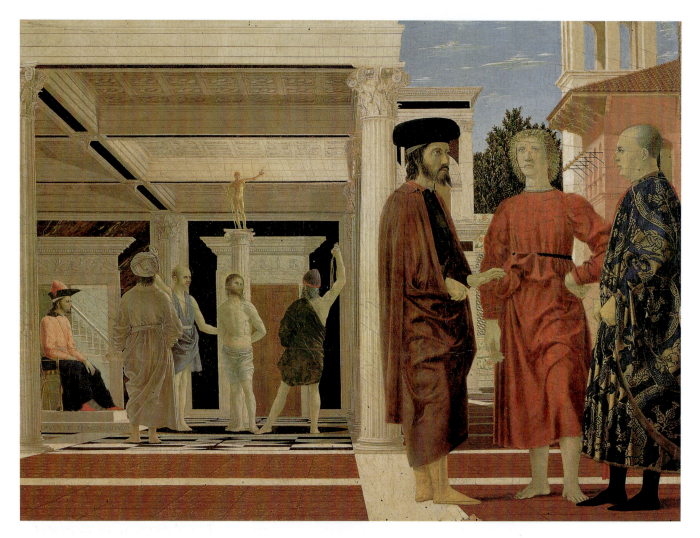

members of the **Cubist** movement; here her Cubist **style** breaks apart a scene and re-creates it from a variety of different angles. In this image, she shows us the seltzer bottle from the side, while we look down at the tabletop from above. The entire work becomes unified, however, because the artist paints a variety of different viewing angles using flat areas of color and pattern throughout, rather than relying on a more realistic representation. Even though we view the **still life** from many different angles, the artist was able to unify the composition by using similar elements. The texture of the paint, the hard diagonal angular lines, and the dominant gray-brown color all work together to counteract the potentially excessive variety that could have come from the many points of view presented.

The great masters of the **Renaissance** understood the importance of unity in their works. They also appreciated the value of putting limits on the number of different elements they introduced into a design, as Piero della Francesca (c. 1415–92) does in *The Flagellation* (**1.6.6**). He concentrates on two major areas, **foreground** and **background**, where two different groups of figures stand. The organic human shapes in the foreground are balanced against the geometric lines of the background. The two groups complement each other and create an order that is reinforced by the strong horizontal and vertical lines throughout the work. This scene depicts Christ, before his crucifixion, being flogged by his captors. The figures in the foreground—whose identities are not known—seem oblivious to what is going on behind them. Rather than communicating a feeling of tension and violence, the composition is quiet and logical, emphasizing the mood of detachment and contemplation. This work has invited many interpretations of who the figures are and what they stand for because Piero della Francesca did

1.6.6 Piero della Francesca, *The Flagellation*, c. 1469. Oil and tempera on panel, 23 × 32". Galleria Nazionale delle Marche, Urbino, Italy

---

Cubism, Cubist: a twentieth-century art movement that favored a new perspective emphasizing geometric forms; the Cubists were artists who formed part of the movement. "Cubist" is also used to describe the painting style they used
Style: a characteristic way in which an artist or group of artists uses visual language to give a work an identifiable form of visual expression
Still life: a scene of inanimate objects, such as fruits, flowers, or motionless animals

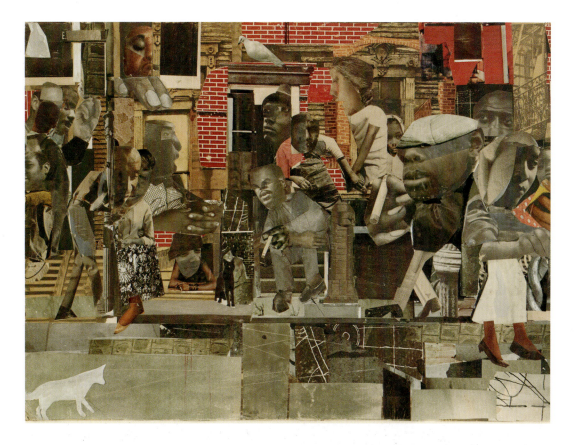

1.6.7 Romare Bearden, *The Dove*, 1964. Cut-and-pasted printed papers, gouache, pencil, and colored pencil on board, 13⅜ × 18¾". MoMA, New York

Renaissance: a period of cultural and artistic change in Europe from the fourteenth to the seventeenth century
Foreground: the part of a work depicted as nearest to the viewer
Background: the part of a work depicted furthest from the viewer's space, often behind the main subject matter
Collage: a work of art assembled by gluing materials, often paper, onto a surface. From the French *coller*, to glue

not identify them or their role in the scene. One possibility that art historians have considered is that the figure in the background on the far left, observing the flagellation of Christ, could be Pontius Pilate, who may symbolize a Byzantine emperor witnessing the suffering of the Church during the Fall of Constantinople in 1453.

Some artists create compositional unity while gathering together bits and pieces of visual information. The African-American artist Romare Bearden (1911–1988) captures the unity of New York in the fragments that make up his **collage** *The Dove* (**1.6.7**). In this work we see snippets of faces and hands, city textures of brick walls and fire escapes, and other associated images assembled into a scene that, at first glance, seems frenetic and chaotic. We may feel this pace of life when we visit a big city, but if we look beyond our first impressions, we often notice the orderly grid of streets and the organization that underpin city life.

Bearden reflects this order in an underlying grid of verticals and horizontals in the street below, and in the vertical streetposts and buildings in the upper section of the work.

The hectic composition is subtly coordinated by an implied triangular shape that runs from the cat in the lower left and the woman's feet in the lower right to the dove (hence the title) at the top center. These three points create a sense of depth while stabilizing the lively image of a bustling street scene.

Conceptual Unity

Conceptual unity refers to the cohesive expression of ideas within a work of art. Ideas can come to us in haphazard and unpredictable ways. Sometimes the expression of these ideas may not look organized, but an artist can still communicate them effectively by selecting images that conjure up a single notion. For example, an artist wishing to communicate the feeling of flight can use such symbols as feathers, kites, or balloons. Each of these has different visual attributes, but they all have an idea in common. That common idea is emphasized when they are placed together in the same work. The artist links images that, although different—perhaps even drastically different—in their appearance, have an idea, symbol, aspect, or association in common. Sometimes, on the other hand, an artist may deliberately break or contradict linkages between ideas to freshen up our tendency to find conventional—even boring—connections between them.

Artists bring their own intentions, experiences, and reactions to their work. These ideas—conscious and unconscious—can also contribute to the conceptual unity of a work and are understood through the artist's style, attitude, and intent. In addition, the conceptual links that artists make between symbols and ideas derive from the collective experiences of their culture: this too influences both the means that artists use to create unity and the viewer's interpretation of the work.

American **Surrealist** sculptor Joseph Cornell (1903–1972) created boxes that contain compositions of **found objects**. His works seem to suggest mysterious ideas and elusive feelings. The disparate shapes, colors, and other characteristics of everyday things come together to form distinctive images. Cornell's works are like a complex game with the viewer, a game that reveals and conceals—just as in a dream or psychoanalysis—the artist's personality. In *Untitled (The Hotel Eden)*, Cornell has collected objects from life and sealed them in a box (**1.6.8**). Although the interior of the box is a protected place, the bird is caged and unable to get out. A yellow ball sits trapped on two rails that limit its freedom of movement to roll back and forth. Neither the bird nor the ball is free. Placed together, all the different objects in the box make an idea greater than any one of them could create on its own. The artist has fused (and deliberately confused) his memories, dreams,

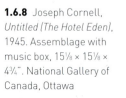

1.6.8 Joseph Cornell, *Untitled (The Hotel Eden)*, 1945. Assemblage with music box, 15⅛ × 15⅛ × 4¾". National Gallery of Canada, Ottawa

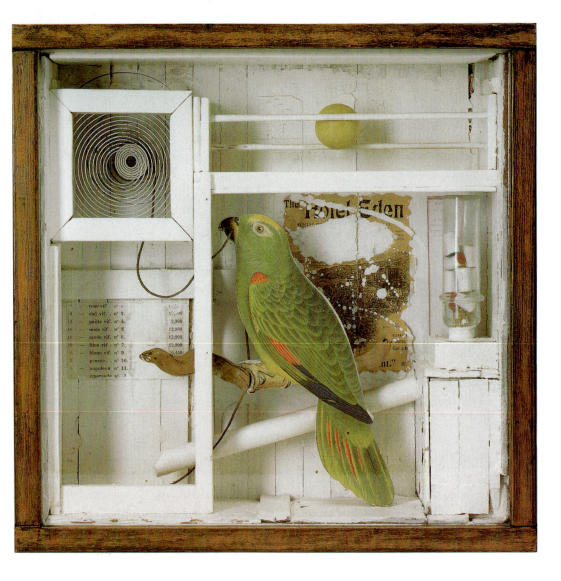

Surrealism, Surrealist: an artistic movement in the 1920s and later; its works were inspired by dreams and the subconscious
Found image or **object:** an image or object found by an artist and presented, with little or no alteration, as part of a work or as a finished work of art in itself

and visualizations; the resulting artwork is a rich and complex visual expression of Cornell's personality and methods.

Gestalt Unity

Gestalt, a German word for form or shape, refers to something (here a work of art) in which the whole seems greater than the sum of its parts. The composition and ideas that go to make a work of art—as well as our experience of it—combine to create a gestalt. We get a sense of gestalt when we comprehend how compositional unity and conceptual unity work together.

We can discover the many faces of gestalt by examining the ancient Hindu relief *Vishnu Dreaming the Universe* (**1.6.9**). In this stone carving, an abundance of human figures surrounds a much larger reclining figure; this is the god Vishnu dreaming. The repetition of the human shapes that attend Vishnu creates compositional unity: these similar shapes link to each other visually.

According to some texts written in the ancient Indian language known as Sanskrit, the existence of the universe, and its creation, are directly dependent on the god Vishnu, who is sheltered by the great serpent Ananta and sleeps on the Cosmic Sea. Through his sleep, the universe is reborn over and over into eternity. Hindu pantheism (the unity of many gods as one) is elegantly illustrated in this work. Brahma is the upper figure seated on a lotus that has sprouted from Vishnu's navel. Here he becomes the active agent of creation. The god Shiva, riding a bull (Nandi), is at Brahma's left. Lakshmi, Vishnu's wife, attends her sleeping husband. Their unity of male and female creates a partnership that results in the birth of a new universe and many other universes into eternity. The dualities of male/female, life/death, good/evil are illustrated in the complex stories of the gods. Shiva, for example, is both creator and destroyer, destruction being necessary for creation—yet another unifying duality.

As is often the case, a religious idea provides profound conceptual unity. The image, the religious idea that the image illustrates, and the

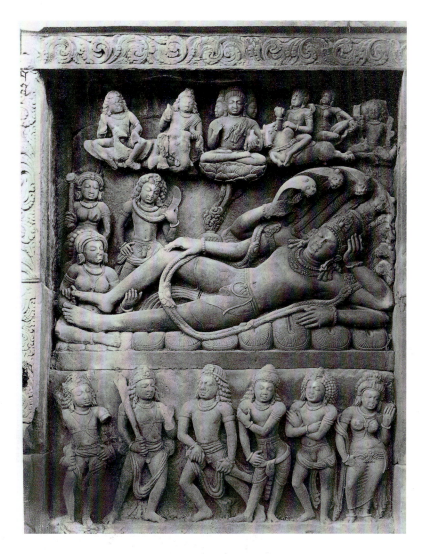

1.6.9 *Vishnu Dreaming the Universe*, c. 450–500 CE. Relief panel. Temple of Vishnu, Deogarh, Uttar Pradesh, India

fervent belief of the artist who created the work interconnect through a symbolic representation in carved stone. As we come to appreciate how these aspects combine so completely in an artwork, we experience a sense of gestalt, an awakened understanding of the whole. This is a goal in any artwork.

Variety

If "variety is the spice of life," it is also the spice of the visual world. In art, variety is a collection of ideas, elements, or materials that are fused together into one design. Inasmuch as unity is about repetition and similarity, variety is about uniqueness and diversity. Artists use a multiplicity of values, textures, colors, and so on to intensify the impact of a work. It is unusual to see a good composition that has just

Value: the lightness or darkness of a plane or area

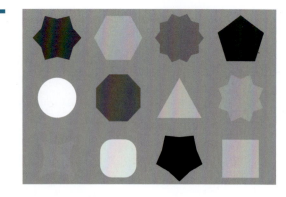

1.6.10 Variety of shapes and values set into a grid

1.6.11 Robert Rauschenberg, *Monogram*, 1955–59. Mixed media with taxidermy goat, rubber tire, and tennis ball, 42 × 63¼ × 64½". Moderna Museet, Stockholm, Sweden

one type of **value**, shape, or color. Variety can invigorate a design. The example in **1.6.10** shows a composition of shapes set into a rectangle on a grid. Even though the grid structure is predictable, the variety of shapes and values counteracts the

rigid structure. Many artists use this kind of variety to express an energy that would be lost if there were too much unity. Variety is the artist's way of giving a work of art a jolt.

The American Robert Rauschenberg (1925–2008) used variety to energize his artwork and challenge his viewers. In the work *Monogram*, Rauschenberg has used all kinds of different things to form his composition (**1.6.11**). The work features a stuffed goat with a tire around its middle standing on a painting. By combining these objects, Rauschenberg creates an outlandish symbol of himself as a rebel and outcast. The goat, an ancient symbol of male lust and a Christian symbol of souls cast out from salvation, becomes the totem of Rauschenberg's

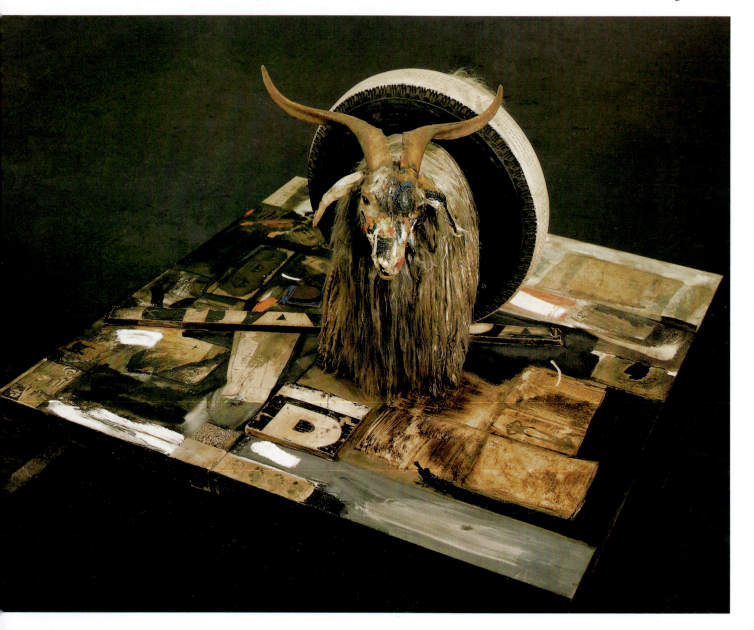

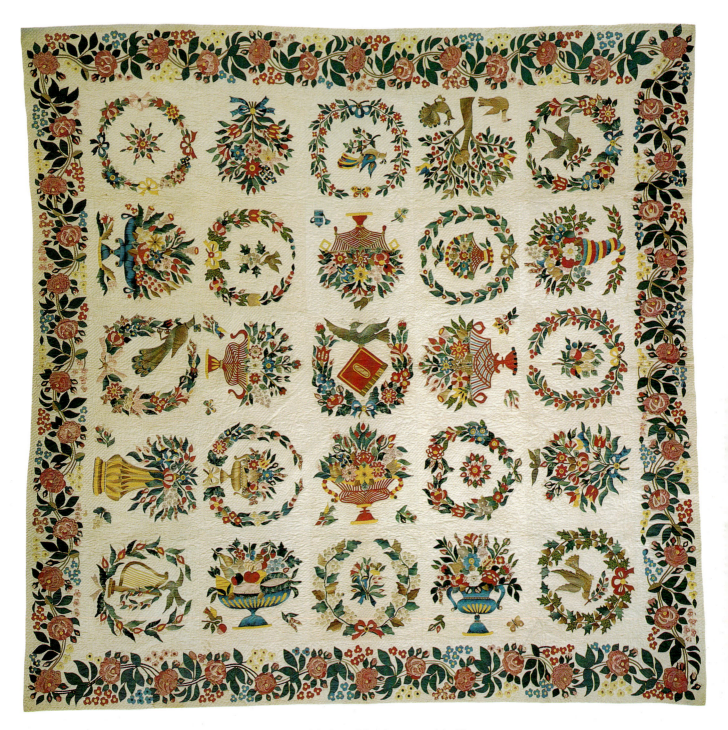

own provocative behaviors and his violation of art-world conventions. The stuffed goat penetrates the tire and stands atop a symbol of the established art world (painting) while defecating a dirty tennis ball on it. For the first time in modern art, too, Rauschenberg breached the divide between painting and sculpture and took painting "off the wall." By using a variety of non-traditional art materials and techniques, the work becomes a transgression against traditional art and morals.

Using Variety to Unify

Although it might seem contradictory, variety can be unifying. Even while using a variety of different shapes, colors, values, or other elements, an artist can create visual harmony. This can be seen in Baltimore album quilts, created by such Maryland artists as Mary Evans in the nineteenth century (**1.6.12**). These carefully sewn quilts are named after the scrapbooks kept by Baltimore girls, although

1.6.12 Album quilt, probably by Mary Evans, Baltimore, Maryland, 1848. Appliquéd cottons with ink work, 9 × 9'. Private collection

rather than being constructed from scraps of leftover material, as many quilts are, these fiber works were made from new pieces of fabric, a reflection of the wealth of this port city. Like a scrapbook, however, these quilts use a variety of images and fuse them together into a finished work. Because a strong structure is imposed on the many different shapes through the use of a grid, the work holds together as a unified whole. The quilted surface is an arrangement of shapes that form a unified composition.

Balance

Just as real objects have physical weight, parts of a work of art can have visual weight, or impact; these need to be balanced to achieve a sort of visual equilibrium. We can identify visual balance in a form or composition, the same as we can with weighted objects, by noting differences between the two halves we are looking at. If the amount of visual weight does not have a reasonable counterweight on the opposite side, the work may appear to be unsuccessful or unfinished. If there are reasonable visual counterweights the work seems complete, and balance has been achieved. Even placing a visual weight in the center of a composition can impose a strong balance on a design.

Finding visual weight and counterweight is a challenge for the artist; balance in a work is not always easy to define. But there are some situations that often arise. For example, dark and light, although opposites, can act as counterbalances. Large shapes or forms can be countered by groups of smaller shapes or forms. For many artists this process is intuitive; they make decisions about the work based on what looks right, rather than on a rigid set of rules.

Symmetrical Balance

If a work can be cut in half and each side looks exactly (or nearly exactly) the same, then it is symmetrically balanced. Near-perfect symmetry exists in the human body. For example, each side of our face has half a nose, half a mouth, half a chin, and so on. The same is true for most animals and a number of geometric shapes, such as circles and squares. Because it is a part of our physical body, symmetry can seem very natural and we can make natural connections to it.

Artists of ancient China designed a creature born of symmetry called the *t'ao t'ieh*. The image of the creature in an artwork is not immediately apparent, because its form is "hidden" amongst many separate symmetrical shapes and forms. It is as if a symmetrical collection of elements coalesces to reveal a monster mask. The image of the t'ao t'ieh has been used widely in Chinese art since the Shang Dynasty (*c.* 1600–*c.* 1050 BCE), when it appeared on ceremonial bronze objects. The meaning of this **motif** is mysterious, but it may symbolize communication with the gods. According to some accounts, the t'ao t'ieh mask represents a monster that, through its own gluttony, is devouring itself: a warning against overindulgence.

The t'ao t'ieh can be found on the bronze ritual container in **1.6.13** by identifying a pair of perfectly round "eyes" on either side of the central vertical ridge. On each side of this central ridge are patterns that mirror each other. Some of these signify horns, claws, fangs, ears, and even smaller images of animals. If you look carefully you may see two rams' heads in profile

Motif: a design or color repeated as a unit in a pattern

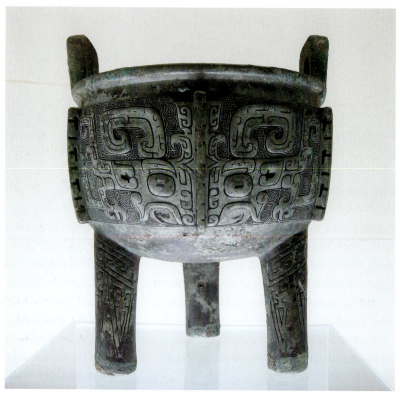

1.6.13 *Liu Ding* (ritual container), China, late Shang Dynasty, *c.* 1600–*c.* 1050 BCE. Bronze. Shanghai Museum, China

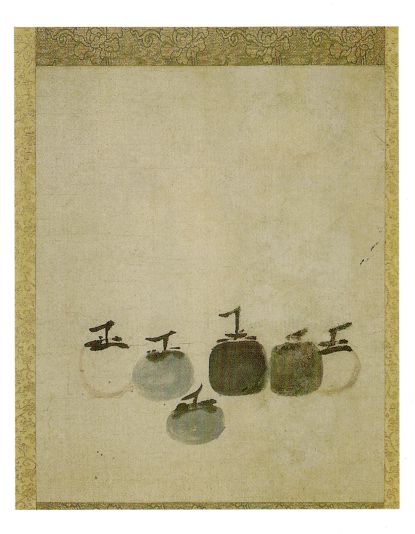

1.6.14 Muqi, *Six Persimmons*, Southern Song Dynasty, *c.* 1250. Ink on paper, 14¼ × 15". Ryoko-in, Dailoxu-ji, Kyoto, Japan

as they butt heads along the vertical central **axis**. The "monster" of symmetry lurks amongst the many parts of the image and waits for us to discover its hiding place.

Asymmetrical Balance

On an old-fashioned scale, the kind with a long arm centered on top of a vertical support, a single heavy object on one side can be balanced by several lighter objects on the other side as long as the weight on both sides is the same. Similarly, when artists organize a composition they often use different visual "weights" on each side of the composition. This is asymmetrical balance, also called dynamic balance; it applies when the elements on the left and right sides are not the same, but the combination of elements counters each other.

Chinese artists have used asymmetrical balance to reflect on life and spirituality. The thirteenth-century Zen Buddhist monk Muqi

expresses balanced asymmetry in his work *Six Persimmons* (**1.6.14**). In this work, dark, light, and the subtle differences in shape are not distributed evenly between the left and right sides of the work. Muqi creates subtle variations in the placement of the persimmons on each side of the central axis. On the right are two large dark shapes with a heavy visual weight, one of which partially overlaps a light shape. On the left there is one light shape and two dark shapes, one of which is placed lower in the picture. Muqi brilliantly counteracts the visual "heaviness" of the right side by placing one shape lower on the left. The lower placement of the smallest persimmon adds visual weight to the left side and counters the visual weight of the largest fruit just above it. For Muqi, the use of brush and ink was a form of meditation, through simple, thoughtful actions, in search of higher knowledge. This work may look simple, but the thoughtful arrangement of the shapes cannot be changed without undermining its "perfect" asymmetry.

Axis: an imaginary line showing the center of a shape, volume, or composition

Gateway to Art: The Taj Mahal
Love and Perfection

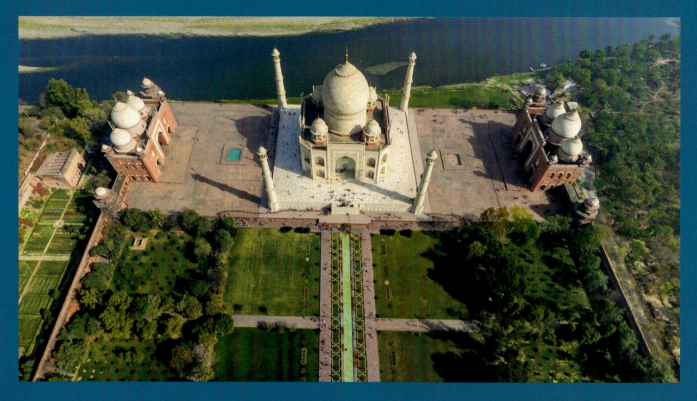

1.6.15 Ustad Ahmad Lahauri, Abd al-Karim Ma'mur Khan, Makramat Khan, commissioned by Shah Jahan, The Taj Mahal, marble architecture, Agra, India

The building that we know as the Taj Mahal is an exemplary and enduring study in pure symmetry (1.6.15). It was commissioned by the grieving Shah Jahan (1592–1666), the fifth Mughal Emperor of India, as a memorial to his third and beloved wife, Mumtaz Mahal (1593–1631). She and Shah Jahan were devoted to each other, and in recognition of their love and as an expression of his admiration for her, he

1.6.16 Plan of the tomb of Mumtaz Mahal

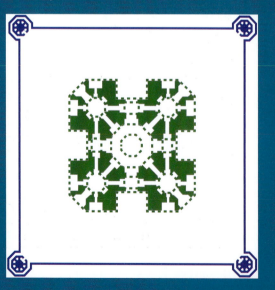

sought after her death to create a building that would, through its visual perfection, honor her memory and stand as a testament to the transcendent power of timeless love.

In art, symmetrical balance is created when harmony unites all the elements, just as Shah Jahan and Mumtaz felt united in their relationship based on requited love. A stable visual form is achieved when opposite sides of a design mirror each other exactly, creating this perfect balance. In most cases symmetry suggests pleasing tranquility, order, and numerical perfection to the viewer, so its use in the proportions and design of the Taj Mahal carries associations of beauty and stability.

The Taj Mahal uses both bilateral and radial symmetry in the design of the central tomb building (1.6.16) and the surrounding complex in which it stands. The entire complex includes the central mausoleum and four minarets, a meeting house, a mosque, two pavilions, a gatehouse, two plaza areas, and a grand garden (1.6.17), all of which can be bisected to reveal identical components on the

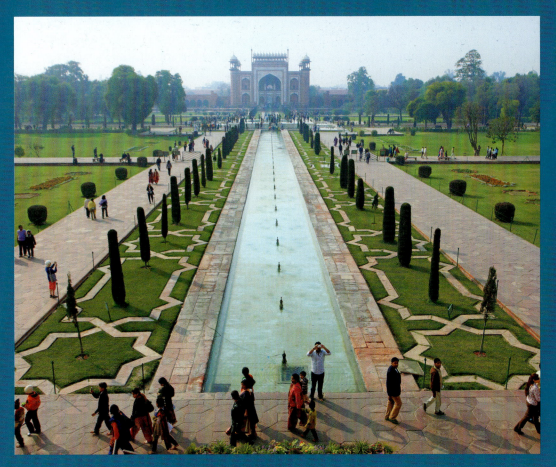

1.6.18 (below) Plan of the charbagh (Mughal garden)

opposite side. There are even some additional areas adjacent and across the Yamuna River that also share the same characteristics. The entire plan, if bisected parallel to its longest axis, would find an exact replication in its opposite side. The carefully apportioned symmetrical balance in this plan expresses a sense of perfection.

Radial balance exists in both the main building and the adjacent *charbagh* (Mughal garden) (1.6.18). Both are planned in such a way that each design element is repeated equidistant to a central point. So the symmetry exists along not only the bilateral axis, but also the principal intersecting axis. The multiple repetition of this balance in the design is a deliberate affirmation, in its sustained artistry, of the depth of Shah Jahan's love. Similarly, the complete design itself reflects his overarching commitment to perfection, shared by his architects Abd al-Karim Ma'mur Khan, Makramat Khan, and Ustad Ahmad Lahauri, as an expression, and indeed a proof, of the timelessness of true love.

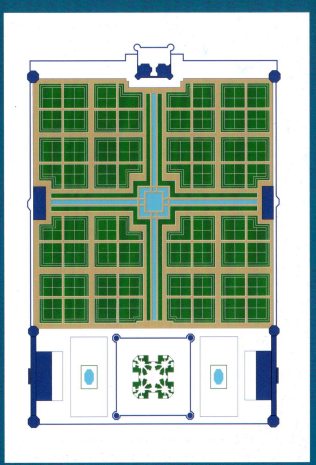

Radial Balance

Radial balance (or symmetry) is achieved when all elements in a work are equidistant from a central point and repeat in a symmetrical way from side to side and top to bottom. Radial symmetry can imply circular and repeating elements. Although the term "radial" suggests a round shape, in fact any geometric shape can be used to create radial symmetry. Artists can employ this kind of balance when it is necessary to depict an element more than twice. It is sometimes used in religious symbols and architecture where repetition plays an important role in the design.

The Tibetan sand painting shown in **1.6.19** is a diagram of the universe (also known as a **mandala**) from a human perspective. The Tibetan Buddhist monks who created this work have placed a series of symbols equidistant from the center. In this mandala the colors vary but the shapes pointing in four different directions from the center are symmetrical. The square area in the center of the work symbolizes Amitayus, or the Buddha of long life, and surrounds a central lotus blossom. The creation of one of these sand paintings is an act of meditation that takes many days, after which the work is destroyed. The careful deconstruction of the work after it has been completed symbolizes the impermanence of the world.

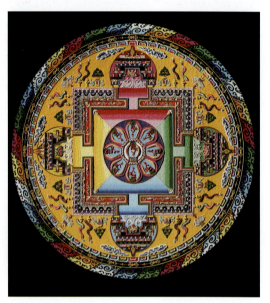

1.6.19 Amitayus Mandala created by the monks of Drepung Loseling Monastery, Tibet

Active Learning Exercises

1. When an artist unifies a design, he or she places elements with similar characteristics into a visual relationship. The simple act of organizing your desk can create unity in the visual space of your desktop. Even making a list is a way of creating a visual unity that organizes information. Collect sixteen small objects of varying shape and color, each of which will fit in the palm of your hand. On a clean sheet of white paper, lay them out in a way that seems regulated and harmonious. Take a picture of the completed composition. What kind of system did you use? Are there patterns that you see now that you may have overlooked before?

2. Find pictures of four objects that have no visual relationships: if one is long and thin, there should not be another long, thin object in the group, and so on. Be conscious of height, width, length, color, value, texture, orientation, symbolism, etc. Once you have collected these pictures, distribute and adhere them on a piece of white paper, making sure that they are not organized in a repetitive system. Have another person look at your collection and find as many similarities as he or she can. Do you think that it is possible to avoid having some unity in a work of art? Why, or why not?

3. Asymmetrical balance is achieved in a work of art when the two halves of a work, when bisected vertically, are not exactly the same but there are elements in each half that offset the visual "weight" of the other. Find online an image of an artwork that uses asymmetrical balance, and print it out. On the printed image, create a vertical line through the middle of the work. Using your drawing tool, circle the element on each side that is balanced against those on the opposite side. Make sure to consider such aspects as negative spaces balanced against positive shapes. Do you think that the work is balanced? Why, or why not?

Images Related to 1.6:
Unity, Variety, and Balance

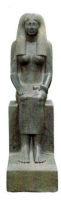

2.4.1 Sculpture of Lady Sennuwy, Egypt, 1971–1926 BCE, p. 249

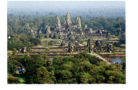

3.3.24 Angkor Wat, Cambodia, 12th century, p. 430

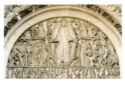

4.2.10 Gislebertus, *The Last Judgment, c.* 1120–35, p. 581

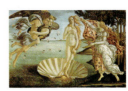

4.9.5 Sandro Botticelli, *The Birth of Venus, c.* 1482–86, p. 662

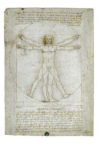

4.4.1 Leonardo da Vinci, *Vitruvian Man, c.* 1490, p. 599

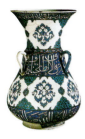

1.4.21 Mosque lamp from the Dome of the Rock, 1549, p. 112

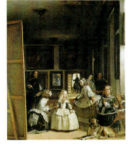

1.10.11a Diego de Silva y Velázquez, *Las Meninas, c.* 1656, p. 190

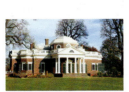

3.7.13 Thomas Jefferson, Monticello, Virginia, 1769–1809, p. 502

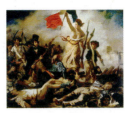

3.7.16 Eugène Delacroix, *Liberty Leading the People* 1830, p. 504

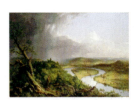

3.7.19 Thomas Cole, *View from Mount Holyoke*, 1836, p. 506

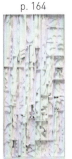

1.8.10 Ando Hiroshige, "Riverside Bamboo Market, Kyōbashi," 1857, p. 164

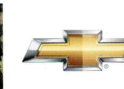

4.5.16 Édouard Manet, *A Bar at the Folies Bergère*, 1882, p. 623

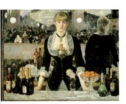

2.7.8 Chevrolet logo, first used 1913, p. 311

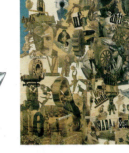

2.8.21 Hannah Höch, *Cut with the Kitchen Knife ...*, 1919–20, p. 333

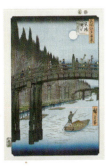

1.2.3 David Smith, *Cubi XIX*, 1964, p. 69

0.0.3 Louise Nevelson, *White Vertical Water*, 1972, p. 28

1.1.23 Miriam Shapiro, *Baby Blocks*, 1983, p. 61

4.10.10 Carrie Mae Weems, "You Became a Scientific Profile," 1995, p. 682

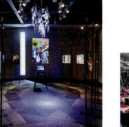

3.9.17 Jolene Rickard, *Corn Blue Room...*, 1998, p. 552

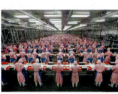

2.8.26 Edward Burtynsky, "Manufacturing #17...," 2005, p. 336

1.7

Scale and Proportion

The nineteenth-century French poet Charles Baudelaire wrote that "All that is beautiful and noble is the result of reason and calculation." Baudelaire was speaking of cosmetics and makeup, and not referring specifically to works of art, but his statement neatly summarizes the care with which artists determine **scale** and **proportion**. Artists use these key **principles** of design to control how they implement the basic **elements** of art, just as grammar controls how words work in a sentence.

We perceive scale in relation to our own size. Art objects created on a **monumental** scale appear larger than they would be in normal life. This monumentality imposes itself on us. In a work created on a human scale, its size corresponds to the size of things as they actually exist. Work at this scale often surprises us. Small-scale objects appear smaller than our usual experience of them in the real world. Often, scale is used to indicate importance, yet this is not always the case: sometimes the smallest thing is the most significant.

Proportion is a core principle in the **unity** of any art object. Usually, an artist ensures that all the parts of an object are in proportion to one another. Alternatively, an artist can create a contradiction by portraying objects or figures out of proportion. For example, a cartoonist may portray a figure with disproportionately large nose or ears to exaggerate the prominent facial features distinctive to a famous personality. Careful proportion is a sign of technical mastery; discordant proportions can express a wide range of meanings.

Scale

The scale of a work of art communicates ideas. A small work communicates something very different than a larger one. Small-scale pieces force viewers to come in close to experience the artwork. A small-scale work implies intimacy, like whispering in someone's ear or admiring a ring on his or her finger. Large-scale works can be experienced by groups of viewers, and usually communicate big ideas directed at a large audience. Artists and designers make conscious choices about the scale of a work when they consider the message they want to convey.

Artists may also consider scale as they make more practical choices about a work. Considerations of cost, the time it will take to execute the piece, and the demands that a specific location may place on the work: all come into play in decisions about scale.

Scale and Meaning

Usually a monumental scale indicates heroism or other epic virtues. War monuments, for example, often feature figures much larger than lifesize in order to convey the bravery of the warriors. The Swedish-born artist Claes Oldenburg (b. 1929), however, uses monumental scale to poke fun while expressing admiration for the little things of everyday life. Oldenburg believes that the items of mass culture, no matter how insignificant they might seem, express a truth about modern life. So he restyles small, often overlooked objects on a monumental

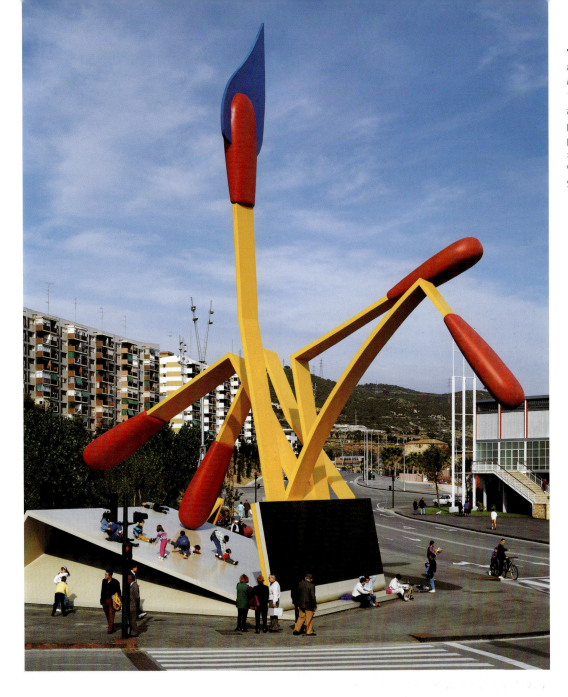

1.7.1 Claes Oldenburg and Coosje van Bruggen, *Mistos (Match Cover)*, 1992. Steel, aluminum, and fiber-reinforced plastic, painted with polyurethane enamel, 68' × 33' × 43'4". Collection La Vall d'Hebron, Barcelona, Spain

scale, giving clothes pins and ice cream cones a grandeur and significance they do not usually have. In the process, Oldenburg transforms the essence of these everyday things as he magnifies their sculptural form. Look at, for example, the enormous book of matches in **1.7.1**, a collaboration between Oldenburg and his wife, the Dutch-born sculptor Coosje van Bruggen (1942–2009).

The American Robert Lostutter (b. 1939) uses small scale to enhance the character of his work. Lostutter likes to create his works on the scale not of a human but of a bird. He paints the plumage of exotic birds in great detail onto human faces, while the tiny size evokes the bird from which the plumage was copied (**1.7.2**). The small scale of Lostutter's work—only one person at a time can see it properly—forces us to come closer; looking at it becomes an intimate experience.

1.7.2 Robert Lostutter, *The Hummingbirds*, 1981. Watercolor on paper, 1¾ × 5⅝". Collection of Anne and Warren Weisberg

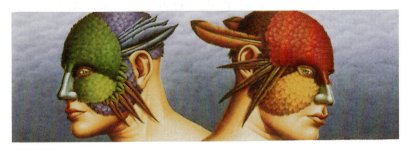

Hierarchical Scale

Artists can use size to indicate the relative importance of figures or objects in a composition: almost always, larger means more important, and smaller means less important. Hierarchical scale refers to the deliberate use of relative size in a work in order to communicate differences in importance. **1.7.3a** and **b** show the use of hierarchical scale in a **relief** sculpture from ancient Egypt. In the art of ancient Egypt, the king, or pharaoh, was usually the largest figure depicted because he had the highest status in the social order. Here, the largest figure (A) represents the pharaoh; he is visually more dominant than the others. This scene depicts

1.7.3a and **b** (below) Hierarchical scale: Relief from the northern wall of the great temple of Amun, 19th Dynasty, c. 1295–1186 BCE. Karnak, Egypt

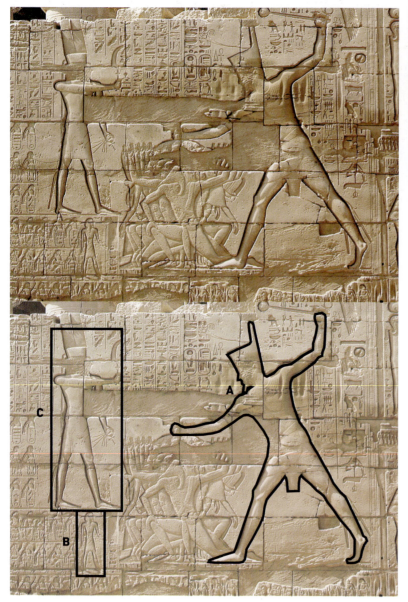

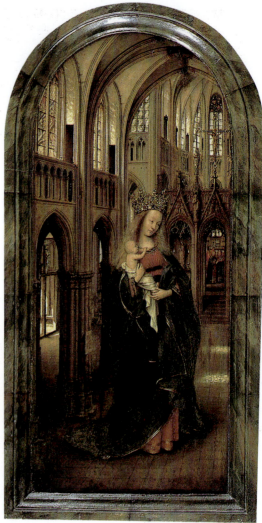

1.7.4 (above) Jan van Eyck, *Madonna in a Church*, 1437–38. Oil on wood panel, 12⅝ × 5½". Gemäldegalerie, Staatliche Museen, Berlin, Germany

the military campaign of Seti I against the Hittites and Libyans.

The Flemish artist Jan van Eyck (c. 1395–1441) uses hierarchical scale to communicate spiritual importance. In his painting *Madonna in a Church*, Van Eyck enlarges the scale so that the enormous mother and child fill the massive space of a **Gothic** church (**1.7.4**). In his effort to glorify the spiritual importance of Mary and the Christ child, Van Eyck also separates them from normal human existence. Their gigantic appearance, relative to the interior, makes these figures appear to be larger than normal human beings. Van Eyck has scaled them to symbolize their central importance in the Christian religion.

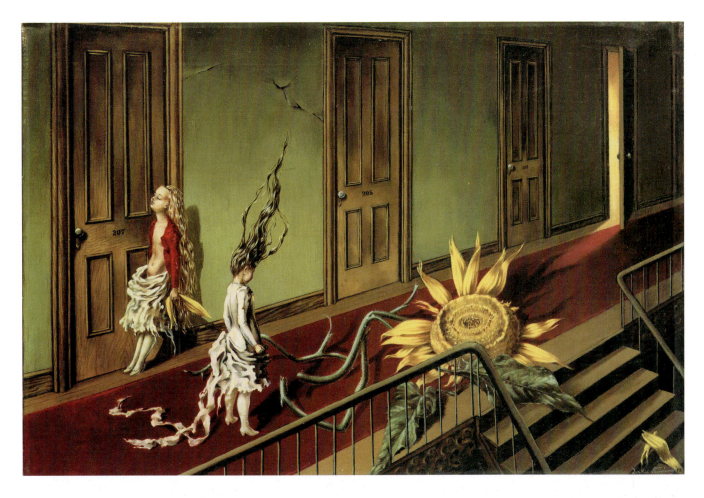

Distorted Scale

An artist may deliberately distort scale to create a supernatural effect. In the twentieth century, artists known as **Surrealists** created works that use dreamlike images to subvert our conscious experiences. The American Surrealist artist Dorothea Tanning (1910–2012), in *Eine Kleine Nachtmusik*, paints a sunflower at a scale that contradicts its surroundings (**1.7.5**). The flower seems huge in relation to the interior architecture and the two female figures standing on the left. By altering our ordinary experience of scale, Tanning invites us into a world unlike the one we know: a realm of childhood dreams and nightmares where odd things happen, such as the strangely "alive" sunflower and the unexplained wind that lifts the hair of one figure. The title, *Eine Kleine Nachtmusik* ("A Little Night Music"), derives from a lighthearted piece of music by the eighteenth-century Austrian composer Wolfgang Amadeus Mozart, but ironically Tanning's scene exhibits a strange sense of dread.

Proportion

The relationships between the sizes of different parts of a work make up its proportions. By controlling these size relationships an artist can enhance the expressive and descriptive characteristics of the work.

As size relationships change, proportions change. For example, **1.7.6** shows the profile of a Greek vase. If we change the width (B) or the height (C), the overall proportions change. Each of these vase profiles communicates a different

1.7.5 Dorothea Tanning, *Eine Kleine Nachtmusik*, 1943. Oil on canvas, 16⅛ × 24″. Tate, London, England

Surrealism, Surrealist: an artistic movement in the 1920s and later; its works were inspired by dreams and the subconscious

1.7.6 Examples of how proportion changes on vertical and horizontal axes

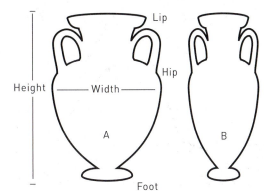

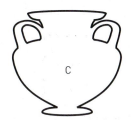

feeling simply because the ratio of height to width is different. When the width is reduced, the vase seems elegant and light. Reducing the height makes the opposite true: the vase seems clumsier and weightier than the original profile (A).

For a two-dimensional work, the artist chooses an area, or **format**, on which to make a drawing, painting, print, or design. The format's dimensions—its height and width—dictate a great deal about what kind of image can be created. For example, a format that is only 2 in. tall and 10 in. across will require that the artist create an image that is short and wide. Artists must plan ahead and choose the format that best fits their intended image.

Human Proportion

As we saw when discussing **1.7.6**, carefully chosen proportion can make an art object seem pleasing to the eye. As it happens, the parts of a vase are given names based on the human body: the lip, hip, and foot. Just as the body of a vase can have agreeable or disagreeable proportions, the same is true of the human body.

In ancient Egypt, the palm of the hand was a unit of measurement (**1.7.7**). Six palm widths equaled a unit of measurement called a cubit. The height of an average man was estimated at 4 cubits or 24 palms: the proportion of the man's palm to the height of his body was therefore 24:1.

The ancient Greeks were especially interested in proportion. Greek mathematicians investigated, in the visual arts and in other art forms, such as music, the mathematical basis of beauty and of ideal proportions. The Greek sculptor Polykleitos wrote a treatise describing how to create a statue of a human being with ideal or perfect proportions. In the first century BCE the Roman writer Vitruvius wrote his book *On Architecture*, in which he claimed to set out the rules that Greeks and Romans applied to the design of architecture.

The Greeks sought an ideal of beauty in the principle of proportion. Figures made during the **Classical period** of Greek sculpture share similar proportions. To the Greeks, these proportions embodied the perfection of the gods. In contrast, fifteenth-century

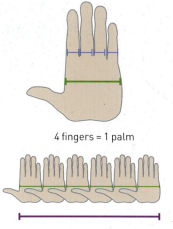
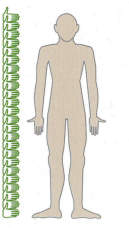

4 fingers = 1 palm

6 palms = 1 cubit

4 cubits = 1 man's height (24 palms)

1.7.7 Ancient Egyptian system using the human hand as a standard unit of measurement

African sculptors preferred to show status and individuality. Pictured in **1.7.8** is a sculpture of the Oni of Ife in **cast** brass. The Oni, or Monarch, of the Ife Dynasty of the Yoruba people is shown standing in full regalia (ceremonial clothing and adornments). The Oni is the most powerful and important figure in this culture, yet his proportions here are neither realistic nor idealized. The head—about a quarter of the entire figure—is large; the Yoruba believe that the head is the seat of a divine power from whence a life source emanates to control personality and destiny. This figure, like Ife kings, represents a direct descendant of Oduduwa, the heroic leader whose children became the great leaders of the Yoruba. The facial features are idealized, suggesting that a personal heritage shapes one's destiny as a great leader. Many African sculptures exaggerate the head and face as a way to communicate status, destiny, and a connection to the spiritual. Both the Yoruba and the Greeks were concerned with creating a connection to the spiritual world, but African artists celebrated the importance of history (inheritance) and one's unique affiliation or office, while the Greeks sought an impersonal, ideal model.

The models used by the Greeks for calculating human proportion were later adopted by artists of ancient Rome and then by the artists of the **Renaissance**. Raphael used them in *The School of Athens* (see Gateway Box:

Format: the shape of the area an artist uses for making a two-dimensional artwork
Classical period: a period in the history of Greek art, c. 480–323 BCE
Cast: a sculpture or artwork made by pouring a liquid (for example molten metal or plaster) into a mold
Renaissance: a period of cultural and artistic change in Europe from the fourteenth to the seventeenth century

1.7.8 Nigerian Ife artist, Figure of Oni, early 14th–15th century. Brass with lead, 18⅜″ high. National Museum, Ife, Nigeria

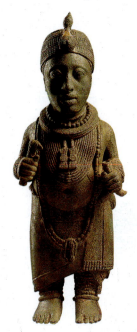

Gateway to Art: Raphael, *The School of Athens*
Scale and Proportion in a Renaissance Masterpiece

The Italian painter Raphael's (1483–1520) sensitivity to proportion reflects his pursuit of perfection, an ideal of Renaissance artists. Raphael indicated the importance of his masterpiece by creating it on a magnificent scale: it measures 200 × 300 in. (16 ft. 8 in. × 25 ft.) (**1.7.9**). The figures inhabit a well-proportioned interior that makes them seem human despite the large size of the work.

An analysis of the dimensions of *The School of Athens* may provide a viewer with some insight into how proportion plays a role in the creation of a design. Because this work measures exactly 200 × 300 in., it can be visually subdivided, horizontally, into three one-hundred in. increments from left to right (A). When the work is subdivided in this way, we can perceive some recognizable divisions in the composition. For example, the central vertical area that is highlighted by coffered arches in the ceiling falls into the middle third of the work. Another interesting correlation is made when we subdivide the work into thirds vertically (B). When we view the vertical divisions, it appears that the vast majority of figures in the foreground area (in front of the steps) are positioned in the bottom third of the design. Interestingly enough, the figures in the background (in the elevated section) fall just beneath one-third of the second vertical division (C) when we subdivide the central horizontal section.

These clear divisions seem intentional and lead one to assume that Raphael was working with a proportional system when he first designed *The School of Athens*. The format appears to reflect a system that some artists call the Rule of Thirds because it organizes the spatial area of a composition according to regular units of one- or two-thirds. The Rule of Thirds is used by artists, designers, photographers, and architects to provide pleasing proportional associations.

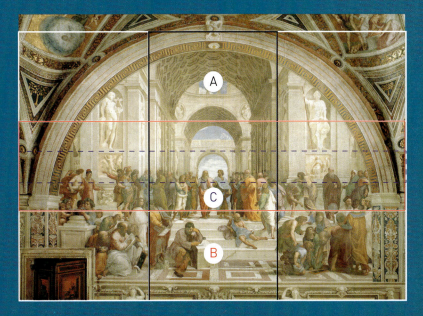

1.7.9 Raphael, *The School of Athens*, with overlaid diagram showing proportional structure

Within this carefully structured composition, Raphael further enhances the impression of Classical harmony and grace in the artwork by using perspective to give the architectural elements of the painting a sense of depth and to draw our eyes to the center of the work, in which he has also placed the two key figures of Greek philosophy, Plato (in the center, left) and Aristotle (center, right). Plato (c. 428–347 BCE) and Aristotle (384–322 BCE), the two greatest philosophers of ancient Greece whose thinking directly influenced the culture of the Renaissance, stand side by side. In Raphael's painting Plato points to the sky. He is the idealist who seeks truth in the world of ideas. Aristotle, who bases his thinking on the study of the material world (and who influenced the scientific method as we know it today) points to the ground. In this way, Raphael brilliantly deploys artistic techniques that perfectly express and complement his subject matter.

Raphael, p. 151) to ensure that the figures in his composition had the ideal human proportion used in the ancient world.

The Golden Section

The Greeks' interest in the use of mathematical formulas to determine perfect proportions has fascinated artists ever since. One of the best-known formulas is what has become known since the Renaissance as the **Golden Section** (**1.7.10**) (also referred to as the Golden Mean or Golden Ratio), a proportional ratio of 1:1.618, which occurs in many natural objects. It turns out that real human bodies do not have exactly these proportions, but when the ratio 1:1.618 is applied to making statues, it gives naturalistic results. It is likely that Greek sculptors used much simpler methods than the Golden Section to calculate the proportions of their sculptures, but the resulting proportions are often very close to the Golden Section. The sculpture of Poseidon (some art historians say it is Zeus) is a famous example (**1.7.11a**). Poseidon, a Greek god, had to be portrayed with perfect proportions. The Greek sculptor applied a conveniently simple ratio, using the head as a standard measurement. In **1.7.11a** and **1.7.11b** you can see that the body is three heads wide by seven heads high.

1.7.10 The Golden Section

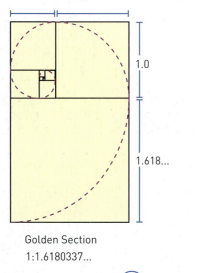

Golden Section
1:1.6180337...

1.0

1.618...

1

1.6180337...

Proportional Ratios

Artists have learned other ways to apply proportional formulas to organize their compositions and ensure that their work is visually interesting. One such technique is known as "Golden Rectangles," because it is based on nesting inside each other a succession

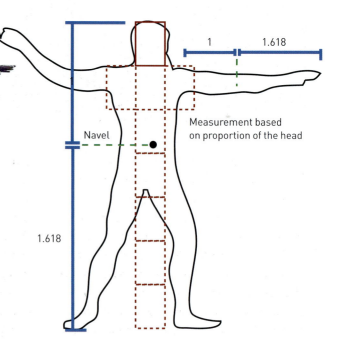

1.7.11a *Poseidon* (or *Zeus*), *c.* 460–450 BCE. Bronze, 6'10½"high. National Archaeological Museum, Athens, Greece

1.7.11b Diagram of proportional formulas used in the statue

Navel

1.618

1

1.618

Measurement based on proportion of the head

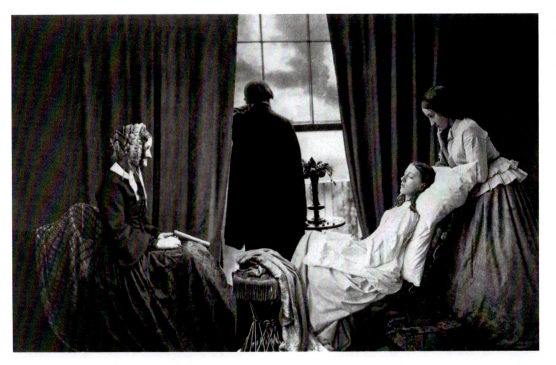

1.7.12a Henry Peach Robinson, *Fading Away*, 1858. Combination albumen print, 9½ × 15½". George Eastman House, Rochester, New York

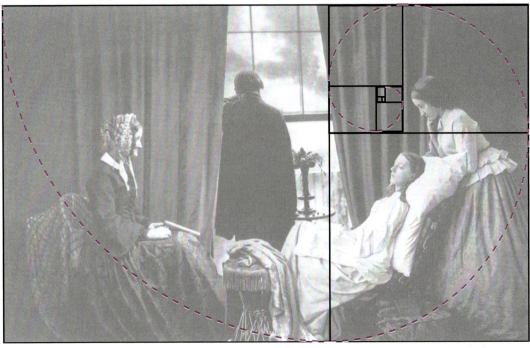

1.7.12b Proportional analysis of the photograph

of rectangles based on the 1:1.618 proportions of the Golden Section. The shorter side of the outer rectangle becomes the longer side of the smaller rectangle inside it, and so on. The result is an elegant spiral shape. In 1858 the English photographer Henry Peach Robinson (1830–1901), one of the great innovators of the photographic arts, used this idea to compose a photograph titled *Fading Away* (**1.7.12a** and **1.7.12b**). Robinson was well known for his work

in fusing many different **negatives** to create a new image. This image shows his attention to the coordinated ratios in artistic composition. Notice how the right-hand drape divides the photograph into two Golden Rectangles and how the spiral draws our eye to the dying young woman.

The Greeks applied their proportional systems to architecture as well as to sculpture. By applying the idealized rules of proportion for

Negative: a reversed image, in which light areas are dark and dark areas are light (opposite of a positive)

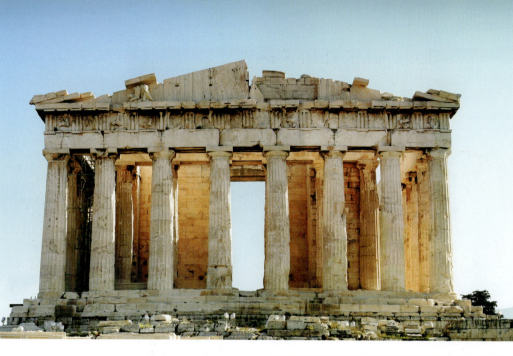

1.7.13a Iktinos and Kallikrates, Parthenon, 447–432 BCE, Athens, Greece

the human body to the design of the Parthenon, a temple of the goddess Athena, the Greeks created a harmonious design. As it happens, the proportions correspond quite closely to the Golden Section (**1.7.13a**). The vertical and horizontal measurements work together to create proportional harmony (**1.7.13b**).

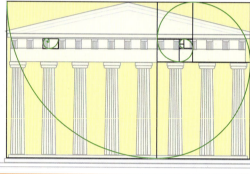

1.7.13b The use of the Golden Section in the design of the Parthenon

Active Learning Exercises

1. Scale changes the experience of the viewer in a work of art. When something is massive it communicates differently than if it were small. To understand this experience fully, look at the same work in a small format and a large one. Using your school identification card or driver's license picture, photocopy your picture and reduce the size to half. Using the same picture, enlarge the image until it fills an entire page. For an even better effect, you could also project the image on a screen. Now compare the images. How are they best viewed? Do they change the way that someone else may respond to your picture? How would that affect other types of subjects?

2. Proportion is especially noticeable when we view images of the human form. We are so familiar with human physical proportions that we notice even slightly pronounced facial features, such as a large nose or ears. Make three photocopies of your school identification or driver's license picture. Each copy should be enlarged or reduced from the original. Cut out facial features from all three, such as the nose, ears, eyes, mouth, and the head, and reconstruct your face using select features from each copy. How do you react to the distorted proportion of your face? Can you think of examples where an artist has changed the facial proportion? Why do you think he or she did so?

3. The ancient Greeks discovered that the proportional ratio called the Golden Section applies to many living things, including the human body. An ancient Greek philosopher named Protagoras reportedly wrote, "Man is the measure of all things," attributing human proportions to the works and objects we create with the human hand. To get a feel for what that ratio looks like, draw a rectangle 5 in. × 8³⁄₃₂ in. on a piece of plain paper. Partition off a 5-in. × 5-in. square at one end. You will see that you have created a smaller rectangle with the proportions of the Golden Section at one end. Are there objects you use daily that feature similar proportions? If so, what are they? If not, was Protagoras wrong?

Images Related to 1.7:
Scale and Proportion

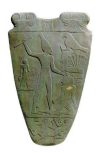

4.7.6b Palette of Narmer (back), Egypt, *c.* 2950–2775 BCE, p. 639

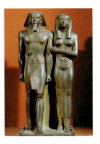

4.9.3b *Menkaure and Khamerernebty*, Egypt, *c.* 2520 BCE, p. 661

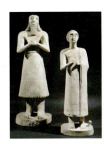

1.10.5 Sumerian Votive Figures, c. 2500 BCE, p. 185

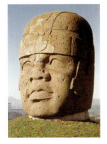

1.2.13 Colossal Olmec Head, 1500–1300 BCE, p. 75

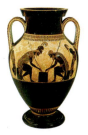

3.1.28 Exekias, Amphora of Achilles and Ajax Playing Dice, 530 BCE, p. 384

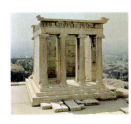

2.5.10 Kallikrates, Temple of Athena Nike, Athens, Greece, *c.* 421–415 BCE, p. 271

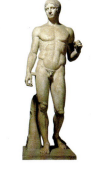

3.1.25 Polykleitos, *Doryphoros* (Roman version), 120–50 BCE, p. 382

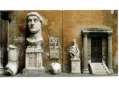

4.6.10 Remnants of colossal statue of Constantine, 325–26 CE, p. 631

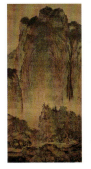

1.3.10 Fan Kuan, *Travelers among Mountains and Streams*, 11th century, p. 88

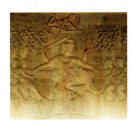

3.3.25 *Vishnu Churning the Ocean of Milk*, 12th century, p. 431

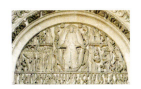

4.2.10 Gislebertus, *The Last Judgment*, *c.* 1120–35, p. 581

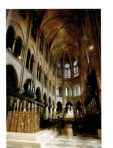

4.1.1 Notre Dame Cathedral, Paris, France, 1163–1250, p. 563

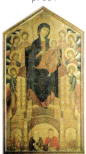

3.2.26 Cimabue, *Virgin and Child Enthroned*, *c.* 1280, p. 409

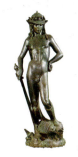

3.6.20 Donatello, *David*, *c.* 1430, p. 482

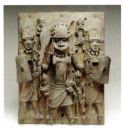

4.7.10 Benin Plaque with warrior and attendants, 16th–17th century, p. 642

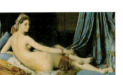

1.10.8 Jean-Auguste-Dominique Ingres, *Grande Odalisque*, 1814, p. 187

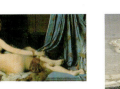

2.4.15 Robert Smithson, *Spiral Jetty*, 1969–70, p. 25

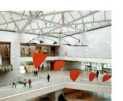

1.5.12 Alexander Calder, *Untitled*, 1976, p. 126

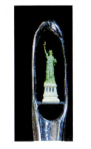

4.4.7 Willard Wigan, *Statue of Liberty*, p. 603

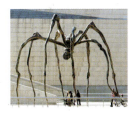

1.2.18 Louise Bourgeois, *Maman*, 1999 (cast 2001), p. 79

1.8

Emphasis and Focal Point

When we emphasize something, we draw attention to it. This is a valuable part of communication that allows us to set some things apart. In art, **emphasis** is the **principle** by which an artist draws attention to particular content.

An entire work, a broad area within a work of art, multiple areas, and even specific points can be emphasized. The term **focal point** can be used both to describe a particular place of visual emphasis in a work of art or design, and to refer to another of the principles of art which, similarly to emphasis, is a way of highlighting certain locations in a work.

An artist can emphasize focal points through the use of line, implied line, value, color—in fact, any of the **elements** of art can help to focus our interest on specific areas. In a way that is similar to the effect of the bull's-eye on a target, focal points concentrate our attention. Even though our field of vision is fairly wide, at any given moment we can focus our vision only on a small area. The physiology of vision underlies the principle of focal point.

The opposite of emphasis is **subordination**: subordination draws our attention away from certain areas of a work. Artists choose carefully—in both two- and three-dimensional works—which areas to emphasize or subordinate in order to heighten the impact of their artworks.

Emphasis and focal point usually accentuate concepts, themes, or ideas the artist wants to express: they signal what the artwork is about.

Emphasis

Broad Emphasis

Sometimes an artist is interested in emphasizing an entire work in its wholeness. When he or she wants to do this, the artist will intentionally create a composition that does not have a dominant area of emphasis. For example, *Starlight* by Canadian-born artist Agnes Martin (1912–2004) has an overall field of a soft, nebulous blue **color** with a superimposed grid that is so uniform that no one area of the work dominates (**1.8.1**). Martin, who grew up in Vancouver, became interested in Eastern philosophy, especially **Taoism**, and for many years lived a life of solitude and simplicity in New Mexico. She explored the idea that art could enable people to experience a profound sense of calm and so "leave themselves behind." In the work *Starlight*, Martin's Taoist ideas about the importance of harmony in the universe are reflected in the emphasis on the work as a whole, held together by the essential simplicity of the grid, the structure of which, with its faint but regular and insistent lines, permeates the entire painting. The resulting effect allows us to immerse ourselves in the work, as if it were a place for reflective meditation.

Emphasis can also be used to draw attention to a large portion of a work. Sometimes an artist wants the emphasis to encompass a significant area, but not quite the entire surface. The African-American sculptor Martin Puryear (b. 1941) makes connections between a

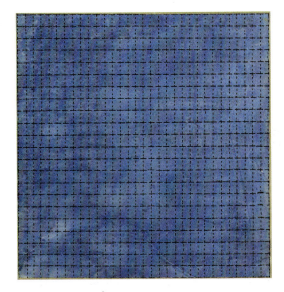

1.8.1 Agnes Martin, *Starlight*, 1963. Watercolor and ink on paper, 11¾ × 10½". Private collection

nineteenth-century trading company and African masks in his work *C.F.A.O.* (**1.8.2**). The Compagnie Française de L'Afrique Occidentale, or CFAO, was a company that connected Europe to ports in Sierra Leone in Africa, where Puryear also worked as a member of the Peace Corps. Using vertical and horizontal axes made of pine strips that fill the **background**, all supported by a discarded wheelbarrow, Puryear frames our attention on the elongated white heart shape in the center of the work. The wheelbarrow and the pine structure, by being more neutral and having more geometric lines, both support and highlight by contrast the large area of emphasis— the white, blank, mask-like shape in the center.

1.8.2 Martin Puryear, *C.F.A.O.*, 2006–7. Painted and unpainted pine and found wheelbarrow, 8´4¾" × 6´5½" × 5´1". MoMA, New York

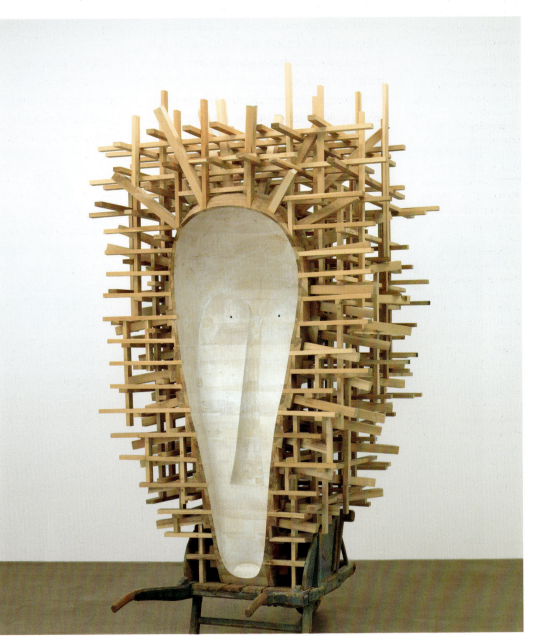

Background: the part of a work depicted as behind the main figures

Composition: the overall design or organization of a work

Line: a mark, or implied mark, between two endpoints

Implied line: a line not actually drawn but suggested by elements in the work

Contrast: a drastic difference between such elements as color or value (lightness/darkness) when they are presented together

1.8.3 Jacob Lawrence, "John Brown Remained a Full Winter in Canada, Drilling Negroes for His Coming Raid on Harpers Ferry (no. 17)", from Jacob Lawrence, *The Life of John Brown* (22 prints), 1977. Gouache and tempera on paper, 20 x 14"

Puryear created the mask to mimic the designs of the Fang tribe of Gabon, West Africa, and the piece is intended to recall French colonialism in the region by associating it with the CFAO. It invites the viewer to lift the wheelbarrow and peer through the two eye-holes in the mask, encouraging him or her to see things from the point of view, or assume the role, of the colonized instead of the colonist.

Broad emphasis can occur when there are multiple elements within a work, but no one element dominates. For example, in a print from the series *The Life of John Brown* by the African-American artist Jacob Lawrence (1917–2000), each of the twelve figures shown (one facing away from the viewer) attracts enough attention so that none stands out as most significant (**1.8.3**). The John Brown to whom Lawrence refers in the title of the work is the Civil War era abolitionist who believed that slavery could be eradicated only through armed insurrection. Brown is not depicted in

the work, but the solemn poses of the figures imply an homage to this anti-slavery militant who was hanged for leading a violent revolt against the US government at Harpers Ferry, West Virginia. In the print, Lawrence's visual balancing of the figures is complemented by his creation of separate areas of emphasis, for example the figure on the right in the yellow coat is immediately emphasized in contrast to the dark figure in the foreground, as is the white rifle held by the figure in brown on the left side of the work. These areas are also evenly balanced, unifying all of the parts into a larger whole. This methodical counter-balancing is critical to the composition because it implies equality amongst the men, thus subtly supporting the ideals for which John Brown fought and died.

Focal Point

Focal point is a tool that artists use to give specific emphasis to an important symbol,

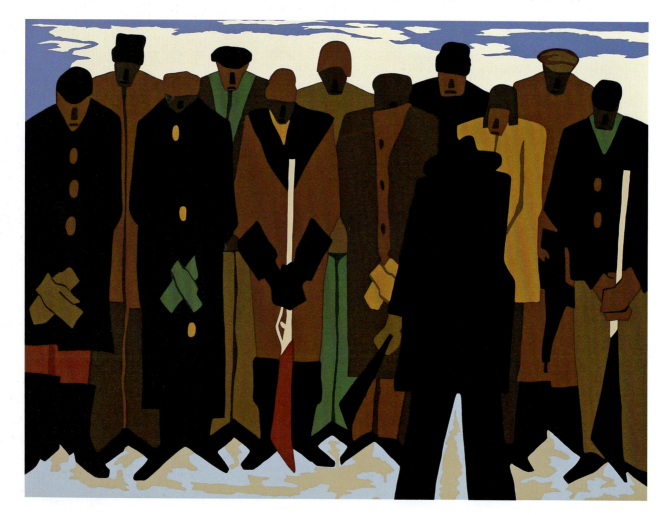

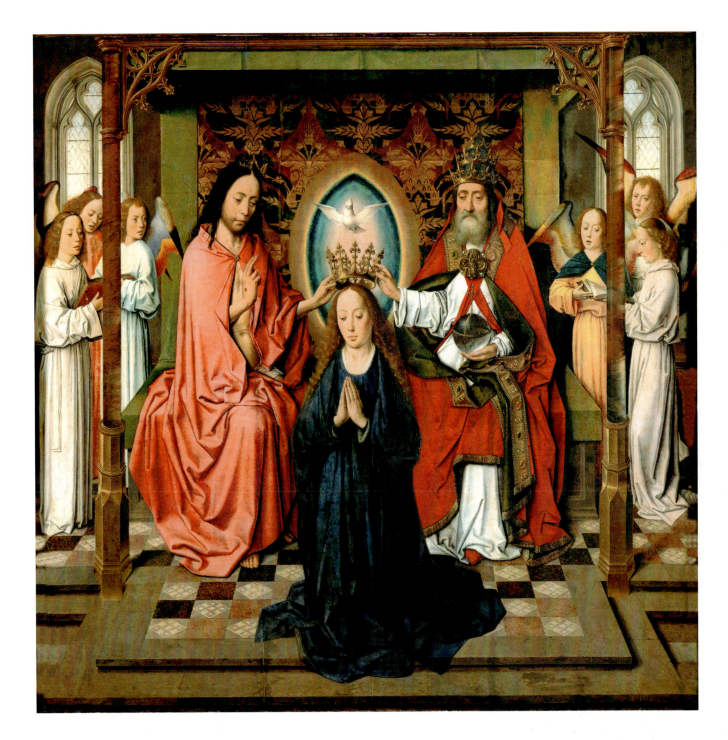

1.8.4 Dieric Bouts (the Elder), *The Coronation of the Virgin Mary*, 1455/60. Tempera on oak panel, approximately 32⅞″ × 33½″. Akademie der Bildenden Künste, Vienna, Austria

event, or distinguishing feature in a work. In any **composition**, a focal point is the place in an area of emphasis to which the artist draws our eye. He or she can do so by using **line**, **implied line**, or **contrast**. These techniques focus our gaze on that point in the work. We can see an intensely dramatic use of focal point in Artemisia Gentileschi's ferocious painting, *Judith Decapitating Holofernes* (see Gateway Box: Gentileschi, p. 163).

Directing the viewer's gaze to a specific location in a work of art is especially important when the subject of the painting, and its purpose, involve a hierarchy that must be observed. In the Dutch artist Dieric Bouts's (1415–1475) painting *The Coronation of the Virgin Mary* (**1.8.4**), it is critical that the viewer's gaze is drawn to a particular point in the design. As the artist, it was Bouts's responsibility to highlight the Virgin Mary even when she was in the presence of the Holy Trinity: God the

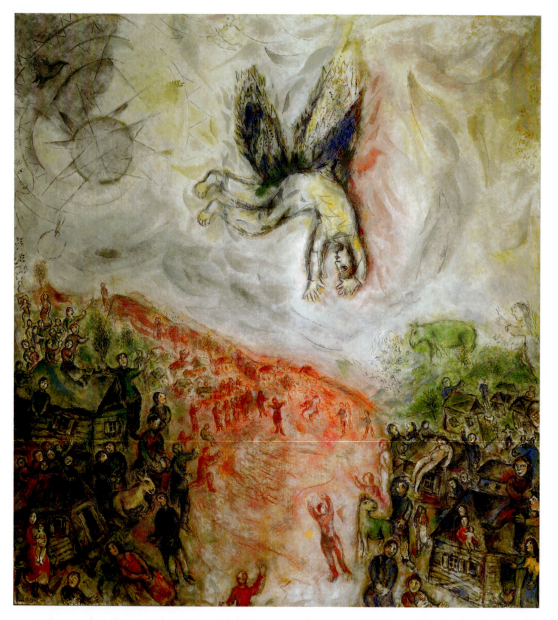

1.8.5 Marc Chagall, *The Fall of Icarus*, 1975. Oil on canvas, 6'11⅞" × 6'6". Musée National d'Art Moderne, Centre Georges Pompidou, Paris, France

Father, Jesus, and the Holy Spirit (pictured here as a dove). Bouts, who lived at a time when great piety was an essential part of life, is able to render the Holy Trinity with appropriate reverence, but skillfully focus attention primarily on Mary, who is being crowned in the foreground. The artist does this by orienting the eyes of all in attendance on the Virgin, who is centrally placed with a light oval shape behind her head. Although the composition features many heads, it is clear to where the viewer's attention is being beckoned. Mary's face, with eyes cast downward in humble respect, is framed by the crown above her head and her folded hands below, and the dove hovering over her provides a further visual clue to where we should

look. In this way Bouts invites the viewer to share in this majestic, solemn, and otherworldly event.

In his painting *The Fall of Icarus*, Marc Chagall (1887–1985) draws attention to and illustrates a critical moment from a haunting story from Greek mythology (**1.8.5**). Icarus and his father Daedalus had been imprisoned on the island of Crete by its ruler, Minos. In order to escape, Daedalus fashioned two sets of wings from feathers and wax. As father and son flew away from their prison, Icarus became overly exuberant. Although his father had warned him not to, Icarus, recklessly enjoying his new wings, flew too high and close to the sun. The wax in his wings melted, and he fell to his death in the sea below. In Chagall's version, Icarus is the focal

Primary colors: three basic colors from which all others are derived

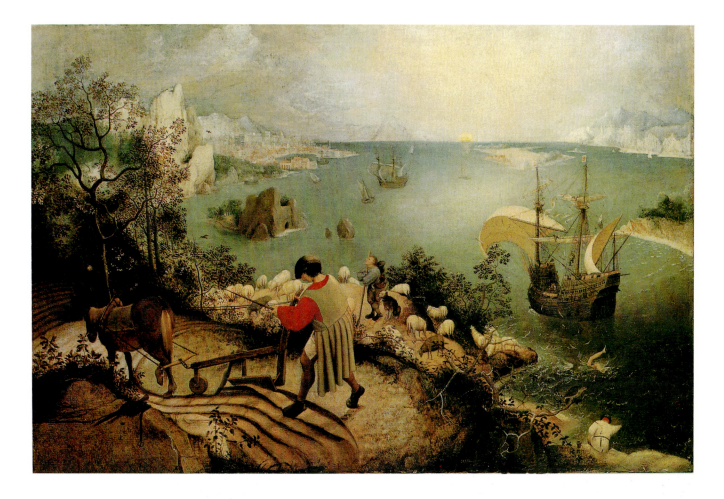

1.8.6 Pieter Bruegel the Elder, *Landscape with the Fall of Icarus, c.* 1555–58. Oil on canvas, mounted on wood, 29 × 44⅛". Musées Royaux des Beaux-Arts de Belgique, Brussels, Belgium

point, distinctly set apart from the light sky not only by his position at the top and center of the work, but also by the use of bold red, yellow, and blue **primary colors** to depict the flailing figure. Using the contrast between the brightly colored wings and the dull, pale-gray sky isolates and draws attention directly to the poor boy, whose futile fluttering is captured in Chagall's energetic brushstrokes. Even though there are many figures in this work, the main emphasis is clearly on the tumbling one in the sky.

Subordination

Subordination is the use of emphasis to draw the viewer's attention away from a particular part of a composition. We are so attuned to looking for emphasized areas and focal points that some artists can use this technique to redirect our attention cleverly from one area of an artwork to another. Subordination can also involve deliberately reducing the impact of certain details.

In direct contrast to Marc Chagall, who in his painting wanted to place the attention of the viewer on Icarus as he fell to Earth (**1.8.5**), in the work *Landscape with the Fall of Icarus*, by Flemish artist Pieter Bruegel the Elder (*c.* 1525/30–1569), the artist deliberately diverts our attention so that we barely notice Icarus plunging to his doom (**1.8.6**): a fine example of subordination. In Bruegel's version of this story, our attention is drawn first to the figure in the foreground, in his eye-catching scarlet smock, plowing his field, unaware of the tragedy. As the painting's title suggests, several other areas of emphasis—the tree on the left, the sunset, the fanciful ships—also capture our interest. We hardly notice poor Icarus, whose legs are disappearing into the sea just in front of the large ship on the right, his feet hardly distinguishable from the whitecaps and the tiny seabirds circling near the vessel. Because Bruegel has gone to such lengths to draw attention away from the plight of his subject, art historians think he is illustrating the Flemish proverb, "No plough stands still because a man dies." Or, as we might say, "Life goes on." Either way, it is a brilliant example of using emphasis and subordination to direct and control the way in which the viewer perceives the painting.

Emphasis and Focal Point in Action

Artists can use direction, dramatic contrasts, and placement relationships to organize the elements in a work and draw our attention to areas of emphasis and focal points.

Contrast

Artists look to create effects of contrast by positioning elements next to one another that are very different, for example areas of different **value**, color, or size. Value is an effective and frequently used means of creating emphasis and focal point. It also has the advantage that it can be used in subtle ways. In *The Funeral of St. Bonaventure*, a painting by Spanish artist Francisco de Zurbarán (1598–1664), most of the lightest values are reserved for the clothing adorning the dead body of St. Bonaventure (**1.8.7**). They create a central focal point that stands out in contrast to the surrounding dark values. We are drawn to the whiteness (symbolic of Bonaventure's chaste and spotless reputation) before we look at the surrounding characters. Enough light value is distributed to the other figures to allow our eyes to be drawn away from Bonaventure's body, making the composition more interesting.

Line

Line is an effective way to focus our attention in an artwork. In Mughal India (the period from 1526 until the mid-nineteenth century), a garden was considered a work of art, one that symbolized the promise of paradise. Zahir ud-Din Muhammad bin Omar Sheikh, nicknamed Babur, founded the Mughal empire in India when he conquered most of

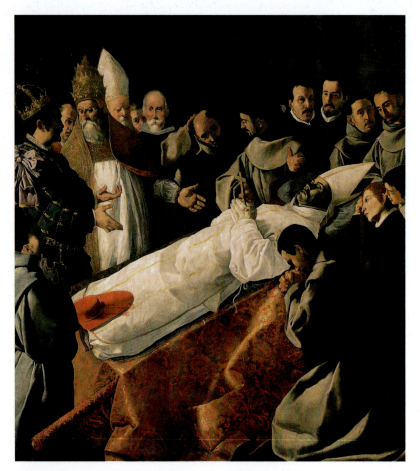

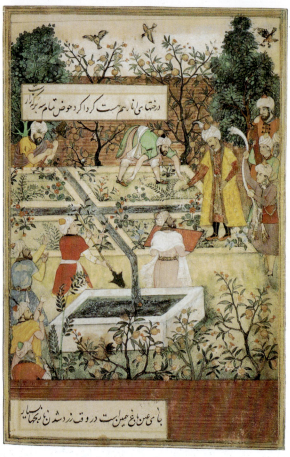

1.8.7 (above) Francisco de Zurbarán, *The Funeral of St. Bonaventure*, 1629. Oil on canvas, 8'2" × 7'4". Musée du Louvre, Paris, France

1.8.8 (left) *The Emperor Babur Overseeing His Gardeners*, India, Mughal period, *c.* 1590. Tempera and gouache on paper, 8¾ × 5⅝". Victoria and Albert Museum, London, England

Value: the lightness or darkness of a plane or area

Gateway to Art: Gentileschi, *Judith Decapitating Holofernes*
Using Focal Point for Dramatic Emphasis

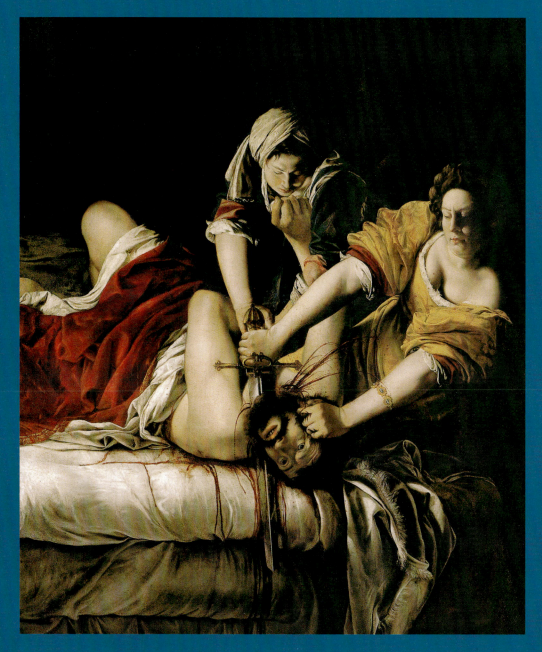

1.8.9 Artemisia Gentileschi, *Judith Decapitating Holofernes*, *c.* 1620. Oil on canvas, 6'6⅜" × 5'3¾". Uffizi Gallery, Florence, Italy

Artists often take advantage of the strength of a single focal point to force us to give our attention to the crux or pivot of the work. Although a composition can have several focal points, the Italian Baroque painter Artemisia Gentileschi (1593–*c.* 1656) uses just one in her *Judith Decapitating Holofernes* (**1.8.9**). Through Gentileschi's use of directional line and contrasting values we are drawn irresistibly to the point where the climax of the story is unfolding. Bright light emphasizes Judith's arms and those of her maidservant (visually connected to the sword itself) as they stretch toward the dark values of their victim's head. The light values of the five bare arms create strong directional lines that lead to the focal point where blood spurts from the violent attack on Holofernes' neck. This double emphasis (contrast of values and directional line) freezes our stare upon the fatal blow, even as it obscures it in darkness.

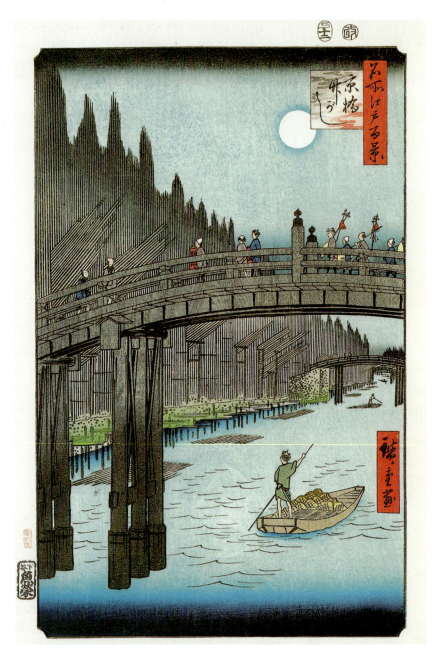

1.8.10 Ando Hiroshige, "Riverside Bamboo Market, Kyōbashi," from *One Hundred Famous Views of Edo*, 1857. 15 × 10⅜". James A. Michener Collection, Honolulu Academy of Arts, Hawaii

Rhythm: the regular or ordered repetition of elements in the work
Outline: the outermost line or implied line of an object or figure, by which it is defined or bounded
Woodcut: a print created from an incised piece of wood

Central Asia and northern India. In **1.8.8**, the gardener/artist Babur is pointing to a feature that channels water in four directions. The life-giving properties of water and the four cardinal directions were important symbols of life and eternity. Because the garden was based on the perfect geometry of a square, it could be expanded an infinite number of times without disturbing the original plantings. In this image of the garden, water is the focal point both conceptually and visually.

We tend to notice diagonal lines because they appear to be more visually active than either horizontal or vertical lines. The strong diagonal of the channel draws our attention to the water as it runs toward us. The central cross-shaped confluence of the waters in the middle of the garden becomes the focal point of the composition.

Placement

The placement of elements within a composition controls **rhythm** and creates multiple focal points. In the print "Riverside Bamboo Market, Kyōbashi," the Japanese artist Ando Hiroshige (1797–1858) has oriented three shapes; all of them are visually independent of each other (**1.8.10**). The positions of the moon, the bridge, and the figure in a boat form three separate focal points. Each shape commands our attention and draws more of our focus to the right side of the work. Even though the bridge is the largest shape, and so naturally catches our attention, the light value and hard geometry of the moon divert our gaze, and the moon becomes a secondary focal point. We look at the figure under the bridge because of its careful placement under the moon, and because it has a definite **outline** that contrasts strongly with the flat color of the water. The varying distances between the placements of the three focal points also create rhythm, which adds visual interest. Hiroshige, a master of **woodcut** printing, uses placement to emphasize specific points in the work and enliven the composition.

Active Learning Exercises

1. Sometimes an entire work of art is emphasized to bring attention to the whole. Works created in this way can bring a new emphasis to the materials and techniques used by the artist. Create an 8 × 8-in. paper square and fill it with marks. These can be dots, lines, strokes, etc., made with any kind of marking or drawing tool. Fill the space so that there is little of the white paper still visible. What kind of mark did you use? Do you think a viewer could interpret your mood from the way that you filled the space? Does the order, or disorder, of the marks that you created reflect anything about your personality?

2. A focal point can be created by using contrast effectively. Even simple repetition or cluttered compositions can be given a dynamic design using focal points. Create an 8 × 8-in. square of white paper and fill it with 16 2-in. squares of black paper. What happens when you remove just one square? Put the first one back and remove one from another location in the square. Is there a difference in the effect, and do some square locations create a stronger focal point? Why? What might the result be if more than one square was removed? What if all but one is taken away?

3. *The Last Supper* by Leonardo da Vinci is a classic example of focal point in a work of art. The figure of Christ in the center of the composition is emphasized by contrast, placement, and line. The use of line is especially effective because the lines that make up the architectural surroundings conspire to draw attention to Christ. Print a copy of *The Last Supper* and, using a marker or highlighter, show where the lines are being used to direct your attention to the image of Christ. Are there lines that don't lead a viewer to the focal point? If so, what do they contribute?

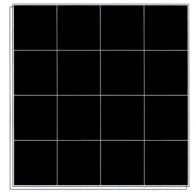

Arrange sixteen 2-inch squares on an 8-inch square

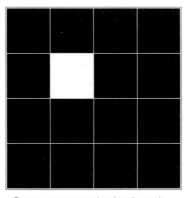

Remove one square and analyse the result

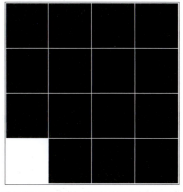

Does the amount of emphasis change if the square is taken from a different location?

Images Related to 1.8:
Emphasis and Focal Point

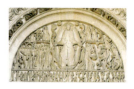

4.2.10 Gislebertus, *The Last Judgment*, c. 1120–35, p. 581

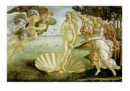

4.9.5 Sandro Botticelli, *The Birth of Venus*, c. 1482–86, p. 662

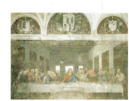

3.6.6 Leonardo da Vinci, *The Last Supper*, c. 1497, p. 468

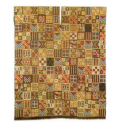

3.4.7 Tunic, Peru, *c.* 1500, p. 437

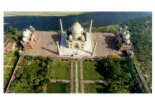

1.6.15 Ustad Ahmad Lahauri, Taj Mahal, Agra, India, 1632–43, p. 142

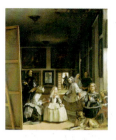

1.10.11a Diego de Silva y Velázquez, *Las Meninas*, c. 1656, p. 190

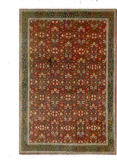

1.9.4 Pashmina carpet, northern India, 2nd half of 17th century, p. 169

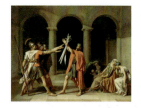

3.7.10 Jacques-Louis David, *The Oath of the Horatii*, 1784, p. 499

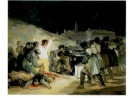

1.9.10 Francisco Goya, *The Third of May, 1808*, 1814, p. 174

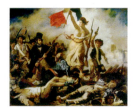

3.7.16 Eugène Delacroix, *Liberty Leading the People*, 1830, p. 504

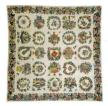

1.6.12 Album quilt, 1848, p. 139

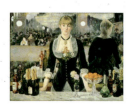

4.5.16 Édouard Manet, *A Bar at the Folies Bergere*, 1882, p. 623

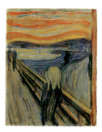

1.10.10 Edvard Munch, *The Scream*, 1893, p. 188

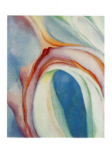

1.1.27 Georgia O'Keeffe, *Music–Pink and Blue II*, 1919, p. 63

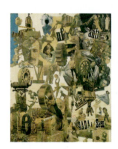

2.8.21 Hannah Höch, *Cut with the Kitchen Knife...*, p. 225

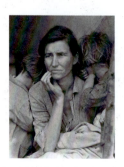

1.5.13f Dorothea Lange, *Migrant Mother*, 1936, p. 127

1.5.7 Bridget Riley, *Cataract 3*, 1967, p.123

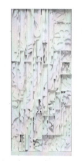

0.0.3 Louise Nevelson, *White Vertical Water*, 1972, p. 28

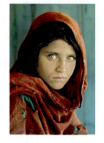

2.8.14a Steve McCurry, *Afghan Girl at Nasar Bagh Refugee Camp*, 1984, p. 327

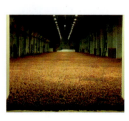

2.4.23b Antony Gormley, *Asian Field*, 2003, p. 263

1.9

Pattern and Rhythm

Space: the distance between identifiable points or planes
Pattern: an arrangement of predictably repeated elements
Elements: the basic vocabulary of art—line, form, shape, volume, mass, color, texture, space, time and motion, and value (lightness/darkness)
Unity: the imposition of order and harmony on a design
Rhythm: the regular or ordered repetition of elements in the work
Composition: the overall design or organization of a work
Shape: a two-dimensional area, the boundaries of which are defined by lines or suggested by changes in color or value
Value: the lightness or darkness of a plane or area
Color: the optical effect caused when reflected white light of the spectrum is divided into separate wavelengths
Contrast: a drastic difference between such elements as color or value (lightness/darkness) when they are presented together

Each day the sun rises and sets; we believe it will do so again tomorrow. Patterns and rhythms in nature help us make sense of the world. They express the order and predictability of our lives. Artists use pattern and rhythm to bring order to **space** and to create a dynamic experience of time.

When events recur, this creates a **pattern**. But other patterns are more regular, more predictable. In art, we can see patterns as the recurrence of an art **element**. In a work of art, the repetition of such patterns provides a sense of **unity**.

Rhythm arises through the repetition of pattern. It adds cohesiveness in artistic **composition** because it links elements together. Rhythm affects our vision as we study a work of art. The rhythm of a series of linked elements guides the movement of our eyes across and through a design. The artist can also use rhythm to add variety.

Pattern

The use of repetition in a work of art usually results in the creation of a pattern. These patterns are sometimes based on occurrences in nature, such as the regular repetition of fish scales, or the pattern created by the cracks that open as mud dries in the desert. Other patterns may be derived from the repeated shapes of mass-produced human-made objects, such as stacked tin cans or the warp and weft of woven cloth. Artists often create unity in works of art by repeatedly using a similar **shape**, **value**, or **color**, for example.

An artist can use repetition of a pattern to impose order on a work. But simple repetition can become more complex and make a work even more interesting when the pattern changes. Sometimes artists use alternating patterns to make a work more lively. The area covered by pattern is called the field; changes in the field can invigorate visual forms. The pattern in **1.9.1** shows a series of star shapes set on alternating black and white backgrounds on a rectangular field. The drastic difference in value combined with the active shape causes a visual vibration.

A variety of different colors and patterns enlivens work by the French painter Suzanne Valadon (1865–1938). In *The Blue Room*, she includes three **contrasting** patterns (**1.9.2**, p. 168). In the blue bed covering, in the lower

1.9.1 Vertical alternating pattern

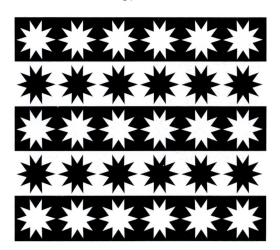

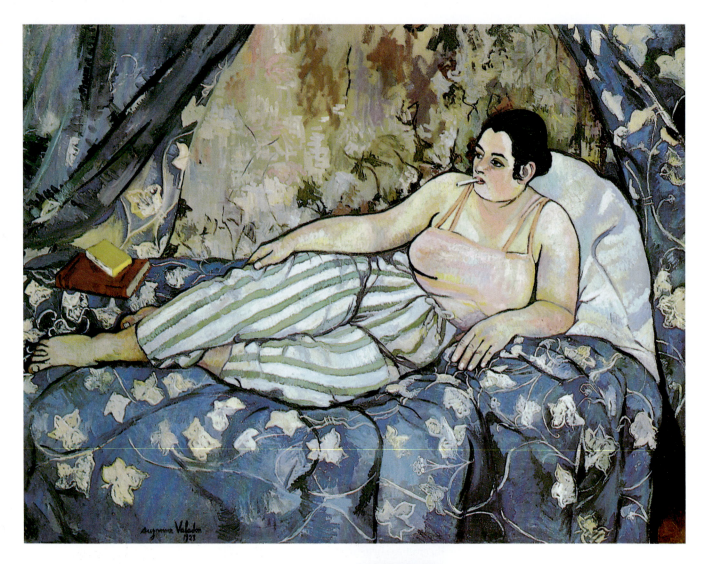

portion of the painting, Valadon has used an organic pattern of leaves and stems. The green-and-white striped pattern in the woman's pajama bottoms dominates in direct contrast to the blue bed covering. Above the figure is a mottled pattern that again contrasts with the other two. The differences in these patterns energize the work.

Motif

A design repeated as a unit in a pattern is called a motif. Motifs can represent ideas, images, and themes that can be brought together through the use of pattern. An artist can create a strong unified design by repeating a motif.

A single motif can be interlaced with others to create complex designs. Many Islamic works use complex interlaced

1.9.2 Suzanne Valadon, *The Blue Room*, 1923. Oil on canvas, 35½ × 45⅝˝. Musée National d'Art Moderne, Centre Georges Pompidou, Paris, France

1.9.3 Huqqa base, India, Deccan, last quarter of 17th century. Bidri ware (zinc alloy inlaid with brass), 6⅞ × 6½˝. Metropolitan Museum of Art, New York

motifs, as two objects created in seventeenth-century India demonstrate. The huqqa base (a huqqa is a water pipe used for smoking) in **1.9.3** may at first glance appear to use little repetition. Nevertheless, as we study the overall design we discover that elements, such as the flowers and leaves of the plants, recur at intervals. Similarly, in the detail of a carpet (**1.9.4**), repeated flower-like motifs are arranged in a pattern in the center. Islamic artists delight in the detail of pattern, as these two works show.

The American artist Chuck Close (b. 1940) uses motif to unify his paintings. Close uses a repeated pattern of organic concentric rings set into a diamond shape as the basic building blocks for his large compositions. These motifs, which appear as **abstract** patterns when viewed closely, visually solidify into realistic portraits

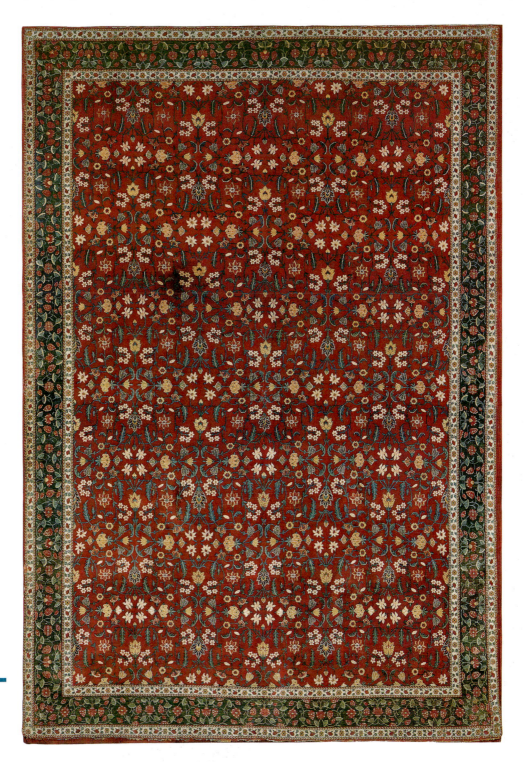

1.9.4 Pashmina carpet with millefleur pattern, northern India, Kashmir or Lahore, second half of 17th century. Pashmina wool (pile), silk (warp and weft); pile dyed and knotted, 83 × 57⅞". Ashmolean Museum, Oxford, England

Abstract: art imagery that departs from recognizable images from the natural world

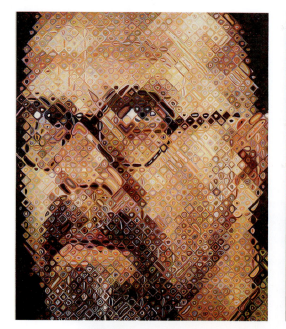

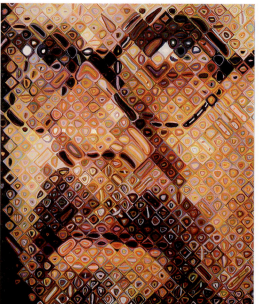

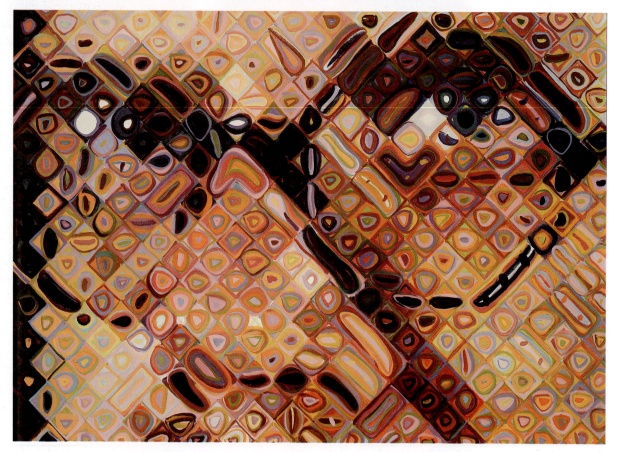

Texture: the surface quality of a work, for example fine/coarse, detailed/lacking in detail

of the model. In his *Self Portrait*, there is a distinct difference between a close-up view of the painting and the overall effect when we stand back from this enormous canvas (**1.9.5a–1.9.5c**). The motif unifies the work and allows Close the freedom to control the color, **texture**, and value. In this case, the motif that Close uses is the result of a technical process. When applied to the larger image, however, it almost disappears because each unit that makes up the whole is so tiny in size. A grid that subdivides the entire image organizes the placement of each cell. In this way Close uses an intricate system of patterns within patterns to achieve a dramatic effect.

Rhythm

Rhythm is something you either have or don't have, but when you have it, you have it all over.

(Elvis Presley)

Rock and roll icon Elvis Presley might as well have been speaking about visual art when he was talking about musical rhythm. Rhythm is something that visual art has "all over." Rhythm gives structure to the experience of looking, just as it guides our eyes from one point to another in a work of art. There is rhythm when there are at least two points of reference in an artwork. For example, the horizontal distance from one side of a canvas to the other is one rhythm, and the vertical distance from top to bottom, another. So, even the simplest works have an implicit

rhythm. But most works of art have shapes, colors, values, lines, and other elements too; the intervals between them provide points of reference for more complex rhythms.

In Flemish painter Pieter Bruegel's work, we see not only large rhythmic progressions that take our eye all around the canvas, but also refined micro-rhythms in the repetition of such details as the trees, houses, birds, and colors (**1.9.6**). All these repetitive elements create a variety of rhythms "all over."

In *Hunters in the Snow*, the party of hunters on the left side first draws our attention into the work. Their dark shapes contrast with the light value of the snow. The group is trudging over the crest of a hill that leads to the right; our attention follows them in the same direction, creating the first part of a rhythmic progression. Our gaze now traverses from the left **foreground** to the **middle ground** on the right, where figures

1.9.6 Pieter Bruegel, *Hunters in the Snow*, 1565. Oil on panel, 46 × 63¾". Kunsthistorisches Museum, Vienna, Austria

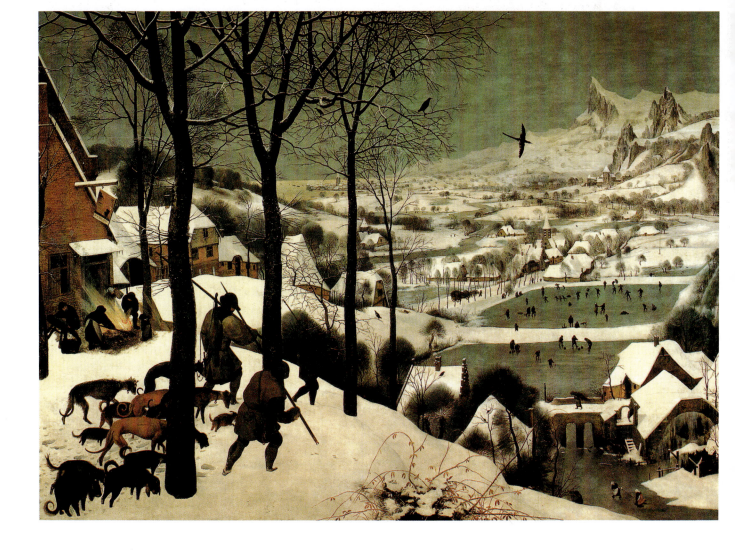

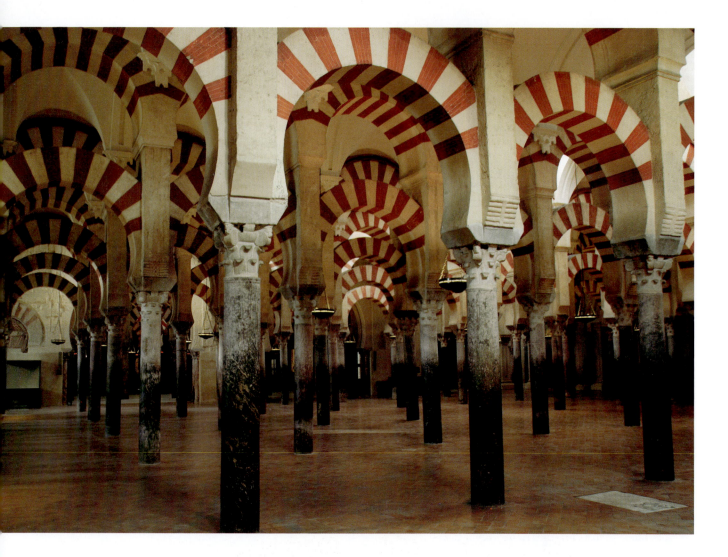

1.9.7 Great Mosque of Córdoba, prayer hall of Abd al-Rahman 1, 784–86, Córdoba, Spain

---

Background: the part of a work depicted furthest from the viewer's space, often behind the main subject matter

Focal point: the center of interest or activity in a work of art, often drawing the viewer's attention to the most important element

Facade: any side of a building, usually the front or entrance

---

appear to be skating on a large frozen pond. Thereafter, the color of the sky, which is reflected in the skaters' pond, draws our attention deeper into the space, to the horizon. We then look at the **background** of the work, where the recession of the ridgeline pulls the eye to the left and into the far background. As a result of following this rhythmic progression, our eye has circled round and now returns to re-examine the original **focal point**. We then naturally inspect details, such as the group of figures at the far left making a fire outside a building. As our eye repeats this cycle, we also notice subsidiary rhythms, such as the receding line of trees. Bruegel masterfully orchestrates the winter activities of townspeople in sixteenth-century Flanders (a country that is now Belgium, The Netherlands, and part of northern France) in a pulsating composition that is both powerful and subtle at the same time.

Simple Repetitive Rhythm

Artists create repetition by using the same shape, color, size, value, line, or texture over and over again. A repeating "pulse" of similar elements sets up a visual rhythm that a viewer can anticipate. Such regularity communicates reassurance.

The design of buildings is often intended to reassure us about the stability and durability of the structure. Stability was so important to the ancient Romans that when the builders finally removed the temporary support structures for archways, the architects who had designed them were made to stand underneath. If the arch failed, the architect would be crushed. Like Roman architects, we want reassurance that our structures will endure. For this reason, architectural designs often incorporate simple repetition.

The main hall of the Great Mosque of Córdoba in Spain is full of seemingly endless rows of identical columns and arches made from alternating red and white voussoirs (stone wedges that make up the arch) (**1.9.7**). Each of these repeating elements—columns, arches, and voussoirs—creates its own simple rhythm. The accumulation of these simple repetitions also enhances the function of the space and becomes a part of the activity of worship, like prayer beads, reciting the Shahada (profession of faith), or the five-times-a-day call to prayer. Our trust in the permanence of architecture is combined with the timelessness of prayer in the repetitions of the Great Mosque of Córdoba.

Progressive Rhythm

Repetition that regularly increases or decreases in frequency creates a progressive rhythm as the eye moves faster or slower across the surface of the work. In the photograph *Artichoke Halved*, by American Edward Weston (1886–1958), the outer layers (bracts) of the artichoke bud are closer together nearer the center (**1.9.8**).

Then, as they form the triangular center of the bud, a second progressive rhythm begins and the small bracts below the triangle form a third rhythm. The highly focused close-up view and strong photographic contrasts of black and white accentuate the sense of speeding up.

Alternating Rhythm

Artists can intertwine multiple rhythms until they become quite complex. The addition and alternation of rhythms can add unpredictability and visual excitement. On the island of Belau in the western Pacific, a traditional men's long house, called the *bai*, serves as a place for meeting and ritual (**1.9.9**). The imagery above the entry of this bai begins, at the bottom, with the regular rhythms of horizontal lines of fish, but the images above become increasingly irregular as they change to other kinds of shapes. The edges of the roof display a regular series of symbolic icons that, together with the building's horizontal beams, frame the composition and give the building's **facade** a dynamic feel.

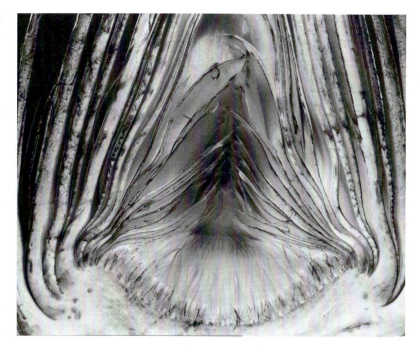

1.9.8 (above) Edward Weston, *Artichoke Halved*, 1930. Silver gelatin print, 7⅜ × 9⅜″. Collection Center for Creative Photography, University of Arizona, Tucson

1.9.9 (below) Bai-ra-Irrai, originally built *c.* 1700 and periodically restored, Airai village, Airai State, Republic of Palau

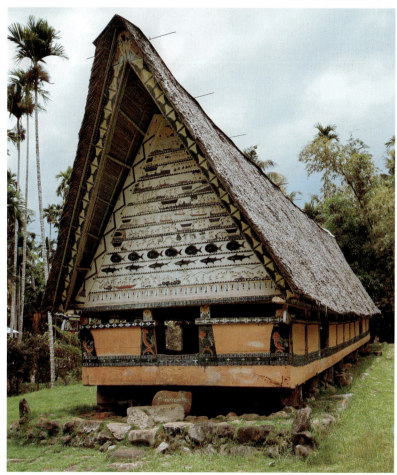

Gateway to Art: Goya, *The Third of May, 1808*
Visual Rhythm in the Composition

Spanish painter Francisco Goya's *The Third of May, 1808* shows an image of Napoleon's troops executing Spanish citizens during the French occupation of Madrid in 1808 (**1.9.10**). Goya, a Spanish citizen who lived through the Napoleonic occupation, had complex views about the political situation as he watched it unfold, but in this work he made choices about how the image needed to be organized to evoke the horror of this event. The work can be vertically bisected to reveal two distinct rhythmic groups that Goya invites us to interpret as engaged in a positive struggle (the figures on the left) and dominating and oppressive (the soldiers on the right). Goya does not allow the "good" victims on the left to overpower the "bad" occupiers in number, but keeps a numerical balance to steady the work. Yet although the number of figures in each group is the same, they are distributed very differently, rhythmically. The group of French soldiers on the right stands in a pattern so regulated it is almost mechanical. Each soldier adopts the same stance, and the strong horizontal barrels of the guns repeat in machine-like uniformity. On the left side, the rhythms are much more irregular and unpredictable. The figures are not organized so rigidly: some are lying on the ground, some standing, and some kneeling. The pose (with arms held high) of the standing figure in white is repeated in the dead figure on the ground, highlighting their helplessness and mortality. The alternating rhythm here leads our eye from the figure in white through a group of figures downward to the victims on the ground. Goya uses the subtleties of rhythm to communicate suggestions of good and evil; the unarmed vulnerability and disarray of those being attacked invites the viewer to sympathize with the plight of the artist's countrymen (the Spaniards) as they face systematic elimination by Napoleon's "war machines," depicted here as an unflinching line of relentless killers.

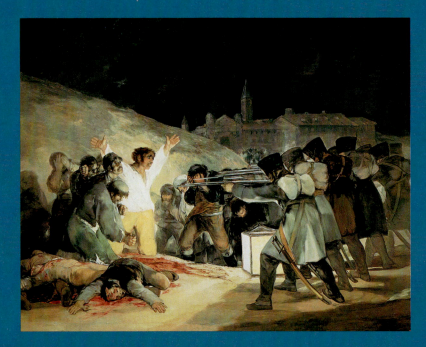

1.9.10 Francisco Goya, *The Third of May, 1808*, 1814. Oil on canvas, 8'4⅜" × 11'3⅞". Museo Nacional del Prado, Madrid

Goya also uses differing visual rhythms to communicate notions of good and evil in the work *The Sleep of Reason Produces Monsters* (**1.9.11**). The box in the lower left corner stabilizes and anchors the image with the straight and regular lines of a square. The visual rhythm created through the vertical and horizontal lines is predictable and logical, symbolizing reason as a guarantee of safety and goodness. The evil monsters that dominate the upper portion of the image are more haphazard, active, and threatening in their placement within the work, rising as if to overwhelm the sleeper below. It is interesting to compare this work with *Third of May*; in *Sleep of Reason* the way in which Goya uses regularity of line and shape to create a stable rhythm has a benign effect, quite unlike the rigid, sinister, machine-like rhythm of the soldiers in *Third of May*.

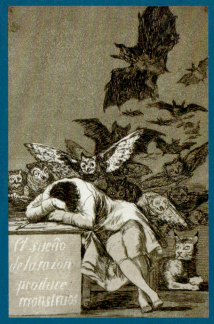

1.9.11 Francisco Goya, *The Sleep of Reason Produces Monsters*: Plate 43 from *The Caprices (Los Caprichos)*, 1799. Etching, aquatint, drypoint, and burin, 8⅛" × 5⅞". Museo Nacional del Prado, Spain

An alternating rhythm can also communicate chaos and make viewers feel uncomfortable. In Spanish painter Francisco Goya's *The Third of May, 1808*, the alternating rhythms help define our ideas about humanity and inhumanity (see Gateway Box: Goya).

Rhythmic Design Structure

The idea of rhythmic structure helps us understand how artists divide visual space into different kinds of sections to achieve different kinds of effects. In her painting of 1849 *Plowing in the Nivernais: The Dressing of the Vines*, the French artist Rosa Bonheur (1822–1899) creates a horizontal structure that leads our eye in sequence from one group of shapes to the next

(**1.9.12a** and **1.9.12b**). Bonheur expertly organizes the composition, emphasizing the cumulative effect of the rhythm of the groupings as they move from left to right. Because the composition is so horizontal, the design **emphasis** directs our gaze sideways using a linear direction and rhythm. By changing the width of the gaps between the animals, Bonheur suggests their irregular movement as they plod forward, drawing the heavy plow. Each group also has a different relative size and occupies a different amount of space, creating a visual rhythm and energy that pulls our attention from left to right.

The careful composition and rhythmic structure in such paintings give an air of respectability and nobility to laborers of the field and the hard work they had to do. Bonheur

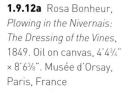

1.9.12a Rosa Bonheur, *Plowing in the Nivernais: The Dressing of the Vines*, 1849. Oil on canvas, 4′4¾″ × 8′6⅜″. Musée d'Orsay, Paris, France

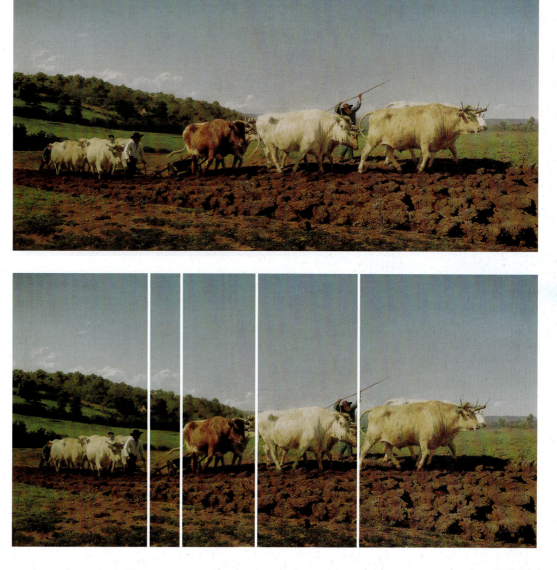

1.9.12b Rhythmic structural diagram of **1.9.12a**

Emphasis: the principle of drawing attention to particular content in a work

may have been sympathetic toward those who worked outside of the stuffy social order of the time, since her gender may have been a disadvantage in a traditionally male profession. Yet her effort to bring respectability to such lives and labor did not seek to glamorize her subject: in this painting she insistently reminds us of the slow physical rhythms created by the brute strength of these beasts and the irregularity of the plowmens' steps as all of them, men and cattle, work together to turn the weighty soil.

Active Learning Exercises

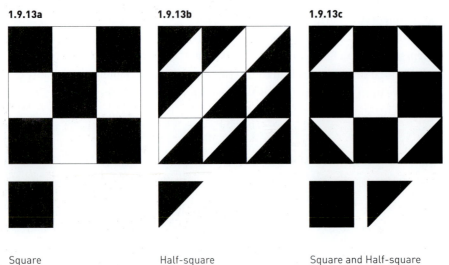

1.9.13a	1.9.13b	1.9.13c
Square	Half-square	Square and Half-square

1. Traditional quilt designs often use repetitive patterns to create a design. These patterns are set into squares that have been subdivided into a grid of nine smaller squares (**1.9.13a**). The nine smaller squares in their turn are then divided in various ways to create a pattern. Using a 6 × 6-in. white paper square and 9 black 2-in. squares, create a checkerboard pattern. Take the leftover black squares and divide them in two, cutting from corner to corner. Now remove the whole black squares and create a pattern with the half-squares (**1.9.13b**). How many combinations can you create when you orient the half-squares? What advantages would the designer of a simple quilt have if he or she limited the shape of the components?

2. Motif is the creation of a pattern or design that is reused in a composition. In Active Learning Exercise 1, a pattern was created using squares and half-squares of black on a white ground. A motif would appear if any of the patterns shown in **1.9.13a** and **b** were repeated in a larger grid structure. For example if you used the square and half-square design four times in a larger square, the design would become a motif or repeating design (**1.9.13c**). Combine your pattern with that of others to use it as a motif. Are there examples of motifs that you have experienced when looking at everyday items, such as wallpaper, quilts, or clothing?

3. Rhythm in visual design has a great deal in common with rhythm in other art forms. For example, the sound of a series of musical notes changes in duration (length), tone (width), and frequency (space between) in ways that can be translated to visual art. Some composers, such as Arnold Schoenberg, even created music based on visual associations. Listen to a short (five-second or less) segment of music: make a horizontal mark for each note, and leave a space for each pause between notes. What visual form did the sound create? Are there other ways that you can make this translation even more specific, for example by widening and thinning the marks? What does this process reveal about rhythm?

Images Related to 1.9:
Pattern and Rhythm

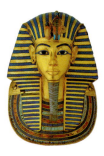

3.1.17 Mask of Tutankhamun, Egypt, 1333–1323 BCE, p. 377

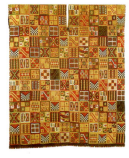

3.4.7 Tunic, Peru, *c.* 1500 CE, p. 437

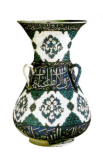

1.4.21 Mosque lamp from the Dome of the Rock, 1549, p. 112

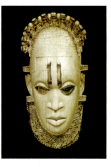

0.0.22 Benin hip pendant, mid-16th century, p. 43

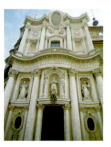

3.6.29a Francesco Borromini, Church of San Carlo, Rome, begun 1665–78, p. 488

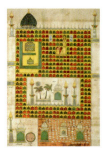

3.2.18 Drawing of sanctuary at Medina, 17th or 18th century, p. 403

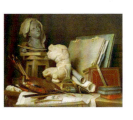

3.7.11, Anne Vallayer-Coster, *Attributes of Painting, Sculpture, and Architecture*, 1769, p. 500

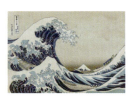

3.3.14 Katsushika Hokusai, "The Great Wave off Shore at Kanagawa," 1826–33, p. 423

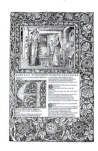

1.6.12 Album quilt, 1848, p. 139

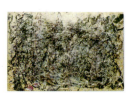

2.7.12 William Morris and Edward Burne-Jones, page from Kelmscott *Chaucer*, 1896, p. 312

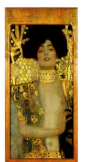

3.8.15 Gustav Klimt, *Judith I*, 1901, p. 523

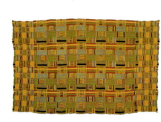

3.5.5 Asante textile wrapper (*kente*), 20th century, p. 453

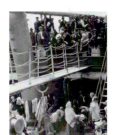

2.8.19 Alfred Stieglitz, *The Steerage*, 1907, p. 331

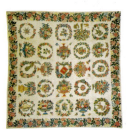

3.8.37 Piet Mondrian, *Composition with Yellow and Blue*, 1932, p. 537

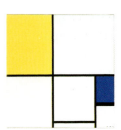

3.9.2 Jackson Pollock, *Number 1A*, 1948, p. 542

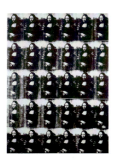

3.9.4 Andy Warhol, *Thirty Are Better than One*, 1963, p. 544

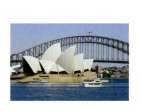

2.5.34 Jørn Utzon, Sydney Opera House, Australia, 1973, p. 286

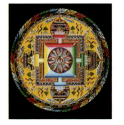

1.6.19 Amitayus mandala, Drepung Loseling Monastery, Tibet, p. 144

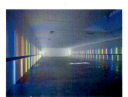
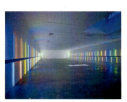

3.9.9 Dan Flavin, *Untitled* (installation), 1996, p. 547

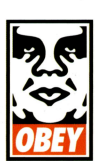

1.1.26a Shepard Fairey, *Obey*, 1996, p. 62

1.10

Content and Analysis

Artworks communicate visual ideas, just as speaking and writing communicate verbal ideas. For the transfer of thought to take place through art, we must interpret the visual language of the artist. This involves analysing the way he or she has created the artwork, as well as thinking about its subject matter and meaning—or content. There are a number of different ways in which we can analyse art (see Box: Types of Analysis, p. 184), and in this chapter we look at the ones that are most frequently used and effective.

Formal Analysis

Artists have many tools at their disposal, which we call the **elements** and **principles** of art (discussed throughout Part I of this book). The elements include line, shape, form, mass, volume, color, texture, space, time and motion, and value. Artists use the principles, such as contrast, balance, unity, variety, rhythm, emphasis, pattern, proportion, scale, and focal point, to organize the elements. A work of art is therefore a product of the dynamic interrelationships between the various art elements and principles.

The process of analysing the elements and principles used by the artist is called **formal analysis**. Making a formal analysis— a visual study—of a work of art is one way to understand more clearly the language used by an artist and to grasp how he or she applies elements and principles in a particular artwork.

To analyse a work of art fully, formally, one describes in specific detail how each element and principle is utilized within an artwork. The examples given on pp. 179–80 focus on specific aspects of the chosen works in order to highlight the elements and principles most prominently used by the artists. For a more complete formal analysis, see the "Combined Analysis" of *Las Meninas* later in this chapter (pp. 190–92).

In order to analyse a **three-dimensional** sculpture formally, you need to see the piece from all sides. As the separate photographs of the *Bust of Queen Nefertiti* (**1.10.1a** and **b**) show, different aspects of the sculpture emerge as we view it from various angles, yet as a whole, it is a vision of an elegant and confident woman. Seen from in front, the face of the Egyptian queen is symmetrically balanced, except for the missing pupil in one eye, and she holds her head high. In addition to the sculpture being three-dimensional, its volume and lifelike quality are further enhanced by the queen's painted skin. The sculpture itself is smooth, but **texture** is implied by the use of **color** in the rich headdress and in the necklace that drapes her graceful neck. Nefertiti's marked cheekbones, full red lips, well-defined eyes, and strongly defined eyebrows portray her as an ideal beauty.

The edges of the tall, flat-topped crown create two sides of a triangle. Two points of the triangle are the upper corners of her crown, and the third point is slightly below her neck. This triangle of her crown has a central vertical line, originally a complete cobra, which helps to enhance the elongation of her neck. The

Elements: the basic vocabulary of art—line, form, shape, volume, mass, color, texture, space, time and motion, and value (lightness/darkness)

Principles: the "grammar" applied to the elements of art—contrast, balance, unity, variety, rhythm, emphasis, pattern, scale, proportion, and focal point

Formal analysis: analysis of the form or visual appearance of a work of art using the visual language of elements and principles

Three-dimensional: having height, width, and depth

Texture: the surface quality of a work, for example fine/coarse, detailed/lacking in detail

Color: the optical effect caused when reflected white light of the spectrum is divided into separate wavelengths

Implied line: a line not actually drawn but suggested by elements in the work

Composition: the overall design or organization of a work

patterned ribbon that crosses under the broken cobra encircles her head, making one want to circle the sculpture, and on either side, the end of the ribbon is placed right above the ear.

When looking at Nefertiti in profile, one sees that the ribbon tips function like **implied lines** that point to the queen's eyes. From the side, the dramatic height and angle of her crown meet the nape of her neck to create a sideways "v." This "v" functions like a directional arrow that creates an implied line from the right to Nefertiti's chin, highlighting the formal symmetry of her beauty. Her long, thin neck lends the queen grace and femininity.

Nighthawks (**1.10.2**, p. 180), by the American artist Edward Hopper (1882–1967), conveys a sense of absence and loneliness. When making a formal analysis of a two-dimensional work,

such as this painting, useful aspects you can consider are the locations of objects, the colors used, and the relationships between the parts of the **composition**. In this scene, we see a darkened building in the background, with large shop windows on the bottom floor and five tall windows on the red-brick upper story. Together, these form repeated dark gulfs that communicate a sense of hollowness, gloom, and vacancy. We notice that even though the scene takes place in a city, the streets around are devoid of people and activity, creating a slightly eerie sense of stillness and quiet.

In front of this building, the sidewalk wraps around a curved diner on the street corner, cutting off the group of people inside, whom we see through the glass outer walls. The struts dividing the panes, and the solid walls above

1.10.1a and 1.10.1b
Thutmosis's workshop, *Bust of Queen Nefertiti* from Amarna, Egypt, *c.* 1350 BCE (New Kingdom, 18th Dynasty). Painted limestone, gypsum, crystal, and wax, 19¾" high. Aegyptisches Museum, Staatliche Museen zu Berlin, Germany

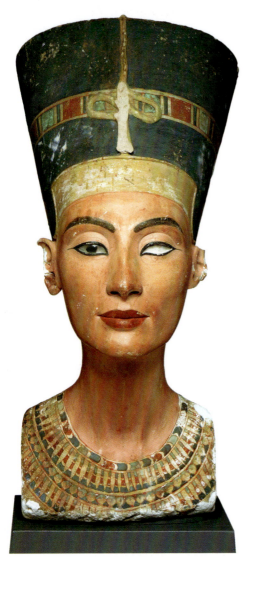

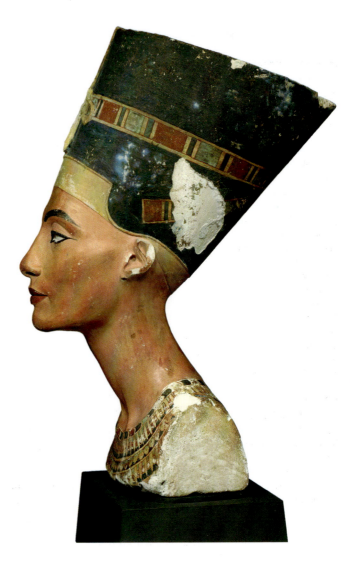

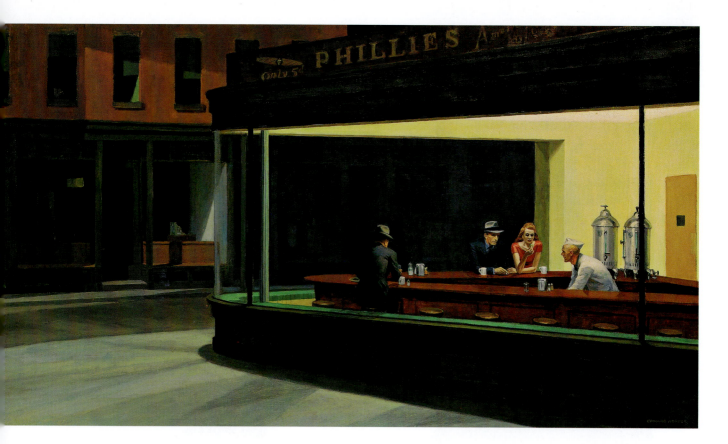

and below, create a strong framework through which we focus on the four figures. The inside is brightly lit, in **contrast** to the streets outside. This makes the room a particular area of **emphasis** in the picture: it further draws our attention to the people, and, together with the use of brilliant color in the yellow wall behind the counter, exposes them clearly to us, showing how isolated they are. The stark contrasts between the woman's red dress and hair, the black suits and hats of the two male customers, and the white uniform of the waiter make the figures more distinct, both within the scene and from one another.

The artist remarked some time after finishing the work, "Unconsciously, probably, I was painting the loneliness of a large city," and if we look more closely, within this careful use of formal devices we see that he intensifies the painting's effect through his choice of specific details. Despite being gathered together, the figures are not smiling and have very little interaction with one another; these individuals appear to be alone in their own thoughts. One cannot tell whether the man and woman sitting together are actually a couple—they do not look

at each other: he stares ahead, while her eyes are downcast. Their hands are close, but do not touch. These figures echo the two drink urns to the right: set very nearly together, but apart. The man and woman are further separated visually by the line of her right arm. The waiter is enclosed on his own within the triangular space of the bar and the other customer sits with his back to us, surrounded by six empty barstools. Although the waiter is in an active pose, it appears that time has stopped. This stillness only further enhances the sense of quiet, as if these lives are frozen, sealed off in their separate loneliness.

Stylistic Analysis

We recognize style in our own lives: the way we dress and arrange our hair reflects our personal style. Artworks also have **style**, or specific characteristics that make them look the way they do. Style allows us to recognize that an artwork was made by a particular artist. A group of artists might share a style because they all used similar techniques, worked at the same time, or

1.10.2 Edward Hopper, *Nighthawks*, 1942. Oil on canvas, 33⅛ × 60". Art Institute of Chicago

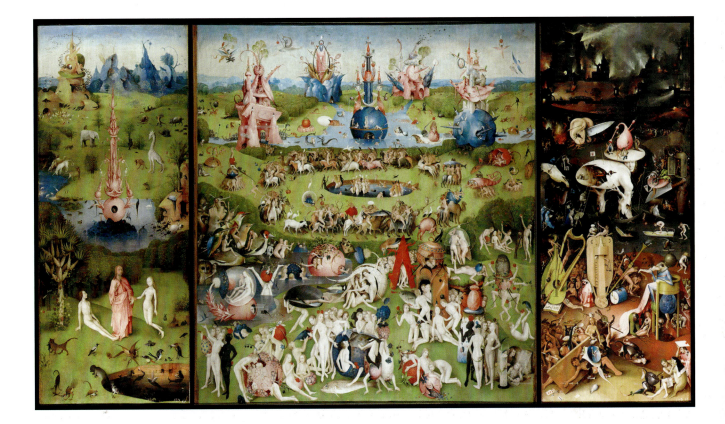

1.10.3 Hieronymus Bosch, *The Garden of Earthly Delights*, 1500–1505. Oil on wooden panel, central panel 7'1⅝" × 6'4¾", wings 7'1⅝" × 38¼". Museo Nacional del Prado, Madrid, Spain

Triptych: an artwork comprising three painted or carved panels, normally joined together and sharing a common theme

studied in the same place. The characteristics that contribute to style include the use of formal elements (line, shape, color, texture, and so on), the use of design principles (symmetry or asymmetry, for example), and the level of abstraction or representation used. Style can be related to the brushstrokes or marks an artist makes, the way light shines brightly on one part of the picture while the rest is in darkness, or the consistent use of a particular color in a certain way.

Style can be individual or shared by a group, school, time period, or movement. Analysing style allows us to make connections between artworks. We can use style as a way to categorize them or to identify who made a work of art, where it came from, or when it was created.

Known for his unique style, Netherlandish artist Hieronymus Bosch (*c.* 1450–1516) is most famous for his painted **triptych** *Garden of Earthly Delights* (**1.10.3**). Unlike many other artists working in Europe in the sixteenth century, Bosch was not interested in convincing realism or perfect proportion. His works are known for their fantastical quality: humans, fruits, and futuristic-looking objects (all in

various distorted sizes) mingle in odd, erotic, and nonsensical ways. The specific meanings of the activities in Bosch's work are uncertain, but on the whole scholars agree that he is expressing a religious condemnation of immorality, particularly in regard to sexual behavior. In this sense his style has something in common with medieval biblical sermons and folkloric sources, which also suggested that sinful actions are reflected in distortions of human anatomy. As a Spanish monk, José de Sigüenza, wrote upon studying the work in 1605, "other artists depicted people as they appear outwardly, but only Bosch had the audacity to paint them as they are on the inside."

The left panel of *Garden of Earthly Delights* shows God's presentation of Adam and Eve before the Fall; the center panel shows elongated nude figures inhabiting the false paradise of Earth, seduced by the ephemeral pleasures of frolicking and eroticism. The right panel shows the consequences of their behavior, with endless forms of tortured damnation for the sinners. Bosch's distinctive style may look quite modern in some ways, but he was an artist of the late medieval period.

1.10.4a Hans Holbein the Younger, *Jean de Dinteville and Georges de Selve ("The Ambassadors")*, 1533. Oil on oak, 6'9½" × 6'10⅓". National Gallery, London, England

Iconographic Analysis

Identifying and interpreting the symbolic meanings of the objects and elements in artworks often reveals previously unsuspected insights into their content (see "Iconographic Analysis," p. 184). *The Ambassadors*, by

The ambassadors are surrounded by books and scientific instruments, objects that testify to the men's intellectual prowess, learning, and wisdom, and to their wealth (only the prosperous could afford such things at this time)

German artist Hans Holbein the Younger (1497–1543), was painted while the artist was at the court of King Henry VIII of England, and is extraordinarily rich in symbolic significance (**1.10.4a**). We can begin by identifying the broader meanings of what the work includes. It shows Jean de Dinteville and the bishop Georges de Selve, Frenchmen who served as ambassadors

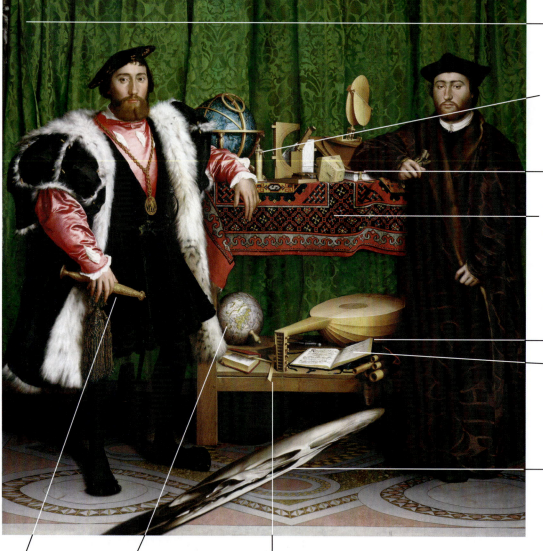

The cylindrical sundial gives the date (April 11, 1533) the painting was completed

The upper shelf, symbolically nearer to Heaven, features devices to understand the heavens and measure time, including a celestial globe, sundial, and compasses. These objects indicate both how learned these men are and that they are well-traveled, as their occupation would demand

29, the age of Dinteville, is engraved on his dagger

The center of the globe on the lower shelf shows Rome, hub of the Catholic faith

The lower shelf, which is concerned with more earthly matters, includes—painted in meticulously precise detail—secular and religious objects including musical instruments, a hymn book, a mathematical book, and a terrestrial globe to England. In 1533, when the work was made, England was on the brink of breaking with the Catholic Church and becoming a Protestant country, and art historians who have been able to study the painting close up have revealed how its iconography reflects this religious predicament: the globe, hymn book, crucifix, and lute all carry specific religious meanings (**1.10.4a–c**).

Most symbolic of all is the large, distorted skull in the foreground, which signifies human mortality, and the inclusion of which indicates that the painting as a whole is what is known as a ***memento mori***—a symbolic reminder of the inevitability of death (**1.10.4d**). Despite the ambassadors' success, wealth, and youth, they are aware of the fleeting nature of life. The strange, haunting form of the skull, facing away from their worldly possessions and toward the half-hidden crucifix, affirms that the men believe their salvation, and eternal life, depend on God.

Anamorphosis: the distorted representation of an object so that it appears correctly proportioned only when viewed from one particular position

1.10.4b

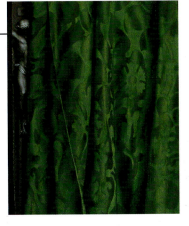

In the upper left corner, partially concealed by the green curtain, is a crucifix

25, the age of de Selve, is inscribed along the top of the page of the book he is leaning on

1.10.4a, b, and c Hans Holbein the Younger, *Jean de Dinteville and Georges de Selve ("The Ambassadors")*, 1533 (details)

1.10.4c

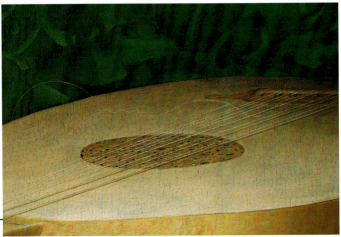

The lute has a broken string: this may be a reference to the religious discord that was occurring at the time—harmony (hence the musical instrument) was a key idea in the sixteenth century

The hymn book, which is so exactly painted that it is possible to read the verses by Martin Luther, the German pioneer of Protestantism, inscribed on its pages, may be included to encourage the restoration of religious concord

1.10.4d

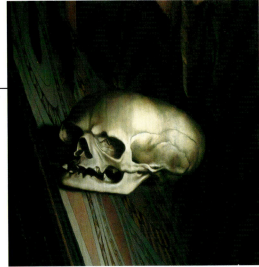

The large, distorted skull in the foreground, painted using **anamorphosis**, a type of optical illusion, signifies human mortality

This skull looks realistic only when the viewer stands in one specific spot, in front and to the right of the canvas

Types of Analysis

There is no single right way to analyse a work of art, and, as we shall see later on in this chapter, different methods can be combined to develop a more complete interpretation. Here is a summary of some important types of analysis.

Formal analysis

Formal analysis involves looking closely and in detail at the work in order to consider how the formal elements and principles of art are used to create it and to convey meaning.

Stylistic analysis

Style in art is the particular combination of characteristics that make a work (or works) of art distinctive. Stylistic analysis focuses on these characteristics in a way that clearly identifies how they typify the work of an individual, are shared by a group of artists to create a movement, or are concentrated in a particular place or time period.

Iconographic analysis

Iconography—"image writing" or "writing with images"—refers to the visual images and symbols used in a work of art as well as to the interpretation of the work's meaning. Iconographic analysis identifies objects and figures in an artwork as signs or symbols that can reflect religious or historical contexts, and the meaning of which was often more directly understood at a particular time by a specific culture, but may now be less apparent to us.

Contextual analysis

Contextual analysis looks at the making and viewing of the work in its context: it studies the atmosphere and ideas, often from a particular time or culture, which the artwork itself includes and reflects. Various aspects of context can be considered; for example, religious, historical, and biographical analysis are all types of contextual analysis.

Religious analysis considers the artwork in relation to the religious context in which it was made; this method often includes identification of narratives, key symbolism, and important figures.

Historical/social analysis considers historical events, either past or present, and the way they appear in an artwork.

Biographical analysis considers whether the artist's personal experiences and opinions may have affected the making or meaning of the artwork in some way.

Feminist analysis

Inspired—as its name suggests—by feminism, feminist analysis considers the role of women in an artwork as its subjects, creators, patrons, and viewers. It can reflect the intentions of an artist, the perspective of a viewer, the interpretation of a critic, or a combination of two or three of these.

Gender Studies analysis

Gender Studies analysis expands the considerations raised by feminist analysis to explore ways in which the work reflects experience based on a person's gender. It can also reflect the intentions of an artist, the perspective of a viewer, the interpretation of a critic, or all three.

Psychological analysis

This type of analysis investigates an artwork through consideration of the state of the artist's mind. Sometimes such interpretations make use of important psychological studies, such as those of Sigmund Freud or Carl Jung.

Contextual Analysis

The **content**, or meaning, of a work of art varies greatly between artworks. Both artists and viewers play roles in providing this meaning. An artwork may convey a particular message to those who view it in the context in which it was made, but the same artwork may convey a different meaning to someone living in another time and place. In order to understand the context of a work of art fully, you will usually have to undertake some research (see Box, p. 189), as well as looking very closely at the artwork itself. Analysis involves gathering information (sometimes from multiple sources). There are numerous types of contextual analysis that you can use to decipher the meaning of a work of art.

Analysis of Religious Context

The powerful feelings behind religious belief have often been a motivator for creating art. The rituals of the Sumerians (4000–1000 BCE) included bringing to their temples offerings for the gods. A dozen small praying figures were found under a Sumerian temple in modern-day Iraq; the two largest ones are shown here (**1.10.5**). The location in which the figures were found gives us a sense of the religious context in which they were created and used. Their wide-eyed upward glances and clasped hands, together with inscriptions on some of them, tell us that they are in eternal prayer. All the figures have similar conical forms and face stoically forward with hands intertwining slightly above the waist. Yet each is unique as well: the sizes, hairstyles, and gender vary, and, while not being precise portraits, every one loosely represents the human who brought it to the temple. Each of these figures holds a goblet for a votive—an offering made in accordance with a vow—to the gods, and would remain in the temple to offer continual prayer when the actual people represented in the statues could not be there.

1.10.6 Palmer Hayden, *Midsummer Night in Harlem*, 1936. Oil on canvas, 25 × 30". Museum of African American Art, Los Angeles, California

Analysis of Historical Context

In the 1920s and 1930s African-American history, cultural traditions, and ways of life were widely explored in literature, music, and the visual arts. The Harlem Renaissance movement, as it was known, flourished in Northern US cities, as many people had moved from the rural south to find better opportunities and escape persecution. Harlem, New York, became an important center for African-American cultural growth that American artist Palmer Hayden (1890–1973) wanted to celebrate. In *Midsummer Night in Harlem* (1936), he highlights the strong sense of community in his subject matter by showing people in the neighborhood gathering on stoops and sticking their heads out of apartment windows. Most people are shown awake and lively, with large smiles and bright eyes (**1.10.6**). The prominent location of the church at the end of the street to our left, and the dresses and hats people are wearing, indicate that they have just returned from an evening at church. The artist makes this, one of many daily-life scenes

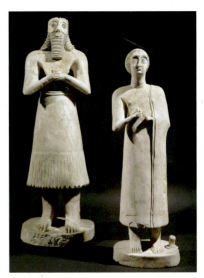

1.10.5 Votive Figures from the Temple of Abu, Eshnunna (Tell Asmar), *c.* 2700 BCE (?). Gypsum, male figure 28⅜" high, female figure 23¼" high. Iraq Museum, Baghdad, Iraq

Content: the meaning, message, or feeling expressed in a work of art

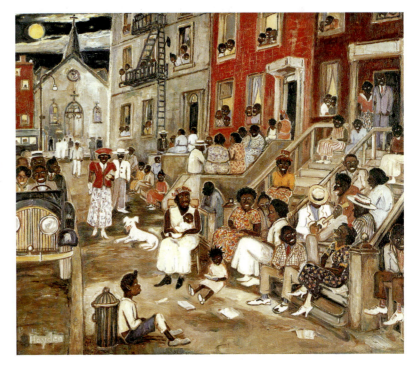

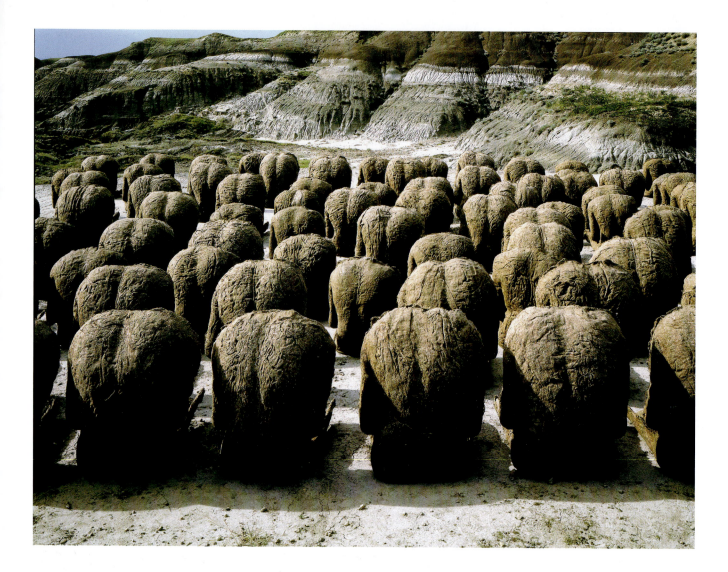

he painted, accessible by emphasizing realistic details of the gathering, such as the clothing, the car, the fire hydrant, and the fire escape. Hayden captures the time and place of this New York community by depicting joyful activity and the bonding of the people collectively under the full moon. At the same time, his use of flat, bright **hues** is a deliberate reference to the colors commonly found in traditional African art and also in modern artworks Hayden had encountered during his artist's training in Paris in the late 1920s.

Analysis of Biographical Context

Polish artist Magdalena Abakanowicz (b. 1930) uses as her source material her personal life experiences, Polish heritage, and imagery derived from Poland during World War II, and

we can only fully understand her work if we know about her life. When she was nine years old, at the beginning of World War II, her village was occupied by invading German troops, and she witnessed at first hand the violent consequences of those events. At the end of the war, Poland spent the next forty-five years as a Soviet-Union-dominated Communist state. Abakanowicz chose to become a weaver and, instead of making realistic depictions of heroic workers, the style of art favored and indeed demanded by the ruling Soviet Union, she made abstract sculpture that explores issues of dignity, courage, and a will to survival under a totalitarian government. In *80 Backs* (**1.10.7**), the fragile, perishable fiber materials reflect her keen awareness of the human vulnerability to which she was so exposed during the war and its aftermath, and also the fact that in the early years of her career, she had no conventional materials from which to sculpt: burlap sacks were some of the few things available to her. She also had no studio in which to work, and soft, pliable materials were useful in that they could be easily folded and stored.

Abakanowicz has often created works involving multiple, repeated figures. This reflects her experience of the Communist regime's emphasis on the collective over the individual, and its attempts to control personal expression. In *80 Backs,* the burlap fabric is shaped into recognizable but abstracted human forms without heads or faces. A few years after making *80 Backs,* Abakanowicz said, "A human being turned into a crowd loses his human qualities. A crowd is only a thousand-times duplicated copy, a repetition, a multiplication. Amongst such a great number, one person is extremely close and at the same time terribly distant."

Feminist Analysis

Biographical analysis usually takes gender, race, and societal position into account. Feminist analysis is a subset of biographical analysis when it studies the life experience of women artists in relation to their work. Feminist analysis has been expanded to include gender studies, which also considers the perspective toward gender of viewers, the treatment of women as subjects, and the role of women at the time the artwork was made.

Grande Odalisque by the French artist Jean-Auguste-Dominique Ingres (1780–1867) was made in 1814 for a male French audience (**1.10.8**). Feminist analysis might compare this artwork to others made at the time and find that female nudes were often depicted as objects of desire and beauty. The woman is dressed as an odalisque (a woman in a harem), and so a feminist analysis might study the French view of women in Near Eastern society, who were considered fascinating for their exotic sensuality. Feminist analysis could seek an explanation for the interest in harem women in art during this period, and might find that women in France were demanding equal rights, causing men to pine for docile females.

A feminist might also study this subject's demure gaze, whereby she accepts her status as an object of beauty. At the time when the picture was painted, critics complained that

1.10.8 Jean-Auguste-Dominique Ingres, *Grande Odalisque*, 1814. Oil on canvas, 35⅞ × 63¾". Musée du Louvre, Paris, France

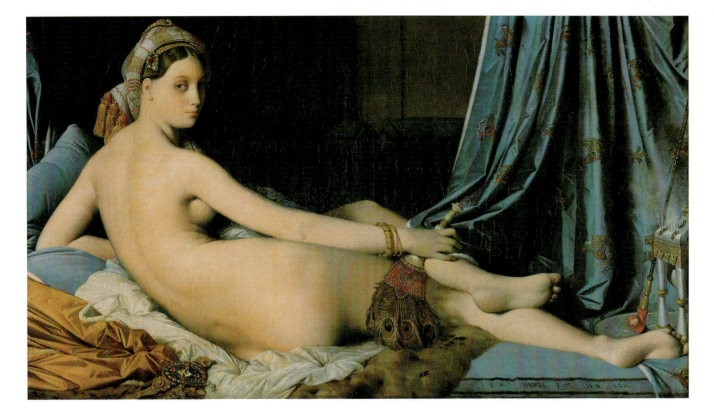

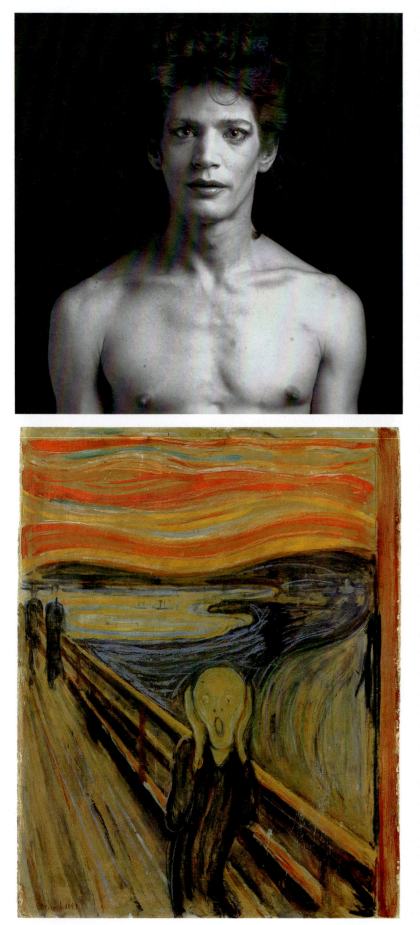

the figure's body parts were disproportionate: her back was too long, and her hips too wide. A feminist analysis would point out that Ingres believed that the back was a very sensual part of a woman's body, and that the painter claimed he could not stop himself, when painting, from adding what appear to be extra vertebrae.

Gender Studies Analysis

American artist Robert Mapplethorpe (1946–1989) used his own lifestyle as inspiration for his photographs. The issue of gender affects his imagery because he chose subjects that were highly sexualized and often related to his own interests as a gay man. His photographs are carefully composed, elegantly lit, and technically perfect, making subjects that might previously have been seen as deviant appear normal, even beautiful. A national controversy was sparked by the exhibition of Mapplethorpe's work that traveled to several museums across the US shortly after the artist died of AIDS-related illness in the late 1980s. Some museum officials and politicians considered the graphic sexual nature of Mapplethorpe's photographs to be problematic because the artist had been awarded a grant from public funds. Mapplethorpe, however, did not see a significant difference between a flower, a Classical sculpture, or a nude male figure.

Mapplethorpe's non-conformist view can be seen in his 1980 *Self-Portrait (#385)* in which his hair is curled and he wears eye shadow, blush, and lipstick (**1.10.9**). If one looks solely at his face, he seems to be a woman. His bare chest, however, tells us that he is a man. Mapplethorpe's appearance raises many questions about the assumptions we make based on the way people look. It also reveals the degree to which gender is a construction and suggests that not all people fit the conventional distinctions between the sexes. Mapplethorpe photographed what he wanted to see, the things that he considered visually interesting but did not find elsewhere in the art world. Interpreting Mapplethorpe's photograph from the perspective of gender studies encourages us

Research and Interpretation

The most effective research will include both primary and secondary sources.

Primary sources include:
- Artworks themselves (the most important primary source)
- Artists' statements
- Interviews with the artist
- Manuscripts, correspondence, and reviews written at the time that exhibitions of the artist's work were held
- Artists' own accounts of their life and work: autobiographies, memoirs, and oral histories recorded later
- Even the title of an artwork is verbal information, provided sometimes by the artist and sometimes by someone else.

Secondary sources include interpretations and analyses of primary sources by someone else, such as:
- Reference books (dictionaries of art, encyclopedias)
- Books by scholars
- Scholarly journal articles
- Book reviews
- Museum websites.*

* The Internet is a rich source of information, but you need to be very careful to evaluate the legitimacy of the sites. In general, websites are unreliable if it is unclear who wrote the information or what contributors' qualifications are. Many of the great museums around the world have their own websites, however, which are excellent and trustworthy sources of fascinating information. These websites are generally considered secondary sources, but may include primary source information, too.

Once you have done your research, you need to pull it all together to present a coherent **interpretation** of the artwork that shows that you understand the content and context. This interpretation should include your own opinion, carefully developed by considering your research findings. The strongest interpretations of an artwork combine the viewer's formal analysis, factual evidence from primary and secondary sources, and support from the work of specialists who know about the topics being covered.

Interpretation: explaining or translating a work of art, using factual research, personal response, or a combination of the two

---

1.10.9 (opposite, above) Robert Mapplethorpe, *Self-Portrait (#385)*, 1980. Gelatin silver print, 20 × 16"

1.10.10 (opposite, below) Edvard Munch, *The Scream*, 1893. Casein and tempera on cardboard, 35⅞ × 29⅛". Munch Museum, Oslo, Norway

Expressionism, Expressionist: an artistic style at its height in 1920s Europe, devoted to representing subjective emotions and experiences instead of objective or external reality

to take his intentions into account, and to think about how gender affects our experience.

Psychological Analysis

Psychological analysis considers the artist's state of mind when creating an artwork.

The Norwegian artist Edvard Munch (1863–1944) used the realm of his own mind as inspiration for *The Scream* (**1.10.10**). As a child he endured the death of his mother and sister, and throughout his life the artist suffered from physical illness and depression. These tragic experiences and psychological disturbances motivated his work. Munch reported that he felt psychologically driven to make art. His painting

The Scream presents a ghoul-like figure on a bridge, with a vibrant red sky in the background. At first glance it appears to be a fictional scene. Entries in Munch's diary, however, indicate that his painting in fact represents his interpretation of an actual event. While walking on an overlook road with two friends (the figures looming in the distance), Munch saw the sky turn red, and he froze with anxiety. Some scholars have suggested Munch witnessed an incredibly intense sunset caused by the dust thrown into the atmosphere during a volcanic eruption that had occurred years before he made the painting. Others believe he experienced an attack of agoraphobia, or fear of open spaces. Like many **Expressionist** artworks, this painting does not depict what Munch actually saw, but what he felt.

Combined Analysis of *Las Meninas*

While it is rare to be able to use every method discussed in this chapter on every artwork, we can often consider one artwork in many ways. Using the modes of analysis discussed earlier, we can arrive at a better and more rounded understanding of the famous painting *Las Meninas* (*The Maids of Honor*) by Diego de Silva y Velázquez (1599–1660).

A *formal analysis* tells us about what the artist has communicated using a visual language. This kind of detailed description often enhances our awareness of the appearance of a work of art. *Las Meninas* shows members of the court of the Spanish King Philip IV gathering in a room in the Alcázar Palace (**1.10.11a**). The painter depicts himself on the left, painting a large canvas. The Princess Margarita is posed in the center, with her ladies-in-waiting ("las meninas") surrounding her. Court workers, including dwarfs, are present as well.

The implied lines suggested by the black frames on the right wall and the ceiling fixtures converge on the chest of the man standing in the doorway. This is the **vanishing point** required in

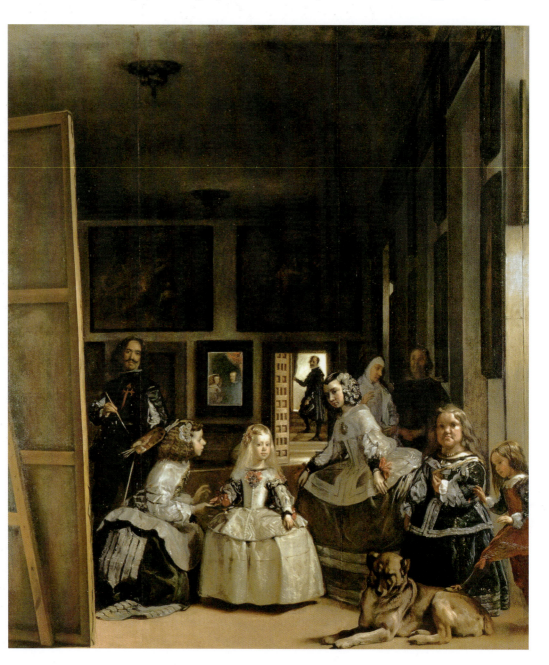

1.10.11a Diego de Silva y Velázquez, *Las Meninas*, c. 1656. Oil on canvas, 10'5¼" × 9¾". Museo Nacional del Prado, Madrid, Spain

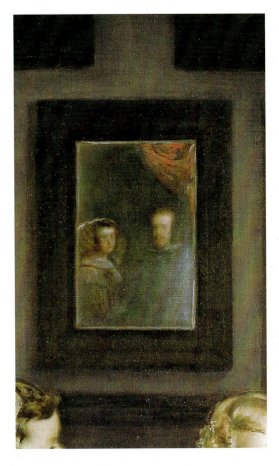

1.10.11b Detail of Diego de Silva y Velázquez, *Las Meninas*

linear perspective to create an illusion of **depth**, as if the viewer is looking into a real room. All the figures in the painting have a realistic sense of **volume** and are arranged to emphasize further the illusion of looking into a real space. Notice how they overlap one another, and that those toward the back of the room are smaller than those at the front. The painting is more than 10 ft. tall, which allows Velázquez to make the figures lifesize, further reinforcing the illusion of three-dimensional space. Finally, most of the **colors** in the painting are **neutral**. The color **palette** of brown, gray, beige, and black creates the impression of a dark space the depth of which is emphasized by the light coming in from a window on the right and the door at the back.

Velázquez highlights several areas he wants to emphasize. The young princess is in the central **foreground**, the part of the painting nearest to us, well lit, and shown attended by her maids. In the **background**, the mysterious male figure is emphasized because his black form contrasts with the light coming through the doorway.

Balance: a principle of art in which elements are used to create a symmetrical or asymmetrical sense of visual weight in an artwork
Focal point: the center of interest or activity in a work of art, often drawing the viewer's attention to the most important element
Rhythm: the regular or ordered repetition of elements in the work

The painter himself stands proudly at his work. And we notice the mirror on the back wall because of its blurry shiny surface: whom does it reflect? (**1.10.11b**). Touches of red lead our eye around the painting to significant points of interest: from Margarita's flowers, to the cross on Velázquez's chest, to the red curtain in the mirror on the back wall.

The painting is **balanced** in various ways. All of the figures are placed in the bottom half of the canvas, balanced by the sparseness of the wall and ceiling that take up the top half. While the figures at first appear to be arranged chaotically, they are actually placed in several stable pyramidal arrangements. One triangle highlights three of the composition's **focal points**: the mirror, Margarita, and the man in the doorway. The frames on the back and side walls form a framework of rectangles that stabilize the space of the room. The figures are of different heights and arranged so that our eye is led in a rhythmic line from Velázquez on the left through to the right of the painting: if you trace the heads of the figures in the foreground with your finger, you will sense the visual **rhythm**.

A *contextual* analysis gives us a better understanding of the content of the work of art by providing information about the time in which this work was made. The young girl is the Spanish princess Margarita Habsburg; the couple in the mirror are her parents, King Philip IV of Spain and Marianna of Austria. The mysterious man in the doorway is Nieto, the queen's chamberlain. Velázquez uses the mirror and this portrayal of an essential aide to the queen subtly to indicate the presence of the royal couple without violating etiquette, which did not permit the showing of the king and queen in a portrait with lesser court members.

A *biographical* analysis suggests why Velázquez placed himself in a painting that obliquely shows the presence of the king. One reason was that he was the king's favorite painter and assistant. It was extremely bold of him to paint himself into a scene with the royal family; by doing so, he wished to show his closeness with the king, and to raise his own status.

An *iconographic* analysis tells us that the cross on Velázquez in *Las Meninas* is the cross of the Order of Santiago. Velázquez had a lifelong ambition to become a knight of the order, but the order challenged his membership for decades. Their bylaws stated that: (1) only those from families of nobility could join, (2) members might have no Moorish (Muslim) ancestry, and (3) a craftsman could not become a member. The members saw painting as simply a manual craft rather than a liberal (or highminded) art. In truth, Velázquez did not meet any of these criteria, but after hundreds of supportive interviews, and with the support of both the king and the pope, Velázquez was finally knighted in 1659, three years after he painted *Las Meninas*.

Why, then, is the cross painted here when Velázquez was not knighted until after this painting was completed? Historians have found evidence that the king ordered the cross painted on after Velázquez's death, to honor the artist for having achieved his lifelong goal.

What Is the Meaning of *Las Meninas*?

After considering the various methods of analysis discussed above, scholars have arrived at a hypothesis as to what Velázquez wanted to say. They suggest that the artist was defending the nobility of painting itself. In order to be accepted as a knight, he needed to prove that his skill was not mere craft, but an intellectual endeavor. Therefore Velázquez created a brilliant illusion of space through his mastery of atmosphere and perspective. Even more boldly, he included the king in a painting that also featured a self-portrait of the artist, demonstrating the king's clear support for the painter. Velázquez's painting is an intentional effort to raise the status of painters, and to raise his own status in Spanish society.

1.10.12 Pablo Picasso, *Las Meninas*, first in a series, 1957. Oil on canvas, 6'4⅜" × 8'6⅜". Museo Picasso, Barcelona, Spain

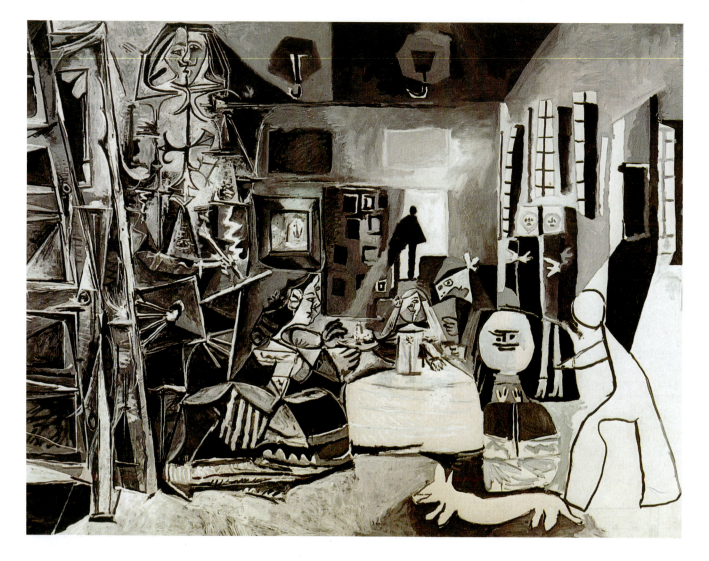

The Influence of *Las Meninas*

Artists often study and copy the work of artists they admire, and may use such studies to create works in their own individual style. On these two pages we see reimagined versions of *Las Meninas*, one by the Spanish painter Pablo Picasso (1881–1973; **1.10.12**), and the other by the contemporary German photographer Thomas Struth (b. 1954; **1.10.13**).

Pablo Picasso did not come to admire Velázquez until late in his own career, when he began to set his skills against the great artists of the past. At the age of seventy-six, Picasso locked himself in a room with a poster of *Las Meninas* and created forty-five paintings in response to Velázquez's masterpiece. In the first work in the series, Picasso alters the size of the canvas

(**1.10.12**). While mimicking Velázquez, he uses the elements and principles differently. For example, although Picasso does not use linear perspective, he creates a sense of depth by making Nieto small in scale and placing his dark figure in the bright doorway. Velázquez now appears to be floating up to the ceiling, leaving his paintbrushes and palette below. Is Picasso removing the old master to make room for himself?

Other figures are mere suggestions of the forms they were in the original painting. Picasso has broken them down into **abstract** parts. Margarita is outlined with no sense of volume, and the heads of the figures on the right are just black lines on white circles. The play of light on the figures is similar to the original, but Picasso's approach is more abstract: on the right, he lines up a row of windows that shine a bright white on the figure there (which correlates to the child

Abstract: art imagery that departs from recognizable images from the natural world

1.10.13 Thomas Struth, *Museo del Prado 7, Madrid 2005*, 2005. Chromogenic print, 5⅞" × 7'2"

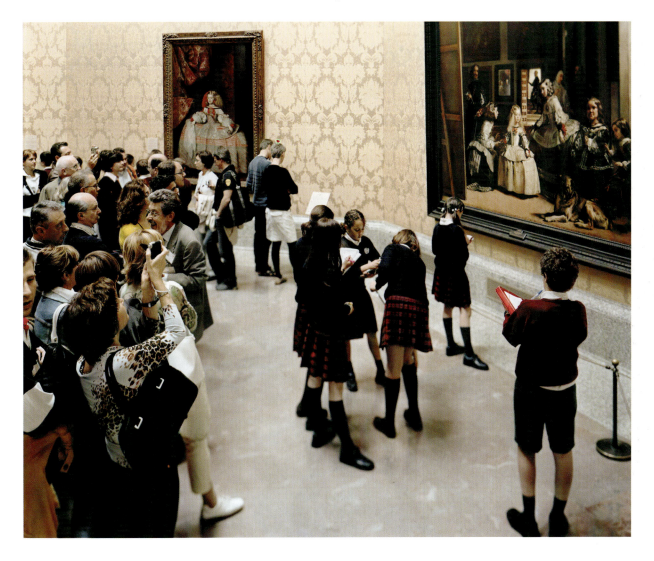

dwarf in the original). Margarita, highlighted in Velázquez's painting, is of a much lighter value than the other figures in Picasso's version, emphasizing that she is the most important person in the group. The majority of the rest of the series, in fact, are studies of Margarita specifically. This may relate to Picasso's own life. He first saw *Las Meninas* as a boy, just after his younger sister had died; she had been about the same age as Margarita here. Picasso has totally reinterpreted this artwork to make it his own; he has even replaced the large mastiff in Velázquez's painting with his own dog.

Thomas Struth used photography to create his view of *Las Meninas*. In **1.10.13** (p. 193), he shows a group admiring the painting at the Prado Museum in Madrid, Spain. There are multiple ways to interpret Struth's artwork. We can study his use of lighting and composition. We can consider which image is the "true" artwork: the photograph of the gallery visitors, or the painting. We can notice the boy sketching on the right, creating his own work of art. Lastly, we could pay attention to the multiple layers of looking and reflecting in Struth's photograph. It portrays people looking at art—exactly what we are doing as we look at the photograph. In this way, the artwork can be seen as a portrait of art appreciation. In 2007, Struth exhibited it at the Prado, hanging it right next to *Las Meninas*.

Active Learning Exercises

1. The tools of formal analysis are the starting point for understanding any work of art; this will help you realize how it was made and develop a deeper appreciation of it. Choose a work of art from another chapter in this book, for example **2.5.26** (p. 280), **2.4.16** (p. 258), or **3.1.30** (p. 385). Begin by taking a long look at the artwork and then use Part I of this book to make a list of the elements and principles of art as they relate to your chosen work. Use your list to write a thorough, detailed description of it. After you have finished, switch papers with a classmate and draw what the other person has described. Compare results and talk about what you learned from doing the drawing.

2. Use the other methods of analysis (besides formal analysis) that are discussed in this chapter to guide your research in order to understand why an artwork was made and what its message is. You could try analysing **1.3.6** (p. 85), **4.5.15** (p. 622) or **4.10.3** (p. 677). Consider the artist's life when the work was created. Delve into the time and place in which he or she lived. What symbols did the artist use, and what was his or her state of mind? Recognize that some artworks are meant to convey distinct messages, which were clear to their contemporary audiences. Organize your findings into a Combined Analysis paper.

3. When looking at a work of art for the first time, it is a good idea to sketch out what is called a compositional diagram. Compositional diagrams vary greatly because they convey an individual's interpretation of what is most striking about an artwork. They are not meant to re-create the work, but instead are used as a tool to capture its points of emphasis and to determine how the elements and principles are used to that effect. In this compositional diagram of *Las Meninas*, the student finds the mirror on the wall to be the most dominant element, and makes it darker. The second-darkest spot, and therefore another point of emphasis in this student's eyes, is the head of Velázquez. This student finds many shapes in the framed artworks and the grouping of the figures, and observes the triangle created by Nieto in the doorway, little Margarita, and the mirror. The diagram also explores the use of perspective and implied line. Creating a compositional diagram can help you to write a thorough and engaging formal analysis. Select a work of art that intrigues you and try creating your own diagram.

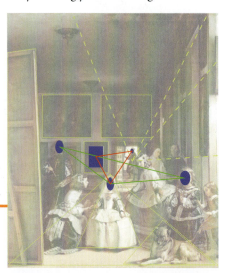

Images Related to 1.10: Content and Analysis

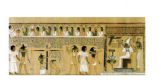

4.2.9 *Book of the Dead*: Last Judgment before Osiris, c. 1275 BCE, p. 580

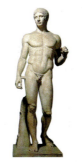

3.1.25 Polykleitos, *Doryphoros* (Roman copy), original *c.* 460–50 BCE, p. 382

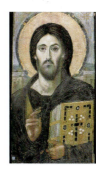

3.2.6 Christ icon, Byzantine, 6th century CE, p. 395

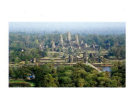

3.3.24 Angkor Wat, Cambodia, 12th century, p. 430

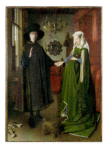

3.6.11a Jan van Eyck, *The Arnolfini Portrait*, 1434, p. 474

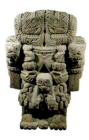

3.4.16 *The Mother Goddess, Coatlicue*, Aztec, *c.* 1487–1520, p. 442

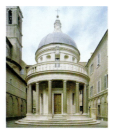

2.5.25 Donato Bramante, Tempietto, San Pietro in Montorio, Rome, Italy, *c.* 1502, p. 279

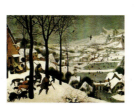

1.9.6 Pieter Bruegel, *Hunters in the Snow*, 1565, p. 171

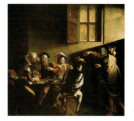

1.3.6 Caravaggio, *The Calling of St. Matthew*, *c.* 1599–1600, p. 85

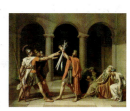

3.7.10 Jacques-Louis David, *The Oath of the Horatii*, 1784, p. 499

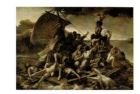

4.8.1 Théodore Géricault, *Raft of the Medusa*, 1819, p. 649

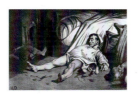

2.3.16 Honoré Daumier, *Rue Transnonain*, April 15, 1834, p. 242

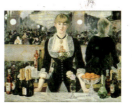

4.5.16 Édouard Manet, *A Bar at the Folies-Bergère*, 1882, p. 623

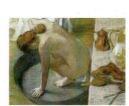

2.1.14 Edgar Degas, *The Tub*, 1886, p. 206

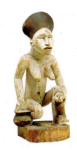

4.3.6 Kneeling female figure with bowl and child, 19th–20th century, p. 591

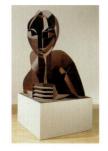

2.4.16 Naum Gabo, *Constructed Head No.2*, 1916, p. 258

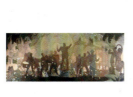

3.8.41 Aaron Douglas, *Aspects of Negro American Life: Slavery through Reconstruction*, 1934, p. 539

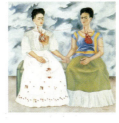

4.10.3 Frida Kahlo, *The Two Fridas*, 1939, p. 677

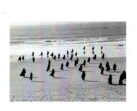

3.9.20b Shirin Neshat, *Rapture series*, 1999, p. 554

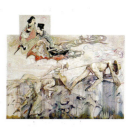

2.2.12 Hung Liu, *Interregnum*, 2002, p. 223

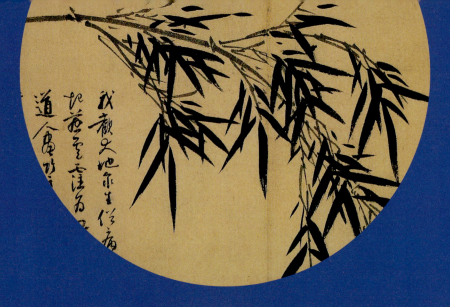

MEDIA

Art is a form of visual communication: artists make art because they want to express something. Just as writers consider carefully the form that best expresses what they want to say (a long novel, a brief poem, a play or film script, for example), artists consider carefully the materials and processes available to communicate their visual ideas. In fact, art can be made from almost anything: one contemporary artist has used elephant dung in his paintings. There are certain media and processes that have been commonly used by artists, some of them for thousands of years, but others that have been developed more recently. In this part you will learn how most of the art that you will encounter has been made.

PART 2

AND PROCESSES

THE MAIN MEDIA AND PROCESSES OF ART ARE:

Drawing

Painting

Printmaking

Sculpture

Architecture

The Tradition of Craft

Visual Communication Design

Photography

Film/Video and Digital Art

Alternative Media and Processes

2.1

Drawing

Sketch: a rough preliminary version of a work or part of a work

He who pretends to be either painter or engraver without being a master of drawing is an imposter.

(William Blake, English artist and poet)

As William Blake suggests, drawing—defined as the depiction of shapes and forms on a surface, primarily by means of lines—is a fundamental artistic skill. Even before we learn to write, we learn to draw; we draw the shape of a cat before we can write the word. Drawing is spontaneous, a convenient way for us to "make our mark" on the world. Like the instinctive crayon marks children make as they explore and develop their fine motor skills, drawing provides a primal outlet for artistic energy and ideas.

Artists draw for many reasons: to define their ideas, to plan for larger projects, to resolve design issues in preparatory **sketches**, and to record their visual observations. Of course,

drawings can also be finished works of art in their own right.

Drawing is the basis of all visual communication. Most artists and designers continue to develop their drawing skills throughout their lives.

Functions of Drawing

Because drawing is a fundamental skill it is used, to some degree, in every artistic medium. Leonardo da Vinci (1452–1519) used drawing to examine the world. His sketchbooks are full of ideas and images, illustrating both his speculative thought and his careful observations. Amongst his explorations, Leonardo dissected human bodies and then drew what he saw. He also studied the works of other artists, and observed the effects of light and shadow on a form. He investigated the mechanics of a bird's wing, and considered whether humans might also be able to fly if such mechanics were re-created on a human scale. His drawing of a flying machine illustrates a concept that had never been considered in this way before (**2.1.1**). Drawing enabled Leonardo to express his ideas beyond what could be said in words.

Some of Leonardo's most revolutionary drawings depict the interior anatomy of the

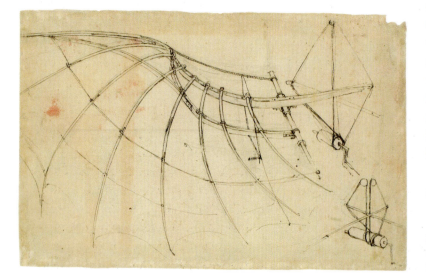

2.1.1 Leonardo da Vinci, *Drawing for a wing of a flying machine*, from the *Codice Atlantico*, fol. 858r. Pen and ink. Biblioteca Ambrosiana, Milan, Italy

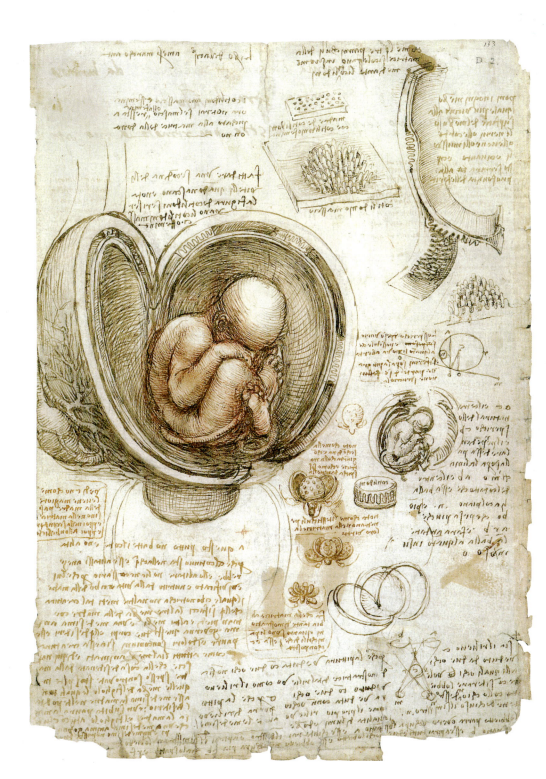

2.1.2 Leonardo da Vinci, *Studies of the fetus in the womb, c.* 1510–13. Pen and ink and wash over red chalk and traces of black chalk, 12 × 8¾″. Royal Collection, London, England

Fresco: a technique where the artist paints onto freshly applied plaster. From the Italian *fresco,* "fresh"

human body (**2.1.2**). These drawings are especially rare because the Church banned all acts that desecrated the body, including dissection. Leonardo may have been allowed to record his observations because he practiced his drawing methodically and with great care. Some speculate that the Church was interested in Leonardo's observations as possible evidence of how the human soul resides in the body.

All artists draw for the same reasons as Leonardo: as an end in itself, to think, and to prepare and plan other works. Drawing played an essential role in Raphael's planning of his **fresco** *The School of Athens* (see Gateway Box: Raphael, p. 200, **2.1.3a** and **2.1.3b**).

Like Raphael, contemporary artists still use drawing as a way to prepare for larger, more involved works. African-American artist John

Gateway to Art: Raphael, *The School of Athens*
Drawing in the Design Process

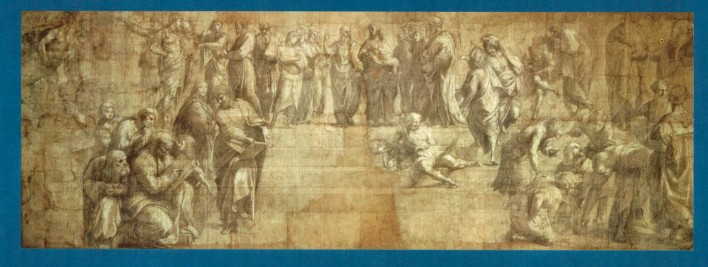

2.1.3a Raphael, Cartoon for *The School of Athens*, *c.* 1509. Charcoal and chalk, 9'4¼" × 26'4⅝". Biblioteca Ambrosiana, Milan, Italy

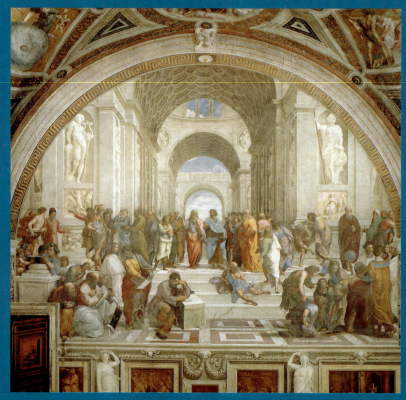

2.1.3b Raphael, *The School of Athens*, 1510–11. Fresco, 16'8" × 25'. Stanza della Segnatura, Vatican City, Italy

When the Italian painter Raphael (1483–1520) prepared to paint *The School of Athens*, he drew the image in advance (**2.1.3a**), practicing before he tackled the larger work (**2.1.3b**).

His preliminary drawings allowed Raphael to refine his ideas and perfect the image at a smaller scale before investing in the more expensive painting materials he used for the final version.

The artist began the painting process by creating a large drawing of the work, almost the same size as the final painting, to use as the design for a mural. This design, called the cartoon, was perforated with small pinholes all along where the lines were drawn. It was then positioned on the wall where Raphael intended to paint the work, and powdered charcoal dust was forced through the small holes in the cartoon's surface, leaving behind an impression of the original drawing. These marks would aid Raphael in drawing the image onto the wall. He applied a thin layer of plaster, repowdered the charcoal dust through the cartoon if necessary, and then began to paint *The School of Athens*.

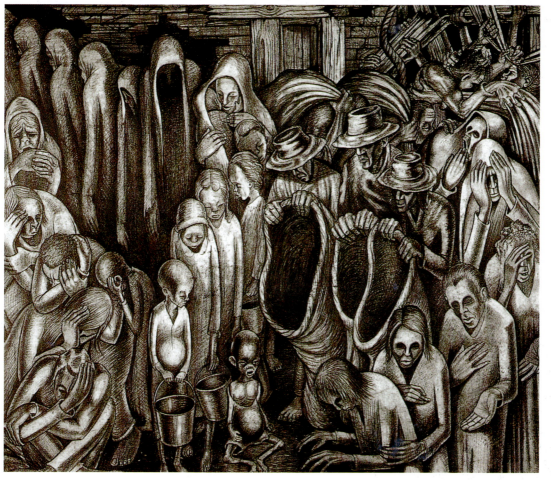

2.1.4 John Biggers, *Night of the Poor*, 1949. Preparatory study for mural, Pennsylvania State University

Biggers (1924–2001) used pencil drawing in his preparation process, leading to large, permanent mural works. Such works as *Night of the Poor* (**2.1.4**) highlight how denial of education to the poor has a chilling effect on their future prospects. The finished painting was installed in Burrowes Hall, where Penn State's School of Education is housed. Even though it is a preparatory drawing, Biggers approaches it with the same energy and resolve that an artist might reserve for a grand painting, so the drawing stands as a great work in its own right.

The Materials of Drawing: Dry Media

When creating a drawing, an artist must first choose whether to draw using dry **media** or wet media. Dry media offer the artist some unique and versatile properties.

Silverpoint

Almost every metal will leave a mark on a fibrous surface. Artists during the Italian **Renaissance** used lead, tin, copper, and silver to draw images. The most common of these drawing metals was silverpoint.

Silverpoint is a piece of silver wire set in some type of a holder, usually wood, to make the wire easier to hold and control. The artist hones the end of the wire to a sharp point. Because of the hardness of the silver, artists can create finely detailed drawings. Historically, artists have drawn with silverpoint on wood primed with a thin coating of bone ash. This creates a white **ground** for the light **value** of the silver. Because silver tarnishes, the drawing becomes darker and the image more pronounced over time. Working on colored paper creates distinctive effects and was particularly popular in Renaissance Italy (*c.* 1400–1600).

Medium (plural **media**): the material on or from which an artist chooses to make a work of art, for example canvas and oil paint, marble, engraving, video, or architecture
Renaissance: a period of cultural and artistic change in Europe from the fourteenth to the seventeenth century
Ground: the surface or background onto which an artist paints or draws
Value: the lightness or darkness of a plane or area

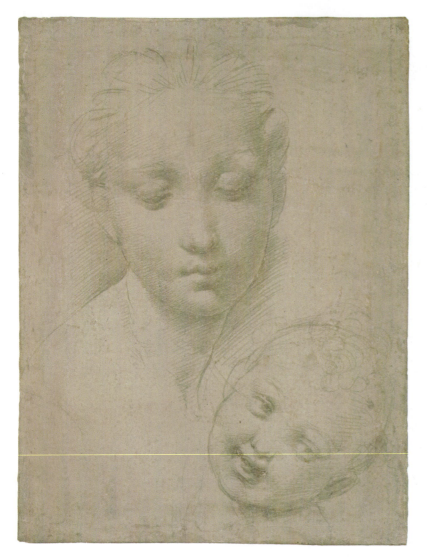

2.1.5 Raphael, *Heads of the Virgin and Child*, c. 1509–11. Silverpoint on pink prepared paper, 5⅝ × 4⅜". British Museum, London, England

In *Heads of the Virgin and Child*, a silverpoint drawing by Raphael, the artist uses **hatching** and **cross-hatching** to create a stronger dark value (**2.1.5**). Because silverpoint has such a light value and is usually drawn with very thin lines, much of the white paper is exposed. By closely overlapping many parallel lines across each other, Raphael covers more of the paper, creating the illusion of a darker value. Many artists use this technique to darken values and create the effect of shading (**2.1.6**).

Pencil

Everyone knows what pencils are. We like them because we can erase and correct errors. This makes the pencil a valuable tool for artists as well. Most artists' pencils differ from those used for writing and are categorized by their relative hardness or softness.

A deposit of solid graphite—which looks and writes like lead, but without its weight—was discovered in the mid-1500s and gave rise to the manufacture of the basic pencil we know today.

Pencils have different degrees of hardness (**2.1.7**). The softer the pencil, the darker the mark, or grade, and the quicker the pencil loses its point. The B or black graphite pencils are softer and darker than the H series. Number 2 (HB to be precise) pencils are the writing tools used by nearly every American elementary-school student. The H or hard graphite pencils create a relatively light mark. This type of pencil is useful when an artist is doing layout work and does not want pencil lines to show in the final product. Artists carefully choose the grade of the pencil lead they use.

The self-portrait by Hungarian artist Ilka Gedö (1921–1985) shows how an artist can vary the pressure of a pencil line to suggest **texture** and create **emphasis** in a drawing (**2.1.8**). Gedö

2.1.6 How hatching and cross-hatching lines are used to create the effect of shading

2.1.7 Pencil hardness scale from 9H to 9B

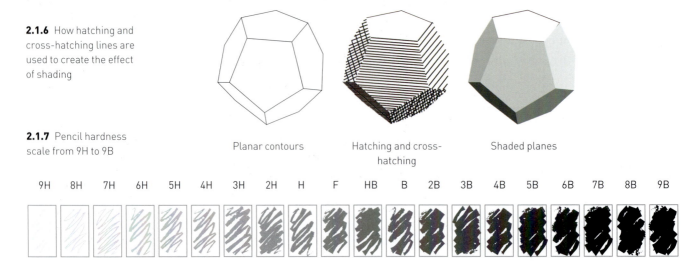

Planar contours

Hatching and cross-hatching

Shaded planes

9H	8H	7H	6H	5H	4H	3H	2H	H	F	HB	B	2B	3B	4B	5B	6B	7B	8B	9B

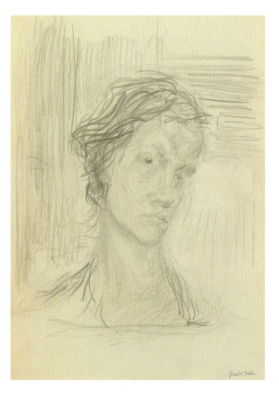

2.1.8 Ilka Gedö, *Self-portrait*, 1944. Graphite on paper, 11⅝ × 8⅜". British Museum, London, England

attention on the artist's face, while the different sets of straight horizontal and vertical lines recede into the **background**. In further contrast, notice how softly the artist handles the graphite in the areas representing the skin compared with the hair or clothing. Gedö was a survivor of the Holocaust; this drawing records her gaunt features shortly after her internment.

Color Pencil

Color pencil is manufactured much like the traditional graphite pencil, but the mixture that makes up the lead contains more wax and **pigment**. Color pencils are used just like graphite pencils, although their marks may be harder to erase or alter. The California artist D. J. Hall (b. 1951) exploits the richness of colored pencil when she creates a work. In *Piece of Cake* (**2.1.9**) the artist pushes the waxy shaft of **color** into the fibers of the paper to achieve maximum richness. By pushing color this aggressively and leaving some strong white areas, Hall implies a sense of the intense light of a California afternoon.

2.1.9 D. J. Hall, *Piece of Cake*, 1987. Colored pencil on paper, 30 × 39½". Metropolitan Museum of Art, New York

has used thick dark lines to imply darkness and thin light lines to suggest lightness. The dark value of the eye and wavy hair, where the pencil has been pressed hard, concentrates our

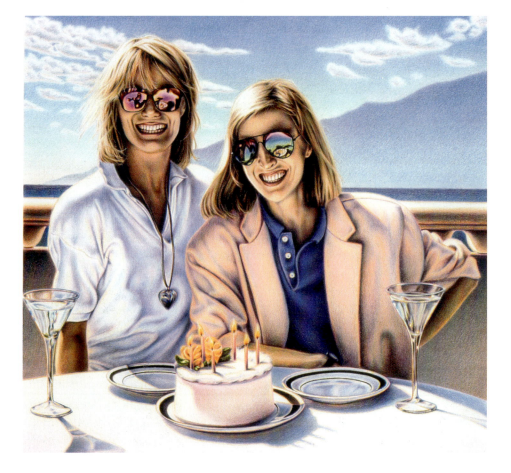

Hatching: the use of non-overlapping parallel lines to convey darkness or lightness
Cross-hatching: the use of overlapping parallel lines to convey darkness or lightness
Texture: the surface quality of a work, for example fine/coarse, detailed/lacking in detail
Emphasis: the principle of drawing attention to particular content in a work
Background: the part of a work depicted as behind the main figures
Pigment: the colorant in art materials. Often made from finely ground minerals
Color: the optical effect caused when reflected white light of the spectrum is divided into separate wavelengths

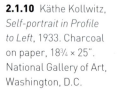

2.1.10 Käthe Kollwitz, *Self-portrait in Profile to Left*, 1933. Charcoal on paper, 18¾ × 25". National Gallery of Art, Washington, D.C.

Charcoal

Charcoal has long been an important material in the history of drawing: samples from cave drawings in France have been dated back to 30,000 BCE. Unlike pencils and silverpoint, charcoal smudges easily, creates lines that can be easily shaped and altered, usually has strong dark value, and is soft compared to metal-based drawing materials. Artists choose charcoal as a drawing material when they want to express strong dark tones, add interest to a surface, and make something look solid rather than linear.

Two types of charcoal are common. Vine charcoal is made from thin vine branches and is very soft and easily erased. Compressed charcoal, to which a binding agent, such as wax, is sometimes added, is much denser.

To make charcoal, finger-length pieces of wood (often dried willow) are placed inside an airtight container (to prevent the loss of important binding chemicals) and heated in an oven until all the wood has been burned.

To draw with charcoal, an artist drags the stick across a fibrous surface, usually paper, leaving a soft-edged line. By using just the end, an artist can create thin strokes; by using the side, he or she can cover a lot of surface quickly. The amount of pressure an artist exerts while drawing controls the lightness or darkness of the stroke. Sandpaper can be used to sharpen the stick for more detail. An artist can achieve a soft visual effect by rubbing the newly charcoaled drawing surface with a bare finger, some tissue paper, or a rolled-paper cone called a tortillion, made expressly for this purpose.

Charcoal is so soft that the texture of the paper surface—even the drawing board's texture below the paper—profoundly affects the image. Charcoal works best on paper with a fairly rough texture (known as **tooth**), which catches the charcoal better in its fibers.

Charcoal portraits by German artist Käthe Kollwitz (1867–1945) and French artist Léon Augustin Lhermitte (1844–1925) show how artists work with the characteristics of the medium (**2.1.10** and **2.1.11**).

In Kollwitz's self-portrait, we feel a sense of energy from the way she applies the charcoal. Although she renders her own face and hand realistically, in the space between we see the nervous energy connecting the eye to the hand. Kollwitz draws with a spontaneous burst of charcoal marks along the arm, in **expressive contrast** to the more considered areas of the head and hand.

In *An Elderly Peasant Woman*, Lhermitte works with the characteristics of charcoal to describe his **subject** carefully. Each line and blemish on this woman's face has been carefully rendered. The charcoal's dark value accentuates the contrast between the **highlights** in the face and the overall darkened tone of the work. It even carefully preserves the light reflected in her eye. Lhermitte has controlled charcoal's inherent smudginess to offer an intimate view of the effects of ageing.

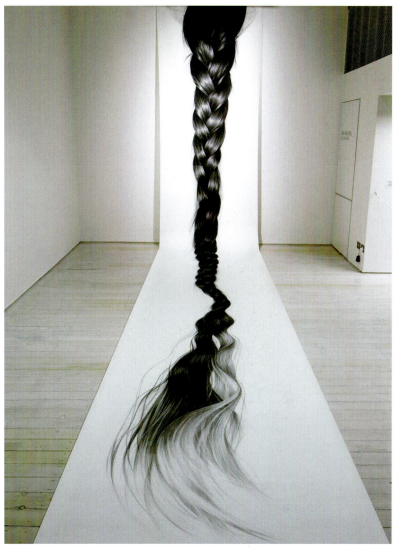

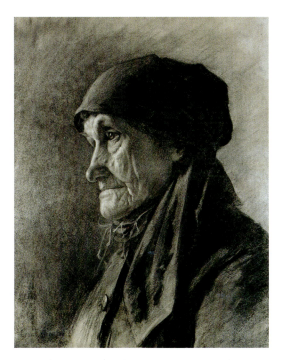

2.1.11 Léon Augustin Lhermitte, *An Elderly Peasant Woman*, *c*. 1878. Charcoal on wove paper, 18¾ × 15⅝″. National Gallery of Art, Washington, D.C.

Although there is precise detail in both drawings, each artist allows the "personality" of the charcoal into the softened background through smudges and irregular soft marks.

The Chinese-born artist Zhang Chun Hong (b. 1971) utilized both charcoal and graphite for dramatic effect in the work *Life Strands* (**2.1.12**). In this work, charcoal provides the deep, dark values that describe a long strand of braided hair. Because charcoal has a rich, dark softness, the tightly interlocked braid can cascade down the page into a scatter of gestural marks where the hair has been unleashed from its binding. The strand metaphorically represents the passage of time from the dark, full hair of childhood to the grayed and thinning hair of old age. In this drawing Zhang masterfully uses drawing on a long Chinese scroll to make parallels between life and art.

2.1.12 Zhang Chun Hong, *Life Strands*, 2004. Charcoal and graphite on paper, 38′ × 4′11″. Private collection

Tooth: the textural quality of a paper surface for holding drawing media in place
Expressive: capable of stirring the emotions of the viewer
Contrast: a drastic difference between such elements as color or value (lightness/darkness) when they are presented together
Subject: the person, object, or space depicted in a work of art
Highlight: an area of lightest value in a work

Binder: a substance that makes pigments adhere to a surface

Foreground: the part of a work depicted as nearest the viewer

Composition: the overall design or organization of a work

Focal point: the area in a composition to which the eye returns most naturally

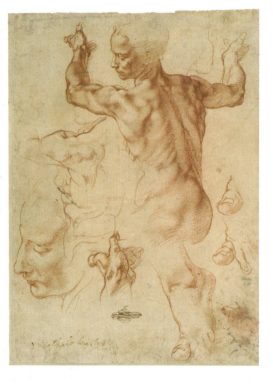

2.1.13 Michelangelo, *Studies for the Libyan Sibyl*, 1510–11. Red chalk, 11⅜ × 8⅜". Metropolitan Museum of Art, New York

Chalk, Pastel, and Crayon

Sticks of chalk, pastel, and crayon are made by combining pigment and **binder**. Traditional binders include oil, wax, gum arabic, and glues. The type of binder gives each material a unique character. Chalks, pastels, and crayons can be prepared in any color. Chalk is powdered calcium carbonate mixed with a gum arabic (a type of tree sap) binder. Pastel is pigment combined with gum arabic, wax, or oil, while crayon is pigment combined with wax. Conté crayon, a variation invented by Nicolas-Jacques Conté, who was a French painter and army officer, is a heavily pigmented crayon sometimes manufactured with graphite.

For their preparatory sketches, artists of the Renaissance used colored chalks, in particular a red chalk known as sanguine. The Italian artist Michelangelo Buonarroti (1475–1564) used this red chalk for his *Studies for the Libyan*

2.1.14 (below) Edgar Degas, *The Tub*, 1886. Pastel, 23⅝ × 32⅝". Musée d'Orsay, Paris, France

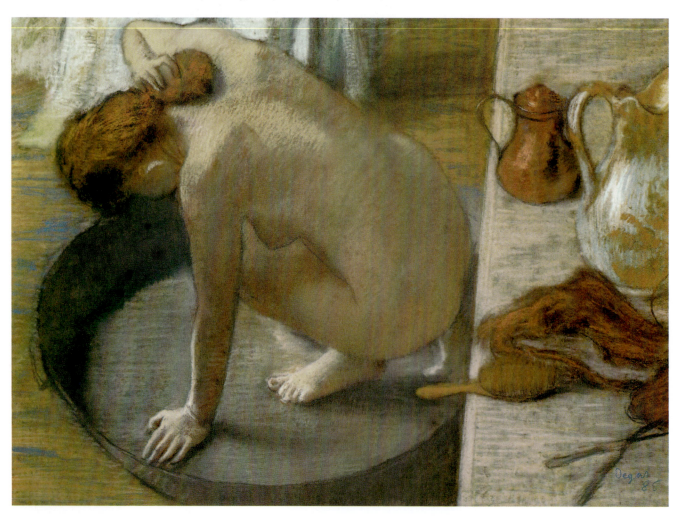

Sibyl (**2.1.13**), which he made in preparation for painting the Sistine Chapel ceiling in Rome. Michelangelo uses hatching and cross-hatching (**2.1.6**, p. 202) to build up the values and give the figure depth. The artist's study concentrates on the muscular definition of the back and on the face, shoulder, and hand, and gives repeated attention to the detail of the big toe. These details are essential to making this twisting pose convincing, and Michelangelo spent extra time refining them.

The French artist Edgar Degas (1834–1917) is noted for pastel studies that stand as finished works of art. In *The Tub*, Degas lays down intermittent strokes of different-color pastel (**2.1.14**). He takes advantage of the charcoal-like softness of the material to blend the colors together, thus giving them a rich complexity and creating a variety of contrasting textures. In pastel as in painting, Degas was a master at re-creating the effects of light and color seen in nature.

In the Conté crayon drawing *Trees on the Bank of the Seine*, the French artist Georges Seurat (1859–1891) uses hatching and cross-hatching, as Michelangelo did, to build up value and create depth (**2.1.15**). Seurat designates the **foreground** by using darker values; he allows the color of the paper to be more dominant in areas he wants to recede into the distance. Because this drawing was a study for a subsequent work, Seurat also took special care in organizing the **composition**. For example, the darkest large tree on the left is the **focal point** of this drawing and leads our eye to the right, where Seurat places a curved tree to direct our attention to the nearby river in the background.

Erasers and Fixatives

Erasers are not only used for correction but also to create light marks in areas already drawn. In this way the artist can embellish highlights by working from the dark to light.

Erasers can be used to create works of art by destroying the marks made by an artist. In 1953 the artist Robert Rauschenberg created a new work of art by erasing a drawing by Willem de Kooning (**2.1.16**). Rauschenberg, a

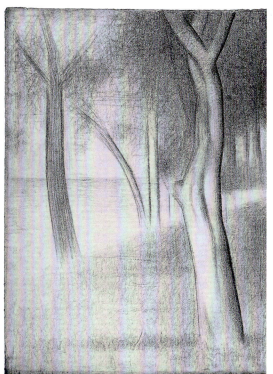

2.1.15 Georges Seurat, *Trees on the Bank of the Seine* (study for *La Grande Jatte*), 1884. Black Conté crayon on white laid paper, 24½ x 18½". Art Institute of Chicago

2.1.16 Robert Rauschenberg, *Erased de Kooning Drawing*, 1953. Traces of ink and crayon on paper, in gold-leaf frame, 25¼ × 21¾ × ½". San Francisco Museum of Modern Art

young, unknown artist at that time, approached the famous de Kooning and asked if he could erase one of his drawings. De Kooning agreed, understanding what the younger artist had in mind. But, in order to make it more difficult, de Kooning gave Rauschenberg a drawing made with charcoal, oil paint, pencil, and crayon. It took Rauschenberg nearly a month to erase it, but he did so, leaving a drawing on the back of the work intact. Some in the art world dubbed him "L'Enfant Terrible," which means a young person who behaves badly, but Rauschenberg's idea was to create a performed work of **conceptual art** and display the result.

A fixative is a coating that can be applied to a drawing to preserve its appearance by making the dry medium adhere to the surface of the paper. Once an artist has applied a dry medium and manipulated it by smudging, marking, or erasing, he or she can apply a fixative to set the image. Because artists usually need to make changes throughout the drawing process, most use a "workable" fixative that can be removed by erasing the surface of the coating. Most commercial fixatives used today are available in an aerosol can or spray bottle for easy and even application.

The Materials of Drawing: Wet Media

The wet media used in drawings are applied with brushes or pens. Wet media dry or harden as the liquid evaporates.

Ink

Ink is a favorite of artists because of its permanence, precision, and strong dark color. There are many types of ink, each with its own individual character.

Carbon ink, made by mixing soot with water and gum, has been in use in China and India since around 2500 BCE. This type of ink tended to discolor over time and could become smudged in moist or humid environments. A contemporary version of carbon ink, called India (or Indian) ink, is a favorite of comic-book artists.

Most European ink drawings from the Renaissance to the present day are made with iron gall ink. Gall ink is prized for its near-permanence and rich black color. It is manufactured from a mixture of tannin (from oak galls—parasitic growths on oak trees), iron sulfate, gum arabic, and water. Gall ink is not entirely lightfast, however, and tends to lighten to brown after many years.

Other types of fluid media include bistre, which is derived from wood soot and usually a yellow-brown color, and sepia, a brown medium that is derived from the secretions of cuttlefish.

Brush Drawing

Because ink is a liquid medium, it can also be applied with a brush. The ancient Chinese used brush and ink for both writing and drawing. Even today, children throughout east Asia who are learning to write must learn to control a brush effectively, in much the same way students in the West learn to use pens and pencils.

East Asian artists use the same brush for writing and drawing. These brushes are made with a bamboo shaft and either ox, goat, horse, or wolf hair. Traditionally, Asian artists use a stick of solid ink that they hold upright and grind on a special ink stone with a small amount of water. As the ink reaches the desired consistency, it is pushed into a shallow reservoir at the rear of the stone. Artists wet the brush by dipping it into this reservoir, and then adjust the shape and charge of the brush by stroking it on the flat of the grinding stone. They can readily adjust the dilution of the ink with water to create an infinite range of grays. This is called a wash, and it allows the artist to control value and texture.

In **2.1.17** the fourteenth-century Chinese artist Wu Zhen (sometimes spelled Wu Chen) (1280–1354) uses brush, ink, and wash to create a masterpiece of simplicity. This finely planned design contains carefully controlled brushstrokes as well as loose, freer ink applications, thereby bringing together two opposing influences and reflecting the central

2.1.17 (opposite top) Wu Zhen, Leaf from an album of bamboo drawings, 1350. Ink on paper, 16 × 21". National Palace Museum, Taipei, Taiwan

Conceptual art: artwork in which the ideas are most important to the work

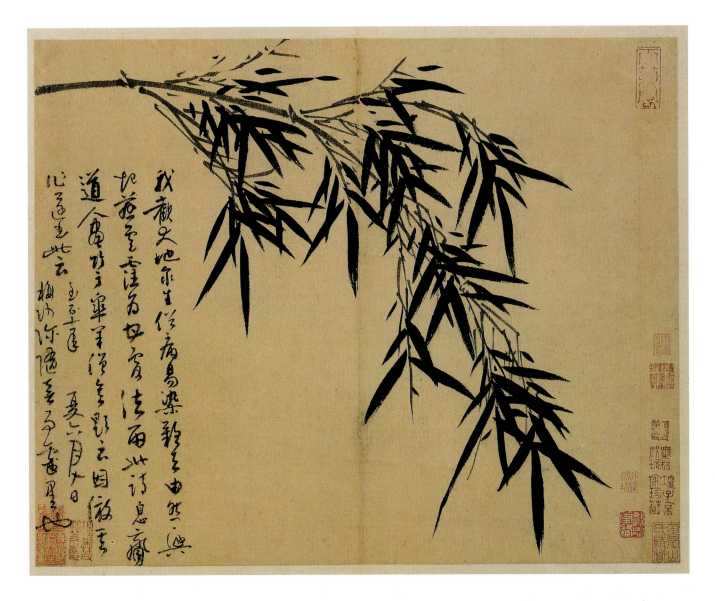

principle of Taoism, a belief in the importance of balanced opposites. Because the artist uses only a few shapes, the arrangement of the bamboo leaves becomes like a series of letters in a word or sentence. Wu achieves the changing dark and light values by adding water to create a wash and lighten the ink. This work was intended as a model for Wu's son to follow as he learned the art of brushwork from his father.

In his image of the landscape just north of Rome, *The Tiber from Monte Mario Looking South*, the French artist Claude Lorrain's (1604/5–1682) thoughtful brushstrokes give us a feeling of the great expanse of the Italian countryside (**2.1.18**). The wash that Lorrain uses creates a sense of depth by making the values of the foreground areas both the darkest and lightest of the whole drawing.

2.1.18 (below) Claude Lorrain, *The Tiber from Monte Mario Looking South*, 1640. Dark-brown wash on white paper, 7⅜ × 10⅝". British Museum, London, England

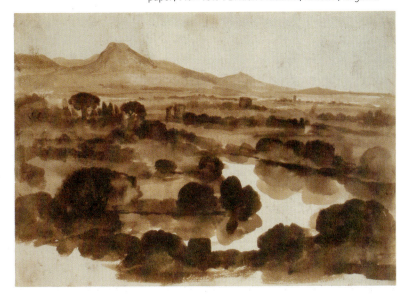

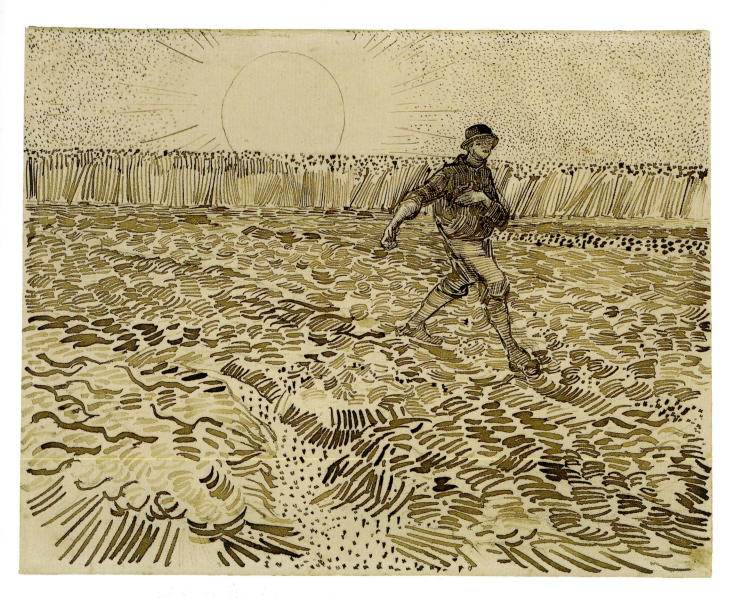

Quill and Pen

Traditionally a quill—the shaft of a bird's feather, or a similarly hollow reed—is carved to a point to apply the ink. A slit, running parallel to the shaft, helps control its rate of flow. The modern version is a pen with a metal nib. The artist can control the flow of the ink by pressing harder or more softly. Apart from choosing different widths of nib, the artist can further increase or decrease the width of the drawn line by holding the pen at different angles. Often, pen-and-ink drawings employ hatching and cross-hatching to create variations in value (**2.1.6**, p. 202).

Dutch artist Vincent van Gogh (1853–1890) uses a reed pen and brown ink for his *Sower with Setting Sun* (**2.1.19**). By changing the way he applies his pen strokes and by controlling their width, he creates an undulating, restless design. Van Gogh's emphatic direction of line expresses the characteristic energy of his work.

Paper

Before the invention of paper, drawings were made on papyrus (a plant material), cloth, wood, and animal hide (parchment and vellum). Paper was invented in China by Cai Lun, who manufactured it from pounded or macerated plant fibers, at around the end of the first century CE. The image in **2.1.20**, even though it was made more than 1,500 years later, shows how this was done. The fibers are suspended in water and then scooped up into a flat mold with a screen at the bottom, so that the water

2.1.19 Vincent van Gogh, *Sower with Setting Sun*, 1888. Pen and brown ink, 9⅝ × 12⅝". Van Gogh Museum, Amsterdam, The Netherlands

Cast: a sculpture or artwork made by pouring a liquid (for example molten metal or plaster) into a mold
Contour: the outline that defines a form

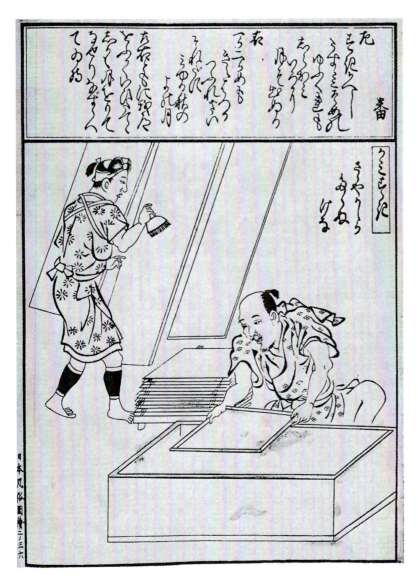

2.1.20 Hishikawa Moronobu, *Papermaking in Japan*, showing the vatman and the paper-drier, 1681. Woodblock print from the four-volume *Wakoku Shōshoku Edzukushi*, 1681

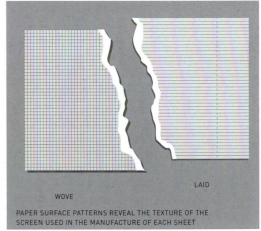

WOVE

LAID

PAPER SURFACE PATTERNS REVEAL THE TEXTURE OF THE SCREEN USED IN THE MANUFACTURE OF EACH SHEET

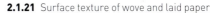

2.1.21 Surface texture of wove and laid paper

can escape. The fibers are now bonded enough to each other to keep their shape when they are taken out. The sheet is then pressed and dried.

Over the centuries, improvements were made to the construction of the mold to speed up times for papermakers to flip out molded sheets of paper and reuse the mold. Hand-made papers are still manufactured this way in many countries, mostly from cotton fiber, although papers are also made of hemp, abaca (a leaf-based fiber derived from a banana-like plant), flax, and other plant fibers.

In addition to their fiber content, papers are classified by their surface texture and weight. Depending on the construction of the mold, the paper usually has a surface texture described as either wove or laid. The laid texture derives from a screen (bottom of the mold) composed of many parallel rods, like a bamboo mat, whereas the wove texture derives from the use of a grid-like mesh of metal wire or cloth (see **2.1.21**).

Paper in bulk is normally measured by the ream (a quantity of 500 sheets). The standard measurement for defining the character of paper is its weight per ream in the paper's basic sheet size. (For cotton rag paper, the sheet size is usually 17 × 22 in.) For example, if 500 sheets of 17 × 22-in. paper weigh 20 lbs., the paper is referred to as "20 lb." Heavier papers are stronger and usually better to work with, but cost more.

Life Drawing

Life drawing is the practice of drawing from a live model, as opposed to using photographs, plaster **casts**, or other existing artworks as source material. We associate this process with nude models, but life drawing can also involve animals, plants, and architecture. Life drawing is one of the core skills that art students learn. In addition to the extended study of live models, two types of introductory drawing methods are popular in the teaching of life drawing: gesture and **contour**.

Gesture Drawing

Gesture drawing aims to identify and react to the main visual and expressive characteristics of a form. Since artists often confront changing

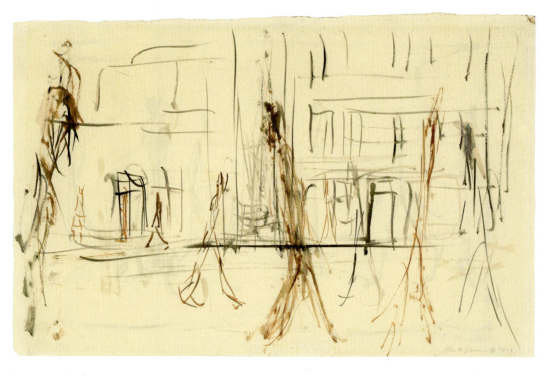

2.1.22 Alberto Giacometti, *The City Square*, 1949. Ink and colored ink on paper, 12⅜ × 20⅛", MoMA, New York

subjects and situations, capturing the energy of the moment is the essential goal of gesture drawing.

The Swiss artist Alberto Giacometti (1901–1966) practiced gesture drawing in a way that exemplifies its function. Giacometti would capture a moment in time by focusing on the action that took place in front of him. Such gesture drawings as *The City Square* (**2.1.22**) are a record of figures moving in space. The abrupt marks give indications of architectural features, the surrounding landscape, and figures milling about. This process of looking at a scene holistically challenges an artist to capture many related forms in one composition.

The energy of the human figure is evident in *Muscular Dynamism* (**2.1.23**), by the Italian artist Umberto Boccioni (1882–1916). In this gestural drawing, the movement of the body is implied by the undulating strokes of the chalk and charcoal. The **rhythms** of the composition lead our eye through a series of changing curves and values that give us a feeling of the energy of the figure. Like Giacometti, Boccioni is primarily interested in capturing the essence of movement by reacting to the subject and employing gestural movement of the human hand.

Contour Drawing

Contour drawing aims to register the essential qualities of three-dimensional form by rendering the **outline**, or contour, of an object. An artist uses contour drawing to sharpen hand–eye coordination and gain an intimate understanding of form, increasing his or her sensitivity to essential detail. For example, contour drawing can help an artist copy the

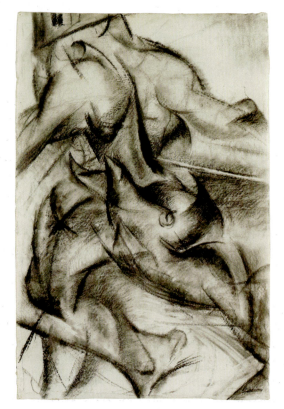

2.1.23 Umberto Boccioni, *Muscular Dynamism*, 1913. Pastel and charcoal on paper, 34 × 23¼". MoMA, New York

shape of a leaf as faithfully as possible by forcing him or her to focus on the subtleties of the object's shape. Because the artist concentrates his or her attention on a single point and incrementally progresses slowly along the visible edge, attributes of the subject may be slightly exaggerated, bringing attention to otherwise-overlooked visual cues.

A wonderful example of contour drawing is illustrated by **2.1.24**, *Mutter und Kind* ("Mother and Child" in German), by the Austrian artist Egon Schiele (1890–1918). If you look carefully at the long line that describes the right side of the woman's back, you will see many subtle changes in line direction, indicating stretching muscles that the mother is using as she embraces her child. The economy of this single line carries so much descriptive information that the artist brilliantly opts to allow it to support the entire right side of the composition.

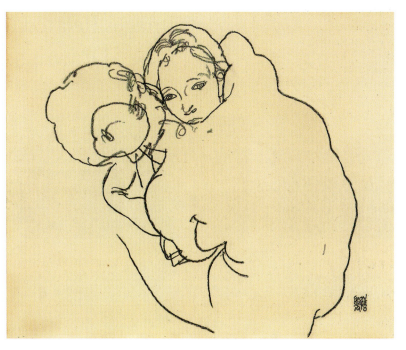

2.1.24 Egon Schiele, *Mother and Child*, 1918. Black Conté crayon on paper, 11¾ × 14⅝".

Active Learning Exercises

1. Hatching and cross-hatching are effective ways to create the effect of shading using lines. Renaissance artists used these techniques when drawing with silverpoint, to give a sense of dark or light. Using Figure **2.1.6**, photocopy the planar contour line graphic of the dodecahedron. Enlarge the image if possible. Then, using a pencil, place your own hatching and cross-hatching lines in the image. Try changing the values by using fewer or more parallel lines than the example. How does the image change? What if you used curved or wavy lines?

2. Brush and ink were used in ancient China for writing and drawing. Because ink has such a rich, dark value, many artists throughout history have employed this medium to create dynamic drawings. One of the challenges in using ink is to create a range of values from light gray to black, which is done by diluting the ink with water. Using some black ink, a brush, a small container of water, and a piece of paper, make four simple strokes, each of a different value of gray. The light tones are sometimes hard to get because they require a great deal more water. Are the values that you have created very different from one another? Do they represent a wide value range (light gray, medium gray, dark gray, and black)? Now try re-creating the shaded planes dodecahedron in Figure **2.1.6**.

3. If you have ever traced an image by placing a piece of paper over another image and following its shape, you have done a contour drawing. You focused on a single point (the end of the pencil) and moved it over the shape beneath to transfer a skeleton of the other shape to your paper. But what if you wanted to transfer a person's face to a paper? To do this you can use a piece of transparency film (transparent drawing surface) and a marker. With one hand hold up the film so that you can see a person's face through it. Then close one eye and focus on the tip of the marker, tracing the features as it follows the basic outlines of that person's face. Try to keep a long, continuous line. If necessary use a support, such as a piece of Plexiglas, so that the film does not bend and sway. Is the result a good likeness of the person? Can you think of other ways this process could be used?

Images Related to 2.1: Drawing

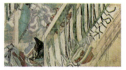

3.3.21 Scene from the *Tale of Genji*, 1st half of 12th century, p. 427

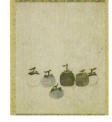

1.6.14 Muqi, *Six Persimmons*, c. 1250, p. 141

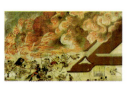

4.7.8 *Night Attack on the Sanjo Palace*, late 13th century, p. 641

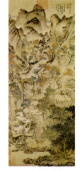

3.3.13 Wang Meng, *Ge Zhichuan Moving His Dwelling*, c. 1360, p. 421

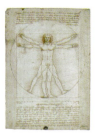

4.4.1 Leonardo da Vinci, *Vitruvian Man*, c. 1490, p. 599

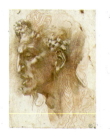

1.3.8 Michelangelo, *Head of a Satyr*, c. 1520–30, p. 86

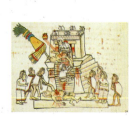

3.4.15 Aztec human sacrifice, from *Codex Magliabechiano*, 16th century, p. 442

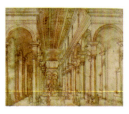

1.1.2a Giovanni Dosio, *Church of Santo Spirito at Florence*, c. 1576–90, p. 50

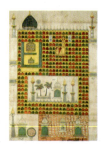

3.2.18 *View of the sanctuary at Medina*, 17th or 18th century, p. 403

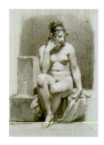

1.3.5 Pierre-Paul Prud'hon, *Study for La Source*, c. 1801, p. 84

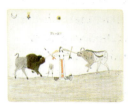

3.4.21 Wo-Haw, *Wo-Haw between Two Worlds*, c. 1875–77, p. 446

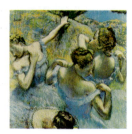

3.8.9 Edgar Degas, *Blue Dancers*, 1897, p. 520

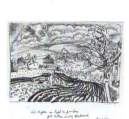

1.1.8 George Bellows, *Woodstock Road*, 1924, p. 53

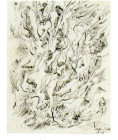

1.1.6 André Masson, *Automatic Drawing*, 1925–26, p. 53

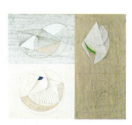

1.1.5 Barbara Hepworth, *Drawing for Sculpture*, 1941, p. 52

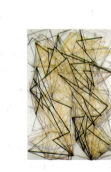

1.1.7 Jean Dubuffet, *Suite Avec 7 Personnages*, 1981, p. 53

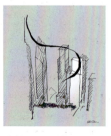

1.1.4 Mel Bochner, *Vertigo*, 1982, p. 52

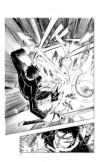

2.5.2 Fumihiko Maki, *Sketch of Four World Trade Center*, 2006, p. 267

1.1.3 CLAMP, page from the Tsubasa RESERVoir CHRoNiCLE, 2007, p. 51

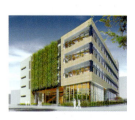

4.4.9 Perkins+Will, CIRS building, Vancouver, Canada, 2011, p. 604

2.2

Painting

When most of us think of art, painting is the **medium** that most often comes to mind. Perhaps this is not surprising, since artists have painted surfaces of many kinds for tens of thousands of years. In prehistoric times, artists painted on the walls of caves. The temples of ancient Greece and Mexico were painted in bright **colors** that look, to our contemporary tastes, garish. About five hundred years ago, artists began painting on linen cloth, a surface that was lighter and easier to handle. Modern muralists and graffiti artists also paint on walls. Of course, artists also paint on a much smaller and more intimate **scale**, on a stretched canvas or a sheet of paper. The artistic possibilities paint offers are almost limitless, and the effects achieved are often amazing.

There are many kinds of paints, suitable for different purposes, but they all share the same components. Paint in its most basic form is composed of **pigment** suspended in a liquid **binder** that dries after it has been applied. Pigment gives paint its color. Traditionally, pigments have been extracted from minerals, soils, vegetable matter, and animal by-products. The color umber, for example, originated from the brown clay soil of the Umbria region in Italy. Ultramarine—from the Latin *ultramarinus*, beyond the sea—is the deep, luxurious blue favored for the sky color in some **Renaissance** painting; it was ground from lapis lazuli, a blue stone found in Afghanistan. In recent times, pigments have been manufactured by chemical processes. The bright cadmium reds and yellows, for instance, are by-products of zinc extraction.

Pigments by themselves do not stick to a surface. They need a liquid binder, a substance that allows the paint to be applied and then dries, leaving the pigment permanently attached. Just as there are many kinds of pigments, there are many binders, traditionally beeswax, egg yolk, vegetable oils and gums, and water; in modern times, art-supply manufacturers have developed such complex chemical substances as **polymers**. Painters also use solvents for different reasons, for example adding turpentine to oil paint to make it thinner.

Artists use many kinds of tools to help them paint. Although historically brushes have been the most popular, some artists have used compressed air to spray paint onto their chosen surface; others have spread it around with a palette knife as if they were buttering toast. Sometimes they have poured it from buckets, or have ridden across the canvas on a bicycle the wheels of which were covered in it; others have dipped their fingers, hands, or entire body in it so they can make their marks.

Paint is an attractive and versatile material with a long and fascinating history; artists have continually experimented with and developed it as a medium. In turn, such developments have reflected the changing pace and values in people's way of life. In the prehistoric era, with little scientific knowledge and no technology available to them, artists used saliva or animal fat to fix pigment made from colored mineral soil and ash from fires to mark and decorate their dwellings. As civilizations became more settled, domestic, and sophisticated, artists employed

Medium (plural **media**): the material on or from which an artist chooses to make a work of art, for example canvas and oil paint, marble, engraving, video, or architecture

Color: the optical effect caused when reflected white light of the spectrum is divided into separate wavelengths

Scale: the size of an object or artwork relative to another object or artwork, or to a system of measurement

Pigment: the colored material used in paints. Often made from finely ground minerals

Binder: a substance that makes pigments adhere to a surface

Renaissance: a period of cultural and artistic change in Europe from the fourteenth to the seventeenth century

Polymer: a chemical compound commonly referred to as plastic

wax (**encaustic**) and egg (**tempera**) as binding agents for mineral pigments; eventually, artists who wanted their work to endure developed **fresco** techniques, using pigment with plaster to embed their paintings permanently in the walls of buildings. In the East, artists painted using the delicate medium of ink to express the complexities of human experience. In the fifteenth and sixteenth century, as the great explorers around the world and travel became more common and widespread, Western artists moved from painting principally on wood panels with tempera, to painting with oil on linen canvases, which could be transported much more easily and could support larger works. Oil was the dominant paint type used by artists until the quickening pace of the modern world, and the industrialization of life, encouraged artists to favor such quick-drying paint types as watercolor and acrylic (a modern, chemical invention), which proved both flexible in application and durable.

This chapter will survey the most common forms of paint, and the many methods and tools used in creating paintings. It will also introduce some notable painters and paintings.

The First Paintings

Researchers have discovered that some images on the cave walls of Pech Merle (**2.2.1**) near Cabrerets, France, were made of a saliva-and-pigment solution that was applied with a small tube. The application of this paint (with saliva as binder) took place 25,000 years ago and the images are mostly of animals, although some human imagery is also present. The two spotted horses in one room at Pech Merle were painted by blowing the solution, which held a pigment that was probably derived from charcoal, through a tube onto the stone cave walls. There have been many discoveries of cave paintings in southern France and Spain, and in each example, the same medium, saliva, has been used as the binding agent.

It seems likely that there were both men and women creating ancient cave art. Recent findings at Pech Merle, involving the finger lengths from handprints that surround the spotted horse paintings, lead researchers to believe that most of the artists involved in this work were female.

2.2.1 Cave paintings from Pech Merle cave, *c*. 23,000 BCE. Pigment with saliva. Near Cabrerets, Lot département, France

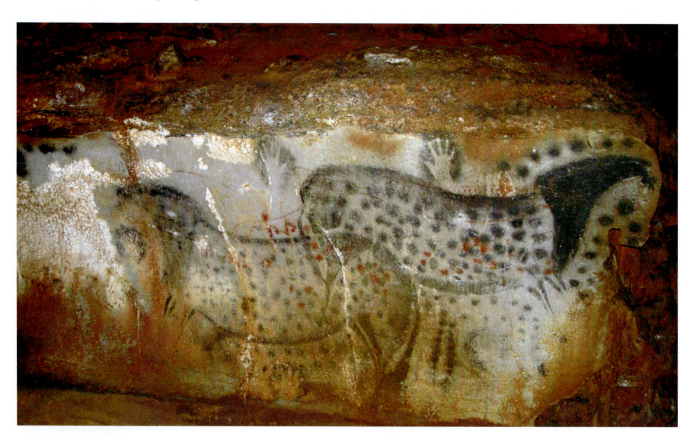

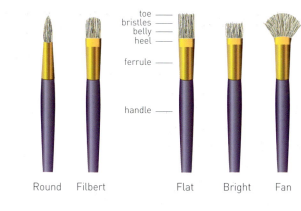

toe —
bristles —
belly —
heel —

ferrule —

handle —

Round   Filbert   Flat   Bright   Fan

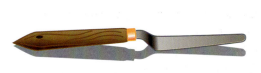

2.2.3 Palette knife, a tool that can be used by the painter for mixing and applying paint

2.2.2 Commonly used brush types, and the parts of an artist's brush: Round: sketching and thinned paint application, can be rolled in hand for special effect; Filbert: for applying color, short bristles for more control and softened edges; Flat: for long, fluid strokes and sharp edges; Bright: for controlled detailing and applying areas of color; Fan: for blending slow-drying paint and softening edges

Encaustic

Another binding technique that was perfected many centuries ago is encaustic, a relatively semi-transparent paint medium that was used by the ancient Greeks and Romans. Encaustic continues to be chosen by some artists today because of the unique character of beeswax. To use encaustic, an artist must mix pigments with hot wax and then apply the mixture quickly. He or she can use brushes (**2.2.2**), palette knives (**2.2.3**), or rags, or can simply pour it. A stiff-backed **support** is necessary because encaustic, when cool, is not very flexible and may crack. The Greeks and Romans typically painted encaustic on wood panel.

2.2.4 Portrait of a boy, *c.* 100–150 CE. Encaustic on wood, 15⅜ × 7½". Metropolitan Museum of Art, New York

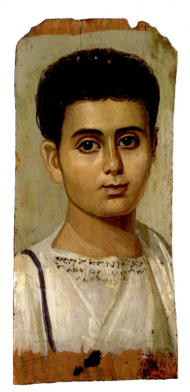

Support: the material on which painting is done
Naturalism, naturalistic: a very realistic or lifelike style of making images

Ancient Roman painters showed great ability in controlling encaustic paint and produced beautiful results. The image of a boy in **2.2.4** was made by an anonymous artist during the second century CE in Roman Egypt. This type of portrait would have been used as a funerary adornment that was placed over the face of the mummified deceased or on the outside of the sarcophagus in the face position. The artist took great care to create a lifelike image and probably captured a fairly **naturalistic** likeness of the deceased boy. Encaustic portraits from this era are referred to as Fayum portraits, after the Fayum Oasis in Egypt where many of them were found.

Fresco

Fresco is a painting technique in which the artist paints onto freshly applied plaster. The earliest examples of the **fresco** method come from Crete in the Mediterranean (the palace at Knossos and other sites) and date to *c.* 1600–1500 BCE. Frescoes were also used later, to decorate the inside of Egyptian tombs. The technique was used extensively in the Roman world for the decoration of interiors, and its use was revived during the Italian Renaissance. The pigment is not mixed into a binder, as it is in other painting techniques. Instead, pigment mixed with water is applied to a lime-plaster surface. The plaster absorbs the color and the pigment binds to the lime as it sets. Once this chemical reaction is complete, the color is very durable, making fresco a very permanent painting medium.

There are two methods of fresco painting: *buon fresco* (Italian for good fresco) and *fresco*

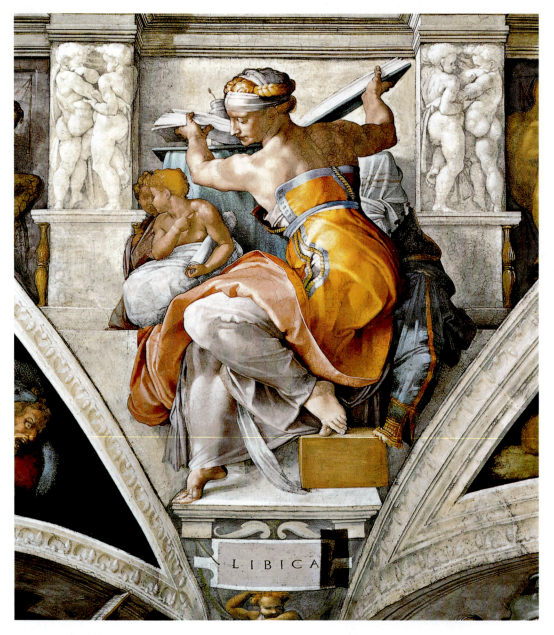

2.2.5 Michelangelo, *The Libyan Sibyl*, 1511–12. Fresco. Detail of the Sistine Chapel ceiling, Vatican City, Italy

secco (dry fresco). When artists work with buon fresco, they must prepare the wall surface by **rendering** undercoats of rough plaster containing sand, gravel, cement, and lime. The artist adds a further (but not final) layer of plaster and allows it to dry for several days; he or she then transfers onto it the design from a full-scale drawing (referred to as a cartoon) in preparation for the final painting. Next, the artist applies the last finishing layer of plaster, re-transferring onto it the required part of the cartoon. Onto this, he or she will paint pigment suspended in water. Because there are just a few hours before the lime plaster sets, only a portion of the wall is freshly plastered each day.

If the artist makes a mistake, the plaster must be chiseled away and the procedure repeated. These technical challenges are offset by the brilliance of color for which fresco is renowned.

Many of the Renaissance fresco paintings were made to decorate the interiors of churches. The Italian artist Michelangelo Buonarroti (1475–1564) used the buon fresco method to decorate the ceiling of the Sistine Chapel in Rome (**2.2.5**). For this monumental undertaking, requiring four years to complete, Michelangelo needed to craft a strategic approach in order to disguise the seams between separate days' work. For example, in one section, called *The Libyan Sibyl*, he plastered only the area where the leg

Rendering: to apply plaster to a wall

Perspectives on Art: José Clemente Orozco
Fresco Painting Inspired by the Mexican Revolution

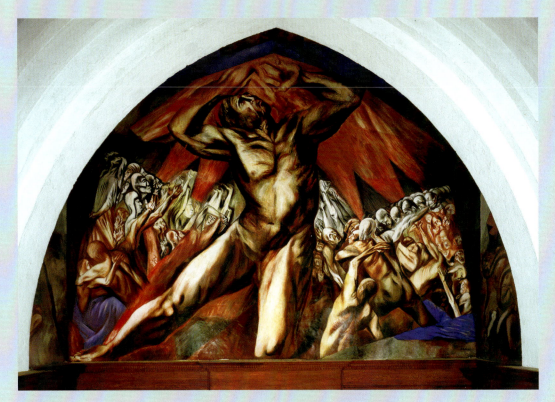

2.2.6 José Clemente Orozco, *Prometheus*, 1930. Fresco mural (central panel), approx. 20 x 28½'. Frary Hall, Pomona College, Claremont, California

For more than thirty years Porfirio Díaz ruled Mexico as a dictator. This was a time of injustice and great divisions between the powerful rich and the poor masses. In 1911, the Mexican people rebelled and forced Díaz to resign. For ten years revolutionary groups led the fight for social justice, and from the 1920s to the mid-1930s, in an outpouring of national creativity, Mexican mural artists painted the walls of public buildings with works that expressed their aspirations for social justice and freedom, and revived the art of fresco painting. Subsequently, scholars termed this period the Mexican Mural Renaissance. One of the most famous mural painters of this time was José Clemente Orozco (1883–1949), who lost his left hand and had his sight and hearing damaged in an explosion during his childhood. Despite these disabilities, he went on to become a significant and radical artist who struggled for the rights of peasants and workers in revolutionary Mexico. His writings about art emphasize his interest in the medium of fresco painting and in its formal aspects: as he wrote, he saw art as visual poetry.

"Fresco painting is free from the inconveniences of oils and varnishes, but the wall upon which the painting is done is subjected to many causes of destruction, such as the use of the wrong kind of building materials, poor planning, moisture from the ground or from the air, earthquakes, dive bombing, tanking or battleshipping, excess of magnesia in the lime or the marble dust, lack of care resulting in scratches or peeling off, et cetera. So, fresco must be done only on walls that are as free as possible from all these inconveniences.

There is no rule for painting al fresco. Every artist may do as he pleases provided he paints as thinly as possible and only while the plaster is wet, six to eight hours from the moment it is applied. No retouching of any kind afterwards. Every artist develops his own way of planning his conception and transferring it onto the wet plaster...Or the artist may improvise without any previous sketches.

A painting is a Poem and nothing else. A poem made of relationships between forms..."

in the **foreground** was to be painted (**2.2.5**). This was probably a day's work, and the seam of the plaster could be camouflaged because the surrounding edges (the purple drapery in particular) change color and **value**.

If an artist cannot finish painting a section within a day of plastering, or needs to retouch a damaged fresco, he or she employs the dry fresco method (fresco secco). To encourage absorbency, wet rags moisten the lime plaster that has already set, and the wall is then painted. The once-dry lime surface soaks up some of the pigment. Frescoes painted using the fresco secco method tend to be less durable than buon fresco, because the surface is less absorbent.

Tempera

If you have ever scrubbed dried egg off a plate while washing dishes, you know how surprisingly durable it can be. Painters who use egg tempera have different ideas about what parts of the egg work best for tempera painting, but many artists have favored the yolk. Despite its rich yellow color, egg yolk does not greatly affect the color of pigment; instead, it gives a transparent soft glow. Tempera is best mixed fresh for each painting session.

Tempera is usually applied with a brush and dries almost immediately. The earliest examples of egg tempera have been found in Egyptian tombs. From the fifth century CE onward, painters of icons (**stylized** images of Jesus and saints) in what we know today as Greece and Turkey perfected the use of the medium and transmitted the technique to early Renaissance painters in Europe and the Middle East.

As in many Italian paintings of the fourteenth century, the paint of the *Entry into Jerusalem*, from the back of the **altarpiece** called the *Maestà*, consists of pigment and egg yolk (**2.2.7**). For the *Maestà*, Duccio di Buoninsegna (c. 1255–1319) created a large, freestanding construction made up of many paintings that can be viewed from both front and back, with the latter comprising a series of images that depict important moments in the life of Christ, of which the *Entry into Jerusalem*

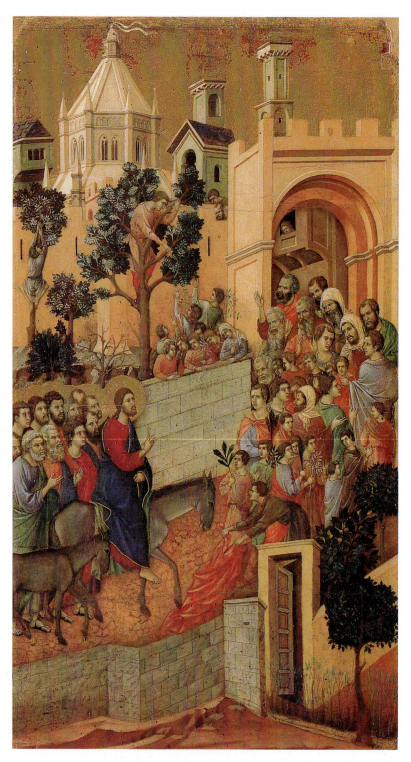

2.2.7 Duccio di Buoninsegna, *Entry into Jerusalem* (from the back of the *Maestà* altarpiece, Siena Cathedral), 1308–11. Tempera and gold leaf on wood, 3'4½ × 1'9⅛". Museo dell'Opera Metropolitana del Duomo, Siena, Italy

is one. Although egg tempera can be challenging because it dries so quickly, Duccio's mastery of the medium, which demanded short, thin strokes, resulted in brilliant detail to enlighten a population of believers.

Foreground: the part of a work depicted as nearest to the viewer
Value: the lightness or darkness of a plane or area
Stylized: art that represents objects in an exaggerated way to emphasize certain aspects of the object

Islamic artists also enjoyed the sensitive detail that can be achieved with tempera, and some used tempera with gold leaf to create rich images for the ruling class. In *Two Lovers* by the Persian miniaturist Riza Abbasi (1565–1635), we see the rich gold-leaf finish combined with the high detail of tempera (**2.2.8**). Riza, who worked for Shah Abbas the Great, has used the transparency of the medium to make the plant life look delicate and wispy. The intertwined lovers stand out proudly from the softness of the plants in the **background**.

The appeal of tempera painting continues today. It has been used to create some of the most recognizable works in American art. Andrew Wyeth (1917–2009), loved by Americans for his sense of realism and high detail, chose tempera to create works that provide a glimpse into American life in the mid-twentieth century. The **subject** of *Christina's World* (**2.2.9**) is a neighbor of Wyeth's in Maine who had suffered from polio and could not walk. Wyeth has chosen to place her in a setting that expresses (in Wyeth's words) her "extraordinary conquest of life." The scene appears placid and bright, reflecting Wyeth's great admiration for her. The high degree of detail creates a sense of mystery that stimulates our imagination.

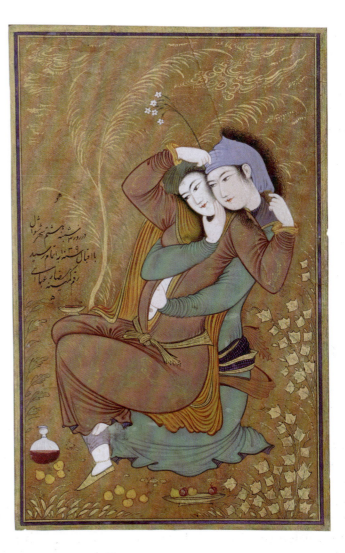

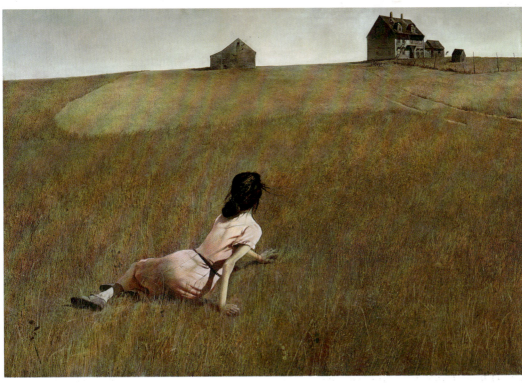

2.2.8 (above) Riza Abbasi, *Two Lovers*, Safavid period, 1629–30. Tempera and gilt paint on paper, 7⅛ × 4¾". Metropolitan Museum of Art, New York

2.2.9 (left) Andrew Wyeth, *Christina's World*, 1948. Tempera on gessoed panel, 32¼ × 47¾". MoMA, New York

Altarpiece: an artwork that is placed behind an altar in a church
Background: the part of a work depicted as furthest from the viewer's space, often behind the main subject matter
Subject: the person, object, or space depicted in a work of art

2.2.10 Jan van Eyck, *The Madonna of Chancellor Rolin*, 1430–34. Oil on wood, 26 × 24⅜". Musée du Louvre, Paris, France

Oil

Painting with oil is a relatively recent invention compared to encaustic, tempera, and fresco. Artists used oil paint during the Middle Ages, but have done so regularly only since the fifteenth century, particularly in Flanders (modern-day Belgium, The Netherlands, and northern France). The oil used as a binder there was usually linseed oil, a by-product of the flax plant from which linen cloth is made. Giorgio Vasari, an Italian Renaissance writer and artist, credits the fifteenth-century Flemish painter Jan van Eyck (*c.* 1395–1441) with the invention of oil paint. In fact, Van Eyck did not invent it, but he is its most astonishing early practitioner. His virtuosity with the medium is apparent in his work known as *The Madonna of Chancellor Rolin* (**2.2.10**).

Because it is so flexible, oil paint readily adheres to a cloth support (usually canvas or linen)—unlike encaustic, which is usually painted onto a stiff panel. Painters like oil paint because its transparency allows the use of thin layers of color called glazes. In the hands of such artists as Van Eyck, glazes attain a rich **luminosity**, as though lit from within. This happens because many layers of transparent and semi-transparent color are applied, allowing light to pass through, then reflect light back, creating an impression that light is emanating from behind the glass-like paint. Because oil paint is slow drying, artists can blend it and make changes days after the initial coating has been applied, thereby achieving smooth effects and a high level of detail.

The use of transparent pigment in glaze painting also encouraged the use of **underpainting**. An underpainting is a preliminary layer of paint that is intended to support the final version of the work. It does this by setting up favorable conditions that allow the artist to achieve particular effects. For example, a **grisaille** (from the French term meaning to turn gray) is a black-and-white underpainting (in appearance similar to a black-and-white photograph) that establishes the light and dark values of the work. A **verdaccio** (from the Italian word for green), or green underpainting, creates conditions that, for example, were well suited to realizing the light flesh tones often used in Renaissance portraiture. Although underpainting became more popular for use with oils, painters have used this technique with many other painting media. Grisaille can also be used as a technique to create a finished work of art rather than just for underpainting.

Oil painting gained another surge in popularity when the American artist John G. Rand (1801–1873) invented a new way of storing and transporting paint. In the late nineteenth century, the collapsible tube replaced the use of pig bladders as the favored container for oil paints. Whereas the pig bladder was sealed with string and the artist would poke a hole in to access the paint, a collapsible tube could be reclosed using a screw-on cap, and was less likely to burst at inopportune moments. The French **Impressionist** movement, in particular, benefitted greatly from this advance, because it became much easier to transport a large variety of colors when painting outdoors.

Modern and contemporary artists have used oils to achieve quite different **expressive** effects.

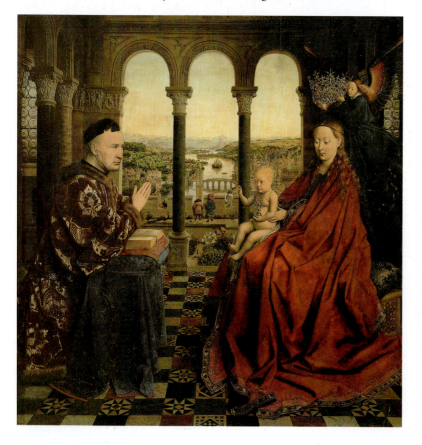

The San Francisco artist Joan Brown (1938–1990) used oil in an **impasto** (thickly painted) fashion (**2.2.11**). Because oil paint is normally thick enough to hold its shape when applied to a surface, the paint can pile up, giving Brown's work a **three-dimensional** presence.

The Chinese-born artist Hung Liu (b. 1948), who grew up in Communist China before emigrating to the United States, utilizes the different qualities of oil paint to achieve her own unique **style**. Hung's images express her Chinese roots. Her work *Interregnum* juxtaposes images and styles (**2.2.12**). The traditional Chinese style is reflected in the idyllic figures in the upper part of the work, in contrast with the back-breakingly hard reality of life under the Communist leader Mao Zedong in the lower part. Hung's work shows the discontinuity between reality and the ideal. It also reflects the meaning of the title: an interregnum is a period when normal government is suspended, especially between successive reigns or regimes.

Expressive: capable of stirring the emotions of the viewer
Impasto: paint applied in thick layers
Three-dimensional: having height, width, and depth
Style: a characteristic way in which an artist or group of artists uses visual language to give a work an identifiable form of visual expression

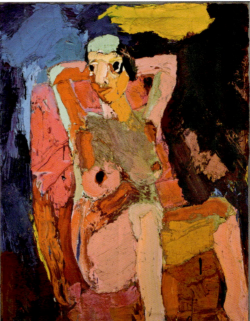

2.2.11 Joan Brown, *Girl in Chair*, 1962. Oil on canvas, 5 × 4'. LACMA, California

2.2.12 Hung Liu, *Interregnum*, 2002. Oil on canvas, 8' × 9'6". Kemper Museum of Contemporary Art, Kansas City, Missouri

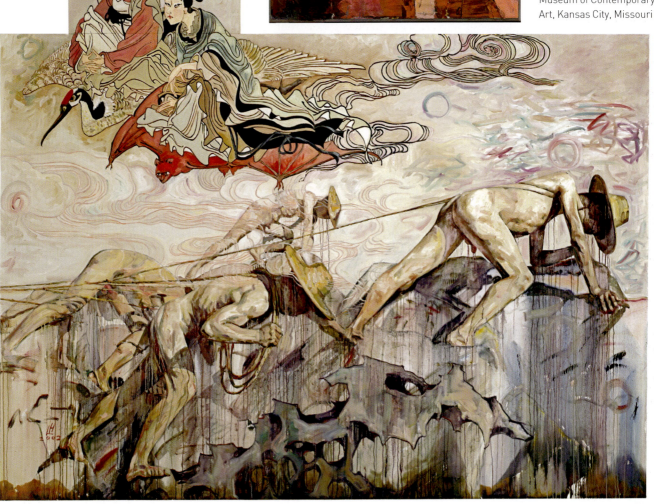

Gateway to Art: Gentileschi, *Judith Decapitating Holofernes*
Paintings as Personal Statements

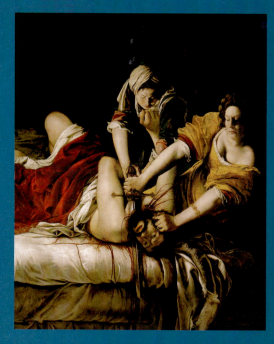

2.2.13 (above) Artemisia Gentileschi, *Judith Decapitating Holofernes*, c. 1620. Oil on canvas, 6'6⅜" × 5'3¾". Uffizi Gallery, Florence, Italy

At a time when there were very few women working as professional artists, Italian **Baroque** artist Artemisia Gentileschi (1593–*c.* 1656) earned a reputation as a talented and accomplished painter. Women were not allowed to follow the traditional avenues of apprenticeship to complete their training as painters, but Gentileschi was the daughter of an artist, and her talent was recognized and fostered by her father. Unlike her male contemporaries, Gentileschi often depicted strong female figures with emotion, intensity, and power, as exemplified in *Judith Decapitating Holofernes* (**2.2.13**); but she also painted many portraits, some of which were in oil paint, including the self-portrait shown here (**2.2.14**).

Artists have always made self-portraits to show off their skill and define themselves as they wish others to see them. In *Allegory of Painting*—"allegory" here meaning an image of a person that represents an idea or abstract

quality—Gentileschi depicts herself at the moment she begins to paint, holding a brush in one hand and her palette in the other. The mask pendant around her neck signifies that painting is an illusion only an inspired master can produce. She shows painting as a physical, energetic act; she is about to be inspired to paint upon the blank canvas before her. Just as *Judith Decapitating Holofernes* portrays strong female figures, Gentileschi's self-portrait shows her succeeding in the male-dominated world of the professional artist.

2.2.14 (below) Artemisia Gentileschi, *Self-portrait as the Allegory of Painting (La Pittura)*, 1638–39. Oil on canvas, 38 × 29". Royal Collection, London, England

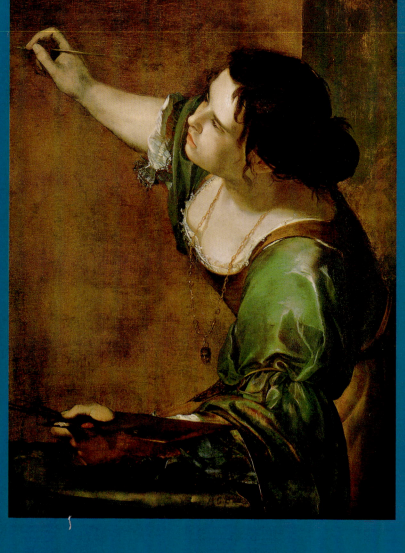

Ink Painting

Although artists often use ink with a pen on paper, they also use it for painting. Different surfaces require differences in ink. If you are drawing on a surface that is not fibrous enough, you need to modify the ink. Ink is commonly used on paper because the fibers hold the pigment, but a slicker surface needs an additional binder. Painting inks are slightly different from drawing inks because they have a binder, usually gum arabic, rather than simply being suspended in water.

Japanese artist Suzuki Shōnen (1849–1918) makes good use of the expressive rich blackness of ink in his *Fireflies at Uji River* (**2.2.15**). The luscious darkness of the ink on the silk scroll supports the retelling of a night scene from the eleventh-century Japanese novel *The Tale of Genji*, when a young man tries to overhear the conversation of two young women. The rushing waters of the Uji obscure their words from the eager ears of the would-be suitor. The artist emphasizes the power of the rushing water with strong brushstrokes and powerful diagonals.

Watercolor and Gouache

Ink can be painted in much the same way as watercolor; artists sometimes incorporate it into their watercolor paintings to give extra richness and darker values. Watercolor and **gouache** suspend pigment in water with a sticky binder, usually gum arabic (honey is used for French watercolor), which helps the pigment adhere to the surface of the paper when dry. Watercolor is transparent, but an additive (often chalk) in gouache makes the paint **opaque**. Usually watercolor and gouache are painted on paper, because the fibers of the paper help to hold the suspended pigments in place. The portability of watercolor (all the artist needs is brushes, small tubes or cakes of paint, and paper) has made it vastly appealing, especially to artists who paint **en plein air**, or outdoors, using the landscape as subject matter.

Baroque: European artistic and architectural style of the late sixteenth to early eighteenth century, characterized by extravagance and emotional intensity
Gouache: a type of paint medium in which pigments are bound with gum and a white filler added (for example, clay) to produce a paint that is used for opaque watercolor
Opaque: not transparent
En plein air: French for "in the open air"; used to describe painting out of doors from start to finish rather than working in a studio for all or part of the process

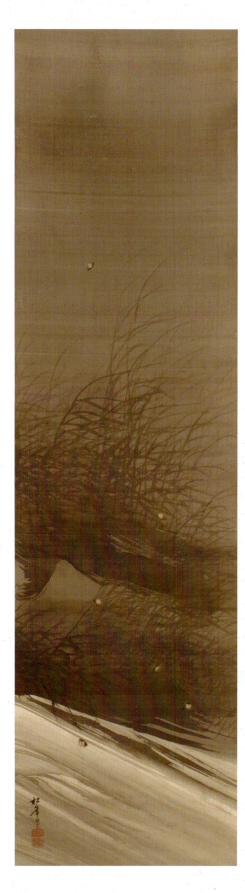

2.2.15 Suzuki Shōnen, *Fireflies at Uji River*, Meiji period, 1868–1912. Ink, color, and gold on silk; hanging scroll, 13¾ × 50˝. Clark Family Collection

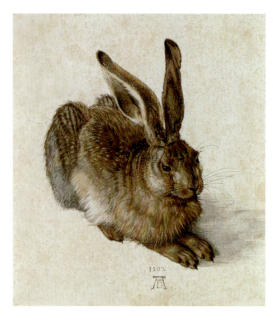

2.2.16 (left) Albrecht Dürer, *A Young Hare*, 1502. Watercolor and gouache on paper, 9⅞ × 8⅞". Graphische Sammlung Albertina, Vienna, Austria

2.2.17 (right) Sonia Delaunay, *Prose of the Trans-Siberian Railway and of Little Jehanne of France*, 1913. Watercolor and relief print on paper, support 77 × 14". Tate Gallery, London, England

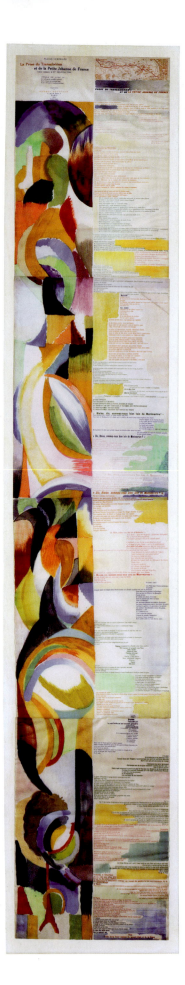

Watercolor's ease of use poses one inherent challenge. Watercolor is transparent, but there is no white transparent pigment; any white area in a watercolor is simply unpainted paper. If an artist paints a white area by mistake, one solution is to paint it over with opaque white gouache.

The watercolors of the German Albrecht Dürer (1471–1528) are noted for their masterful naturalism. Dürer's works, such as *A Young Hare*, reflect direct observation of a natural subject (**2.2.16**). Above all, the artist conveys a sense of the creature's soft, striped fur through a combination of watercolor with opaque white heightening.

French artist Sonia Delaunay (1885–1979), the first woman to have her work shown at the Louvre Museum in Paris, France, during her lifetime, mastered the art of watercolor. *Prose of the Trans-Siberian Railway and of Little Jehanne of France* (**2.2.17**), an **artist's book**, was part of a collaboration with the poet Blaise Cendrars (1887–1916). If all 150 copies of the first edition were placed end to end, it was intended they would stretch the height of the Eiffel Tower. The book was also meant to be folded like a roadmap, and it recounts a trip from Russia to Paris. Delaunay's work is a "simultaneous book" in which her watercolor illustration on the left is set next to the Cendrars poem on the right. She used the bright colors that watercolor affords to create an illustration that progressively changes as the reader advances down the page.

Artist's book: a book produced by an artist, usually an expensive limited edition, often using specialized printing processes

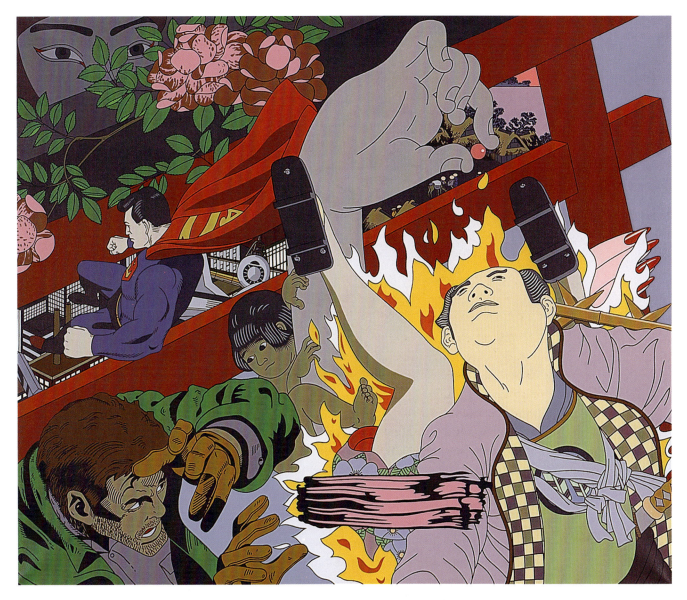

2.2.18 Roger Shimomura, *Untitled*, 1984. Acrylic paint on canvas, 5'1½" × 6'¼". Kemper Museum of Contemporary Art, Kansas City, Missouri

Acrylic

Acrylic paints are composed of pigments suspended in an acrylic polymer resin. They dry quickly and can be cleaned up with relative ease. Latex house paint is made of acrylic polymer. These paints have been in use only since about 1950, but they have become popular with artists because of their versatility and practicality. Unlike oil paints, which dissolve only in turpentine or mineral spirits, acrylics can be cleaned up with water. When dry, however, they have similar characteristics to those of oil paint, although they can also be used in ways that mimic the soft effects of watercolor. They also set easily on a variety of different artistic supports, from paper through to canvas and wood.

Many professional artists, including the contemporary Japanese-American artist Roger Shimomura (b. 1939), prefer acrylics as their primary painting medium. Shimomura uses them to create works that investigate the relationships between cultures. He merges traditional Japanese imagery, such as a Samurai warrior, with popular culture and typically American subjects, such as Superman. This combination of styles reflects the mixing of cultures resulting from contact between nations. In *Untitled* (**2.2.18**) Shimomura refers to the internment of Japanese-Americans during World War II. The painting explores the effects of conflict between two cultures.

Artists will sometimes choose a painting medium that helps to support the idea

Found image or object: an image or object found by an artist and presented, with little or no alteration, as part of a work or as a finished work of art in itself

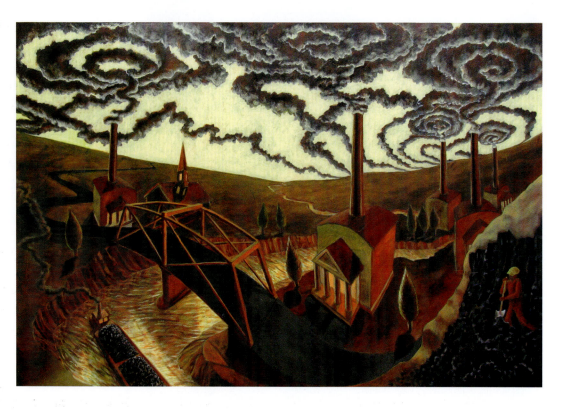

2.2.19 Ralph M. Larmann, *Coalopolis*, 2010. Acrylic on canvas, 40 × 60". Collection Indiana State University, Terre Haute, Indiana

being communicated in the work. Ralph M. Larmann (b. 1959) chose to use acrylic paint for his work, *Coalopolis* (**2.2.19**), because the plastic quality of the polymer reflects and is derived from contemporary manufacturing processes. In Larmann's industrial, menacing landscape, twisting clouds of coal soot rise in dark coils to fill the sky over a fictional town, emphasizing the uncomfortable relationship between economic progress and ecological damage. Even though this message of impending

environmental disaster and the acrylic medium are contemporary, Larmann employs an old-fashioned glaze process that is similar to that of such early Dutch painters as Van Eyck, which in this case gives the image a strange glow or luminosity.

Mixed-Media Painting

The traditional boundaries between art media have been blurred as artists explore new ways to express themselves. Mixed-media and collage work have become popular ways of integrating imagery into a painted artwork. One of the first leading female practitioners of mixed-media painting was the American artist Jane Frank (1918–1986). In her work *Frazer's Hog Cay #18* (**2.2.20**) the artist incorporates oil paint and stones together to create an association to a quiet Bahamian island. Even though Frank, who had studied under the abstract artist Hans Hofmann, did not represent a recognizable landscape, she alludes to it through the use of the **found objects**. The added natural sand and stones influence our senses so that we can more easily imagine the island where they may have been discovered.

2.2.20 Jane Frank, *Frazer's Hog Cay #18*, 1968. Mixed media: oil paint and stones, 38 x 46". Smithsonian American Art Museum, Washington, D.C.

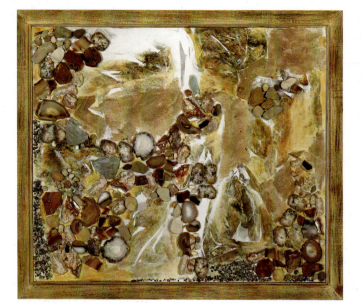

Mural Art and Spray Paint

The Mexican Muralists, who espoused ideas about social justice and freedom in their works, believed that a painting should belong to all the people of a community, so they often worked outside, usually on a large scale so all could share (see Perspectives on Art Box: José Clemente Orozco, p. 219). This idea of collaborating on a painted work with an entire neighborhood has become an important tool for urban renewal and community. Judy Baca's (b. 1946) *Danza de la Tierra* (**2.2.21**), was painted in 2008 for an interior wall in the Dallas Latino Cultural Center. Baca created this work using influences from the surrounding community and local traditions. It is intended to offer the viewer a vibrant and energetic expression of Latino culture. Baca will often employ members of the local area to help create her wall paintings, encouraging strong community involvement.

Spray paint can be applied using a spray gun or spray can, a favorite of tag and graffiti artists. Graffiti artists prefer to use spray enamel, a commercially produced paint, packaged in an aerosol can and generally used for applying an even coating on a slick surface. A propellant forces the paint out in a fine mist when the user pushes down on the valve button. Graffiti artists often cut into the spray nozzle with a knife to alter the spray stream, for example to spread a wider mist.

Practitioners of spray-painted graffiti art are considered vandals and criminals by local governments when they paint places without the permission of the property owners. Because of this, many keep their identity secret and sign their work with an alias, called a tag. Even so, many graffiti artists have become known, even celebrated.

The British graffiti artist known as Banksy (b. 1973?) uses **stencils** as a quick way of transferring his designs to surfaces. (Speed of application is important to graffiti artists, who often risk being arrested for defacing private property.) In *Graffiti Removal Hotline*, Banksy, who carefully guards his identity and personal information, skewers and taunts the authorities who seek to curb his street art activities (**2.2.22**, p. 230). Banksy's street art is full of such lampooning, and he often also points out the absurdity of modern life. In this work the boy pictured on the right has applied pink paint to "deface" a wall that carries a dull and

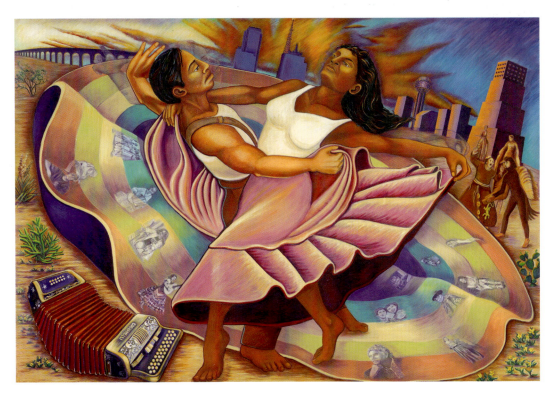

2.2.21 Judith F. Baca, *Danza de la Tierra*, 2008. Acrylic on canvas, 10 × 15'. Dallas Latino Cultural Center, Texas

rigid message. Banksy captures the irony of the moment by using pink, traditionally a "passive" color, as a tool of criminal vandalism.

As we have seen, the ancient artists who created the Spotted Horses at Pech Merle (**2.2.1**, p. 216) did so by blowing a saliva-and-pigment solution through a small tube. Although today's spray paint comes in a can, the technique closely resembles that method, used 25,000 years ago. Because the spray spreads out in a fine mist, the ancient spray-paint artist, like today's spray painters, would **mask** out areas to create hard edges. Ancient artists may even have done this with the edge of their hand, covering the wall where they did not want the paint to fall. The contemporary street artist Banksy and the ancient women and men of Pech Merle may seem worlds apart, but they share a common technique, attesting to the timelessness of painting.

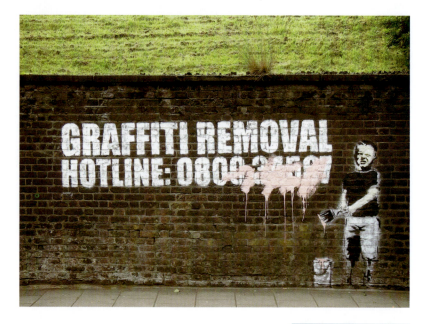

2.2.22 Banksy, London, England, 2008

Mask: in spray painting or silkscreen printing, a barrier the shape of which blocks the paint or ink from passing through

Active Learning Exercises

1. Paint consists of pigment suspended in a binder that helps to adhere it to a surface. Tempera paint (*not* egg tempera) can be purchased in dehydrated and liquid form. The binder used is gum arabic, a sticky tree sap that holds the colored pigment to a surface, such as paper. Using tempera paint, brushes, paper, a pear, and a cup of water for cleaning up, do a painting of the pear. Since the pear shape is organic and irregular, it will be easy to make it look like a pear, even if it does not look like that specific one. Try to mix color and be as exact as you can: color is one of the most important elements of art to a painter. What attributes of this medium did you notice as you worked? Try painting the background and a shadow under the pear. How does this change your composition?

2. Watercolor painting is popular because the materials are simple and cleaning up is easy, but it can be challenging because the artist must plan ahead. The key to making a good watercolor is to anticipate where the white areas will be, because once painted, the color cannot be removed. So leave the white paper as the highlights, and layer more in the darker areas. Using a simple, inexpensive watercolor kit and a piece of watercolor paper (a heavy textured paper), paint an apple that you have polished to a fine gloss. You should note a light highlight that will not be painted on your paper. Leave the light tones and paint the dark spots first, then overlap those areas and work into the medium-toned areas next, always leaving the white highlights alone. What do you notice when you paint over a section that was previously painted? What happens when you moisten the paper, then paint?

3. To control the intensity of value or color when creating an ink painting, the artist must dilute the ink with water. Before you create an ink painting, practice controlling the lightness or darkness of the ink. Using black ink, a brush, and a cup of water, paint three cherries on a piece of good drawing paper. One should be dark in value, the next should be medium, and the last should be light. See if you can impose control over the value. Is it easier to make the light values or the dark? Try dipping the brush in water before you add ink. Then try another painting, working from light to dark. Which were the easier values to make?

Images Related to 2.2: Painting

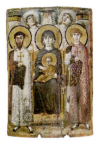

3.2.7 *Icon of Virgin and Child Surrounded by Saints*, 6th century, p. 396

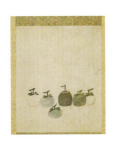

1.6.14 Muqi, *Six Persimmons*, c. 1250, p. 141

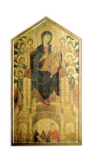

3.2.26 Cimabue, *Virgin and Child Enthroned*, c. 1280, p. 409

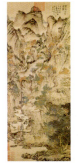

3.3.13 Wang Meng, *Ge Zhichuan Moving His Dwelling*, c. 1360, p. 421

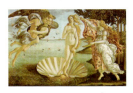

4.9.5 Sandro Botticelli, *The Birth of Venus*, c. 1482–86, p. 662

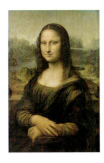

0.0.11 Leonardo da Vinci, *Mona Lisa*, c. 1503–6, p. 35

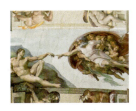

3.6.7b Michelangelo, Detail of *Creation of Adam*, 1508–12, p. 469

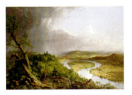

3.7.19 Thomas Cole, *View from Mount Holyoke, Massachusetts*, 1836, p. 506

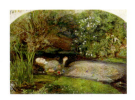

3.7.22 John Everett Millais, *Ophelia*, 1851–52, p. 508

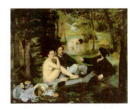

3.8.2 Édouard Manet, *Le Déjeuner sur l'Herbe*, 1863, p. 514

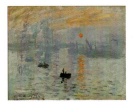

3.8.4 Claude Monet, *Impression, Sunrise*, 1872, p. 516

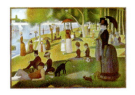

4.4.14 Georges Seurat, *Sunday on La Grande Jatte*, 1884–86, p. 607

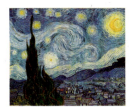

3.8.10 Paul Cézanne, *Mont Sainte-Victoire*, 1886–88, p. 521

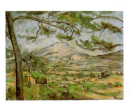

3.8.12 Vincent van Gogh, *Starry Night*, 1889, p.522

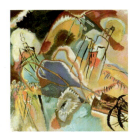

3.8.27 Vasily Kandinsky, *Improvisation #30*, 1913, p. 531

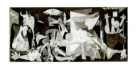

4.7.5 Pablo Picasso, *Guernica*, 1937, p. 638

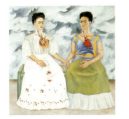

4.10.3 Frida Kahlo, *The Two Fridas*, 1939, p. 677

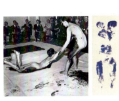

4.9.11a, 4.9.11b Yves Klein, *Anthropométries de l'époque bleue*, 1960, p. 666

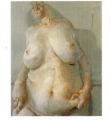

4.9.19 Jenny Saville, *Branded*, 1992, p. 672

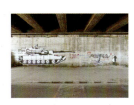

4.7.13 Ganzeer, *Tank vs Bike*, 2011, p. 644

2.3

Printmaking

Edition: all the copies of a print made from a single printing

Relief: a print process where the inked image is higher than the non-printing areas

Intaglio: any print process where the inked image is lower than the surface of the printing plate; from the Italian for "cut into"

Lithography, lithographic: a print process done on a flat, unmarred surface, like a stone, in which the image is created using oil-based ink with resistance from water

Serigraphy: printing that is achieved by creating a solid stencil in a porous screen and forcing ink through the screen onto the printing surface

Matrix: an origination point, such as a woodblock, from which a print is derived

Impression: an individual print, or pull, from a printing press

Incised: cut

Woodblock: a relief print process where the image is carved into a block of wood

Woodcut: a print created from an incised piece of wood

Before the invention of printing, artists who wanted to have multiple copies of their work needed to copy it over by hand, one reproduction at a time. Printing with inks, first used in China to print patterns on fabrics in the third century CE, changed all that. Printing allowed the same designs to be more easily reproduced and distributed to many people. In the world of art, however, printmaking is much more than a way of copying an original. There are many different techniques, and each one gives a unique character to every work it creates. Artists may well choose a particular technique because they think it will suit the kind of effect they want to achieve.

Although artists may not always do the production work themselves, if they create the master image, supervise the process, and sign the artwork, it is considered an original print. This differs from a commercial reproduction of an artwork, where the artist may not be involved in the process. The production of two or more identical images, signed and numbered by the artist, is called an **edition**. When an artist produces only one print, it is called a monoprint. The method used to create a print may dictate the number of works that can be produced. There are four main printing processes: **relief**, **intaglio**, **lithography**, and **serigraphy**. Each process involves a different **matrix**, or point of origination from which the print is derived— for example, the plate used in etching, or the woodblock used to make a woodcut.

In relief printmaking, the artist cuts or carves into a workable surface, such as wood or linoleum, to create the image. The printmaker rolls ink onto the raised surface that remains, and presses a sheet of paper or similar material onto the image to make what is known as an **impression**.

Intaglio printing requires the artist or printmaker to cut or scrape (in many different ways) into what is usually a metal plate. Ink is applied and then wiped off the surface, leaving ink in the lines or marks made by the artist. The pressure of the printing press transfers the image from the plate to the paper.

In the printing process known as lithography, the image is drawn with an oily crayon onto a special kind of limestone. The non-image area of the stone absorbs a little water, but enough so that when the printmaker applies oil-based ink to the whole stone, the ink remains only on the image area. In the printing press the image transfers to the paper.

Serigraphy, more commonly called silkscreen printing, physically blocks out non-image areas so that ink passes through the screen only where required.

Context of Printmaking

Ancient civilizations in Egypt and Mesopotamia reproduced images by rolling cylindrical **incised** stones across clay or pressing them into wax. These early relief impressions were used as a tamper-proof seal to show if the contents of a sack had been opened. Elsewhere, in ancient China, Chinese craftspeople used wooden stamps to print patterned designs into textiles.

The earliest existing printed artworks on paper (itself invented in China in the second or first century BCE) were created in China and date back to the eighth century CE. By the ninth century, printed scrolls containing Buddhist *sutras* (scriptures or prayers) were being made across east Asia. Over the ensuing centuries, paper technology spread across the Islamic world as clever entrepreneurs created small prints that were sold as if they were handwritten charms. **Woodblock** printing and papermaking workshops became common throughout Europe by the beginning of the fifteenth century, and paper was no longer an expensive, exotic commodity.

While the woodblock print remained the primary vehicle for the development of the print in Asia (especially Japan), in the West a number of additional techniques developed over time.

Relief Printmaking

Relief prints are made by carving away from a block of a suitably workable material, such as wood or linoleum, a certain amount of it, to create a raised image. The artist then applies ink to the raised surface and transfers the image to paper or similar material by applying pressure in a printing press (see **2.3.1**). The areas of the block that remain print the image because the carved areas are recessed and are not inked.

Traditionally, wood has been used for relief prints because it is readily available, familiar to work with, and holds up under the pressure exerted by the printing process; these prints are known as **woodcuts**. Today, for linocuts, printmakers use linoleum, an inexpensive material that cuts easily and can produce a clean, sharp image.

Woodblock

The German artist Albrecht Dürer (1471–1528) combined images and the printed word (with text printed on the reverse) when he illustrated the final book of the Bible, the Book

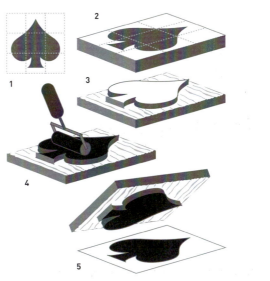

2.3.1 A brief overview of the relief printing process:
1. An image is designed and is prepared for transfer to the block surface.
2. The image is now transferred to the block.
3. The surface area that will not be printed is carved away.
4. The remaining protruding surface is carefully inked.
5. The raised inked area is transferred to the surface to be printed.

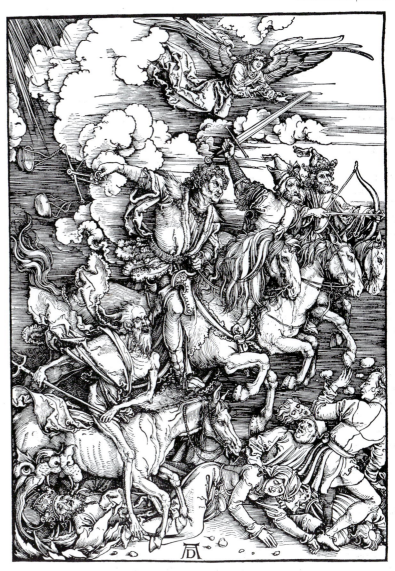

of Revelation. *Four Horsemen of the Apocalypse* (**2.3.2**) is the most famous image in this series of fifteen illustrations and was made from

2.3.2 Albrecht Dürer, *Four Horsemen of the Apocalypse*, c. 1497–98. Woodcut, 15⅜ × 11"

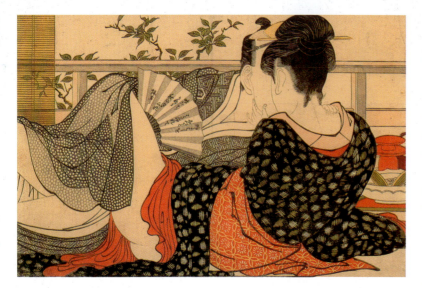

2.3.3 Kitagawa Utamaro, *Lovers in an Upstairs Room*, from *Uta Makura (Poem of the Pillow)*, 1788. Color woodblock print, 10 × 14½". British Museum, London, England

a specially prepared woodblock. In this process, unlike cutting from a solid block of wood, a print craftsman stacks and glues a series of thin, sliced layers of wood to create a more stable printing block (similar to plywood) that will be less likely to splinter or crack. Dürer commissioned professional block cutters to perform the layering, and they also cut the highly detailed lines of his original drawing into the block. This technique resulted in thin lines and detail that could withstand the compression of repeated printings. Because it required expert craftsmen, the labor was very expensive. But the series of works was so popular it made Dürer wealthy. The Book of Revelation is a symbolic piece of writing that prophesies the Apocalypse, or end of the world. The horsemen represent Death, Plague, War, and Famine.

Many great masters of woodblock printing were active in eighteenth- and nineteenth-century Japan. Kitagawa Utamaro's (1753–1806) print, entitled *Lovers in an Upstairs Room*, uses multiple **colors** and shows great graphic skill in controlling the crisp character of the print and the interplay of multiple blocks in different colors (**2.3.3**).

To create a color woodblock print, an artist must produce a separate relief block for every color. Utamaro uses at least three colors to create *Lovers in an Upstairs Room*: red ocher (a shade of red-brown), black, and green. In color woodblock printing, each block must be accurately carved and planned, because each individual color is printed in sequence on the

same sheet of paper. Care must be taken to align each print color perfectly (this is called registration); this is done by carving perfectly matching notches along two sides of each block to guide the placement of the paper. Utamaro is regarded as one of the greatest Japanese printmakers. He made images for the Japanese middle and upper classes of figures, theaters, and brothels, in a **style** known as *ukiyo-e* printmaking. Ukiyo-e means "pictures of the floating world," a reference to a young urban cultural class who separated themselves from the agrarian life of traditional Japan by indulging in a fashionable and decadent lifestyle. The people of the "floating world" were the celebrities of their time.

In his woodcut *Prophet*, the German artist Emil Nolde (1867–1956) uses the natural character of the wood to suggest the hardships and austerity of the life of his **subject** (**2.3.4**). The crude carving of the block has produced splintering, and the printing has revealed the grain of the wood. The print's lack of refinement reflects the raw hardness of the **ascetic** life that one might associate with a prophet. This

2.3.4 Emil Nolde, *Prophet*, 1912. Woodcut, printed in black, composition 12⅝ × 8¾". MoMA, New York

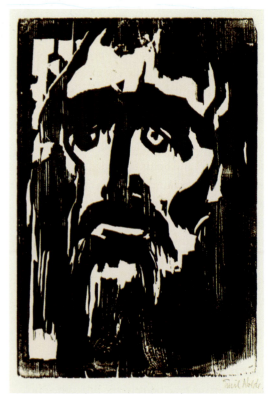

Gateway to Art: Hokusai, "The Great Wave off Shore At Kanagawa"
Using the Woodblock Printing Method

Katsushika Hokusai's woodblock print "The Great Wave off Shore at Kanagawa" (**2.3.5**) uses multiple colors and shows great graphic skill. It is a fine example of the printmaker's art. Hokusai (1760–1849) was not solely responsible for the production of this print: he relied on skilled craftsmen. Hokusai made a drawing of his subject, which a print craftsman then transferred face down onto a block of cherry wood. When the drawing was peeled away, the image remained, and the craftsman then carved the image into the wood. To create a color woodblock print, a printer must produce a new relief block for each separate color. (Incidentally, "The Great Wave" was one of ten prints in the series *Thirty-Six Views of Mount Fuji* to use a new blue color, imported from Europe, known as Prussian blue.) Nine blocks were used to print "The Great Wave." Each block had to be carefully carved, and the printmaker had to carry out the sequence of printing skillfully, because each new color was printed directly on top of the same sheet of paper. If all nine blocks were not printed in

exactly the correct position, the print would be discarded because it did not match the others in the edition. The blocks of wood were used so many times that the carving eventually deteriorated. Although it is unknown how many prints were made, it is estimated there were more than 5,000.

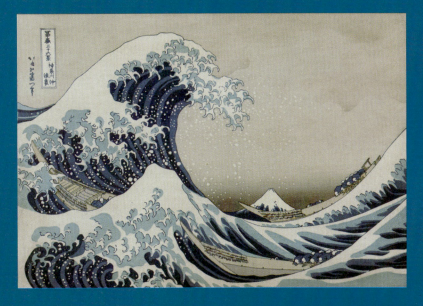

2.3.5 Katsushika Hokusai, "The Great Wave off Shore at Kanagawa," from *Thirty-Six Views of Mount Fuji*, 1826–33 (printed later). Print, color woodcut. Library of Congress, Washington, D.C.

print also demonstrates one of the principal advantages of relief printmaking: it favors dark images that involve strong **contrast**, as here.

Linocut

Linoleum ("lino") printmaking, similarly to the woodblock method, is done by carving into the surface of a material, then printing the raised surface left behind. The resulting prints are commonly known as linocuts. Because linoleum is softer than most woodblocks and does not show a wood grain, many contemporary printmakers prefer it for relief printing. One such artist is Stanley Donwood (real name: Dan Rickwood; b. 1968), who is best known for his creation of artwork for the rock band Radiohead. Donwood produced a series, or

group of associated works, which depicts the last days of the city of Los Angeles, titled *Lost Angeles* (**2.3.6**). To create these works, he cut into sheets of linoleum to create the image, then printed the results on fine Japanese paper. The soft linoleum

2.3.6 Stanley Donwood, "Hollywood Limousine," from the *Lost Angeles* series, 2012. Black screenprint on a silver foil layer, 22 x 35³/₄"

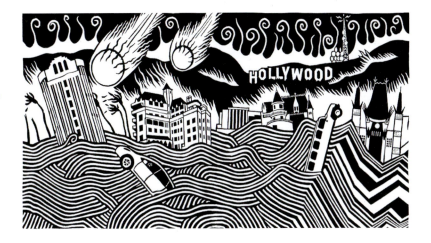

allowed Donwood to capture the myriad of fictional events in great detail, with the kind of clarity that a storybook illustration might have.

Intaglio Printmaking

Intaglio is derived from an Italian word that means "cut into" a surface. Usually the artist uses a sharp tool (a burin) to cut or gouge into a plate made of metal (or sometimes acetate or Plexiglas). Intaglio printing differs from relief printmaking because little of the base material is removed. The ink on the raised surface is also wiped away before printing, leaving ink in the scarred surface of the plate. The pressure of the printing press squeezes the plate against the paper, transferring the ink. There are several variations of intaglio printing, all of which give the resulting artwork a different visual character (see **2.3.7**).

Engraving

Albrecht Dürer printed from a woodblock for his *Four Horsemen of the Apocalypse* but chose a different technique, **engraving**, for *Adam and Eve* (**2.3.8**). The intaglio engraving method is based on the careful scoring of a metal plate so that clean gouges are created in the surface. An engraving can achieve fine detail, making the resulting print more like the artist's original

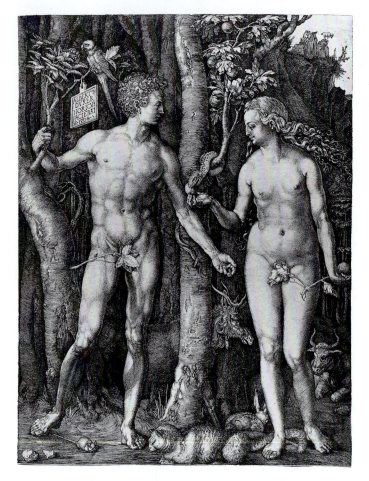

drawing. Dürer also had a business reason for choosing to engrave his work. He had to pay engravers to make his printing plate, and because the metal plate is much more durable than the woodblock, he could make and sell many more copies.

2.3.8 Albrecht Dürer, *Adam and Eve*, 1504. Engraving on paper. Victoria and Albert Museum, London, England

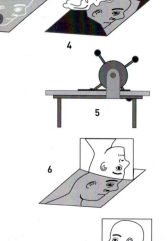

2.3.7 A brief overview of the engraving process (intaglio):

1. An image is designed for the plate.
2. Using a sharp tool, the artist incises the image into the plate.
3. The plate is inked.
4. The surface of the plate is wiped, removing all ink except in the grooves.
5. Paper is placed on the plate and it is pressed.
6. The paper lifts the ink out of the grooves and the ink is imprinted on the paper.
7. The final image is complete. (In most printmaking methods the final image is reversed from the plate or block.)

Engraving: a printmaking technique where the artist gouges or scratches the image into the surface of the printing plate

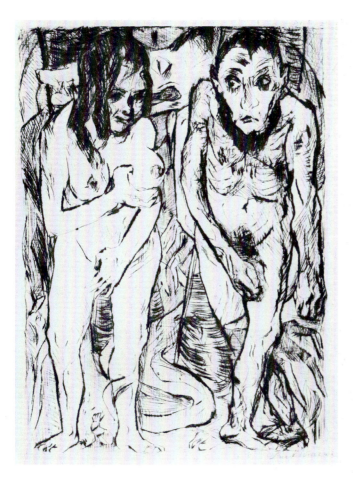

2.3.9 Max Beckmann, *Adam and Eve*, 1917, published 1918. Drypoint, 9⅜ × 7". Private collection, New York

as nakedness was their natural state), covering their genitals with their hands. They know that they will be punished, and this uncertainty about their future, together with their growing worldliness, is captured in the rougher, less finished-looking lines created by using drypoint.

Etching

Dutch artist Rembrandt Harmenzoon van Rijn (1606–1669) was a master of intaglio printmaking, especially **etching**. Etching is a process in which a metal plate is covered with an acid-resistant coating, into which the artist scratches the design. The plate is then immersed in a bath of acid. The acid "bites" into the metal where the covering has been removed, making grooves that hold the ink. Unlike engraving and drypoint, the artist does not score a hard metal plate but makes small incisions, which allows for greater control in incorporating subtle changes of dark or light lines that affect **value**. In his etching *Adam and Eve*, Rembrandt brings out details by marring the plate surface more in the areas that will appear darker in the print (**2.3.10**).

2.3.10 Rembrandt van Rijn, *Adam and Eve*, 1638. Etching, 9¾ × 7". Kupferstichkabinett, Museen Preussiches Kulturbesitz, Berlin, Germany

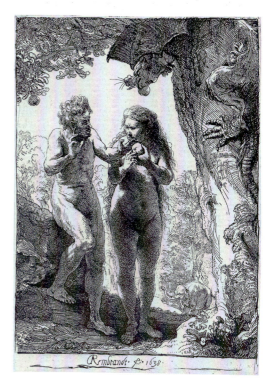

Drypoint

For his *Adam and Eve*, Max Beckmann (1884–1950) chose the **drypoint** intaglio method rather than engraving (**2.3.9**). In engraving, the burin is pushed across the surface, but in drypoint it is pulled, leaving a rough edge, or burr. When the plate is wiped the ink is caught under the burr. The result is a less precise line that has more irregularities. Artists can use this irregularity to add new dimensions to a work. For example, in Beckmann's *Adam and Eve* the lines appear more irregular than those in Dürer's version of the same subject. Beckmann, a German **Expressionist** artist, probably chose drypoint because its slightly uneven quality of line expresses unpredictability and an organic naturalness—two attributes that suit his choice of subject matter. In this image, Adam and Eve have eaten the apple from the Tree of the Knowledge of Good and Evil. We can tell this because they are beginning to express a sense of shame at being naked (in the Bible, they felt no shame before they had eaten from the tree,

Drypoint: an intaglio printmaking process where the artist raises a burr when gouging the printing plate

Expressionism, Expressionist: an artistic style, at its height in 1920s Europe, devoted to representing subjective emotions and experiences instead of objective or external reality

Etching: an intaglio printmaking process that uses acid to bite (or etch) the engraved design into the printing surface

Value: the lightness or darkness of a plane or area

Aquatint

Another process that requires the use of an acid bath to etch the surface of the plate is **aquatint** (from its Italian name *acqua tinta*, meaning "dyed water"). Despite the name, water does not play a role in aquatint printmaking. The image is created in a coating of powdered **rosin** (a tree sap), or spray paint, on the surface of the plate. When heated, the rosin melts onto the surface of the plate, creating a mottled, acid-resistant barrier into which the design is etched. Since the rosin leaves irregular areas of the plate exposed, a soft **organic** texture (similar to that created when one uses brush and ink) dominates the image. The artist can even use a brush to push around the dry rosin (before heating) to draw the original design, adding to the watery effect. Francisco Goya (1746–1828) utilizes the wash-like appearance of aquatint in his print *Giant* (**2.3.11**). Goya probably used a rosin box, a device that allows the artist to control the distribution and amount of powder that falls onto the plate, then he scraped away the heated rosin in the areas where he wanted the dark values of the final printed image to appear. The artist can progressively scrape more and more to get darker values. The **implied texture** of the aquatint print is soft and rich, giving a softness and subtlety to the contours of the giant's body that communicate the sense of its being a fantastical, unreal creature.

2.3.11 Francisco Goya, *Giant*, c. 1818. Burnished aquatint, first state, sheet size 11¼ × 8¼". Metropolitan Museum of Art, New York

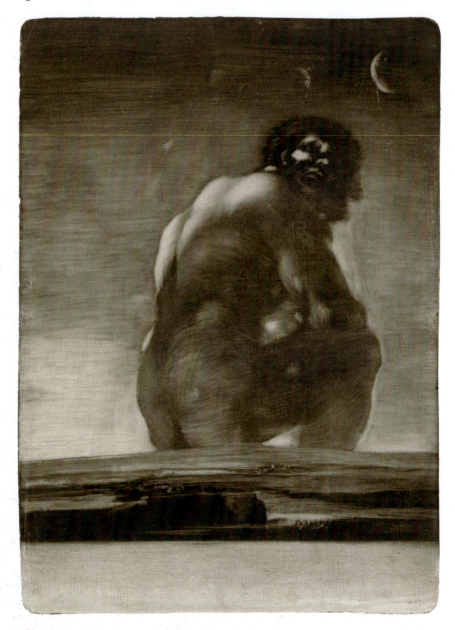

Aquatint: an intaglio printmaking process that uses melted rosin or spray paint to create an acid-resistant ground

Rosin: a dry powdered resin that melts when heated, used in the aquatint process

Organic: having irregular forms and shapes, as though derived from living organisms

Implied texture: a visual illusion expressing texture

Composition: the overall design or organization of a work

Directional line: implied line within a composition, leading the viewer's eye from one element to another

Gateway to Art: Goya, *The Third of May, 1808*
Prints as Art and as Creative Tools

The Spanish artist Francisco Goya (1746–1828) painted *The Third of May, 1808* (**2.3.12a**) in 1814, six years after the event it memorializes. During the French occupation of Spain (1808–14), Goya also sketched scenes of the occupation by Napoleon's troops. These **sketches** were published in 1863 as a series of prints called *Disasters of War*. *The Third of May, 1808* is often considered to be the most dramatic of Goya's studies of the Spanish War of Independence. In it, we can see aspects of the **compositions** of the prints in *Disasters of War*.

Compositionally, there are similarities between the print and the later painting. In "And There Is No Remedy" (**2.3.12b**), the firing squad about to shoot its helpless targets is arranged in a strikingly similar way to the firing squad in *Third of May*. The light area on the left is echoed in the small hill behind the

martyr in *Third of May*. The vertical post to which the victim is tied in the print also draws the viewer toward the center of the work; this device was repeated with the church tower in the painting. The horizontal rifles on the right side of the print create a **directional line** drawing attention toward the victim, a technique Goya repeats in *Third of May*. "And There Is No Remedy" is a good example of the way in which an artist reworks a visual idea over a period of time to develop ideas and refine the composition. Goya's masterpiece evolved after years of trial and practice in his prints.

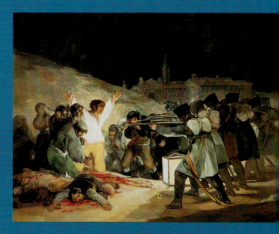

2.3.12a Francisco Goya, *The Third of May, 1808*, 1814. Oil on canvas, 8'4⅜" × 11'3⅞". Museo Nacional del Prado, Madrid, Spain

2.3.12b Francisco Goya, "And There Is No Remedy," from *Disasters of War*, c. 1810

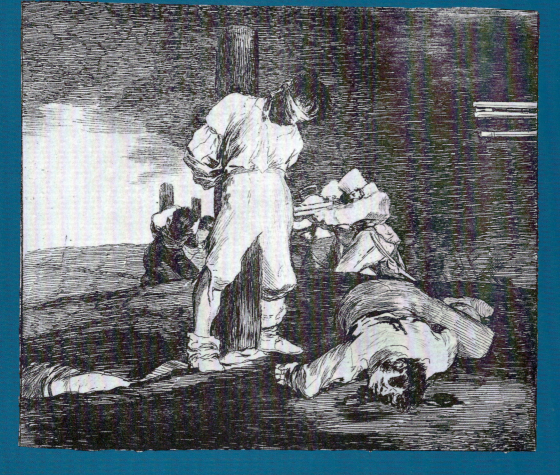

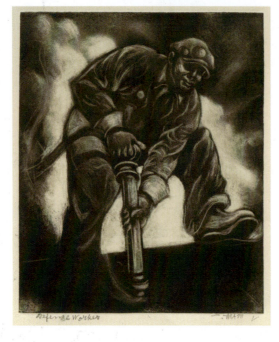

2.3.13 Dox Thrash, *Defense Worker*, c. 1941. Carborundum mezzotint over etched guidelines, 9¾ × 8". Print and Picture Collection, Free Library of Philadelphia

Mezzotint

Because each intaglio method leaves its own unique mark on the plate, many artists have opted to use more than one method when making a print. In his *Defense Worker*, the African-American artist Dox Thrash (1893–1965) uses **mezzotint** over etched guidelines (**2.3.13**). Mezzotints often produce dark, rich values because the ink has many places to settle. To make a mezzotint, the entire surface is roughened with a heavy rocking tool, which is a metal object with a spiked, curved bottom. This can be rocked back and forth across the surface of the plate so that it is completely covered in burrs. The burrs are then smoothed in the areas where the printmaker wants the light tones. Ink is removed from the smoothed areas when the plate is wiped: the inked areas create dark tones, and the smoothed areas hold less ink, to create light tones. Thrash wanted to use this dark mood to reflect the drama and seriousness of the war effort at home. This work was sponsored by the Works Projects Administration, a government program originally created during the Great Depression to employ Americans at a time when jobs were hard to find. Artists, writers, musicians, and others contributed to American culture and infrastructure by applying their skills, first in support of rebuilding America and

then, during World War II, in support of the war effort. Thrash, like other artists of the time, uses the dark values afforded by the medium to express the spirit and strength of the American worker.

Collagraphy

Relief and intaglio printmaking rely on a compromised surface—in a printmaking context, one that has been cut into in order to fashion an image. The ink is then applied to the surface and transferred to paper. But **collagraphic** prints are created by building up (rather than cutting into) a surface that can be inked for the purpose of transfer to paper. The artist glues materials to a rigid support, such as wood or heavy cardboard; this effectively "**collages**" the image to that surface. The image can then be printed by inking the materials with printing ink, and pressing paper onto them.

The artist most closely associated with the development of the collagraph was Glen Alps (1914–1996), a longtime faculty member at the University of Washington in Seattle. Alps first used the term **collagraph** to describe the process. In his work *Roll-Up #2* (**2.3.14**), pieces of material are glued in a way that allows the printmaker more freedom because the surface can be easily manipulated. Although Alps did not invent the collagraphic technique, he was the first printmaker to succeed in mastering and promoting the process.

Lithography

Lithography (from the Greek for stone writing) is traditionally done on stone. It is what is known as a **planographic** printmaking technique, that is, the print is made from an entirely flat surface, rather than one that is carved or otherwise modified. German author Alois Senefelder (1771–1834), out of money and looking for a cheaper method to print his newest play, devised the lithographic printing process in 1796. The complex presses used nowadays by commercial printers for producing newspapers,

Mezzotint: an intaglio printmaking process based on roughening the entire printing plate to accept ink; the artist smoothes non-image areas

Collagraphy, collagraphic, collagraph: a type of relief print that is created by building up or collaging material on or to a stiff surface, inking that surface, then printing

Collage: a work of art assembled by gluing materials, often paper, onto a surface. From the French *coller*, to glue

Planography: a print process—lithography and silkscreen printing—where the inked image area and non-inked areas are at the same height

2.3.14 Glen Alps, *Roll-Up #2*. Collagraph, 26¼ × 32½".

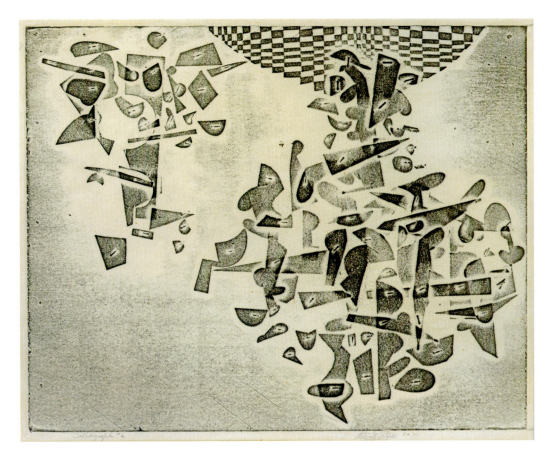

2.3.15 A brief overview of the lithography process:

1. The artist designs the image to be printed.
2. Using a grease pencil, the design is drawn onto the limestone, blocking the pores.
3. The stone is treated with acid and other chemicals that are brushed onto its surface. Then the surface is wiped clean with a solvent, such as kerosene.
4. The stone is sponged so that water can be absorbed into the pores of the stone.
5. Oil-based ink is repelled by the water and sits only on areas where the oil crayon image was drawn.
6. Paper is laid on the surface of the stone and it is drawn through a press.
7. The print is removed from the stone.
8. The completed image appears in reverse compared with the original design.

magazines, and brochures ("offset lithography") use thin sheets of zinc or aluminum instead of stone, but the basic principles are the same as Senefelder's original discovery.

Contemporary artists' lithographic prints are still made on the kind of stone used by Senefelder. Some artists like lithography because it allows them to draw a design in the same way they do a drawing. Successive stages in the process are illustrated in **2.3.15**. An artist first draws a design, using a grease pencil or other oil-based drawing material, directly onto a piece of specially selected, cleaned, and prepared limestone. Next, the artist applies a number of materials to the stone, including a gum arabic and nitric acid solution that makes the image more durable. Then he or she wipes the surface clean using kerosene. Even though the image appears to have been obliterated by the kerosene (this is a most unnerving moment for novice printmakers!), the stone is now ready to be printed. The surface is sponged with water,

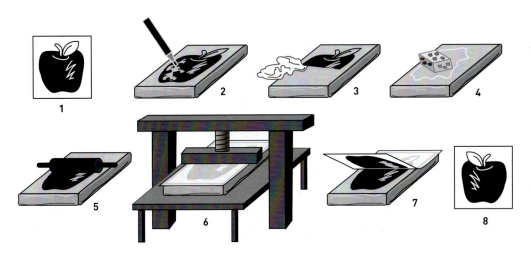

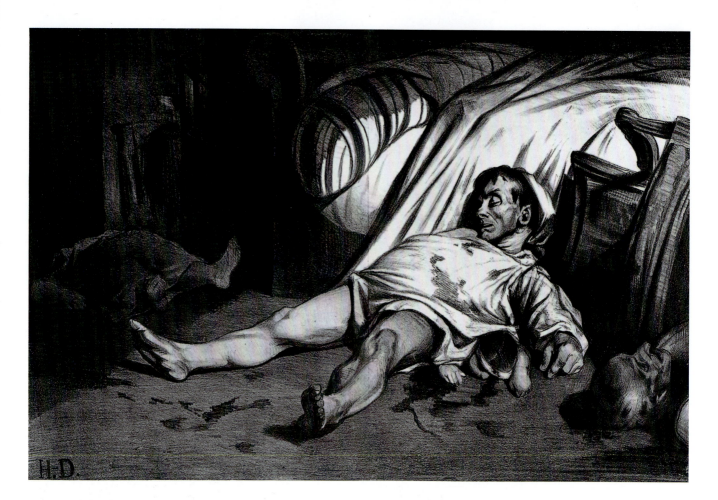

which is repelled by the greasy areas of the drawing, and rolled with oil-based ink. In the ungreased regions the water repels ink, leaving only the image covered with ink. At this point the artist carefully places paper over the stone and lightly presses down, usually by passing it through a printing press.

In 1834, the French artist Honoré Daumier (1808–1879) used his skills combined with the lithographic process to tell the citizens of Paris about an incident of police brutality. Daumier, who worked for the monthly magazine *L'Association Mensuelle*, depicted the aftermath of a horrible incident that took place at Rue Transnonain on April 15, 1834 (**2.3.16**). That night, police responded to a sniper attack they believed had come from that street by entering a property there, no. 12, and ruthlessly killing everyone inside. Daumier, a great critic of the French government's treatment of workers, drew the massacred in gruesome detail, including placing the most shocking—the dead child—in the center, under its father's body.

Stencil: a perforated template allowing ink or paint to pass through to print a design

Mask: in spray painting or silkscreen printing, a barrier the shape of which blocks the paint or ink from passing through

Serigraphy (Silkscreen Printing)

Serigraphy, also known as silkscreen printing, is another planographic printing process, as well as one of the most versatile, capable of placing a heavy coverage of ink on a wide variety of surfaces, from printed circuit boards to packaging, from solar panels to T-shirts. Artists value, amongst its many other virtues, its potential for printing strong colors.

Unlike all the other printing processes discussed in this chapter, only silkscreen printing produces "right-reading" reproductions of the original artwork. Relief, intaglio, and litho prints all make mirror images, so an artist making such a print needs to think in reverse.

Silkscreen printing was first developed in China during the Song Dynasty (960–1279) and uses a **stencil** process. A stencil **masks** out areas so that ink will take on the shape of the unmasked, open parts. It can be used to create a large number of prints. The silkscreen itself is nowadays a fine mesh, usually made out of nylon. The image area of the screen is open and allows ink to pass through, while the rest of the screen is masked off. As the printmaker moves the squeegee (like a heavy flat windshield wiper) over the screen, the mask prevents ink from passing through in unwanted areas. The mask can be a kind of thick glue painted on with a brush, or it can be a physical barrier, such as tape. Photographic silkscreen prints can be produced using a photosensitive masking material.

The American artist Andy Warhol (1928–1987) utilized photographic silkscreen techniques over aluminum paint to create a distinctive style, seen in his work *Four Marilyns* (**2.3.17**). Warhol reproduces a sultry image of

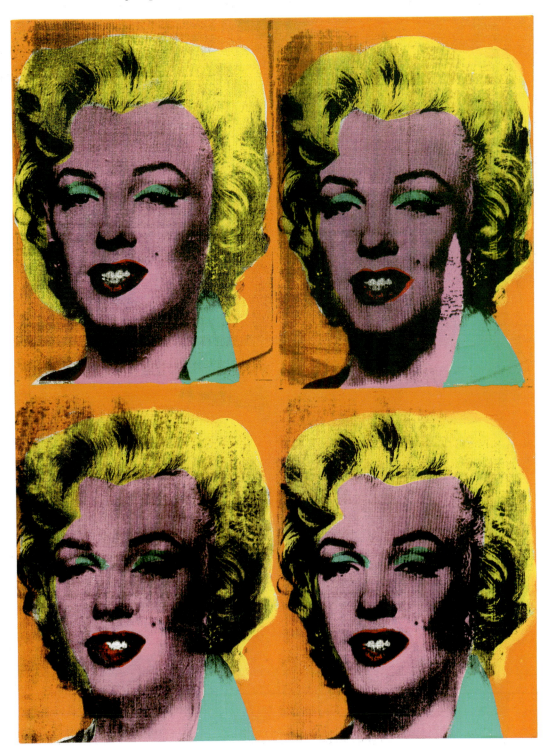

2.3.17 Andy Warhol, *Four Marilyns*, 1962. Acrylic, silkscreen ink, pencil on linen, 29 x 21½". Sold at Phillips, New York 2014

Marilyn Monroe from a photograph taken at the height of the actress's career, deliberately repeating her image to comment on the nature of mass-produced images in advertising. Public figures market their image the same way food companies promote cans of soup. Silkscreen printing is particularly suited to printing large areas of flat, heavy color, and by using this technique, Warhol emphasizes the flatness and lack of depth in the image of Marilyn, showing how it has become a commodity rather than a genuine attempt to capture her individuality. The repeating "clones" of Marilyn also accentuate the degeneration that occurs when an original is copied.

Editions

Prints are produced in limited numbers of identical impressions, called editions. The printmaker has the ethical responsibility for making sure each print is similar enough to the others so that each person who buys a print has a high-quality image. When a print is deemed identical to others in the edition, it is assigned a number in the production sequence. For example, a print marked 2/25 is the second print in an edition of twenty-five. Some unnumbered prints bear the letters A/P. These prints, called artist's proofs, are used by the printmaker to check the quality of the process and are not intended to be part of the edition. Some artist's proofs are sold as one-of-a-kind works, rather than as part of an edition, because variations in the process may produce visually engaging results. Even though most artists could create more prints than they do, they usually decide to print a set number: a limited edition. The artist afterward destroys the original plates so it is impossible to make any more copies. Destroying the plates protects the integrity of the edition, because no more can be made. It also limits the number in the edition so that each print is rarer and therefore more valuable.

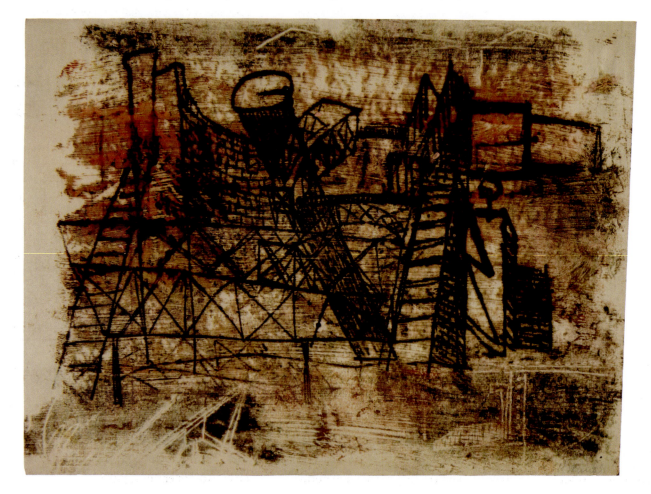

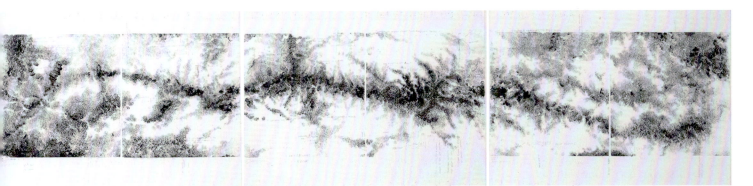

Monotypes and Monoprints

Nearly all printmaking is done in editions, or multiple impressions, but some artists who like the way a printed image looks will opt to create unique prints. Monotypes and monoprints are print techniques that enable an artist to produce an image that is one of a kind.

A monotype image prints from a polished plate, perhaps glass or metal. The artist puts no permanent marks on it. He or she makes an image on it in ink or another medium, then wipes away the ink in places where the artist wants the paper to show through. The image is then printed. Only one impression is possible.

Hedda Sterne (1910–2011) was the sole woman in a group of **abstract** painters called the Irascibles. Although abstract, Sterne's *Untitled (Machine Series)* monotype makes associations with architectural and mechanical images (**2.3.18**). Sterne probably employed a straightedge to maintain the regularity of line in the print.

Monoprints can be made using any print process. The artist prepares the image for printing as described previously in this chapter, but will ink or modify each impression in a unique way. This includes varying colors, changing the spread of the ink across the image area, and adding features by hand. The individual modifications possible are as infinite as for any hand-made work of art. Artists choose to make monoprints to explore "themes and variations," where some elements of the work remain the same but others are different. If two prints are identical, they are not monoprints.

Kathy Strauss's (b. 1956) monoprint *Kepler Underneath 1* painstakingly depicts the Milky Way Galaxy (**2.3.19**). The artist has first incised a series of calculus problems into the metal plate. As with any other intaglio print, the plate was then completely covered with ink and wiped. Ink stayed in the incised grooves. Strauss has then painted the image of the Milky Way in ink directly onto the same plate; when the inking was complete, she centered the paper over the image and ran it through the press. Because Strauss painted the ink on by hand, she cannot re-create the result exactly in a second print, so it is not part of an edition (see p. 244).

Print Shops and Digital Reproduction Services

Contemporary printmakers sometimes rely on the technical expertise of craftsmen who may not be artists themselves, but have developed the knowledge and expertise to bring creative ideas to a well-crafted artwork. For example, Printmakers Chicago is a commercial printing service that works with artists and other creative professionals to re-create original imagery. This studio, like many others, works with the individual artist to find the right paper, surface appearance, and archival qualities that meet his or her high standard. Although some print shops will provide traditional printmaking tools and equipment along with their expertise, Printmakers Chicago provides digital reproductions that replicate the character of the original work, be it a print, painting, or other two-dimensional piece.

Abstract: an artwork the form of which is simplified, distorted, or exaggerated in appearance. It may represent a recognizable form that has been slightly altered, or it may be a completely non-representational depiction

Active Learning Exercises

1. A relief print is a print that is created by carving away material from a flat surface, then inking the raised surface, then transferring the image to paper, usually by pressing. This process has been done with wood and linoleum, but can also be created from any semi-hard pliable material. For example, a potato can be used to create a simple relief print. To do this one would cut a flat surface into one side of the potato, then carve away any excess to reveal the image. To print, simply ink the raised surface with water-based printing ink and press into a paper surface. This is one of the most common ways that children are introduced to printmaking, but the same process can be used to make complex images. Have you ever done a potato print? Are simple processes, like potato prints, viable for creating works of high art or are they simply a tool for introductory learning? Why do you think this is?

2. A collagraph can be produced by gluing objects to a rigid surface, inking them with printing ink, then transferring the image to paper. Try creating a collagraph with some cardboard pieces, some craft glue and a rigid board. Glue cardboard shapes to the rigid board, then use more glue to "draw" some texture on the shapes. Allow it to dry, then ink the surface with a water-based printing ink. You can use a brayer (a roller tool) or a brush to apply the ink. Leaving the inked surface face up on a tabletop, slowly lower a piece of paper until it makes contact with the print surface. Press the back of the paper with your hand and smooth it with the back of a spoon so that it makes good contact with the paper. Remove the paper with the printed image. What kind of differences occurred between the cardboard shapes and the glue lines? How can you modify the print surface to create other effects?

3. A monotype is a print that is produced as a unique work of art. The artist applies ink to a slick surface, such as Plexiglas or metal, with a brush. The artist creates the image more like a painting, but will press the inked surface onto the paper. Try producing a monotype by brushing printing ink onto a rigid slick surface, then transferring it to paper. What effect does the pressing have on the look of the image? Based on your experience, what advantages or disadvantages does a monotype provide an artist?

Images Related to 2.3:
Printmaking

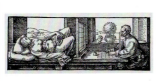

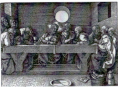

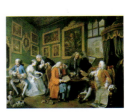

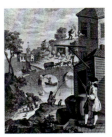

3.6.15 Albrecht Dürer, *The Last Supper*, 1523, p. 479

1.3.24 Albrecht Dürer, *Draftsman Drawing a Recumbent Woman*, 1525, p. 98

3.6.2 Giorgio Vasari, *Lives*, Portrait of Michelangelo, 1568, p. 465

3.7.8 William Hogarth, *The Marriage Settlement*, c. 1743, p. 497

4.5.6 William Hogarth, *False Perspective*, 1754, p. 615

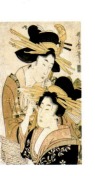

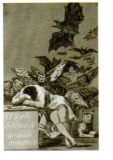

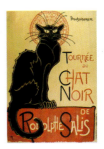

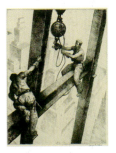

3.3.22 Kitagawa Utamaro, *Two Courtesans*, 2nd half of 18th century, p. 428

1.9.11 Francisco Goya, *The Sleep of Reason Produces Monsters*, 1799, p. 174

1.8.10 Ando Hiroshige, "Riverside Bamboo Market," 1857, p. 164

3.8.16 Théophile-Alexandre Steinlen, *Tournée du Chat Noir poster*, 1896, p. 524

1.1.14 James Allen, *The Connectors*, 1934, p. 57

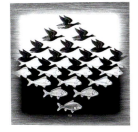

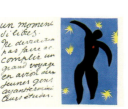

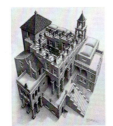

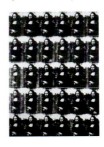

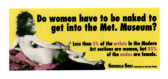

1.1.29 M. C. Escher, *Sky and Water I*, 1938, p. 64

4.9.18 Henri Matisse, *Icarus*, 1943–47, p. 671

1.3.23 M. C. Escher, *Ascending and Descending*, 1960, p. 97

3.9.4 Andy Warhol, *Thirty Are Better than One*, 1963, p. 544

4.10.8 Guerilla Girls, *Do Women Have to Be Naked to Get into the Met. Museum?*, 1989, p. 681

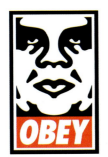

1.1.26a Shepard Fairey, *Obey*, 1996, p. 62

2.4

Sculpture

A great sculpture can roll down a hill without breaking.

(Michelangelo Buonarroti,
Italian sculptor, painter, and architect)

Michelangelo is generally regarded as one of the finest sculptors in the Western tradition—some would say the greatest (see Box: Michelangelo, p. 252). When the **Renaissance** Italian artist made the humorous remark above, he probably had in mind most of his own sculptures: statues chiseled out of durable marble. This might be the first response of most of us when asked to define what we mean by sculpture, although we might broaden our definition to include other materials, such as metal, ceramics, and wood. But, as we will see in this chapter, sculpture can be made from many materials: for example, glass, wax, ice, plastic, and fiber. In fact, the materials of modern sculpture can include, for example, neon lights and even animals. Sculptors' methods today still include chiseling (as Michelangelo did), carving, molding, assembling, and constructing, but inventive sculptors are finding new ways to create their art, and new materials to make it with.

It is probably because artists are so inventive that it is difficult to define sculpture exactly. Look up the word in a dictionary and then check whether the definition fits all the works in this chapter; it probably will not. But we can agree on a few things that are true of all sculptures. They exist in three dimensions and occupy physical space in our world. And

they invite us to interact with them: by looking at them, by walking round them, or by entering them and being immersed in an environment created by the sculptor, including sights, sounds, textures, and other sensory experiences.

Approaches to Three Dimensions in Sculpture

Sculptors planning new sculptures have two basic options for displaying them. The first approach invites us to examine them on all sides; sculpture made to be enjoyed in this way is known as freestanding, or sculpture **in the round**. Many freestanding sculptures are made so that we can move around them, but sculptures in the round can also be displayed in a way that prevents a viewer seeing every side of them. Sculptures can be made, for example, to be placed in a niche or standing against a wall. In such cases, the location of the statue determines the vantage points from which it can be viewed, and the sculptor will design his or her work with the viewer's position in mind.

The second fundamental approach to the **three-dimensional** nature of sculpture is **relief**, a type of sculpture specifically designed for viewing from one side. The image in a relief either protrudes from or is sunk into a surface. It can have very little depth (**bas-relief**) or a great deal (**high relief**).

Renaissance: a period of cultural and artistic change in Europe from the fourteenth to the seventeenth century
In the round: a freestanding sculpted work that can be viewed from all sides
Three-dimensional: having height, width, and depth
Relief: a raised form on a largely flat background. For example, the design on a coin is "in relief"
Bas-relief: a sculpture carved with very little depth
High relief: a carved panel where the figures project with a great deal of depth from the background

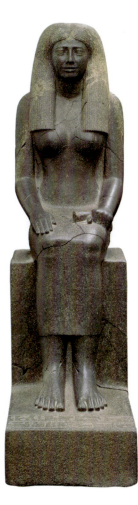

2.4.1 *Sculpture of the Lady Sennuwy*, 1971–1926 BCE. Granite, 67 × 45¾ × 18". Museum of Fine Arts, Boston, Massachusetts

Freestanding Sculpture

Some freestanding sculpture is not intended to be experienced from every point of view. The Egyptian sculpture (1971–1926 BCE) of the Lady Sennuwy, wife of the very powerful governor of an Egyptian province, was designed to be seen from the front (**2.4.1**). (Many Egyptian sculptures were made to be displayed with their backs to a wall or a pillar.) In this work we can get a sense of the original block of granite from which the work was chiseled. Egyptian figure sculptures often sit, as this one does, very straight and upright on the stone from which they were carved, with the arms and legs drawn in close to the body.

Giambologna (1529–1608), a Flemish artist working in Florence, Italy, designed the *Rape of a Sabine* at the request of Florence's ruler, Francesco de' Medici (**2.4.2a** and **2.4.2b**). The

2.4.2a, 2.4.2b
Giambologna, *Rape of a Sabine*, 1583 (post-restoration). Marble, 13'6" high. Loggia dei Lanzi, Piazza della Signoria, Florence, Italy

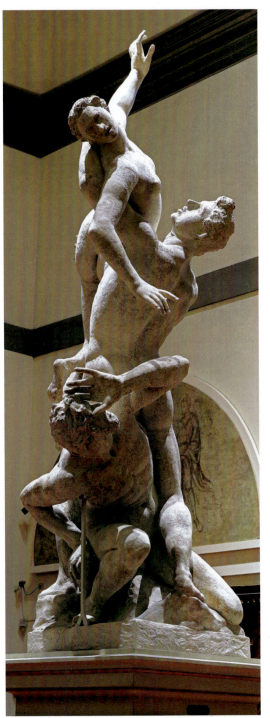

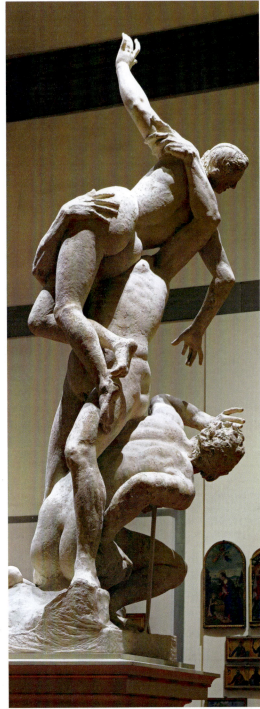

sculpture forms a kind of spiral that draws the viewer around to view its many changing **planes**. With each step, the viewer can discover unexpected details as the surfaces spiral upward. This is a powerful and beautiful work, but Giambologna had more in mind when he created it than just a dramatic design. His statue was a piece of political propaganda. It re-creates an ancient story about the foundation of Rome around 753 BCE. Most of the early founders of Rome were male. For the city to grow, the Romans needed wives. They solved this problem by inviting their neighbors the Sabines to a festival, during which the Romans seized the Sabine women and forced them to marry. This story symbolized the ability of a small community to become the most powerful city in Italy—as Rome was by Giambologna's time—and with this dramatic sculpture Francesco announced to the Florentines and their enemies that, like Rome, Florence had risen to become a force to be reckoned with.

Bas-Relief and High Relief

In bas-relief (the French word *bas* means "low"), the sculptor's marks are shallow. An example of this kind of sculpted surface was found in the North Palace of the Assyrian king Ashurbanipal in the ancient city of Nineveh in Mesopotamia (modern-day Iraq). Assyrian kings ruled over a large territory and had powerful armies. They decorated the interior walls of their palaces with images depicting their strength and power. The artist who carved away the stone to create *Dying Lioness* intended to reflect the great strength and bravery of King Ashurbanipal as he hunted and killed the most fearsome beast known to the Assyrians (**2.4.3**).

The symbol of the lion is also used to represent power and bravery in the *Memorial to King Leopold of the Belgians*, created to commemorate the death of Belgium's first king (it declared independence from the Netherlands in 1830) in 1865 (**2.4.4**). The British sculptor Susan Durant (1827–1873) chose to incise the surface more deeply for the figures closer to the viewer; this means that they are in high relief. Thus these figures—the lion and the reclining

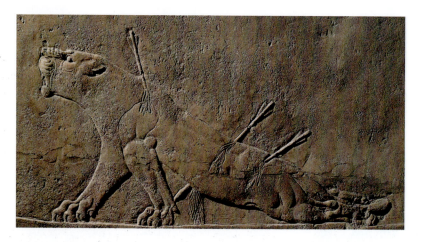

image of Leopold—protrude from the surface more than the angels in the **background**, which have been carved in low relief. The illusion of depth emphasizes Leopold's bravery in accepting the Belgian National Congress's invitation to become king. Durant was unusual in being a successful sculptor in nineteenth-century England at a time when it was not easy for women to break into such a profession; she was in demand for her portraits, which included a **bust** of Harriet Beecher Stowe, the author of the anti-slavery novel *Uncle Tom's Cabin*. Durant became a favorite sculptor to the British royal family, and her memorial to King Leopold I was originally installed in his niece Queen Victoria's chapel at Windsor Castle in 1867 but was moved to Christ Church, Esher, in 1879.

2.4.4 Susan Durant, *Memorial to King Leopold of the Belgians*, 1867, in Christ Church, Esher, England

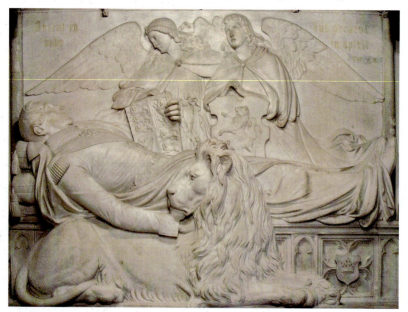

2.4.3 *Dying Lioness*, limestone relief from the North Palace of Ashurbanipal, Nineveh, Assyrian period, *c*. 650 BCE. British Museum, London, England

Plane: a flat surface, often implied in the composition
Background: the part of a work depicted furthest from the viewer's space, often behind the main subject matter
Bust: a statue of a person depicting only his or her head and shoulders
Subtractive: the methodical removal of material to produce a sculptural form

Methods of Sculpture

Sculptural methods are either **subtractive** or additive. In the subtractive processes, a sculptor uses a tool to carve, drill, chisel, chip, whittle, or saw away unwanted material. In the additive processes of modeling, **casting**, or constructing, sculptors add material to make the final artwork.

Carving

The most ancient works of art that still exist were made using subtractive methods of sculpture. Most of these were made of stone or ivory (because wood eventually decays, we have few ancient wooden sculptures) and were worked by chipping, carving, sanding, and polishing.

Casting: a sculpture or artwork made by pouring a liquid (for example molten metal or plaster) into a mold
Form: an object that can be defined in three dimensions (height, width, and depth)
Additive (sculpture): a sculpting process in which the artist builds a form by adding material

Gateway to Art: Colossal Olmec Heads
Sculpture in Stone and Clay

The Olmec artist who sculpted this colossal head (2.4.5) probably worked the way most subtractive sculptors do even today. After choosing a stone that best resembles the desired shape, the artist works around it, knocking off large chunks of material until the final **form** has been established. Then the sculptor begins to bore into the surface, refining and establishing the main details of the work. In the case of the colossal head, the stone carver was working with an extremely hard material, so making a subtractive sculpture by carving away from the existing block of basalt was the only way the head could be created. This would probably have involved cutting deep into the stone to fashion the eyes, while ensuring enough material was left to make the nose and mouth. Then the artist would carefully hone the details, and finish by polishing the surface to eliminate the marks made by the cutting tools. The achievement of the Olmec sculptors was especially impressive since the Olmec had no metal tools; archaeologists believe this head was made using stone hammers and wooden drills.

The Olmec were experienced potters as well as being skilled stone carvers. Along with carving colossal stone works, they made sculptural figurines in clay. One well-known ceramic sculpture is called *Baby Figure* (2.4.6). One of the most striking differences from the colossal heads (2.4.5) is the scale of

2.4.5 Colossal Head #10, Olmec. Basalt, 5'11" × 4'8¼" × 3'. San Lorenzo, Veracruz, Mexico

this figure. At just over a foot tall, it is closer to the size an actual baby would be. By contrast, a person's head is about the size of one of the eyes on a colossal head. The Baby Figure shows the whole body instead of focusing only on the head. The rolls of flesh and the gesture of putting the hand to the mouth seem very intimate and personal, with a careful attention to detail. Another major difference between the colossal heads and this figurine is the materials used to make them. The fine, white clay, called kaolin, was molded while it was still wet. The ceramist was able to take advantage of the softness of the clay to add and take away material to create the desired form: the figurine is an example of both **additive** and subtractive sculpture. The ceramic sculpture is also hollow, while the stone head is solid.

2.4.6 (below) *Baby Figure*, between 12th and 9th centuries BCE. Ceramic, cinnabar, red ocher, 13⅜" high. Metropolitan Museum of Art, New York

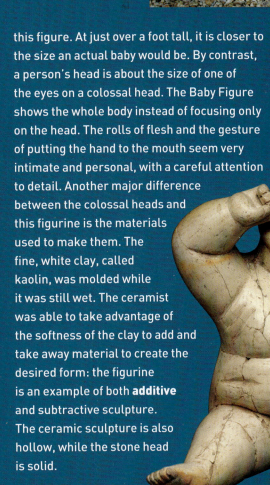

Michelangelo

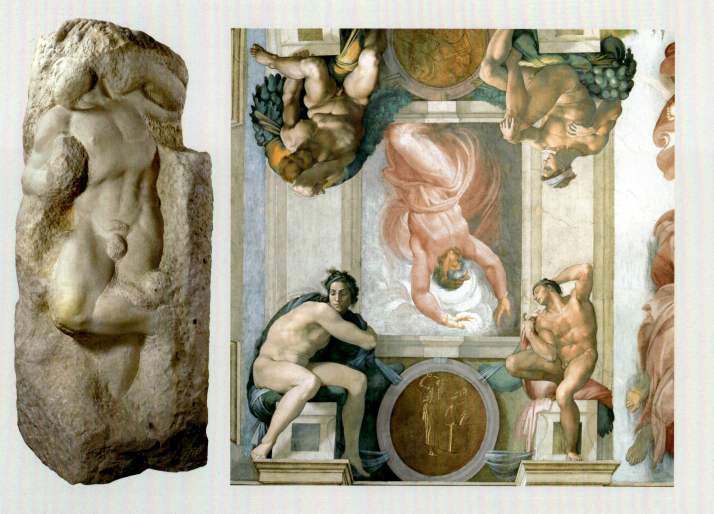

One artist in history stands out because of his unique mastery of the materials and methods of sculpture. Michelangelo (b. Michelangelo Buonarroti, 1475–1564) used an unconventional technique to "release" the figure, as he saw it, from the stone. Rather than remove stone progressively from all sides, as most sculptors do, Michelangelo began on one side of the stone and sculpted through to the other side. He felt that he was freeing the figure from the stone in which it had been trapped. His unfinished sculpture, *Awakening Slave*, gives an insight into the artist's technique (**2.4.8**).

Michelangelo excelled in architecture and painting as well as sculpture. Yet he saw these arts through the eyes of a sculptor; he believed sculpture itself was the finest, the most challenging, and the most beautiful of all the visual arts. While painting the Sistine Chapel ceiling (**2.4.9**—*Separation of Light and Darkness*), which many see as his grandest work, Michelangelo dreamed of finishing the ceiling quickly so that he could get back to work on several large sculptures intended for the tomb of Pope Julius II. He made many **sketches** of the figures intended for the nude male sculptures (which he called *ignudi*, from the Italian word for nude) that he planned would cover the tomb. Unfortunately, the tomb was never completed in the way that Michelangelo intended, but some sculptures carved for the project survive. Figure **2.4.10**—*Moses*—is one example, and if we compare this polished statue with the *Awakening* Slave (**2.4.8**), we can see how much refining of his sculptural work the artist did after the initial carving stage.

2.4.8 (above left) Michelangelo, *Prisoner*, known as the *Awakening Slave*, 1519–20. Marble, 8'9⅛" high. Accademia, Florence, Italy

2.4.9 (above right) Michelangelo Buonarroti, *Separation of Light and Darkness*, 1508–12, detail of the vault, Sistine Chapel, Vatican City, Italy

The muscular figures painted on the Sistine Chapel ceiling have led many viewers to believe they are looking at sculptures. The figures have the appearance of **mass**, particularly the nudes, which really seem to be men perched on architectural platforms. The ceiling is smooth, however; the illusion of these three-dimensional forms was created through the use of shading. Michelangelo painted darker shades in the areas that would have been carved more deeply if the figures had been sculptures. Thus, even when he painted, he thought like a sculptor.

2.4.10 Michelangelo, Tomb of Julius II, detail of *Moses*, 1513–16. Marble, 7'8½" high. San Pietro in Vincoli, Rome, Italy

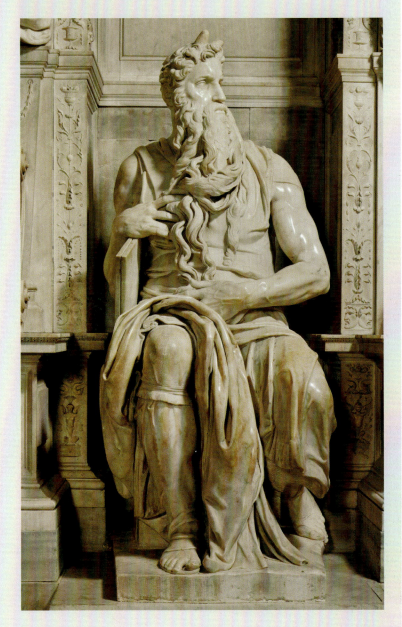

Sketch: a rough preliminary version of a work or part of a work
Mass: a volume that has, or gives the illusion of having, weight, density, and bulk

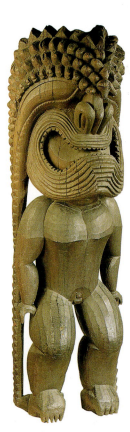

2.4.7 Figure of the war god Ku-kaʻili-moku, Hawaii, 18th or 19th century. Wood, 8'11" high. British Museum, London, England

The nearly nine-foot-tall figure of the Hawaiian war god Ku-kaʻili-moku was carved (the subtractive method) from large pieces of wood (**2.4.7**). The sculpture represents a god whose name translates from Hawaiian as "Ku, the land-grabber." Originally created for the powerful King Kamehameha I, the image of the god exhibits an open mouth (a disrespectful gesture) and was probably intended to gain divine favor. Another god, Lono (god of prosperity), is also symbolized by pigs' heads in Ku's hair. The combination of the two gods may have represented Kamehameha's invasions and conquests of adjacent kingdoms.

Modeling

Modeling in clay and wax (for example) is an additive process; the artist builds up the work by adding material. Clay and wax are pliable enough for sculptors to model them with their hands; sculptors also use specialized tools to manipulate them. Because such materials as clay often cannot support their own weight, sometimes an artist will employ a skeletal structure, called an **armature**, to which the clay will be added; the armature will then later be removed (or burned away) when the work is dry. Permanent sculptures created from clay will most often be dried, then fired in a kiln until the chemical structure of the clay changes. Because this process produces a very dry and hard material, many clay works from antiquity still exist.

Large sculptures, such as the Etruscan sarcophagus (a kind of coffin) in **2.4.11**, are built from multiple pieces fired individually. Four separate terra-cotta (baked clay) pieces make up this sarcophagus, which contains the ashes of the deceased. The sculptor paid particular attention to the gestures and expressions of the couple, shown relaxed and enjoying themselves at an Etruscan banquet, although the expressions are **stylized** and not a likeness of the deceased. The **plastic** character of clay allowed the artist to make images that are **expressive** and capture the mood of the event.

The way the sculptor interpreted the figures tells us two interesting things about their culture. Women actively participated in social situations; this woman is shown gesturing, and even reclines in front of her husband. And, since this sculpture is part of a tomb, it suggests that celebrations took place upon the death of loved ones, although the figures' joyful expressions may simply indicate the deceased in an eternal state of happiness.

Casting

Casting, another additive process, involves adding a liquid or pliable material to a mold. It is done in order to set a form in a more durable material, or to make it possible to create multiple copies of a work. The first step in casting is to make a model of the final sculpture. This is used to make a mold. A casting liquid (often molten metal, but other materials, such as clay, plaster, acrylic polymers, or glass are also used) is poured into the mold. When it hardens, the result is a detailed replica of the original model.

Plaster casts are often used to create models and finished products. To create a plaster cast,

the artist makes a clay original, coats it with a release agent (usually a slick, oily substance), then creates a plaster coating to go over the original. The artist is careful to make divisions so that the plaster mold can be easily separated,

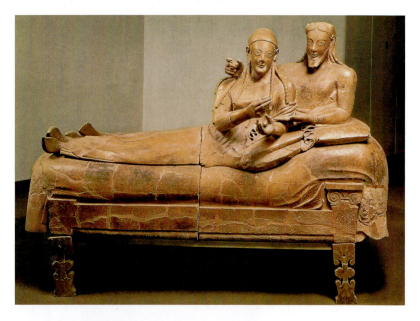

2.4.11 Sarcophagus from Cerveteri, *c.* 520 BCE. Painted terra-cotta, 3′9½″ × 6′7″. Museo Nazionale di Villa Giulia, Rome, Italy

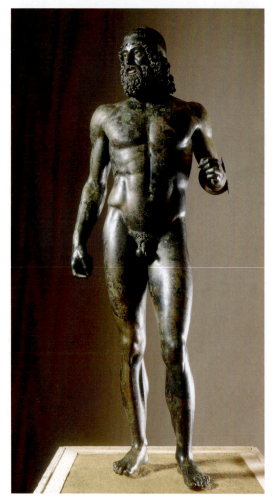

2.4.12 *Riace Warrior A*, *c.* 460 BCE. Bronze with copper, silver, and ivory, 6′6″ high. Museo Nazionale della Magna Grecia, Reggio di Calabria, Italy

Armature: a framework or skeleton used to support a sculpture
Stylized: art that represents objects in an exaggerated way to emphasize certain aspects of the object
Plastic, plasticity: referring to materials that are soft and can be manipulated, or to such properties in the materials
Expressive: capable of stirring the emotions of the viewer

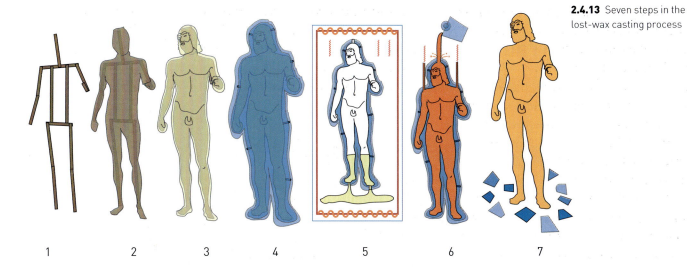

1   2   3   4   5   6   7

in sections, from the clay original. After the plaster has cured—set in a permanent state—the sections are carefully detached, the inside of the parts of the mold coated with release agent, and the mold reassembled. Plaster, or another pliable casting material, can then be poured into the mold, allowed to set, and the cast form removed.

The ancient Greeks cast bronze to produce many of their sculptures. Bronze is an alloy, or mixture, of copper and tin. It melts at a relatively low temperature (an average of 1,750°F depending on the composition of the alloy) and is comparatively easy to cast. Once formed and cooled it is light (compared to stone) and durable. The so-called *Riace Warrior A* is a fine example of the casting skills of ancient Greek artists (**2.4.12**). It is one of two sculptures found in 1972 by divers off the coast of Riace, Italy. This sculpture reflects great attention to detail and was made at a time when the Greeks emphasized the perfection of the human body. The figure is posed in a **contrapposto** (Italian for "opposite"), which uses the natural curvature of the body to enliven the design. By shifting the weight to the right leg, the hips are set at a slight angle, which is countered by small shifts in the shoulders, with the head fractionally tilted. The work may have been cast to celebrate the victory of the Athenians over the invading Persians, and the relaxed contrapposto reflects strength and confidence.

Riace Warrior A was created using the lost-wax method of casting. (Each numbered stage refers to **2.4.13**.) The artist begins by building an armature (1) and then adds clay to it to create the form (2). A thick layer of wax is added to the armature, and any detail the sculptor wishes to see in the final work is carved into the wax (3). Clay, sand, and ground-up pieces of old molds are used to cover the surface of the wax form, preserving all the detail. This hard coating, which needs to be strong enough to bear the heat and weight of the metal until it cools, will be the mold (4). Small holes are drilled in the bottom of the mold, which is then placed in a kiln. In the oven, the wax melts out through the holes in the bottom of the mold, leaving a hollow space inside the mold (5). Immediately after the mold has been removed from the kiln, very hot molten metal—in this case, bronze—is poured into it (6). When the metal has cooled, the mold is removed (usually by breaking it with a hammer) to reveal the work—which is still not finished (7). The artist cuts off any extra metal, then sands and polishes. Over time, exposure to the elements can add surface color, called a **patina**, to bronze sculpture. Such a patina can enhance the beauty of the work. Nowadays it is commonly applied more artificially, by using chemical preparations.

Lost-wax casting is called a substitution process because the molten metal takes the place of the wax. Other materials, such as foam or wood, are occasionally used as substitution materials instead of wax, because they can be burnt out of the mold.

Contrapposto: a pose in sculpture in which the upper part of the body twists in one direction and the lower part in another
Patina: surface color or texture on a metal caused by ageing

Pushing beyond Traditional Methods

The traditional processes used for sculpting were ideal for the creation of static objects, but artists have found other ways to enliven the medium that go beyond conventional additive and subtractive techniques.

Earthworks

Prehistoric artists of the Americas made **monumental** sculptures that used the surface of the Earth itself as material: this was additive sculpture on a very large scale. The most prominent of these is the Great Serpent Mound near Locust Grove, Ohio. As can be readily seen from the air, it resembles a snake with its mouth open, ingesting an egg (**2.4.14**). The identity of

the people who created it is still debated. The head of the serpent and the egg are aligned to the position of the setting sun on the summer solstice (the longest day of the year), suggesting that the Great Serpent Mound was used in making solar observations. The original artists heaped piles of earth to "sculpt" this work onto the Ohio landscape.

In the 1960s artists again became interested in earthworks. The best-known modern earthwork is Robert Smithson's (1938–1973) *Spiral Jetty* in the Great Salt Lake in Utah (**2.4.15**). Smithson chose a spiral, a shape naturally found in shells, crystals, and even galaxies. The coiled artwork was made by dumping 6,550 tons of rock and dirt off dump trucks, gradually paving a spiraling roadbed out into the salt lake. The artwork is not static in the way it interacts with nature. Over the years the lake has repeatedly submerged and then revealed the sculpture. The

2.4.14 Great Serpent Mound, *c.* 800 BCE–100 CE, 1330 × 3', Locust Grove, Adams County, Ohio

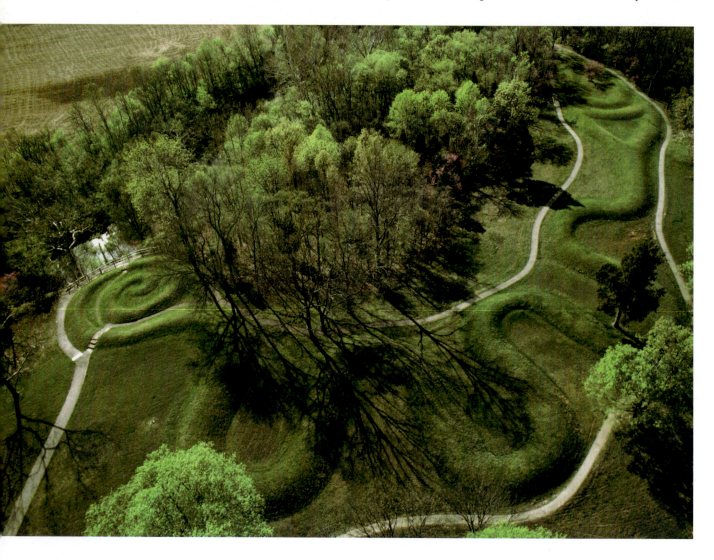

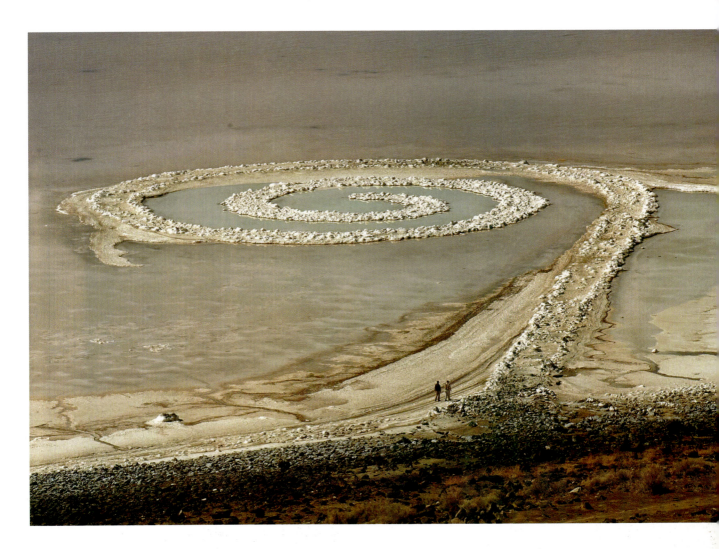

2.4.15 Robert Smithson, *Spiral Jetty*, 1969–70. Black rock, salt crystals, and earth, 160' diameter, coil length 1500 × 15'. Great Salt Lake, Utah

artwork is constantly evolving as it drowns and then rises with a new encrustation of salt crystals.

Because of their enormous size, earthwork projects need the collaboration of many artists and workers. Such works as the Great Serpent Mound required a community effort. Today, earthwork projects are obliged to have permits and community approval, and to involve large groups of workers and heavy equipment. Artists do not earn money from their artworks, but create them as a service to the community. Many contemporary artists believe that earthworks should represent a harmony between nature and humanity.

Construction

When engineers make a piece of machinery, they use a variety of methods to create and put together its components. Some of the parts will be made by sawing, grinding, milling, and using other ways of removing material; others will be modeled, molded, and cast. All the components will then be assembled. Some artists construct sculptures in a similar way.

The idea of constructing sculptures is relatively new. Methods for doing so have proliferated with the growth of standardized, engineered materials, such as sheet metals and plastics. In the late nineteenth century, sculptors began to look beyond traditional carved or cast forms to the process of constructing. The artists of the **Constructivist** movement in the Soviet Union created an entire art movement based on sculptural construction techniques associated more with a factory than with an art studio. Constructivists considered art to be a scientific investigation of the social needs of the time. One of the group's members, Naum Gabo (b. Naum Neemia Pevsner, 1890–1977), had studied physics, mathematics, and engineering

2.4.16 Naum Gabo, *Constructed Head No. 2*, 1916. Cor-ten steel, 69 × 52¾ × 48¼". Tate, London, England

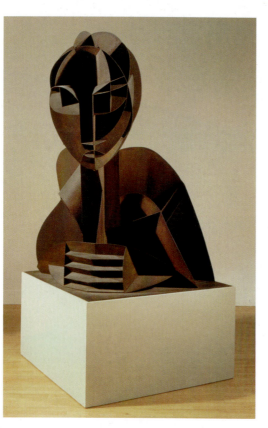

2.4.17 (below) Damien Hirst, *The Physical Impossibility of Death in the Mind of Someone Living*, 1991. Glass, painted steel, silicone, monofilament, shark, and formaldehyde solution, 7'1½" x 17'9⅜" x 5'10⅞"

in college. His *Constructed Head No. 2* (**2.4.16**) investigates the sense of **space** and form implied by flat planes, in contrast to the solid mass of conventional sculpture. Here Gabo is more interested in showing the interior construction of the work than the exterior surface. He has welded the intersecting planes of metal together more as if he were a mechanic or engineer.

Contemporary artists have adopted modern-day industrial techniques and unconventional materials to create their sculptures. They have challenged traditional notions of what sculptures can be. Today's sculptors can use anything to communicate their message. British artist Damien Hirst (b. 1965) made his work *The Physical Impossibility of Death in the Mind of Someone Living* out of quite unconventional materials (**2.4.17**). This constructed work is made with a large tank full of formaldehyde, in which the artist has suspended a dead shark. Of course, not every part of this work was constructed; Hirst did not construct the shark, he had it caught by fishermen. The entire work resembles a dissection specimen from a biology class.

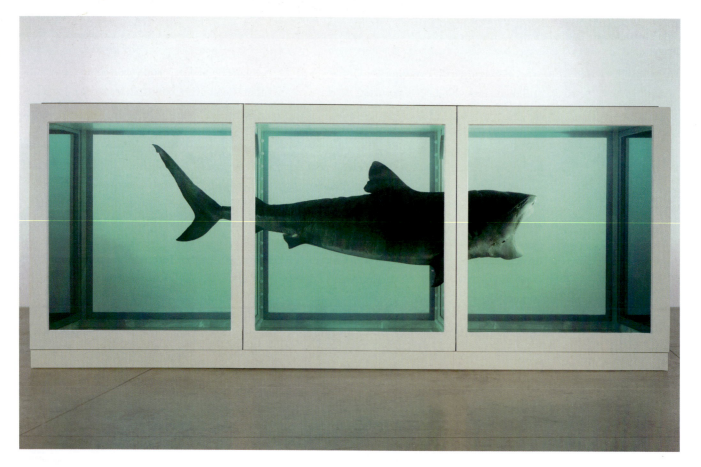

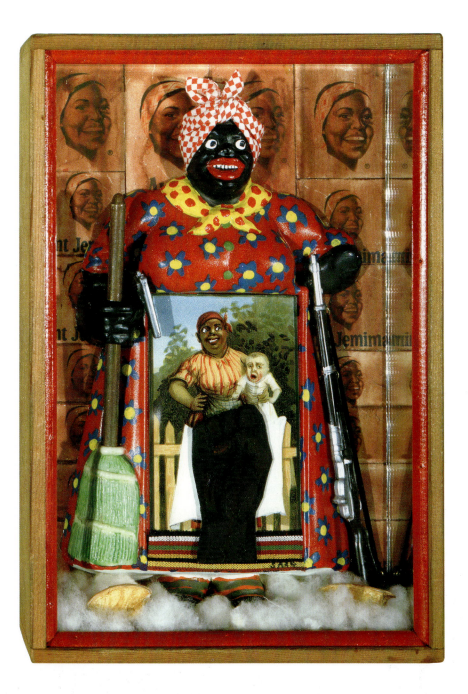

2.4.18 Betye Saar, *The Liberation of Aunt Jemima*, 1972. Mixed media assemblage, 11¾ x 8 x 2¾". Collection University of California, Berkeley Art Museum, California

Hirst is known for creating his sculptures from unusual objects that contrast life and death.

Assemblage

The practice of gathering objects and fabricating them into a work of art is called **assemblage**. The gathered objects, sometimes called **found objects**, are repurposed so that they support the visual ideas and compositions of the artist. When the contemporary African-American artist Betye Saar (b. 1926) created the work *The Liberation of Aunt Jemima* (**2.4.18**), she collected a variety of different found objects, such as cotton, syrup-bottle labels, and a stereotypical "Mammy" doll, and assembled them in a wooden box. The objects symbolize the relics and memorabilia of both personal and societal history as it relates to issues of gender and race; these pieces represent influences that were important to traditional African groups. Saar is interested in exploring themes of personal and communal identity: her art examines the survival of African traditions in black culture and often challenges stereotypes, for example those represented by such figures as "Aunt Jemima."

Space: the distance between identifiable points or planes

Assemblage: artwork made of three-dimensional materials, including found objects

Found image or **object:** an image or object found by an artist and presented, with little or no alteration, as part of a work or as a finished work of art in itself

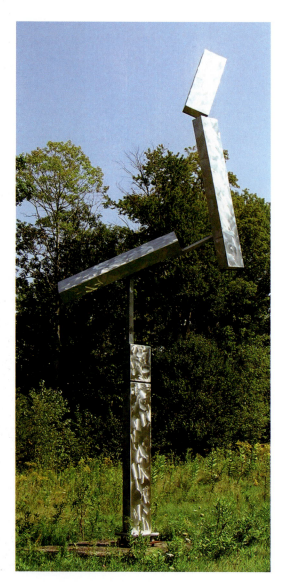

2.4.19 Pablo Picasso, *Bull's Head*, 1942. Assemblage of bicycle seat and handlebars, 13¼ × 17⅛ × 7½". Musée Picasso, Paris, France

2.4.20 (right) George Rickey, *Breaking Column*, 1986 (completed by the artist's estate, 2009). Stainless steel, 9'11⅜" × 5½". Contemporary Museum, Honolulu, Hawaii

Artifact: an object made by a person
Readymade: an everyday object presented as a work of art
Appropriation: the deliberate incorporation in an artwork of material originally created by other artists
Kinetic art: art, usually three-dimensional, with moving parts, impelled by wind, personal interaction, or motors
Medium (plural media): the material on or from which an artist chooses to make a work of art, for example canvas and oil paint, marble, engraving, video, or architecture
Installation: originally referring to the hanging of pictures and arrangement of objects in an exhibition, installation may also refer to an intentional environment created as a completed artwork.

Readymades

In the early twentieth century, a few artists began to create works using as raw materials **artifacts** that already existed. Sometimes, they simply decided that found objects were works of art. Pablo Picasso (1881–1973) once took the handlebars and the seat of a bicycle and combined them to make his *Bull's Head* (**2.4.19**). Such artworks are known as **readymades**. Although Picasso did not make the individual parts, he arranged them in such a way that they resemble a bull's head, yet they are also readily recognizable as parts of a bicycle. The artist's intent was both a serious and a humorous attempt to redefine art.

Picasso was following in the footsteps of the French artist Marcel Duchamp (1887–1968), who pioneered a practice known as **appropriation**, as a way of challenging traditional ideas about art. Duchamp argued that any object, by virtue of being chosen and presented by an artist, can become a work of art. This way of making art is known as appropriation, because the artist appropriates (takes over) a pre-existing image or object and alters its appearance in a way that changes its original meaning or purpose. For Duchamp, the

act of discovery (of conceiving the artwork) was the most important part of the artist's process; he believed that it is the artist's original interpretation of the appropriated object that makes it art. "I chose it!" Duchamp exclaimed, creating endless possibilities for artists to redefine art as ideas, and help us see things differently.

Kinetic and Light Sculpture

Technological advances in our society have created more opportunities for creativity. Sculptors who work with movement and light express their ideas in ways that would not have been possible just a century or two before. These moving and lighted sculptural works, similarly to those of the Constructivists, rely on

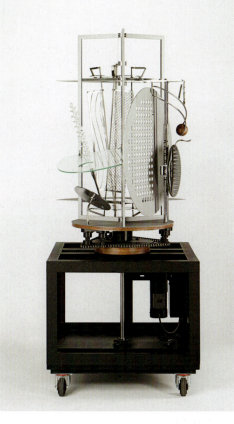

2.4.21 László Moholy-Nagy, *Light Prop for an Electric Stage*, 1929–30. Exhibition replica, constructed 2006, through the courtesy of Hattula Moholy-Nagy. Metal, plastics, glass, paint, and wood, with electric motor, 59½ × 27⅝ × 27⅝″. Harvard Art Museums, Busch-Reisinger Museum, Cambridge, Massachusetts

2.4.22 Athena Tacha in collaboration with EDAW of Alexandria, Virginia, *Star Fountain* (night view), 2009. Sandstone, cast stone, granite, brick, glass, animated RGB-LEDs. Muhammad Ali Plaza, Louisville, Kentucky

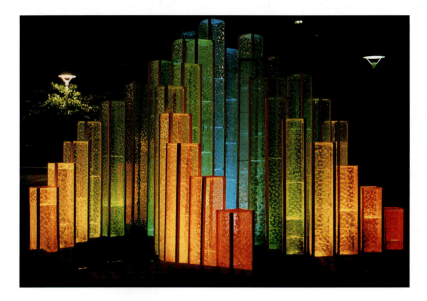

mechanical engineering as well as the creative input of the artist.

Sculpture that moves is called **kinetic** sculpture. The American artist George Rickey (1907–2002) designed works that were carefully balanced so that they could pivot in a variety of directions and provide an infinite number of constantly changing views. His *Breaking Column* is moved by the slightest current of air; it also has a motor, and moves even when there is no wind (**2.4.20**).

One of the first artists to merge movement, lighting, and performance into a single work was the Hungarian László Moholy-Nagy (1895–1946). Moholy-Nagy was interested in the work of the Constructivists and wanted to incorporate technology into his art. The sculpture *Light Prop for an Electric Stage*, initially created as a stage lighting device, eventually became the main character in a film, also by Moholy-Nagy. The work has a motor that moves a series of perforated discs so that they cross in front of the lighting unit (**2.4.21**). This creates a constantly changing sculptural object, and the changes in lighting also influence the surrounding environment.

Moholy-Nagy's investigations into the use of light influenced artists who were interested in effects produced by controlling the lighting of an interior space. Through the use of light an artist can change how a viewer perceives a three-dimensional space. Carefully organized light projection can create the illusion that a surface exists in three dimensions even if it has only two.

Installations

Modern artists have explored many ways of expanding the range of sculpture as a **medium**. **Installation** sculpture involves the construction of a space or the assembly of objects to create an environment; we are encouraged to experience the work physically using all our senses, perhaps entering the work itself.

An installation work by the Greek-born artist Athena Tacha (b. 1936) deals with action. The movement in Tacha's work implies the action of dance, as the rhythms of her installations flow and repeat in graceful patterns. One gets the fullest impression of these rhythms at night, as her works are infused with constantly changing colored lighting. *Star Fountain* (**2.4.22**) is a series of vertical glass columns organized into a spiraling shape, with color changes over a four-minute time span. The reflecting water and the adjacent *Dancing Steps* enliven the surrounding plaza, enveloping those near by.

Perspectives on Art: Antony Gormley
Asian Field

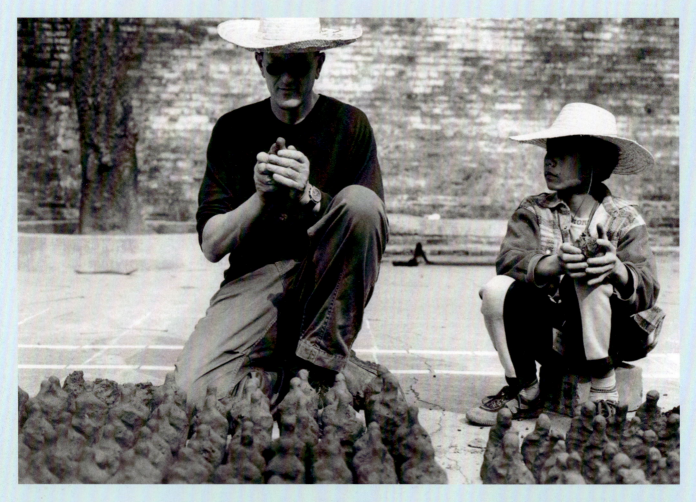

2.4.23a Antony Gormley, *Asian Field*, work in progress, 2003. Clay from Guangdong Province, China. Hand-sized clay elements made in collaboration with people from Xiangshan village. Xiangshan, China

Antony Gormley (b. 1950) is a British sculptor whose work is concerned with the human form (**2.4.23a**). *He developed the vast installation,* Asian Field *(1991–2003), as an art project beginning in 1983* (**2.4.23b**).

Traveling to communities around the world, Gormley handed out fist-sized balls of clay and instructed participants to form them into an image of their own bodies, working as quickly as possible. Then participants were told to place the figure in front of them, at arm's length, and give it eyes. Gormley explains his approach to the human form and to Asian Field *in particular.*

The figures in my work are not portraits, they are corpographs: a three-dimensional equivalent of a photograph but which is left as a negative, as a void. They don't do anything, they don't represent anything, they are simply still objects in a moving world. And their meaning, if they have one, comes only when they act as a response to the lived time that surrounds them.

To make a work I have to stand very still and concentrate. One of the most direct ways to re-establish direct first-hand experience is to close your eyes and be in whatever that space is that you find yourself in. I've called this experience lots of things: the space of the body, the space behind appearance, the darkness of the body, the space of embodied consciousness.

My work is at its best when inserted into the stream of everyday life—whether that's in rooms, standing on walls or ceilings, or on the street. They may look at first hand like statues, but in fact they are simply lived moments made into matter. They identify a space that was occupied at a particular time by a particular body, and by implication can be occupied by anyone.

I am working in the most direct way I can to build a bridge between art and life. What the effect of my works is on their environment and on the internal condition of others I have no control over. I think of my works as objects that act on the space in which they are placed, allowing it to become a space for imagination and reflection.

The *Field* works were made differently from much of my work, in collaboration with large numbers of people. In each rendition of the installation there are thousands of clay figures, each modeled by an individual hand. The figures have empty voids for eyes. This is because sight is itself a form of blindness. It wraps us in a world of names and forms that are immediately translated into symbols, signs, emblems.

2.4.23b Antony Gormley, *Asian Field*, 2003. 210,000 hand-sized clay elements, installation view, warehouse of former Shanghai No. 10 Steelworks, China

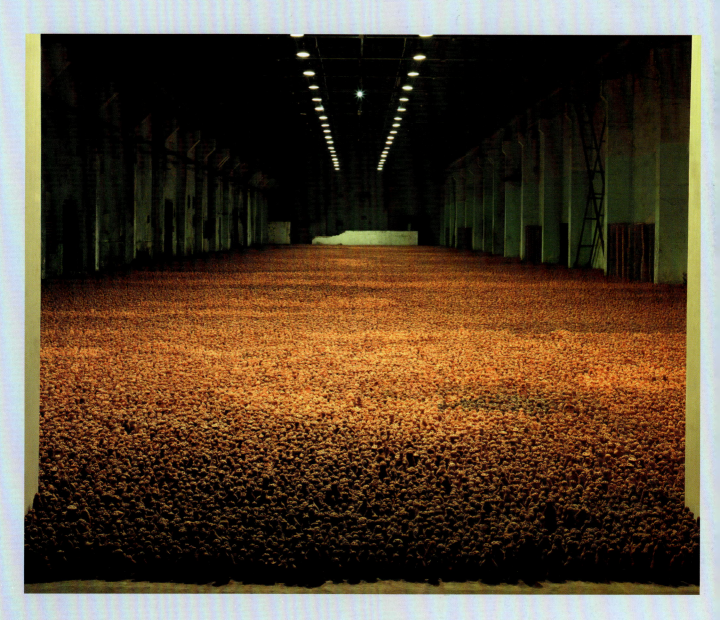

Active Learning Exercises

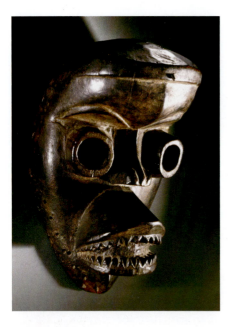

2.4.24 A mask of the Dan or neighboring peoples (Dan/Guere culture, E. Liberia, W. Guinea, Ivory Coast) *c.* 19th century. Wood and paint. Robert Sainsbury Collection, England

1. A relief sculpture is often a raised surface that is intended to be viewed from one side. Using cardboard, glue, a pencil, and a utility knife, a relief sculpture of a face can be made. Start by considering **2.4.24**, an African mask, and use it as a guide. Cut out a shape similar to the overall shape of the mask and use it as your base. Next, cut out shapes that define the shape and size of the other facial features—eyes, nose, and mouth—and glue them into place. To define these facial features even more, cut out smaller versions of the previous and glue them, centered on the larger features, on the same mask. Do this again, two more times, each time making the shape smaller. Hang this object on the wall and look carefully at the shadows that are created. How do light and shadow affect the relief? How do you think painting the object white or black would change it?

2. A constructed sculpture is one that uses common building practices, such as nailing or bolting, to connect the parts. Using cardboard, glue, tape, a pencil, and scissors, re-create *Constructed Head No. 2* (**2.4.16**, p. 258). You will need to look closely and cut out the individual pieces, then construct them in a way that is similar to that used by the artist. Feel free to tape and glue them into place. Remember that Gabo was interested in giving the feeling of a three-dimensional object using **two-dimensional** planes. Could this process be used for other shapes?

3. Readymades are works of art that are created by changing the purpose of an existing object. For example, Picasso used bicycle parts to create a sculptural bull's head. Try looking for objects that could be repurposed into readymades, and think about what kinds of objects produce the most interesting or effective works of art.

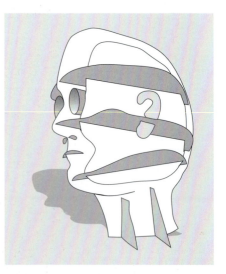

Two-dimensional: having height and width

Images Related to **2.4**: Sculpture

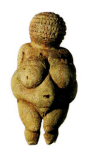

4.9.1 *Woman from Willendorf, c.* 24,000–22,000 BCE, p. 659

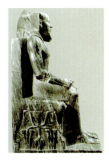

3.1.15 Statue of Khafre with Horus, Egypt, *c.* 2500 BCE, p. 375

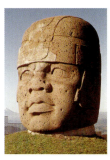

1.2.13 Colossal Olmec Head, 1500–1300 BCE, p. 75

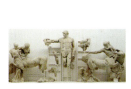

4.2.1 Apollo, Centaur, and Lapith, *c.* 460 BCE, p. 575

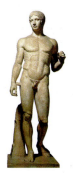

3.1.25 Polykleitos, *Doryphoros*, (Roman version) 120–50 BCE, p. 382

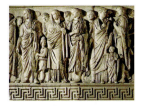

1.2.6 Imperial Procession from the Ara Pacis Augustae, 13 BCE, p. 71

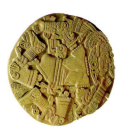

3.4.17 *Aztec stone disc with Coyolxauhqui*, 1400–1520, p. 443

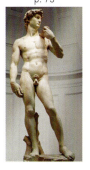

3.6.21 Michelangelo, *David*, 1501–4, p. 483

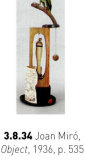

0.0.22 Benin hip pendant, mid-16th century, p. 43

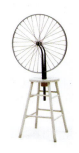

1.5.4 Gianlorenzo Bernini, *Apollo and Daphne*, 1622–24, p. 121

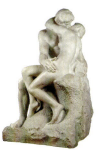

3.8.7 Auguste Rodin, *The Kiss*, 1886, p. 519

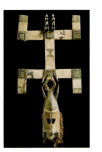

3.5.6a Kanaga mask, Mali, early 20th century, p. 454

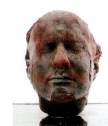

3.8.30 Marcel Duchamp, *Bicycle Wheel*, 1913, p. 533

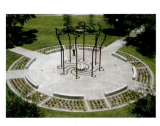

3.8.34 Joan Miró, *Object*, 1936, p. 535

1.2.19 Méret Oppenheim, *Object*, 1936, p. 80

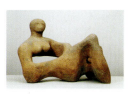

4.9.15 Henry Moore, *Recumbent Figure*, 1938, p. 670

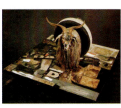

1.6.11 Robert Rauschenberg, *Monogram*, 1955–59, p. 138

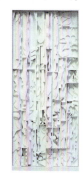

0.0.3 Louise Nevelson, *White Vertical Water*, 1972, p. 28

0.0.15 Marc Quinn, *Self*, 1991, p. 38

1.5.2 Nancy Holt, *Solar Rotary*, 1995, p. 120

2.5

Architecture

Architecture communicates important ideas; it has a special place in our lives. Architecture—design that surrounds and influences us—represents the safety of home, the strength of government, the energy of commercial enterprise, and the power of human innovation. It connects us to our history in a very real way: a historic building shows us how people lived in the past, while a new building adapts design ideas from previous eras to a contemporary context. Architecture suggests feelings of permanence and place. It is no wonder we all have an opinion about a new building, because a building inevitably affects all who see or enter it, whether or not they are aware of this.

Architectural space is the result of thoughtful design by an artist, or by a team of artists working to a common idea. The architect is the master planner who creates a building's overall design. Thoughtful design reflects a building's function and its intended role in the community. For example, an architect designing a college building will consider its users—the instructors and students—and will design classroom spaces that are well lit and flexible. Sometimes an interior designer is responsible for making the space inside appropriate for the building's intended use. In the case of a college classroom, an interior designer will choose colors and furnishings and plan the organization of the space in a way that reflects the needs of students and teachers. A landscape architect may be employed to organize the outdoor spaces around the building. This designer will plan the landscaping, parking, and entry and exit routes to be consistent with the rest of the structure. The architect, interior designer, and landscape architect actively communicate with the building contractors to ensure that the final construction will accord with the design team's intentions.

Structure, Function, and Form

Architecture is principally concerned with structure, function, and **form**. The engineering and science of architecture strives to understand and control the forces pushing or pulling the structure of the building. These forces, called stresses, are constantly at work. When stresses pull they create tension, which lengthens and stretches the materials of the building. When stresses push they create compression, which can squash and shorten the same materials. Architectural engineers work to create balances between tension and compression so that the amount of push equals pull. Each kind of building material resists the stress of compression or tension differently. Architects measure the strength of the material so that they can anticipate and control the balance of forces at work. If balanced correctly, a building can stand for many thousands of years; if not, it may collapse.

The Turkish architect Sinan (1489–1588) was chief architect to the Ottoman court under Sultan Süleyman, who commissioned him to design the magnificent mosque shown in **2.5.1**. Sinan's visionary ingenuity and grasp of engineering

Form: an object that can be defined in three dimensions (height, width, and depth)
Texture: the surface quality of a work, for example fine/coarse, detailed/lacking in detail

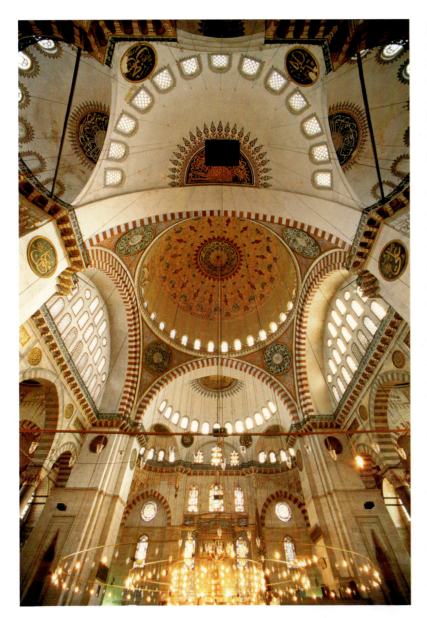

2.5.1 Sinan, Süleymaniye mosque, 1557, Istanbul, Turkey

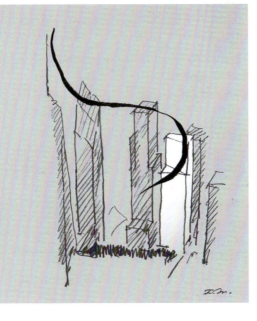

2.5.2 Fumihiko Maki, Sketch of Four World Trade Center, 2006

principles enabled him to develop new ways of opening up the architectural space and creating this extraordinary building, which includes not only the principal dome but also four half-domes around it. The skillful design, perfectly balancing all of the different parts, has enabled this elaborate and complex structure to endure for more than 500 years.

The engineering of a building, or its structural integrity, dictates some of the design decisions. Wood-frame buildings may require waterproof external cladding to protect the timber from damp and rot. Tall office buildings may need to have a strong steel frame (or an alternative) to bear the combined weight of the whole structure (see p. 282).

An architect collects information about the planned location of the building, its place in the community, and its purpose; selects the appropriate building techniques; and decides which materials are needed to construct it.

The location, or site, influences the design. Is the building going to sit on a plain or a mountainside, in a city or a rural community, on a waterfront or in a desert? Each of these sites presents different challenges the design must try to answer. For example, a building facing the sea might need to be strong and resilient to resist the effects of storms, while one in a desert must be made of materials that can help keep the building cool.

Artists must consider the availability and cost of building materials when they plan their projects. The unique character of these materials—for example their flexibility, strength, **texture**, and appearance—also affects the architect's choices.

Although buildings can be some of the largest and most complicated man-made objects, they usually begin from the simplicity of a drawing. Fumihiko Maki (b. 1928) created a simple drawing as he began working on a design for the New World Trade Center in New York City (**2.5.2**). The drawing shows how his building was designed to fit in with other buildings on or around the site by continuing a spiral design.

In a successful architectural work, the final appearance of a building's structure will also reflect—in some way—the community. In

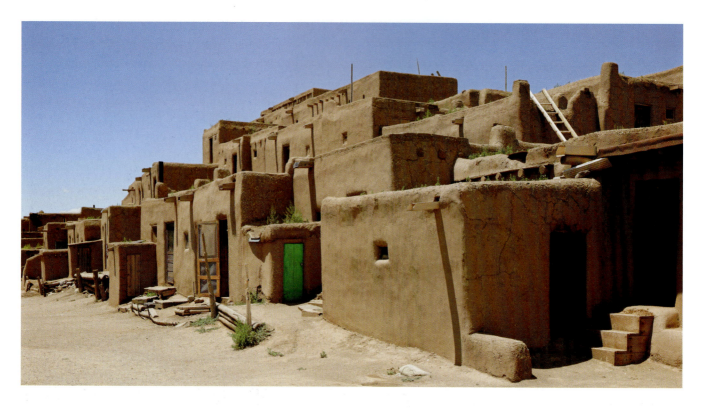

2.5.3 Taos Pueblo, New Mexico, pre-1500

Taos Pueblo, New Mexico, for instance, many buildings are made of adobe brick (**2.5.3**). Their character derives from the available materials, such as the abundance of sand and clay; perhaps the community has traditional standards, such as the building methods and styles of the native Pueblos and Spanish settlers. The architecture of New York City looks very different, but is based on similar principles. Generations of people have admired the coherent **composition** of the forms of the skyscrapers, like a **Cubist** painting, as if the community had somehow combined together as a single artist to make something beautiful (**2.5.4**).

2.5.4 SoHo lofts, New York City

Composition: the overall design or organization of a work

Cubism, Cubist: a twentieth-century art movement that favored a new perspective emphasizing geometric forms; the Cubists were artists who formed part of the movement. "Cubist" is also used to describe their painting style

Monumental: having massive or impressive scale

Span: the distance bridged between two supports, such as columns or walls

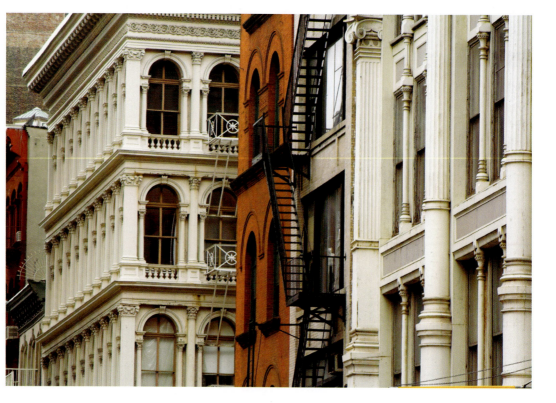

Ancient Construction

Ancient cultures derived their building materials from the Earth. Stone, wood, and clay are plentiful and easily available, but they must be modified for use in architecture. When shaped and used with great care and skill, these raw materials can result in architecture that transcends time.

Basic Load-Bearing Construction

Probably the most direct way to build something is the apparently simple process of piling one stone or brick on top of another, as for example in a Maya pyramid. Such massive load-bearing works have occurred throughout history. Protruding out of the Guatemalan rain forest at Tikal are hundreds of such pyramids that rise sharply toward the sky, emphasizing their role as gateways to the gods (**2.5.5**). Maya pyramids primarily served as platforms for temples. The pyramid that makes up the support for Temple I (**2.5.5**) is basically a carefully organized stack of stones. The weight of the temple structure at the top, which is a three-room building where Maya priests conducted religious rites, bears down on the stone platform beneath it, which, in turn, bears down on the stone platform beneath *it*, and so on, holding all the stones securely in place (**2.5.6**). Construction on this scale required sophisticated engineering and mathematical skills to ensure that such an enormous structure formed a perfectly symmetrical shape that would stand for thousands of years. The ability of the ancient Maya to engineer these massive structures using only stones, with the few tools available at the time, has always been a cause of wonder.

Post-and-Lintel Construction

The **monumental** quality of ancient pyramids stands as a testament to the ingenuity and will of humankind. But these impressive structures did not provide the spacious interiors we have come to expect in everyday architecture. In order to create an interior space, an architect must create a **span**, or a distance between two supports in a structure. One of the oldest and most effective ways of doing this is a system called post-and-lintel construction.

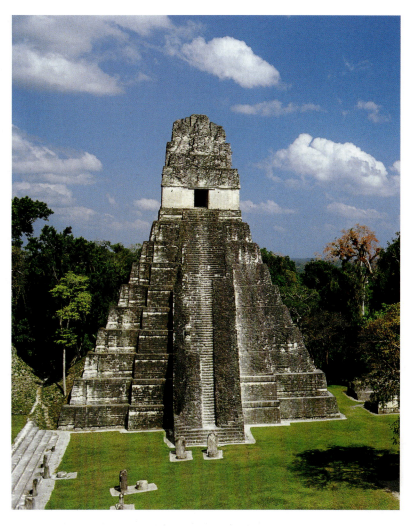

2.5.5 Temple I in the Great Plaza, Maya, *c.* 300–900 CE, Tikal, Guatemala

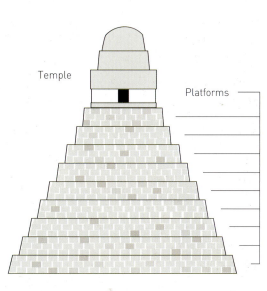

Temple

Platforms

2.5.6 Basic load-bearing architecture: Maya pyramid

Post-and-lintel construction: a horizontal beam (the lintel) supported by a post at either end
Column: freestanding pillar, usually circular in section

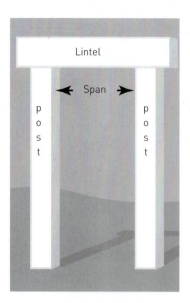

2.5.7 Post-and-lintel construction

2.5.8 Great Court at Temple of Amun-Re, Middle Kingdom, c. 950–730 BCE, Karnak, Egypt

In basic **post-and-lintel construction** (**2.5.7**) the lintel rests on top of two posts. Ancient Egyptian architects built the Temple of Amun-Re at Karnak by placing a series of post-and-lintel spans side by side to create a spacious interior, as seen in the Great Court (**2.5.8**). The temple also includes an architectural space known as a hypostyle hall, a room created by using a series of **columns**, or a colonnade, to support a flat ceiling. The hall was used by Egyptian priests for rituals to worship the god Amun-Re, while ordinary people stood outside in an open courtyard. Amun-Re's temple, still one of the largest religious structures in the world, is just one of many at Karnak.

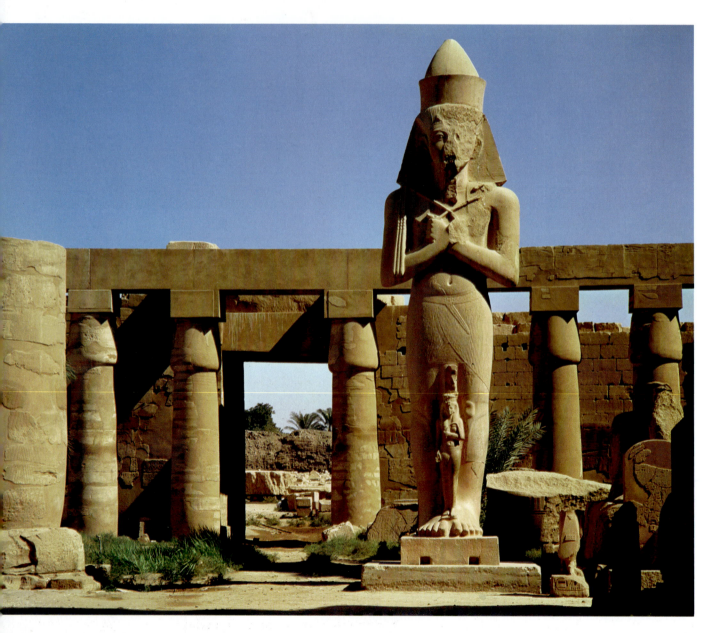

Post-and-Lintel in Classical Greek Architecture

The architects of ancient Greece must have been aware of the majestic architecture of the Nile valley, where such monuments as the Temple of Amun-Re (**2.5.8**) can be found. The Greeks adapted the systems invented by the Egyptians and became some of the world's greatest practitioners of post-and-lintel construction. They standardized the basic post, or column (**2.5.9**), an essential point of compression to support the weight of a building. Classical Greek architecture is dominated by the use of columns, a structural element with three basic parts: **capital**, **shaft**, and **base**. The capital, or uppermost part of the column, supplies the transition point from the lintel to the shaft, or main vertical attribute of the post. The base acts as a stabilizing point where the building's weight is concentrated.

The most notable examples of Greek architecture were dedicated to religious use. The decorative styling of Greek temple architecture, like Greek post-and-lintel construction, was standardized into three basic orders: Doric, Ionic, and Corinthian. The Doric order features a simple, round "pillow" capital, a wide, heavy shaft, and the original form had no base. The Ionic order is capped with a scroll-like shape called a volute, and has a thin shaft and an ornate base. The Corinthian order's showy capital is made up of two rows of acanthus leaves with four volutes that protrude near the top. Corinthian columns are slender and have an ornate base.

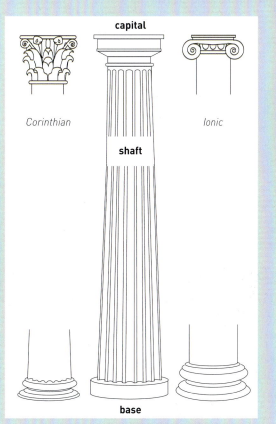

capital

Corinthian

Ionic

shaft

base

2.5.9 Parts of a column: capital, shaft, base

The Temple of Athena Nike (**2.5.10**) is attributed to the Greek architect Kallikrates (active from *c.* 450 BCE). It employs an elegant, thin variant of the Ionic column (so-called from its origin in Ionia, east of the Greek mainland). By using thinner columns, the architect made the statue of the goddess Athena inside the temple seem larger. The building was dedicated to Athena, the patron of the city of Athens where this temple stands.

The ancient Greeks made a lasting impact on Western traditions in architectural style. The Romans quickly adopted Greek orders while adding their own new stylistic accents. Rome's architectural innovations then influenced later styles of the **Renaissance** (see p. 279) and **Baroque**, even being revived again in the eighteenth century to celebrate the rise of democratic government, especially in the US and France. The architectural character of Washington, D.C., with its many columns (the White House is a good example), reflects the ideals of democracy that the ancient Greeks instituted to free citizens of Athens to decide their own destiny.

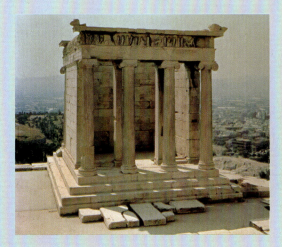

Capital: the architectural feature that crowns a column
Shaft: the main vertical part of a column
Base: the projecting series of blocks between the shaft of a column and its plinth
Renaissance: a period of cultural and artistic change in Europe from the fourteenth to the seventeenth century
Baroque: European artistic and architectural style of the late sixteenth to early eighteenth century, characterized by extravagance and emotional intensity

2.5.10 Kallikrates, Temple of Athena Nike, *c.* 421–415 BCE, Acropolis, Athens, Greece

Arches in Ancient Architecture

A limitation of early post-and-lintel architecture is that the lintels could not span large spaces. Stone, while enormously strong in compression, is fairly weak in tension. Since stone cannot stretch, its use risks creating a weakness in the middle of a span that can snap under heavy pressure. Architects who want to design large interior spaces in stone have to be aware of the weight of the building constantly pressing down. The ancient Babylonians in Mesopotamia (modern-day Iraq) and the Mycenaeans of early Greece both employed the **corbeled** arch (**2.5.11**) as a solution to this problem. The stepping inward of successive layers of stonework over the doorway allows for the compression created by the weight of the building to be directed outward through **cantilevered** (secured at only one end) stones, rather than downward. This reduces the pressure on the structure and allows the architect to design and span larger spaces.

Early inhabitants of the Greek coastline experimented with ways to open up interior spaces through the use of corbeled arches. The entrance to the Treasury of Atreus (also called the Tomb of Agamemnon: **2.5.12**), built around 1250 BCE, provides a glimpse into ancient

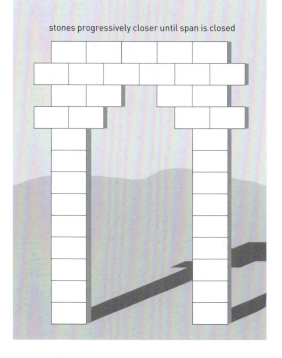

2.5.11 Corbeled arch

stones progressively closer until span is closed

construction using a corbeled arch. Although a lintel interrupts the space between the doorway and the arch above, the progressive cantilevering of stones above the lintel provides an additional opening so that more light can enter the chamber beyond.

The Romans perfected the rounded arch (**2.5.13**), which was a more efficient way of

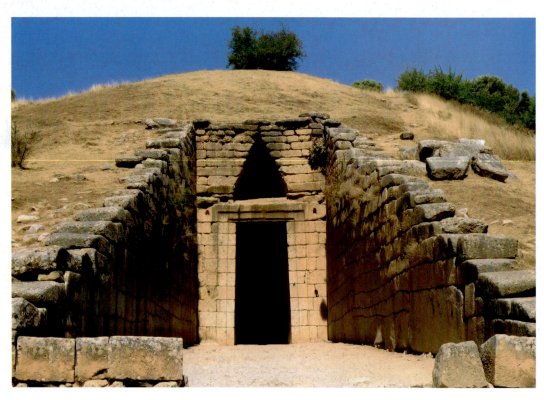

2.5.12 Entrance, Treasury of Atreus, *c.* 1250 BCE, Mycenae, Greece

Corbeled: with a series of corbels—architectural feature made of stone, brick, wood, etc.—each projecting beyond the one below
Cantilever: a long support that projects out from a structure

2.5.13 (right) Arch construction

2.5.14 (bottom) Pont du Gard, first century CE, Nîmes, France

2.5.15 (below, right) Barrel vault

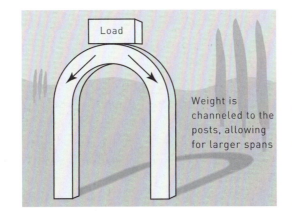

Load

Weight is channeled to the posts, allowing for larger spans

Aqueduct: a structure designed to carry water, often over long distances
Vault: an arch-like structure supporting a ceiling or roof

distributing compressive stress over the whole of the structure by spreading the weight of the building outward along the entire span of the arc. Its efficiency helped them span wider spaces than any previous architects had managed. The upper level of the Pont du Gard, in southern France, is a Roman **aqueduct**, built to move fresh water from mountain springs 30 miles away to the populated territories recently conquered by Rome (**2.5.14**). The lower level is a bridge across the river. The goal of the aqueduct was to create a consistent downhill path for the water: 1 in. down for every 33 in. along. The Romans made this impressive structure without any mortar holding the stones together, so perfectly were they cut to fit. After conquering an area, the Romans often built aqueducts and roads. These structures benefitted the local community, projected Roman imperial power, and enabled the army to move quickly across its new territory.

Vaults

Roman architects used three important architectural structures: the arch, vault, and dome. A **vault** is an arch that has been extended like a long hallway to create an open space overhead. The most common type of vault, the barrel vault, consists of a long, semicircular arch (**2.5.15**). The vault helped to span larger

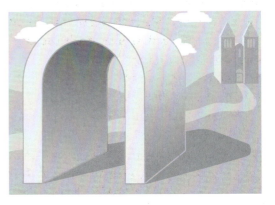

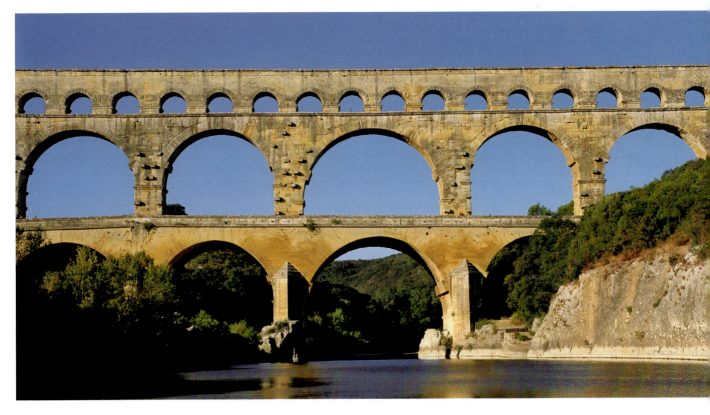

Abbot Suger and the Dynamics of Gothic Architecture

The somber, austere interiors of Romanesque churches led one particular church leader to seek innovations in the prevailing architectural style. Abbot Suger (1081–1151) had the Abbey Church of Saint-Denis, near Paris, France, rebuilt from its original Romanesque style to provide a much grander place for worship. The Abbey Church of Saint-Denis was the national church of France; it housed the remains of the country's patron saint, Saint Denis, and many French kings. Suger decided that the existing church was too small and lacked sufficient grandeur. Two ideas were central to Suger's new church: the worshiper should be bathed in divine light, and should feel lifted up toward heaven.

Adding larger windows to the structure could provide more light, but that would weaken the walls and increase the chance of a collapse. The walls of Saint-Denis had to be supported by external structures. Suger's plan incorporated an architectural structure called a **flying buttress** (see **2.5.17a** and **2.5.17b**), designed to transfer the weight of the ceiling outward beyond the walls. This idea worked well: as the walls no longer needed to bear the weight of the building, the windows could be much larger to allow light into the interior. Suger was still not satisfied, however, because the light was not yet "divine."

Suger had seen small colored-glass windows in German churches and decided that the methods used to make these smaller

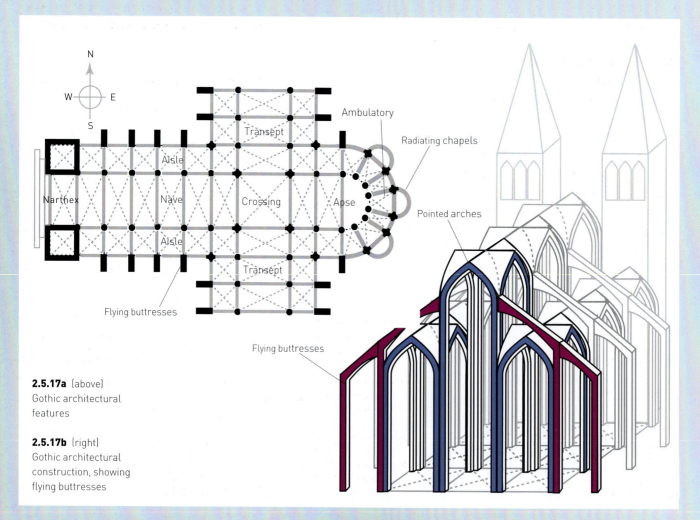

2.5.17a (above)
Gothic architectural features

2.5.17b (right)
Gothic architectural construction, showing flying buttresses

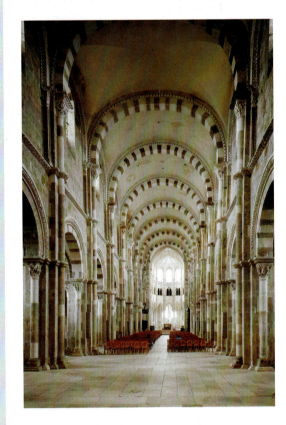

2.5.18 Stained-glass window, Abbey Church of Saint-Denis, France

areas of an interior space; this was an especially important point during the European Middle Ages, as churches became more significant centers of community activities.

The Church of Sainte-Madeleine at Vézelay (**2.5.16**) in France was a stop along the Christian pilgrimage route to the holy church Santiago de Compostela in Spain. The builders of the **Romanesque** church at Vézelay needed to create a space that could accommodate large numbers of visitors. Their solution was to use the barrel vault, but they had to deal with an important limitation of vault construction. Because the weight of the vault thrusts outward, the walls supporting it must be massive so as not to collapse. Vaulted **aisles** counteract this outward pressure on the walls and support both sides of the **nave**. Even though Romanesque churches are large enough for plenty of pilgrims and worshipers, the thick walls have only small windows, creating dark and gloomy interior spaces. One visionary, named Abbot Suger, was not satisfied with the dreariness of Romanesque architecture and embarked on the formulation

2.5.16 Church of Sainte-Madeleine, Vézelay, France

windows could be applied on a larger scale. By dividing up the window spaces into components of a larger design, Suger's glaziers were able to make enormous **stained-glass** windows (**2.5.18**). The light would pass through images based on biblical narratives and be projected onto the worshiper. This was Suger's "divine light."

What about Suger's other requirement, that the worshiper feel lifted up toward heaven? The rounded arch of Romanesque churches tended to appear squat, and Suger wanted an arch that would raise the worshiper's gaze upward. He achieved this by adding a point to the arch. **Pointed arches** are structural features that help conduct the downward thrust of the vault outward, but they also have a strong upward visual **emphasis**. They could be arranged so that two vaults intersected to form **rib vaults**, which could be repeated in rows to open up long areas. Often associated with pointed arches, rib vaults appear in some earlier structures, but they were used throughout Saint-Denis. Suger, through his role in creating this remarkable building, was pivotal in establishing this highly influential architectural style, which came to be known as Gothic.

Romanesque: an early medieval European style of architecture based on Roman-style rounded arches and heavy construction
Aisles: in a basilica or other church, the spaces between the columns of the nave and the side walls
Nave: the central space of a cathedral or basilica

of a new, more dynamic style that was to become one of the most important and influential movements in Western architecture (see Box: Abbot Suger and the Dynamics of Gothic Architecture, pp. 274–75).

Domes

Abbot Suger had said he wanted his church to be more impressive than the Church of Hagia Sophia (Holy Wisdom) in Constantinople (modern Istanbul, Turkey). Hagia Sophia is a magnificent Byzantine (Late Roman, with Eastern influences) structure that had already been standing for more than 500 years by Suger's

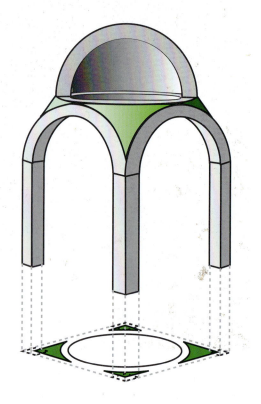

2.5.20 Pendentives

2.5.19 Hagia Sophia, 532–35 CE, Istanbul, Turkey

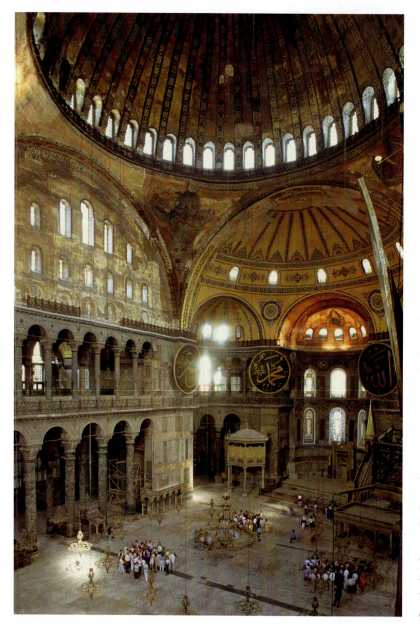

time. Its most impressive feature is its enormous **dome** roof (**2.5.19**). Structurally, a dome is like an arch rotated 360 degrees on its vertical **axis**. Shaped like an umbrella or a ball cut in half, it is a very strong structure. Domes can span large areas, because, as in other arch structures, the weight of the dome is dispersed outward toward the walls. Most dome constructions require the support of thick walls or some other system for distributing the weight. The dome of Hagia Sophia is so large and high that, for nearly 1,000 years, it was the largest interior space of any cathedral in the world.

The inside of Hagia Sophia is illuminated by a series of **clerestory windows** in the lower portion of the dome and in the walls just below it. The dome rests on four arches. **Pendentives** (**2.5.20**) elegantly transfer the load of the circular dome to the four massive pillars of the square building beneath it. It is no wonder that Suger admired and revered the architecture of this building.

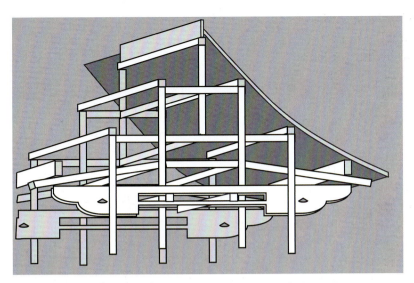

2.5.21 Post-and-beam architecture

2.5.22 Horyu-ji (Horyu Temple), Kondo and pagoda, *c.* 7th century, Nara, Japan

Post-and-Beam (Wooden) Architecture

The post-and-beam construction technique (**2.5.21**) has been used to build some of the world's finest wooden architecture. Two of the oldest wooden buildings in the world are in the grounds of the Buddhist Horyu-ji (Horyu Temple) in Nara, Japan (**2.5.22**). The construction of the Horyu-ji complex was the idea of the Japanese emperor Yomei, who hoped to gain spiritual favor so he could recover from illness, but he died before work started. In 607 Empress Suiko and Crown Prince Shotoku fulfilled the emperor's dying wish and built the first temple in the complex. Since then it has withstood the ravages of time, and is an example of the durability of well-constructed wooden buildings.

These buildings use a complex post-and-beam design that is both beautiful and structurally sound. Crossbeams and counter-beams create a series of layers supporting the elaborate curved roof. The main building of the complex, the Kondo, is almost 61 ft. long by 50 ft. wide. This same structural design also enabled the architects to construct buildings that were very tall: the Goju-no-To (Five-story Pagoda) is 122 ft. tall. The pagoda's height was designed to impress rather than serve any practical purpose, since it is not possible to enter the top four floors.

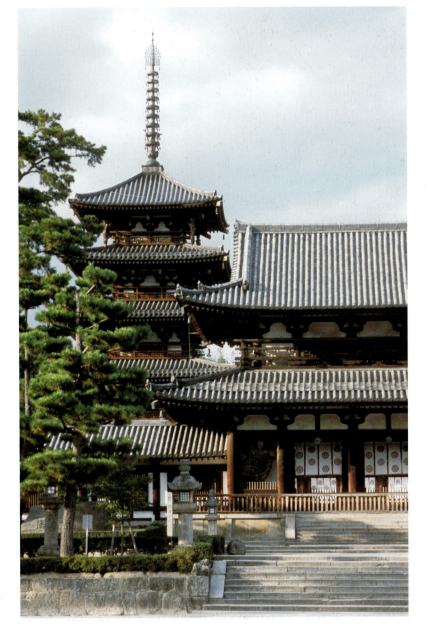

Gateway to Art: The Taj Mahal
Engineering Eternity

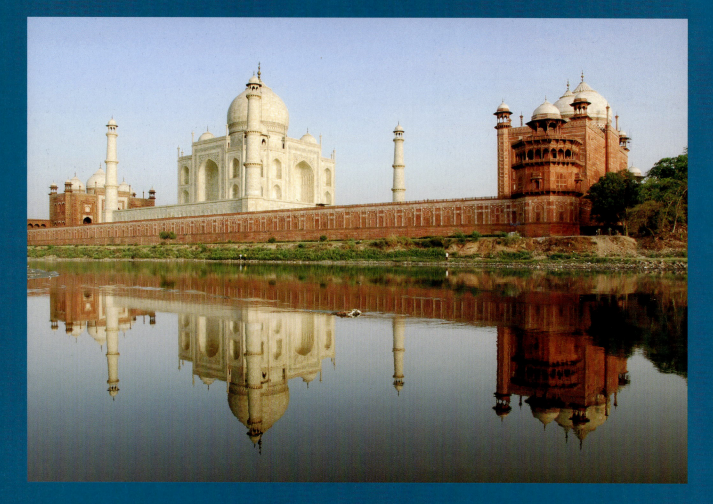

In 1631, the Mughal Emperor Shah Jahan experienced a terrible personal tragedy when his third wife, Mumtaz Mahal, died in childbirth. Mumtaz, a Persian princess, had devoted her life to Shah Jahan, even, while pregnant, accompanying him on multiple military campaigns. The Shah's grief was so profound he dedicated all of his vast resources to the creation of a mausoleum complex in her honor that would endure throughout eternity.

The Shah assembled a team of architects and engineers who, under his supervision, would build a symbol of his love that could defy the instability of this world. The lead architect was probably Ustad Ahmad Lahauri, who borrowed design elements from Persia, India, and Turkey, incorporating them into a masterpiece of Islamic symmetry. The Taj Mahal (2.5.23) was built of white marble with a unique crystalline character that absorbs and radiates the light of northern India. When it was first constructed, many artists created lavish decorative work for the buildings on the site, including mosaic inlays, relief carvings, gold details, and inlaid precious stones.

2.5.23 View of the Taj Mahal from the Yamuna River, Agra, India

2.5.24 Diagram illustrating the support structure of the Taj Mahal

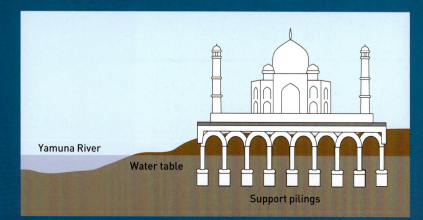

The central dome is 58 ft. in diameter and 213 ft. tall. The structure is completely symmetrical both when viewed from above and from any of its four sides. Four domed chambers emanate from this central dome, balanced on an octagon-shaped platform. Four towers called minarets, each 162 ft. high, frame the corners of the large structure. The minarets and pointed domes are characteristic of Islamic art.

Because Shah Jahan wished for a pastoral site, the complex was built next to the Yamuna River, away from the hustle and bustle of nearby Agra. Because the building was so close to the river, which would rise and fall with the seasons, a clever combination of stone filler material and wooden supports was constructed to hold the foundation in place.

The promise of a masterwork that would endure throughout eternity has been challenged in recent years, as experts have reported threats to the longevity of the building. Discoloration of the marble has led some to believe that polluted air, produced as India grows into a world economic power, is causing a yellowing of the marble surfaces. That concern is dwarfed by more serious issues regarding the integrity of the structure's foundation-support system as river conditions change. The support structure (**2.5.24**), which incorporates submerged sal (a teak-like timber) and ebony wood, may be in jeopardy as river levels drop, allowing the wood to dry out and contract. Recent water-management projects leave the riverbed nearly dry for months. Cracks have been observed in the Taj Mahal's marble structure and many fear that this building, which has so far transcended time, may not be able to survive the realities of the mortal world for ever.

Central-plan church: church design, often in the shape of a cross with all four arms of equal length

Classical Architectural Styles

Since the fall of the Roman Empire, architects of Western civilization have sought to revive the majesty displayed in the architectural style of the Greeks and Romans. The Romans had incorporated the unique architectural designs of the Greeks into their own after conquering Greek territory by 46 CE. These buildings endured a millennium of disrepair, surviving the ravages of time to a significant degree and affirming the great architectural engineering of the ancients. As Italian city-states, such as Florence, gained greater economic power in the fourteenth century, it became possible to erect large architectural projects in homage to the monumental Classical ruins that dotted the Italian and Greek landscapes. So, it was natural that the architects of the Renaissance looked to the Greeks and Romans for inspiration.

One of the great architects of the High Renaissance who drew inspiration from the ancients was Donato Bramante (1444–1514). Bramante is credited with introducing the architectural style of the High Renaissance when he built a memorial at the place where St. Peter was believed to have been crucified. The Tempietto (Italian for "small temple") is a **central-plan** church with a dome in Rome, Italy (**2.5.25**). The circular plan and dome reflect

2.5.25 Donato Bramante, Tempietto of San Pietro, *c.* 1502. Montorio, Rome, Italy

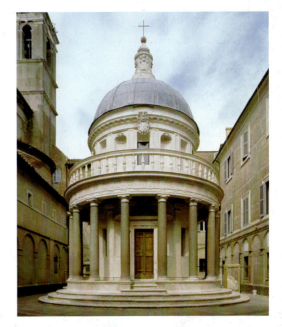

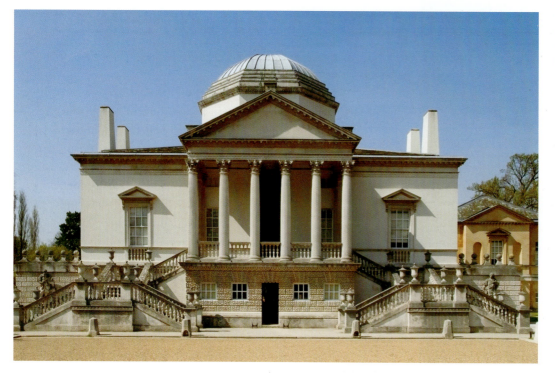

2.5.26 Lord Burlington, Chiswick House, 1729. Chiswick, London, England

influences from Roman domed structures, for example the remains of Hadrian's villa at Tivoli, and colonnaded Greek temples. Bramante, like many Renaissance architects, particularly sought to design works that used geometric shapes and forms, such as circles, spheres, and cylinders.

The architectural style of the Greeks and Romans was once again revived during the mid-eighteenth century. This renewed Classical style was a reaction against the more opulent and ornamented Baroque and **Rococo** styles that had dominated the previous two centuries. Appropriately labeled Neoclassicism, it sprang from the orderly attention to simple geometric shapes and forms that had characterized the architectural styles of the ancients. One of the first expressions of Neoclassical architecture was designed by an English aristocrat named Richard Boyle, better known as Lord Burlington. His design for Chiswick House (**2.5.26**) exemplifies the character of earlier Classical styles, but also integrates more contemporary elements, such as the chimneys that straddle the domed central roof. The design reflects an interest in the historical beginnings of Western architecture combined with the practical concerns of the eighteenth century.

The Emergence of the Methods and Materials of the Modern World

In the nineteenth century, iron, steel, and concrete became both less costly and more

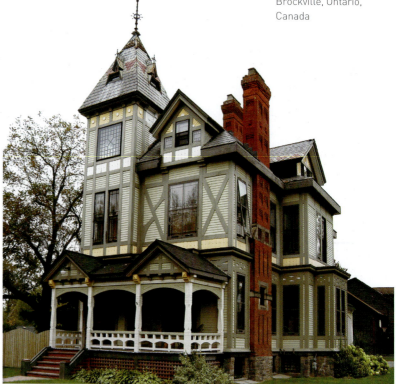

2.5.27 Stick Style house using balloon framing, Brockville, Ontario, Canada

widely available, and so came into common architectural use. New possibilities emerged as architects began to examine innovative ways to control tension and compression. Buildings could be built taller and in different configurations. Architects found exciting new ways to distribute the stress forces in their buildings. New types of building emerged, and the use of previously untried materials made buildings look radically different.

An entirely different type of wooden construction was invented in the United States in 1832. Balloon framing (**2.5.27**) involves the fabrication of lightweight wooden frames to support the structure, instead of utilizing heavy timbers. It was introduced when the advent of power sawing could efficiently and economically produce smaller cross-section lumber from saw logs. The Stick Style took advantage of balloon framing to support a decorative design that often used asymmetry with steep roofs to create a dynamic visual statement. Originally balloon framing was a derisive term used by builders who stayed with traditional building methods and felt the new method was too fragile to support a building. Today, however, most houses in America are built using this method.

Cast-Iron Architecture

Cast iron has been available to humankind since ancient times. Iron is a more flexible material than stone. Molten iron can be cast in a mold to almost any shape, but it was not until the eighteenth century that it could be smelted in large enough quantities to play a significant role in building. An important example of the use of cast iron during the Industrial Revolution was the Crystal Palace, designed by Sir Joseph Paxton (1803–1865) for the Great Exhibition of 1851 in London (**2.5.28**). This event was intended to promote trade, and to showcase Great Britain's goods, services, and technical innovation— for which the building was a very good advertisement. The walls and roof were of glass, supported by the skeletal cast-iron structure.

Rococo: decorative artwork style featuring elaborately curved lines and organic forms of ornament

2.5.28 Joseph Paxton, Crystal Palace, 1851, London. 19th-century engraving

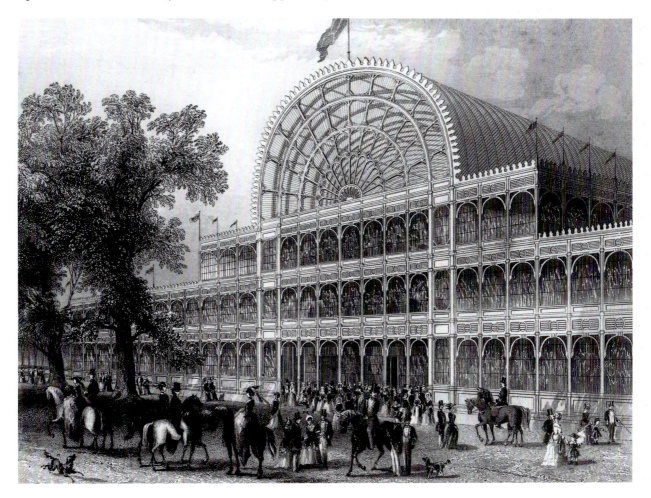

The building was more than a third of a mile long; it was completed in only eight months by 2,000 men; and it used 4,500 tons of cast iron and 990,000 square feet of glass.

The Crystal Palace inspired other architects to work with iron, including French engineer Gustave Eiffel. It was eventually dismantled and reassembled in south London, where it became an exhibition center and concert hall. It was destroyed by fire in 1936.

Steel-Frame Construction

The use of cast iron for construction opened up new possibilities for architects. Cast iron was stronger than wood and more flexible than stone. It could be shaped into any form and was cheap, since iron ore was plentiful. Steel, a material made from iron and a small quantity of carbon, was stronger than pure iron and had even greater potential.

One architect who noted the advantages of steel was Louis Sullivan (1856–1924), called the "father of **Modernism**," who became a pioneer in the creation of the modern skyscraper. Sullivan, who attended Massachusetts Institute of Technology at the age of sixteen and took his first architect job at seventeen, participated in the rebuilding of Chicago after the Great Fire of 1871. Chicago provided fertile ground for creative young architects, and Sullivan pushed the use of steel frame to new heights.

Although Sullivan was based in Chicago, one of his masterpieces is in St. Louis, Missouri. The

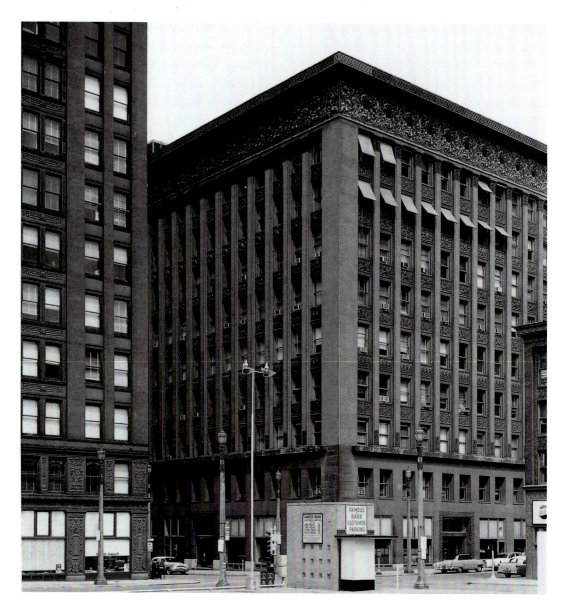

2.5.29 Louis Sullivan, Wainwright Building, 1890–91, St. Louis, Missouri

Wainwright Building, a ten-story office building, is one of the world's oldest skyscrapers (**2.5.29**). In this building Sullivan obeys his famous phrase, "form follows function," by providing versatile interior space. Because the steel frame supports the building, and because it is mostly located at its outer edges, the space of the interior can easily be reconfigured to meet the specific needs of the user.

The skyscraper was a completely new idea, and architects like Sullivan had no precedents on which to base their design. The Wainwright Building reflects the elements of a column (base, shaft, capital [**2.5.9**, p. 271]) in the organization of the exterior. Representing the capital, at the top of the building, is a **cornice**, or protruding ledge, which is highly ornamented with designs derived from Gothic cathedrals. The middle and tallest area shows strong vertical emphasis, with its projecting rectangular-section shafts and high, narrow windows. The lower section (base) shows little ornamentation and reflects ideas of the time about the frivolous nature of ornament. Later architects would avoid ornament altogether and rely on the **aesthetic** characteristics of the structure to provide excitement and interest in their design.

Because steel frames carry the load of the building, many Modernist architects realized there was no need to use a facing material, such as brick; the entire side of the building could be sheathed in glass. The simplicity of this idea captured the imagination of such remarkable architects as Germany's Ludwig Mies van der Rohe (1886–1969) (**2.5.30**), who proclaimed "less is more," and the Swiss Le Corbusier (1887–1965), who called a building a "machine for living." (See Box: Contrasting Ideas in Modern Architecture, p. 284.) A building could now reflect its surroundings while also giving people inside it a spectacular view of the landscape.

When it opened on January 4, 2010, the Burj Khalifa (**2.5.31**) became the most impressive piece of steel-frame construction in the world, as well as the tallest man-made structure. Designed and built by the architecture and engineering firm Skidmore, Owings & Merrill under the supervision of American architect Adrian Smith (b. 1944) and engineer Bill Baker (b. 1953),

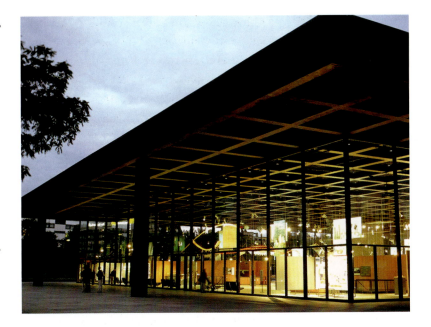

the Burj Khalifa is the tallest building in the world. Its design was derived from the spiraling minarets—towers that surround mosques and are used to call the faithful to prayer—of Islamic architecture. The structural framing that supports the building is created from tubular steel to make the support lighter without compromising the integrity.

2.5.30 Mies van der Rohe, Neue Nationalgalerie, 1968, Berlin, Germany

2.5.31 Adrian Smith and Bill Baker (Skidmore, Owings, and Merrill), Burj Khalifa, 2010. Dubai, United Arab Emirates

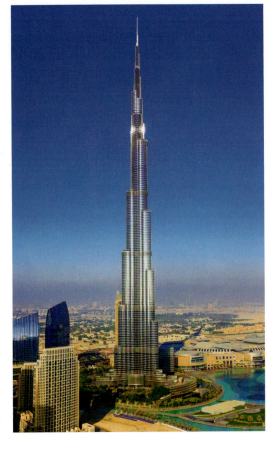

Contrasting Ideas in Modern Architecture:
Le Corbusier's Villa Savoye and
Frank Lloyd Wright's Fallingwater

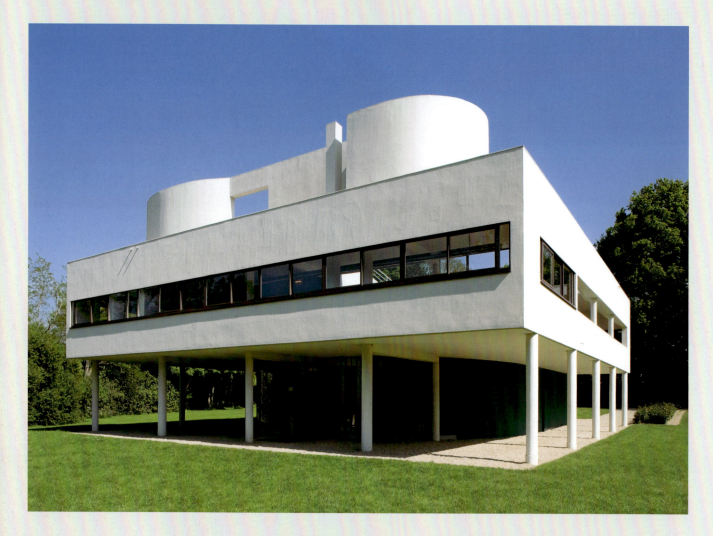

2.5.32 Le Corbusier, Villa Savoye, 1928–31, Poissy, France

Architecture is one of the most visible expressions of the Modernist movement.

A building's appearance can be a visual expression of an idea the architect wants to communicate. Two buildings constructed about the same time, the Villa Savoye and Fallingwater, share certain similarities, but are based on radically different ideas about architecture.

The Villa Savoye in Poissy, France, was completed in 1931 as a weekend residence for a family that lived in Paris during the week. It is one of Le Corbusier's finest expressions of his architectural philosophy (**2.5.32**). Le Corbusier (1887–1965) was a Swiss-French

architect (also a designer and painter) who saw architecture as a "machine for living": the architecture of a building should be designed around the lifestyle of the occupants. Le Corbusier's architectural designs were part of the International Style, promoted as a universal aesthetic form that could be built in any geographical or cultural environment relatively inexpensively. This style emphasized industrial and (in theory) cheap materials, such as steel, glass, and concrete. It also favored a strongly geometric visual organization of spaces and elements of the building, including the shapes of the windows, roofline, and walls. With its preferences for unadorned, open interiors, the International Style claimed its rational approach to design could (and should) be used universally, for rich and poor alike.

Five years later, the American architect Frank Lloyd Wright (1867–1959) was commissioned to build Fallingwater in Bear Run, Pennsylvania, as a weekend getaway for the Kaufmann family (2.5.33). It was completed in 1939. The profile of the house features vertical and horizontal elements much like those of the Villa Savoye, but Wright did not think that a house should be a machine. He believed the design of a house should respond **organically** to its location.

Rather than position the house so that the Kaufmanns could view the waterfall from inside, Wright placed the house right on top of it. He made the house so integral to the environment that the bottom step of one of the stairways hovered just above the creek. Wright believed so strongly in the organic relationship between site and building that he had many of the materials collected from the surrounding countryside. The stone was quarried nearby and the wood for the supports between the windows came from the surrounding forest. The design mimics the layers in the rocks around the site, and the reinforced concrete is colored to fit in as well. Sometimes underlying rock juts into the living space of the house so that the occupants may take pleasure in stepping over or around the stone.

Le Corbusier's design was inexpensive compared with Wright's, particularly since Wright's building materials needed to be specially collected from the surrounding countryside. Each design creates a beautiful modern space. In Wright's work, architecture becomes part of the natural surroundings, whereas Le Corbusier wants nature to be viewed from a comfortable vantage point.

Organic: having irregular forms and shapes, as though derived from living organisms

2.5.33 Frank Lloyd Wright, Fallingwater, 1939, Bear Run, Pennsylvania

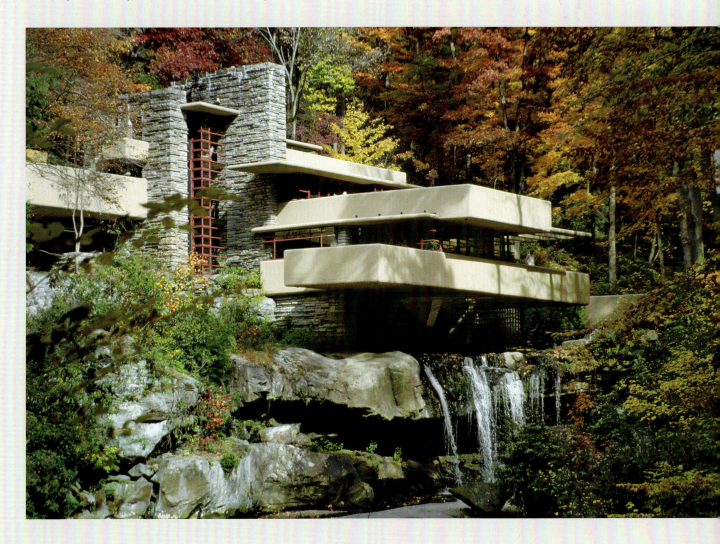

Reinforced Concrete

The character of architecture comes from its use of building materials, the sourcing or manufacture of which determines much of modern buildings' visual form. Steel and glass are produced in rectangular shapes that are a vital part of the visual aesthetic prizing the integration of form and function. But what aesthetic form would a material have if its raw manufactured state was liquid?

Architects began to use reinforced concrete as a way of avoiding the hard, right-angled edges of buildings made from blocks or bricks. Like steel and cast iron, reinforced concrete did not come into widespread use in architecture until the nineteenth century. Concrete is a mixture of cement and ground stone. It is reinforced through the use of either a fibrous material (such as fiberglass) or steel rods called rebars. The inclusion of fibrous or metal reinforcing helps the concrete resist cracking. In architecture, steel rebar is shaped to the architect's design specifications; builders make a large wooden mold, and then pour the concrete into the "form." Reinforced concrete gave rise to shell architecture, which is the use of a solid shell that also provides support for the structure.

When the Danish architect Jørn Utzon (1918–2008) designed the Sydney Opera House, overlooking the harbor of Sydney, Australia, he broke away from Modernist rectangular designs (**2.5.34**). The structure is a testament to the **expressive** character of reinforced concrete. The rooflines resemble billowing sails, a reference to the building's harbor location. The "sails" were created over precast ribs and then set into place, allowing the architect more freedom in the creation of the design and (in theory) reducing the cost. In fact, owing to a succession of technical problems with this innovative building, the project cost fourteen times its intended budget. As controversy surrounding the project escalated, Utzon resigned nine years before its completion.

2.5.34 Jørn Utzon, Sydney Opera House, 1973, Sydney, Australia

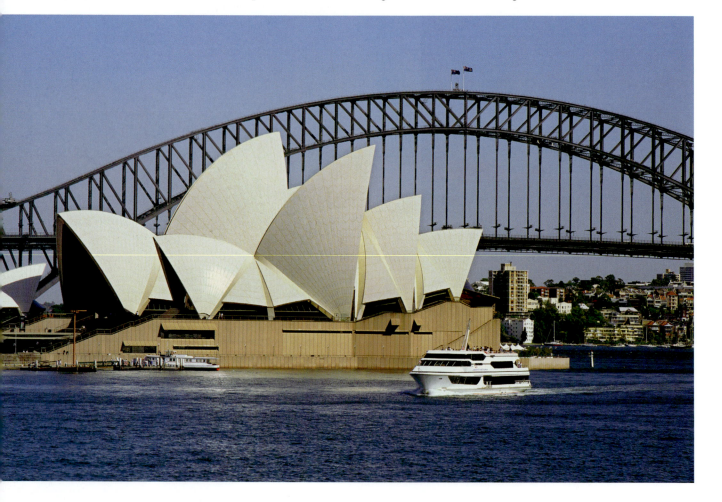

The Postmodern Reaction to Modernism

Beginning in the 1980s, a new approach to architecture, known as **Postmodernism**, combined the hard, pure rectangles of Modernism with unusual materials and features of styles from the past. Postmodernism took hold as architects sought new ways to reflect a complex and changing world.

The Humana Building in downtown Louisville, Kentucky, designed by American Michael Graves (1934–2015), is an intriguing mix of historical styles and references (**2.5.35**). The **facade** onto the street has a **stylized** Greek **portico**. The **negative space** of large windows and openings implies columns that rise up to support a cornice and triangular glass structure similar to the triangular **pediment** of a Greek temple. The upper portion of the building (set back from the street) suddenly changes from simple right angles to a series of curved

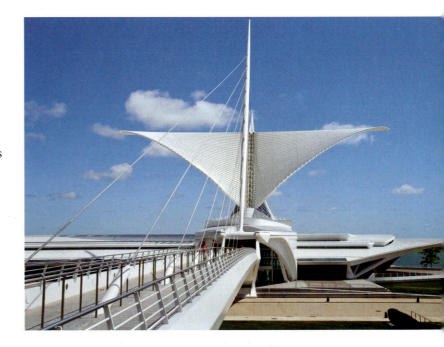

surfaces that undulate like the architecture of the Baroque period. Graves also artfully varies the facing material, changing its color and texture at different intervals, seeking to avoid the austere simplicity and purity of Modernism. A piece of Modernist architecture would not include influences from Greek or Baroque architecture because the Modernist idea was to create a new style that was not based on the past.

In Postmodernist architecture, form no longer follows function with the same dedication as it did during the Modernist period. In fact, sometimes the building seems like a huge toy, a playful exploration of what we expect a building to be. The Quadracci Pavilion at the Milwaukee Art Museum was designed by Spanish architect Santiago Calatrava (b. 1951) to express the character of the site (**2.5.36**). Built on the shores of Lake Michigan, the pavilion reminds us of ships passing by; a cable-suspended bridge over a beautiful expanse of water also connects the museum to downtown Milwaukee. The building becomes a **kinetic sculpture** when a large moveable sunscreen atop the structure slowly rises and lowers throughout the day, like the flapping wings of the many species of birds that flock near the lake. The inside is reminiscent of the curved interior of a sailing ship. The Quadracci Pavilion provides an exciting exhibition space for the display of contemporary art.

2.5.36 Santiago Calatrava, Quadracci Pavilion, Milwaukee Art Museum, Wisconsin, 2001

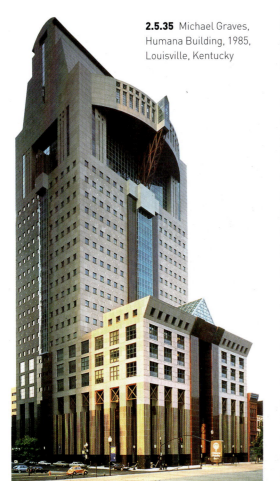

2.5.35 Michael Graves, Humana Building, 1985, Louisville, Kentucky

Postmodernism, Postmodernist: a late-twentieth-century style of architecture and art that playfully adopts features of earlier styles
Facade: any side of a building, usually the front or entrance
Stylized: art that represents objects in an exaggerated way to emphasize certain aspects of the object
Portico: a roof supported by columns at the entrance to a building
Negative space: an empty space given shape by its surround, for example the right-pointing arrow between the **E** and the **x** in the **FedEx** logo (see p. 29)
Pediment: the triangular space, situated above the row of columns, on the facade of a building in the Classical style
Kinetic sculpture: three-dimensional art that moves, impelled by air currents, motors, or people

Perspectives on Art: Zaha Hadid
A Building for Exciting Events

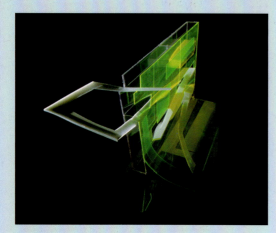

Zaha Hadid (b. 1950) was born in Iraq and trained as an architect in London. She has designed notable buildings in Europe and the United States. Here she describes how an architect thinks about a new building for art exhibitions, performances, and installations in downtown Cincinnati, Ohio.

The new home for the Contemporary Arts Center is located on a small space in downtown Cincinnati (**2.5.37a** and **2.5.37b**). Our challenge was to design for a prominent location an exciting new building that would provide spaces for many different activities: temporary exhibitions, site-specific installations and performances, an education facility, offices, art-preparation areas, a museum store, a café, and public areas.

We designed the gallery spaces as a three-dimensional "jigsaw puzzle" of interlocking solids and voids suspended above the lobby. The unique geometry, scale, and varying heights of the gallery spaces offer organizational flexibility to accommodate and respond to the size and media of the contemporary art that will be displayed.

We wanted to draw visitors into the building from the surrounding areas by creating a dynamic public space. Pedestrians enter the building and move around it through an "urban carpet" of polished undulating surfaces that curves slowly upward. As it rises and turns, the urban carpet leads visitors up a suspended mezzanine ramp through the full length of the lobby, which functions during the day as an open, daylit artificial park. The urban carpet also connects to zigzag ramps that take visitors to the galleries.

Seen from the street, the building appears to be made up of stacked horizontal blocks of glass, metal, and concrete, suspended above the glass at ground level. We wanted to give the building a weightless quality, as if it were a sculpture, not just a building. The public and administrative spaces are glass, so that those outside are invited to look into the building, and those inside to look out at the cityscape. In this way the center's building is connected to the city it serves.

2.5.37a (left) Zaha Hadid, Contemporary Arts Center, Cincinnati, Ohio. Study model by the architects, experimenting with different structural ideas

2.5.37b (below) Zaha Hadid, Contemporary Arts Center, 2003, Cincinnati, Ohio

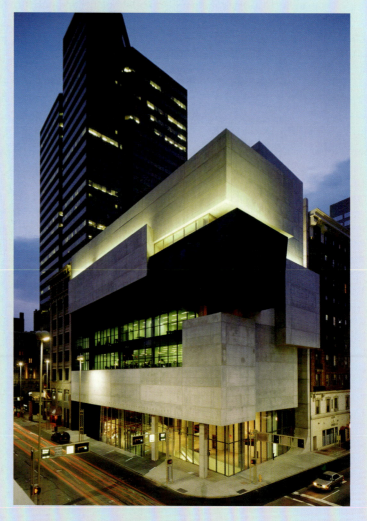

The Future of Architecture

Architecture faces both challenges and opportunities as the twenty-first century unfolds. Concerns over limited resources, energy conservation, and sustainability have become important issues. American husband-and-wife team Gail Vittori (b. 1954) and Pliny Fisk III (b. 1944) have been considering the problems of sustainability and use of architecture for decades.

Since 1991 Vittori and Fisk have been co-directors of the non-profit Center for Maximum Potential Building Systems (founded by Fisk in 1975), which works to make new buildings more environmentally friendly. The center's design of a model village in Longju, China, is part of a larger vision that includes helping farmers to develop sustainable methods of farming (**2.5.38**). The design involves not just the buildings but also the working methods and entire lifestyle of the community. Fisk has created greener ways to raise crops and livestock so that each village can be more efficient and environmentally friendly. Vittori is on the board of directors of the US Green Building Council, which promotes the LEED (Leadership in Energy and Environmental Design), a program and rating system that encourages building with renewable materials and appropriate technology. Because each building's location and unique needs can dictate energy use, the LEED provides guidance on the methods and materials that would best fit the structure.

2.5.38 Architectural illustration of an urban block for a Szechuan Chinese village (Longju), Center for Maximum Potential Building Systems, 2005

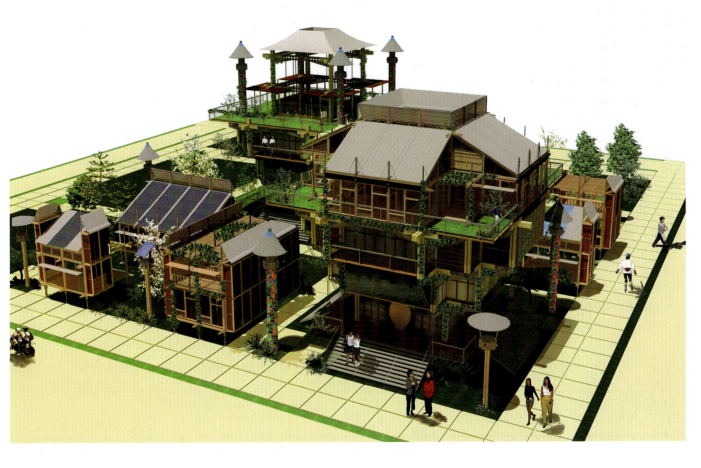

Active Learning Exercises

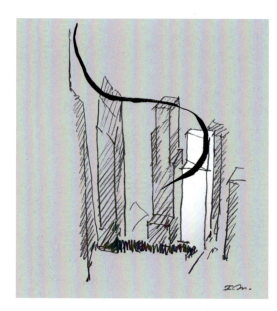

2.5.2 Fumihiko Maki, Sketch of Four World Trade Center, 2006

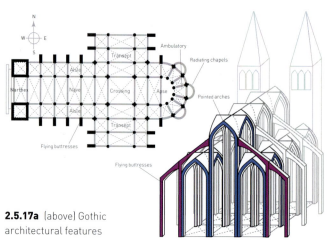

2.5.17a (above) Gothic architectural features

2.5.17b (right) Gothic architectural construction, showing flying buttresses

1. Architecture, like any other design process, begins by creating a drawing that illustrates a central idea. For example, the concept drawing created by Fumihiko Maki (**2.5.2**) for a new World Trade Center illustrates how the spiraling design would fit with other buildings in Manhattan. Maki's drawing was an expression of his idea, not a realistic representation. Using a pencil and paper, create a drawing of a monument to the Greek philosopher Plato that will be placed on your college campus. What visual elements and styles did you use? Why? How was your design integrated into the campus environment?

2. Gothic architecture came into existence because Abbot Suger wanted to design around the experience of the visitor when he or she entered a church. In order to do this, he created a system that balances tension and compression so that they work to stabilize the architectural framework of the church. This framework was based on the use of columns, pointed arches, and flying buttresses, all organized so that the weight of the building was transferred through the system, making the walls less structurally critical. Using a pencil and paper, draw the system that Suger created, labeling the pointed arches, columns, and flying buttresses, and using arrows to indicate how the weight is being transferred. Feel free to look at **2.5.17a and b** as a guide. Why was this system so innovative in its time? Why was the experience of the visitor so important to Suger?

3. Architectural style influences, and is influenced by, the surrounding environment, so that environment is a major concern for designers. Understanding how a building will fit is a challenge for even the most visionary architect. Print or photocopy pictures of various buildings, some private residences and some large public buildings. Using scissors, cut out the buildings from the environment that surrounds them, then photocopy them at 50 percent of their original size. Now print several background environments, a cityscape, a countryside, and a beach area. Once again, cut out the individual buildings from the paper they are on and place them in each of these environments. What environments work best for your buildings? Why?

Images Related to 2.5: Architecture

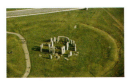

4.1.6 Stonehenge, England, *c.* 3200–1500 BCE, p. 566

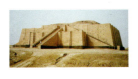

4.1.5 Ziggurat at Ur, ancient Sumer, *c.* 2100 BCE, p. 565

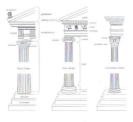

3.1.21 Diagram of Classical architectural orders, p. 380

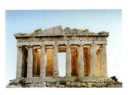

1.7.13a Iktinos and Kallikrates, Parthenon, Athens, 447–432 BCE, p. 154

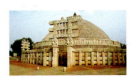

3.3.2 Great Stupa, Sanchi, India, *c.* 150–50 BCE, p. 414

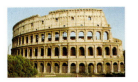

4.1.2 Colosseum, Rome, Italy, 72–80 CE, p. 563

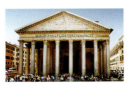

3.1.34 Pantheon, Rome, Italy, *c.* 118–125, p. 387

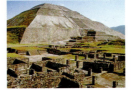

3.4.11 Pyramid of the Sun, Teotihuacan, *c.* 225, p. 440

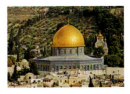

3.2.15 Dome of the Rock, Jerusalem, 688–91, p. 401

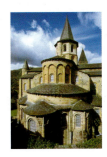

3.2.20 Sainte-Foy, Conques, France, *c.* 1120, p. 404

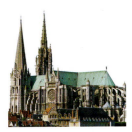

3.2.24 Chartres Cathedral, France, 1260, p. 407

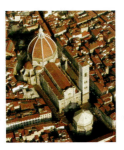

3.6.3 Arnolfo di Cambio and others, Florence Cathedral, begun 1296, p. 466

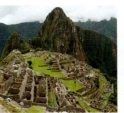

3.4.5 Machu Picchu, Peru, 1450–1530, p. 436

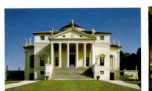

3.6.9a Andrea Palladio, Villa Rotunda, begun 1565/6, p. 471

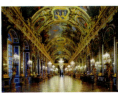

3.7.2 Jules Hardouin-Mansart, Hall of Mirrors, Versailles, France, 1678–84, p. 491

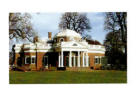

3.7.13 Thomas Jefferson, Monticello, 1769–1809, p. 502

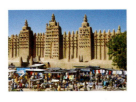

3.5.7 Great Mosque, Djenné, Mali, 1907, p. 455

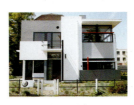

3.9.15 Gerrit Rietveld, Schröder House, 1924–25, p. 551

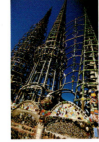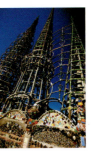

0.0.8 Simon Rodia, Watts Towers, 1921–54, p. 32

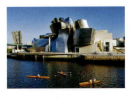

1.2.17 Frank Gehry, Guggenheim Museum, Bilbao, Spain, 1997, p. 78

2.6

The Tradition of Craft

Life is so short, the craft so long to learn.

(Geoffrey Chaucer, English poet)

In Geoffrey Chaucer's (*c.* 1340–1400) time, the makers of the fine objects we can see today in the world's great art museums learned their trade in associations called guilds. Fourteenth-century aspiring craftsmen trained with masters, a process that lasted many years, as Chaucer's comment suggests. In medieval Europe, painting (for example) was not considered to be of higher status than the work of either turning ceramics into fine vessels or weaving exquisite tapestries.

Things gradually changed after 1400 during the **Renaissance**, and by the eighteenth century, certain **media**, notably painting and sculpture, came to be considered as art, while ceramics, weaving, and embroidery were termed crafts. Other materials, such as metals, were used to make fine sculpture (which was "art") as well as practical and household objects ("craft"). Crafts came to mean the disciplines that produced hand-made items to be used rather than simply looked at. This view was generally accepted, even though utilitarian objects require technical skill to produce, and craftspeople devote years to mastering their craft. Indeed, some hand-crafted objects, because of their ingenuity and refinement, stand out as artworks that transcend mere utility.

The distinction between art and craft was unique to Western culture, and it has now broken down in the twentieth and twenty-first century, as this chapter will show. As for the rest of the world, the maker of a bronze vessel in China during the Shang Dynasty (1300–1045 BCE), the maker of a fine embroidered wool tunic in Paracas, South America (600–175 BCE), and the **ceramist** who made lamps for the Dome of the Rock in Jerusalem (sixteenth century) probably did not consider themselves any less skillful or "artistic" than painters or sculptors. Craftspeople working today still produce works using traditional craft materials and techniques, but have updated their methods and subjects to reflect a changing world; they also sometimes apply traditional skills but use new, contemporary materials to create their work. Examples of contemporary artists working in this way include Hyo-In Kim (p. 293) and Toshiko Horiuchi (p. 303).

In this chapter we will examine both craft objects and works of art, each made with the same materials. If we try to define precisely the difference between art and craft we will discover it is difficult, perhaps impossible. As you read this chapter, ask yourself whether you think the objects discussed can be considered art or craft. At the same time, think about whether the makers of the objects, and the people they made them for, could tell the difference either. In the hands of skillful designers, great craft objects such as those discussed here possess artistry equal to great works of art.

Renaissance: a period of cultural and artistic change in Europe from the fourteenth to the seventeenth century

Medium (plural **media**): the material on or from which an artist chooses to make a work of art, for example canvas and oil paint, marble, engraving, video, or architecture

Ceramist: a person who makes ceramics

Perspectives on Art: Hyo-In Kim
Art or Craft: What's the Difference?

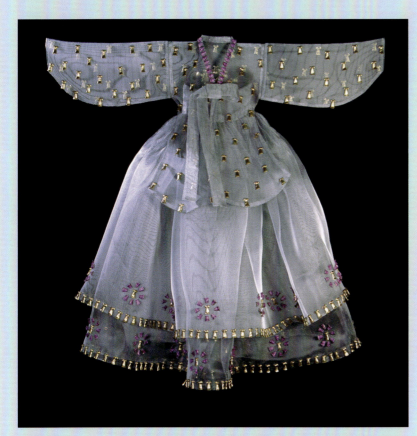

2.6.1 Hyo-In Kim, *To Be Modern #2*, 2004. Metal screen, wire, porcelain, acrylic paint, and found objects, slightly over lifesize

2.6.2 Hyo-In Kim

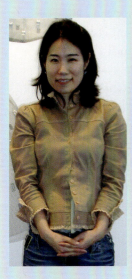

When we look at a fine painting we will almost certainly describe it as being art. But is a fine example of clothing, for example, art or craft? If craft is something that has a useful function, then presumably a dress is craft. Here, however, Professor Howard Risatti, an art historian at Virginia Commonwealth University, examines a work based on a traditional Korean dress that transforms a practical piece of clothing to comment on our modern globalized world (2.6.1). He asks: What makes something a work of art rather than a work of craft?

Only by understanding something essential about a work of art can we begin to appreciate its richness and complexity as an aesthetic object. So to begin, we must ask, "What is essential to a work of craft?" To my thinking, it is that craft is an object constructed around the idea of function, say the way a container functions to hold water, or a chair to support

a person, or clothes to cover someone's body. The work shown here is from a series by the young Korean-American artist Hyo-In Kim. It is a *hanbok*, a traditional Korean dress worn with shoes and a hairpin by women of the upper and royal classes. Its gold-colored decoration indicates its prestige; such expensive materials were costly and well beyond the means of commoners, who mostly wore plain white garments.

The title, *To Be Modern #2*, however, suggests the artist has something more in mind than simply a fondness for traditional Korean clothes. Kim is faithful to the original dress design; she wants it to be correct to tradition. But she also wants it to indicate something important about tradition. That is why she has subtly transformed it by making it out of silver-colored wire mesh (instead of cloth) and by molding the decorative details out of porcelain, which she has then painted gold. And in keeping with the idea of transformation, instead of displaying it on a manikin like a dress in a store window, like something to be bought and sold, she decided to suspend it with its sleeves outstretched so that its transparency and weightlessness would be emphasized.

Kim intends us to see through the material so that the dress, like the hairpin, appears to float like a ghostly, disembodied figure—something almost there and yet not quite. This apparitional effect, enhanced by the glittering gold of the decoration, is then undercut when, upon close-up inspection of the dress, the decoration turns out to be tiny versions of fashionable Western clothing: jeans, skirts, shoes, purses. What Kim wants us to see and appreciate, both literally and figuratively, is that those traditional cultural values that give structure and form to people's lives, including our own, are fading away and disappearing as globalization spreads.

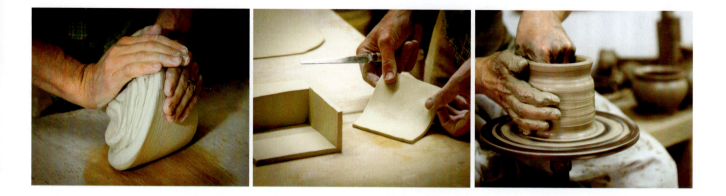

Ceramics

Our word ceramic comes from the Greek word *keramos*, meaning "pottery," which was probably derived from a word in Sanskrit (a language of ancient India) meaning "to burn." The accepted interpretation of the word, burnt earth, aptly describes the ceramic process. The manufacture of a ceramic object requires the shaping of clay, a natural material dug from the earth, which is then baked at high temperatures to make it hard.

We know that the basic techniques used to make ceramics date back thousands of years because archaeologists investigating the earliest known civilizations have found potsherds, small pieces of ancient ceramics.

The first step in making a ceramic object is to choose a clay. Ceramists can choose from a variety of clays, each with unique characteristics; they often select a mixture they have developed themselves that fits their own working methods. Clay used to make earthenware has good **plasticity**, or pliability, but it can be somewhat brittle after firing. Earthenware is often red in color and hardens at a lower temperature than other clays. Stoneware clays are less plastic than earthenware clays. Stoneware (as its name implies) is much harder than earthenware and is fired at a higher temperature. Stoneware is a good clay for the creation of items for everyday use, such as mugs and bowls. Porcelain, a durable, high-temperature ceramic commonly used for fine dinnerware, is made of a mixture of three clays: feldspar, kaolin, and silica. Porcelain is strong but sometimes hard to manipulate. Fine white china, bathroom fixtures, and dental crowns are made of porcelain.

When the ceramist has selected the clay, the next step in the making process is called wedging. This means the clay is kneaded to work out pockets of air (which can destroy a piece of ceramic ware when it is heated) and make the clay easier to work. Next, the ceramist uses one of a number of hand methods to shape the clay into the form of the finished object. For example, the artist can build up an object using slabs or coils of clay, or by modeling a lump of clay into the desired shape by pressing or pinching. Another method is to shape the clay as it turns on a rapidly turning potter's wheel, a process known as **throwing**.

Once it has been shaped, the clay is left to dry. The dried clay, called **greenware**, is very fragile. It is ready to be loaded into an oven called a kiln, and to be fired at a high temperature (between 2,000 and 3,000°F). The firing process takes an entire day of slowly raising the temperature to the appropriate level, then another day to allow for a slow cool-down to prevent cracking. The fired object, called **bisqueware**, is now permanently a hard ceramic and cannot be wetted and returned to a soft-clay state.

To add the finishing touches to a ceramic object, artists apply a glaze, a liquid mixture of clay, water, and chemical compounds that will give the object a glass-like finish and that adds color, **texture**, and protection to the object's surface. (A glaze can also make an object more watertight.) Some ceramists opt for a more matte finish, so they use a thin liquid clay called slip. The artist usually applies the slip or glaze with a brush. The object is again placed in the kiln and fired to melt and harden the glaze or slip, which fuses with the clay body.

Plastic, plasticity: referring to materials that are soft and can be manipulated, or to such properties in the materials
Throwing: the process of making a ceramic object on a potter's wheel
Greenware: a clay form that has been shaped and dried, but not yet fired to become ceramic
Bisqueware: a ceramic form that has been fired but not glazed or that has not received other surface finishing
Texture: the surface quality of a work, for example fine/coarse, detailed/lacking in detail

2.6.4 (right)
Seated Figure, Oaxaca, Mexico, Zapotec style, 300 BCE–700 CE. Ceramic, 12⅝ × 7 × 7⅜". Cleveland Museum of Art, Ohio

2.6.5 (below right)
Porcelain flask with decoration in blue underglaze, Ming Dynasty, 1425–35. Palace Museum, Beijing, China

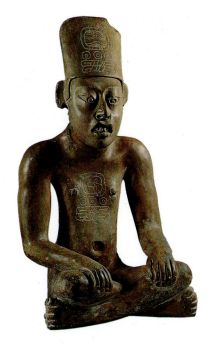

Coil Method

The art of using coils to create a clay object has been a common hand-building method since ancient times. A coil is created by rolling the clay on a flat surface so that it extends into a long, rope-like shape. When making a round vessel, the artist wraps the coil around upon itself and then fuses the sections together by smoothing.

Seated Figure, a work from the Zapotec culture of Mexico, was made using the coil method (**2.6.4**). This figure was made to be buried in the tomb of a Zapotec ruler, and may portray a god or possibly a companion for the deceased. On its headdress and chest the artist has carved two calendar dates in Zapotec writing. Most of the pottery made by native American cultures was carefully crafted by hand. The coil method was preferred for constructing rounded objects because the **organic** line of the coil could be controlled in a way that would complement the piece's essence or spirit.

Throwing

The use of a potter's wheel probably began when an artist, in order to make the process of coiling more efficient, placed his or her clay object on a round mat and turned it while adding coils of clay to a piece of pottery. A potter's wheel consists of a round disk that revolves while the ceramist shapes the object. No one is sure exactly when such wheels were invented, but by 3000 BCE the Chinese were using them to produce ceramic objects.

The process of making pottery on a wheel is known as throwing. The potter centers a mound of clay on the turning wheel and then shapes a pot by poking a hole in the middle of the mound, and then pushing and pulling the wall of the pot up and out with both hands as it turns. To finish the surface of the pot, the potter can employ sponges and scrapers as it spins, or simply let the natural grooves made by the fingertips remain. Finally, a piece of wire is used to cut the finished piece from the wheel.

The ceramic artists of China invented porcelain and used a greater variety of high-quality glazes than any ceramic tradition in the world, many of which are still in use today. The porcelain flask (**2.6.5**) was produced on a potter's wheel during the Ming Dynasty almost 600 years ago. Chinese ceramists of the Ming Dynasty were known for their use of multiple glaze layers. Their wares were so fine that the users of Ming Dynasty porcelain included the emperor of China himself. In this piece the artist used, first, a blue glaze and then a clear glaze over that to complete the work. The clear glaze gave the flask a luxurious glossy finish.

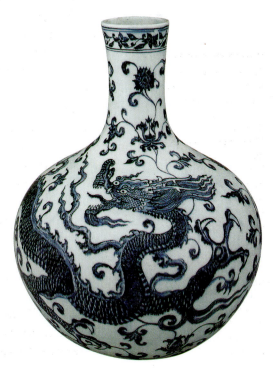

Organic: having irregular forms and shapes, as though derived from living organisms

San Ildefonso-Style Pottery

Native American pottery is regarded as some of the most distinctive in the world. Ceramic objects created in the Americas were constructed using hand-building methods, rather than with a potter's wheel, yet the pottery created possesses great symmetry.

One family of Native American potters revived and perfected the pottery traditions of the Tewa people in Southwestern North America from the early twentieth century. Dr. Edgar Lee Hewett discovered sherds of pottery near San Ildefonso Pueblo in New Mexico and asked a local potter to produce replicas of the originals. That potter, Maria Martinez (1887–1980), whose Tewa name was Po've'ka ("Pond Lily"), and her husband Julian (1879–1943) re-created ceramic objects that their distant ancestors had made. They were asked to demonstrate the process at the Panama California Fair in 1915, and then in other major public venues.

Maria and Julian Martinez went on to develop their own distinctive San Ildefonso style, which became internationally famous. Maria would carefully craft the pottery objects from the volcanic ash-laden clays of the region, then Julian would apply the designs. Different slips are painted on the surfaces, which have either a glossy or matte finish. Then the pieces are fired in a mound of wood and manure that gives the piece its rich black color.

One of the favorite designs used is that of the *avanyu* (**2.6.8**). An avanyu is a water guardian serpent god of the Tewa peoples. The image is common in the many caves that dot the canyons in this area. It bears a close resemblance to the **Mesoamerican** serpent god Quetzalcoatl. Avanyus are frequently used as decorative motifs in Southwest pottery.

Mesoamerican: an archaeological term referring to people or objects from the area now occupied by Mexico and Central America

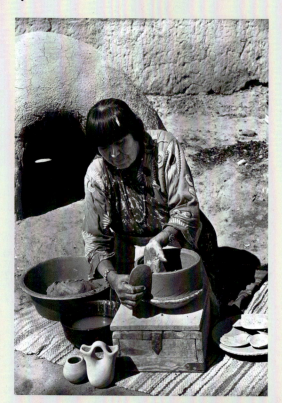

2.6.6 (left) Maria Martinez, San Ildefonso Pueblo, New Mexico, *c.* 1930–40 (?)

2.6.7 (right) Julian Martinez, San Ildefonso Pueblo, New Mexico, *c.* 1925-45 (?)

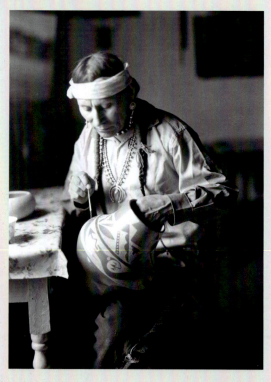

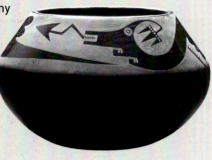

2.6.8 (left) Maria Martinez and Julian Martinez, Bowl with plumed serpent, *c.* 1925. Coiled and burnished earthenware, 6" x 9½". Newark Museum, New Jersey

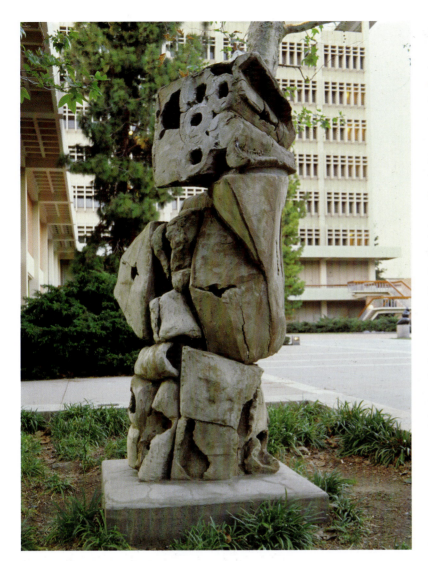

2.6.9 (above) Peter Voulkos, *Gallas Rock*, 1960. Stoneware with slip and glaze, 84 × 37 × 26¾". University of California at Los Angeles, Franklin D. Murphy Sculpture Garden

2.6.10 (right) Portland Vase, Roman, *c.* 1–25 CE. British Museum, London, England

Three-dimensional: having height, width, and depth
Expressionism, Expressionist: an artistic style at its height in 1920s Europe, devoted to representing subjective emotions and experiences instead of objective or external reality
Plane: a flat surface, often implied by the composition

Slab Method

When artists use slab construction to make a ceramic object they first roll out a flat sheet of clay. They then cut this clay into the shapes they need to make the object. To make a **three-dimensional** object, the ceramist takes care to join the corners. This style of working lends itself to making boxes and other forms that have large flat sides.

In *Gallas Rock*, by American sculptor Peter Voulkos (1924–2002), we see slab construction (and wheel throwing) used in an organic and **Expressionist** way (**2.6.9**). The slabs are evident in the flat **planes** that dominate this 8-foot-tall sculptural object. Voulkos is known for using clay's naturalness—its tendency to take on organic forms—and plasticity.

Glass

As with ceramics, the manufacture of glass objects relies on heat, and materials dug from the earth. The process of applying intense heat to melt silica (usually sand) together with lead (historically used to help the melted silica to flow) is the basis for most glass production. As in the making of ceramics, slow cooling of heated objects is critical to avoid serious cracking.

Glass was probably first used in ancient Mesopotamia (modern-day Iraq) and Egypt around 3500 BCE. At that time, glass was cast in small molds and core formed, that is, molten glass was wrapped around a lump of clay or dung attached to the end of a metal rod. The ancient Egyptians valued glass as highly as gold. Glassblowing, the process of forming a glass vessel by forcing air into molten glass, usually by blowing through a tube, was in use by the first century BCE in Syria and was later adopted and perfected by the Romans.

The Portland Vase, named after one of its owners, Margaret Bentinck, Duchess of Portland, is a stunningly beautiful vessel, created in the Roman Empire during the first century CE (**2.6.10**). Recent research has shown that it was made by the dip-overlay method: an elongated bubble of blue glass was partially dipped into a crucible of white glass, before the two were

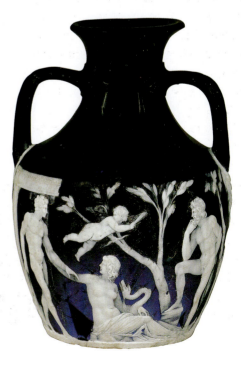

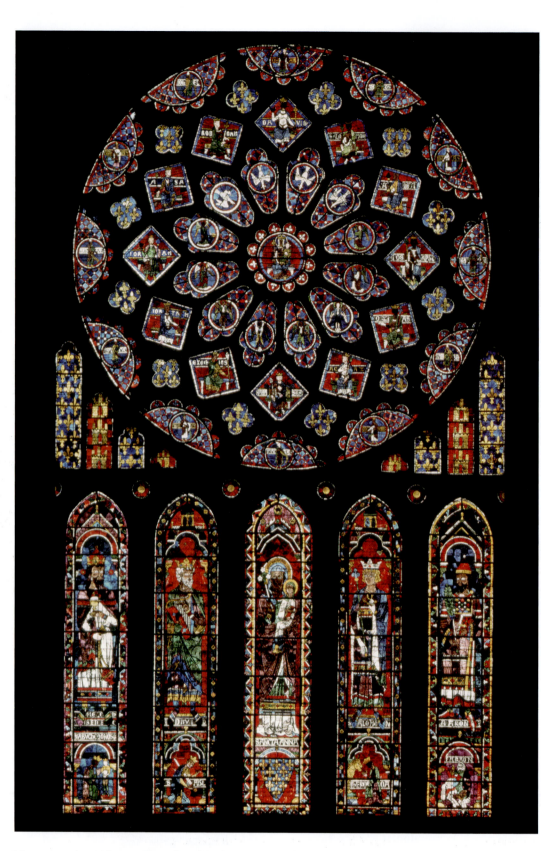

blown together. After cooling, the white layer was cut away to form the design. The cutting was probably performed by a skilled gem-cutter. The blue glass forms the **background** to the figures picked out in white. The amazing degree of detail attests to the artist's skill, as we can see from the four figures and a tree-like plant.

The designers of the **Gothic** cathedrals of medieval France adopted a type of colored glass, known as **stained glass**, which had been used

2.6.11 Rose window and lancets, north transept, 13th century. Chartres Cathedral, France

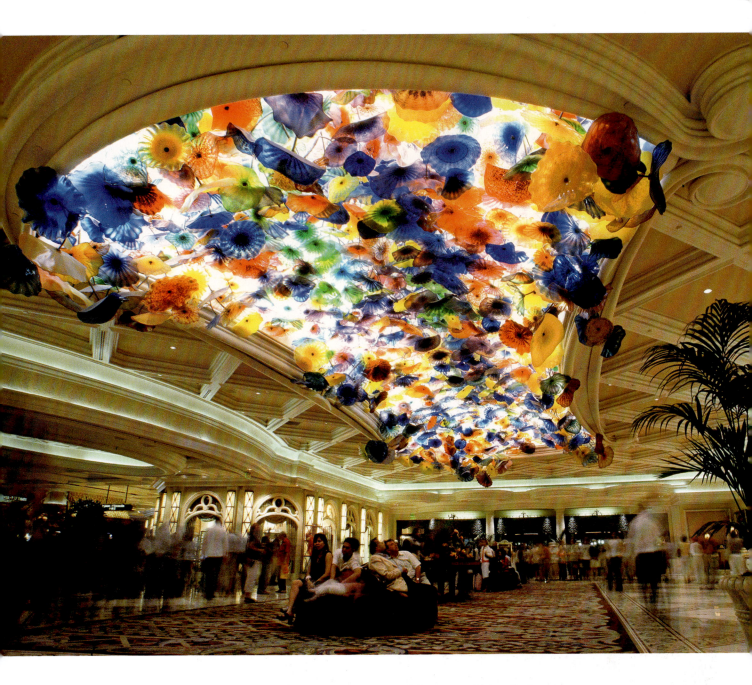

previously on a smaller scale in northern Europe. But the French did something extraordinary with stained glass by using it to make enormous decorative windows that bathed the cathedral in colored light. The windows of the cathedral in the northern French town of Chartres are magnificent examples of stained glass (**2.6.11**). The large (43 ft. in diameter) circular windows are accented by the **contrast** with smaller, tall thin windows with pointed tops. The brilliant blue color in these windows stands apart as one of the most extraordinary achievements of the early thirteenth century. They are so valued that to prevent them from

being damaged during World War II, they were removed and placed in storage until after the war had ended.

The contemporary American glass artist Dale Chihuly (b. 1941) makes comparable use of the kind of **aesthetic** experience that glass can bring to an interior. To enhance the reception area at the Bellagio Hotel in Las Vegas, Chihuly has created a dazzling ceiling made of 2,000 individually blown glass flowers (**2.6.12**). The strong color, reminiscent of stained glass, enlivens and invigorates the interior and becomes an inviting and memorable symbol of the hotel. The effect is mesmerizing.

2.6.12 Dale Chihuly, *Fiori di Como*, 1998. Hand-blown glass and steel, 70' × 30' × 12'. Bellagio Hotel, Las Vegas, Nevada

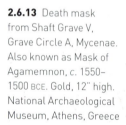

2.6.13 Death mask from Shaft Grave V, Grave Circle A, Mycenae. Also known as Mask of Agamemnon, c. 1550–1500 BCE. Gold, 12" high. National Archaeological Museum, Athens, Greece

Metalwork

As with ceramics, the use of metal in the creation of objects goes back to ancient times. Metal has been so important in human history that some archaeological periods, such as the Bronze Age (more than 5,000 years ago) and Iron Age (more than 3,000 years ago), are named for the metal most commonly used at that time. The working of metal has been a measure of human development and, like most traditional crafts, an important medium for utilitarian purposes.

The properties of a metal object are derived from its basic components. Some metals, such as iron or copper, are natural materials and can be dug from the ground and then refined. Others are **alloys**, or combinations of two or more naturally occurring metals, combined to take advantage of the specific properties of each. For example, if tin is mixed with copper, it produces bronze. As a result of the addition of tin, the bronze is harder and has a lower melting point than copper, so it is easier to manipulate. Other common alloys include pewter, brass, and steel.

Metal can be heated to a liquid state and poured into molds. It can also be heated and then hammered into shape, or it can be worked (usually, again, by hammering) when it is cold. Most metals are strong but malleable, and can be bent or stretched to fit the needs of the artist. Gold is particularly well suited for decorative metalwork because it is comparatively soft (for a metal) and easy to shape.

The gold mask in **2.6.13** was created by laying a thin piece of metal over an object carved to resemble a human face. The artist then carefully hammered the surface of the thin metal, a process called **chasing**, until the shape and texture of the design was imprinted in the metal. The artist has deftly given us the impression of a human face by placing objects, such as cowrie shells for the eyes, under the surface of the metal and forcing the gold sheet into its final shape. This process would have been repeated with different textures and objects to create the detailed ears, eyebrows, beard, and so on. This type of mask was used as a burial mask to cover the face of the departed.

The process of chasing utilizes hammering the front of a metal surface with a form beneath to create a relief design, but reversing the process can have equal impact. This technique is known as **repoussé**. Take for example the *Chalice with Apostles Venerating the Cross* (**2.6.14**), a silver cup that was created in around 600 CE. In order to create this precious object, the artist hammered a blunt tool against the back of the image. Consequently the opposite side was systematically pushed out to form the images of figures, columns, crosses, and arches. These symbols were used by Early Christians to represent elements of their belief system.

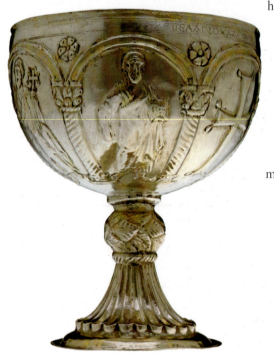

2.6.14 *Chalice with Apostles Venerating the Cross*, c. 600 CE, Syria (Byzantine). Silver repoussé, partial gilt, 6⅝ × 5½" diameter at rim. Walters Art Museum, Baltimore

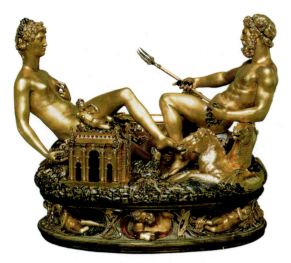

2.6.15 Benvenuto Cellini, *Salt Cellar of Francis I*, 1540–43. Gold, enamel, ebony, ivory, 11¼ × 8½ × 10⅜". Kunsthistorisches Museum, Vienna, Austria

An artist with good technical skills can control metals to make almost any object he or she can imagine. The Italian goldsmith Benvenuto Cellini (1500–1571) created the *Salt Cellar of Francis I* as an extremely elaborate object to go on the dining-table of the king of France (**2.6.15**). To make this salt cellar, Cellini first sculpted wax models of Neptune (the Roman god of the salty sea) and Mother Earth (whence table salt was extracted) in harmony and at rest. Cellini then covered the wax model with a strong material, perhaps sand and lime, to make a mold. The mold was then heated so that the wax melted and left the center of the mold empty. Once the metal had reached the required 2,000°F, Cellini poured the molten gold into the mold. When it was cool, the artist could remove the mold and then carefully finish off the piece. The salt was held in a bowl shape next to Neptune, and the pepper inside the small triumphal arch next to the symbolic image of Earth. This magnificent example of Renaissance metalwork took more than two years to make.

Fiber

Fibers are threads made from animal or vegetable materials (such as fur, wool, silk, cotton, flax, or linen) or, more recently, synthetic materials (for example nylon or polyester). Fiber art is most often associated with the creation of textiles. The fibers can be spun into yarn, string, or thread, then woven or knitted into lengths of textiles. In the case of embroidery, the thread, string, or yarn is applied using stitching techniques. Relatively stiff fibers, such as grass and rushes, can be woven together to make baskets and similar objects. Processing plant fibers begins with separating the fiber from the plant, then preparing it for use by spinning the fiber into a long thread. In the case of cotton, once the cotton bolls are collected, the fibers are separated and washed; then the individual fibers are spun, or twisted, into thread. Wool is sheared from sheep in the spring, washed and separated, then spun into yarn. Silk fibers are very fine and are the product of silkworms, which spin cocoons. Once the cocoons are complete, they are harvested. They are softened in warm water to loosen the gum that binds the fibers together. The silk can then easily be removed and spun into an exquisite fabric.

Alloy: a mixture of a metal combined with at least one other element
Chasing: a technique of hammering the front of a metal object to create a form or surface detail
Repoussé: a technique of hammering metal from the back to create a form or surface detail

2.6.16 Mary Linwood, detail from *Hanging Partridge*, late 18th century. Crewelwork embroidery, approximately 24½ × 28". Private collection

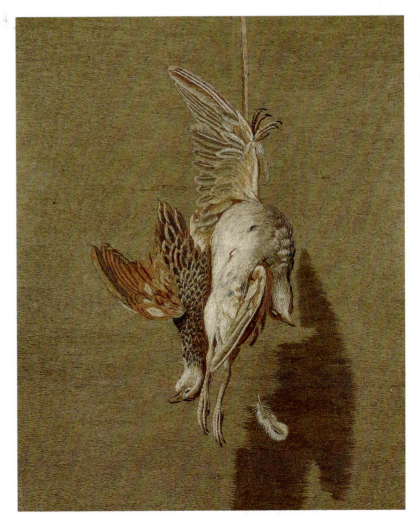

Faith Ringgold, Tar Beach

"There once was a little girl named Cassie who lived in an apartment in New York. On warm summer evenings, she and her family would lay out blankets and have picnics under the stars on their tar beach. The roof was a wonderful place to lie back and look at the city and its lights, and dream about wonderful things like flying through the sky. She could dream that her father, who had helped to build the building where she lived, could join the union, even though being half-Black and half-Indian made it impossible. She could dream that her mother owned an ice-cream factory and was able to eat ice cream every night for dessert."

In this artwork, the African-American artist Faith Ringgold (b. 1930) tells a story of a child called Cassie (**2.6.17**). Ringgold relates the African-American experience, her personal history, and her family life by presenting her own childhood memories in a work that combines painting on canvas with the quilting skills of her family and ancestors. Ringgold began to paint on fabrics in the 1970s. As she did, the works evolved into a collaborative effort with her mother, who was a dressmaker and fashion designer. Ringgold would create the painted part of the work, and her mother would stitch the edges and sew patches of cloth and quilted areas together to form a border. Her great-great-great-grandmother had been a slave who made quilts for plantation owners in the South. Ringgold's works thus possess many layers of meaning that relate to this history and these craft skills. Together these layers communicate the richness of human experience.

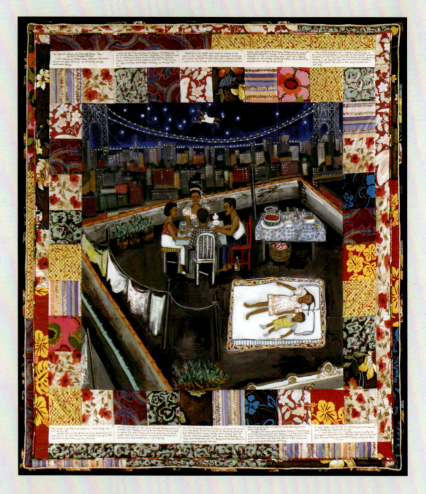

2.6.17 Faith Ringgold, *Tar Beach*, 1988. Acrylic on canvas, bordered with printed, painted, quilted, and pieced cloth, 6′2⅝″ × 5′8½″. Solomon R. Guggenheim Museum, New York

Embroidery is the process of stitching an image into a fabric surface using a needle and thread (or yarn). An embroiderer attaches the thread to the fabric by way of a variety of stitches, each with its own function in a design. British artist Mary Linwood (1755–1845) practiced the art of crewel embroidery, a process that uses freeform, fine wool thread stitching on a drawn design. The detail from *Hanging Partridge* (**2.6.16**, p. 301) shows the process is a lot like "painting with thread," as the artist applies the thread colors the way a painter would apply color in a painting. This kind of needlework is intricate and slow (one of Linwood's pieces reportedly took ten years to complete), but it shows exceptional patience and skill. Linwood's work was held in high esteem, and indeed she was popular with royalty in England and Russia.

The Tlingit people, who live on the western coast of Canada and Alaska, combine both animal and plant material in their fiber art. The blanket shown in **2.6.18** has been woven

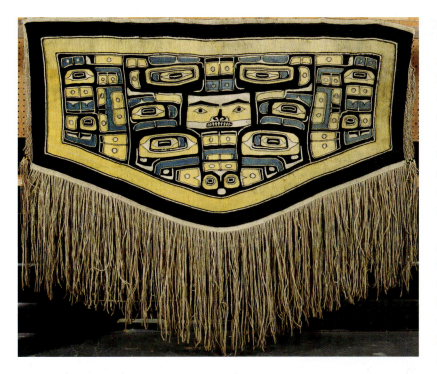

entirely by hand (without a loom) from goat wool and cedar bark in their traditional **Chilkat** style. As Chilkat weaving is intended to be a two-dimensional portrayal of totem carving, the designs for the blankets come from pattern boards developed by wood carvers who use symbols that convey subjects of significance to their tribe or family. In many cases these designs are **abstract** depictions of animals. The central figure here looks like a bear or raccoon. Note the large eyes on either side of the image, which imply the presence of even bigger creatures. Blankets like this are worn on civic and ceremonial occasions by high-ranking tribal members, their long fringe intended to sway against the body in both dances and rituals. They are very expensive, and the prized possessions of anyone fortunate enough to inherit or purchase one.

Knitting is a process of creating a fabric using loops and stitching. Various materials can be knitted, including wool, cotton, nylon, and so on. The Japanese artist Toshiko Horiuchi MacAdam (b. 1940) knits entire environments where viewers are invited to touch the artwork. Her early work in architectural fabric structures led her to create interactive environments. For example, *Knitted Wonder Space II* (**2.6.19**) is a knitted structure designed to be a children's playground. MacAdam builds these large-scale fiber constructions in her studio in Canada, and installs them as required: her work can be found in many countries worldwide. These works challenge preconceived ideas of what fiber art can be, as do others in which artists have knitted metals and plastics as if they are also fibrous.

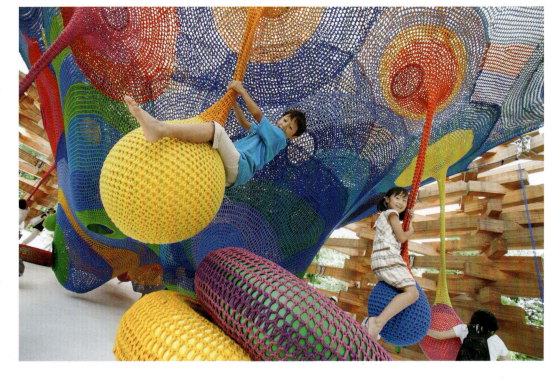

Intarsia: the art of setting pieces of wood into a surface to create a pattern
Illusionism, Illusionistic: the artistic skill or trick of making something look real
Value: the lightness or darkness of a plane or area
Warp: the pieces of thread or yarn that are held in place lengthwise in the weaving process
Weft: the pieces of thread or yarn that are passed over and under the warp to create a textile

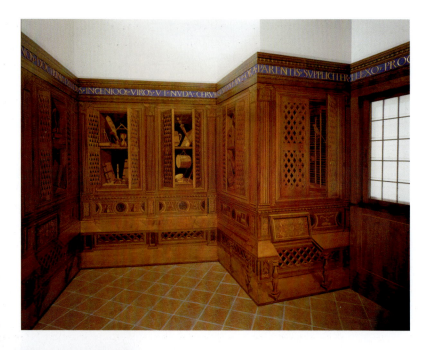

2.6.20 Detail of *studiolo* from the Ducal Palace in Gubbio, Italy, Giuliano da Maiano, after a design by Francesco di Giorgio Martini, *c.* 1480. Walnut, beech, rosewood, oak, and fruit woods in walnut base, 15'11" × 16'11" × 12'7¼". Metropolitan Museum of Art, New York

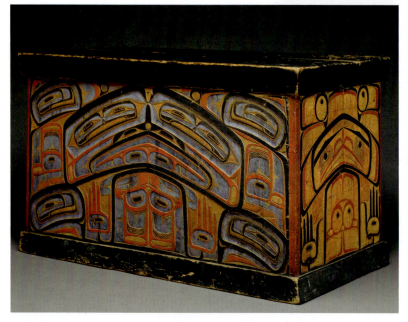

2.6.21 Captain Richard Carpenter, Bent-corner chest, *c.* 1860. Yellow cedar, red cedar, and paint, 21¼ × 35¾ × 20½". Seattle Art Museum, Washington

Wood

Wood, an organic plant-based material, deteriorates over time, so we have few ancient examples of art objects made from it. But we know that wood has been utilized for objects and architecture throughout history. Trees provide many colors and hardnesses of wood, the innate beauty of which can be brought out by cutting and carving. Sanding and polishing a piece of wood gives its surface a mesmerizing beauty.

Around 1480, the Italian artist Francesco di Giorgio Martini (1439–1501) used a decorative wood technique called **intarsia** in his design for a *studiolo* (a private room, often a library or study) in Gubbio, Italy. Intarsia is a kind of wood mosaic using woods of different colors. Giuliano da Maiano, who executed the work, took very thin, shaped pieces of wood and organized them to create a masterpiece of **illusionistic** depth and **value** (**2.6.20**). To the casual viewer, because the artists employed such skill, it is not clear where reality ends and the illusion begins. Federico da Montefeltro, the Duke of Urbino, who commissioned Martini to create this work, wanted the symbols in this magnificent design to reflect his achievements as a ruler, military commander, collector of books, and patron of the arts.

A Native American artist of the Heiltsuk tribe worked with wood to make the bent-corner chest shown in **2.6.21**. To create this vessel, a plank of cedar was smoothed, notches known as kerfs were cut at three corners, and then the wood was made flexible by exposing it to steam created by fire-baked rocks and water. The plank was then bent at the kerfs and joined at the juncture of the last corner. After that, the chest was carved and painted with an elaborate, symmetrical design that fills the whole surface. A separate base and top were then fitted to the whole.

The practice of wood turning, or fashioning a wooden object using a lathe (a power-driven spinning support), has grown in popularity recently. The artist who practices this craft must, naturally, be knowledgeable about wood and its attributes; prepare the wood by seasoning (careful ageing and drying); and control the orientation of the grain of the wood on the turning axis. Andrew Early, a South African wood turner who was taught this craft by his father, John, has become one of today's most collected and exhibited wood turners. Early places emphasis on selecting and preparing the wood to capture its natural organic character, often ageing the wood for many years. He leaves voids and irregularities that naturally occur in the lumber to preserve its rich innate "personality" or character. Such works as the turned wood bowl in **2.6.22** reflect the sensitivity to the material that most craftspeople and artisans possess after having spent long hours in the study and execution of excellence. Early would probably agree with Chaucer that "life is so short, the craft so long to learn."

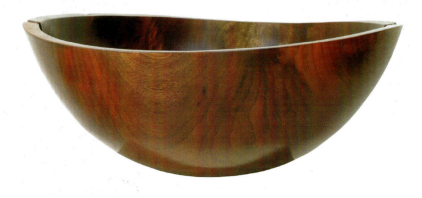

2.6.22 Andrew Early, turned bowl, 2010. Indian mahogany, 13¾" x 29½"

Active Learning Exercises

1. Clay is a natural material that can be found along riverbeds or even simply in the earth below our feet. Using a ball of artist's firing clay (other types of clay may be used if the work will not be fired), approximately the size of a baseball, mold it into a cup-like form. Objects like this are simple manipulations called pinch pots. If you allow this object to dry and then fire it, it will become ceramic. What problems did you encounter when creating your pinch pot? Are there modifications that you would like to see? What kinds of simple tools could you use to improve your craftsmanship?

2. The coil method was used by many ancient cultures to create everyday pottery. The ancient Greeks created impressive containers by simply layering a series of rope-like strands of clay one on top of another and building these into an upward spiral until they reached the desired height.

   To create a simple coil cylinder, you will need a ball of clay about the size of a softball, a cup of water, a plastic fork, and a clean flat surface to work on. Roll the clay into long ropes about ¾ in. thick. Score both sides of the clay rope with the plastic fork, then form a circle with the clay on the flat surface or tabletop. Using the water, moisten the roughened clay, and place another circle of clay on top of the previous. Fuse the two circles together by smoothing the clay until it appears that no joint exists between the coils and there is one low, solid cylinder. Repeat this process until a solid cylindrical form has been created. How high can you take this cylinder? Now consider that Greek amphorae, often more than 3 ft. tall, were made using this method. What kind of problems do you think these ancient craftsmen encountered?

3. Weaving is an ancient craft used to create cloth and other textiles. It is achieved by interlacing rows of material, usually fiber, until the desired size and shape are completed. To make a simple piece of weaving, use 18 strips of paper that are 11 in. long and ¾ in. wide. Tape down 9 strips, laying them parallel and next to each other: this will be the **warp**. Now take one strip and, at a right angle to the warp, insert it so that it crosses under, then over, the warp strips. This is the first of our **weft**, or filling, for the weaving. For the second strip we want to use the same process, but alternate it so that the second strip goes over and under the opposite warp than the first. We will complete the weaving by repeating the weft process, always alternating from strip to strip until all 9 are in place.

   When using fibers, a loom aids the weaver by holding the warp in place. Try incorporating color into another weaving. How could you achieve patterns? Can you think of ways that this process could be applied to other materials, such as metal?

Images Related to 2.6: The Tradition of Craft

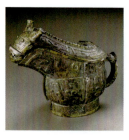

3.3.10 Ritual wine vessel, China, *c.* 1700–1050 BCE, p. 419

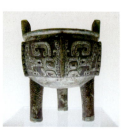

1.6.13 *Liu Ding* (ritual container), Shang dynasty, China, 1600–1100 BCE, p. 140

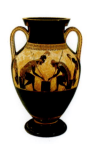

3.1.28 Exekias, amphora of Achilles and Ajax Playing Dice, 530 BCE, p. 384

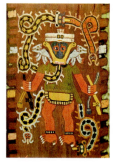

3.4.3 Paracas textile, Peru, 3rd century BCE, p. 435

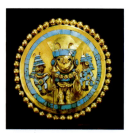

3.4.4 Earspool, *c.* 300 CE, Peru, p. 435

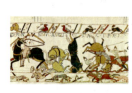

4.7.7 Detail of the Battle of Hastings, *Bayeux Tapestry*, *c.* 1066–82, p. 640

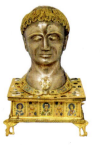

3.2.14 Reliquary of the Head of St. Alexander, 1145, p. 400

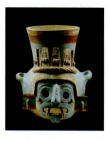

4.3.14 Aztec vessel with mask of Tlaloc, *c.* 1440–69, p. 596

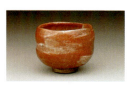

3.4.7 Tunic, Andes, *c.* 1500, p. 437

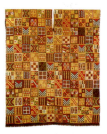

0.0.10 Tea bowl, Japan, 16th century, p. 34

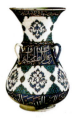

1.4.21 Mosque lamp from the Dome of the Rock, Jerusalem, 1549, p. 112

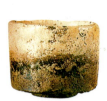

3.3.19 Hon'ami Koetsu, Tea bowl, early 17th century, p. 426

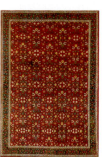

1.9.4 Pashmina carpet, northern India, 2nd half of 17th century, p. 169

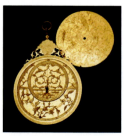

4.4.6 Muhammad Mahdi al-Yazdi, Astrolabe, 1659–60, p. 602

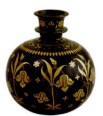

1.9.3 Huqqa base, India, last quarter of 17th century, p. 168

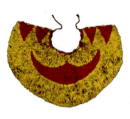

3.5.13a Feather cloak, Hawaii, 18th century, p. 459

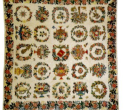

1.6.12 Album quilt, 1848, p. 139

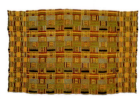

3.5.5 Textile wrapper (kente), Africa, 20th century, p. 453

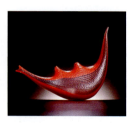

1.2.5 Lino Tagliapietra, *Batman*, 1998, p. 70

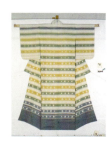

3.3.16 Sonoko Sasaki, *Sea in the Sky*, 2007, p. 424

2.7

Visual Communication Design

The essence of visual communication design is the use of symbols to communicate information and ideas. Traditional communication design was known as graphic design: the design of books, magazines, posters, advertising, and other printed matter by arranging drawings, photographs, and type. Advances in printing processes, television, the computer, and the growth of the Web have expanded graphic design to include many more design possibilities. A better and more complete term for it now is visual communication design. Furthermore, while graphic design was the responsibility of specialists, the typographical power of the computer—both for print and the Web—means that many more people can, with a little practice, create an effective and even innovative design work, provided they understand the principles of visual communication design.

This chapter will discuss the development of the **media**, systems, and processes used in visual communication design. While based on simple ideas, visual communication design enables us to express our ideas with increasing clarity, style, and sophistication—valuable qualities in a rapidly changing world.

The Early History of Graphic Arts

The graphic arts probably started when a prehistoric person spat pigment through a reed to **stencil** a handprint on the wall of a cave. The ancient Mesopotamians, in what is now Iraq, were the first people (*c.* 3400 BCE) to employ picture symbols in a consistent language system. The ancient Egyptians later created their own version of picture symbols, known as hieroglyphics, as a written form of communication. In particular, the Egyptians wrote them on scrolls made of a paper-like substance created from the pith of the papyrus plant (see, for example, **2.7.1**). While early Chinese written characters also frequently

2.7.1 Section of papyrus from *Book of the Dead of Ani*, *c.* 1250 BCE. British Museum, London, England

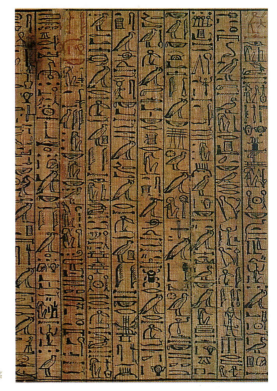

Medium (plural **media**): the material on or from which an artist chooses to make a work of art, for example canvas and oil paint, marble, engraving, video, or architecture

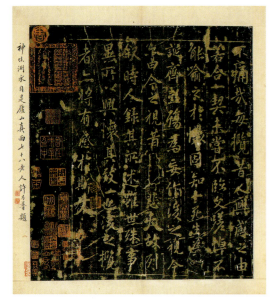

2.7.2 Rubbing of stela inscription, *Preface of the Lanting Gathering*, Ding Wu version (Inukai version), original by Wang Xizhi, Eastern Jin Dynasty, dated 353. Album, ink on paper, 9⅝ × 8⅞". Tokyo National Museum, Japan

fine specimens of writing were carved on large standing stone tablets, from which visitors could take copies by making rubbings—a rudimentary printing technique (**2.7.2**).

During the Middle Ages, European artists combined calligraphy and illustration to craft **illuminated manuscripts** (for example **2.7.3**). Illuminated manuscripts were executed in monasteries on prepared animal skins, called parchment. After being painted and lettered by hand, they were bound as books. This kind of design was very time consuming and produced only one copy of the book. The invention of printing technology simplified the design process and made it possible to print multiple copies. In other words, printing made graphic design possible.

Abstract: art imagery that departs from recognizable images from the natural world
Calligraphy: the art of emotive or carefully descriptive hand lettering or handwriting
Illuminated manuscript: a hand-lettered text with hand-drawn pictures

2.7.3 *Dutch History Bible*, copied by Gherard Wessels van Deventer in Utrecht, 1443, fol. 8r. National Library of the Netherlands, The Hague

resembled the subject they identified, later forms of picture writing became increasingly **abstract**. The Western alphabet has followed the same trajectory; while originally (for example) the letter A was supposed to be derived from the shape of a house, and B from a cow, it has now lost any of its earliest connections with the representations of things.

Wherever literacy takes hold, **calligraphy** usually develops as a form of art concerned to express layers of meaning and feelings by means of the shape of written letterforms. For example, handwritten wedding invitations are created using calligraphy because the flowing line and distinctive character of the lettering communicate the upcoming event in an elegant and romantic way. In oral communication, changes in tone, volume, facial expression, hand gestures, and body movement work together; in calligraphy, the physical act of writing, the thought expressed, and the visual form of the text become one. Chinese culture particularly exalts calligraphy executed in black ink with a brush. The Chinese calligrapher Wang Xizhi defined the art of calligraphy in China during the Jin Dynasty (265–420 CE). Although none of Wang's originals still exists, other calligraphers copied his work through the ages, perpetuating his ideal of perfect form. In ancient China,

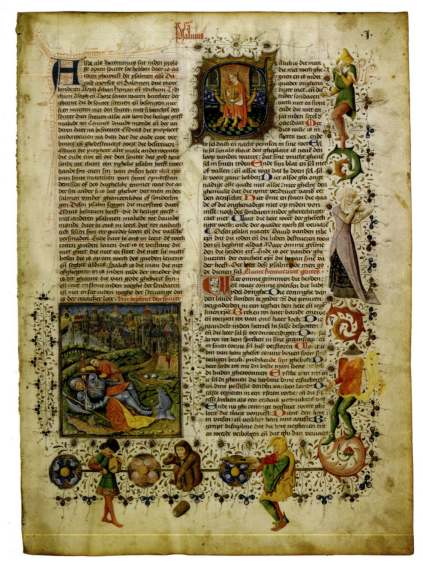

Graphic Design

Graphic design is the art of improving visual communication. As you read this text, you may have noticed the way the information is organized. Headings, page numbers, illustrations, and the definitions of terms in the margin have all been carefully considered with you in mind. The use of **boldface** type and columns of text helps you read and understand. In other visual arts it may be preferable to invite a viewer to consider and contemplate. But in graphic design, the communication is intended to be instantaneous, clear, and direct.

Typography

The visual form of printed letters, words, and text is called **typography**. Type, a word derived from a Greek word meaning "to strike," first came into existence with Johannes Gutenberg's (c. 1398–1468) invention of the printing press in Germany around 1450. Gutenberg also created a technique for producing small cast-metal letter shapes, known as letterforms, that could be set next to each other in a row, inked, and then printed in relief on paper using his press. Gutenberg's letterforms have angled thick and thin strokes that mimic the pen calligraphy used in illuminated manuscripts (called Black Letter). Scholars believe his intention was to emulate handwritten texts; his first Bibles used the exact same letterforms as those used in manuscripts, and the pages even included illustrations drawn by hand.

The German master printmaker Albrecht Dürer (1471–1528) wrote systematically on the subject of typography in order to teach others. In *The Painter's Manual: A Manual of Measurement of Lines, Areas, and Solids by Means of Compass and Ruler* (1525; republished 1538), Dürer sought to create a set of rules for the design of letter shapes (**2.7.4**). His was the first text to standardize how to create each letter using such geometric elements as squares, circles, and lines. Through these careful instructions, a typographer could create letterforms similar to those used by the ancient Romans.

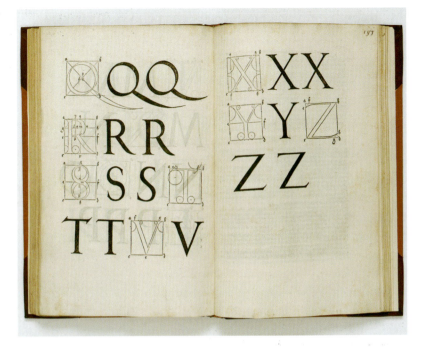

Dürer's Roman alphabet is notably different from Gutenberg's letterforms. A complete alphabet of letterforms and matching punctuation is called a font. A font is a group of letterforms designed to have a unified appearance. Roman-style fonts were derived directly from the letters chiseled into stone on the buildings and monuments of ancient Rome. Those characters had a vertical or horizontal mark at the edges of some letters. These marks, called serifs, were integrated into many early typefaces. The differences between these kinds of fonts are shown in **2.7.5**.

2.7.4 Albrecht Dürer, pages from *Course of the Art of Measurement with Compass and Ruler*, 1538. Victoria and Albert Museum, London, England

Boldface: a darker and heavier typeface than its normal instance
Typography: the art of designing, arranging, and choosing type

𝕲𝖚𝖙𝖊𝖓𝖇𝖊𝖗𝖌 𝕭𝖎𝖇𝖑𝖊

Roman Serif Font

Sans Serif Font

2.7.5 Some font styles:
1. Replica of Black Letter style used in Gutenberg's 1454 Bible
2. Times New Roman with some serifs circled
3. Helvetica font with no serifs (sans serif)

Influence of the Bauhaus on Visual Design

The Bauhaus was a German school of art and design that operated in the early twentieth century. From about 1919 to 1933, the students at the school were immersed in the creation of art and design relating to every object and idea that could be addressed using **Modernist** theory, or the idea that the design of an object and the material from which it is made should be determined by its purpose ("form follows function"). Although the Bauhaus was initially conceived as a school of architecture by its founder, Walter Gropius, the school worked to establish design ideals that could be applied universally with no constraints on culture or medium. Bauhaus artists designed and redesigned furniture, kitchenware, and household items, and set a new standard for visual communication design.

The mission of the school was to create designs that fit the modern world. Using inexpensive and common materials, the artists of the Bauhaus sought to imagine a style that was universal and did not favor one culture over another. This was evident in the printed materials that were generated by such professors as Herbert Bayer. Bayer created a sans serif typeface that he named "Universal" (**2.7.6a**). Bayer's typeface had its own character that could not be immediately associated with any one culture, but that was easy to read and facilitated visual communication. This same typeface was used to spell out the name of the Bauhaus on the outside of the building (**2.7.6b**).

After the rise of the Nazi Party in Germany and the subsequent closure of the school in 1933, a number of artists and designers relocated outside of Europe, many moving to the United States. Among them was Ludwig

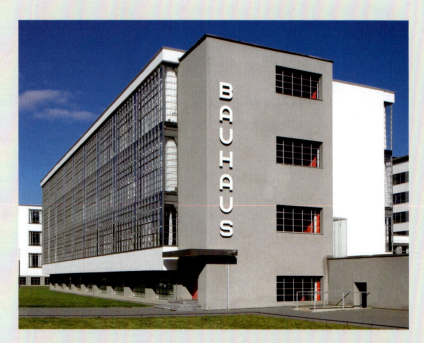

Mies van der Rohe (1886–1969), who had been Head of the Bauhaus. He re-established the school and continued its ideals by founding the Armour Institute of Technology (later called the Illinois Institute of Technology) in Chicago. Mies van der Rohe is often best remembered for his emphasis on simplicity of design, and his quips, "Less is more" and "God is in the details," expressed two key ideas that inspired an entire generation of architects and designers in the mid-twentieth century, whose influence can still be seen in design practice today.

2.7.6a (above top)
Herbert Bayer, *Universal* typeface, 1925

2.7.6b (above)
Walter Gropius, Bauhaus building, 1925–26, Dessau, Germany

In books and newspapers, serif fonts are traditionally used in the main text because they are considered easier to read. Typographers often use a sans serif font, or a font without serifs, in headings. (Sans serif derives its name from the French word *sans*, meaning "without," and perhaps from the Dutch word *schreef*, meaning a stroke of a pen.) In the twenty-first century, sans serif has become the standard font style in electronic media, as tiny serifs may not fully appear in comparatively low-resolution electronic displays.

Typographers follow some simple rules to make sure a written message is clear. When using multiple fonts, the fonts must be different enough to avoid confusion between the typefaces. The visual weight, or thickness, of the letters can be used for **contrast** and to emphasize a section of the text simply by changing type to bold. The choice of larger or smaller font sizes also adds another level of contrast and **emphasis**. Finally, even more emphasis and contrast can be gained through the choice of **color**. Typographers use these options carefully to "keep it simple" and to create a message that is clear, concise, and easily understood.

Logos and Icons

Businesses and other organizations use logos as communication tools. A logo (from the Greek *logos*, meaning "word") is often simply a carefully designed piece of type, called a logotype, that is unique and easily identified. The logo design of the Ford Motor Company has become universally recognized (**2.7.7**). In 1903

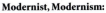

2.7.8 Chevrolet logo, first used in 1913

an engineer and Ford executive named Harold Wills created the original logo, which read "Ford Motor Company Detroit, Mich.," from the lettering style used on his business cards. His original design was later simplified into a plainer writing style that was common at the time. This particular font, known as Spencerian script, was derived from the style of handwriting that was practiced in America in the nineteenth century.

Sometimes a designer communicates an idea using a pictorial symbol instead of type. The Chevrolet logo was first used in 1913 and has been an identifying mark for the company ever since. Originally, the name "Chevrolet" was written across the simple stylized cross (called the "bowtie"). Over time, the symbol became associated in people's minds with the name, which was then removed from the design. It now communicates the company name without using one letter of the alphabet (**2.7.8**).

The immediacy and universal communicative properties of logos have become the basis for a new kind of labeling system that is now used worldwide. Icons, or simple symbolic graphic shapes, are being used in place of written labels because they provide an

Modernist, Modernism: a radically new twentieth-century architectural movement that embraced modern industrial materials and a machine aesthetic
Contrast: a drastic difference between such elements as color or value (lightness/darkness) when they are presented together
Emphasis: the principle of drawing attention to particular content in a work
Color: the optical effect caused when reflected white light of the spectrum is divided into separate wavelengths

2.7.7 Ford Motor Company logo, *c.* 1906

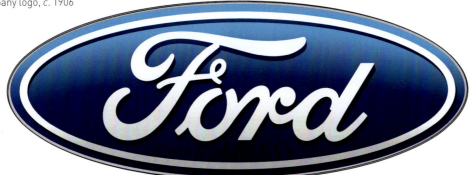

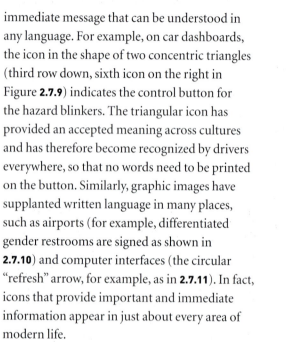

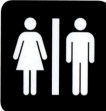

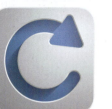

immediate message that can be understood in any language. For example, on car dashboards, the icon in the shape of two concentric triangles (third row down, sixth icon on the right in Figure **2.7.9**) indicates the control button for the hazard blinkers. The triangular icon has provided an accepted meaning across cultures and has therefore become recognized by drivers everywhere, so that no words need to be printed on the button. Similarly, graphic images have supplanted written language in many places, such as airports (for example, differentiated gender restrooms are signed as shown in **2.7.10**) and computer interfaces (the circular "refresh" arrow, for example, as in **2.7.11**). In fact, icons that provide important and immediate information appear in just about every area of modern life.

Illustration

Illustrations are images created to inform as well as to embellish the printed page. Good illustration is critical in such fields as medicine and science, where it may communicate essential information more effectively than text or a photograph.

The nineteenth-century English artists and designers William Morris (1834–1896) and Edward Burne-Jones (1833–1898) believed society should reject rampant industrialization and restore hand craftsmanship. Their illustrated book of the works of the medieval poet Geoffrey Chaucer was hand-crafted so that each page contained illustrations, **illuminated characters**,

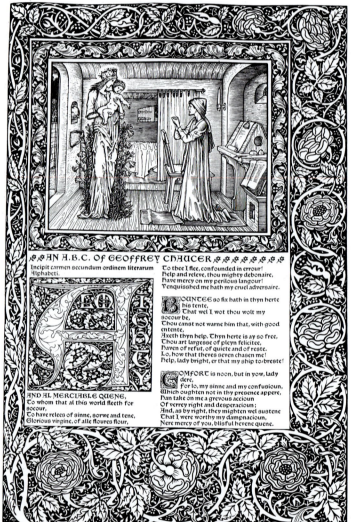

and patterns (**2.7.12**). The illustrations allow readers to experience and understand the works of Chaucer more richly. They support and enhance the written words.

The American illustrator James Montgomery Flagg (1877–1960) brought a patriotic literary

![I Want You for U.S. Army recruitment poster](...)

I WANT YOU
FOR U.S. ARMY
NEAREST RECRUITING STATION

printed design. Digital drawings are produced through the use of computer applications that use mathematical formulas dependent on the relative placement of points. In these math-based applications, the computer generates an image, called a vector graphic, from a series of lines plotted from the relationship between individual points. Since points and lines are the basic units of this system, it bears a resemblance to drawing processes. Most of the line art in this book was created using this type of digital illustration application.

The Portuguese-born illustrator Jorge Colombo (b. 1963) creates drawings digitally, using his iPhone in the streets of New York City. His images have become well known, having graced several covers of *The New Yorker* magazine (**2.7.14**). The artist likes to create his work this way because passersby think that he is just checking his e-mail and do not disturb him as he works. The results are fresh and spontaneous enough to capture the vibrant energy of New York.

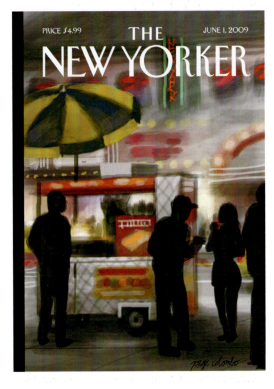

2.7.13 James Montgomery Flagg, *I Want You for U.S. Army,* recruitment poster, *c.* 1917

figure to life and created a memorable icon of the United States when he drew the first image of "Uncle Sam." Although Uncle Sam was a fictional character from the early nineteenth century, it was Flagg who brought him to life and, in his poster of 1917, "I Want YOU for U.S. Army," created an image that would become a representation of the US government (**2.7.13**). The poster, which was inspired by a similar British poster featuring Lord Kitchener, helped to recruit soldiers for World Wars I and II. Flagg designed the image of Uncle Sam using his own face, its intimidating authoritarian stare and the outstretched pointing finger intended to confront and single out the viewer and challenge his commitment to the defense of the nation.

Digital illustration has become a popular way for designers to incorporate illustrations into a

2.7.14 Jorge Colombo, *Finger Painting. The New Yorker* magazine cover, June 1st, 2009. Digital sketch using iPhone

Layout Design

Layout design is the art of organizing type, logos, and illustrations in traditional print media. Good layout design is essential if information is to be easily understood. One of the main considerations in layout design is spacing. Designers are very aware of **white space**—the **voids** that lie between text areas and images—and are careful in its organization and distribution in their layouts.

If you examine the way this page is designed, you will notice the relationships between columns of text, images, and other features, such as page numbers. The designer responsible for this page has made sure each feature has enough white space around it to be easily identified and understood, but is close enough to related elements, such as the pictures, so that the text and images complement each other.

The French artist Henri de Toulouse-Lautrec (1864–1901) created posters for his favorite

2.7.15 Henri de Toulouse-Lautrec, *La Goulue at the Moulin Rouge*, 1891. Lithograph in black, yellow, red, and blue on three sheets of tan wove paper, 6'2½" × 3'9⅝". Art Institute of Chicago

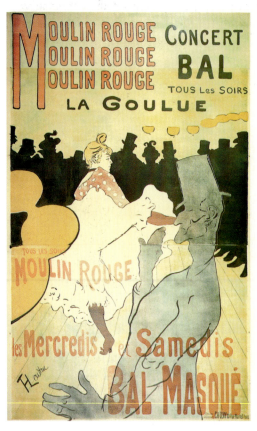

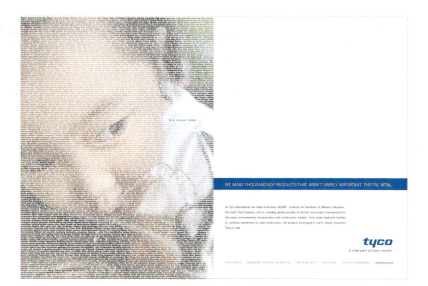

Parisian nightspot, the Moulin Rouge. In *La Goulue at the Moulin Rouge*, Toulouse-Lautrec uses a free, rounded writing style that is as casual as the spectators in the nightclub scene, as they watch La Goulue (the nickname, meaning "The Glutton," of the dancer Louise Weber) dance the can-can (**2.7.15**). Here, the text is calligraphy rendered by hand directly (in mirror-writing) on the lithographic stone from which it is printed. Toulouse-Lautrec's great skill as an illustrator and typographer is apparent in the excellent hand-rendered text and images.

Effectively controlling type and layout can produce amazing results. In the Tyco "Vital" advertising campaign, the designer carefully controls the color and size of the fonts so that the list of Tyco products and services reveals the face of a young child (**2.7.16**). The designer effectively communicates the suggestion that Tyco's products and services are vital to her and others' survival.

Color in Visual Communication Design

Artists who design images for commercial printing or to display on video screens take a different approach to color than painters or other kinds of artists. In this section we will look at how color is used in print and electronic displays.

2.7.16 Hill, Holliday, Connors, Cosmopulos advertising agency, Boston, Massachusetts, *Tyco—A Vital Part of Your World*, 2005

White space: in typography, the empty space around type or other features in a layout
Void: an area in an artwork that seems empty
Primary colors: three basic colors from which all others are derived

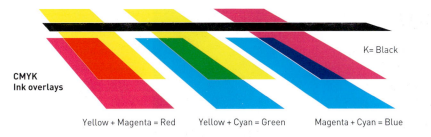

2.7.17 Cyan, Magenta, Yellow, and Black ink overlays, showing the resulting secondary color when they are combined

CMYK
Ink overlays

K= Black

Yellow + Magenta = Red   Yellow + Cyan = Green   Magenta + Cyan = Blue

Color in Print

Most printed color images—from posters, to magazines, to this book—rely on four separate colors to create the range of colors that we see. Commercial printers use three **primary colors**—cyan (a kind of light blue-green), magenta (a light red-violet), and yellow—plus black, or key; the color system for printing is referred to as CMYK (**2.7.17**). An image is scanned and separated into the four colors. Figure **2.7.18** shows a typical set of color separations. The image is re-created when the separated colors are printed in sequence, overlapping each other. The four colored inks are printed on paper as dots in a regular pattern ("screen"): the smaller the dot, the less of each color is printed. In the darkest colors the dots are nearly joined together. If you look very closely (using a magnifying lens) at the pictures in this book, you will be able to see the dots. This color printing process, called offset printing, saves time and money, but still provides good color quality for a viewer. Like

other aspects of visual communication, the perception of color is important to support comprehension, because color provides more levels of information by attracting attention and differentiating visual data.

Color in Electronic Displays

A computer-generated image produces color very differently. First, the digital display is illuminated by three different colored light cells, called phosphors, which project the primary colors of red, green, and blue (this color system is referred to as RGB) (**2.7.19**). Then, the electronic monitor turns a combination of phosphors on or off to produce the colors the designer wants. For example, if the red and blue phosphors are on, the color on the display will be magenta. If all three of the primaries are on, the combination will result in white light. Complex combinations of these color lighting cells will result in millions of color possibilities.

The brilliant illuminated color of a video display is a seductive medium for video game

2.7.18 Color separation for a commercially printed reproduction of an artwork by Van Gogh. The image on the extreme left is Van Gogh's original; the other four show how it reproduces in each of the separate, different-colored ink printing screens

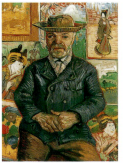

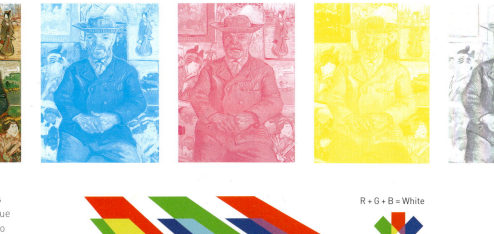

2.7.19 Combinations of Red, Green, and Blue (RGB) light, overlaid to reveal mixtures

RGB
Light overlays

R + G + B = White

Red + Green = Yellow   Green + Blue = Cyan   Red + Blue = Magenta

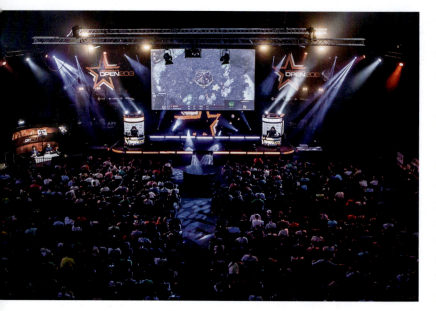

2.7.20 Dreamhack Gaming Conference, Bucharest, Romania, 2013

developers. Blizzard Entertainment developed the game Starcraft using RGB primaries to create a dazzling illuminated array of colors reminiscent of a modern-day stained-glass window. Starcraft's rich colors are displayed for a large audience each year at the annual Dreamhack (**2.7.20**) computer gaming conference in Bucharest, Romania. Teams of professional game players generate vivid animated scenes for audiences that fuse the experience of an animated movie with that of

a sporting event. Digital works have a glow and rich color that bring new sensations to art and design, and they attract a growing number of artists and game developers.

Web Design

In the past twenty-five years, visual communication design has been dramatically influenced by the Internet. The use of text and image in mass communication has evolved from the motionless design of print publications to the interactive designs used on the World Wide Web. The Web allows designers more freedom to add interactivity so that text and image can change as the reader progresses through the information presented.

In a website design created at the 2008 Carolina Photojournalism Workshop, the communicated message is enhanced by the integration of text, image, and interactivity (**2.7.21**). The artist, Seth Moser-Katz (b. 1984), has placed a large, photographic background image, illustrating the important issue of beach erosion, into the page design. The central location of the gray text box, combined with the open space around it, draws attention to the written message. Moser-Katz has also cleverly created a series of rectangular images as hyperlinks at the bottom of the design. When a user moves a cursor over one, new text appears in the gray text box. When clicked, a new page opens that plays a recorded message and presents a series of photos related to an important issue for those who live in the region. By employing a good visual communication design, Moser-Katz makes the message more direct, clear, and engaging.

Contemporary website designers try to connect the subject to the design by incorporating interesting features. The web design group Hello Monday did just that when it created a website for an exhibition of the Belgian artist René Magritte's work (**2.7.22a** and **2.7.22b**) at the Museum of Modern Art in New York and the Art Institute of Chicago. In this design the designers have programmed the interactivity so that sounds, movement, and other features

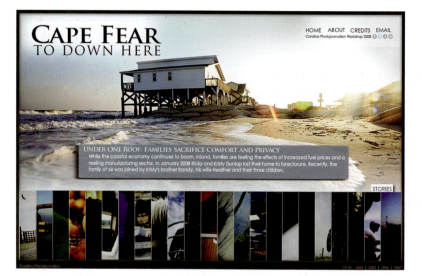

2.7.21 Screenshot from Carolina Photojournalism Workshop, Seth Moser-Katz (design) and Emily Merwyn (programming). Photo Eileen Mignoni. School of Journalism and Mass Communication at the University of North Carolina at Chapel Hill, 2008. http://www.carolinaphotojournalism.org/cpjw/2008

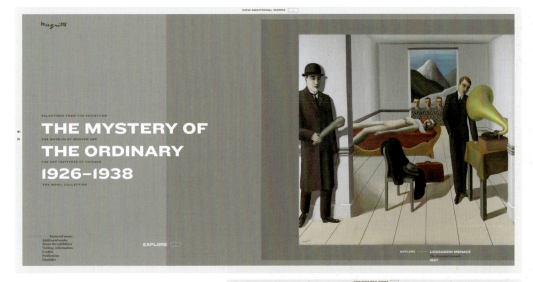

2.7.22a "Magritte: The Mystery of the Ordinary, 1926–1938," The Museum of Modern Art, New York, 2013. Screenshot from exhibition website, design by Hello Monday, 2013. Featuring detail of René Magritte's *The Menaced Assassin*, Brussels, 1927

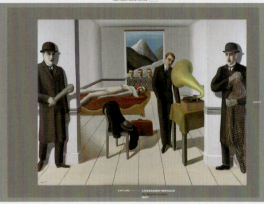

2.7.22b René Magritte, *The Menaced Assassin*, Brussels, 1927. Oil on canvas, 4′ 11¼″x 6′ 4⅞″. MoMA, New York. Screenshot from "Magritte: The Mystery of the Ordinary, 1926–1938" exhibition website, MoMA, 2013

are revealed as the viewer enters the site and is invited to discover new aspects of it while being introduced to the artist's work. Magritte's art possesses a mysterious character that the designers have captured in the intriguing ways that windows open (often from the side and center of the screen) and the media (various sounds are activated as the user selects content) are experienced by the viewer.

Active Learning Exercises

1. Typography is the visual form of printed letters, words, and text. Good typography is the art of using type in a way that is interesting and communicative. A good rule of thumb in typography is to limit the number of fonts to just a few that contrast with each other. For example, a funky typeface, like Comic Sans, would make a great heading font because it can attract attention, but it works best when complemented by a more readable font, like Times New Roman. Look through your list of fonts and create some combinations by writing a short paragraph with a title. Which combinations are easiest to read and which are hardest? Ask one of your peers. What other ways can you improve the visual form of your written work?

2. The illustrator Jorge Colombo created cover-worthy illustrations using his iPhone. There are quite a few apps for sketching available, and some of these are free. Try out a sketching app and see what kind of image you can make. After you have done some sketching look at Jorge Colombo's work (**2.7.14**). Can you imagine how he could create this work? Make a few notes of how you think he achieved it, and then, if you have access to the Internet, you can compare your notes with the artist's own videos of his process, which he has posted on the Web (http://www.jorgecolombo.com/covers/tny_20091116_mov.htm and http://www.jorgecolombo.com/covers/tny_20090921_mov.htm).

3. The color that appears on a computer monitor can be quite different than what emerges when a design is printed. The illumination of the screen can enliven the color in ways that pigment on paper cannot. Use your writing program (for example, Word) to create some color shapes. Print out the images and compare them to the image on your monitor. What are the main differences? The color on the screen is probably lighter and more vivid: can you darken it there so it matches the printed color better?

Images Related to 2.7:
Visual Communication Design

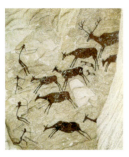

1.5.16 Cave paintings, Valltorta Gorge, Spain, *c.* 20,000 BCE, p. 129

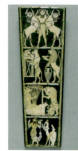

3.1.10 Sumerian Lyre panel, 2500–2400 BCE, p. 371

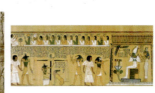

1.7.3 Relief from Temple of Amun, Egypt, 1295–1186 BCE, p. 148

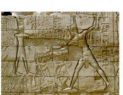

4.2.9 Book of the Dead, Egypt, 1275 BCE, p. 580

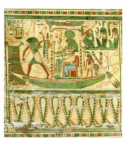

0.0.1 Detail of sun god Re from coffin, Egypt, 990–969 BCE, p. 26

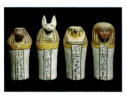

3.1.16 Hieroglyphs on Canopic jars, Egypt, 700 BCE, p. 376

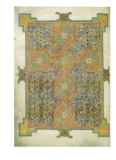

3.2.11a Cross-carpet page, Lindisfarne Gospels, 710–721 CE, p. 399

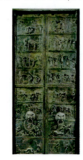

4.2.2b Doors, Church of St Michael's, Hildesheim, Germany, 1015, p. 576

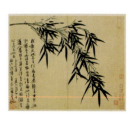

3.2.10 Page from the Koran, late 12th century, p. 398

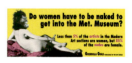

2.1.17 Wu Zhen, Leaf from an album, 1350, p. 209

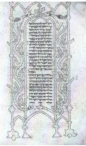

1.1.10 Franco-German hand, *Pentateuch*, 13th–14th century, p. 54

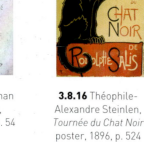

3.8.16 Théophile-Alexandre Steinlen, *Tournée du Chat Noir* poster, 1896, p. 524

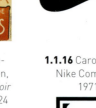

1.1.16 Carolyn Davidson, Nike Company logo, 1971 p. 57

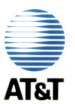

1.1.25 Saul Bass, Bass & Yager, AT&T logo, 1984, p. 61

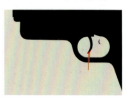

4.10.8 Guerilla Girls, *Do Women Have to be Naked to Get into the Met. Museum?*, 1989, p. 681

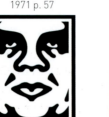

1.6.4 I. Michael Interior Design, Interior design, 1990s, p. 130

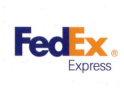

0.0.5 FedEx Express logo, 1994, p.29

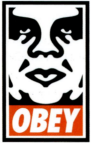

1.1.26a Shepard Fairey, *Obey*, 1996, p.62

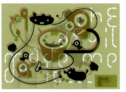

1.1.12 Sauerkids, *The Devil Made Me Do It*, 2006, p. 55

1.1.28 Noma Bar, *Gun Crime*, 2010, p.64

2.8

Photography

Recording the Image

The word photography derives from two Greek words, *photos*, meaning "light," and *graphein*, meaning "to draw": together, they mean "drawing with light." Before the digital era, traditional photographic processes recorded an image onto a light-sensitive material, usually film, which darkened when it was exposed to light. Because this produces what is known as a **negative** (a piece of film in which the lights and darks are the opposite of what we see in life, with the tones reversed), the image is repeatable. This negative can be reversed again, with chemicals or by re-exposure to light, to make an infinite number of **positive** prints, called photographs. Until the 1980s, this was how most photographs were created.

With the development of digital cameras in the 1980s, it became possible to record images in the form of pixels, which can then be stored as files on a computer. Today, digital photography is the most common way of creating photographic images. The portability of digital devices, and the fact that they make it easy and quick to capture images directly and instantly review them, whether indoors or out, have made them hugely popular. Additional adjustments, often quite complex and involving a lot of skill, can be made afterward to produce the final image on a monitor or in the form of a print.

While an iPhone, a Polaroid, and an antique camera may look very different to one another, the mechanics of all cameras are very similar to those of the human eye. Light enters the eye through the pupil; similarly, light enters the camera through a small opening, the aperture. In both eye and camera the lens adjusts, or is adjusted, to bring things into focus and give a clear vision of what is being viewed.

We now encounter photography everywhere. Many of us regularly take photographs and snapshots, and we have also become familiar with the idea and fact of photographers producing enduring works of art. But—perhaps surprisingly—when photography was invented in the nineteenth century, its reliance on mechanical and chemical processes led many to refuse to consider it an art form. Photography seemed to be a simple recording of the real world by a machine, not the result of an artist's creative imagination and highly developed skill. In fact a photographer can express ideas in many ways, for example by deciding the way the **subject** is photographed, by manipulating the image after it has been captured, or by combining the photograph with other images.

The invention of photography had an enormous impact on the development of modern art because of its ability to record reality in a way that seems to replicate the world precisely as we see it, something that had previously only been possible through an artist's rendering. Photography's ability to record directly even the most minute visual details opened up additional possibilities for art. As photography became widely practiced and accepted, artists working in any medium, including photography itself, no longer felt obliged to restrict their work to depicting reality

Negative: a reversed image, in which light areas are dark and dark areas are light (opposite of a positive)
Positive: an image in which light areas are light and dark areas are dark (opposite of a negative)
Subject: the person, object, or space depicted in a work of art

Color: the optical effect caused when reflected white light of the spectrum is divided into separate wavelengths

Fixing: the chemical process used to ensure a photographic image becomes permanent

Cyanotype: photographic process using light-sensitive iron salts that oxidize and produce a brilliant blue color where light penetrates and remain white where light is blocked; a variant of this process was used historically to copy architectural drawings

convincingly: many began to experiment with other approaches that would revolutionize art from the late nineteenth century onward.

The History of Photography

The basic principles of photography were known long before modern photographic processes were invented. A simple kind of camera called the camera obscura (Latin for dark room) had been used by artists for several centuries as an aid to drawing. It was not until the nineteenth century, however, that inventors discovered a number of ways to make permanent camera images that could be reproduced: in other words, photography.

The first cameras were indeed room sized, and the projections they created were used as guides for making drawings. An early illustration of a camera obscura shows the basic principles of all cameras today (**2.8.1**). When a small hole, or aperture, is placed in an exterior wall of a darkened room, light rays project the outside scene onto the opposite wall inside the room. A person could stand inside a camera obscura and trace over the image projected onto the wall. Inside the camera the image, no matter what size it was, continued to appear in **color**, but upside down and backward. Smaller, portable

models that often reversed the image using mirrors became widely available in Europe in the eighteenth century.

The images projected in a camera obscura are not permanent, but looking at the work of a contemporary artist allows us to see what a camera obscura image looks like. Cuban-American photographer Abelardo Morell (b. 1948) records camera obscura images in his photographs. He turned an entire hotel room into a camera obscura to project an upside-down image of the dome of the Panthéon, a building in Paris, France (**2.8.2**). The image projected in Morell's hotel room was only temporary until he took a picture of it, showing that the principles of the camera obscura are the same as those in a photographic camera.

The earliest images projected in the camera obscura were limited because they were transient and could be recorded only when traced over by hand. Photography could not exist until the image could be **fixed** (as photographers say). Some of the first photographic images made using a camera obscura came to be known as daguerreotypes. This process was developed and invented during the 1820s and 1830s by two Frenchmen—a painter and stage designer, Louis-Jacques-Mandé Daguerre (1787–1851) and a chemist, Joseph Nicéphore Niépce (1765–1833)—who worked together to establish a method of producing and fixing a camera image. They placed a polished metal plate, made light sensitive by silver iodide, inside the camera. The camera's shutter was opened to expose the plate to sunlight and record an image on its surface. Mercury vapors revealed the image before it was chemically fixed with table salt (later, as the process became more refined, daguerreotypes would be fixed with sodium thiosulfate, commonly known as hypo). While the daguerreotype process created very detailed images captured through a camera, these single, positive images on metal plates could not be readily reproduced (see **2.8.11** on p. 326).

2.8.1 *Optics: the principle of the camera obscura,* 1752. Engraving, 3¾ x 6½"

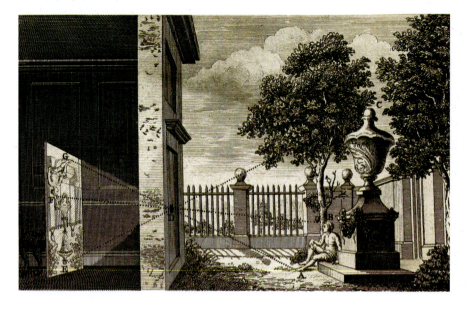

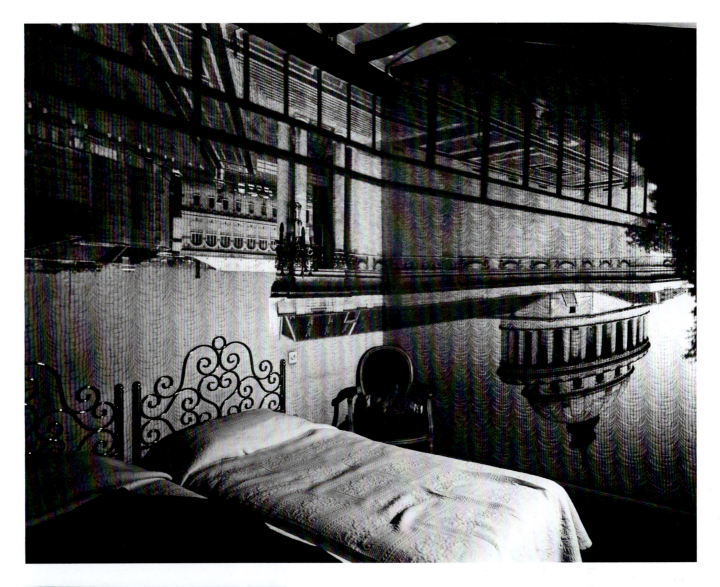

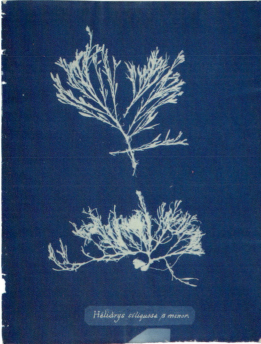

Hélidrys siliquosa β minor

In 1839, English scientist John Herschel (1792–1871) discovered a chemical compound that could fix, or make permanent, camera obscura images. Using another of Herschel's processes, English botanist and photographer Anna Atkins (1799–1871) made **cyanotype** images in 1843–44. She placed pieces of algae directly on paper that had been treated with a special light-sensitive solution, and exposed the sensitized paper to direct sunlight (**2.8.3**). The areas of the paper exposed to the light turned dark, but in the places where the plant's leaves and stems created a shadow, the paper remained white. Although Atkins made this image without a camera, the same principles are at work when a film camera is used, and her images look exactly like film negatives.

2.8.2 (above) Abelardo Morell, *Camera Obscura Image of the Panthéon in the Hotel des Grands Hommes*, 1999. Gelatin silver print, 20 × 24˝

2.8.3 (left) Anna Atkins, *Halydrys Siliquosa*, 1843–44. Plate 19 from Volume 1 of *Photographs of British Algae*. Cyanotype, 5 × 4˝. British Library, London, England

Traditional and Alternative Darkroom Methods

Once a photographer captures an image on film inside a camera, he or she must develop the film to produce a negative, and can then make photographic prints. A darkroom prevents any further light from reaching the light-sensitive materials and damaging the image during the process. Shining a light from an enlarger through the negative reverses the tones and projects a positive image onto light-sensitive paper. At this point the photographer chooses what size to make the image, but it is not yet visible on the paper. The paper then goes through a series of chemical solutions: first, a fluid called the **developer** reveals the image; next, placing the paper in the stop bath halts the development process; then fix, or fixer—a compound that also stops and stabilizes the photographic image— makes it permanent. Finally, the print is washed and dried.

In 1995 Scott A. Williams, PhD, and his Technical Photography class at Rochester Institute of Technology, New York, discovered that successful negatives and photographic prints could be made using a coffee-based developer. The ingredients are simple: caffeinated instant coffee, washing soda, and vitamin C. The development time is longer but no chemical stop bath is required. While no alternatives for chemical fix exist, using the Caffenol process, as it is now called, greatly reduces the environmental toxicity of traditional darkroom photography. In recent years environmentally conscious photographers, such as Maia Dery (2.8.6), have begun to use Caffenol as an alternative to more toxic chemical developer.

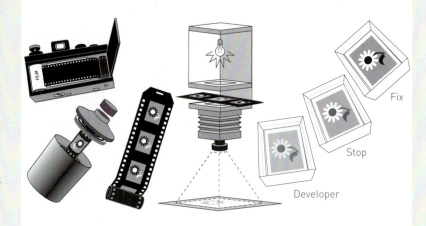

2.8.5 Diagram of film photography darkroom

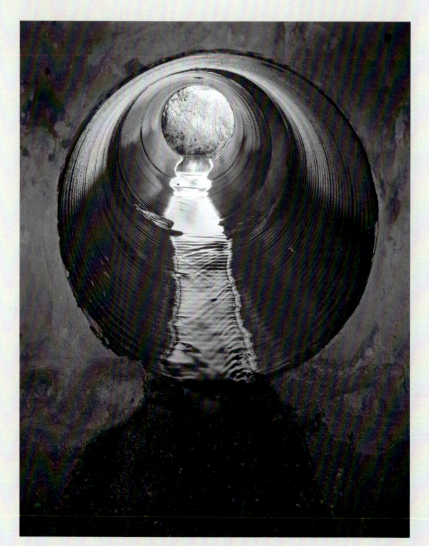

2.8.6 Maia Dery, *Storm Drain–Cape Fear River Basin*, 2013. Caffenol negative/Caffenol silver gelatin print, 9¾ × 7½"

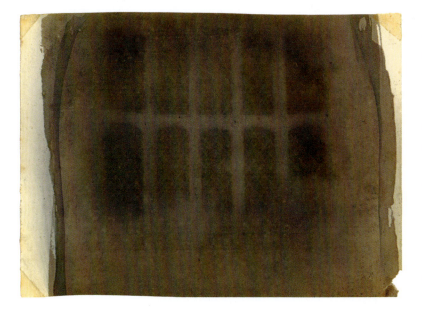

2.8.4 (above) William Henry Fox Talbot, *The Oriel Window, South Gallery, Lacock Abbey*, 1835 or 1839. Photogenic drawing negative; 3¼ x 4¼". Metropolitan Museum of Art, New York

Developer: after an image has been recorded on light-sensitive film or photographic paper (usually in a camera), immersion in this liquid substance chemically transforms a latent (or invisible) image into a visible one
Value: the lightness or darkness of a plane or area
Genres: categories of artistic subject matter, often with strongly influential histories and traditions
Portrait: image of a person or animal, usually focusing on the face
Still life: a scene of inanimate objects, such as fruits, flowers, or motionless animals
Style: a characteristic way in which an artist or group of artists uses visual language to give a work an identifiable form of visual expression

At about this time, the Englishman William Henry Fox Talbot (1800–1877) captured on light-sensitive paper a negative image of a window (**2.8.4**). This image, known as a calotype, resembled Atkins's botanical specimens. Talbot eventually discovered how to reverse the negative to make numerous positive prints, in which the places that appeared light in the negative, such as the window frames, would be dark in the print, while the dark areas, such as the sky, would change to light. The resulting print contained shades of gray that matched the **values** of the original scene. This negative/positive process is the basis of film photography (see Box: Traditional and Alternative Darkroom Methods).

These early processes were central to photography until the invention of digital cameras, first available around 1985, which record images not on film but in the form of pixels (tiny square dots arranged in a grid). Images recorded as pixels can be stored as digital files and printed on paper or projected on a screen or computer monitor. Some photographers present these images as they were originally taken, but many make alterations to them on a computer.

Photographic Genres

As photography became widely used in the nineteenth century, the English art critic John Ruskin argued that "a photograph is *not* a work of art" because only art "expresses the personality, the activity, the living perception of a good and great human soul." Photographers create images in the same **genres** as painters, however, making **portraits**, landscapes, and **still lifes**; although some photographs are factual records, others clearly explore ideas similar to the more traditional ones favored by Ruskin in the 1850s.

Portraiture

From the earliest days of photography, portraiture has been one of its most popular uses. Before photography was invented, the only way to get a portrait was to have an artist paint one—an expensive and time-consuming process. Photography changed all that. Eventually, camera technology allowed people to take their own pictures and to select and capture their own memories. Many photographic portraits follow the conventions for portraiture established in painting, while others take advantage of the camera's immediacy and its documentary potential to make new **styles** of portraits.

French photographer Nadar (1820–1910) made portraits of many well-known artists,

2.8.7 (below right) Nadar, *Sarah Bernhardt*, 1865. Albumen print, Bibliothèque Nationale, Paris, France

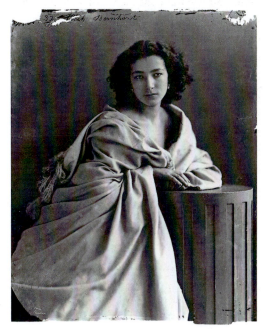

Gateway to Art: Lange, *Migrant Mother*
How the Famous Photograph Was Created

In 1936 Dorothea Lange (1895–1965) was working as a photographer for the federal Farm Security Administration when she took a photograph that would become a symbol of the hardships of the Great Depression. Lange wrote about the experience in the following passage:

"I saw and approached the hungry and desperate mother, as if drawn by a magnet. I do not remember how I explained my presence or my camera to her but I do remember she asked me no questions. I made five exposures, working closer and closer from the same direction. I did not ask her name or her history. She told me her age, that she was thirty-two. She said that they had been living on frozen vegetables from the surrounding fields, and birds that the children killed. She had just sold the tires from her car to buy food. There she sat in that lean-to tent with her children huddled around her, and seemed to know that my pictures might help her, and so she helped me. There was a sort of equality about it.

The pea crop at Nipomo had frozen and there was no work for anybody. But I did not approach the tents and shelters of other stranded pea-pickers. It was not necessary; I knew I had recorded the essence of my assignment."

Shooting documentary photographs involves many ethical issues, and Lange's photograph has been the subject of much discussion about the moral responsibilities of photographers. For example, did Lange consider Thompson's feelings when she had the photograph published? Should the photograph have been published without identifying the mother and her children? Lange was doing the job the federal government had hired her to do, however, and her photo made a difference to the lives of many poor and hungry people: after the picture was published, food was rushed to the migrant camp.

We are now very aware that photographs can be reproduced and manipulated, but we still tend to assume a photograph shows us what is "real." Such documentary images as *Migrant Mother* also raise the ethical questions of how the image presents the actual people it depicts; whether they have any say in their portrayal and its impact on viewers' perceptions of them; whether the photograph should be used later, and if so, how. For example, although Florence Thompson is now dead, Lange's photograph continues to be an enduring symbol of people struggling against poverty and deprivation. It reflects the lasting power of art, but this image also makes us wonder: is it fair for an artist to turn a real person into such a symbol?

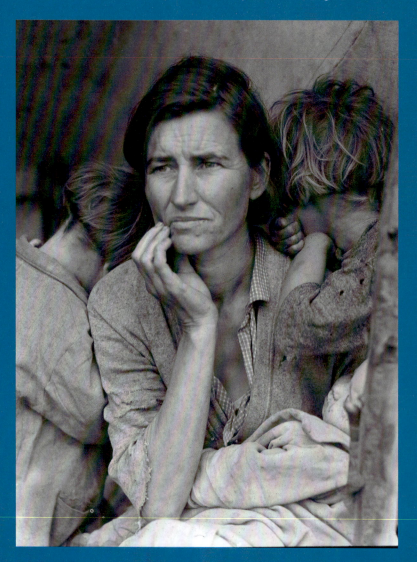

2.8.9 Dorothea Lange, *Migrant Mother*, 1936. Library of Congress, Washington, D.C.

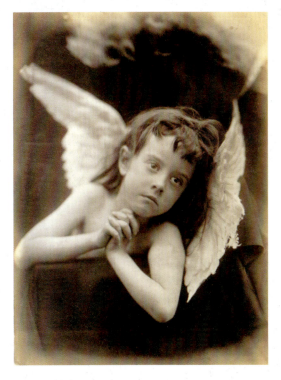

2.8.8 Julia Margaret Cameron, *Angel of the Nativity*, 1872. Albumen print, 12⅞ x 9½". The J. Paul Getty Museum, Los Angeles, California

Landscape

While portrait photographers capture images of individuals, landscape photographers take pictures of the land and its natural features. American Ansel Adams (1902–1984) is known for his landscape photographs of the American West. In *Sand Dunes, Sunrise—Death Valley National Monument, California*, Adams captures black, white, and gray tones that create a balanced effect (**2.8.10**). For Adams, a balanced photograph contains a range of tones that help us see the subject the way the artist wants us to, with everything in the picture clearly in focus. He was also deeply involved with the Sierra Club, which is dedicated to preserving America's wilderness. Such landscape photographs as these can raise awareness of nature's grandeur.

Foreground: the part of a work depicted as nearest to the viewer
Soft-focus: deliberate blurring of the edges or lack of sharp focus in a photograph or movie
Baroque: European artistic and architectural style of the late sixteenth to early eighteenth century, characterized by extravagance and emotional intensity

2.8.10 Ansel Adams, *Sand Dunes, Sunrise— Death Valley National Monument, California*, c. 1948. Gelatin silver print, 19½ × 14¾"

writers, and politicians. His photograph of the actress Sarah Bernhardt illustrates his straightforward style (**2.8.7**). Rather than showing the actress posed with elaborate props, which was the norm for portraits at the time, Nadar placed her in the **foreground**, surrounded only by luxurious fabric and leaning on a plain column. By focusing his attention on the sitter, Nadar creates an image that highlights the actress's elegance and an introspective aspect of her personality.

Also known for her portraits of celebrities, British photographer Julia Margaret Cameron (1815–1879) intentionally avoided sharp focus in order to emphasize spiritual and literary content in her work. Cameron believed that photography could show, in addition to what was visible, allegorical, poetic, and intuitive aspects of life that we may not readily see in the course of our daily lives. In order to achieve these aims, she used specially designed lenses as well as long exposure times to create a **soft-focus** look. In *Angel of the Nativity* (**2.8.8**) her characteristic technique helps transform her niece into a cherub, similar to those commonly featured in Renaissance and **Baroque** paintings.

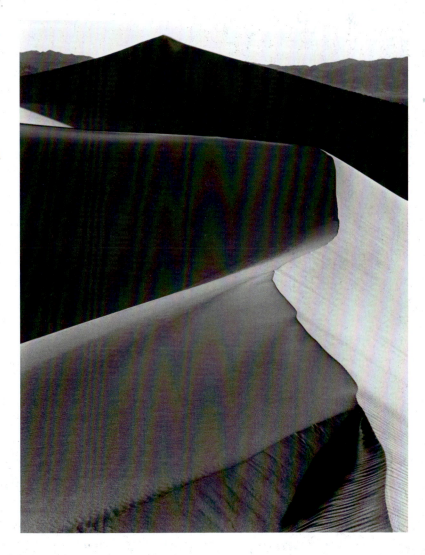

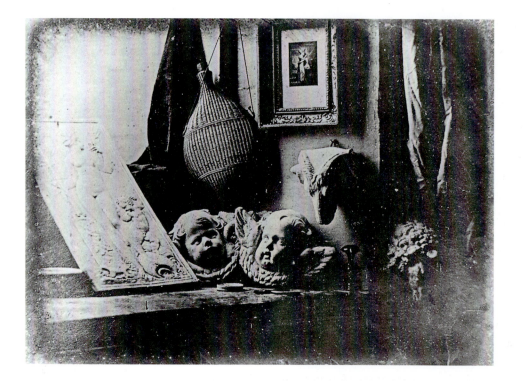

2.8.11 (left) Louis-Jacques-Mandé Daguerre, *The Artist's Studio*, 1837. Whole-plate daguerreotype. Collection of the Société Française de Photographie, Paris, France

2.8.12 (below) Edward Weston, *Pepper No. 30*, 1930. Gelatin silver print, 9⅜ × 7½". Collection Center for Creative Photography, University of Arizona

Still Life

One of the earliest surviving photographs is of a collection of objects in the photographer's studio. Daguerre, who was a painter as well as a photographer, used the genre of still life in much the same way that he did when he painted. A still life, or artistic arrangement of objects, allowed him to study the formal relationships of light, shadow, and **texture**. At this time many artists worked with live models in their studios, but in *The Artist's Studio* Daguerre used plaster **casts** instead, because his exposure times were then generally more than eight minutes, much too long to photograph a living person (**2.8.11**).

In the early twentieth century, photographers took a slightly different approach to still lifes. By focusing so closely on an object that it became almost **abstract**, such photographers as the American Edward Weston (1886–1958) were able to create a new visual experience. Weston believed in photographing a subject as he found it, creating sharply focused prints on glossy paper, and framing images with white mats (cardboard surrounds in which a window for the image was cut) and simple frames. Weston's *Pepper No. 30* concentrates the viewer's attention on the **form** and texture of the vegetable, so it begins to look like something other than itself,

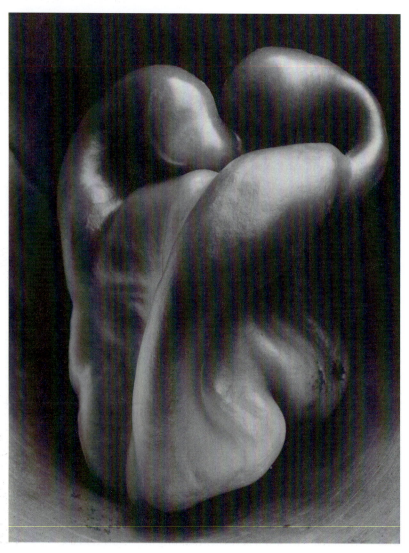

taking on qualities similar to those of a human form; at the same time it clearly represents what it is, a pepper (**2.8.12**).

Photojournalism

Photojournalism is the use of photography to tell a news story. Some of the earliest examples of photojournalism date back to the Civil War, when photographic equipment was portable enough to be used in the field. Although we now readily accept that photographs can distort, exaggerate, and even lie—because they can be manipulated, altered, cropped in particular ways, and only ever give a partial view—the medium was once believed to be inherently truthful. This credibility, even today, is crucial for news reportage.

American Lewis Wickes Hine (1874–1940) used photography to expose the injustice of child labor in the early 1900s (**2.8.13**). He went into factories and mines under the guise of a salesman, repairman, or safety investigator, and then took photographs as well as detailed notes about the ages of the children he found there. When he later published his findings, the public

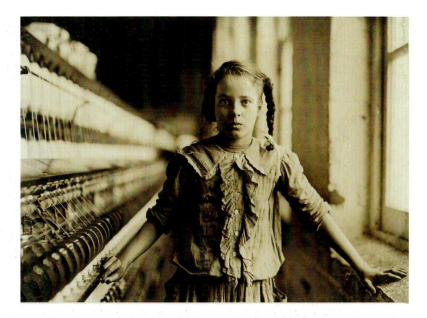

was shocked by his photos of these children and their often grueling and dangerous working conditions. His efforts eventually led to the establishment of laws preventing children from working at such young ages.

Many years after Hine, American Steve McCurry (b. 1950) also focused his lens on the plight of a child. He took his photograph called *Afghan Girl* in a refugee camp in 1984 after the Soviet invasion of Afghanistan (**2.8.14a**).

2.8.13 Lewis Wickes Hine, *Ten Year Old Spinner, Whitnel Cotton Mill*, 1908. Photographic print. Library of Congress, Washington, D.C.

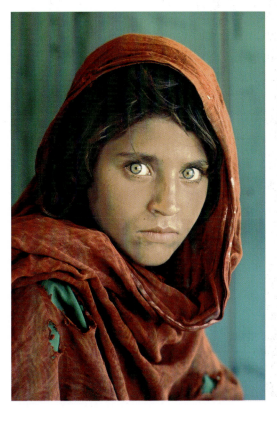

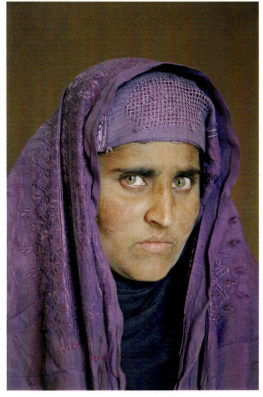

2.8.14a (far left) Steve McCurry, *Afghan Girl at Nasar Bagh Refugee Camp, Peshawar, Pakistan*, 1984

2.8.14b (left) Steve McCurry, *Sharbat Gula, Peshawar, Pakistan*, 2002

Texture: the surface quality of a work, for example fine/coarse, detailed/lacking in detail

Cast: a sculpture or artwork made by pouring a liquid (for example molten metal or plaster) into a mold

Abstract: art imagery that departs from recognizable images from the natural world

Form: an object that can be defined in three dimensions (height, width, and depth)

Perspectives on Art: Steve McCurry

Steve McCurry is a photographer who launched his photojournalism career by entering Afghanistan disguised in native clothing shortly before the Russian invasion in 1978. He estimates that during his career he made more than 800,000 photographs, including the famous Afghan Girl (2.8.14a), on Kodachrome film. For 75 years Kodachrome film was known for its rich, vibrant colors; archival durability; poetic rendition of reality; and being what McCurry called "probably the best film ever made." As a result of the digital revolution in photography, however, Kodak stopped manufacturing the film in 2009. McCurry decided to mark the demise of the film by launching a project to use the last roll of Kodachrome film to come off the assembly line. In a National Public Radio interview with Audie Cornish (July 24, 2010) and a National Geographic documentary about the making of the project, McCurry talked extensively about his process and the challenges he faced.

Discussing the pressure associated with taking photographs on the last-ever 36 frames of Kodachrome, McCurry said, "What do you photograph? . . . I need to find iconic situations and iconic people that are going to be kind of a great celebration of this last roll of film."

McCurry decided to make a series of portraits because it was the final roll of film and he could not take as many risks as outdoor settings and street scenes would require. He started the project in New York City, where he lived; then traveled to India, "where color is culturally important," as evidenced by its symbolic importance and prominence in religion, politics, festivals, and celebrations; went to Rajasthan because he felt a personal connection with people he had recently photographed there; and ended up in Parsons, Kansas, the location of the last Kodachrome-processing lab in the world.

Along the way McCurry worried about technical mishaps common with film as opposed to digital cameras: "it was really nerve-wracking because . . . you load [the film] in and, heaven forbid, somebody opens the back by mistake. You know, going through security . . . I was worried sick that there was going to be X-ray damage . . ." Opening

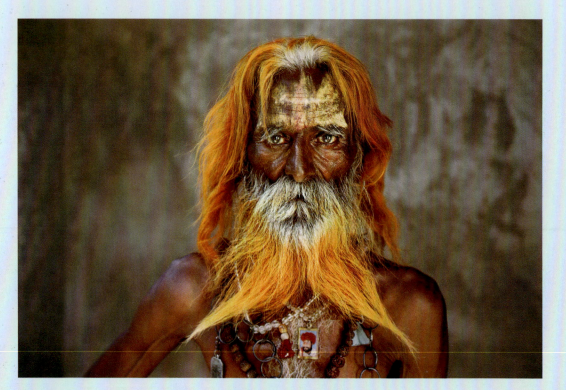

2.8.15 Steve McCurry, *Rabari Tribal Elder*, India, 2010

the camera outside of a darkroom can ruin unprocessed film by exposing it to light, while subjecting it to X-ray screening can cause fogging and discoloration. "[And then . . .] am I getting the right moment? . . . is it in focus, is the exposure right?" While many of these challenges exist when McCurry uses a digital camera, with digital photography, being able to see the results immediately (rather than having to wait until the film is developed) affords the opportunity to take another picture. McCurry used his digital camera to set the lighting, determine the composition and design, and make test photos before shooting any film with his analog (traditional) camera.

During his week in Rajasthan, McCurry photographed an ancient tribe of nomads. He felt it was especially fitting to "honor the film . . .with the memory and history of these Rabari shepherds" whose migratory way of life is coming to a close extremely rapidly due to modernization and land development. Like the *Magician* (**2.8.15**), some of the nomads are entertainers. These snake charmers, storytellers, and fortunetellers will have to find new ways to make a living. McCurry's powerful and compelling portrait demonstrates his belief that it is "the whole face that tells a story, not just the eyes . . . all the features work together."

At twelve years old, this young girl, Sharbat Gula, had already lost both parents, fled from her home with her grandmother, brother, and sisters, and walked over snow-covered mountains to Pakistan. For McCurry, pictures of individuals tell the story of conflict. This girl was just one of the people McCurry encountered on his trip, but her eyes made her unforgettable. In 2002, using the original photograph, McCurry again found Sharbat Gula, then in Afghanistan, and confirmed her identity by iris-pattern identification. When they met for the second time, custom dictated she could not smile or even look at a man who was not her husband. Both times their encounter was through the lens of the camera (**2.8.14b**).

Today, photojournalism communicates events almost immediately on television and the Internet, but those same images can also be used to record events for posterity. Photographs made during the attack on the World Trade Center on September 11, 2001, were published all over the world right after the event. In the days following 9/11, a group of photographers organized an exhibition called *Here Is New York: A Democracy of Photographs on the Streets of SoHo in New York City* (**2.8.16**). The collection of photos gave voice to almost 800 people who had experienced the attack at first hand, whether they were professional photographers or people who just happened to be carrying a camera that day. The exhibition traveled all over the world and was later donated to the New York Historical Society.

2.8.16 Hiroko Masuike, *Here Is New York: A Democracy of Photographs*, exhibition at the New York Historical Society, September 2007

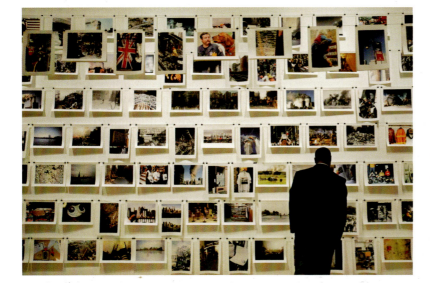

The Art of Photography

Photojournalists often focus on documenting a real event as accurately as possible, while artists use photography for a variety of creative purposes. Soon after it was invented, there were heated debates about whether photography worked best for recording reality or as a way to make works of art. Even though photographs have been collected in major fine art museums since the early twentieth century, the immediacy of the medium still causes some people to have trouble considering photography as "art." But a

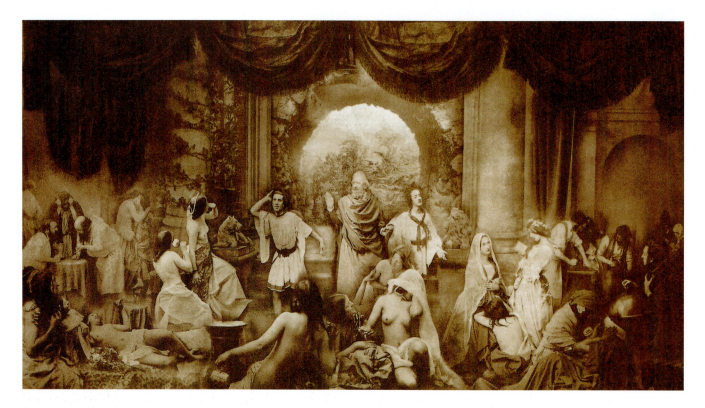

2.8.17 Oscar Gustav Rejlander, *The Two Ways of Life*, 1857. Albumen silver print, 16 × 31". Royal Photographic Society, Bath, England

2.8.18 Loretta Lux, *The Waiting Girl*, 2006. Ilfochrome print, 11⅞ × 15⅞"

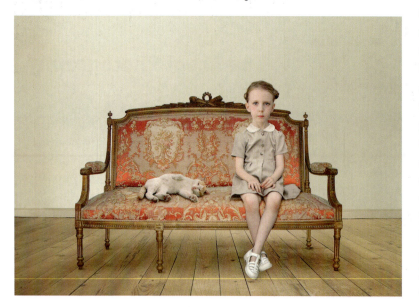

walk through today's galleries in any major city will show that photography is a favored medium of many contemporary artists.

Making "Artistic" Photographs

Swedish photographer Oscar Gustav Rejlander (1813–1875) worked in a labor-intensive, time-consuming way, just like traditional artists. By emulating the appearance and process of painting, Rejlander hoped his photographs would earn the respect that at that time was reserved for painting. His *Two Ways of Life* was made with thirty separate negatives, which were cut out like puzzle pieces (**2.8.17**). He exposed the negatives one at a time, covering the rest of the print every time he exposed another negative. The resulting image, which took him six weeks to make, looks like one seamless scene.

While Rejlander used manual methods to create his images, German photographer Loretta Lux (b. 1969) uses digital technology to assemble the elements in her compositions. She takes pictures of her friends' children and then subtly manipulates the colors and **proportions**, making the subjects look as if they just stepped out of a fairy tale. Sometimes she also paints **backgrounds**, which she then photographs and retouches digitally to contribute to the otherworldly effect. She works on each photograph for anywhere from several months to a year. *The Waiting Girl* shows a little girl and a cat on a vintage sofa (**2.8.18**). The girl's severely knotted hair, her uniform-like dress with its prim collar, and the emptiness of the background give the impression she spends her time in a confined environment, likely with people much older than herself. This picture, like the one Rejlander created, shows a scene that did not exist before the artist made it. Lux's subtle use of digital technology, though, allowed her to alter certain attributes, such as **scale** and proportion, to create the effect she wanted.

Recording Detail and Stopping Time

At a time when other photographers were trying to imitate traditional painting, the American Alfred Stieglitz (1864–1946) was amongst the first to emphasize what he considered to be the particular strengths of the photographic medium: its clarity and realism. In addition to making artistic photographs, Stieglitz actively promoted photography as a fine art medium in the journal *Camera Work* (first published in 1902) and in his New York galleries. *The Steerage* shows the decks of a passenger ship in the cheapest accommodations, separate from the first-class passengers, including Stieglitz himself (**2.8.19**). Stieglitz was struck by the **composition** of **shapes** and **rhythms** in the photograph, including the straw hat on the upper deck near the center, the crossed suspenders on the man

2.8.19 Alfred Stieglitz, *The Steerage*, 1907. Chloride print, 4⅜ × 3⅝". Alfred Stieglitz Collection, Art Institute of Chicago, Illinois

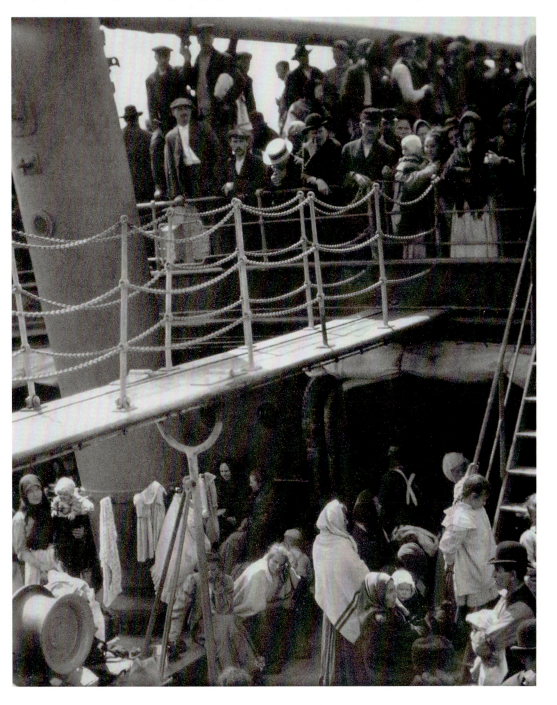

Proportion: the relationship in size between a work's individual parts and the whole

Background: the part of a work depicted furthest from the viewer's space, often behind the main subject matter

Scale: the size of an object or an artwork relative to another object or artwork, or to a system of measurement

Composition: the overall design or organization of a work

Shape: the two-dimensional area the boundaries of which are defined by lines or suggested by changes in color or value

Rhythm: the regular or ordered repetition of elements in the work

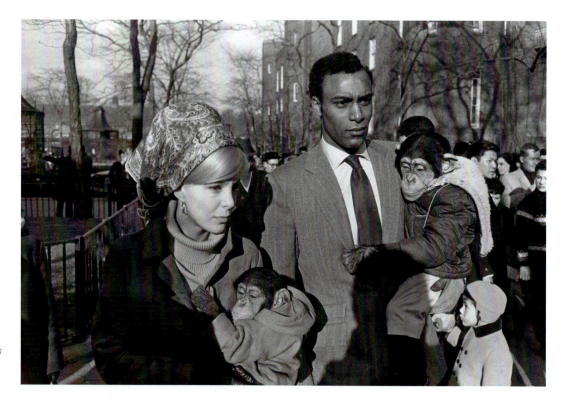

2.8.20 Garry Winogrand, *Central Park Zoo, New York City*, 1967. Gelatin silver print, 11 × 14"

below, the funnel leaning left, the stairway on the right, and the shapes of round machinery, draping chains, and the triangular mast. This composition seemed thoroughly modern and reminiscent of the abstract paintings of that era.

In contrast to Stieglitz's concern with sharp focus and formal composition, American Garry Winogrand (1928–1984) was more interested in photography's ability to capture a fleeting moment in time honestly. Winogrand used a small camera he could easily carry around. He generally did not pose his subjects or set up shots beforehand. Many of his photographs seem spontaneous, as in *Central Park Zoo, New York City*: he walked the city's streets and captured what he found there (**2.8.20**). Winogrand's approach, known as the snapshot aesthetic, seems casual, but he intended his photographs to be serious and artistic.

Photocollage and Photomontage

A **collage** is a composition created by gluing together fragments of separate materials to form an image. Collage is the name for both the technique and the resulting artwork. A photocollage is made from photo-based

images and pre-printed materials, or combines photographs and text. A collage is a unique artwork, like a drawing or a painting, that is not generally reproduced. By contrast, a **photomontage** is made to be reproduced. In photomontage, the artist combines smaller photographic images (using prints or negatives), then rephotographs or scans the result.

German artist Hannah Höch (1889–1978) was one of the first to make photomontages. She used them to protest social conditions, especially during and after World War I. In *Cut with the Kitchen Knife through the Last Weimar Beer-Belly Cultural Epoch of Germany*, Höch's **Dada** combination of text and images, and the image title, is at once complex and apparently nonsensical (**2.8.21**). The disorder of the image, which comprises pictures of political figures and modern technology from mass-media publications, reflects the chaos of life at that time. Höch also expresses her concern about women's issues in post-war Germany, highlighting their traditional tool of the kitchen knife and also including, in the lower right corner, a map showing where women had obtained the right to vote.

The American photographer Stephen Marc (b. 1954) manipulates and juxtaposes images so

Collage: a work of art assembled by gluing materials, often paper, onto a surface. From the French *coller*, to glue

Photomontage: a single photographic image that combines (digitally or using multiple film exposures) several separate images

Dada: anarchic anti-art and anti-war movement, dating back to World War I, that reveled in absurdity and irrationality

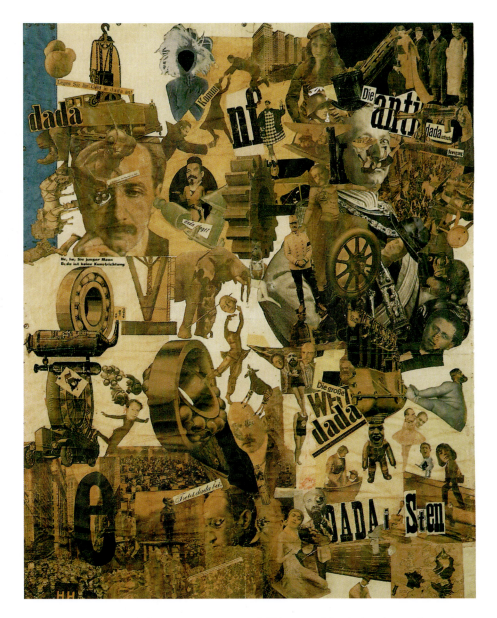

2.8.21 Hannah Höch, *Cut with the Kitchen Knife through the Last Weimar Beer-Belly Cultural Epoch of Germany*, 1919–20. Photomontage and collage with watercolor, 44⅞ × 35½". Nationalgalerie, Staatliche Museen, Berlin, Germany

they take on new meaning. In *Untitled—Passage on the Underground Railroad,* he interweaves pictures from various sources to create layers that are visually interesting (**2.8.22**). They also communicate complex ideas about how the past informs the present. Highlighting the dark and powerful history of the Cedar Grove Plantation in Vicksburg, Mississippi, Marc photographed the slave quarters there; he also includes an extract from a slave-owner's letter defending his decision not to emancipate his slaves. The rhythms of the fence, antique hoe, and cotton

2.8.22 Stephen Marc, *Untitled—Passage on the Underground Railroad*, 2002. Digital photomontage, archival pigment inkjet print, 9 × 26". Arizona State University, Phoenix

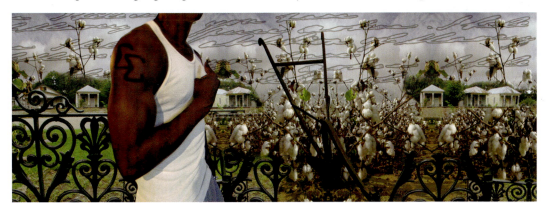

plants are punctuated by the young man who stands, displaying his Phi Beta Sigma fraternity brands, a voluntary celebration of fraternal commitment. The artist sees these markings as a contemporary crossover of African scarification and body marking, and the branding of livestock and slaves. The historical backdrop for this contemporary African-American enhances our understanding of the image.

Black and White versus Color

Although color processes were invented around the end of the nineteenth century, they were not used widely in photography until much later. Some artists hand-tinted their photographs or used complicated methods to make color photographs before color film became commercially viable in the 1930s. Even after that, some preferred to use black and white because it makes elements of the composition clearer, specifically the lines, contrast, and overall design. Today, so many of the images we see are in color that black-and-white photographs sometimes give the impression of being old-fashioned.

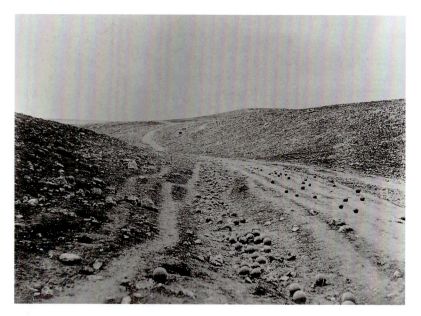

But whether the image is captured in black and white or color, digital technology now makes it easy to alter the tonality of photographs, using a number of effects that replicate the results of early photographic processes, including black-and-white and sepia tones.

We can see in the work of British artist Roger Fenton (1819–1869) some of the haunting

2.8.23 Roger Fenton, *Valley of the Shadow of Death*, 1855. Salted paper print from a paper negative. Gernsheim Collection, Harry Ransom Humanities Research Center, University of Texas at Austin

2.8.24 Sally Mann, "The New Mothers," from series *Immediate Family*, 1989. Gelatin silver print, 8 × 10"

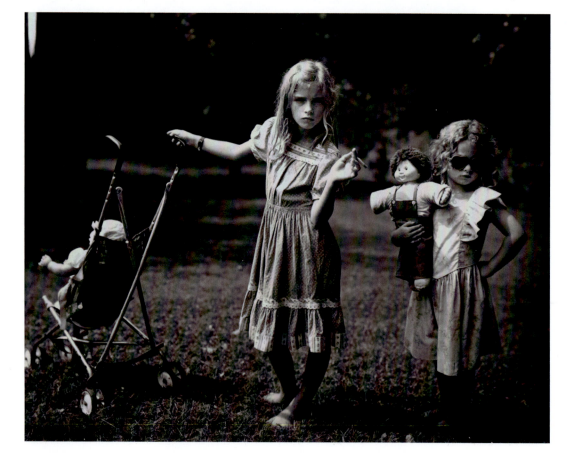

effects achieved by early practitioners of photography. Fenton was hired by a publisher to photograph the Crimean War (1853–56). Because his mission was to help counteract unfavorable public perceptions about the British government's involvement in the war, none of his photographs shows casualties or dead bodies. The title, *Valley of the Shadow of Death*, seems to derive from a passage from Psalm 23 in the Bible, referring to the comfort God offers for life's suffering, but in fact Fenton chose it some time after he had taken the photograph, as a result of the popularity of a now-famous poem by Alfred, Lord Tennyson. "The Charge of the Light Brigade" contains the refrain "Into the Valley of Death/Rode the six hundred," echoed in Fenton's title (**2.8.23**). In black and white, the cannonballs littering the battlefield seem eerie, and look like human skulls. Fenton captures the emptiness and desolation of the aftermath of combat in a poetic and thought-provoking scene.

The series *Immediate Family* by American photographer Sally Mann (b. 1951) uses black and white to transform ordinary moments into nostalgic and provocative statements. Parts of childhood experience and family interactions that might have passed by without note are captured in honest and refreshing ways. The images also reveal how children sometimes predict adult behaviors in their innocent mannerisms. Mann collaborated with her children to make the photographs: sometimes she came up with the ideas, sometimes they did. *The New Mothers* shows the artist's daughters at play, believably taking on the guise of women much older than themselves (**2.8.24**).

The color photograph *Radioactive Cats* by American Sandy Skoglund (b. 1946) is a carefully organized **narrative tableau**, or arrangement (**2.8.25**). Skoglund makes all the objects in her photographs, arranges them herself, then hires actors to pose with them, and records the resulting scene. Sometimes she also exhibits the tableau. In *Radioactive Cats*, the outlandish color contributes to a **surreal** combination of factual and fictional elements that make us question whether seeing really should be believing.

Canadian Edward Burtynsky (b. 1955) prints his powerful color photographs on a large scale, about 3 × 4 ft., so that small details create an

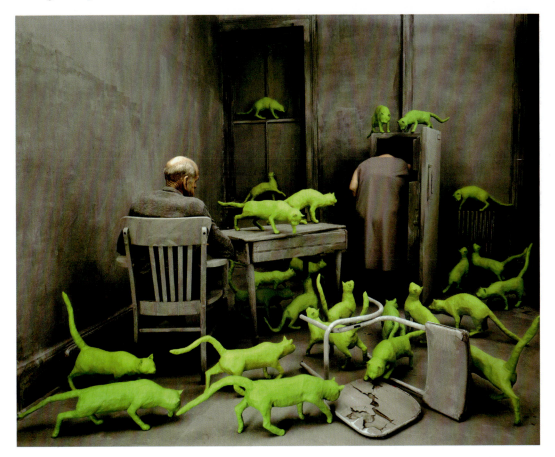

2.8.25 Sandy Skoglund, *Radioactive Cats* © 1980. Cibachrome or pigmented inkjet color photograph, 25⅝ × 35"

impression of the vast scale of urban landscapes and the relative smallness of humankind. His series called *Manufacturing* focuses on factories in China, where raw and recycled materials are brought to be turned into commercial products and shipped all over the world. "Manufacturing, #17: Deda Chicken Processing Plant" shows a vista of workers in a chicken-processing plant (**2.8.26**). The vivid pinks of the uniforms, the white boots, and the bright-blue aprons punctuate the industrial grimness of the warehouse. Without passing judgment, Burtynsky's arresting images call attention to things not usually in our consciousness. Burtynsky has said he wants viewers to come to their own conclusions about civilization's impact on the planet because "it's not a simple right or wrong. It needs a whole new way of thinking."

Expressive: capable of stirring the emotions of the viewer

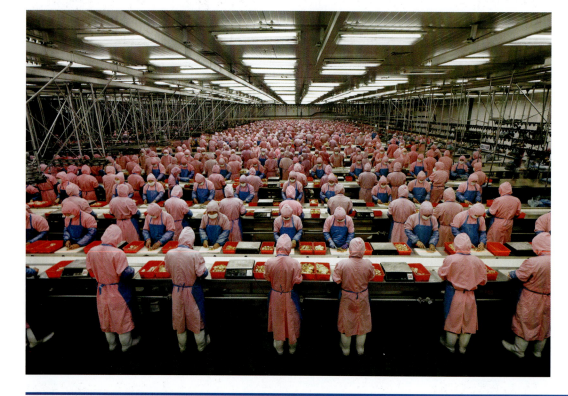

2.8.26 Edward Burtynsky, "Manufacturing, #17: Deda Chicken Processing Plant, Dehui City, Jilin Province, China, 2005"

Active Learning Exercises

1. The medium of photography is unique because it contains a direct connection to both a particular moment in time (a reality existing in the external world captured by the camera) and the creative and **expressive** choices in the mind of the artist. Find three photographs not in this chapter that represent a) connection to a specific moment in time, b) obvious creative alterations from reality, and c) a balanced combination of the two.

2. Choose five of the photographic categories from this chapter (e.g. portrait, snapshot, photojournalism, abstraction, photomontage). Using a cell phone or digital camera and/or iPad, take a photograph corresponding to each of your chosen categories. Present your chosen photographs to the class with a brief explanation of how each one relates to the relevant category.

3. The medium of photography introduced many perspectives on "truth." Considering both formal appearance and underlying content, choose three artworks that show different notions of "truth" that are relevant to historic or contemporary photography. Is a photograph more truthful than a painting or sculpture? Why, or why not? How has our understanding of truth changed due to the invention of photography? How might people be more skeptical about visual reality based on their experience with photographs in popular culture?

Images Related to 2.8:
Photography

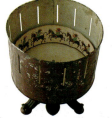

1.7.12a Henry Peach Robinson, *Fading Away*, 1858, p. 153

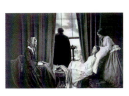

1.5.8 Zoetrope, 19th century, p. 124

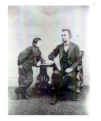

4.7.1 Timothy O'Sullivan, *Harvest of Death, July 1863*, 1863, p. 635

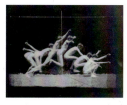

3.7.23 Alexander Gardner, *Abraham Lincoln and His Son Thomas (Tad)*, 1865, p. 509

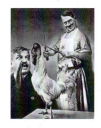

3.8.3 Thomas Eakins, *Motion Study: Male Nude, Standing Jump to Right*, 1885, p. 515

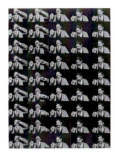

1.5.3 Thomas Edison and W. K. Dickson, *Fred Ott's Sneeze*, 1894, p. 121

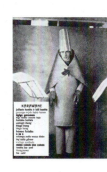

3.8.29 Hugo Ball, Performance of "Karawane" at Cabaret Voltaire, 1916, p. 532

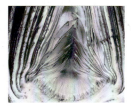

3.8.25 *Man Ray, Gertrude Stein with Portrait by Picasso*, gelatin silver print, 1922, p. 530

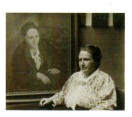

1.9.8 Edward Weston, *Artichoke Halved*, 1930, p. 173

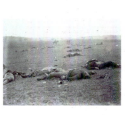

3.8.31 John Heartfield, *Have No Fear, He's a Vegetarian*, 1936, p. 533

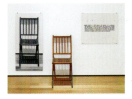

3.9.10 Joseph Kosuth, *One and Three Chairs*, 1965, p. 547

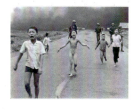

4.7.2 Nick Ut, *Vietnamese Girl Kim Phuc Running after Napalm Attack*, June 8, 1972, p. 636

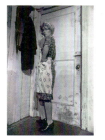

4.10.4 Cindy Sherman, "Untitled Film Still #35", 1979, p. 678

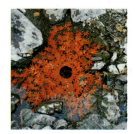

3.9.12 Andy Goldsworthy, *Japanese Maple Leaves*, 1987, p. 548

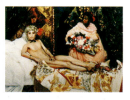

4.9.10 Yasumasa Morimura, *Portrait (Futago)*, 1988–90, p. 665

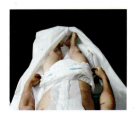

4.3.4 Andres Serrano, *The Morgue (Gun Murder)*, 1992, p. 590

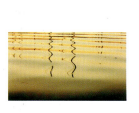

4.4.16 Marcia Smilack *Cello Music*, 1992, p. 608

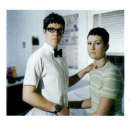

4.10.13 Catherine Opie "Melissa and Lake," 1998, p. 684

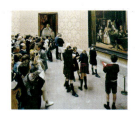

1.10.13 Thomas Struth, *Museo del Prado 7*, 2005, p. 193

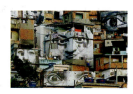

4.8.2 JR, *Women Are Heroes*, 2008, p. 650

2.9

Film/Video and Digital Art

Of all the **media** chosen by artists, the moving image is one of the youngest and most widely used. The products of film, video, and digital art include home movies, artworks, independent films, and major motion pictures. For most of its history to date, the dominant process for making movies has been film: flexible, celluloid, and light-sensitive. A movie camera captures movement by taking many separate **frames** per second, all exposed in sequence onto the same strip of film. After being developed and edited, the moving film passes in front of a bright light in a projector that shines the image onto a screen.

Because of the high costs of the medium, making a full-length movie requires serious, usually commercial, investment. While digital cameras are widely used by individuals, at present, 35mm film remains a dominant technology for professional productions, partly because until recently, digital cameras could not match the resolution, or detail, possible with film cameras, due to the number of megapixels required. But a number of talented and high-profile directors have brought digital filmmaking into the mainstream. It has the considerable advantages of streamlining workflow for the director and editor; eliminating the costs of film and film processing; giving greater access to footage; and increasing the possibilities for more accessible and affordable manipulation than 35mm film.

While films are made using a movie camera and viewed with a projector, videos are generally made with small, hand-held cameras. Video, in which images consist of pixels, was initially an **analog** technology, like film. Analog recordings, usually on tape, can be shown on the camera's screen or a television. When made using the analog process, videotapes can be edited by splicing (joining) together separate recordings to maximize the impact of every scene. The analog nature of films and videotapes requires them to be viewed from beginning to end, although sections can be skipped by fast forwarding, or replayed by rewinding.

More common today, however, is the use of digital video cameras, first commercially available in 1986, to record images as files on a DVD or computer hard drive. Digital videos are viewed on a computer monitor, or on a screen using a digital projector. Video has the advantages of being less expensive and highly portable, yet the quality is still generally lower than film. Often, moving images are recorded on film and transferred to a digital format for the purposes of editing and presentation.

These recent technological developments in both film- and video-making processes mean that, while viewing motion-picture productions once required a dedicated room, projector and screen, over time they have transitioned to broadcasts and recordings seen on televisions in businesses and people's homes. Today, they can be viewed on a variety of devices and screen sizes, almost anywhere at any time: so much so, that it is hard now to imagine a time when they did not exist.

Medium (plural **media**): the material on or from which an artist chooses to make a work of art, for example canvas and oil paint, marble, engraving, video, or architecture
Frame: a single image from the sequence that makes up a motion picture; on average, a 90-minute film contains 129,600 separate frames
Analog: photography or movie made using a film camera that chemically records images using a continuous gradation of value ranges from light to dark so that they directly match the actual appearance of the object or scene

Moving Images before Film

How is the illusion of movement created? The principle was understood long before the invention of still or moving film images. An antique child's toy called a zoetrope (**2.9.1**) contains a rotating cylinder with a sequence of images on the inside. By looking through the outer ring of the cylinder, which has slots cut into it, and spinning the zoetrope, the viewer gets the impression of a single image in continuous **motion**. The illusion of movement created in this way is the basis of modern film and video technique.

A theory known as persistence of vision explains that this illusion results from the presentation to the eye of separate images at regular intervals so that they appear to be a continuous sequence. Because visual sensations persist even after the seen object is no longer there, the mind connects them together. This concept is illustrated in a rudimentary way by a flip book with separate still images in a sequence that, when flipped, become visually connected and appear to move. Images captured in the camera use the same concept: the faster the succession of images, the smoother the impression of movement. In the earliest film projectors there was a visible "blink" between frames. A modern movie will show images at twenty-four frames per second; **IMAX** high-definition films can show forty-eight, to provide a heightened sense of reality.

As strange as it may seem, in order to make moving pictures it was first necessary to freeze movement in the form of still images. After many failed attempts, the English photographer Eadweard Muybridge (1830–1904) arranged a line of twelve cameras to take a sequence of twelve pictures of a running horse. The cameras, connected to cables stretched across the racetrack, were tripped as the horse passed.

Muybridge's experiments cost about $42,000 and resolved a wager that a galloping horse has all four of its legs off the ground at once. The camera proved what the naked eye could not see: the horse does (see the third frame of **2.9.2**). Before then, people thought the legs of the horse were extended, like those of a rocking horse, when off the ground. When prints of Muybridge's photographs were published in *Scientific American* magazine, they were accompanied by instructions to cut them out and place them in a zoetrope.

2.9.1 Diagram of a zoetrope

Series of changing images

Look

Spin

2.9.2 Eadweard Muybridge, *The Horse in Motion*, June 18, 1878. Albumen print. Library of Congress, Washington, D.C.

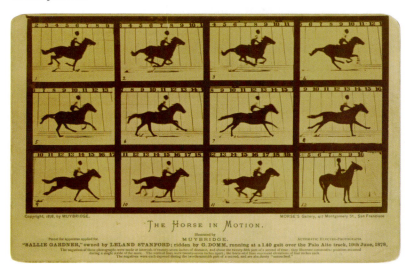

Silent and Black-and-White Film

The very earliest films were short clips usually documenting single instances of everyday occurrences—feeding the baby, doing a dance, leaving the factory gate at closing time, watching the arrival of a passenger locomotive. The earliest motion pictures were black and white and silent: they had no soundtrack. They were shown in nickelodeons, small storefront movie theaters popular in the early years of the twentieth century. Nickelodeons provided musical accompaniments with live piano and drums, and some provided lecturers to explain the action as the moving pictures, or movies, played. As movies grew into a business, they were shown in huge, ornate movie palaces that might also feature a pipe organ.

By 1896, movies were being shown all over Europe and the United States. Georges Méliès (1861–1938), a French magician and filmmaker, began showing films as part of his theatrical magic show. His silent science-fiction and fantasy films featured trick effects and humor. In *A Trip to the Moon* (1902), Méliès's most famous film, a group of astronomers flies to the moon in a spaceship launched from a cannon (**2.9.3**). Their vessel crashes into the man-in-the-moon's right eye, and then the astronomers encounter wondrous sights and moon inhabitants called Selenites. Méliès was one of the first to use multiple settings, repeated scenes, and cuts to establish a sense of time moving forward.

The American filmmaker D. W. Griffith's (1875–1948) silent film *Birth of a Nation* (1915) was Hollywood's first blockbuster and one of the first films to tell an epic story (**2.9.4**). The film introduced a number of new techniques, including original editing **styles** to make transitions between scenes and vary the sense of pace. *Birth of a Nation* uses symbolism, gesture, and intertitles (onscreen text), rather than spoken dialogue, to move the story along. The film is now controversial for its reinforcement of racist views and stereotypes of the Old South; in fact, the Ku Klux Klan used it for recruitment. Despite this unpleasant history, *Birth of a Nation* is important for the epic scale of its production, its stylistic and technical innovations, and its use of the film medium as a **propaganda** tool.

Another American filmmaker, Orson Welles (1915–1985), wrote, directed, and starred in *Citizen Kane* (1941), a film that was a box-office failure but hailed by critics as brilliant (**2.9.5**).

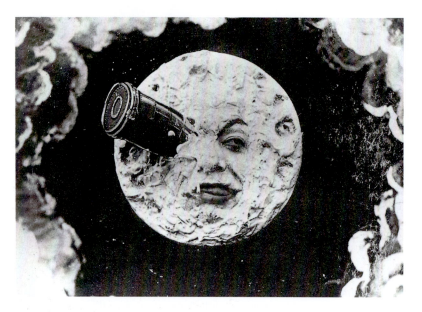

It is now widely considered one of the most important films of all time. Welles's film tells the story of Charles Foster Kane, a character modeled on the real-life newspaper tycoon William Randolph Hearst. To tell Kane's story, Welles used what were then highly innovative techniques, including fabricated newspaper headlines and newsreels that give the impression of following a factual story. Other parts of the plot are told using flashbacks, which was then a new mode of storytelling; these are

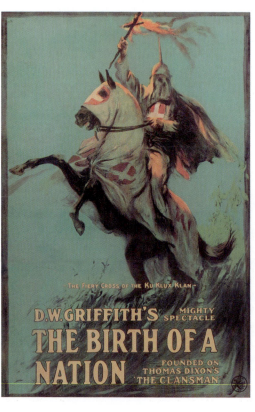

2.9.3 Georges Méliès, scene from *A Trip to the Moon (Le Voyage dans la Lune)*, 1902, 14 minutes, Star Film

2.9.4 D. W. Griffith, *Birth of a Nation*, 1915, publicity poster

THE FIERY CROSS OF THE KU KLUX KLAN

D.W. GRIFFITH'S MIGHTY SPECTACLE
THE BIRTH OF A NATION
FOUNDED ON THOMAS DIXON'S THE CLANSMAN

Style: a characteristic way in which an artist or group of artists uses visual language to give a work an identifiable form of visual expression
Propaganda: art that promotes an ideology or a cause
Color: the optical effect caused when reflected white light of the spectrum is divided into separate wavelengths

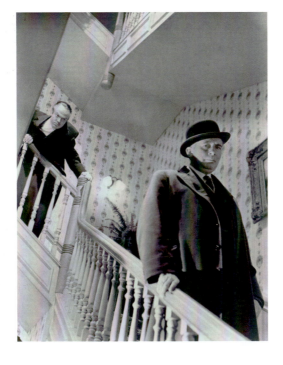

2.9.5 Orson Welles, scene from *Citizen Kane*, 1941, 112 minutes, RKO Pictures

2.9.6 Victor Fleming, scene from *The Wizard of Oz*, 1939, 101 minutes, Metro-Goldwyn-Mayer (MGM)

now commonplace. *Citizen Kane* also features additional techniques that were revolutionary for the time, such as dramatic lighting, innovative editing, natural sound, elaborate sets, moving camera shots, deep focus, and low camera angles. The movie questions the values of the American Dream and was controversial for its criticism of Hearst, a powerful public figure.

Sound and Color

From the late 1920s, movie studios promoted **color** as a novelty to attract audiences. One of the first popular films to make use of color combined both the new and old approaches. In *The Wizard of Oz* (1939), Dorothy Gale is transported by a cyclone from Kansas to the Technicolor Land of Oz (**2.9.6**). The story's two separate locales are distinguished by the use or absence of color. The film opens with Dorothy in the black-and-white world of her home on a Kansas farm. Later, the brilliant colors of the Land of Oz transport us into a fantasy world clearly far removed from Kansas. Color features prominently throughout the film: Dorothy wears ruby slippers as she travels with her companions—her dog Toto, the Scarecrow, the Tin Man, and the Lion—along the yellow-brick road to the Emerald City to find the wizard.

Before 1927, any sound in cinemas was performed live by musicians in the theater building. After that, integrated sound made it possible to build dialogue, background noise, and music into the film itself. *Singin' in the Rain*, made in 1952, looked back to the silent era by telling the story of a silent-film

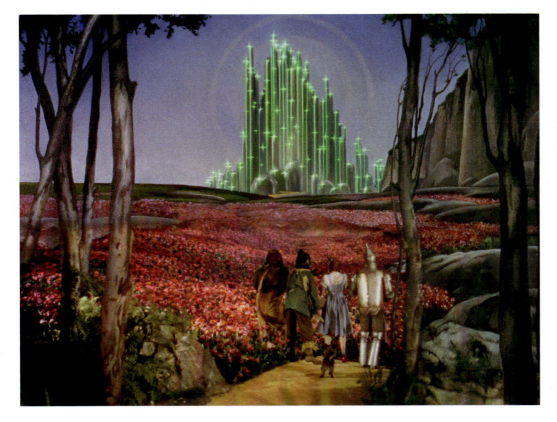

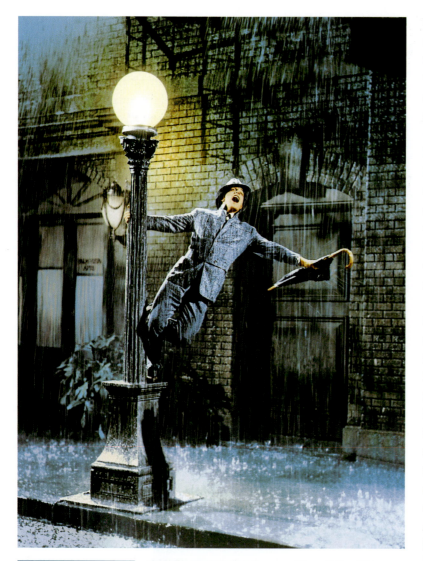

Musical: genre of film in which the story is told through song, usually combined with dialogue and dancing

2.9.7 (above) Stanley Donen and Gene Kelly, still from *Singin' in the Rain*, 1952, 103 minutes, produced by Loew's Incorporated, distributed by MGM

2.9.8 (below) Michel Hazanavicius, still from *The Artist*, 2011. 100 minutes, Studio 37

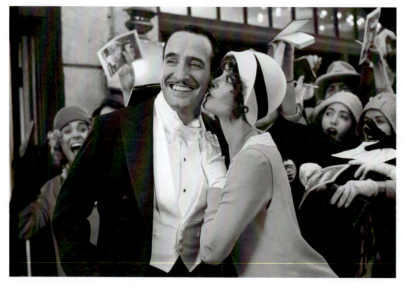

company making the difficult transition to sound. Synchronizing sound with the actors' lip movements and dubbing was one of the great technical challenges of early sound movies, as songs could not be performed on camera by the actors, but had to be recorded separately. *Singin' in the Rain* finds much humor in this situation. In the movie's most famous scene, actor Gene Kelly jubilantly performs the title song in the rainy streets. **Musicals** usually tell their story in a combination of dialogue, songs, and dance, with song being their dominant characteristic. Frequently, as in this scene, dialogue stops completely, and song and dance move the story along (**2.9.7**).

In 2011 the French film director Michel Hazanavicius achieved a huge success with his modern film, *The Artist*, which harks back to the impact of sound on the silent-film industry. In the words of one critic, the film "uses old technology to dazzling effect to illustrate the insistent conquest of a new technology." All of the technical details, including lenses, lighting, and camera moves, were calculated to match the look of original silent films of the 1920s and 1930s as closely as possible. *The Artist* won eighteen major awards, including the Academy Award for Best Picture, for its witty, stylish, and ingenious story, which was told almost entirely in silence and in black and white. It shows how vividly actors can communicate through gesture, expression, and dance, without relying on a soundtrack. The film's extraordinary success proved that cinema's appeal remains primarily visual, and that, despite all of the technological progress that has been made in the industry in the past century, audiences are still nostalgic for the "good old days" of black-and-white movies.

Animation and Special Effects

Animation creates the illusion of movement in films by taking a still image of an object or drawing, changing it slightly for each new frame, and then projecting all the images in sequence. The many thousands of images in modern

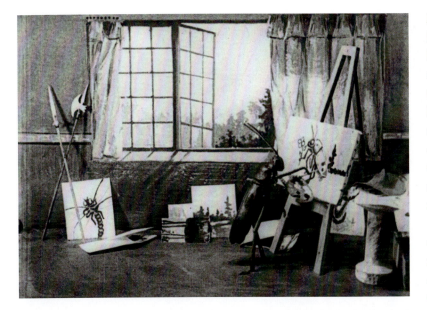

2.9.9 (above) Wladyslaw Starewicz, *Mest Kinematograficheskogo Operatora* (*The Cameraman's Revenge*), 1912, 12 minutes, produced by Khanzhonkov Company, Moscow, Russia

2.9.10 (below) Hayao Miyazaki with Kirk Wise (English version), still from *Spirited Away*, 2001, 125 minutes, Studio Ghibli

Animation: genre of film made using stop-motion, hand-drawn, or digitally produced still images set into motion by showing them in sequence

Background: the part of a work depicted furthest from the viewer's space, often behind the main subject matter

animations, such as those from Pixar Studios, are generated and manipulated on computers.

Special effects can be created by using models, props, or makeup during filming, or by the use of digital technology during or post-production.

Some of the earliest film animations were made using puppets or dolls. In stop-motion animation, the figures are photographed in a pose, moved very slightly, and then photographed again; the process is repeated until the desired sequence of movements has been acted out. Russian animator Wladyslaw Starewicz (1882–1965) created a stop-motion animation movie about infidelity, with a twist: the characters in *The Cameraman's Revenge* (1912) are bugs (2.9.9). Mr. Beetle has gone to the city on business. He meets a dancer at the Gay Dragonfly, a burlesque parlor. A grasshopper cameraman at the burlesque also has designs on

Miss Dragonfly. He is so jealous that he films Mr. Beetle and the dancer. When Mr. Beetle returns home, he finds his wife in the arms of an "artist" cricket. Mr. Beetle, after beating up the lover, forgivingly takes his wife to the movies, where his own indiscretions are projected onto the big screen. This film is surprising for the physical expressiveness of the bugs as well as for the wit that gives the plot a slapstick quality. Like many animated films, *The Cameraman's Revenge* was made more for adults than children.

In hand-drawn animation, a separate drawing must be created for each frame. For much of the twentieth century, the most common technique for making animated films was cel animation, which uses a sequence of drawings called cels (originally on celluloid, then acetate). **Backgrounds** and stationary sections were overlaid by the moving parts on transparent sheets, greatly reducing the number of images that had to be generated. Though some directors still use cel animation, for the most part it has been replaced by digital technology. Digital animation more efficiently generates all the individual frames on a computer, but original images may still be made using stop-motion or hand drawings. Digital processes also provide more options for the creation and inclusion of imagery, sound, and narrative components of the sequence or movie, because using digital technology enables these elements to be imported and then manipulated.

The Oscar-winning film *Spirited Away* (2001), written and directed by Hayao Miyazaki (b. 1941), tells the story of a ten-year-old girl named Chihiro who is unhappy about moving to a new town with her family. After she is introduced to a world filled with spirits from Japan's mythology, she discovers that her parents have been transformed into pigs by a witch (2.9.10). She must go on a quest to conquer her fears in order to find the strength to bring her family back together. Miyazaki personally created detailed storyboards, or series of drawings, to be used as the basis for the animations, which were then completed by a team of artists, with a separate drawing made for each stage in the movement of any moving object in a scene. At least twelve drawings, and

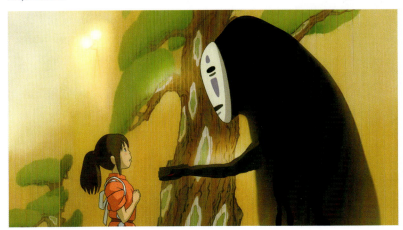

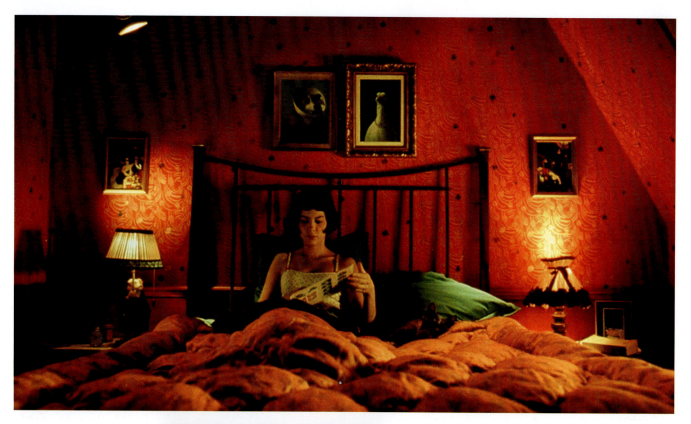

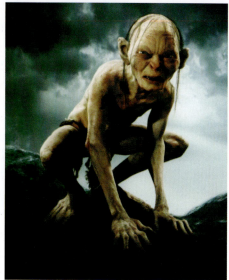

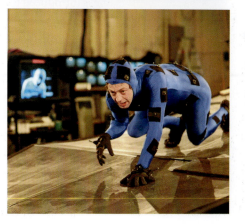

2.9.11 (above) Jean-Pierre Jeunet, still from *Amélie (The Fabulous Destiny of Amélie Poulain)*, 2001, 122 minutes, Claudie Ossard Productions

2.9.12a (right) Gollum from Peter Jackson's *The Lord of the Rings: The Return of the King*, 2003. 201 minutes, New Line Cinema

2.9.12b (below) Andy Serkis playing Gollum in *The Lord of the Rings: The Two Towers*, 2002

Impressionism, Impressionist: a late nineteenth-century painting style conveying the impression of the effects of light; Impressionists were artists working in this style
CGI: computer-generated imagery

sometimes thirty, were required for every second of *Spirited Away*. Thus a film of this length (125 minutes) requires a minimum of 90,000 drawings, and perhaps as many as 200,000.

The French director Jean-Pierre Jeunet (b. 1953) adds animation and special effects to live-action film to tell the story of *Amélie* (2001), a shy twenty-three-year-old waitress (**2.9.11**). Amélie's heart beats out of her chest at one point; in another scene, when her crush Nino walks away, she melts into a puddle on the floor. Inanimate objects, such as the **Impressionist** artist Pierre-Auguste Renoir's painting *Luncheon of the Boating Party*, take on so much significance that they almost function as additional characters. Jeunet creates an environment in which fantasy, reality, and rich color are mixed together to reveal the magical qualities of ordinary life.

Cutting-edge visual effects in the *Lord of the Rings* film trilogy (2001–3, **2.9.12a** and **b**) brought to life the fictional world of J. R. R. Tolkien's novels by combining live action and **computer-generated imagery (CGI)**. Directed by Peter Jackson (b. 1961), these adventure/fantasy films won many Oscars, including Best Picture and Best Visual Effects. One of the most remarkable actors from the series was deemed ineligible for the Best Supporting Actor award, though, because his character was computer generated. Andy Serkis (b. 1964) was responsible for the facial expressions, bodily movements, and distinctive voice of Gollum. Serkis acted out all of the scenes twice: once on set, which allowed him to interact directly with the other actors and greatly assisted the animators; and again on the performance-capture stage. Combining traditional acting, **motion capture** (also known as mo-cap or performance capture), and the skills of animators enabled the transformation of Serkis into a fictional character. The motion-capture process involved putting dots on Serkis's face and body suit to track and record his movements with twenty-five cameras in order to register as much information as possible so the software could replicate the movements digitally. The animators then used **key-frame animation** to edit Gollum into the movie. Because Tolkien wrote that the character was called Gollum for the gurgling sound his voice made, Serkis based the voice on the sounds and motions his cat made coughing up a furball. Serkis's method of intense psychological and emotional character development, and his dedication to realizing the physicality of the character, make Gollum believable and haunting.

2.9.13 Robert Wiene, still from *The Cabinet of Dr. Caligari*, 1920, 80 minutes, Steiner

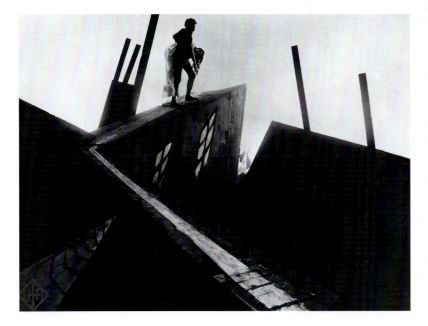

Film Genres

Over time, certain **genres**, or categories, of film have developed their own conventions, plot lines, and stock characters. As we have seen, musicals interweave singing and (usually) dancing into the narrative flow; animation and **science-fiction** films explore fantasy in a context of space and time beyond the everyday. Romantic comedies and Westerns have evolved to explore changing views of relationships and US history. Additional popular film genres include action; comedy; crime thriller; **drama**; film noir (from the French meaning "black film": that is, films that take a dark, cynical view of life); horror; war; history; **documentary**; and art films.

One of the earliest horror films, *The Cabinet of Dr. Caligari* (1920), creates a creepy, nightmarish world. Directed by Robert Wiene (1873–1938), the film tells the story of a psychiatrist, Dr. Caligari, and his servant Cesare, who can foretell the future. Another character, Francis, suspects Caligari and Cesare of a series of murders, including that of his friend. In one scene Cesare abducts Francis's fiancée, Jane. (He is shown carrying her away on the wall in **2.9.13**.) The film ends with a twist when Francis turns out to be a patient of Dr. Caligari, and the entire film is apparently one of his delusions.

The Cabinet of Dr. Caligari is famous for its plot development, its character types, the strange, shifting mood of the film, and the way its scenic design expresses this psychology. The costumes, makeup, gestures, and music combine to create a dark and mysterious atmosphere. The film's **Expressionist** sets were designed by German artists and include crooked walls, angular buildings, and jarring plant **forms** that mimic the narrator's tortured mind.

Documentaries seek to inform us about actual subjects, events, or people. Some documentaries present the story directly, filming events as they occur through people's own voices and actions. Other documentaries edit past, present, and future events together to tell a story. Some documentaries use voiceover commentary to narrate or interpret the action or events. Most documentary films combine such approaches,

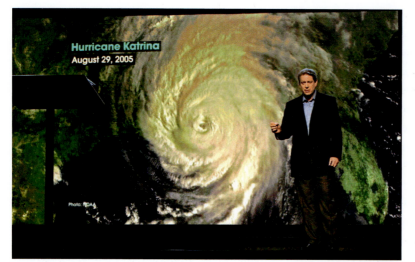

shaping factual information to express a point of view.

An Inconvenient Truth (2006), directed by Davis Guggenheim (b. 1963), presents startling facts about global warming. The film interweaves former Vice President Al Gore's public lectures on climate change with narratives about his life, family, and political career (**2.9.14**). With graphs, charts, and photographs, Gore describes the impact of pollution and carbon emissions on our planet. In one of the most startling examples of global climate change, photographs show the recession of glaciers and the melting of the ice shelves of Antarctica.

Animated maps of Florida, San Francisco, Beijing, Bangladesh, and Manhattan show the projected effects on shorelines if the sea level rises 20 ft., as it will if the ice masses of major sections of Antarctica continue to melt.

Film as Art
Auteur Films

Auteur theory, from the French word for "author," considers films to be works of art due to the fact that they are the realization of a director's creative vision. This theory, focusing on the director or screenwriter, has been controversial due to the collaborative nature of movies and the fact that it does not acknowledge the creative contribution of actors, cinematographers, set and costume designers, and the many other people who help to make a film. Proponents of the theory, though, cite the films of François Truffaut, Jean-Luc Godard, Akira Kurosawa, Alfred Hitchcock, Jean Renoir, Woody Allen, Jane Campion, Julie Taymor, and Wes Anderson as especially guided by the artistic vision of their directors.

The distinctive vision of Chinese director Wong Kar-Wai (b. 1958) permeates *Chungking Express* (**2.9.15**). In the crowded urban

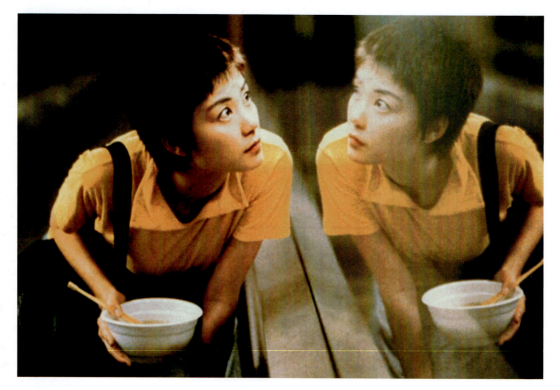

Auteur theory/auteur films: from the French word for "author," refers to films that notably reflect the director's creative vision above other criteria
Aesthetic: related to beauty, art, and taste

metropolis of Hong Kong, we follow the stories (one after the other) of two police officers. Two tales overlap, like the strangers who brush past each other in a Hong Kong crowd depicted at the beginning of the film. In both cases the officers are transitioning from one romance to another, but the future of each new romance remains uncertain. The suspenseful story of drug dealing in the first tale in some ways contrasts with the odd comedy of the second; in other ways, however, the two stories resonate poetically, each evoking the other in its depiction of lost love and longing. Wong's work is characterized by complicated narratives in addition to a stylized, color-rich, impressionistic cinematography (by Christopher Doyle) that highlights the fast pace and isolation of contemporary life.

Experimental Films

Experimental films analyse and extend the medium of film by using new technology or subject matter, and by exploring new **aesthetic** ideas. They tend to be visually compelling and poetic, notable for their unusual content and idiosyncrasy. They are often the production of a single person or small group, and experimental filmmakers use inexpensive equipment and low-budget formats to create desired effects. Such films frequently do not have integrated

2.9.16 Maya Deren, still from *Meshes of the Afternoon*, 1943, 14 minutes, 16mm black-and-white silent film

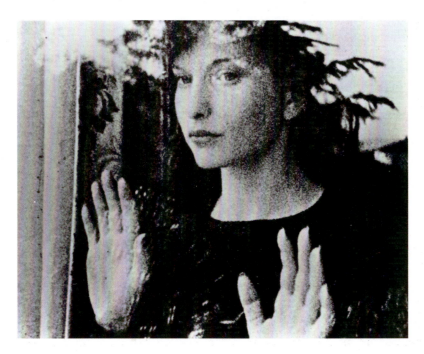

sound, or use it in unnatural ways. Experimental filmmakers tend to adopt innovative approaches, including dream sequences and fantastic imagery created by manipulating the filmstrip. Their films are also often autobiographical.

American dancer, choreographer, and filmmaker Maya Deren (1917–1961) wrote *Meshes of the Afternoon* (1943) and co-directed it with her husband, cinematographer Alexander Hammid. The short (14-minute) film follows a woman's experience of an afternoon, shuffled together with her dreams after she has drifted off to sleep (**2.9.16**). Two sequences are repeated: in one, a cloaked woman with a mirror over her face walks down the road; in the other, the woman (played by Deren) enters a house and walks up the stairs. These sequences seem to be replaying themselves in the woman's mind rather than representing actual events. Several objects are shown again and again: a flower, a key, a telephone, a knife, a record player, billowy curtains, rumpled sheets. Elements change each time the sequences occur. For instance, one moment the flower is placed on the pillow, the next the knife appears in the same position. Toward the end of the film a man replaces the female figures, one moment entering the house and the next walking on the road.

Time is circular in this film, and the overall effect mimics a dream in which events that make sense to the dreamer seem illogical to others. Each object seems to have an unnamed symbolic significance, and it is impossible to separate actual occurrences from memories or fiction. Ultimately, the film reflects a state of mind, and can be best understood as visual poetry.

Video

Typically, video artworks are made to be presented in art galleries or at art events. They may be shown on television monitors or projected onto walls. Sometimes artists incorporate video displays (along with other media) in a darkened area in ways that transform the space and create a total environment of sight and sound. Because high-quality video equipment is relatively inexpensive, artistic experimentation with video is widespread.

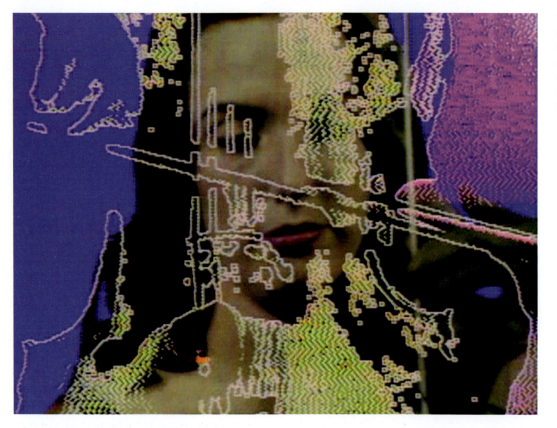

2.9.17 Nam June Paik and John J. Godfrey, still from *Global Groove*, 1973, single-channel videotape, color with sound. Courtesy Electronic Arts Intermix (EAI), New York

Korean-American artist Nam June Paik (1932–2006) was a pioneer of video art. In 1969 Paik worked with Shuya Abe, an engineer from Tokyo, to modulate video signals with a device called the Paik-Abe Synthesizer. The results combined both recognizable and distorted pictures that were recorded and could be replayed later. Paik's *Global Groove* (1973), a 30-minute video recording, comments on the increasing role of media and technology in daily life.

Global Groove replicates the variety of topics available on television at the time the video was made, from Pepsi commercials to news footage to game shows to President Richard Nixon's face. All these scenes are interspersed, like glimpses of changing channels. Most of the clips integrate music and visuals, consisting of either performers or dancers. For example, Charlotte Moorman is shown playing several experimental cellos designed by Paik. The close-up of her face (**2.9.17**) is surrounded by visual noise, static translated into changing designs that correspond to the rhythms of the music she is playing. *Global Groove* draws on contemporary culture, and foreshadows music video by integrating visual and musical inputs.

Interactive Technology

Artists and designers create installations, websites, video games, and television shows that provide new possibilities for sharing and accessing creative expressions. Recent developments in digital technology have allowed artists to involve viewers as active participants in the artwork by, for example, determining the appearance of the work or choosing different paths to follow.

Once seen as an inferior medium to film and cinema, television has created its own set of entertainment criteria. *House of Cards* (2013) (**2.9.19**) represents a new genre of television series broadcast on the Internet. Netflix created the miniseries (based on a highly successful British series of the same title and with a similar plotline, but broadcast, like most TV shows, with each episode in sequence and always at a fixed time on scheduled dates) following a model used on cable TV in 1984. The streaming format and release of all thirteen episodes simultaneously allow viewers to decide whether to watch the show all at once or over time. This gives the viewer much more control over the viewing experience, and puts Netflix in a better position to compete

Perspectives on Art: Bill Viola
How Did Video Become Art?

Bill Viola, one of the world's leading video artists, has been working in video since the 1970s. In 2005 he gave the following explanation for why many contemporary artists prefer video as an art form.

I first touched a video camera in 1970 as a first-year art student. In those politically charged times, making art took on a renewed urgency, and the new electronic communication technologies played a central role in re-imagining not only what a work of art could be but also how it could reach beyond the art world to engage life and society directly and transform the world. By the early 1970s, political and social activists, documentary filmmakers, and artists of all disciplines were using video and showing their work together in art museums, film festivals, community centers, universities, and on television.

Video as art exists somewhere between the permanence of painting and the temporary existence of music. Technically, the video system of camera and recorder mimics the human eye and memory. The so-called video "image" is actually a shimmering energy pattern of moving electrons vibrating in time. To exist, the fabric of the image needs to be in a constant state of motion. The electronic image is not fixed to any material base, and as digital data it is infinitely reproducible. It can be copied, stored, and transferred onto new formats in a continuous chain of eternal life. As an electronic signal it can travel at the speed of light around the Earth and beyond, and it can appear in multiple places at the same time. As an international technical standard, the image exists in the same form as the dominant mass media, allowing artists the potential to address the global culture. Since the production and distribution of images is now accomplished by the same technological system, today's artists have the freedom to work within existing institutions or become their own producers and distributors.

Technology is the imprint of the human mind onto the material substance of the natural world. Like the Renaissance, today's technological revolution is fueled by a combination of art, science, and technology, and the universal human need to share our individual ideas and experiences in ever-new ways. The medium of video, where images are born and die every instant, has brought a new humanism to contemporary art. The digital image has become the common language of our time, and through it living artists are once again emerging from the margins of the culture to speak directly to the people in the language of their experience.

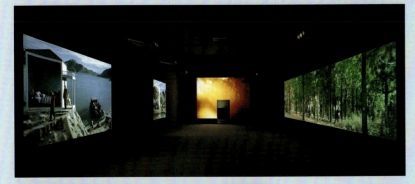

2.9.18a Bill Viola, *Going Forth by Day*, 2002. Installation view, video/sound installation, five-part projected image cycle

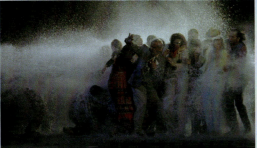

2.9.18b Bill Viola, *The Raft*, May 2004. Video/sound installation, color, High-Definition video projection on wall in darkened space, screen size 13' × 7'3⅜"

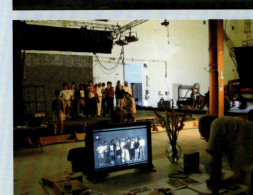

2.9.18c Bill Viola (on the right) in production for *The Raft*, Downey Studios, Downey, California, 2004

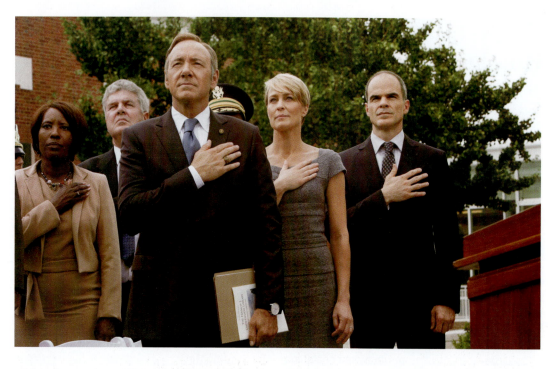

2.9.19 David Fincher, still from *House of Cards*, Netflix original television series, 2013–

with industry giants HBO (Home Box Office) and Showtime, which delay releasing digital content long after the filming (HBO a full year later). The show, a political drama, has been highly successful, with critics praising its intense characters and impressive acting, especially from Kevin Spacey as the lead. Actress Robin Wright won a Golden Globe for her performance as Claire Underwood. Wright described her character as "very stoic, like a bust in a museum . . . a beautiful Lady Macbeth that starts to erode into a true human."

Active Learning Exercises

1. Film and video evolved from the sequencing of still images to replicate the appearance of life moving in front of our eyes. As an illustration of the concepts behind moving images, make a flip book. Choose an action or motion and break it down into 10 discrete parts (e.g. jumping off the ground, a bird flying, the sun moving across the sky, etc.). Draw (or photograph) each part of the sequence on a 1 in. × 1 in. piece of paper. Put your pictures together and hold or staple one side to make the flip book. Share your flip book with the class. What kinds of changes effectively create the illusion of continuous motion in the flip books? Which ones do not?

2. Choose one of the formal elements of film and video discussed in this chapter to investigate further: sound, color, animation, or special effects. Using the Internet or your own past experience, find three film stills (or segments from films, or entire films) not in this chapter that show a selection of approaches for your chosen element. You may choose to seek similar results (the color blue used to evoke a sad mood) or various applications (the same song used in very different ways). Share your results with the class.

3. This task involves comparing the conventions for two of the genres of film or television shows discussed in this chapter (or two other genres of your own choosing). To do this, you will also need to consider at least two examples for each genre in your comparison, in order to establish patterns. Describe the characters, plotlines, settings, and so on, for each of your chosen genres. What similarities and differences do you note? Are you drawn to one genre over another? If so, why? If you are interested in both genres, explain why. How does analysing a film in this way affect your experience of it? How might this experience affect your future viewing habits?

Images Related to 2.9:
Film/Video and Digital Art

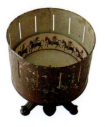

1.5.8 Zoetrope, 19th century, p. 124

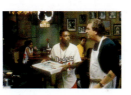

4.10.9 Spike Lee, *Do the Right Thing* (still), 1989, p. 682

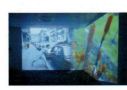

3.9.21 Pipilotti Rist, *Ever Is Over All*, 1997, p. 555

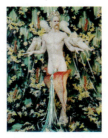

3.9.22 Matthew Barney, *Cremaster 5*, 1997, p. 556

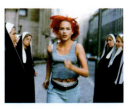

1.5.10 *Run Lola Run* (still), Tom Tykwer, 1998, p. 125

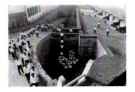

3.9.20a Shirin Neshat, *Rapture*, 1999, p. 554

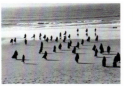

3.9.20b Shirin Neshat, *Rapture*, 1999, p. 554

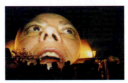

4.1.13 Krzysztof Wodiczko, *Tijuana Projection*, 2001, p. 573

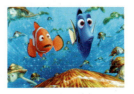

1.5.9 Walt Disney Pictures, Frame from *Finding Nemo*, 2003, p. 124

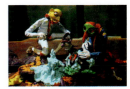

3.9.23 Natalie Djurberg, *I Wasn't Made to Play the Son* (video still), 2011, p. 556

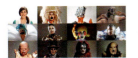

4.3.7 Jillian Mayer, *I Am Your Grandma* (stills), 2011, p. 592

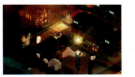

1.3.16 Screenshot from *Transistor* game, 2014, p. 91

2.10

Alternative Media and Processes

Artworks made using alternative **media** and processes break down the traditional boundaries between art and life. They draw our attention to actions or ideas rather than to a physical product. The creative process produces events, ideas, and experiences that are artworks in and of themselves. Many artworks that are interactive or involve the viewer in unusual and significant ways fall into this category. In addition, many alternative processes incorporate more than one type of medium (often several) and make categorization of artworks much more complicated.

In **conceptual art**, the idea behind an artwork is more important than any visible subject or material product. Artists generally plan the piece and make all of the major decisions beforehand; the execution of the piece itself is secondary. Conceptual art often produces no permanent artwork and very little that can be promoted and sold: sometimes a set of instructions, a documentary photograph, or nothing at all remains as evidence that the piece existed.

For example, if an artist printed a set of instructions for the viewer, the actual, tangible result of the piece would be the actions that person performed. Yoko Ono's *Wish Tree* artworks (**2.10.3**—see p. 355) existed only in a potential state when the artist first made them. Each piece requires the viewer's participation to be realized. In Vito Acconci's *Following Piece* (**2.10.8**, see p. 358), there was no audience at the time, but the artist took pictures of each "following" he made.

Performance art has some similarities to theater because it is performed in front of a live audience; it includes varying amounts of music,

dance, poetry, video, and multimedia technology. Unlike traditional theater, however, there is rarely an identifiable story and the performance takes place in consciously artistic venues. The actions of the artist, or individuals chosen by the artist, become the focus. These actions, which occur in a gallery, on a stage, or in a public place, may last from a few minutes to a few days and are rarely repeated.

When artists design an entire exhibition space as an artwork, usually in a gallery or museum, it is called an **installation**. Installations might consist of props and sets to transform the space into a room in a house or a place of business; they might incorporate electronic displays or video projections; or they might involve artworks arranged in relation to one another in a sequence or series. Often installations are designed to fit the dimensions or environment of a particular location: these installations are called "site-specific." The artist plans the space, considers how people will move through it, and arranges the elements to create a certain effect. Whether they are designed for an interior or exterior space, installations immerse viewers in the artwork.

Context of Alternative Media

During the twentieth century, a way of making art emerged that focused on modes of creation, such as actions, texts, and environments. These approaches differed from the traditional Western practices of "fine art," narrowly defined as

Medium (plural **media**): the material on or from which an artist chooses to make a work of art, for example canvas and oil paint, marble, engraving, video, or architecture
Conceptual art: artwork in which the ideas are most important to the work
Performance art: a work involving the human body, usually including the artist, in front of an audience
Installation: originally referring to the hanging of pictures and arrangement of objects in an exhibition, installation may also refer to an intentional environment created as a completed artwork

paintings on canvas and sculptures on pedestals. American artist Jackson Pollock's (1912–1956) **action paintings** of the 1950s brought the canvas off the easel and onto the floor to become a surface around which the artist moved as he splashed, dripped, and flung his paint. His unusual and exciting painting techniques galvanized public interest in "difficult" modern art. Pollock rocketed to popular fame following an article of August 8, 1949 in *Life Magazine* that even asked, "Is he the greatest living painter in the United States?" Not long after Pollock's early death in a car crash, though, there was a sense that artists had exhausted all they could say with paint on canvas. Artists began to turn to performance, conceptualism, and installations to explore radical new ideas about art.

Because this chapter focuses on the ideas expressed in the making of artworks rather than the finished objects themselves, we shall also look at the documentation about them—instructions used to plan an activity, notes taken by the artist related to a piece, or photographs or video made during a performance. The works themselves tend to last for a relatively short period of time.

Conceptual Art

Conceptual art is a form of art that emphasizes ideas and radically downplays the importance of the work of art as craft object. It has flourished from the 1960s onward. In some ways conceptual art is similar to **Dada** absurdist events in Zürich in 1916, where artists performed nonsense poetry as a release from and savage commentary on the events of World War I. Dadaist Marcel Duchamp (1887–1968) also made artworks that challenged traditional notions of art. One of his works, *Fountain*, was rejected for an art exhibition in New York in 1917 because it was simply a factory-made white porcelain urinal, signed "R. Mutt." While the group hosting the exhibition was outraged, it missed Duchamp's entire point: the meaning of the artwork transcends its medium. An artist can communicate worthwhile ideas using any sort of material because the message is what matters. As the first artist truly to promote this kind of art,

Duchamp was very influential for many artists later in the twentieth century. His approach opened up possibilities of making art from everyday things and materials, imagery from popular culture, or even simply *ideas.*

Duchamp was also one of the first artists to experiment with **kinetic art**, or art with moving pieces, although his works of this kind are less well known than his **readymades**. Similarly, Swiss artist Jean Tinguely (1925–1991) was interested in exploring impermanence, accident, and uncertainty as legitimate forces within the creation and experience of a work of art. His 1960 *Homage to New York* (**2.10.1**), a mechanized **assemblage** of discarded junk, was designed to mimic the automatic processes and spontaneous painting techniques that had become popular amongst artists (methods such as those used by Jackson Pollock, see p. 542). Once set in motion, in the sculpture garden of the Museum of Modern Art, the piece behaved unpredictably in its one-off "performance." In addition to the crashing, whirring, and smoke that the artist intended it to produce, flames shot out from a piano, where a can of gasoline had been set to overturn on a burning candle; a small carriage also hurtled out, making a shrieking noise and heading straight for the audience (a journalist sent it back in another direction); and eventually a fire fighter, afraid that the piece would endanger the museum, put out the flames. This

Action painting: application of paint to canvas by dripping, splashing, or smearing that emphasizes the artist's gestures
Dada: anarchic anti-art and anti-war movement, dating back to World War I, that reveled in absurdity and irrationality
Kinetic art: art, usually three-dimensional, with moving parts activated by wind, personal interaction, or motors
Readymade: an everyday object presented as a work of art
Assemblage: technique of creating artworks that challenged traditional art practice in the late twentieth century by using found objects, junk, and other non-art materials

2.10.1 Jean Tinguely, *Homage to New York*, The Museum of Modern Art, New York, March 17th, 1960. Photo David Gahr

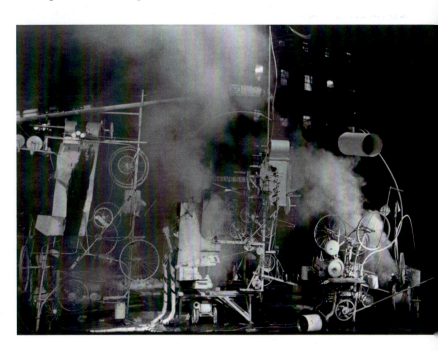

piece revived many of Dada's (and Duchamp's) rebellious and humorous antics, in the form of a huge self-destructing sculpture.

Many examples of conceptual art consist of words on a page or background. These words cut to the chase, not only directing our attention to the core concept but also allowing us to make the words meaningful for ourselves. American artist Barbara Kruger (b. 1945) uses her training and experience as a graphic designer to combine **found images** and words to give them new meanings. Her pieces address the powerful institutions of society and stereotypes that are often seen in graphic design and museum display. As in *Untitled (Your Gaze Hits the Side of My Face)* (1981–83), there is often a feminist overtone to her work, taking the institutions to task for their treatment of women (**2.10.2**).

2.10.2 Barbara Kruger, *Untitled (Your Gaze Hits the Side of My Face)*, 1981–83. Photograph, 55 × 41"

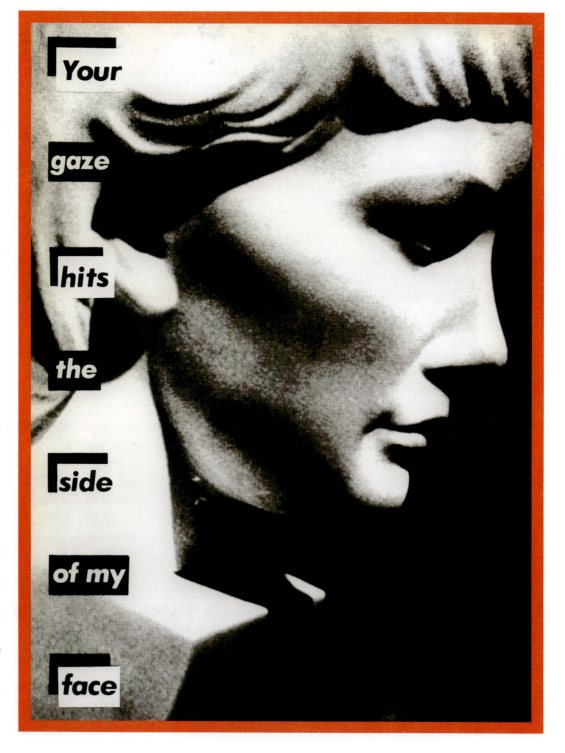

Found image or object: an image or object found by an artist and presented with little or no alteration as a work of art

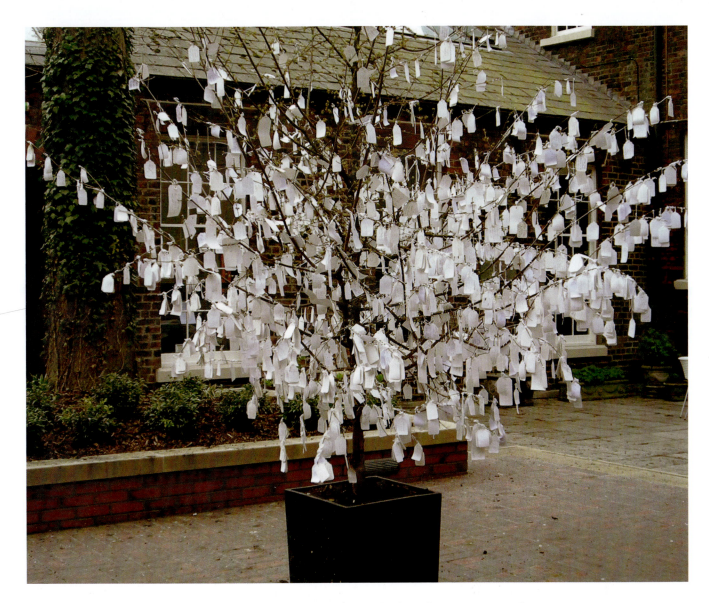

Because the text is written in the first person, the sculpture in the picture seems to be speaking, addressing the viewer directly. In this piece, beauty is shown to be just a coating or surface, and the viewer realizes that when we gaze at beauty, we run the risk of objectifying the beautiful person, that is, considering her as an object rather than a living being.

Yoko Ono (b. 1933), a Japanese-born American artist and musician, began making conceptual artworks in the early 1960s. Her first pieces were poetic instructions to be performed or just imagined. Sometimes they were typescripts framed and put on the wall. Other times, Ono painted right on the museum or gallery wall (highlighting the transient nature of some of these pieces: when the exhibition ended, those instructions would disappear).

She then started to ask viewers to complete her pieces by, for example, burning or walking on the paintings. Eventually she made "Instruction Paintings," consisting of typed instructions, rather than finished works of art. The instructions are open-ended and serve as a beginning point rather than a final product. They rely heavily on the interaction and participation of the viewer. The instructions for *Wish Tree for Washington D.C.* (2007) state: "Make a wish, Write it down on a piece of paper, Fold it and tie it around the branch of a Wish Tree, Ask your friends to do the same, Keep wishing Until the branches are covered with your wishes." Inspired by the Japanese practice of tying prayers to a tree, Ono has made *Wish Trees* like the one in **2.10.3** all over the world.

2.10.3 Yoko Ono, *Wish Tree for Liverpool*, 2008. Bluecoat Arts Centre, Liverpool, England

Perspectives on Art: Mel Chin
Operation Paydirt/Fundred Dollar Bill Project

*Mel Chin (b. 1951), an American conceptual artist, challenges the traditional role of the artist and the expected outcomes of artworks. Here Chin describes how a collective work of art (**2.10.4 and 2.10.5**) made by children and adults across the United States (and interested people from other countries) is being used to raise awareness and support for an important environmental initiative.*

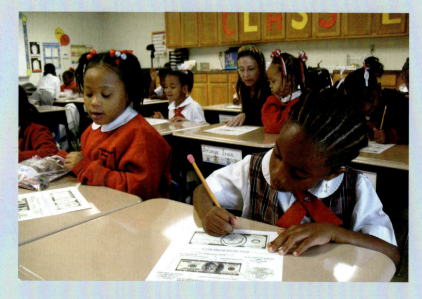

Following Hurricane Katrina, I was invited to contribute to rebuilding the social, cultural, and physical infrastructure of New Orleans. Researching the impact of the storm and the pre-existing conditions in the city, I found New Orleans to be the second most lead (Pb)-contaminated city in the United States, and that the elevated levels had existed in the soil before the storm. The contamination exists in thousands of properties and contributes to the high percentage of the inner-city childhood population that suffers from lead poisoning. Scientific studies have linked lead poisoning to elevated rates of violent criminal activity and poor academic performance in schools. The presence of polluted soil and the absence of capital to respond to the situation motivated the creation of this dual-layered project. Paydirt/Fundred is a method to respond to this condition—through art—and to transform—through science—an environment that compromises human health.

Operation Paydirt offers a pragmatic, scientifically proven method of neutralizing hazardous lead that contaminates soil and compromises the health of children. This plan, focused on solution, has the potential for creating a model for all cities and counteracting an environmental factor that undermines the health of society.

Supporting Operation Paydirt is the Fundred Dollar Bill Project, a collective artwork, created by children and adults across the country, of original interpretations of the US $100 bill. Through Fundred, a childhood population most threatened has a means to respond. These unique artworks will be delivered to the steps of Congress where an even exchange of this "creative capital" will be requested to obtain funding for implementation of Operation Paydirt.

We started in 2008 with fewer than 100 *Fundreds* in the Safehouse in New Orleans, now we have nearly 450,000 from across the country. *Operation Paydirt* continues to raise awareness, to collaborate with scientists, to move in the direction of policy change, and to bring forth the voices of people as a catalyst in lead-poisoning prevention. We remain determined to deliver Operation Paydirt and the Fundred Dollar Bill Project.

2.10.4 Mel Chin, Operation Paydirt/ Fundred Dollar Bill Project. Children making Fundreds at Langston Hughes Charter, New Orleans, 2008

2.10.5 Mel Chin, Operation Paydirt/ Fundred Dollar Bill Project. Examples of the fundreds drawn by students in New Orleans, Louisiana (top left and right); Marfa, Texas (bottom left); and Collowhee, Tennessee (bottom right)

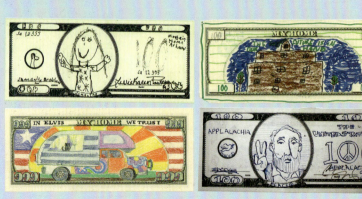

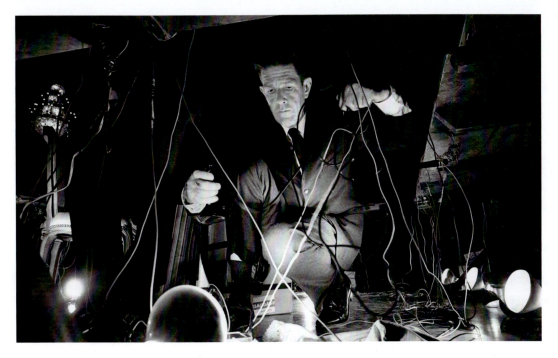

2.10.6 John Cage, during his concert held at the opening of the National Arts Foundation, Washington, D.C., 1966

Performance Art

During the 1960s and 1970s, artists all over the world began exploring theatrical actions or performances as a new form of creative activity they termed performance art. American composer John Cage (1912–1992) incorporated into his music chance operations, experimental techniques, and even silence. Heavily influenced by Zen Buddhism, Cage wanted to jolt his audiences into paying attention to the life all around them. He was one of the first artists to conduct **happenings**, or impromptu art actions. *Theater Piece No. 1* (1952) was an unrecorded collaboration in poetry, music, dance, and paintings by the faculty and students at Black Mountain College in North Carolina. The performers mingled with the members of the audience, and the piece relied for its outcome on improvisation and chance rather than a script or musical score. Its lasting influence comes from its emphasis on performance rather than documentation. Happenings expanded the scope of art to include the lived moment— actions as they happen, here and now.

The work of German artist Joseph Beuys (1921–1986) explores his own German heritage and wider issues of social identity. Beuys's early life under the Nazis, especially his compulsory

membership of the Hitler Youth and volunteer service as a fighter pilot in the German Air Force, strongly influenced his artwork. He claimed that nomads rescued him in North Africa after a plane crash he sustained in World War II, and prevented him from freezing to death by wrapping him in fat and felt. Hence those materials became symbolic elements in many of his sculptures and performances.

A large piece of felt was one of the major props in his piece *Coyote, I Like America and America Likes Me* (**2.10.7**). The piece is mysterious. Because Beuys did not speak or interact with anyone during the five-day

2.10.7 Joseph Beuys, *Coyote, I Like America and America Likes Me*, May 1974. Living sculpture at the René Block Gallery, New York

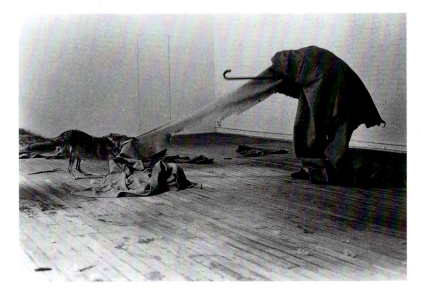

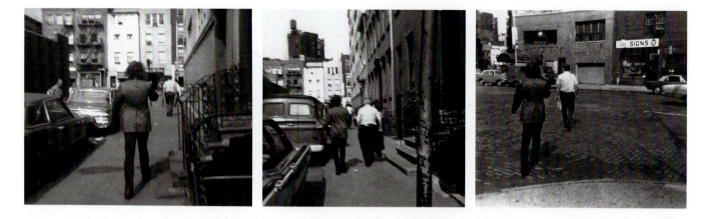

performance, a sense of myth surrounds the events that actually took place. Upon arrival in America, Beuys was transported from the airport to the gallery in an ambulance. He was wrapped in felt, covered in hospital blankets, and carried on a gurney so he could not see his surroundings or touch American soil. During the performance he was confined in the gallery with a coyote, a trickster or mischievous figure in native American mythology, and symbolic of the spirit world. Beuys's action (as he called his performances) was intended to activate a process of spiritual healing and reconciliation, to make amends for the desecrations caused by the coming of Europeans to the New World.

When he was finished with his performance, the artist was wrapped up and whisked away by ambulance in the same manner as he had come. Beuys saw his actions as a way to make art more connected to society, incorporating commitments to activism and political reform.

Early in his career, American artist Vito Acconci (b. 1940) was known for art actions and performances. These works consisted of situations he set up for himself, and records of how he completed them. His stated intentions for *Following Piece* (**2.10.8**) were: "Choosing a person at random, in the street, a new location, each day. Following him wherever he goes, however long or far he travels. (The activity ends when he enters a private place—his home, office, etc.)." Acconci performed this activity for twenty-three days; the longest following lasted nine hours. An exhibition of *Following Piece* includes documents of the events, such as the artist's handwritten note cards, and photographs

of Acconci walking behind the person being followed. *Following Piece* examines both the relationship between the artist and the viewer and the way an artist's actions create interactions with another person. In this sense, Acconci's work is a conceptual performance: it is about ideas and a set of actions as much as about the production of a work of art. It is interesting to note how our view of such works can change through time. In 1969, when the piece was first developed, it was regarded as a new idea, but nowadays, we might look on the artist's actions in following and photographing someone without their knowledge as disturbing or even menacing.

Some performances put the body through extremes of endurance, as Serbian artist Marina Abramović (b. 1946) has done in a number of works dating back to the 1970s. In one piece she lay in a ring of fire until she fainted from asphyxiation (and had to be rescued by onlookers). In another, one of her longest pieces (it took almost three months), she and her partner Ulay started at opposite ends of the Great Wall of China and met in the middle after walking more than 1,242 miles.

In 2010, Abramović performed the longest-lasting work of her solo career so far, *The Artist is Present*, for three months at the Museum of Modern Art, New York (MoMA) (**2.10.9**). Every day during that period she sat quietly at a table in the museum's gallery all day, from before it opened until after it closed. Museum visitors were invited to sit—one at a time, for as long as they wished—in the chair opposite her. The title of the piece poignantly calls attention to its purpose: for the artist to be personally in the

2.10.8 Vito Acconci, *Following Piece*, 1969. Street Works IV, 23-day activity

space and engage with people, creating what she has called an "energy dialogue," without talking, touching, or otherwise overtly communicating. Through this engagement, Abramović put her mental and physical abilities to the test. At the same time, the audience experienced the intensity of this seemingly simple interaction. Portraits were made of each person who sat in the chair, showing most of them staring intently forward, some of them smiling, and a number of people crying.

This piece was a part of a retrospective exhibition of Abramović's work, which was the first major performance exhibition at MoMA. The show revealed the numerous challenges institutions must deal with when displaying performance art, such as the unpredictability of audience members who have been invited to participate. Crowd control took on epic proportions for this retrospective, with around 1,400 museum visitors per day and an estimate of more than 500,000 over the whole course of the exhibition. In addition to photographs, video documentation, and written accounts of performance pieces made throughout Abramović's career, for the first time, performers reenacted her earlier pieces so that visitors could experience them first hand, and visitors shared their perspectives on personal blogs and through social media.

2.10.9 Marina Abramović, *The Artist Is Present*, Performance, 3 months. The Museum of Modern Art, New York, 2010

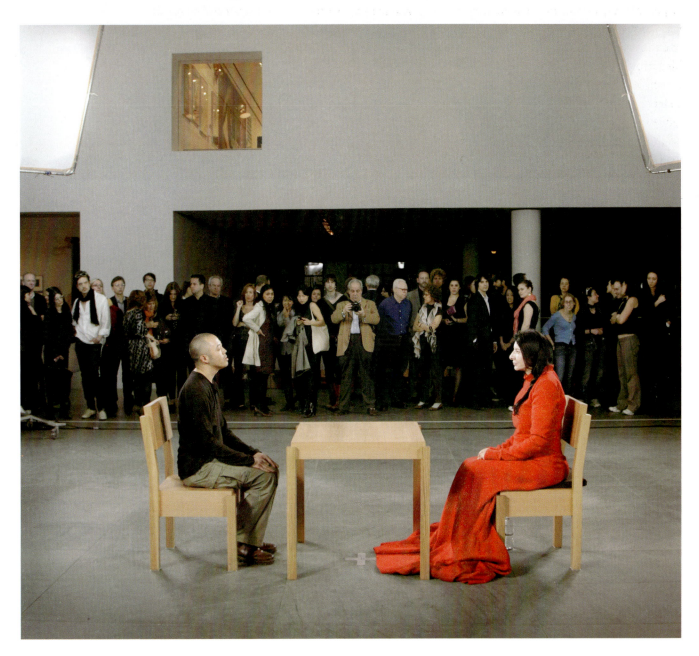

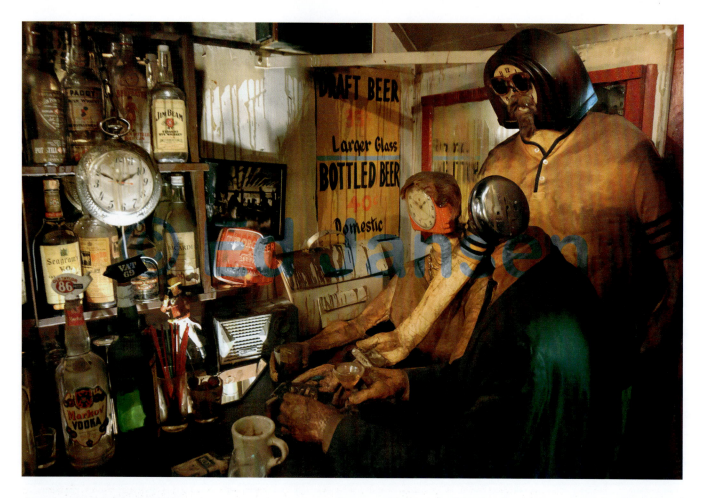

Installation and Environments

The Beanery by American Ed Kienholz (1927–1994) reflects the artist's desire to break down barriers between art and life (**2.10.10a** and **b**). Kienholz meticulously replicated the interior of his local bar, Barney's Beanery, complete with lifesize figures inspired by people he knew. This very specific place has been transformed into an assemblage through the products, interior design, technology, clothing, newspapers, music, and even odors it contains.

2.10.10a Edward Kienholz, Detail of *The Beanery*

2.10.10b Edward Kienholz, *The Beanery*, 1965 (restored 2012). Installation, 8′3 ½″ x 21′11¾″ x 6′2 ¾″. Stedelijk Museum, Amsterdam, The Netherlands

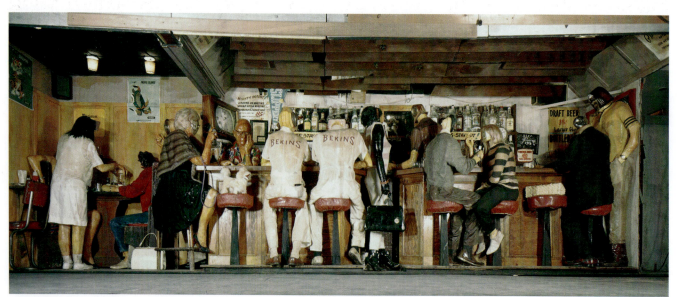

To keep the experience as true to the artist's intentions as possible, the original soundtrack on tape has recently been converted to CD, and "odor paste" that smells like a bar is replenished by the museum. By placing clocks in place of the faces, Kienholz reiterated the fact that time now stands still in this sculptural **tableau**.

American (with African, native American, and European ancestry) Fred Wilson (b. 1954) draws on his background as an art educator to rearrange objects in museum collections. He takes on the role of the **curator**—the person responsible for overseeing, preserving, and exhibiting objects in a particular collection— and converts the role into an art action. Wilson's work at the Metropolitan Museum of Art, the American Museum of Natural History, and the American Crafts Museum gave him insight into the ways in which museum displays create certain experiences that have specific effects on audiences. In his own art, Wilson looks critically at the assumptions behind the ways museum exhibitions work.

In *Mining the Museum* at the Maryland Historical Society, Wilson selected and presented objects from the museum's own collection (**2.10.11**) in unusual ways, and included objects rarely seen because they were usually in storage. He also provided provocative wall labels, and installed audio loops to accompany certain pieces. One section of the installation displayed five "cigar store Indians" with their backs to the viewer. (Since the nineteenth century, "cigar store Indians" have been used as sidewalk displays for tobacco shops in America.) The title, *Portraits of Cigar Store Owners*, is ironic because native Americans would never have owned cigar stores at that time; it is also critical of the degradation of the dignity of native Americans that is involved in turning them into advertising signs. Throughout *Mining the Museum*, the museum's unconscious racial biases are exposed. As a result of this installation the Maryland Historical Society realized it had never staged an exhibition about slavery or institutionalized racism, even though eight out of ten Baltimore residents are African-American.

Tableau: a stationary scene arranged for artistic impact
Curator: a person who organizes the collection and exhibition of objects/ artworks in a museum or gallery; and negotiates interactions between artists, artworks, institutions, and the public

2.10.11 Fred Wilson, *Portraits of Cigar Store Owners*, from *Mining the Museum*, installation April 4, 1992–February 28, 1993

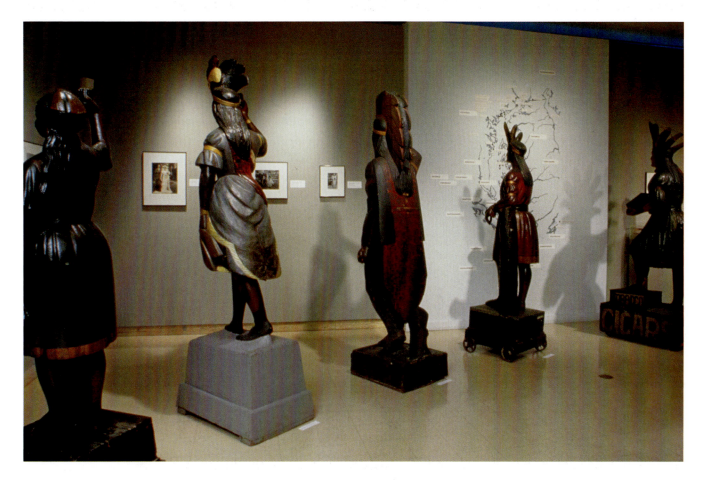

The installations of American artist Kara Walker (b. 1969) also address overlooked history: the pre-Civil War South. Walker adopts the nineteenth-century technique of **silhouette** cutouts, in which an artist makes a likeness of the sitter by tracing the shadow cast from a strong light source. The silhouettes in Walker's installations provide a glimpse of the **subject** in an indirect way, a trace of history that seems to have existed. She has recently incorporated overhead projectors in her installations to cast additional shadows on the walls, including those of viewers in the room. As the viewer's shadow appears on the wall, he or she is included and even implicated in the events unfolding there. The combined projections and silhouettes can be seen in *Insurrection! (Our Tools Were Rudimentary, Yet We Pressed On)*, which presents a story that combines fact and fiction (**2.10.12**). Walker explains that this scene is intended to show "a slave revolt in the antebellum South where the house slaves got after their master with their instruments, their utensils of everyday life."

Each grouping of figures highlights the bodies of the individuals, the stories they represent, and the scenarios of which they become a part.

2.10.12 Kara Walker, *Insurrection! (Our Tools Were Rudimentary, Yet We Pressed On)*, 2000. Projection, cut paper, and adhesive on wall, 4'8¾" × 29'1⅞". Solomon R. Guggenheim Museum, New York

Silhouette: a portrait or figure represented in outline and solidly colored in
Subject: the person, object, or space depicted in a work of art

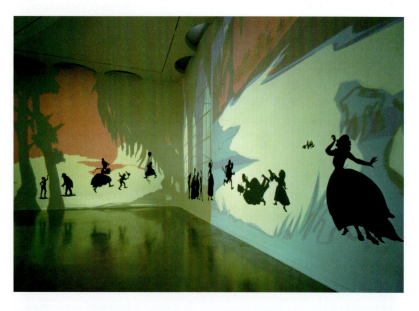

Active Learning Exercises

1. Performance art enlivens moments that were once replicated in other art forms. Review examples of performance art in this chapter and elsewhere in the book (the Images Related to 2.10 section on p. 363 will help you find other works featured). What characteristics do these artworks share with music performances, plays, movies, or other types of popular culture? In what ways are they different? What does making this comparison reveal to you that you had not considered before?

2. Conceptual art concentrates on ideas, and installations consciously arrange an environment for the viewer to engage with. These types of artworks celebrate the perceptions and understanding of those who respond to them as much as the skills of the artists who made them. How do these practices compare with "traditional" media, such as painting, sculpture, and drawing? What are your feelings about these "alternative" art forms? Which, if any, artworks from this chapter do you have trouble understanding or accepting as art? Why? Which, if any, do you find refreshing or inspiring? Share your thoughts with your classmates.

3. The art in this chapter emphasizes the lived moment, or actions as they are happening, by focusing on the processes involved. Take this practice as an inspiration for making your own process art piece. Begin by listing or documenting as many actions as you can for a three-hour period during your day. Now make an art piece, in any format, that seems to express that small segment of your life effectively. Keep in mind that artworks made using alternative media and processes draw our attention away from art that tells a story, or that seems to be a picture of something, and toward the acts of making, thinking, and experiencing. What do you notice when you reflect on your list? Which things reflect normal, mundane, parts of your daily routine? Which things are unusual? How can you effectively convey or communicate your experience for this time period? Consider artworks in this chapter or elsewhere in the book for inspiration.

Images Related to 2.10: Alternative Media and Processes

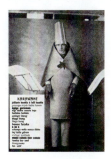

3.8.29 Hugo Ball, Performance of "Karawane" at Cabaret Voltaire, 1916, p. 532

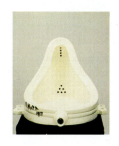

3.9.7 Marcel Duchamp, *Fountain*, 1917, p. 546

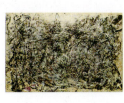

3.9.2 Jackson Pollock, *Number 1A*, 1948 , p. 542

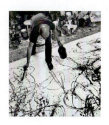

3.9.1 Hans Namuth, Photograph of Jackson Pollock painting, 1950, p. 542

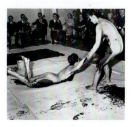

4.9.11a Yves Klein, *Anthropométries de l'époque bleue*, 1960, p. 666

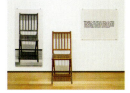

3.9.10 Joseph Kosuth, *One and Three Chairs*, 1965, p. 547

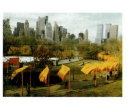

4.1.7 Christo and Jeanne-Claude, *The Gates*, 1979–2005, p. 567

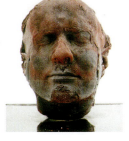

0.0.15 Marc Quinn, *Self*, 1991, p. 38

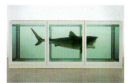

2.4.17 Damien Hirst, *The Physical Impossibility of Death in the Mind of Someone Living*, 1991, p. 258

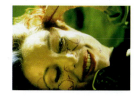

4.9.20a ORLAN, Seventh surgery-performance, entitled *Omnipresence*, 1993, p. 673

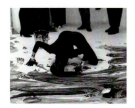

4.9.12 Janine Antoni, *Loving Care*, 1993, p. 667

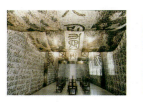

4.1.10 Wenda Gu, *United Nations—China Monument*, 1998, p. 569

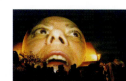

4.10.12 Nikki S. Lee, *Hip Hop Project (25)*, 2001, p. 683

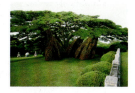

4.1.13 Krzysztof Wodiczko, *Tijuana Projection*, 2001, p. 573

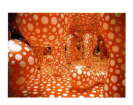

4.3.17 Patrick Dougherty, *Na Hale 'o waiawi*, 2003, p. 597

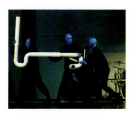

1.5.11 Blue Man Group performance, Nevada, 2005, p. 126

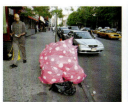

1.4.30 Adrian Kondratowicz, TRASH project, 2008, p. 117

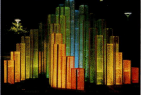

2.4.22 Athena Tacha with EDAW, *Star Fountain*, 2009, p. 261

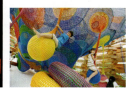

2.6.19 Toshiko Horiuchi McAdam, *Knitted Wonder Space II*, 2009, p. 303

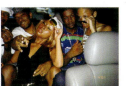

4.4.18 Yayoi Kusama, Installation at the Tate Gallery, London, England, 2012, p. 609

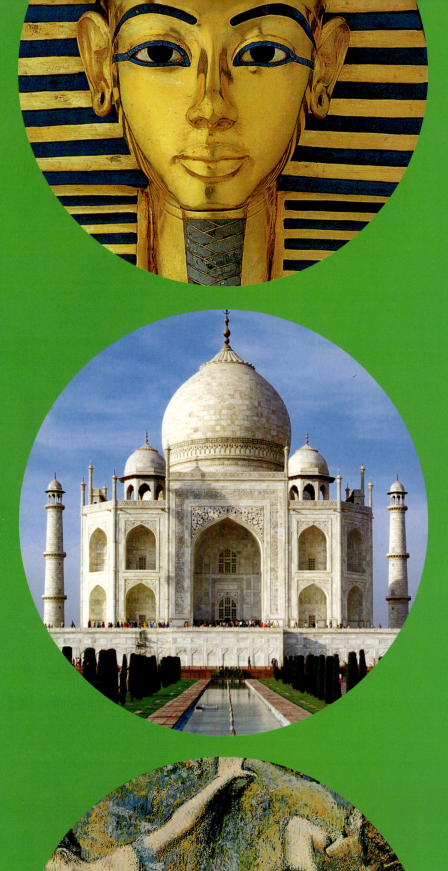

HISTO

The history of art is an important aspect of the many ways in which we can understand a work. Art is not just the skillful application of design concepts and materials to produce an impressive work. Inevitably, an artwork is influenced by the time and place in which it was created. This influence is known as the context in which the art was made. In this part, as well as learning about context, you will discover how history has influenced art and how art, in its turn, reflects history.

PART 3

RY AND CONTEXT

IN THIS PART YOU WILL STUDY:

The Prehistoric and Ancient Mediterranean

Art of the Middle Ages

Art of India, China, Japan,
and Southeast Asia

Art of the Americas

Art of Africa and the Pacific Islands

Art of Renaissance and Baroque Europe
(1400–1750)

Art of Europe and America (1700–1865):
Rococo to Realism

The Modern Aesthetic: Manet in 1863
to the American Scene in the 1930s

Late Modern and Contemporary Art:
From Abstract Expressionism in the
1940s to the Present Day

3.1

The Prehistoric and Ancient Mediterranean

Human prehistory is the long period during which humans and their ancestors developed societies for which no written record has been found. We know about the achievements of these early people from the material traces they left behind. In Europe, this takes us back thousands of years—even 2.5 million years, if we include tools. These ancient people survived by gathering wild plants and hunting, and some found time to produce what we admire today as prehistoric art. Prehistoric art has been discovered in this region from as early as *c.* 40,000 BCE.

As humans formed larger communities, the Mediterranean region—the ancient Near East, northern Africa, and southern Europe—

3.1.1 Map of prehistoric Europe and the ancient Mediterranean

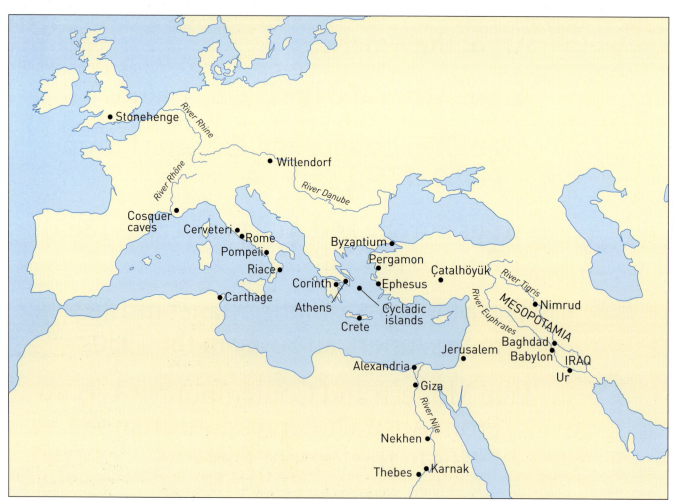

flourished as an area of trade. The region thrived because of being surrounded by bodies of water; frequently, the most powerful were those who controlled access to the seas. Here, a succession of civilizations arose that continue to shape the ways we live, even in the twenty-first century. It was here that humans first invented agriculture, started to live in urban settlements, and eventually planned cities; it was here that people invented writing, and produced works of art we still regard as great wonders of the world. The achievements of these people remain evident in our own lives. We write with an alphabet refined by the ancient Romans of Italy. Farmers who raise wheat crops today can do so because other farmers domesticated wheat and barley nearly 10,000 years ago.

These achievements, which we generally describe as the beginning of civilization, were matched independently elsewhere, for example in Asia and the Americas. The developments in the Mediterranean, however, are also part of the history of the Americas because of the arrival there of Europeans more than 500 years ago. This chapter first tells the story of the sculptures, cave paintings, and palaces made by prehistoric Europeans. Then we will look at the emergence of early civilizations in the ancient Near East and the rise of a great civilization in Egypt. Lastly we will study the powerful societies of ancient Greece and Rome and the beautiful sculptures, paintings, and buildings they produced.

Prehistoric Art in Europe and the Mediterranean

As long as 40,000 years ago, prehistoric people painted the interiors of caves; and sculptures still survive from 5,000 years after that. Not surprisingly, such art is preoccupied with the basics of life: procreation and sources of food. Prehistoric artworks are particularly important records of the lives of our early ancestors, because written records of these cultures do not exist. Often what we know about their

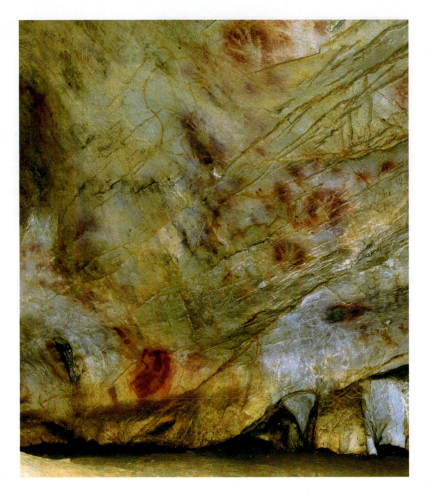

3.1.2 Hand stencils, from El Castillo Cave, Cantabria, Spain, c. 37,300 BCE

lives is based upon archaeological finds, and our modern interpretations of these discoveries.

The earliest paintings in Europe are found on walls in El Castillo Cave in Spain (**3.1.2**). Dating is possible through scientific study of the calcite (a carbonate mineral frequently found in caverns) that has formed on top of the paintings. The calcite in El Castillo is at least 40,000 years old, so the paintings underneath may date from much earlier. Prehistoric humans often painted over previous images already on the wall. The very earliest paintings in this cave were red spheres, made by blowing pigment, in this case red **ocher**, through a reed. Humans often blew the **pigment** around their hand, creating an effect similar to a **stencil**. Later, people would use the same method to create images of animals they hunted.

The most common type of prehistoric artworks found throughout the world are small female sculptures that suggest a preoccupation with fertility. Like other such "fertility figures,"

Ocher: a pigment found in nature containing hydrated iron oxide
Pigment: the colored material used in paints. Often made from finely ground minerals
Stencil: a perforated template allowing ink or paint to pass through to print a design

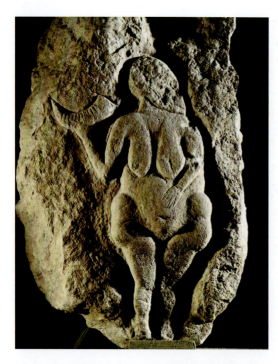

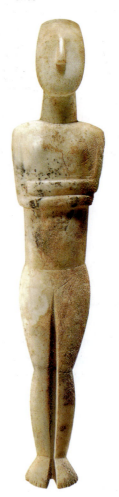

3.1.3 (left) Venus of Laussel, found in Marquay, Dordogne, France, c. 23,000 BCE. Low relief on limestone block, 18⅛" high. Musée d'Aquitaine, Bordeaux, France

the Venus of Laussel (**3.1.3**) shows a faceless woman with large breasts, belly, and vulva, signifying her fertility. Made approximately 25,000 years ago, the figure was carved into limestone and originally painted with red ocher. The carving is unique in that the woman holds a horn-shaped object that has thirteen short lines carved on it, which have led scholars to develop different opinions about the work. For example, the figure may represent a **shaman** and the horn could have been used for a ritual designed to ensure a successful hunt, or as a musical instrument. Other experts have suggested the horn may be a phallic symbol, emphasizing the woman's role for procreation. Further, as the number thirteen corresponds to the number of menstrual cycles a woman may have in a year, some scholars have speculated that the horn may symbolize a waning crescent moon, which, with the number of stripes, could be intended to represent a woman's monthly cycle.

On the Cycladic Islands, now part of modern-day Greece, a number of human figures, carved out of white marble, have been found, many of them at grave sites (**3.1.4**). Cycladic sculptures of females far outnumber those of males. Curiously, however, the female Cycladic figures look similar to their male counterparts, with barely noticeable breasts and only minimal anatomical detail. The figures usually have a long head and protruding nose; they are generic renderings of females, rather than individual portraits. Originally, these figures were painted in black, red, and blue to show some facial details, body ornamentation, and probably jewelry. Because of the sculptor's emphasis on parts of the body related to reproduction, such as the slight swelling in the belly, many scholars believe these objects are fertility figures. It is thought that the smaller of these figurines, which would fit in one's hand, may have been carried around as a kind of talisman, or charm against bad luck. Little is known about the Cycladic culture because it did not have a written language, but these expressive, almost geometric figures are some of the most intriguing in the history of art.

Other significant early works of art from the Mediterranean region come from Çatalhöyük, Turkey. Here, fragments of wall paintings remain from a large building complex that stood between *c.* 7000 and 5700 BCE. Inhabitants of the Çatalhöyük settlements lived in mud-brick homes, which they entered from the rooftops; there was no organized street system. The deceased were buried beneath the floors, and sometimes homes were demolished to create a higher base from which to build new ones.

3.1.4 (above) Attributed to the Steiner Master, Reclining female figure of the Late Spedos variety, Cyclades, 2500–2400 BCE. Island marble, 23⅜" high. The J. Paul Getty Museum, Villa Collection, Malibu, California

3.1.5 Landscape with erupting volcano, detail of watercolor copy of a wall painting from Level VII, Çatalhöyük, Turkey, c. 6150 BCE. Wall painting: Ankara Museum of Anatolian Civilizations, Turkey. Watercolor copy: Private collection

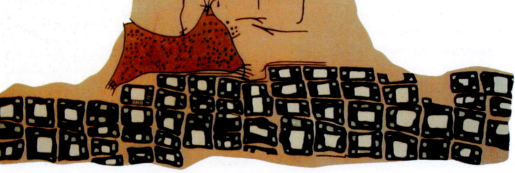

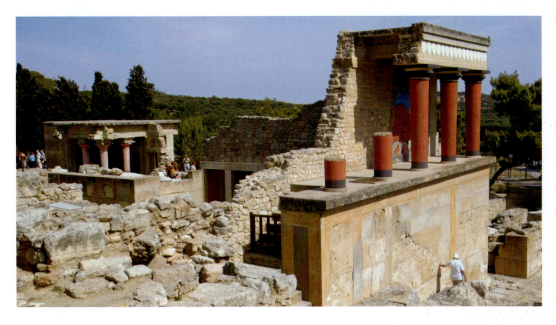

Shaman: a priest or priestess regarded as having the ability to communicate directly with the spiritual world

Fresco: painting made on freshly applied plaster

3.1.6 Ruins of Palace of Knossos, Crete, Greece, c. 1700–1400 BCE. From 1900, parts of the palace were reconstructed, as seen here

More than twelve layers of building have been discovered at the site.

While many paintings from Çatalhöyük depict humans and animals (often in hunting scenes), one intriguing but faint wall painting re-creates the design of the town (reproduced here in a watercolor copy for ease of reading), with rectangular houses closely aligned side by side (**3.1.5**). In the background is the double-peaked volcano, Hasan Da, which in reality is 8 miles away. The volcano appears to be erupting; lava falls in droplets down the mountain, and smoke fills the sky. Scholars have not determined an exact volcanic eruption that could be the one referred to in this image: this makes it possibly the first "pure" landscape (a picture of a setting in its own right, without life and narrative) ever created in the history of mankind.

Just over 100 miles south of the Cyclades and dating from a little later in time, there is ample archaeological evidence of a sophisticated and complex civilization, the Minoan, on the island of Crete from about 2700 to 1400 BCE. Minoan cities, with their powerful fleets and location at the hub of the eastern Mediterranean, grew wealthy as centers of trade. Some of our written evidence of Minoan culture comes from the Greeks. According to their legend, King Minos was the stepfather of the Minotaur, half man, half bull, a man-eating creature trapped in a labyrinth. The powerful Minos required the Athenians to send seven young men and seven young women as tribute each year to satisfy the Minotaur's appetite.

The Minoans built palaces in the center of their cities, the largest being King Minos's Palace of Knossos (**3.1.6**). This complex—up to five stories high—was a maze of some 1,300 rooms, corridors, and courtyards. These spaces were used for governmental and ceremonial functions, as accommodation for the king's family and their servants, as large storerooms, and even as a theater. The palace complex was so full of twists and turns that it is easy to see how the Greeks developed a myth about the labyrinth.

The importance of bulls in Minoan culture can be seen from their inclusion in the Minotaur myth and in much of Minoan art. Several sculptures and **frescoes** with scenes of bulls were found throughout the Palace of Knossos, including the lively *Bull-Leapers* (**3.1.7**). In this scene, three young acrobats are jumping

3.1.7 *Bull-Leapers*, from Palace of Knossos, Crete, Greece, c. 1450–1375 BCE. Archaeological Museum, Heraklion, Crete, Greece

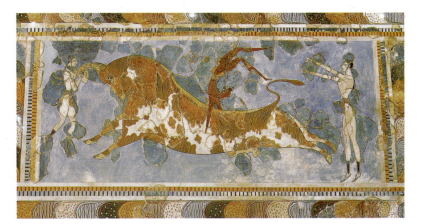

a spirited bull. The boy flips over the beast as a young woman on the left—lighter-skinned to identify her gender—prepares to take the next leap. The girl on the right has apparently just landed. The creature is depicted with great energy, yet the Cretans seem able to match it. Bull-leaping, boxing, and acrobatic scenes were common **subjects** in Minoan art, evidence of an athletic people; these activities may have been for pleasure, or for more ritualistic ceremonies.

Minoan civilization suffered a variety of upheavals, natural and man-made, from around 1500 BCE, when, as some believe, a volcanic eruption on the nearby island of Thera created a huge tidal wave that destroyed the Minoans' cities and fleets. Some decades later, Mycenaean invaders from mainland Greece overran Crete, taking over such palace sites as Knossos.

Mesopotamia: The Cradle of Civilization

Mesopotamia, from the Greek for "the land between the rivers" (a reference to the Tigris and Euphrates rivers), includes the regions of modern Iraq and portions of Syria, Turkey, and Iran. Ancient Mesopotamia is often called the "Cradle of Civilization," for it was here that urban centers first developed as early as 4000 BCE. The earliest forms of writing, using pictograms, also developed in Mesopotamia in the fourth millennium BCE. Here too, in the rich land of the Fertile Crescent, complex irrigation systems enabled people to produce plentiful crops. Mesopotamia was frequently conquered by rulers desiring the wealth of its farmland. Amongst the many cultures that battled for control of the region were the Sumerians, Akkadians, Assyrians, and Babylonians.

Sumerians

The Sumerian civilization was the first great power in Mesopotamia. By the third millennium BCE, under the Sumerians, a writing system evolved from pictograms: it was called cuneiform, and consisted of wedge-shaped symbols drawn with a reed "pen" in soft clay. The

Sumerians also seem to have invented the wheel, which was probably first used to help potters make circular pots. The people of Mesopotamia worshiped many gods and goddesses (a practice known as **polytheism**) in temples or shrines located on huge ziggurats—stepped pyramid structures made of baked and unbaked mud bricks—which they constructed in the center of their communities.

Ur was an important city of Sumer, and the treasures found at its Royal Cemetery reveal the wealth of the Sumerian elite. Buried with the bodies were gold jewelry and daggers inlaid with **lapis lazuli**. Whether the dead were royalty or religious leaders is unknown, but the chariots, weapons, and musical instruments buried with them indicate their importance. Servants and soldiers were also interred with their leaders, perhaps to protect and serve them in the afterlife.

The artists of Sumer excelled in the art of inlaying ivory and shell in wood, as seen in the *Standard of Ur* found in the Royal Cemetery of Ur (**3.1.8a and b**). When it was first discovered, scholars thought it must have been carried on the end of a pole, like a standard, but there is no

Subject: the person, object, or space depicted in a work of art
Polytheism: the worship of more than one god or goddess
Lapis lazuli: bright-blue semiprecious stone containing sodium aluminum silicate and sulphur

3.1.8a and 3.1.8b *Standard of Ur*, c. 2600–2400 BCE. (a: top) War and (b: bottom) Peace. Wood inlaid with shell, lapis lazuli, and red limestone, 7⅞ × 18½". British Museum, London, England

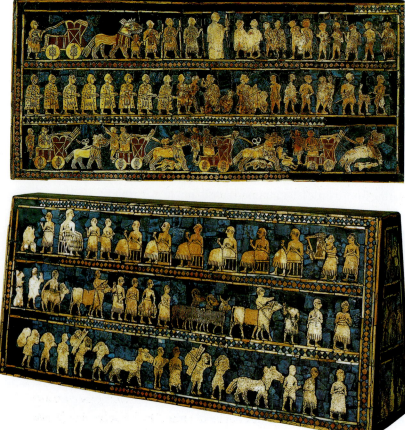

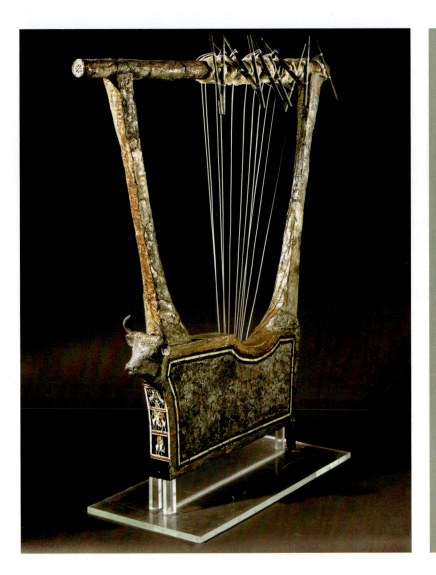

3.1.9 Sumerian bull lyre, *c.* 2550–2450 BCE. Wood, lapis lazuli, gold, silver, shell, bitumen, in modern wood support, 46 × 55". From the King's Grave, Royal Cemetery, Ur, Iraq. British Museum, London, England

---

Register: one of two or more horizontal sections into which a space is divided in order to depict the episodes of a story
Hierarchical scale: the use of size to denote the relative importance of subjects in an artwork

---

real evidence for this. The wooden box is only 8 in. high and decorated with inlaid pieces of shell, lapis lazuli, and red limestone. One side of the box shows war scenes (**3.1.8a**), while the other shows life during times of peace (**3.1.8b**). Each side is divided into three sections, known as **registers**. The bottom register of the war side shows chariots running over the bodies of the enemy. In the middle register, the box shows soldiers (from left to right) marching, shaming their enemies by stripping them of their clothing, and forcing them to continue walking. In the center of the top register is the ruler. His larger size indicates his importance, a convention known as **hierarchical scale**. His status is reinforced by the fact that all the surrounding people are facing him. He has stepped out of his chariot while prisoners are brought before him. On the peace side (**3.1.8b**),

3.1.10 Inlaid panel from a Sumerian lyre's sound box, showing mythological figures, *c.* 2550–2400 BCE. Gold, silver, lapis lazuli, shell, bitumen, and wood, 13" high. From the King's Grave, Royal Cemetery, Ur, Iraq. University of Pennsylvania Museum of Archaeology and Anthropology, Philadelphia

animals, fish, and other foods are brought to a banquet where seated figures drink while a musician playing a lyre entertains them. The standard is a fine example of narrative art and a source of evidence about what food the Sumerians ate, their clothing and weapons, their musical instruments, and their success in war.

Three lyres, stringed instruments similar to a harp, were found amongst the magnificent objects in the Royal Cemetery of Ur. Lyres were popular musical instruments in ancient Sumer, but the example in **3.1.9** is more elaborate than most. As it was found in a grave, it seems to have

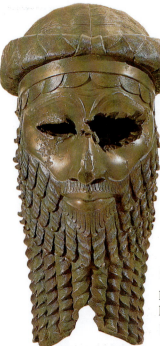

3.1.11 Head of an Akkadian ruler, *c.* 2300–2200 BCE. Bronze, 15" high. National Museum of Iraq, Baghdad

been intended as a suitable burial offering for a powerful person. Although the body of the instrument disintegrated long ago, the wooden section of the lyre has been reconstructed to give an idea of its appearance. The original panels on the sound box of another of the lyres, made of lapis lazuli and shell, have survived (**3.1.10**, see p. 371). They reveal that the lyre, which played music we can no longer hear, was also covered in symbols that we now do not entirely understand. The panels show animals engaged in such human activities as dancing, walking on two legs, and bringing instruments and drinks to a ceremony, probably much like the ones in which this lyre was used. The fusion of humans and beasts, such as the scorpion man below and the human-headed bulls above, suggests a sacred event, perhaps a marriage or a funeral procession. Some scholars, however, suggest that the scenes decorating the lyre show activities in the supernatural realm of the dead.

Akkadians

The next Mesopotamian empire was founded by the Akkadian king Sargon, who ruled between *c.* 2334 and 2279 BCE. He conquered the Sumerian city-states. Before King Sargon, most rulers of Mesopotamia were believed to be merely representatives of the gods on Earth. The Akkadian rulers who followed Sargon, however, elevated themselves to divine status. The bronze, lifesized Akkadian Head (**3.1.11**) is the portrait of a great king, probably Sargon's grandson Naram-Sin (*c.* 2254–2218 BCE). The figure's expression is one of proud majesty. The artist paid particular attention to the texture and patterning of the hair on the ruler's beard, eyebrows, and head. The eye sockets have been damaged from violent gouging, either to remove the materials (probably shells or lapis lazuli) used to make the eyes, or to make the figure's presence less powerful. The head was originally discovered in Nineveh in northern Iraq, and was one of the many objects missing after the looting of the National Museum of Iraq in Baghdad in 2003 during the US invasion of Iraq. More than

15,000 artifacts were stolen, of which fewer than half have been recovered—this Akkadian head being one of them.

Assyrians

The Assyrians, who had intermittently enjoyed considerable power in the second millennium BCE, ruled much of Mesopotamia during the Neo-Assyrian period (883–612 BCE). The first great Assyrian king, Ashurnasirpal II (who ruled between 883 and 859 BCE), used slave labor to build the large city of Nimrud (near modern Mosul, Iraq), which became the capital of Assyria.

Ashurnasirpal II's grand palace was covered with **relief** sculptures of battles, hunting scenes, and religious rituals. An accompanying

3.1.12 Human-headed winged lion (*lamassu*) from gateway in Ashurnasirpal II's palace in Nimrud, Mesopotamia, Neo-Assyrian, 883–859 BCE. Alabaster (gypsum), 10'3½" high. Metropolitan Museum of Art, New York

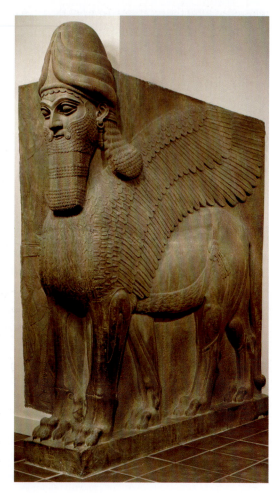

inscription refers to guardian figures (called *lamassu*) at gateways and entrances throughout the palace: "Beasts of the mountains and the seas, which I had fashioned out of white limestone and alabaster, I had set up in its gates. I made it [the palace] fittingly imposing."

These figures were meant to show the fearsome power of the Assyrian ruler and the authority given to him by the gods (**3.1.12**). Almost twice as tall as a human, this lamassu combines the head of a man with the body and strength of a lion and the wings and all-seeing eyes of an eagle. The horned cap signifies divinity, representing the gods' support and protection of the rulers of Assyria. Lamassu often have five legs, so they appear to be standing still when viewed from the front and striding forward when seen from the side. The lion is an animal that is often associated with kingship, and at this time in this civilization, only Assyrian kings were considered powerful enough to protect the people from the lions that roamed the areas outside the cities, and only kings were allowed to hunt the creatures. Some of the reliefs decorating Ashurnasirpal II's palace show the king hunting lions.

Babylonians

In the late seventh century BCE the Babylonians defeated the Assyrians and re-emerged as a powerful force in Mesopotamia. The ruler Nebuchadnezzar II (605–562 BCE) built a grand palace famous for its Hanging Gardens. Around the city, he built fortified walls with eight gateways. The dramatic Ishtar Gate was the main entrance to the streets and temples of Babylon (**3.1.13**). This enormous ceremonial entrance was actually two arched gates, the shorter of which (shown here) stood 47 ft. high. Golden reliefs of animals that symbolize Babylonian gods project out from a background of blue glazed bricks.

A Processional Way ran through the Ishtar Gate, leading to the ziggurat on the south side of the city, which some believe to be the inspiration for the Old Testament story of the Tower of Babel. Walls on either side of the Processional Way were covered with 120 glazed reliefs of lions (60 on each side), symbols of the goddess Ishtar.

The Ishtar Gate was taken to Germany in pieces in the early twentieth century and is now reconstructed at the Pergamon Museum in Berlin. In the same museum, next to the Gate, is

Relief: a sculpture that projects from a flat surface

3.1.13 Ishtar Gate from Babylon (Iraq), reign of Nebuchadnezzar II (602–562 BCE). Colored glazed terracotta tiles, 48'4" x 51'6" x 14'3¾". Vorderasiatisches Museum, Staatliche Museen, Berlin, Germany

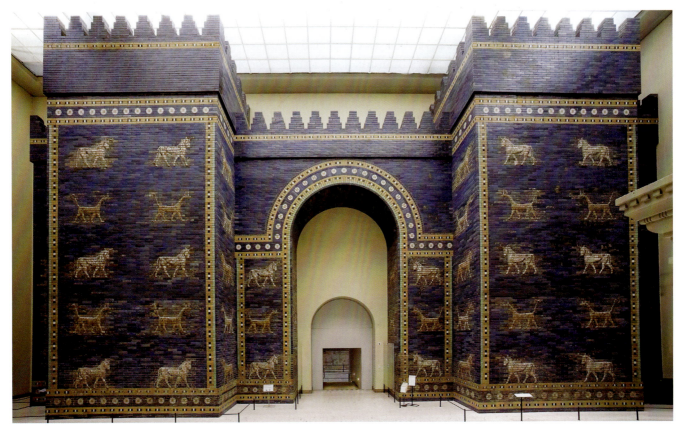

a wall from the entrance to Nebuchadnezzar's throne room, which shows **stylized** palm trees above lions that are similar to those that covered the walls of the Processional Way.

Ancient Egypt

At the time of the pharaohs, or Egyptian kings, the African land of Egypt traded with peoples throughout the Mediterranean, and thus many of the ideas and techniques invented by Egyptian artists were taken up by Mediterranean civilizations. Indeed, some thousands of years after they were made, the ancient Egyptians' extraordinary artistic and architectural achievements continue to be a source of wonder and astonishment worldwide.

It is perhaps appropriate that our fascination with Egyptian art should be so longlasting when so much of early Egyptian culture focused on eternity and the afterlife. The Egyptians believed that their pharaohs ruled with the authority of gods, and as a result, the Egyptian people took great care to ensure that, when a pharaoh died, his needs in the afterlife—where it was believed a person would require everything he or she had needed when living—would be met. So in the pharaohs' tombs were buried furniture, weapons, jewelry, and food. Family and servants were even killed to accompany the

dead pharaohs, although as time went on the Egyptians came to believe that art portraying these objects and people would be enough.

When a pharaoh died, in order to preserve his body for its afterlife, it was mummified, a process that took several months. The heart was left inside the body; Egyptians believed it to be the organ of thought and therefore necessary for the body to exist in the afterlife. The brain was deemed to be of no value and was removed through the nostrils. The liver, lungs, intestines, and stomach were also removed, and preserved in containers called canopic jars (**3.1.16**; see Box: Hieroglyphs, p. 376). The body was then soaked in a salt preservative called natron (a hydrated carbonate of sodium, found on some lake borders) for forty days and was finally wrapped in linen. An elaborate funerary mask was placed upon the face of the pharaoh, and he was buried inside layers of **sarcophagi**. These complex burials were meant to protect the treasure and life force, or *ka*, of the buried.

The great investment of time, labor, and wealth that was involved in creating the pyramids demonstrates further the importance the Egyptians placed on the afterlife. The three pyramids at Giza (**3.1.14**) were built to house the tombs of three Egyptian pharaohs: Khufu, his son Khafre, and Menkaure, son of Khafre. Construction on Khufu's pyramid, the largest of the three at 481 ft. high and 750 ft. per side,

Stylized: art that represents objects in an exaggerated way to emphasize certain aspects of the object

Ka: in Egyptian belief, the spirit of a person that leaves the body upon death and travels to the afterlife

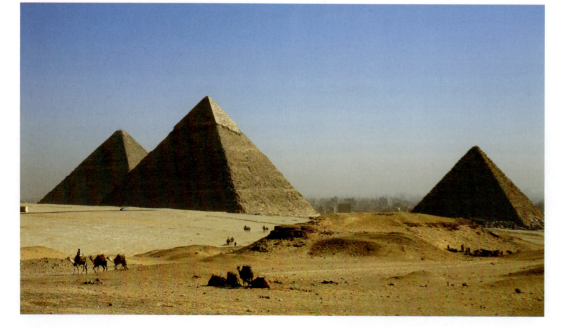

3.1.14 Pyramids at Giza, Egypt: from left to right, the pyramids of Khufu, Khafre, and Menkaure

began about 2551 BCE, and all three were completed over three generations. The sides of each pyramid are precisely the same length and all are placed precisely at the **cardinal points**, revealing the Egyptians' mastery of engineering and mathematics.

The pyramids were built of carefully stacked stones clad in white limestone. The pyramid of Khufu contains about 2,300,000 blocks of stone that have been calculated to weigh on average 2.5 tons. The methods used by the Egyptians to move such massive stones are still debated today, although scholars have suggested that they probably used the Nile for transportation, then either dragged the stones across the sand or rolled them over a series of logs. Once the stones made it to the site, tumbling, systems of levers, and ramps were likely used.

Connected to Khafre's pyramid through an underground walkway is Khafre's temple, next to which is a colossal stone sculpture of a Sphinx, a mythical creature with the body of a lion and the head of a human ruler (see Images Related to 3.1, p. 389). As in Assyrian culture, the image of the lion was in part an expression of royal power,

but for the Egyptians it was also a symbol of the sun god, Re, who was believed to carry away in his boat the dead to their afterlife. One theory is that the pyramids themselves may also have been seen to represent Re; for when the sun could be seen at the apex of a pyramid, the pyramid glistened and reflected the light of the sun. According to this theory, the corners of the pyramid extended the rays of the sun, and thus symbolically represented a ladder for the pharaoh to ascend to the afterlife. The funerary temples of these three pharaohs were placed on the east side of the pyramids, to symbolize that, just as the sun rises again in the east, they would be reborn into the afterlife.

The image **3.1.15** shows the statue of the pharaoh Khafre, which was found in the pharaoh's temple. When Khafre died, his body was taken to his temple and mummified (see p. 374) before being taken to his pyramid. In this statue, Khafre and the chair in which he sits have been carved from a single block of hard stone called diorite. He seems to sit stiffly, as if attached to his throne. Egyptian sculptures portrayed people with gracefully proportioned bodies, but they only subtly suggested movement, in this case by showing one hand clenched in a fist. To signify the pharaoh's importance, the powerful sky god Horus, symbolized as a falcon, perches on the throne behind his head. In Egyptian belief, Khafre's statue provides a place for his ka to rest during the afterlife. In fact, in Egyptian writing, "sculptor" translates as "he who keeps alive."

The Egyptians invented a system of writing using **hieroglyphs** and often carved or painted them on their artworks. Egyptian hieroglyphs were gradually deciphered after the finding of the Rosetta Stone in 1799 (see Box: Hieroglyphs, p. 376). This single discovery made possible a much greater understanding and appreciation of the art and culture of Egypt. More than 100 years later, the revelation in 1922 of the extraordinary riches hidden within the tomb of Tutankhamun fueled renewed interest in the ancient dynastic culture (see Perspectives on Art Box: The Golden Mask of King Tutankhamun, p. 377).

Portraits of rulers were common in ancient Egypt, as is exemplified by this portrait of

3.1.15 Khafre with the falcon god Horus embracing the back of his head, *c.* 2500 BCE. Diorite, 5'6⅛" high. Cairo Museum, Egypt

Sarcophagus (plural **sarcophagi**): a coffin (usually made of stone or baked clay)
Cardinal points: North, South, East, and West
Hieroglyph: written language involving sacred characters that may be pictures as well as letters or signifiers of sounds

Hieroglyphs

We can understand Egyptian art largely because we can translate hieroglyphs, the written language of the ancient Egyptians. This was made possible in 1799 through the discovery of the Rosetta Stone, which was found by the French army led by Napoleon during the course of his invasion of Egypt. The lettering on the stone is dated to 196 BCE and repeats the decrees of Ptolemy V, the Greek ruler of Egypt, in three separate forms of writing. Hieroglyphic and Demotic were different written forms of the Egyptian spoken language; Greek was familiar to many scholars and was the key to deciphering the other two. Hieroglyphs are often images of recognizable objects, but the image can represent the object itself, an idea, or even just a sound associated with that object. In 1822 Frenchman Jean-François Champollion was finally able to claim that, thanks to studying the Rosetta Stone, he understood the meaning of the complex hieroglyphic writing of the ancient Egyptians.

We know quite a bit about the burial practices of the Egyptians from the hieroglyphs written on the objects buried with the dead. Canopic jars like the ones shown here (**3.1.16**), each only 12 in. high, were designed so that each would hold an organ of the deceased. The hieroglyphic inscription painted down the vertical band on the front of each canopic jar identifies the figure it portrays and the organ it was meant to protect. Each jar represents one of the sons of Horus, who protects the organ contained within: the baboon-faced Hapy guards the lungs, the jackal-headed Duamutef guards the stomach, the falcon-headed Qebhsenuef guards the intestines, and the human-looking Imsety guards the liver.

3.1.16 Painted wooden canopic jars, *c.* 700 BCE (25th Dynasty). Painted sycamore fig wood, 12¼ " high. British Museum, London, England

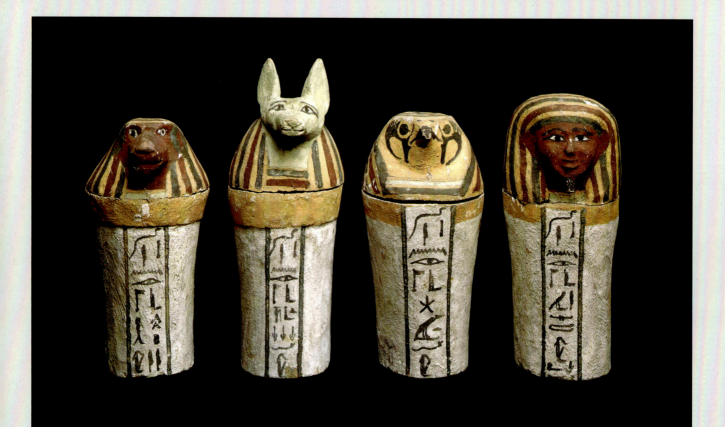

Perspectives On Art: Zahi Hawass
The Golden Mask of King Tutankhamun

Faience: quartz or sand ground and heated to create a shiny, glasslike material

3.1.17 Funerary mask of Tutankhamun, reign of Tutankhamun (1333–1323 BCE). Solid gold, semiprecious stones, quartz, and vitreous paste, 21¼" high. Cairo Museum, Egypt

Zahi Hawass is an Egyptian archaeologist and was formerly Secretary General of the Supreme Council of Antiquities. Amongst his responsibilities was the care of the fabulous treasures of King Tutankhamun, discovered by the English archaeologist Howard Carter in 1922. Dr. Hawass is one of the few people to have studied the famous mask of the king up close. Here he describes how the mask was made.

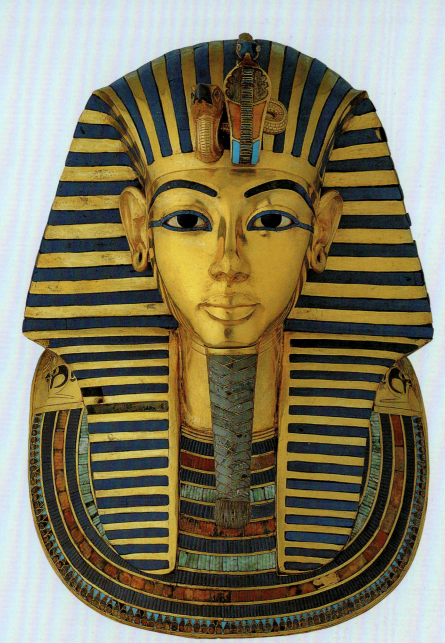

Whenever a television program wants to interview me about the golden king, I go directly to the mask (**3.1.17**). While the film crew is setting up the cameras, I have a chance to look again at the mask and I always discover something new. Each time, its beauty makes my heart tremble.

This spectacular mask represents an idealized portrait of the king. Intrinsically beautiful owing to the precious materials and masterful workmanship that went into its creation, it was also an essential item of the royal burial equipment, serving as an image that the soul could enter and occupy during the afterlife if something happened to the body.

The artisans who crafted this masterpiece began by hammering together two thick sheets of gold, thought by the ancient Egyptians to echo the flesh of the gods. They then shaped this metal into the likeness of the king wearing the striped nemes headcloth, using inlays of semi-precious stones and colored glass to add color and detail. The whites of the eyes were inlaid with quartz, and obsidian was used for the pupils. Red paint was lightly brushed into the corners of the eyes, subtly increasing their realism.

The vulture and cobra adorning the king's brow, images of the protective goddesses of Upper and Lower Egypt respectively, were made of solid gold with inlays of lapis lazuli, carnelian, **faience**, and glass. The long curled beard on the king's chin, emblematic of divinity, is made of blue glass laid into a golden framework.

On the shoulders and the back of the mask is a magical text that refers to the different parts of the body and mask, and their connection to particular gods or goddesses. This served to protect the king's body and render it functional for the afterlife.

Deify: to worship and make into a god or goddess

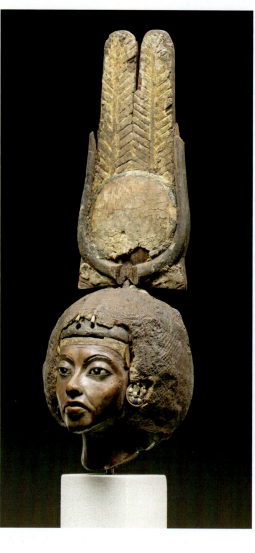

3.1.18 *Queen Tiye of Egypt* portrait head, *c.* 1355 BCE, (18th Dynasty), from Medinet el-Gurob, Egypt. Yew wood, ebony, gold, silver, lapis lazuli, textiles, faience. Head 4 × 3 × 3¼", base 4 × 4¾ × 4¾". Ägyptisches Museum, Staatliche Museen zu Berlin, Germany

3.1.19 (below) Fowling scene, from the tomb of Nebamun, Thebes, Egypt, 18th Dynasty, *c.* 1350 BCE. Painted plaster, 38⅝ × 8¾". British Museum, London, England

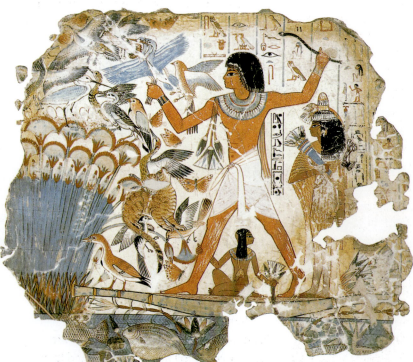

Tutankhamun's grandmother, Queen Tiye (**3.1.18**). This object is extraordinarily well preserved, considering it was made out of wood thousands of years ago. Its preservation is due to the fact that it was found buried underground in Gurob, and protected by the dry Egyptian desert. The portrait was made when Tiye was wife to the pharaoh; it originally had a gold crown, the remnants of which still cover the queen's forehead. One of her gold-and-blue earrings is visible in her left ear. When her husband died, Tiye's son Akhenaten became pharaoh, and she was one of his main advisors. Her son formally **deified** her, and several additions were made to this sculpture to signify Tiye's new identity as an eternal goddess. The earlier gold crown was covered with a finely woven linen cap and decorated with blue faience beads. The tall headdress with a gold disk framed by horns, along with two long gold feathers, also signified her new status. The inclusion of the disk, a symbol of Re, the sun god, is significant because Tiye's son worshiped only the Aten, the disk or orb of the sun, rejecting the polytheism of the pharaohs who ruled before him.

Paintings made during the time of the ancient Egyptians are rich in details that tell us about the way people lived. Wealthy people filled their tombs with paintings showing what they wished to take with them into the afterlife. The image in **3.1.19** is from the tomb-chapel of Nebamun, a "scribe and grain accountant in the granary of divine offerings" in the Temple of Amun-Re at Karnak. The hieroglyphic writing (see Box: Hieroglyphs, p. 376) on the right identifies him and tells us that he enjoyed hunting. Nebamun is depicted hunting several species of birds; a cat holding birds in its mouth is shown underneath his right elbow. The artist included an Egyptian boat and the rich, lush growth of the reed-like papyrus plant. This scene highlights the importance of the River Nile to the Egyptians, and how the flooding of the Nile symbolized a cycle of regeneration and new life each year, just as Egyptians believed that after death they would be reborn. The artist depicted the figures in hierarchical scale, that is, in proportion to their importance: Nebamun is shown the largest, his wife is smaller, and their daughter is the smallest of all. Nebamun's legs are shown in profile while his torso is shown frontally, and although his face is in profile, his eye looks straight at the viewer. This method of depicting figures is known as **twisted perspective**, also called **composite view**.

Art of Ancient Greece

"Man is the measure of all things."

(Protagoras, Greek philosopher)

The Greeks, like the civilizations that came before them, worshiped gods. But, as the quote from Protagoras indicates, they also valued humanity. Although their gods were portrayed as idealized and beautiful beings, they looked like humans and had some human weaknesses. The emphasis on the individual led the Greeks to practice democracy (the word means rule by the

demos, or people), although their society did not give equal rights to women or slaves. Their great advances in philosophy, mathematics, and the sciences continue to influence our thinking up to the present day.

Athleticism was important in Greek culture and the Greeks held sporting contests, the origins of the modern Olympic Games, at which individuals competed for glory and money. Sculptures of men were predominantly of the nude body, shown with ideal proportions. For the Greeks, the idealized human form represented high intellectual and moral goals. Indeed, Greek architecture was based on mathematical systems of proportion similar to those applied to the human form. Greek pride in their own physical and intellectual achievements is evident in the art they produced.

Every large city in Greece had its own government and was protected by its own god. Each had an acropolis, a complex of buildings on the highest point in the city that was both a fortress and a religious center, dedicated to the city's patron deity. The best-known acropolis is in Athens, and is dedicated to Athena, the goddess of war, wisdom, and the arts (**3.1.20**). According to Greek mythology, the city was won by the goddess in a competition with Poseidon, god of the sea. Legend says that the goddess grew an olive tree, giving Athenians a source of wealth and defeating Poseidon, who had created a spring by striking the earth with his trident.

The original temple complex to Athena on the acropolis was burned by the Persian army in 480/479 BCE, less than a decade after it was begun. A new temple was built on the site because, according to legend, a new olive tree grew from the ashes of the old temple. This new temple, the Parthenon, was both the main temple to Athena and a war treasury. After the Persian attack the Athenians formed an alliance with other Greek cities to protect one another from further attacks by the so-called "barbarians." The cities contributed funds to prepare for future wars; these were housed in the Parthenon.

The new Parthenon was so important that it was made of glistening white marble transported several miles to Athens, and then

3.1.20 Reconstruction view of the Acropolis, Athens, Greece, at the beginning of the 4th century BCE

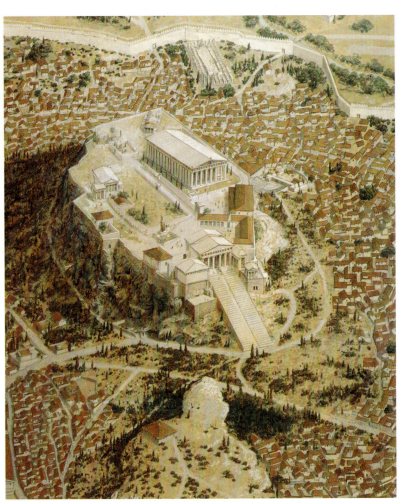

Classical Architectural Orders

The Greeks developed three types of designs, called **architectural orders**, for their temples. Elements of Greek temple design have been used in government buildings throughout the United States, particularly in state capitols and in Washington, D.C. See if you can recognize aspects of Greek architecture on the buildings near where you live. The Doric and Ionic orders were first used as early as the sixth century BCE.

The Parthenon is unusual in that it combines the two: its exterior columns and **frieze** are Doric, while the inner frieze (as viewed from the outside) is Ionic. The reason for this is debated, but it is likely that the blending of two styles popular in different parts of Greece marked a unity between different Greek cities. The Corinthian order was invented toward the end of the fifth century BCE. It was used for very few Greek buildings, but was widely applied by the Romans. The easiest way to recognize which order was used in a building is to look at the columns, and more specifically the **capitals**. Ionic and Corinthian columns both have a more decorative and slender quality than the bolder, more masculine Doric order. The Doric column has the least amount of ornamental detail. The Ionic column has the most noticeable fluting (vertical grooves) on the **shaft** and a volute (inverted scroll) on the capital. The Corinthian column is the most ornate, with layers of acanthus leaves decorating the capital. The **entablatures** of the three architectural orders are also quite distinct. The Doric frieze is divided by triglyphs (a kind of architectural decoration so named because it always has three grooves) that alternate with metopes (panels often containing relief sculpture). The Ionic and Corinthian friezes have relief sculpture along the entire frieze, and do not contain metopes or triglyphs.

3.1.21 Diagram of the Classical architectural orders, differentiating between the Doric, Ionic, and Corinthian. Key parts of Greek temple design, such as the pediment, entablature, frieze, capital, column, shaft, and base are also identified

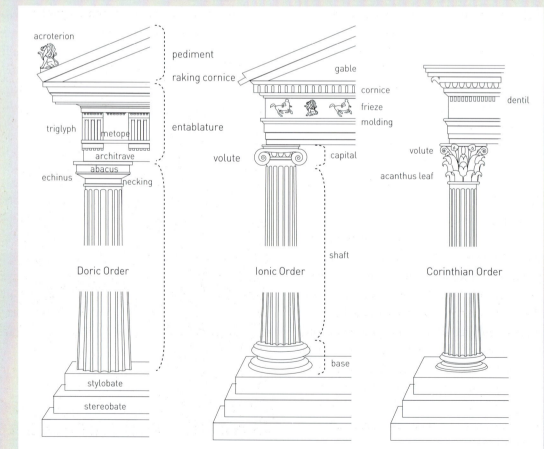

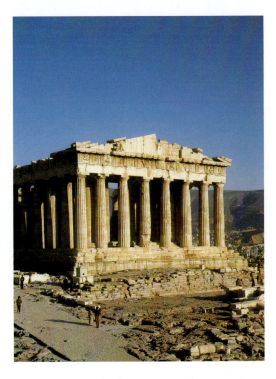

3.1.22 Iktinos and Kallikrates, Parthenon, 447–432 BCE, Acropolis, Athens, Greece

Placed in the metopes of the frieze in the Parthenon were sculptural reliefs of the battle in which the Lapiths, a legendary people in Greek mythology, tried to prevent the centaurs (creatures that are half man and half horse) from kidnapping the Lapith women (**3.1.23**). The scenes are intensely energetic, yet neither side seems to win. This subject was chosen as a metaphor for the Athenians (represented by the civilized Lapiths) who were always at war with the Persians (represented by barbaric centaurs). The sculptural scenes of gods that filled the **pediments**, and the reliefs in the metopes, were taken away between *c.* 1801 and 1805 by the British Ambassador Lord Elgin, who was given permission to do so by the Turks then in control of Athens. The Parthenon or Elgin Marbles reside today in the British Museum in London, although the Greeks have asked for their return.

The *Aphrodite of Knidos* by Praxiteles was the first Greek sculpture to show a completely nude woman; while the original no longer exists, dozens of Roman copies and adaptations still survive (**3.1.27**; and see also Box: Stylistic

carried up the steep slope to the acropolis. Its design was thought to epitomize ideal proportions, symbolizing for the Athenians their achievements as an enlightened society. Modern visitors to the Parthenon can see the basic architectural structure of the building, but can gain only a slight impression of its original appearance (**3.1.22**). Originally it had a timber roof covered with marble tiles, but this was destroyed in 1687, when Turkish army munitions stored there exploded. When it was first made, the structure was covered with sculptures. Both building and sculptures were painted in red, yellow, and blue. The bright paint has fallen off or faded over time, giving modern viewers the incorrect impression that Greek architecture and sculpture were intentionally made the natural color of marble. In several places there were statues of Athena to receive offerings and prayer. One enormous statue of the goddess, 38 ft. tall and made of gold and ivory, dominated the interior space. For many, the Parthenon is the iconic example of **Classical** architecture (see Box: Classical Architectural Orders, p. 380). The sculpture that covered the Parthenon was in a Classical style (see Box: Stylistic Changes in Sculpture of Ancient Greece, p. 382).

3.1.23 Metope of a Lapith and centaur in combat, from the south side of the Parthenon, designed by Pheidias, *c.* 445 BCE. Marble, 52⅝″ high. British Museum, London, England

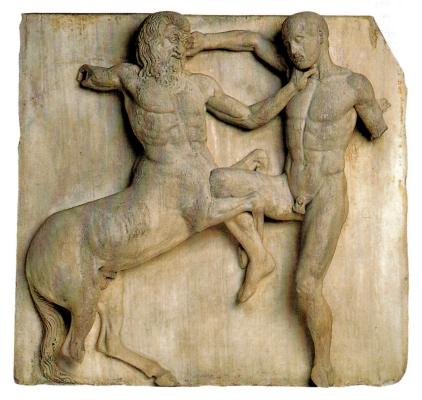

Stylistic Changes in the Sculpture of Ancient Greece

Greek sculptures are categorized generally in three types, referring to both the date of their making and to their style. **Archaic** works were produced from the late seventh to early fifth century BCE. Art from *c.* 480–323 BCE is labeled Classical. Later works are known as **Hellenistic**. A comparison of sculptures from these three periods demonstrates the main differences between them.

The name for one of the earliest Archaic types of Greek statues is *kouros*, or "male youth" (**3.1.24**). Compare this work with the Egyptian sculpture of Khafre (**3.1.15**, p. 375). The Greek sculptor subtly suggests movement by placing one foot in front of the other, whereas the seated statue of Khafre seems bound to the block of diorite from which it was carved. Unlike the distant stare of Khafre, which suggests he is in the spiritual world of the dead, the kouros has lively energy and seems to be part of the world of the living. He wears nothing more than an Archaic smile, which conveys innocence and serenity. Statues like this were grave markers and offerings at sanctuaries. Statues of young maidens were called *korai*; interestingly, these were all clothed, as were most Greek statues of females at the time. It was not until the end of the Classical period that women were portrayed in the nude (see **3.1.27**, p. 383).

Sculptors of the Classical period tried to give their work the idealized proportions of a perfect human form. The subjects of most Greek sculptors are heroes or gods. The *Doryphoros* (Spear Bearer) is a famous example of the work of Polykleitos; unfortunately, only a Roman copy of the original survives (**3.1.25**). Polykleitos developed a canon, or set of rules, for creating a harmoniously proportioned

human body using a set of mathematical ratios. Polykleitos also gave his statue a new stance, called contrapposto, which imitates the way humans balance their own weight. The *Doryphoros* portrays a man who stands naturally with his left knee bent and whose weight is shifted to his right hip. His raised

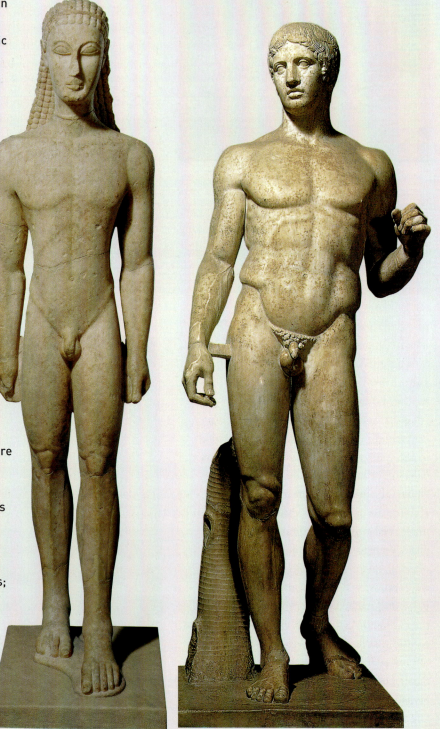

3.1.24 Statue of a *kouros* (youth), Naxian, *c.* 590–580 BCE. Marble, 6´4⅝" high. Metropolitan Museum of Art, New York

3.1.25 Roman version of the *Doryphoros* of Polykleitos, 120–50 BCE, after a bronze original of *c.* 460 BCE. Marble, 6´6" × 19" × 19". Minneapolis Institute of Arts, Minnesota

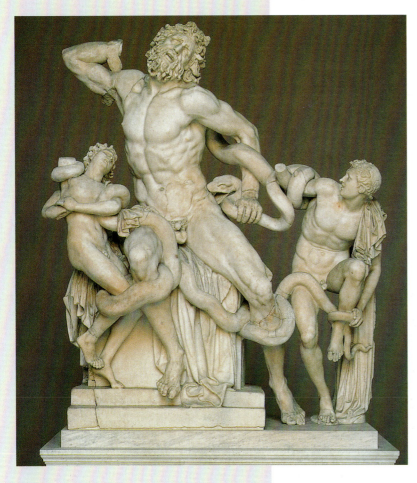

3.1.26 *Laocoön and His Sons*, copy of bronze original probably made at Pergamon *c.* 150 BCE. Marble, 6'½" high. Vatican Museums, Vatican City

left arm balances this shift in weight. Such poses made figures appear less stiff than the earlier kouros.

One of the most compelling Hellenistic sculptures is the *Laocoön*, in which the priest Laocoön and his sons are shown struggling in agony as they are attacked by twisting sea serpents, sent by the god Poseidon (**3.1.26**). Hellenistic sculpture shows the same idealized muscular bodies as earlier Greek sculptures. Hellenistic artists, however, chose subjects that involved creating figures in dramatic poses, challenging the artist to convey an even greater sense of movement and heightened emotion. **Renaissance** artists were often impressed by the balanced forms from the Classical period, but this dynamic Hellenistic sculpture, discovered in Rome in 1506, inspired such artists as Michelangelo and Bernini to imbue their art with similar drama and movement.

3.1.27 (right) Praxiteles, *Venus of Cnidus (Knidos)*, Roman copy, 2nd century CE, after a Greek original of the 4th century BCE. Marble, 6'8¼" high. Museo Pio-Clementino, Vatican City, Italy

Archaic: Greek art of the period *c.* 620–480 BCE
Hellenistic: Greek art of the period *c.* 323–100 BCE
Renaissance: a period of cultural and artistic change in Europe from the fourteenth to the seventeenth century
Contrapposto: a pose in sculpture in which the upper part of the body twists in one direction and the lower part in another
Three-dimensional: having height, width, and depth

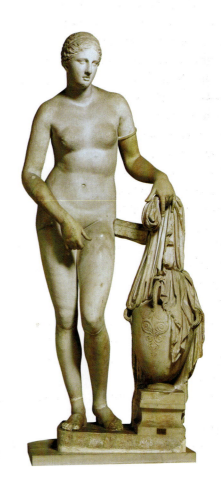

Changes in Sculpture of Ancient Greece). The goddess's **contrapposto** stance shows her in the act of getting ready to take a bath, having just removed her clothing, which is hanging on the water vase beside her. This type of sculpture, in which Venus (the Roman name for Aphrodite) is seen covering her genital area with her right hand, is called "*Venus Pudica*" or "modest Venus." The believable consistency of her flesh, and the curvature of her body, made this sculpture both shocking and erotic to viewers in ancient Greece.

Ancient accounts tell us that Greek paintings were remarkably convincing scenes with **three-dimensional** figures that seemed to come to life. Unfortunately, only incomplete fragments survive. Several Roman mosaics were made as copies of Greek paintings, however. We can also surmise the skill of Greek painters by looking at the scenes painted on pottery.

The vase in **3.1.28** (see p. 384) shows the Greek warriors Achilles and Ajax playing a game while waiting to battle with the Trojans. Through the layering of clothing, body parts, and even facial hair, the Athenian artist Exekias

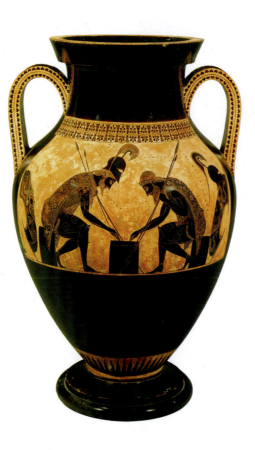

3.1.28 Exekias (potter and painter), black-figure amphora with Achilles and Ajax Playing Dice, Vulci, *c.* 530 BCE. 24" high, diameter at mouth 11". Vatican Museums, Vatican City, Italy

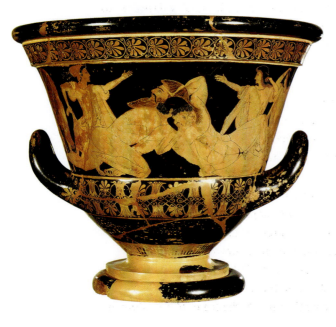

3.1.29 Euphronios (painter) and Euxitheos (potter), attic red-figure calyx-krater showing Heracles and Antaios in battle, *c.* 515–510 BCE. 17⅝" x 21⅝". Musée du Louvre, Paris, France

the vase, and a master painter. The two worked together closely, as the painting technique was intricately connected with the process of firing the pot. Exekias was particularly talented in that he was both a skilled painter and potter. There were two main types of Greek vase painting: black-figure and red-figure. To make a black-figure vase the painter used slip (watered-down clay) to paint the design on the pot; he then incised the details into the slip. A three-phase firing method then turned the slip-covered areas black, while the rest of the pot remained the original red color.

The red-figure technique was invented around 530 BCE, after the time of Exekias. It used the reverse process to black-figure: the slip was used to outline the figures and paint in the details. This can be seen on a *krater*, a type of vessel, showing Heracles and Antaios in Battle (**3.1.29**). The red-figure method had the advantage of making the figures appear slightly more three-dimensional, which is advantageous for showing these two muscular figures actively struggling. Very close attention is also paid to their facial expressions and hair. Depth and space are created by the two smaller female figures in the background, who frame the scene with comparative calmness as they raise their arms. Kraters are containers for mixing wine with water, into which cups can then be dipped to ladle out the diluted wine for drinking. As the Greeks developed a strong trade market through ports throughout the Mediterranean, a variety of Greek vases and pots have survived in great numbers outside of Greece, particularly in Etruscan tombs, where they were collected and buried with their owners.

Etruscan Art

During the sixth century BCE, the Etruscans were successful seafarers and traders who lived in central Italy, and formed the first urban civilization in the northern Mediterranean. Despite their prosperity, the Etruscans were eventually conquered by the Romans around 280 BCE. We understand much about Etruscan funerary customs because they built

was able to represent figures that seem to fill a real space. The shields perched behind the figures also help to create a sense of depth. The long body of the pot and its two handles identify this as an *amphora*, a type of pot that was used to carry and store such goods as wine or olive oil.

Greek pots were made in large workshops headed by both a master potter, who formed

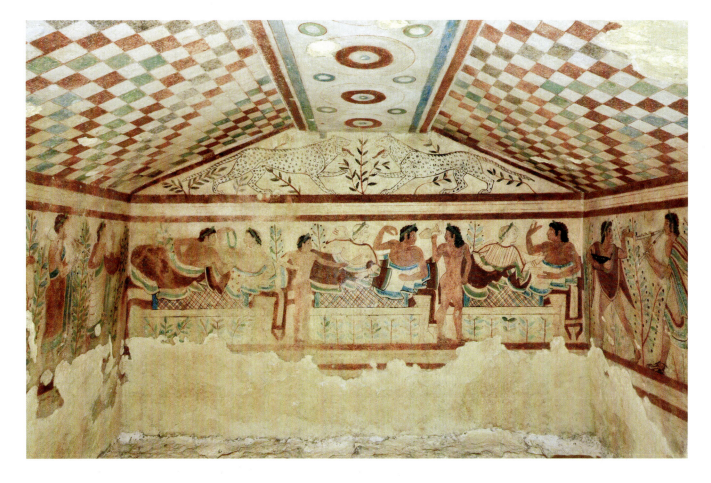

necropolises, or large cemeteries, containing hundreds of tomb chambers, which were filled with sculptures, or decorated with images of objects. The Etruscans were also very talented metalworkers; many intricate objects for personal use, such as gold jewelry and bronze mirrors, have also been found in the tombs in Italy, and must have been buried with the deceased. These indicate that, like the ancient Egyptians, the Etruscans believed that all of these things would be needed in the afterlife.

Large Etruscan tomb chambers, often containing the remains of generations of one family, were buried within mounds made of raised dirt and limestone. The tomb chambers were designed to mimic Etruscan houses, and portrayed settings in which celebrations could be held in the afterlife. The painting in the Tomb of the Leopards (**3.1.30**) shows a banquet in which men (portrayed as dark-skinned) and women (portrayed as light-skinned) are enjoying music, food, and drink. Etruscan women held a higher status within their own culture than other women were afforded in the ancient world. This

is reflected here by their placement as equals, lounging with their husbands.

Roman Art

The first evidence of a settlement at Rome dates back to about 900 BCE. This small village grew to become the center of an enormous empire that, by the year 117 CE, covered much of Europe, northern Africa, and large parts of the Middle East. In the process of conquering such large territories, the Romans absorbed many cultures, frequently adopting the gods of other peoples but giving them Latin names. The Roman emperors often associated themselves with qualities of the gods, and successful leaders were often deified after they died.

Another example of Roman absorption of other cultures was their adoption of the Corinthian architectural order developed by the Greeks (see p. 380). The Romans also used Greek methods to create ideal proportions in their architecture. At the center of each Roman

3.1.30 Tomb of the Leopards, c. 530–520 BCE. Monterozzi Necropolis, Tarquinia, Italy

Bust: statue of a person depicting only his or her head and shoulders
Facade: any side of a building, usually the front or entrance
Coffered: decorated with recessed paneling
Oculus: a round opening at the center of a dome

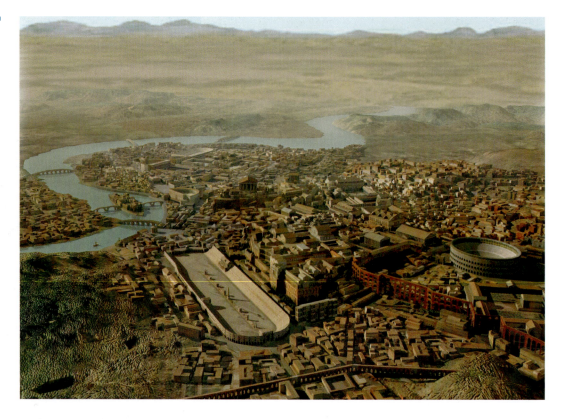

3.1.31 Reconstruction illustration of ancient Rome. In this image, the River Tiber can be seen flowing by the city. The enormous stadium, the Circus Maximus, and the great arena, the Colosseum, stand out as an oblong and circular shape respectively

3.1.32 A Roman citizen carrying death masks of his ancestors, c. 80 BCE. Marble, lifesize. Barberini Museum, Rome, Italy

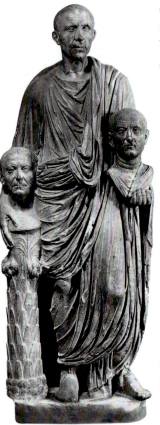

city was a forum, or marketplace, which was surrounded by temples, basilicas, and civic buildings (**3.1.31**). Emperors made a public show of their power by commissioning architects to create grand arches and tall columns, which usually celebrated the rulers' triumphs in battle. Statues of the current emperor were also distributed throughout the empire.

The Romans greatly admired Greek bronze sculptures and often remade them in marble. While the Greeks celebrated the idealized human body and mostly portrayed nude gods and mythological heroes, Roman art focused instead on emperors and civic leaders, who were usually portrayed clothed in togas or wearing armor. Roman sculpture often portrayed the individual character of its subject with recognizable, rather than ideal, facial features. Aged members of Roman society were portrayed—and viewed—as wise and experienced, particularly in political settings.

Roman artists recognized individuals' accomplishments with naturalistic, lifelike portraits often made from death masks. Family members treasured such portraits as recording their loved one's likeness and character. In **3.1.32**

a Roman citizen proudly displays the **busts** of his ancestors in order to reinforce his own social standing. His face shows individuality, and he wears clothing appropriate to his status.

The catastrophic eruption of Mount Vesuvius in 79 CE buried the buildings of the Roman cities of Pompeii and Herculaneum in a matter of hours under some 60 ft. of volcanic ash. This unique act of accidental preservation has given us, centuries later, an incomparable opportunity to witness how Romans lived in their homes. Frescoes covered the walls of many rooms in the houses in Pompeii. Some of the paintings offer convincing illusions of landscape scenes. Some of the interiors are covered with what appear to be marble panels, but which in reality are only painted. One such room is covered with scenes believed to describe rituals relating to the worship of Dionysus, the god of wine, ecstasy, agriculture, and the theatre (**3.1.33**). Excavation of Pompeii began in the eighteenth century, and the remarkable discoveries there stimulated interest in ancient art throughout Europe.

One of the Romans' most impressive works of architecture is the Pantheon ("Temple of all the Gods"). It was originally constructed in the

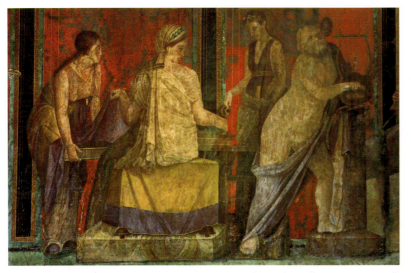

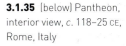

3.1.35 (below) Pantheon, interior view, c. 118–25 CE, Rome, Italy

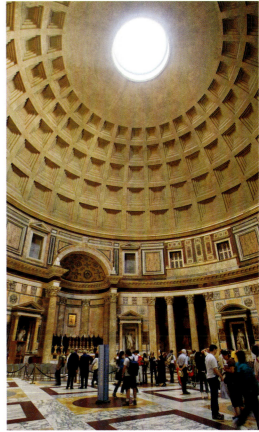

first century BCE. Emperor Hadrian had it rebuilt from c. 118 to 125 CE in order to enhance his own status. The entrance **facade** is a pediment atop Corinthian columns (**3.1.34**). Once inside, one is standing under a spectacular **coffered** dome 143 ft. in diameter and 143 ft. from the ground (**3.1.35**). The dome was made possible by the Romans' revolutionary use of concrete and their engineering genius. In the center of this dome is an **oculus**, or eye, open to the skies. One can tell the season and time of day by where

3.1.33 (above) Detail from Dionysiac mystery frieze in Room 5 of the Villa of the Mysteries, Pompeii, Italy, c. 60 BCE. Wall painting, 5'4" high

3.1.34 (bottom) Pantheon, entrance porch, c. 118–125 CE, Rome, Italy

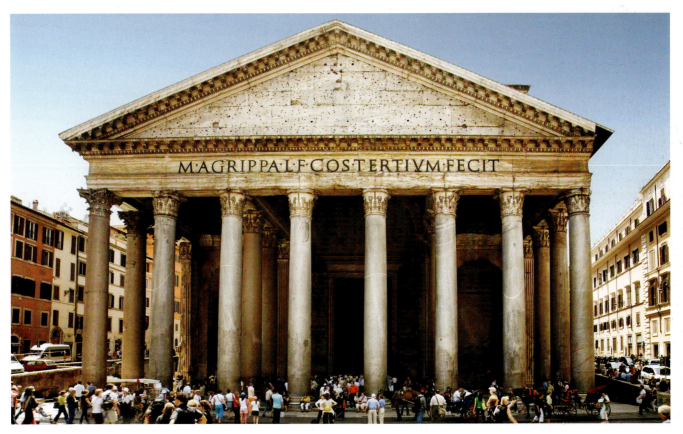

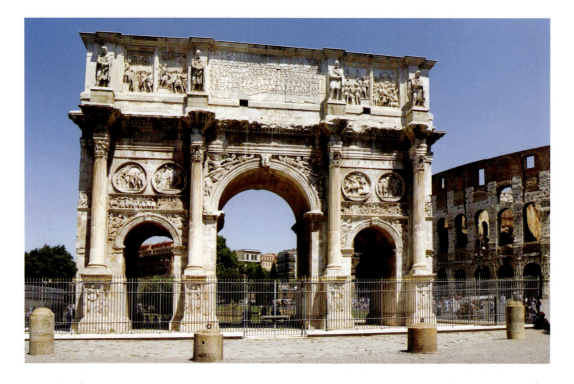

3.1.36 Arch of Constantine, south side, 312–15 CE, Rome, Italy

the sunlight hits the interior. Any rain coming in runs quickly away into a central drain because the entire floor slopes gradually.

The enormous Arch of Constantine (**3.1.36**) was built between 312 and 315 CE by the Emperor Constantine to commemorate the military victory (the Battle of the Milvian Bridge) that would ensure his future position as sole ruler of the empire. Constantine proclaimed his place in history, and therewith his greatness, by placing the arch close to the famed Colosseum, built by an earlier family of powerful emperors. Constantine also had sculpture removed from other imperial monuments, often erasing the faces of previous emperors from such statues and replacing them with his own likeness; he then had the sculptures placed upon the triumphal arch. By doing so, he proclaimed both his lineage to previous great emperors and his belief in his superiority over them. Constantine associated himself with Apollo and other pagan gods, as well as with Christianity. He became known as Constantine the Great, and would eventually make it legal to practice all religions, opening the doors for Christianity to grow into the primary religion of the empire. He was baptized as a Christian on his deathbed.

Discussion Questions

1. Compare the way females were portrayed in different periods of the prehistoric and ancient world. For example, consider the form and emphasis of prehistoric sculptures (*Woman of Willendorf*, p. 389, or *Venus of Laussel*), Cycladic female figures, or sculptures from Classical Greece (korai, or the *Aphrodite of Knidos* by Praxiteles).

2. Discuss the architecture of the ancient Greeks and Romans. What advancements did each culture make in building, and why are these works still considered such marvels today?

3. How did the natural environment of the people of the ancient Mediterranean affect the style, materials, and subject matter of their art?

Images Related to 3.1:
The Prehistoric and Ancient Mediterranean

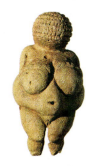

4.9.1 *Woman from Willendorf, c.* 24,000–22,000 BCE, p. 659

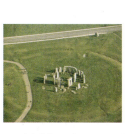

4.1.6 Stonehenge, England, *c.* 3200–1500 BCE, p. 566

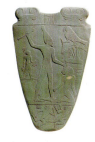

4.7.6b Palette of Narmer (back), Egypt, *c.* 2950–2775 BCE, p. 639

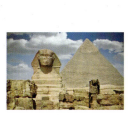

1.2.2 Great Sphinx of Giza, *c.* 2500 BCE, p. 68

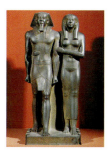

4.9.3b *Menkaure and Khamerernebty,* Egypt, *c.* 2520 BCE, p. 661

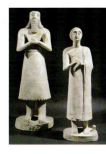

1.10.5 Sumerian Votive Figures, from the Temple of Abu. *c.* 2500 BCE, p. 185

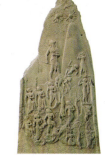

4.2.6 Stela of Naram-Sin, *c.* 2254–2218 BCE, p. 578

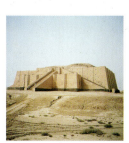

4.1.5 Ziggurat, Ur, *c.* 2100 BCE, p. 565

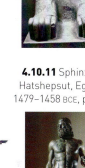

4.6.9 Stela of Hammurabi, *c.* 1792–1750 BCE, p. 631

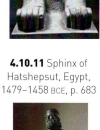

4.10.11 Sphinx of Hatshepsut, Egypt, 1479–1458 BCE, p. 683

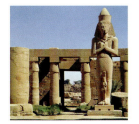

2.5.8 Temple of Amun Re, Egypt, 1417–1379 BCE, p. 270

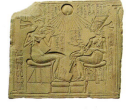

4.6.7 Akernaten, Nefertiti, and three daughters, relief sculpture, Egypt, *c.* 1353–1335 BCE, p. 630

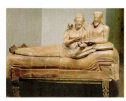

2.4.11 Sarcophagus from Cerveteri, *c.* 520 BCE, p. 254

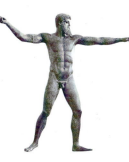

1.7.11a *Poseidon* (or *Zeus*), *c.* 460–450 BCE. p. 152

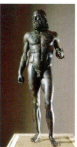

2.4.12 *Riace Warrior A, c.* 450 BCE, p. 254

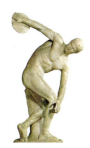

4.9.4 Myron, *Discus Thrower (Discobolos), c.* 450 BCE, p. 662

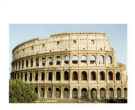

4.1.2 Colosseum, Rome, 72–80 BCE, p. 563

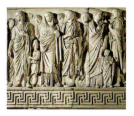

1.2.6 Imperial Procession from the Ara Pacis Augustae, 13 BCE, p. 71

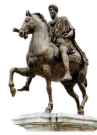

0.0.19 Equestrian statue of Marcus Aurelius, *c.* 175 CE, p. 42

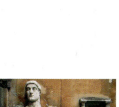

4.6.10 Remnants of colossal statue of Constantine the Great, 325–26 CE, p. 631

3.2

Art of the Middle Ages

The Roman empire dominated the Mediterranean region from the second century BCE, later extending its control of Western Europe and the Middle East, but by the fourth century CE the empire was crumbling in the west. In 330 the Roman Emperor Constantine I (272–337 CE) moved the center of the Roman empire from Rome to Byzantium, which he renamed

Constantinople (today's Istanbul, Turkey). The eastern part of the empire became known as the Byzantine empire and lasted a millennium, until Constantinople fell to the Turks in 1453. In the west, however, a series of invasions had ended the Roman empire by 476. The period that followed is known as the Middle Ages, or the medieval period, because it comes between the time of the

3.2.1 Map of Europe and the Middle East in the Middle Ages

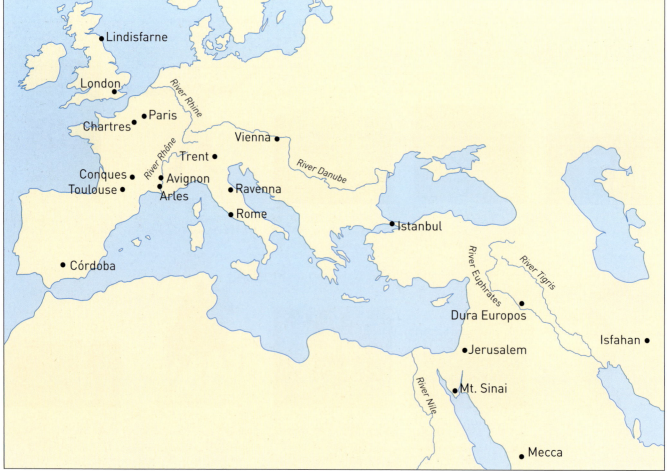

ancient civilizations of the Mediterranean region and the rebirth, or **Renaissance**, of Greek and Roman ideals in the fifteenth century.

In the study of the history of art, the Middle Ages is often broken down further because of the stylistic variations of its art, particularly its architecture. Beginning in the eleventh century, large stone churches, heavily ornamented with sculpture inside and out, were built throughout the Christian world. These churches were later given the name **Romanesque** for their similarity to the heavy round-arched style of the Romans. This comparison is not obvious, but the term Romanesque was meant as a contrast to the architectural style that followed it, from around 1150, in which great **Gothic** cathedrals, the spires of which reached toward the heavens, were built. Religious belief was integral to the lives of the people—whether Christian, Jew, or Muslim—who lived in Europe and the Middle East during the Middle Ages (see Box: Three Religions of the Middle Ages, p. 394). Much of the art from the period reflects their beliefs.

Art of Late Antiquity

Jewish culture thrived periodically during the Middle Ages, although this was also a time of persecution. Partially as a result of the constant displacement of many Jews, few examples of Jewish art from the Middle Ages survive. The oldest surviving Jewish artwork (other than coins) can be found in a synagogue in the ancient Roman city of Dura Europos, on the River Euphrates in modern Syria. Here, more than fifty stories are displayed in **fresco** paintings on the wall. The synagogue paintings were used to teach the stories upon which Jewish history and belief are based. The **didactic** nature of these images explains why figures are shown, a feature that is uncommon in later Jewish art. On the center of the west wall facing Jerusalem is a shrine containing the Torah, the most important part of the Jewish Bible, which contains the commandments given to Moses by God (**3.2.2**).

3.2.2 Interior west wall of synagogue at Dura Europos, Syria, 244–45 CE. Reconstruction in National Museum, Damascus, Syria

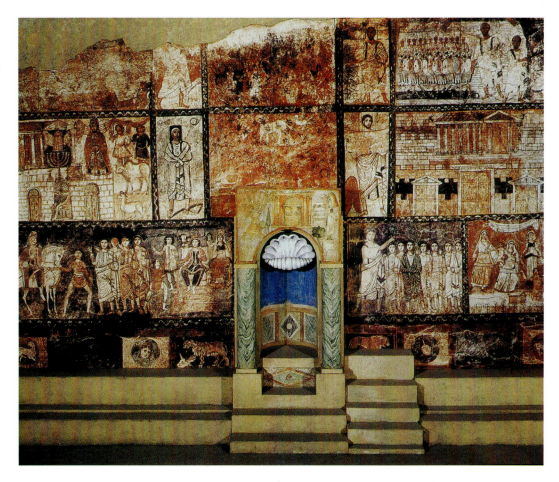

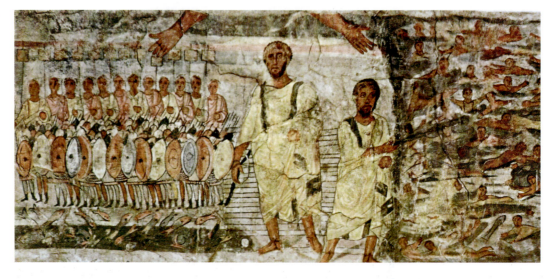

3.2.3 *Exodus and Crossing of the Red Sea*, panel from west wall of synagogue at Dura Europos, Syria, 244–45 CE. Reconstruction in National Museum, Damascus, Syria

The fresco painting of the scene in **3.2.3** does show God, but not his face; only his hands are seen, reaching down from the sky. In the passage from the Book of Exodus in the Torah, God tells Moses to guide the Israelites out of Egypt toward Mount Sinai, where Moses will receive the Ten Commandments. When they arrive at the Red Sea, God tells Moses to place his rod in the water. This action parts the sea, creating a safe crossing for Moses and his people. When they are safely on the other side, Moses again places his rod in the water. The Red Sea floods, drowning the Egyptian soldiers who have been chasing the Israelites. The Exodus painting is a **continuous narrative**, in which different points in time in the story are shown within the same scene. Moses is shown in the center, while the soldiers on the left are lined up to follow him. A second Moses is shown slightly in front and to the side of the first. Behind the second Moses on the right side of the scene, the soldiers have been washed away as the sea has flooded.

3.2.4 Painted ceiling, late 3rd–early 4th century CE. Catacombs of Saints Peter and Marcellinus, Rome, Italy

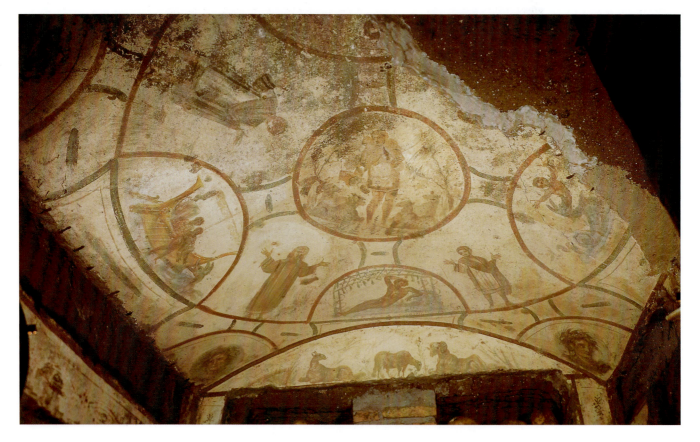

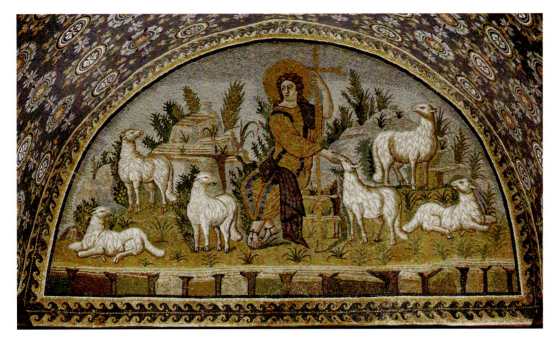

3.2.5 *Good Shepherd*, 425–26. Mosaic in lunette. Mausoleum of Galla Placidia, Ravenna, Italy

The Christian Church, which had been unified under Roman rule, split in 1054. The result was a Greek Orthodox Church in the east and a Roman Catholic Church in the west, each ruled by separate leaders and following different doctrines and practices. The earliest examples of Christian art date from the early third century. From 200 CE to the sixth century, it was common practice amongst Christians, Jews, and others in Italy to bury the dead in underground cemeteries known as catacombs. The catacombs may also have served as sites for Christian worship. Scenes were often painted on burial-room walls and ceilings. One such scene in a catacomb in Rome shows Jesus as the Good Shepherd in the center and tells the Old Testament story of Jonah in the semicircular areas around the central image (**3.2.4**). Christians believe that the story of Jonah, who was swallowed by a whale and then spat out alive three days later, foreshadows the death and resurrection of Jesus.

In their depiction of Christian themes, early Christian artists often used motifs and figures adapted from pagan cultures. Under the Roman empire, religious **syncretism**—the blending of multiple religious or philosophical beliefs— was common; as Christianity spread, rituals, symbols, and even objects were assimilated from the pagans. For example, statues of the Egyptian goddess Isis, mother to the god Horus, were altered and used as models for images of the Virgin Mary. The Good Shepherd in **3.2.4** was adapted from images of several pagan figures, including the Greek hero Orpheus (who could charm animals with his songs) and the Greek god Apollo (god of music, the sun, and healing, who was always shown as a beardless youth).

A century later, the depiction of Christ changed. Christian artists developed a range of symbols that were more varied and elaborate. The **mosaic** in **3.2.5** was made for the building known as the Mausoleum of Galla Placidia, which was the family tomb of the Roman Emperor Flavius Honorius. We can see that Christ is still portrayed as a Good Shepherd, here flanked by three lambs on each side, but he is seated and more mature. Compared to the image on the catacomb ceiling, Christ's appearance is regal. He wears a fine gold robe with a purple (the traditional color for royalty) cloth draped over his shoulder; he holds a golden cross. His hair is long, and a prominent gold halo shines behind him; the **tesserae**, small pieces of glass that make up the mosaic, create a beautiful glow that glitters and reflects light. Unlike figures in Roman art, Christ's body is sharply delineated and flat-looking rather than fully **three-dimensional**. These stylistic qualities foreshadow the art of Byzantium, the Christian empire that continued in the east after the fall of the western Roman empire.

Continuous narrative: when different parts of a story are shown within the same visual space
Syncretism: the blending of multiple religious or philosophical beliefs
Mosaic: a picture or pattern created by fixing together small pieces of stone, glass, tile, etc.
Tesserae: small pieces of stone or glass or other materials used to make a mosaic
Three-dimensional: having height, width, and depth

Three Religions of the Middle Ages

> You shall not make for yourself an idol, whether in the form of anything that is in heaven above, or that is on the Earth beneath, or that is in the water under the Earth. You shall not bow down to them or worship them.
>
> (Second Commandment, Exodus 20:4–5)

Judaism, Islam, and Christianity all have their origins in the Middle East. They have some similar beliefs—each religion considers Abraham to be a prophet, for example, and each considers their God to be the one true God. Importantly for the study of art, each also warns against the worship of false idols. Understanding some basic beliefs of followers of these faiths can help us to understand better some of the art produced during the Middle Ages.

- Judaism began with a contract between Abraham and God (Yahweh) in *c.* 2000 BCE. Abraham promised to exalt Yahweh as the one true God, and in exchange Yahweh promised Abraham many descendants, who are the Jewish people of today. The Torah (or "Teaching") was written by Moses under divine inspiration and is the core of Jewish belief and law. Jewish art does not show any more than the hands of Yahweh, and rarely shows human figures. Instead, it usually depicts objects used in acts of worship—scroll holders, candelabra, and the like.

- Christians worship Jesus Christ (a Jew who lived from *c.* 7–2 BCE to *c.* 30–36 CE), who they believe was the son of God. The Bible contains both the writings of the Jewish Bible ("The Old Testament") and what Christians see as their fulfillment in the life of Jesus ("The New Testament"). For Christians, Jesus was a great teacher who demonstrated how to lead a good and pious life, but who also suffered, was sacrificed and then rose again to show that the sins of humanity could be forgiven and that for those who were true believers, eternal life could be achieved after death. Christians have interpreted the Second Commandment in different ways, at times causing great conflict and even the destruction of images (see Box: Iconoclasm, p. 396).

- Muslims (followers of Islam) call their one true God Allah. They believe that Jesus was a prophet but that Muhammad (*c.* 570–632 CE) was the primary messenger of Allah. The Koran is the word of Allah given to Muhammad and is Islam's primary sacred text. Islamic art never depicts the figure of God. Also, human figures are not shown within the holy space of a mosque. The majority of Islamic art is decorative and often makes beautiful use of **calligraphy** to show the word of Allah.

Byzantine Art

The Byzantine Emperor Justinian I (483–565) was a devoted **patron** of the arts. He funded hundreds of churches, mosaics, and paintings throughout his empire, including Hagia Sophia in the center of Constantinople. One of Justinian's greatest achievements was his protection of more than 2,000 icons at the monastery of St. Catherine, Mount Sinai,

in Egypt (see Box: Iconoclasm, p. 396). **Icons**, paintings of religious figures on wooden panels, are still used in the Eastern Orthodox Church for meditation and prayer. Many early Christians believed icons had special healing powers; therefore, icons that survive are often faded from being kissed and touched by numerous worshipers.

The sixth-century icon of Christ (**3.2.6**) from the St. Catherine Monastery is intended

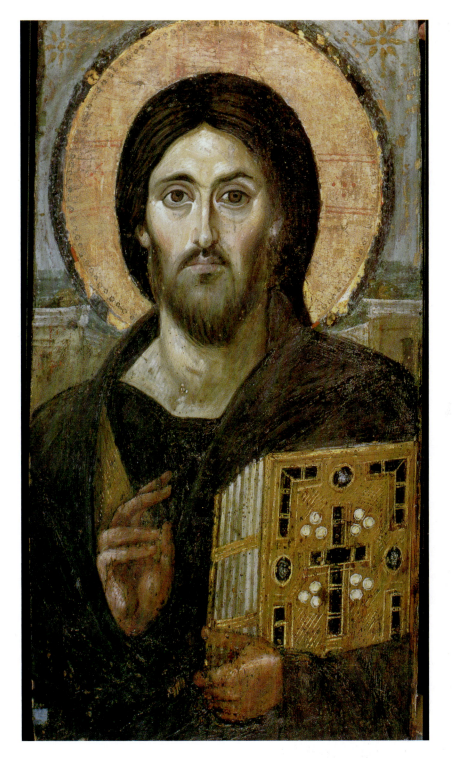

3.2.6 Christ icon, 6th century. Encaustic, 33 × 18". St. Catherine Monastery, Mount Sinai, Egypt

to show the dual nature of Christ as both human and God. As in the Good Shepherd mosaic (**3.2.5**), here Christ is shown as a regal figure, wearing a rich purple robe. He is now represented with a beard and long hair, which became the convention in subsequent Christian art. Christ's duality is brilliantly portrayed here by the differences made to each side of his face; his right side (the viewer's left) represents his heavenly half, and his left side his human half. The right side of Christ's face is ideally proportioned, with a healthy glow, and his hair is in place. By comparison, his left side seems to sag slightly, his eyes and mouth have wrinkles, and his hair is somewhat disheveled. His right hand forms into a gesture of holy blessing, while his left hand holds scripture, sacred writings read by those on Earth.

Iconoclasm: Destruction of Religious Images

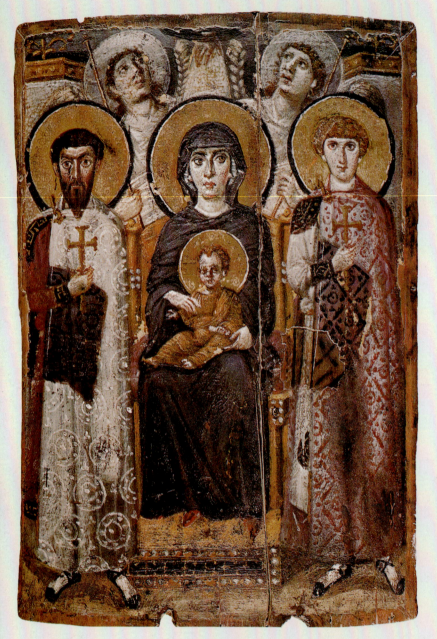

3.2.7 *Virgin and Child Surrounded by Saints*, 6th century. Encaustic, 27 × 19⅝". Monastery of St. Catherine, Sinai, Egypt

Iconoclast: someone who destroys images, often out of religious belief

Icons, or religious images, are designed to create a state of meditation, in which the artworks are studied for long periods, inspiring worship. Iconoclasm, or the destruction of religious images, shows the power art can have, and the fear its power can generate.

The Byzantine empire's iconoclastic controversy in the eighth and ninth centuries was provoked by divisions amongst Christians over the interpretation of the Bible's Second Commandment: "You shall not make for yourself an idol, whether in the form of anything in heaven above, or that is on the Earth beneath, or that is in the water under the Earth. You shall not bow down to them or worship them." Some Christians took this commandment to mean that icons, which might inspire too much worship, should be prohibited.

A study of the icon *Virgin and Child Surrounded by Saints* (**3.2.7**) can help us understand why the **iconoclasts** were so concerned that Christians might confuse worship of an image with worship of the holy figures themselves. In the icon, Mary initially attracts our attention because she sits in the center, wearing a dark purple gown (the imperial color), and presents Christ, who sits on her lap. The bearded St. Theodore and the beardless St. George stand slightly in front of the Virgin's throne. The saints are closest to us because they are human and therefore most like us. A hierarchy is thus created as we "enter" the picture through them and become closer to Mary, who is herself an intercessor for Christ. The two figures behind the enthroned Mary are angels looking up at heaven. Their gaze reminds Christian believers that the figures in the icon will bring them closer to the heavens above.

Iconoclasts believed that the faithful were worshiping icons of religious figures rather than worshiping Mary and Jesus directly. This fundamental disagreement led to the destruction of thousands of Byzantine icons, including almost all portrayals of Christ and Mary. Most of the surviving icons from before the ninth century are in St. Catherine's Monastery at the foot of Mount Sinai, where they were protected by their location in the Egyptian desert.

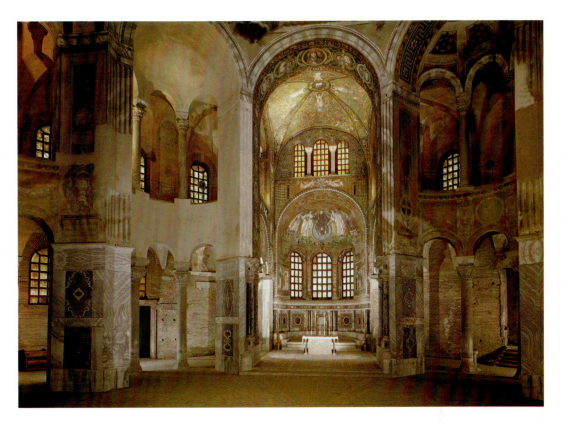

3.2.8 Church of San Vitale, *c.* 547 CE, Ravenna, Italy

One of the most beautiful Byzantine churches was built in Ravenna, Italy, in the sixth century (**3.2.8**). **"Central-plan" churches** were a common style in the Eastern Orthodox tradition, as opposed to the Latin cross design of the West (see **3.2.21** on page 405). The floor plan of the Church of San Vitale is based on two octagons, one inside the other. The smaller octagon, the **nave**, is a space nearly 100 ft. high, filled with windows, and covered by a dome. Natural light glistens off the glass mosaics that cover the walls. Eight semicircular bays emanate from the center, with the **apse** that contains the **altar** on the southeast side; above the altar is a mosaic of Christ enthroned on Earth. Flanking either side of the apse are glorious mosaics of the Emperor Justinian and the Empress Theodora. The mosaic of Theodora and her attendants is filled with rich details, such as the Three Magi on the hem of the empress's stunning purple robe (**3.2.9**). It is characteristic of Byzantine art that figures and their clothing are often boldly **outlined**. Such delineation creates a flatness to the figures and decreases their three-dimensionality. This lack of volume or mass, along with the way the figures seem to float, gives

3.2.9 *Theodora and Attendants, c.* 547. Mosaic on south wall of apse, 8'8" × 12'. Church of San Vitale, Ravenna, Italy

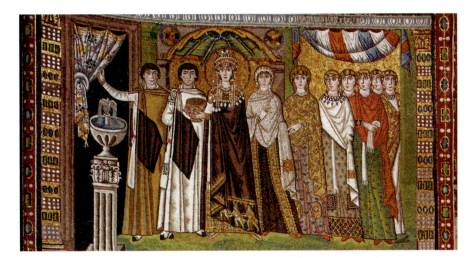

a timeless, spiritual quality to the image, as if it belongs somewhere between the heavenly and Earthly realms. It is important to remember that this mosaic is placed in a very sacred part of the church. The empress carries a jeweled chalice of wine that she raises up in the direction of the actual altar, which is located directly to the left of the mosaic. The figures in the image are even layered so that their repetition creates a sense of movement toward the altar. On the opposite wall is a mosaic of the Emperor Justinian holding bread (see Images Related to 3.2, p. 411); the bread and wine are symbols of the important religious ceremony of the **Eucharist**, which took place in this church.

It is also significant that Theodora is depicted outdoors, shown by the green grass, canopies, and fountain. The artist was clarifying that Theodora and her ladies were not in as sacred a realm as the emperor and his men in the opposite mosaic, who are surrounded by a solid gold **background**. Creating such different backgrounds was a way for the artist to show that women were allowed only in the courtyard of the church or on the second-story balcony surrounding the nave. In reality, the Empress Theodora would not have been allowed near the altar (where this mosaic was placed), not just because she was a woman, but also because she was from the lower classes, having been an actress and a prostitute when she met Justinian.

Manuscripts and the Middle Ages

Manuscripts (books written and decorated by hand) are some of the richest and most detailed artworks made by Muslims and Christians in the Middle Ages. The production of manuscripts was intensely laborious, from making the pages out of animal hides to copying painstakingly in careful handwriting. Manuscripts were the work of many artists (usually monks and sometimes nuns), some specializing in decorative lettering (scribes), and others in painting images (illuminators). Jewelers and workers in fine metals often contributed to decorating the

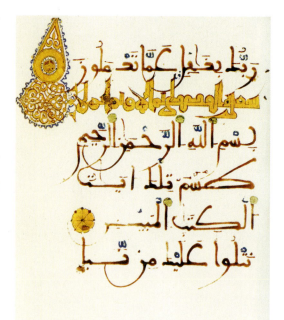

3.2.10 Page from the Koran, probably late 13th century, *Maghribi* on vellum, 7½ × 7½". British Library, London, England

covers. The great effort required to create a manuscript was considered a tribute to God.

Islamic manuscripts rarely show human figures, and never the image of Allah (God). Rather, attention is paid to the word of Allah, recorded in the Koran, and revealed in elegant script. Islamic artworks often have an **arabesque** quality, and this is particularly apparent in manuscripts.

Surah (chapters) from the Koran are written in Arabic, from right to left, but the script varies from region to region. In a beautiful page of the Koran from thirteenth-century Spain (**3.2.10**), the oldest Arabic script, *kufic*, is used for the headings, while the script *maghribi* is used for the rest of the text. This regional script derived its name from its popularity in the region of Maghreb, which in the Middle Ages included northern Africa and Islamic areas of Spain. The areas in the manuscript where the text is thicker and in gold signify the heading for a new chapter. The ornamental circular designs in gold break the reading into appropriate sections.

The Lindisfarne Gospels are an illuminated manuscript book of the Christian gospels of Matthew, Mark, Luke, and John (known as the Four Evangelists). They were made during the early eighth century. Each gospel is decorated with a "cross-and-carpet" page (named for its similarity to a carpet design). The design in the cross-and-carpet page at the beginning of

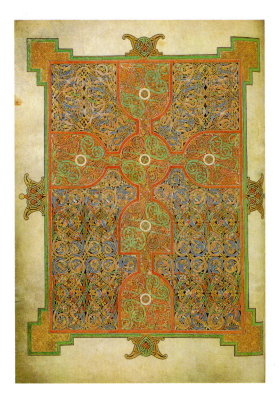

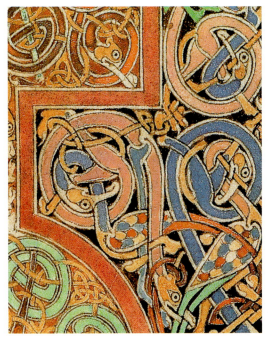

3.2.11a Cross-and-carpet page introducing the Gospel according to St. Matthew. Lindisfarne Gospels, fol. 26b, 710–721. Illuminated manuscript, British Library, London, England

3.2.11b Detail of **3.2.11a**

St. Matthew's gospel appears to be made up of numerous intertwining lines (**3.2.11a**). Upon closer inspection, however, tiny animal heads can be seen twisting throughout (**3.2.11b**). While the specific meaning of these animals is unclear, this decorative element was common in the Middle Ages, particularly in northeast England, where the Lindisfarne Gospels were made.

The Lindisfarne Gospels were scribed fully or in part by a bishop named Eadfrith, who signed his name to the manuscript. The pages, written in Latin, would have taken him at least five years to complete. Such beautiful pages as these are often called **illuminations** because their rich colors recall light shining through **stained glass** in a cathedral. (Similarly, because of their didactic nature, stained-glass windows have been called "books in glass," and the sculpture around cathedrals "books in stone.") Both the Lindisfarne Gospels and the Spanish Koran were made to be studied and enjoyed over long periods of contemplation.

Manuscripts often illustrated religious stories or the visions of spiritual leaders. Hildegard of Bingen was a Christian mystic and visionary; she advised kings and popes, who often traveled long distances to meet with her. Born into an aristocratic family and educated as a nun,

she eventually became abbess of a convent in Germany. Her visions included insights into medicine, astronomy, and politics, which she shared in a book called *Scivias* (*Know the Ways*), which was read throughout Europe. The original manuscript was destroyed during World War II; however, from copies of *Scivias* we know that Hildegard was repeatedly portrayed in the act of receiving a vision. Her assistant is also usually shown transcribing her vision (**3.2.12**). This misleadingly suggests that the scribe wrote on the pages after they were bound. In reality, the

3.2.12 *The Fifth Vision of Hildegard of Bingen*, frontispiece for *Scivias*, c. 1230, original manuscript lost. Biblioteca Governativa, Lucca, Italy

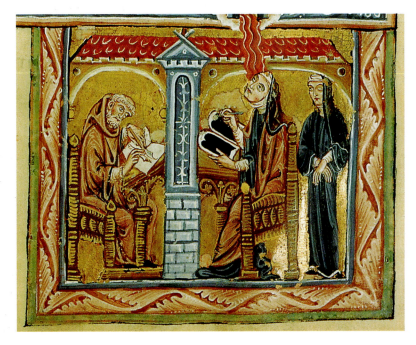

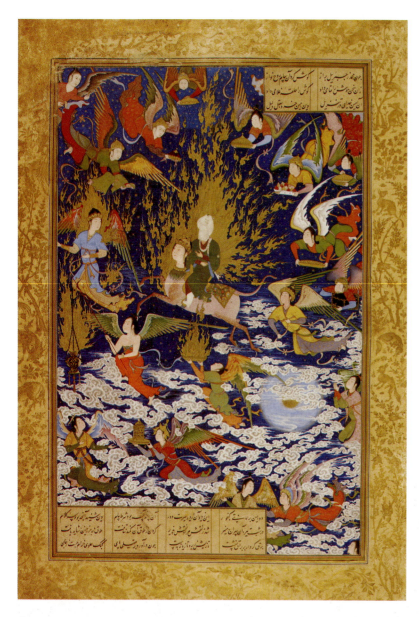

his holiness, as he rides his half-human horse Buraq toward the heavens. On the left, guiding Muhammad, is the angel Gabriel (Jibra'il), whose head is also surrounded by flames. Manuscripts in the Middle Ages are richly detailed objects that reflect the piety of the time.

Pilgrimage in the Middle Ages

Pilgrimages were integral to the practice of Christianity, Islam, and Judaism. In medieval Europe, devout Christian pilgrims journeyed to holy sites where significant religious events had occurred or where relics were kept. Relics were holy objects (such as a piece of the wooden cross on which Christ was crucified), or body parts of saints or holy figures. Elaborately decorated containers called reliquaries were made to house individual relics, and they were designed to look like the relic they contained. Thus, such a reliquary as that of the Head of St. Alexander

3.2.14 (below) Reliquary of the Head of St. Alexander, 1145. Silver repoussé, gilt bronze, gems, pearls, and enamel, 7½" high. Musées Royaux d'Art et d'Histoire, Brussels, Belgium

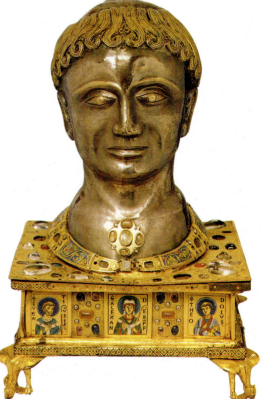

3.2.13 (above) *The Ascent of the Prophet Muhammad on His Steed, Buraq, Guided by Jibra'il and Escorted by Angels*, 1539–43. Miniature painting from a manuscript of Nizami's *Khamsa (Five Poems)*, originally produced in Tabriz, Iran

Repoussé: a technique of hammering metal from the back to create a form or surface detail

manuscript took months to make: it was carefully graphed out on pieces of paper before being put together as a book. Hildegard described the experience of receiving visions as "a fiery light, flashing intensely, which came from the open vault of heaven and poured through my whole brain," an apt description for what is taking place in the manuscript shown here.

Islamic manuscripts often depict events from the life of Muhammad, the main prophet of Allah. The manuscript painting in **3.2.13** shows the ascension of Muhammad, which Muslims believe took place at the Dome of the Rock in Jerusalem (see **3.2.15**). Muhammad's face is not shown, but is covered with a veil. He is surrounded by blinding flames, which signify

(**3.2.14**) houses a skull. This reliquary was made in 1145 for the Abbot Wibald of Stavelot in Belgium. The face is made of beaten silver (**repoussé**), with the hair made from gilded bronze. The emphasis on the portrait itself recalls the Roman heads of antiquity. The head is placed upon a base covered with gems and pearls. Small plaques painted in enamel show a portrait of the sainted Pope Alexander in the center, flanked by two other saints.

Jerusalem

Throughout the Middle Ages, devout people made pilgrimages to the city of Jerusalem; a shining gold dome still marks a site in the city that is sacred to Jews, Christians, and Muslims alike (**3.2.15**). The Dome of the Rock surrounds the sacred Foundation Stone, which Jews believe is the site of the beginning of the world, and Muslims believe is the rock from which Muhammad ascended to heaven. To Jews and Christians, this site is also thought to be the place where Adam was created and where Abraham was asked to sacrifice his son.

The Dome of the Rock was built as a site for pilgrims (not as a mosque) between 688 and 691 under the order of Abd al-Malik, who wanted it to surpass all Christian churches in the Middle East. Although al-Malik was a caliph (an Islamic ruler), the Dome of the Rock was probably built by Christian laborers; its proportions, octagonal shape, dome, and mosaic designs show a clear Byzantine style.

The glorious dome that crowns the shrine was originally solid gold, but was rebuilt in the twentieth century with aluminum. In 1993, King Hussein of Jordan spent more than $8 million of his own money to gild the aluminum with gold. The height and diameter of the dome are approximately 67 ft. each, as is the length of each of the eight walls. The walls of the octagon are covered with verses in Arabic calligraphy from the Koran. Since 2006, although all religions are permitted on the Temple Mount, only Muslims have been allowed within the domed shrine.

3.2.15 Dome of the Rock, 688–91, Jerusalem, Israel

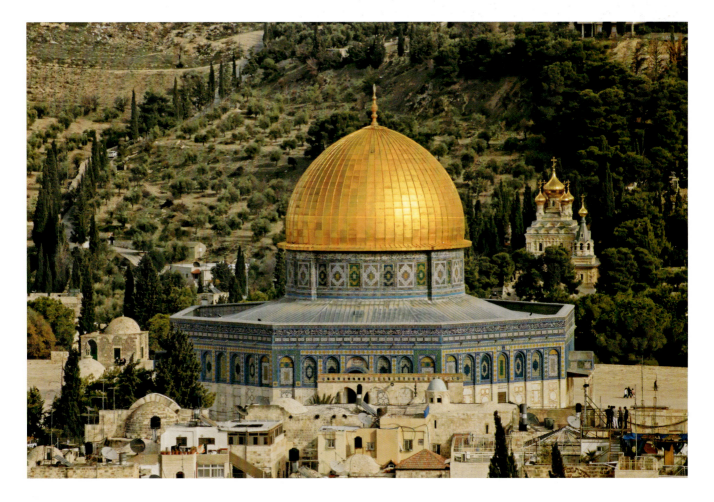

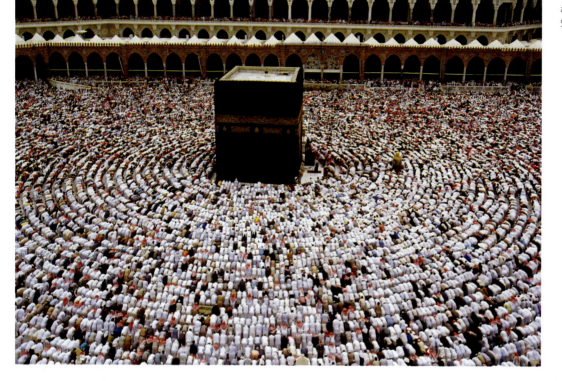

3.2.16 Kaaba, Al Masjid al-Haram, Mecca, Saudi Arabia

Mecca and Mosques

Mecca, Saudi Arabia, is the most important pilgrimage site for Muslims. The prophet Muhammad was born in Mecca around 570. Mecca is also the site of the Kaaba, a large cube-shaped building (today draped in black-and-gold cloth), built by Abraham for God (**3.2.16**), which is surrounded by a large mosque. Like Christian churches, mosques are designed

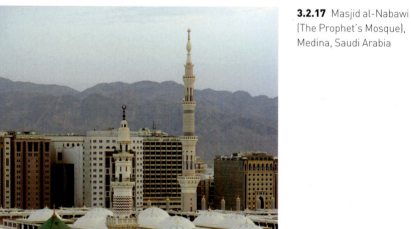

3.2.17 Masjid al-Nabawi (The Prophet's Mosque), Medina, Saudi Arabia

Minaret: a tall slender tower, particularly on a mosque, from which the faithful are called to prayer
Mihrab: a niche in a mosque that is in a wall oriented toward Mecca
Qibla: the direction to Mecca, toward which Muslims face when praying

to reflect religious belief and practice. In the center of each mosque complex is usually a large courtyard with a pool where the faithful can cleanse themselves before entering the mosque itself to pray. Muslims must pray five times a day in the direction of Mecca. They are called to prayer from the mosque's large towers (**minarets**) that rise above the city: nine distinctive minarets surround the mosque in Mecca. One of the five important commitments of the Muslim faith (known as the Five Pillars of Islam) is the obligation to visit Mecca once in one's lifetime, unless sickness or some other factor makes this impossible, to honor the house of Allah. Although pilgrimage is important to many Christians, it has never been an obligation as it is in Islam.

Unlike Christians, Muslims do not worship relics of holy figures and saints since for Muslims there is only one God, called Allah, and the Prophet Muhammad specifically forbade the worship of idols. Nevertheless, one holy place in addition to Mecca, Medina, is a destination for Muslim pilgrims because it is the location of the tomb of Muhammad himself. Many pilgrims do visit the mosque (**3.2.17**), often before or after a visit to Mecca, in order to "greet" the Prophet, but limit themselves to a greeting as Islam prohibits worship of any other than Allah.

The original mosque on the site was built by Muhammad himself and was his house as well as a place of worship. The building measured 100 cubits (about 183 ft.) on all sides, and was built of mud-brick, with palm trunks to support a flat roof over the northern part of the building, where worshipers prayed toward Jerusalem. In 624, however, Allah revealed to Muhammad that the direction of prayer (known as the *qibla*) should be redirected to the south, toward Mecca. In the eighth century a curved prayer niche, called a *mihrab*, was built into the southern wall. All mosques include a mihrab within them, placed on the wall facing Mecca (known as the qibla wall). This enables Muslims to pray toward Mecca from any mosque in which they may happen to be.

Subsequent rulers have greatly enlarged the mosque, making it one hundred times bigger than the original. They have added a courtyard, school, resting places for pilgrims, ten minarets and twenty-four domes. The slightly taller green dome marks the spot of Muhammad's tomb (**3.2.17**). Within the mosque, the most sacred spot is the Riad-ul Jannah. Placed between the prophet's **minbar** (pulpit) and his tomb, it is believed to be a piece of the Garden of Paradise.

A two-dimensional diagram, including labels (**3.2.18**), shows the sanctuary at Medina. Both the sanctuary and Mecca were quite often depicted in this way. This image shows the tomb chamber of the Prophet (identifiable by its green dome) in the upper left-hand corner. A textile covering patterned in green and white chevrons is visible on the grille and tomb within the chamber. At the center of the image is the garden that Fatima, the daughter of the Prophet, planted

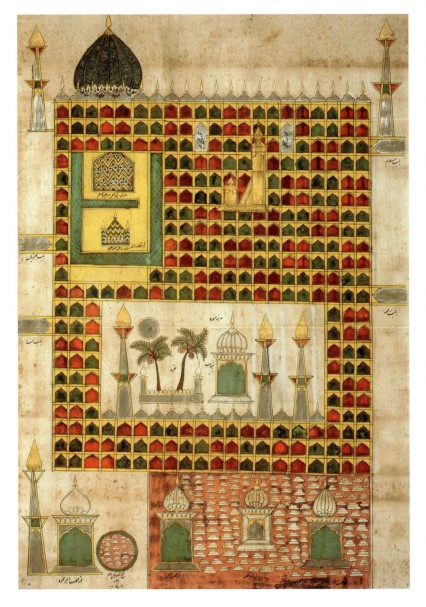

3.2.18 *View of the sanctuary at Medina*, 17th or 18th century. Opaque watercolor, gold, silver, and ink on paper, 25½ × 18¼". Nasser D. Khalili Collection of Islamic Art

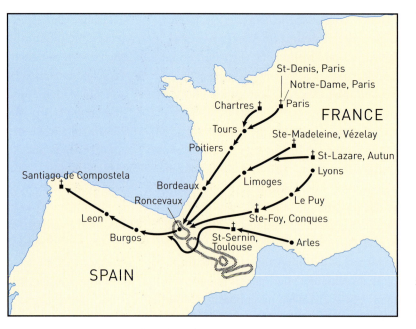

3.2.19 Pilgrimage map showing the routes from France toward Santiago de Compostela, with important churches including Sainte-Foy at Conques

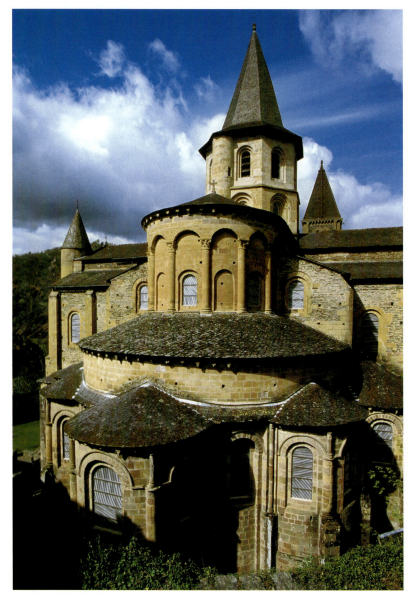

3.2.20 (below) Church of Sainte-Foy, Conques, France

with two palm trees; her tomb is also shown there, while others—belonging to some of the Prophet's companions—can be seen outside the walls of the sanctuary. To the right of the diagram, standing in the **arcades**, we can see the Prophet's minbar, from which he preached.

Romanesque Art and Christian Pilgrimages

One of the most traveled pilgrimage journeys in the Middle Ages was to the burial site of St. James at the Cathedral of Santiago de Compostela in Galicia, Spain. The official paths to the cathedral (The Way of St. James) started at four important sites in France (**3.2.19**), each of which held a religious relic. During the journey, which could take several months, pilgrims would stop at other important sites for rest, food, and spiritual nourishment. Along the way large churches were built, even in small towns that could not otherwise have funded such expansive construction, in order to accommodate the crowds of pilgrims.

One such small town was Conques in France. Conques was a stop along one of the French routes to Santiago de Compostela, but was also a pilgrimage destination in its own right. In the ninth century, a monk from Conques stole the relics of Sainte Foy (Saint Faith) from their original resting place in the much larger town of

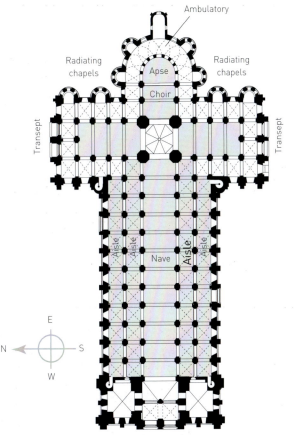

Ambulatory

Radiating chapels

Radiating chapels

Apse

Choir

Transept

Transept

Aisle

Aisle

Nave

Aisle

Aisle

E

N ← → S

W

West portal

Agen. According to legend, Sainte Foy was a young woman who lived in Agen in the third century. She was tortured to death with a red-hot brazier during the persecution of Christians in about 290 or 303. A number of miracles attributed to the relics made Conques a famous pilgrimage site, and by the eleventh century the numbers of pilgrims made a new church to house the relics necessary.

Sainte-Foy is a characteristically Romanesque church. Its **arches**, **vaults**, and **columns** recall architectural elements from ancient Rome. For example, the exterior arches are rounded.

Churches in the Middle Ages in the Western tradition were often designed, as Sainte-Foy was, in the shape of a Latin cross (**3.2.21**). In this kind of plan the main and longer **axis** (the nave) usually runs from west to east, with a shorter axis (the **transept**) at right angles across it nearer the east end. Cathedral floor plans were designed to guide the flow of visiting pilgrims and the congregation during services. Worshipers entered at the west end and walked eastward down the nave toward the altar. The **choir** continued the nave on the other side of the crossing. As it was closest to the apse, which contained the altar, it was reserved for the clergy and, as its name suggests, the choir of singers. Pilgrims could also circle around behind the apse through the **ambulatory** and visit individual chapels, most of which held sacred relics.

The west–east orientation of churches, like the shape of the cross, also has symbolic meaning. The crucifixion is often depicted in a painting or sculpture at the east end, while an artwork of the Last Judgment is displayed at the western **portal**, where parishioners and pilgrims would enter and exit. The orientation of the church also mimics the natural course of the sun: thus to the east, Christ, as "light of the world," rises like the sun in the morning, while to the west, the setting sun reminds worshipers of their own mortality and the impending Judgment Day.

Most people in the Middle Ages were illiterate, so pictures taught religious stories to

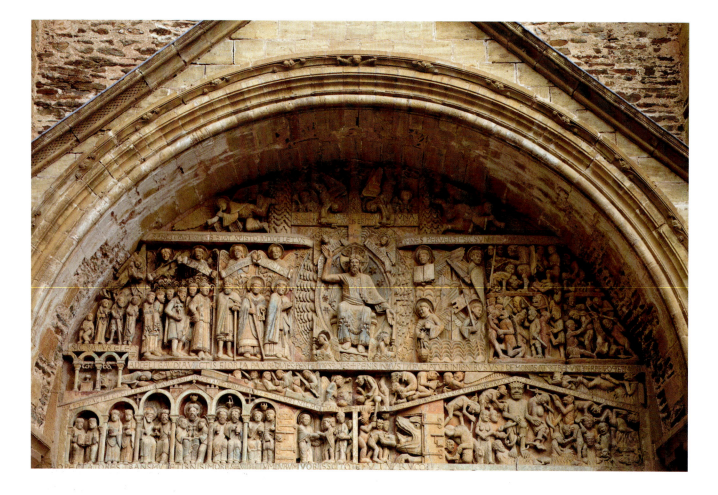

3.2.22 Tympanum of the west portal of Sainte-Foy, Conques, France

3.2.23 Diagram of the west portal tympanum in **3.2.22**

Tympanum: an arched recess above a doorway, often decorated with carvings

Lintel: the horizontal beam over the doorway of a portal

Trumeau: within a portal, a central column that supports a tympanum

Door jamb: vertical sections, often containing sculpture, that form the sides of a portal

Relief: a sculpture that projects from a flat surface

Hierarchical scale: the use of size to denote the relative importance of subjects in an artwork

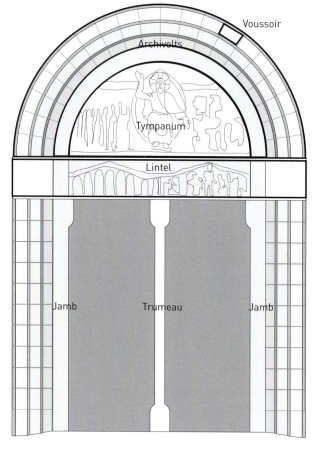

pilgrims and parishioners alike, and thus reinforced their faith. Portals, or gateways, served as both entrances and exits to the church for the public (see diagram, **3.2.23**). In many Romanesque churches, the **tympanum**, **lintel**, **trumeau**, and **door jambs** were all covered with **relief** sculptures, often of scenes from the Bible, and originally colorfully painted. The tympanum above the entryway to Sainte-Foy (**3.2.22**) shows the Last Judgment, using **hierarchical scale** to highlight the importance of Christ in the center; he is larger than the angels, prophets, and ancestors that surround him. He raises his right hand to show the salvation of those to his right, and lowers his left hand, marking the damnation of those to his left. He is enclosed within a **mandorla**, an oval, pointed, full-body halo that is a decorative hallmark of the Romanesque style.

The entire scene is divided into three **registers**. The top register contains four angels, two of whom hold the cross and two who herald the Last Judgment with their horns. In the middle register, Christ is surrounded by more angels. To the left of Christ (Christ's right) are the Virgin Mary, with a faint amount of surviving blue paint, and St. Peter holding his keys. The other figures are historical people who played an important role in the history of the monastery of Conques, including King Charlemagne, who was its most significant patron.

Sainte Foy is shown on the left side, between the middle and bottom register, slightly to the right of some arches. She is bowing down, praying before a large hand, which represents God. To the right of Christ (Christ's left) are the damned, suffering a variety of tortures, often

based on the kind of sin the damned person performed during his or her lifetime. Below Christ are scenes of souls being guided either to heaven, through an arched doorway, or to hell, represented by the head of a monster and a door designed to bolt in the damned for eternity.

The Rise of the Gothic

New construction methods heralded a new style: Gothic cathedrals, which were first built in the twelfth century, are distinguished by their great height and glorious stained-glass windows. The grand interior of Chartres Cathedral in France (**3.2.25**) combines all of the characteristic elements of Gothic architecture. The vaulted ceiling is 118 ft. above the floor and the nave is more than 50 ft. wide, surrounding receptive visitors with height and light to transport them beyond the cares and concerns of the mundane world.

Rib vaults make the great height of Gothic cathedrals possible: the weight of the structure is spread through the ribs of the ceiling vaults (see **3.2.25**, p. 408), before further dividing the burden between the walls and **flying buttresses** (see **3.2.24**). Flying buttresses function like many long, outstretched fingers to prevent the walls from falling outward. Because these engineering achievements distributed the weight previously

3.2.24 Chartres Cathedral, completed 1260, France

carried by very thick walls, it was possible to build with walls that became progressively thinner. In addition, large stained-glass windows now filled cathedrals with light, as the walls no longer needed to bear all the weight of the structure. The cathedral at Chartres is famous for the beautiful blue cast from its stained-glass windows.

Cathedrals were built by hired mason-workers headed by one main architect. Funding for the cathedral was donated by townspeople

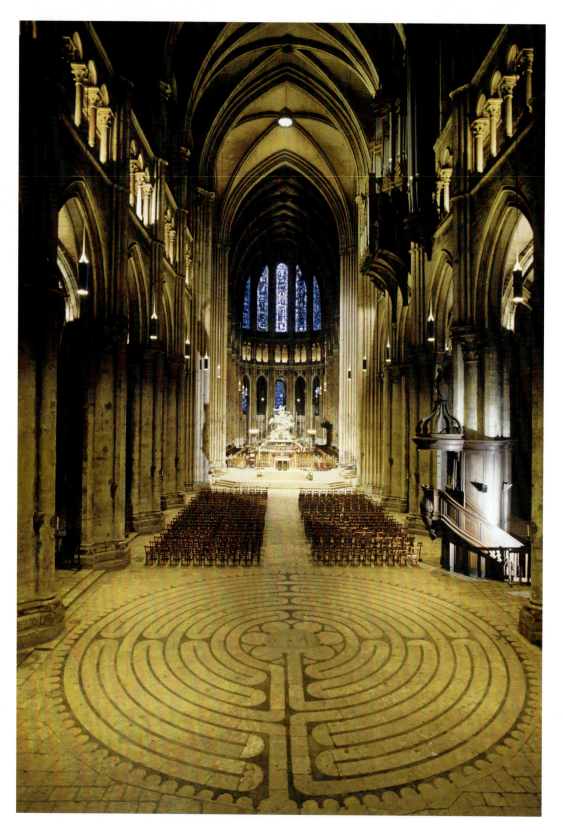

3.2.25 Chartres Cathedral, interior view showing labyrinth

Stylized: art that represents objects in an exaggerated way to emphasize certain aspects of the object
Composition: the overall design or organization of a work

and pilgrims, but part of the money came from bishops, the centralized Catholic Church, and wealthy individuals. By offering gifts to the Church, benefactors were not only acknowledged by others, but would also often be pardoned by religious officials for their sins.

Upon entering Chartres, pilgrims walked the labyrinth on the floor, symbolic of their physical and spiritual journey (**3.2.25**). Again, as at Sainte Foy, the architects created a pathway through the cathedral that guided the pilgrims to the numerous chapels containing relics. The site of Chartres was particularly important for holding the tunic worn by the Virgin Mary at Christ's birth. When the tunic survived a fire in 1194, the townspeople believed this to be a sign that Mary continued to protect them and wished for them to rebuild the cathedral.

The current popularity and proliferation of new church labyrinths, particularly in the United States, is evident in Grace Episcopal Cathedral in San Francisco, which replaced its indoor tapestry replica of the Chartres labyrinth with one made of stone, outside on its terrazzo. Labyrinths have since been re-introduced into Christian churches throughout the United States and worldwide, as relevant spiritual tools. For example, in the days following the terrorist attacks of September 11, 2001, more than 2,000 people walked the labyrinth at Grace Cathedral to pray and search for solace.

From the Gothic to Early Renaissance in Italy

How did artists represent in two dimensions the equivalent of the soaring spirituality of the Gothic style of architecture? And how did this evolve into a new style of painting that would come to be known as Renaissance art? Two paintings of the Virgin Mary and Christ Child, one by Cimabue (c. 1240–1302) and the other made thirty years later by his student Giotto di Bondone (c. 1266–1337), illustrate some of the characteristics that mark the transition from the Gothic to the early Renaissance style.

Cimabue's Gothic painting is reminiscent of Byzantine icons, with the rich gold throughout,

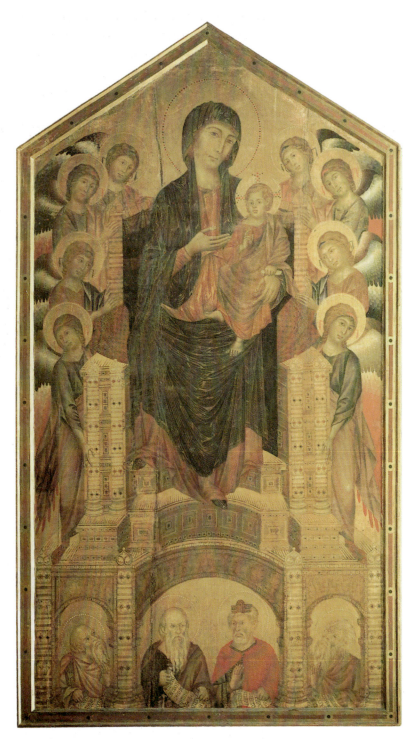

the **stylized** quality of Mary's robe, the organization of the angels' faces and halos in orderly rows, the elongation of the bodies, and the flatness of the figures appearing somewhat like paper cutouts (**3.2.26**). Cimabue's figures seem to float in space and rise up toward the top of the **composition** in much the same way that Gothic cathedrals emphasized height to inspire worshipers to look up toward the heavens.

3.2.26 Cimabue, *Virgin and Child Enthroned*, c. 1280. Tempera and gold on wood, 12'7½" × 7'4". Uffizi Gallery, Florence, Italy

While Giotto's *Virgin and Child Enthroned* (**3.2.27**) clearly shows architectural elements that recall Gothic churches (such as the pointed arch on Mary's throne), his painting makes many innovations, such as the three-dimensionality of his **forms** and the emphasis on creating a believable sense of the space in which Mary sits. We can also see through the spaces in the framework of the throne: the figures nearer to us overlap those that are behind them, and light seems to shine in a natural way and cast consistent shadows, helping to create the illusion that this is a three-dimensional space. Mary, Jesus, and the angels all also look more three-dimensional than the more delineated figures in Cimabue's painting. Cimabue's *Virgin and Child Enthroned* seems to focus only on the spirituality of the scene; Giotto seems to wish to create a realistic space, more like the world in which we live. This shift in approach was revolutionary, and Giotto's artistic inventions were at the forefront of the stylistic changes that would take place in the fifteenth and sixteenth century.

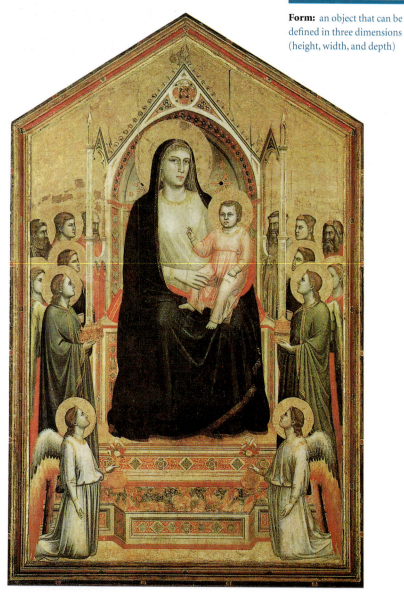

Form: an object that can be defined in three dimensions (height, width, and depth)

3.2.27 Giotto, *Virgin and Child Enthroned*, c. 1310. Tempera on wood, 10'7" × 6'9". Uffizi Gallery, Florence, Italy

Discussion Questions

1. The Middle Ages was a time of strong religious belief. Select two artworks, each made for believers of a different religion, and contrast how the artist has emphasized the religious elements of the artwork.

2. Compare the architecture of a Gothic cathedral with that of an Islamic mosque. How does the architecture of each reflect the beliefs and rituals of its worshipers?

3. Select one two-dimensional artwork (paintings, mosaics, manuscripts) from the Western and one from the Byzantine tradition. Contrast the form and content of the two artworks.

Images Related to 3.2:
Art of the Middle Ages

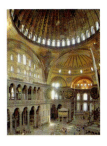

2.5.19 Hagia Sophia, Istanbul, Turkey, 532–35 CE, p. 276

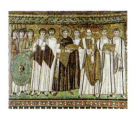

4.6.5 Mosaic depicting Emperor Justinian, c. 547 CE, p. 629

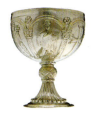

2.6.14 *Chalice with Apostles Venerating the Cross*, Byzantine, c. 600 CE, p. 300

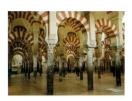

1.9.7 Great Mosque of Córdoba, Spain, 784–86, p. 172

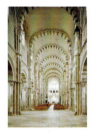

2.5.16 Church of Sainte-Madeleine, Vézelay, France, 9th–13th century, p. 275

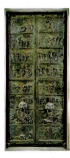

4.2.2b Doors, Abbey Church of St. Michael's, Hildesheim, Germany, 1015, p. 576

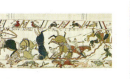

4.7.7 Detail of the *Bayeux Tapestry*, c.1066–82, p. 640

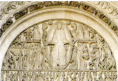

4.2.10 Gislebertus, *The Last Judgment*, c. 1120–35, p. 581

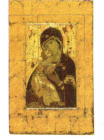

4.2.7 *Virgin of Vladimir*, 12th century (before 1132), p. 579

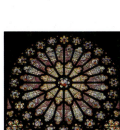

2.5.18 Stained-glass window, Abbey Church of Saint-Denis, France, 12th century, p. 275

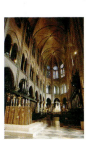

4.1.1 Notre Dame Cathedral, Paris, France, 1163–1250, p. 563

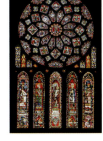

2.6.11 Rose window with lancets, Chartres Cathedral, France, 13th century, p. 298

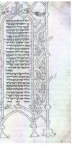

1.1.10 Franco-German hand, *Pentateuch*, 13th–14th century, p. 54

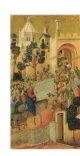

2.2.7 Duccio di Buoninsegna, *Entry into Jerusalem* from the *Maestà*, 1308–11, p. 220

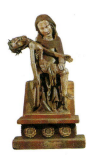

1.2.4 *Roettgen Pietà* (*Vesperbild*), Germany, c. 1330, p. 69

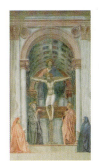

1.3.20 Masaccio, *Trinity*, c. 1425–26, p. 95

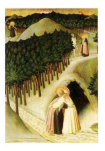

1.5.1 Workshop of the Master of Osservanza, *The Meeting of St. Anthony* and *St. Paul*, c. 1430–35, p. 119

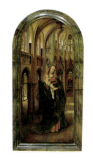

1.7.4 Jan van Eyck, *Madonna in a Church*, 1437–38, p. 148

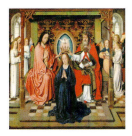

1.8.4 Dieric Bouts, *The Coronation of the Virgin Mary*, 1455/60, p. 159

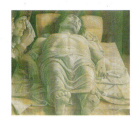

4.3.3 Andrea Mantegna, *Dead Christ*, c. 1480, p. 590

3.3

Art of India, China, Japan, and Southeast Asia

Asia is home to artistic traditions that date back many thousands of years. India and China are large landmasses, both bordered by land and by great expanses of ocean. Southeast Asia lies east of India and south of China; the arts of the region have been influenced by these large neighbors. Japan, on the other hand, is a country of more than 3,000 islands off the eastern coast of mainland Asia. Trade by sea and along the famed Silk Road—a network of trade routes between Asia and the Mediterranean world—led to the spread of cultural ideas and a sharing of religious and philosophical beliefs.

Religion and philosophy have been integral to the art of the entire region (see Box: Philosophical and Religious Traditions in Asia), yet certain stylistic characteristics make the art of each of these cultures distinctive. In Indian art,

3.3.1 Map of Asia

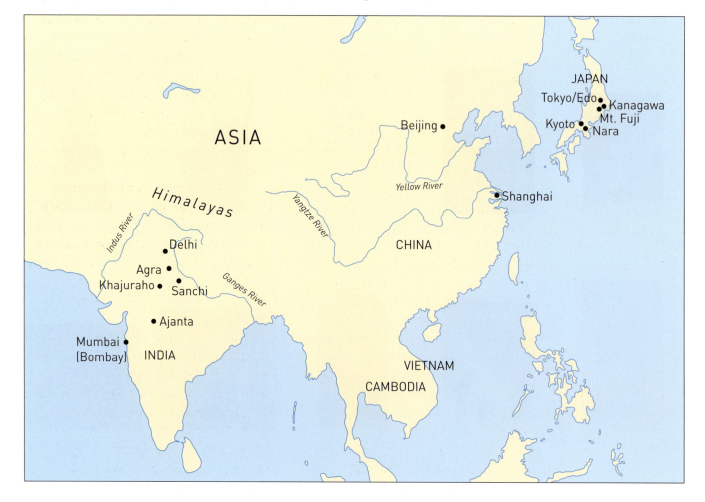

there is a noticeable tendency toward elaborate decoration and an emphasis on the human body, frequently showing sensual movement and suggesting fertility. Chinese art combines an interest in religious subject matter with a great respect for Chinese heritage and ancestors.

In general, Chinese artworks are also very precise and symmetrically balanced; Chinese artists desire to create uniformity and convey control of their material. In contrast, Japanese artworks tend to be more asymmetrical, organic, individual, and to convey spontaneity. Japanese

Philosophical and Religious Traditions in Asia

The arts of India, China, Japan, and Southeast Asia can be fully understood only in relation to each country's religions and philosophies. All have a long tradition of religious pluralism, in other words the acceptance of beliefs from different religions and philosophies. They could also be described as **syncretic**: their religions blend two or more belief systems. As one example, it is common in Japan to be a follower of Shinto, and a Buddhist, and to practice Confucianism all at the same time. This is possible partly because of the similar values of the various religions and philosophies. For instance, many of these religions strive for harmony with nature, and have a component of ancestral worship.

Buddhist beliefs are founded on the teachings of Buddha (563–483 BCE). Buddhism emphasizes an acceptance of the difficulties of life and of samsara (the cycle of birth, death, and reincarnation). Once one attains Enlightenment, the ultimate wisdom, one arrives at nirvana, the end of suffering for eternity. Zen Buddhism, native to Japan, promotes meditation and introspection, which can be attained through focus on individual moments and daily tasks.

Confucianism is based on the philosophy of Chinese Master Kong (Confucius) (551–479 BCE), who promoted the use of ethics to attain social order. His teachings emphasize self-discipline, moral duty, and paying respect both to one's ancestors and (by extension) to the elders of society. Confucianism is common in China and Japan.

Daoism (The Way) comes from the teachings of Lao Zi (b. 604 BCE), who explained in *Dao de jing* ("The Book of the Way") how to live in harmony with nature and the universe.

Yin and yang is the concept that seemingly opposing forces are interconnected and need each other for balance. Such opposing forces might be male and female, or light and dark. Daoism is found throughout Asia, but most prominently in China.

Hinduism encompasses a number of beliefs, including reincarnation, rebirth of the soul or of the body, and karma, the idea that one's actions will cause a reaction or consequence in the universe. Hindus believe that while on Earth their main goals should be to practice righteous living (*dharma*), acquire wealth, achieve physical and emotional love, and attain spiritual salvation. Hindus believe in the existence of several gods (including Brahma, Shiva, and Vishnu), although individual practice and worship vary greatly amongst adherents. Hinduism originated in India and has been adopted throughout Asia, although India still holds the largest Hindu population.

Islam: Muslims base their beliefs on a sacred text called the Koran that records the will of Allah (God) as revealed to the prophet Muhammad (*c.* 570–632 CE). Islam originated at the birthplace of Muhammad (Mecca, Saudi Arabia) but today is practiced worldwide, with many followers in Asia, including India and China.

Shinto is a native religion of Japan. Its name means The Way of the Gods. Shinto worships several gods and emphasizes respect for nature and ancestors. Followers believe that non-human entities (animals, plants, and inanimate objects) all possess a spiritual essence. *Kami*, for example, are believed to be forces in nature (such as wind or trees), or spirits of ancestors.

art is also distinctively contemplative and reveals a great reverence for nature. Southeast Asia is an immensely diverse region; strong influences of Hinduism and Buddhism, from India, often feature in Southeast Asian art and architecture. For example, many Hindu temples were built to represent cosmic mountains, homes for Hindu gods who were believed to support local rulers. This chapter highlights both the individuality of these countries and the themes and ideas that unite their artistic traditions.

India

The landmass of India occupies a peninsula in southern Asia that is bordered on the north by the Himalayan mountains. It is about one-third the size of the United States. Buddhist and Hindu beliefs have been important influences on India's rich visual history. The shrines and temples built for both of these religions are designed to be small replicas, or microcosms, of the universe, places to meditate and worship the gods. In the early twelfth century, Muslim invaders from what is now Afghanistan began centuries of rule in India. These Islamic rulers were responsible for magnificent works of art, including India's best-known landmark, the Taj Mahal (see Gateway box: The Taj Mahal, p. 418).

Buddhism in Indian Art

Siddhartha Gautama (563–485 BCE), who would become the Buddha or "The Enlightened One," was born a prince in what is now Nepal.

Traditions tell how Siddhartha was raised in comfort in the royal palace, but at the age of twenty-nine, he witnessed the lives of the poor and sick and became an **ascetic**, rejecting his wealth and worldly pleasures. Buddhists believe that he achieved Enlightenment through meditation and self-discipline; he spent the second half of his life teaching others to try and do the same. After his death, his life and teachings were spread by word of mouth throughout India. The Buddha's remains were cremated and buried within eight large dirt mounds, called **stupas**, the locations of which were relevant to important periods in his life.

The Great Stupa in Sanchi, India, was built by King Ashoka as part of a large Buddhist monastery (**3.3.2**). Ashoka (304–232 BCE) was emperor of India in the mid-third century BCE. He was born a Hindu, but it is said that he became a Buddhist after feeling ashamed of the murderous destruction caused by a war in which his army killed more than 100,000 people. He became known as "the pious Ashoka" and gained a reputation as a charitable and peace-loving ruler who built hospitals and schools throughout India. When Ashoka converted to Buddhism, he disinterred the Buddha's remains and distributed them to be reburied within thousands more stupas he built throughout India.

Surrounding the Great Stupa at Sanchi are four gateways, or **toranas**, placed at the four cardinal points surrounding the large mound. Sensual female figures of tree spirits hang from the brackets on some of the toranas (**3.3.3**). These figures symbolize procreation, abundance, and the source of all life. At a height of 35 ft., the columns and horizontal cross beams of these toranas are covered with scenes of the Buddha's multiple lives (**jatakas**). The Buddha himself is not shown, but there are signs of his presence, such as an empty throne and his footprints. In this way, Buddhists are invited to follow in the footsteps of the Buddha. Pilgrims enter through the east gate and circle the stupa in a clockwise direction, following the path of the sun. Stone railings added after Ashoka's time allow pilgrims to climb higher safely as they encircle the mound

3.3.2 Great Stupa, third century BCE, enlarged under the Sunga and Andhra Dynasties, c. 150–50 BCE, Sanchi, India

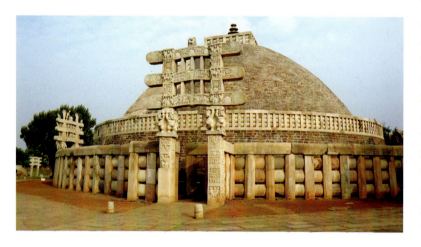

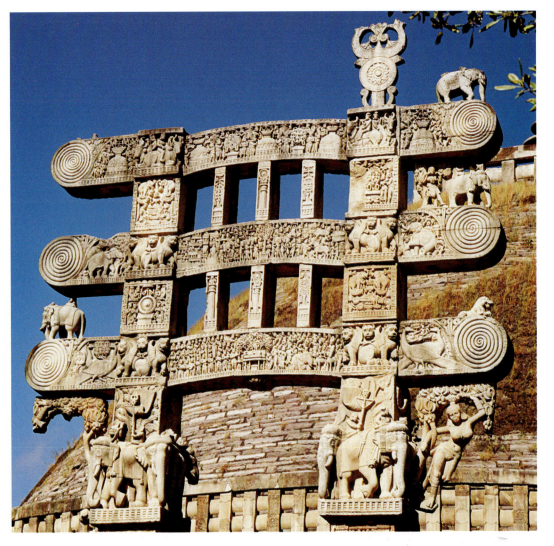

in which the Buddha's remains are interred, a ritual that emulates Buddha's path toward Enlightenment. The stupa and its four gateways represent a three-dimensional **mandala**, or a re-creation of the universe.

This seated Buddha from the Gupta period (320–550 CE) (**3.3.4**) is in a meditative, serene pose, with his eyes closed, spiritually turning inward to develop inner strength and enlightenment. His body is graceful, with a solid posture and elegantly crossed legs. The soft facial features and overall ideal beauty of the sculpture are typical of the Gupta period. Buddha is represented here as a compassionate teacher, with the orb of the sun, representing the Wheel of Law (Buddha's teaching of the path to nirvana), behind him.

The meaning of sculptures of Buddha is often communicated through the hand

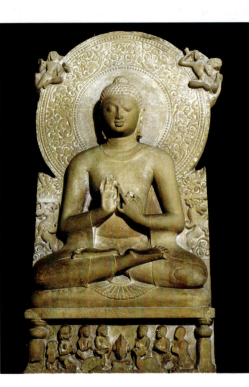

3.3.4 Seated Buddha from the Gupta period (5th century CE). Stone, 61 × 34¼ × 10⅝". Sarnath Museum, Uttar Pradesh, India

Mandala: a sacred diagram of the universe, often involving a square and a circle

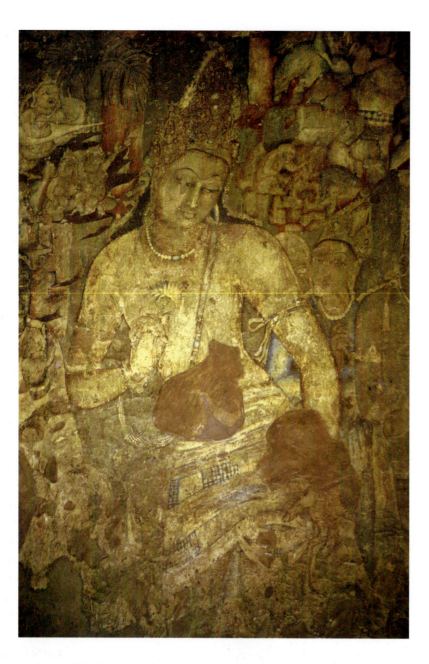

3.3.5 Bodhisattva Padmapani, Cave 1, Ajanta, India. Cave painting, second half of 5th century CE

gestures of the figure. In this case, Buddha is setting the Wheel of Law into motion while teaching the principles of his Eightfold Path of Righteousness; the sculpture also represents his eternal guidance. This statue was found in Sarnath, the site of Buddha's first sermon, and the figures carved below the Buddha are his disciples, giving him their rapt attention.

During the fifth century CE, in Ajanta, western India, along the Silk Road, twenty-nine caves were carved into the side of a horseshoe-shaped cliff and were filled with Buddhist sculptures and paintings. Although only fragments of the mural paintings survive, the beauty of individual figures and the complexity of the scenes are apparent. Most scenes depict portions of the jatakas, scenes of contemporary rulers, or Buddhist teachings. Several paintings are of *bodhisattvas*, beings who could have achieved nirvana but who chose instead to sacrifice themselves and help others work toward Enlightenment (**3.3.5**). In one cave painting, Padmapani, a bodhisattva who embodies compassion, is dressed as a prince with a glorious crown and a pearl necklace, and poses gracefully with a serene gaze that suggests contentment and enlightenment. He is shown holding a lotus flower, a common symbol in Buddhist art for its ability to grow from the mud and become beautiful.

3.3.6 (below) Kandariya
Mahadeva temple, c. 1000,
Khajuraho, Madhya
Pradesh, India

3.3.7 (right) Detail
of exterior sculpture,
Kandariya Mahadeva
temple

Hinduism in Indian Art

Hinduism has been practiced at least as far back as 1000 BCE. Today, it is the world's third largest religion, with the majority of its followers living in India. The kinds of personal practices and gods that are worshiped vary greatly amongst Hindus, but Hindus all share the belief that one's spirit is eternal. Just as Buddhism grew because powerful people promoted it, the increase in popularity of Hinduism was largely due to the efforts of rulers to encourage Hindu worship, particularly by building religious temples.

Around 1020 CE, King Vidyadhara built a large complex containing Hindu temples in Khajuraho, in northern India. The largest of these, the Kandariya Mahadeva, is dedicated

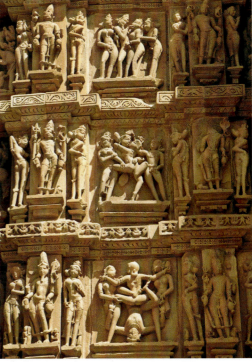

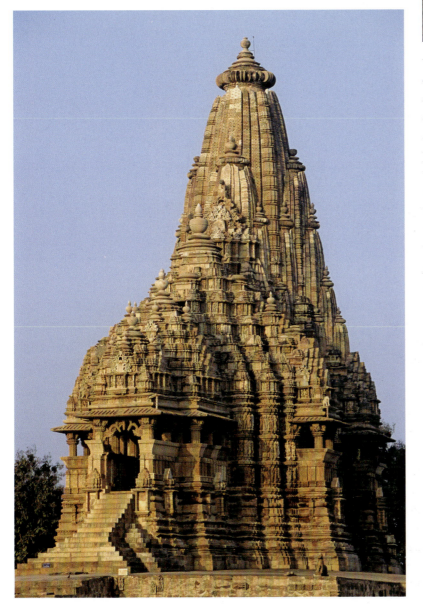

to Shiva, the Hindu god of creation and destruction (**3.3.6**). Hindus see their temples as "cosmic mountains," links between heaven and Earth. The large towers on Hindu temples are called *shikhara*s and represent mountain peaks. The vertical towers pull the eye upward to the heavens, suggesting to Hindus a desire for nirvana, or the final end of suffering. Every temple has a central room underneath the shikhara that contains an image of the god to whom the temple is dedicated. A Hindu priest's job is to maintain the sculpture (which embodies the god itself) through prayer, meditation, incense burning, feeding and clothing the sculpture, and pouring milk or honey on it.

The temple is aligned with the rising and setting of the sun, with stairs for entrance on the east. Horizontal decoration encourages the viewer to walk around the temple and view the intricate carving and relief sculpture. The exterior is covered with more than 600 sculptures in poses that suggest dancing, which creates a rhythmic pulsing effect over the entire structure (**3.3.7**). Many of the scenes are sensual and erotic, depicting the physical union of males and females. The sexual joining of these male and female forces represents the balance of opposing elements in the universe, or the unity of the cosmos.

Gateway to Art: The Taj Mahal
The Gardens of Paradise in the Taj Mahal

By the mid-sixteenth century, the Mughals (distant Muslim descendants of the historic Mongolian conqueror Genghis Khan) had conquered part of northern India and were based in Delhi. In the Islamic faith, gardens are symbolic of the paradise of heaven, and the Mughal emperor Akbar (1542–1605) created a garden for the site of his own tomb, which was completed by his son Jahangir. Akbar's garden is vast and square, and enclosed by high walls. Red sandstone causeways divide it into quarters, which link the tomb to the gates into the garden (3.3.8).

Following in the footsteps of his grandfather, Akbar, in the seventeenth century Shah Jahan created his own vision of heaven for the burial site of his beloved wife, Mumtaz (3.3.9). The immense gardens that cover the Taj Mahal complex are designed to represent the paradise of the afterlife for those of Muslim faith. Forty-two acres are divided by four rivers that extend from a raised central pool that contains five fountains. The channels of water represent the promised rivers of Paradise, that is, rivers of water, milk, wine, and honey. The pool represents the water from which the deceased will drink upon immediately entering Paradise. Each of these sections is then subdivided by walkways into quadrants, creating sixteen sections in all. Trees and flowers are planted in beds raised higher than the river. Cypress trees (representing death or immortality) and roses and fruit trees (representing life) originally filled the grounds, which are placed precisely between the tomb and the gateway entrance (*darwaza*) that separates the worldly atmosphere of the market from the heavenly gardens.

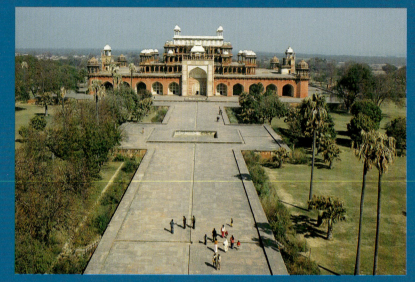

3.3.8 Gardens of the Tomb of Akbar, Sikandra, India

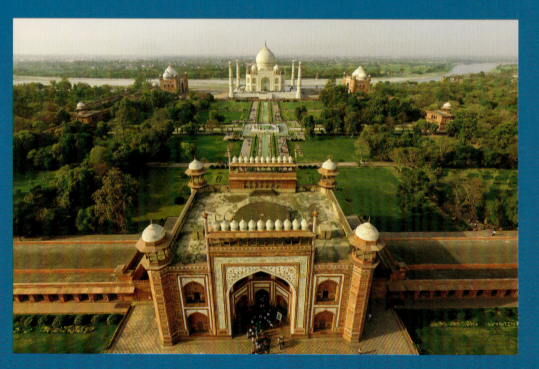

3.3.9 Aerial view of the gardens of the Taj Mahal, Agra, India

China

The earliest traces of civilization in China have been found along the Yellow and Yangtze rivers. The first Chinese emperor, Qin Shi Huangdi, established the first unified Chinese dynasty in 221 BCE. China's boundaries have changed throughout its subsequent history according to its military success or failure, but today it is approximately the same size as the United States.

Buddhism and Daoism are the largest religions in China. Each faith integrates the beliefs of the other and of Confucianism (see Box: Philosophical and Religious Traditions in Asia, p. 413) as well: the Chinese believe a person may practice more than one belief system. This affects the whole of Chinese culture. In Chinese art, for example, scroll paintings are intended to enhance meditation, and respect for nature and one's elders—virtues that are valued by all three faiths. Many great Chinese artworks have been discovered in tombs, providing evidence both of a widespread reverence for ancestors, and of the importance of the idea of the afterlife.

Death and the Afterlife

For thousands of years, Chinese people have worshiped their ancestors, who they believe are transformed after death into supernatural entities with the power to communicate with the gods and protect the living. To show the ancestors due respect, and so that the deceased would have what they needed in the afterlife, both valuable and everyday items were buried with them in their tombs (**3.3.10** and **3.3.11**). Humans and animals were also sacrificed, in the belief that they would serve the dead in the next realm. Today, similar customs persist: the Chinese often burn money, food, and other objects in the hope that these will reach their ancestors in the spirit world.

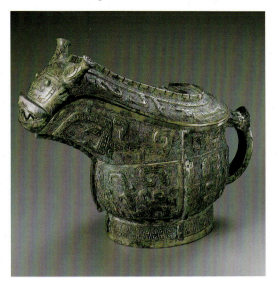

3.3.10 (left) Ritual wine vessel (*guang*), late Shang Dynasty, *c.* 1600– *c.* 1050 BCE. Bronze, 6½ × 3¼ × 8½″. Brooklyn Museum, New York

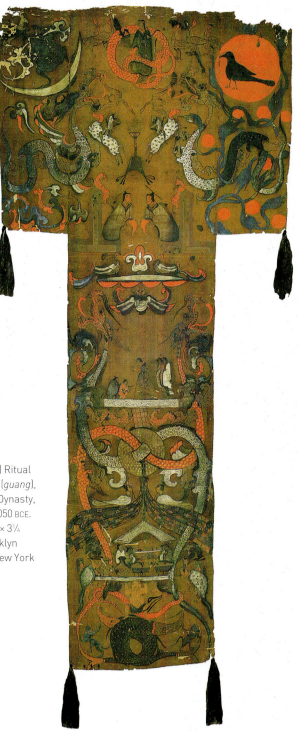

3.3.11 Painted banner from tomb of Lady Dai Hou Fu-ren, Han Dynasty, *c.* 168 BCE. Silk, length 80½″, width at top 36″, width at bottom 18¾″. Hunan Museum, Changsha, China

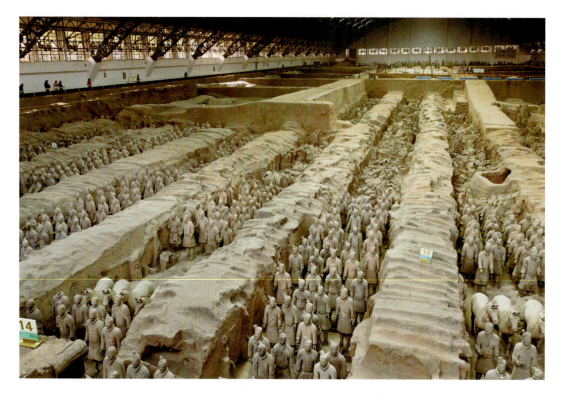

3.3.12a Building housing pit number 1 of the terra-cotta army, mausoleum of Qin Shi Huangdi, *c.* 210 BCE. Xi'an, Shaanxi Province, China

As early as the Shang Dynasty (*c.* 1600– *c.* 1050 BCE), Chinese people placed objects in tombs. The tombs of the Shang Dynasty's rulers have preserved many lavishly made items in jade, gold, ivory, and, in particular, bronze. The bronze sculptures of this period were made using a process known as **piece mold casting,** which involves cutting the mold into sections and then reassembling it before pouring in the molten bronze.

The bronze guang (lidded vessel; **3.3.10**, see p. 419) was found buried in a tomb. It was used to pour wine during a ritual. The container depicts a horn-headed dragon with sharp teeth at its spout. The dragon was one of the most commonly used **motifs** in Chinese art, symbolizing good fortune, power, and immortality. The mazelike **abstract** design on the side of the vessel is called a *t'ao t'ieh* (monster mask). It warded off evil spirits and protected the ancestral soul.

The tomb of Lady Dai (died 168 BCE), a noblewoman of the Han Dynasty (206 BCE–220 CE), was excavated in 1972, revealing a wealth of objects intended to accompany her into the afterlife. A stunning richly painted silk textile (**3.3.11**, see p. 419) had been placed over Lady Dai's coffin, protected by several additional layers of wooden coffins. The silk banner is in the shape of a T; the wide horizontal section represents heaven with twisting dragons, a toad on a gold moon, and a crow on a red sun. At the top in the center, surrounded by a red serpent, is probably an imperial ancestor. Lady Dai stands upon a central white platform about halfway down the banner, awaiting her ascent to the heavenly realm. Above her is a bird and, at the cross of the T, two kneeling figures who are thought to be guardians or guides of some kind. A jade circle, crossed by two writhing dragons and known as a *bi*—frequently used as a symbol for heaven—sits below Lady Dai on her platform. Scholars have hypothesized that this banner either shows Lady Dai's funeral and her journey to heaven, or views of the three spiritual realms of heaven, Earth, and the underworld.

Similarly to the Shang kings before them, the emperors of ancient China also sought to take their riches with them to the afterlife. Ancient records described how the first emperor of China, Qin Shi Huangdi, prepared for his death by constructing a burial mound with a vast underground city palace that matched the one he occupied in life. These accounts were believed to be sheer legend until 1974, when, in a spectacular archaeological discovery, excavations

Piece mold casting: A process for casting metal objects in which a mold is broken into several pieces that are then reassembled into a final sculpture

Motif: a distinctive visual element, the recurrence of which is often characteristic of an artist's work

Abstract: an artwork the form of which is simplified, distorted, or exaggerated in appearance. It may represent a recognizable form that has been slightly altered, or it may be a completely non-representational depiction

Terra-cotta: iron-rich clay, fired at a low temperature, which is traditionally brownish-orange in color

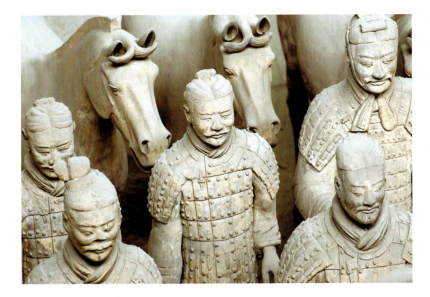

3.3.12b Soldiers from the mausoleum of Qin Shi Huangdi, *c.* 210 BCE. Terra-cotta and pigment, figures approximately lifesize. Xi'an, Shaanxi Province, China

of a tomb mound revealed evidence that the ancient stories were true (**3.3.12a and b**).

Soon after he came to the throne at the age of thirteen, Qin Shi Huangdi began overseeing the elaborate preparations for his own resting place, which continued for thirty-six years until his death in 210 BCE. Artisans filled the complex surrounding Qin Shi Huangdi's tomb with the treasures he would need in the afterlife, including an army of **terra-cotta** soldiers, chariots, and horses, all of which were originally painted.

The 8,000 lifesize figures found in the largest pit were intended to guard the body of the emperor. They have similar rigid and upright poses because molds were used for the various body parts and then pieced together. The unique portions of each soldier (clothing, weaponry, and facial features) were added on individually, however, with a layer of moist clay.

Chinese Scroll Painting

The earliest known painting in China dates back some 10,000 years. Archaeologists have found painted pots, and paint on the walls and floors of caves and huts. From 200 BCE until today, however, many Chinese paintings have been made with ink on silk or paper, the same materials used in the arts of **calligraphy** (fine hand lettering) and poetry. These three arts are inextricably linked for the Chinese (see Box: The Three Perfections: Calligraphy, Painting, Poetry, p. 422). Most Chinese paintings are made

Calligraphy: the art of emotive or carefully descriptive hand lettering or handwriting

as hanging or hand scrolls; their subject matter includes battles, scenes of daily life, landscapes, and animals. Chinese scroll paintings are meant to be experienced as though we are on a slow, contemplative journey. Artists who paint scrolls do not intend their work to be viewed from one position, as is usual in artworks created in the European tradition. Instead, the complexity and (in the case of a hand scroll) length of a painting invite us to view one portion of it at a time.

The calligraphy in the upper right of the hanging scroll shown in **3.3.13** tells us that *Ge Zhichuan Moving His Dwelling* is a historical

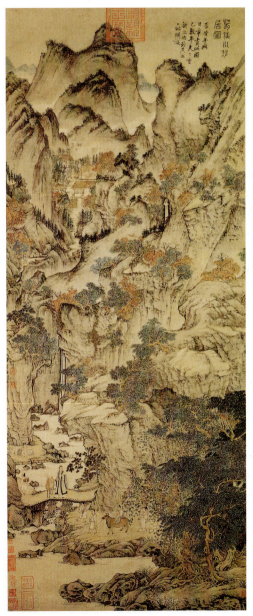

3.3.13 Wang Meng, *Ge Zhichuan Moving His Dwelling*, *c.* 1360. Hanging scroll, ink and color on paper, 54¾ × 22⅞". Palace Museum, Beijing, China

The Three Perfections: Calligraphy, Painting, Poetry

In Chinese society, talented calligraphers are accorded the highest respect. The Chinese script used today goes back to at least the Qin Dynasty (221–207 BCE). Chinese calligraphers can convey a mood through the handling of a brush, the thickness of a line, the quickness of a stroke. Skilled calligraphers can communicate through their script elegance, formality, sadness, or joyful exuberance. Historically, many poets became calligraphers so that they could express most eloquently the moods of their poems. Many painters, too, were calligraphers, because both art forms require great skill in the handling of the brush.

During the Song Dynasty (960–1279), painters called literati wrote poems—either their own or the work of other poets—next to their paintings. The tradition continues to this day. Room for calligraphic inscriptions is often left on paintings, not only for the artist's signature but also to describe a scene, dedicate the painting, or add poetry.

The Chinese believe that any inscriptions on a painting become part of the work, whether or not they are written by the painter. Frequently, red seals or stamps are pressed onto part of a work to claim authorship, or to show admiration for that part. **Colophons** are inscriptions—often poems or historical information about the artwork—usually written in black ink by the artist or admirers of the work. Therefore, a scroll painting with many inscriptions and colophons is one that has been much enjoyed, and this becomes part of the story of the painting.

scene from the life of a well-known Chinese writer. Ge Zhichuan was one of the first alchemists (someone who seeks to make gold or silver from lead or iron). He is also considered a great teacher of Daoism. In the painting, Ge Zhichuan is traveling to Guangzhou to find the red, mercury-based mineral cinnabar. He is shown in the lower left on a bridge. His family follows in the lower center. The scene shows the power of nature compared to the small scale of man.

The fantastic landscape, full of twisting trees, steep cliffs, and high waterfalls, shows the mystical nature of Ge Zhichuan's journey; it also symbolizes the wondrous path we all take through life. We cannot view the entire scroll at one time, just as we cannot see everything going on around us. This is a metaphor for the Zen-like philosophy that one can comprehend the universe in its entirety only through the mind, thus achieving Enlightenment. As Ge Zhichuan follows his meandering path, he will eventually arrive at a new village, seen in the upper left. His destination is higher in the scroll than his present location; this is a device used in Daoist painting to symbolize the growth that the subject will experience on his spiritual path. Just like the

people in the painting, the viewer may wander in any direction, exploring new territory and facing challenges; all of this is a metaphor for the journey of life. The mountain ridges high in the distance speak of the journeys yet to come.

Japan

Japan is a country of many islands off the eastern coast of Asia. In size, it covers about the same area as California. Combining its own cultural and religious traditions with influences from mainland Asia, Japanese art reflects stories of Buddha and of emperors, and (in modern times) the lives of ordinary people as well. Vulnerable to frequent tsunamis, earthquakes, and volcanic eruptions, the Japanese have a great respect for nature. According to the Shinto religion, spirits called kami are present everywhere, including within nature. Many Japanese combine aspects of Shinto with a belief in Buddhism. The Japanese reverence for nature, their desire for meditation, quiet reflection, and mental discipline, are all seen in the art they create (see Box: Sonoko Sasaki, pp. 424–25).

Colophon: comment written on a Chinese scroll by the creator, owner, or a viewer

Gateway to Art: Hokusai, "The Great Wave Off Shore at Kanagawa"
Mount Fuji: The Sacred Mountain of Japan

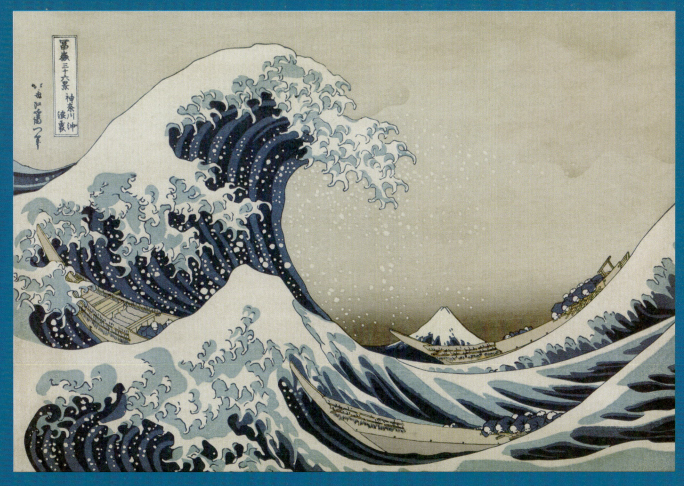

3.3.14 Katsushika Hokusai, "The Great Wave off Shore at Kanagawa," from *Thirty-Six Views of Mount Fuji*, 1826–33 (printed later). Print, color woodcut. Library of Congress, Washington, D.C.

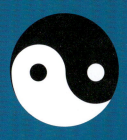

3.3.15 Yin and yang symbol

Katsushika Hokusai's series *Thirty-Six Views of Mount Fuji* was so popular in his time that he made forty-six scenes. Mount Fuji is the largest mountain in Japan (12,388 ft. high), and has become a recognizable symbol of the country. The mountain is sacred to believers of both Buddhism and Shinto. Because it is an active volcano, it is believed to have a particularly powerful kami, or spirit, although it has not erupted since 1708. In one print from Hokusai's series, "The Great Wave off Shore at Kanagawa" (3.3.14), the mountain is the only part of the scene that is not in motion; it is therefore a powerful stabilizing force. Indeed, the fierce movement of the wave thrashing the boats around contrasts markedly with the eternal and still form of the mountain. As one looks at the print, an abstract yin and yang (3.3.15), symbolic of the belief that the forces

may seem opposed, but are dependent on each other (see Box: Philosophical and Religious Traditions in Asia, p. 413), appears in the intertwining of the large wave with the sky. Two smaller focal points then become Mount Fuji, the reduced size of which serves to make the curling wave seem to tower even higher, and the boat on the left.

All of the views in this series contrast the stable form of Mount Fuji with the daily actions (fleeting life) of people. In "The Great Wave," Hokusai shows the hard lifestyle of the fishermen who worked in the area of Edo, and their courage in the face of the power of nature. Just as their lives were at risk, Hokusai was also likely thinking of his own mortality: he was in his seventies when he made this print. Here, he demonstrates the balance and harmony of man and nature.

Perspectives on Art: Sonoko Sasaki
Arts and Tradition in Japan

In an effort to protect the skills needed to preserve Japan's traditional art forms, the Japanese government designates outstanding traditional artists "Important Intangible Cultural Property Holder" (popularly known as National Living Treasures). Sonoko Sasaki was named a National Living Treasure for her skills in weaving a traditional textile known as tsumugi-ori. Here she explains her work.

I work with *tsumugi-ori* textiles because the touch and look of the material are very

3.3.16 Sonoko Sasaki, *Sea in the Sky*, 2007. Tsumigi-ito silk thread and vegetable dyes, 70⅞ × 51¼". Collection of the artist

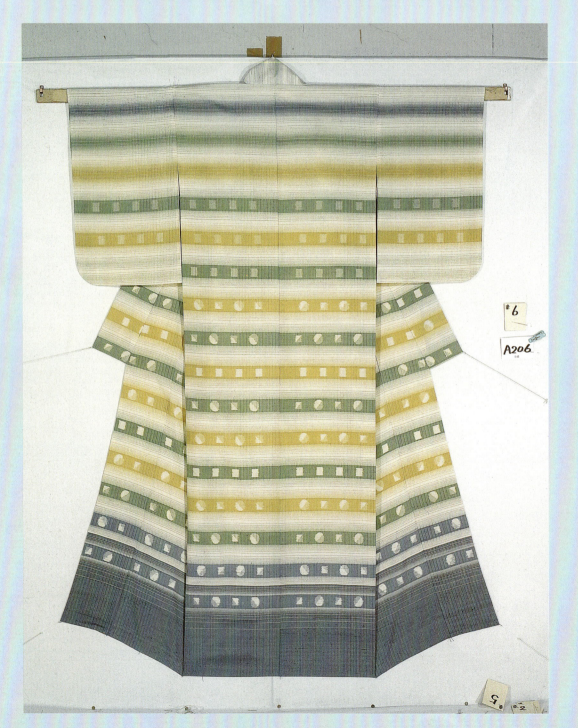

attractive to me. Tsumugi thread is different from cotton thread because it consists of extremely long fibers that are tough, waterproof, and glossy.

Actually, tsumugi-ori was originally quite a rustic textile made by women involved in silk cultivation after their farming work. As a result, tsumugi-ori has always had a strong connection with the Earth and nature, and with the cycle of the four seasons that in Japan shows us the beautiful scenes of the natural world. I always try to sharpen my sense of color with all five of my senses, which helps me give a variety of colors to my work. The colors I use also come from nature. The dyes I use to color my textiles come from roots, flowers, and fruits of plants of every season.

Water, light, and wind are also essential for tsumugi-ori textiles. Water is important for me, and fills me with awe, since the threads must be boiled in a dye and then washed. Sunlight and wind are needed to dry the dyed thread.

I weave my textiles using a hand-loom and then tailor the material to make kimonos, a traditional Japanese dress. In other words, my works have meaning and value only if someone wears them. Here the key is again the four seasons. I delicately change the color of the textiles according to the seasons. At the same time, people who wear my kimonos place a high value on their sense of the seasons. In this way the artist and the wearer share their consciousness of the seasons, a tradition, inherited by generations of women, that I think is special to Japan.

I do not have any idea why I have been designated as a National Living Treasure, but I understand that I have accepted a responsibility to work on and protect the art

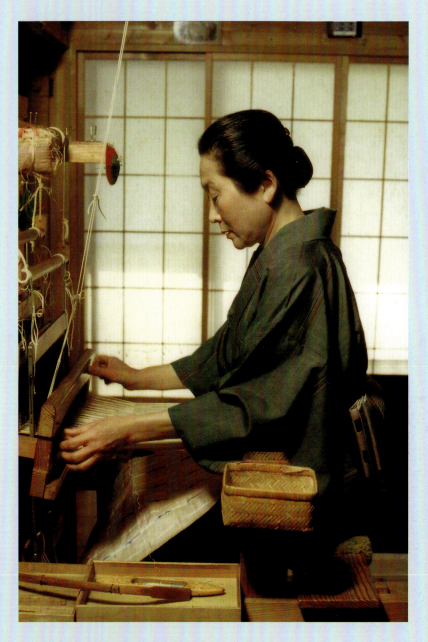

and culture of tsumugi-ori for the rest of my life. I am truly happy to pursue my "road of coloration" and "road of weaving" now and forever. Even if I were born again, I would still like to choose tsumugi-ori, as, for me, nothing is more glamorous than dyeing and weaving.

3.3.17 Sonoko Sasaki at work at her loom

The Japanese Tea Ceremony

Chanoyu (Way of the Tea) is the Japanese word for the traditional tea ceremony. Rooted in Zen Buddhism, chanoyu is a set of rituals that helps one find peace and solace from the ordinary world. It is a tenet of Buddhism that disciplined observation of the mundane things in life leads one toward Enlightenment, and chanoyu is designed to facilitate such observation. It also helps create an environment for intense concentration. Tea masters train for many years in the practice of creating a meditative environment through the serving of tea and the preparation of the teahouse. In the sixteenth century, the tea master Sen no Rikyu developed an influential tea ritual; the Taian tearoom in Kyoto is the only remaining teahouse by this master (**3.3.18**). The modest room is made with natural materials, such as mud for the walls, and bamboo and other wood for the trim and ceilings. The windows are made of paper, and the *tatami* (floor mats) are made of straw. The simple room has no decoration except for a simple scroll or small floral arrangement, placed in a niche called a *tokonoma*.

Chanoyu can take hours. It involves preparing and drinking the tea, and quiet conversation. The ceremony begins as one removes one's shoes and enters the house on hands and knees, showing humility. The contemplative environment invites participants to enjoy conversation, and also to appreciate each object involved in the ceremony. In **3.3.19** the tea bowl called Mount Fuji is so named for its abstract suggestion of snow above and a landmass below, bringing to mind the famous mountain. The tea bowl shows the integration of forms drawn from nature with a man-made object. This type of Japanese ceramics, known as **raku**, is an example of wares used in the tea ceremony. Each piece has its own irregular **texture** and pattern, yet is simple, to encourage participants in the ceremony to notice small details. Users of the tea bowl consider how it was made from Earthly elements, admire the abstract design, and enjoy the way the object feels in their hands. By doing so, they train themselves to slow down and take note of every moment in their lives.

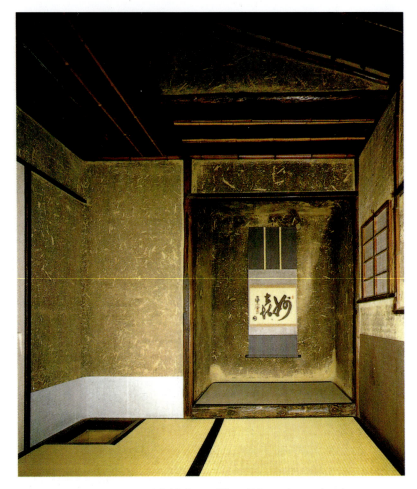

3.3.18 Sen no Rikyu, Taian teahouse, interior, *c.* 1582. Myoki-an Temple, Kyoto, Japan

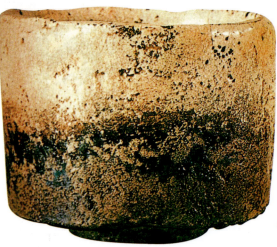

3.3.19 Hon'ami Koetsu, Tea bowl (called Mount Fuji), Edo period, early 17th century. Raku ware, 3⅜" high. Sakai Collection, Tokyo, Japan

Raku: hand-made and fired ceramic, made for a tea ceremony
Texture: the surface quality of a work, for example fine/coarse, detailed/lacking in detail
Continuous narrative: when different parts of a story are shown within the same visual space

Storytelling

One of the oldest examples of storytelling in Japanese art appears on a wooden shrine in the Buddhist Horyu-ji Temple in Nara (**3.3.20**). One side of the shrine is painted with a jataka (a story from the life of Buddha) known as *The Hungry Tigress*. The painting is a **continuous narrative**, meaning that it shows multiple scenes of a story in one pictorial space. In this story, Buddha sacrificed his own body to save a starving tigress and her cubs. Buddha is shown first at the top of a cliff carefully hanging his clothes from a tree, his slender body reflecting the curves of the natural elements that surround him. He then jumps off the cliff, and is finally devoured by the tigers in the valley below.

The *Tale of Genji* is one of the great works of Japanese literature. Written in the eleventh century by Murasaki Shikibu, a noblewoman at the court of the emperor at Heian-kyo (modern-day Kyoto), it tells of the love affairs of Prince Genji. The chapters are filled with undercurrents of sadness, reflecting the Buddhist view that Earthly happiness is fleeting, and that there will always be consequences of our actions. Some of the earliest surviving Japanese painting illustrates the *Tale of Genji*, including the scroll section shown in **3.3.21**.

The scroll is designed so that different portions of the tale are revealed as the scroll is unrolled from right to left. In this scene we

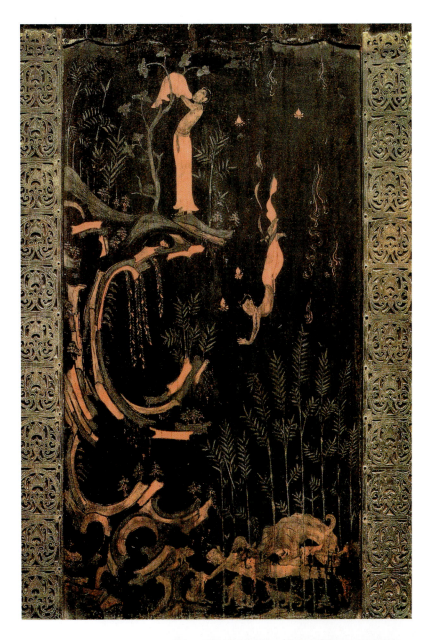

3.3.20 (above) *The Hungry Tigress*, panel from the Tamamushi Shrine, Horyu-ji Temple, Nara, Asuka period, *c.* 650. Lacquer on wood, shrine 7'7¾" high. Horyu-ji Treasure House, Japan

3.3.21 (right) Scene from the *Tale of Genji*. Heian period, first half of 12th century. Hand scroll, ink and color on paper, 8⅝ × 18⅞". Tokugawa Art Museum, Nogoya, Japan

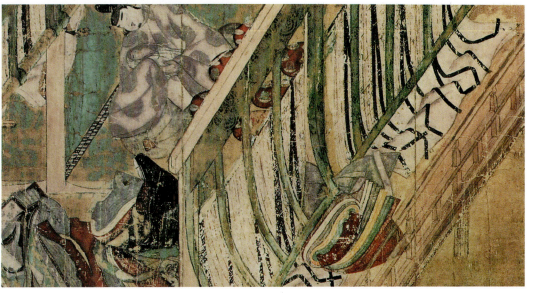

see the prince from a so-called "blown-off roof" perspective, in which we as viewers peer, almost voyeuristically, into the private space of the palace. The flat figures and use of strong **diagonal** lines to guide the viewer through the scene are both qualities frequently used in Japanese painting. The strict diagonal and vertical lines not only powerfully divide the space within the scene, but also create a sense of drama and tension.

This scene specifically shows Genji at the naming ceremony for his first son. Unbeknownst to anyone but Genji and his wife, however, the baby he holds is actually his father's son, and Genji is being forced to raise the child as his own. The claustrophobic positioning of Genji, trapped between two rows of curtains and crushed against the top edge of the page, reflects the trapped feeling of the character in the story. In the tale, he is being punished for his past deeds because he had an affair with one of his father's wives.

Ukiyo-e

Ukiyo, a Japanese word that means "floating world," is an idea that grows out of the Buddhist thought that life is fleeting and that each moment should be enjoyed. *Ukiyo-e*, or "pictures of the floating world," were **woodblock** prints that when first produced in the seventeenth century showed characters and scenes from the entertainment districts of Edo, modern Tokyo. The subject matter therefore included brothels, geisha, and theater actors; later ukiyo-e included landscapes and images of different classes of women. The Japanese printmaker Kitagawa Utamaro (1753–1806) specialized in *bijinga*, or images of beautiful women (**3.3.22**). Ukiyo-e artists chose woodblock printing because it made possible the mass production of inexpensive images for a popular market. From the 1860s onward, ukiyo-e prints also became extremely popular imports in Europe and America (see *Japonisme*: The Influence of Ukiyo-e on Western Artists). Katsushika Hokusai's series *Thirty-Six Views of Mount Fuji* remains a popular ukiyo-e series (see Gateway Box: Hokusai, **3.3.14**, p. 423).

Diagonal: a line that runs obliquely, rather than horizontally or vertically
Woodblock: a relief print process where the image is carved into a block of wood
Impressionism: late nineteenth-century painting style conveying the impression of the effects of light

Composition: the overall design or organization of a work
Background: the part of a work depicted as behind the main figures
Space: the space between identifiable points or planes

Modeling: the representation of three-dimensional objects in two dimensions so that they appear solid
Volume: the space filled or enclosed by a three-dimensional figure or object
Value: the lightness or darkness of a plane or area

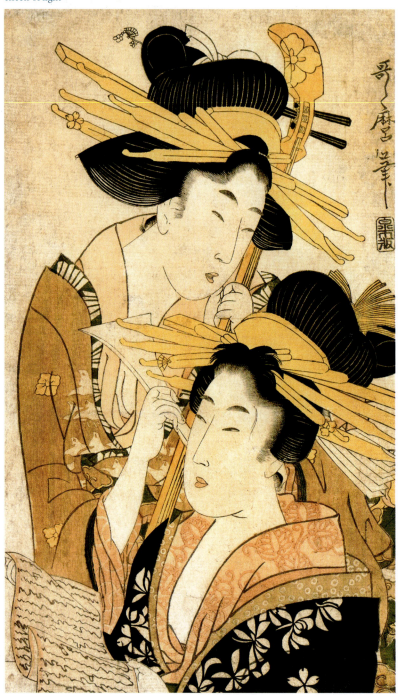

3.3.22 Kitagawa Utamaro, *Two Courtesans*, second half of 18th century. Woodblock print, 12⅝ × 7½". Victoria and Albert Museum, London, England

Japonisme: The Influence of Ukiyo-e on Western Artists

Japonisme is a term used to describe the way in which the work of Japanese artists influenced many artists in Europe. Japanese prints often depicted space, cropped scenes, and flattened objects through the use of line rather than shadows. After studying Japanese prints, such **Impressionist** painters as Claude Monet, Camille Pissarro, and Edgar Degas began to incorporate slanted viewpoints, bright colors, and busy patterns into their work. Likewise, Henri de Toulouse-Lautrec made prints that were influenced by Japanese techniques, while Édouard Manet and Vincent van Gogh included copies of Japanese prints in their paintings.

The American painter Mary Cassatt (1844–1926) lived most of her life in France and exhibited with the Impressionists. After seeing more than a hundred of the Japanese printmaker Kitagawa Utamaro's prints exhibited in Paris in 1890, Cassatt wrote to friends raving about him; later, she began creating prints very much in the style of Utamaro. Cassatt herself had always focused on the daily lives of women in her paintings. A comparison between one of Utamaro's prints (see **3.3.22** opposite) and a painting by Cassatt (**3.3.23**), made three years after she had seen the Japanese artist's work in Paris, highlights the techniques Cassatt emulated.

The **composition** of the two scenes is very similar. Each has a form that creates a strong diagonal line from the upper right to the lower left. The musical instrument is gently being played by the beautiful lady in the **background** of Utamaro's print, while the foot of the child in Cassatt's painting is gently stroked by her mother's hand. The mother's right arm and that of the musician are both, in contrast to the objects they hold, strictly vertical.

Both artists use bold lines to create a flattening of **space** and absence of **modeling**. In Utamaro's print, lines in the ladies' dresses suggest folds, but also make the women appear as two-dimensional as the writing on the paper one of them holds. Cassatt creates a similar effect with the striped lines on the

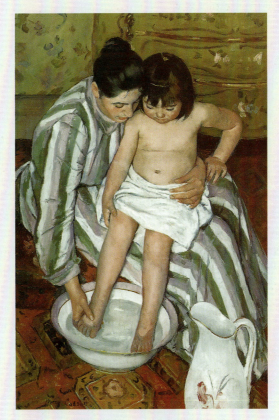

3.3.23 Mary Cassatt, *The Child's Bath*, 1893. Oil on canvas, 39½ × 26". Art Institute of Chicago, Illinois

mother's dress, which lengthen the figure but give her body less **volume** than the child she holds. The child, in contrast, has softer outlines and a range of **values** on her skin.

The background of Utamaro's print is mostly empty, creating an absence of space behind the ladies apart from some twisting flowers on one of the robes, and crowded calligraphy in a music book. Cassatt fills her background space, but her busy floral patterns echo the flowers in the Japanese work.

Lastly, Japanese prints often look at their subject from multiple vantage points. Utamaro's ladies are being viewed from up close and at the same height, but the bottom of the rearmost lady's dress, the music, and parts of the instrument are seen from above. Similarly, in Cassatt's painting, the scene is depicted from various vantage points. For example, the viewer looks at the child's torso, the dresser in the background, and at the pitcher in the lower right corner from directly in front at the same height. Yet, simultaneously, the bowl of water and the rug are viewed from above.

Southeast Asia: Cambodia

Covering more than 500 acres (three-quarters of a square mile, or some 380 football fields), the largest religious monument in the world is in Cambodia, Southeast Asia (**3.3.24**). Angkor Wat was created in the twelfth century by Suryavarman II, ruler of the Khmer empire. The temple complex was built to worship the Hindu god Vishnu, believed to be the preserver of the universe who restores the balance of good and evil during difficult times, and as a burial site for the king. Therefore, the temple is oriented toward the west where the sun sets (representing the end of life). Angkor Wat was designed as a re-creation of the heavens on Earth: the site is tiered, with the center being the highest point. In the center is a temple mount, in which five towers represent Mount Meru, in Hindu belief the home of the gods. Each of the towers resembles a lotus flower, a plant often associated with Vishnu. The massive moat that surrounds this complex symbolizes the ocean, encompassing the water-floating lotus flowers. Emanating from the temple mount is a richly modeled complex built of sandstone and covered with **bas-reliefs**.

The bas-reliefs that adorn Angkor Wat show military and religious scenes, all designed to convey Suryavarman's power. *Vishnu Churning the Ocean of Milk*, which is 161 ft. long, depicts the story of the creation of a potion for reinvigorating the life force (**3.3.25**). Vishnu is in the center, with two arms holding weapons (a sword and disk). The gods, on the right, and the demons, on the left, struggle against one another as they each pull on one side of a serpent wrapped around the mountain that is behind Vishnu. Vishnu utilizes the tortoise shell on his back to help hold up the mountain as it churns. The movement of the serpent causes the mountain to move and release Amrita, the magical potion, or elixir, of eternal life, to rise from the depths of the ocean. In the original story that inspired the bas-reliefs, this is how Vishnu and the gods trick the demons into helping them release the powerful elixir, which transforms the ocean into milk. Milk, of course, gives nutrients and life to newborns. In fact the process of churning milk into buttermilk is very similar to the scene shown here.

Angkor Wat is an example of the way in which, commonly throughout Asia, different religions have, over time, been expressed

Bas-relief: a sculpture carved with very little depth

3.3.24 Angkor Wat, Siem Reap, Cambodia

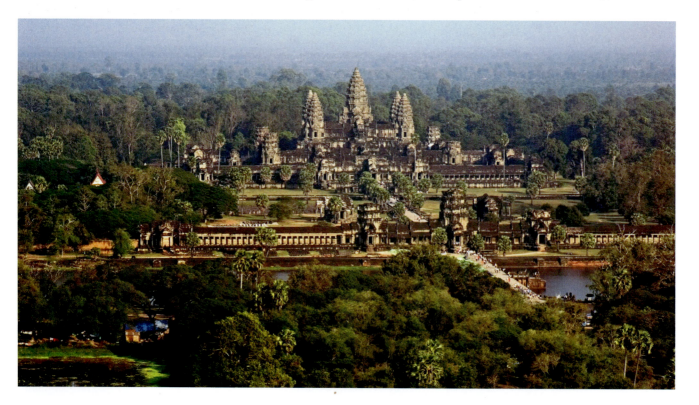

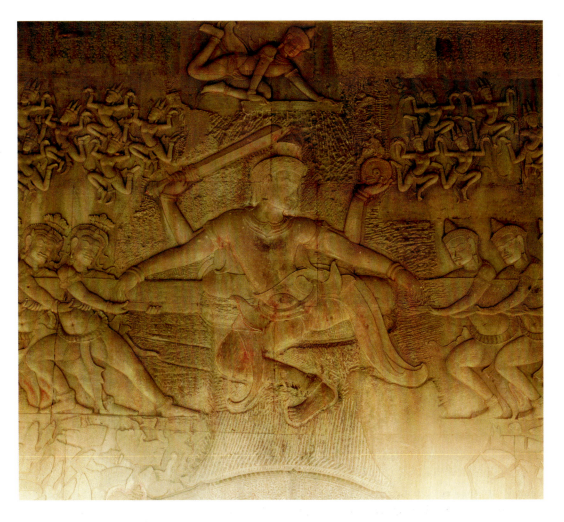

3.3.25 *Vishnu Churning the Ocean of Milk*, relief sculpture, Angkor Wat, Siem Reap, Cambodia

and blended in architectural sites: what is often described as their syncretic nature. Although Angkor Wat was originally built under Hindu rule, Cambodia has been primarily Buddhist since 1200. The lotus-shaped towers hold a different symbolic meaning for Buddhists, for whom the lotus flower represents strength and beauty in the face of adversity, since it must grow through the muck of the earth in order to bloom into a work of beauty. Similarly, Buddhists experience difficulties and struggles in life in order to gain Enlightenment. During the fourteenth century, because of the many Buddhist pilgrims who visited Angkor, statues of Buddha were added to the artworks of Vishnu there.

Discussion Questions

1. In what ways are religion and philosophy reflected in artworks from Asia? Cite examples from India, China, and Japan.

2. Humankind's relationship with nature is a strong element in many artworks from Asia. Consider the artist's interpretation of nature in three artworks introduced in this chapter.

3. Chinese scroll paintings are a unique kind of artwork. Discuss the format of a scroll, how it is viewed, and the skills needed by the artist. How do these characteristics of scroll paintings differ from other kinds of painting you have studied?

4. Religious and political leaders often influence the kinds and quantities of artworks made in a certain time or culture. Cite two examples in which a ruler or leader impacted the art of Asia. What role did he or she play?

Images Related to 3.3:
Art of India, China, Japan, and Southeast Asia

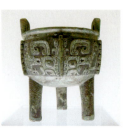

1.6.13 *Liu Ding* (ritual container), China, *c.* 1600–*c.* 1050 BCE, p. 140

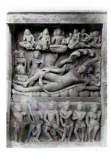

1.6.9 *Vishnu Dreaming the Universe*, India, *c.* 450–500 CE, p.137

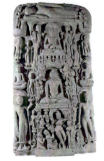

4.2.3 Life of Buddha, stela, Gupta period, India, *c.* 475 CE, p. 577

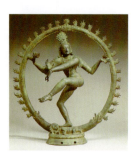

4.3.11 *Shiva Nataraja*, Chola period, India, 11th century, p. 594

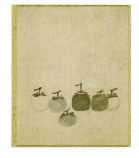

1.6.14 Muqi, *Six Persimmons*, *c.* 1250, p. 141

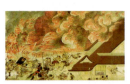

4.7.8 *Night Attack on the Sanjo Palace*, from *Heiji Monogatari*, Japan, late 13th century, p. 641

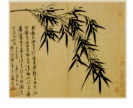

2.1.17 Wu Zhen, Leaf from an album of bamboo drawings, 1350, p. 209

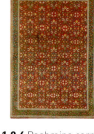

2.6.5 Porcelain flask, Ming Dynasty, China, 1425–35, p. 295

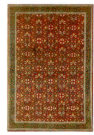

1.8.8 *The Emperor Babur Overseeing His Gardeners*, India, *c.* 1590, p. 162

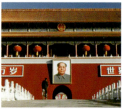

1.9.4 Pashmina carpet, northern India, 2nd half of 17th century, p. 169

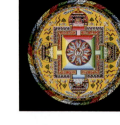

1.9.3 Huqqa base, India, last quarter of the 17th century, p. 168

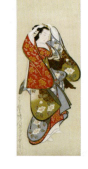

4.9.7 Kaigetsudo Dohan, *Beautiful Woman*, 18th century, p. 663

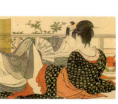

2.3.3 Kitagawa Utamaro, *Lovers in an Upstairs Room*, 1788, p. 234

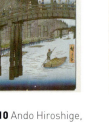

1.8.10 Ando Hiroshige, "Riverside Bamboo Market, Kyōbashi", 1857, p. 164

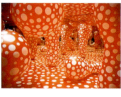

4.6.11 Mao Zedong's portrait, Tiananmen, Beijing, China, p. 632

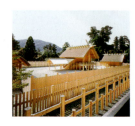

1.6.19 Amitayus Mandala, Drepung Loseling Monastery, Tibet, p. 144

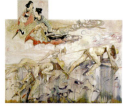

4.2.15 Ise Jingu (shrine), Japan, 4th century, rebuilt 1993, p. 585

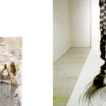

2.2.12 Hung Liu, *Interregnum*, 2002, p. 223

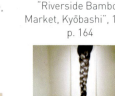

2.1.12 Zhang Chun Hong, *Life Strands*, 2004, p. 205

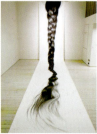

4.4.18 Yayoi Kusama, *Dots Obsession*, 2009, p. 609

432 HISTORY AND CONTEXT

3.4

Art of the Americas

When's the Beginning?

We can never be sure when the first human arrived in the Americas, but scholars believe that there were no humans there at all until 15,000 to 18,000 years ago, when groups of people crossed a land bridge that linked Asia to North America. Expertly made mammoth-bone spear points, discovered on a farm in Clovis, New Mexico, in 1929, are dated to 11,500 years ago. Similar Clovis points, as they are called, have been found all over North America, indicating that the continent was populated with people using the same type of hunting technologies. More recent discoveries in Chile (dating perhaps to 12,500 years ago), Oregon (14,300 years ago), and Virginia (possibly 15,000 years ago) have convinced many scholars that the Americas were inhabited long before the Clovis spear points were made.

We can trace the early civilizations of South America, ancient Mexico and Central America (Mesoamerica), and North America through their art and architecture. Some descendants of these people still live in the Americas, speaking their own languages, continuing ancient cultural practices, and following artistic traditions hundreds of years old. The arrival of Europeans from the fifteenth century onward drastically altered the ways of life of the native peoples. European settlers destroyed many great cities and magnificent works of art, especially those made of gold and silver, which they melted down for their monetary value. Enough remains, however, to tell us much about how people lived

in the Americas. Although they were spread over the two continents and their cultures were enormously varied, these people shared some common interests. Their art reflects the ways in which their societies were organized; their cultural and spiritual beliefs; and their connections with nature.

As is the case when looking at all prehistoric and ancient art, understanding the art of the ancient Americas requires the careful interpretation of a variety of clues. In addition to the artwork itself, scholars use scientific testing and written accounts to piece together the story of ancient American artifacts. Indigenous accounts include oral histories, handwritten accounts with painted pictures and glyphs in bark books, and inscriptions on

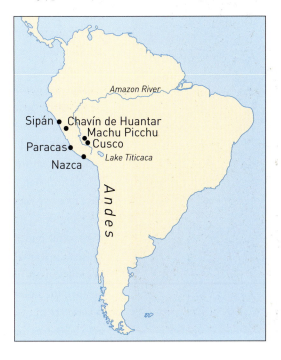

3.4.1 Map showing sites of ancient South America

3.4.2a Raimondi Stela, Chavín de Huantar, 7th century BCE. Granite, 6'5 x 2'5". Museo Nacional de Arquelogía Anthropologia e Historia del Perú, Lima, Peru

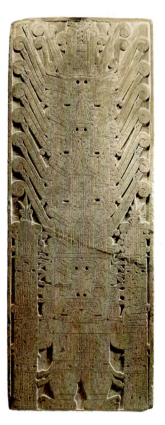

stone monuments that have survived for many generations. The intricate writing of the Maya has been deciphered and has provided vast amounts of information about their beliefs and the ways they lived their lives. European explorers wrote firsthand accounts, translated indigenous writing, and continued to interpret the art and culture well after the conquest.

South America

From about 3000 BCE, the region around the Andes Mountains was home to a host of cultures, including the Chavín, Paracas, Nazca, Moche, Tiwanaku, and Inca. The objects created by Andean artists frequently reflected the local environment and resources, with animals, plants, and people represented, often in a **stylized** form. Beliefs about the relationship between humans and the parallel supernatural realm were communicated both in myths about the origin of the world and in the images that artists created.

The Chavín and the Paracas

The Chavín culture is one of the oldest in South America. The Chavín established a pilgrimage center in Chavín de Huantar, Peru, around 900 BCE. This site is marked by remarkable temples and elaborate stone monuments.

The Raimondi Stela (**3.4.2a**) contains a complex depiction of a deity with both human and animal attributes. (The carving on the stone surface is so delicate that the design is easier to see in drawings; see **3.4.2b and 3.4.2c**.) At the bottom of the **stela** is a creature with eagle talons for feet. The figure's hands hold two staffs, which have faces, snakes, swirls, and vegetation tangling along their surfaces. A headdress, with scroll-ended projections, takes up more than half of the composition. Its eyes are looking up, like a stalking jaguar. When we turn the stela upside down, though, the second creature seems to descend from above; its eyes look down over a crocodile

snout with an additional face above it with thin eyes, a scroll nose, and fanged smile. What was formerly the headdress repeats the crocodile face menacingly. Such designs, with lines that describe more than one object at the same time, possess what is known as **contour rivalry**. They allow a figure to serve a dual purpose and to project multiple readings.

The Chavín culture's principal deity, known as the Staff God, has a close connection to nature, agriculture, and fertility, as does the crocodile. In Chavín culture generally and in this artwork in particular, animals feature prominently and are strongly associated with all three realms of the

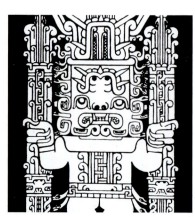

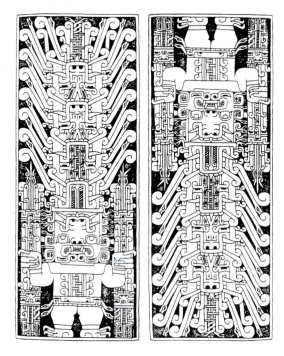

3.4.2b and **3.4.2c** Drawings of details from the Raimondi Stela

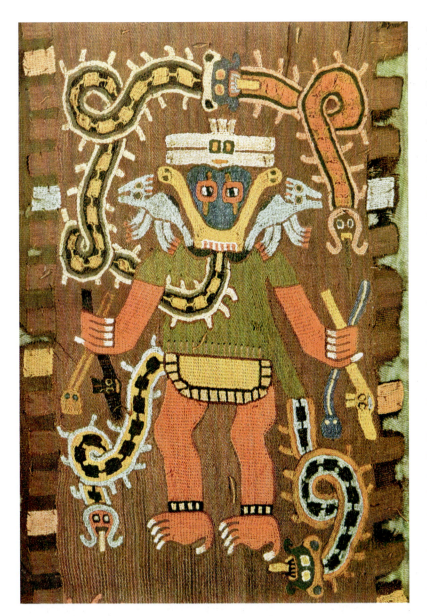

developed by the Chavín culture. A Paracas textile (**3.4.3**) is a detail from a **mantle**, a cape-like garment often made by the Paracas people for burial purposes. Intricately **embroidered** stitches form each figure; their repetition creates a pattern. Outlines merge into body parts, and costumes resemble animals (in **3.4.3**, a kind of mythical being with deer on its shoulders—a shaman with its animal self as a disguise). Plant forms and animals appear frequently in Paracas imagery, and deer shown here represent revered creatures associated with the hunt.

The Moche

Visually and conceptually intricate designs were also common for the Moche culture of northern Peru. Moche art, made from about 200 BCE to 600 CE, tells us much about their society. The earspool (a large-gauge ornament worn through the earlobe) in **3.4.4** was found in a royal tomb at Sipán. It shows a figure dressed almost exactly like the man found buried in the tomb, who is believed to be a warrior-priest. Pictured standing next to him on the earspool (and also lying next to him in the tomb) are two attendants dressed for battle. The detailed depiction includes replica turquoise-and-gold earspools, a war-club and shield, a necklace of owls' heads, and a crescent-shaped helmet. Although gold was not considered as valuable as textiles in the ancient Andes, its symbolic associations with the sun's energy and power made it nonetheless very important.

3.4.3 (above) Paracas textile, embroidered with mythological figure, 3rd century BCE. Wool embroidery. Museo Arqueología, Lima, Peru

3.4.4 (right) Earspool, c. 300 CE. Gold, turquoise, quartz, and shell, 5" diameter. Royal Tombs of Sipán Museum, Sipán, Peru

cosmos: snakes with the earth, crocodiles, or caymans, with the watery underworld, and birds with the celestial realm of the sky.

Andean textile design is closely related to carved stone **relief** sculpture, such as the Raimondi Stela. They both use contour rivalry to create complex patterns that encourage multiple interpretations. Some of the most spectacular textiles were made by the Paracas people, who lived on the coast of Peru from about 600 to 200 BCE. The dry conditions of their **necropolis** have preserved a great number of these textiles. They show a continuation of the style (single lines describing more than one thing and readable in more than one direction) and content (natural life and mythical beings)

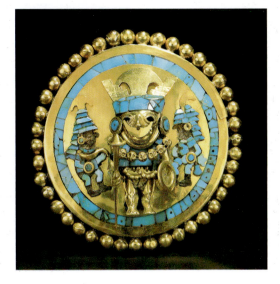

The Inca

The Inca, like the Moche metalworkers who integrated into their designs the world they saw around them, were inspired by nature. The Inca culture may have existed as early as 800 CE. It became an empire when the powerful Inca ruler Pachacuti centralized the government. By the early 1500s a series of rulers had increased the area of land under their control until it covered more than 3,000 miles of the western coast of South America, thus becoming the largest empire in pre-Columbian America. Pachacuti selected a ridge high on a mountaintop in Peru for Machu Picchu, his private estate and religious retreat (**3.4.5**). The location, on what is now known as the Inca trail, offered privacy and protection as well as breathtaking views; the site is now one of the world's most popular tourist destinations. The condor, a majestic bird of prey, is depicted throughout the site, which includes a building known as the Condor Temple, and a stone carved in the shape of a curved beak. The walls, terraces, platforms, and buildings are constructed of huge stones precisely stacked and fitted together without mortar. Machu Picchu was abandoned around 1527, probably after a devastating smallpox epidemic caused by contact with Europeans. Because of its elevated location, the site was not excavated until 1911, when Yale archaeologist Hiram Bingham led an expedition to the Inca trail. After more than 100 years in the collection of Yale University, the artifacts gathered by Bingham and his crew with the approval of the Peruvian government were returned to Peru from 2011 to 2012. When collected artifacts are returned to indigenous cultures (a process known as repatriation), the focus is usually on legal rights. This case is different: with the return of these items, the focus has been on stewardship (careful and responsible management), preservation, research, and exhibition of the materials, rather than ownership.

3.4.5 Machu Picchu, 1450–1530, Peru

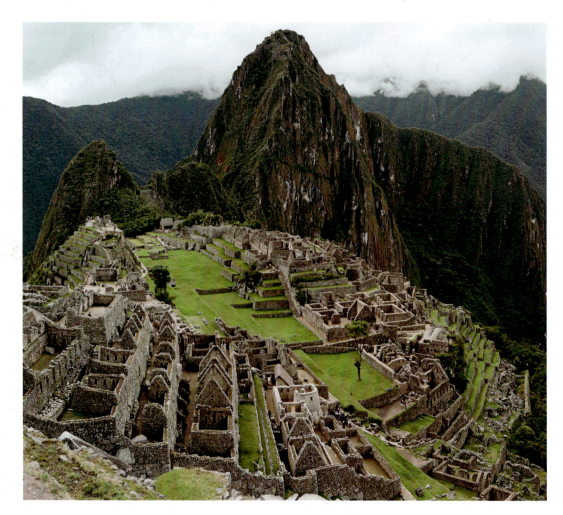

The Importance of Wool

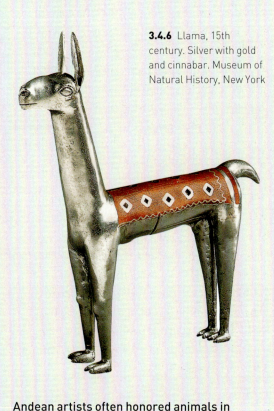

3.4.6 Llama, 15th century. Silver with gold and cinnabar. Museum of Natural History, New York

such, but through the complexity and variety of designs, they stand for the conquest of all possible ethnicities. The tunic refers to an important Inca creation myth, when the great god Viracocha sent out all the different peoples with their ethnic patterns painted on their bodies.

In the Andes, textiles were made exclusively by women. Weaving was such a sacred art that it had its own god, Spider Woman, who featured prominently in the Inca creation story. Textiles were not only considered sacred, but were also more valuable than gold or silver. This scale of values was not shared by the Spaniards who conquered Peru in the sixteenth century: they demanded gold and silver from the Inca and melted down fine works of art to ship the precious metals home to Spain.

3.4.7 Tunic, c. 1500. Interlocked tapestry of cotton and wool, 35⅞ × 30⅛". Dumbarton Oaks Research Library and Collections, Washington, D.C.

Andean artists often honored animals in their artworks. Here, a small silver llama figurine (**3.4.6**) seems to wear on its back a red blanket—made of inlaid cinnabar edged with gold. This sculpture was probably a burial offering and was wrapped, along with the body, in actual textiles. It indicates the crucial role the llama played in supplying wool for weaving. Cloth not only served the practical function of warmth and protection, but also identified the wearer's social status as part of a particular group. For instance, the clothing worn by an unmarried woman would easily distinguish her from a married woman in her own group, as well as from members of another social group.

The checkerboard tunic in **3.4.7** was worn by an Inca ruler. Its square designs contain a number of patterns that together indicate the high status and importance of the person who wore it. The little checkerboard designs would have decorated tunics worn by warriors serving the ruler; similarly, the diagonal lines and dots indicate the clothing of administrators. The other patterns do not directly represent specific roles or people as

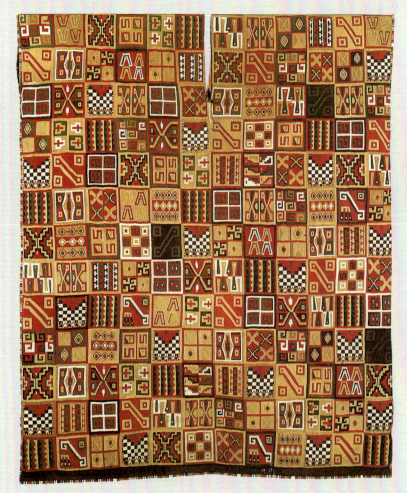

Mesoamerica

"Mesoamerica" is the name given by archaeologists to the area occupied by modern-day Mexico and Central America. The many different peoples and cultures that inhabited the region founded powerful city-states and produced diverse artworks. Skilled astronomers and mathematicians, Mesoamericans developed an accurate calendar that they used to calculate the dates of important ceremonies and rituals and to predict astronomical events. They shared similar religious beliefs and many cultural traditions, including a ball game played with a hard rubber ball (see **3.4.13**, p. 441).

The art and architecture of the Olmecs (**3.4.9**, p. 439), who lived on the fertile lowlands of Mexico's Gulf Coast from *c.* 1200 to 400 BCE, influenced later Mesoamerican people, for example the inhabitants of the city of Teotihuacan, the Maya, and the Aztecs. The Olmecs used images to record information, a tradition also common amongst other people of Mesoamerica. Eventually the Olmecs, and later the Teotihuacanos, used images as a form of writing, although scholars have not yet been able to interpret their scripts. The Maya also developed a system of writing, called **hieroglyphs**, much of which can now be read. Some Aztec **pictographs**, too, can be deciphered.

Teotihuacan

The main components of the Olmec site at La Venta are a pyramid and a plaza, a layout that also features, on a much larger scale, at Teotihuacan, in the Central Highlands of Mexico about 30 miles from modern-day Mexico City. Teotihuacan was one of the largest cities in the world at the time. Around 500 CE, at the peak of its power, it had 600 pyramids and 2,000 apartment compounds (**3.4.10a** and **3.4.10b**).

3.4.8 Map of Mesoamerica

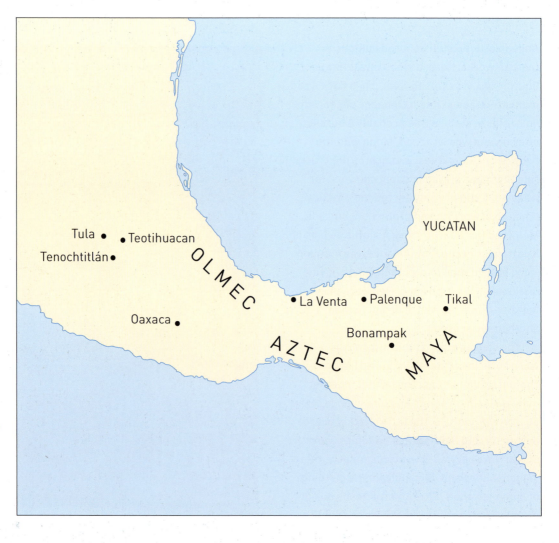

Hieroglyph: written language involving sacred characters that may be pictures as well as letters
Pictograph: picture used as a symbol in writing

Gateway to Art: Colossal Olmec Heads
The Discovery of Monumental Portraits at La Venta

Today we often see Olmec art in modern museums, but centuries ago these massive monuments were displayed in the ceremonial centers of Olmec cities. They were then forgotten for hundreds of years as they lay buried in remote locations. David Grove, an archaeologist and an expert on the Olmec, recounts the discovery in 1940 of four Olmec heads and other Olmec wonders at La Venta by the archaeologists Matthew and Marion Stirling:

It had taken the Stirlings five days to reach La Venta, and they would spend a total of ten days exploring the site . . . However, even after reaching the site's ruins, the stone monuments were not immediately visible to them.

The primary purpose of their visit was to locate, study, and photograph the eight stone monuments that had been reported by the scholars Frans Blom and Oliver La Farge in 1925. The narrow four-mile-long island was heavily forested . . . To assist them they recruited seven local men [who] were happy to show Matt and Marion the stones they knew of—if they could find them again . . .

Eventually, one of the workers recalled seeing some stones in another area of the forest . . . As Stirling relates the tale, the worker "cut his way through the dense growth for no more than fifty yards when we came to a large hemispherical stone almost completely concealed by vines and growth. I looked at it closely. Lo and behold, here was Blom's colossal head that we had almost given up hope of locating! . . . Less than twenty yards away a large stela lay on its back. This I immediately recognized as Blom's Stela 2.

"While this work was going on, a small boy who happened to be standing by remarked that he had seen some stones . . . I went with him to a point in the forest about a half mile away, and one after another he showed me three round projecting stones in a line about thirty yards apart." When excavated, those stones turned out to be three more colossal stone heads! They were positioned about 100 yards north of the pyramid, and occurred in an east–west row (3.4.9). The new discoveries received the labels Heads 2, 3, and 4.

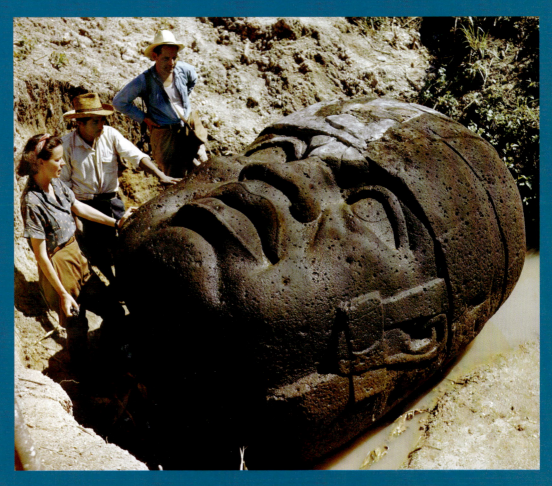

3.4.9 With the help of local villagers, the archaeologists Matthew Stirling and his wife, Marion, discovered this 8-foot-tall colossal head (Monument 1) in San Lorenzo in the state of Veracruz, Mexico, in 1945, a few years after their discoveries in La Venta

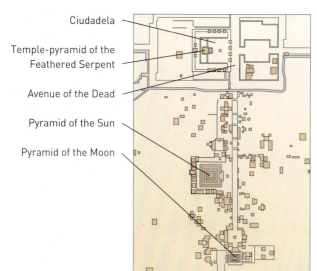

Ciudadela

Temple-pyramid of the
Feathered Serpent

Avenue of the Dead

Pyramid of the Sun

Pyramid of the Moon

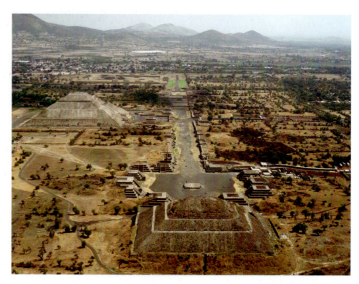

3.4.10a and **3.4.10b** Plan and aerial view (from Pyramid of the Moon) of the ceremonial center, Teotihuacan, Mexico

A wide street, the Avenue of the Dead, runs north–south and is about 3 miles long. At its northern end lies the Pyramid of the Moon. The Pyramid of the Sun lies on its east and the Temple of the Feathered Serpent is located to the south (**3.4.10a** and **3.4.10b**).

The Pyramid of the Sun, Teotihuacan's largest structure, is a **stepped pyramid** (**3.4.11**). Covering 13 acres, its base is about 700 ft. across on each side; it is 210 ft. tall. The location of the Pyramid of the Sun was of utmost importance. It faced west—toward the setting sun and the

Avenue of the Dead—and was built on top of a cave and a spring. Caves had religious significance throughout Mesoamerica because they were thought to connect the world of humans with the world of the gods. The Aztecs, who established a powerful empire in central Mexico about 800 years after Teotihuacan was abandoned, admired the cultural achievement of the Teotihuacanos. In fact, the name Teotihuacan is Aztec for "The Place of the Gods," and the Pyramid of the Sun was a place of pilgrimage for the Aztecs.

3.4.11 Pyramid of the Sun, *c.* 225 CE, Teotihuacan, Mexico

Stepped pyramid: a pyramid consisting of several rectangular structures placed on top of one another

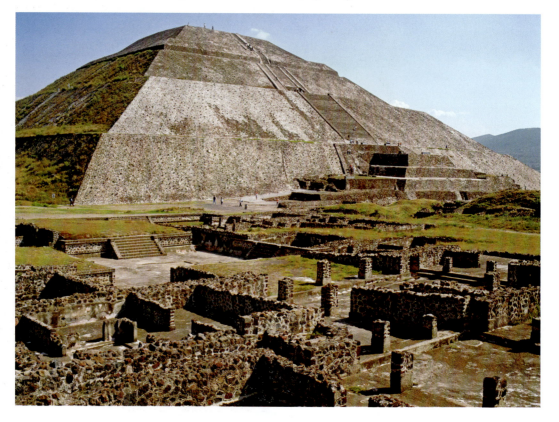

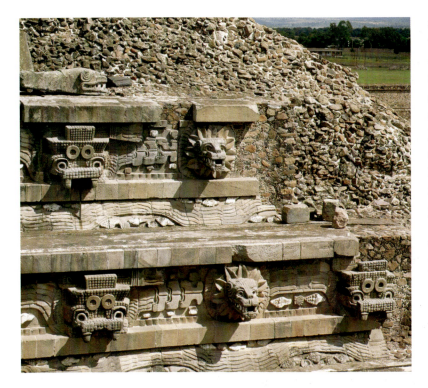

3.4.12 Architectural sculpture with serpent heads and masks on the Temple of Quetzalcoatl at Teotihuacan, Mexico (also known as the Temple of the Feathered Serpent)

The Temple of the Feathered Serpent at Teotihuacan is located in an enclosed compound. The plaza next to it is below ground level, to symbolize the underworld. Sculpted heads on the temple depict serpents with feathers and jaguar features alongside square heads with goggle eyes and fang-like teeth (**3.4.12**). To the Aztecs, these sculptures looked like images of their gods Quetzalcoatl, the feathered serpent, and Tlaloc, the goggle-eyed rain god. These figures symbolized warfare and fertility, or perhaps cycles of wet and dry seasons.

The Maya

The dates for Maya civilization are from about 2000 BCE to 1500 CE. At the peak of the Maya empire, from about 300 to 900 CE, there were Maya centers in Mexico, Guatemala, Belize, Honduras, and El Salvador. By 900 most of them had faded away, but the civilization continued to exist in isolated locations. Surviving Spanish colonization, the Maya continue to speak their own language and now number an estimated seven million.

Mythology and cosmology and their associated rituals were important to Maya society. The ballgame was a common ritual event in Mesoamerica and could also be played for

sport, gambling, or as a gladiatorial contest to the death (**3.4.13**). The rubber ball, magnified on the cylindrical vessel shown here, was about 8 in. in diameter. The game was played on a court; the objective was to get the ball through a ring or into a goal area without using one's hands. The rings were very high off the ground and virtually impossible to get the ball through. Players wore protective gear, including yokes, fitted round the waist to strike the ball and protect the body. They used *hachas* or *palmas* (thin flat stones) to guide and deflect the ball. The elaborate quality of the yokes and helmet-like headdresses of the players on the vessel in **3.4.13** indicate that this was a ceremonial game played for the purposes of ritual.

Mesoamerican ballgames often served as the arena for the final stages of warfare in which captured enemies met their fate. The murals at the Maya city of Bonampak in southern Mexico show the victory of the Lord of Bonampak, Chaan Muan, in 790 CE, and the treatment of his defeated opponents. The wall illustrated in **3.4.14** (see p. 442) shows the ritual presentation of captives on the steps of a temple. Chaan Muan is shown at the center of the composition, wearing a headdress with long green feathers; his ministers and aides stand beside him, well armed and in full regalia. The prisoners have been stripped of their own clothing and

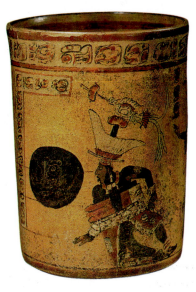

3.4.13 Cylindrical vessel with ritual ballgame scene, *c.* 700–850. Ceramic, 6¼ × 4″. Dallas Museum of Art, Texas

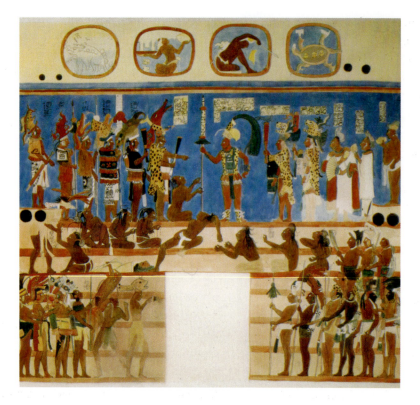

3.4.14 Bonampak mural, copy of fresco from Room 2, original 8th century. Peabody Museum, Harvard University, Cambridge, Massachusetts

weapons, and are naked and vulnerable. They have been tortured, perhaps starved, and likely made to play a fixed and fatal ballgame in which the losers are eventually executed. The man sprawled out at the ruler's feet has an incision in his side, indicating that he is already dead. To the left of this figure are several prisoners with blood dripping from their fingers, their fingernails recently ripped out. The Maya considered blood on the steps a sign of their triumph and a sacrifice to please the gods, and they wanted as much of it on the building as could be spilled.

The Aztecs

The Aztecs formed a powerful empire in Mesoamerica, which they dominated at approximately the same time the Inca were in power in South America (from 1400 until Spanish occupation in the 1520s and 1530s). At its peak, the empire covered Central Mexico, Guatemala, El Salvador, and Honduras; the Aztecs were conquered by Cortés in 1524.

In a manner similar to the Olmec, Teotihuacan, and Maya societies before them, the Aztecs placed pyramid structures in the center of their cities, emphasizing their importance as the site of rituals. Amongst the

most notorious of these rituals was the practice of sacrificing a person by extracting from the body his or her still-beating heart (**3.4.15**). Sacrifices to the gods were performed at specific times of the year, such as planting season, and at certain points in the ceremonial calendar, for example the end of a 52-year cycle. Important events, such as the dedication of a new temple, might also be the occasion for sacrifices. Capturing victims for this purpose was one of the major goals of warfare, another being to

3.4.15 A human sacrifice, fol. 70r of the *Codex Magliabechiano*, 16th century. European paper, 6½ × 8⅞″. Biblioteca Nazionale Centrale, Florence, Italy

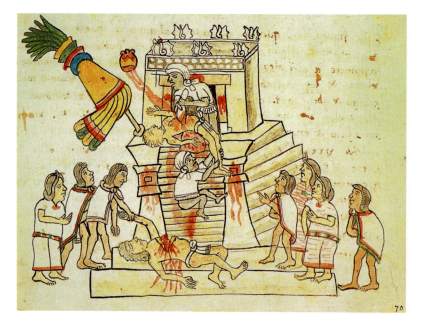

expand the empire. People sometimes sacrificed members of their own community. In some cases it was considered an honor to die by the sacrificial blade; other individuals were selected because they had been born on an "unlucky" day.

The Aztecs based some of their sacrifice rituals on the story of their origins, which they traced to a mythical place called "Aztlan." The Aztecs believed that their ancestors had journeyed from Aztlan to their future capital at Tenochtitlán (modern Mexico City). During their journey they met Coatlicue, or "Serpent Skirt," the guardian at Serpent Mountain. Coatlicue had been impregnated by a ball of feathers that fell from the sky; her son Huitzilopochtli, the god of war, was miraculously born fully armed. When Coatlicue's other children attempted to murder their dishonored mother, Huitzilopochtli defended her by attacking his sister Coyolxauhqui, or "She of the Golden Bells." Coyolxauhqui's dismembered body was rolled in pieces down Serpent Mountain.

The events of Huitzilopochtli's birth are the source for many Aztec artworks, including a colossal sculpture of Coatlicue (**3.4.16**). A

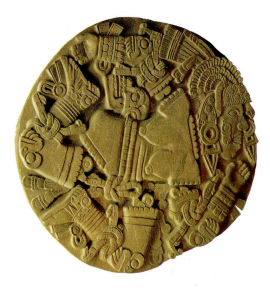

3.4.17 *The Dismemberment of Coyolxauhqui, Goddess of the Moon*, late postclassic. Stone, 9′10⅛″ diameter. Museo del Templo Mayor, Mexico City

ferocious face, created by the profiles of two facing serpent heads, enhances her imposing presence. She also has a necklace made of human hearts and hands, with a skull pendant. Coatlicue was the Mother Goddess, associated with the Earth, fertility, and transformation, who was seen as both creator and destroyer.

Coyolxauhqui's dismemberment was commemorated on a stone disk (**3.4.17**) placed at the base of an early temple built on the site of the Great Temple of the Aztecs in Tenochtitlán. The goddess is shown in a simplified but realistic way, with parts of her body scattered across the circular surface. Each limb, like her waist, is tied with a rope that has snake heads on the ends. The incorporation of skulls throughout the scene—at her waist, elbows, and knees—evokes her violent murder. The placement of the disk also symbolized the treatment of sacrificial victims: as a sign of their defeat, their bodies were thrown down the steps of the Great Temple to land where the disk of Coyolxauhqui lay.

This story poetically explains astronomical phenomena observed by the Aztecs. Coatlicue (the Earth) gives birth to Huitzilopochtli (the sun), who then slices up his sister (the moon), as their siblings (the stars) stand by. It is a metaphor for the phases of the moon, when the sun—with the help of the Earth's shadow—appears to slice up the moon during an eclipse.

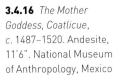

3.4.16 *The Mother Goddess, Coatlicue*, c. 1487–1520. Andesite, 11′6″. National Museum of Anthropology, Mexico

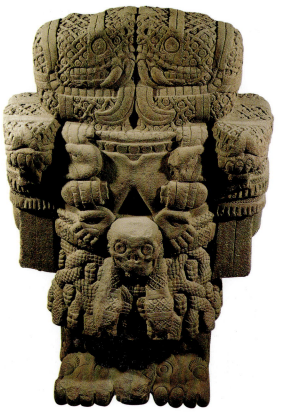

North America

During the thousands of years before Europeans arrived, the people who lived in the North American continent occupied arctic regions, ocean coasts, dry desert lands, semi-arid plains, and lush forests. The resources available to these original Americans were therefore very diverse. In modern Arizona, New Mexico, and Colorado, some groups lived in permanent dwellings made of adobe. Other people, from the Midwest to modern-day Mississippi and Louisiana, constructed settlements of wood and earth and made large ceremonial mounds. On the northwest coast, fishing communities built villages, using abundant local wood. Still others lived nomadic lives, moving to find their food and other essential materials. Not surprisingly, the people of North America spoke many different languages and developed diverse cultural traditions. Their structures and domestic objects met their practical needs, but many were so beautifully decorated that today we call them "art." Although European invaders killed many native people and displaced others, some survived, maintained their cultural traditions, and continued to make fine artworks.

Ancient Puebloans (The Anasazi)

The people of North America used local materials to build practical structures that provided shelter. Late in the twelfth century (*c.* 1150 CE), a drought forced the Ancient Puebloans, also referred to as the Anasazi, to abandon their homes, called **pueblos**, on the canyon floors of New Mexico, and move north to what is now southwestern Colorado. When they arrived at Mesa Verde they constructed communal dwellings of stone, timber, and adobe (sun-dried bricks made of clay and straw) in ridges high on cliff faces, often hundreds of feet above the canyon floor (**3.4.19**). These locations took advantage of the sun's orientation to heat the pueblo in the winter and shade it during the hot summer months. Exactly why or even how the cliff dwellings were constructed we do not know. Similarly, we do not know what happened

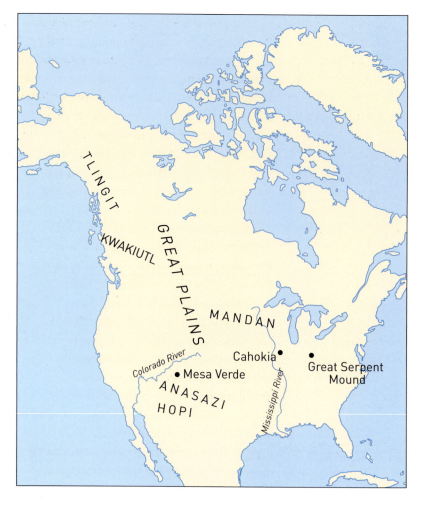

3.4.18 Map of North America

3.4.19 Cliff Palace, 1100–1300, Mesa Verde, Colorado

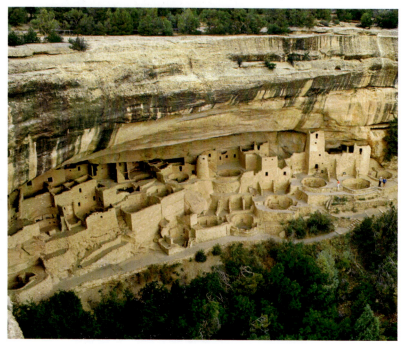

to the Ancient Puebloans after the four-corners area (the place where today Utah, Colorado, New Mexico, and Arizona meet) was abandoned between about 1300 and 1540. Although modern descendants of the Ancient Puebloans—the Hopi, Zuni, Tewa, and Taos Indians—have many cultural and symbolic connections with their ancestors, even they do not know the full story.

Plains Indians

Pushed westward by European expansion, many native Americans were forced into the Great Plains region. Groups belonging to the Sioux clan, such as the Lakota and Crow, became nomadic, living in portable homes called **tipis** (also spelled **teepees**), made of wooden poles covered with bark or deer and buffalo hides. The Mandan had been living on the Plains in what is now North and South Dakota for more than a thousand years. They had established permanent villages, but they used tipis when hunting or traveling. The painted buffalo hide in **3.4.20a** and **3.4.20b** shows a detailed, **naturalistic** representation of a battle in 1797 between the Mandan of North Dakota and the encroaching Sioux. Sixty-four combatants, twenty of them on horseback, are engaged in battle with spears, bows and arrows, tomahawks, and guns. This

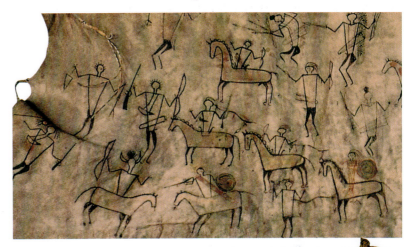

3.4.20a (above) Detail of Robe with battle scene

3.4.20b Robe with battle scene, 1797–1800. Tanned buffalo hide, dyed porcupine quills, and pigments, 37 × 40¼". Peabody Museum of Archaeology, Harvard University, Cambridge, Massachusetts

Pueblos: word meaning "town" that refers to Anasazi settlements throughout the Four Corners area of Utah, Colorado, New Mexico, and Arizona; also the name of groups descending from the Anasazi
Tipi or teepee: portable dwelling used by Plains groups
Naturalistic: a very realistic or lifelike style of making images

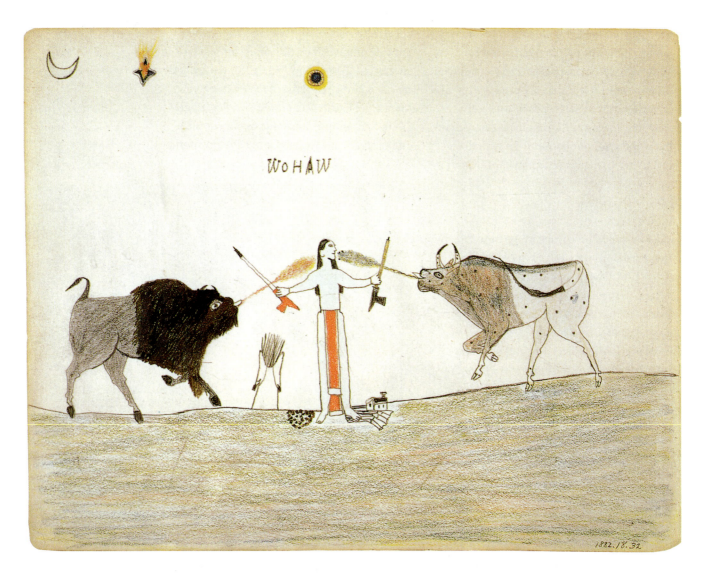

WOHAW

1882./8.32.

hide was meant to be draped over the shoulders of its wearer, likely someone who played a key role in the battle it depicted. Hides used for tipis and as garments were decorated with different **motifs**. This narrative scene would have served a commemorative purpose for the individual wearer, and as an aid to the oral storytelling tradition of the Mandan people.

While the Mandan robe tells us something of a battle between two native North American tribes, *Wo-Haw between Two Worlds* offers a window into the changing existence of one individual as a result of westward European expansion (**3.4.21**). It is a drawing from a sketchbook kept during the artist's imprisonment in Fort Marion, Florida, between 1875 and 1878. Wo-Haw was one of about seventy Kiowa, Cheyenne, and other Plains individuals arrested in Oklahoma for allegedly

committing crimes against white settlers. Twenty-six of the men made art while they were in captivity. No traditional materials, such as the buffalo hide and mineral pigments used in the Mandan robe, were available, so they used the pencils and paper provided for them.

Wo-Haw's self-portrait shows him caught between the two worlds referenced in the drawing's title: that of his ancestry on his right side (our left) and the new presence of European settlers on his left. His Kiowa heritage is represented by a buffalo and a tipi underneath a crescent moon and a shooting star. The world of whites is represented by a domesticated bull, cultivated fields, and a European-style frame house. Wo-Haw holds peace pipes toward both the Native American and European worlds, expressing the hope that they can learn to live in peace.

3.4.21 Wo-Haw, *Wo-Haw between Two Worlds*, 1875–77. Graphite and colored pencil on paper, 8½ × 11". Missouri Historical Society, St. Louis

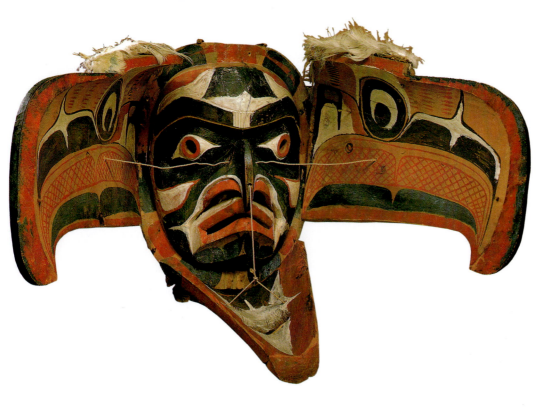

3.4.22 *Eagle Transformation Mask* from Alert Bay, British Columbia, late 19th century. Wood, feathers and rope, 58 × 33". American Museum of Natural History, New York

The Kwakiutl

The Kwakiutl, native Americans in southern British Columbia, Canada, continue to practice ceremonies passed down through the generations. They are known for their masks, which they use ceremonially in different ways, depending on the time of year. The late-nineteenth-century *Eagle Transformation Mask* (**3.4.22**) was probably used in a public summer performance for a coming-of-age ceremony. The eagle was likely the spirit guardian revealed during a vision quest undertaken at the onset of puberty. As such, the *Eagle Transformation Mask* showed the deep, inner reality of the wearer, who used the strings to open and close the mask, giving the impression he was transforming into an animal. In flickering firelight the mask's movement created an impressive spectacle as its human aspects, such as the large nose, combined with animal features, in this case a curved beak. The dancer thus transformed himself from human to eagle and back again as he danced. This performance served a ritual function, highlighting the powerful nature of the eagle, transferring that bravery and strength to the human wearer and his community. It also represents the ancestral connections between humans and eagles. The transformation that was enacted during the performance also symbolized the changes the wearer experienced during initiation.

The Great Basin and California Indians (Coast Miwok,-Kashaya Pomo)

Basket-making, a long-standing tradition for California Indians, served functional, symbolic, and metaphorical purposes for their communities. Although in the past several groups developed unique approaches in isolation, many of today's basket-weavers share their techniques with each other and work to revive the practices used by their ancestors. **Coiling** and **twining** are the two most common methods of construction.

Understanding a basket requires consideration of the materials, construction, form, design, and intended use. Baskets of different shapes were made to be balanced on the head, worn on the back, or carried to help transport items including water, food, supplies, and even babies. Other functions include storage, fishing, and cooking. Baskets woven to contain clothing and building materials provided protection, and some baskets have

Motif: a distinctive visual element, the recurrence of which is often characteristic of an artist's work
Coiling: basket-weaving technique using a central foundation that is spiraled or coiled, and wrapped with another fiber that is stitched back into the previous row
Twining: basket-weaving technique consisting of twisting two strands of material around a foundation of parallel sticks

been used for ceremonial purposes. Native American weavers even made baskets, such as the one shown in **3.4.23**, that were watertight and could be filled with boiling water to cook acorn mush, a staple in the diet of California Indians for centuries.

The plants chosen for a basket's construction were often determined by what grew in the region, but also by the characteristics of the material that made it suitable for its purpose. For example, willow bark was commonly used for storage containers and for baskets for other uses in the home because it contains salicin, a natural insect repellant (which would help protect the contents from the ravages of mites and weevils) and an agent that would prevent the basket from catching fire if placed near a stove or other source of heat.

The names of many weavers of the baskets in museum collections are unknown because little information was recorded when they were collected. Julia Parker (b. 1928), a Coast Miwok-Kashaya Pomo weaver, learned from talented elders, including her husband's grandmother Lucy Telles, how to make baskets like the one in **3.4.23**. The collective nature of basket-making is reflected in Parker's practice, which she has taught to her family (her daughter, granddaughter, and great-granddaughter are

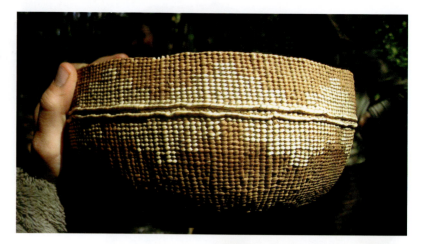

also basket-weavers) and shared with the public as a cultural specialist at Yosemite Museum, giving basket demonstrations and workshops. Because it is so time-consuming, basket-making has become increasingly rare, though it is now highly valued for its intricacy, craft, and visual appeal.

3.4.23 (above) Julia Parker, basket for cooking acorns, *c.* 2011. Collection Julia Parker

3.4.24 (below) Julia Parker holding one of her baskets

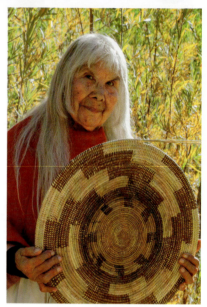

Discussion Questions

1. Select three artworks from the Americas that deal with supernatural beings or gods. What do you think they tell us about the importance of the supernatural to ancient Americans? You might choose one work from another chapter in this book, for example: **1.2.7**, **2.6.18**, **4.2.5**.

2. Select three examples of artworks that incorporate aspects of nature or the environment in their imagery, and discuss why artists of the ancient Americas were so interested in these themes. You might choose one work from another chapter in this book, for example: **1.1.1**, **4.3.14**.

3. Choose three artworks that represent the power of rulers, and discuss how that power is represented visually. You might choose one work from another chapter in this book, for example: **4.3.10**, **4.6.6**.

4. The arrival of European settlers on the American continent had a profound impact on indigenous beliefs and cultural practices. Select three works of art from the Americas that in different ways would have clashed with European viewpoints, or that expressed the views of indigenous Americans about the European settlers. You might choose one work from another chapter in this book, for example: **4.3.1**.

Images Related to 3.4:
Art of the Americas

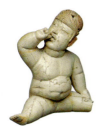

2.4.6 Olmec, *Baby Figure*, 12–19th centuries BCE, p. 251

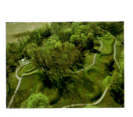

2.4.14 Hopewell Culture, Great Serpent Mound, *c.* 800 BCE–100 CE, p. 256

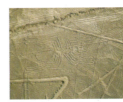

1.1.1 Spider, Nazca, Peru, *c.* 500 BCE–500 CE, p. 49

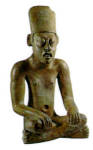

2.6.4 Zapotec *Seated Figure*, 300 BCE–700 CE, p. 295

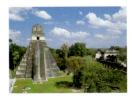

2.5.5 Maya Temple I, Tikal, Guatemala, *c.* 300–900 CE, p. 269

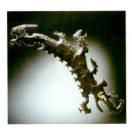

4.4.4 Maya Culture, Flint depicting crocodile canoe, 600–900, p. 601

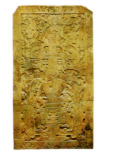

4.3.10 Maya Sarcophagus Lid, tomb of Lord Pacal, *c.* 680, p. 594

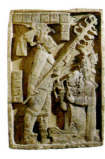

4.6.6 Maya Lintel with Shield Jaguar and Lady Xoc, *c.* 725, p. 629

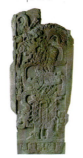

1.2.7 Maya Stela with Supernatural Scene, 761, p. 71

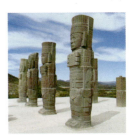

4.7.9 Tula Warrior Columns, 900–1000, , p. 642

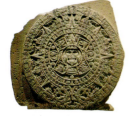

4.4.5 Aztec Calendar Stone, 900–1521 CE, p. 602

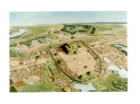

4.1.8 Monk's Mound, Cahokia, Illinois, *c.* 1150, p. 568

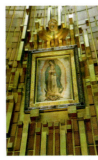

4.3.14 Aztec Vessel with Mask of Tlaloc, *c.* 1440–69, p. 596

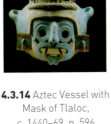

0.0.17 *The Virgin of Guadalupe*, Tepeyac, Mexico City, 1531, p. 40

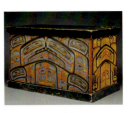

2.6.21 Captain Richard Carpenter, Bent-corner chest, *c.* 1860, p. 304

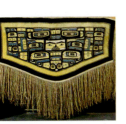

2.6.18 Tlingit Chilkat dancing blanket, 19th century, p. 303

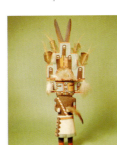

4.3.13 Hopi kachina doll, *c.* 1925, p. 595

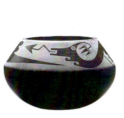

2.6.8 Maria Martinez and Popovi Da, *Bowl with Avanyu Motif*, *c.* 1950–71, p. 296

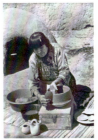

2.6.6 Maria Martinez at work, *c.* 1960s, p. 296

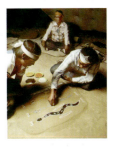

4.2.5 Navajo medicine man in healing ceremony, photo 20th century, p. 578

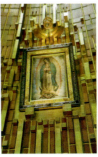
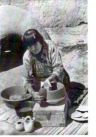

3.5

Art of Africa and the Pacific Islands

As diverse as they may at first seem, the artworks produced on the expansive continent of Africa and in the remote islands of the Pacific Ocean have some intriguing similarities. In both areas art integrates and responds to the environment, incorporates important mythological beliefs, and follows traditional methods of construction and decoration.

Both of these regions' artistic traditions rely on such natural materials as wood, reeds, shells, and earth. For example, cowrie shells feature prominently in the *nkisi nkonde* (see p. 452) from the Democratic Republic of Congo and the decoration of the Abelam cult house in Papua New Guinea (see **3.5.16**, p. 462). In both parts of the world, the shells are symbols of fertility. Natural materials often have symbolic significance, but because they—wood in particular—are usually perishable, few examples of ancient artworks made from such substances remain.

As we find elsewhere in the world, artists in Africa and the Pacific Islands tend to serve as communicators for and within their communities. They record events and relate important cultural beliefs, such as rules for acceptable behavior, or fables that seek to explain the mysteries of the world. In both areas, ritual is an integral part of their creations. Special objects are produced for ceremonies to celebrate birth, to mark a child's passage into adulthood, and to remember those who have died.

Perhaps the most striking similarity between art made in Africa and that of the Pacific Islands is the continuity of traditional techniques. Artists usually have to undergo an apprenticeship lasting several years. In these cultures, learning traditional ways to make objects is more important than building an individual reputation. Although some artists have become legendary, the names of most have been forgotten over time.

Art of Africa

Modern Africa includes 54 different countries, more than 1.1 billion inhabitants, and at least 1,000 different languages. Archaeological evidence from about 200,000 years ago suggests that the first modern humans lived on the African continent, before moving to other parts of the world. As regards more recent records of human activity, oral history has been more important for African communities than written documentation; records of specific events do not exist in many areas, especially south of the Sahara. Art has therefore been a particularly important form of communication and cultural expression. Among the earliest examples of African art are portable objects, such as beads made from shells that date back to 75,000 years ago. Wooden sculpture and architecture also have long traditions, although ancient examples have perished.

Portraits and Power Figures

For thousands of years, people have used art to tell stories about and create images of their

Figurative: art that portrays items perceived in the visible world, especially human or animal forms

Terra-cotta: iron-rich clay, fired at a low temperature, which is traditionally brownish-orange in color

Coiling: the use of long coils of clay—rather than a wheel—to build the walls of a pottery vessel

Firing: heating ceramic, glass, or enamel objects in a kiln, to harden them, fuse the components, or fuse a glaze to the surface

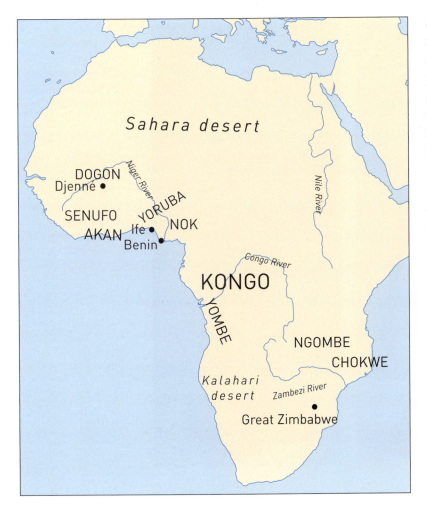

3.5.1 Map of Africa

strong physical presence. The Nok of Nigeria made hollow, life-sized **terra-cotta** figures with a **coiling** technique commonly used to make pottery vessels. The features and details of the sculptures were carved in a manner similar to woodcarving. Because clay is a durable but breakable material, very few of the sculptures have been found undamaged. In many cases only the heads remain intact.

Like many Nok heads, the piece in **3.5.2** has a distinctive hairstyle or headdress, with three conical buns on top. Also characteristic of Nok sculpture, the head has triangular-shaped eyes and holes in the pupils, nostrils, mouth, and ears, which probably facilitated air flow during **firing**. In the lifesized sculptures that have survived, Nok figures are shown standing, kneeling, and sitting, wearing detailed jewelry and costumes. The heads are proportionally much larger than the bodies, a feature that is also common in later traditions in African art: the head, because of its association with knowledge and identity and the fact that it is often considered the location of a person's spirit, is emphasized in many figurative sculptures.

daily lives. African rulers, like elites everywhere, have used art to assert and reinforce their power, and some of the art they have commissioned has also emphasized their connection with the supernatural realm, thereby encouraging a sense that gods or ancestor spirits have bestowed upon them the authority to rule. It is also believed that artworks can act as conduits to the spirit world, and permit supernatural forces entry into the human world, to bestow good or ill fortune.

The objects themselves are invested with power, and a certain amount of power is also associated with the owner. Often objects or artworks communicate the rules and customs that members of society are expected to follow. These objects can be symbolic, related to a particular position or role; or they can tell a tale, illustrating a proverb or a story with a specific message.

Although we do not know the exact meanings and uses of some of the oldest known **figurative** sculptures in Africa, they have a

3.5.2 Head from Rafin Kura, *c.* 500 BCE–200 CE. Terra-cotta, 14¼"high. National Museum, Lagos, Nigeria

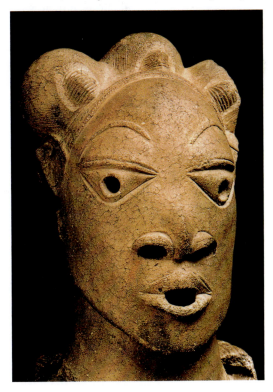

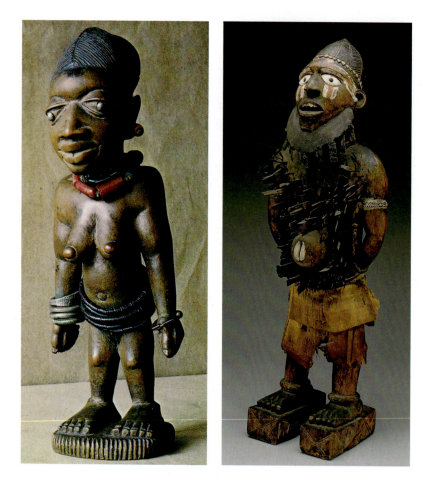

3.5.3 (far left) Twin figure, probably from Ado Odo in Yorubaland, pre-1877 (probably 19th century). Wood, 10" high. Linden Museum, Stuttgart, Germany

3.5.4 (left) Standing male figure (nkisi Mangaaka), late 19th century. Wood, iron, raffia, ceramic, kaolin pigment, red camwood powder (*tukula*), resin, dirt, leaves, animal skin, and cowrie shell, 43¾ × 15½ × 11". Dallas Museum of Art, Texas

The Yoruba of western Nigeria contributed much to the rich tradition of figurative sculpture in Africa. Sculptors working in the Yoruba city of Ile-Ife produced impressive terra-cotta and metal sculpture; and the twin figure in **3.5.3** displays Yoruba skill at woodcarving. Its features, characteristic of the regional style, include small size, large eyes, and elongated breasts. Such figures, known as *ere ibeji*, were sometimes carved when a twin died at birth or in infancy, in order to harness the life force of the deceased and bring prosperity to their families. This twin figure shows how Yoruba hand-made objects are invested with spiritual powers of their own.

Also known for a strong sculptural tradition, the Yombe use power figures as reminders of social obligations and enforcers of proper behavior. Objects called *minkisi nkondi* (the singular *nkisi* means "sacred medicine"; *nkondi* comes from *konda*, "to hunt") could take the form of shells, bags, pots, or wooden statues. Substances, or actual medicines, might be placed inside the minkisi to give them certain properties. In carved figures, these medicines were placed in the head or stomach area. A particular type of nkisi, called *nkisi Mangaaka*, is a standing figure with a beard that served as an additional reservoir for magical properties (**3.5.4**). White kaolin clay, shells, and other reflective objects on figures like this one symbolized contact with the supernatural. Ritual specialists, believed to have the power to release the spiritual presence within the object, activated all minkisi.

Each figure served a specific function, but generally an nkisi Mangaaka was responsible for making sure that oaths sworn in its presence were honored. Each time the figure was needed, the ritual specialists would drive nails, blades, and other metal objects into its wooden surface to make it "angry" and "rouse it into action." As a mediator between the ancestral spirit world and the living world of human beings, the nkisi Mangaaka was able to bring protection and healing to the community. The nkisi Mangaaka shown here has been activated many times by iron blades. The giant cowrie shell on its abdomen is a symbol of fertility and wealth for

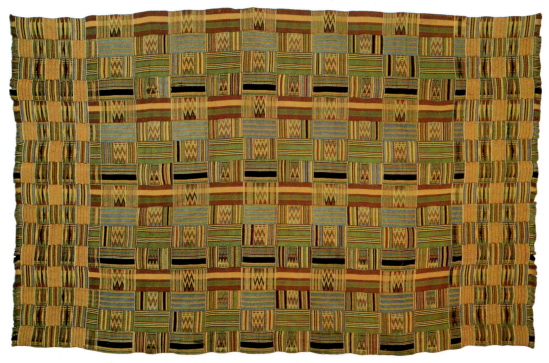

the Yombe people as well as other cultures; such shells are also widely used as currency. This nkisi Mangaaka has wide, staring eyes and an imposing stance to help ensure that no other forces will interfere with the fulfillment of its ritual function.

Personal Stories and Symbolism

Because many kinds of information have traditionally been communicated visually rather than verbally in Africa, objects are often made with a specific purpose or even a specific person in mind. Artworks that contain **abstract** designs and patterns can convey information that is just as important, recognizable, and specific as **representational** images. They can also communicate a great deal about the maker or the user of an object. The symbols that decorate utilitarian objects, from clothing and pipes to bowls and chairs, and the care that went into making them, give them significance.

The colors, materials, and designs of textiles can indicate a person's age, station

in life, and cultural connections. In the West African kingdom of Asante in Ghana, woven fabrics called *kente* were traditionally worn only by royalty and state officials: they were too expensive for ordinary people to wear the cloth. More recently kente have become accessible to the general public, though they are typically reserved for special occasions.

Making kente requires a loom that allows the weaver to integrate vertical and horizontal designs in a strip ranging from 2 in. to 4 in. wide. The strips are sewn together to make a complete cloth of geometric shapes and bright colors. Women wear the cloth in two parts, as a floor-length skirt and a shawl over the shoulder, while men drape it around themselves like a toga. The kente in **3.5.5** contains yellow, representing things that are holy and precious; gold, a symbol of royalty, wealth, and spiritual purity; green, for growth and good health; and red, for strong political and spiritual feelings.

In museums, masks are often presented as lifeless objects on display, isolated from the vibrant sights, sounds, smells, and movements of the masquerade. For African groups, though,

Abstract: an artwork the form of which is simplified, distorted, or exaggerated in appearance. It may represent a recognizable form that has been slightly altered, or it may be a completely non-representational depiction
Representational: art that depicts figures and objects so that we recognize what is represented

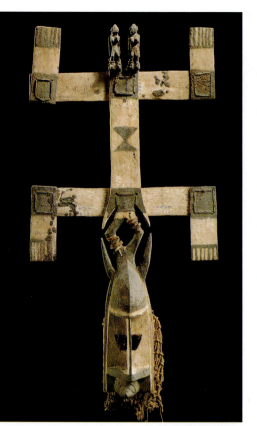

the mask is most meaningful when being performed. In fact, sometimes masks are created for a particular event and discarded afterward because they are no longer "alive." In other cases, masks are maintained from year to year and generation to generation by the performers and their apprentices.

The Dogon of Mali in West Africa traditionally used the Kanaga mask in ceremonies designed to assist the deceased in their journey into the spiritual realm (**3.5.6a** and **3.5.6b**). According to one interpretation, the two cross bars on the mask represent the lower earthly realm and the upper cosmic realm of the sky. In performance, dancers swoop down and touch the mask to the ground; loud noises, like the crack of gunfire, scare away any souls that might be lingering in the village. Today such funeral rituals, called *dama*, continue to be performed, though rarely, and still include masks.

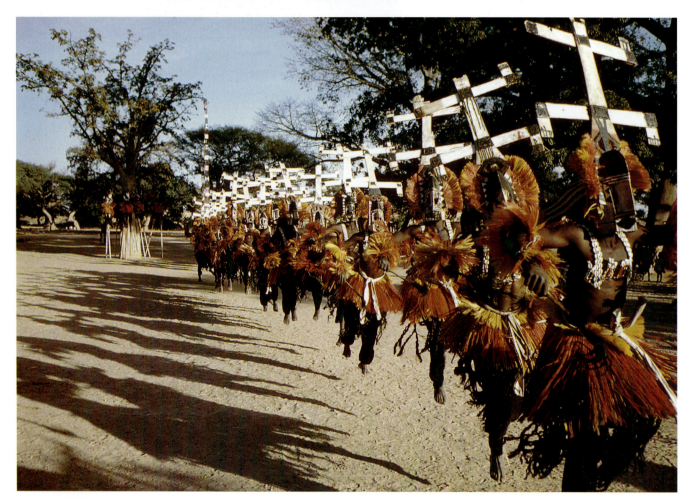

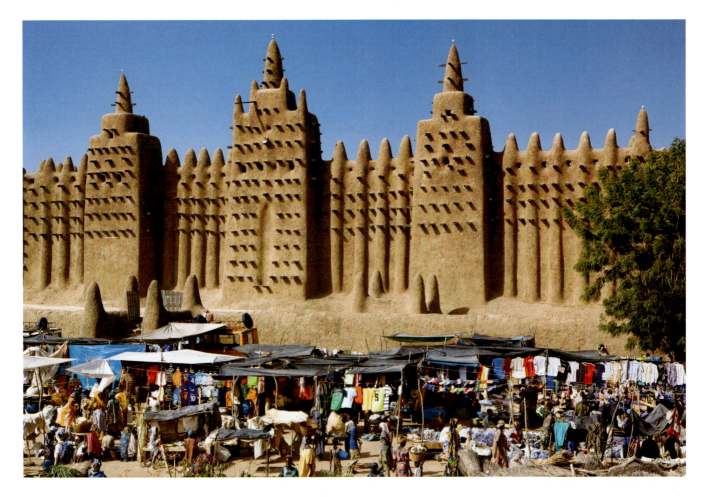

3.5.7 Monday market, Great Mosque, Djenné, Mali

African Architecture

The history of architecture in Africa is difficult to track because so many buildings were made of perishable materials, such as mud-brick and wood. Some ceremonial structures, places of worship, and royal residences have been maintained over time, but others have fallen into ruin, creating only a mysterious sense of the past. The symbolism of the structures and ornamentation of the buildings communicate to us the importance of spiritual concerns, ties to ancestors, and connections with nature.

The town of Djenné in Mali has long been a trade center and site of Islamic learning and pilgrimage. The town's Great Mosque (**3.5.7**) is located next to Djenné's bustling marketplace. An earlier building on this site was a mosque adapted from the palace of Koi Konboro when he converted to Islam in 1240. Several centuries later, in 1834, Sheikh Amadou Labbo ordered that the mosque be demolished. He considered the original too lavish, and built a more modest

one on the site. The current building, more in keeping with the thirteenth-century version, was finished around 1907 while Mali was under French occupation. It is considered the largest mud-brick structure in the world.

The Great Mosque combines characteristics of Islamic mosques with West African architectural practices. The **qibla**, or prayer wall, faces east toward Mecca. Three **minarets**, or towers, are used to call the faithful to prayer. Spiral staircases inside the minarets lead to the roofs, which feature cone-shaped spires topped by ostrich eggs. These ostrich eggs are important symbols of fertility and purity for the people of Djenné.

The clay-mud and palm-wood exterior of the building is similar to the houses of Mali. Numerous wooden beams line the mosque's surface, not only to give it a distinctive look, but also to serve functional purposes. Some beams structurally support the ceiling, but most are used to access the walls for annual maintenance. The area's hot climate has also affected the

Qibla: the direction to Mecca, toward which Muslims face when praying
Minaret: a tall slender tower, particularly on a mosque, from which the faithful are called to prayer

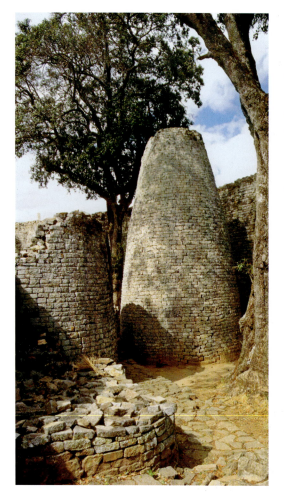

3.5.8 Conical tower, *c.* 1350–1450, Great Zimbabwe, Zimbabwe

building's design, with roof ventilation to cool the building, and mud-brick walls to regulate the temperature. The walls' thickness ranges from 16 to 24 in.; they are thickest where they are tallest. They absorb heat to keep the interior cool during the day, and release it at night to keep it warm.

Amongst the largest and most impressive examples of architecture south of the Sahara Desert are the massive stone walls of Great Zimbabwe, built and expanded from the thirteenth to the fifteenth century in southern Africa (**3.5.8**). The name Zimbabwe comes from the Shona phrase for "houses of stone" or "royal court," indicating that the modern-day Shona believe the site may have been used formerly by elite inhabitants. The remnants of altars, stone **monoliths**, and soapstone sculptures found at Great Zimbabwe suggest that it served as both a political and religious center for the Shona state. During its prime, from about 1350 to 1450, this

site functioned as an important cattle farm and trade center. Exports of gold, copper, and ivory went to the Indian Ocean region and East Africa; cloth, glass beads, and ceramics were imported from India, China, and Islamic countries. It is estimated that at least 10,000 people lived in the city's surrounding area, with several hundred elite residing inside the walls of the Great Enclosure. But by the end of the fifteenth century, when centers of trade moved to the north, the site had been abandoned.

Many of the original mud-and-thatch buildings and platforms have long since disintegrated, but the sturdily built stone walls and structures remain. The walls likely served as a symbolic display of authority, a way to distinguish the areas used by royalty from the rest of the village. The curving walls were built without mortar from slab-like pieces of granite quarried from the nearby hills. They range in thickness from 4 to 17 ft., and are about twice as high as they are wide. The stability of the walls is increased by their design, which slopes slightly inward at the top. The purpose of the Conical Tower, an imposing structure that is completely solid and rises above the high wall of the Great Enclosure, remains a mystery.

Sculptures are often integrated into buildings as decoration and to invest the space with symbolic meaning. Eight carved pieces of soapstone, each about 16 in. tall, were found on top of columns at Great Zimbabwe. The image of the creature in **3.5.9** combines the features of a human-like bird and crocodile (the crocodile's eyes and zig-zag mouth are visible just below the bird's leg and tail feathers). The bird's beak has been replaced with human lips, and its claws look more like feet, suggesting that these figures have supernatural significance. In fact, the Shona believe that royal ancestral spirits visit the living world through birds, especially eagles. Birds are considered messengers from the spirits because they traverse freely between the realms of the sky and the Earth. These sculptures reflect some of the core beliefs in many African cultures: the symbolic use of emblems of royal authority, reminders of familial relationships, and expectations of spiritual reward in the afterlife.

Monolith: a monument or sculpture made from a single piece of stone

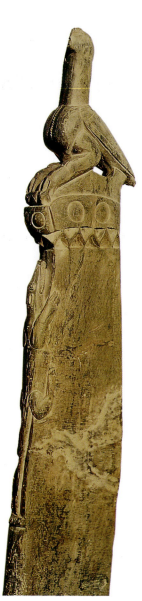

3.5.9 Bird on top of stone monolith, 15th century. Soapstone, 14½" high (bird image). Great Zimbabwe Site Museum, Zimbabwe

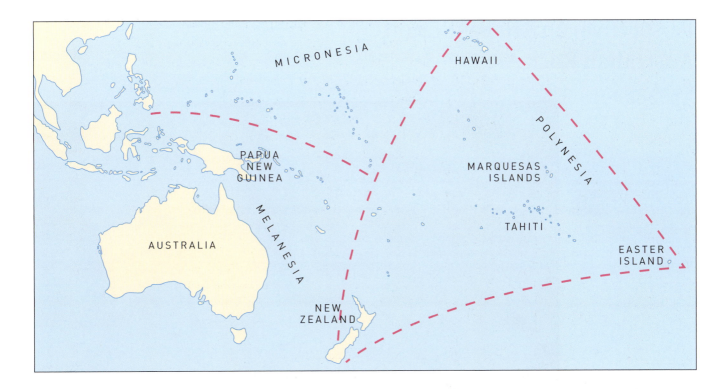

Art of the Pacific Islands

The geographic area of the Pacific Islands includes Polynesia, Melanesia, Micronesia, and Australia (see Perspectives on Art: Australian Rock Art). The islands are separated by enormous expanses of ocean, but since ancient times the people living there have been connected by shared beliefs, languages, and similarities in their cultures, which strongly value customary ways of life and behavior, such as farming, ancestor worship, and the preservation of social and artistic traditions.

The art of the Pacific Islands includes such portable objects as jewelry, furniture, and weapons; body ornamentation; wooden sculpture; paintings on rock; monumental sculptures; masks; and ceremonial architecture. The works often combine practical usefulness with sacred significance, thus linking the everyday world and living people with their ancestors and gods.

New Zealand

The Maori of New Zealand have one of the most elaborate traditions of tattooing in the world. Their words for it are *ta moko*. **Tattoos** (or moko) are made by injecting a pigment or dye under the skin so that a permanent mark is left on the body. It is not known when the first tattoos were made. The earliest preserved tattooed bodies date back to *c.* 3300 BCE and feature abstract tattoos composed of designs with dots and line patterns; Maori designs are part of this tradition (**3.5.11**).

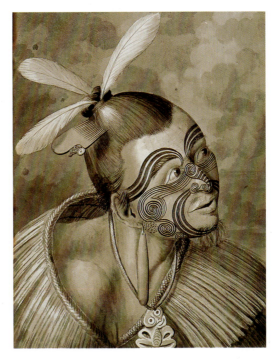

3.5.10 Map of the Pacific Islands

3.5.11 Sydney Parkinson, Drawing of traditional Maori tattoo, from *A Journal of a Voyage to the South Seas* (1784), pl. 16

Tattoos: designs marked on the body by injecting dye under the skin

Perspectives on Art: Paul Tacon
Australian Rock Art

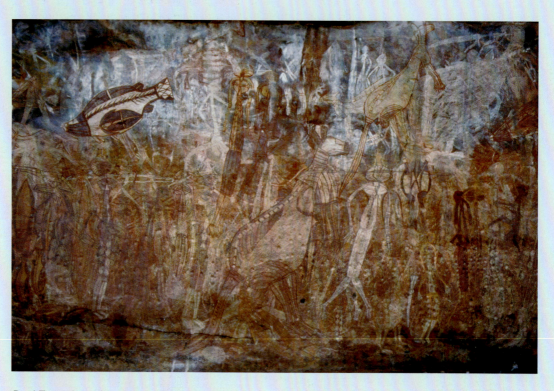

3.5.12 X-ray kangaroo rock painting, *c*. 1900. Ocher and kaolin paint, 6'9½" high. Kakadu National Park, Northern Territory, Australia

Paul Tacon is an Australian anthropologist and archaeologist who specializes in the art of the Aboriginal people of Australia. Here he describes how Aboriginal rock paintings thousands of years old served communal purposes. He also connects them to the practice of contemporary Aboriginal artists.

Rock art subject matter in Australia is often derived from the life experience of the Aboriginal people and from nature, but it also has much mythological content. In many cases it is intimately linked to oral history and storytelling, singing, and performance. Hunting kangaroos would have been a familiar activity, but the slender figure, a "Mimi," is one of the spirits who taught humans to hunt and paint during one of the early eras of the "Dreaming," or the creation period. Paintings of this type from Arnhem Land in Australia's north are less than 4,000 years old. They often show figures with aspects of internal or "X-ray" detail, such as an indication of the spine and some internal organs, in addition to the exterior **contour** lines. Although these paintings could be used to teach young people about hunting and food-sharing practices, it seems most paintings were not used as a magical aid to hunting. Rather, both X-ray and solid infill animals were more often painted after they were caught and as part of storytelling.

Aboriginal Australian designs are tremendously variable across the country and over time. Some form of art has been practiced for at least 40,000 years, although most surviving prehistoric art is less than 15,000 years old. It is estimated there are well over 100,000 surviving rock art sites—places with paintings, drawings, stencils, carvings, and figures made out of beeswax; these artworks have been made on the walls and ceilings of rock shelters, in caves, on boulders, and on rock platforms. Today, Aboriginal artists paint on such surfaces as sheets of bark, paper, canvas, bodies, houses, cars. They use cameras, make films, and produce multimedia and computer-manipulated works. A concern for the land, people, and other creatures has always been important for all Aboriginal groups.

Contour: the outline that defines a form

The designs mark specific events in the wearer's life, such as reaching puberty, becoming a warrior, making a kill, getting married, having a child, and so on. Tattoos covering the entire face and body were originally worn by chiefs and their families, indicating lineage and social status. The patterns may seem to be the same at first: however, upon closer inspection, no two designs are exactly alike. In fact, elaborate facial designs were so distinctive and specific to an individual that at times they were used as a form of legal signature.

Hawaii

The first inhabitants of Hawaii (*c.* 600 CE) were Polynesians from the Marquesas Islands, more than 2,000 miles away. Five hundred years later, Tahitian settlers introduced a strict social hierarchy based on a system of *kapu* (or taboo) and a new host of gods and demigods. King Kamehameha unified the islands' warring factions during the eighteenth century. In modern times Hawaii became the fiftieth state of the United States in 1959, though it has also kept cultural connections with its Polynesian and Tahitian roots.

The ceremonial and warfare attire for Hawaiian nobility included thickly woven cloaks called *ahu'ula*, made of feathers (**3.5.13a** **and 3.5.13b**). These garments were used as a kind of armor in hand-to-hand combat; more importantly, however, they were believed to offer the protection of the gods. Ahu'ula cloaks were generally made by men. This was a time-consuming task that required a great degree of

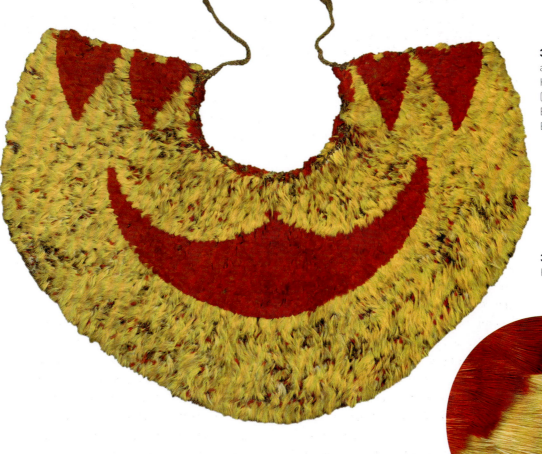

3.5.13a Cloak of red and yellow feathers, Hawaii, 18th century (?). Width 26³⁄₈ x 12¼". British Museum, London, England

3.5.13b Detail of Hawaiian feather cloak

skill, and was by and large considered a sacred activity. The feathers were tied to a plant-fiber netting with cording, based on an ancient belief that knots reflected a metaphorical binding between humans and gods.

The cloak in **3.5.13a** (see p. 459) is decorated with geometric designs, and identifies the wearer as a high-ranking member of society. The red feathers on ahu'ula came from the 'i'iwi bird, and the yellow feathers from the 'o'o bird. Because the yellow birds were very rare, cloaks with more yellow feathers were considered more valuable, and all-yellow cloaks were the most valuable of all.

These feather cloaks were prized possessions that were passed from generation to generation, unless they had been collected by enemies as war trophies or presented as political gifts. One famous cloak was presented by King Kamehameha III to American naval officer Lawrence Kearny as a gesture of gratitude for his diplomatic service on behalf of Hawaii.

Easter Island

Easter Island is small, measuring 15 miles long and 7½ miles wide. It is also extremely isolated, almost 1,300 miles off the nearest inhabited landmass, the coast of Chile. Easter Island's famous stone sculptures are called *moai* (meaning "seamount," "image," "statue," or "bearers of the gift"). The term refers to

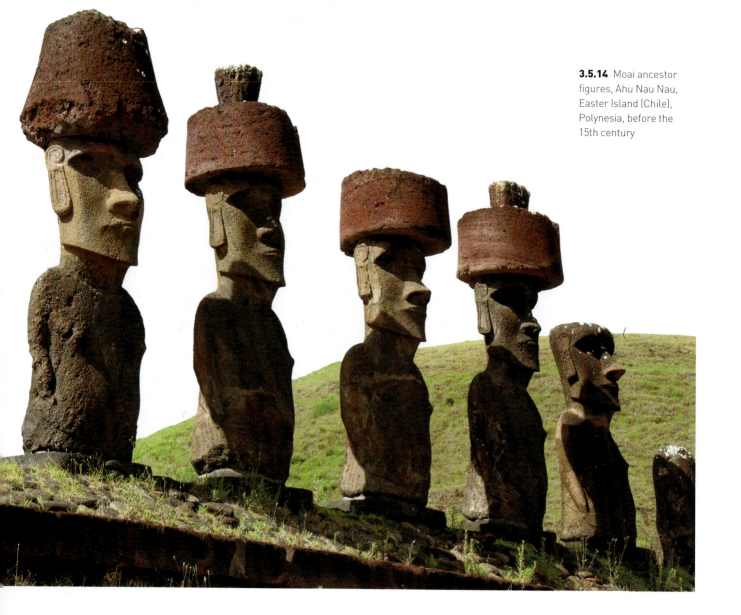

3.5.14 Moai ancestor figures, Ahu Nau Nau, Easter Island (Chile), Polynesia, before the 15th century

abstract monolithic stone sculptures found throughout Polynesia (**3.5.14**). Between 900 and 1500 CE, about a thousand of these huge figures were carved out of volcanic rock and scattered around the island, especially along the coast. They represent deified ancestors who were chiefs. The large quantities and size of the moai also suggest some kind of ritual, ceremonial, or cultural importance. Measuring from 10 to 60 ft. in height and weighing as much as 50 tons, these figures have unique individual features as well as common general characteristics.

While their heights and body shapes vary, they all have deep eye sockets (perhaps originally inlaid), angular noses, pointed chins, elongated earlobes, and an upright posture; their arms are by their sides, and they have no visible legs. Many of the moai (887 documented to date) were originally placed on platforms along the coastline, facing inland; a small number of them wore flat cylindrical hats of red volcanic stone, each weighing more than 10 tons. Scholars believe it likely that the hats on the sculptures represented crowns, identifying them as ancestor chiefs and thus providing a connection between the present and the past, the natural and the cosmic realms. During a period of civil strife from 1722 to 1868, all of the moai on the coastline were torn down by islanders. Thanks to recent archaeological efforts, many of the statues have been put back in their original place, and appear to emerge from the sea.

Papua New Guinea

The Abelam live in the wetland areas of the northern part of Papua New Guinea. One of the principal activities of their society is farming, especially yams, taro, bananas, and sweet potatoes. Yams are the main crop of Abelam society. Symbolically, they are associated with male fertility. The Abelam hold yam festivals each year to display the most impressive yams, with the grower of the largest yam achieving higher social status and helping to secure the prosperity of the village as a whole. In the festivals associated with these contests, the yams actually wear masks made of baskets and wood (**3.5.15**).

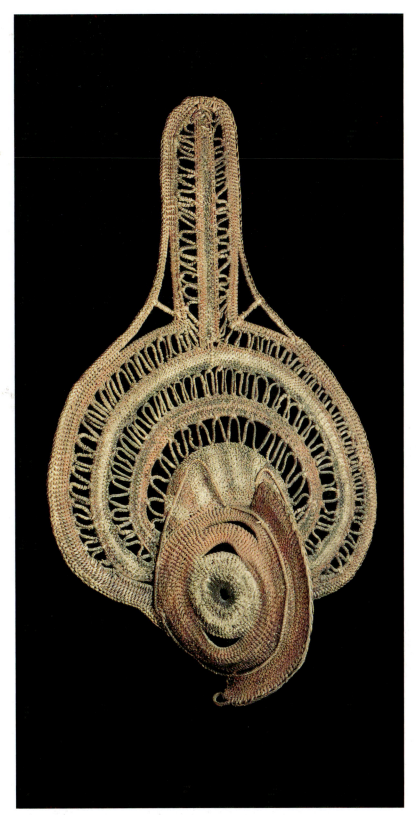

3.5.15 Yam mask, Abelam, Maprik district, Papua New Guinea. Painted cane, 18⅞" high. Musée Barbier-Mueller, Geneva, Switzerland

3.5.16 Interior of Abelam cult house, Bongiora, Maprik, Papua New Guinea, Melanesia. Museum der Kulturen, Basle, Switzerland

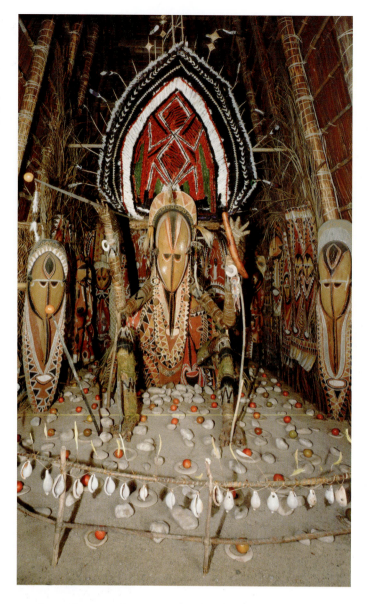

Another important ceremony for the Abelam has traditionally been the initiation cycle for male members of the community. Eight separate rituals take place over the course of twenty or thirty years before a man is fully initiated. The elaborate ceremonial houses where some rites of passage take place are meant to impress the initiate with the power and intrigue of Abelam deities and traditions (**3.5.16**). The interior space is filled with detailed wooden figures representing supernatural beings, and with meaningful objects.

Colors and shapes have symbolic meaning in Abelam art; for example, white is believed to make long yams grow, and the pointed oval shape represents the belly of a woman. The use of yellow, red, and white is common. Certain objects, such as large cowrie shells, represent fertility and prosperity. Abelam see individual carvings, as well as the entire ceremonial houses, as temporary. They are important during use but to be discarded afterward. Because of the powerful nature of the objects and imagery, they must be taken far away from the village, and are sometimes abandoned in the jungle or sold to collectors or museums.

Discussion Questions

1. Discuss three artworks that have been used in a ritual context. Consider how they were made and why they might have been made that way. You might choose one work from another chapter in this book, for example: **1.9.9, 4.2.4, 4.3.5**.

2. Consider the ways in which inanimate objects have been imbued with power. What has to be done to them for their power to be activated? What happens to that power over time? You might choose one work from another chapter in this book, for example: **2.4.18, 4.2.7, 3.9.7, 1.4.21**.

3. Choose three artworks connected with family or ancestors. Consider how the artworks express ideas about family and ancestors and why these concepts might be important. You might choose one work from another chapter in this book, for example: **3.1.32, 4.3.6, 4.3.9, 4.8.3**.

4. Mythology and legend have been very informative to the makers of art in these areas. Consider the stories that are being told according to the evidence we have about the artworks in this chapter. What kinds of information are we missing? How might we fill in the blanks?

Images Related to 3.5:
Art of Africa and the Pacific Islands

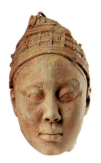

4.9.6 Ife culture, Head, possibly a king, West Africa, 12th–14th century, p. 663

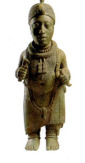

1.7.8 Ife culture, Figure of Oni, early 14th–15th century, p. 150

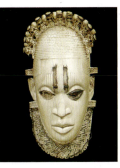

0.0.22 Benin hip pendant, mid-16th century, p 43

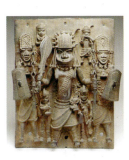

4.7.10 Benin Plaque with warrior and attendants, Benin, 16th–17th century, p. 642

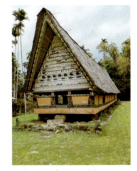

1.9.9 Bai-ra-Irrai, Republic of Palau, c. 1700, p. 173

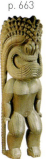

2.4.7 Figure of the war god Ku-ka'ili-moku, Hawaii, 18th or 19th century, p. 253

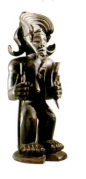

4.6.8 *Chibinda Ilunga*, Chokwe (Central Africa), mid-19th century, p. 630

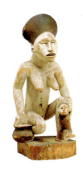

4.3.6 Kneeling female figure, Yombe (possibly Kongo), late 19th–early 20th century, p. 591

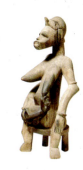

2.4.24 Unidentified Dan or We artist, Mask, Ivory Coast, before 1914, p. 264

4.2.4 Mother-and-child figure, West Africa, late 19th–mid-20th century, p. 577

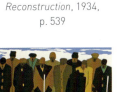

3.8.41 Aaron Douglas, *Aspects of Negro American Life: Slavery through Reconstruction*, 1934, p. 539

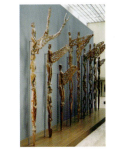

4.3.5 Asmat culture, Bis ancestor poles, late 1950s, p. 591

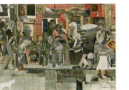

1.6.7 Romare Bearden, *The Dove*, 1964, p. 135

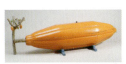

1.4.14 Kane Kwei, *Coffin in the Shape of a Cocoa Pod*, c. 1970, p. 108

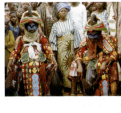

4.1.9 Yoruba culture, Gèlèdé masqueraders in Benin, 1971, p. 569

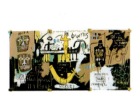

1.8.3 Jacob Lawrence, "John Brown Remained a Full Winter in Canada...," 1977, p. 158

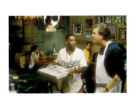

3.9.19 Jean-Michel Basquiat, *The Nile*, 1983, p. 553

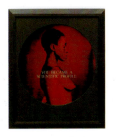

4.10.9 Spike Lee, still from *Do the Right Thing*, 1989, p. 682

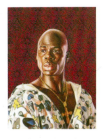

4.10.10 Carrie Mae Weems, "You Became a Scientific Profile," 1995, p. 682

4.8.4 Kehinde Wiley, *Portrait Bust of Cardinal Richelieu*, 2009, p. 652

3.6

Art of Renaissance and Baroque Europe (1400–1750)

The thousand years of European history known as the Middle Ages were followed by the period known as the **Renaissance** (1400–1600). The term means "rebirth," a reference to a renewed interest in the Classical world of Greece and Rome. The influence of Classical subject matter is evident in the numbers of nudes and mythological figures in Renaissance art. Yet artworks from the Renaissance, even those with Classical subjects, often have a Christian message.

The Renaissance was also marked by an interest in education and the natural world. Improved literacy, means of travel, and printed books (made possible by the invention of moveable type in the 1400s) expanded the transmission of ideas and artistic developments throughout Europe. Humanism became influential as a philosophical approach to life that stressed people's intellectual and physical potential to achieve personal success and contribute to the betterment of society.

3.6.1 Map of Renaissance and Baroque Europe

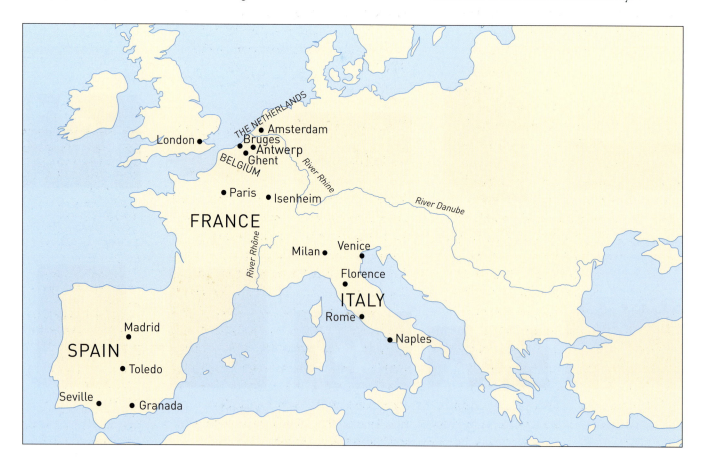

Religion continued to be a large part of people's lives. The Reformation (beginning in 1517) resulted in Protestants breaking away from the Catholic Church. The Catholic Church's Counter-Reformation (1545–1648) was an attempt to define further the beliefs of Catholics in opposition to the Protestants. Both the Reformation and the Counter-Reformation had a great impact on the way art was made. Generally, Catholic artwork highlighted the power of intermediaries—such as saints and the Church—between Christians and God. Since the Catholic leadership was based in Rome, much of the artwork of the Italian Renaissance reflects Catholic doctrine. By contrast, in northern Europe, artworks inspired by Protestant beliefs were common. Protestantism is based on a more individual and direct relationship with God rather than one strictly guided by and through the Church. As a result, northern Renaissance imagery often includes intimate scenes and intricate details (see **3.6.11a and b**, pp. 474–75; **3.6.12**, p. 476; and **3.6.13a–d**, p. 477).

Italian artist and historian Giorgio Vasari (1511–1574) used the term Renaissance (*rinascità*) in the first art history book, *The Lives of the Most Excellent Painters, Sculptors, and Architects* (sometimes known as *Lives of the Great Artists*). Published in 1550, it includes a significant discussion of the great Renaissance artist Michelangelo (**3.6.2**). Vasari's text emphasized the intellectual ability needed to make paintings, sculptures, and architecture. Around this time artists began to be seen as creative geniuses, even divinely inspired, rather than manual makers of craft works. The art of the Renaissance can be divided into chronological and stylistic periods: early, high, late, and Mannerist. All are discussed here.

The period that followed the Renaissance is known as the **Baroque** (1600–1750). Like the word Renaissance, Baroque refers to both a historical period and a style of art. The seventeenth century is noted for an increase in trade, advancements in science, and the permanent division between the Roman Catholic Church and Protestants. Baroque art draws on much of the same subject matter as the Renaissance, but Baroque images tend to include

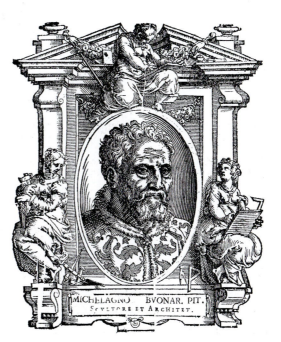

3.6.2 Portrait of Michelangelo from Giorgio Vasari's *Lives of the Great Artists*, second edition, 1568. Engraving

more motion and emotion. The Renaissance and Baroque periods were both marked by constant warfare throughout Europe, and art was often used to memorialize battles or to inspire people to support their rulers. Throughout this time, artworks were commissioned by wealthy **patrons**, often a church or ruling family, who determined such things as the size, subject matter, and even how much of an expensive **pigment**, such as ultramarine blue, the artist could use.

The Early Renaissance in Italy

Following the renewed interest in the Classical past and the influence of humanist thought, Italian artists during the early Renaissance were preoccupied with making pictures that their viewers would find entirely believable. The real, however, was balanced by the **ideal**, especially when the subjects were mythological or religious. Whereas, during the Middle Ages, depictions of the nude body had been avoided except to show the weakness and mortality of such sinners as Adam and Eve, during the Renaissance, artists portrayed the idealized nude figure as the embodiment of spiritual and intellectual perfection.

Renaissance: a period of cultural and artistic change in Europe from the fourteenth to the seventeenth century
Baroque: European artistic and architectural style of the late sixteenth to early eighteenth century, characterized by extravagance and emotional intensity
Patron: an organization or individual who sponsors the creation of works of art
Pigment: the colored material used in paints. Often made from finely ground minerals
Ideal: more beautiful, harmonious, or perfect than reality; or exists as an idea

Toward the end of the Middle Ages, the works of Giotto created a more believable, human space. They were part of a transition from spiritual Gothic art to the **three-dimensional** space that became characteristic of the Italian Renaissance. In art, although religious **subjects** remained popular, the emphasis switched from a belief in faith as the only factor in attaining immortality after death, to a concentration on how human actions could enhance the quality of life on Earth. Mathematics and science, derived from a renewed study of Classical Greek and Roman works, encouraged the systematic understanding of the world. Renaissance artists used and refined new systems of **perspective** (discussed below) to translate their careful observations more consistently into realistic artistic representations. These influences inspired Renaissance artists to combine existing subject matter and techniques with innovative approaches.

The Italian sculptor and architect Filippo Brunelleschi (1377–1446) is famous for solving an architectural problem in Florence. More than a century after construction started, Florence Cathedral was still unfinished because no one had figured out how to build its enormous 140-foot-diameter **dome**. In 1419 a competition was held and Brunelleschi's radical proposals won (**3.6.3**). He not only designed the dome but also devised the machinery used to build it, and oversaw the construction itself, thus earning himself the right to be called the first Renaissance architect.

The dome was a great technological challenge. Existing construction techniques required temporary wooden scaffolding to form the dome shape (170 ft. above the ground at its top) until the stonework was finished—which in this case would have been too costly and heavy. The enormous weight of the bricks and stone could not be held up by external stone supports either, because of the existing buildings around the cathedral. Brunelleschi invented equipment to hoist the building materials and came up with an ingenious system that used each stage of the structure to support the next as the dome was built, layer by layer (**3.6.4**). The dome's construction began in 1420 and took sixteen years to complete.

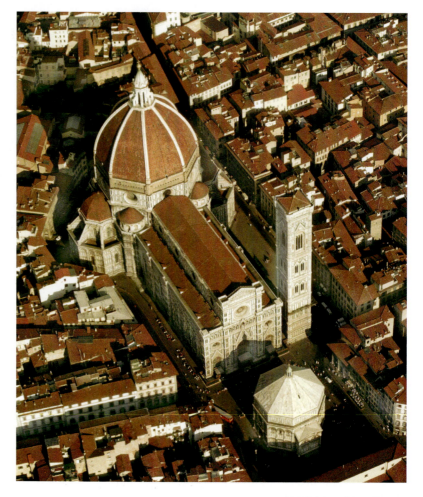

3.6.3 (above) Arnolfo di Cambio and others, Florence Cathedral (Italy), begun 1296, view from south

3.6.4 (left) Modern diagram showing Filippo Brunelleschi's dome of Florence Cathedral, 1420–36

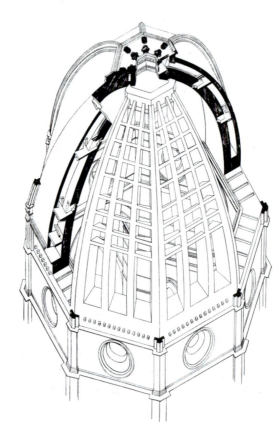

Three-dimensional: having height, width, and depth
Subject: the person, object, or space depicted in a work of art
Perspective: the creation of the illusion of depth in a two-dimensional image by using mathematical principles
Dome: an evenly curved vault forming the ceiling or roof of a building
Linear perspective: a system using converging imaginary sight lines to create the illusion of depth

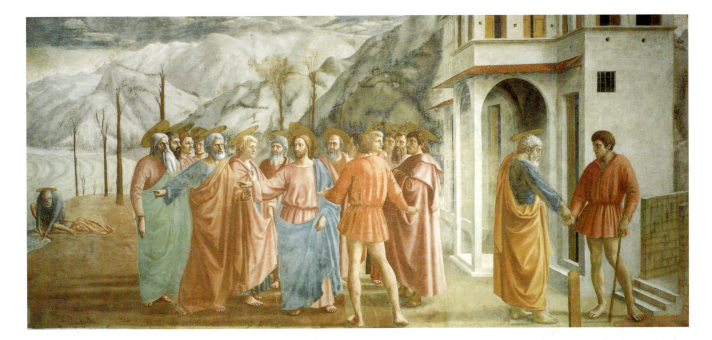

3.6.5 Masaccio, *Tribute Money*, c. 1427. Fresco, 8'1" × 19'7". Brancacci Chapel, Santa Maria del Carmine, Florence, Italy

Fresco: paintings made on freshly applied plaster
Scale: the size of an object or artwork relative to another object or artwork, or to a system of measurement
Naturalism: a very realistic or lifelike style of making images
Vanishing point: the point in a work of art at which imaginary sight lines appear to converge, suggesting depth
Focal point: The area in a composition to which the eye returns most naturally
Atmospheric perspective: use of shades of color to create the illusion of depth. Closer objects have warmer tones and clear outlines, while objects set further away are smaller and become hazy
Chiaroscuro: the use of light and dark in a painting to create the impression of volume
Narrative: an artwork that tells a story
Continuous narrative: when different parts of a story are shown within the same visual space

Brunelleschi is also credited with inventing a new method for drawing, known as **linear perspective**, a technique for creating the illusion of three-dimensional space. He shared the process with other Florentine artists, including his close friend, a painter nicknamed Masaccio, or "Big Clumsy Tom" (1401–1428). Leon Battista Alberti (1404–1472) wrote in his treatise *On Painting* (1435) about the theories of perspective that were already being put into practice by Brunelleschi and Masaccio, and the technique spread.

Masaccio applied the rules of linear perspective in several large-scale **fresco** paintings, including *Tribute Money* (**3.6.5**). This painting depicts the biblical story from the gospel of Matthew, in which, as advised by Jesus, St. Peter has to pay the local tax collector. Here, figures, architecture, and landscape are integrated into a believable scene. The buildings in the foreground appear on the same **scale** as the group of figures standing next to them. As the buildings and people get further away from us, they get smaller, and lead, in a **naturalistic** way, toward a **vanishing point** on the horizon. The **focal point** converges on Jesus, and the vanishing point lies behind his head, making him the visual and symbolic center of the scene. Masaccio uses **atmospheric perspective** to show the distant landscape, where the mountains fade from greenish to gray.

Innovations in this painting include consistent lighting throughout, a wide range of colors, and the use of **chiaroscuro** (extremes of light and dark) to enhance the illusion of three-dimensional form. *Tribute Money* is one of Masaccio's most original paintings: it also shows three scenes in a sequence within one setting. While the fresco maintains the medieval tradition of **narrative** painting, the composition deviates from the earlier practice in an important way. Rather than showing each scene on a separate panel, events that take place at different times are shown together in a unified space, or a **continuous narrative**. In the center, the tax collector, with his back to us, demands the Jewish temple tax as the disciples look on. Jesus tells Peter to retrieve the money from the mouth of the first fish he catches. We see Peter doing so in the middle ground on our left. On our right, Peter pays the collector double the amount owed, using the money miraculously obtained from the fish's mouth. This story would have been particularly relevant for contemporary Florentines, who were required to pay a tax for military defense in 1427, the same year the painting was made.

Like other Early Renaissance artists, Masaccio used both linear and atmospheric perspective to convince viewers they were looking at reality rather than a symbolic representation. He incorporated an understanding of the movement of the human bodies beneath the drapery to increase the sense of **volume**. This series of frescoes, which was displayed in the Brancacci family chapel, was a major influence on later artists, including Michelangelo (**3.6.7**), who specifically went to the chapel to study Masaccio's paintings.

The High Renaissance in Italy

The Italian artists Leonardo da Vinci (1452–1519), Michelangelo Buonarroti (1475–1564), and Raphael (1483–1520) dominated the art world at the beginning of the sixteenth century. All three of them utilized the rules of perspective and illusionism, but willingly departed from exact mechanical precision in order to create desired visual effects.

Leonardo was the eldest amongst them. He was known not only as a great painter but also as a scientist and engineer. Leonardo invented a painting technique he called **sfumato**, which consisted of applying a hazy or misty glaze over the painting to create blended areas rather than harsh outlines. In Leonardo's *Last Supper*, the best-known depiction of Christ sharing a last meal with his disciples before his crucifixion, the artist used an experimental mixture of **media** (**3.6.6**).

Leonardo was commissioned by Dominican friars to paint *The Last Supper* for their dining hall in the monastery of Santa Maria delle Grazie in Milan, Italy. Leonardo emphasizes Christ as the most important figure in four ways. First, Christ is depicted in the center of the painting. Second, he is shown as a stable triangular form, in contrast with the agitated activity of the other figures. Third, his head is framed by the natural light of the middle of the three windows behind him. Finally, Leonardo arranged the linear perspective of his painting so that the vanishing point is directly behind Christ's head.

This work is not simply a representation of a meal, however, for Leonardo highlights two important aspects of religious doctrine related to this event: the Eucharist, or communion ceremony, and the betrayal of Judas. Here Leonardo portrays the tradition accepted by Catholics, who believe that the communion bread and wine are the body and blood of Christ. The artist also invites the viewer to locate Judas:

Volume: the space filled or enclosed by a three-dimensional figure or object
Sfumato: in painting, the application of layers of translucent paint to create a hazy or smoky appearance and unify the composition
Medium: (plural **media**): the materials on or from which an artist chooses to make a work of art
Pedestal: a base upon which a statue or column rests

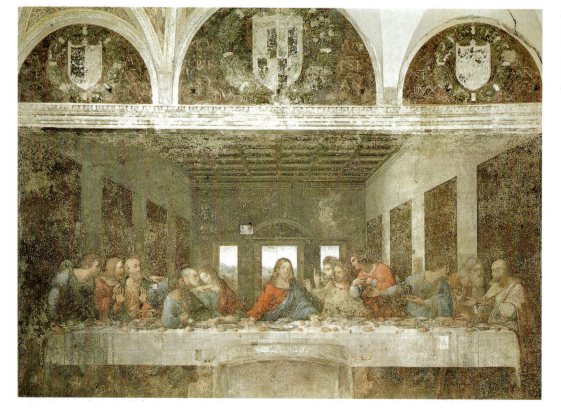

3.6.6 Leonardo da Vinci, *The Last Supper, c.* 1497. Fresco: tempera on plaster, 15'1" x 28'10½", Refectory of Santa Maria delle Grazie, Milan, Italy

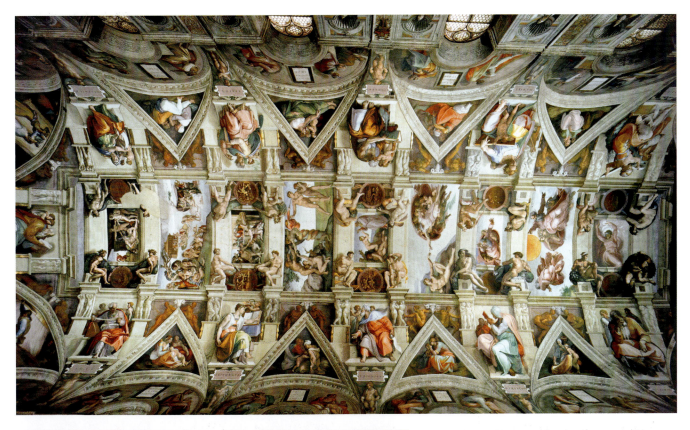

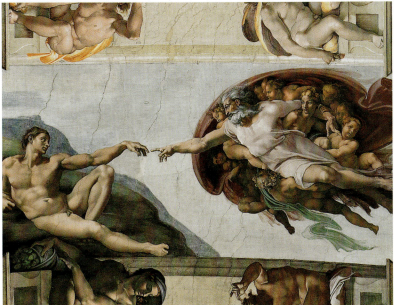

3.6.7a (above top)
Michelangelo, View of the
ceiling frescoes in the
Sistine Chapel, 1508-12.
Vatican City, Italy

3.6.7b (above)
Michelangelo, Detail
of *Creation of Adam*,
Sistine Chapel ceiling

by depicting the moment when Christ has just
announced, "One of you is about to betray me"
(Matthew 26:21), Leonardo shows, through
gesture and facial expression, the individual
reaction of each of the disciples. Judas has his
elbow on the table and is in the group of three
to Christ's right (our left). The deceiver clutches
a money bag in his right hand and has just
knocked down a salt dish, which is a bad omen.

The Catholic Church was an important
patron of the arts. Like the Dominican friars
who hired Leonardo in Milan, Pope Julius II
(1443–1513) also commissioned significant
artworks. As part of Julius's campaign to restore
Rome and the Vatican to its ancient grandeur,
he had Michelangelo painting the ceiling of
the Vatican's Sistine Chapel while Raphael was
working on the *School of Athens* fresco nearby
in the Vatican apartments between 1510 and
1511 (see Gateway Box: Raphael, **3.6.10,** p. 472).
Michelangelo's enormous painting, which took
the artist four years to complete, is so believable
we could be fooled into thinking the beams,
pedestals, and structural elements are real
(**3.6.7a**). Michelangelo preferred stone carving
to painting, which perhaps explains why he
painted the ceiling with such apparently three-
dimensional figures and surrounded them
with architectural elements and sculpture. The
nine panels at the ceiling's center detail the Old
Testament stories of Genesis, from the creation
of the heavens and Earth, to the creation and
fall of Adam and Eve, and ending with scenes
from the Great Flood. The ceiling is covered with
detailed figure studies, Michelangelo's specialty.

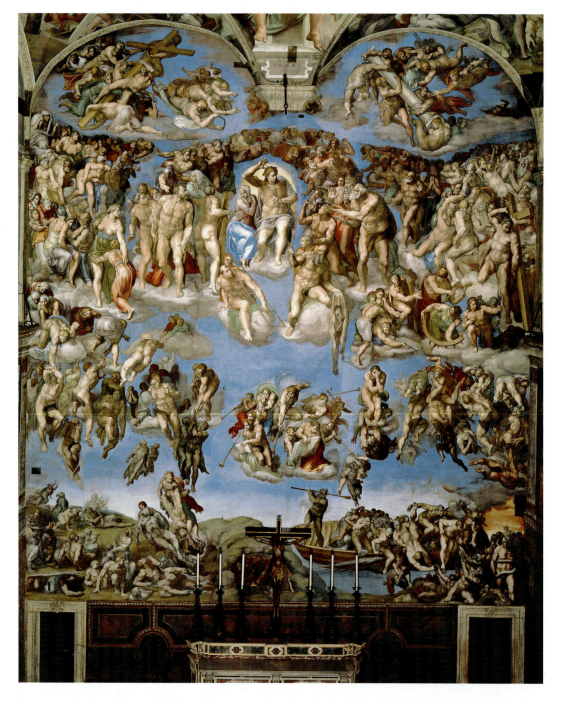

3.6.8a Michelangelo, *Last Judgment*, 1534–41. Sistine Chapel, Vatican City, Italy

Humanism, humanist: the study of such subjects as history, philosophy, languages, and literature, particularly in relation to those of ancient Greece and Rome
Column: freestanding post, usually circular when seen in section

In the *Creation of Adam* panel, for example, human nudity could be associated with the perfection of man (**3.6.7b**, p. 469).

Michelangelo also worked on another famous commission in the Sistine Chapel more than twenty years later. When the artist was in his sixties, Pope Clement VII requested that Michelangelo paint the Last Judgment on the wall behind the altar (**3.6.8a**). As during the earlier commission, Michelangelo was forced to delay sculptural projects that captivated him more fully. His muscular, dynamic figures on both the ceiling and the altar wall highlight Michelangelo's first love of sculpting the nude male body. After years of wishing he could be sculpting rather than painting, and of enduring frequent unsolicited advice regarding his compositions and choice of nude figures, Michelangelo painted the mask on St. Bartholomew's flayed skin within *The Last Judgment* as a self-portrait of the tortured artist who would have preferred his chisel and hammer (**3.6.8b**). Some scholars speculate that the location of Bartholomew

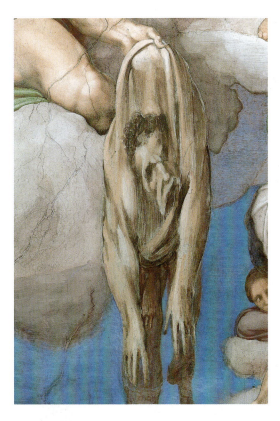

(and Michelangelo's self-portrait) on the side of the damned are a cloaked reference to the artist's homosexuality because, at that time, the Catholic Church considered homosexuality a sin. The energetic, whirlpool effect of the judgment scene is much more chaotic and psychologically dark than many other Last Judgment scenes made by previous artists. The nude figures within it, which took the artist seven years to complete, represent blessed and damned souls as they face their last moments on Earth. *The Last Judgment* reflects the uncertainty of the late Renaissance and points to the preoccupations of the Baroque era to come.

The Classical past, especially ancient Rome, directly influenced the appearance of and theories behind Renaissance architecture in Italy. Not only did Renaissance architects travel to Rome to see the Colosseum and the Pantheon, but they also read the writings of the Roman architect Vitruvius and studied **humanism**, which is a philosophy that emphasizes the worth and importance of the individual as crucial to the development of a civilized society. This emphasis in turn led to Renaissance artists and architects gaining greater social status as creative, intelligent individuals.

In their designs, Renaissance architects combined mathematical principles with Classical architectural features including **columns**, **pediments**, semicircular arches, and **hemispherical** domes. The design of the Villa Rotunda (also called Villa Capra, **3.6.9a**) by Italian architect Andrea Palladio (1508–1580) reflected Renaissance principles in its use of circles, squares, and rectangles to create a visual balance that radiates in all four directions. Palladio's designs were tremendously influential in the design of churches and domestic architecture in sixteenth-century Italy and subsequently.

The bishop Paolo Almerico commissioned Palladio to build him a retirement home in the Venetian countryside. The location of this

3.6.8b Michelangelo, Detail of *Last Judgment* showing self-portrait in St. Bartholomew's skin, 1534–41. Sistine Chapel, Vatican City, Italy

3.6.9a Andrea Palladio, Villa Rotonda, Vicenza, Italy. Completed after 1580 by Vincenzo Scamozzi

Pediment: the triangular space situated above the row of columns on the facade of a building in the Classical style
Hemispherical: having half the form of a spherical shape divided into identical, symmetrical parts

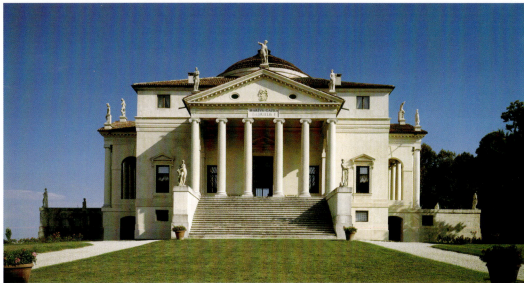

Gateway to Art: Raphael, *The School of Athens*
Past and Present in the Painting

Apollo: god of music and lyric poetry; made to look like Michelangelo's *Dying Slave*

Socrates, in green, engaging youths in debate, talking to Alexander the Great

Plato, a great Classical philosopher, modeled after Leonardo da Vinci

Aristotle holding *Nicomachean Ethics* and pointing to the ground—the material world

The sky (and Plato pointing to it) as a reference to the heavens as the realm of the ideal

Architecture and coffered ceiling use rules of perspective as a reference to man's design ability and perhaps dominance over nature

Athena: Goddess of Wisdom

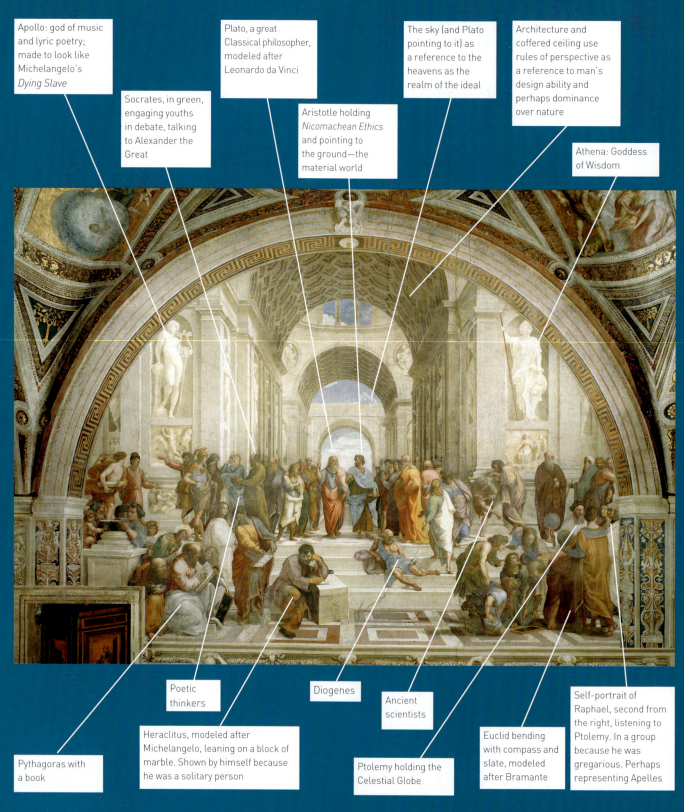

Poetic thinkers

Diogenes

Ancient scientists

Self-portrait of Raphael, second from the right, listening to Ptolemy. In a group because he was gregarious. Perhaps representing Apelles

Heraclitus, modeled after Michelangelo, leaning on a block of marble. Shown by himself because he was a solitary person

Pythagoras with a book

Ptolemy holding the Celestial Globe

Euclid bending with compass and slate, modeled after Bramante

3.6.10 Raphael, *The School of Athens*, 1510–11. Fresco, 16'8" × 25'. Stanza della Segnatura, Vatican City, Italy

In *The School of Athens*, Raphael links a gathering of great philosophers and scientists from the Classical past—Plato, Aristotle, and Pythagoras, for example—to sixteenth-century Italy by using people he knew as models for the figures from ancient Greece and Rome. The two figures in the center combine spiritual and intangible thought, represented by Plato pointing toward the heavens, and the study of things observable in nature, represented by Aristotle, whose hand is open toward the ground. During the Renaissance, writings by Plato (c. 427–347 BCE) were combined with Christian doctrine to form a philosophy termed Neoplatonism. Renaissance humanists believed that individuals' achievements in the arts and sciences reflected the beauty of God.

By using the Renaissance painter Leonardo da Vinci as the model for the Greek philosopher Plato, Raphael expresses admiration for Leonardo's accomplishments. Using the face of Leonardo also allows us to see Plato in the flesh as a believable individual. Raphael pays homage to his contemporary Michelangelo, too, who is shown sitting by himself on the steps, in the guise of the pessimistic philosopher Heraclitus. This is a reflection of Michelangelo's solitary personality. Raphael subtly includes a self-portrait of himself as the Greek painter Apelles in the group on the right listening to the mathematician and astronomer Ptolemy (holding a globe), showing himself to be a gregarious, intellectual person.

The thinkers on the left represent the Liberal Arts of grammar, arithmetic, and music, while those on the right are involved with the scientific pursuits of geometry and astronomy. The setting for this symposium is a grand Roman building with majestic **arches** and **vaults** that open up to the heavens. The Classical past is further invoked through the sculptures of Apollo (on our left) and Athena (on our right) in the niches behind the crowd. Despite its sixteenth-century references, the scene is utterly convincing, with calm, orderly groups of scholars and thinkers from throughout history gathered according to Raphael's carefully organized plan.

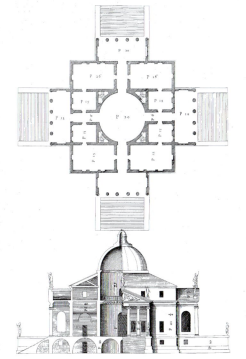

3.6.9b Andrea Palladio, Plan and part elevation/section of the Villa Rotunda, Vicenza, Italy, begun 1565/6. From the *Quattro Libri*, Book II

Arch: structure, usually curved, that spans an opening
Vault: an arch-like structure supporting a ceiling or roof
Facade: any side of a building, usually the front or entrance
Symmetrical balance: an image or shape that looks exactly (or nearly exactly) the same on both sides when cut in half
Proportion: the relationship in size between a work's individual parts and the whole

aristocratic refuge on a hilltop with panoramic views inspired Palladio, who said:

> The place is nicely situated and one of the loveliest and most charming that one could hope to find; for it lies on the slopes of a hill, which is very easy to reach. The loveliest hills are arranged around it, which afford a view into an immense theatre . . . ; because one takes pleasure in the beautiful view on all four sides, loggias were built on all four facades.

The plan of the building consists of a square, made up of a number of rectangles and other symmetrical shapes, surrounding a circle in the center (see **3.6.9b**). This configuration creates a clear, balanced design that allows a visitor to look out from a central point in the circular courtyard toward the four different views Palladio mentioned. In addition, people approaching the building would see four identical **facades** (see **3.6.9a**, p. 471), each with a stately set of stairs topped by six columns that hold up a triangular pediment. The central plan and repeated facades create a building that expresses **symmetrical balance**, **proportion**, and clarity.

The Renaissance in Northern Europe

3.6.11a Jan van Eyck, *The Arnolfini Portrait*, 1434. Oil on panel, 32⅜ × 23⅝". National Gallery, London, England

The Renaissance that took place in northern Europe in the countries we now know as the Netherlands, Germany, France, and Belgium differed significantly visually from the developments in Italy. Throughout the fifteenth century, the artists of the Netherlands continued using the traditional methods established in medieval manuscript illumination painting. At that time they had a reputation for producing much of the best art in Europe, and their work influenced the visual arts elsewhere on the Continent.

Unlike early Renaissance works from Italy, Northern Renaissance artworks are less

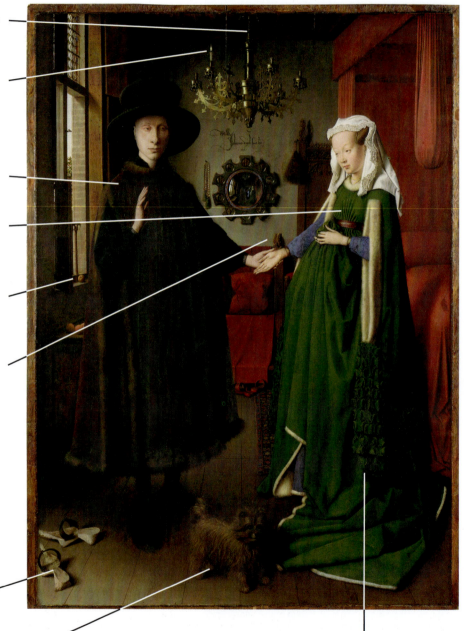

Chandelier is very ornamental and expensive, a clear sign of wealth

Single candle burning in the chandelier: possibly a symbolic reference to Christ; or a unity candle used in a marriage ceremony; or a sign of a legal event

Man stands near the window to show that he is part of the world outside

Woman stands near the elaborate bed to indicate her domestic role and the hope that she will bear children

Fruit on the windowsill: sign of fertility. Indicates wealth (oranges and lemons were expensive because they had to be imported from Spain); also a reference to innocence and purity before humans sinned in the Garden of Eden

Figure carved on the chair: St. Margaret, protector of women in childbirth

Shoes/clogs: given to a woman as a wedding gift; symbol of stability; removed to show that the event taking place here is sacred and makes the ground sacred, too

Dog: sign of fidelity and wealth

Full-skirted dress: fashion of the day because the current queen was pregnant (the woman in the painting is not pregnant herself, because she never had children)

Symbolism: using images or symbols in an artwork to convey meaning; often obvious when the work was made but requiring research for modern viewers to understand
Oil paint: paint made of pigment floating in oil
Tempera: fast-drying painting medium made from pigment mixed with water-soluble binder, such as egg yolk
Texture: the surface quality of a work, for example fine/coarse, detailed/lacking in detail
Glazing: in oil painting, adding a transparent layer of paint to achieve a richness in texture, volume, and form

concerned with idealized figures and precise perspective, but often contain messages expressed through **symbolism** (see **3.6.11a and b**, *The Arnolfini Portrait* and Box: Pieter Bruegel: A Sampling of Proverbs, p. 477). Artists in the northern countries are known for their skilled use of **oil paint** as opposed to the more common use of fresco and **tempera** painting in Italy. While a fresco painting has to be completed quickly (it dries within a day), the slow drying process of oil paint allowed artists to create fine details and **texture** in their work. The development of oil paint was attributed to Dutch artist Jan van Eyck (*c.* 1395–1441) by Giorgio Vasari, but it was actually used in the Middle Ages to decorate stone, metal, and, occasionally, plaster walls. The technique of **glazing**, which Van Eyck developed with such virtuosity, was widely adopted throughout Europe after 1450.

One of the most important northern Renaissance paintings, *The Arnolfini Portrait* by Jan van Eyck, has been a source of mystery for scholars for generations (**3.6.11a**). Like many works from this time and region, it depicts an intimate, domestic scene, and the young couple and the room in which they stand are painted in such detail that viewers feel as if they are looking

into a real room with real people. Indeed, since the nineteenth century, the portrait was thought to depict Giovanni Arnolfini, a wealthy merchant, and his wife. In 1934, the art historian Erwin Panofsky (1892–1968) suggested it could have been some kind of legal document, perhaps certifying their wedding ceremony. An inscription on the wall above the mirror says "Johannes de eyck fuit hic 1434," or "Jan van Eyck was here 1434," which Panofsky argued announces the painter's presence and suggests he was declaring himself as one of two witnesses, visible in the convex mirror behind the principal figures, at the event (**3.6.11b**). Fifteenth-century viewers would probably have paid careful attention to the mirror, with its circular mini-pictures, or roundels, depicting scenes from the crucifixion of Christ, since such an object would have been very expensive, a truly luxurious possession. The mirror helps extend the illusion of reality by showing in its reflective surface the room in front of them, which is otherwise not in the picture.

Through intense study of the culture in which this artwork was made, Panofsky argued that numerous objects in this painting had symbolic meanings that are lost to modern viewers, and

3.6.11b Detail of Jan van Eyck, *The Arnolfini Portrait*

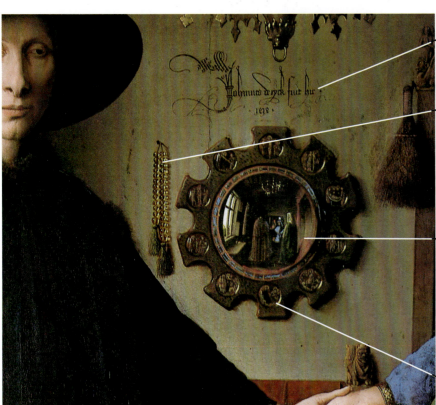

"Johannes de eyck fuit hic 1434": innovative signature of the artist (seen by some as evidence that this is a legal contract)

Crystal prayer beads beside the mirror: indicate the couple's piety

Reflection in the mirror includes the entire room and likely the artist

Roundels around the mirror show scenes from the Passion of Christ

3.6.12 Rogier van der Weyden, *Saint Luke Drawing the Virgin*, c. 1435–1440. Oil and tempera on panel, 54⅛ x 43⅝". Museum of Fine Arts, Boston, Massachusetts

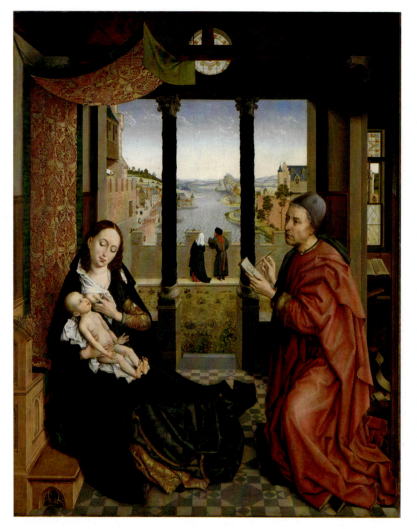

that the image is about the sacramental nature of marriage. For example, the shoes on the left can be interpreted as having been taken off because the ground is considered sacred for the event; the dog is, traditionally, a sign of fidelity; the single candle lit in the chandelier suggests unity; and the exotic, ripe fruit near the window indicates the hope of fertility.

While Panofsky's **iconographic analysis** has been adopted as a valid approach by many art historians, scholars still debate the meaning of this painting. Recent discoveries prove that not all of the above interpretation can be true. In 1997, documents were found that show that the Arnolfini couple were not married until 1447, six years after the death of Van Eyck. The artist, therefore, cannot have painted this portrait as a depiction of their wedding, and it seems that the scene must be of some other event. Although the original meaning may not yet be known, Van Eyck has created a masterpiece of illusion.

Artists in fifteenth-century Flanders in Belgium were not simply paid workers or craftsmen, but considered themselves highly accomplished professionals. This belief is made clear in a work by Rogier van der Weyden (c. 1400–1464), *Saint Luke Drawing the Virgin* (**3.6.12**). The subject of the painting is based on a legend from the sixth century, which claimed that the Virgin Mary appeared miraculously, with her baby Jesus, to St. Luke so that he could record their accurate likeness. The Virgin is seen in a touching domestic scene, feeding her infant son, while St. Luke draws a **sketch**: a preliminary step to creating a final oil painting. That the Virgin chose to appear to St. Luke, seen here as an artist, would seem to endorse the role of the artist as an inspired creative figure, worthy of recording sacred visions. Consequently, some scholars have argued that the painting was commissioned by the Guild of Saint Luke, the association that in early modern Europe controlled the training of all professional artists, for its chapel. Others consider the painting to be Van der Weyden's own statement of his professional status as an artist: this interpretation sees St. Luke as a self-portrait. It is possible that both interpretations are valid: in any case this is a clear assertion of the artist's importance.

Many northern Renaissance artists also explored explicitly religious subject matter in the form of painted **altarpieces** with multiple framed panels. In contrast to the quiet, intimate atmosphere of Van der Weyden's painting (**3.6.12**), the German artist Matthias Grünewald (c. 1475/80–1528) painted a complex and explicit altarpiece for the chapel in a hospital that cared for patients with skin diseases, the Abbey of St. Anthony in Isenheim (in what is now northeastern France). The Crucifixion scene, which forms the center panel when the altarpiece is closed, is one of the most graphic images of Christ's crucifixion in the history of art (**3.6.14**, see p. 478). The vivid details offered patients who were suffering from a variety of serious diseases a way to identify with Christ in his human form, as well as comfort that they were not alone in their own suffering. St. Anthony, shown on the right wing of the

Pieter Bruegel: A Sampling of Proverbs

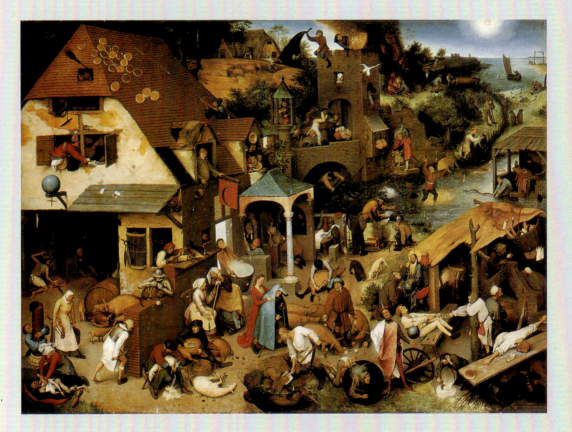

3.6.13a Pieter Bruegel the Elder, *Netherlandish Proverbs*, 1559. Oil on oak, 3'10" × 5'2". Gemäldegalerie, Staatliche Museen, Berlin, Germany

3.6.13 b, c, d Details of Pieter Bruegel the Elder, *Netherlandish Proverbs*

Pieter Bruegel the Elder (*c.* 1525/30–1569) was an artist from the Netherlands who became famous for his landscapes and humorous scenes of peasant life. His work comments on the beliefs and customs of his day. The painting *Netherlandish Proverbs* depicts recognizable types, such as farmers and townspeople (**3.6.13a** and **3.6.13b–d**). The people are general and universal figures, rather than specific or idealized portraits.

The examples shown here identify a selection of the more than one hundred proverbs that Bruegel illustrated in this painting. A few of the proverbs that are still familiar to us include the "world turned upside down"; the man who is "beating his head against a wall"; and "no use crying over spilt milk," which is depicted in the man trying to ladle the remains of the overturned bucket between the table and the cart.

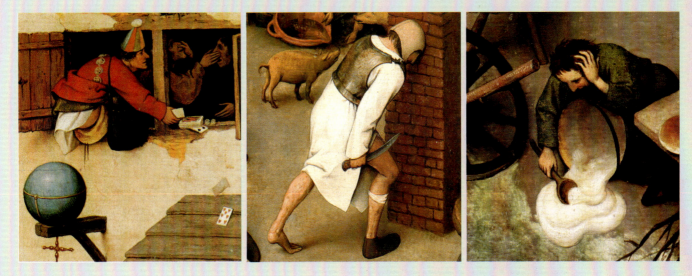

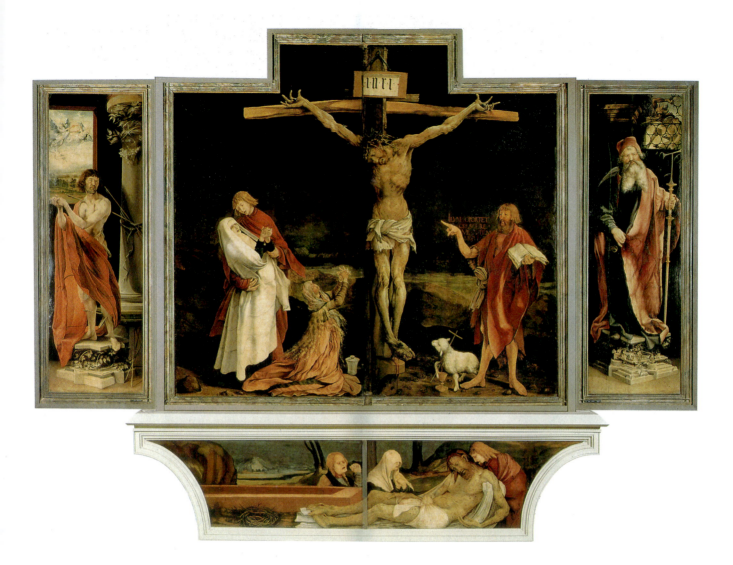

3.6.14 Matthias Grünewald, *Isenheim Altarpiece* (closed), *c.* 1510–15. Oil on panel, center panel: Crucifixion, 8′9⅝″ × 10′; predella: Lamentation, 29⅞″ × 11′1⅞″; side panels: Saints Sebastian and Anthony 7′6⅝″ × 29½″each. Musée d'Unterlinden, Colmar, France

Composition: the overall design or organization of a work
Predella: platform or base on which an altar stands, often decorated with scenes related to the main panels

altarpiece, was the patron saint of sufferers from skin disease. Indeed, a common disease that caused a swollen stomach, convulsions, gangrene, and boils on the skin was named "St. Anthony's Fire." When patients prayed before this altarpiece they saw the green pallor of Christ's skin, the thorns that drew blood from his body, and the deformations of his bones caused by hanging on the cross for so long. The altarpiece could be opened to reveal additional scenes inside that also relate to St. Anthony.

Christ's suffering was further emphasized when the altarpiece was opened on certain occasions, such as Easter Sunday. When the left door was swung open, Christ's arm would appear to separate from the rest of his body. Similarly, opening the left side of the Lamentation scene at the bottom of the altarpiece would make his legs appear to be cut

off. As limbs were often amputated to prevent the further spread of disease, many patients could directly identify with Christ's experience.

A quarter of a century after Leonardo's famous painting of the Last Supper, the woodblock print of the same subject made by the German artist Albrecht Dürer (1471–1528) offers a different interpretation. Dürer was a talented draftsman and one of the first painters to work seriously on woodcuts, etchings, engravings, and printed books. Two study trips that he made to see the paintings of Renaissance Italy were deeply influential. They encouraged him to depict Classical subject matter and to calculate carefully his depictions of the human form and its environment. Like Leonardo, Dürer draws attention to Christ in his **composition** by placing him centrally and surrounding his head with white light (**3.6.15**). Only eleven

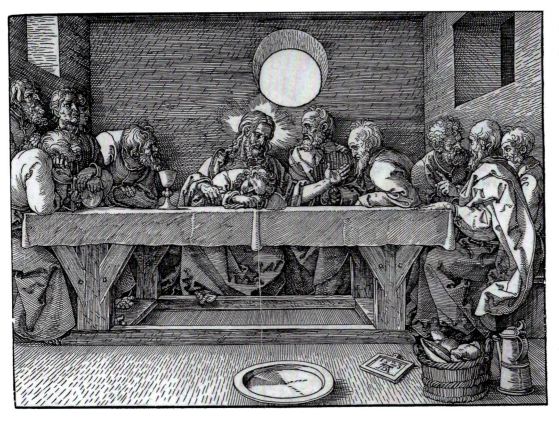

3.6.15 Albrecht Dürer, *The Last Supper*, 1523. Woodcut, 8⅜ × 11⅞". British Museum, London, England

disciples are there; the absence of Judas tells us that he has already gone out to betray Jesus to the authorities. Dürer's print reflects the ideas of the Protestant Reformation and, in particular, the doctrine of the Lutheran Church. While Lutherans accepted the Communion ceremony, they insisted it was only a re-enactment of the Last Supper, not a literal receiving of Christ's body and blood. To emphasize this important doctrinal point, Dürer displays an empty plate in the foreground, signifying that the meal has already taken place.

Late Renaissance and Mannerism

Pope Julius II's building campaign and patronage of the arts had helped make Rome the center of artistic and intellectual activity in Italy. The Sack of Rome by the troops of Charles V of Spain in 1527 brought the high Renaissance to a close, and forced many artists to flee the city. When Pope Clement VII, one of Julius's successors, humiliatingly had to crown Charles as Holy Roman Emperor in 1530, it

was further evidence of the end of those days of supremacy and assuredness. The disorder of the period was reflected in its art.

Compared to the art that came before it, the late phase of the Renaissance (*c.* 1530–1600) tends to feature compositions that are more chaotic and possess greater emotional intensity. The successes of the high Renaissance could not be rivaled: Leonardo, Raphael, and Michelangelo were thought to have achieved perfection in the arts. Artists were faced with the predicament of where to go from there. In reaction, instead of harmony, many artworks stressed **dissonance**. Imagination often took the place of believable reality. Distortion and disproportion, rather than mathematically precise depictions, were intentionally used to emphasize certain anatomical features and themes. During the late Renaissance period, a style called **Mannerism** developed, characterized by sophisticated and elegant compositions in which the accepted conventions of poses, proportions, and gestures became exaggerated for emotional effect.

The Italian Mannerist artist Sofonisba Anguissola (*c.* 1532–1625) achieved a level of success rarely enjoyed by women during the Renaissance. Known primarily for her portraits,

Dissonance: a lack of harmony
Mannerism: from Italian *di maniera*, meaning charm, grace, playfulness; mid- to late sixteenth-century style of painting, usually with elongated human figures elevating grace as an ideal

she gained an international reputation that led to an official appointment at the court of the Queen of Spain. Anguissola emphasized emotion and heightened the realism in her artworks. *Portrait of the Artist's Sisters Playing Chess* (**3.6.16**) shows an everyday scene in the outdoors, as indicated by the tree behind the girls, and the landscape in the distance. Anguissola concentrates on the rich details of the textures of the girls' clothing, jewelry, and hair. Rather than focusing on creating a unified and mechanically precise scene, Anguissola has emphasized the individuality of each one of her sitters, from the expressions on their faces to the elegant placement of their fingers. As the older sisters play their game, the clear sense of joy in the youngest sister's face is balanced by the expression of the maid, who looks on with care and concern.

The Last Supper is a traditional biblical subject; Leonardo's famous version was painted eighty years before the one shown in **3.6.17**. But Paolo Caliari of Verona, known as Veronese (1528–1588), took a new and unconventional approach. His painting combines the strict **rhythm** of the prominent, Classical architectural features, especially the three Roman arches that frame and balance the scene, with the chaos and activity common in later Renaissance art.

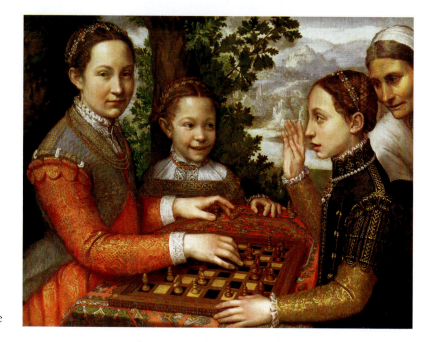

Overall, the composition is formally balanced and detailed in an elegant architectural setting, but the artist included characters not traditionally shown in this scene. Along with Christ and the disciples, Veronese includes members of the Venetian elite, and entertainers.

This approach proved controversial with Church officials. They objected to Christ, in this key moment in the gospels, being shown so near such unsavory characters as clowns, dwarves, and dogs. The Inquisition, a religious court

3.6.16 (above) Sofonisba Anguissola, *Portrait of the Artist's Sisters Playing Chess*, 1555. Oil on canvas, 28⅜ × 38¼". National Museum, Poznań, Poland

3.6.17 (below) Veronese, *Christ in the House of Levi*, 1573. Oil on canvas, 7'3⅜" × 16'8⅞". Galleria dell'Accademia, Venice, Italy

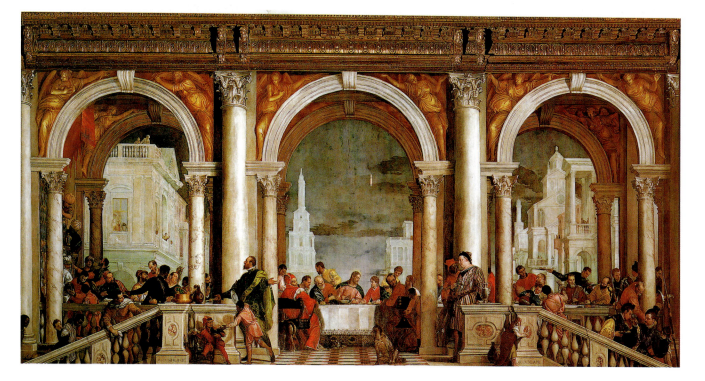

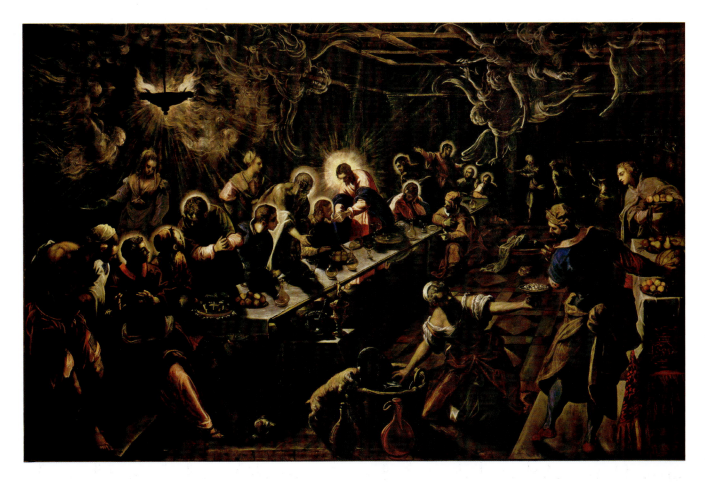

that could punish heresy with death, charged Veronese with irreverence. To avoid making painstaking changes to his painting, he retitled it to portray the Feast in the House of Levi, based on a story in the Bible in which Jesus scandalized the Jewish priests by eating with sinners.

The surge of Protestantism at this time led in its turn to the Counter-Reformation, in which the Catholic Church powerfully reasserted core Catholic values and enforced them through the Inquisition. Catholicism had long believed that images should be used as powerful teaching tools, and this belief now became more apparent in the art of the time. For example, the intensely dramatic quality of *The Last Supper* by the Venetian artist Tintoretto (1519–1594) highlights the urgency of the Catholic mission to encourage believers to remain in the Church rather than converting to Protestantism (**3.6.18**). Tintoretto depicts the Last Supper as a glorious and spiritual event. There are many ordinary people busy in service and discussion—we can almost hear the buzz of conversation and clatter of dishes. At the same time, the heavens seem to

be opening up to send down angels, depicted as otherworldly, turbulent figures, twisting through the darkness overhead, to witness the event.

This scene is a marked change from the **symmetry** and emotional **balance** of both Leonardo's (**3.6.6**; see p. 468) and Dürer's (**3.6.15**; see p. 479) versions. Tintoretto still makes Christ the focal point by placing him in the center with the largest and brightest halo, reaching out with a glass to one of the disciples; Judas is easy to find, too, alone without a halo on the opposite side of the table from Jesus. But Tintoretto's picture conveys a dynamic—even disturbed—sense of motion and drama, with the table placed at an angle pointing off-center deep into space, dramatic contrasts of lighting, and the theatrical gestures of the characters. The combination of the domestic, earthly setting with the hovering, shadowy angels above hints at the imminent spiritual crisis that is about to occur when Judas, tempted by the worldly offer of money, will betray Jesus to his death.

In Jacopo da Pontormo's (1494–1556) Mannerist painting of the Deposition, the

3.6.18 Tintoretto, *The Last Supper*, 1592–94. Oil on canvas, 11'11¾" × 18'7⅝". San Giorgio Maggiore, Venice, Italy

---

Rhythm: the regular or ordered repetition of elements in the work
Symmetry: the correspondence in size, form, and arrangement of items on opposite sides of a plane, line, or point that creates direct visual balance
Balance: a principle of art in which elements are used to create a symmetrical or asymmetrical sense of visual weight in an artwork

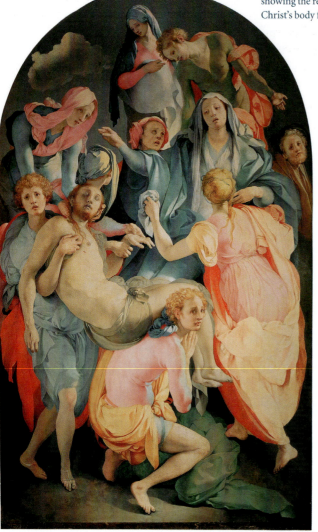

Deposition: a scene showing the removal of Christ's body from the cross

3.6.19 Jacopo da Pontormo, *Deposition*, 1525–28. Oil on wood, 10'3¼" × 6'3⅝". Capponi Chapel, Santa Felicita, Florence, Italy

arrangement of the group of figures appears to be very unstable (**3.6.19**). Pontormo has stacked the figures vertically and placed them in an oddly swirling pattern, almost as if they are supported by the figure at the bottom of the composition, who is crouching unsteadily on tiptoe. Far from being a realistic depiction of observable reality, the figures are overly muscular and the colors are striking. We would expect to see grief and sorrow in a **deposition** scene, but here the faces show expressions of loss and bewilderment. Everything contributes to a sense of anxiety and disorder.

Depictions of David

The biblical story of David and Goliath inspired three renowned Renaissance and Baroque sculptors in three centuries. Donatello, Michelangelo, and Bernini each took a different approach to the appearance of the hero, David. Each work displays the characteristic cultural and artistic concerns of their respective eras. In the Bible, David is a young Israelite who battles the giant Goliath. Goliath challenges the Israelites to send a champion to fight in single combat. Only David is brave enough to face him. Armed with just his shepherd's hook, slingshot, and a handful of stones, he fells Goliath with a single slingshot to the forehead and then uses the giant's own sword to cut off his head. David's triumph against a powerful opponent became an emblem for the city of Florence after its forces defeated a much stronger army from Milan in 1428. Our comparison of statues of David considers two sculptures made for Florence and one made in Rome.

Donatello (c. 1386/87–1466) was a skilled sculptor of both bronze and marble. At the time he made *David*, he was reinvigorating the ancient technique of bronze casting. His *David*, the first nearly full-scale male nude since antiquity, also reflects the sculptor's familiarity with and admiration for the Classical ideal depictions of the human body (**3.6.20**). Rather than emphasizing the mortal and corruptible nature of the body, as was common during the Middle Ages, Donatello follows the idealized nude model used by Greek and Roman sculptors. His statue reveals the artist's careful observation of physical posture. David stands with his weight on his right leg, leaving the left leg relaxed, his left shoulder higher and his right lower as a result—a pose known as **contrapposto**. Donatello's understanding of human anatomy makes his *David* look mobile and lifelike.

3.6.20 Donatello, *David*, c. 1430. Bronze, 5'2¼"high. Museo Nazionale del Bargello, Florence, Italy

Michelangelo's *David* was carved from a single block of marble (**3.6.21**). It was originally intended to be placed in a high niche of Florence Cathedral as a symbol of the city's power and (temporary) freedom from the tyranny of the Medici. The sculpture was so popular that on its completion in 1504 it was instead placed near the entrance to the main piazza, or plaza, where it could be viewed by masses of people. Its Classical attributes include athletic musculature and essentially ideal proportions. By presenting David as nude, with a scarcely noticeable slingshot over his shoulder—the only reference to his identity—Michelangelo creates a sculpture of a man as well as a hero. David's facial expression is idealized and calm, but his gaze, which is purposefully directed off to the side, reveals a mood of concentration and intensity.

Gianlorenzo Bernini (1598–1680) created his *David* in the Baroque period. It is a dynamic, three-dimensional sculpture that emphasizes movement and action (**3.6.22**). Whereas Donatello's sculpture shows David as triumphant and Michelangelo's sculpture shows him as contemplative, Bernini's sculpture shows David at a moment of dramatic, heightened tension, when he is about to launch the stone. The energy of David's entire body is focused on the physical movement he is about to make. Even the muscles in his face tighten. Bernini is said to have studied his own reflection to create the perfect facial expression for such an energetic feat. Unlike Michelangelo's and Donatello's sculptures, which are meant to be viewed from the front, Bernini's is intended to be seen and understood **in the round**.

These three sculptures are clearly different in several ways. Michelangelo's sculpture is more than twice the size of the other two, in order to allow viewers to see all of the detail had the sculpture been installed in its originally planned location, high above the ground. Donatello's sculpture is the only one to include weaponry other than a slingshot: his David holds the sword with which he has just beheaded his opponent, whose head lies at his feet. Bernini's sculpture, like Michelangelo's, features the slingshot, but it is in action, and a pile of cast-off armor lies beneath. Such a prop was necessary to allow for the wide stance and gesture of the figure, as marble sculptures are prone to snap if their weight is unsupported.

The moment each artist chose to depict has a strong influence on the resulting appearance and effect of their sculptures. Donatello shows a triumphant, boyish David standing in calm repose after the fight. Michelangelo presents David as an adult: the sheer size and mass of his form are much more manlike than Donatello's slim, youthful figure. Michelangelo's David stands poised at a moment of anticipation and determined contemplation before the battle; a concentrated expression is visible on his face. Bernini's David, more mature, is dynamically focused on casting a lethal strike at the giant Goliath—the time of calculation and reflection has passed; now it is time for action.

Religious stories were common subjects for artworks during the Renaissance and Baroque. Instead of having to invent something completely new, these three artists' David sculptures show their originality in their treatment of the subject.

Contrapposto: a pose in sculpture in which the upper part of the body twists in one direction and the lower part in another

In the round: a freestanding sculpted work that can be viewed from all sides

3.6.21 (below left) Michelangelo, *David*, 1501–4. Marble, 14'2⅞"high. Galleria dell' Accademia, Florence, Italy

3.6.22 (below right) Gianlorenzo Bernini, *David*, 1623. Marble, 5'7"high. Galleria Borghese, Rome, Italy

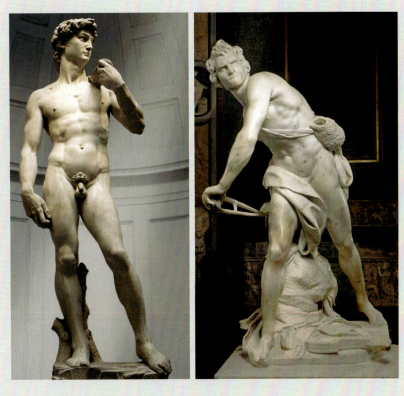

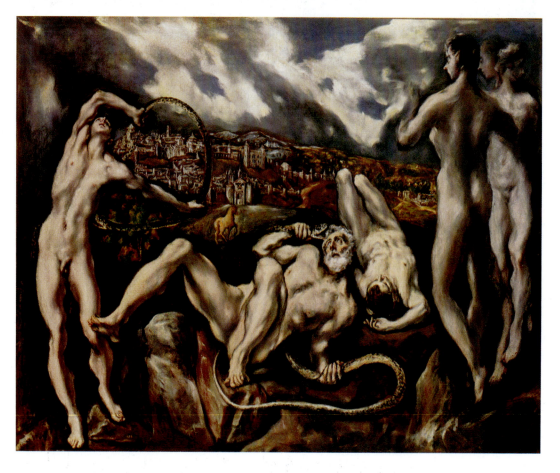

3.6.23 El Greco, *Laocoön*, c. 1610/14. Oil on canvas, 54⅛ × 68". National Gallery of Art, Washington, D.C.

Expressionistic: devoted to representing subjective emotions and experiences instead of objective or external reality
Color: the optical effect caused when reflected white light of the spectrum is divided into separate wavelengths
Outlines: the outermost line or implied line of an object or figure, by which it is defined or bounded
Modeling: the representation of three-dimensional objects in two dimensions so that they appear solid
Genre: categories of artistic subject matter, often with strongly influential histories and traditions
Tenebrism: dramatic use of intense darkness and light to heighten the impact of a painting

Another Mannerist, Domenikos Theotokopoulos (*c.* 1541–1614), called El Greco ("The Greek"), worked in Venice and Rome before moving to Spain. *Laocoön* is a subject from Greek mythology (see Images Related to 3.6, p. 489). The Trojan priest Laocoön attempted to warn the inhabitants of Troy that Greek soldiers were trying to infiltrate their fortifications by hiding inside the Trojan Horse, seen in the middle ground at the center of this painting. El Greco shows the priest and his sons being attacked by snakes sent by the god Poseidon (who supported the Greeks) to stop Laocoön's warning (**3.6.23**). The landscape in the background is a view of Toledo, Spain, where El Greco lived and made his best-known works late in his life. El Greco combined Mannerist exaggeration, seen in the elongated forms and distorted figures, with his own **expressionistic** use of **color**, **outlines**, and **modeling**. Like other Mannerist artworks, this intricate composition combines carefully observed factual information with mythological stories according to the dictates of the artist's imagination.

The Baroque

The **Baroque** period was a time of exploration, increased trade, and discovery in the sciences. The Western world now accepted the theory of astronomer Nicolaus Copernicus that the Sun, rather than the Earth, was the center of the universe—a theory the Catholic Church had previously rejected. Light, both heavenly and otherwise, became a prominent feature in many Baroque artworks (see Gateway Box: Gentileschi and Caravaggio). The seventeenth century was also a time of battles throughout Europe, largely the result of the divisions in the Catholic Church after the Reformation. Baroque artworks give us a sense of this turmoil: their theatrical, dynamic compositions feature dramatic movement and light. Some Baroque artists, such as Nicolas Poussin, continued the high Renaissance interest in carefully ordered calmness. Others, such as Gianlorenzo Bernini (see pp. 482–483: Depictions of David), displayed heightened emotion and created figures that seem to be in action, breaking into the viewer's personal space.

Gateway to Art: Gentileschi, *Judith Decapitating Holofernes*
The Influence of Caravaggio

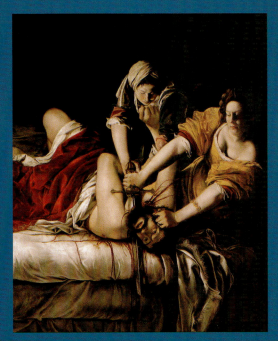

3.6.24 Artemisia Gentileschi, *Judith Decapitating Holofernes*, c. 1620. Oil on canvas, 6′6⅜″ × 5′3¾″. Uffizi Gallery, Florence, Italy

3.6.25 Caravaggio, *Judith Decapitating Holofernes*, 1599. Oil on canvas, 4′9″ × 6′4¾″. Galleria Nazionale d'Arte Antica, Rome, Italy

Along with many other artists in Europe in the seventeenth century, Artemisia Gentileschi (1593–c. 1656) imitated the artistic style of Italian artist Caravaggio (1571–1610). In addition to being an accomplished painter, Caravaggio led a tumultuous existence. By the time he was in his late twenties, Caravaggio's innovative approach to painting had earned him an impressive reputation and he was receiving Church commissions. At the same time, he was involved in brawls; he eventually killed a man in a fight over a tennis match. While on the run from these charges, he died of unknown causes at the age of thirty-nine.

Caravaggio's paintings, although often of religious stories, look like everyday **genre** scenes, filled with people from the lower classes, shown unidealized and wearing unkempt clothes. This naturalistic, down-to-earth approach offended some viewers who believed religious figures in artworks should be presented as idealized individuals to signify their holiness. Caravaggio's talent, however, was also greatly appreciated by many art lovers and patrons. His development of **tenebrism** was adopted by other painters during his lifetime and by later artists as well.

In Caravaggio's *Judith Decapitating Holofernes* (**3.6.25**), a strong beam of light seems to stop time as Judith's knife slices through the general's neck. The light emphasizes the drama of this particular moment and shows the main characteristics of Caravaggio's style. The scene seems to emerge into the light from a darkened background with an effect similar to a modern spotlight. Because the background is so dark, the action takes place in a shallow, stage-like space, again reinforcing dramatic effect. The details Caravaggio has focused on, such as the seventeenth-century clothing, emphasize the ordinary aspects of this biblical event.

Artemisia Gentileschi's style was greatly influenced by Caravaggio's detailed realism and dramatic use of **tenebrism**. In their paintings of Judith decapitating Holofernes (see **3.6.24** and **3.6.25**), both artists use extreme darks and lights for dramatic effect, emphasize the violence of the scene through spurting blood and blood-stained sheets, and show the female characters with a marked determination that was not typical at the time.

Gentileschi also infused her Judith image with active physical strength on the part of the women in a way that allows the viewer to sense the sheer effort required to sever the brute's head. By contrast, Caravaggio's Judith, apart from having powerful forearms, appears quite delicate, and shocked at her deadly deed. Similarly, Caravaggio shows Judith's maidservant as an old woman who seems to take no active part in the murder; Gentileschi's servant, however, physically restrains the Assyrian general as Judith severs his head.

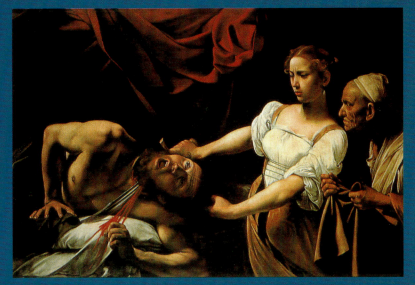

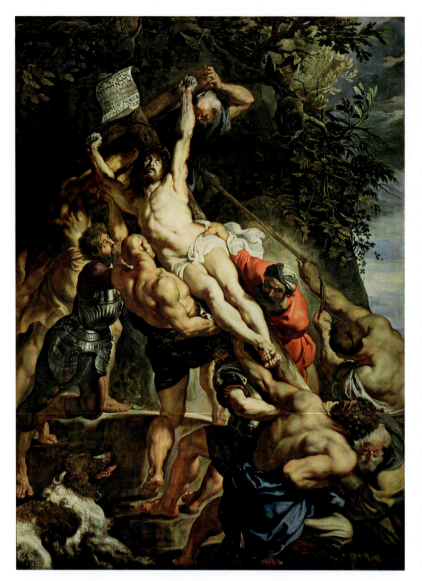

3.6.26 Peter Paul Rubens, centre panel from *The Raising of the Cross* triptych, 1610-11. Oil on panel, 15'1⅞" x 11'1½". Onze Lieve Vrouwkerk, Antwerp Cathedral, Belgium

Peter Paul Rubens (1577–1640) produced about 2,000 paintings in his lifetime, an impressive output made possible because he operated a large workshop in Antwerp (in modern-day Belgium). His assistants were responsible for producing some of his paintings, but Rubens generally finished works for important clients himself. His *The Raising of the Cross* was one of several paintings commissioned by wealthy merchants to be installed in churches (**3.6.26**).

In *The Raising of the Cross*, we can sense the physical exertions of these muscular men to raise Christ on the cross. A dynamic tension is created along the diagonal line of the cross that visually connects the men at its base as they strain to pull Christ up toward the right side of the painting. Although, in fact, Christ would have been

tortured and close to death at this point, the artist has painted his flesh as almost immaculate, and lighter than that of those around him. In this way, and by bathing him in light, Rubens makes Christ the focal point and emphasizes his holiness.

Rembrandt Harmensoon van Rijn (1606–1669) was an extremely popular painter who also had a large workshop at one point in his life. Yet, despite his impressive reputation, he filed for bankruptcy in old age. In *The Night Watch*, the gathering of officers and guardsmen likely commemorates a visit by Queen Marie de'Medici to Amsterdam in 1638 (**3.6.27**). The painting was commissioned by the civic militia, and scholars believe that all of those portrayed in this scene contributed financially to the artist's fee. *The Night Watch* is a fine example of Rembrandt's innovative approach to a group portrait. His painting is not only convincing but also full of the vitality and energy typical of a group getting ready for an important occasion. The various members of the company are shown busily organizing themselves. This painting came to be known as *The Night Watch* because its dark atmosphere made it look like a night scene. Rembrandt made skillful use of chiaroscuro, tenebrism, and dramatic lighting to enliven his composition, but the impression of night-time was actually created by years of accumulated dirt and layers of varnish. The painting was revealed to be a daytime scene when it was cleaned after World War II.

French artist Nicolas Poussin (1594–1665) specialized in paintings of subjects from Classical antiquity. Everything in his paintings was carefully constructed and positioned. He would even arrange miniature figures on a small stage when choreographing the scenes for his landscapes. Yet, though these and his buildings look detailed and realistic, their appearance and placement were always invented from his imagination. *The Funeral of Phocion* depicts two men carrying the deceased Phocion, an Athenian general, over a winding road that leads away from the city (**3.6.28**). Phocion had been executed after being falsely accused of treason; because he was considered a traitor, he was buried outside the city.

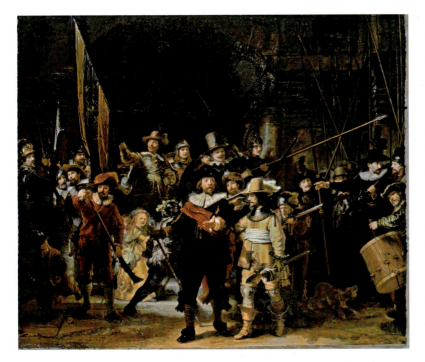

3.6.27 Rembrandt van Rijn, *The Company of Frans Banning Cocq and Willem van Ruytenburch (The Night Watch)*, 1642. Oil on canvas, 11'11" × 14'4". Rijksmuseum, Amsterdam, The Netherlands

3.6.28 Nicolas Poussin, *The Funeral of Phocion*, 1648. Oil on canvas, 44⅞" × 68⅞". National Museum of Wales, Cardiff

Foreground: the part of a work depicted as nearest to the viewer

Implied line: a line not actually drawn but suggested by elements in the work

The composition highlights the tragedy of Phocion's burial as a traitor, when he was in fact a hero who should have been honored. The two figures carrying Phocion's body, covered with a white sheet, are prominently placed in the **foreground**. The large tree to the right arches over and creates an **implied line** from the pallbearers through the figures, trees, and buildings that gradually become smaller as

they recede into space. The winding road both emphasizes the distance of Phocion's burial from the city and creates a sense of deep space, skillfully guiding our gaze into the landscape. The carefully structured sense of the landscape continues the Renaissance emphasis on balance and order. Similarly, the Classically designed buildings and figures dressed in antique clothing call our attention to the past.

During the seventeenth century, popes and powerful royal patrons commissioned numerous important buildings in Italy. Architecture at this time evolved so that, instead of the harmonious proportions and austere simplicity that were common in Renaissance designs, architectural works now incorporated much more ornate decorations and more complex forms. The result was that Baroque buildings became stages for dramatic expressions of the architect's art.

One example is the Baroque Church of San Carlo alle Quattro Fontane (**3.6.29a**, see p. 488), in Rome, designed by Italian architect Francesco Borromini (1599–1677). Borromini, like his Renaissance predecessors, incorporated geometric shapes into his design, but he did not aim to achieve the perfectly balanced symmetry of such buildings as Palladio's Villa Rotunda (**3.6.9b**). Instead, this church takes on the

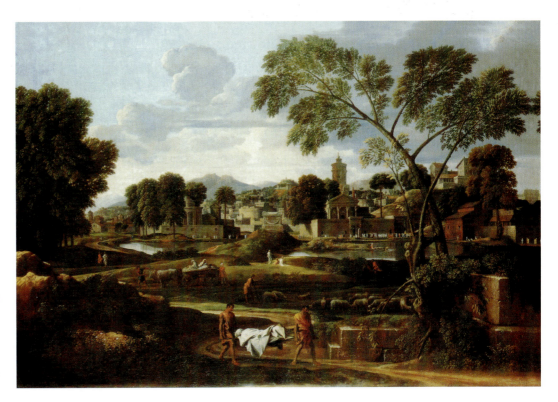

qualities of a dramatic sculpture. At the center of the plan is an oval (**3.6.29b**), which is less symmetrical than the flawless equilibrium of a central circle found at the heart of Renaissance designs. In the interior of the building, columns divide the walls into undulating spaces. The irregular shapes of the interior are echoed in the curving, wavelike walls of the facade (**3.6.29a**). Because the walls are curving instead of flat, they create dramatic shadows. The surfaces and spaces of this church are typically Baroque in that they are very ornamental and spectacular. The complexity of this design influenced later Baroque architects. In addition to the new emphasis on opulence, light was emphasized both through the use of windows and in the imagery of painted frescoes in Baroque church interiors.

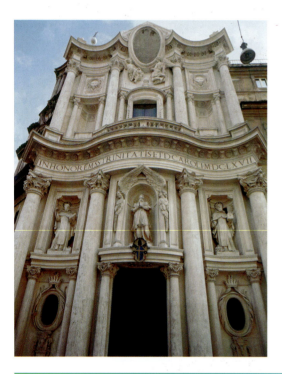

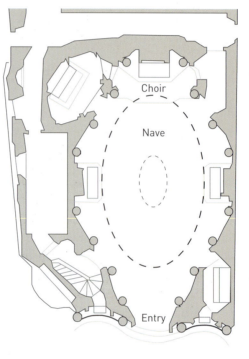

3.6.29a (far left) Francesco Borromini, Church of San Carlo alle Quatro Fontane, Rome, Italy, 1638–46. Facade added c. 1677

3.6.29b (left) Plan of the Church of San Carlo alle Quattro Fontane

Discussion Questions

1. Find two examples of artworks in this chapter in which linear perspective plays an important part. Point out the parts of the composition that use linear perspective to create the desired illusion. Discuss what the artist wants to communicate by using linear perspective.

2. From this chapter, choose a northern Renaissance artwork and an Italian Renaissance artwork. List the prominent characteristics of each work, including information about their form and content.

3. Select three artworks that deal with subject matter from the Bible. Consider how they portray their biblical themes: examine style, medium and technique, content, and any other aspects that the artist emphasizes. You might want to consider works from other chapters, such as **2.4.9** and **4.10.1**.

4. Select a Renaissance artwork and a Baroque artwork from this chapter. List their similarities and differences. Consider their subject matter, style, content, and emotional impact.

5. Select three Renaissance artworks that draw on the artistic and intellectual heritage of Classical Greece and Rome. Make a list of the ways in which they use the Classical past. Make another list of any Renaissance innovations, either in terms of form or of content. You might choose one work from another chapter in this book, for example: **4.9.5**, **4.9.8**.

Images Related to 3.6:
Art of Renaissance and Baroque Europe (1400–1750)

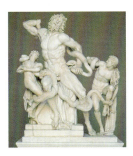

3.1.26 *Laocoön and His Sons*, Hellenistic Greece, 150 BCE, p. 383

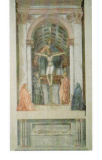

1.3.20 Masaccio, *Trinity*, c. 1425–26 CE, p. 95

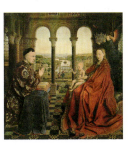

2.2.10 Jan van Eyck, *The Madonna of Chancellor Rolin*, 1430–34, p. 222

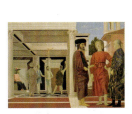

1.6.6 Piero della Francesca, *The Flagellation*, c. 1469, p. 134

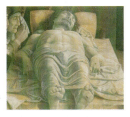

4.3.3 Andrea Mantegna, *Dead Christ*, c. 1480, p. 590

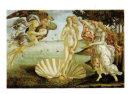

4.9.5 Sandro Botticelli, *The Birth of Venus*, c. 1482–86, p. 662

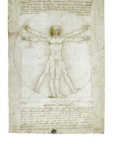

4.4.1 Leonardo da Vinci, *Vitruvian Man*, c. 1490, p. 599

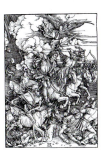

2.3.2 Albrecht Dürer, *Four Horsemen of the Apocalypse*, c. 1497–98, p. 233

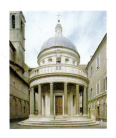

2.5.25 Donato Bramante, Tempietto, Cloister of San Pietro, Rome, Italy, c. 1502, p. 279

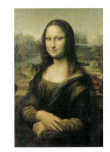

0.0.11 Leonardo da Vinci, *Mona Lisa*, c. 1503–6, p. 35

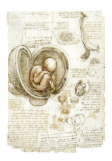

2.1.2 Leonardo da Vinci, *Studies of the fetus in the womb*, c. 1510–13, p. 199

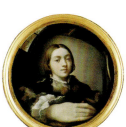

4.5.4 Parmigianino, *Self-portrait in a Convex Mirror*, c. 1524, p. 614

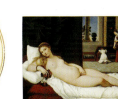

4.9.8 Titian, *Venus of Urbino*, 1538, p. 664

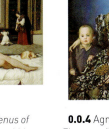

0.0.4 Agnolo Bronzino, *Eleonora di Toledo and Her Son Giovanni*, c. 1545, p. 29

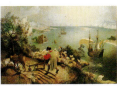

1.8.6 Pieter Bruegel the Elder, *Landscape with the Fall of Icarus*, c. 1555–58, p. 161

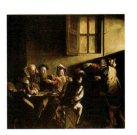

1.3.6 Caravaggio, *The Calling of St. Matthew*, c. 1599–1600, p. 85

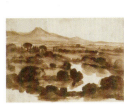

2.1.18 Claude Lorrain, *The Tiber from Monte Mario Looking South*, 1640, p. 209

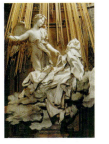

4.2.8 Gianlorenzo Bernini, *The Ecstasy of St. Teresa*, 1645–52, p. 579

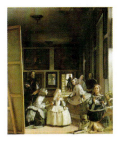

1.10.11a Diego Velázquez, *Las Meninas*, c. 1656, p. 190

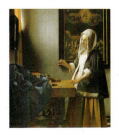

4.2.11 Johannes Vermeer, *Woman Holding a Balance*, c. 1664, p. 581

3.7

Art of Europe and America, 1700–1865: Rococo to Realism

The eighteenth and nineteenth centuries in Europe are characterized by concerns about social equality, and a transition in power from the wealthy to the growing middle class. Thus this period is often called an Age of Revolutions, beginning with the American Declaration of Independence in 1776. There were three revolutions in France during this period (1789, 1830, and 1848), all of which called for government by and for the people and equality for the lower classes, and all of which inspired revolutions elsewhere in Europe. At the same time, the Industrial Revolution, instigated by advancements in technology, began in Britain and spread throughout Europe, creating a shift from agrarian societies to more urban ones offering new working opportunities for the majority of people. Within Europe, the development of the telegraph in the 1830s allowed for ever-quickening communication, and the invention of the steam engine in 1869 led to expansive railroads, enabling more people to travel greater distances faster. Europe and America therefore became more aware of the world at large. As a result of all of these factors, as well as through colonization and trade, the Western art world was influenced by other cultures.

This was an age also known as the **Enlightenment**, sometimes called the Age of Reason. Enlightenment thinkers called for reason over faith, liberty over oppressive systems of government, and equal rights for all men. The English philosopher John Locke promoted a theory of empiricism, according to which humans are born with minds (blank slates) that are influenced by their experiences, rather than being innately functioning. This notion had large ramifications for better understanding the importance of education and the impact of social experience on individuals.

In his treatise called *The Social Contract* (1762), the writer and political theorist Jean-Jacques Rousseau (1712–1778) states that, "Man is born free, and everywhere he is in chains." Influenced by the ideas of John Locke, Rousseau believed that society should be governed by the consent and involvement of all the people. For this kind of community to work, Rousseau argues, society must support equal rights and education.

Artworks of this time both reflect and promote contemporary changes in economics, politics, and personal expression. While art historians have determined stylistic tendencies, it is important to note that the various styles in this period often overlapped; that is, each style did not strictly follow another chronologically. At times, artworks possess qualities of more than one style, or will not seem to fit easily into any single category. This complexity reflects the richness of ideas that were being exchanged in the eighteenth century.

Absolute Monarchy

At the beginning of the eighteenth century, most European countries were governed by **absolute** monarchs—rulers who, it was believed, derived

Enlightenment: historical period, also called the Age of Reason, in which reason was prized above faith, liberty above oppression, and there was a movement to secure equal rights for all men

Absolute, Absolutism: when applied to a ruler or monarch, the belief that he or she holds the ultimate power and that this derives from the will of God

Baroque: European artistic and architectural style of the late sixteenth to the early eighteenth century, characterized by extravagance, movement, and emotional intensity

their power and authority from God. Some artworks of the time are evidence of the extreme wealth and frivolous attitude of these rulers. The extravagance of the monarchy in France was epitomized by King Louis XIV (1638–1715), whose grandiose view of himself and his role in the world demonstrated the power of the absolute monarch. Louis called himself the Sun King to associate himself with the Greek sun god Apollo, and to imply that the activities of France began when—like the sun—Louis arose in the morning, and stopped when he retired at night. The exaggerated self-regard, even pomposity, of the royal circle would eventually prove their downfall and lead to their demise by the end of the eighteenth century.

The regal portrait by Hyacinthe Rigaud (1659–1743) is meant to demonstrate the king's power (**3.7.1**). Louis is dressed in royal attire, the gold fleur-de-lis (or "lily-flower," the symbol of the French monarchy) embroidered on a rich blue velvet gown, lined in expensive white fur known as ermine. Insisting on the finest of everything, Louis XIV dressed himself in the most opulent textiles from around the world. He invented the high heels shown here, which he used to increase his height (5 ft. 4 in.) and to show off his trim legs. This painting was made when the monarch was in fact in his sixties. It was common practice for painters to depict royal figures in the best light, often portraying them decades younger than they actually were.

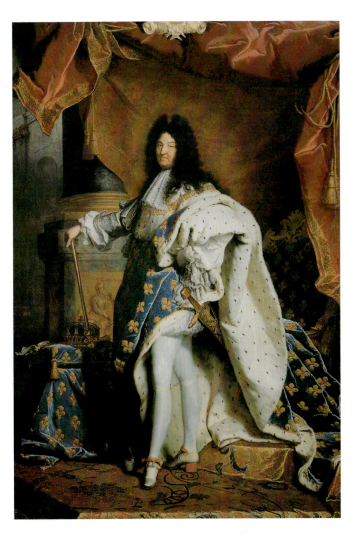

The Sun King stands at the entrance to the famed **Baroque** Hall of Mirrors (**3.7.2**), an opulent chamber filled with mirrors (highly expensive at the time) that reflect the gardens

3.7.1 Hyacinthe Rigaud, *Louis XIV*, 1701. Oil on canvas, 9'1" × 6'4⅜". Musée du Louvre, Paris, France

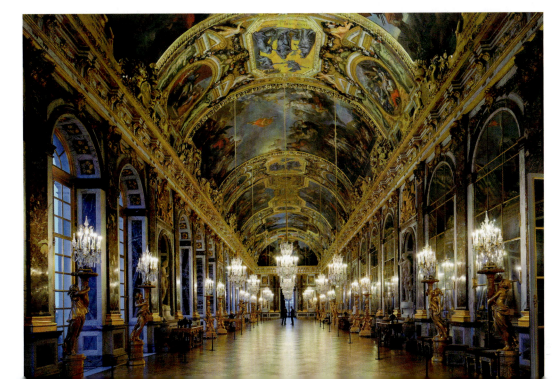

3.7.2 Jules Hardouin-Mansart, Château de Versailles, Hall of Mirrors (Galerie des Glaces), 1678–84, Versailles, France

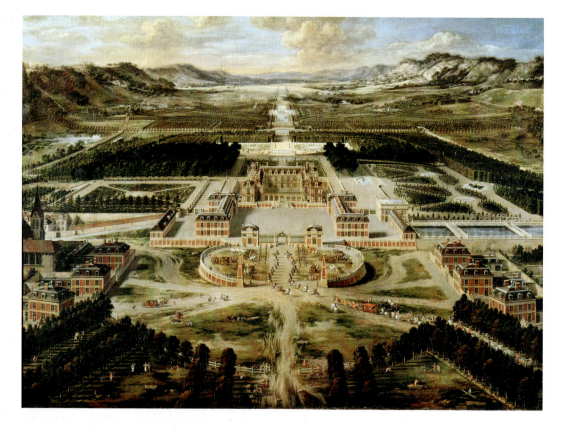

surrounding his grand new palace of Versailles, near Paris. Louis XIV was a great **patron** of the arts, and had commissioned the finest artists in Europe to construct and decorate Versailles to be the largest palace in the world. The Hall of Mirrors was used for greeting dignitaries, for formal celebrations, and as a ballroom. The 239-foot-long hallway is lavishly decorated with gilding, chandeliers, sculpture, and paintings depicting scenes of Louis XIV's political successes. The bright light that fills the room and is reflected in the numerous mirrors symbolizes Louis's identity and power as the Sun King.

Vast gardens surround the palace, covering almost 2,000 acres, with manicured geometric shapes carved into the landscape (**3.7.3**). Originally the garden was filled with 200,000 trees and 210,000 flowers, which were replanted frequently, and with 2,100 sculptures, many of them placed on the spectacular fountains, of which there are more than fifty. There was not enough water to run them all at once, though, and servants used a system of whistles to alert one another to turn on the fountains whenever the Sun King was within viewing range, giving him the impression that they ran continuously.

The King's commitment to the arts was a serious one, and when he decided to build Versailles, he turned the old royal palace in Paris, the Louvre, into a residence for the artists who worked for him. During his reign he approved the foundation of the Royal Academy of Painting and Sculpture. Academies offered artists their best opportunities to display and sell their work, and were therefore very influential, but also insisted on strict guidelines for the artworks they supported (see Box: European and American Art Academies, **3.7.9**, pp. 498–99).

Rococo

The undisputed power of the European ruling classes during the seventeenth and much of the eighteenth century inspired a period of extravagance amongst the very wealthy. Desiring the finest in everything, the ruling classes financed endless commissions of artworks in a style known as the Rococo. Stylistically, in its abundance of rich decoration, the Rococo is an outgrowth of the Baroque, but while the Baroque's subject matter was

Patron: an organization or individual who sponsors the creation of works of art
Organic: having irregular forms and shapes, as though derived from living organisms

very formal and moralistic, the Rococo's was more whimsical. Rococo artworks tend to be lighthearted, indulgent, and even somewhat superficial, featuring elaborately curved lines and **organic** forms.

Rococo paintings were often commissioned by the aristocracy and are playful in mood, sometimes with erotic undertones. The delicate brushstrokes and pastel colors create a sense of lightness and ease, and the frequently

frivolous subject matter suggests that those who commissioned such artworks had ample time to amuse themselves.

At first sight, *The Swing*, by Jean-Honoré Fragonard (1732–1806), appears to be an innocent scene of a refined young lady enjoying her swinging (**3.7.4**). Upon closer inspection, however, we see that the woman has flirtatiously kicked her shoe into the air, which allows the "gentleman" (thought by some to be the patron

3.7.4 Jean-Honoré Fragonard, *The Swing*, 1766. Oil on canvas, 31⅞ × 25¼". Wallace Collection, London, England

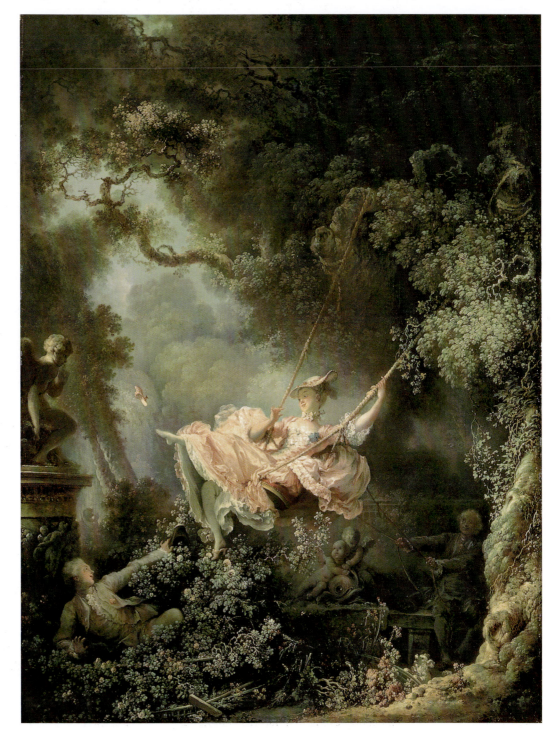

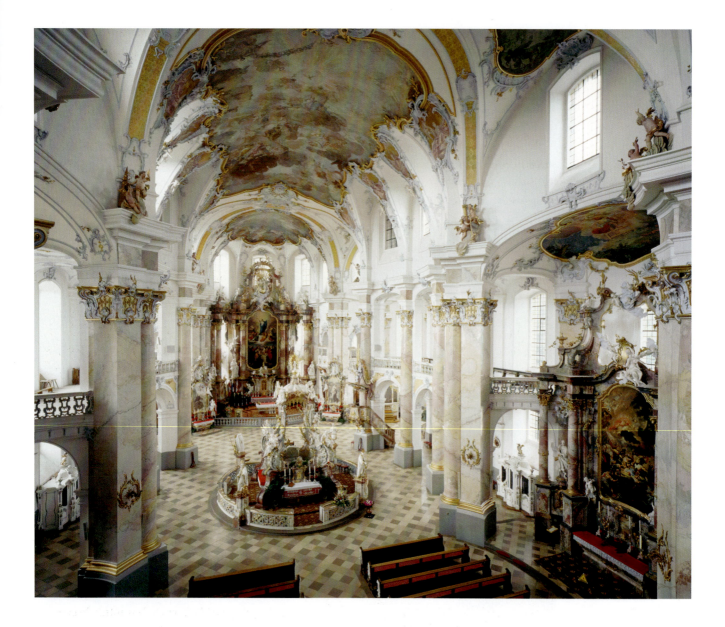

of this painting) in the bushes below a view up her skirt. In a statue on the left side of the canvas, Cupid puts his finger to his lips, suggesting a secret love tryst between the young couple. The feathery brushstrokes, pastel colors, and abundance of flowers support the romantic and trivial nature of the subject matter. A bishop, standing in the shadows in the lower right-hand part of the canvas, holds a rope that controls the swing, and he appears to be completely unaware of the couple's mischievous behavior. The artist's inclusion of this figure has been interpreted by some as a comment on the Church's ignorance of immoral behavior, and by others as a chiding of the Catholic Church for not condemning such conduct.

Rococo palaces and churches throughout Europe also convey the desire of the time that art should stimulate the eyes with pleasure. The German architect Johann Balthasar Neumann (1687–1753) built churches with predominantly bright white interiors, as if to reflect Germany's glistening winter snow. The basilica of Vierzehnheiligen ("Fourteen Holy Ones") near Bamberg, in Bavaria, southern Germany, has fourteen statues around the altar, depicting Catholic saints; believers pray to the saints for protection against sickness. These saints are venerated in this region for the help they are thought to have given during the severe suffering caused by the Black Plague centuries before. Yet although this is a place of worship, there

3.7.5 Johann Balthasar Neumann, Basilica of Vierzehnheiligen, 1743–72, near Bamberg, Germany

is constant interest and vivacity in the ornate decoration of the church's brightly lit interior. From the subtle pink and yellow in the columns, to the paintings on the recesses in the ceilings, to the gilded touches throughout, rich detail creates a luxurious and fanciful space (**3.7.5**).

By the late eighteenth century, the wasteful spending and frivolity of the monarchy had caused such popular opposition that the monarchy itself took notice. Marie Antoinette, the wife of King Louis XVI (1754–1793) (great-great-grandson of the Sun King), had become the symbol of the royal family's extravagance. While the French state suffered financial strain and the people went hungry, the queen decorated herself with expensive clothes and jewels and was given her own chateau, or palace, which she decorated extravagantly. The French directed much of their anger at the queen; many considered her promiscuous, even incestuous,

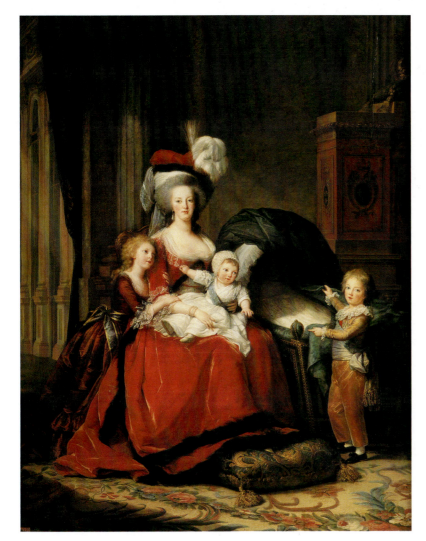

3.7.6 Elisabeth-Louise Vigée-Lebrun, *Marie-Antoinette and Her Children*, 1787. Oil on canvas, 9'1½" × 7'⅝". Musée National du Château de Versailles, France

although historians find that some of the accusations against her were greatly exaggerated.

One portrait of Marie Antoinette and her children (**3.7.6**) was painted to improve the queen's reputation. She is shown seated in Versailles with the Hall of Mirrors (**3.7.2**) behind her right shoulder, in a manner that is similar to the portrait of Louis XIV standing at the entrance to the same place. While her rich velvet dress shows her status as Queen of France, her wardrobe is neither overly revealing nor lacking in French style and taste, which had been a criticism of previous portraits. In dramatic opposition to her growing reputation as promiscuous and unavailable to the king, she is shown as a loving mother adored by her children, who cling to her. Her somber expression suggests sorrow over the recent loss of her youngest daughter, for whom the empty cradle was intended. In fact, the artist Elisabeth-Louise Vigée-Lebrun (1755–1842), who painted this and many other portraits of Marie Antoinette, wrote in her diary of the kind nature of the queen, and of the latter's sympathy for the painter when she herself was pregnant and when she faced challenges as a female artist in the Royal Academy of Painting and Sculpture. The portrait did not, however, assuage the growing anger of the French people. It was removed from public display shortly after being exhibited in 1788, for fear that it would be attacked. The following year, the French Revolution began. Three years later, in 1792, the monarchy was overthrown, and in 1793 Louis XVI and Marie Antoinette were beheaded.

Rejecting the Rococo: Sentimentality in Painting

The Rococo's lighthearted subject matter did not appeal to all eighteenth-century artists: some were interested instead in creating art with moral messages that often pulled on the heartstrings of the audience. Jean-Baptiste Greuze (1725–1805) was known for his images that idealized the virtue of the simple life of the lower classes. In *The Marriage Contract* a young loving couple, whose arms are intertwined, is about to be married (**3.7.7**). A notary on the right documents the formal agreement. The bride's humble father has just given the young man her dowry, and the members of her family are crying over how much they will miss her. The scene emphasizes the rustic surroundings of the family, highlighting their lack of financial wealth and suggesting that the poor are closer to nature. The family's situation is echoed by the hen feeding her chicks in the lower portion of the canvas. One chick goes off to the right to sit upon a saucer, just as the young bride is about to go off to start her own family. While the family is financially poor, it is rich in love. The simplicity and purity of the setting and the people contrast with the frivolous materialism of the Rococo.

The works of British painter and **engraver** William Hogarth (1697–1764) were also a reaction to the aristocratic classes of the Rococo era. Hogarth's **narratives** criticized the morals of his time. Many of his paintings were reproduced as **prints**, which were released one at a time to spur interest and curiosity; these were the soap operas of the eighteenth century. Hogarth's prints (often engraved by others) made his work affordable for the lower and middle classes, who were a receptive audience for his satirical series. The prints were incredibly popular and forged copies were rampant, so much so that he requested protection for his original creations from Parliament, leading to the Engraving Copyright Act of 1734, also called Hogarth's Act.

The series *Marriage à-la-Mode (A Fashionable Marriage)* includes six paintings on which the highly successful engravings were based. *The Marriage Settlement* is the first in the series (**3.7.8**), and shows a quite different marriage arrangement than that in Greuze's depiction (**3.7.7**). The betrothed couple sits together on the left, completely uninterested in each other. The miserable bride toys with her handkerchief while her father's lawyer, Silvertongue, flirts with her. The bridegroom admires himself in a mirror, too much of a snob even to look at his bride. The two dogs

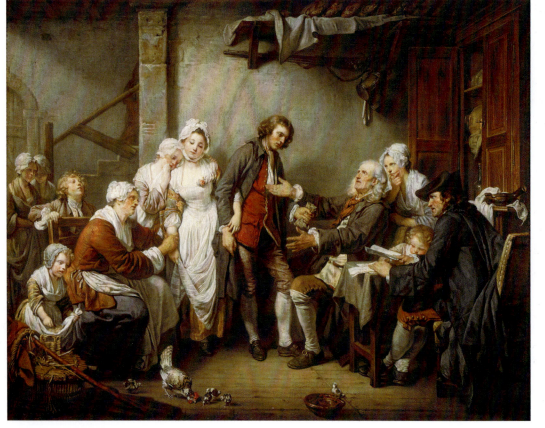

3.7.7 Jean-Baptiste Greuze, *The Marriage Contract*, 1761. Oil on canvas, 25¼ × 31½". Musée du Louvre, Paris, France

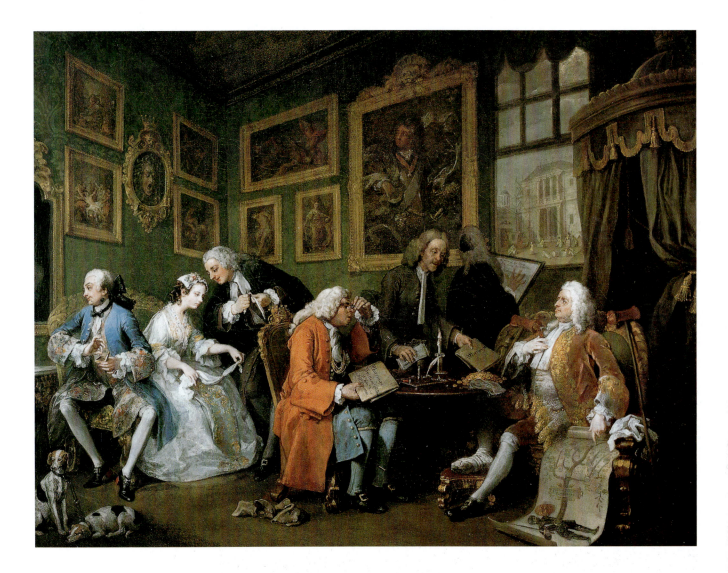

shackled together in the foreground echo the attitudes of the bride and groom. The marriage contract is being arranged by their fathers. The groom's father, on the far right, proudly displays in his family tree his aristocratic lineage as Earl Squander. The bride's father, a successful merchant, offers a fine dowry in the form of a pile of coins placed in front of the earl. Out the window above the earl can be seen his building project, which will be financed by the dowry. In the rest of the series, both husband and wife have affairs and gradually fritter away their fortune; the wife finally poisons herself after Silvertongue, who has become her lover, has been executed for the murder of her husband. Much of Hogarth's artwork addresses the need for social change, and the *Marriage à-la-Mode* series condemns the devastating effect of immorality on society.

Neoclassicism

Those marks of heroism and civic virtue presented to the eyes of the people will electrify the soul, and sow the seeds of glory and loyalty to the fatherland.

(Jacques-Louis David)

This statement by the French painter David summarizes the moral objectives of Neoclassical (literally, "new Classical") art. This was a movement that developed during the late eighteenth century as an even bolder reaction against the artificiality of the Rococo. Neoclassical artworks recall, in their imagery and subject matter, the ancient **Classical** cultures of Greece and Rome. This interest in the ancient world was fueled by such archaeological discoveries at about this time as the remains of

3.7.8 William Hogarth, *The Marriage Settlement*, *c.* 1743. Oil on canvas, 27½ × 35¾". National Gallery, London, England

Classical: ancient Greek and Roman; art that conforms to Greek and Roman models, or is based on rational construction and emotional equilibrium

European and American Art Academies: Making a Living as an Artist

Throughout the eighteenth century and for much of the nineteenth, in Europe, government-sponsored art academies provided the main outlet for European artists to exhibit their work. Since patrons often chose artists who were members of an academy, such academies influenced an artist's ability to earn a living. France was the artistic center of Europe at this time, and the French Academy of Painting and Sculpture, founded in 1648 (renamed the Academy of Fine Arts in 1816), was vastly influential in determining artistic success. Its strict curriculum required artists to copy ancient works of art before they were allowed to study a living model. Students also studied history, mythology, literature, and anatomy—important subjects of academic art. The Academy thrived on the notion of competition. The winner of the most important competition, the Prix de Rome (Rome Prize), was sent to Rome to study Classical works and the **Renaissance** masters. Following the French model, Britain's Royal Academy of Arts was founded in 1768. The first Art Academy in America was founded in 1805 in Philadelphia, Pennsylvania.

The French Academy also developed a hierarchy that determined the relative importance of the subject matter of a painting. History paintings (**3.7.12**, **3.7.16**), which depicted historical, biblical, or mythological scenes, usually containing large groups of people, were considered to be the finest of the genres. Portraits (**3.7.6**) were the next most valued paintings, then scenes of the lower class (**3.7.7**, **3.7.20**), landscapes (**3.7.19**), and finally still life paintings (**3.7.11**). History paintings highlighted an artist's use of academic training in that they showed subjects, often with **idealized** nude bodies, that the artists had studied in their readings. Artists who painted other **genres** would often try to increase the importance of their artworks by including elements important to the Academy, such as references to human beings, Classical stories, and messages of morality. While artists who excelled in any of these subjects could belong to the Academy, only those who were considered history painters were allowed to teach there.

During the eighteenth and nineteenth centuries only four women were allowed into

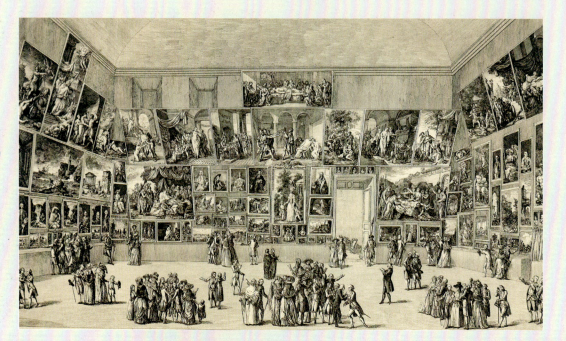

3.7.9 Pietro Antonio Martini, *The Salon*, 1785. Musée du Château de Versailles, France

Renaissance: a period of cultural and artistic change in Europe from the fourteenth to the seventeenth century
Idealized: represented as perfect in form or character, corresponding to an ideal
Genre: categories of artistic subject matter, often with strongly influential histories and traditions

the French Academy. It was very difficult for women to become artists because of a lack of training venues and because women were not allowed to study nude models, which was considered a critical skill in the Academy, particularly in the creation of history paintings. The female artists who did become successful academic painters did so in one of the "lesser" genres, and thanks to extra familial or royal support (**3.7.6**, **3.7.11**). In European society in general, women had fewer rights than their male counterparts, but wealthy women did wield power through social gatherings in their private homes. Through these societal parties, hostesses would inspire intellectual exchange between artists, writers, musicians, and critics.

The Royal Academy of Painting and Sculpture held an exhibition called the Salon in Paris, held every one or two years, which was highly competitive, and the public flocked to this social event. In Pietro Antonio Martini's print of the Salon of 1785 (**3.7.9**), paintings fill the walls from floor to ceiling. The history paintings (always much larger in scale) were given prominent places, and the lowest of the genres, the still lifes, were usually hung lower. Martini's print highlights the prominent placement (at the center of the middle wall) of David's history painting *Oath of the Horatii* (**3.7.10**) in the 1785 Salon. Critics from around the world reviewed the exhibition, making or breaking artists' reputations.

After the French Revolution (1789), the French Academy continued, but it was apparent that its rules and organization no longer fulfilled the needs of artists in the modern world, and that it needed to transform to survive. Previously, enormous and expensive history paintings had been popular with the aristocracy. Now, the emerging middle classes began to see the value of the lesser genres; they could afford to buy them, and had room to hang them in their homes. The expanding and increasingly prosperous middle class in turn fueled a growth in independent dealers and enabled artists to exhibit in venues the Academy did not control, most famously the Impressionist exhibitions from 1874 to 1886. As options expanded for the artists to exhibit and sell artworks, the control the Academy had wielded now waned. In 1881, organization and control of the official Salon was put in the hands of individual artists, and the government withdrew its support.

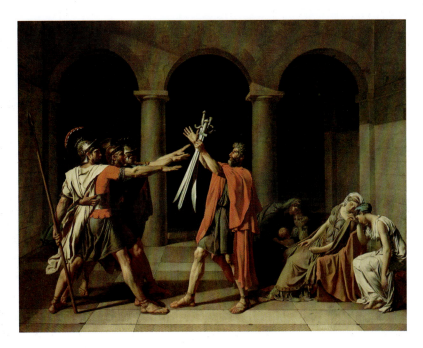

3.7.10 Jacques-Louis David, *The Oath of the Horatii*, 1784. Oil on canvas, 10'10" × 13'11⅜". Musée du Louvre, Paris, France

the Roman city of Pompeii. Ancient Greece and Rome were thought to embody such virtues as civic responsibility and an emphasis on rational thought. At a time of public unrest, Neoclassical artworks used historical or mythological stories to convey a moral message, and sought to convey rationalism and stability through structure and stillness, creating visions of balance and order.

Jacques-Louis David (1748–1825) lived through one of the most tumultuous periods in French history. He made paintings purchased by the monarchy, then supported revolutionary leaders who opposed the king, and later painted numerous portraits of the French Emperor Napoleon. Although David's painting *The Oath of the Horatii* (**3.7.10**), because of its promotion of civic duty, or accepting personal sacrifice in the service of one's nation, is often linked with the ideas that fueled the French Revolution of 1789, in fact the image was made for King Louis XVI, five years before the revolution that removed him from the throne.

The painting shows a scene from early Roman history in which three brothers make a vow to their father to fight for Rome. The scene is Neoclassical in its serious subject matter, its muscular Classical figures, and its stable, balanced composition, created in part by the pyramidal groupings of the figures. The three Roman archways divide the scene with the brothers on the left, the father in the center, and the women of the family on the right. While the soldiers stand heroically, the women mourn the losses they know will come.

Anne Vallayer-Coster (1744–1818), trained by her father and other artists, was a brilliant painter of still lifes. Although she often painted fruits or flowers, she chose the subject of *Attributes of Painting, Sculpture, and Architecture* (**3.7.11**) to gain entrance into the Academy (see Box: European and American Art Academies, pp. 498–99). The painting, Neoclassical in its powerfully structured composition, was sized to be an "overdoor," meaning that it would have been hung high above a doorway. The dynamism of the composition is enhanced when one stands below the work and feels a sense of anxiety that the precariously arranged objects could fall. Vallayer-Coster chose objects referencing intellectualism in other artistic endeavors, including architectural plans, tools, and a Classically styled sculpture that seems to point its missing head to the upper left. Unlike other paintings of the attributes of the arts, however, the artist includes an unfinished bust. We know it is unfinished because of its darker shade, signifying that the clay is moist, and

3.7.11 Anne Vallayer-Coster, *Attributes of Painting, Sculpture and Architecture*, 1769. Oil on canvas, 35½ × 47¾". Musée du Louvre, Paris, France

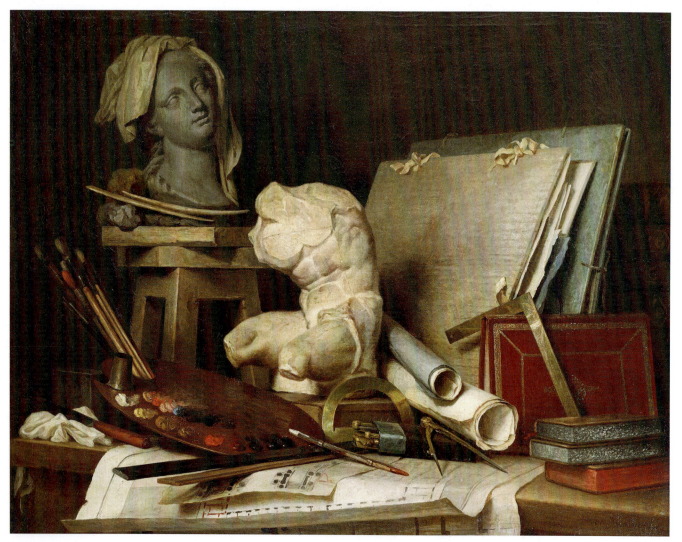

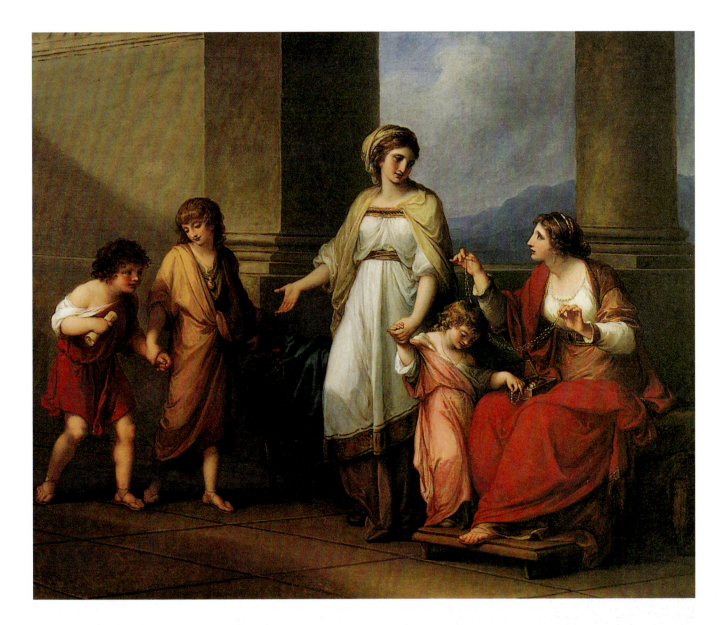

3.7.12 Angelica Kauffmann, *Cornelia Pointing to Her Children as Her Treasures*, c. 1785. Oil on canvas, 40 × 50". Virginia Museum of Fine Arts, Richmond

the temporarily removed cloth that is used to prevent it drying. The bust might be interpreted as a self-portrait, in which the artist is presenting herself as an unfinished work, ready to be molded by the Academy.

The Swiss-Austrian Angelica Kauffmann (1741–1807) used purely Neoclassical elements, such as Classical subject matter and Classical architecture, in her paintings. Kauffmann was one of only two women amongst the thirty-four original members of the British Royal Academy of the Arts. Founded in 1768, it was the British version of the French Academy of Painting and Sculpture (see pp. 498–99). Kauffmann was trained in painting by her father in her youth, and became a well-respected artist with commissions from international patrons. Her

best-known works are Neoclassical scenes that portray strong female characters. In *Cornelia Pointing to Her Children as Her Treasures*, a Roman woman is represented as a model of motherhood and morality (**3.7.12**). While the woman on the right displays her fine jewelry, Cornelia gestures to her sons as her source of pride, her own jewels; they will grow up to be the political leaders Tiberius and Gaius Gracchus. Cornelia's daughter, curious, strokes the woman's jewels, but Cornelia holds her hand firmly and models strength of character rather than pride in material wealth.

Neoclassicism represented the ideals of Americans in the late eighteenth century: equality, patriotism, and civic responsibility. The new American cities chose Neoclassicism

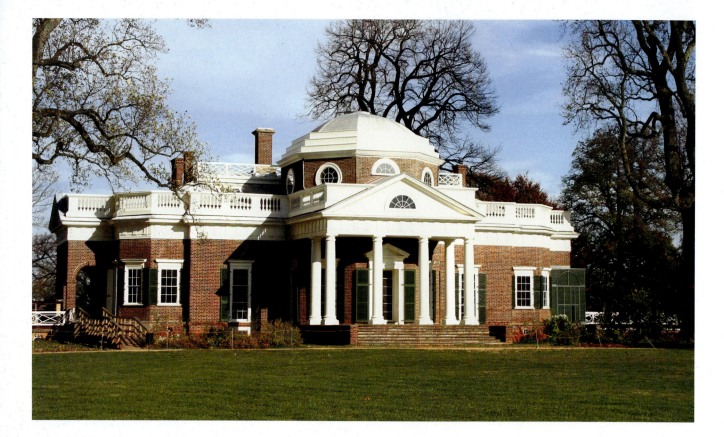

as their preferred architectural style. Thomas Jefferson (1743–1826), author of the Declaration of Independence and America's third president, designed a Neoclassical home for himself in Charlottesville, Virginia; he named it Monticello (**3.7.13**). He was inspired by the Renaissance architect Andrea Palladio's use of Classical elements, such as **arches**, **domes**, and **pediments**, all of which can be seen in the design of Monticello. Its central dome has an **oculus**, like the Classical Roman Pantheon. The house has forty-three rooms, eight fireplaces, and thirteen skylights. It was begun in 1769, but Jefferson continued to make changes and additions to it until his death, more than fifty years later.

Romanticism

While the style and subject matter of Neoclassical art were designed to express rationalism, stability, and traditional notions of duty, Romantic artworks, by contrast, emphasize individuality, and surge with drama, fantasy, and heightened emotion. Additionally, many Romantic images portray the power and beauty of nature and man's relationship with it, both as a rejection of the encroaching industrialization of the period and as a symbol for the natural impulses and creativity of humans. Romantic artists valued emotion over reason, and **Romanticism** in art, which emerged in the first half of the nineteenth century, reflects the turmoil of the European and American revolutions, when the people rose up against the ruling classes and demanded their freedom. One of the most shocking and moving Romantic images is Francisco Goya's *Third of May, 1808* (see Gateway Box: Goya, **3.7.15**), commemorating the Spanish resistance to Napoleon's occupation of Madrid. Romantic art challenged the traditional norms and structures of society and often showed citizens' sacrifices for ideals of liberty, equality, and humanity, in images charged with energy created by the use of **implied lines** in all directions, frequent **asymmetry**, and visual movement and **rhythm**.

Liberty Leading the People, by Eugène Delacroix (1798–1863), depicts the French people bravely rising up against their government in the three-day July Revolution of 1830 (**3.7.16**). In the painting, the bare-breasted

3.7.13 Thomas Jefferson, Monticello, 1769–1809, Charlottesville, Virginia

Arches: structures, usually curved, that span an opening
Dome: an evenly curved vault forming the ceiling or roof of a building
Pediment: the triangular space, situated above the row of columns, on the facade of a building in the Classical style
Oculus: a round opening at the center of a dome
Romanticism: movement in nineteenth-century European culture, concerned with the power of the imagination and greatly valuing intense feeling
Implied line: a line not actually drawn but suggested by elements in the work
Asymmetry: a type of design in which balance is achieved by elements that contrast and complement one another without being the same on either side of an axis
Rhythm: the regular or ordered repetition of elements in the work

Gateway to Art: Goya, *The Third of May, 1808*
The Artist and the Royal Family

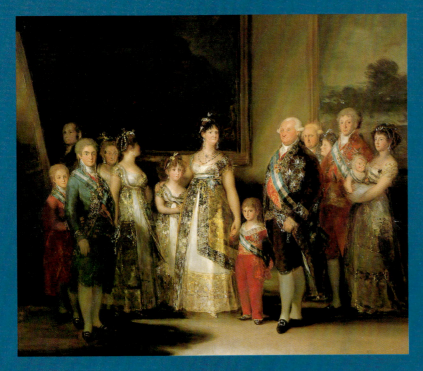

3.7.14 Francisco Goya, *Family of Charles IV*, c. 1800. Oil on canvas, 9'2¼" × 11'⅜". Museo Nacional del Prado, Madrid, Spain

The Spanish royal family commissioned paintings from Goya before and after the French occupation of Spain (1808–14). An examination of *The Third of May, 1808* (**3.7.15**) and Goya's portrait *The Family of Charles IV* (**3.7.14**) poses interesting questions about Goya's personal views and the turbulent history of the time.

In his portrait of 1800, Goya shows the royal family ornately dressed. The king wears black military attire and many gold medals. Yet critics commented on how Goya represented the less flattering aspects of the royal family, one describing them as "a shopkeeper and his family after they have won the lottery." The king and queen are both shown as ageing and overweight, the king's bulging paunch the antithesis of what one expects from a nation's military leader. The queen is prominent in the center, somewhat obtrusively stealing the stage from her husband and children. Her position perhaps reflects the fact that she was the most powerful person in the family; that she arranged the individual sittings for the painter; and that she approved the final work.

The royal couple's two younger children stand on either side of her while the eldest, Prince Ferdinand (later Ferdinand VII), is shown on the far left in a rich regal blue. He holds hands with a young lady; her face is not visible because she represents the prince's bride, who has not yet been chosen. Behind them is the grandmother with a large mole, which the painter made no effort to hide, on her face.

There is no evidence, however, that Goya intended to insult or make fun of the royal family. The painting may reflect his respect for truth and nature; and the sitters seemed quite pleased with the portrait, even allowing the artist to include his self-portrait in the shadows on the far left of the canvas. Goya's inclusion of himself in the painting is a reference to *Las Meninas*, a famous royal portrait of the family of an earlier Spanish monarch, Philip IV, by Velázquez (see **1.10.11a**, p. 190).

Eight years after he appeared in Goya's portrait of his family, Ferdinand VII helped the French to overthrow his father. The Spanish people had mixed responses to the French occupation; some hoped it would bring an end to the tyranny of the Inquisition, which enforced religious orthodoxy. Goya's painting *The Third of May, 1808* documents and memorializes the ill-treatment of the Spanish people who initially rose up against the French. Interestingly, the painting was commissioned in 1814 by Ferdinand VII, who had replaced his father as King of Spain.

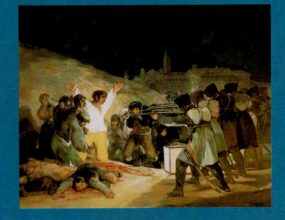

3.7.15 Francisco Goya, *The Third of May, 1808*, 1814. Oil on canvas, 8'4⅜" × 11'3⅞". Museo Nacional del Prado, Madrid, Spain

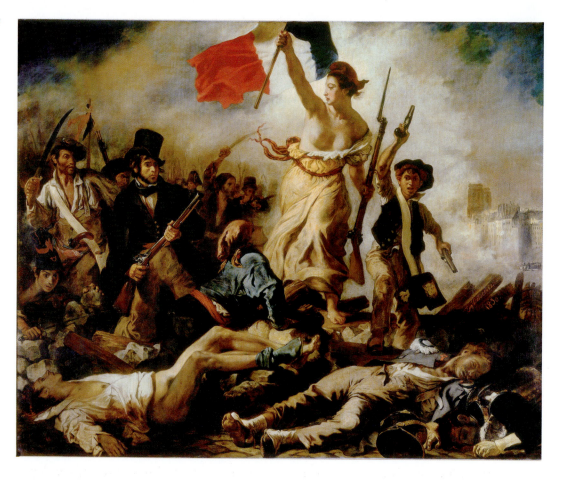

3.7.16 Eugène Delacroix, *Liberty Leading the People*, 1830. Oil on canvas, 8′6⅜″ × 10′8″. Musée du Louvre, Paris, France

3.7.17 William Blake, *Elohim Creating Adam*, 1795. Color print finished in ink and watercolor on paper, 17 × 21⅛″. Tate, London, England

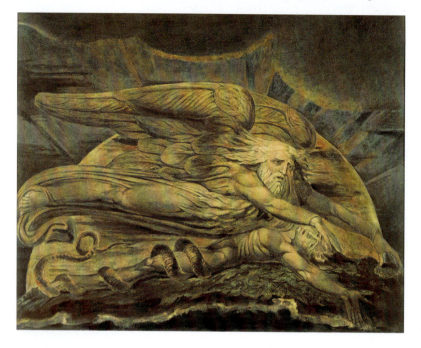

symbol of freedom, Liberty, carries the flag of the revolution in one hand and a musket in the other. The depiction of this **personification** of France's symbol of Liberty was shocking at the time for its portrayal of a modern, dirty figure rather than an idealized goddess. Although partly an imagined scene, the painting accurately shows the sacrifice of people of all ages and social classes. A little boy fearlessly marches forward carrying two pistols, while an upper-class gentleman in a top hat holds a rifle. Crowds of people with muskets and swords follow Liberty as she climbs over those who have died, signifying that such sacrifice is worth the greater good. In contrast to David's *Oath of the Horatii* (**3.7.10**), which glorifies a Roman story for a modern purpose, Delacroix's Romantic image highlights the emotion felt by many Parisians about a contemporary event.

The British artist and poet William Blake (1757–1827) conveys in both his visual and literary works emotionally charged messages about his beliefs in personal and creative freedom. In *Elohim Creating Adam* (**3.7.17**), Blake transforms Michelangelo's famous *Creation of Adam* from the Sistine ceiling in Rome into a Romantic image filled with anguish and struggle. In Blake's vision, God ("Elohim" in Hebrew) has enormous wings that seem to grow from the tendons in his shoulders. The process of creation is shown to be painful for both

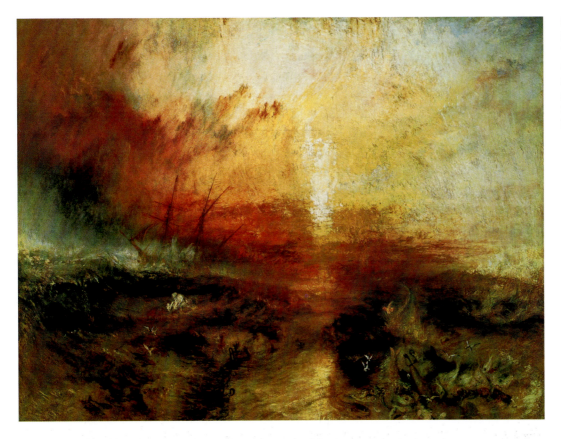

3.7.18 J. M. W. Turner, *Slave Ship (Slavers Throwing Overboard the Dead and Dying, Typhoon Coming On)*, 1840. Oil on canvas, 35¾ × 48¼". Museum of Fine Arts, Boston, Massachusetts

creator and created, rather than a cause for joy and celebration. The sadness evident in Elohim's face may convey his knowledge that the creation of man will inevitably bring about humanity's fall from grace, implied in the image by the presence of a snake. Blake believed that man's spiritual freedom was suppressed on the day of his creation, and his painting shows it: Adam's body is restrained by the serpent, while his mind is restrained by the hand of God. Blake resisted any controls on either his creativity or behavior, rejecting many of the accepted Christian values of the time and rebelling as well against the philosophies of the British Royal Academy.

Some fifty years after Blake's work, another British painter, J. M. W. Turner (1775–1851), also used his art to express his views, in the instance shown here as a force for social protest. In his dramatic painting in the Romantic style, *Slave Ship (Slavers Throwing Overboard the Dead and Dying, Typhoon Coming On)* (**3.7.18**), Turner condemns the slave trade. Although slavery was illegal by this time throughout Britain, Turner was highlighting the injustice of the slave trade and protesting against any consideration of its renewal. His powerful canvas portrays an infamous incident aboard the slave ship *Zong* in 1781. It was common practice for slave-ship captains to fill their vessels with more slaves than they would need, knowing that disease might spread amongst them. The captain of the *Zong* knew that he would be paid for any slaves lost at sea, but not for those who were sick when they arrived. He therefore had sick slaves thrown overboard while still far from land.

Turner's chaotic canvas displays several aspects of the Romantic style. Man versus nature was a common theme in Romantic art, and here the immense power of nature, expressed as a fierce storm, overpowers the slaves. Body parts, still shackled and being attacked by sharp-teethed fish, can be seen in the central and right foreground. Turner uses intense colors and turbulent brushstrokes to convey the heightened emotion and fearful horror of the event. His canvas also has an **abstract** quality, making its subject matter difficult to understand. Turner placed beside his painting a quotation from the book that had inspired it, in order to help viewers understand his artwork's meaning.

Abstract: an artwork the form of which is simplified, distorted, or exaggerated in appearance. It may represent a recognizable form that has been slightly altered, or it may be a completely non-representational depiction

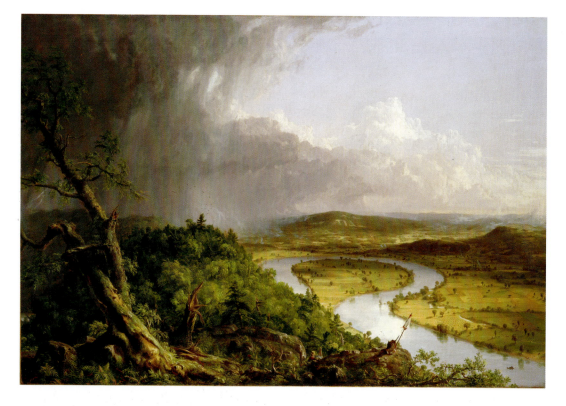

3.7.19 Thomas Cole, *View from Mount Holyoke, Massachusetts, after a Thunderstorm—The Oxbow*, 1836. Oil on canvas, 4'3½" × 6'4". Metropolitan Museum of Art, New York

Sublime: feeling of awe or terror, provoked by the experience of limitless nature and the awareness of the smallness of an individual

Realism: nineteenth-century artistic style that aimed to depict nature and everyday subjects in an unidealized manner. "Realism" is also used to describe a historical movement from the same period, which tried to achieve social change and equality by highlighting, in art and literature, the predicament of the poor

Illusionism, illusionistic: the artistic skill or trick of making something look real

Born in England, the painter Thomas Cole (1801–1848) emigrated to America at the age of seventeen and went on to found the Hudson River School, a group of Romantic American painters who painted the American landscape as an expression of pride in the expansion of the developing nation and its great natural beauty. This group's paintings embody the idea of the **sublime**, where the awe-inspiring power of nature overwhelms the smallness of man. In his painting *The Oxbow*, Cole views the twisting Connecticut River from a dramatic vantage point (**3.7.19**). A tree in the foreground has been battered by weather, while the river is far below in the valley. Above are fierce thunderclouds, but in the distance we can see the sky after the storm has passed. The only trace of man in this scene, hard to pick out against the dense trees, is the artist, wearing a hat. We can just glimpse him, engulfed by the grandeur of the landscape, in the lower center of the canvas.

Realist Tendencies

Show me an angel, and I'll paint one!

(Gustave Courbet, French painter, defending realism)

Beginning around the mid-nineteenth century, a significant shift took place in the objectives of the visual arts and in the way art looked. To varying degrees, a number of artists broke away from the traditions of earlier eighteenth- and nineteenth-century art to create objective representations of the real world. The movement called **Realism** refers specifically to writers and artists in France who were concerned about achieving social change after the Revolution of 1848. They created depictions of individuals in modern society, with underlying political messages about the inequality of the poor. Realism in general, however, can also refer to artists (in France and elsewhere) who observed their modern subjects in great detail yet did not have a social or political agenda. Realist artists also began to allow the process of creating art to show through in their final works, and were less concerned with **illusionistic** surfaces.

Gustave Courbet (1819–1877) is credited with first using the term "realist" to describe his own work. As a reaction to the Neoclassical, moralizing images of historic scenes, or the extremely emotional paintings of the Romantics, Courbet argued that it was more meaningful to paint people and things in everyday life.

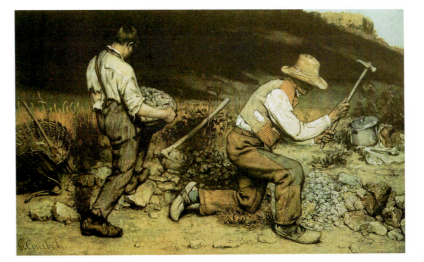

3.7.20 Gustave Courbet, *Stonebreakers*, 1849. Oil on canvas, 5'3" × 8'6". Formerly in the Gemäldegalerie, Dresden, Germany; believed to have been destroyed in 1945

The painting *Stonebreakers* was shocking for its depiction of working-class people on a large-sized canvas, a scale normally reserved for the heroic subject matter of history paintings (**3.7.20**). Courbet's painting highlights the backbreaking, monotonous work of the poor. The breaking of stones was a job taught by older generations to young men, and it was a job a man would have for a lifetime. The painting shows an older worker and his young assistant as powerful and unrelenting—qualities that alarmed the upper classes: a year before Courbet painted this work, in the Revolution of 1848, workers throughout Europe had rebelled and demanded an end to bad working conditions and to low pay.

The desire to portray realistic subject matter that reflected the everyday life of the lower classes was taken up by painters in the United States as well. Henry Ossawa Tanner (1859–1937) was born into a middle-class African-American family. He was educated at the Pennsylvania Academy of the Fine Arts, where his professor, the painter Thomas Eakins, encouraged him to study anatomy and observe nature closely. Later Tanner moved to Paris, where he was influenced by French painters, including Courbet.

Just as Courbet's *Stonebreakers* showed an older man training a younger worker, Tanner's *Banjo Lesson* shows the passing of knowledge between generations (**3.7.21**). In a humble home, a young African-American boy is patiently being taught by his grandfather to play the banjo. Tanner's painting challenges the stereotype then common in America, of smiling black men as simple-minded entertainers. Tanner creates a dignified image of a poor black family by showing a thoughtful black man as a teacher, and an intelligent black child engaged in

3.7.21 Henry Ossawa Tanner, *The Banjo Lesson*, 1893. Oil on canvas, 48 × 35½". Hampton University Museum, Hampton, Virginia

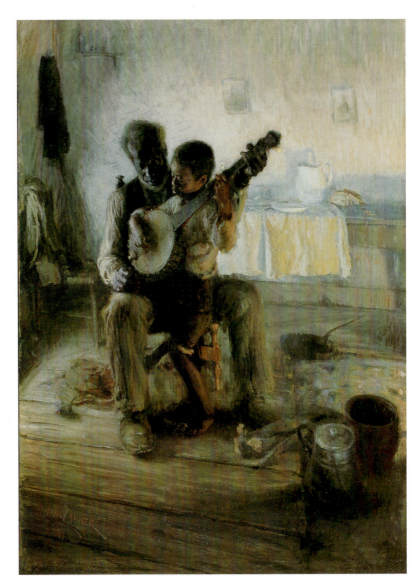

Pre-Raphaelite Brotherhood: English art movement formed in 1848 by painters who rejected the academic rules of art, and often painted medieval subjects in a naïve style

learning. Tanner sets a calm scene with natural objects and earthy colors, but he symbolizes the boy's spiritual and mental growth with the light coming in through the window, creating a soft rhythm, which can be likened to the act of playing the banjo.

Realist tendencies took a different form in the case of a group of English painters and writers, formed in 1848, who called themselves the **Pre-Raphaelite Brotherhood**. While many realist painters in France were rejecting the traditions of their Academy, the Pre-Raphaelites, as they became known, were opposed to the values of the Royal Academy of Arts in Britain, which promoted artwork inspired by artists of ancient Greece and Rome and of the Renaissance. Pre-Raphaelite artists were instead inspired by medieval subject matter. They were realist in their intense attention to visual details and their true-to-life depictions of nature and people.

Ophelia (**3.7.22**) by the Pre-Raphaelite John Everett Millais (1829–96) is a scene from Shakespeare's tragedy *Hamlet*, in which the young female character, Ophelia, drowns herself because her lover Prince Hamlet has rejected her and accidentally killed her father. Millais's depiction of nature is painstakingly detailed. To make this painting, he selected a single spot on a nearby river and painted the plants growing there so carefully that botanists can identify every one. He worked at the site almost every day over a five-month period. Millais also included flowers that were not growing by the river but that are mentioned in *Hamlet*. He then took realism to the extreme by having his model pose for the painting in a filled bathtub so that he could study the way her hair and dress floated. Although she often had oil lamps around her to keep her warm, the model caught a severe cold from spending so many hours in the water in the middle of winter.

3.7.22 John Everett Millais, *Ophelia*, 1851–52. Oil on canvas, 30 × 44". Tate, London, England

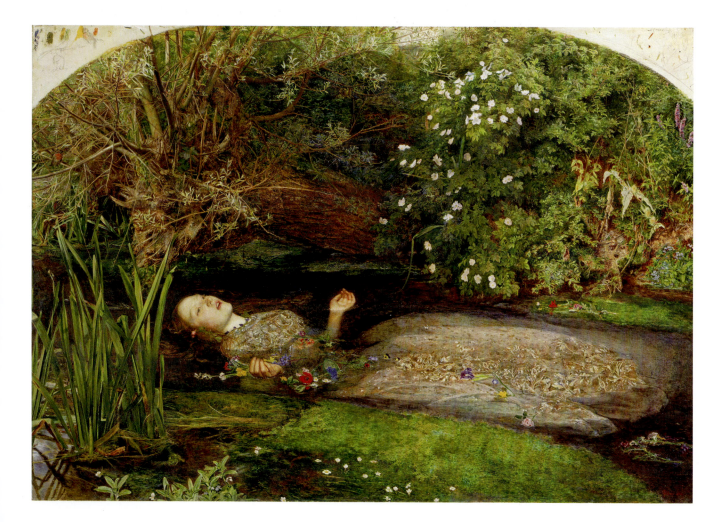

A Revolutionary Invention: Photography and Art in the Nineteenth Century

Realism was partly inspired and fueled by the invention of photography in the first decades of the nineteenth century, which led many artists to feel pressured to capture the truth of everyday life the way that photographers could. The advent of photography also affected artists directly in terms of their income. A client who wanted, for example, a portrait, had previously had only one option: to pay a portrait artist to paint a likeness, which was a time-consuming task for both the artist and the **sitter**, expensive for the client, and lucrative for the artist.

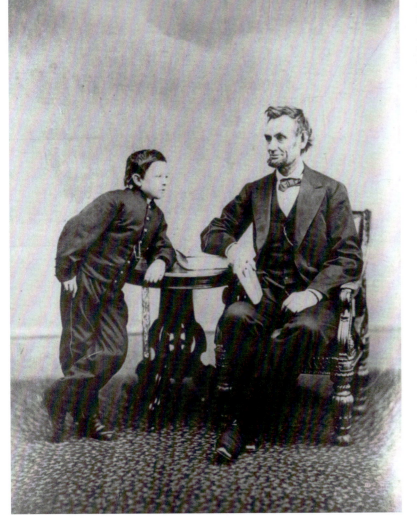

3.7.23 Alexander Gardner, *Abraham Lincoln and His Son Thomas (Tad)*, 5 February 1865. Silver gelatin print, 8 × 10". Library of Congress Prints, Washington, D.C.

Photography provided another, much less laborious and less expensive way to record a likeness or an event in a very realistic manner.

By the 1860s, portraits were commonly taken of celebrities, and portraits of families were common. Exposure times, while still taking several seconds, no longer took minutes, so sitters did not have to be still for very long. President Lincoln had more than forty individual photographic portraits taken of himself while in office, and credited these photos, often reproduced in small sizes for the public, with helping Americans feel like they knew him, and with fueling support for his political decisions. Figure **3.7.23** shows Lincoln, donning a rare, slight smile, sitting with a book while one of his sons stands casually nearby.

Since portraits had long been produced by professionally trained painters and sculptors, the ability of the camera to record such scenes as Lincoln's portrait raised some important questions. Could portraits made with a camera be considered art? In other words, were photographers artists, or simply technicians creating reproductions? The notion that photographers could replace the role of painters sparked a debate that raged during the second half of the nineteenth century.

Thomas LeClear's *Interior with Portraits* at first seems to be self-explanatory (**3.7.24**, see p. 510). A young brother and sister are posed before a painted landscape while a photographer on the far right snaps their picture. LeClear, however, is highlighting the tension between photographers and painters as they competed for patrons in this period. While photographs are often thought to be accurate accounts of reality, LeClear shows that in some ways paintings can be more truthful.

The date of the painting, 1865, marks the year of the death of the young boy shown, James Sidney. Yet Sidney did not die as a child, but as a firefighter at the adult age of twenty-six. His sister, Parnell, however, died years prior, in 1849. Therefore, the children shown in the painting were not this age nor even alive when this canvas was painted. The scene is effectively a memorial to the lost pair, and the painting is able to create an apparent reality and transcend time in a way

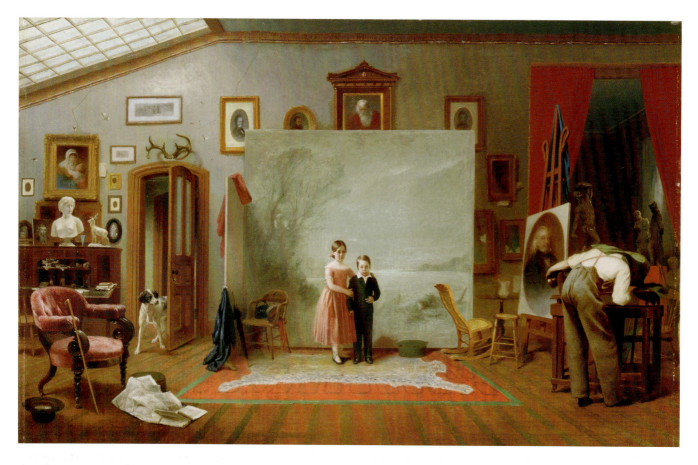

that the camera, used to capture particular real-life moments, could not. While post-mortem photographs of deceased children, which helped the bereaved remember their loved ones' faces, were common during this period, LeClear shows that, in this case, a painting could keep these children alive in the memory of their loved ones better than a photograph.

In the decades that followed LeClear's painting, some artists responded to the advent of photography and the restrictions of their traditional academic training by continuing to question what the purpose of art should be. They did not come up with a single answer to this fundamental question, but this exploration by many artists would change the very nature of art.

3.7.24 Thomas Le Clear, *Interior with Portraits*, c. 1865. Oil on canvas, 25⅞ × 40½". Smithsonian American Art Museum, Washington, D.C.

Discussion Questions

1. Find in this chapter three artworks that reflect new political ideas or revolutionary turmoil. List the ways in which the composition and content of each artwork express political ideas.

2. Enlightenment thinkers in the eighteenth and nineteenth centuries emphasized liberty and equal rights, and the importance of reason, rather than faith. Find an artwork in this chapter that reflects such ideas, and discuss how it expresses Enlightenment thinking.

3. Choose one Rococo, one Neoclassical, and one Romantic artwork. Discuss and compare the visual characteristics of the three works. You might choose one work from another chapter in this book, for example: **4.8.1**, or see Images Related to 3.7 (opposite).

4. In the eighteenth and nineteenth centuries many artists were trained in Academies. Find a work in this chapter made by an artist who had an academic training, then find an artwork made by an artist who rejected the methods of the Academy. Compare and contrast the two works and suggest how the artists sold their work.

Images Related to 3.7:
Art of Europe and America, 1700–1865

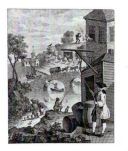

4.5.6 William Hogarth, *False Perspective*, 1754, p. 615

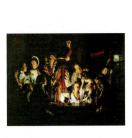

4.4.2 Joseph Wright of Derby, *An Experiment on a Bird in the Air Pump*, 1768, p. 600

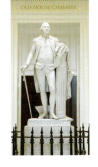

4.6.2 Jean-Antoine Houdon, *George Washington*, 1788–92, p. 626

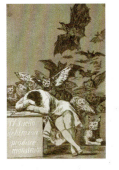

1.9.11 Francisco Goya, *The Sleep of Reason Produces Monsters*, 1799, p. 174

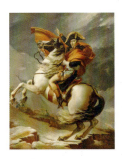

4.6.3 Jacques-Louis David, *Napoleon Crossing the Alps*, 1801, p. 627

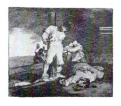

2.3.12b Francisco Goya, "And There Is No Remedy," from *Disasters of War*, c. 1810, p. 239

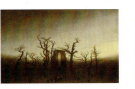

4.3.16 Caspar David Friedrich, *Abbey Among Oak Trees*, 1809–1810, p. 597

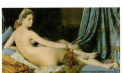

1.10.8 Jean-Auguste-Dominique Ingres, *Grande Odalisque*, 1814, p. 187

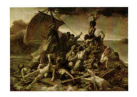

4.8.1 Théodore Géricault, *Raft of the Medusa*, 1819, p. 649

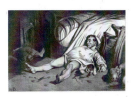

2.3.16 Honoré Daumier, *Rue Transnonain*, 1834, p. 242

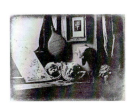

2.8.11 Louis-Jacques-Mandé Daguerre, *The Artist's Studio*, 1837, p. 326

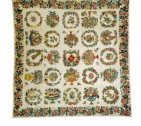

1.6.12 Album quilt, 1848, p. 139

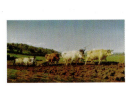

1.9.12a Rosa Bonheur, *Plowing in the Nivernais*, 1849, p. 175

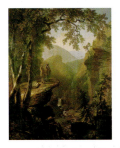

1.3.13 Asher Brown Durand, *Kindred Spirits*, 1849, p. 90

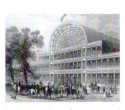

2.5.28 Joseph Paxton, Crystal Palace, London, 1851, p. 281

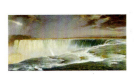

0.0.2 Frederic Edwin Church, *Niagara*, p. 27

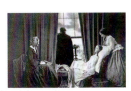

1.7.12a Henry Peach Robinson, *Fading Away*, 1858, p. 153

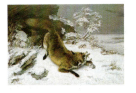

4.3.15 Gustave Courbet, *Fox in the Snow*, 1860, p. 596

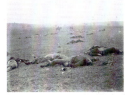

4.7.1 Timothy O'Sullivan, *Harvest of Death*, Gettysburg, 1863, p. 635

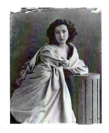

2.8.7 Nadar, *Sarah Bernhardt*, 1865, p. 323

3.8

The Modern Aesthetic: Manet in 1863 to the American Scene in the 1930s

Print: a picture reproduced on paper, often in multiple copies

Plane: a flat surface, often implied by the composition

Representational: art that depicts figures and objects so that we recognize what is represented

Formal: in art, refers to the visual elements and principles in a work

Symbolist: artist or artistic style belonging to the movement in European art and literature, *c.* 1885–1910, that conveyed meaning by the use of powerful yet ambiguous symbols

Expressionism, Expressionist: an artistic style at its height in 1920s Europe, devoted to representing subjective emotions and experiences instead of objective or external reality

Abstract: art imagery that departs from recognizable images from the natural world

Modernism, Modernist: a radically new twentieth-century art and architectural movement that embraced modern industrial materials and a machine aesthetic

Dada, Dadaist: anarchic anti-art and anti-war movement, dating back to World War I, that reveled in absurdity and irrationality

In the second half of the nineteenth century, art entered a period of great experimentation. European and North American cultures and lifestyles were changing radically: railways expanded rapidly, steamships crossed the world's oceans, and industrial growth brought the rural poor to cities. Increasingly, the city, which offered modern forms of transport, such as the tram, and new technologies, such as electricity, became the center of economic activity and growth. The expanding economy, in turn, created a prosperous middle class who had the time and money to devote themselves to leisure and cultural pursuits. Those who could not afford hand-painted or -drawn portraits of themselves could purchase mass-produced photographic **prints**; for the first time in history, the culture people consumed became a central part of their identity, and an indication of their desired status. Economic prosperity also had political consequences: powerful European nations conquered empires worldwide and entered into competition for territory and resources. These tensions culminated in the cataclysm of World War I from 1914 to 1918.

Photography, invented and refined in the middle of the nineteenth century, was a new technology that influenced art directly. Some commentators argued that, because it recorded reality with mechanical precision, photography was the enemy of art. The French poet Charles Baudelaire declared that "As the photographic industry became the refuge of all failed painters with too little talent, or too lazy to complete their studies . . . the badly applied advances of photography . . . have greatly contributed to the impoverishment of French artistic genius." Others, however, saw positive opportunities, and experimented with the artistic potential of the new medium. Photography's tendency to flatten the illusion of depth, its sharp framing and cropping of the world it portrayed, and its lack of even focus across the picture **plane**, suggested different, novel ways of portraying the world in paintings and drawings too.

Artists responded to the rapid and continuing pace of change in society with multiple forms of experimentation. Some, such as the Impressionists and Post-Impressionists, continued to be interested in **representational** art, but chose to explore the impact of the **formal** qualities of their artwork. They sought to capture the impression of the fleeting moment through quick brushstrokes, dabs of paint, and the use of vibrant color and light. Then there were artists who did the complete opposite. **Symbolists** and **Expressionists** attempted to portray what could be felt but not seen, venturing into the realm of the **abstract**.

Although experiments in **Modernism** occurred on both sides of the Atlantic in the first decades of the century, the devastation of World War I spurred the creation of European movements in the 1920s that were very distinct from those inspired by the impact of the Great Depression in America in 1929. The art of the European **Dadaists** and **Surrealists** reacted against the evils of war and what these artists saw as the corruption pervading modern society by making attacks on art itself and by exploring the psyche, while **American Scene** artists chose to respond to the suffering surrounding them through the portrayal of subjects and spaces close to their heart.

Art Academies and Modernism

Much of the art of the late nineteenth and the early twentieth century that is most familiar to us today is often from experimental artists, pushing traditional boundaries and fighting against long-held artistic conventions with a view toward conveying the spirit of their time. Modernism itself is often defined as a movement that essentially broke with tradition. It is important to remember that much of the art respected today was considered shocking in its time, particularly to those who admired artists using classic conventions established and maintained by the Art Academies. Often, these were government-sponsored institutions, set up to train artists to produce work in a particular

style and following certain prescribed ideas about what was suitable subject matter for artworks. Indeed, modern artists were often held up for comparison, frequently in a negative manner, with those who were supported and exhibited by the academic system. By the end of the nineteenth century, this division led to artists establishing new avenues for selling and exhibiting their artworks outside of the traditional **Salon**.

The contrast between art produced within the traditions established by the Academy and the work of artists experimenting with other forms of representation can be understood by comparing two very different French paintings from 1863. Alexandre Cabanel's *Birth of Venus* (**3.8.1**) is an example of the kind of work that was highly appreciated in academic circles. A nude Venus, the mythical Greek goddess of love, lounges invitingly on the ocean, her sensual body on full display, offered submissively to the viewer's gaze, her eyes almost covered by her arm, and barely open. Flying young boys, known as *putti*, accompany her, creating a fluttering decorative "ribbon" above her reclining form.

Surrealism, Surrealist: an artistic movement in the 1920s and later; its works were inspired by dreams and the subconscious; work in the style of that movement
American Scene: naturalistic style of painting in the US from the 1920s to the 1950s that celebrated American themes, locations, and virtues
Salon: official annual exhibition of French painting, first held in 1667

3.8.1 Alexandre Cabanel, *Birth of Venus*, 1863. Oil on canvas, 51⅛ × 88 ½" Musée d'Orsay, Paris, France

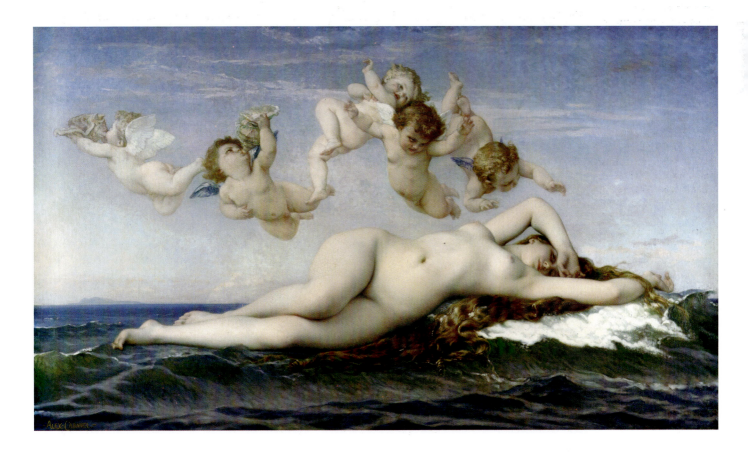

The French painter Édouard Manet's (1832–1883) *Le Déjeuner sur l'Herbe* (*Luncheon on the Grass*: **3.8.2**) also includes a naked woman, but a very different one from Cabanel's Venus. Manet's nude is completely awake, self-possessed, and looks self-confidently and directly at the viewer. She is accompanied, not by naked putti, but by fully clothed, middle-class men with whom she appears to be having a picnic. Far from being submissive, Manet's woman sits up, at ease with her nudity—she has casually discarded her clothes—and her businesslike gaze suggests she may be a modern prostitute, or perhaps an artist's model, rather than a mythological goddess. Viewers were shocked to see two men dressed in contemporary clothing casually placed in a local park next to a naked woman who (despite the speculation about her profession) does not seem to be portrayed for the erotic pleasure of the audience—her body is much less fully displayed than the Venus Cabanel depicted.

The artworks of Cabanel and Manet also differ in their painting and **compositional** techniques. Cabanel's artwork has a sense of depth and illusionism: for example, **atmospheric perspective** is used to show the land in the far distance. His Venus is fully rounded to give maximum appeal to the viewer. Manet, instead, flattens the visible space in his scene. In the small area of distant landscape in the center of the painting, he further destroys the illusion of depth by using thick brushstrokes and obscuring access to the objects in the distance with trees and the figure of an enigmatic woman stooping in the stream.

Manet's figures appear almost as cutouts, much less volumetric than Cabanel's erotic and fleshy nude, and whereas Cabanel uses different degrees of **value** to model the flesh of his Venus, Manet's female appears as if sitting in an unnatural spotlight: unlike Cabanel's painting, there is no gradual, soft gradation from light to dark, and the **outline** of her body is harsh. Although shocked by the composition, contemporary viewers would have realized that Manet had based both his arrangement of figures and the fact that some were naked

Composition: the overall design or organization of a work
Atmospheric perspective: use of shades of color and clarity to create the illusion of depth. Closer objects have warmer tones and clear outlines, while objects set further away are cooler and become hazy
Value: the lightness or darkness of a plane or area
Outline: the outermost line or implied line of an object or figure, by which it is defined or bounded

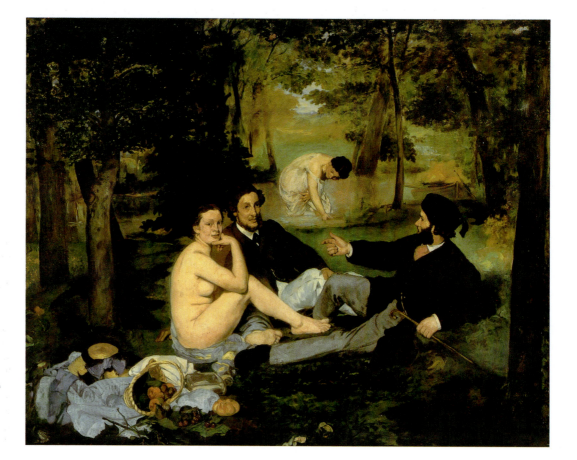

3.8.2 Édouard Manet, *Le Déjeuner sur l'Herbe* (*Luncheon on the Grass*), 1863. Oil on canvas, 6'9⅞" × 8'8⅛". Musée d'Orsay, Paris, France

and some were clothed on already esteemed artworks, depicting mythological themes, in the Louvre museum. Manet is not interested in re-creating a mythological subject in an idealized way, however, but rather in portraying figures from his own era, and reflecting on the act of painting itself. By thinly disguising his use of Classical models to portray a controversial scene of leisure, Manet highlights in *Luncheon on the Grass* how distant the artistic standards of the Academy were from the styles adopted by modern painters.

Alexandre Cabanel had been supported by the Academy throughout his career, having been sent to study in Rome, and winning awards at previous Salons. His *Birth of Venus* was praised by critics in the Salon of 1863 and purchased by Emperor Napoleon III for his personal collection. In contrast, in the same year, Manet's *Luncheon on the Grass* was not accepted for the Salon but was instead placed in an exhibition called the Salon des Refusés (Salon of the Rejected), which was arranged by Napoleon III to address the many complaints that year about the large number of artworks not accepted in the official Salon. Installed near the Salon, this second exhibition was designed to appease artists who felt unfairly excluded from that show. The Academy also anticipated that visitors to the exhibition would heap ridicule upon the artists and works its jury had rejected, but in this it was not entirely successful. Such paintings as Manet's *Luncheon on the Grass* were indeed mocked by some critics, but the public was now exposed to art that had not been approved by the Academy, and artists were emboldened to exhibit independently in venues throughout Paris. With this painting Manet proved that it was possible for an artist to create arresting work that did not conform to convention, and to break away from or alter traditional subjects and modes of representation. It is regarded by some as the work that marks the beginning of modern art, and Manet himself came to epitomize the notion of a modern painter.

Yet the hold of the Academy persisted, even as both European and American artists struggled against its academic standards in their attempts

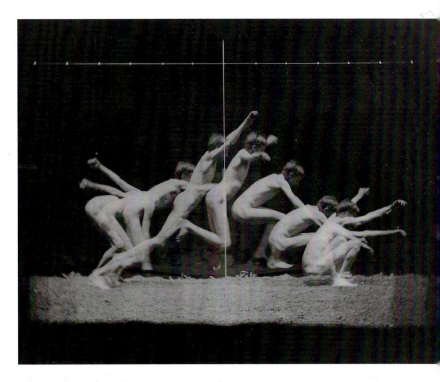

3.8.3 Thomas Eakins, *Motion Study: Male Nude, Standing Jump to Right*, 1885. Dry-plate negative, 3⅝ × 4½". Pennsylvania Academy of Fine Arts, Philadelphia

to create works that captured the modern sensibility. For instance, the American artist Thomas Eakins (1844–1916) was a student and later a teacher at the first American art academy, the Pennsylvania Academy of Fine Arts. Eakins also studied in France and criticized the French Academy's obsession with **Classicism** and **idealism**, much preferring to study the nude in a **Realist** manner. When he started teaching at the Pennsylvania Academy in 1876, and later became its director in 1882, his methods were controversial because of their deviation from traditional European approaches. Rather than follow the standard artistic norm—that of the intense study of the nude figure, Classical statuary and the work of earlier artists—Eakins promoted the study of anatomy through photographs and through observation of dissections. Influenced by the photography of Eadweard Muybridge and his study of horses and humans in motion, he, too, observed the human body in motion through photography. In **3.8.3**, Eakins superimposed several exposures of a jumping man onto one negative, creating a tool to improve his understanding of anatomy for his paintings. Due to his unconventional teaching methods, including allowing women to study the full male nude, Eakins was forced to resign in 1886.

Classical, Classicism: art that conforms to Greek and Roman models, or is based on rational construction and emotional equilibrium
Idealism: elevating depictions of nature to achieve more beautiful, harmonious, and perfect depictions
Realism, Realist: artistic style that aims to represent appearances as accurately as possible

Impressionism: a late nineteenth-century painting style conveying the impression of the effects of light; **Impressionists** were painters working in this style

Style: a characteristic way in which an artist or group of artists uses visual language to give a work an identifiable form of visual expression

En plein air: French for "in the open air"; used to describe painting out of doors from start to finish rather than working in a studio for all or part of the process

Three-dimensional: having height, width, and depth

Texture: the surface quality of a work, for example fine/coarse, detailed/lacking in detail

Palette: a smooth slab or board used for mixing paints or cosmetics

Impressionism

The artists who came to be called **Impressionists** worked in individual, sometimes very different, **styles**, but they were united in rejecting the formal approach of the art taught in the Academy. Their art attempted not so much to portray exactly and realistically such scenes as a landscape or life in a city (although they did depict those subjects), as to capture the light and sensations produced by the scene. The Impressionists formed a group to show their work together outside the official Salon, in eight exhibitions held between 1874 and 1886. Their subject matter was scenes of everyday life: rural landscapes, and life in the modern and growing cities of France—especially scenes of the middle classes engaged in leisure pursuits, as seen in Manet's *Luncheon on the Grass* (see p. 514). The Impressionists were often intent on capturing the essence of moments in time, and many of them painted **en plein air** (outdoors), made possible by the advent of tubed containers for oil paint.

Before the Impressionists, artists who followed traditional methods of painting gave their work a smooth surface, often finishing paintings with a topcoat of varnish, so that the application of the paint was not evident. Impressionists, on the other hand, chose to reveal their brushstrokes. The almost sketchy, unfinished appearance of many Impressionist works breaks away from the academic tradition of simply creating an illusion of **three-dimensional** space on the canvas. Instead, Impressionists flattened space, welcomed visible **texture**, and often allowed the canvas to be seen beneath the painting.

The Impressionists lived during a time in which great strides were made in the studies of optics and color theory, which changed the way these artists painted. They discovered that if they applied individual colors in their purest form on the canvas, rather than mixing them beforehand on the **palette**, the colors remained more intense. Through observation they realized that objects are not one single color, but are made up of many variations of color; to imitate this, Impressionist artists placed brushstrokes

3.8.4 Claude Monet, *Impression, Sunrise*, 1872. Oil on canvas, 19½ × 25½". Musée Marmottan, Paris, France

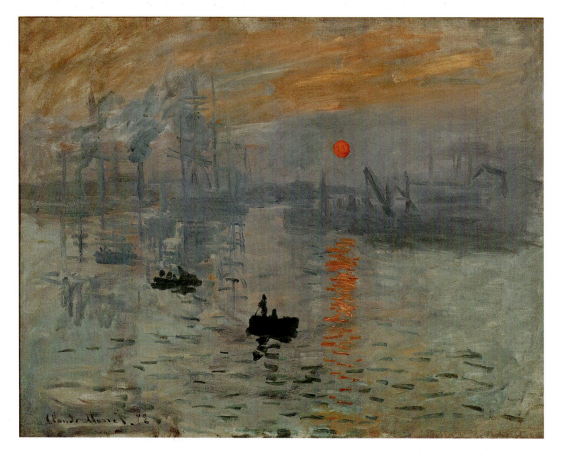

of different colors next to one another, knowing that the viewer's eye would blend disparate **hues**, a process known as **optical mixture**. Often, too, Impressionists reinterpreted the bright natural light of day in their paintings by applying a layer of white paint as a base coat.

The Impressionists were also influenced by photography and Japanese **woodblock** prints. They adopted unusual vantage points and **cropping** of scenes in ways that were similar to both of these media, including new ways of arranging space within an image using **asymmetry** and the layering of objects. While photographers could capture a single moment in time, the Impressionists tried to capture the sensations of such moments: the atmosphere, colors, light, and individual impressions.

At the first of the Impressionist exhibitions, in 1874, hung a painting by Claude Monet (1840–1926) called *Impression, Sunrise* (**3.8.4**). Monet's title was meant to convey that he had somehow captured the essence of light glittering on water in the harbor of Le Havre. A critic described Monet's painting—which indicated with only a few brushstrokes the sea, the reflection of the sun, and the boats in the background—as merely "an Impression indeed!," thus giving the group of painters their famous name. This same critic claimed that even gazing at the work had caused a man to go stark raving mad and run out into the street.

Many Impressionist paintings do indeed have an apparently unfinished quality, because the artists are interested in capturing instantaneous moments rather than creating a highly finished, technically flawless effect. Monet would later make series of paintings of different subjects, such as cathedrals, haystacks, poplars, and train stations. In addition to focusing on the subject, each artwork within a series is slightly different in the way it captures the impressions of mood, light, and color.

Whereas many painters in the past, working within their studios, had taken the upper classes as their subject, the Impressionists instead often painted outdoors and chose to capture the urban middle classes in such places as bustling cafés. In a period when people had more leisure time than ever before, the Impressionists depicted

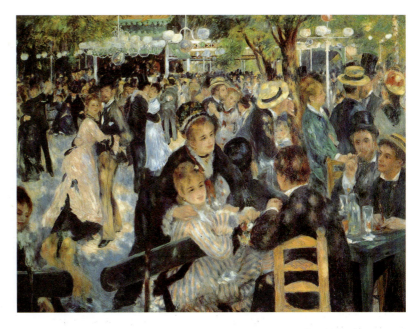

Parisians, for example, dancing, drinking, swimming, and attending the opera or the ballet. Such paintings as *Bal du Moulin de la Galette* by Pierre-Auguste Renoir (1841–1919) were intended to transport viewers into a world of beauty and pleasure (**3.8.5**). Renoir shows people at a popular outdoor café in the Montmartre district of Paris. At the end of the nineteenth century this venue was also a dance hall and gathering-place for artists and intellectuals. The absence of strong outline, almost as if the artist painted with a cotton ball, and his use of dark blues and purples instead of black, are characteristic of Renoir's style. The spontaneous brushstrokes he used and the cheerful gathering he chose to depict reflect his belief that life was, or should be, a perpetual holiday.

Another perspective on the life of the urban middle class can be seen in a painting by Gustave Caillebotte (1848–1894), a wealthy lawyer as well as a painter, who supported other Impressionists financially. Caillebotte's *Paris Street: Rainy Day* (**3.8.6**, see p. 518) shows the results of the massive rebuilding of Paris organized by Baron Haussmann, the prefect or state representative of the region. Under the direction of Napoleon III, Haussmannization involved tearing down much of the medieval city, an action that displaced thousands, and building glorious new boulevards, townhouses, and parks. Caillebotte makes use of linear perspective to show how the modern boulevards extend in every direction,

3.8.5 Pierre-Auguste Renoir, *Bal du Moulin de la Galette*, 1876. Oil on canvas, 51⅝ × 68⅞". Musée d'Orsay, Paris, France

Hue: general classification of a color; the distinctive characteristics of a color as seen in the visible spectrum, such as green or red
Optical mixture: when the eye blends two colors that are placed near one another, creating a new color
Woodblock: a relief print process where the image is carved into a block of wood
Cropping: trimming the edges of an image, or composing it so that part of the subject matter is cut off
Asymmetry: a type of design in which balance is achieved by elements that contrast and complement one another without being the same on either side of an axis

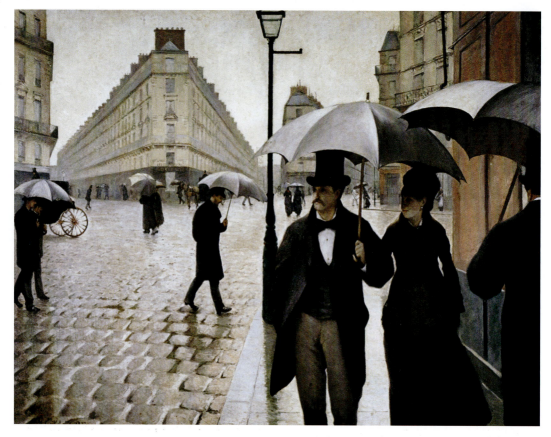

like spokes on a wheel. A green lamppost and its shadow extend beyond the height of the canvas, creating a strong vertical line that divides the composition. To the left of the post is a **facade** added to an apartment building. To the right is a well-dressed couple who, although surrounded by the different classes of people in the city, seem to be alone and in their own world. Caillebotte's use of perspective makes us feel as if we are part of the busy city and will soon collide with the strolling couple.

Edgar Degas (1834–1917) was a prolific artist who reveled in experimentation in a variety of media, including pastel, charcoal, oil, photography, **lithography**, and sculpture. He was interested in the careful observation of characters from daily life, and also studied anatomy through photography using methods similar to Eadweard Muybridge and Thomas Eakins (**3.8.3**, see p. 515). Degas is well known for his paintings and pastels of female subjects, including laundresses, prostitutes, singers, and bathers. One of his favorite subjects was ballet dancers, whom he studied not only during performances, but also during practice,

stretching, and backstage (**3.8.9**, see p. 520). Degas's scenes of dancers, in both public and private settings, evoke the everyday quality of a dancer's life, and his composition gives the impression of immediacy, as if the viewer has caught the dancers off guard, primping before their performance. The artist masterfully uses the medium of pastel, essentially drawing on the surface (rather than using a paintbrush), to create a rich texture in which light bounces off the flesh of the dancers and their dresses.

Degas's *Blue Dancers* also demonstrates a fascination with Japanese prints, which he shared with other Impressionists. By the time this painting was made, in 1897, French steamships had begun to import artworks from places previously unknown, as far away as Japan, which had only just opened its borders to trade in 1853. The woodblock prints by Japanese masters, for sale in Paris, featured sections of solid color and a lack of shading, as well as flat, rather than three-dimensional, images. These prints inspired Impressionists to flatten the visual depth in their works also, through the use of cropping, asymmetry, texture, unique or

Modern Sculpture: Auguste Rodin and Camille Claudel

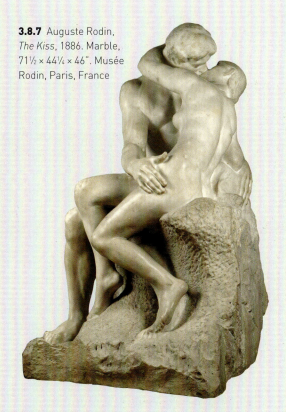

3.8.7 Auguste Rodin, *The Kiss*, 1886. Marble, 71½ × 44¼ × 46". Musée Rodin, Paris, France

The Frenchman Auguste Rodin (1840–1917) epitomizes the modern sculptor. Rather than copying from Classical busts and using traditional poses, as had been done for centuries, Rodin used live models and depicted energetic and passionate figures. By the beginning of the twentieth century, Rodin was one of the most famous living artists. He had a large workshop of sculptors who produced his works in both bronze and marble. Rodin was careful to maintain his individual style, however, and frequently completed the final work on his sculptures himself.

The Kiss is a sculpture of two nude lovers embracing, engaged in a passionate kiss (**3.8.7**). The couple was originally conceived to be part of Rodin's *Gates of Hell*, two large bronze doors depicting scenes from a masterpiece of medieval Italian literature, Dante's *Divine Comedy*. *The Kiss* is based upon the story of Paolo and Francesca, lovers from Dante's time who were killed by Francesca's husband (Paolo's brother). Rodin did not include them in the final door composition, and

instead made several copies of *The Kiss*, one of which was a marble commissioned by the French government.

Camille Claudel (1864–1943) worked in Rodin's workshop, and quickly became his lover as well. A talented sculptor in her own right, Claudel was able, through Rodin's connections, to meet important people, and to receive commissions she might not otherwise have had. *The Waltz* shows two dancers intertwined as they move as one (**3.8.8**). The woman's dress has fallen off her body and blows to the side, expressing the energetic movement of the couple. One writer proclaimed, "In this group of a waltzing couple, they seem to want to finish the dance so they can go to bed and make love." A government representative who had purchased many of Rodin's erotic nudes remarked that *The Waltz* was too erotic, and suggested that Claudel should put clothes on the figures.

There is a clear discrepancy in the way gender affected how Claudel was treated professionally. While there is no evidence that either of these sculptures was made in reference to the love affair between the two sculptors, Claudel's work was often disproportionately seen as an emotional response to her relationship with Rodin, while no one ever thought to view his work in such a light. Camille Claudel's family forcibly placed her in an insane asylum for the last thirty years of her life. The degree and legitimacy of her mental illness is difficult for scholars to determine, but the fact she was institutionalized has further clouded all interpretations of her work.

3.8.8 Camille Claudel, *The Waltz*, Bronze (posthumous edition), 16⅞ × 14⅜ × 6¾". Private collection

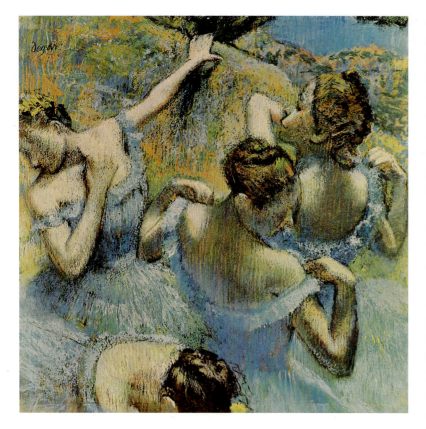

3.8.9 Edgar Degas, *Blue Dancers*, c. 1897. Pastel on paper, 25½" × 25½", The Pushkin State Museum of Fine Arts, Moscow, Russia

unusual vantage points, and layering of objects. The Japanese tradition of delineation (bold outlining) of forms also proved revolutionary in the works of the Impressionists.

Influence from Japanese prints is evident in Degas's dynamic composition, which uses diagonal lines to guide the viewer's eyes around the scene. The head of the girl on the left and the body of the girl at the bottom of the composition are cropped. Likewise, Degas's scene is viewed from slightly above (a device known as **bird's-eye view**). His experimentation with such foreign techniques, along with his desire to capture the spontaneity of modern daily life, was shared by all the Impressionists.

Post-Impressionism

By the 1880s, the once-revolutionary Impressionism had gained great public popularity amongst the newly risen middle class. Yet the Academy critics accused the Impressionists of lacking discipline and training, and of having no intellectual substance other than a shallow preoccupation with the

Bird's-eye view: an artistic technique in which a scene or subject is presented from some point above it

depiction of beauty. Impressionist artists responded to these criticisms in different ways: Monet developed his serial approach, in which he analysed atmosphere rather than subject matter; Renoir returned to Classical models and created a series of bathers. The movement that resulted, that of Post-Impressionism, consisted of artists who had been exposed to, and often participated in, the Impressionist movement, but who wanted to differentiate themselves from what was then perceived to be the simplicity of the Impressionists. They preferred instead to emphasize abstract qualities or subjective content in their artworks.

The French painter Paul Cézanne (1839–1906) developed a new type of landscape painting through intense study of Mont Sainte-Victoire, a mountain he could see from his studio (and childhood home) in Aix-en-Provence, where he worked for much of his adult life. Cézanne made several paintings of this mountain, working on some of them for years. By gradually adding brushstrokes to reflect the mountain's changing atmosphere and weather conditions, Cézanne sought to construct the essence of the mountain as it appeared over time, rather than at a single moment.

Cézanne created the structure of his landscape in a very different way from earlier painters. He conceived a view of nature in which the subject was analysed from multiple views, forms became abstracted, and planes shifted. For example, Cézanne utilized his understanding of atmospheric perspective to blend warm and cool colors within the same structure, as in the mountain (**3.8.10**). This creates a push–pull effect for viewers, as the warm hues of the mountain come toward us, and cool colors recede. The tree in the foreground creates a similar experience as we look at it, a feeling of being pulled into the depth of the painting and then being pushed forward, as if the image has been flattened. The upper branch seems to echo the outline of the distant mountain, bringing it closer to us.

The French painter Paul Gauguin (1848–1903) was a successful stockbroker, but at the age of thirty-five gave up his career to become a painter. Modern civilization was, in Gauguin's

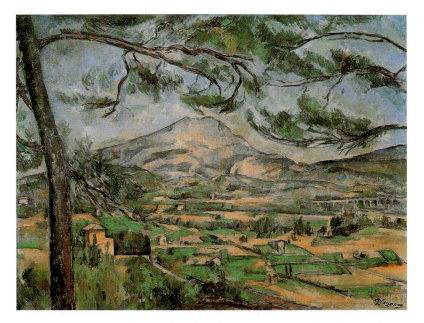

3.8.10 Paul Cézanne, *Mont Sainte-Victoire*, c. 1886–88. Oil on canvas, 26 × 36¼". Courtauld Gallery, London, England

3.8.11 Paul Gauguin, *The Vision after the Sermon (Jacob Wrestling with the Angel)*, 1888. Oil on canvas, 28½ × 35⅞". Scottish National Gallery, Edinburgh, Scotland

view, materialistic and lacking in spirituality. This belief led him to seek to portray people whom he considered pure, untouched by materialistic values. *The Vision after the Sermon* shows the pious people of the small town of Pont-Aven dressed in their Sunday clothes (3.8.11). The scene in the upper right depicts the sermon the townspeople have just heard, that of the biblical story of Jacob wrestling with the angel. The spaces are abruptly flattened, the figures lack volume and are closely cropped. Yet rather than just showing a scene from everyday life, Gauguin expresses what is in these people's minds: a vision. The way the tree slices the scene

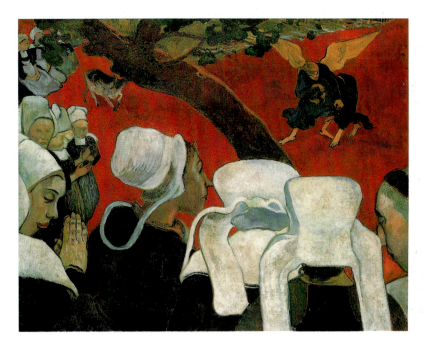

in two (one section for the dreamers and one for the dream) is a device Gauguin observed in Japanese prints. Some scholars believe that Gauguin depicted himself as the figure with closed eyes in the lower right of the canvas, as if he too is experiencing a vision. Gauguin once said, "I shut my eyes in order to see." The bold red charges this image with a vivid power that speaks to the intense spirituality of the women and the drama of their vision, but also suggests the violence of the struggle they are witnessing between Jacob and the angel. Gauguin's ability to use color as an expressive element would greatly influence later artists, particularly the Symbolists (see pp. 522–23).

After leaving Pont-Aven in 1888, Gauguin shared a house with the Dutch painter Vincent van Gogh (1853–1890) for two months in the southern French town of Arles. The two artists challenged and annoyed one another. While Van Gogh envisioned an artistic exchange, a brotherhood of painters, Gauguin made it clear that he felt his work was superior to the gentler Van Gogh's. Van Gogh's mood fluctuated between pure joy in their working closely alongside each other and frustration at Gauguin's intense bouts of criticism and anger. Shortly before Christmas of the same year, Vincent van Gogh was hospitalized for slicing off his left ear lobe, and after this, he and Gauguin never spoke again. Gauguin took his desire to study people of a pure and "primitive" nature to Tahiti, while Van Gogh remained in France.

Famous to us now, yet largely unremarked upon in their time, the paintings of Vincent van Gogh express strong emotions. Yet, unlike Gauguin, Van Gogh claimed he could not invent images, but instead painted emotion into what he saw. He once stated:

I cannot work without a model. I won't say that I don't turn my back on nature to transform a study into a picture, arranging the colors, exaggerating, simplifying, but when it comes to form I'm too fearful of departing from the possible and the true . . . I exaggerate, sometimes I make changes . . . but I do not invent the whole picture.

Van Gogh, who struggled with mental illness all his life, painted *Starry Night* during a stay in an asylum; the scene includes elements of the real-life view from his window (**3.8.12**). The artist infused the scene with his own emotions: one can sense the very physical act of applying the thick paint (**impasto**), and Van Gogh's energy, in swirls that show movement in the sky and the light emanating from the stars. A cypress tree, resembling flames reaching up to the sky, fills much of the left side of the canvas. The church in the distance may hint at Van Gogh's personal trials with religion; some believe it relates to his childhood church in The Netherlands. His use of color and form expresses his emotional suffering; in 1890, the year after this painting, Van Gogh shot himself in the chest with a revolver and died two days later.

It may seem incredible now, but Van Gogh considered himself an artistic failure, having sold only one artwork his entire life; his great popularity did not occur until long after his death. It is thought that his brother's wife, Johanna, was principally responsible for ensuring his art became recognized: she kept a complete collection of his works for almost twenty years after he died. By 1906 Van Gogh's art was beginning to be exhibited more frequently, and by the 1950s he was acknowledged to be an important artist. His fame grew, and by the late twentieth century his paintings had become amongst the highest-priced artworks in history, selling for up to $82.5 million.

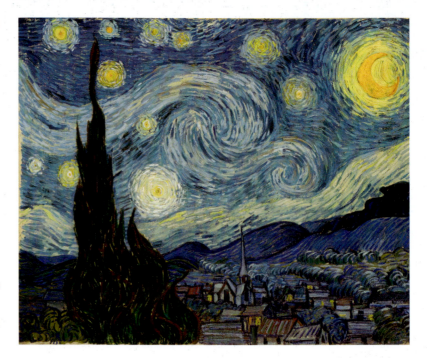

Henri Rousseau's (1844–1910) *The Sleeping Gypsy* (**3.8.13**) portrays a sleeping woman lying in the middle of a desert as she is approached by a powerful lion. The scene is at once mysterious and jarring, as one cannot help but fear for the safety of the sleeping gypsy. She is presented in an unrealistic manner, as if floating in front of the land rather than lying on it, and covered in stripes that seem to hide her form. She lies both above and beside her instrument and a vessel for water. The bizarre presence of the lion, the perfect full moon, and the abstraction of form suggest that the scene itself may be a dream.

Impasto: paint applied in thick layers
Baroque: European artistic style of the late sixteenth to early eighteenth century, characterized by extravagance and emotional intensity

3.8.13 Henri Rousseau, *The Sleeping Gypsy*, 1897. Oil on canvas, 51 × 79½". MoMA, New York

The Era of Symbolism

Symbolist painters were inspired by the use of emotionally potent and often dreamlike images. Although they frequently made use of widely recognized symbols, such as mythological subjects, and women in the guise of virgin or seductress (see Gateway Box: Gentileschi, p. 523), they also engaged in individual explorations of otherworldliness. In sum, they used their medium to express emotion instead of as a means to describe situations, relying on abstraction and the distortion of form and color.

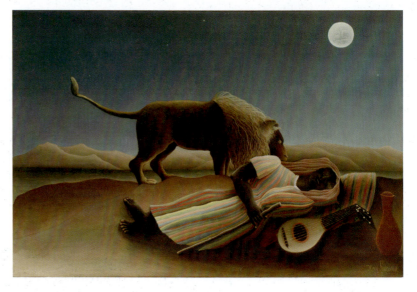

Gateway to Art: Gentileschi, *Judith Decapitating Holofernes*
Variations on a Theme

Artemisia Gentileschi's *Judith Decapitating Holofernes* (**3.8.14**), from the **Baroque** era, and Gustav Klimt's *Judith I* (**3.8.15**) are both paintings based on the biblical story of Judith beheading Holofernes, an Assyrian general who was planning to attack her homeland—but the two images clearly reveal striking differences in style and approach. While Gentileschi's work displays Baroque qualities, Klimt (1862–1918) was a founding member and first president of the Vienna Secession, a group of artists in Vienna, Austria, who, like the Impressionists, wanted to create and exhibit art outside of academic constraints. If we compare the two works, we can see how far the style of such Symbolist artists diverged from what had gone before.

Gentileschi's scene is staged for maximum dramatic effect, like a theatrical performance, shining a spotlight on the gory beheading of Holofernes, making the portrayal of Judith that of a powerful, surprisingly physical being. She is shown in the act of attacking the general, sword in hand and with her sleeves rolled up.

In Gustav Klimt's *Judith I*, on the other hand, the artist fills his scene with fantasy and eroticism, qualities favored by the Symbolists. His Judith appears as a glamorous seductress, or *femme fatale*—a woman whose sexual allure is believed to be dangerous to men—dripping with gold, her lush black hair piled high, heavy-lidded eyes half shut, body half exposed. The model for Judith in real life was Adele Block-Bauer, a wealthy, married patron with whom Klimt was madly in love, and Judith's seductive quality is the focus of his work, which we absorb firstly as the portrait of a beautiful, sensual woman. The artist seems to trap her, visually, with the thick gold choker round her neck, a device that also hints at the beheading that has just occurred.

Contrary to Gentileschi's painting, where the wounded head is in the center, Klimt's version lures us in with Judith's beauty,

and then shocks us with the realization that she is clasping the severed head victoriously in her hands. This attitude lends the work its sinister, disturbing power; instead of grappling with her victim, as in Gentileschi's version, Judith here seems almost to be caressing his dead head. The lavish use of gold, both in the frame and the decorative gold leaf that surrounds and nearly engulfs Judith, is characteristic of Klimt's art, and of the Art Nouveau style (see p. 524). Its rich, gleaming appeal, so much at odds with the grim subject matter, intensifies the strange, spell binding quality of the painting.

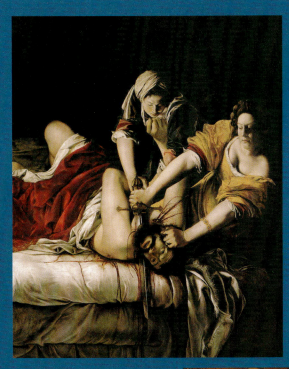

3.8.14 Artemisia Gentileschi, *Judith Decapitating Holofernes*, c. 1620. Oil on canvas, 6'6-3/8" × 5'3¾". Uffizi Gallery, Florence, Italy

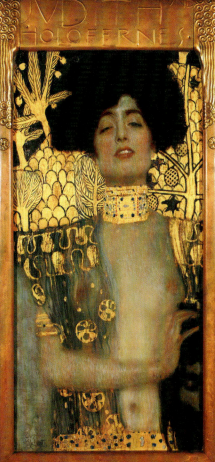

3.8.15 (below) Gustav Klimt, *Judith I*, 1901. Oil and gold plating on canvas, 33 × 16½". Österreichische Galerie Belvedere, Vienna, Austria

Fin de Siècle and Art Nouveau

Fin de siècle (from the French, "end of the century") refers to the period from the end of the nineteenth century to the start of World War I in 1914. This was a time of great social change in Europe. A growing middle class had sufficient income to enjoy the pleasures that life had to offer. As they faced the new century, some were anxious, however (and rightly, in view of the war that ensued a decade later), about the changes it would bring. Others devoted themselves to self-indulgence, pushing the traditional boundaries of etiquette and challenging the standards laid down by society. In art and design, the **Art Nouveau** style emphasized decorative pattern and applied it to the traditional "fine arts" (such as painting and sculpture), the decorative arts (such as furniture, glass, and ceramics), and architecture and interior design. Art Nouveau is characterized by **organic** flowing lines, gold decoration, and the simulation of forms in nature.

The tremendous rise in commercial entertainment in this period led many artists

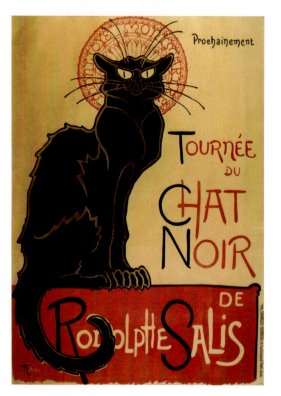

3.8.16 Théophile-Alexandre Steinlen, *Tournée du Chat Noir de Rodolphe Salis*, 1896. 37¾ × 53½". Collection Zimmerli Art Museum at Rutgers University, New Brunswick, New Jersey

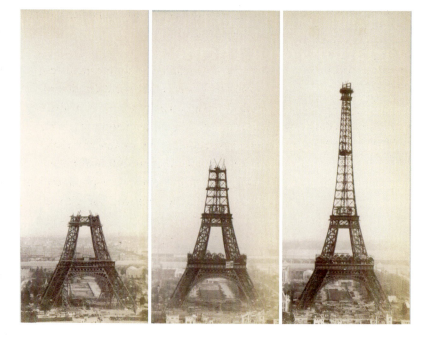

3.8.17 Gustave Eiffel, Eiffel Tower, 1889, Paris, France

to make a living making posters to promote products, celebrities, and clubs. A poster by Théophile-Alexandre Steinlen (1859–1923) promoted a tour of the performers from the nightclub Le Chat Noir (The Black Cat) then located in Montmartre, Paris (**3.8.16**). Louis Rodolphe Salis (1851–1897) was the owner of the club and made Le Chat Noir the first cabaret, a nightclub for drinking while watching short performances. Using hues of rich gold, red, and black, the artist conveys the sense that the entertainment at this establishment is mysterious and decadent. A striking black cat, with a body more like a panther, stares at the viewer hypnotically with his delightful whiskers and the moon motif framing his head. The stylized quality of this device, of the lettering, and in the curvature of the tail that mimics the 'S' in Salis, are typical of the Art Nouveau style.

Fin-de-siècle artists favored new, modern materials, such as cast iron. This was the material chosen for the construction of the Eiffel Tower, made to welcome visitors to the 1889 World's Fair (**3.8.17**). While it was being built, many Parisians considered it a monstrosity that was ruining the skyline of their city. For its critics, the tower symbolized the decadence of the modern

Art Nouveau: French for "new art," a visual style of the late nineteenth and early twentieth century, characterized by organic flowing lines, simulating forms in nature and involving decorative pattern

Organic: having irregular forms and shapes, as though derived from living organisms

generation, who were destroying French history and long-held traditions:

> We, writers, painters, sculptors, architects, passionate lovers of the beauty, until now intact, of Paris, hereby protest with all our might, with all our indignation, in the name of French taste . . . in the name of French art and history under threat, against the construction, in the very heart of our capital, of the useless and monstrous Eiffel Tower.

Yet the engineer Gustave Eiffel (1832–1923) pushed on regardless, and the criticism declined after the tower was completed. Today, the Eiffel Tower is a beloved and iconic symbol of Paris.

The Revolution of Color and Form

Much as the Eiffel Tower is emblematic of the city of Paris, Henri Matisse (1869–1954) and Pablo Picasso (1881–1973) are very important figures now permanently associated with the development of modern art. Matisse, a Frenchman, had already earned some professional notoriety by the time the young Picasso moved from Spain to Paris in 1904. Picasso left behind his academic training in representational art to embrace the brave new world of experimental approaches he found there. Meanwhile, Matisse was working in Paris, exploring the expressive potential of **color** and its relation to **form**—as he was to do throughout his career. Over their long creative lifetimes, Matisse and Picasso developed a mutual respect for each other, but they were also rivals because each one wanted to be considered the leader of the progressive art world. As it turns out, both artists enjoyed extremely productive careers and have been extraordinarily influential: Matisse for his expressive forms, decorative style, and bold use of color; Picasso for his radical handling of form and shape.

Henri Matisse

The colors in Matisse's *Joy of Life*—orange and green bodies, pink trees, a multicolored sky—are not strictly **naturalistic** (**3.8.18**).

3.8.18 Henri Matisse, *Joy of Life*, 1905–6. Oil on canvas, 5'9⅛" × 7'10⅞". Barnes Foundation, Merion, Pennsylvania

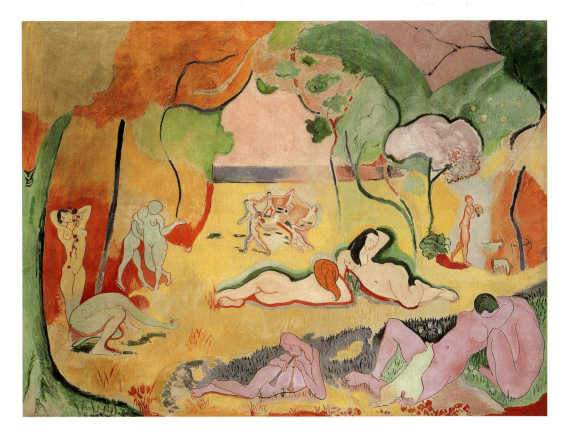

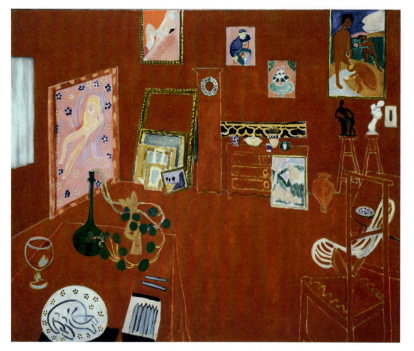

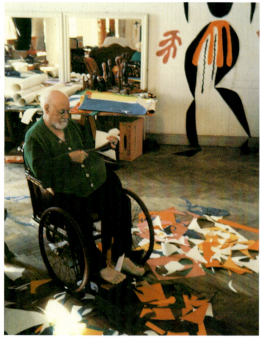

3.8.19 Henri Matisse, *The Red Studio*, 1911. Oil on canvas, 5'11¼" × 7'2¼". MOMA, New York

3.8.20 Henri Matisse in his studio, 1953

Fauvism: early twentieth-century art movement that emphasized bold, exaggerated colors and simplified forms to favor creative expression over accuracy

Sketch: a rough preliminary version of a work or part of a work

Cubism, Cubist: a twentieth-century art movement that favored a new perspective emphasizing geometric forms

Renaissance: a period of cultural and artistic change in Europe from the fourteenth to the seventeenth century

Composite view: representation of a subject from multiple viewpoints at one time

These departures from everyday appearances are intentional. An artist's inspired choice of colors varies according to what he or she sees or imagines. For Matisse, color was principally a way to express emotions. In fact, Matisse founded a movement now known as **Fauvism** (from French *fauve*, "wild beast"). The group's name derived from a comment by a critic who found their work a little mad, especially in comparison to Classical approaches, because the bold colors the Fauves used did not correspond to natural appearances. Matisse continued to explore the potential of pure color throughout his career. He often emphasized colors and made them vibrant and intense rather than rendering them as subdued or blending them to make a scene look more natural. Matisse was interested in making an artwork, not in imitating nature or copying external appearances. He was not trying, as many artists from earlier times had principally done, to persuade us into believing that we are looking through a window onto a "real" world. In response to a viewer who complained that one of his portraits did not resemble the dimensions of an actual woman, Matisse said, "I did not create a woman. I made a picture."

In *The Red Studio* Matisse has included a lot of information about his working environment, but he has also left a lot out (**3.8.19**). He accurately shows a number of the paintings,

sculptures, and ceramics he had been working on. The space is filled with an intense red; this makes the artworks stand out against the walls and floor, which have been collapsed into a single flat plane. The furniture is also red, with subtle gold outlines indicating the edges and details. Matisse is keenly concerned with the use of color to convey his experience of place.

When Matisse worked on a painting he generally started with complex **sketches** and, over time, simplified the image by eliminating details and paring down the composition. He also used paper cutouts as preparatory sketches, pinning them on a canvas to help him place the figures in a composition. In early 1941 Matisse was diagnosed with cancer of the intestines. After his treatment, he was permanently confined to a wheelchair (**3.8.20**), making painting any large-scale work impossible. So Matisse began to present the cutouts as the completed works themselves. He created his cutouts from paper his assistants would paint in bright colors; the artist would then use scissors as if "drawing" the elegant lines of the shapes he was making, creating images filled with movement and life.

There seems to have been no limit to the ideas Matisse could fashion in this way. He used cutouts to design tapestries, the interior decoration of buildings, and stained-glass windows. His final cutout compositions were on a large scale, some covering an area of more than 87 square feet. Toward the end of a long career Matisse found that simple scissors and paper offered a way to help him continue, once again, finding new ways to experiment with line and color.

Picasso, Braque, and Cubism

In the early twentieth century, shortly after Matisse was experimenting with new ways of using color in the 1900s, Picasso and the French artist Georges Braque (1882–1963) revolutionized the way artworks were made. They concentrated on their underlying geometric form and the construction of pictorial space, and together eventually developed the style known as **Cubism**. Instead of showing conventionally realistic objects in the illusion of three-dimensional space in the way that had fascinated Western artists since the **Renaissance**, they enabled us to see what an object might look like if we could see more than one side of it at the same time. They broke up objects and figures into geometric shapes and changed them according to their own conception of deeper truth.

Picasso explored new methods of depicting the human figure in his painting *Les Demoiselles d'Avignon* (**3.8.21**). Rather than re-creating the way we actually see a room with people standing in it, Picasso has treated the space in the picture, and the figures within it, in a truly revolutionary way. He has simplified the forms into abstract planes, made the figures more angular, and broken down the individual faces and bodies into geometric pieces. The blue and white planes of what would usually be called the background clash violently with the angular pink figures of the women, in a complex struggle for dominance.

The three figures on the left are shown in historical, even Classical poses. The forms of the two women near the center of the painting are simplified, with almond-shaped eyes, triangular noses, and outlines for bodies, but they are still recognizable as female figures. The heads of the standing figures on the far left and far right have been dramatically replaced by African masks. Picasso, along with Matisse and other European artists in the early twentieth century, studied and collected art from outside the Western tradition, especially Africa and the Pacific Islands, and this interest is reflected in the masked faces.

The crouching figure at the bottom right has the most abstract features. Her body is splayed out, and the geometric shapes that make up the woman's face do not correspond to the usual orientation. The eye on our left is shown from the front, while the eye on our right is in profile. The nose is also in profile with the mouth off to the side and a crescent shape in place of the jawline. The **composite view** of this figure shows us more parts of her body than we could see from one vantage point. In this painting, the figures are still fairly recognizable. Picasso's later Cubist pieces become far more abstract, yet always intentionally retain a connection to the visible world.

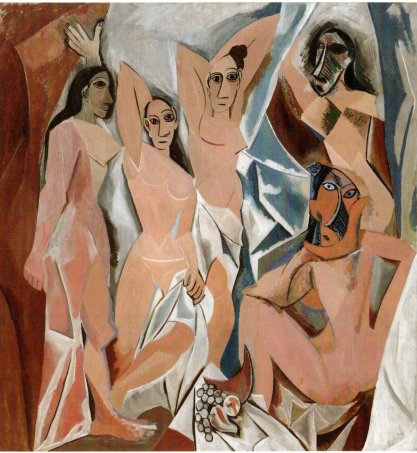

3.8.21 Pablo Picasso, *Les Demoiselles d'Avignon*, 1907. Oil on canvas, 8′ × 7′8″. MoMA, New York

Gateway to Art: Picasso, *Girl before a Mirror*
Picasso's Women

Pablo Picasso made figure studies and portraits throughout his career, using the groundbreaking abstraction developed through Cubism. The presence of bold geometric shapes, heavy outlines, and saturated non-natural color are hallmarks of his style. While the women in *Les Demoiselles d'Avignon* (see **3.8.21** on p. 527) are not necessarily meant to be identifiable (though one is said to have been modeled after his lover), even his most abstract paintings represent specific women in his life.

Scholars have connected various phases and styles in Picasso's career to the women with whom he had relationships at the time. Marie-Thérèse Walter is the subject of *Girl before a Mirror* (**3.8.22**). Her physical features, including cobalt-blue eyes, blonde hair, and a voluptuous body, are not the focus in this painting. She was said to be sweet, demure, and innocent, perhaps explaining why Picasso tended to use pastel colors and pleasing organic shapes in his pictures of her. In this painting, the lavender profile of her face and body on the left side of the canvas make her seem graceful and ideal, an impression that is reinforced by the white halo around her head. The adjacent frontal face is more roughly painted in yellow with darkly rouged cheeks,

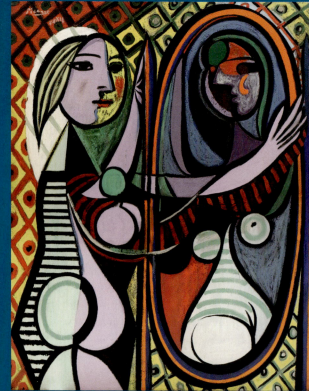

3.8.22 Pablo Picasso, *Girl before a Mirror*, Boisgeloup, March 1932. Oil on canvas, 64 × 51¼. MoMA, New York

suggesting another side to Walter's persona. The diamond shapes in the background can be understood as an abstract self-portrait. They come from the costume of Harlequin, a character from the Italian Renaissance comedy drama called *commedia dell'arte* that Picasso repeatedly painted. Over time he used the diamond pattern as a shorthand symbol for himself; thus, in this portrait, he subtly infuses his presence into the work.

Abstraction: the degree to which an image is altered from an easily recognizable subject

Collage: a work of art assembled by gluing materials, often paper, onto a surface. From the French *coller*, to glue

An early Cubist painting, Georges Braque's *Houses at L'Estaque*, emphasized the geometry of the setting (**3.8.23**). In this painting, inspired by the style of the Post-Impressionist artist Paul Cézanne (see p. 521), the houses become stacked golden cubes and pyramids surrounded by the slightest suggestion of trees and shrubs. By eliminating the details and making all of the houses the same color, Braque focuses attention on the underlying shapes and overall pattern of the picture. The shading is applied in a decorative way to give the shapes more definition. The bold treatment of this painting's forms might seem to come solely from the artist's imagination. Photographs taken at this site, however, indicate that, in fact, Braque was surprisingly true to the configuration and placement of the trees and houses. The changes he made to the colors and shapes make the painting an **abstraction** based on nature.

During the second phase of Cubism, artists used newspaper and wallpaper as well as fine art papers to make paper **collage**. The papers were cut into shapes and glued to a support. This kind of construction is very familiar to us today, but in the early twentieth century it was a completely

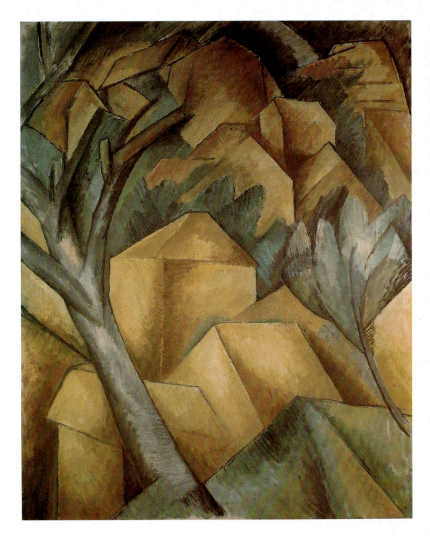

3.8.23 Georges Braque, *Houses at L'Estaque*, 1908. Oil on canvas, 28⅜ × 23½". Kunstmuseum, Bern, Switzerland

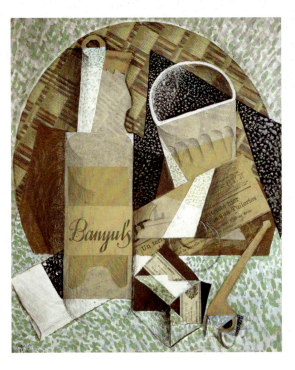

3.8.24 Juan Gris, *Bottle of Banyuls*, 1914. Pasted papers, oil, charcoal, and gouache, and pencil on canvas, 21½ × 18". Kunstmuseum, Bern, Switzerland

new technique for making art. *Bottle of Banyuls* (**3.8.24**) by Spanish painter and sculptor Juan Gris (1887–1927) includes some shapes that relate to a table (the patchwork circle around the objects near the center), glass (suggested by the transparent paper he used), and a bottle (the layered rectangular shape on the left). By using an actual bottle label from the southern French wine Banyuls, the artist is able to identify the shapes as a bottle and to bring everyday materials into the picture.

Expressionism

The raw emotionality of *Les Demoiselles d'Avignon* was not emphasized in the Cubists' coolly analytical studies concentrating on form and space. In the meantime, from around 1905 to around 1920, other artists evolved a style that came to be known as Expressionism, in which they chose to explore ways of portraying emotions to their fullest intensity by exaggerating and emphasizing the colors and shapes of the objects depicted.

Expressionists, like the Impressionists and Cubists, were concerned with the representation of objects and the world. But as Expressionists depicted their subjects, they emphasized inner states of feeling. Expressionist artists tried to depict what they felt rather than what they saw, with sometimes unconventional results.

The making of self-portraits was central to Expressionism because artists could explore a great variety and intensity of emotions through repeated studies. Self-portraits also allow artists to express both the inner and outer worlds that they know most fully. For instance, when making a portrait of someone else, an artist could only guess at the other person's mood, thoughts, or motivations. While making a self-portrait, however, he or she could decide which moods or motivations to show and how best to do so.

The German Expressionist artist Paula Modersohn-Becker (1876–1907) made several self-portraits (**3.8.26**, see p. 531). She also has the distinction of being one of the first women to make nude self-portraits. Her style reflects the flattened forms, reduced details, heavy outlines,

Gertrude Stein as an Art Patron

The American writer Gertrude Stein (1874–1946) and her brother Leo (1872–1947), who lived together in Paris from 1904 to 1913, began to collect art by **avant-garde** artists, and eventually had an outstanding collection of modern art. They were amongst the first art **patrons** to support progressive artists, a major boost for these artists at a time when their work was not well received by the general public. The weekly **salons** Gertrude held in her studio apartment provided a meeting place for both artists and writers. In fact, the Steins introduced Picasso and Matisse to one another, sparking their friendship and artistic rivalry.

In 1905, two years before *Les Demoiselles d'Avignon*, Gertrude Stein commissioned Picasso to paint her portrait (seen in Man Ray's photograph of her, **3.8.25**). She wrote that she sat for Picasso ninety times: he worked on the painting for months but was never satisfied. Eventually he abandoned the naturalistic approach and painted out the details of her facial features after seeing ancient Iberian sculptures in Spain and at the Louvre museum in Paris. When comparing Stein's actual appearance with her painted likeness in Man Ray's photograph of 1922, we see that Picasso replaced the soft contours of her cheeks,

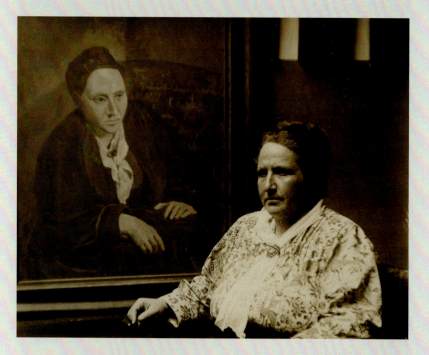

eyes, and mouth with mask-like forms. The painting is now famous, not only because it represents their interaction, but also because it inspired a new phase of Picasso's work that relied on his personal vision rather than on what he observed, starting him on the path toward Cubism. When someone remarked that Gertrude Stein did not look like her portrait, Picasso responded, "She will."

3.8.25 Man Ray, *Gertrude Stein and Picasso's Portrait*, 1922. Vintage gelatin silver print, 3¾ × 4¾". The Richard and Ellen Sandor Art Foundation

---

Avant-garde: early twentieth-century emphasis on artistic innovation, which challenged accepted values, traditions, and techniques
Patron: an organization or individual who sponsors the creation of works of art
Salon: a social gathering for writers, artists, and musicians, usually hosted by wealthy and influential women

and solid geometry she saw in earlier avant-garde styles of such artists as Paul Cézanne and Paul Gauguin in Paris (see p. 521). At the same time, her work balances delicate details in gesture and mood with a portrayal of the physical substance of her body.

Russian Vasily Kandinsky (1866–1944) was one of the first artists to make **non-objective**, or completely abstract, paintings. Inspired from an early age by a love of color, he became part of the German Expressionist group **Der Blaue Reiter**. These artists rejected Classical approaches in favor of radical experimentation. Non-objective art makes no reference to recognizable subjects;

there are only abstract shapes, designs, and colors. Kandinsky's abstract paintings can be thought of as a visual equivalent for the non-verbal experience of instrumental music. He frequently used such titles as "improvisation" or "composition" for his paintings, a reference to the work of contemporary composers whose music he admired. Kandinsky said his *Improvisation #30* was inspired by talk of war in 1913, a year before World War I began (**3.8.27**). The chaotic and energetic forms reflect the turmoil of the time, though they do not illustrate any particular event. While the artist made the painting spontaneously, with no specific

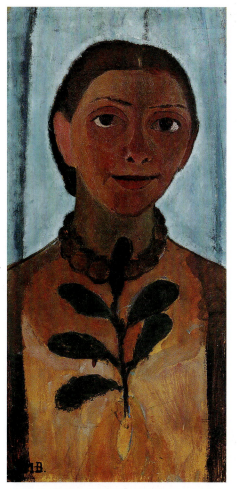

3.8.26 (right) Paula Modersohn-Becker, *Self-Portrait with Camellia*, 1906–7. Oil on canvas, 24¼ × 12". Museum Folkwang, Essen, Germany

3.8.27 (below left) Vasily Kandinsky, *Improvisation #30 (Cannons)*, 1913. Oil on canvas, 43¾ × 43¼". Art Institute of Chicago, Illinois

scene in mind, as we look at it we can make out some leaning buildings, a crowd of people, and a cannon firing. Many of Kandinsky's later pieces avoid such recognizable objects because, as he famously wrote in his book *Concerning the Spiritual in Art*, instead of expressing any outward and visible content, art should express an inner spiritual necessity. This book has become a major document reflecting art's move away from material reality in the early twentieth century.

German artist Ernst Ludwig Kirchner (1880–1938) used a deliberately raw painting style in his search for meaning beyond surface appearance. Kirchner used flat planes of intense color, simplified forms, and rough, even aggressive, brushwork. Kirchner's painting *Potsdamer Platz* reflects his belief that art should come from direct experience (**3.8.28**). The figures he saw in this street scene appear very civilized and dressed for a night on the town, but their similar clothing and mask-like faces drain them of individuality, almost turning them into clones. In this painting Kirchner seems to ask why these people lack purpose and why they

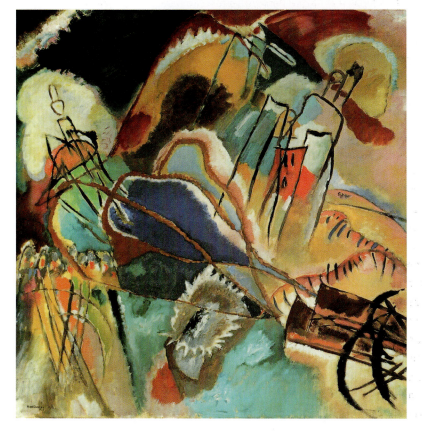

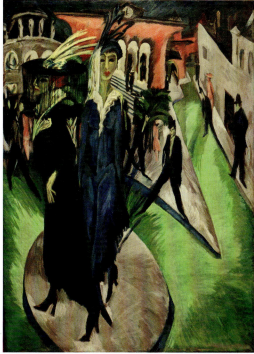

3.8.28 (above) Ernst Ludwig Kirchner, *Potsdamer Platz*, 1914. Oil on canvas, 78¾ × 59". Nationalgalerie, Berlin, Germany

all appear to be the same. He had been part of a group of artists, called **Die Brücke** ("The Bridge"), who intended their new mode of expression to form a bridge between the past, present, and future. According to these artists, the decadence and dehumanization of society could only be counteracted by the younger generation—such artists as themselves.

Dada

The devastating effects of World War I had a profound impact on how people thought about the world, "progress," and civilization. Improvements in science and industrial manufacturing may have led to some positive developments in life, but to many people they seemed primarily to have resulted, disastrously, in arms production on an unprecedented scale, and in mass slaughter in the trenches of northern Europe. The war inevitably also affected artists and the way they made art. Artists who adopted the term Dada for their art protested the kinds of "rational" thought processes that had led to war. Dadaism also took the Impressionists' and Cubists' questioning of representation still further and radically rejected the notion of art altogether.

The name Dada was notoriously chosen at random from the dictionary. It is both a nonsense word and one that has contradictory meanings in several languages. Dada was anti-art and refused to call itself a movement. It was founded by a group of artists and writers who avoided the draft by taking refuge in the neutral country of Switzerland. Dada soon spread to the United States and later to Berlin, Cologne, Paris, Russia, Eastern Europe, and Japan. Dada works, performances, and publications were critical and playful. They emphasized individuality, irrationality, chance, and imagination.

In keeping with its activist nature, Dada was inspired by revolutionary thinking and initially took the form of events, posters, and pamphlets. In February 1916 German actor and anarchist Hugo Ball (1886–1927) opened the Cabaret Voltaire in Zürich, Switzerland, with his future wife, Emmy Hennings (1885–1948). The Cabaret

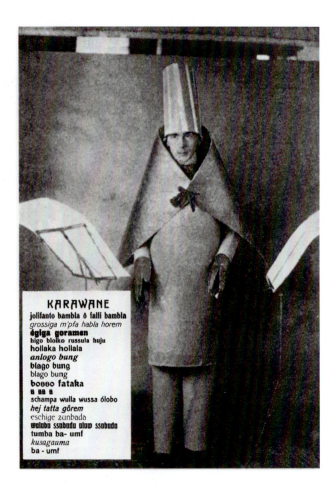

3.8.29 Hugo Ball, Performance of "Karawane" at Cabaret Voltaire, Zürich, Switzerland, 1916

was a **bohemian**, avant-garde nightclub that provided artists and writers with a place to meet, perform, and be entertained. Ball organized and promoted many of the events. The performances were lively and highly theatrical. At a particularly flamboyant recital of one of his sound poems, "Karawane," Ball wore a costume that made him look like a figure from a Cubist painting (**3.8.29**). His poems were made of nonsense words and sounds, intended to be chanted, screamed, and howled. Sometimes several poets would recite at the same time while others yapped like dogs.

The French artist Marcel Duchamp (1887–1968) was a key figure in the New York branch of Dada (he became an American citizen in 1955). Following his early career as a painter (see **3.8.36**, *Nude Descending a Staircase, No. 2*, p. 536), one of his first and most enduring anti-art statements was his *Bicycle Wheel* (**3.8.30**). Its date of production, 1913, shows that the spirit of Dada pre-dates the war. This **assemblage** of **found objects** resembles a sculpture, with a stool serving as the base, and the wheel itself as the main subject. Duchamp first made the

Die Brücke: German Expressionist movement of painters and printmakers formed in Dresden (1905–13) with the aim to defy anything Classical and to use art as a bridge between the past, present, and a utopian future

Bohemian: derived from the gypsies of the former Czech kingdom of Bohemia who moved around; a wanderer; an artist or writer who functions outside the bounds of conventional rules and practices

Assemblage: artwork made of three-dimensional materials including found objects

Found image or **object:** an image or object found by an artist and presented, with little or no alteration, as part of a work or as a finished work of art in itself

Readymade: an everyday object presented as a work of art

Kinetic art: art, usually three-dimensional, with moving parts activated by wind, personal interaction, or motors

Conceptual art: artwork in which the ideas are most important to the work

Photomontage: a single photographic image that combines (digitally or using multiple film exposures) several separate images

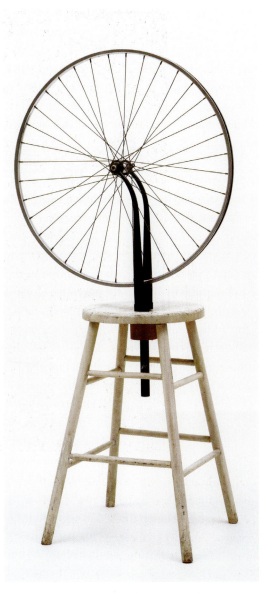

3.8.30 Marcel Duchamp, *Bicycle Wheel*, 1951. Metal wheel mounted on painted wood stool, 50½ × 25½ × 16⅝". MoMA, New York

piece for his own pleasure, because he "enjoyed looking at it, just as I enjoy looking at the flames dancing in the fireplace."

The original *Bicycle Wheel* was lost when Duchamp moved to the United States in 1915. Usually, an artwork's value partly depends on the existence of "an original" creation that is unique, but Duchamp unflinchingly re-created the piece for an exhibition in 1916. This version, too, was lost. According to the Museum of Modern Art in New York, the *Bicycle Wheel* in its collection is the third re-make. Duchamp, in true Dada style, subverts the institution and originality of art.

Duchamp was responsible for three major innovations in art in the twentieth century: **readymades** (ordinary objects turned into artworks simply by the decision of the

artist), **kinetic** sculptures (sculptures with moving parts), and what came to be known as **conceptual art** (see chapter 3.9, p. 547). For Duchamp, the making of the work and its appearance were secondary. What mattered were the choices of the artist and art's effects in our mind.

A member of Berlin Dada, German John Heartfield (born Helmut Herzfeld, 1891–1968) made political statements using the medium of **photomontage**. He boldly published works criticizing the then leader of Nazi Germany, Adolf Hitler. As a result, Heartfield eventually had to flee to Prague (in what is now the Czech Republic) and later to England to escape arrest and persecution. He distributed his work on posters and in magazines. His piece *Have No Fear, He's a Vegetarian* powerfully warns about Hitler's plans for conquest (**3.8.31**). It foreshadows many of the disasters, from widespread starvation to genocide (the deliberate mass killing of a specific race or group of people), that were to take place throughout Europe. Hitler was a vegetarian, but he is shown here wearing a blood-spattered apron. He also grins maniacally while he sharpens a large carving knife to kill a cock as French Prime Minister Pierre Laval looks on. The cock symbolizes France, a country Hitler would invade four years later.

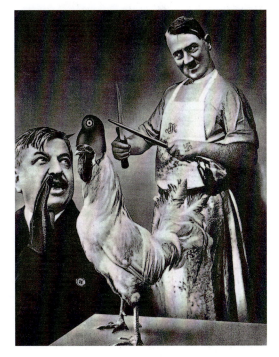

3.8.31 John Heartfield, *Have No Fear, He's a Vegetarian*, published in *Regards*, no. 121 (153), Paris, May 7, 1936. Stiftung Archiv der Akademie der Künste, Berlin, Germany

Surrealism

Like Dada, Surrealism was opposed to rationality and convention. Surrealists believed that art was a model for human freedom, meaning, and creativity in an absurd world. The movement began in the early 1920s amongst a group of writers and poets in Paris, and developed during the time between the two World Wars; the group's ideas were then taken up by visual artists. Surrealism was the first artistic style based directly on the ideas of Austrian psychoanalyst Sigmund Freud. Surrealists used techniques that Freud had originally pioneered to access his patients' unconscious minds in order to make artwork that was not fully under their conscious control: dreams and dreamlike images were therefore very important to their work. Sometimes the Surrealists used extremely realistic images in surprising ways to jolt our expectations. Surrealists challenged the very idea of objective reality, which they considered nonsense.

One artist whose work influenced the Surrealists was the Greek-born Italian Giorgio de Chirico (1888–1978). He was not a member of the Surrealist movement, but, as the Surrealists later would be, he was interested in intuitive and irrational approaches to art. In his work *The Melancholy and Mystery of the Street*, de Chirico creates a dreamlike environment in which more questions are posed than resolved (**3.8.32**). The little girl with the hoop, herself a shadow, seems unaware of the figure with a pole looming around the corner. Although the **narrative** remains unclear, a vague sense of threat fills the still air. The crisp clarity of the forms, the Classical architecture, and the gradation of colors in the otherwise empty sky are all characteristic of de Chirico's work and enhance the enigma.

Max Ernst (1891–1976) was a German-born artist who was first involved with Dada and then Surrealism. For him, the process of making art was of utmost importance. Ernst used different techniques—such as collage, rubbing, and scraping—to encourage chance events that would reduce his conscious control over his work. These processes, as he stated, would liberate the human imagination. He deliberately embraced the bizarre, strange, and irrational to express truths that he believed were buried by logic in the conscious mind. In Ernst's *Surrealism and Painting* the figure shown painting is not a human being but an amorphous blob (**3.8.33**). This shapeless being can be interpreted in different ways. It may refer to the general difficulty of understanding or explaining creativity. Perhaps it depicts the chance processes Ernst used in making art. The painting on the easel is a representation of the equally uncertain results, here seen as abstractions that seem vaguely cosmic, like planets and intergalactic matter in the uncharted territory of outer space. Overall, Ernst made a strong statement about how liberating it can be to allow the imagination to wander in the mysterious realm of creativity.

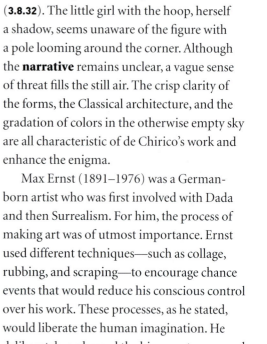

3.8.32 Giorgio de Chirico, *The Melancholy and Mystery of the Street*, 1914. Oil on canvas, 34¼ × 28⅛". Private collection

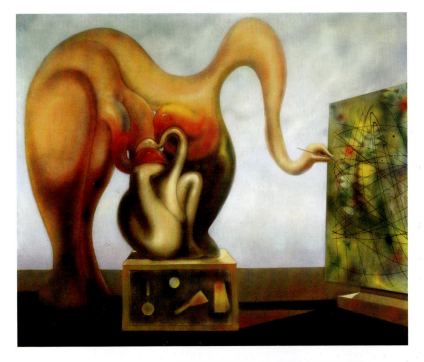

3.8.33 Max Ernst, *Le Surréalisme et la Peinture (Surrealism and Painting)*, 1942. Oil on canvas, 6'5" × 7'8". The Menil Collection, Houston, Texas

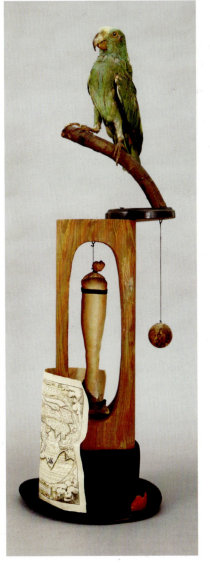

3.8.34 Joan Miró, *Object*, 1936. Assemblage: stuffed parrot on wood perch, stuffed silk stocking with velvet garter and doll's paper shoe suspended in hollow wood frame, derby hat, hanging cork ball, celluloid fish, and engraved map, 31⅞ × 11⅞ × 10¼". MoMA, New York

Using the technique of assemblage, Surrealists created the three-dimensional equivalent of collage. These assemblages were principally intended to be playful and nonsensical and to reflect new ways of thinking. Spanish artist Joan Miró (1893–1983) compiled an unexpected assortment of items in his sculpture called *Object* (**3.8.34**). A derby hat, which serves as the sculpture's base, has a map placed on one side of its brim and a red plastic fish on the other. A block of wood sits on the hat with a perch on top of it that supports a stuffed parrot. Miró fashioned a miniature woman's leg by stuffing a silk stocking in a shapely manner, placing a doll's shoe on one end, and wrapping a band for a garter on the other. This leg is hanging in an oval-shaped opening of the wooden block. A cork ball hangs from the parrot's perch beside the leg. The objects have the whimsical quality of toys. When viewed together, as the artist has arranged them, they also have an air of mystery, as if they are clues to an unsolved crime or random items that make sense only to their owner.

The Influence of Cubism

Cubism's ground-breaking approach to art (see pp. 527–529 above) had a huge impact throughout Europe. Many artists adopted the Cubist style, while others explored ways of making art and representing objects that had not been conceived of before Cubism.

Futurism

In Italy, during the period from 1909 to the late 1920s, some artists were influenced by Cubism's clashing planes and geometry to develop a style known as Futurism. Unlike Cubist artworks, though, Futurist works celebrated dynamic movement, progress, modern technology, and political beliefs that were later to be known as Fascist. They also expressed contempt for the past. Italian Umberto Boccioni (1882–1916) explored some of these concepts in his Futurist sculpture *Unique Forms of Continuity in*

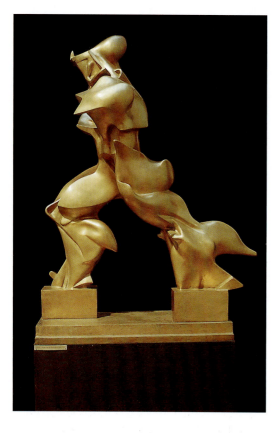

3.8.35 Umberto Boccioni, *Unique Forms of Continuity in Space*, 1913 (cast 1931). Bronze, 49¾ × 35 × 16". Private collection

3.8.36 Marcel Duchamp, *Nude Descending a Staircase, No. 2*, 1912. Oil on canvas, 57⅞ × 35⅛". Philadelphia Museum of Art, Pennsylvania

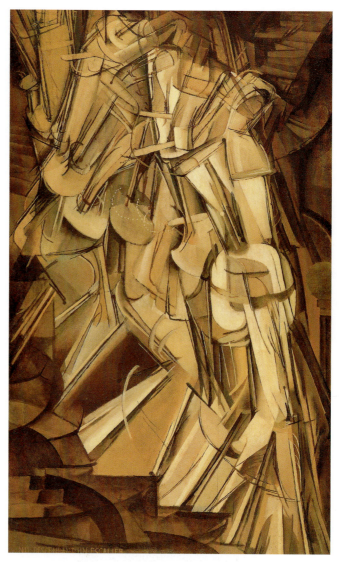

Space (**3.8.35**). Looking like a flame, the figure forcefully strides through space. Boccioni made the sculpture in plaster; it was not cast in bronze during his lifetime. The shiny, golden appearance of the metal version embodies the words of the founder of Futurism, Filippo Marinetti: "War is beautiful because it inaugurates the long dreamed-of metallization of the human body." Nonetheless, the figure has heroic **monumentality** as it leaves behind the artistic traditions of the past.

As we have seen, Marcel Duchamp (see pp. 532–33) had a huge impact on the development of modern art. It was his *Nude Descending a Staircase, No. 2* and the scandal it caused at the Armory Show in New York in 1913 that earned him an international reputation (**3.8.36**). For this short period in his career Duchamp combined Cubism's figures—

broken into geometric planes—with Futurism's emphasis on movement. The mechanization of the figure in this painting reflected a widespread contemporary interest in machines, industrial progress, and stop-motion photography. Like many other works at the Armory Show, this painting shocked an audience familiar only with representational imagery, or pictures "of" something. Because today we are more familiar with abstract imagery, *Nude Descending a Staircase, No. 2* no longer seems to us outrageous, shocking, or criminal, yet certain people saw it that way in 1913.

Abstraction

The road to abstraction began with the Impressionist emphasis on the immediate effects

Monumental: having massive or impressive scale

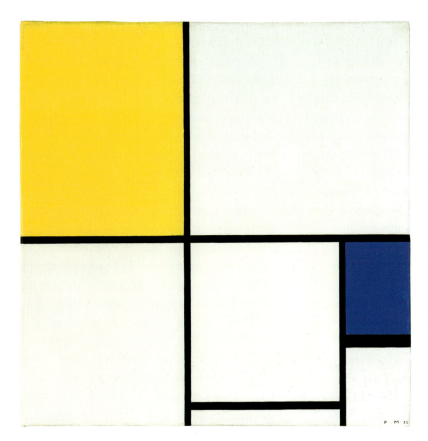

3.8.37 Piet Mondrian, *Composition with Yellow and Blue*, 1932. Oil on canvas, 21⅝ × 21⅝". Beyeler Collection, Beyeler Foundation, Riehen/Basel, Switzerland

of color and light instead of details in line work and shading. From there, Post-Impressionists emphasized visual structure and emotion, Matisse and the Fauvists released color from its representational obligations, Expressionists explored nonrepresentational approaches, and the Cubists revolutionized form by showing multiple viewpoints at one time. Early twentieth-century abstract artists continued where these avant-garde pioneers left off.

The Dutch painter Piet Mondrian (1872–1944) was the founder of the movement called **De Stijl** ("The Style") in the Netherlands. He painted in a naturalistic style early in his career and was influenced by avant-garde movements, including Cubism, to move away from directly depicting visible reality. Always interested in the underlying structure in his subjects, Mondrian increasingly began to concentrate on creating non-representational works. In 1914 he began making compositions entirely of intersecting lines, right-angled shapes, and linear planes. In 1921 he restricted his palette to the **primary colors**, and black, white, and gray. Using these select formal elements for decades, Mondrian is known for his geometric abstractions (**3.8.37**).

The subtle adjustments in the proportions and arrangements in his paintings result from mathematical principles and the ratios of the **Golden Section**. Mondrian believed that the clarity and organization of his compositions reflected rational beauty that is objective and appeals to the mind in a universal way, as opposed to subjective beauty, which appeals to the senses.

Russian Kazimir Malevich (1878–1935) was, like Kandinsky (p. 530), one of the first artists to make completely non-objective paintings. Unlike Kandinsky, Malevich concentrated solely on direct geometric forms. He called his approach Suprematism because he considered it morally, spiritually, and aesthetically superior to what had been done in the past. Malevich believed that recognizable objects were a burden for the viewer and that geometric abstraction helped to free the mind from the thoughts of politics, religion, and tradition that were so much on people's minds in the early twentieth century, partly as a result of the cataclysmic conflict of World War I. Most of Malevich's Suprematist works consist of rectangular shapes floating on a white **ground**. While they look like Cubist collages, the shapes are actually painted. In *Suprematist Painting (White on White)* the palette has been reduced to two shades of white, and the inner square is tilted to suggest movement (**3.8.38**).

3.8.38 Kazimir Malevich, *Suprematist Composition: White on White*, 1918. Oil on canvas, 31¼ × 31¼". MoMA, New York

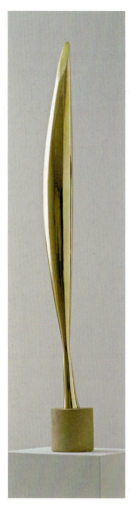

3.8.39 Constantin Brancusi, *Bird in Space (L'Oiseau dans l'Espace)*, 1928. Bronze, 54 × 8½ × 6½". MoMA, New York

The Romanian-born French sculptor Constantin Brancusi (1876–1957) devoted his working life to finding the very simplest and most elegant way to express the essence of his chosen subject. His *Bird in Space* distills the vital qualities of a bird to what, at first sight, looks like a totally abstract form (**3.8.39**). The shape exquisitely reminds us of a bird's body, a feather, or even the soaring quality of flight.

This sculpture, with the polished bronze form stacked on top of a small stone cylinder with a lighter-colored stone rectangular prism underneath, shows Brancusi's careful consideration of even the *base* of the sculpture. He chose the materials of the base—usually wood, metal, stone, or marble—to contrast in texture with a different material used for the rest of the sculpture. In this case, the solidity and bulk of the stone suggest heaviness and earth, while the contrasting thinness of the smooth and shiny bronze makes it look as if it would slip easily through the air.

Early Twentieth-Century Art in America

The move toward abstraction in the US happened after the 1913 Armory Show in New York City, when the American public was introduced to the work of such artists as Matisse, Picasso, Kandinsky, and Duchamp. While European artists and some Americans continued experiments with abstraction during the 1930s, another group, inspired by the harsh realities presented by the advent of the Great Depression in 1929, chose to focus on distinctly American subjects and representational styles. This came to be known as American Scene painting. A sense of disconnection from the radical European style in this time of hardship made the American Scene artists retreat to subjects familiar to them. And while the two branches of American Scene took slightly different approaches, they shared nationalistic sentiments about the movement. The Regionalists focused on rural environments and promoted American virtues, such as patriotism and hard work, while the Social Realists were interested in promoting social justice through their artwork.

An American Regionalist, Grant Wood (1891–1942) studied in Europe but realized that his inspiration came from his home in the Midwest and the places he knew best. Wood's sister and his dentist were the models for the farmer and his daughter in Wood's now-famous *American Gothic* (**3.8.40**). They stand in front of an Iowa farmhouse built in a style called Carpenter Gothic, inspiring the painting's title. Their full-frontal posture and the clarity of detail and light come from Flemish Renaissance art (see chapter 3.6) that Wood had studied while in Europe. While this painting has been the subject of many artistic parodies, it was meant to be a serious reflection of hope in spite of the Depression, and an affirmation of the American values of individuality, morality, and hard work.

Beginning in the 1920s and 1930s, the Harlem Renaissance or "New Negro" movement specifically focused on the expression of African-American experience through music, writing, and visual art. Interested in art at an early age, American Aaron Douglas (1899–1979) moved to New York City and soon became a leading figure of the movement. As seen in *Aspects of Negro American Life: Slavery through Reconstruction* (**3.8.41**), Douglas's work depicts African-American life and post-slavery/pre-

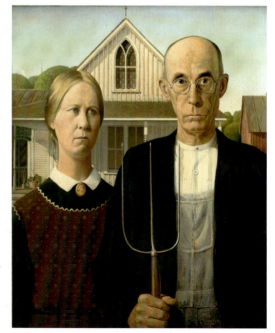

3.8.40 Grant Wood, *American Gothic*, 1930. Oil on beaverboard, 30¾ × 25¾". Art Institute of Chicago, Illinois

Silhouette: a portrait or figure represented in outline and solidly colored in

Civil Rights struggles. Part of a series of four paintings commissioned by the Works Progress Administration (WPA) for the 135th St. branch of the New York Public Library, each panel depicts a different aspect of black life, from Africa to the migration to northern US cities. The *Slavery to Reconstruction* panel combines the past and the present—jungle plants and animals referencing Africa alongside a trumpet and drum referencing jazz and its importance

to society at the time the painting was made. The **silhouettes**, which became a signature aspect of Douglas's work, were created from the combined influences of Egyptian wall paintings, Art Deco (a style similar to Art Nouveau) designs, African art, and Modernist abstraction. The lively atmosphere, dancing, and jazz music shown here also represent the intersections of African heritage, African-American culture, and nationalistic identity.

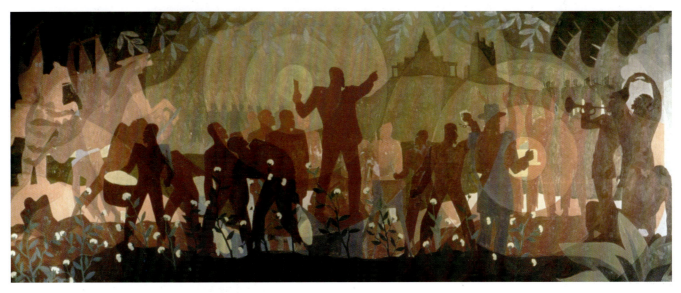

3.8.41 Aaron Douglas, *Aspects of Negro American Life: From Slavery to Reconstruction*, 1934. Oil on canvas, 57¾ × 108¼". The New York Public Library, Schomburg Center for Research in Black Culture, New York

Discussion Questions

1. Select one Realist, one Impressionist, and one Post-Impressionist work of art. Discuss how the Impressionist work both built on and deviated from the Realist style. Next, discuss how the Post-Impressionist work built on and deviated from the style of the Impressionist work.

2. Select a biblical or mythological topic. Compare how it was depicted by three different artists from three different times. How do the personal circumstances of the artist and the time in which he or she lived impact the way in which each artist chose to depict your subject?

3. Choose the artwork from this chapter that you have the most trouble relating to visually or conceptually. Write a statement "justifying" this artwork to the best of your ability. Pretend you are taking a family member to a museum and he or she asks you to explain what this work is about. Rather than simply saying, "I don't get it, either," come up with what you would say to help this person understand.

4. Matisse and Picasso were artistic rivals who challenged one another throughout their careers. Select two artworks (one by each artist) that were painted the same year. Make a formal analysis on each artwork and study the biography of its artist. Write an essay comparing the two works and artists.

Images related to 3.8:
The Modern Aesthetic: Manet in 1863 to the American Scene in the 1930s

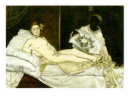

4.9.9 Édouard Manet, *Olympia*, 1863, p. 665

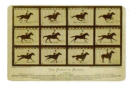

2.9.2 Eadweard Muybridge, *The Horse in Motion*, 1878, p. 339

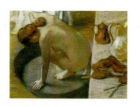

2.1.14 Edgar Degas, *The Tub*, 1886, p. 206

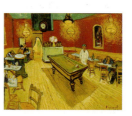

1.4.26 Vincent van Gogh, *The Night Café*, 1888, p. 114

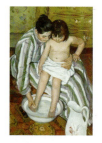

3.3.23 Mary Cassatt, *The Child's Bath*, 1893, p. 429

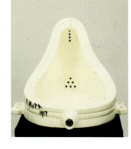

1.4.18 André Derain, *The Turning Road, L'Estaque*, 1906, p. 110

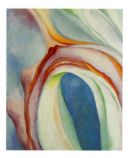

3.9.7 Marcel Duchamp, *Fountain*, 1917, p. 546

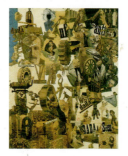

1.1.27 Georgia O'Keeffe, *Music—Pink and Blue II*, 1919, p. 63

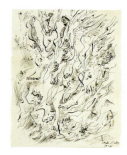

2.8.21 Hannah Höch, *Cut with the Kitchen Knife...*, 1919–20, p. 333

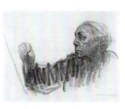

1.1.6 André Masson, *Automatic Drawing*, 1925–26, p. 53

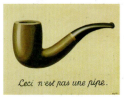

1.3.1 René Magritte, *The Treachery of Images*, 1929, p. 82

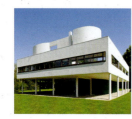

2.5.32 Le Corbusier, *Villa Savoye*, 1928–31, p. 284

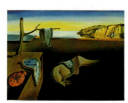

4.4.17 Salvador Dalí, *Persistence of Memory*, 1931, p. 608

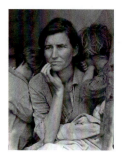

2.1.10 Käthe Kollwitz, *Self-Portrait in Profile to Left*, 1933, p. 204

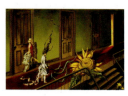

2.8.9 Dorothea Lange, *Migrant Mother*, 1936, p. 234

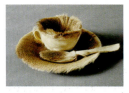

1.2.19 Méret Oppenheim, *Object*, 1936, p. 80

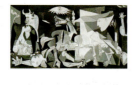

4.7.5 Pablo Picasso, *Guernica*, 1937, p. 638

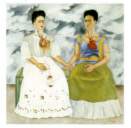

4.10.3 Frida Kahlo, *The Two Fridas*, 1939, p. 677

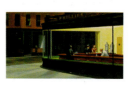

1.10.2 Edward Hopper, *Nighthawks*, 1942, p. 180

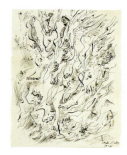

1.7.5 Dorothea Tanning, *Eine Kleine Nachtmusik*, 1943, p. 149

3.9

Late Modern and Contemporary Art: From Abstract Expressionism in the 1940s to the Present Day

The world that emerged from World War II was radically changed. The tragedy of the Holocaust left millions dead as the German military systematically slaughtered innocent civilians considered "inferior" by the Nazis, including six million Jews. When the war was over, the great powers of Europe—Great Britain, Germany, France, and Italy—found their societies devastated by the destruction of years of war. Two new super-powers now dominated the world. The United States had become an economic powerhouse based on free enterprise and capitalism. On the other hand, the Soviet Union, which now dominated much of central Europe, adopted a centrally planned system of economic management, Communism, and focused on rivaling the industrial might of America in what came to be called the Cold War.

After World War II the global expansion in commerce and politics was paralleled by the fact that territories that until then had been colonized by European countries (for example India under Britain, Africa under France and Britain) gained political independence to become new nations in their own right. These developing and expanding nations promoted their own cultural traditions, including Muslim, Hindu, and Buddhist religions. People emigrated (forcibly or by choice) from Africa, Asia, Latin America, and throughout Europe, bringing their belief systems and customs to countries the populations of which had previously been unfamiliar with them.

During the later part of the twentieth century, far-off places became more accessible to Western and industrialized countries by means of new communication technologies (radio, television, computers) and advancements in air travel (high-speed jets, space exploration). Goods, people, and ideas could now circulate around the globe faster than ever before.

In art, the Modern period (c. 1860–1960) continued, and was followed by the Contemporary period (1960–present). Artists responded to events occurring in the wider world as well as to developments in the world of art. During this time period, some artists continued the formal experiments, such as **abstraction** and experimental ways of depicting the world or expressing their ideas, which had been pioneered by early **Modernist** artists. While the latter had rejected the use of recognizable imagery in their art, as well as the **styles** and approaches of artists from earlier eras, contemporary artists experimented seemingly without limit and in a variety of ways. Some indeed reintroduced realistic imagery into their artworks and often referred to past artistic styles. For others, the ideas or concepts expressed in art took precedence over the physical objects they created. Artists looked to a wide range of influence, from current popular culture to traditional cultural identity, for inspiration.

Additionally, while museums and galleries have continued to play important roles in the art world, artists can now also show their work to international audiences via the Internet, whether they live in such urban centers as New York, Los Angeles, Paris, and Tokyo, or far from a modern city. In recent years art has taken on a distinctly

Abstraction: the degree to which an image is altered from an easily recognizable subject
Modernism, Modernist: a radically new twentieth-century art and architectural movement that embraced modern industrial materials and a machine aesthetic
Style: a characteristic way in which an artist or group of artists uses visual language to give a work an identifiable form of visual expression

international character, with renewed interest in engaging audiences and making an impact on the world around us.

Abstract Expressionism

European refugees including numerous artists, intellectuals, and scientists came to the US during World War II to escape persecution. Many of them settled in New York City, which became a globally important cultural center. Whereas the **avant-garde** artistic developments described in chapter 3.8 began in Europe, **Abstract Expressionism** was the first Modernist art movement to originate in the US. This movement, which evolved in the 1940s and 1950s, was a sign of increasing national self-confidence in America after the end of the war. Abstract Expressionist artists wanted to create, with energy and emotion, a universal visual experience that anyone could respond to, without needing to refer to their own life experience, religious or political beliefs.

To make his enormous paintings, American artist Jackson Pollock (1912–1956) started by unrolling the canvas onto the floor. Then

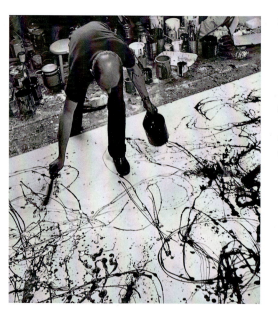

3.9.1 (left) Jackson Pollock painting in his Long Island studio, 1950. Photo by Hans Namuth

3.9.2 (below) Jackson Pollock, *Number 1A*, 1948. Oil and enamel paint on canvas, 5'8" × 8'8". MoMA, New York

he could move about freely, almost dancing around and over the piece (**3.9.1**). Pollock also used sticks as well as brushes to drip and pour the paint onto the surface. The absence of any recognizable **subject** fixes our attention on the actions and gestures of the artist. The process becomes the subject, making the painting about the act of creation itself. The results of Pollock's process, known as **action painting**, are complex abstract paintings so large that when we stand before them they completely dominate our field of vision. Pollock's artworks evolved organically

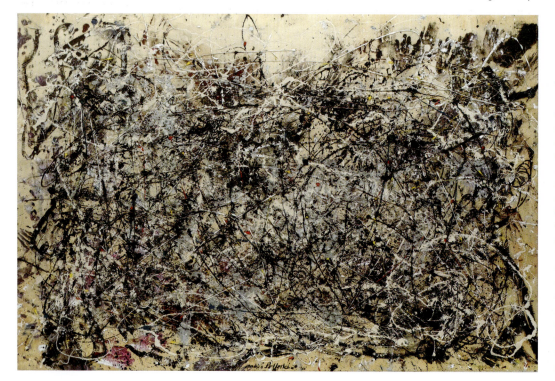

Avant-garde: early twentieth-century emphasis on artistic innovation, which challenged accepted values, traditions, and techniques
Abstract Expressionism: a mid-twentieth-century artistic style characterized by its capacity to convey intense emotions using non-representational images
Subject: the person, object, or space depicted in a work of art
Action painting: application of paint to canvas by dripping, splashing, or smearing that emphasizes the artist's gestures

and spontaneously rather than from precise pre-planning. The improvisational process and the tension between the **rhythms** and cross-rhythms of Pollock's paintings also have some similarities to jazz music, which he liked to listen to as he worked (**3.9.2**).

American artist Mark Rothko (1903–1970) emigrated to the US from Russia with his family. He became interested in **Surrealist** art as a way to move beyond depicting familiar subjects and to explore **archetypes** and mythic **narratives** that might generally appeal to any viewer regardless of his or her background.

Eventually, Rothko entirely eliminated **representation** from his compositions, and concentrated on **form** and color. For about twenty years, from *c.* 1950 to 1970, his works consisted of luminous rectangles floating in fields of color, such as *No. 5/No. 22* from 1950 (**3.9.3**). This painting includes subtle color shifts, not only in the oranges and variations of yellows in the large fields, but also within the undertones, with a greenish shade in the golden-yellow background to heighten contrast with the red band. Rothko chose not to give his works narrative titles and to allow us to respond deeply and individually. He wanted to create an opportunity for viewers to be transported away from the specificity of scenes from daily life and lose themselves in contemplation. Rothko famously said, "I'm not an abstractionist. I'm not interested in the relationship of color or form or anything else. I'm interested only in expressing basic human emotions: tragedy, ecstasy, doom, and so on."

Pop Art

Unlike the Abstract Expressionists, the artists who began producing **Pop art** in the late 1950s embraced everyday subject matter in their work. Americans and Europeans were surrounded by consumer culture and futuristic high-tech gadgets that promised ways for "everyone" to live a life of plenty and leisure. In reality, however, middle-class suburban living was out of reach for people who lived in the inner cities—primarily African Americans at the time—not to

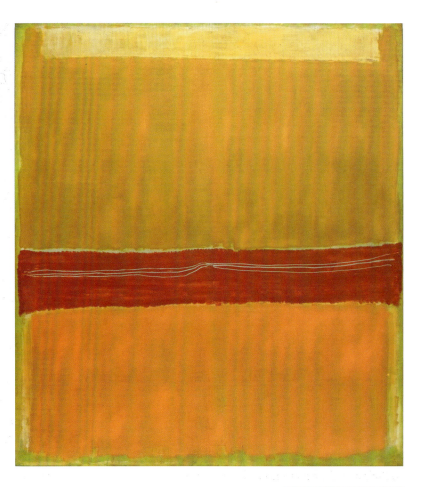

3.9.3 Mark Rothko, *No. 5/No. 22*, 1950 (dated 1949 on reverse). Oil on canvas, 9'9" × 8'11⅛". MoMA, New York

mention countries outside the West. In addition, no matter how hard society tried to tune out the constant threat of atomic war with the latest movie idols and pop music playing on the radio, it could not be ignored.

Pop art embraced the objects and experiences of daily life in a way that was entirely new to the art world at the time. Jasper Johns (b. 1930) and Robert Rauschenberg (1925–2008), who believed that Abstract Expressionist art was too obscure and personal, served as inspiration for Pop artists by highlighting common objects taken directly from the life they were living (see Images Related to 3.9, p. 559). Because Pop artists wanted their subjects to be immediately familiar to their audiences, they borrowed their imagery from popular culture, including famous artworks, comic-books, commercial advertising, car design, television, movies, and the news. At the time there was a division between fine art (a supposedly sophisticated part of "high" culture)

Rhythm: the regular or ordered repetition of elements in the work
Surrealism, Surrealist: an artistic movement in the 1920s and later; its works were inspired by dreams and the subconscious
Archetype: psychoanalytical term used to describe very typical kinds of people that originated long ago, serve as patterns, and can be recognized in later groups or individuals, for example, mothers, heroes, and villains
Narrative: an artwork that tells a story; the story that the artwork expresses
Representation: the depiction of recognizable figures and objects
Form: an object that can be defined in three dimensions (height, width, and depth)
Pop art: mid-twentieth-century artistic movement inspired by commercial art forms and popular culture

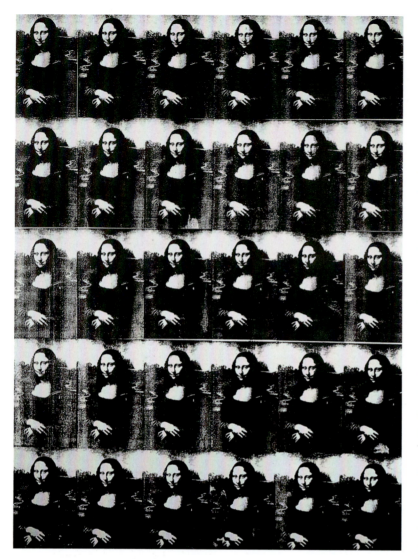

3.9.4 Andy Warhol, *Thirty Are Better than One*, 1963. Silkscreen ink on synthetic polymer paint on canvas, 9'2" × 7'10". Private collection

and its opposite, popular culture (considered unrefined and ordinary). Pop artists bridged this gap by combining fine art materials with commercial elements, such as pictures from magazines, sometimes printing by **silkscreen** (which is used for printing packaging), and then selling their pieces in fine art galleries.

American Andy Warhol (1928–1987) began his professional career as an illustrator and graphic designer in advertising. Around 1960, using the expressive brushwork and drips of paint that were characteristic of Abstract Expressionism, Warhol made **acrylic** paintings of the comic-book heroes Superman, Batman, and Dick Tracy. He then quickly turned to the imagery of advertising, using as his subjects such familiar products as Campbell's soup and Coca-Cola. He also began using the silkscreen technique. This process allowed him not only

to make art more quickly, but also to give it a depersonalized and mass-produced quality very different from some art's emphasis on personal expression or technique. Warhol even borrowed, or appropriated, the famous image of the Italian Renaissance artist Leonardo da Vinci's *Mona Lisa* (see Images Related to 3.9, p. 559). The title of this piece, *Thirty Are Better than One*, clearly echoes the language of advertising and consumerism—"more is better" (**3.9.4**). It refers to the multiple reproductions of the painting in Warhol's work while also undermining the "high art" tendency to value an artwork financially and aesthetically only if it is "original" and unique.

The American artist Roy Lichtenstein (1923–1997) also made works based on comics. Lichtenstein challenged traditional notions of the subject matter and appearance of fine art painting by embracing everyday subjects. In his painting *Girl in Mirror* he uses strong black **outlines** filled with bold **primary colors** (**3.9.5**). In order to create gradations of a color, Lichtenstein borrowed a technique from older kinds of newspaper printing and comics. The regular pattern of dots, called **Ben-Day dots**, emulates the screen visible on printed pictures, where areas of light **value** have small dots, and those of dark value have large ones nearly joined together. Lichtenstein's dots give a commercial edge to the technique of **pointillism**, while his use of black, white, and primary colors references the color **palette** of such geometric abstract artists as Piet Mondrian (see Images Related to 3.9, p. 559). It is also interesting to compare and contrast his very different treatment of his subject, the girl with a mirror, with that of Pablo Picasso in the latter's painting *Girl before a Mirror* (see Images Related to 3.9, p. 559).

Warhol's and Lichtenstein's work used appropriation to bring recognizable and familiar imagery into galleries and museums. By combining the practices of what was then considered "high art" at the time with the "low art" of **graphic design**, these artists were able to bridge the gap between the two and expand the boundaries of acceptable fine art practices to include popular imagery and commercial printing processes.

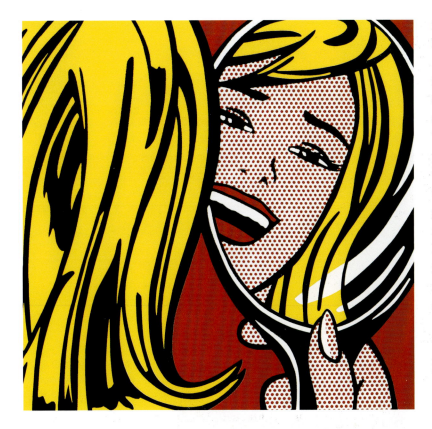

3.9.5 Roy Lichtenstein, *Girl in Mirror*, 1964. Enamel on steel, 42 × 42". Private collection

---

Primary colors: three basic colors from which all others are derived

Ben-Day dots: printing process named for its inventor

Value: the lightness or darkness of a plane or area

Pointillism: a late nineteenth-century painting style using short strokes or points of differing colors that optically combine to form new perceived colors

Palette: the range of colors used by an artist

Graphic design: the use of images, typography, and technology to communicate ideas for a client or to a particular audience

Minimalism, Minimalist: a mid-twentieth-century artistic style characterized by its simple, unified, and impersonal look, and often employing geometrical or massive forms

Minimalism

Minimalist artists in the 1960s reacted against both what they saw as the excessive emphasis on the artist's personality in Abstract Expressionism, and the commercial nature of Pop. Minimalism is an approach to making art that by its very nature is non-representational. Minimalists sought instead to use neutral textures, geometric shapes, flat colors, and even mechanical construction in order to strip away any traces of emotion or underlying meaning in their work.

American sculptor Donald Judd (1928–1994) produced Minimalist pieces that were totally abstract, usually rectangles and cubes. Although during the early stages of his career Judd was a painter, and he did go on to paint some of his sculptures, he generally preferred the medium of sculpture to painting because it existed in "actual space." According to Judd, any painting, no matter how abstract, shows something, whereas a sculpture *is* something, in real space. His sculptures had an industrial appearance and were commercially manufactured to allow the artist to focus on new materials rather than

fine art conventions, which he believed had become limiting.

For his *Untitled* piece (**3.9.6**), Judd ordered from a factory ten boxes made with stainless steel around the edges and Plexiglas on the top and bottom, each measuring 9⅛ × 40 × 31 in. Then, when the piece was installed, it was placed according to his specifications. Even though the work includes multiple pieces, they are spaced in an orderly way to focus the viewer's attention on "the thing as a whole, its quality as a whole." Judd preferred to have his pieces made in this way because it made them stand on their own, limited the role of the artist as creator, and downplayed any underlying message.

American artist Dan Flavin's (1933–1996) work, like that of other Minimalists, is made from industrial materials and has a clean,

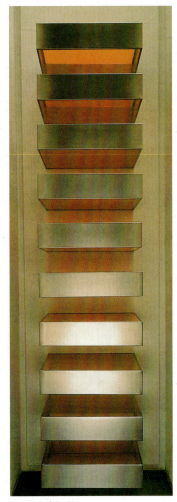

3.9.6 Donald Judd, *Untitled*, 1967. Stainless steel and Plexiglas, 190⅛ × 40 × 31". Modern Art Museum of Fort Worth, Texas

Borrowing an Image

Many artworks are personal statements, and those statements can take many forms. Some artworks are created by borrowing objects, figures, or entire compositions from the work of other artists. This practice, known as **appropriation**, can be traced to the invention by French artist Marcel Duchamp (1887–1968) of **readymades** (3.9.7), which consist of ordinary objects transformed into artworks simply by a decision taken by the artist. When Duchamp introduced such readymades as *Fountain* into the realm of art, he was challenging existing artistic practice and shifting the focus to the ideas behind the work rather than its physical appearance.

Duchamp appropriated such objects as urinals, bicycle wheels, snow shovels, and even existing artworks as viable material for his art. Over time, other artists followed in his footsteps by continuing to appropriate artworks (including ones by Duchamp). Some also borrowed images from the realms of popular culture, advertising, and even social stereotypes. Thus an artist can make a personal statement by appropriating the work of another.

The American artist Sherrie Levine (b. 1947) is known for her appropriation of famous paintings, sculptures, and photographs from the past. These pieces raise many questions: Who can be an artist? What role does the artist play? How has that role changed over time? What is originality? Who can be original? The pieces Levine appropriates are generally by male artists who worked at a time when there were very few women in the art world, as has been the case throughout most of history. Levine's work leads us to reconsider the structures of art institutions as they existed in the past. Her sculpture *Fountain (After Marcel Duchamp: A. P.)* (3.9.8) recalls Duchamp's famous porcelain urinal from 1917. Unlike Duchamp, though, who took an existing urinal and declared it to be art, Levine had a urinal cast in bronze, a material traditionally used for fine art sculptures. Levine encourages the viewer not just to interact with her own piece, but also to consider his or her attitude toward Duchamp's urinal; so her quotation of a past artwork makes Levine's sculpture most meaningful for viewers who are familiar with Duchamp's work.

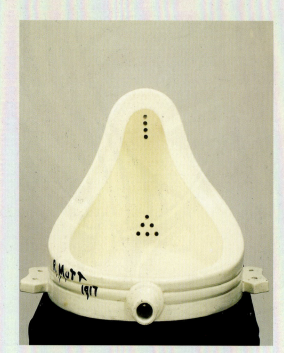

3.9.7 Marcel Duchamp, *Fountain*, 1950. Replica (original of 1917 lost). Porcelain urinal, 12 × 15 × 18". Philadelphia Museum of Art, Pennsylvania

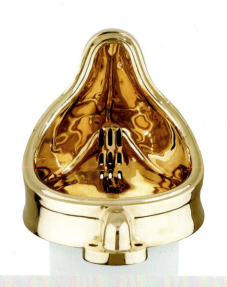

3.9.8 Sherrie Levine, *Fountain (After Marcel Duchamp: A. P.)*, 1991. Bronze, 26 × 14½ × 14"

geometric quality. Flavin created individual artworks and **installations** with fluorescent light tubes. The sculptures have a physical aspect (the fixtures and tubes), but they also focus our attention on the use of light itself as a means to impact the space. The light from the bulbs, which are commonly used in offices, stores, and even homes, takes on a new significance in the form of a sculpture on the walls of an art gallery. When the fluorescent tubes are placed together in an installation (see **3.9.9**), the noticeable glow transforms the space. Flavin's work promotes the idea that a simple object that has been commercially purchased can become a work of art and cause us to look at such familiar objects in new ways.

Conceptual Art

Conceptual art takes the non-representational tendencies that are apparent in Minimalism even further, often eliminating the art object altogether. Instead of painting a canvas or carving a block of marble, for example, an artist might arrange certain objects together in a way that makes people reconsider each one in a new light. Some conceptual artists focused their efforts on planning, rather than producing, artwork. The results of conceptual art include documentation, **sketches**, **artist's books**, photographs, performances, and mail art (any artwork, often in the form of postcards or small packages, distributed through the mail).

The work of American Conceptual artist Joseph Kosuth (b. 1945) provokes questions in the minds of viewers. His processes, approach, and materials were inspired by Marcel Duchamp's readymades (see Box opposite) as well as by his interest in art that appeals to the mind rather than the senses. On one level, Kosuth's *One and Three Chairs* simply presents three things that a chair could be: on our left, a photographic representation of a chair; in the center, an actual wooden chair; and on our right, an enlarged dictionary definition of the word "chair" (**3.9.10**). On another level, this piece represents a sophisticated

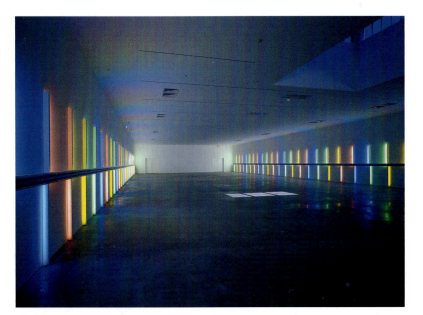

investigation into how we know and understand the world around us. Which of these chairs is more familiar? Which is more "real"? Which one provides us the most information? Ultimately, our experience of a "chair," its meaning, our awareness of how we communicate ideas, and the way all these things impact art is changed after seeing this piece.

3.9.9 (above) Dan Flavin, *Untitled*, 1996. Installation of 4' fixtures in two opposing banks for the east and west interior walls of Richmond Hall. Pink, yellow, green, blue, and ultraviolet fluorescent tubes and metal fixtures, two sections, each 8' high, approx. 128' wide. Menil Collection, Houston, Texas

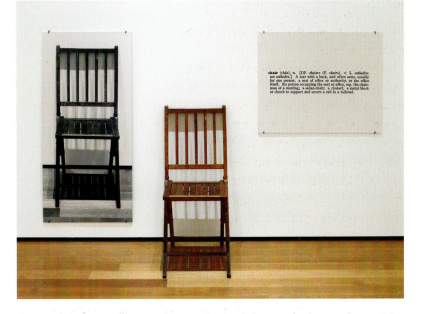

3.9.10 Joseph Kosuth, *One and Three Chairs*, 1965. Mounted photograph of a chair, wooden folding chair, and photographic enlargement of a dictionary definition of "chair," photographic panel 36 × 24⅛", chair 32⅜ × 14⅞ × 20⅞", text panel 24 × 24⅛". MoMA, New York

Performance and Body Art

The Cuban-born artist Ana Mendieta (1948–1985) is known for using her own body as an integral part of her art-making. Her performances and art actions explore personal themes (such as the displacement she experienced by moving away from the country of her birth to the United States). She also incorporates references to natural elements (water, earth, fire, blood) and biological cycles (life, death, spiritual rebirth). For her *Silueta* series of 1973–80 (see **3.9.11**), Mendieta situated her body in various outdoor environments: on the ground, in front of a tree, on a sandy beach. In the example shown here, the artist's body is camouflaged by the flowers and mud that cover it. Whether her body or its **silhouette** is shown in the photograph, the images of this series reinforce the powerful connection between a woman's body and nature, and show them as sources of strength, endurance, and nourishment.

Earthworks

Minimalist and Conceptual art expanded the existing notion of art. Similarly, artists who created earthworks (a term coined by Robert Smithson [1938–1973], see Images Related to 3.9, p. 559), or land art, made art that was so large that it could not be displayed in commercial art galleries. This art was hard (but not quite impossible) to sell and required a great effort to see. These works unite art and life, sculpture with nature. The media earthwork artists have used range from collections of natural materials, big and small, to expanses of mesas in Nevada, lakes in Utah, fields in New Mexico, and beyond. Since almost all land art is in a specific location, it cannot be shown in traditional art venues, although photographic documentation and fragments of an earthwork can be displayed in galleries and museums.

Not all earthworks are made on an enormous scale, however. In fact, British artist Andy

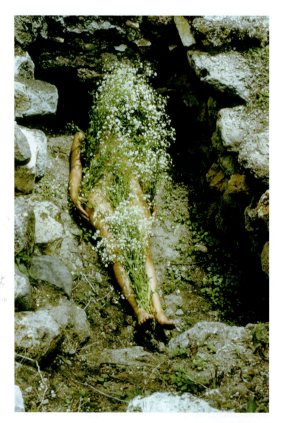

3.9.11 (above) Ana Mendieta, "Untitled" (*Silueta* series, Mexico). Color photograph from 35 mm slide, 20 × 16"

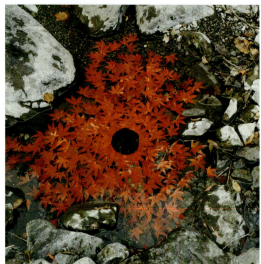

3.9.12 Andy Goldsworthy, *Japanese maple / leaves stitched together to make a floating chain / the next day it became a hole / supported underneath by a woven briar ring / Ouchiyama-Mura / Japan, 21–22 November / 1987.* Print size 24 × 24"

Goldsworthy (b. 1956) creates both intimate and larger-scale site-specific structures out of grass, rocks, leaves, flowers, bark, snow, ice, and water. *Japanese maple leaves ...* (**3.9.12**) consists of a ring of leaves stitched together, placed in a rocky pool supported by a briar ring. This piece draws attention to the splendor of nature in the unrivalled vibrancy of the leaves' red hue, configured to **contrast** with the gray of the stones, almost as if they had arranged themselves. An environmentalist as well as an artist, Goldsworthy meticulously creates his

Silhouette: a portrait or figure represented in outline and solidly colored in

Contrast: a drastic difference between such elements as color or value (lightness/darkness) when they are presented together

Postmodernism, Postmodernist: a late twentieth-century style of architecture and art that playfully adopts features of earlier styles

Collage: a work of art assembled by gluing materials, often paper, onto a surface. From the French *coller*, to glue

Medium (plural **media**): the material on or from which an artist chooses to make a work of art, for example canvas and oil paint, marble, engraving, video, or architecture

3.9.13 Romare Bearden, *Three Folk Musicians*, 1967. Collage of various papers with paint and graphite on canvas, 50⅛ × 60". Private collection

pieces, then photographs them before, through the passage of time and the weather, they disintegrate and return to nature.

Postmodernism, Identity, and Multiculturalism

Art and society in the second half of the twentieth century responded to earlier political and cultural events, including the atrocities resulting from the Nazis' totalitarian regime, the Cold War, and debates over US involvement in Vietnam. Those who in the past had been oppressed or discriminated against began to claim their rights. The Civil Rights movement in the US claimed equality for African Americans, while feminism asserted the right of women to the same treatment, privileges, opportunities, pay, and status as men. Reacting against the principally Eurocentric, "white male" perspective of Modernism, some artists and scholars promoted the idea that meaning is ultimately unreliable and that truth arises from multiple sources. A disillusionment with big government inspired some **Postmodernist** thinkers to suggest that power does not come from a single leader, but instead from the masses. As a result,

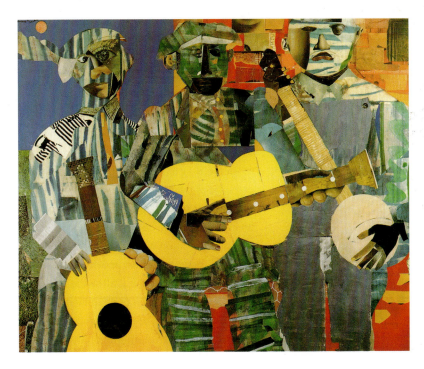

art became noticeably concerned with social issues and with addressing the concerns of a multicultural world.

Postmodern artworks and architecture are often complex and even ambiguous, incorporating visual references to earlier artworks or buildings, philosophical ideas, or political issues (see Box: Modern and Postmodern Architecture, pp. 550–51). The Postmodern movement, part of the Contemporary period (*c.* 1960 to the present), constitutes both a reaction to and a continuation of ideas developed during the Modern period (*c.* 1860–1960). While artists continued explorations of form and content that were prominent in the mid- to late twentieth century, additional influences were also introduced. Artists included references to their own personal history or the history of the nation or culture with which they were connected. By the 1980s artists and art institutions recognized the need to be more inclusive in their consideration of artists from all cultural backgrounds. Postmodern artists are driven by a desire to have their voices heard so that their artwork reveals the specificity of their cultural backgrounds and identity, rather than a reflection of the old Modernist ideal of shared, universal experience.

African American artist Romare Bearden (1911–1988) trained in both the US and Europe. His work incorporates many artistic influences, including abstraction from Modernist Cubism and traditional African masks. Bearden was also inspired by his childhood spent growing up in Harlem in New York City. This was the time of the Harlem Renaissance (*c.* 1918–37), an artistic, literary, and musical flowering of the African-American community that fostered cultural pride and racial consciousness. Prominent African-American cultural figures, for example jazz musician Duke Ellington, poet Langston Hughes, and novelist and critic Ralph Ellison, were close family friends who instilled in the young Bearden a lifelong connection to literature and jazz. In such pieces as *Three Folk Musicians* (**3.9.13**), Bearden brings all his diverse interests together in the form of **collage**, the **medium** for which he is best known. In this work we see a rhythmic interpretation of a common, everyday scene using disjointed fragments of paper. Here collage has been used by Bearden to express African-American experience.

Intrigued by the impact of African art on contemporary culture, American Xenobia Bailey (b. *c.* 1955) established her reputation initially by making crocheted hats. After her designs were featured in *Elle* magazine, they appeared as props in Spike Lee's film *Do the Right Thing* (see Images Related to 3.9, p. 559) and on US television's *Cosby Show*. Over time, Bailey's work has expanded to include costumes, wall hangings, and full-blown museum installations. The forms, shapes, and colors she uses are inspired by African hairdos, architecture, and headdresses; Hindu religious figures; and Chinese opera headpieces. Her work *(Re)Possessed* (**3.9.14**) is a teepee-like structure that, in addition to looking like an enlarged version of one of her hats, references

3.9.14 Xenobia Bailey, *(Re)Possessed* (installation view, John Michael Kohler Arts Center, Sheboygan, Wisconsin), 1999–2009; mixed-media environment; dimensions variable. Photo courtesy of John Michael Kohler Arts Center © the artist and Stefan Stux Gallery, New York. Components include the following: Xenobia Bailey, *Mandalas*, 1999–2009 and *Sistah Paradise's Great Walls of Fire Revival Tent*, 1993; Doughba H. Caranda-Martin, *Teas*, 2008; Barbara Garnes, *Tea Service*, 2006

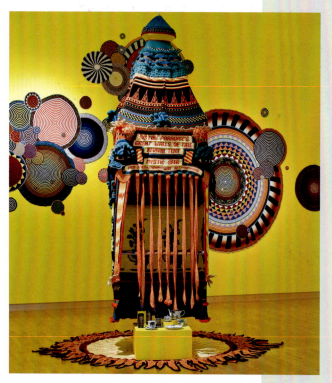

De Stijl: a group of artists originating in The Netherlands in the early twentieth century, associated with a utopian style of design that emphasized primary colors and straight lines

Three-dimensional: having height, width, and depth

Asymmetry: a type of design in which balance is achieved by elements that contrast and complement one another without being the same on either side of an axis

Aesthetic: related to beauty, art, and taste

Classical: ancient Greek and Roman; art that conforms to Greek and Roman models, or is based on rational construction and emotional equilibrium

Facade: any side of a building, usually the front or entrance

Capital: the architectural feature that crowns a column

Modern and Postmodern Architecture

In order to understand Postmodern architecture, it is necessary to consider it in contrast to Modernism, the predominant architectural style from the late nineteenth century until the 1960s. Modernist architecture was characterized by straight lines and geometric shapes (see, for example, Le Corbusier's Villa Savoye in Images Related to 3.9, p. 559). Its designs were intended to be direct, clean, uncluttered, and progressive. As early as the 1960s, Postmodernist architects reacted against the Modernists' use of lines, severe geometry, and subdued colors, considering the aims of Modernists to be too idealistic and inaccessible. As a result, Postmodern designs often combine dynamic forms (for example, Frank Gehry's [b. 1929] Guggenheim Museum, Bilbao, see "Images Related to 3.9," p. 559) and incorporate familiar elements from different historical periods, such as columns reminiscent of buildings in ancient Greece.

Like his fellow Dutch **De Stijl** artists, Modernist designer Gerrit Rietveld (1888–1964) emphasized geometric shapes, horizontals and verticals, and a limited color palette of black, white, and primary colors. His Schröder House, created in 1924–25, integrates Modernist design into a building that served the specific needs of Rietveld's client (**3.9.15**). The lower floor consists of traditional kitchen, dining, and living areas, while upstairs Rietveld took an innovative approach to the bedrooms. Modular partition walls separate the areas of the upper floor, providing private quarters for sleeping but allowing a more open space to be used during the day. The balconies, windows, concrete planes, and linear elements on the

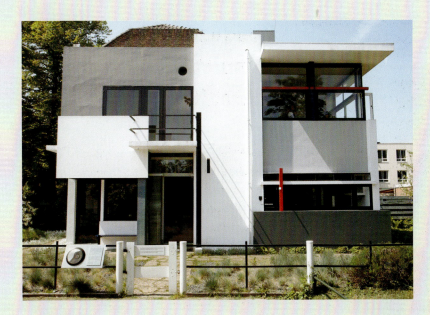

building's exterior, which resembles a **three-dimensional** version of an abstract painting, show how architects achieve balance through **asymmetry**. Rietveld's emphasis on geometry and function influenced the International Style of architecture, developed in the 1920s and 1930s, which stressed logical planning, followed an industrial or machine **aesthetic**, and eliminated all arbitrary decoration.

By the 1960s architects began to react to the severity of International Style Modernism by incorporating references to earlier buildings and including ornamentation that was not required by the structural design. This new approach marked the beginning of the Postmodern style. The Portland Public Services Building, designed by American Michael Graves (1934–2015) in 1980–82, was the first public building to employ the Postmodern approach (**3.9.16**). Its distinctive design includes a brightly colored exterior, small square windows, and **Classical** architectural forms. Columns have been extended up to ten stories tall on either side of the entrance and on the sides of the building. On the **facade**, the shape of the exaggerated **capitals** has been repeated on the upper floors. While this building has generated some controversy due to the strong negative opinions about its appearance, and claims of shoddy workmanship, it stands as a significant example of Postmodern ingenuity and of Postmodernism's potential to integrate diverse ideas. More recently, Graves has become well known for a line of kitchenware and domestic merchandise available exclusively at J. C. Penney stores. The line of household products, which Graves originally designed for Target, features sleek shapes and stylish colors that incorporate many Postmodern design principles and integrate distinctive design into functional items.

3.9.16 (below) Michael Graves, Portland Public Services Building, 1980–82, Portland, Oregon

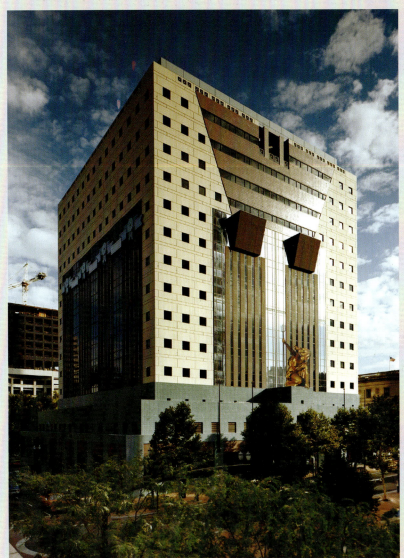

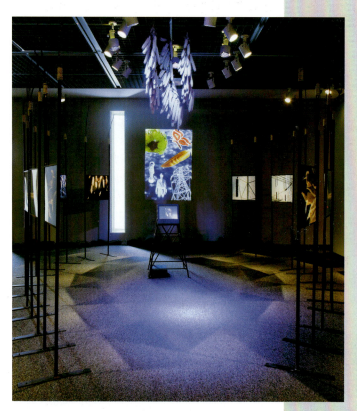

the absence of historical information about enslaved Africans in America. Bailey created Sistah Paradise, a mythological individual, as a reminder of colonization and as a figure to inspire the continued pursuit of justice and equality for African Americans.

Throughout her artistic career, native-American artist Jolene Rickard (b. 1956) has also told complex stories as she examines her heritage through myths, stories, cultural practices, and experiences, both past and present. As a member of the Tuscarora nation (from the Iroquois language family), Rickard creates work that often combines spiritual experiences and events from daily life, which are familiar to the Tuscarora, but less so to outside audiences. Her installation *Corn Blue Room* (**3.9.17**), part of an exhibition called "Reservation X: The Power of Place," explores the importance of home in the formation of identity, and also the changing nature of the reservation as a community and home. Ears of corn hang from above, saturated with blue light. The photographs and CD-ROM in the space relate to nature on one side (corn, the seasons, community) and technology on

Inside, Outside, Upside Down: Ideas Recontextualized

Contemporary artists often defy expectations by blurring the boundaries between elements that had once seemed very separate, even in opposition to one another. They mix such **genres** as fiction and non-fiction, such categories as craft and fine art, and such media as painting and sculpture. Instead of believing that their art represents a universal voice, artists embrace the fact that their personal point of view impacts the art that they make. Artists also emphasize the fact that the meaning in their works is open-ended and ultimately requires the viewer to decide what it might be.

Visionary artist and American James Hampton (1909–1964) worked as a janitor in Washington, D.C. and in his spare time made what he called his "life's work," *The Throne of the Third Heaven of the Nations' Millennium General Assembly* (**3.9.18**). Hampton constructed about 180 pieces for *The Throne* with found materials, including furniture, jelly jars, cardboard, construction paper (originally deep purple, now faded to tan), and electrical wire, which he transformed with coverings of gold and silver foil. Hampton arranged the pieces into a large **tableau** suggesting the Kingdom of Heaven at the second coming of Christ on Judgment Day, as described in the Book of Revelation in the Bible. There are what appear to be lecterns at the back, while the wall plaques along the sides represent the Ten Commandments. Crowns (a sign of spiritual kingship), wing shapes (suggesting angels), and light bulbs (symbolic of God as the light of the world) also express Hampton's vision. Though he hoped to open his own church one day, very few people saw this piece during his lifetime.

American Jean-Michel Basquiat (1960–1988) was also an outsider of sorts, because he was not formally trained, and started as

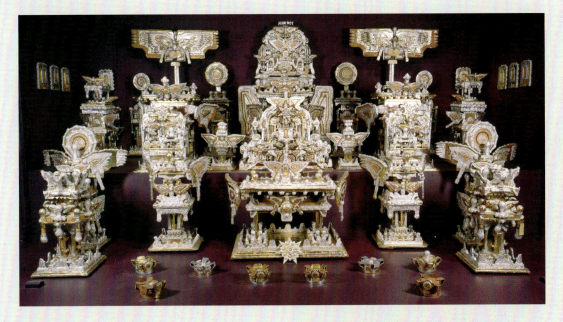

3.9.18 James Hampton, *The Throne of the Third Heaven of the Nations' Millennium General Assembly*, 1950–64. Gold and silver aluminum foil, colored kraft paper, and plastic sheets over wood, paperboard, and glass, 180 pieces, 10½ × 27 × 14½". Smithsonian American Art Museum, Washington, D.C.

3.9.19 (below) Jean-Michel Basquiat, *The Nile*, 1983. Acrylic and oilstick on canvas mounted on wood supports, triptych, 5'8" × 11'11". Private collection

a graffiti artist. His style has been called **Neo-Expressionist** because, like earlier Expressionists, it used aggressive lines, rough **textures**, and personal narrative. His painting *The Nile* (**3.9.19**), also known as *The History of Black People* or *The Grand Spectacle*, is an expansive collage of images inspiring us to reconsider many potentially outsider groups with which Basquiat was connected. The scribbled text and intentionally primitive figures bring into the art world his beginnings as an untrained artist tagging buildings, or anonymously signing them with recognizable marks, on the streets of New York. Numerous references to Egypt, including a female figure in the center, the boats, pharaoh, and guard dog to the right, together with the African masks on the left, connect to African heritage. By referring to Memphis both in connection with Thebes (Egypt) and Tennessee, Basquiat reinforces the spread of African culture and traditions into other parts of the world, a development known as the "African Diaspora." Spanish words filtered throughout refer to his immigrant parents, who came from Puerto Rico and Haiti. Notably, the word "slave" written on the figure to the right has been crossed out, suggesting that, while the sufferings of slavery cannot be erased or ignored, new terminology and expectations beyond its history are needed.

Genres: categories of artistic subject matter, often with strongly influential histories and traditions
Visionary art (also **Outsider Art**): art made by self-taught artists following a personal vision
Tableau: a stationary scene arranged for artistic impact
Neo-Expressionist: a broad term, first used in the late 1970s to early 1980s; describes figurative and allegorical, not totally abstract, art with materials used aggressively to give clear evidence of the artist's gestures
Texture: the surface quality of a work, for example fine/coarse, detailed/lacking in detail

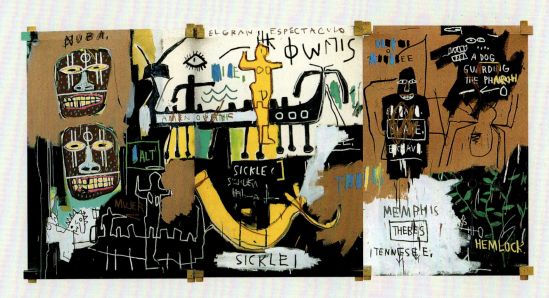

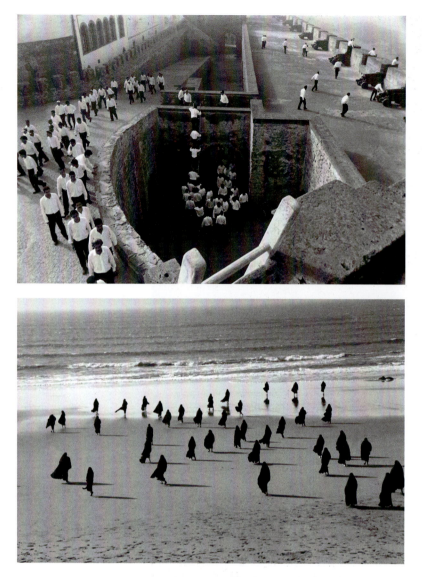

Islamic Revolution, the country had become a conservative, theocratic republic. One of the most striking changes was the requirement for women to wear the *chador*, a loose robe that covers them from head to toe, leaving only their faces and hands exposed. Neshat made art as a way to process her feelings of displacement, exile, and loss. Over time her work has taken a more critical stance against the erosion of individual freedom in the extremist environment she knows the people of her country are enduring.

In such artworks as the film *Rapture* (**3.9.20a and 3.9.20b**) Neshat projects two images into the space at the same time. One screen shows men wearing white shirts and black pants in a stone fortress. The motivation behind their collective actions is never explained, but they seem to revolve around the cannons located on the building's rooftop. On the other screen, women wearing black chadors are shown making their way to a beach where they push a small group of women out to sea in a rowboat. Whether the women are being persecuted or liberated, whether they chose to leave or were forced to go, is unclear. Because she deals with social, political, and cultural issues in a very poetic way, Neshat's work has a broad appeal to audiences all over the world.

3.9.20a (above, top) Shirin Neshat, *Rapture*, 1999. Production still

3.9.20b Shirin Neshat, *Rapture* series, 1999. Gelatin silver print, 42½× 67½"

the other (the towers of a hydroelectric plant owned by the New York Power Authority), both of which have significantly impacted the Tuscarora community's land in upper New York State. The installation invites viewers to walk into the space and interact with it. By looking at the photographs and the CD-ROM, they can experience the importance of songs and dances as ways of expressing kinship and of passing knowledge from one generation to the next.

Iranian-born artist Shirin Neshat (b. 1957) has lived in the United States since 1974, when she was seventeen years old. Her photographs and films explore the experience of a woman caught between the tradition and heritage of her native Iran and her perspective as a woman living outside that culture. When she was allowed to return to Iran in 1990, following the

Navigating Fact and Fiction

In the late twentieth and early twenty-first centuries, computers, televisions, and smartphones bombard us with an increasing and overwhelming number of images and ideas twenty-four hours a day, seven days a week. Many contemporary artists acknowledge and embrace the complexity and chaos of the world in which we live. The Internet and increasingly easy international travel make the world seem smaller, and have hugely expanded our awareness of and interest in other cultures. Some artists have brought order to their experiences of this global culture by creating their own systems of symbols and signs. Others incorporate widely

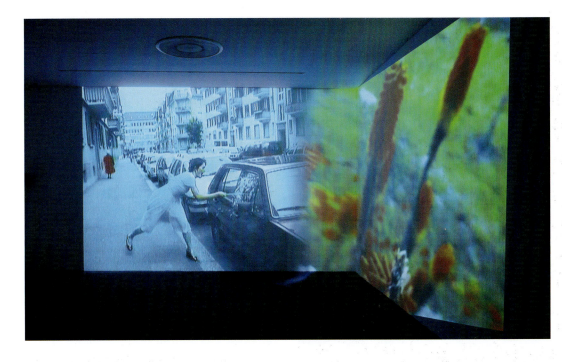

3.9.21 Pipilotti Rist, *Ever Is Over All*, 1997. Video installation with two monitors, dimensions variable. MoMA, New York

ranging styles, techniques, and messages into single artworks. Reflecting the experience of living in the twenty-first century, contemporary artists assimilate approaches from all kinds of sources, past and present, real and imagined. Artworks made in response to the complexity of today's world, not surprisingly, contain many elements that operate on more than one level. The more you learn, the more each individual element makes sense and comes alive. Many artists navigate this complexity by integrating and fusing the once-distinct realms of fact and fiction.

A captivating video installation called *Ever Is Over All* (**3.9.21**), by Swiss artist Pipilotti Rist (b. 1962), creates a multi-sensory experience that subtly comments on decorum and the breaking of the rules that normally govern society. A two-part projection into the corner of the room, it also has an ambient sound component that pulses throughout the gallery or museum space. On one screen we see a fictional woman whose brilliant aquamarine dress and ruby-red slippers contrast with the drab backdrop of an urban street. On the other screen, the brilliant oranges, yellows, and greens of a very real field of torch lilies, also called red-hot pokers, directly illuminate the room.

In her princess attire, the woman carries a torch lily like a staff. As she saunters down the street, she occasionally stops to smash out a car window with her flower. The violence of her vandalism does not have any effect on her happy-go-lucky demeanor. In fact, she does not even react when a police officer passes her on the sidewalk. The police officer does not react to her apparent vandalism either. They just exchange a pleasant greeting. Because the artist herself plays the part of the window-smasher, this piece could be seen as a self-portrait. Ultimately Rist has created for the contemporary viewer an enigmatic fairy tale in which we feel a release as the character's aggressions are acted out in unlikely ways, while the story that this piece tells empowers her (and us) to maintain or restore a sense of beauty in the world.

From 1994 to 2002 American artist Matthew Barney (b. 1967) produced, created, and starred in five full-length films called the *Cremaster* cycle. "Cremaster" literally refers to the set of muscles that control the height of male testicles. Barney adopted the cremaster as a metaphor because it expresses the sense that identity changes over time: from prenatal sexual differentiation (in *Cremaster 1*) to a fully formed, or "descended," being (in *Cremaster 5*). The films do not use narrative or dialogue in the conventional sense, but visually and conceptually incorporate the history of the place where the films are set, episodes of invented

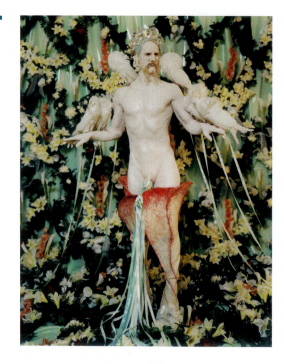

3.9.22 Matthew Barney,
Cremaster 5, 1997.
Production still

own wandering interests and the way he absorbs things on a day-to-day basis. The intricate symbolism that Barney invests in the people, places, and things in the films recalls all the simultaneous meanings that these elements can have (whether we are aware of them or not), and suggests that we can access them at the touch of a button or the whim of an artist.

A joyous splash of vibrant color is the first sensation upon seeing the installation and narrative claymation work of Swedish artist Nathalie Djurberg (b. 1978). Claymation is a form of **stop-motion animation** using figures and objects made of plasticine clay. Each frame of the video involves slight adjustments to the objects and figures, such that when they are played in sequence, they appear to change and move. The ambient and dramatic music contributed by Djurberg's collaborator, Hans Berg (who is also Swedish; b. 1978), enhances the feeling of whimsy and intrigue that infuses the carnivalesque atmosphere. Just like carnival, though, there is a darker side as the work takes sinister turns to include mutilation, destruction, and death.

mythology, Barney's personal interests, and a symbol system that he has developed.

In the still from *Cremaster 5* (**3.9.22**), Barney plays a fictional character known as the Queen's Giant, who is undergoing the final stages of his transformation to a fully formed man. In an interview in 2004, Barney explained that he was not searching for coherence in the *Cremaster* cycle, but that the films' ambiguity mimics his

I Wasn't Made to Play the Son (**3.9.23**), one of five videos in Djurberg's installation called *The Parade*, is no exception. After meandering

3.9.23 Nathalie Djurberg,
*I Wasn't Made to Play the
Son* (video still), 2011. Clay
animation, digital video,
music by Hans Berg,
6 minutes 27 seconds

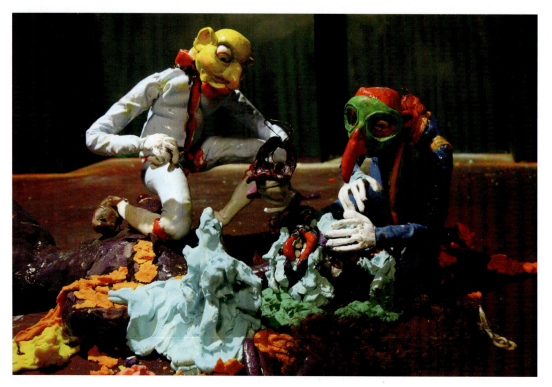

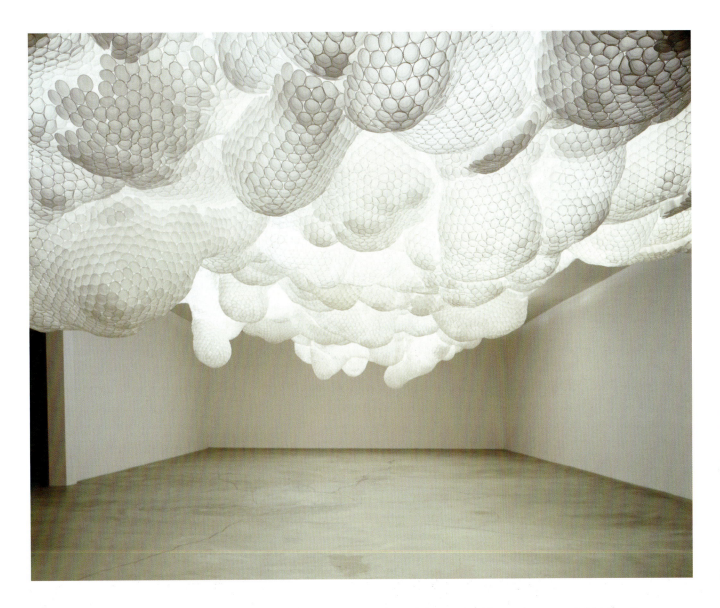

through the gallery space filled with more than eighty brilliant hand-made birds of all sizes, shapes, and colors, one begins to take in the narratives of the videos. Many of the artist's characters are in fact caricatures, identifiable by their excessive traits. The physical violence of the pieces—often sexual in nature, perpetrated against women, or occurring between humans and animals—is so blatant that it becomes almost ludicrous. The contrast of brutality (albeit in clay) in the context of jubilant entertainment, with bright colors and whimsical music, creates distinct and conflicting feelings of attraction/repulsion. A cynical viewer might leave thinking that art has, once again, imitated the tragedies of life and made them palatable. For a politically minded observer, the installation might raise questions about the treatment of

women, or inspire activism against domestic violence. Though the intentions and message are far from clear, Djurberg's work might be seen as similar to fairy tales, offering a release from the challenges and stresses of daily life.

Many contemporary artists continue practices from previous artistic styles, movements, or individual approaches. Minimalism comes to mind when viewing the work of American Tara Donovan (b. 1969), both in the materials and the aesthetic effect. The experience of her work changes dramatically depending on the viewer's proximity to a piece. Donovan's sculptures have been installed inside walls (seen through transparent sections), in outdoor courtyards, and, more frequently, filling a whole gallery or room. When one stands far

3.9.24 Tara Donovan, *Untitled*, 2003. Styrofoam cups and hot glue, 16' × 16'. Installation: Ace Gallery, Los Angeles, 2005

away from *Untitled* (**3.9.24**) and takes in the panorama of the space, one notices, uncertain whether they are created by fabric or a giant lamp, the contours of cloud-like shapes that fill the ceiling. Upon closer inspection, the details of the medium become clear: this shape is formed from simple Styrofoam cups—lots of cups. The artist has also made sculptures out of toothpicks, pencils, tar paper, paper plates, short pieces of wire, buttons, and plastic straws (more than two million of them in another piece called *Haze*). Donovan states that the value of mass-produced objects in an art context is now widely accepted; the excitement comes from what happens to them. Donovan calls her work "site-responsive" because she selects her materials for their unique properties—here, the soft white color and curves of the cups—and the way in which these interact with aspects of a given space—for example, the ceiling, lighting, and shape of the room—to produce a very specific effect on the viewer.

Discussion Questions

1. Choose an artwork from this chapter by Marcel Duchamp, Jackson Pollock, or Andy Warhol. Find an artwork in the chapter (or in another) that was influenced or inspired by the work you have chosen. Discuss the way that the progression of ideas from one artist to another can be seen in your chosen examples.

2. Choose two artworks from this chapter in which an artist has incorporated imagery from the media and popular culture or modern technology. Discuss the relationship between form and content in these examples.

3. Find two artworks from the period studied in this chapter in which the artists approach the same subject in different ways. Compare your artworks in terms of formal appearance, the artists' intentions, and how you respond to their different approaches. You might choose one work from another chapter in this book, for example compare the self-portrait of Ana Mendieta with **1.9.5a** or **4.10.3**; or consider depictions of Egypt in Basquiat's piece alongside the Pyramids (**3.1.14**) or *The Journey of the Sun God Re* (**0.0.1**).

4. Select two artworks that address questions relating to identity. Compare the media used by the artists and explain which artwork most impressed you and why. You might choose one work from another chapter in this book, for example: **1.10.10, 2.10.12, 2.6.1, 3.1.32, 3.5.5**, or **4.3.7**.

Images Related to 3.9:
Late Modern and Contemporary Art

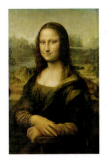

0.0.11 Leonardo da Vinci, *Mona Lisa*, c. 1503–6, p. 35. This work inspired Andy Warhol (see p. 544)

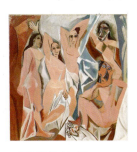

3.8.21 Pablo Picasso, *Les Demoiselles d'Avignon*, 1907, p. 527

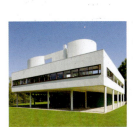

2.5.32 Le Corbusier, Villa Savoye, 1928–31, p. 284

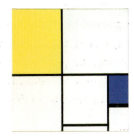

3.8.37 Piet Mondrian, *Composition with Yellow and Blue*, 1932, p. 537

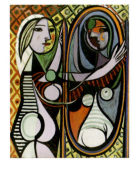

3.8.22 Pablo Picasso, *Girl before a Mirror*, 1932, p. 528

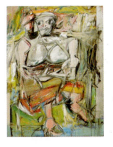

4.9.2 Willem de Kooning, *Woman I*, 1950–52, p. 660

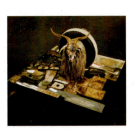

1.6.11 Robert Rauschenberg, *Monogram*, 1955–59, p. 138

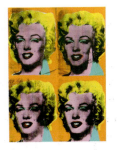

2.3.17 Andy Warhol, *Four Marilyns*, 1962, p. 243

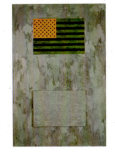

4.4.15 Jasper Johns, *Flag*, 1965, p. 607

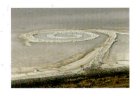

2.4.15 Robert Smithson, *Spiral Jetty*, 1969–70, p. 257

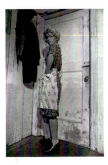

4.10.4 Cindy Sherman, "Untitled Film Still #35," 1979, p. 678

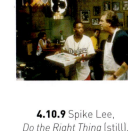

4.10.9 Spike Lee, *Do the Right Thing* (still), 1989, p. 682

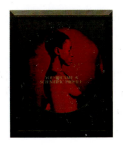

1.7.1 Claes Oldenburg and Coosje van Bruggen, *Mistos (Match Cover)*, 1992, p. 147

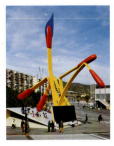

4.10.10 Carrie Mae Weems, "You Became a Scientific Profile...," 1995, p. 682

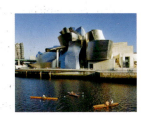

1.2.17 Frank Gehry, Guggenheim Museum, Bilbao, Spain, 1997, p. 78

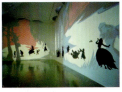

2.10.12 Kara Walker, *Insurrection! (Our Tools were Rudimentary, Yet We Pressed On)*, 2000, p. 362

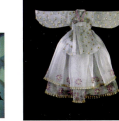

2.6.1 Hyo-In Kim, *To Be Modern #2*, 2004, p. 293

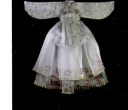

2.10.9 Marina Abramovic, *The Artist Is Present*, 2010, p. 359

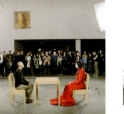

4.3.7 Jillian Mayer, *I Am Your Grandma* (stills), 2011, p. 592

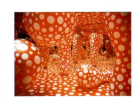

4.4.18 Yayoi Kusama, Installation at the Tate Gallery, London, England, 2012, p. 609

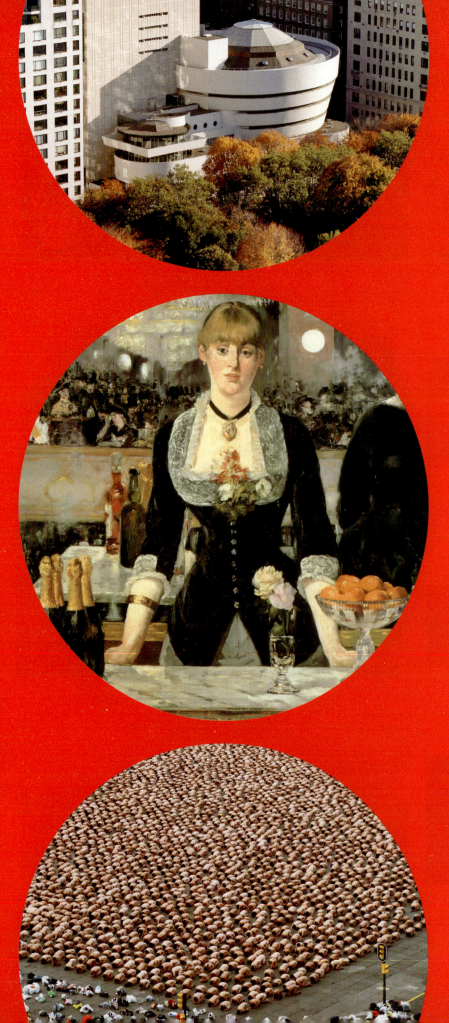

Artworks reveal the concerns of humanity. Throughout the world, similar issues, or themes, are explored by artists. By comparing artworks in terms of their meaning, we come closer to understanding the uniqueness of different cultures and artists. Exploring topics commonly addressed by artists throughout space and time, and through a variety of methods and materials, also makes us more aware of shared concerns. Artworks deal with belief systems, survival, the natural world, and technology; and with issues related to status, power, identity, and creative expression. By studying art in this way we can better understand various cultures and ourselves.

PART 4

THEMES

IN THIS PART YOU WILL STUDY:

Art and Community

Spirituality and Art

Art and the Cycle of Life

Art and Science

Art and Illusion

Art of Political Leaders and Rulers

Art, War, and Revolution

Art of Social Conscience

The Body in Art

Identity, Race, and Gender in Art

4.1

Art and Community

> The community mural process makes art more accessible; it brings art into the lives of people who didn't have it.
>
> (Susan Cervantes, San Francisco muralist)

> This is a way of getting your art on the street. Lots of people stop to look at it. It's not like being famous, but it's a way of getting your art looked at. You have an audience.
>
> (Aliseo Purpura-Pontoniere, urban youth arts student)

We tend to think of art as the work of a single individual. Art, however, often involves large numbers of people, even whole communities. As the statements above by professional artist Susan Cervantes and a student who worked with her demonstrate, artists can create art not just for the enjoyment and benefit of a single **patron**, or for a larger audience in an art gallery, but also for an entire community. Community art may require numerous people to become involved in its construction. Other times, artworks play important roles for performers in ceremonies and group events. Still other community artworks, situated in public places, are there to be contemplated by countless viewers. A community—whether a small rural town, an apartment complex, a college campus, or an Internet discussion group—shares a common interest, if not a physical space. Studying the art made by and for communities throughout history tells us a great deal about the interaction between artists and their environments.

In this chapter we will examine the many ways in which art has been used to pursue community objectives. Because buildings have such a direct impact on shaping a community, often becoming symbols of a particular place, we will look at several examples of architecture as well as at paintings and ritual performances. We will look first at an example of architecture built to unite communities through religion. We will then turn our attention to other types of community art, including artworks made by, for, and about the community; those that reflect shared beliefs or experiences; and art made to exist in public places.

Civic and Ceremonial Places: The Heart of the Community

Structures designed to house ceremonies, civic events, and entertainments often draw crowds of people, whether they were originally intended to or not (see Box: Art, Super-Sized, pp. 566–67). Throughout history and in places as varied as ancient Rome, medieval France, and present-day New York City, communities have come together to build, visit, or acknowledge important locations. Whether because of their distinctive features, or because they reflect the concerns and practices of the communities that use them, buildings often become iconic destinations that people want to see when they travel.

The magnificent interior spaces found in **Gothic** cathedrals, which were built in many European countries between the twelfth and

Patron: an organization or individual who sponsors the creation of works of art

Gothic: Western European architectural style of the twelfth to the sixteenth century, characterized by the use of pointed arches and ornate decoration

Passion: the arrest, trial, and execution of Jesus Christ, and his sufferings during them

Arches: structures, usually curved, that span an opening

Stained glass: colored glass used for windows or decorative applications

Vaulted: covered with an arch-shaped ceiling or roof

Nave: the central space of a cathedral or basilica

Concrete: a hard, strong, and versatile construction material made up of powdered lime, sand, and rubble

Travertine: light-colored limestone deposited in mineral springs and used as a building material

sixteenth centuries, were intended to inspire masses of worshipers to religious devotion. Today, Christians still visit cathedrals for worship and prayer, but the beauty and religious significance of these buildings also attract visitors who do not share the Christian faith. These spectacular churches, built using the resources of the entire community, were and remain a source of great civic pride. Pilgrims traveled to Notre Dame Cathedral (**4.1.1**) in Paris, France, to worship and to experience a sense of religious community, both because the building was so impressive and because it held relics Christians considered sacred, such as a piece of the True Cross on which Jesus Christ was crucified, a fragment of the Holy Lance used to pierce his side, and the Crown of Thorns that the Romans made to mock Christ as King of the Jews. Pilgrims curious to see these items from Christ's **Passion** also hoped to benefit from their mystical power. Notre Dame's grand interior combines all of the characteristic elements of Gothic architecture, including pointed **arches** and **stained-glass** windows. The **vaulted** ceiling is 102 ft. above the floor and the **nave** is more than 39 ft. wide, surrounding receptive visitors with soaring height and spiritual light to transport them beyond the cares and concerns of the ordinary world.

While cathedrals, churches, and other places of worship have become noteworthy as centers of community activity, buildings designed to gather together and entertain whole communities have existed since antiquity. Amongst the most famous arenas of the ancient world was the Colosseum, one of imperial Rome's largest public buildings and an extraordinary feat of architecture and engineering (**4.1.2**). Measuring 615 ft. long by 510 ft. across and standing 159 ft. tall, the Colosseum could hold between 45,000 and 55,000 people. The Romans were the first to exploit fully the structural possibilities of **concrete**, which they used to construct the Colosseum's massive foundations and parts of its vaulted ceilings. The exterior was covered with marble and **travertine** limestone (a light-colored form of limestone deposited in mineral springs) and decorated with columns

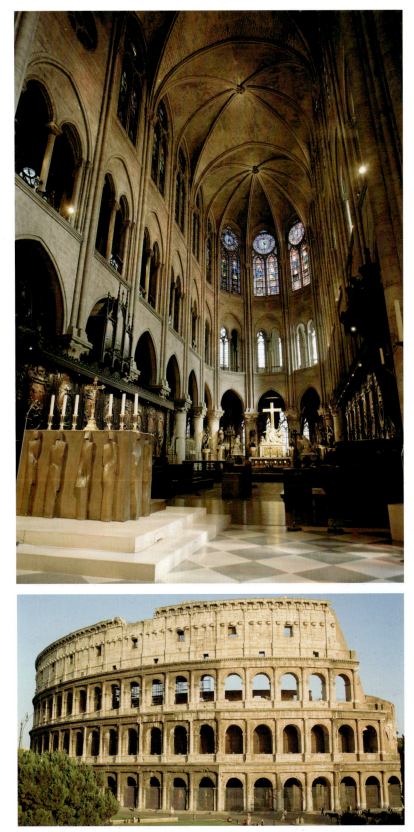

4.1.1 Notre Dame Cathedral, interior, 1163–1250, Île de la Cité, Paris, France

4.1.2 Colosseum, 72–80 CE, Rome, Italy

and with **pilasters** made of another type of local limestone. There were 76 entrance doors, called *vomitoria*, a word that offers a vivid mental image of the crowds spilling from the doors after an event. Roman citizens flocked to the Colosseum to see mock sea battles and gladiatorial fights with both man and beast.

The Colosseum was designed almost 2,000 years ago for the entertainment of enormous crowds, but today's stadiums are built to hold far more people. The AT&T Stadium (**4.1.3**) was built in Arlington, Texas in 2009 to be the home of the Dallas Cowboys. It has the fourth largest seating capacity in the NFL, 80,000, with a maximum capacity of 105,000 including standing room. A true community venue, this stadium is city owned and supported by taxpayers. Cowboys owner Jerry Jones funded much of the $1.15 billion construction cost and the NFL loaned a considerable amount toward the project. With a 3-million-square-foot interior, AT&T Stadium is the world's largest domed structure and column-free interior. The roof retracts and glass doors at the endzones can be opened. A true feat of twenty-first-century engineering, the building boasts LCD screens throughout and had the world's largest HDTV at the time of its construction. To attract an even wider audience, the building also houses an art museum with site-specific works commissioned from eighteen contemporary artists.

In addition to attracting members of the public seeking entertainment, cultural instruction, and reflection, museums also serve as centers of local distinction, in much the same way as cathedrals and sports arenas do. In a bid to keep pace with the expanding attractions of other destination sites, many art museums, such as the Solomon R. Guggenheim Museum in New York City (**4.1.4**), have broadened their own appeal by hosting community programming, including festivals, concerts, and film screenings. The design of the Guggenheim Museum employs strong geometric shapes, which is characteristic of many modern buildings. This white, circular building is distinctive amongst the city's rectangular blocks and glass skyscrapers, however, and for many visitors its design is as much of an attraction as the art collected inside. Architect Frank Lloyd Wright (1867–1959) sought to provide what the director of the museum had asked for, "a temple of spirit, a monument." The interior is open, with a continuous spiral ramp around the central **atrium** connecting each successive floor. The space is filled with light from the domed skylight above.

Pilaster: a vertical element, square in shape, that provides architectural support for crossing horizontal elements in post-and-lintel construction; also used for decoration

Atrium: a central, normally public, interior space, first used in Roman houses

Pyramid: ancient structure, usually massive in scale, consisting of a square base with four sides that meet at a point or apex with each side forming a triangular shape

Ziggurat: Mesopotamian stepped tower, roughly pyramid-shaped, that diminishes in size toward a platform summit

4.1.3 AT&T Stadium, Arlington, Texas, 2009

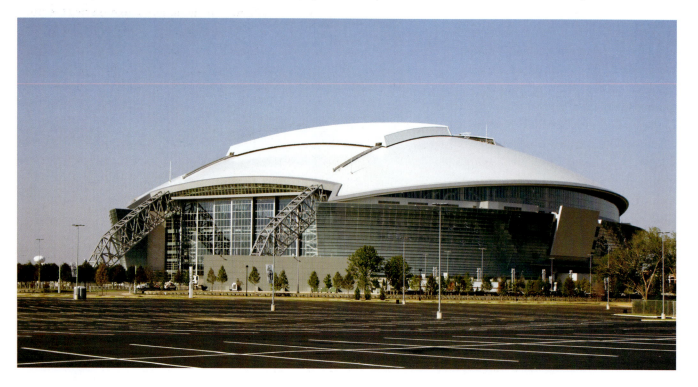

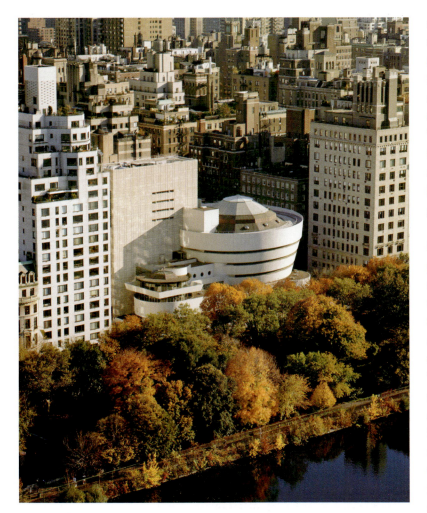

4.1.4 Frank Lloyd Wright, Solomon R. Guggenheim Museum, 1956–59, New York

Man-Made Mountains

Buildings and other constructions intended to shape and dominate the environment—as Wright surely intended with his design for the Guggenheim (**4.1.4**)—have been made since

ancient times. Earthen mounds and **pyramids** are amongst the most intriguing kinds of architecture. Mysteries surround their creation, function, and symbolic significance. Why were such substantial human and material resources devoted to these man-made mountains? Whether they were built as memorials for the dead, for administrative purposes, or for religious worship and rituals, these structures had a dramatic and lasting impact on the geography of their locations.

While they resemble the Egyptian pyramids in their form (see Images Related to 4.1, p. 574) the **ziggurats** of the ancient Near East, such as the one in the city-state of Ur in Sumer (now part of Iraq), were built for the benefit of the living community rather than to bury the dead (**4.1.5**). The ziggurat was part of a temple complex with civic and ceremonial purposes. The mud-brick structures are made up of at least three stepped levels, accessed by stairways or ramps. The lowest level is about 50 ft. high and about 210 by 150 ft. in area, with the others decreasing in size as they get closer to the heavens. The topmost platform, more than 100 ft. high, served as an elevated stage for the priest, who was one of the few people allowed access to that part of the ziggurat, and who served both as the principal human intermediary to the god who protected the city, and the chief administrator of the ziggurat. The city of Ur and its ziggurat were dedicated to the moon god Nanna, one of the three important sky deities in Sumerian religion. Festivals were

4.1.5 Ziggurat, Ur (near Nasiriyah, Iraq), originally built *c.* 2100 BCE and heavily restored

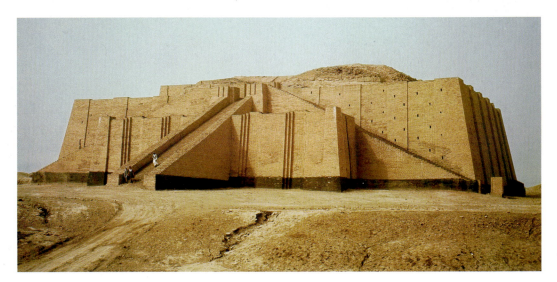

Art, Super-Sized

Two famous works of art, made more than 4,000 years apart, occupied public spaces used by large numbers of people. Both structures were created by the efforts of masses of laborers. Considering these enormous works together can help us understand how a work of art can change a public place and how people interact with such works.

Very little is known about the makers of Stonehenge (4.1.6), but the creators of *The Gates* (4.1.7), Christo (b. 1935) and Jeanne-Claude (1935–2009), explained themselves in countless statements and interviews. We know about the construction methods of Christo and Jeanne-Claude from descriptions and from video documentation, but the techniques used to erect Stonehenge, and the intentions of its builders, remain shrouded in mystery. Stonehenge is still standing after thousands of years, while *The Gates* was designed to be in place only temporarily.

Despite their differences, both works share a common aim: to focus the attention and movements of crowds of people in directions calculated by the artists who designed them.

The oldest parts of Stonehenge, on Salisbury Plain in England, are the circular embankment and ditch that surround the monument. This site was used for hundreds of years before the stones were imported from as far as 23 miles away. The massive stones in the **sarsen** circle weigh up to 50 tons apiece, each one equaling the weight of 500 people or 5 buses. We will probably never know how the builders moved those stones. Most scholars believe Stonehenge, 106 ft. in diameter and up to 20 ft. tall in places, served as a giant observatory or calendar. People who gathered at Stonehenge on the longest day of the year, the summer solstice, would have seen the sun rise precisely over the great stone known as the Heelstone, which stands outside the circle. For a farming community, such as the one

4.1.6 Stonehenge, *c.* 3200–1500 BCE, Salisbury Plain, Wiltshire, England

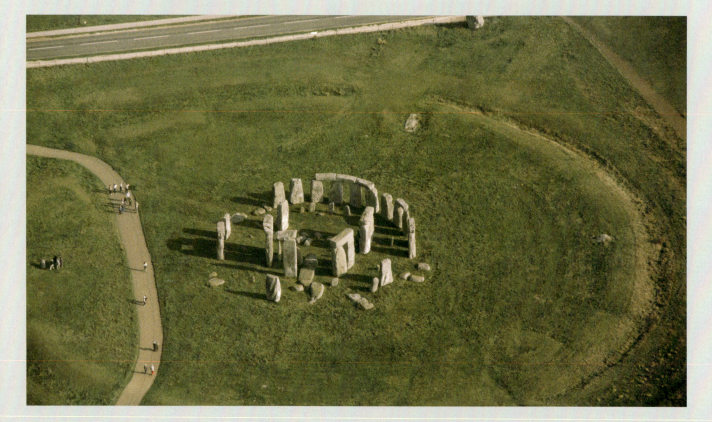

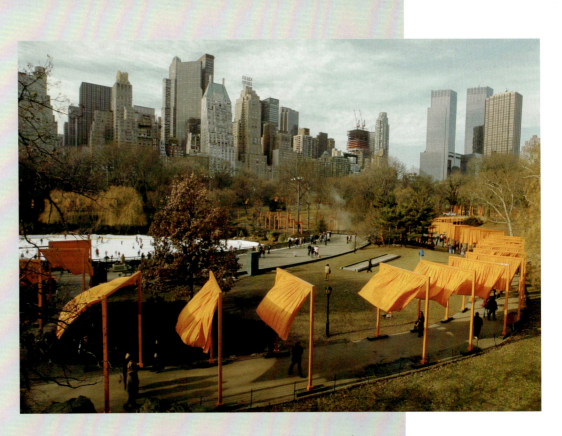

4.1.7 Christo and Jeanne-Claude, *The Gates*, Central Park, New York City, 1979–2005. Steel, vinyl tubing, and nylon fabric, *c.* 16' high

that built Stonehenge, the precise date of the summer solstice was important: it signaled the time to prepare for the fall harvest.

The Gates, installed in 2005, meandered through the 23 miles of walkways in New York's Central Park for just sixteen days. The installation was intended for public enjoyment, and an estimated four million people visited Central Park during the exhibition. The piece required community support garnered through petitions and meetings between the artists and New York City officials. Discussions about *The Gates* began in 1979 and the project was finally approved in 2003. The negotiation process was integral to the production of Christo's and Jeanne-Claude's installation, emphasizing the important role that the community plays in the conception and creation of their artworks.

Facts and figures provided on the artists' website indicate the mind-boggling amounts of material and labor involved in the making of *The Gates*. A total of 60 miles of saffron-colored nylon fabric hung from 7,503 gates. Each gate was 16 ft. tall, with fabric coming down to approximately 7 ft. above the ground. The gates ranged from about 5 ft. to 18 ft. across, depending on the width of the walkway.

The artists employed engineers; project directors; fabricators for the materials in the US and Germany; 600 paid workers to install, monitor, and remove the pieces; and security guards to protect the work at night. After *The Gates* was taken down the materials were recycled, reflecting the artists' environmentally sustainable practices.

Although these two works were made at different times on different continents, they have in common the fact that their construction required the efforts of significant numbers of people and that they were used or viewed by an entire community. While it is uncertain how or why Stonehenge was built, it is clear that a highly organized social structure must have been in place to see such a venture through. *The Gates* similarly required teams of experts and construction crews to carry out the artists' vision. Keen on involving the community and having their work enliven public spaces, but interested in maintaining creative freedom, Christo and Jeanne-Claude did not accept any government or public funding and themselves paid for the creation, installation, and maintenance of the work.

Sarsen: a type of hard, gray sandstone

Masquerade: performance in which participants wear masks and costumes for a ritual or cultural purpose
Gèlèdé ritual: ritual performed in Nigeria's Yoruba society to celebrate and honor women

organized around the phases of the moon, especially when it appeared as a crescent, and offerings were left on the high platform to please Nanna and ensure the abundance of such sacred liquids as water, milk, and blood.

More than 3,000 years after the construction of the ziggurat at Ur, builders made the largest earthen mound ever discovered in North America (**4.1.8**). Cahokia, located in what is now southern Illinois, near St. Louis, covered 6 square miles and had an estimated population of 10,000–20,000. As with other communities that built such impressive structures, there is evidence of a highly organized society, advanced engineering knowledge, and a productive work force at this site.

The focal point of the settlement at Cahokia was Monks Mound, which was originally surrounded by about 120 smaller mounds. The base of Monks Mound measures 1,080 by 710 ft. and is topped by two smaller platforms. Though its exact purpose is uncertain, Monks Mound likely served as an elite residence, a temple, a burial structure, or perhaps all three. Monks Mound is aligned with the sun at the equinoxes, the two times of the year (in spring and fall) when day and night are exactly the same length. These alignments suggest that it may have functioned as a calendar and also served a ceremonial purpose. The site was abandoned around 600 years ago due to climate changes and the depletion of natural resources. Because Monks Mound has suffered from slumping and erosion, the huge earthen mound's appearance is much less dramatic and impressive than it must have been at the height of Cahokia's occupation.

Rituals of Healing and Community Solidarity

The production of art is often deeply connected to philosophical, religious, and ideological beliefs. Artworks made to be used in a ritual context often have symbolic meanings in addition to their appearance and visual impact. With such artifacts as temporary constructions, and masks, it is important to keep in mind that the way they were experienced in their original context would have been very different from the way we now see them in the pages of a book or inside glass museum cases. The objects themselves are suggestive of sights, sounds, and even smells to which we no longer have access.

Masks and **masquerades** serve the important communal function of mediating between the human and spiritual realms. Masquerades enable humans to communicate with the spirit world, as the masker's personality is temporarily replaced with that of the spirit being evoked. The spirit's message will then have

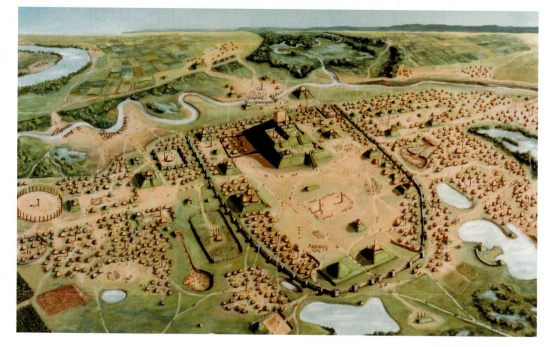

4.1.8 Monk's Mound, Cahokia, Illinois, c. 1150 (reconstruction drawing)

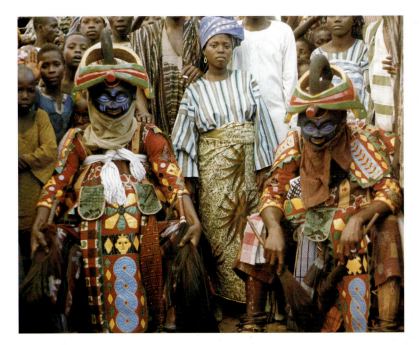

4.1.9 Pair of Gèlèdé masqueraders wearing appliquéd cloth panels, Ketu area, town of Idahin, Benin. Photo by Henry John Drewal, 1971

a direct impact upon the functions and behavior of the community. At the same time, the ritual performance of masquerades is often designed to reinforce the cultural beliefs of a community. While the mask is generally the focal point of the performance, it must be combined with costumes, music, and dance in order to invoke a particular spirit. **Gèlèdé rituals** performed by the Yoruba in Nigeria, Africa celebrate female strength, honor women as mothers,

and commemorate their life-giving powers in the hope that they will continue to use them to help sustain and improve the community (**4.1.9**). These ceremonies also acknowledge the important part played by female ancestors in Yoruba society and promote general spiritual well-being and social harmony.

The Chinese artist Wenda Gu (b. 1956) says that he makes his so-called "hair monuments" in an effort to unite the people of the world through a chain of artworks. The monuments are made of walls or screens woven from human hair donated by people from countries around the globe. Gu then paints what appear to be ideograms (symbols that convey the meaning of words, such as numerals or Chinese characters) with a brush that is itself made from human strands of hair. The signs he paints are suggestive of particular cultures rather than literal transcriptions. *China Monument: Temple of Heaven* (**4.1.10**) is reminiscent of a Buddhist temple in which one partakes of a tea ceremony, and includes ancient-looking Chinese tables and chairs. Video monitors in the seats of the chairs show clouds and poetic text by the artist, so that the people experiencing this artwork are given the sense that they have entered a spiritual realm.

4.1.10 Wenda Gu, *United Nations—China Monument: Temple of Heaven*, 1998. Mixed media, 52 × 20 ×13'. Hong Kong Museum of Art, China

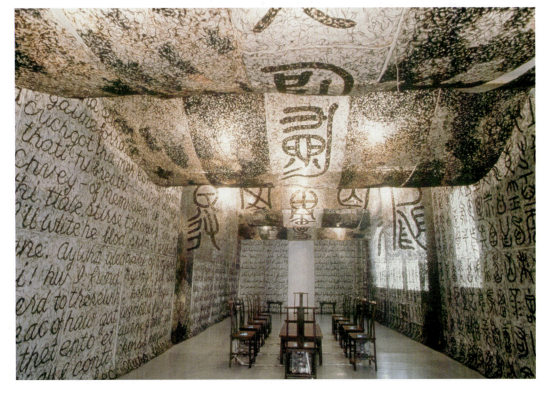

The space also unites a variety of cultures by including symbols that imitate Arabic, Hindi, and Chinese, as well as the Latin alphabet used by Western languages. Gu's *United Nations* series of hair monuments has been made in more than twenty countries on five continents. More than a million people have contributed their hair to it. Gu has therefore been able to unite humans from all over the world in his work, through their common biology. The artist hopes someday to create monuments in every country in the world, linking all the different human cultures.

Art in the Public Sphere

Not all art exists in galleries and museums. Public art generally appears in plazas and parks, or on the exterior walls of buildings. Public artworks are therefore accessible to a wide audience, as we have seen on pp. 566–67, and they are often much beloved by the community. But they can also cause problems. Sometimes public art can be taken out of context or misunderstood. Sometimes people can have different views about what should be seen in public or is appropriate in a particular environment. Public artworks can provoke strong reactions, both favorable and disapproving, and can sometimes spark fierce controversies.

Tilted Arc, by the American Minimalist sculptor Richard Serra (b. 1939), was commissioned by the federal General Services Administration (GSA) and installed on Federal Plaza in downtown New York City in 1981 (**4.1.11**). It became the subject of controversy shortly after it was installed. The 12 by 120 ft. sculpture, a curving wall of **Cor-ten steel**, cut across the plaza. Some of the people who worked in the GSA building complained that it interfered with their use of the plaza and caused a safety hazard as well, attracting graffiti artists, rats, criminals, and potentially even terrorists. Although the majority of testimonies at a public hearing to decide whether or not to leave the sculpture in place were in favor of keeping the work, it was ordered to be removed. The artist's lawsuit against the GSA failed to reverse the decision and the sculpture was dismantled

Perspectives on Art: Richard Serra
A Sculptor Defends His Work

In 1979 the General Services Administration (GSA) contracted the American sculptor Richard Serra to install a work on Federal Plaza in New York City. The sculpture, Tilted Arc, *was erected in 1981. The work proved controversial and in 1985 Serra had to defend his sculpture at a public hearing.*

My name is Richard Serra and I am an American sculptor.

I don't make portable objects. I don't make works that can be relocated or site adjusted. I make works that deal with the environmental components of given places. The scale, size, and location of my site-specific works are determined by the topography of the site, whether it be urban, landscape, or an architectural enclosure. My works become part of and are built into the structure of the site, and they often restructure, both conceptually and perceptually, the organization of the site.

My sculptures are not objects for the viewer to stop and stare at. The historical purpose of placing sculpture on a pedestal was to establish a separation between the sculpture and the viewer. I am interested in creating a behavioral space in which the viewer interacts with the sculpture in its context.

One's identity as a person is closely connected with one's experience of space and place. When a known space is changed through the inclusion of a site-specific sculpture, one is called on to relate to the space differently. This is a condition that can be engendered only by sculpture. This experience of space may startle some people.

When the government invited me to propose a sculpture for the plaza it asked

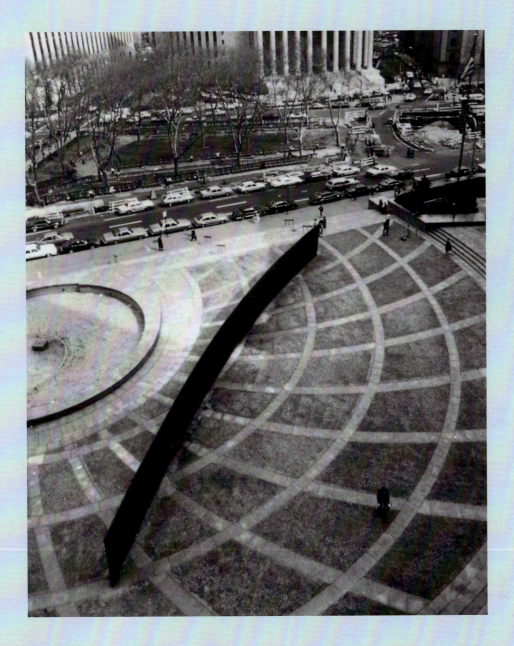

4.1.11 Richard Serra, *Tilted Arc*, 1981 (destroyed March 15, 1989). Weatherproof steel, 12′ × 120′ × 2½″. Collection General Services Administration, Washington, D.C. Installed at Federal Plaza, New York

for a permanent, site-specific sculpture. As the phrase implies, a site-specific sculpture is one that is conceived and created in relation to the particular conditions of a specific site, and only to those conditions.

To remove *Tilted Arc*, therefore, would be to destroy it . . .

It has been suggested that the public did not choose to install the work in the first place. In fact, the choice of the artist and the decision to install the sculpture permanently in the plaza were made by a public entity: the GSA. Its determination was made on the basis of national standards and carefully formulated procedures, and a jury system ensured impartiality and the selection of art of lasting value.

The selection of this sculpture was, therefore, made by, and on behalf of, the public.

The agency made its commitments and signed a contract. If its decision is reversed in response to pressure from outside sources, the integrity of governmental programs related to the arts will be compromised, and artists of integrity will not participate. If the government can destroy works of art when confronted with such pressure, its capacity to foster artistic diversity and its power to safeguard freedom of creative expression will be in jeopardy.

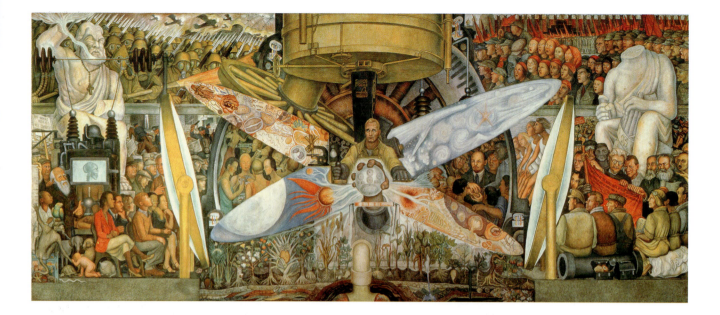

4.1.12 Diego Rivera, *Man, Controller of the Universe*, or *Man in the Time Machine*, 1934. Fresco, 15′ × 37′6⅞″. Full composite view of the fresco. Palacio de Bellas Artes, Mexico City, Mexico

in 1989. Serra had argued that *Tilted Arc* was designed specifically for Federal Plaza and that relocating it was the equivalent of destroying it, so the metal was sent to a scrap yard (see Perspectives on Art Box: Richard Serra: A Sculptor Defends His Work, pp. 570–71). Even though the sculpture was demolished, the artist's hope of making people aware of their environment, pay attention to the path they follow on the way to work, and think about their surroundings was in some ways achieved by the attention generated by the controversy.

The dispute over Serra's *Tilted Arc* raises many questions that have a bearing on the form and functions of all public art. What is the desired impact of public art? Does it need to please its audience, or can it be used as a tool to challenge their beliefs and experiences? How much weight should be given to the artist's freedom of expression? Should consideration be given to whether the artwork is in keeping with the kind of work an artist is known to produce? How much power should public voices be given, whether they belong to specialists in the art world or members of the general community? What bearing does the issue of funding—which may come from the government through special programs aimed at promoting public art or from individual patrons—have on how one answers such questions?

The subject matter of public art, especially when it has political implications, has also been a source of debate. One of the most infamous scandals surrounding a public art project occurred in 1932 when the Mexican artist Diego Rivera (1886–1957) was commissioned by American businessman and millionaire Nelson Rockefeller to paint a **mural** in the Radio Corporation Arts (RCA) Building at Rockefeller Center in Manhattan. Rivera was inspired by Mexico's tradition of adorning walls with paintings and sculptures, which originated long before European contact. Such murals create an environment rich with stories related to all aspects of life. Rivera's written plan for *Man at the Crossroads Looking with Hope and High Vision to the Choosing of a New and Better Future*, which Rockefeller approved, included depictions of forces of nature as well as technology, and looked forward to "the liquidation of Tyranny" and a more perfect society. In the course of painting, however, Rivera made some changes inspired by his Communist inclinations. The most notable was on the right side of the mural, where he included a portrait of the Russian revolutionary Vladimir Lenin leading a demonstration of workers in a May Day parade.

When he was asked to remove Lenin's portrait, Rivera refused, and offered instead to balance it with a depiction of Abraham Lincoln. Rockefeller rejected this proposal, paid Rivera his full fee, and banned him from the building. Rockefeller then made plans to remove

Mural: a painting executed directly onto a wall

the mural. An outpouring of public support for the project followed: picket lines were formed, newspaper editorials were published, and Rivera made a speech at a rally outside City Hall. Despite suggestions that the mural be moved a few blocks away to the Museum of Modern Art, it was ultimately demolished with pickaxes in February 1934. That same year Rivera re-created the mural, with the new title *Man, Controller of the Universe*, in Mexico City (**4.1.12**). Rivera rather bluntly described the conflict that can arise between the vision of artists with strong opinions and their audiences: "[The artist] must try to raise the level of taste of the masses, not debase himself to the level of unformed and impoverished taste."

Over the course of his career, the Polish-born artist Krzysztof Wodiczko (b. 1943) has created more than eighty video projection pieces intended to draw attention to situations of social injustice around the world. Images and text telling the stories of individuals who have been overlooked or mistreated are projected onto architectural facades and monuments, which were made by or for powerful figures in the community. The projections of socially conscious messages about human rights and democracy onto public buildings associated with collective memory and history reclaim these spaces for the people and build community solidarity. *Tijuana Projection* (**4.1.13**) gave voice to women in the maquiladora industry, which consists of assembly plants and factories close to the border between Mexico and the United States, where cheap labor can be hired, and is notorious for substandard

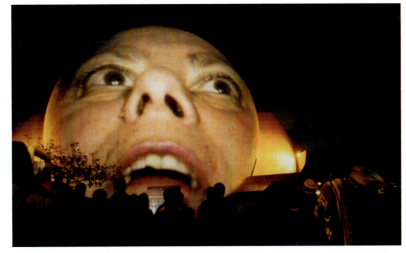

working conditions. The women were recorded recalling a traumatic event and their testimonies were projected live for two consecutive nights on the spherical Centro Cultural Tijuana to a public plaza filled with more than 1,500 people. They told of terrible home and working conditions including rape, incest, poisoning in the factories due to exposure to toxic chemicals, and police abuse. Wodiczko commented, "Their situation is incomparably worse than anything I have tried to understand before." His hope, though, was that this project would be a catalyst for them to move out of this situation and toward a better life.

We can see from the work of Serra, Rivera, and Wodiczko that art displayed in public places often raises our awareness, either by drawing our attention to existing spaces and specific ideas, or by reflecting issues that resonate for the community and need to be addressed.

4.1.13 Krzysztof Wodiczko, *Tijuana Projection*, 2001. Public video projection at the Centro Cultural Tijuana, Mexico. Organized as part of the event InSite 2000

Discussion Questions

1. In this chapter you have studied artworks that in different ways reflect the importance of community. What does community mean to you? Think of an artwork in your community (a building, painting, or sculpture for example). Discuss the ways in which it conveys (or perhaps contradicts) your own ideas of the importance of community.

2. Research a public artwork that interests you. Consider art in public buildings, parks, schools and colleges, churches, etc. Do you consider the work controversial? Explain your reasons. Was the artwork publicly funded? Are you in favor of such works receiving public funding? Compare the artwork to a controversial artwork discussed in this chapter.

3. Choose a work in this chapter that was the result of the combined efforts of a number of people. Then find three other collaborative works elsewhere in this book (**1.1.1**, **1.6.19**, **2.10.5**) or by searching the Internet. Compare the ways in which collaboration affected the works and how the results were innovative or inspiring.

Images Related to 4.1: Art and Community

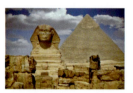

1.2.2 Great Sphinx of Giza, Egypt, *c.* 2500 BCE, p. 68

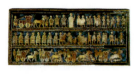

3.1.8a *Standard of Ur,* *c.* 2600–2400 BCE, p. 370

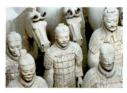

3.3.12b Soldiers from the mausoleum of Qin Shi Huangdi, China, *c.* 210 BCE, p. 421

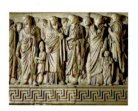

1.2.6 Imperial Procession from the Ara Pacis Augustae, 13 BCE, p. 71

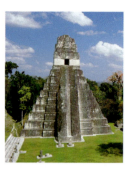

2.5.5 Temple I in the Great Plaza, Maya, *c.* 300–900 CE, p. 269

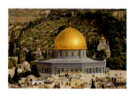

3.2.15 Dome of the Rock, Jerusalem, 688–91, p. 401

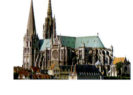

3.2.24 Chartres Cathedral, France, completed 1260, p. 407

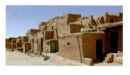

2.5.3 Taos Pueblo, New Mexico, pre-1500, p. 268

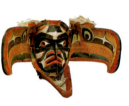

3.4.22 *Eagle Transformation Mask* from British Columbia, late 19th century, p. 447

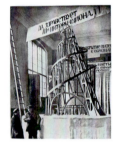

1.2.11 Vladimir Tatlin, Model for *Monument to the Third International,* 1919, p. 74

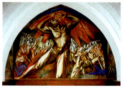

2.2.6 José Clemente Orozco, *Prometheus,* 1930, p. 219

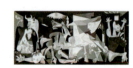

4.7.5 Pablo Picasso, *Guernica,* 1937, p. 638

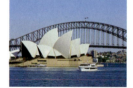

2.5.34 Jørn Utzon, Sydney Opera House, Australia, 1973, p. 286

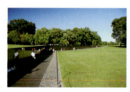

4.7.15 Maya Lin, Vietnam Veterans Memorial, Washington, D.C., 1981-83, p. 646

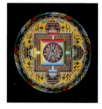

1.6.19 Amitayus Mandala, Drepung Loseling Monastery, Tibet, p. 144

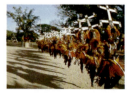

3.5.6b Dogon culture Kanaga Mask Ceremony, late 20th century, p. 454

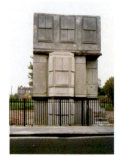

1.2.14 Rachel Whiteread, *House,* 1993, p. 76

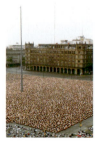

4.9.13a Spencer Tunick, Installation at Zócalo, Mexico, 2007, p. 668

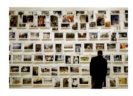

2.8.16 Hiroko Masiuke, *Here Is New York: A Democracy of Photographs,* 2007, p. 329

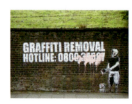

2.2.22 Banksy, London, 2008, p. 230

4.2

Spirituality and Art

For as long as art has been made, there have been artworks inspired by beliefs in ancient deities, spirit beings, and the sacred figures of the world's religions. Through these works artists have sought to express things that cannot be seen and are little understood. In this chapter we use the term spirituality to examine the ways in which beliefs, including both narrative stories and their interpretations, have generally inspired artists for thousands of years. Spirituality encompasses our sense of being connected to others, our awareness of both mind and body, and our wish to understand life's meaning in and beyond the world in which we find ourselves. Spirituality serves as a source of inspiration and a way for us to share our beliefs. This chapter investigates five broad categories of artworks with a spiritual context: those that incorporate specific gods or deities; those that refer to the spirits of the natural world or ancestors; suggestions of communication with the spirit world; depictions of judgment at the end of an Earthly life; and reactions to places that have a sacred resonance.

Deities

Artists communicate the stories of specific religious figures or deities to help explain their importance. Depictions of individuals considered divine in Greek mythology, the Christian Bible, and Buddhist scripture can make those individuals more accessible and memorable.

The ancient Greeks often made artworks to honor their gods and deities. The sculptures in **4.2.1** are from the west **pediment** of the temple dedicated to the god Zeus at Olympia, Greece, where the Olympic Games were born. The scene depicts the legendary battle between the Lapiths of Thessaly and the centaurs—half-human and

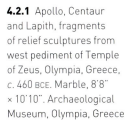

4.2.1 Apollo, Centaur and Lapith, fragments of relief sculptures from west pediment of Temple of Zeus, Olympia, Greece, *c.* 460 BCE. Marble, 8'8" × 10'10". Archaeological Museum, Olympia, Greece

Pediment: the triangular space, situated above the row of columns, on the facade of a building in the Classical style

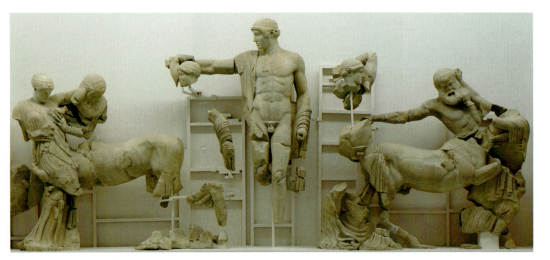

4.2.2a (below) Detail of Hildesheim Doors: Temptation in the Garden of Eden

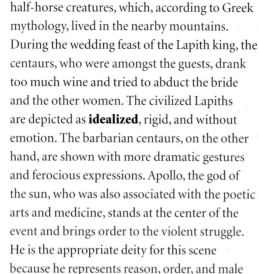

half-horse creatures, which, according to Greek mythology, lived in the nearby mountains. During the wedding feast of the Lapith king, the centaurs, who were amongst the guests, drank too much wine and tried to abduct the bride and the other women. The civilized Lapiths are depicted as **idealized**, rigid, and without emotion. The barbarian centaurs, on the other hand, are shown with more dramatic gestures and ferocious expressions. Apollo, the god of the sun, who was also associated with the poetic arts and medicine, stands at the center of the event and brings order to the violent struggle. He is the appropriate deity for this scene because he represents reason, order, and male beauty. The centaurs, who are associated, by their drinking, with Dionysus, the god of wine, represent the opposite attributes of change, chaos, and even madness.

In Christian Europe in the eleventh century, visual artists often illustrated themes and events from the Bible. Bishop Bernward, who directed the building of the Abbey Church of St. Michael's at Hildesheim, Germany, commissioned a set of doors that depict scenes from the book of Genesis on the left side and scenes from the life of Christ on the right. In chronological order the doors are read counterclockwise, beginning at the top of the left door. But the panels are also arranged so that events from the Old Testament are paired with related episodes from the New Testament (**4.2.2 a–c**).

For example, the third panel from the top matches the Tree of Knowledge on the left with the Tree of Life on the right. In the left scene the original sin is committed. Because Eve accepted the forbidden fruit from the Tree of Knowledge, she and Adam were expelled from the Garden of Eden into the world of suffering and death. On the right, the cross on which Jesus was crucified, understood as the Tree of Life, offers eternal life to believers who ask for forgiveness of their sins and accept Christ as their savior. The elongated and frail appearance of the figures and the

4.2.2b (right) Doors depicting scenes from Genesis and the Life of Christ, commissioned by Bishop Bernward for the Abbey Church of St. Michael's, Hildesheim, 1015. Bronze, 16'6" high. Dom-Museum, Hildesheim, Germany

4.2.2c (far right) Diagram with identification of panels on Hildesheim Doors

	Old Testament	New Testament	
Paradise Lost	Formation of Eve	Noli Me Tangere	Paradise Gained
Salutations	Eve Presented to Adam	The Three Marys at the Tomb	Salutations
Tree of Knowledge (sin)	Temptation and Fall	The Crucifixion	Tree of Life, The Cross, Salvation
Judgment	Accusation and Judgment of Adam and Eve	Judgment of Jesus by Pilate	Judgment
Separation from God	Expulsion from Paradise	Presentation of Jesus in Temple	Reunion with God
Firstborn Son of Eve (Cain) and Poverty	Adam and Eve Working	Adoration of the Magi	Firstborn Son of Mary (Jesus) and Wealth
Abel's Sacrificial Lamb	Offerings by Cain (grain) and Abel (lamb)	The Nativity	Jesus, Lamb of God
Despair, Sin, Murder	Cain Slaying Abel	The Annunciation	Hope and Everlasting Life

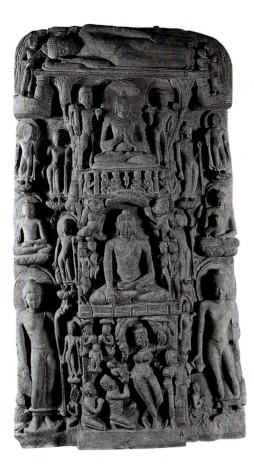

4.2.3 Life of Buddha, stela, Gupta period, c. 475 CE. Sandstone, 41" high. India Museum, Calcutta, India

non-naturalistic settings reflect the Christian emphasis on internal, spiritual matters and themes instead of the exterior, physical world.

The subject matter of Buddhist art is the life of Buddha and his teachings and beliefs, which are considered pathways to achieving spiritual perfection. Buddha, or the Awakened One, was a Hindu prince named Siddhartha Gautama who lived in Nepal and northern India from about 563 to 483 BCE. The larger panels of the **stela** in **4.2.3** show the cycle of Buddha's life. In the bottom section we see his miraculous birth as he emerges from his mother's right side. The second section, above the birth scene, is the moment of his enlightenment as he touches the Earth with a symbolic gesture of strength and renewal. In the third section he is shown giving his first sermon, seated with his legs crossed and his hands posed in prayer, with the wheel of law behind him. At the top of the sculpture he is shown reclining as he achieves tranquility, called nirvana. The smaller carvings along the sides of the stela show

noteworthy moments after he decided to leave his princely life at the age of thirty to become a holy man.

Spiritual Beings and Ancestors

In African cultures, artworks often reflect beliefs in the spirits of gods and ancestors. According to these cultures' customary views, objects are infused with a spiritual presence. They help to continue and preserve cultural practices, ideas, and family ties. Contemporary artists who examine black history often refer to traditional African art, customs, and rituals in their artwork.

The religion of the Senufo people of West Africa is centered on a creator deity, nature spirits, and ancestors, including a female ancestral spirit called "ancient mother" or "ancient woman." These spirits can be beneficial or harmful. They are often depicted as beings with an anatomy very different from that of humans. The head, legs, and detailed features of the Senufo sculpture in **4.2.4** are relatively small while the arms and breasts are exaggerated. The inclusion of a nursing baby suggests that this is one of the female ancestral spirits. Such an "ancient woman" would serve as a guiding spirit for adult males of the Poro society, who were responsible for male initiation and maintaining religious practices, historical traditions, social customs, and political control.

Ancient rituals passed from generation to generation often reflect ideas that are central to that community's belief system. One example of this practice is the sand painting ritual of the Navajo of New Mexico. Navajo **sand paintings** are temporary works of art, constructed as part of a prayer or

4.2.4 Senufo mother-and-child figure, late 19th–mid 20th century. Wood, 25" high. Cleveland Museum of Art, Ohio

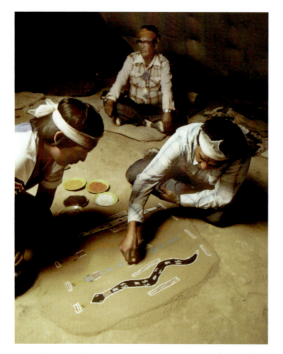

4.2.5 (above) Navajo man in healing ceremony

4.2.6 (right) Stela of Naram-Sin, c. 2254–2218 BCE. Pink sandstone, 6'7" × 3'5". Musée du Louvre, Paris, France

ceremony (**4.2.5**). The paintings are closely connected to nature, both in materials used (such as corn, pollen, charcoal, sand, and powdered stones) and imagery. The subject matter comes from Navajo creation mythology and includes logs, holy plants, animals, and deities. After an image has been meticulously created over the course of days or weeks, a healing ceremony takes place, overseen by a **shaman** or medicine man (rarely a woman). The person to be healed sits in the painting's center in order to absorb power from Navajo ancestors and from the gods, whose images are depicted in the painting. The careful production of sand paintings and the choice of an impermanent medium express the belief that the powerful forces of nature and ancestry are ultimately out of human control, but that they can tapped to benefit the community in the physical realm by promoting food, health, harmony, and well-being.

Connecting with the Gods

Communication with the gods has been an important subject for art in many cultures. Sometimes special individuals serve as intermediaries between people and a deity. Christian saints and mythological figures interact with God (or the gods) to provide role models or to help educate viewers about religious practices. Rulers have also been depicted interacting directly with divine beings or traveling into supernatural realms. Artworks showing such interactions reinforce the power of rulers by convincing their people that they are blessed, aided by the gods, and worthy of their exalted position.

Human interaction with a deity is the focal point of the Stela of Naram-Sin (**4.2.6**). Naram-Sin, an Akkadian king who ruled central Mesopotamia (part of modern Iraq) around 2254–2218 BCE, was both a religious figure and a military leader. His stela commemorates the Akkadian victory over the Lullubi people. The lower portions of the scene show signs of the battle that has taken place on a mountain. Above, Naram-Sin stands victorious near the summit, his horned helmet and larger size emphasizing his importance. The sun god is not depicted in human form but appears symbolically as a sunburst. Naram-Sin's location as close as possible to the sun god illustrates his own supreme, divine status in society and suggests that he was looked upon with approval by the gods. In the ancient Near East there was a close relationship between people and the gods. Because humans were imperfect and in need of assistance from a higher being, prayers were offered, and rituals and sacrifices performed, to keep the gods happy. As the deified representative of his community, a ruler like Naram-Sin needed to maintain a favorable

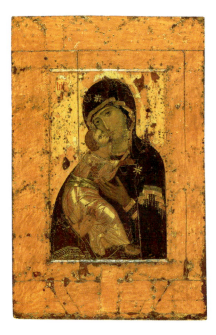

4.2.7 *Virgin of Vladimir*, 12th century (before 1132). Tempera on panel, 30¾ × 21½". Tretyakov Gallery, Moscow, Russia

4.2.8 Gianlorenzo Bernini, *The Ecstasy of St. Teresa*, 1647–52. Polychromed marble, gilt, bronze, yellow glass, fresco, and stucco, 4'11" high (figures only). Cornaro Chapel, Santa Maria della Vittoria, Rome, Italy

connection with the supernatural realm to ensure continued prosperity for his kingdom.

During the Middle Ages, Christians in the Eastern Orthodox Church used small portable religious images, called **icons**, depicting holy figures as a focus of devotion and a source of inspiration. Icons were believed to be able to communicate with God and sometimes even to have other miraculous powers. Many were painted on wood panels, so they could be carried around, although some were attached to chapel screens in churches.

The portable icons were more accessible for ordinary people. They could also be transported from Byzantium to distant places, such as Russia, in order to help spread and support Christian beliefs. Although icons themselves were not worshiped as divine, they became the subjects of intense veneration because they depicted individuals whose saintliness meant they were close to God, and therefore able to spread goodness.

The Orthodox Church required the form and content of icons to follow traditional rules. As a result, although each painting is unique, it has a family resemblance to other icons: gold backgrounds, **linear outlines**, and **stylized** but believable poses. It was important that the figures in the icons could be recognized by anyone who saw them. Thus the Madonna and Child were always shown with haloes to represent their holiness. The *Virgin of Vladimir* portrays Mary as the "Virgin of Loving Kindness," with her face touching Jesus to emphasize her virtue (**4.2.7**). This icon, probably made in the city of Constantinople, was intended to bless and protect the city in which it was housed (it has been in Moscow almost continuously since 1395). Only the faces are original; the rest of the panel, probably damaged by people touching it, has been repainted.

The Ecstasy of St. Teresa by Gianlorenzo Bernini (1598–1680) is another Christian artwork that is meant to inspire devotion and reverence (**4.2.8**). It was made between 1647 and 1652 to decorate a funerary chapel for the Cornaro family in the Church of Santa Maria della Vittoria in Rome, Italy. This massive sculpture (more than 11 ft. tall) depicts one of St. Teresa of Ávila's mystical visions: she is about to be pierced by an angel's arrow that will infuse her with divine love. The theatrical staging and the emphasis on dramatic light—created by the use of gilt bronze rays behind the figures and by the light falling from a hidden window above the sculpture—are typical of the Baroque style. Bernini's sculpture is executed with great attention to detail. The whole scene seems to take place in the clouds and the angel almost hovers above St. Teresa. Marble is made to suggest several different textures including smooth skin, gauzy fabric, clinging draperies, and the heavy wool of the **nun's habit** worn by the saint. The combination of accurate and believable details with an exaggerated picture of devotion reflects the Catholic Church's new emphasis at that time on believers establishing a strongly personal relationship with Christ. In Bernini's sculpture Christ's **Passion** is relived in the intensity of St. Teresa's piety, which serves as an example to be followed by the devout.

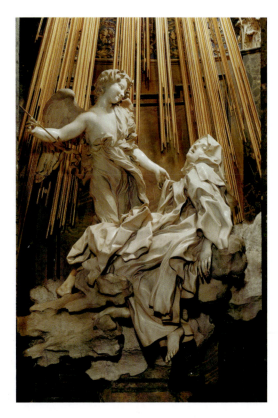

Judgment and the Afterlife

As we live our lives, our choices determine the impact we will have and how we will be perceived. In many belief systems, the moral implications of our decisions have lasting consequences. As a result, the act of judging a life before the deceased is allowed to pass into the afterlife has been the theme of numerous artworks. In many judgment scenes, including those discussed here, scales are featured as a symbol of justice in which a life is "held in the balance" before the soul is allowed to pass on.

In ancient Egypt, the deceased were buried with a set of belongings that reflected their position in life. One of the most important of these possessions was a Book of the Dead, a scroll with spells and incantations designed to help the deceased navigate the passage into the afterlife. As we can see in the Book of the Dead that belonged to a scribe named Hunefer, who lived over 3,000 years ago, a successful journey required proof that one had lived an honorable life and that proper respect had been paid to the gods (4.2.9).

At the top of the scroll, Hunefer pleads his case to the forty-two judges of the dead, represented here by just fourteen mummified deities because the artist did not have room to show them all. In the bottom panel, Hunefer is escorted by Anubis (the jackal-headed god associated with mummification and the afterlife) to the scales where his soul will be weighed. As Ammit ("Eater of the Dead," with the head of a crocodile, mane and forequarters of a lion, and hindquarters of a hippopotamus) anxiously looks on, Anubis determines that Hunefer's soul, in the form of his heart in a canopic jar, is lighter than the ostrich feather it is weighed against. Having been proven worthy, Hunefer is presented by Horus (falcon-headed god of the sun, sky, and war) to Osiris (god of goodness, vegetation, and death), who is seated on his throne. This book of the dead was placed in Hunefer's coffin in the hope that its script would be followed and he would successfully gain immortality in the afterlife.

In twelfth-century Europe, depictions of the Last Judgment took on an ominous tone in scenes showing the fate of the blessed and the damned side by side. In Gislebertus's version of *The Last Judgment* (4.2.10), the **lintel** underneath the main panel contains a row of figures awaiting judgment. The Romanesque characteristic of elongated and somewhat angular figures on the sculpture throughout the whole portal creates a visually dynamic tension.

A pair of hands comes down from above to gather the sixth figure from the right for

4.2.9 *Book of the Dead*: Last Judgment before Osiris, *c.* 1275 BCE. Painted papyrus, 15 ⅜" high. British Museum, London, England

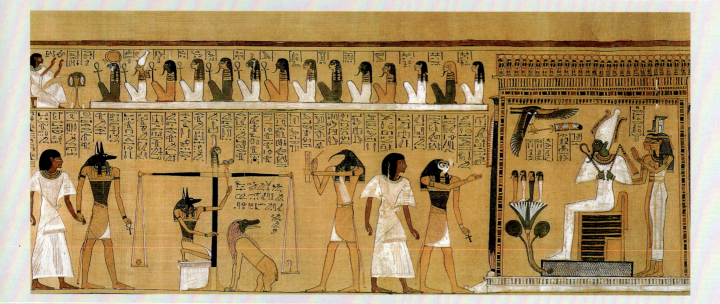

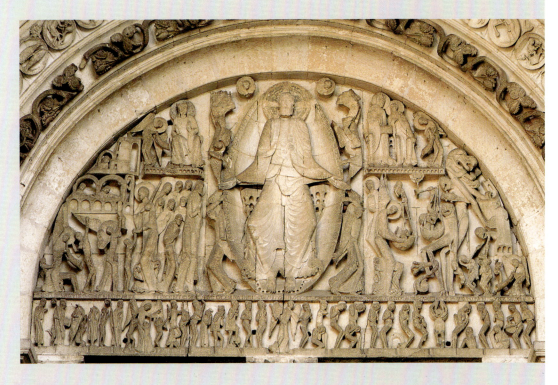

Lintel: the horizontal beam over the doorway of a portal
Tympanum: an arched recess above a doorway, often decorated with carvings

4.2.10 Gislebertus, *The Last Judgment*, *c.* 1120–35. Tympanum from West Portal, Cathedral of Saint-Lazare, Autun, France

4.2.11 Johannes Vermeer, *Woman Holding a Balance, c.* 1664. Oil on canvas, 16¾ × 16˝. National Gallery of Art, Washington, D.C.

his weighing. In the center of the carved **tympanum** Christ is shown as larger than all the rest of the figures, indicating his key role in the judgment of humankind. On his right (our left) are the angels and the souls of the blessed, who will go on to live out eternity in heaven. Their bodies are smooth, elegant, and peaceful. On Christ's left are the scales in which souls are weighed, and the ravaged bodies of the damned. Their horrid, grotesque appearance was meant to send a strong message to churchgoers about the consequences of living a sinful life and give them a glimpse of the misery of spending the afterlife in Hell.

The Dutch painter Johannes Vermeer (1632–1675) subtly includes religion in a scene from everyday life in his *Woman Holding a Balance* (**4.2.11**). Following a style that was popular at the time, Vermeer focuses on an ordinary moment, in which the woman is standing at a table by a window near her open jewelry boxes. The painting on the wall behind her provides a symbolic backdrop for her actions. It shows the Last Judgment, with Christ in the sky above and the souls to be judged below, and serves as a reminder that life is short and that it is important to be honest and decent. The scales the woman

holds are empty, but perfectly balanced, suggesting that one's actions rather than one's possessions are the true indication of a person's worth.

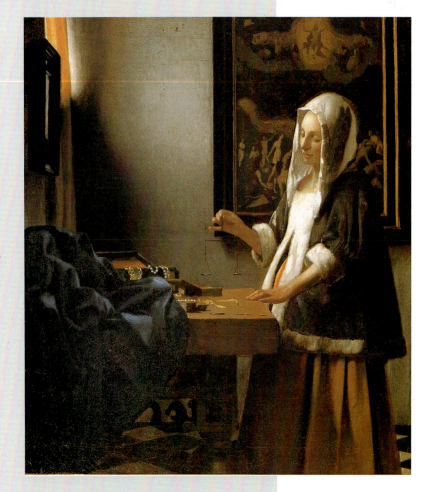

Sacred Places

We all have places that restore our souls. Whether it is the mountains, the beach, or the family dinner table, there are places that allow us to feel connected and at peace. Certain artworks are found in places of personal retreat or communal worship as sites of reverence, renewal, and contemplation. By marking these sites and communicating these experiences, artists and architects give us a sense of their connectedness to nature, religion, or community.

Places that people returned to again and again, like the **prehistoric** caves of Lascaux and the **catacombs** of Rome, were clearly important for their users. When such places, which had been created for memorial or religious purposes, were adorned with artworks, their sacred nature took on a new dimension.

4.2.12a (below, top)
Plan of Lascaux Caves, Dordogne, France

4.2.12b (below, bottom)
Hall of the Bulls. Pigment on limestone rock. Lascaux Caves

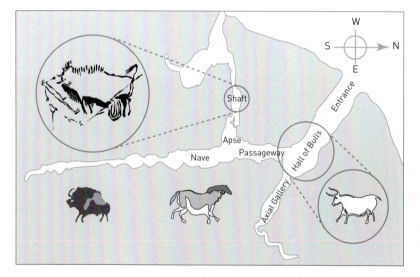

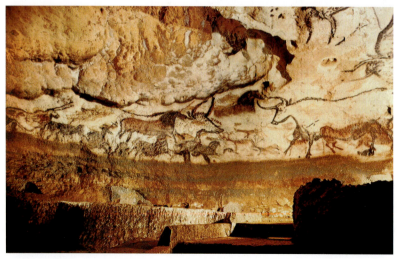

The walls of the Lascaux Caves in southern France (**4.2.12a**) were painted sometime between around 17,000 and 15,000 BCE. One section is densely packed with paintings of animals (**4.2.12b**). The effort required to adorn the walls of the caves with so many images suggests that these depictions of animals that were encountered on a daily basis were incredibly important. Some of the most magnificent paintings are contained in the Hall of the Bulls in the main cave, which is 66 ft. wide and 16 ft. high. The hall is located near the entrance to the system of caves. The hall, as its name suggests, is decorated with outlines and realistic details of numerous bulls—one of them more than 15 ft. long. The paintings in this area overlap, indicating that the site was visited repeatedly, that it was decorated over a period of time, and that making these paintings in this particular place was significant. They mark it as a location that was sacred in some way to the people who used it.

Because the makers of the paintings at Lascaux had no system of writing, we must deduce the stories of these images from the pictures themselves. In addition to telling a story, which was one likely purpose of the images, prehistoric cave paintings may also have been used to teach hunting and to represent shamanic or ritual practices. Paintings similar to those at Lascaux have been found in other places in France and also in Spain, indicating that these paintings were part of a widespread cultural practice by people who either moved from place to place or shared ideas with others.

The human desire to paint important or sacred places is equally evident in the catacombs constructed outside the city of Rome, Italy, between the second and fourth centuries CE (**4.2.13a and b**). An underground system of tunnels measuring between 60 and 90 miles in length and containing the ancient remains of 4 million people, the catacombs were sacred spaces for Romans, who held different religious beliefs and went there to visit their ancestors' burial places. While pagan Romans practiced both cremation and burial of the dead, burial was especially important for Jews and Christians. The catacombs were also used as temples for

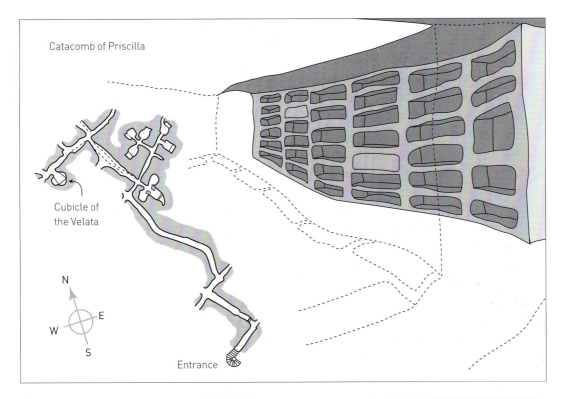

Catacomb of Priscilla

Cubicle of
the Velata

N
E
W
S

Entrance

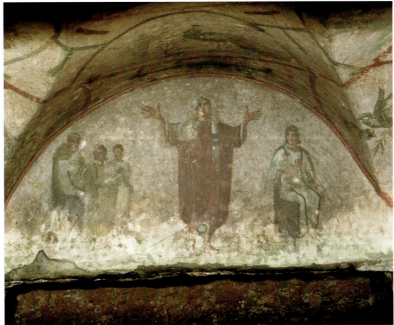

4.2.13a (above) Plan and section through the main gallery of the oldest region of the catacomb of Callixtus, 2nd century CE. Rome, Italy

4.2.13b (right) Catacombs of Priscilla, 2nd and 3rd centuries CE. Via Salaria, Rome, Italy

religious observances, a space where Christians could gather, and hiding places for fugitives.

Like Lascaux, the catacombs contain paintings in different types of areas. In the catacombs, **frescoes** ornament both the places used for burial and the rooms in which people could congregate. The paintings consist of pagan, Jewish, and Christian scenes. Although the same imagery was seen by Romans of all three faiths, particular subjects, such as banquet scenes or shepherds, would be interpreted differently according to the viewer's religion. For example, the central figure in the Christian fresco from the catacombs of Priscilla is shown standing in a praying position (**4.2.13b**). Such a pose appears in pagan art, but it has a distinct meaning for Christians, who understand the figure to be praying to their God. Using imagery, such as this prayerful person, that was familiar to practitioners of other religions probably helped

Prehistoric: dating from the period of human existence before the invention of writing

Catacombs: an underground system of tunnels used for burying and commemorating the dead

Fresco: a technique where the artist paints onto freshly applied plaster. From the Italian *fresco*, "fresh"

win potential converts to Christianity while also conveying a clear message to existing believers.

A mosque is a building where Muslims gather to pray to Allah. Because mosques are often the largest structures in a city, they have also played a significant role in community activities when used as schools or hospitals. In addition to the Taj Mahal (see Images Related to 4.2, p. 587), Shah Jahan was responsible for the building of Masjid-i-Shah, also known as The Mosque of the Imam in Isfahan (present-day Iran). This mosque has four *iwan*s, or vaulted entrances, between the courtyard and the mosque's interior. Large towers (minarets) rise above the city to call citizens to prayer. Pointed arches, a characteristic feature of Islamic architecture, crown the *mihrab* (a special prayer niche), iwans, and decorative walkways throughout the mosque. In its central courtyard there is a large pool for cleansing before prayer. Muslims must pray five times a day facing the direction of the city of Mecca. The mihrab, placed on the wall oriented toward Mecca (*qibla* wall), indicates the correct direction for worshipers' prayers.

The walls of the mosque are decorated with the intricate blue tilework, calligraphic texts, and foliage designs commonly found in Islamic architecture. A fine example of complex Islamic geometric patterning can be seen in the honeycomb design of the *muqarna*s in one iwan entrance to the Mosque (**4.2.14**). The muqarnas (or stalactite vaults) are decorative elements originally used to cover the tombs of holy men. The shape of the muqarnas in the pointed vault resembles a series of small domes lined up in rows and stacked on top of one another. One description suggests that the muqarnas sanctify the space by symbolizing "the rotating dome of heaven."

Marking a site as sacred is a common practice in the long-standing Japanese religion called Shinto, which emphasizes the ways such natural elements as the sun, mountains, water, and trees are connected to well-being. Unlike Christianity and Islam, Shinto focuses on the here and now and reveres nature itself as a deity. For example, Shinto recognizes a mountain as a sacred object because it is the source of water for rice cultivation. Such a mountain was once worshiped directly, but over time shrines were built as places to worship a god, known as a *Kami*, that was important to a particular area or community. These sites, like the Grand Shrine of Ise, or Ise Jingu, started with small piles of stones in an area surrounded by stone enclosures, which have gradually evolved to include buildings, fences, and gates.

Ise Jingu is one of thousands of shrines throughout Japan dedicated to the sun goddess Amataerasu Omikami. Local residents visit the shrine to revere the goddess and seek her assistance. The site is now marked by a stately **A-framed** wooden building that is simple in

4.2.14 Main entrance portal (*iwan*) with *muqarna*s vaulting. Masjid-i-Shah, early 17th century, Isfahan, Iran

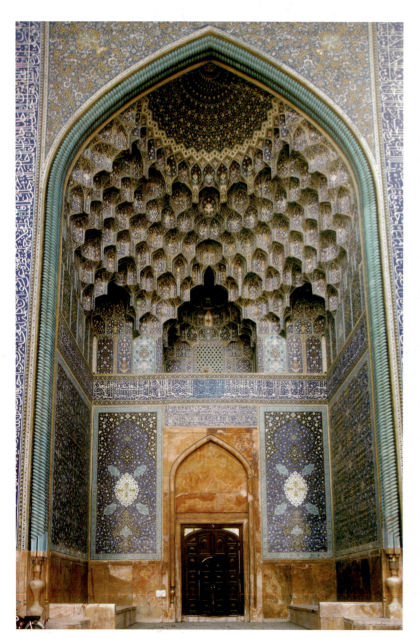

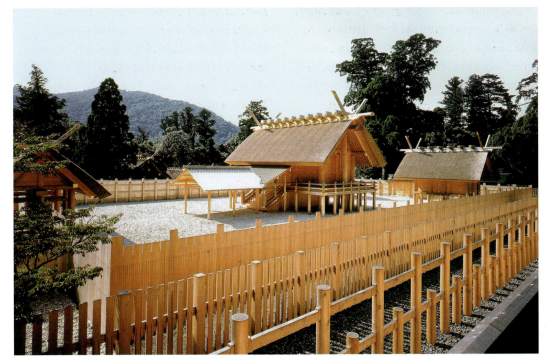

design and made with natural materials (**4.2.15**). Because nature is cyclical, the shrine must also be renewed and refreshed. Since 690 CE, Ise Jingu has been rebuilt every twenty years with a special ceremony in which meals are shared with the Kami, infusing the everyday act of eating with ritual significance.

The Rothko Chapel in Houston, Texas, is a place of worship open to people of all beliefs (**4.2.16**). The chapel's **octagonal** interior walls hold fourteen paintings by the Russian-born American **Abstract Expressionist** painter Mark Rothko (1903–1970). Rothko worked closely with the architects on the designs for

4.2.16 Rothko Chapel, 1966–71. Menil Collection, Houston, Texas

A-frame: an ancient form of structural support, made out of beams arranged so that the shape of the building resembles a capital letter A
Octagonal: eight-sided
Abstract Expressionism: a mid-twentieth-century artistic style characterized by its capacity to convey intense emotions using non-representational images

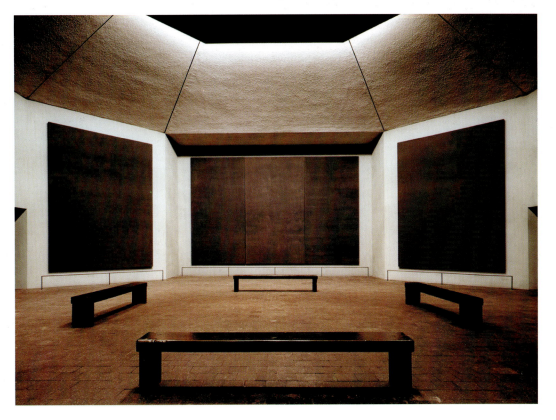

the chapel. He wanted his paintings to be hung a certain distance from the floor, presented in low lighting, and shown together in a group in order to create an environment that enveloped and transported viewers beyond their everyday experience.

The canvasses at the Rothko Chapel employ a restricted, dark palette of colors ranging from maroon and plum to black. The fields of color are intense and powerful, creating a tranquil and contemplative atmosphere. The chapel marks a culmination in the artist's search for the simplest means to express universal truths that are spiritual in nature but unconnected to any particular religious experience or doctrine. The Rothko Chapel has become a sacred place for worship and religious services, a site for performances and scholarly lectures, and a space for visitors to contemplate while immersed in an experience that integrates Rothko's paintings with architecture.

Discussion Questions

1. Find three works of art that deal with spirituality (in other chapters in this book, in your community, or any other examples that you know about). Into which category of works in this chapter do they fit? If they do not seem to fit any of these sections, how would you categorize them?

2. Review the sacred places covered in this chapter and then think of a building, public space, or sculpture that is important to you. Choose a place or artwork that you are comfortable discussing with others and that is personally significant and connected in deep ways to your sense of self. Describe it as fully as possible (the function of the space, what you do there, what it looks like, how you feel when you are there, whether other people have similar experiences there, and so on). Be sure to consider how your experience could best be shared with someone unfamiliar with your personal sacred space.

3. In this chapter you have encountered some spaces that have been sacred to a large community and even to a global body of followers. Alone or in groups describe a sacred space with universal appeal, or invent and design one. Sacred spaces often harmonize with nature or feature geometric forms, and include sacred symbols. Will your space include any of these elements? Try to make your chosen space reflect feelings and/or physical attributes that are important to you.

Images Related to 4.2:
Spirituality and Art

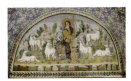

3.2.5 *Good Shepherd*, mosaic, Ravenna, Italy, 425–26, p. 393

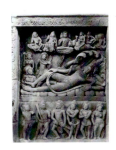

1.6.9 *Vishnu Dreaming the Universe*, India, c. 450–500 CE, p.137

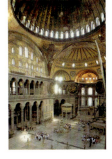

2.5.19 Hagia Sophia, Istanbul, Turkey, 532–35 CE, p. 276

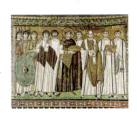

4.6.5 Mosaic depicting Emperor Justinian, c. 547 CE, p. 629

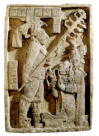

4.6.6 Maya lintel showing Shield Jaguar and Lady Xoc, c. 725 CE, p. 629

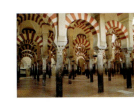

1.9.7 Great Mosque of Córdoba, Spain, 784–86, p. 172

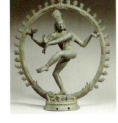

4.3.11 *Shiva Nataraja*, Chola period, India, 11th century, p. 594

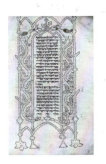

4.1.1 Notre Dame Cathedral, Paris, France, 1163–1250, p. 563

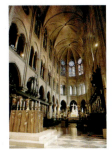

1.1.10 Franco-German hand, *Pentateuch*, 13th–14th century, p. 54

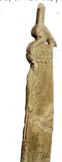

3.5.9 Bird on top of stone monolith, Great Zimbabwe, Africa, 15th century, p. 456

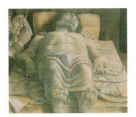

4.3.3 Andrea Mantegna, *Dead Christ*, c. 1480, p. 590

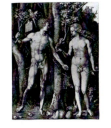

2.3.8 Albrecht Dürer, *Adam and Eve*, 1504, p. 236

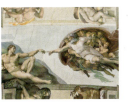

3.6.7b Michelangelo, Detail of *Creation of Adam*, 1508–12, p. 469

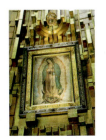

0.0.17 *The Virgin of Guadalupe*, 1531, Basilica of Our Lady of Guadalupe, Mexico City, Mexico, p. 40

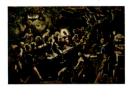

3.6.18 Tintoretto, *The Last Supper*, 1592–94, p. 481

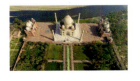

1.6.15 Ustad Ahmad Lahauri et al, Taj Mahal, India, 1632–43, p. 142

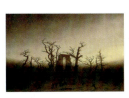

4.3.16 Caspar David Friedrich, *Abbey Among Oak Trees*, 1809–10, p. 597

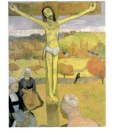

1.4.27 Paul Gauguin, *The Yellow Christ*, 1889, p. 116

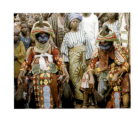

4.1.9 Pair of Gèlèdé masqueraders, Idahin, Benin, 1971, p. 569

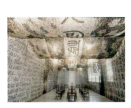

4.1.10 Wenda Gu, *United Nations—China Monument*, 1998, p. 569

4.3

Art and the Cycle of Life

> How strange is the lot of us mortals! Each of us is here for a brief sojourn; for what purpose he knows not, though he senses it. But without deeper reflection one knows from daily life that one exists for other people.
>
> (Albert Einstein, physicist and Nobel Prize winner)

Human cultures from the earliest times to the twenty-first century have been deeply concerned with fundamental questions of existence: where do we come from? What happens when we die? What lies beyond death? These persistent concerns, not surprisingly, have also been a frequent subject of works of art.

In this chapter, we look at the ways in which artists have examined the cycle of life. Visual artists have dealt with topics as unfathomable as the beginning of human existence, as miraculous as the birth of a child, as enduring as natural forces or the passage of time, and as overwhelming as the finality of death. The examination of life's mysteries takes the form of mythical visions, narrative accounts, and direct portrayals of life's beginnings, its endings, and what happens in between.

Renaissance: a period of cultural and artistic change in Europe from the fourteenth to the seventeenth century
Foreshortening: a perspective technique that depicts a form at a very oblique (often dramatic) angle to the viewer in order to show depth in space

Life's Beginnings and Endings

Stories about the beginning of civilization and the creation of humankind are found throughout history in cultures across the globe.

Creation myths can help us come to grips with concepts that we may not understand intellectually, such as the fact of life itself. Equally important are stories that tell about the process of childbirth and emphasize how we are connected to our family members. Artworks with such subjects often reflect the beliefs of an entire community.

For some cultures, such as the Aztecs of central Mexico, it was important to mark the physical, if still mystical, beginnings of human life. For the Aztecs, a woman giving birth was seen as a female warrior going to battle on behalf of the state. Women who died in childbirth were afforded the same respect as men who died on the battlefield; they resided in the same final resting place as heroes, accompanying the sun on its daily journey through the sky. The goddess Tlazolteotl, an Earth Mother and patron of childbirth, was known as the "filth eater" because she visited people at the end of their lives and absolved or ate their sins. She was responsible for bringing disease as well as curing it. A stone sculpture of Tlazolteotl shows her in the act of giving birth (**4.3.1**). The grimace on her face resembles a skull, and a tiny figure, a miniature adult, emerges from her body. Female deities worshiped by the Aztecs, such as Tlazolteotl, often had dual personalities. Not only were they acknowledged as life-givers, but they were also feared as powerful and terrifying.

While the Tlazolteotl sculpture shows a symbolic representation of childbirth, the Dutch artist Rineke Dijkstra (b. 1959) highlights some of the stark realities of birth in her *Mothers*

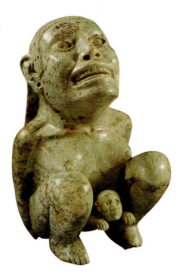

4.3.1 Tlazolteotl giving birth to the maize god, *c.* 1500. Aztec granite carving, 8 × 4¾ × 5⅞". Dumbarton Oaks Museum, Washington, D.C.

series. "Julie" (**4.3.2**) captures a mother and her newborn baby just one hour after delivery, at a time and in a way that defies most expectations of mother-and-child imagery. They are standing against a cold, anonymous wall. Their position starkly exposes the vulnerability, even shock, that both mother and baby probably feel. Dijkstra makes public a time in a woman's life that is now generally considered private and personal. Inspired by watching the birth of a friend's baby, Dijkstra's photographs capture the awkwardness and enduring strength of the early moments of a new life.

In addition to life's beginnings, artists have also pondered physical death, creating images of the deceased. Christian artists during the **Renaissance** often depicted the damaged body of Christ after his crucifixion. Such images were important because they emphasized the miraculous nature of Christ's later resurrection, and also the concept of eternal life after death at the core of Christianity. The Italian artist Andrea Mantegna (*c.* 1431–1506) created a direct and intimate view of the body in *Dead Christ* (**4.3.3**, see p. 590). Because Mantegna has **foreshortened** the scene, we are first confronted by the stigmata (the wounds Christ suffered while hanging on the cross) in his feet and, further into the picture, in his hands. His body, covered in carefully depicted drapery, extends away from us on a marble slab. Beyond

the muscular torso, we see his lifeless face. By Christ's side are the Virgin Mother and Mary Magdalene, who are mostly cropped out of the picture. While their grief adds to the atmosphere of the scene, the artist focuses our attention on the immediacy of Christ's body and the fact that he is no longer alive.

Perhaps because we are somewhat detached from death, or perhaps out of a sense of propriety, contemporary images of the deceased are not as common as they were during the Renaissance. Photographs of the dead can be especially shocking because today we no longer have such a direct relationship with the dead as people did in the past. Then, loved ones died at home, not in hospitals; bodies were laid out for burial by family members, not by funeral homes. The American artist Andres Serrano (b. 1950) made a series of photographs in a morgue in

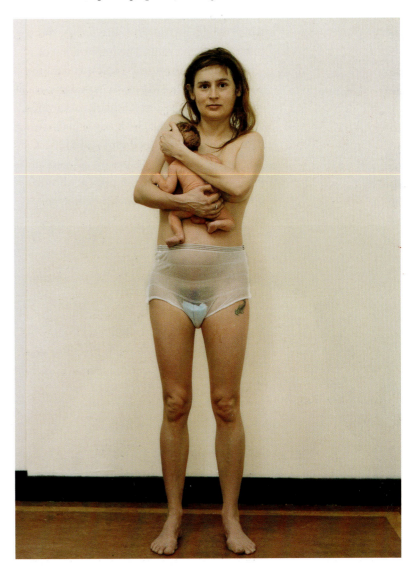

4.3.2 Rineke Dijkstra, "Julie, Den Haag, The Netherlands, February 29, 1994," from the *Mothers* series. C-print, 60¼ × 50¾"

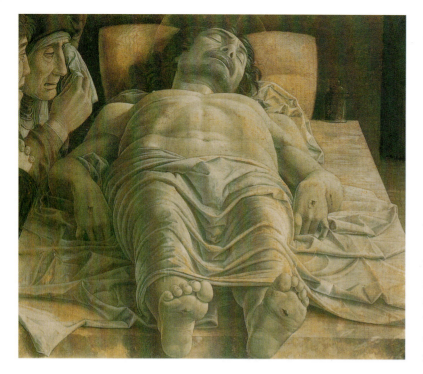

4.3.3 Andrea Mantegna, *Dead Christ*, c. 1480. Tempera on canvas, 26¾ × 31⅞". Pinoteca di Brera, Milan, Italy

4.3.4 Andres Serrano, *The Morgue (Gun Murder)*, 1992. Cibachrome print, 50 × 60"

which the subjects are identified only by the manner of their deaths. The composition of *The Morgue (Gun Murder)* (**4.3.4**), with the feet pointing away from the viewer, is the opposite of Mantegna's *Dead Christ*. The dark background, the white bandages and body bag, and the strong lighting create a sense of drama and contrast. The formal beauty of the image itself contradicts the shocking reality that this person, whose identity we will never know, was murdered.

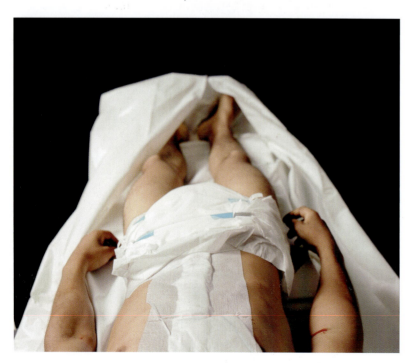

As Serrano's photograph demonstrates, the visceral quality of art can often challenge us intellectually. Even if we do not find the imagery pleasant, it can convey a powerful message and provide us with a deeper understanding of difficult subjects.

Lineage and Ancestors

One way to make sense of one's place in the world is to explore connections with the past. Some people use family albums to chronicle their own life stories and consult pictures to find out about what their ancestors looked like and what events and details occurred during their lifetimes. Artists have explored similar connections, sometimes factual and sometimes fabricated. In addition to telling stories and satisfying curiosity, artworks related to family lineage can serve to legitimize a person's status and rank in society.

The Asmat people live on the island of New Guinea in the southern Pacific Ocean. They trace their origins to the mythical figure called Fumeripits, who carved the first humans from wood and brought them to life by playing a drum. Woodcarving is thus an esteemed tradition amongst the Asmat, and sculptures are often made to represent and honor people who have recently died and the ancestors they are joining in the afterlife.

Ancestor poles known as *bis* (**4.3.5**) represent both stories about the cyclical nature of human life and the social and family ties that connect the community. The bis is carved with imagery associated with power, virility, and fertility, including strong bodies, horns used in headhunting (a practice in which the head of a victim is removed, then preserved, after he or she has been killed), and trees where the spirits dwell. At the top, a root from the sago palm tree has been retained, creating a wing-like projection. In the main section of the sculpture, there are representations both of the dead individual for whom the bis was made and also of other ancestors. The lower part of the sculpture, called the "canoe," is believed to carry the deceased into the afterlife.

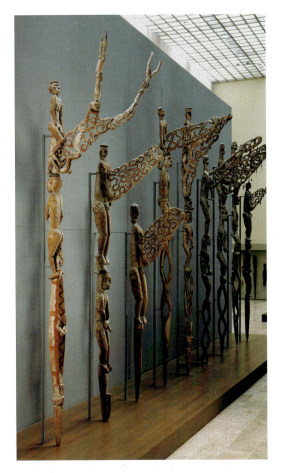

4.3.5 *Bis* poles, late 1950s. Wood, paint, and fiber, 18' × 3'6" × 5'3". Metropolitan Museum of Art, New York

Ancestor poles, such as this one, were once made in connection with headhunting and warfare, and continue to serve a ritual function for male initiation and memorial feasts. A profound bond exists between the figures the Asmat carve and the trees they come from, which are as important as the relationships between generations of ancestors. Once a sculpture has served its ritual function it is returned to the palm groves to decay and strengthen future harvests of the trees.

In many African cultures an important connection between past and present exists in the reverence people show for their ancestors and the nature spirits that influence their lives. The rituals they perform are as crucial to their livelihood as the chores and tasks of daily life. A painted wooden maternity sculpture (called a *pfemba*) from the Yombe (possibly Kongo) people shows a woman kneeling as she holds a bowl in one hand and supports a child with the other (**4.3.6**). This sculpture could be a simple representation of a routine daily event—a woman goes to collect water and takes her child with her—but the artist has given us clues that it has further significance. This example is unlike other pfemba figures, because they usually show the women nursing the child. The bowl and the child may be gifts bestowed by the god, or they may represent sacrifices the woman is prepared to make. White paint (as has been used on this sculpture) often identifies nature spirits, who are associated with the ancestors. Connected to female fertility, such sculptures convey beauty, strength, and dignity. This woman thus provides a role model for the living members of the community: they are to honor their ancestors with gifts of sustenance and with children who will continue the traditions they have worked so hard to establish.

Inspired by a family member who was obsessed with genealogy, contemporary

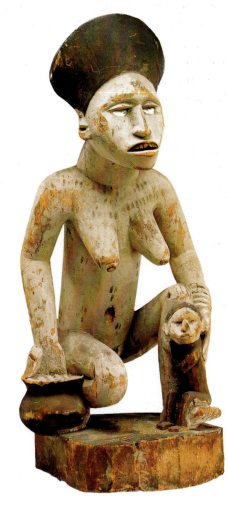

4.3.6 Kneeling female figure with bowl and child, late 19th/early 20th century. Wood, pigment, and glass. 21½ × 10 × 9½". Dallas Museum of Art, Texas

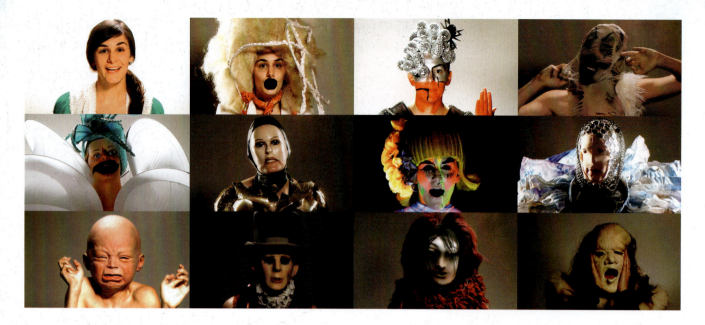

4.3.7 Jillian Mayer, *I Am Your Grandma* (selected video stills), 2011. Duration 1 min. 3 secs. Music by Jillian Mayer and Michael-John Hancock

Vanitas: a genre of painting that emphasizes the transient nature of earthly materials and beauty; often seen in still-life painting
Still life: a scene of inanimate objects, such as fruits, flowers, or motionless animals
Trompe l'oeil: an extreme kind of illusion meant to deceive the viewer that the objects included are real
Memento mori: the Latin phrase that means "remember that you must die." In artworks, symbols are used to represent the transient nature of life on Earth; examples of such symbols include skulls, flowers, and clocks
Baroque: European artistic and architectural style of the late sixteenth to early eighteenth century, characterized by extravagance and emotional intensity
Cubism, Cubist: a style of twentieth-century art that favored a new perspective emphasizing geometric forms

American artist Jillian Mayer (b. 1984) began to wonder what her descendants would know about her in the future. As she said, "we only know our grandparents as old." Her musings resulted in *I Am Your Grandma* (**4.3.7**), a minute-long video that went viral on YouTube (more than 2.9 million views at the time of writing). Like a self-portrait in the future tense, the video mixes fast-paced shots of Mayer wearing thirteen different costumes and rapping a catchy tune:

> One day, I'm gonna have a baby, and you will call her mom. That baby will have a baby and you will have this song to know that I am your grandma…This is a gift I give to you, like I already said, that there was a time I was aware that one day I'd be dead. I wish we could have met. I would have loved you so, but you are in the future. You get love by video.
> I am your grandma…

Funny but somewhat unnerving, this "message to [her] future unborn grandchild" shows the artist to be anything but old. Mayer is interested in what she calls "legacy leaving," and she acknowledges the importance of "using technology to deal with identity." In the video, an informed viewer can find visual references to characters from art history—Pablo Picasso's images of the harlequin, a comic figure from European theater tradition—as

well as from popular culture—for example, the singer Lady Gaga's Mother Monster—based on the experience and imagination of the artist. Whether we recognize the specific references or not, *I Am Your Grandma* embraces play, ambiguity, and uncertainty as ways to connect with the real world, a world in which attachments are sometimes made to people we have never met: including distant or long-dead relatives, characters in theater or art, or favorite singers.

Mortality and Immortality

Art and ritual often mark different stages of life. Artists have recorded images of birth and death as ways to consider the fleeting existence of the life force that ultimately defies comprehension. While some artifacts refer to the ceremonies undertaken to ask ancestors or supernatural beings to ensure continued prosperity, others present the lifeless body itself. There are many questions, often unanswerable, that artists confront. After we die, do we leave the world of the living? Is it important for the body to stay intact? Is there a place to which the soul is believed to go? These concerns about life, death, and the afterlife have inspired artists for millennia.

Gateway to Art: Picasso, *Girl before a Mirror*
Vanitas

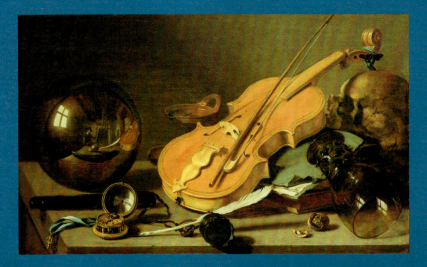

4.3.8 Pieter Claesz (attr.), *Vanitas (Still Life with Glass Globe)*, c. 1628. Oil on panel, 14⅛ × 23¼". Germanisches Nationalmuseum, Nürnberg, Germany

The term **vanitas** refers to a person's vanity, materialism (in terms of physical limitations, and also the desire to own possessions), and inevitable mortality. In art, "vanitas" has come to refer to artworks based on the theme of the fleeting nature of life, which first became popular in the seventeenth century in Dutch **still life** paintings, for example *Vanitas (Still Life with Glass Globe)* (**4.3.8**) attributed to Pieter Claesz (1597–1660).

Still life images, because they depict inanimate objects, give the artist the chance to display a great degree of technical ability by tricking the viewer with ***trompe l'oeil*** techniques that make the scene look very realistic. The passing of time is suggested in *Vanitas (Still Life with Glass Globe)* by the timepiece, and the skull is an obvious ***memento mori*** (literally meaning "remember that you must die"). The tipped glass and cracked walnut tell us that a person was here enjoying wine and food, but is now gone. The instrument reminds us that music is also only transient; it is not fixed in time and will at some point end. Claesz shows his presence by including his own reflection, seen in the glass ball on the left side of the table. Not only does this self-portrait display the artist's virtuosity, but it also presents a challenge to death; the painter lives on through his work.

Spanish artist Pablo Picasso's (1881–1973) keen awareness of the history of art allowed him to pick and choose influences from the past. In addition to the tradition of vanitas still life, Picasso would have known about Renaissance and **Baroque** figure studies depicting the goddess Venus looking at herself in a mirror. This subject connects in a direct way with the concept of vanitas, because beauty is ephemeral and destined to fade over time. Traditionally, the inclusion of a mirror in a painting symbolizes the artist's desire to compete with nature and produce as lifelike an image as possible. While Picasso is more interested in **Cubist** abstraction than *trompe l'oeil* illusion, the vanitas theme plays a large part in his *Girl before a Mirror* (**4.3.9**). As the woman gazes on herself in the mirror she sees a dark, chaotic reflection. Perhaps the deathly head reflecting back at her is a prediction of her inevitable future, a memento mori restating the age-old message that life is short.

4.3.9 Pablo Picasso, *Girl before a Mirror*, Boisgeloup, March 1932. Oil on canvas, 64 × 51¼". MoMA, New York

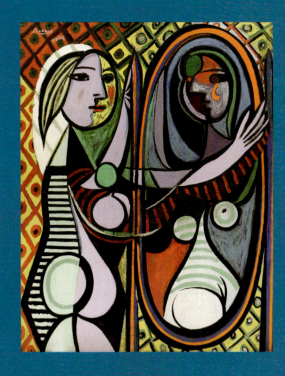

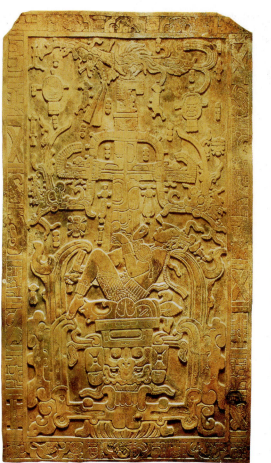

4.3.10 Sarcophagus lid, tomb of the Maya ruler Lord Pacal (Shield 2), 680. Limestone. Temple of the Inscriptions, Palenque, Mexico

Death and the afterlife are inseparably connected with life in many religions and belief systems. A sarcophagus lid made for Pacal, the seventh-century ruler of the Maya city-state of Palenque in southern Mexico, illustrates the king's integral role in the cycle of life (**4.3.10**). The elaborate scene, carved in **low relief**,

4.3.11 *Shiva Nataraja (Lord of the Dance)*, Chola Period, India, 11th century. Bronze, 43⅞" high. Cleveland Museum of Art, Ohio

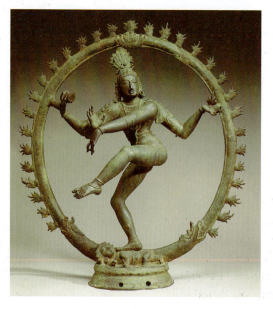

shows Pacal reclining on a slab that marks the intersection of the Earthly realm and the underworld. Just beneath Pacal is the face of the setting sun, representing death. From Pacal's navel sprouts the world tree, which connects the three cosmic realms: its roots are in the underworld, its trunk is in the Earthly world, and its branches are in the sky. The ruler himself serves a similar purpose. By carrying on the lineage of his ancestors, he ensures sustenance and productivity for his people and provides a connection with the gods.

In India, connections between the present life and those before and after it are central to the Hindu belief system. One of the principal Hindu deities, Shiva, embodies a balancing of contradictory qualities: half-male and half-female, benevolent and fearsome, giver and taker of life. As Nataraja, or "Lord of the Dance" (**4.3.11**), Shiva is responsible for dancing the world into existence and generating *samsara*, the endless cycle of death and rebirth in which Hindus believe. The flames surrounding Shiva's agile form represent the periodic chaos and destruction that happen when the dance ceases. During these periods of inactivity, the fire cleanses the physical world while providing a release from samsara. Shiva dances while poised on top of a dwarf who represents the evil and ignorance that are stamped out during the dances. Shiva's dance creates a balance between creation and destruction that, over the course of time, manifests itself in the cycle of life.

The Power of Nature

Artists have long been fascinated by the power of nature to affect humankind. Many cultures believe that natural events are caused by gods.

Zen dry gardens, such as the one at Ryoan-ji in Kyoto, Japan (**4.3.12**), have been popular since the fifteenth century. A microcosm of the larger Earthly landscape, white quartz gravel represents water, and the bigger rocks are surrounded by moss, mimicking islands. The garden is maintained to create a serene space for contemplation. Practitioners of Zen Buddhism cultivate mental calm on the path

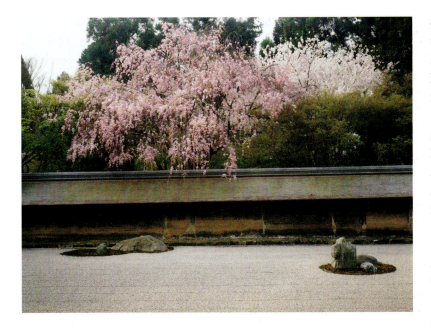

4.3.12 Japanese Zen garden, Ryoan-ji temple, Kyoto, Japan, c. 1480 (Muromachi period). Stone and gravel

effectiveness in bringing rain, and it carries a rattle in one hand and a sprig of Douglas fir (here represented by a feather) in the other. As the first kachina to bring mature corn to the Hopi, this figure helps ensure a successful corn crop.

Because rain is essential to sustain life, rain gods were important to the ancient Mexicans. Many groups in central Mexico, such as the Aztecs, worshiped a rain god known as Tlaloc. Also associated with the Earth's fertility, Tlaloc is represented by the colors blue and white and

4.3.13 (below) Hopi *kachina* doll, c. 1925. Wood, feathers, and pigment, 25¼" high. Gustav Heye Center, New York (National Museum of the American Indian)

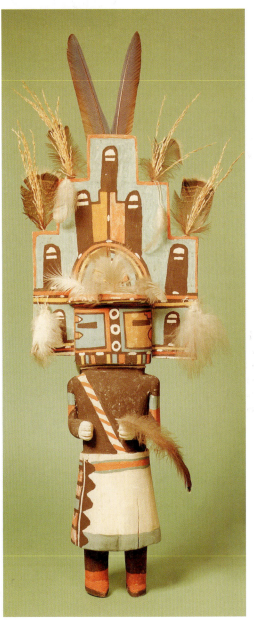

to enlightenment by emphasizing rigorous discipline and personal responsibility, here achieved by raking the gravel regularly. This practice reinforces the impermanence of Earthly existence; any design—however beautiful—that is raked into the garden will soon disappear or be replaced. The garden features fifteen stones of assorted shape and size, but at any one time the viewer can catch sight of only fourteen; only those who have reached enlightenment possess the ability to see all fifteen stones at once. Zen gardens are designed to be places to embrace the present moment and meditate on nature and life.

For the Hopi of the southwestern United States, *kachina*s are supernatural spirits that personify events and natural elements. The phenomena represented by kachinas include the solstices (the longest and the shortest days of the year, which mark the beginning of a new stage in the seasonal ritual cycle), patterns of stars (constellations), plants, and animals. During the planting season, masked dancers embody the kachinas in annual festivals dedicated to rain, fertility, and good hunting. Dolls associated with these spirits are also made. The kachina doll shown in **4.3.13** represents the Jemez kachina, which appears near the end of the season when the kachinas are about to leave the steep-sided, elevated plateaus known as mesas, where the Hopi live, for six months. The elaborate headdress on the Jemez kachina contains cloud symbols, denoting its

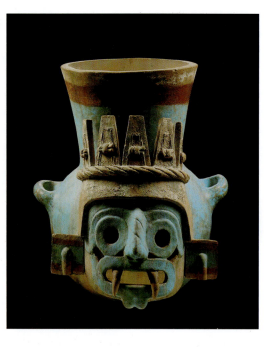

4.3.14 Aztec vessel with mask of Tlaloc, *c*. 1440–69. Fired clay and paint, 13¾ × 14 × 12⅜". Museo del Templo Mayor, Mexico City, Mexico

4.3.15 Gustave Courbet, *Fox in the Snow*, 1860. Oil on canvas, 33½ × 50". Dallas Museum of Art, Texas

by the symbols for raindrops and water plants. A large ceramic vessel representing Tlaloc, which was found at the Templo Mayor in the Aztec city of Tenochtitlan (under present-day Mexico City), exhibits the god's most prominent characteristics: goggle-like circles around his eyes as well as snake-like fangs (**4.3.14**). In Mexico's dry climate, the crops depend on seasonal rains. If there was no rain, people went hungry, so the Aztecs were careful to keep Tlaloc happy. It is likely that offerings were made during ceremonies in which this vessel was used in order to prevent droughts and ensure that rain would nourish the Aztec crops.

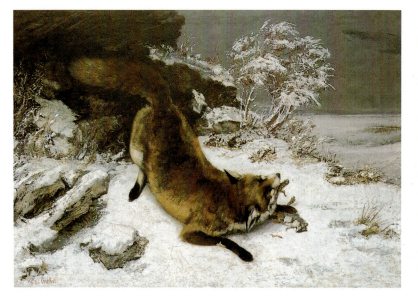

The French artist Gustave Courbet (1819–1877) painted a very different representation of the violent forces of nature (**4.3.15**). Courbet shows an ordinary moment in the wilderness when one life is given for the sake of another. A red fox is devouring a rat that it has caught on a snowy day. Courbet was renowned for his ability to render realistic details: he depicts the fluff of the fox's coat, the coarseness of the rocks, the delicacy of the snow on the grasses, and the intensity of the rat's blood. By choosing this subject, Courbet has captured a moment that emphasizes the fleeting quality of life, in which tomorrow the fox could very well be the hunted instead of the hunter.

For the German painter Caspar David Friedrich (1774–1840), nature reflected the presence of God in the human world. *Abbey Among Oak Trees* (**4.3.16**) conveys an aura of haunted stillness. A procession of people walks in the snow through the ruins of a **Gothic**-style structure based on the remains of Eldena Abbey in Greifswald, northeastern Germany. Surrounded by grave markers and flanked by two oaks where the church's towers would have been, the scene conveys a mood of death, particularly in its wintry landscape. Friedrich places importance on spirituality, rather than organized religion; even though most of the church is ruined, people still come to worship. A master of the **Romantic style**, Friedrich's artworks emphasize emotion and imagination over realism and reason. In a larger sense, *Abbey Among Oak Trees* reveals a sublime awareness that the cycles of nature outlast human constructions, lifespans, and existence.

Rather than being inspired by or representing nature, American artist Patrick Dougherty (b. 1945) directly incorporates natural elements into his large-scale sculptures. Throughout the US, and all over the world, Dougherty's site-specific stickworks transform twigs and branches into something entirely new for a short period of time, usually around two years. Frequently the pieces, which visitors are encouraged to enter, build on ideas of home, architecture, and dwellings. The process of making a stickwork takes about two weeks, and begins by collecting saplings from the location in which the work is to be installed. Dougherty enlists help from community volunteers to build the sculpture using a technique similar to weaving. For *Na Hale 'Eo waiawi* ("Wild Dwellings from Strawberry Guava") (**4.3.17**), Dougherty and his team used native strawberry guava, rosewood, and monkey pod saplings. Situated outdoors, in the grounds of the Contemporary Art Museum in Honolulu, the sculpture looks like a grove of giant tree trunks. Stickworks transform the life of the saplings: in this case the final sculpture comes full circle, recalling the sticks' former existence as living material at the same time as extending their lifespan in the immortal realm of art.

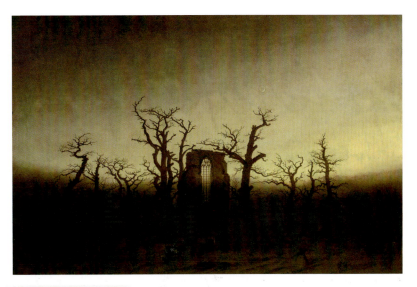

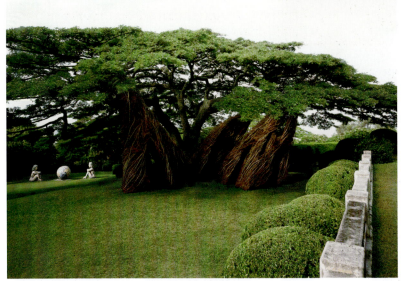

4.3.16 (above) Caspar David Friedrich, *Abbey Among Oak Trees*, 1809–10. Oil on canvas, 43½ × 67⅜". Alte Nationalgalerie, Berlin, Germany

4.3.17 (left) Patrick Dougherty, *Na Hale 'Eo Waiawi*, 2003. Strawberry guava and rose apple saplings, 20 x 30' and 30' high. The Contemporary Art Museum, Honolulu, Hawaii

Gothic: Western European artistic and architectural style of the twelfth to the sixteenth century, characterized by the use of Christian imagery, pointed arches, and ornate decoration

Romantic style: belonging to the nineteenth-century cultural movement Romanticism, which was concerned with the power of the imagination and greatly valued intense feeling

Discussion Questions

1. Choose two artworks from this chapter that fit one of the following criteria: (1) one that depicts a human and one that depicts a mythical being; (2) one personal and one communal; (3) one about birth and one about death. Compare and contrast what the artworks look like and what they are communicating and note at least three points of comparison and contrast. What does this comparison reveal to you about the artworks that you had not considered before?

2. Find several artworks in this chapter or elsewhere in this book (for example, **2.1.2**, **2.4.6**, **3.3.23**, **3.4.15**, **4.3.3**, **4.3.8**, **4.3.15**) from the same cultural tradition that deal with the theme of the cycle of life. What do your chosen artworks have in common? In what ways are they similar? What do they tell you about your chosen culture's attitudes to life and death?

3. Many artworks that deal with the cycle of life are full of symbolic meanings, chosen to make the work memorable. Find two works in this chapter that use symbols in this way and discuss what they hope to communicate to their audience. Then think of an event in your life that could be represented by symbols. What things (colors, scents, feelings) stand out most in your mind? Finally, translate your own personal myth into a picture that can visually communicate the event's importance to others.

Images Related to 4.3:
Art and the Cycle of Life

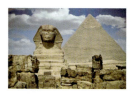

1.2.2 Great Sphinx of Giza, Egypt, *c.* 2500 BCE, p. 68

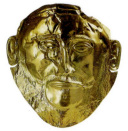

2.6.13 Gold death mask, Mycenae, Greece, *c.* 1550–1500 BCE, p. 300

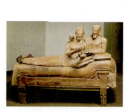

2.4.11 Sarcophagus from Cerveteri, Italy, *c.* 520 BCE, p. 254

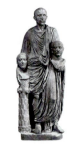

3.1.32 Roman carrying death masks of his ancestors, *c.* 80 BCE, p. 386

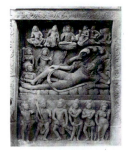

1.6.9 *Vishnu Dreaming the Universe*, India, *c.* 450–500 CE, p.137

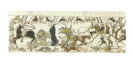

4.7.7 Detail of the *Bayeux Tapestry*, *c.* 1066–82, p. 640

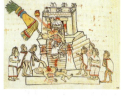

3.4.15 Aztec human sacrifice, *Codex Magliabechiano*, 16th century, p. 442

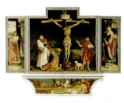

3.6.14 Matthias Grünewald, *Isenheim Altarpiece*, *c.* 1510–15, p. 478

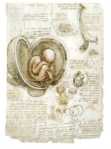

2.1.2 Leonardo da Vinci, *Studies of the fetus in the womb*, *c.* 1510–13, p. 199

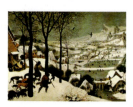

1.9.6 Pieter Bruegel, *Hunters in the Snow*, 1565, p. 171

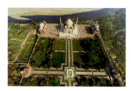

1.6.15 Ustad Ahmad Lahauri et al, Taj Mahal, India, 1632–43, p. 142

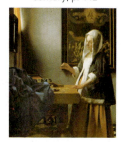

4.2.11 Johannes Vermeer, *Woman Holding a Balance*, *c.* 1664, p. 581

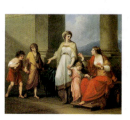

3.7.12 Angelica Kauffmann, *Cornelia Pointing to Her Children*, *c.* 1785, p. 501

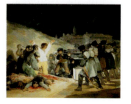

2.3.12a Francisco Goya, *The Third of May, 1808*, 1814, p. 239

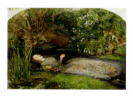

3.7.22 John Everett Millais, *Ophelia*, 1851–52, p. 508

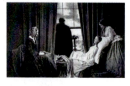

1.7.12a Henry Peach Robinson, *Fading Away*, 1858, p. 153

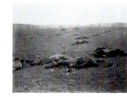

4.7.1 Timothy O'Sullivan, *Harvest of Death*, Gettysburg, 1863, p. 635

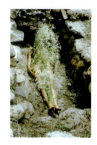

3.9.11 Ana Mendieta, "Untitled" (*Silueta* series), 1973, p. 548

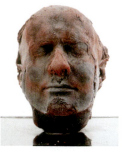

0.0.15 Marc Quinn, *Self*, 1991, p. 38

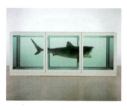

2.4.17 Damien Hirst, *The Physical Impossibility of Death...*, 1991, p. 258

4.4

Art and Science

Some consider science and art to be separate disciplines, even complete opposites. We tend to think of art as intuitive and emotional, and science as rational and objective. Both fields, however, are exploratory in nature and involve extensive trial and error; art and science interact more often than we might suppose. Like scientists, artists are keen observers of phenomena and events, and often artworks contain scientific knowledge and ideas. Sometimes, artworks openly celebrate scientific achievements, and some artists have even used scientific methods to make art. Because of advancements in science and technology, today we are able to study artworks—using such techniques as x-ray—to understand better the practices of past artists, and to preserve and restore artworks for the future. The appreciation of art relies, of course, on the human senses, and artists have always been particularly keen on manipulating the perception of the viewers of artworks. This has involved some artists in the science of **psychology** and the **physiology** of perception.

Art Celebrating Science

The great **Renaissance** artist Leonardo da Vinci (1452–1519) was not only a painter, but also an engineer, anatomist, botanist, and mapmaker. The drawing *Vitruvian Man* (**4.4.1**) shows Leonardo's interest in the proportions of the human body. The **mirror writing** above and below the drawing—readable when reflected—

consists of Leonardo's notes based on the ideas of the first-century BCE Roman architect Vitruvius. Vitruvius was an architect, engineer, and the author of *Ten Books on Architecture*, the only surviving treatise on architecture from the ancient world.

In this treatise Vitruvius outlined the ideal proportions of a man, and argued that architecture should imitate these proportions. Thus, in Leonardo's drawing, the length of both arms combined is equal to the height of a man,

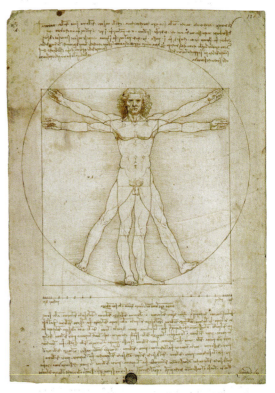

4.4.1 Leonardo da Vinci, *Vitruvian Man: Study of the Human Body*, c. 1490. Pen and ink with wash over metalpoint, 13½ x 10". Gallerie dell'Accademia, Venice, Italy

Psychology: a science that studies the nature, development, and operation of the human mind
Physiology: a science that studies the workings of the body and its organs
Renaissance: a period of cultural and artistic change in Europe from the fourteenth to the seventeenth century
Mirror writing: writing that reads correctly only when reflected in a mirror, as in the case of the journals and other writings of Leonardo da Vinci

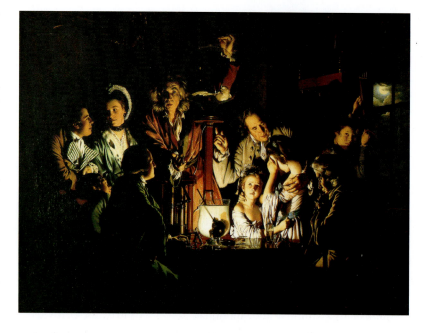

4.4.2 Joseph Wright of Derby, *An Experiment on a Bird in the Air Pump*, 1768. Oil on canvas, 6 × 8'. National Gallery, London, England

the distance from an elbow to the tip of a finger is one-quarter the height, and a man's foot is one-seventh his height. Leonardo also made his own observations of the human body, frequently studying corpses to determine whether the writings of Vitruvius were accurate. Rather than a drawing that simply illustrates the ideas of Vitruvius, Leonardo's work also shows his own exploration of the science of the human body.

The English painter Joseph Wright of Derby (1734–1797) was friendly with members of the Lunar Society, an informal club of scientists, intellectuals, and manufacturers who met monthly to discuss developments in science and technology. Wright lived during the period known as the **Enlightenment**, a time of intense interest in science and reason. He often painted scientific and industrial subjects, employing a notably dramatic use of light and dark, called **tenebrism**.

His painting *An Experiment on a Bird in the Air Pump* shows a traveling scientist demonstrating the creation of a vacuum before an audience (**4.4.2**). If the scientist removes all the air from the glass container in which a bird is imprisoned, the bird will suffocate and die a dreadful death. The artist has chosen to depict the climactic moment of truth. He has increased the drama by his use of shadows and light, which highlights reactions of concern and indifference, contempt and resignation, pity and fear. Strong

light from behind the glass (which contains a skull) in the center of the table shines on the faces of the observers. While light is a symbol of knowledge, the scientist's outward gaze involves us, the viewers of the painting, in the moment's moral dilemma as well. We feel a strong desire to stop the experiment and prevent the bird from suffocating.

Artists study anatomy to learn how to depict figures, and many artists have become interested in dissection and medical procedures. The American painter Thomas Eakins (1844–1916)

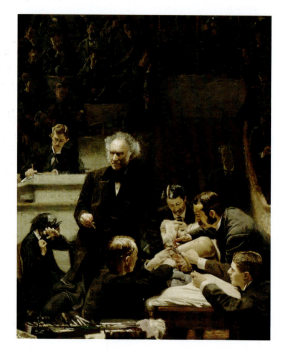

4.4.3 Thomas Eakins, *Portrait of Dr. Samuel D. Gross* (*The Gross Clinic*), 1875. Oil on canvas, 8' × 6'6". Philadelphia Museum of Art and Pennsylvania Academy of Fine Arts

depicted a demonstration he witnessed by a famous surgeon, Dr. Samuel Gross, in Philadelphia (**4.4.3**). Assistants surround the body while the white-haired doctor lectures to medical students, dimly lit in the seating in the background. Eakins's detailed observation of the procedure created such a brutally **realistic** depiction that a critic for the *New York Daily Tribune* commented,

> It is a picture that even strong men find difficult to look at long, if they can look at it at all.

Eakins's meticulous detail makes his painting a useful historical document of early surgical procedure. For instance, he shows us the use of anesthesia (the anesthetist holds a white cloth over the patient's face), a recent invention that had made such surgery as this possible. The artist was not, however, satisfied with mere accuracy; he also wanted to give his painting emotional impact. The lighting is not typical of an operating room, but instead is highly theatrical. Eakins also includes the patient's distraught mother, seen on the left, who in reality was probably not present at the surgery.

Astronomical Knowledge in Art

For millennia, the regular yet ever-changing night sky was a source of endless fascination and study. We know, for example, that in the Middle East, navigation guides called astrolabes, which tracked the skies and the planets, were in use by 500 CE. In another part of the world, in ancient Mexico, amongst the Maya and Aztecs, the planets were regarded as gods, and their movements were closely monitored. Some of the most fascinating artworks of the Maya and Aztecs reflect this interest in astronomy. Careful astronomical observation enabled these people to create remarkably precise calendars.

The **flint** in **4.4.4** incorporates elements of the cosmology (beliefs about the origin of the world) and astronomical knowledge of the

Maya. The delicate carving of this very hard stone reveals a high level of craftsmanship. Light enough to be held in one hand, the flint depicts the story of creation, said by the Maya to have occurred precisely on August 13, 3114 BCE, when the First Father was sacrificed after losing a ball game against the Lords of Death. The First Father's soul is seen riding a crocodile to the Maya underworld (called the Place of Creation, ruled by a water-monster god) accompanied by other Maya lords. The **profiles** of the First Father and two of the lords appear on top of the crocodile, leaning back to suggest the speed of the journey. Two additional figures are shown facing downward toward the underside of the crocodile. The serrated edge on the bottom of the flint represents the forceful waves encountered on the journey. The moment shown here is the transformation of the crocodile into a sacred canoe just before it dives into the rough waters, signifying the death of the First Father. Soon thereafter, the First Father will rise from the waters, transform into the maize god, and become the creator of humans.

The flint, however, is more than a depiction of a Maya story; it is also an instrument for astronomical observations. When held up to the sky on August 13 each year, the five heads on this flint align with the brightest stars of the Milky Way galaxy. For the Maya, the stars re-enact the story of man's creation when, at midnight, the stars of the Milky Way align horizontally

Enlightenment: an intellectual movement in eighteenth-century Europe that argued for science, reason, and individualism, and against tradition, and there was a movement to secure equal rights for all men

Tenebrism: dramatic use of intense darkness and light to heighten the impact of a painting

Realistic: artistic style that aims to represent appearances as accurately as possible

Flint: an object or tool made from the very hard, sharp-edged stone of the same name

Profile: the outline of an object, especially a face or head, represented from the side

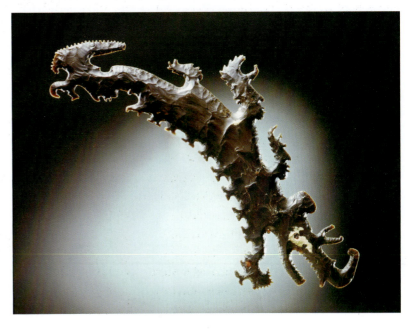

4.4.4 Maya flint depicting a crocodile canoe with passengers, 600–900 CE. 9¾ × 16¼ × ¾". Dallas Museum of Art, Texas

east to west. In the next several hours, the galaxy appears to pivot and fall out of the sky, resembling a canoe diving into water. Then, immediately before the sunrise, the three stars of Orion's belt appear, symbolizing for the Maya the three hearthstones at the site of the First Father's rebirth.

Like the Maya, the Aztecs were skillful observers of the skies. The Aztec Sun Stone in **4.4.5** is a store of astronomical and mathematical knowledge. Originally painted in shades of brown, red, white, blue, and green, the heavy Sun Stone (weighing 24 tons) stood atop the main temple at Tenochtitlan, the capital of the Aztec empire. Later it was buried, to be uncovered again only in 1790 in what is now downtown Mexico City.

The Sun Stone, also known as a calendar stone, reveals how the Aztecs counted time, and illustrates their belief that the Earth endures recurring cycles of destruction and creation. The center of the stone shows the face of Tonatiuh, the sun god to whom Aztecs offered frequent human and animal sacrifices. Each of the four squares emanating from Tonatiuh's face frames a symbol representing the ways in which the Earth previously came to an end: by wind, by fire, by floods, and by wild beasts. The Aztecs believed that the Earth would be destroyed again by an earthquake. In the ring surrounding these symbols are twenty animals, each framed

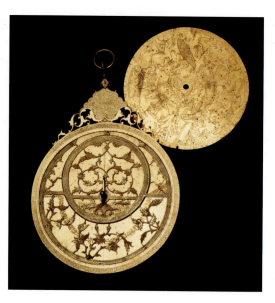

4.4.6 Muhammad Mahdi al-Yadzi, astrolabe, 1659–60. Gilt brass, silvered brass, brass, and glass. 7⅜" diameter. National Maritime Museum, London, England

by a rectangle. These represent the days of the Aztec month. Priests used the calendar stone to determine sacrificial periods.

Used as guides for navigation, astrolabes were made as early as the fifth century CE in the Middle East, and by 800 they had become extremely common in the Islamic world. During the early twelfth century, the technology spread to Europe via Muslims living in Spain. The astrolabe was especially useful to Muslims, who were required to pray while facing toward the city of Mecca five times a day; the astrolabe could find the direction of Mecca as well as calculate the time of day.

An astrolabe is made up of layers of disks or plates that fit into a larger brass dial called a mater. Each of the five plates in the example in **4.4.6** is aligned to a different **latitude**. On the very top is a smaller disk called a rete, which has been cut out almost completely and on which the positions of heavenly bodies are indicated.

The brass astrolabe shown here is an example of fine metalwork. It was made during the seventeenth century in the Safavid empire, in what is now Iran.

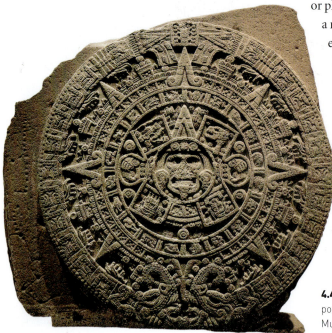

4.4.5 Calendar stone (Sun Stone), late postclassic Aztec. Basalt, 12' diameter. National Museum of Anthropology, Mexico City, Mexico

Latitude: a point on the Earth's circumference measured to the north or south
Tracery: a complex but delicate pattern of interwoven lines

Floral decorations serve as the pointers on the rete. The astrolabe is covered with Persian and Arabic inscriptions. For example, on the outside edge, there are verses about fourteen important Islamic figures. On the rete, there is a series of verses that describe the parts of the astrolabe metaphorically. The **tracery** around the mater contains a dedication inscribed to a Safavid leader. And on the back of the instrument, there is an inscription by the astrolabe's maker, dedicating himself to God.

Using Science to Create Art

Advancements in science enable artists to create new kinds of art. The advent of the microscope enabled one artist to create minuscule artworks, and medical studies have enabled a scientist to preserve bodies and exhibit them as art. Elsewhere, greater awareness of environmental issues has motivated architects to use science in the creation of modern buildings.

The British artist Willard Wigan (b. 1957) has created artworks possible only because he uses a microscope—his creations can barely be seen by the naked eye. He carves individual pieces of sand or grains of rice and places them on equally tiny bases, such as the head of a pin or a strand of human hair. The Statue of Liberty in **4.4.7** was re-created inside the eye of a needle. Wigan then paints his artworks using an eyelash for a brush. To create one of these microscopic works, Wigan puts himself into a very calm state of mind, which slows his heartbeat and decreases hand tremors: "I need to work between heartbeats, or else the pulse in my finger will cause a mistake," he says. He works through the night so that daylight activity, such as cars frequently driving by, will not disturb his steady hand. Wigan found that the intense concentration required for this sculpting helped him come to terms with his difficulties as a dyslexic child. As he recalled:

I became obsessed with making more and more tiny things. I think I was trying to find a way of compensating for my embarrassment at having learning difficulties: people had made me feel small so I wanted to show them how significant small could be.

A German medical scientist, Gunther von Hagens (b. 1945), used his knowledge of anatomy and science to develop a technique, called plastination, which preserves bodies after death and allows them to be arranged in poses. His popular traveling exhibition, *Body Worlds*, has been seen by millions of people, many of whom consider it to be art. The exhibition, however, has been controversial. Although all the bodies featured in it are those of willing donors, many people consider the display irreverent, and complain about the overly theatrical poses of the bodies as well as the fact that the shows are often promoted as art, rather than science

One specimen, *Basketball Player*, is posed as if dribbling a ball down the court (**4.4.8**). The skull has been split so that we can see the brain. This dramatic presentation allows us to see the tension of the inner body and to understand better how we ourselves move. The *Body Worlds* exhibition also includes a body with the damaged lungs of a smoker, and a pregnant woman with her deceased fetus still in her body.

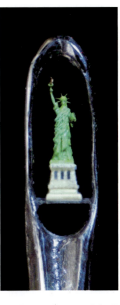

4.4.7 Willard Wigan, *Statue of Liberty*

4.4.8 Gunther von Hagens, *Basketball Player*, 2002. *Body Worlds* exhibition, www.bodyworlds.com

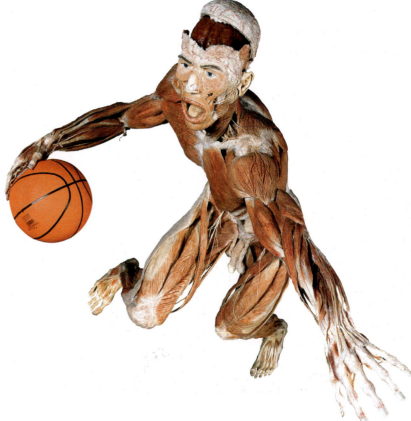

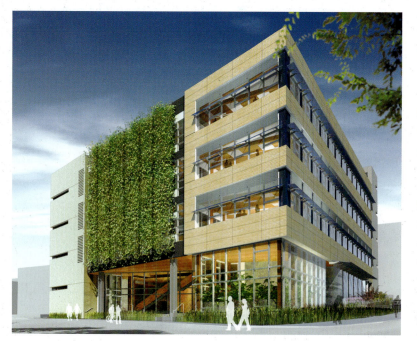

4.4.9 Perkins+Will, Center for Interactive Research on Sustainability (CIRS), University of British Columbia, Vancouver, Canada, 2011

Green practices: Environmentally friendly activities, including energy efficiency and recycling
Fresco: painting made on freshly applied plaster
Pentimento (plural **pentimenti**): Italian for "repentance," evidence of an underlying image showing that an artist changed his or her mind during the painting or drawing of an artwork
Abstraction, abstracted: the degree to which an image is altered from an easily recognizable subject

The Center for Interactive Research on Sustainability (CIRS) in Canada has commissioned an exemplar building (**4.4.9**) at the University of British Columbia, Vancouver, for demonstrating **green practices** and energy savings. The Center is designed as a "living laboratory" for experimentation and the study of environmentally friendly and self-sustaining practices. Through a variety of methods the structure itself produces more energy than it uses. All water used in the building is rainwater, collected from the rooftops and around the building and then treated onsite. Temperature control is achieved largely by a so-called "living wall" on the west facade, on which chocolate vines grow—blocking sun from warming the interior in summer, and then, when the vine leaves fall off in winter, letting the heat in. A garden was also planted in the center of the U-shaped building (on the rooftop of an auditorium that is lower than the rest of the building). Solar panels around the southwest corner and south side can also be closed to function as blinds. Artificial lighting on the inside is programmed to dim or turn off when enough natural light is present. Such technological innovations have earned CIRS the label "greenest building in North America."

The Scientific Restoration of Artworks

Scientific advancements have not only enabled the creation of artworks, but have also helped to improve the way experts can restore and understand them (see Gateway Box: Picasso, opposite). The most momentous restorations in recent times have been the cleaning of the **frescoes** at the Vatican in Rome, Italy. The restoration of Michelangelo's Sistine Chapel ceiling, which began in 1980, took nine years to complete, twice as long as it took Michelangelo to paint the ceiling originally (**4.4.10**).

In order to decide how best to clean the frescoes, restorers first had to determine what was original and what was due to the effects of time, such as candle smoke, the interventions of previous restorers, rain damage, the settling of building foundations, and even bacteria introduced by the visits of millions of tourists. They analysed the chemical composition of minuscule samples of the paint, glue, wax, and

4.4.10 Sistine Chapel ceiling during restoration, Vatican City, Italy, 1980–89

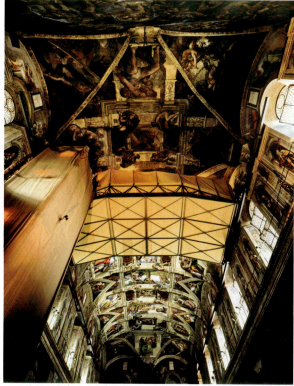

Gateway to Art: Picasso, *Girl before a Mirror*
Understanding Artworks through Science

4.4.12 X-ray photograph taken in 2011 of Pablo Picasso's *Girl before a Mirror*, Boisgeloup, March 1932

4.4.13 Pablo Picasso, *Girl before a Mirror*, Boisgeloup, March 1932. Oil on canvas, 64 × 51¼". MoMA, New York

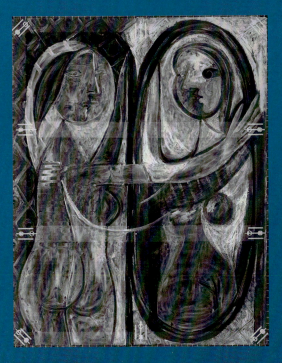

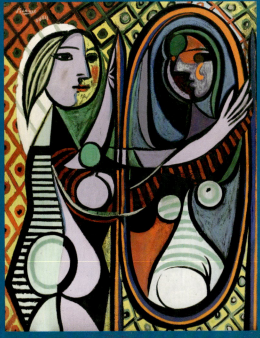

Developments in science have been utilized to understand more about artworks from the past. Chemical analysis of tiny paint chips has led to knowledge about the kinds of paints artists used and how the color of artworks might have changed over time. Such knowledge has helped scientists and historians to envision and sometimes even restore artworks to their original condition.

X-rays allow scholars to view what lies beneath layers of paint on the surface. Frequently, scholars find **pentimenti** that reveal earlier iterations of a painting or preparatory sketches. These can be extremely helpful for scholars trying to understand an artist's working process. Sometimes such discoveries also make one question why an artist might have changed his or her original conception along the way.

An x-ray taken by the Museum of Modern Art of Pablo Picasso's *Girl before a Mirror* reveals some interesting changes made during the early stages of the painting (**4.4.12** and **4.4.13**). Most noticeably, the girl (on the left) looking at herself in the mirror appears more naturalistic and less **abstracted** in the x-ray than she does in the final painting. These two layers of the painting correspond to changes in Picasso's work at the time: the radical reorganization of body parts in his depictions of the nude, seen in the woman herself, and his further expansion into more abstract imagery, seen in the reflection. What ends up as a somewhat pronounced belly looks more like her backside in the under layer. For the finished work, Picasso chose to create a circle, perhaps to represent a womb, put horizontal stripes on the girl's back, and make her more angular, rather than curved, on the lower left. Finished in 1932, the painting foreshadows the future of Picasso and his model, Marie-Thérèse Walter, as she became pregnant with his child in 1935. The advancement of science means that scholars have more data to consider when forming their interpretations of art.

Pointillism: a late nineteenth-century painting style using short strokes or points of differing colors that optically combine to form new perceived colors

Color theory: the understanding of how colors relate to each other, especially when mixed or placed near one another

Optical mixture: when the eye blends two colors that are placed near each other, creating a new color

Afterimage effect: when the eye sees the complementary color of something that the viewer has spent an extended time viewing (also known as successive contrasts)

Palette: the range of colors used by an artist

varnish taken from the many layers they found on the ceiling. This analysis, plus their ability to examine the entire work at close range, led them to believe that Michelangelo had painted the ceiling almost entirely in *buon fresco* (when the plaster was still wet) with only slight corrections executed *a secco* (when the plaster had dried), and that all other layers were later additions.

The most shocking discovery, revealed after centuries of dirt were removed, was the bright colors that Michelangelo had used. Critics denounced the cleaning as a disaster, accusing the restorers of removing Michelangelo's original varnish. An international committee of the world's leading art conservators, however, reviewed the approach taken by the restoration team, and after a lengthy inspection of the restorers' research, methods, and handiwork, the panel declared that the team had been thorough and painstaking, and that their approach was accurate and correct: the original paintings had indeed been this bright.

The cleaning of the Sistine Chapel ceiling paved the way for further restorations at the Vatican, including of Michelangelo's *Last Judgment* (restored 1990–94) on the altar wall of the chapel (**4.4.11**), and, down the hall, four rooms of paintings by Raphael, including *The School of Athens* (restored 1995–96).

The Science of Perception and the Senses

Since art is a visual medium, artists expect viewers to respond to the artwork through their sense of sight. It is not surprising, therefore, that artists have often been keenly aware of scientific studies of visual perception. Some artists have also experimented with ways to use their images to trigger responses from the other senses, such as hearing or smell.

Sunday on La Grande Jatte (**4.4.14**) is a picture of people engaged in the activities of everyday life. But its artist, the Frenchman Georges Seurat (1859–1891), also applied to this artwork recent scientific studies on the way that the human eye perceives color. Seurat developed a process called **pointillism**, a meticulous way of applying **color theory** in his paintings. He relied on two optical effects (**optical mixture** and **afterimage effect**) to create scenes in which the figures are very distinct, almost like cutouts, because of the precise way in which he applied tiny dots of color to the canvas. The colors we see when we view *Sunday on La Grande Jatte* from several feet away are quite different from the colors we see up close. For example, the green grass is made up of dots not only of various shades of green but also of oranges and purples. Seurat took three years to paint this work, meticulously applying dots while considering the effects of color theory on his **palette** choices. To ensure that the optical arrangement would not be disrupted when the painting was framed, Seurat also painted a border using the same pointillist technique.

The American artist Jasper Johns (b. 1930) makes us take a second look at familiar subjects, objects the artist says are "seen but not looked at." He uses such iconic images as numbers, letters, targets, and, perhaps most famously, the American flag, of which he painted several versions. In the version of *Flag* reproduced here, Johns uses his knowledge of color theory to create an optical illusion that forces a viewer to stare intently at an image of the flag (**4.4.15**). The top flag is made up of black and green stripes,

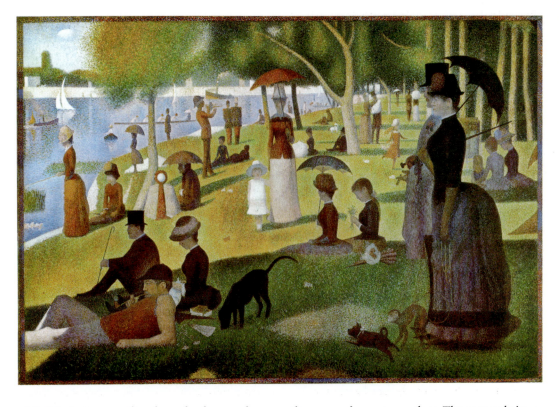

4.4.14 Georges Seurat, *Sunday on La Grande Jatte*, 1884–86. Oil on canvas, 6'9¾" × 10'¼". Art Institute of Chicago, Illinois

while black stars are placed on a background of orange; these colors are complementary to the white, red, and blue colors of the American flag. Johns's optical effect depends on the use of

4.4.15 Jasper Johns, *Flag*, 1965. Private collection

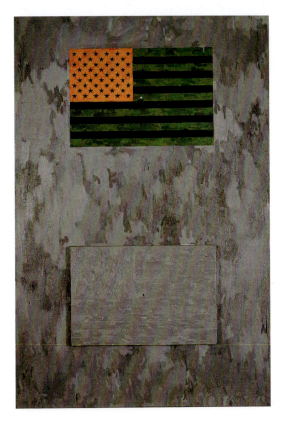

these complementary colors. The rectangle in the bottom half of the painting is just a faded ghost of a flag. For the optical illusion to work, stare at the top flag for a full minute. Focus your attention on the white dot in the center. After a minute has passed, blink and look at the black dot in the center of the lower flag. The red, white, and blue of the American flag will appear. Johns is utilizing the science that lies behind afterimage effect. While looking at the top flag, your eyes became fatigued from the colors. Therefore, when you blinked your eyes and looked at the lower flag, your eyes produced the complementary colors of each aspect of the upper flag.

At times, artists often try to trigger other senses in addition to sight. The process whereby stimulation in one sense causes experiences in a different sense—such as visualizing color when we hear music—is called **synesthesia**. The artist Marcia Smilack (b. 1949) experiences life as a synesthete, and creates artworks that reflect this correspondence between the senses. She describes her experience:

> The way I taught myself photography is to shoot when I hear a chord of color…I hear with my eyes and see with my ears.

Synesthesia: when one of the five senses perceives something that was stimulated by a trigger from one of the other senses

Of the photograph *Cello Music* (**4.4.16**), Smilack says:

> I walked by the water and heard cello…
> I couldn't resist the sound so I gave in and
> aimed my camera at what had elicited it. As
> soon as I let go of my thoughts, the texture of
> the water washed over me in synch with the
> sound and turned to satin on my skin. When
> I felt myself climb into the shadows between
> the folds, I snapped the shutter. I hear
> cello every time I look at it today, though
> I discovered that if I turn it upside down, it
> becomes violin.

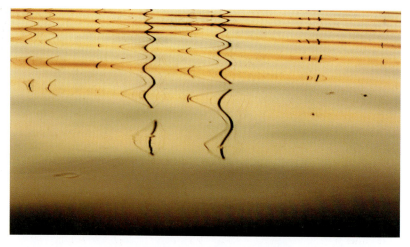

4.4.16 (above) Marcia Smilack, *Cello Music*, 1992. Photograph, 12¾ × 24″. Collection of the artist

Science of the Mind

While some artists have introduced the science of perception and color theory into their works, others have explored different aspects of the science of the mind. Artworks are often portals through which we can learn about an artist's personal struggles, and some artists use psychology and dream theories to try to represent the subconscious world in their work.

Salvador Dalí (1904–1989) was one of a group of artists known as the **Surrealists**, who were inspired by psychology and dream studies, and most particularly by the theories of the father of **psychoanalysis**, Sigmund Freud. Themes of sexual desire and fear are common in Dalí's paintings, which he associated with Freud's studies on sexual urges and behavior.

In *Persistence of Memory* (**4.4.17**), the stretched form in the center (a nose with long eyelashes and a tongue hanging out) is a self-portrait, and the cliffs in the background resemble the Catalan coast in Spain, where Dalí lived. After a late night, Dalí was inspired to paint the work while playing with some melted cheese from dinner. He said the painting was "nothing more than the soft, extravagant, solitary, paranoiac-critical Camembert cheese of space and time." Dalí invented the term paranoiac-critical, which he defined as the

spontaneous method of irrational knowledge based on the critical and

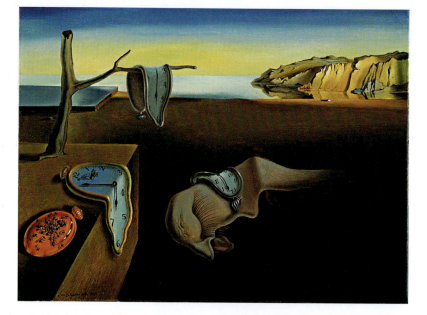

4.4.17 Salvador Dalí, *Persistence of Memory*, 1931. Oil on canvas, 9½ × 13″. MoMA, New York

systematic objectivity of the associations and interpretations of delirious phenomena.

The consistency of the cheese inspired the three warped, dangling watch faces. The limp watches may be interpreted as symbols of both impotence and recent sexual satisfaction.

Scholars have remarked on a link between this work and the physicist Albert Einstein's theory of relativity, which addresses the complexities of time. In Dalí's painting, the clocks each read a different time, conveying a distorted sense of time and space. Dalí also painted a fly on the drooping watch on the ledge, a visual metaphor for the phrase "time flies."

Yayoi Kusama is a Japanese artist who has used art to cope with her personal struggles

Surrealism, Surrealist: an artistic movement in the 1920s and later; its works were inspired by dreams and the subconscious
Psychoanalysis: a method of treating mental illness by making conscious the patient's subconscious fears or fantasies
Installation: originally referring to the hanging of pictures and arrangement of objects in an exhibition, installation may also refer to an intentional environment created as completed artwork

and mental illness. Kusama compares the dots in her artworks to the cosmos; for her, the Earth, moon, stars, and each of us are dots. Like the cosmos, her paintings and **installations** have no boundaries. Upon entering a Kusama installation, the viewer will see dots of various sizes covering the floors, ceiling, and walls. The artist often uses mirrors, which multiply the number of dots experienced by the viewer and emphasize a sense of infinity (**4.4.18**).

Kusama has had hallucinatory episodes in which she sees the world around her covered in a net, and for her, dots also symbolize the "holes" in this net pattern. She has said:

> When I was a child I experienced this state of self-obliteration, so I painted the same motif endlessly. When I was painting I found the same pattern on the ceiling, stairs, and windows, like they were all over. So I went closer and tried to touch them. Then they started to come up my arm as well. It was horrible but now it's over, almost.

Kusama frequently dresses in dots, and usually photographs herself within her

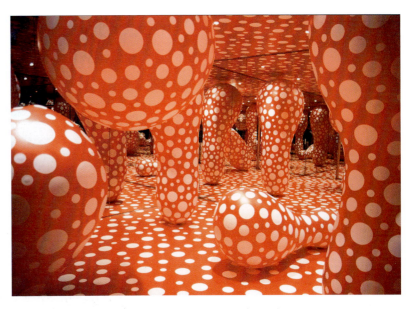

4.4.18 Yayoi Kusama, *Dots Obsession*, 2009. Vinyl balloons, dimensions variable, set of 8 pieces. Installation at Collection Les Abattoirs, Toulouse, France

Happening: impromptu art action, initiated and planned by an artist, the outcome of which is not known in advance

installations wearing a coordinating dress or dot-shaped stickers on her clothes. The blending of the dots on her dress with those of the installation reflect Kusama's belief that by seeing oneself as part of the cosmos, in which the self exists as part of a larger system, the ego is lessened, even neutralized. Kusama has expanded her motif of dots to staging **happenings** around the world, in which she and others are covered in dots in public settings.

Discussion Questions

1. Many artists study synesthesia, are synesthetic themselves, or try to trigger synesthetic responses in the viewer. Study the work of an artist who is known for trying to evoke music in his or her artworks, for example Georgia O'Keeffe (**1.1.27**), Paul Klee (**1.4.20**), Vasily Kandinsky (**3.8.27**), or Piet Mondrian (**3.8.37**). Choose a single painting and, through formal analysis, determine how the artist is trying to inspire sensations that are similar to those stimulated by the playing of music.

2. Elsewhere in this book we have looked at examples of the artwork of the great Italian Renaissance artist Leonardo da Vinci (see for example **0.0.11** and **3.6.6**). Find three scientific studies by Leonardo (**2.1.1** and **2.1.2**, for example) and discuss how they might have contributed to his paintings and other artworks. Would you categorize Leonardo's drawings as art or science, or both? Why? How do you think his scientific studies may have contributed to the making of his paintings?

3. In this chapter we discussed the art of Willard Wigan and Gunther von Hagens. Many contemporary artists create computer-generated artwork or reflect subjects (such as outer space or DNA) influenced by discoveries in science. Can you find any examples of contemporary art that were influenced by such recent technological advancements?

4. Using the Internet, explore how modern science has been used to make or understand one of your favorite artworks. You may want to consider architectural practices utilizing green technology (**4.4.9**); restoration of artworks (**4.4.10**); or the use of technology to comprehend an artist's working methods (**4.4.12**).

Images Related to 4.4:
Art and Science

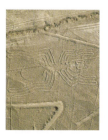

1.1.1 Spider, Nazca, Peru, *c.* 500 BCE–500 CE, p. 49

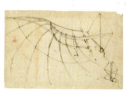

1.7.13b The use of the Golden Section in the design of the Parthenon, p. 154

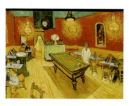

2.1.1 Leonardo da Vinci, *Drawing for a wing of a flying machine*, p. 198

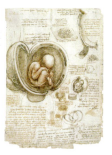

2.1.2 Leonardo da Vinci, *Studies of the fetus in the womb, c.* 1510–13, p. 199

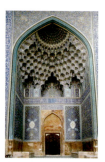

4.2.14 Main entrance portal, Isfahan, Iran, early 17th century, p. 584

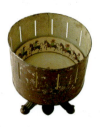

1.5.8 Zoetrope, 19th century, p. 124

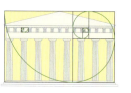

2.9.2 Eadward Muybridge, *The Horse in Motion*, 1878, p. 339

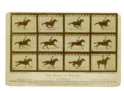

1.4.25 Vincent van Gogh, *The Night Café*, 1888, p. 114

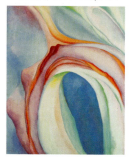

1.1.27 Georgia O'Keeffe, *Music—Pink and Blue II*, 1919, p. 63

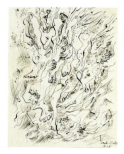

1.1.6 André Masson, *Automatic Drawing*, 1925–26, p. 53

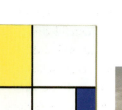

3.8.37 Piet Mondrian, *Composition with Yellow and Blue*, 1932, p. 537

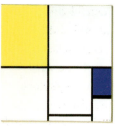

2.4.15 Robert Smithson, *Spiral Jetty*, 1969–70, p. 257

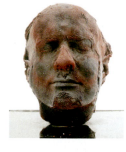

0.0.15 Marc Quinn, *Self*, 1991, p. 38

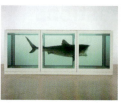

2.4.17 Damien Hirst, *The Physical Impossibility of Death...*, 1991, p. 258

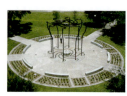

1.5.2 Nancy Holt, *Solar Rotary*, 1995, p. 120

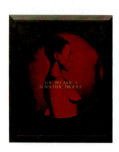

4.10.10 Carrie Mae Weems, "You Became a Scientific Profile," 1995, p. 682

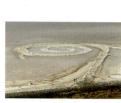

1.9.5a Chuck Close, *Self Portrait*, 1997, p. 170

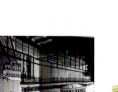

2.8.2 Abelardo Morell, *Camera Obscura Image...*, 1999, p. 321

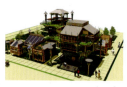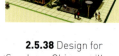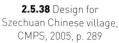

2.5.38 Design for Szechuan Chinese village, CMPS, 2005, p. 289

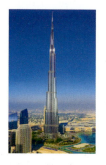

2.5.31 Adrian Smith and Bill Baker, Burj Khalifa, Dubai, 2010, p. 283

4.5

Art and Illusion

Atmospheric perspective: use of shades of color and clarity to create the illusion of depth. Closer objects have warmer tones and clear outlines, while objects set further away are cooler and become hazy
Trompe l'oeil: an extreme kind of illusion meant to deceive the viewer
Two-dimensional: having height and width
Three-dimensional: having height, width, and depth

4.5.1 *Painted Garden*, Villa of Livia, Prima Porta, 30–20 BCE. Fresco. Museo Nazionale Romano, Palazzo Massimo, Rome, Italy

Zeuxis painted a boy carrying grapes, and when the birds flew down to settle on them, he was vexed with his own work, and came forward saying…I have painted the grapes better than the boy, for had I been perfectly successful with the latter the bird must have been afraid.

(Pliny the Elder, *Natural History*)

The ancient Roman author Pliny the Elder tells a story that reveals the millennia-old efforts by artists to create convincing illusions. Pliny describes a contest between two great Greek painters, Zeuxis and Parrhasius, to see who could paint the most realistic picture. As Pliny tells it, Zeuxis's painting of grapes was so realistic that birds flew down to peck at them. Parrhasius in turn painted such a convincing curtain that Zeuxis reached for the drapery, hoping to see the painting on which his rival was working. After being fooled, Zeuxis conceded that Parrhasius had won the competition.

Although the paintings of Zeuxis and Parrhasius have not survived, there are other examples of illusionism from the ancient world that still exist today. One is a garden scene, painted in the underground dining area of a villa built for Livia, the wife of the first-century BCE Emperor Augustus (**4.5.1**). Though it is below ground, visitors to this room are surrounded by the illusion of a green garden filled with numerous kinds of trees, fruit, and birds. One bird, to the right of the oak tree, is in fact eating some luscious hanging fruit, reminiscent of the kind of trickery described in Pliny's story. To create a sense of space, the artist used **atmospheric perspective**, making the trees and objects in the foreground more vivid and crisp than those in background. The low wall in the foreground, shaped to accommodate the tree in front of it, also helps to create a sense of depth.

Many artists since have striven to match and even surpass the achievements of ancient painters, developing techniques that fool us into thinking we are looking at real spaces and objects rather than artworks. ***Trompe l'oeil*** ("fool the eye") is the French term for **two-dimensional** artworks that convincingly appear to be **three-dimensional** objects. Even in three-dimensional art, such as architecture, artists have employed visual tricks to "fool the eye."

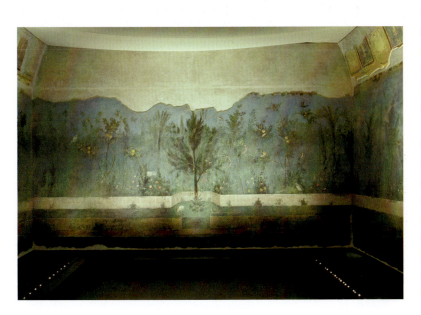

Art as an Illusionistic Window

Artists of the Italian **Renaissance** revived the ideals of the ancient Greeks and Romans, including the desire to impress others with artworks that imitate the real world. The architect and thinker Leon Battista Alberti (1404–1472) wrote in his treatise *On Painting* that artists should design their paintings as illusionary windows through which viewers would be able to perceive a new reality (see Gateway Box: Raphael).

Gateway to Art: Raphael, *The School of Athens*
Architectural Illusion

The Italian artist Raphael (1483–1520) painted *The School of Athens* on one of the walls of the library of Pope Julius II in the Vatican, in Rome, to create the illusion of an architectural space that was separate from the actual room and filled with lifesized figures linking the Classical world with the **humanist** Renaissance (**4.5.2**). The arched frame and sculptural figures (painted by another artist) are all part of the illusion. This **frescoed** wall was designed as part of a larger program including three other paintings, an intricately tiled floor, and a painted ceiling, all choreographed thematically as a backdrop for Pope Julius II's library. The pope's hundreds of books were laid on shelves built directly under the paintings on each of the four walls (these shelves have since been removed).

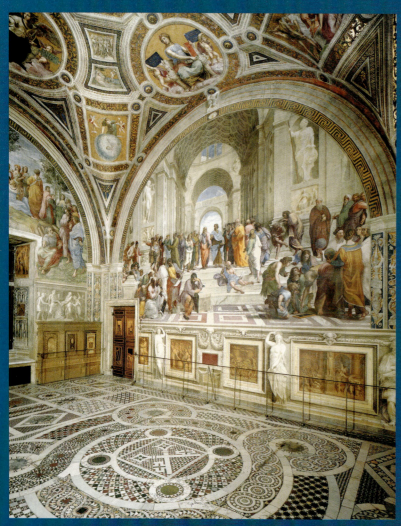

4.5.2 Raphael and assistants, Stanza della Segnatura, Vatican City, Italy, 1509–11

The School of Athens highlights the development of learning in the ancient world, focusing on the great philosophers Plato and Aristotle, who are the central figures in the painting. The other large paintings, turning counterclockwise around the room, are: Parnassus, the mountain sacred to the god Apollo and, in Classical mythology, the home of poetry (on the left wall in **4.5.2**); Disputa, a work that unites Classical ideas with Renaissance Christian theology; and Jurisprudence, which emphasizes law and justice. The thematic decorative scheme reflects the purpose of the room: Julius's books were arranged so their subjects corresponded with the Classical topic of the wall painting above them. Beneath *The School of Athens* were books on philosophy and mathematics; beneath Parnassus, poetry; and so on. The ceiling further unites the themes of the walls through its depiction of four female figures, who personify Philosophy, Poetry, Theology, and Justice. If you stand in the room, the illusion of depth created in *The School of Athens* is even more successful because the paintings on all four walls appear to be separate rooms.

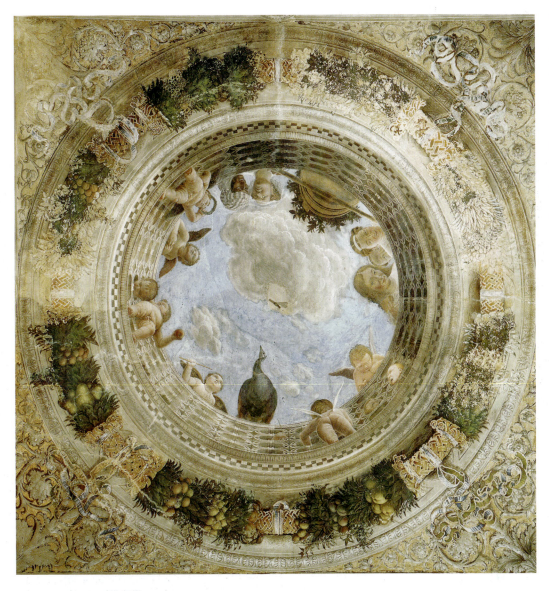

Renaissance: a period of cultural and artistic change in Europe from the fourteenth to the seventeenth century

Oculus: a round opening at the center of a dome

Putto (plural **putti**): a representation of a nude or scantily clad infant angel or boy, common in Renaissance and Baroque art

Balustrade: a railing supported by short pillars

Convex: curved outward, like the exterior of a sphere

Humanism, humanist: the study of such subjects as history, philosophy, languages, and literature, particularly in relation to those of ancient Greece and Rome

Fresco: a technique where the artist paints onto freshly applied plaster. From the Italian *fresco*, "fresh"

4.5.3 Andrea Mantegna, detail of central oculus, ceiling of the Camera degli Sposi. Fresco, 8'9"diameter. Ducal Palace, Mantua, Italy

During the Renaissance, the Italian artist Andrea Mantegna (*c.* 1431–1506) created *trompe l'oeil* paintings for an entire room of the palace of Ludovico Gonzaga, the Duke of Mantua. The chamber, known as the Camera degli Sposi (Room of the Newlyweds), was used both to greet government officials and as a bedroom for the duke and his wife (**4.5.3**). Mantegna painted the walls with scenes of the royal family and of historical victories of the Gonzagas.

In the vaulted ceiling the artist painted the illusion of what seems to be an **oculus** opening onto a blue sky, and surrounded it with figures looking down at the people below. There are **putti** with their chubby baby bodies, some hanging onto the painted **balustrade**, others looking down through the painted oculus. Several young girls peer over the balustrade,

as does an enigmatic turbaned figure. One light-skinned girl wears a white veil, referring to the title of the room and to the duke's recent marriage. Similarly, the prominent peacock symbolizes Juno, the Roman goddess of marriage. All of this activity surprises the viewer below, who may feel particularly nervous about the potted plant precariously held in place with a pole by two smirking young girls.

The Italian artist Francesco Mazzola (1503–1540), known as Parmigianino ("the little one from Parma"), gave a self-portrait to Pope Clement VII in order to attract commissions (**4.5.4**). The painting is on a **convex** piece of wood; holding it, one seems to be looking into a convex mirror—except that one does not see one's own reflection in the artwork, but the portrait of Parmigianino, who studied

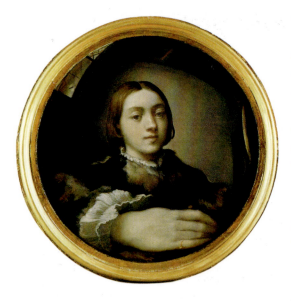

4.5.4 Parmigianino, *Self-Portrait in a Convex Mirror*, *c.* 1524. Oil on wood, 9½" diameter. Kunsthistorisches Museum, Vienna, Austria

himself in an actual convex mirror to create this painting. Parmigianino, however, made one change from what he saw when he studied his reflection. The artist accurately depicted himself as right-handed, but in order to do so he would presumably have had to study his left hand when he actually painted. Parmigianino also featured a portion of the frame of the painting he was creating (visible on the right side of the artwork) in order to heighten the illusion of it being a hand-held mirror. Renaissance painters utilized their skills to create illusions so lifelike that they appeared to be reality rather than art, thus inspiring artists in future generations to create increasingly convincing illusionistic works.

In the nineteenth century, the American painter William M. Harnett (1848–1892) was so skillful at tricking his audiences with *trompe l'oeil* that, when he created a truly convincing dollar bill in one of his paintings, he was investigated for counterfeiting by the US Treasury Department. In *The Old Violin*, Harnett painted a violin and sheet music so that they appear to be hanging from a real wooden door (**4.5.5**). The artist teases viewers, leading us to question what is reality and what is illusion. If we were to read the small piece of torn newspaper so skillfully painted slightly to the left of the bottom of the violin, we would find that the text

is gibberish: it is not a newspaper, but another superb illusion. The only part of the painting that is in fact real is a blue envelope signed by the artist, which he attached to the lower left corner of the painting. When this painting was first exhibited, guards had to be posted around the painting constantly to prevent viewers from reaching out to test if the objects were real. While some artists, such as Harnett, thrived working within the rules of illusionism, others found the obsession with illusion and perspective restrictive and somewhat absurd (see Box: Satirizing Illusionism).

The British artist Julian Beever (b. 1960) applies a special form of *trompe l'oeil* known as **anamorphosis** to his sidewalk art. An anamorphic image is one that is stretched and distorted, but becomes clear and realistic when

Anamorphosis: the distorted representation of an object so that it appears correctly proportioned only when viewed from one particular position

4.5.5 William M. Harnett, *The Old Violin*, 1886. Oil on canvas, 38 × 23⅝". National Gallery of Art, Washington, D.C.

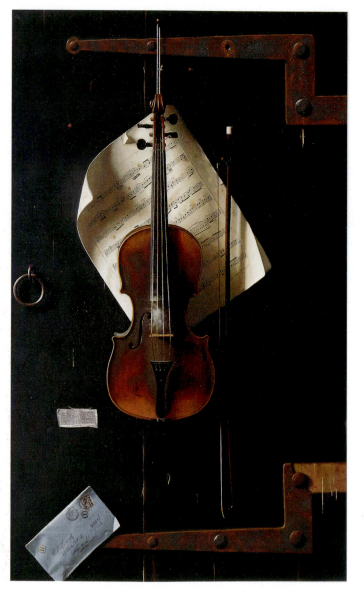

Satirizing Illusionism: Hogarth's *False Perspective*

In this work, William Hogarth (1697–1764), an eighteenth-century British artist, **satirizes** the traditional training of painters who were taught to use the rules of **perspective** to create believable spaces (4.5.6). In this **frontispiece**, Hogarth applies these rules in order to break them. He thus creates the illusion of a space that is, in fact, impossible. On the bottom of the print, he wrote: "Whoever makes a Design without the Knowledge of Perspective will be liable to such Absurdities as are shown in this Frontispiece."

See if you can find these spatial impossibilities:

- The woman in the window of her building is lighting the pipe of the man standing on top of the hill. Lower in the image, we can see a tree, and horses pulling a wagon, between the building and the base of the hill. How can the woman reach the man?
- The man in the right foreground must have quite an extraordinarily long fishing line in order to reach beyond the rod of the man in the distance.
- In the lower left, the sheep closest to us are smaller than those further away.
- Similarly, the trees at the bottom of the hill get larger as they recede into the distance, suggesting that the bird on the furthest tree is improbably big.
- The church in the distance appears to be both grounded on land and floating on water.

- The man in the boat in the center of the scene appears to aim his gun at a swan, but instead shoots the underside of the bridge.
- The sign on the building in the foreground seems to be hanging behind the trees on the hill in the background.
- The barrel behind the large man in the foreground shows both the top and bottom of the container.
- The **vanishing point** of the grid upon which the man in the foreground stands is projecting into the viewer's space, rather than receding into the pictorial space, making it seem as if the man should be falling forward out of the picture.

Satire: work of art that exposes the weaknesses and mistakes of its subjects to ridicule

Perspective: the creation of the illusion of depth in a two-dimensional image by using mathematical principles

Frontispiece: an illustration facing the title-page in a book

Vanishing point: a point in a work of art at which imaginary sight lines appear to converge, suggesting depth

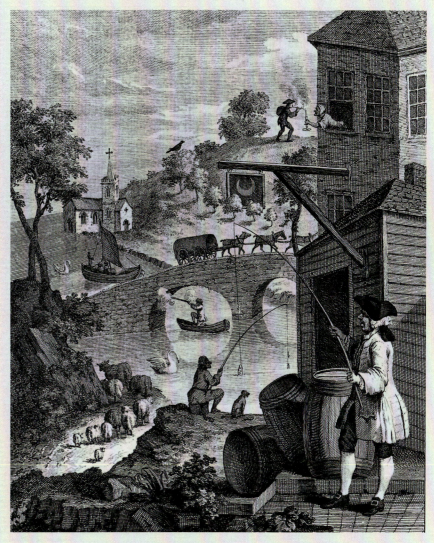

4.5.6 William Hogarth, *False Perspective*. Engraving from *Dr. Brook Taylor's Method of Perspective Made Easy, Both in Theory and in Practice*, 1754

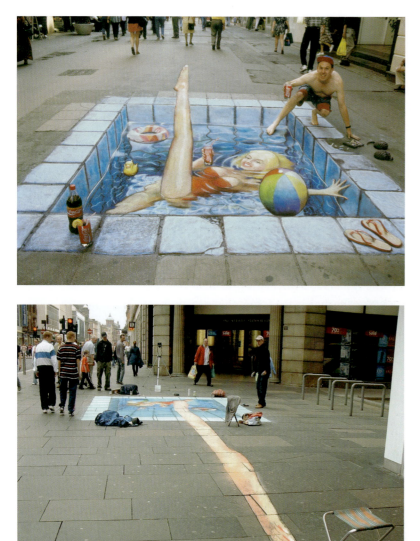

Illusionism as Trickery: Illusion in Three Dimensions

> With wonderful skill, he carved a figure, brilliantly, out of snow-white ivory…and fell in love with his own creation.
>
> (The ancient Roman poet Ovid on Pygmalion's carving of Galatea)

In Classical mythology, the sculptor Pygmalion created a statue of a woman so fine and beautiful that he fell in love with her. He dressed and pampered her, believing her more perfect than any human woman. He begged the gods to grant him a wife as perfect as his statue, and the goddess of love, Venus, granted his wish by bringing the statue to life. The myth suggests that an artist's love for his work, and his skill at re-creating the natural world, can create illusions even more divine than those made by nature.

Like Pygmalion, sculptors can use their skill to create works that appear to be convincingly real, and that share the physical and psychological space of those who observe them. Duane Hanson's (1925–1996) lifesize museum guard tricks many visitors into thinking that he is there to keep a watchful eye on the art, but in truth he is part of the art himself (**4.5.8**). Hanson's sculptures are realistic likenesses of Americans doing everyday activities, such as working, shopping, sunbathing, or sleeping. By choosing to replicate people and actions familiar to the viewer, Hanson elevates the importance of daily life and social situations to that of a subject worthy of contemplation. Although his works are incredibly true to life, all of the figures, including this museum guard, direct their gaze away from the viewer, allowing him or her to observe the sculpture closely without feeling as if the sculpture is staring back.

In ancient Greece, the designers of the Parthenon understood that the human eye could play tricks on the beholder. They used their knowledge of mathematics to ensure that the building would appear just as they wished it to (**4.5.9a**). Because of the great size of the

4.5.7a (above top) Julian Beever, *Woman in Pool*, drawn in Brussels, Belgium, 1992. Colored chalks, 14'9¼" × 13'1½" (correct viewing point)

4.5.7b (above) Julian Beever, *Woman in Pool*, drawn in Glasgow, Scotland, 1994. Colored chalks, 14'9¼" × 13'1½" (incorrect viewing point)

viewed from a single, oblique angle. Beever's chalk drawings confront passersby with what appear to be convincing scenes taking place in three-dimensional space. When his *Woman in Pool* is viewed from the right vantage point, it appears that a woman is lying back in a swimming pool, drink in hand, kicking her leg in the air (**4.5.7a**). But when it is viewed from the opposite direction, the illusion is destroyed and one can see that Beever used extreme **foreshortening** to represent the woman's leg (**4.5.7b**). The only genuinely three-dimensional element in the photograph of the illusionistic drawing (**4.5.7a**) is the artist himself, who is holding a drink and has his foot placed flat on the pavement.

temple, the base and columns would appear warped unless the architects could adjust their design to counteract these naturally occurring optical illusions. For example, the **stylobate**, or platform on which the columns stand, would appear to sag if it were constructed as a precisely straight horizontal structure. To counteract this, the architects created a slight upward swelling in the center of the stylobate, which makes the base of the temple seem perfectly horizontal when we look at it.

Several other visual manipulations were utilized in the design of the columns. For example, the columns of the Parthenon actually swell at about mid-height (**4.5.9b**). This optical trick prevents them from appearing, when looked at from a distance, to be hourglass-shaped, which would happen if the columns were flawlessly straight sided. This swelling at the midpoint of such columns is called **entasis**. In addition, the columns are not perfectly vertical but actually slightly tilted. If they were extended into the air, the implied lines created by the four corner columns would eventually intersect about a mile and a half into the sky. Finally, the columns are not all spaced equidistantly, as they appear to be; those closer to the corners have less space between them. This is another visual trick used to compensate for the optical illusion that makes columns near

Foreshortening: a perspective technique that depicts a form at a very oblique (often dramatic) angle to the viewer in order to show depth in space
Stylobate: the uppermost platform of a Classical temple, on which the columns stand
Entasis: the slight swelling or bulge at the midpoint of a column

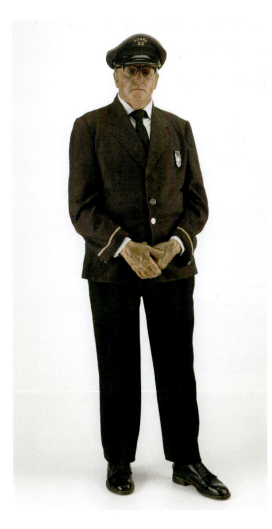

4.5.8 Duane Hanson, *Museum Guard*, 1975. Polyester, fiberglass, oil, and vinyl, 5'9" × 21" × 13". The Nelson-Atkins Museum of Art, Kansas City, Missouri

4.5.9a (below left) Kallikrates and Iktinos, Parthenon, 447–432 BCE, Acropolis, Athens, Greece

4.5.9b (below right) Diagram showing the optical illusions utilized in the Parthenon

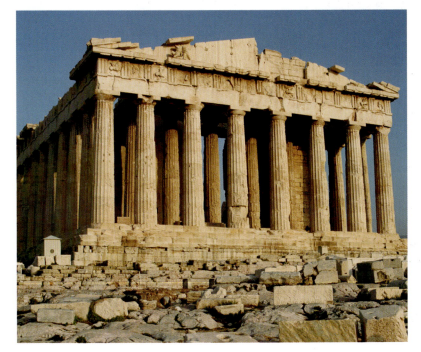

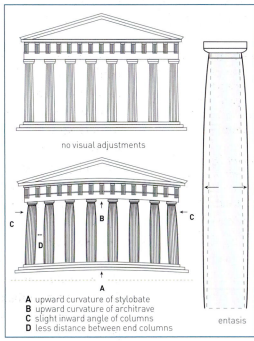

no visual adjustments

A upward curvature of stylobate
B upward curvature of architrave
C slight inward angle of columns
D less distance between end columns

entasis

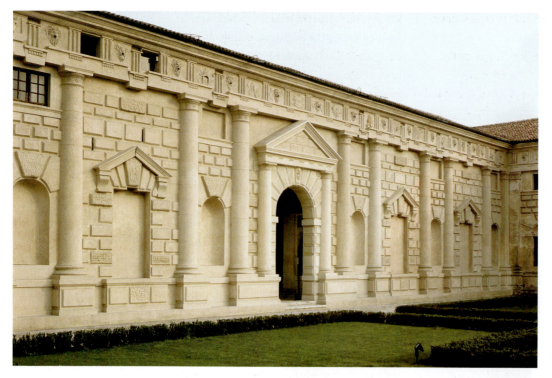

4.5.10 Giulio Romano, Palazzo del Tè, exterior, 1524–34, Mantua, Italy

4.5.11 Giulio Romano, *Fall of the Giants*, 1526–35. Fresco, Sale dei Giganti, Palazzo del Tè, Mantua, Italy

the end of a row appear further apart than ones near the middle.

Architectural and two-dimensional illusory techniques were utilized by the Italian artist and architect Giulio Romano (*c.* 1499–1546), who designed a villa for the same Gonzaga family that had commissioned the decoration of the Camera degli Sposi from Mantegna (see **4.5.3**). As both architect and interior painter for the Palazzo del Tè in Mantua (**4.5.10**), Giulio Romano designed a building that subtly broke many of the rules of Classical architecture, with the result that, when looked at closely, the villa appears to be unstable. Giulio Romano achieved this playful illusion by taking Classical architectural elements used in such buildings as the Parthenon, and arranging them to create the impression of instability rather than the solidity normally expected of architecture. The **architraves** that rest on the columns are narrower than would normally be the case; but, even stranger, they seem to break in the middle rather than reaching from one column to the next, as they should. As a result, some of the **triglyphs** in the **frieze** above the columns appear to be slipping down, as if they might even fall to the ground. The material of the structure itself is also an illusion; rather than marble or stone, which were normally used

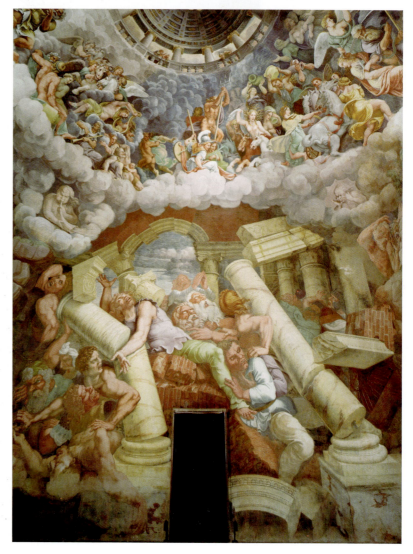

for luxurious buildings, the exterior is **stucco**-covered brick.

The explanation for the odd design of the Palazzo del Tè's exterior becomes apparent when one enters the building (**4.5.11**). A painted scene of the *Fall of the Giants* playfully suggests why the exterior appears to be falling apart. The painting depicts an episode from Greek mythology, when the gods defeated the giants in battle. Having been trained by Raphael, and having worked as his assistant on his paintings for the Vatican (see p. 612), Giulio Romano built on the techniques of his master for this powerful painted illusion. The building in Giulio Romano's painting appears to be tumbling down, crushing the struggling giants below. The powerful wind, shown at the viewer's upper left blowing a trumpet, is controlled by the gods in the clouds of Mount Olympus, and therefore protected from the turmoil below.

Illusion and the Transformation of Ideas

Many twentieth-century artists rejected the earlier ideal that painting should aim to recreate three-dimensional reality (see Box: Cubism: The Fracturing of Illusion, p. 620). In *The Human Condition*, the Belgian artist René Magritte (1898–1967) asks the viewer to question what appears to be a painting of a landscape on an easel, which has been placed before a window that looks out onto the same landscape (**4.5.12**). We realize, however, that the scene outside the window is also an invention; the window and drapes and the painting on the easel are both part of the painted canvas that we behold. The artist explains,

> [The tree] exists for the spectator, both inside the room in the painting, and outside in the real landscape, in thought. Which is how we see the world: we see it as being outside ourselves even though it is only a mental representation of it that we experience inside ourselves.

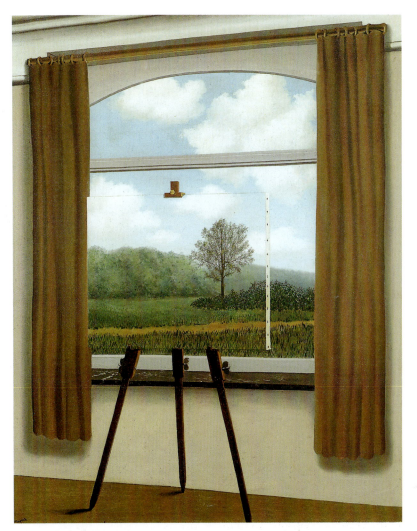

Magritte confronts us with issues of representation and truth and refers directly to the achievements in **linear perspective** made by the artists of the Renaissance. What at first seems an extension of the desire to create a convincing view through a window is shattered when Magritte forces us to consider what is real, and what is only of the mind. Magritte showed that the "illusionistic window" of the Renaissance is indeed only a canvas. By so doing, he opened the door for artists to make paintings with purposes other than the representation of perfect three-dimensional illusions of subjects as if they were real life. As Magritte demonstrated, painting can be a powerful mode for expressing complex ideas, rather than solely re-creating what we see with our eyes.

In a way that is similar to Magritte, certain artists often use intensely realistic illusionistic techniques to inspire the viewer to take a more contemplative approach to looking at art. The

4.5.12 René Magritte, *The Human Condition*, 1933. Oil on canvas, 39⅜ × 31⅞ × ⅝". National Gallery of Art, Washington D. C.

Architrave: a beam that rests on the top of a row of columns
Triglyph: a projecting block carved with three raised bands, which alternates with figurative reliefs in a frieze
Frieze: the strip that goes around the top of a building, often filled with sculptural ornamentation
Stucco: a coarse plaster designed to give the appearance of stone
Linear perspective: a system using converging imaginary sight lines to create the illusion of depth

Cubism: The Fracturing of Illusion

After French artist Georges Braque (1882–1963) saw Spanish artist Pablo Picasso's now-famous painting *Les Demoiselles d'Avignon* (1907) for the first time in 1907, the two artists worked together daily, consciously developing a new style of art. Their objective was to move beyond the traditional depictions of previous centuries, in which paintings were illusionistic renderings drawn using conventional systems of perspective. This style became known as **Cubism**, and its first phase can be described as an analysis and fracturing of **form** and **planes** of depth using only a **monochromatic** palette.

As Braque's *Man with a Guitar* (4.5.13) shows, Cubist art is not totally **non-objective**, or non-representational; some element of the artist's subject is always identifiable. Imagine each object is a cube with a top, bottom, and sides. Cubist artists select portions (or sides) of each object to represent, and Cubist works, including Braque's painting, often show different faces of an object simultaneously. While it is difficult to find in the painting a clear representation of a man or a guitar, lines and shapes suggest the form of a human figure. At the edges of the figure are scrolls recalling parts of an instrument or sheets of music. Braque includes, in the upper left, a seemingly three-dimensional rendering of a rope, the tail of which hangs from a nail. By creating one clear element of illusionism, Braque was able to highlight the intentional breaking down of three dimensions elsewhere in the painting. Cubist artists were interested in emphasizing the two-dimensional painted surface rather than recreating the illusion of three-dimensionality.

4.5.13 Georges Braque, *Man with a Guitar*, 1911–12. Oil on canvas, 45¾ x 31⅞". MoMA, New York

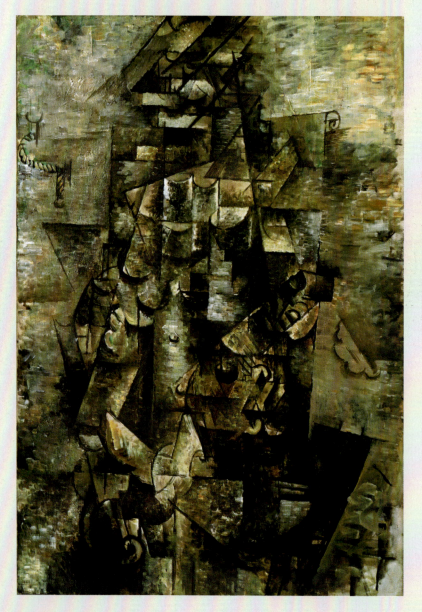

Cubism, Cubist: a twentieth-century art movement that favored a new perspective emphasizing geometric forms
Form: an object that can be defined in three dimensions (height, width, and depth)
Plane: a flat surface, often implied by the composition
Monochromatic: having one or more values of one color
Non-objective: art that does not depict a recognizable subject

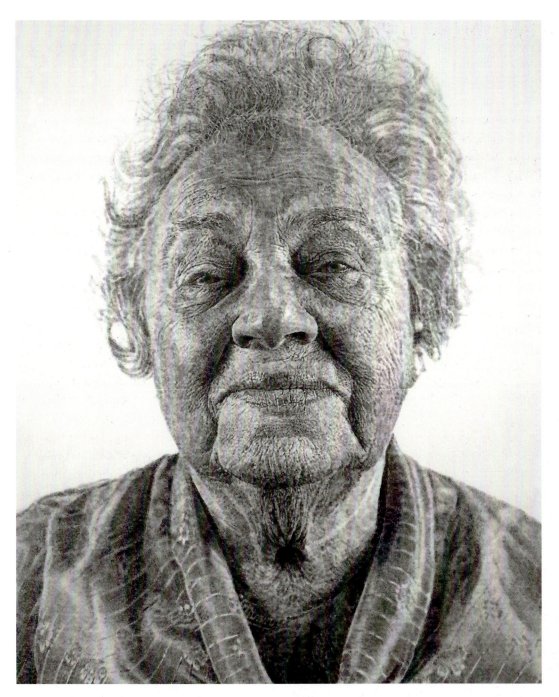

4.5.14 Chuck Close, *Fanny/Fingerpainting*, 1985. Oil on canvas, 8'6" × 7'. National Gallery of Art, Washington, D.C.

Photorealist American artist Chuck Close (b. 1940) creates artworks that inspire us to question what we see. As a child, one of Close's favorite pastimes was to entertain neighbors and schoolmates by doing magic tricks. As an adult artist, he has become known for manipulating portraits of friends and family. He begins his creative process by taking photographs of them, which he then transforms into artworks in another **medium**. For example, although *Fanny/Fingerpainting* looks like a photograph, Close actually hand-painted an image of his wife's grandmother using only his thumb- and fingerprints (**4.5.14**). As with most of his artworks, Close laid a grid over the original photograph of the subject, and then carefully enlarged and copied each block so that the entire image fills an 8 ft. 6 in. by 7 ft. canvas. The original photograph is thus transformed into a much bigger image that appears to be a photographic enlargement produced by technology. Close's process, while still quite mechanical, remains personal because of the use of the artist's own hands in the act of creation.

Medium (plural **media**): the material on or from which an artist chooses to make a work of art

The painting *Marilyn (Vanitas)* (**4.5.15**) by Photorealist Audrey Flack (b. 1931) was made fifteen years after the American film actress Marilyn Monroe died of a drug overdose in 1962; it is a homage to Marilyn as well as a comment on human mortality. A photograph on the right, which is also reflected in the mirror on the left, shows Monroe's public persona as a blonde beauty. Mirrors, a reference to vanity, are often used in art to symbolize the transience of youth, beauty, and life. The calendar, clock, and hourglass also represent the passing of time. As such they too are reminders of the brevity of life—as are the burning candle and the flower and fruit, all of which live only a short time. An artwork that serves to remind us of death and the transience of life is known as a **vanitas**.

The hyper-realistic colors and floating objects within Flack's painting give it an otherworldly quality—a dramatic contrast to the objects that symbolize time. By including a childhood portrait of herself with her brother, the artist further wishes to remind herself that the pleasures of her life are as fleeting as those of the movie idol. The mirrored compact, makeup, and pearls refer to Marilyn Monroe's mask to the world. Although the painting appears to be a photograph, it is an illusion, just like Earthly beauty and the glamorization of famous figures.

The painting *A Bar at the Folies-Bergère* (**4.5.16**), by French artist Édouard Manet (1832–1883), also makes use of a mirror to suggest that the viewer should question whether what he or she sees is real or an illusion. The Folies-Bergère was one of the most popular

4.5.15 Audrey Flack, *Marilyn (Vanitas)*, 1977. Oil over acrylic on canvas, 8 × 8′. Collection of the University of Arizona Museum of Art, Tucson

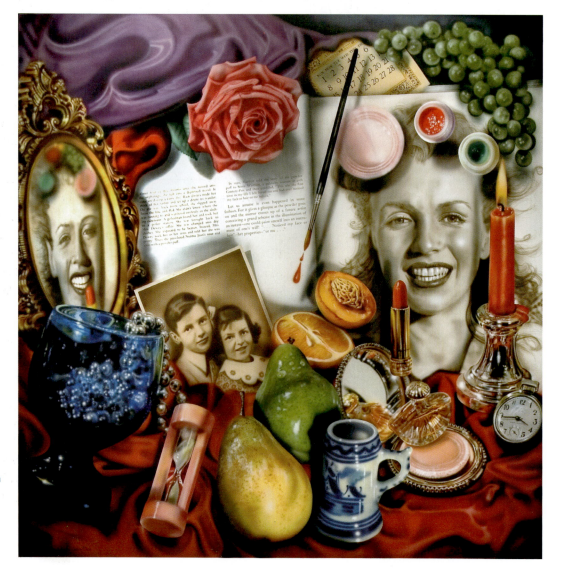

Vanitas: a genre of painting that emphasizes the transient nature of Earthly materials and beauty; often seen in still-life painting

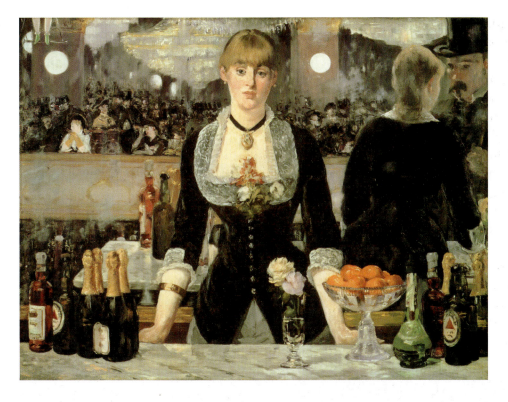

4.5.16 Édouard Manet, *A Bar at the Folies-Bergère*, 1882. Oil on canvas, 37⅞ × 51¼". Courtauld Gallery, London, England

bars and entertainment houses in Paris in the nineteenth century; the club offered entertainment by dancers, singers, and even trapeze artists (a pair of feet can be seen hanging in the upper left of Manet's painting), all dressed in revealing and provocative clothes. The blurry background behind the barmaid suggests she is standing in front of a mirror, which reflects the Parisian club scene she is facing. Discrepancies in the reflection, however, make one question the accuracy of what one sees. For example, the bottles next to the barmaid on the left of the canvas appear to be placed in a different order and in a different place in the reflection behind her. In addition, some viewers question whether the posture of the barmaid on the far right is an accurate reflection of the barmaid looking out at us. Manet certainly had the skill to depict perspective precisely, so one must consider why he chose to create such an ambiguous reflection.

Several interpretations of *A Bar at the Folies-Bergère* have been suggested. If we assume that the figure on the right is indeed a reflection of the barmaid, then we viewers are standing in the place of the man in the top hat to whom she is talking. He is presumably a client. It was common for the female entertainers and barmaids at the Folies-Bergère to be hired by the clientele for sexual favors. Could that be what they are talking about? The ambiguities in the reflection may be a way for the artist to suggest different emotional states in the barmaid, contrasting her personal experience or feelings with her external appearance. Some have argued that she appears to be much more engaged in the reflected image than she is as she stands before us in the center of the painting. Her gaze leaves us questioning her state of mind: is she sad, distracted, or bored? Another interpretation suggests that the artist is depicting a fantasy. By utilizing the tools of illusionism, Manet created a psychological mystery.

Discussion Questions

1. Look at artworks by René Magritte (for example, *The Human Condition* in this chapter (**4.5.12**) and *The Treachery of Images* on p. 82 (**1.3.1**). Write a short essay explaining what Magritte was saying about the Renaissance idea of the "illusionistic window."

2. Select one of the artists in this chapter and study other works he or she has made. Does the artist use illusionism frequently? What do you think is his or her motivation for so doing?

3. Study Hogarth's *False Perspective* (**4.5.6**). Now draw a scene from your imagination and include in it at least three examples of altered visual reality like those included in Hogarth's print.

Images Related to 4.5: Art and Illusion

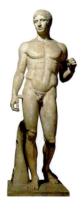

3.1.25 *Doryphoros* (Roman version), 120–50 BCE, p. 382

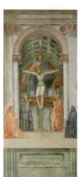

1.3.20 Masaccio, *Trinity*, c. 1425–26, p. 95

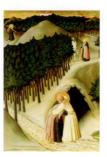

1.5.1 *The Meeting of St. Anthony and St. Paul*, c. 1430–35, p. 119

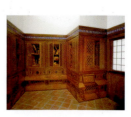

2.6.20 Francesco di Giorgio Martini, *Studiolo*, c. 1480, p. 304

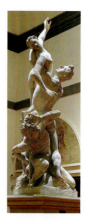

2.4.2a Giambologna, *Rape of a Sabine*, 1583, p. 249

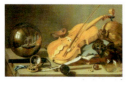

4.3.8 Pieter Claesz (attr.), *Vanitas (Still Life with Glass Globe)*, c. 1628, p. 593

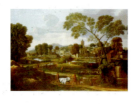

3.6.28 Nicolas Poussin, *The Funeral of Phocion*, 1648, p. 487

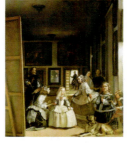

1.10.11 Diego de Silva y Velázquez, *Las Meninas*, c. 1656, p. 190

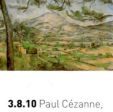

3.8.10 Paul Cézanne, *Mont Sainte-Victoire*, 1886–88, p. 521

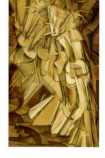

3.8.36 Marcel Duchamp, *Nude Descending a Staircase...*, 1912, p. 536

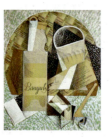

3.8.24 Juan Gris, *Bottle of Banyuls*, 1914, p. 529

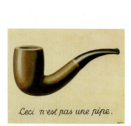

1.3.1 René Magritte, *The Treachery of Images*, 1929, p. 82

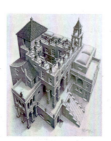

1.3.23 M. C. Escher, *Ascending and Descending*, 1960, p. 97

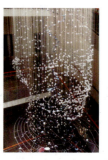

1.2.10a Ralph Helmick and Stuart Schechter, *Ghostwriter*, 1994, p. 73

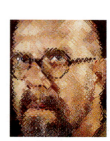

1.9.5a Chuck Close, *Self Portrait*, 1997, p. 170

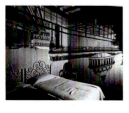

2.8.2 Abelardo Morell, *Camera Obscura Image...*, 1999, p. 321

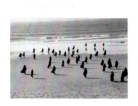

3.9.20b Shirin Neshat, *Rapture*, 1999, p. 554

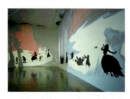

2.10.12 Kara Walker, *Insurrection!*, 2000, p. 362

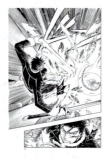

1.1.3 CLAMP, page from *Tsubasa RESERVoir CHRoNiCLE*, 2007, p. 51

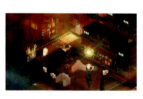

1.3.16 Screenshot from *Transistor*, computer game, 2014, p. 91

4.6

Art of Political Leaders and Rulers

Idealized: represented as perfect in form or character, corresponding to an ideal
Propaganda: art that promotes an ideology or cause
Iconic: Possessing established and widely recognizable characteristics

4.6.1 George Gower, *Elizabeth I* (known as the *Armada Portrait*), 1588. Oil on panel, 41¼ × 52⅜". Woburn Abbey, Bedfordshire, England

Political leaders have always made use of works of art to help define and assert their power and to influence their people. Seeking to demonstrate supreme control, leaders have used artworks to highlight their right to rule, sometimes even to claim that their authority has been granted by the gods. Leaders are often portrayed in an **idealized** way—dressed in elaborate clothing, placed centrally in the composition, depicted larger than other figures, and positioned so that the viewer looks up at them. National leaders have frequently commissioned artworks to reinforce their reputations as skillful commanders and to project an image of military strength. Portraits can be a potent **propaganda** tool for sustaining

a leader's power. Such images are also potentially revealing of what a society might be looking for, or expecting, from its leader. This chapter explores how heads of state and other political leaders have seen themselves and how they wished to be viewed by both friend and foe.

Iconic Portraiture of Leaders

What image comes to mind when you think of a great leader? Artists have endeavored for centuries to develop ways to show leaders as figures with power and authority, deserving the respect and trust of the people they govern. Portraits vary in the degree to which they accurately depict the physical characteristics of the sitter, conveying instead the qualities a leader wants to be perceived to embody. The following portraits of Queen Elizabeth I, George Washington, and Napoleon Bonaparte have become **iconic**—recognizable worldwide for so strikingly depicting the historical impact of the leaders they represent. As you read about them, consider whether there is a difference in the way the woman is portrayed and what the image suggests about her power, and the way the images of male leadership convey their qualities as rulers.

Elizabeth I became queen of England in 1558 and maintained her rule until her death in 1603, despite the challenges of inheriting a religiously divided country and a poor economy,

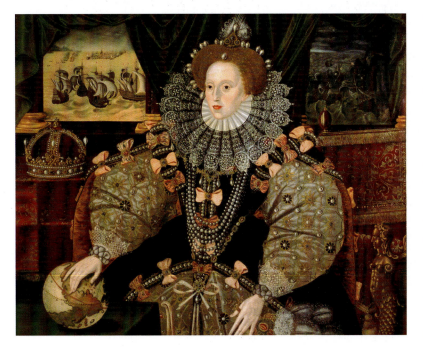

and being declared an illegitimate child of Henry VIII after her mother's execution. For all these obstacles, Elizabeth's reign was relatively peaceful, culturally rich, and saw England united under Protestantism. As an unmarried woman, she risked being seen as weak and unable to rule; however, Elizabeth used her status to her own advantage, and through art she was able to promote her chastity as evidence of her commitment first and foremost to her country. One of the great successes of her reign came in 1588 when the Spanish Armada, a fleet of more than a hundred ships—commanded by Philip II, whose one-time marriage proposal Elizabeth had rejected—tried to invade England only to be defeated by the waiting English navy.

In the *Armada Portrait* (**4.6.1**, p. 625), painted to commemorate the English victory, the queen is shown in a rich gown covered with bows and pearls. The largest pearl hangs over her genital region, symbolizing the chastity she has maintained. She sits next to her royal crown, with her right hand on a globe, signifying English naval might throughout the world, and her desire to expand to the Americas. The scenes behind her depict events from the Armada. On the left, the English ships are stationed ready to attack the arriving Spanish fleet. On the right, in a now stormy sky, we see Spanish ships wrecking along a coastal shore, which in real life many of them did while trying to escape England's fire power.

It was a unique challenge to portray George Washington, the first president of the United States. Initially, attempts had been made to depict Washington in the manner of an ancient god, sculpted in white marble, wrapped in **Classical** drapery, and seated high atop a throne. Washington and many citizens argued that such godlike images of a ruler enthroned and partially nude did not represent the ideals of the young country of America. More fittingly, Washington requested that Jean-Antoine Houdon (1741–1828), one of the most respected sculptors of contemporary figures, carve a portrait of him in his military uniform (**4.6.2**).

Houdon did, however, maintain certain elements adopted from ancient sculpture: white marble was used, and Washington stood using

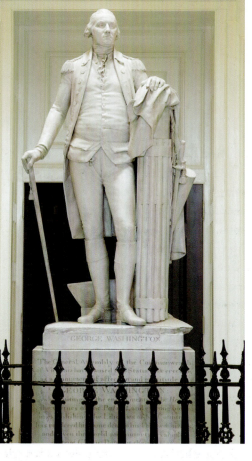

OLD HOUSE CHAMBER

4.6.2 Jean-Antoine Houdon, *George Washington*, 1788–92. Marble, 6'2" high. Virginia State Capitol, Richmond, Virginia

a **contrapposto** stance adopted from ancient Greek figures. Washington's left hand is placed upon a *fasces* (a bundle of wooden rods), which was a symbol of power in ancient Rome. There are thirteen rods, which represent the number of US colonies; they are bound together in unity. Washington is shown with his sword set aside and his cape removed. He resigned from the position of Commander-in-Chief of the Continental Army after the Revolutionary War (1775–83) and returned to his farm (a plow is behind him in this sculpture), before being appointed America's first president in 1789. Washington's gaze—slightly to the left, upward, and into the distance—has become so iconic that it has often been repeated in other portraits, particularly of democratic leaders.

Classical: art that conforms to Greek and Roman models
Contrapposto: a pose in sculpture in which the upper part of the body twists in one direction and the lower part in another
Romanticism: movement in nineteenth-century European culture, concerned with the power of the imagination and greatly valuing intense feeling
Absolute, Absolutism: when applied to a ruler or monarch, the belief that he or she holds the ultimate power and that this derives from the will of God

During his reign as emperor of France, from 1804 to 1815, Napoleon Bonaparte (1769–1821) had painters create hundreds of portraits of him in an effort to persuade the French people of his leadership skills, military might, and humanitarian efforts. Many of these artworks were masterpieces of propaganda, fueling the French peoples' support of the emperor. Jacques-Louis David (1748–1825) became Napoleon's favorite painter, and his portrait *Napoleon Crossing the Alps* (**4.6.3**) became representative of Napoleon's leadership as he conquered much of the world.

In *Napoleon Crossing the Alps*, David displays the powerful force of nature, a characteristic of **Romanticism**, and the French leader's ability to withstand the wind and snow as he leads his troops. Here the painter memorializes an actual event, as Napoleon and his men victoriously crossed the dangerous Alpine pass of St. Bernard to enter and eventually conquer Italy. Although the journey was real, the artist deliberately glamorizes the moment, heightening its dramatic impact. David borrowed the military pose of a ruler atop a horse from the equestrian monument tradition, popular in portraits of the emperors of ancient Rome.

The horse struggles against the powerful wind, yet Napoleon fearlessly points toward the snow-covered mountains that his troops must cross: by implication, the artist suggests the leader can master not only his horse but also nature. Napoleon's name is carved into the rock ("Bonaparte"), above the names of two earlier military leaders—the great Carthaginian general Hannibal and the Holy Roman Emperor Karolus Magnus, also known as Charlemagne—who had crossed the same treacherous path.

Art to Demonstrate Absolute Power

A ruler with **absolute** power is one who has the freedom to govern as he or she pleases. How is such unlimited power achieved? Often, leaders of such regimes—the **Byzantine** emperor Justinian, for example—are believed to have

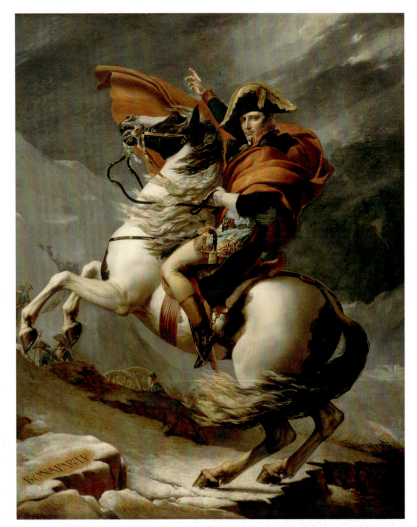

been given their authority by divine powers, and therefore frequently determine the customs, religion, and social structure of the people they rule. Even when rulers seem unjust or extreme, their subjects are less likely to rebel if their authority is believed to have derived from the gods. In ancient Maya culture, ancient Egypt, and many cultures in Africa, including the Chokwe, discussed on p. 630, rulers were also believed to be descendants of the gods. In order to maintain their authority, rulers often use imagery to spread the stories they want their people to remember.

The Byzantine (late Roman) Emperor Justinian used imagery to show the presence of his power throughout his empire. Justinian is remembered as a remarkable military and civil leader, as well as a great **patron** of the arts who funded the building of hundreds of churches. Portraits of Justinian, who ruled in the sixth century, were often placed in these churches to

4.6.3 Jacques-Louis David, *Napoleon Crossing the Alps* (or *Bonaparte Crossing the St. Bernard Pass, 20 May, 1800*), 1801. Oil on canvas, 8'9¼" × 7'3¾". Châteaux de Versailles et de Trianon, Versailles, France

Byzantine: relating to the East Roman empire, centered on Constantinople (modern-day Istanbul) from the fifth century CE to 1453
Patron: an organization or individual who sponsors the creation of works of art

Gateway to Art: Colossal Olmec Heads
Portraits of Powerful Rulers

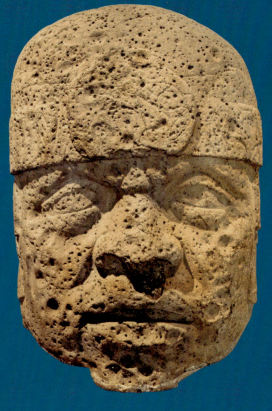

4.6.4 Colossal head, Olmec, 1200–600 BCE. Museo Nacional de Antropología, Mexico City, Mexico

The distinctive facial features and individual headdresses of the seventeen colossal Olmec heads suggest that each one represented a real person (**4.6.4**). Scholars think they probably depict specific Olmec rulers. The effort it must have taken to create each sculpture is evidence of the power of the ruler. The material used to make the colossal heads is a hard volcanic stone known as basalt. In San Lorenzo, Mexico, where ten colossal heads have been found, the stone would have been transported more than 50 miles over rivers and marshy terrain, suggesting that the ruler had a wealth of resources at his disposal. Many Olmec heads have been discovered underground, indicating that they were buried as part of a ritual. In addition, many of the heads have been mutilated or carved from the stone of Olmec "altar-throne" sculptures, leading some scholars to conclude that old sculptures were damaged, buried, or recycled to become different sculptures when a new ruler took power. Scholars cannot say with certainty why this was done, but it seems likely that the burial and mutilation of Olmec monuments occurred when the ruler died. Although there is much we will never know about why these heads were made, it seems clear that they are intended to express the power of mighty rulers.

demonstrate his patronage as well as his power, which was believed to have been granted by God. In the Church of San Vitale, in Ravenna, Italy, there is a glorious colored-glass mosaic of the emperor, which he probably never saw (**4.6.5**).

Justinian stands in the center of the **mosaic**, wearing the imperial color purple. On either side of him are clergy in white robes. To his far right are soldiers, who display a large shield that bears the Greek letters for Christ (*chi-rho*), emphasizing Justinian's role as a Christian military leader. There are other Christian symbols in the mosaic: the men to the left of the emperor hold a cross, a copy of the gospels (the first four books of the New Testament), and a censer used to burn incense in church services. Justinian holds the bread used to represent the body of Christ in the communion service, and the mosaic itself is displayed near the altar where the service would take place. Interestingly, one other figure in this mosaic is given special recognition: the local bishop, Maximianus, who arranged the commission, organized the composition so that his figure was the only one identified in writing on the image (his name is written above his portrait), and so that his feet should be placed slightly in front of the emperor. One wonders what Justinian would have thought, had he seen the mosaic. Justinian himself needed no such label: the imperial robe, in addition to his crown and halo, were enough to identify the ruler.

In ancient Maya culture, a ruler's power was reinforced through prayers and sacrifices to the

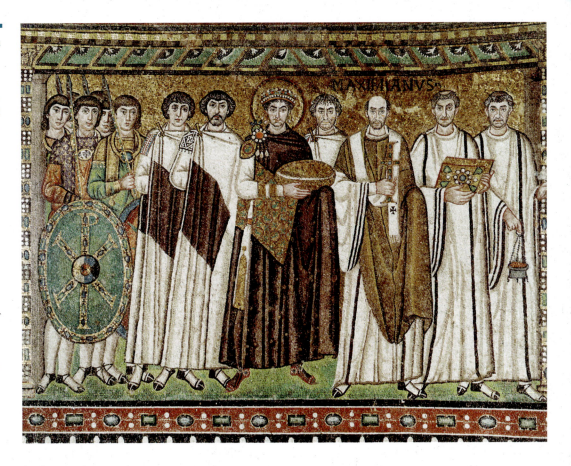

4.6.5 (right) Mosaic depicting Emperor Justinian, *c.* 547 CE. Glass. San Vitale, Ravenna, Italy

4.6.6 (below) Maya lintel showing Shield Jaguar and Lady Xoc, *c.* 725 CE. Limestone, 43 × 30". British Museum, London, England

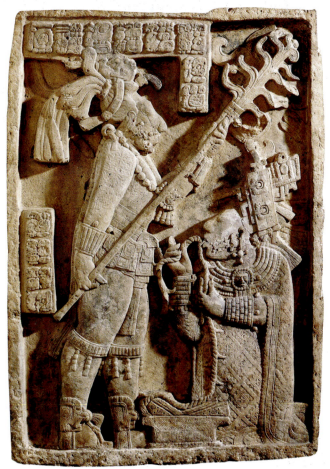

gods. An intricately carved **lintel** from a temple in Yaxchilán in southern Mexico shows Lady Xoc, wife of the ruler Shield Jaguar, kneeling before her husband and pulling a rope covered with thorns through a hole in her tongue in a bloodletting ritual (**4.6.6**). The writing around the edges of the scene tells us the names of the figures and describes what is taking place. According to the symbols above the king's head, this ritual took place on October 28, 709 CE.

Bloodletting led to a hallucinogenic state, in which the participant imagined that he or she was seeing things. The Maya may have enhanced such states by fasting and taking drugs; they believed that these rituals caused spiritual visions. Shield Jaguar and Lady Xoc prayed to the sun god; they both wear his image on their **pectorals**. This ceremony may be related to a specific battle, as Shield Jaguar, dressed as a warrior, wears an elaborate headdress that includes the shrunken head of a victim sacrificed to the gods. He holds a large burning torch to light the evening ritual.

This lintel is one of three that depict specific bloodletting ceremonies undergone by Lady

Xoc (each with different dates); they were placed together over a doorway in a temple dedicated to her. Although Lady Xoc is shown as clearly subordinate to Shield Jaguar, her elaborate costume, her role in the ritual, and the fact that this bloodletting scene was imitated in artworks of later generations, highlight that she too was a person of importance.

The ancient Egyptians believed their kings, known as pharaohs, were descended from the gods. The Pharaoh Akhenaten, like Shield Jaguar, ruled under the authority of a sun god. Although previous pharaohs had worshiped many gods, Akhenaten, who ruled in the fourteenth century BCE, used his supreme power to recognize only the sun god Aten. Akhenaten's beliefs are clearly stated in a **sunken relief**, originally painted, that depicts the pharaoh on the left, his wife and trusted adviser Nefertiti opposite him, and their three daughters cradled on their laps (**4.6.7**). The sun is carved deeper than anything else in the relief, which signifies visually its importance as a god, and its rays emanate toward the family, suggesting the sun god's support of the royal

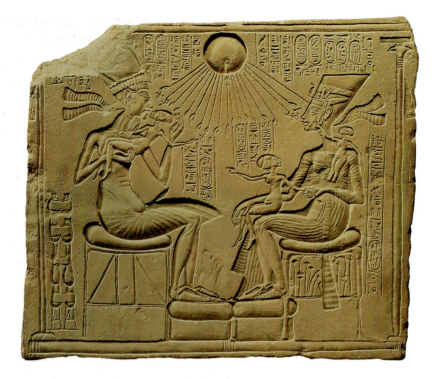

family. The flames at the end of the rays are small hands, some holding an *ankh*, the character that symbolizes life in ancient Egyptian writing. The depiction of Nefertiti as almost the same size as her husband indicates her importance. Some historians believe she ruled the kingdom jointly with Akhenaten.

The sculpture *Chibinda Ilunga*, made by the Chokwe people of Central Africa, depicts a legendary leader from the seventeenth century who was a masterful hunter, a successful king, and a descendant of a deity (**4.6.8**). The sculpted figure wears a headdress of bark cloth supported by a rattan frame, similar in form to the bark-and-fiber masks worn by Chokwe leaders. *Chibinda Ilunga*'s large hands and feet, muscularity, and intense expression show his physical power. He carries a staff, a symbol of prestige that stands for the passage of power from an ancestor to a chief or from one chief to another. His flaring nostrils and the antelope horn he carries identify him as a hunter. The horn was a trophy of his successes in capturing game, and it also served as a container for potent substances or medicines, contributing an additional element to his arsenal of impressive traits. The sculpture conveys the valued attributes of authority, potency, and restraint that made this celebrated hunter a model leader.

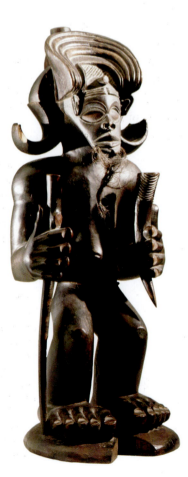

4.6.7 (above) The Egyptian king Akhenaten, his queen Nefertiti, and three daughters, c. 1353–1335 BCE. Limestone, 12¼" high. Ägyptisches Museum, Staatliche Museen zu Berlin, Germany

4.6.8 (left) Chokwe, *Chibinda Ilunga*, mid-19th century. Wood, hair, and hide, 16 × 6 × 6". Kimbell Museum of Art, Fort Worth, Texas

Sunken relief: a carved panel where the figures are cut deeper into the stone than the background

Art as Societal Control

Strong leaders understand the power of art as a tool for propaganda, both to convey their messages and to influence people to obey their laws. The ancient Babylonian king Hammurabi used an image to emphasize his divine connection to the gods in order to persuade his people to follow his decrees. The Roman Emperor Constantine utilized his own portraits to symbolize his political and military strength, and in the twentieth century, Chinese Communist leader Mao Zedong commissioned art to promote his political ideology.

King Hammurabi of Babylon (now part of Iraq) is best known today for the code of law that he established around 1790 BCE. It was innovative for being a set of written statutes, as opposed to unwritten or arbitrary rules, which might vary by region or local authority. His code was carved in **cuneiform** writing into a **stela** for public viewing (**4.6.9**). King Hammurabi's code has often been summarized as "an eye for an eye," because it frequently called for a person to be punished for wrong-doing by suffering in the same way as the person who had been wronged. Yet Hammurabi's laws tended to be more complex and less even-handed when they pertained to people with low status, such as slaves, freedmen, and women. For example, the law did not punish a husband for adultery,

although it did consider the wife's financial well-being if her husband decided to leave her. In contrast, a woman caught in an adulterous affair was thrown into a river, with her hands tied, along with her lover. If her husband only suspected her of adultery, but had no proof, she was required to jump into the river. If she survived, she was deemed innocent.

The scene at the top of the stela shows that Hammurabi's power has been given to him by the gods. Shamash, the god of justice and the sun god, is enthroned and seen with flames radiating from his shoulders. The sun god reaches toward Hammurabi and hands him rings and a scepter, symbols of power, as he dictates to the king the laws he will implement. Written below this scene is a long description of the gods' support for Hammurabi and the king's law code. Monuments similar to this stela were placed throughout Mesopotamia to enforce Hammurabi's judicial system.

Constantine the Great ruled part of the Roman empire from 306 CE and was sole emperor from 324 until his death in 337. Constantine was successful in numerous military campaigns, and he is notable for having been the first Christian Roman emperor. A colossal marble-and-bronze statue of the emperor seated on a throne was made in 325 to be placed in a **basilica** in the center of Rome. Only parts of the statue survive (**4.6.10**), but the head alone, which is more than 8 ft. tall, gives

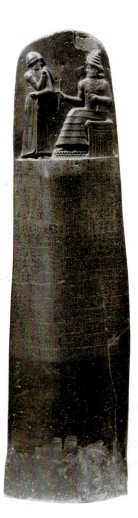

4.6.9 Stela of Hammurabi, c. 1792–1750 BCE. Diorite, 88⅝ × 25⅝". Musée du Louvre, Paris, France

4.6.10 Remnants of colossal statue of Constantine the Great, 325–26 CE. Marble, head 8′6″ high. Palazzo dei Conservatori, Rome, Italy

Cuneiform: a form of writing from ancient Mesopotamia that uses wedge shapes
Stela: upright stone slab decorated with inscriptions or pictorial relief carvings
Basilica: an early Christian church, either converted from or built to resemble a type of Roman civic building

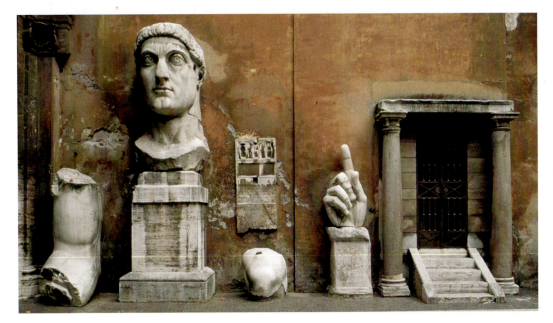

an idea of the imposing force one must have felt standing in the presence of this statue, which was made to enforce Constantine's power even when he was away.

In its youthful features and ideal athletic body, the statue was modeled after portraits of earlier emperors. The emperor was enthroned in a manner similar to seated statues of the Roman god Jupiter, but he held in his hand an orb on which a Christian cross was placed. This statue is one of the earliest examples of how pagan art was often reinterpreted to incorporate Christian symbolism and meaning. Constantine's far-off gaze toward the heavens is also distinct from earlier portraits of Roman emperors and signifies his close connection to God, and the power he therefore derived from the Almighty to rule over the Roman empire.

As we have seen, art is often used by leaders seeking to manipulate the people they govern. Mao Zedong led the Communist Party to power in the Chinese civil war that ended in 1949. Mao, who ruled the most populous country in the world for twenty-seven years, understood the power of imagery and, like leaders for centuries before him, used artwork to promote his political and social agenda to his thousands of subjects. Mao installed a huge portrait of himself at Tiananmen in Beijing, the capital of China, when he declared the country to be the People's Republic of China (**4.6.11**). Tiananmen, the site of many important political and cultural events in China's history, was built in the fifteenth century as a gateway to the Forbidden City, the home of the Chinese emperors for centuries.

4.6.11 Mao Zedong's portrait. The Gate of Heavenly Peace, Tiananmen (south entrance to the old Forbidden City), Beijing, China

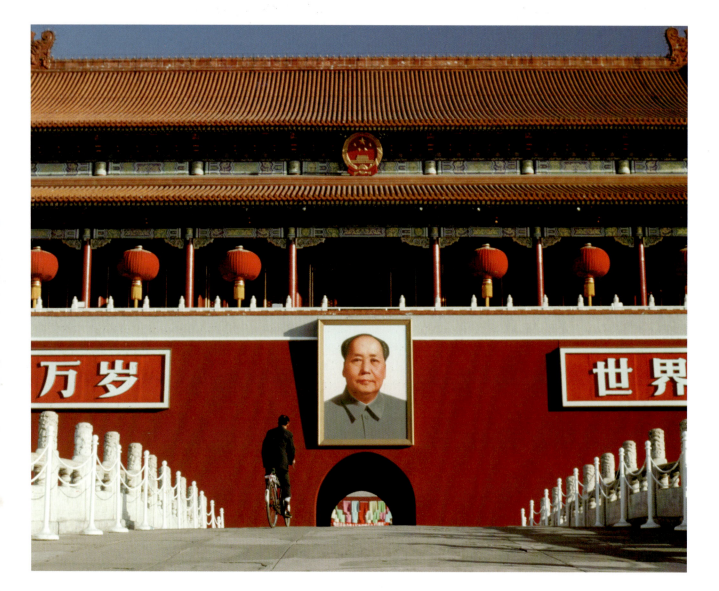

Mao's portrait is a powerful national symbol of China, even though his legacy remains very controversial. His "Great Leap Forward" campaign in 1958, an attempt to transform and industrialize China, resulted in widespread famine, and the Cultural Revolution that followed in 1966 led to the imprisonment and persecution of millions of people. Yet he maintained a hold on the Chinese people in part because of the image he projected as the benevolent leader of the Chinese Republic. Mao's face, typically similar in appearance to the portrait hanging in Tiananmen, decorated bank notes, stamps, statues, posters, and massive portraits in public spaces, conveying the idea that he was always watching over his citizens.

The portrait that hangs over Tiananmen is not the same painting that was placed there in 1949; it has been replaced with near-identical portraits almost yearly. In the mid-1960s Mao's official portrait was altered to show both of his ears, symbolizing that he listened to the needs of his populace. When Mao died in 1976, the large oil painting at Tiananmen was replaced temporarily with a black-and-white photograph to signify China's mourning.

As well as displaying Mao's portrait, Tiananmen Square has also been the site of bloody protests against China's Communist rule. The most famous example took place in 1989, when more than 100,000 people gathered in peaceful protest against government corruption and unfair wages. Sadly, the police responded with violence, and several thousand people were killed. To this day the Chinese government continues to suppress information about the massacre; however, the image of a lone man stepping in front of a row of tanks on June 5, 1989 has become iconic around the world. The identity of the so-called "tank man" and the consequences of his actions have never been determined. Mao's portrait was splattered with red paint during the same pro-democracy protests; in addition, an unemployed man set fire to it in 2007, and in 2014 black paint was thrown across the lower part of the painting. In all cases, the portrait was replaced immediately and the vandals arrested. The continued installation of Mao's portrait in Tiananmen Square is used by today's Chinese leaders to maintain the outward expression of Communist control.

Discussion Questions

1. In this chapter we have examined portrayals of leaders from many cultures and eras. Find another artwork in which a leader is represented. Considering the elements and principles of art discussed in Part 1 of this book, perform a visual analysis of your selected artwork. How does the artist convey the power of the leader?

2. Leaders are often shown as powerful warriors. Select one such work from this chapter and then find another in another chapter in this book (for example, **1.7.8**, **3.1.15**, **4.2.6**): make sure the two are from different cultures or eras. Compare the two representations. In what ways are they similar and in what ways different?

3. Do portraits of leaders tell us what he or she really looked like? Choose four examples from this chapter and for each make a list of aspects of the artwork that seem individual and realistic and those aspects that may exaggerate or idealize the ruler's appearance. Discuss your findings in a short essay.

Images Related to 4.6:
Art of Political Leaders and Rulers

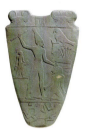

4.7.6b Palette of Narmer (back), Egypt, *c.* 2950–2775 BCE, p. 639

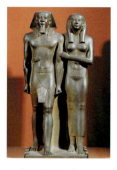

4.9.3b *Menkaure and His Wife, Queen Khamerernebty*, Egypt, *c.* 2520 BCE, p. 661

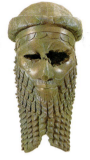

3.1.11 Head of an Akkadian ruler, *c.* 2300–2200 BCE, p. 372

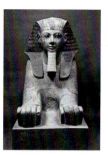

4.10.13 Sphinx of Hatshepsut, Egypt, 1479–1458 BCE, p. 683

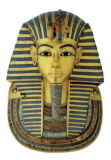

3.1.17 Funerary mask of Tutankhamun, 1333–1323 BCE, p. 377

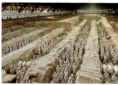

3.3.12b Soldiers from the mausoleum of Qin Shi Huangdi, China, *c.* 210 BCE, p. 421

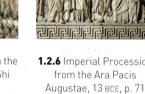

1.2.6 Imperial Procession from the Ara Pacis Augustae, 13 BCE, p. 71

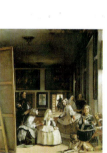

0.0.19 Equestrian statue of Marcus Aurelius, *c.* 175 CE, p. 42

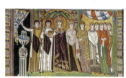

3.2.9 *Theodora and Attendants*, mosaic, Italy, *c.* 547, p. 397

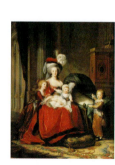

3.3.24 Angkor Wat, Cambodia, 12th century, p. 430

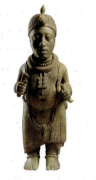

4.9.6 Head, possibly an Ife king, West Africa, 12th–14th century, p. 663

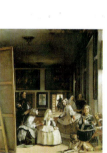

1.7.8 Nigerian Ife artist, Figure of Oni, early 14th–15th century, p. 150

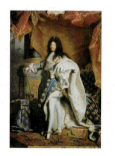

1.10.11 Diego de Silva y Velázquez, *Las Meninas*, *c.* 1656, p. 190

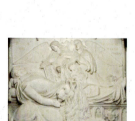

3.7.1 Hyacinthe Rigaud, *Louis XIV*, 1701, p. 491

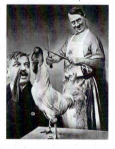

3.7.6 Elisabeth-Louise Vigée-Lebrun, *Marie-Antoinette and Her Children*, 1787, p. 495

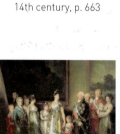

3.7.15 Francisco Goya, *Family of Charles IV*, *c.* 1800, p. 503

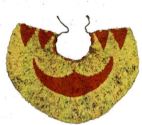

3.5.13a Feather cloak (Ahu'ula), Hawaii, *c.* 1843, p. 459

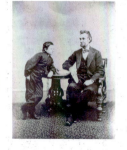

3.7.23 Alexander Gardner, *Abraham Lincoln and His Son Thomas (Tad)*, 1865, p. 509

2.4.4 Susan Durant, *Memorial to King Leopold of the Belgians*, 1867, p. 250

3.8.31 John Heartfield, *Have No Fear, He's a Vegetarian*, 1936, p. 533

4.7

Art, War, and Revolution

War has been a theme of artworks for millennia. Artists re-create the terror of battle, the tragedy of death, the joy of victory, and the sorrow of defeat. Artists choose the subjects of revolution or war for a variety of reasons: to educate us about the realities of conflict, to inspire us through the depiction of heroism, or to shock us into opposing violence. Artworks about historical events can be rich sources of information, skillfully documenting the kinds of weapons used in a particular battle or the uniforms the soldiers wore; but artists may also manipulate scenes in order, for example, to inspire support for one side over another. Art about war, revolutions, or uprisings should therefore be treated with caution, for just as we bring our own biases when we engage with an artwork, so artists may also be promoting a specific political point of view.

4.7.1 Timothy O'Sullivan, *Harvest of Death*, *Gettysburg, Pennsylvania, July 1863*. Photograph. Library of Congress, Washington, D.C.

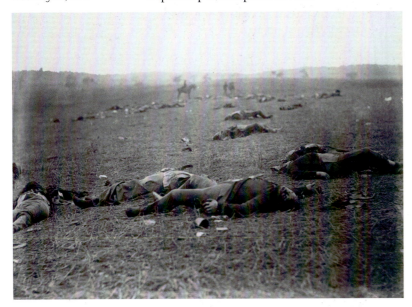

Documenting the Tragedies of War

As a viewer, do you question certain visual documents of history more than others? Do you assume that visual images (such as photographs and video) that show current events are accurate, or do you sometimes think they might have been manipulated?

When artists document actual events, they may try to record exactly what they have seen. More frequently, however, artists tend to infuse their images with the emotions aroused by the sight of death, destruction, and tragedy. An image of battle, therefore, can have a profound impact on the people who see the artwork, even as the artist's emotions sometimes distort the facts of history. Art that seems to be documentary evidence may not be entirely factual. It is important to assess the art of war with great care and attention as to the context in which the work was created. (For two contrasting views of the same conflict, see Gateway Box: Goya, **4.7.3** and **4.7.4**, p. 637.)

American Timothy O'Sullivan (1840–1882) took the famous Civil War photograph *Harvest of Death* after a day at Gettysburg, the battle that caused the most casualties of the entire conflict (**4.7.1**). His photograph shows a field covered with bodies, highlighting the tragic loss of life. The clothes of some of the soldiers have been partly removed, suggesting that thieves have been searching their bodies. O'Sullivan has focused the composition on the face of

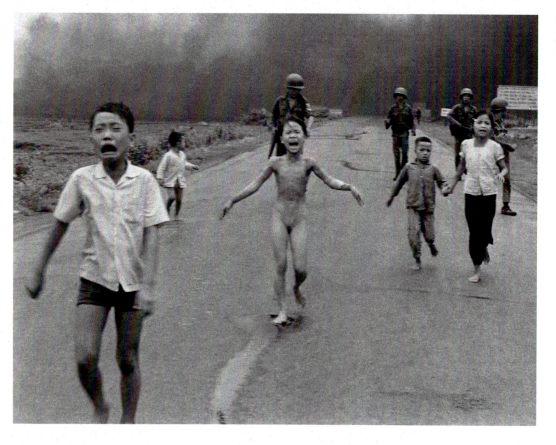

the soldier in the foreground, his arms flung out from his sides. By concentrating on this individual, whose features we can see, O'Sullivan brings home the human aspect of the great loss of life at Gettysburg.

One often assumes that a photograph can be trusted as an accurate documentation of an event. Yet photographers, like other artists, can manipulate their scenes through lighting and **composition**. O'Sullivan was known sometimes to rearrange bodies and otherwise alter the setting before taking his photographs. We do not know if he arranged the corpses or their clothing in order to heighten the emotional impact of this powerful image. If we knew he had staged the scene in some way, would we doubt the truth of the tragedy he represents?

The photograph by the Vietnamese Nick Ut (b. 1951) of children running from their village in Vietnam after a napalm attack was so shocking that some, including the US president Richard Nixon, questioned its authenticity when it appeared in newspapers on June 12, 1972 (**4.7.2**). The image also moved many Americans to question their nation's involvement in the

Vietnam War. The photographer defended its authenticity for years:

> The picture for me and unquestionably for many others could not have been more real. The photo was as authentic as the Vietnam War itself. The horror of the Vietnam War recorded by me did not have to be fixed. That terrified little girl is still alive today and has become an eloquent testimony to the authenticity of that photo.

Although the photograph records an actual event, Ut's disapproval of the war and his concern for its victims influenced the way his shot was composed. He focused on the little girl, Kim Phuc, screaming in terror, running naked, her clothes having been burned off her body. Her two brothers are running on the left side of the image, while her two cousins hold hands behind her on the right. The soldiers in the background appear strangely calm, a dramatic contrast to the horrified expressions of the running children.

The story of the people in the photograph did not end with that moment. The nine-year-

Composition: the overall design or organization of a work

Gateway to Art: Goya, *The Third of May, 1808*
Two Views of a War

Sometimes, we can look at a painting on its own and reach one conclusion; but when we look at it next to another work, our opinion of both paintings changes. If we look at Francisco Goya's painting *The Third of May, 1808* on its own, for example, we might conclude that it is a powerful condemnation of the French Emperor Napoleon and his troops (**4.7.3**). But what happens if we view the work beside another that Goya painted in the same year, *The Second of May, 1808* (**4.7.4**)? Can both paintings be understood better as a condemnation, not of Napoleon in particular, but of war in general?

The Spanish War of Independence (1808–14), the beginnings of which are depicted in *The Second of May, 1808*, was known for its guerrilla fighting and for the heroism of the civilian population (**4.7.4**). Goya's *Third of May* shows the punishment of civilians who had brutally attacked the invading French soldiers on the previous day (the subject of *The Second of May, 1808*).

Unlike *The Third of May*, *The Second of May* does not show sympathy for the Spanish rebels. While the figures in *The Third of May* seem to be still, as if frozen by the horror of the moment, *The Second of May* is full of movement and chaotic action. In fact, when the two paintings are viewed together, we may view the executions on May 3 as inevitable following the violent slaughter of French soldiers the day before. The French general Joachim Murat, angered by the riots, proclaimed, "French blood has flowed. It demands vengeance." At least 400 Spaniards were executed in Madrid, more than 40 on the hill of Príncipe Pío, the location depicted in Goya's *Third of May*.

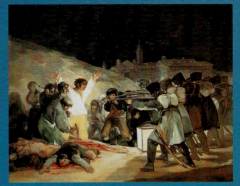

4.7.3 Francisco Goya, *The Third of May, 1808*, 1814. Oil on canvas, 8′4⅜″ × 11′3⅞″. Museo Nacional del Prado, Madrid, Spain

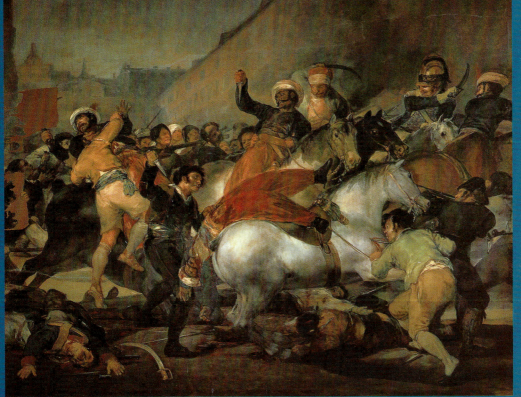

4.7.4 Francisco Goya, *The Second of May, 1808*, 1814. Oil on canvas, 8′9″ × 11′4⅛″. Museo Nacional del Prado, Madrid, Spain

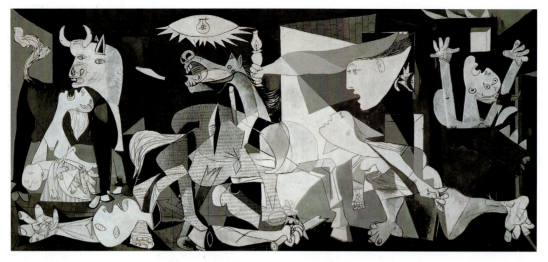

4.7.5 Pablo Picasso, *Guernica*, 1937. Oil on canvas, 11'5½" × 25'5¾". Museo Nacional Centro de Arte Reina Sofia, Madrid, Spain

old girl kept screaming; the photographer gave her his water and rushed her to a hospital. Physicians predicted Phuc would die. But because of the fame of the photograph, money poured in to save her. She underwent seventeen surgical operations and later emigrated to Canada. Nick Ut became "Uncle Nick" to the little girl and the two have remained in close contact throughout their lives. Although this photograph shows the suffering of a small group of people, it symbolizes for many the tragedy of the entire Vietnam War.

The Spanish artist Pablo Picasso (1881–1973) painted *Guernica* as a passionate response to the aerial attack carried out on April 26, 1937, on a small town of that name in northern Spain (**4.7.5**). During the Spanish Civil War, the Nationalist general Francisco Franco, who would later become the country's ruler, allowed German and Italian planes to test their bombing tactics on Guernica and learn about the psychological effects of air warfare. More than 1,000 civilians were killed in three hours of bombing. News of the attack quickly spread to Paris, where Picasso read stories and saw photographs of the devastation.

While the general meaning of *Guernica* is clearly outrage against the violence directed at the citizens of the small Spanish town, Picasso never explained the specific symbolism of the figures in the painting, nor elaborated on his political motivations for the work. Picasso would have accepted multiple interpretations because he believed in viewers making their own reading of an artwork. He stated:

A picture is not thought out and settled beforehand. While it is being done it changes as one's thoughts change. And when it is finished, it still goes on changing, according to the state of mind of whoever is looking at it.

The painting is black, gray, and white, perhaps because Picasso associated the attack with black-and-white newspaper photographs. The small dashes on the body of the horse also seem to recall the print from a newspaper. Expressive faces with distorted necks scream and cry in despair. On the right, a figure reaches to the sky as it escapes from a burning building; flames appear like scales on the back of a dragon. The tortured figure on the left experiences the horror of her child's murder.

The bull, often associated with the violence of Spanish bullfighting, is seen by many as a symbol of Franco. The terrified horse, as it tramples upon a man lying on the ground, may represent the chaos inflicted upon the people by the attack. The lightbulb shining powerfully at the top of the canvas may symbolize awareness and knowledge, as if illuminating the situation.

Picasso exhibited this large protest statement at the Spanish Pavilion during the 1937 World's Fair in Paris, France, and declared that neither he nor the painting would go to Spain as long as Franco ruled. The artwork traveled the world before coming to rest in New York's Museum of Modern Art. Franco died in 1975, two years after Picasso. In 1981, *Guernica* was finally sent to Madrid, Spain, to be exhibited permanently.

Warriors and Scenes of Battle

Artists have often recorded and celebrated the bravery of warriors, both their successes and defeats, in great detail. Although at times, as we have seen, an artist's interpretation of historical events is skewed and presented through an emotional lens, artworks can be valuable records of critical historical moments. They can teach us the significance of certain battles, and provide accurate studies of the weapons used and the uniforms worn by those who took part in them.

The Palette of Narmer, one of the earliest surviving ancient Egyptian artworks, records the unification of Egypt after a great war, and highlights the importance of the first pharaoh, Narmer, who was to rule over all of Egypt and keep the peace (**4.7.6a** and **4.7.6b**). Egyptian civilization survived along the north-flowing river Nile. Before the reign of Narmer, Egypt was divided into Upper Egypt (to the south) and Lower Egypt (in the more fertile north). **Palettes** were used to grind **pigment** that both men and women painted around their eyes to protect them from the sun. The round area on the front of the Palette of Narmer, in which the necks of two creatures intertwine, would have been used for the mixing of the paint.

The front of the palette is divided into four **registers**. The top register shows a pair of horned bull heads, which represent the aggressive strength of the king. In the next register the king is shown larger than the other figures to indicate his importance, a convention known as **hierarchical scale**. On the far right of this register are ten bodies with severed heads between their legs, indicating the scores of enemies Narmer has killed. The intertwining of the fantastical long-necked creatures in the next register embodies the unification of Upper and Lower Egypt. In the bottom register, Narmer is again represented as a bull, who bows his head toward a fortified city and tramples on an enemy.

The back of the palette features a large scene in which the pharaoh, wearing the White Crown that symbolizes Upper Egypt, prepares to club an enemy who kneels before him. The falcon represents the god Horus, suggesting that Narmer was supported by the gods. At the very bottom of the reverse side of the palette is a scene showing two fallen enemies, viewed as if from above. Much of the picture writing on the palette has not yet been interpreted, but it seems to record the names of places conquered by Narmer. Taken as a whole, the palette shows this pharaoh's military might as he unifies all of Egypt under his rule.

Palette: a smooth slab or board used for mixing paints or cosmetics
Pigment: the colorant in art materials. Often made from finely ground minerals
Register: one of two or more horizontal sections into which a space is divided in order to depict different episodes of a story
Hierarchical scale: the use of size to denote the relative importance of subjects in an artwork

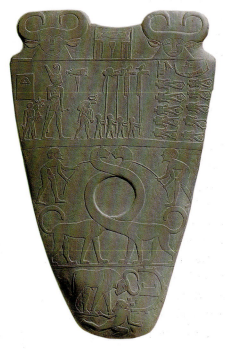
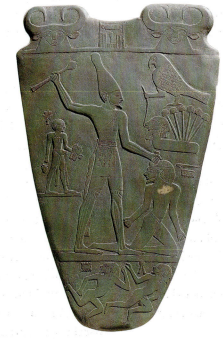

4.7.6a (far left) Palette of Narmer (front), Early Dynastic Period, Egypt, c. 2950–2775 BCE. Green schist, 25¼ × 16⅝". Egyptian Museum, Cairo, Egypt

4.7.6b (left) Palette of Narmer (back), Early Dynastic Period, Egypt, c. 2950–2775 BCE. Green schist, 25¼ × 16⅝". Egyptian Museum, Cairo, Egypt

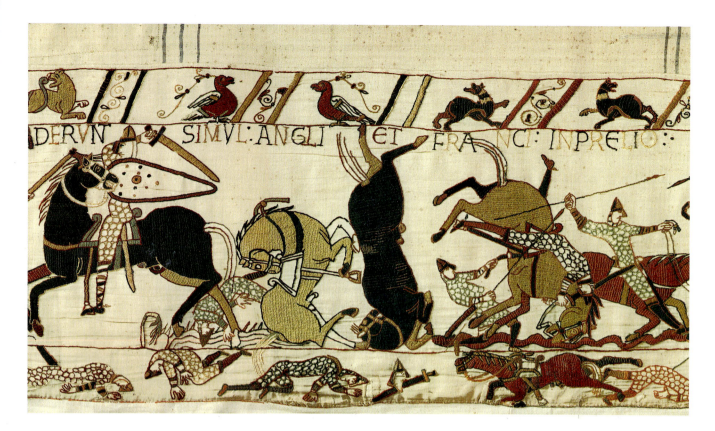

DERVNT　SIMVL·ANGLI　ET FRA NCI· INPRELIO ::

Some artists have focused on the heat of battle, and conveyed the sounds and sensations of war using completely different **media**. Both the *Bayeux Tapestry* and the *Tale of the Heiji Rebellion* (*Heiji Monogatari*) portray rousing battle scenes (**4.7.7** and **4.7.8**). We can almost hear the clanking of weapons and smell the odor of burning flesh. And while a few figures illustrate the courage of the enemy, both artworks are skewed toward celebrating the overwhelming prowess of the victors. Both artworks, too, consist of multiple scenes and are meant to be viewed slowly, unravelling their historical stories one incident at a time. Their very long horizontal formats take the viewer on a visual journey through history.

The 275-foot-long *Bayeux Tapestry* records the events surrounding the Battle of Hastings (1066), in which the Normans, led by William the Conqueror, seized control of England from the Anglo-Saxons. It was probably commissioned by William's brother Odo, the Bishop of Bayeux in France, shortly after the Norman victory. The so-called **tapestry** was embroidered by women (legend says William's wife was one of the embroiderers), and took more than ten years to complete. It shows the

events that led to the battle, the preparations of the Norman fleet, the Battle of Hastings itself, and finally the coronation of William the Conqueror as King of England. More than six hundred men, but only three women, are shown in the fifty scenes on the tapestry. The embroiderers were highly skilled. To establish a sense of depth, each figure is given a border, which is filled in with stitches running in the opposite direction to the rest of the embroidery, and then outlined in boldly contrasting colors. The process creates clearly delineated figures, a flat sense of space (to guide the viewer in a horizontal direction), and, through repeated patterns, a sense of overall **rhythm**.

The *Night Attack on the Sanjo Palace* (**4.7.8**) is one scene from one of five long painted scrolls that depict battles from the *Tale of the Heiji Rebellion*, a Japanese war epic about the short-lived Heiji era (1159–60). In this period several clans fought for control of Kyoto, the historical capital of Japan. This scene shows the burning of the palace by samurai warriors of the Fujiwara and Minamoto clans during the raid in which they captured the Emperor Nijo. Soon afterward, another clan, the Taira, rescued the emperor and regained control of Kyoto.

4.7.7 Detail of Battle of Hastings, *Bayeux Tapestry, c.* 1066–82. Linen with wool, 275' long. Bayeux Tapestry Museum, Bayeux, France

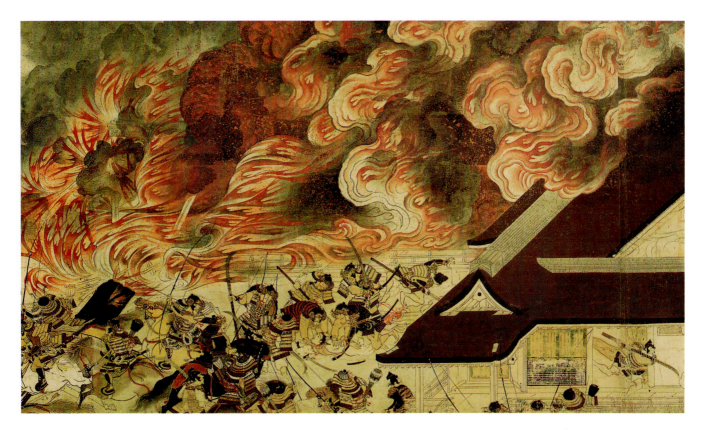

4.7.8 *Night Attack on the Sanjo Palace*, from *Heiji Monogatari*, Kamakura period, late 13th century. Hand scroll, ink and color on paper, 16⅛" × 22'11¼" (whole scroll). Museum of Fine Arts, Boston, Massachusetts

Medium (plural **media**): the material on or from which an artist chooses to make a work of art
Tapestry: hand-woven fabric—usually silk or wool—with a non-repeating, usually figurative, design woven into it
Rhythm: the regular or ordered repetition of elements in the work
Isometric perspective: a system using diagonal parallel lines to communicate depth
Bird's-eye view: an artistic technique in which a scene or subject is presented from some point above it
Pectoral: a large ornament worn on the chest

Like the *Bayeux Tapestry*, the *Night Attack on the Sanjo Palace* is representative of the visual style of its period. The almost 23-foot-long Japanese scroll employs **isometric perspective** from a **bird's-eye view**. The horses and warriors are carefully delineated and detailed. The precise lines and limited use of blurry brushwork (as in the horses' tails and the billowing smoke) demonstrate the artist's skill. The story in the scroll is read from right to left, and the artist guides the viewer in that direction using the diagonal lines of the buildings, the layering of the figures, and the movement of the billowing smoke. In the section of the scroll shown here, the building on the right shows the palace under attack; then, moving left, prisoners are beheaded. The emperor is shown captured on a black cart in the lower left. Later in the scroll the emperor will be imprisoned and the decapitated heads will be displayed on pikes.

The attention to detail in both the Japanese scroll and the Norman tapestry gives us a strong sense of the equipment and weapons used by the warriors of these peoples. The Japanese samurai are shown covered in intricately detailed armor atop their fine and powerful horses. Lengthy bows and arching swords are their weapons of

choice. The soldiers of the Bayeux tapestry wear patterned armor and conical helmets, and carry broadswords, kite-shaped shields, and spears.

Little is known about the militaristic society of the ancient Toltec people of Mexico except what can be learned from the legends of later cultures, such as the Aztecs, who often sought to demonstrate an ancestral link with the Toltec. These legends suggest that the Toltec ruled a substantial empire. It is believed that around 1000 CE the Toltec capital of Tula was the largest city in Mexico at that time, with a population of more than 50,000.

Four large warrior columns, standing between 15 and 20 ft. tall, are some of the few remaining artworks of the Toltec (**4.7.9**, see p. 642). The carved warriors stood high above the city, painted in bright colors. The imposing figures once supported the roof of a temple that stood on a pyramid and was reached by a steep stairway. The carving of the columns gives us some sense of how a Toltec warrior would have looked. The figures are identical, each wearing a feathered headdress, a butterfly-shaped **pectoral**, sandals decorated with symbols of the gods, and a belt supporting a large mirror or shield on their lower back.

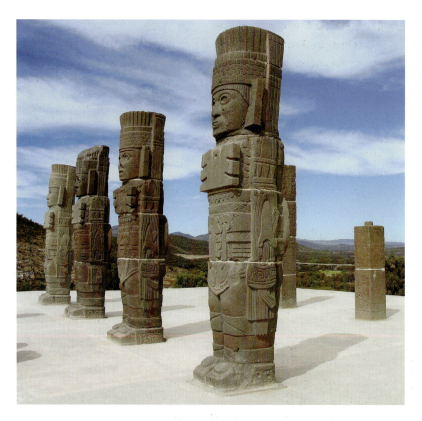

4.7.9 Tula warrior columns, 900–1000 CE. Basalt, 15–20' high. Tula, Hidalgo, Mexico

High relief: a carved panel where the figures project with a great deal of depth from the background

Each warrior holds spears or arrows in his left hand and a spearthrowing device in his right. Similar warriors—ranging from the small scale to the large, and occurring both as freestanding figures and as columns in temples—comprise the majority of the few Toltec sculptures that survive. This suggests that the Toltec probably lived in a time of frequent warfare, and that they revered their warrior rulers.

A plaque from the palace of an African king suggests that military strength is often needed to bring peace to a kingdom (**4.7.10**). The kings, or obas, of Benin, were both military and spiritual leaders of a West African state that was at its height between 1450 and 1700. The obas commissioned hundreds of brass artworks to reflect their power, including plaques to cover the royal palace, many of which depict warriors who followed the orders of the oba. The central warrior in this plaque is larger than the two beside him, signifying his importance; he is in **higher relief** than the others, making him seem closer to us. The ceremonial sword he carries in his left hand, and his elaborate helmet, tell us that he is a high-ranking chief. His spear and the shields of those beside him are imposing, emphasizing their physical power and that of

their ruler, the oba. The chief wears a leopard-tooth necklace and has dotted markings on his stomach and arms resembling the spots of a leopard. Leopards, known for their power and speed, were a symbol of the oba.

4.7.10 Benin plaque with warrior and attendants, 16th–17th century. Brass, 18¾" high. Metropolitan Museum of Art, New York

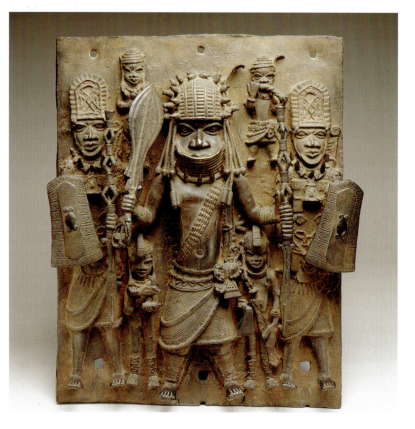

The Artist's Response to War

Artists have often created artworks that attempt to convey their personal experience of war. This is sometimes a cathartic exercise, releasing emotion, and it is sometimes meant to inspire awareness of the realities of war. But by no means all powerful responses to war have been created by artists who actually witnessed the events they portray. Artists can produce powerful visual statements about the horrors of war from both their experiences and their own imagination. (See the Perspectives on Art Box: Wafaa Bilal, *Domestic Tension*: An Artist's Protest against War, p. 645.)

The German painter Otto Dix (1891–1969), who fought in World War I, recorded the horrors he witnessed in the painted **triptych** *The War* (**4.7.11**). The central panel shows death and destruction. A soldier wearing a gas mask, representing Dix himself, witnesses the devastation at first hand. Bloody bodies are piled on top of one another, one with legs in the air. Chaos fills the scene. Arched pieces of metal stretch out across the sky and support a skeletal figure, whose outstretched finger points toward the bullet-ridden body on the right. The arching forms enclose the scene, leaving us feeling

smothered by the horror that is shown. Our anxiety is increased with nothing to calm us or to rest our eyes upon.

The left wing of the triptych shows heavily equipped soldiers, united in their duty and prepared for battle. The scene precedes the horror that will take place in the central panel. The right-hand wing shows a man, a self-portrait of Dix, carrying a wounded soldier. The sky in the triptych symbolizes the increasing danger of the situation, beginning on the left with pale sunlight, moving toward foreboding clouds, and ending with a stormy and destructive sky on the right. Underneath the central panel, in a section called the **predella**, Dix has painted a sleeping or dead soldier, lying in a trench.

The triptych format is traditionally used for religious scenes, with Christ's crucifixion portrayed in the center and his entombment in the predella below. By using this format, Dix elevates the importance of his subject matter. And in associating an ordinary soldier with the soon-to-be-resurrected Christ, he endows him with the status of a martyr.

During World War II, Otto Dix's work was censored by the Nazis for its negative presentation of war. The contemporary German artist Anselm Kiefer (b. 1945) addresses such censorship in his work. Kiefer was born in

Triptych: an artwork comprising three painted or carved panels, normally joined together and sharing a common theme
Predella: the horizontal section on the bottom of a triptych altarpiece that often functions as a support or stand

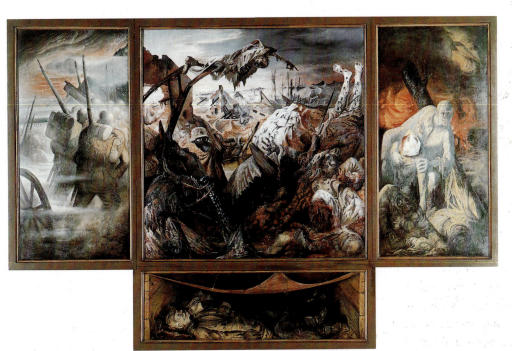

4.7.11 Otto Dix, *The War*, 1929–32. Oil and tempera on wood, central panel 80¼ × 80¼", side panels 80¼ × 40⅛", bottom panel (predella) 23⅝ × 80¼". Staatliche Kunstsammlungen, Gemäldegalerie Neue Meister, Dresden, Germany

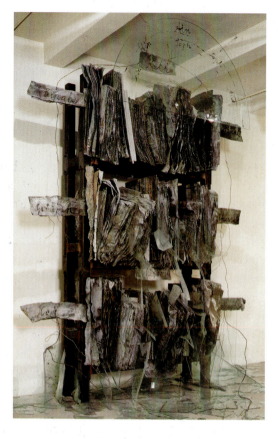

4.7.12 Anselm Kiefer, *Breaking of the Vessels*, 1990. Lead, iron, glass, copper wire, charcoal, and Aquatec, 12'5" × 27'5½" × 17'. St. Louis Art Museum, Missouri

4.7.13 Ganzeer, *Tank vs. Bike*, with graffiti by Sad Panda, 2011. Cairo, Egypt

Germany just months before World War II ended. He grew up in a society ashamed of its past. His artworks force viewers to acknowledge the horrors of the Nazi regime that ruled Germany from 1933 until 1945. His attempts to confront this past have often shocked and angered Germans. For example, he photographed himself making the Nazi salute—a gesture that has been illegal in Germany since 1945.

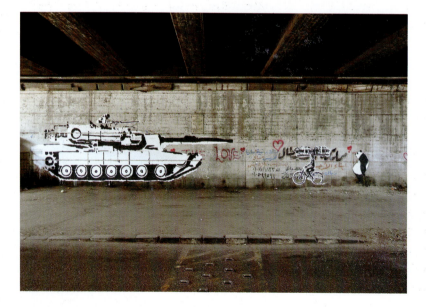

Kiefer's *Breaking of the Vessels* conveys the loss of life and the destruction of knowledge caused by the extermination of millions of Jews during the Holocaust (**4.7.12**). The imposing 27-foot-tall artwork is made of lead and glass. The heavy lead books appear to be scorched, just like the human beings (also holders of knowledge) who were incinerated in concentration camps. The shattered glass also recalls *Kristallnacht* (Night of the Broken Glass), when the Nazis destroyed hundreds of Jewish stores and synagogues in 1938. The splintered glass on the ground makes any access to these books of knowledge a dangerous and frightening proposition. Symbolically, Kiefer has conveyed the fear and pain one must face to confront the past.

In *Breaking of the Vessels*, Kiefer draws upon the Jewish religion and more specifically the Kabbalah, a collection of Jewish mystical writings. The words "Ain-Sof," which mean the infinite presence of God, are written on the arched piece of glass above the bookshelf. Ten lead labels are placed around and on the bookshelf; these represent the ten vessels containing the essence of God as described in the Kabbalah. In this way, the books represent the presence of God even in the midst of human destruction.

The Egyptian artist Mohamad Fahmy, known as Ganzeer, became internationally famous for his graffiti art criticizing the Supreme Council of the Armed Forces (SCAF), a council of senior military officials that ruled his country after the Egyptian Revolution in February 2011. Immediately following the revolution, Ganzeer began a series called the *Martyr Murals*, in which he created portraits of those killed during the revolution. Like much **street art**, this artwork was collaborative, the result of many artists who wished to raise their voices in protest against the massacre. During Mad Graffiti Weekend (May 20–21, 2011) Ganzeer produced his best-known work, *Tank vs. Bike*, in which an enormous tank points its gun at a young Egyptian boy on a pushbike, balancing a huge tray full of bread upon his head (**4.7.13**). Ganzeer was assisted by a team of volunteers to create the stencils for this work. Later, the artist known as Sad Panda added on his trademark figure behind the biker, and

Perspectives On Art: Wafaa Bilal
Domestic Tension: An Artist's Protest against War

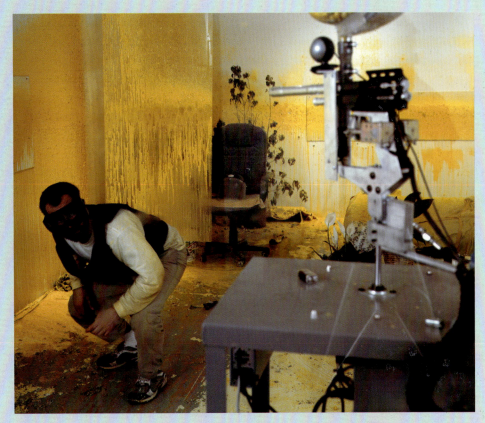

4.7.14 Wafaa Bilal, *Domestic Tension*, 2007. Flatfile Gallery, Chicago, Illinois

Iraqi-born Wafaa Bilal teaches in the Photography and Imaging department at the Tisch School of the Arts at NYU. His art reflects his concerns with the injustices committed in Iraq under the dictatorial regime of Saddam Hussein and, since then, during American military operations in the country.

As an Iraqi artist living in the US since 1992, I have created many provocative works to raise awareness and create dialogue about US–Iraq conflicts. But when my brother Haji was killed by an American bomb at a checkpoint in our hometown of Kufa, Iraq, in 2004, the war became deeply personal.

I had to find an unconventional new approach to translate this tragic event into a work of art that empowered its audience. Not something that lectured the audience, nor something dogmatic, but a dynamic encounter between me and my audience.

A TV news segment about a soldier in Colorado remotely dropping bombs on Iraq highlighted the anonymous and detached nature of this current war, and the complete disconnect between the comfort zone here in the US and the conflict zone in my home country. I needed to create a platform for people to be nudged out of their comfort zone.

The result was an interactive performance entitled *Domestic Tension* (**4.7.14**). I stayed in a Chicago gallery for a month with a paintball gun aimed at me. People could control the paintball gun, and command it to shoot at me, over the Internet.

I wanted to create a virtual and physical platform, turning the virtual to physical and vice versa, and, by putting my body on the line, create a physical impact in viewers by enabling them to identify with the physical effect on my body.

The project generated worldwide attention, with more than 60,000 shots taken and 80 million hits to the website from 137 countries.

I never anticipated how many people would be drawn to the project and how it would become a truly dynamic artwork in which the viewers had control over the **narrative**. It achieved an unexpected goal of democratizing the process of the viewing and the making of the artwork, by enabling the audience to participate.

As evidenced by dialogue on the website's chat room, the experience had a profound impact on many people from all sides of the political spectrum. At the conclusion of the project, I felt fulfilled in my mantra that "Today we silenced one gun; hopefully one day we will silence all guns."

since then other artists have added to the image and it continues to evolve. For example, graffiti artist Khaled painted bodies being crushed under the tank. This recorded an actual event that took place in October 2011, when a group of peaceful civilians, protesting the demolition of a church, were attacked by security forces and the army. Graffiti and other street art has been a major form of protest throughout the uprisings against governments across the Middle East and North Africa, known as the Arab Spring.

Remembrance and Memorials

Art can serve as a way to acknowledge a historical tragedy, mistreatment, or suffering, often in the hope that similar events will not be repeated. Memorials may address the history of a single individual or of many people. While memorials are often designed to promote healing and comfort the grieving, they can also be statements of tragedy, and can fuel uprisings. They can also express hope for a better world in the future.

The Vietnam Veterans Memorial was built in Washington, D.C., to pay tribute to many fallen men and women and in the hope of laying to rest some of the lingering controversy over the war (**4.7.15**). The design itself was immediately controversial, however. The competition to

design the monument—which drew more than 1,400 submissions—was won by a twenty-one-year-old American of Chinese descent studying architecture at Yale University. Maya Lin (b. 1959) envisaged her monument as a place for mourning and healing. A black-granite, V-shaped wall descends into the earth, and then ascends, giving one a sense of coming into the light. The wall also becomes taller as one descends, creating a powerful visual expression for the enormous loss of life during the war. It symbolizes the eternal wound in America caused by the conflict, but also the healing that Lin hoped would take place as those who experienced the monument physically rose again.

The names of the dead are carved into the wall and organized by the date of death. The surface is polished because, the artist explained, "the point is to see yourself reflected in the names." The walls are aligned toward two other monuments, the Washington Monument and the Lincoln Memorial. The integration of the Vietnam Veterans Memorial with these important structures acknowledges the significance of the Vietnam War to American history.

Lin intended the memorial as a tribute, and most visitors are moved upon experiencing it. Some veterans, however, saw it as part of a continued condemnation of the war. They said that rather than uplifting and instilling pride in the soldiers who fought, the monument's descent into the ground symbolized a moral criticism both of the war and its soldiers. The veterans also perceived the choice of black granite, as opposed to the more conventional use of pure white marble for memorials, as a criticism. In response to these protests, a bronze sculpture of three soldiers, more traditional in style, was later placed a short distance from the wall.

On September 11, 2001, the United States suffered the worst terrorist attack in its history. Two hijacked planes destroyed the Twin Towers of New York's World Trade Center, a third plane damaged the Pentagon in Washington, D.C., and a final plane crashed in a Pennsylvania field. The 9/11 attacks traumatized the nation and appalled the world. The perpetrators were members of Al Qaeda, an Islamic fundamentalist group that

4.7.15 Maya Lin, Vietnam Veterans Memorial, Washington, D.C., 1981–83. Granite, each wing 246' long, 10'1" high at highest point

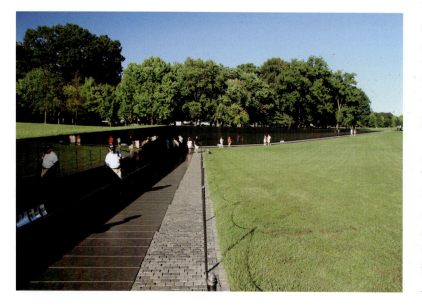

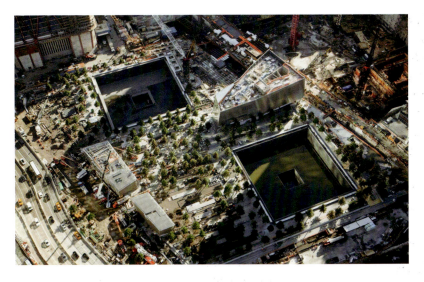

4.7.16 Michael Arad and Peter Walker, 9/11 Memorial, New York. Photo taken 28 July 2011

was born out of the Soviet War in Afghanistan (1979–89). The group's leader, Osama bin Laden, claimed the attacks were motivated by America's support of Israel and of the oppression of Muslims around the world. Hate crimes against Arab-Americans rose dramatically in the United States in the aftermath of 9/11, and many felt as if they were being judged for their race or religion.

Ten years after the 9/11 attacks, a monument was dedicated at the site of the World Trade Center towers to those who lost their lives. Although the memorial was designed with great awareness and respect for the survivors, those who lost loved ones, and those who had been persecuted, it has still been criticized by some.

Perhaps most notably, the remains of many of the deceased are still buried underground at the site, making the site sacred ground in the minds of some family members and therefore inappropriate as a site for a gift shop, admission prices, or gawkers.

Square footprints of the fallen towers, framed in steel, are now filled with waterfalls that represent the loss of so many lives. The edges of the squares are covered with bronze plaques inscribed with the names of the 2,977 who were killed, including those on the hijacked flights on 9/11, those at the Pentagon, and the rescuers who tried to help people escape, as well as victims of the World Trade Center bombing in 1993. Every effort was made to align the names most accurately to the location closest to where they perished in the buildings, and the victims of the other sites were placed together.

Located between and to the side of the tower waterfalls is the entrance to the 9/11 Memorial Museum, which is entirely underground. It contains artifacts from and information about the events of September 11. The entryway is designed so that visitors experience the sadness of the event as they descend underground and are introduced to the personal lives of the victims. When visitors rise above the earth again and visit the sites of the towers, the sound and sight of the rushing waters and trees are meant to invite contemplation and promote healing.

Discussion Questions

1. Find an artwork that depicts a battle. Perhaps choose one from the Revolutionary War, Civil War, or a famous battle from European history. Study the history of the battle and then ask yourself whether the artist recorded the event accurately. Did he or she try to persuade the viewer to support one side in the battle? How?

2. Find a photograph that documents a scene from the Civil War, World War II, or the Vietnam War. Considering the elements and principles of art discussed in Part 1 of this book, perform a visual analysis of the photograph. What does this tell you about the way the artist used the medium of photography to convey a message?

3. Study images of the entirety of the *Bayeux Tapestry* and of the *Heiji Monogatari* scroll. Bearing in mind the format of these works, how do they use their format to convey a narrative? Stylistically, how does each artwork show scenes of battle?

4. Select a war memorial from anywhere in the world. Consider how the artist has used the elements and principles of art to create a space for healing and remembrance.

Images Related to 4.7: Art, War, and Revolution

3.1.8a *Standard of Ur*, *c.* 2600–2400 BCE, p. 370

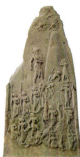

4.2.6 Stela of Naram-Sin, *c.* 2254–2218 BCE, p. 578

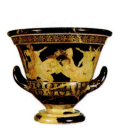

3.1.29 Euphronios and Euxitheos, krater showing Heracles and Antaios, *c.* 515–510 BCE, p. 384

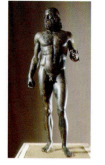

2.4.12 *Riace Warrior A*, *c.* 460 BCE, p. 254

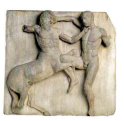

3.1.23 Metope of a Lapith and centaur, Greece, *c.* 445 BCE, p. 381

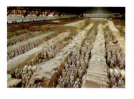

3.3.12a Terra-cotta army, mausoleum of Qin Shi Huangdi, China, *c.* 210 BCE, p. 420

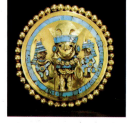

3.4.4 Moche Earspool, Peru, *c.* 300, p. 435

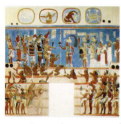

3.4.14 Bonampak mural (copy), Mexico, original 8th century, p. 442

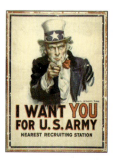

3.6.20 Donatello, *David*, *c.* 1430, p. 482

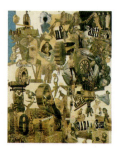

3.4.20b Hide robe with battle scene, US, 1797–1800, p. 445

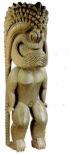

2.4.7 Figure of the war god, Hawaii, 18th or 19th century, p. 253

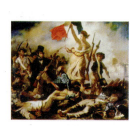

3.7.16 Eugène Delacroix, *Liberty Leading the People*, 1830, p. 504

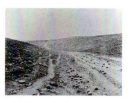

2.8.23 Roger Fenton, *Valley of the Shadow of Death*, 1855, p. 334

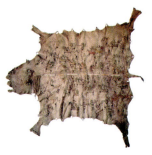

2.7.13 James Montgomery Flagg, recruitment poster, *c.* 1917, p. 313

2.8.21 Hannah Höch, *Cut with the Kitchen Knife...*, 1919–20, p. 333

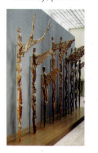

4.3.5 *Bis* poles, Asmat culture, New Guinea, late 1950s, p. 591

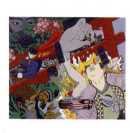

2.2.18 Roger Shimomura, *Untitled*, 1984, p. 227

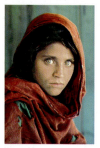

2.8.14a Steve McCurry, *Afghan Girl*, 1984, p. 327

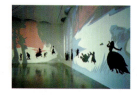

2.10.12 Kara Walker, *Insurrection!*, 2000, p. 362

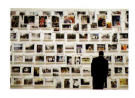

2.8.16 Hiroko Masuike, *Here Is New York: A Democracy of Photographs*, 2007, p. 329

4.8

Art of Social Conscience

The visual language of art can be an extremely effective means of communicating a point of view on social issues. While words can describe an event, art can demonstrate it visually with raw power. Art often reflects historical, social, and political concerns. It can even provoke change. Art is able to arouse such strong emotions that artworks themselves can become the focus of protest, sometimes suffering damage or destruction as a result. Art can also inspire us toward a better and more just world. This chapter is concerned with the ways that artists have expressed their convictions through artworks that have, at times, caused powerful, even violent, reactions.

Art as Social Protest

By creating potent artworks that activate emotional responses, artists can instigate social change. Here we examine artworks that have sought to combat cruelty, poverty, and inequality, for example the injustices of slavery and colonialism. While considering this section's protest artworks, think about your own response. Does the artist inspire you to agree with his or her point of view?

The painting *Raft of the Medusa* (**4.8.1**), by the French artist Théodore Géricault (1791–1824), memorializes on a grand scale a scandalous event in history. On July 2, 1816, the French naval vessel *Medusa* ran aground off the coast of West Africa. While the captain and approximately 250 crew boarded the lifeboats, the rest of the passengers—146 men and one woman, some of them slaves—got onto a makeshift raft that had been built from the wreckage. Although the raft was pulled by the lifeboats initially, the captain soon abandoned it. Left to battle starvation, sunburn, disease, and dehydration, only fifteen men survived the horrors of the sea; some cannibalized their shipmates. Géricault's painting shows with emotional intensity

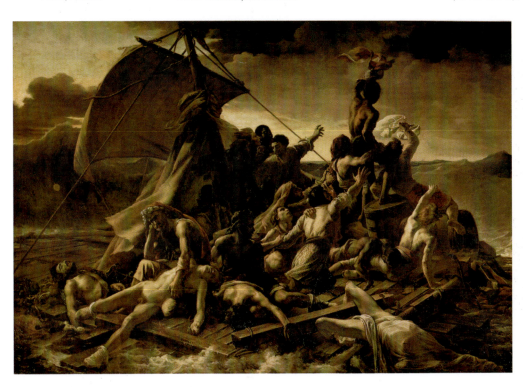

4.8.1 Théodore Géricault, *Raft of the Medusa*, 1819. Oil on canvas, 12'1³⁄₈" x 17'9⁷⁄₈". Musée du Louvre, Paris, France

the moment when the raft's survivors are about to be rescued.

Géricault interviewed the survivors, studied corpses, and even had a replica of the raft built in his studio in preparation for this project. The survivors told him of their despair and madness when they saw a ship on the horizon on the thirteenth day. They had seen ships in the distance before but the ships' crews had not seen them, and many feared this ship, too, would disappear. But the survivors, all close to death, were rescued, and they told the world the story of their abandonment.

In *Raft of the Medusa*, Géricault depicts the emotions of the survivors. Several men, their arms reaching out toward the tiny ship in the distance, convey desperate hope. Another is shown still slouched in despair, and surrounded by corpses; he even holds one on his lap. The artist painted the skin of the men with a green pallor to indicate that they are near to death. Yet the musculature of their bodies gives them nobility. Standing at the painting's apex, atop a pyramid of bodies, a black man waves a piece of his clothing to get the attention of the ship in the distance. The dramatic intensity is heightened by the use of diagonal lines that compose the figures into a large X. From the bottom left corner of the **composition** the bodies of the men are arranged

in a line that leads the viewer's eye to the black man in the upper right. An opposing diagonal is made from the mast in the upper left to the nude male body on the lower right, which appears to be falling from the raft.

Géricault's picture criticizes not only the *Medusa* disaster but also colonization and slavery. Only one African survived the tragic journey, and Géricault includes him as the powerful figure trying to attract the attention of the distant ship.

Art that Raises Social Awareness

Because of the power of visual language, artists can spur people to become involved in a social issue, and can call for the punishment of those responsible for a wrong. These artists have used art to shine light on social, racial, and environmental issues.

The French artist JR visits countries affected by political unrest and mounts colossal photographs of local people on exterior walls to draw attention to a plight shared by humans across the world. In *Women are Heroes* (**4.8.2**) JR brought attention to the conditions of the poor

Composition: the overall design or organization of a work

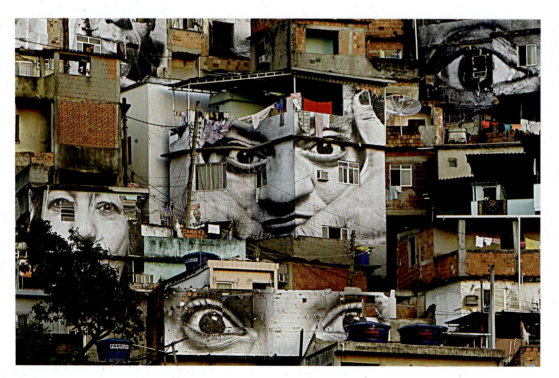

4.8.2 JR, Video still from *Women are Heroes: Favela Morro da Providência*, 2010. Rio de Janeiro, Brazil

Gateway to Art: Lange, *Migrant Mother*
The Impact and Ethics of Documentary Photography

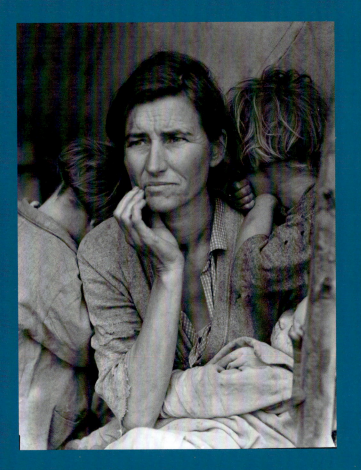

4.8.3 Dorothea Lange, *Migrant Mother*, 1936. Library of Congress, Washington, D.C.

Dorothea Lange's famous photograph of Florence Thompson, known as *Migrant Mother*, was used to demonstrate the plight of the poor and remains a powerful symbol of the struggle against poverty (**4.8.3**). The picture was taken in 1936 when Florence and her children were living in the remains of a Californian pea-pickers' camp. Lange's image had an immediate impact. The photograph was published in several newspapers and *Time* magazine. The federal government sent 20,000 pounds of food to the camp. Unfortunately, the Thompson family had migrated elsewhere before the supplies arrived.

While the photograph had an incalculable effect on people's understanding of the devastation of the Great Depression, Thompson herself was always ashamed and irritated by the portrait. To her mind, it never had a positive effect on her life. When the photograph was taken she was recently widowed, had six children, and worked wherever she could to support her family. She eventually had eleven children, and lived in fear that if the government knew of her financial difficulties they might take her children away. The identity of Thompson was not discovered until 1978, and she was quoted as saying, "I wish she hadn't taken my picture," and complained about never being compensated.

After Thompson's death, her children spoke of the frustration the photograph caused them as well. When they first saw their mother's photograph in a newspaper in 1936, they mistook an inkstain across her forehead for a shot wound, and ran home, where they were relieved to find her alive and well. Additionally, Lange's notes seem to have mixed up the details of the Thompsons with another family. The newspapers never mentioned that Thompson was a native American who became a migrant when she was displaced from her tribal land as a girl. It was not until 1983, when Florence lay on her deathbed, and letters of sympathy poured in, that the children changed their outlook:

> None of us really understood how deeply Mama's photo affected people. . .it gave us a sense of pride.

The experience of the Thompson family raises questions about the role of an artist when depicting an actual event. To what extent should the subject's privacy be protected, and to what extent should he or she be compensated, if at all, when his or her image has demonstrable effects on the social conscience? Almost 100 years after it was taken, Lange's photograph remains a memorable symbol of the plight of the poor, and since 1936 it has been published many times in books and newspapers and has twice featured on US postage stamps.

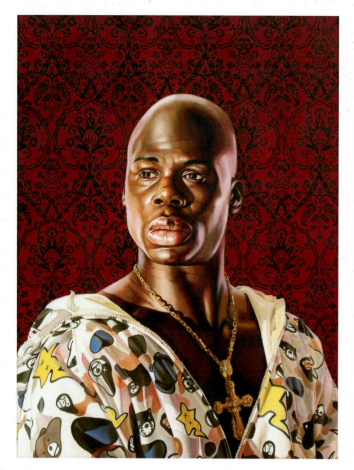

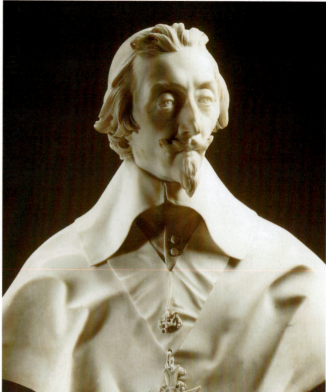

4.8.4 (left) Kehinde Wiley, *Portrait Bust of Cardinal Richelieu*, 2009. Oil on canvas, 48 x 36"

in Rio de Janeiro, Brazil. By displaying enormous photographs showing portions of women's faces, particularly their eyes, JR took a fresh approach to publicizing the problems of poverty and drugs in the severely deprived area. Installing the large photographs was a challenge in itself because of the dilapidation of many of the buildings, the steep climb to get to the structures, and the dangers of a neighborhood blighted by drug trafficking, violence, rape, and hunger. The eighteen women shown in the photographs deal with everyday vulnerability and the trauma of these dangers in their daily lives, yet they try to hold their families together and develop a sense of community.

Kehinde Wiley (b. 1977) is an African-American artist who noticed that the paintings in his local museum rarely showed dark-skinned figures. After studying many seminal **portraits** in the history of European art, he began to make artworks in a similar vein, but with **subjects** that he could relate to. In order to find these subjects for his paintings, he takes photographs

of ordinary people in their own clothing and asks them to re-create poses from famous artworks. Wiley forces the viewer to reconsider the significance of a portrait he or she is familiar with by casting dark-skinned men as the subject in scenes that were originally painted of and for white patrons.

In *Portrait Bust of Cardinal Richelieu* (**4.8.4**), the subject's pose is reminiscent of a white marble bust made by the Italian **Baroque** sculptor Gianlorenzo Bernini (1598–1680) (**4.8.5**). Bernini's sculpture, finished in 1641, is a likeness of the powerful French politician and churchman Cardinal Richelieu (1585–1642), in which the figure is draped in the vestments of a cardinal and wears a highly ornate cross. The cardinal himself was said to have disliked the bust because it showed him as a haughty, scornful figure.

The man in Wiley's painting has broad shoulders and a strong face that is self-assured rather than proud. His body is sculptural, reminiscent of Bernini's original, against a flat,

4.8.5 (above right) Gianlorenzo Bernini, *Bust of Cardinal Richelieu*, 1641. Marble, 33 × 10¼ × 13". Musée du Louvre, Paris, France

Portrait: image of a person or animal, usually focusing on the face
Subject: the person, object, or space depicted in a work of art
Baroque: European artistic and architectural style of the late sixteenth to early eighteenth century, characterized by extravagance and emotional intensity
Background: the part of a work depicted furthest from the viewer's space, often behind the main subject matter

Gateway to Art: Hokusai, "The Great Wave off Shore at Kanagawa"
Using Famous Art to Make a Social Difference

In 2009, contemporary artist Chris Jordan created a likeness of "The Great Wave off Shore at Kanagawa" by Katsushika Hokusai (4.8.6) in a bid to highlight the environmental problem of consumer waste. Jordan assembled more than 2.4 million pieces of plastic to create his artwork, *Gyre* (4.8.7), to reflect the number of pounds of plastic that are estimated to enter the world's oceans every hour. Jordan's artwork attempts to show the inconceivability of that number. The plastic for the artwork was collected from the Pacific Ocean, and the artist named the work after the Pacific Gyre, a thousand-mile whirlpool where enormous quantities of trash collect. By gathering together all the junk we discard, Jordan draws attention to the huge volume of waste that humans create. By using such familiar objects as toothbrushes and combs, the artist hopes to show people how their individual trash contributes to the larger problem.

The artist has recycled trash to create several artworks, and explains the thinking behind these works, which are intended to address American mass consumption in particular:

> The pervasiveness of our consumerism holds a seductive kind of mob mentality. Collectively we are committing a vast and unsustainable act of taking, but we each are anonymous and no one is in charge or accountable for the consequences. I am appalled by these scenes, and yet also drawn into them with awe and fascination. I find evidence of a slow-motion apocalypse in progress.

Jordan's reference to Hokusai's famous scene, which emphasizes the beauty and power of nature, encourages the viewer to reflect whether even the power of nature can survive this massive environmental problem and the threat it poses to the future of our planet.

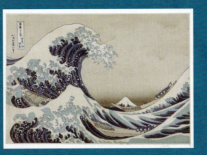

4.8.6 Katsushika Hokusai, "The Great Wave off Shore at Kanagawa", from *Thirty-Six Views of Mount Fuji*, 1826–33 [printed later]. Print, color woodcut. Library of Congress, Washington, D.C.

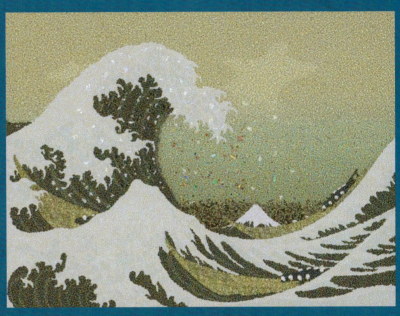

4.8.7a (above) Chris Jordan, "Gyre," from the series *Running the Numbers II: Portraits of global mass culture*, 2009. 2.4 million plastic pieces, digitally assembled, 8 x 11'

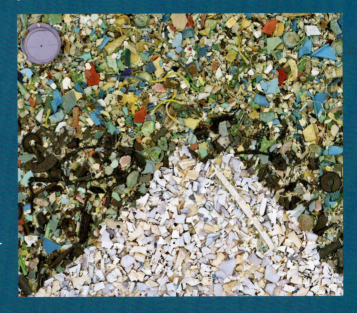

4.8.7b Chris Jordan, "Gyre," 2009 (detail)

decorative **background**, which is in the style favored by Italian painters during the Baroque period. Similarly to the cardinal in Bernini's bust, Wiley's subject wears a heavy cross, suggesting he is pious; this gold cross, however, recalls the modern gold chains frequently worn by ordinary people, and the man's jacket is modern and casual, and unzipped to highlight his dark skin further. His intense facial expression is quietly dignified. Wiley's virtuosity with paint is clear from the way he accurately depicts the play of light and shadows on the **sitter**'s skin. By painting this man in his own clothing, Wiley adapts traditional portraiture to a modern-day context. The artist has traveled the world working on this project, collecting subjects from France, Israel, Brazil, India, and various African countries to add to his portrait series.

Art as the Object of Protest: Censorship and Destruction

Art can inspire a forceful response. When the ideas an artwork represents are considered harmful or incompatible with a desired message or point of view, artworks might be censored or removed from public eyes. Sometimes the impact of a work of art is so powerful that viewers wish to destroy it, along with the message or attitude they see represented in it.

The *Rokeby Venus* (or *The Toilet of Venus*) by the Spanish artist Diego de Silva y Velázquez (1599–1660) (**4.8.8a**) may seem inoffensive to the modern viewer, but in 1914 it was the target of a violent protest. A woman called Mary Richardson, armed with a meat cleaver she had hidden inside her coat, slashed the *Rokeby Venus* seven times (**4.8.8b**). Richardson was a member of the Suffragette movement, which campaigned to give women the right to vote. For her, the painting represented a sexist definition of ideal beauty, showing a woman solely as an object of male desire. Richardson was motivated more specifically to protest against the imprisonment of the Suffragette leader Emmeline Pankhurst. Richardson later explained that she believed justice to be more valuable than art:

> I have tried to destroy the picture of the most beautiful woman in mythological history as a protest against the Government for destroying Mrs. Pankhurst, who is the most beautiful character in modern history.

Richardson's attack on the painting did not have its intended effect on perceptions of the *Rokeby Venus*. The seven slashes were soon completely repaired, and many still consider the painting to be a defining representation of female sensuality and beauty. Richardson was imprisoned briefly after the attack; the incident did not seem to help the Suffragette movement either (although some women did gain the right

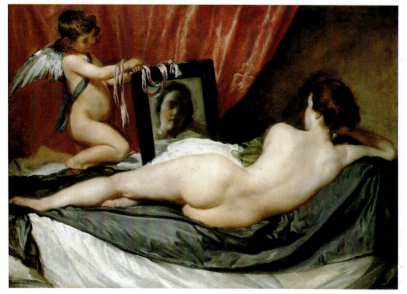

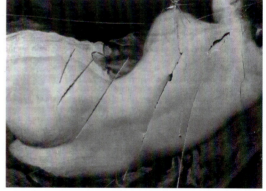

4.8.8a (left) Velázquez, *The Toilet of Venus* (*Rokeby Venus*), 1647–51. Oil on canvas, 48½ × 69¾". National Gallery, London, England

4.8.8b (above) Photograph of damage to the *Rokeby Venus*, 1914

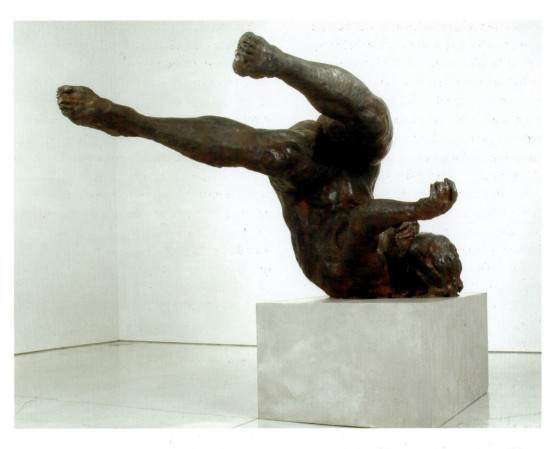

to vote in Britain in 1918). For a while after the incident, in fact, women were forbidden to enter the National Gallery, unless they were accompanied by a male chaperone.

While Velázquez's *Venus* was the subject of protest centuries after its creation, the American artist Eric Fischl's (b. 1948) *Falling Woman* provoked an instantaneous reaction (**4.8.9**). When the bronze sculpture, intended as a tribute to the victims of the terror attacks of September 11, 2001, was unveiled in New York City, it was considered so offensive that it was covered over almost immediately. It shows a woman in freefall, with her legs above her head and her arms flailing. Fischl placed a poem next to his artwork:

> We watched,
> Disbelieving and helpless,
> On that savage day.
> People we love
> Began falling,
> Helpless and in disbelief.

Many New Yorkers had witnessed firsthand the tragedy of desperate victims, trapped in the World Trade Center towers, jumping to their deaths to escape the fire. Perhaps because of this, Fischl's sculpture, displayed only a year after the terrorist attack, was seen as too potent and heart-wrenching. The artwork and the response to it reflect one of the challenges artists face when they address contemporary issues. Would Fischl's sculpture have been accepted if it had been unveiled many years later, when the event was no longer fresh in the minds of so many? Or was it simply too graphic, depicting a moment too shocking and too unbelievable for people ever to want to remember?

Some viewers, however, were upset that the sculpture was covered up, considering it a powerful reminder and a valid, even cathartic (emotionally releasing) response to what happened. "The sculpture was not meant to hurt anybody," said the artist:

> It was a sincere expression of the deepest sympathy for the vulnerability of the human condition. Both specifically towards the victims of Sept. 11 and towards humanity in general.

Censorship of Art: The Nazi Campaign against Modern Art

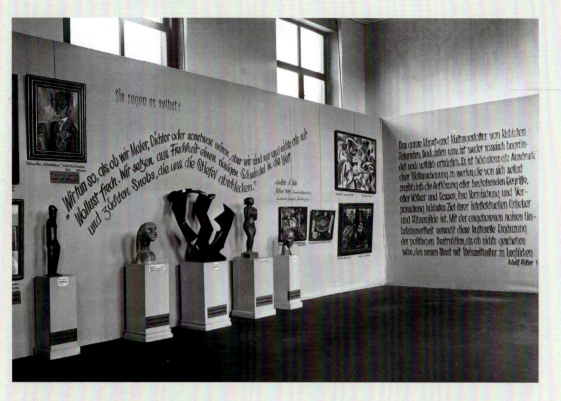

4.8.10 Photograph of the Nazi-curated traveling exhibition "Degenerate Art" (*Enkartete Kunst*) at its first stop at the Hofgarten, Munich, Germany, 1937

We have already discussed art's power to provoke a strong reaction, and, in some cases, to cause shifts in public opinion. For this reason, artworks and the artists who create them are often amongst the first to be targeted by dictatorial governments. They are also some of the first victims in times of war.

In Germany in the 1930s, the National Socialist (Nazi) regime of dictator Adolf Hitler launched a systematic and large-scale attack on modern art that did not conform to Nazi party goals. Although Hitler liked to think of himself as an artist, he abhorred modern art. He understood the power of art to persuade the masses, however.

The Nazis initially confiscated around 5,000 works of art from museums; they later took a further 16,500 from private collections. Some 4,000 of these were burned; others became the property of Nazi collectors, or were sold to foreign collectors for Nazi profit. The artists who made them were banned from working. The Nazis also dismissed museum directors, closed art schools, such as the famous **Bauhaus**, and burned books.

On July 18, 1937 the Nazis opened an exhibition of "Great German Art," which displayed the kind of art approved by the regime. The next day they opened another show of 730 works called "**Degenerate** Art," to suggest that these were the work of mentally deficient artists. Works were deliberately displayed awkwardly, and labels on the walls ridiculed the artworks (**4.8.10**). One read: "We act as if we were painters, poets, or whatever, but what we are is simply and ecstatically impudent. In our impudence we take the world for a ride and train snobs to lick our boots!"

One of the artists whose work was ridiculed in the exhibition was Emil Nolde (1867–1956). His series of nine panels on the Life of Christ were hung together next to writing on the wall that said: "Mockery of the Divine." The *Crucifixion*, the largest of the series (**4.8.11**) was placed in the center. Its unnaturally bright colors, the greenish pallor of Christ and other figures, and the blurry, unfinished look of the paintings made them, in the eyes of the creators of the exhibition, anti-religious.

Bauhaus: design school founded in Weimar, Germany, in 1919
Degenerate: considered to be less than a normal level in physical, mental, or moral qualities

Yet unlike most of the artists mocked at the show, Nolde was himself a member of the Nazi party. He was so appalled to see his work in the exhibition that he wrote to Paul Joseph Goebbels, the Nazi Minister of Propaganda, demanding that the "defamation" against him cease. Nolde's paintings were returned to him but he was ordered to stop making art. He continued to create watercolors in secret, fearing that he would be discovered if he used strong-smelling oil paint. Yet despite the constraints he was under, Nolde was one of the lucky artists. Dozens of others whose work featured in the show fled Germany or committed suicide, and many were later sent to concentration camps.

Attendance at the Degenerate Art exhibition was unparalleled for its time, with more than two million visitors in Munich alone, and one million more when the show went on tour through the rest of Germany and Austria. Although there are records of people spitting on the artworks, there remains little other evidence of what visitors actually thought of the art in this propaganda spectacle.

When the exhibitions ended, the Nazis sold some artworks to raise money for their impending war effort, but most of the artworks were destroyed, along with thousands of others considered degenerate. The freedom to create art and to have opinions about it are emblems of a peaceful society; the Degenerate Art show and the book burnings perpetrated by the Nazis are two examples of how extreme censorship can result in the end of peace and freedom for many.

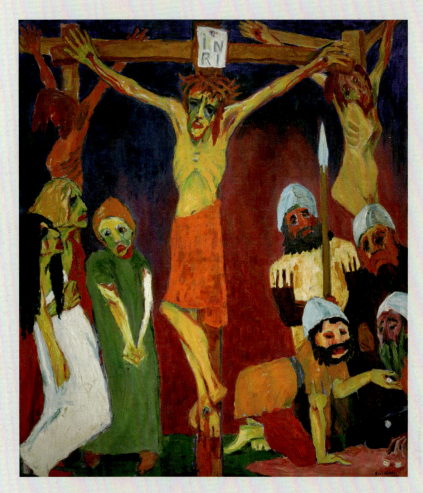

4.8.11 Emil Nolde, *The Crucifixion*, 1912, from a polyptych, *The Life of Christ*. Oil on canvas, 7'2⅝ × 6'3¼". Stiftung Seebüll A. & E. Nolde, Neukirchen, Germany

Discussion Questions

1. In this chapter we have studied many ways in which artists have made a powerful case about an issue that concerned them. Now ask yourself what issue you feel most passionately about, and create an artwork that communicates your ideas. Be persuasive and try to convey the reasons you believe as you do.

2. Study artworks in this chapter that have been censored or in some other way withheld from public view. Are there any other works you have read about that the public has been prevented from seeing? Do you believe that artworks should never be censored, or do you think that there are some subjects that should be banned? Write half a page defending your belief in the limits or freedom of expression in art, using at least two specific artworks as examples to make your point.

3. Which of the artworks in this chapter do you find to be the most moving or persuasive? Considering the elements and principles of art discussed in Part 1 of this book, perform a visual analysis of the artwork and consider what the artist did (in your opinion) so successfully.

Images Related to **4.8**:
Art of Social Conscience

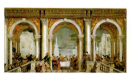

3.6.17 Paolo Veronese, *Christ in the House of Levi*, 1573, p. 480

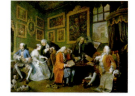

3.7.8 William Hogarth, *The Marriage Settlement*, c. 1743, p. 487

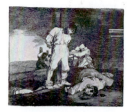

2.3.12b Francisco Goya, "And There Is No Remedy," from *Disasters of War*, c. 1810, p. 239

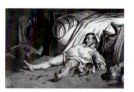

2.3.16 Honoré Daumier, *Rue Transnonain*, 1834, p. 242

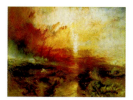

3.7.18 J. M. W. Turner, *Slave Ship*, 1840, p. 505

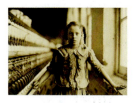

2.8.13 Lewis Wickes Hine, *Ten Year Old Spinner*, 1908, p. 327

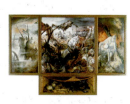

4.7.11 Otto Dix, *The War*, 1929–32, p. 643

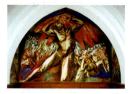

2.2.6 José Clemente Orozco, *Prometheus*, 1930, p. 219

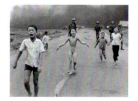

4.7.2 Nick Ut, *Vietnamese Girl Kim Phuc Running after Napalm Attack*, 1972, p. 636

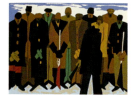

1.8.3 Jacob Lawrence, "John Brown Remained a Full Winter...," 1977, p. 158

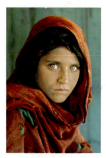

2.8.14a Steve McCurry, *Afghan Girl*, 1984, p. 327

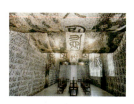

4.1.10 Wenda Gu, *United Nations—China Monument, Temple of Heaven*, 1998, p. 569

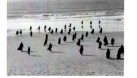

3.9.20b Shirin Neshat, *Rapture*, 1999, p. 554

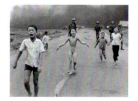

2.10.12 Kara Walker, *Insurrection!*, 2000, p. 362

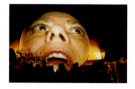

4.1.13 Krzysztof Wodiczko, *Tijuana Projection*, 2001, p. 573

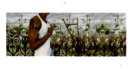

2.8.22 Stephen Marc, *Untitled—Passage on the Underground Railroad*, 2002, p. 333

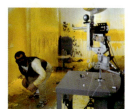

4.7.14 Wafaa Bilal, *Domestic Tension*, 2007, p. 645

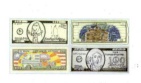

2.10.5 Mel Chin, *Operation Paydirt/Fundred Dollar Bill Project*, begun 2008, p. 356

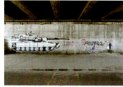

4.7.13 Ganzeer, *Tank vs. Bike*, with graffiti by Sad Panda, 2011, p. 644

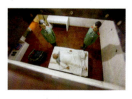

0.0.18b Ai Weiwei, *Entropy* (detail), from *S.A.C.R.E.D.*, 2011–13, p. 41

4.9

The Body in Art

The human **form** is one of the most common **subjects** in art, perhaps because making art about the body allows us to reflect on, come to terms with, and literally express ourselves. Some of the earliest sculptures made during **prehistoric** times depict human figures. Since then, artists have continued to portray the body, both clothed and unclothed, in motion and in repose. The body is not always portrayed as it "actually looks," and it may even be altered so much that it does not resemble a real human body at all. The reality of the body can be distorted to suggest great beauty, or to emphasize such qualities as power, status, wisdom, even godlike perfection. Personal and cultural preferences often determine the way an artist chooses to portray a body. Of course, the body itself can also participate in art: through performances, dances, rituals, and so on. As a subject, it offers endless expressive possibilities.

Archetypal Images of the Body

The Dutch-born American artist Willem de Kooning (1904–1997) made a series of paintings of women that incorporate bold, apparently aggressive, even violent, marks and slashing strokes (see p. 660). De Kooning said that his *Woman* series referred to "the female painted through all the ages, all those idols." The types of ancient figures to which de Kooning alluded, for example the *Woman from Willendorf* (**4.9.1**),

serve as **iconic** artistic models for the idea and image of woman.

The *Woman from Willendorf* is one of the earliest known artworks, dating to about 26,000 years ago. Female figurines have been discovered all over the world. In fact, such sculptures as this are commonly amongst the oldest created objects in a number of societies. The small size

4.9.1 *Woman from Willendorf*, c. 24,000–22,000 BCE. Oolitic limestone, 4⅜" high. Naturhistorisches Museum, Vienna, Austria

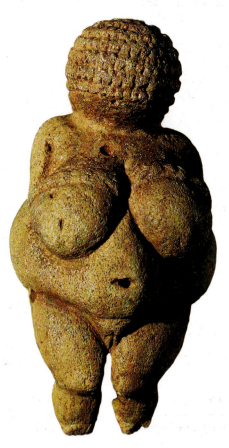

Form: an object that can be defined in three dimensions (height, width, and depth)
Subject: the person, object, or space depicted in a work of art
Prehistoric: dating from the period of human existence before the invention of writing
Iconic: possessing established and widely recognizable characteristics

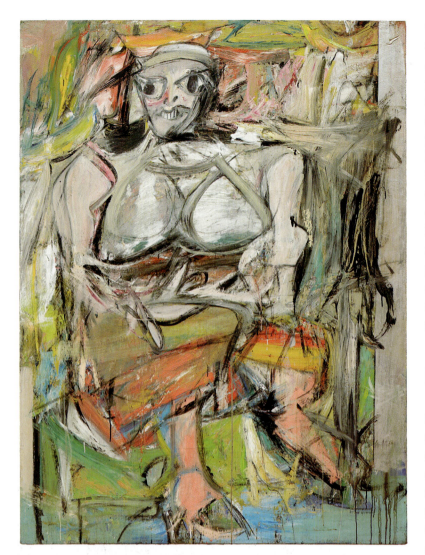

4.9.2 Willem de Kooning, *Woman I*, 1950–52. Oil on canvas, 6'3⅞" × 4'10". MoMA, New York

of this figurine, just over 4 in. tall, made it easily portable, a benefit for nomadic people. Because of the maker's emphasis on female anatomy (breasts, buttocks, and rotund belly), the *Woman from Willendorf* is believed to be a fertility figure. Perhaps it was used as a charm to encourage pregnancy, or as a teaching tool. It almost certainly celebrates the woman as a mother and bringer of life.

The exaggerated form and emphasis on characteristically female elements of human anatomy visually connect the *Woman from Willendorf* with de Kooning's *Woman I* (**4.9.2**). This large painting, made thousands of years after the tiny sculpture was created, features the glaring eyes and grinning mouth of a woman's face at the top of the composition. By contrast, the *Woman from Willendorf* does not include facial features at all. In *Woman I* the most prominent parts of the body are the breasts,

while the arms and legs are minimized in a manner similar to the *Woman from Willendorf*. Although both artworks convey the inherent power of women as givers and protectors of life, they do so very differently. De Kooning's woman seems strong to the point of being ferocious. The painting is physically big, over lifesized, making literal the larger-than-life feeling conveyed by the small sculpture. Both figures have an **abstracted** form, visible in the rough shapes of the *Woman from Willendorf* and the jagged brushstrokes of *Woman I*. Their appearance makes them less representations of individual people and more reflections of a universal idea of powerful women. As de Kooning's statement suggests, *Woman I* embodies "the female… through all the ages."

Ideal Proportion

Long before de Kooning's search to find something universal about the female figure, the ancient Egyptians applied formal mathematical systems in consistent ways to depict their ideal of the human form. They developed a standardized method for depicting men and women, and used it for thousands of years. A similar system of proportion was later adopted by the Greeks for their **figurative** sculpture and influenced European artists during the **Renaissance**. These **idealized** proportions, clearly visible in figurative paintings, reliefs, and three-dimensional sculpture, were applied to architectural construction as well. The **canon of proportions** was developed to make the depicted body match ancient Egyptian notions of perfection.

The Egyptian canon of proportions is calculated in the form of a grid that provides consistent measurements of the parts of the body (**4.9.3a**). Each square of the grid represents a standard small measurement, or a unit, based on the width of the pharaoh's clenched hand. Sometimes other ratios are used to make the grid, resulting in a slightly different but still standardized appearance. The pharaoh's body was used as the standard for measurement because all measure came from the king. In fact, the **hierarchical scale** used in Egyptian depictions of multiple figures shows the pharaoh and nobles as significantly larger than workers, members of lower classes, and animals, because they were viewed as being of greater importance.

Thus, in ancient Egyptian art, the portrayal of the body followed **conventions**, or prescribed methods, which produced consistent results. Egyptian depictions of the human body, as a result, look very similar even when they have been produced thousands of years apart. In sculpture, royal figures are shown either seated or standing, firmly connected to the stone from which they are carved, with their arms and hands close to their sides. In standing poses, the feet are firmly planted on the ground with the legs slightly apart and one foot in front of the other, as if the figure is about to take a step. Any suggestion of movement is potential, however, as

if the figure is frozen; if it were in motion, its weight would shift to one side or the other. In the Egyptian figure, the feet are flat, the hips are even and immobile, and the shoulders are entirely square.

The use of the canon gives the sculpture of *Menkaure and His Wife, Queen Khamerernebty*, an austere strength (**4.9.3b**). Their poses make the figures look rigid, calm, and enduring. They stand close together, as a single unit, his hands close to his sides and hers embracing his arm and torso. Their bodies do not twist and the features are bilaterally symmetrical (meaning that the left side matches the right). The strong, frontal pose suggests that the power of the pharaoh is changeless, unwavering, and eternal. This representation is idealized: the couple's appearance is based on abstract concepts rather than direct observation.

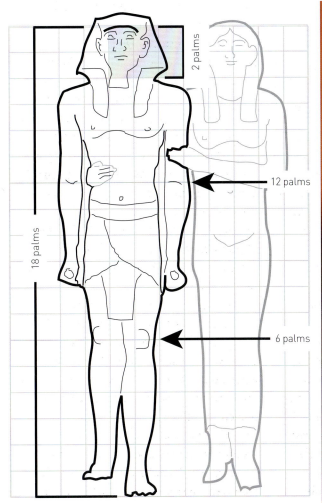

4.9.3a Canon of proportions: *Menkaure and His Wife, Queen Khamerernebty*

18 palms
2 palms
12 palms
6 palms

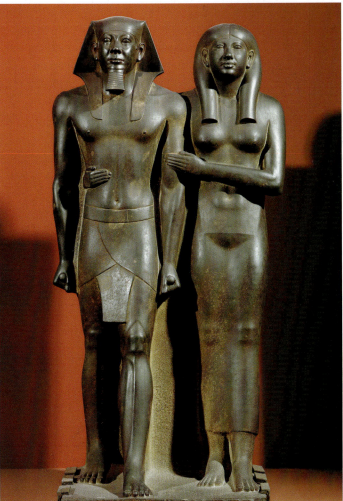

4.9.3b *Menkaure and His Wife, Queen Khamerernebty*, 4th Dynasty, *c.* 2520 BCE. Graywacke, 54¾ × 22½ × 21¼". Museum of Fine Arts, Boston, Massachusetts

Notions of Beauty

Ideal proportions inform many cultural notions of preferred body type. Our notions of beauty are formed by our personal experiences and by the society in which we live. If we look at the ways in which artists have depicted the human form, we soon realize that in different times and places beauty can mean very different things (see Box: Reclining Nudes, pp. 664–665). In some cultures small feet or long necks are admired. Some groups may favor plump, even voluptuous, bodies, while others prefer slender, very thin and angular physiques. Our bodies can also express many things about our personalities: we can appear calm or agitated, elegant or unkempt, smart or stupid, sensuous or intellectual. The complex relationship between internal characteristics and outward appearance has led artists to explore these aspects of beauty through the human form.

The notions of beauty held by the ancient Greeks were based upon the combination of an underlying canon of mathematical proportions with the finely honed physiques possessed by male athletes. It was far more common to see a Greek male than a Greek female figure sculpted in the **nude**. Depicting the body without clothes allowed artists to study musculature and reflect observations and knowledge of the anatomy in a way that a clothed body does not show. Because the Greeks hoped to model themselves after gods, they aimed for perfect balance between mind and body in both their lives and their art. Such sculptures as the *Discus Thrower* demonstrate the ideal musculature of the athletic body (**4.9.4**). Greek athletes competed in the nude, and sculptures of male sportsmen celebrated the strength and virility inherent in the masculine form. The *Discus Thrower* also shows the competitor immersed in concentration, his mind in complete harmony with his physique.

In ancient Greece, although the male nude was certainly more common, the female nude eventually began to gain respectability in the late fourth century BCE. Years later, during the Renaissance, such Italian artists as Sandro Botticelli (*c.* 1445–1510) revived the appearance of the female nude as it had been depicted in antiquity. In Botticelli's day the female nude became an acceptable subject as long as it appeared in a historical or mythological context.

4.9.4 (above) Myron, *Discus Thrower (Discobolos)*, Roman copy of Greek bronze original from *c.* 450 BCE. Marble, 5'1" high. Museo delle Terme, Rome, Italy

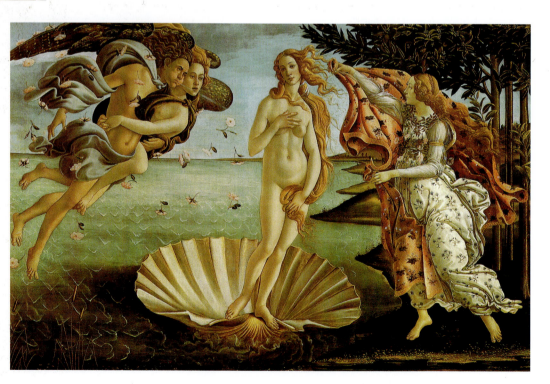

4.9.5 (right) Sandro Botticelli, *The Birth of Venus*, *c.* 1482–86. Tempera on canvas, 5'8" × 9'1⅝". Uffizi Gallery, Florence, Italy

According to Classical mythology, Venus, the goddess of love and beauty, first emerged from the sea as a fully formed adult on a shell. In his painting *The Birth of Venus* (**4.9.5**), Botticelli focuses on the moment when Venus has been blown to shore. She is wafted toward the land by Zephyr, the god of the west wind, who is accompanied by the earth nymph Chloris. Awaiting Venus is a goddess or nymph who will wrap her in a blanket of flowers. Venus has smooth ivory-colored skin, long flowing hair, and an elegant pose. She discreetly covers her nudity, indicating that chastity is part of her appeal. The graceful shape and the flawless quality of her body reflect the purity of the newborn goddess and create a harmonious and pleasing composition. Botticelli has modeled his figure on an ancient sculpture, thus basing his conception of beauty on Classical Greek standards.

In African societies, notions of beauty are often closely tied to the community's core values of composure and wisdom, believed to reflect, even increase, a person's power. In other words, beauty is about more than external appearance. It is also about internal and societal principles. Being calm, wise, and composed were important attributes for the kings of Ife in West Africa. The elegant lines, delicate features, and elaborate headdress of the terra-cotta head in **4.9.6** indicate that it probably represents an Ife king, or *oni*. As the head was considered the seat of intelligence and the source of power, this sculpture's exquisite features draw our attention there. The lifelike details—the folds of the ears, the contours of the nose, and the plumpness of the lips—are extremely naturalistic, but also graceful and refined. The fine lines on the face resemble scarification patterns, or scars created by cutting or branding the skin. Beauty in this case is a balance of invisible internal characteristics and an idealized, visible, outward appearance.

Many cultures determine beauty by a person's ability to conform to expectations, whether through clothes, cosmetics, or body shape. In Japan, traditional female performers called *geisha* are known for their social skills and artistic talents, such as singing, dancing, and serving tea. Geisha, not to be confused with courtesans or prostitutes, have a professional relationship with their clients and are strongly discouraged from becoming too intimate with them. A geisha's appearance changes over the course of her career. Early on she wears dramatic hairstyles, heavy makeup, dark eyeliner, and red lip pencil applied to make her lips look small. As an apprentice, the source of her beauty lies in her appearance, but later it is seen to derive from her maturity and her *gei*, or art. After three years of apprenticeship, a geisha adopts less elaborate kimonos tied with simpler knots, lighter makeup, and a subdued hairstyle, like the one seen in Kaigetsudo Dohan's *Beautiful Woman* (**4.9.7**). Like other Japanese artists, Kaigetsudo Dohan (working 1710–16) celebrated beautiful women, here emphasizing the experienced geisha's impressive attire and relatively natural appearance. In addition to her musical skills and gift for intelligent conversation, this mature geisha would have been appreciated for her inner beauty.

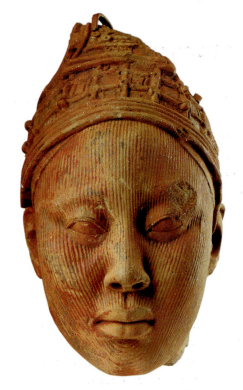

4.9.6 Head, possibly an Ife king, 12th–14th century. Terra-cotta with residue of red pigment and traces of mica, 10½ × 5¾ × 7⅜". Kimbell Art Museum, Fort Worth, Texas

4.9.7 Kaigetsudo Dohan, *Beautiful Woman*, Edo Period, Japan, 18th century. Hanging scroll, ink and color on paper, 64⅜ × 20⅛". Metropolitan Museum of Art, New York

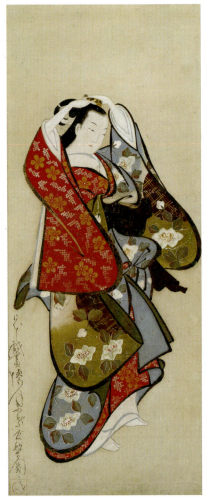

Reclining Nudes

While nudes have long been a subject in the history of art, the tradition of depicting the nude female figure lying down, or reclining, was established during the Renaissance. These types of picture recall the ancient Greek emphasis on the beauty and honesty conveyed by the nude human form. In some cases they also suggest the sensuality of the nude.

The Venetian painter known as Titian (c. 1485/90–1576) was influenced by the Classical tradition when he painted a female nude for the duke of the Italian town of Urbino (4.9.8). The roses in the woman's right hand hint at her identity: they are a symbol of Venus, the Classical goddess of beauty (hence the name by which the painting is commonly known, the *Venus of Urbino*). She looks out from her couch with a coy expression and casually covers her pubic area, at once modest and inviting, as if she exists simply to be looked at. The presence of the maids in the background preparing her clothes, however, connects her to the concerns of a real woman.

But by suggesting that his painting depicted a mythological figure, Titian was able to explore in depth such secular themes as the nature of love and desire.

It is clear that the French artist Édouard Manet (1832–1883) was familiar with the *Venus of Urbino* when he painted his *Olympia* (4.9.9). The **composition** of the paintings and the posture of the women within them are almost identical. Manet, however, has replaced the sleeping dog at the foot of the bed with a hissing black cat. And instead of the maids in the background, there is a black servant who brings Olympia flowers. In this painting, as in others, Manet took a Classical subject and updated it for his own time. In modernizing the reclining nude, Manet considered the reality of the situation. Why would a woman be naked and on display? One obvious answer: because she is a prostitute. Not only was Olympia a common name for a prostitute, but Manet depicted her as a real woman, thin (at least by the standards of the time) and probably poor. Olympia's pose would have seemed

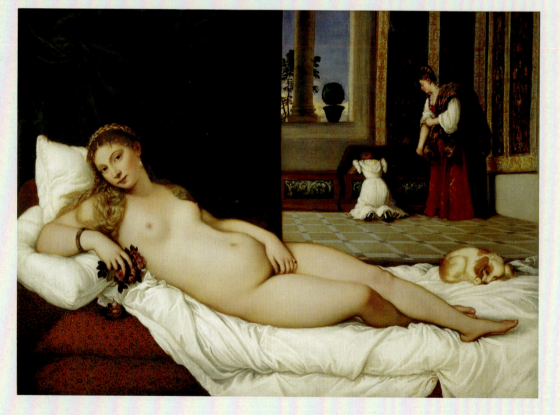

4.9.8 Titian, *Venus of Urbino*, 1538. Oil on canvas, 3'10⅞" × 5'5". Uffizi Gallery, Florence, Italy

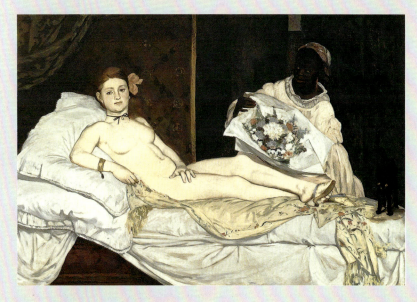

4.9.9 Édouard Manet, *Olympia*, 1863. Oil on canvas, 3'3⅜" × 6'2¾". Musée d'Orsay, Paris, France

confrontational because she stares out at the viewer in an assertive way, while people at that time were used to seeing more passive women with voluptuous bodies and docile expressions similar to the *Venus of Urbino*'s.

In the late twentieth century, the Japanese artist Yasumasa Morimura (b. 1951) revisited the theme of the reclining nude (**4.9.10**). The meaning of this piece, like that of Manet's *Olympia*, gains depth if one knows about the earlier artworks to which it alludes. Morimura employs digital processes, which allow him to play the roles of both Olympia and the servant. The resulting photograph is part of a series that the artist made in which he impersonates famous female icons from Western culture, transcending race, gender, and ethnicity. Here, the act of covering the genitalia with the left hand takes on entirely new significance in disguising the truth of his masculinity. The robes of the earlier pieces are replaced with a kimono and the cat at the foot of the bed is a porcelain Lucky Cat, commonly found in Japanese restaurants and shops as a talisman of good fortune. Morimura's reclining nude updates the theme with current technology and raises pertinent questions about identity, suggesting that appearances can be deceptive, that race and gender are artificial constructions, that we should not make assumptions about identity, and that our understanding of who we are is influenced by the past.

4.9.10 Yasumasa Morimura, *Portrait* (*Futago*), 1988–90. Color photograph, printed in 2 editions at varying sizes

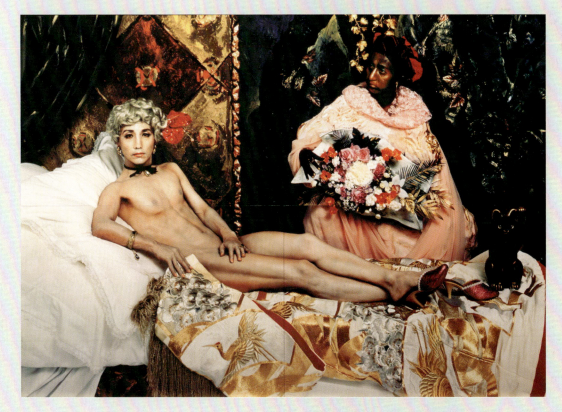

Composition: the overall design or organization of a work

Performance Art: The Body Becomes the Artwork

Geisha are considered living works of art. Similarly, in **performance art**, and in some **installations**, the body and its actions become the artwork (see Perspectives on Art Box: Spencer Tunick: Human Bodies as Installations, pp. 668–69.) A performance by definition involves the human form in action, but by engaging all of a viewer's senses through movement, expression, sound, smell, and so on, it also activates the space itself. The performers share a space with the audience, and the art becomes part of the viewer's lived experience. Because performances are not permanent or static, once they are finished they can be re-experienced only indirectly, through documentation. Written accounts, photographs, and videos taken at the time remind us later of the performances themselves.

Perhaps inspired by his deep interest in the martial art of judo, the French artist Yves Klein (1928–1962) began experimenting with "living brushes," or women using their bodies as the vehicle for applying paint to canvas. In the late 1950s he had been one of the first artists to make **monochromatic**, or one-color, paintings. He used a bright, dense, ultramarine blue, a color that he eventually patented as "International Klein Blue" (IKB). Klein integrated performance in an innovative way to make the blue paintings for which he was known. The first paintings made by the "living brushes" were monochromes that looked like the ones Klein himself had produced. Later, the women left imprints of their bodies on the canvas or paper (**4.9.11b**).

Klein devised the pieces, directed the women, and hired an orchestra for the first public performance of the "living brushes," called *Anthropométries de l'époque bleue* (or *Anthropometries of the Blue Period*) (**4.9.11a**). In order to create a musical accompaniment that was suitable for monochromatic paintings,

4.9.11a (below left) Yves Klein, *Anthropométries de l'époque bleue*, March 9, 1960. Galerie Internationale d'Art Contemporain, Paris, France

4.9.11b (below right) Yves Klein, *Anthropométrie sans titre*, 1960. Pure pigment and synthetic resin on paper mounted on canvas, 50⅞ × 14⅝". Private collection

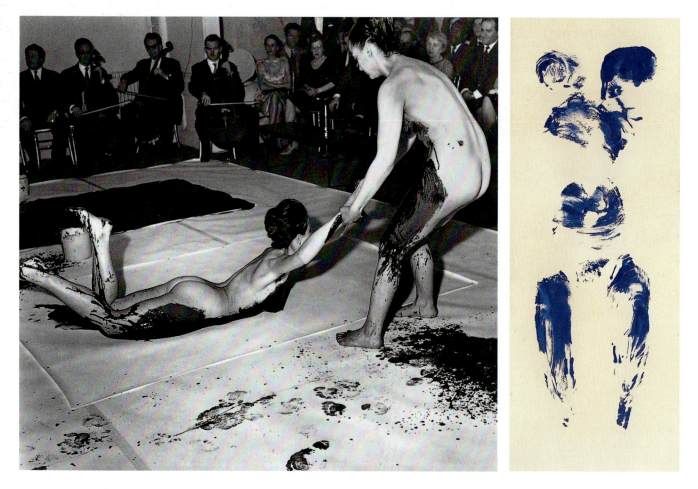

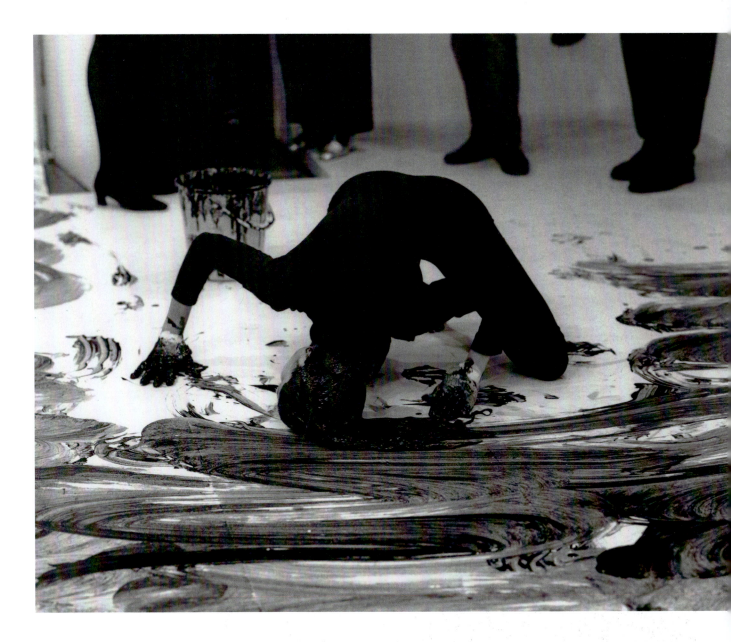

4.9.12 Janine Antoni, *Loving Care*, 1993. Performance with Loving Care hair dye Natural Black, dimensions variable. Photographed by Prudence Cuming Associates at Anthony d'Offay Gallery, London, England, 1993

Monochromatic: having one or more values of one color

Klein had the musicians play a single chord for twenty minutes and then sit in silence for twenty minutes. In an art gallery, works of art are usually inert, still objects and it is the viewers who move around (often in silence). In the case of Klein's performances, the artwork itself moved and made sounds while the audience sat still, giving the work a very physical presence in the usually quiet and austere gallery. At the same time, attention was brought to the odd circumstance of living nude figures as "art," now active in the gallery space instead of represented in artworks, and surrounded by a fully clothed audience.

Unlike Klein, who directed rather than participated in his artworks, artist Janine Antoni (b. 1964 in the Bahamas) uses her own body and her own actions as the basis for most of her performances. In *Loving Care*, named for a brand of hair-care products, Antoni dipped her head in a bucket of hair color and proceeded to mop the floor with it, using her hair as a paintbrush (**4.9.12**). As more and more of the floor became covered with gestural marks, viewers were pushed out of the gallery space. The artwork comments on several typically "feminine" actions, including the domesticity of mopping and the messiness of using cosmetics for beautification. Antoni takes the dynamic creative role here, bringing attention to the actions she is performing as well as to the status of women in the art world and in society.

Perspectives on Art: Spencer Tunick
Human Bodies as Installations

The American photographer Spencer Tunick (b. 1967) is famous for his installations involving crowds of nude people (4.9.13a). He explains how he came to make such work, and how complicated it can be to organize the people.

I didn't start out photographing hundreds or thousands of nude people. From 1992 to 1994 I worked on individual portraits of nudes on the streets of New York. I gained confidence in my ability to work on a public street, to deal with traffic, traffic light intervals, and the police. I switched to multiples when I had so many people to work with. I would carry the photographs round in my wallet and show them to people. By 1994 I had phone numbers for twenty-eight people and I decided to photograph them all at once outside the UN

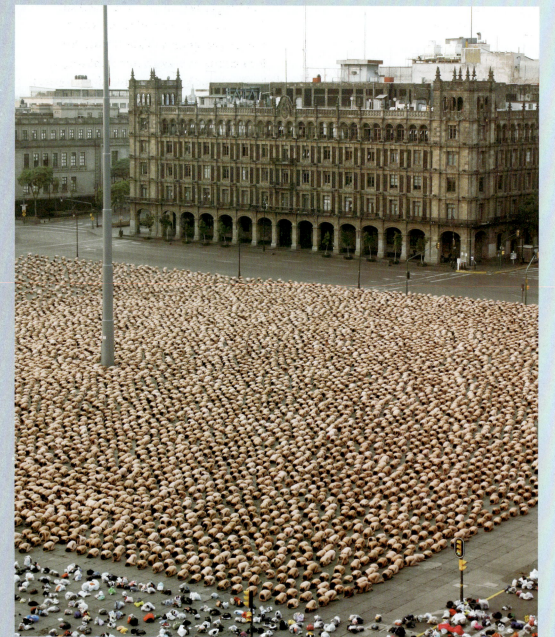

4.9.13a (left) Spencer Tunick, Installation at Zócalo, Mexico City, Mexico, May 6, 2007. More than 18,000 people participated

4.9.13b (opposite above) Spencer Tunick steps through 300 people whom he arranged as a living sculpture near City Hall, Fribourg, Switzerland, 2001

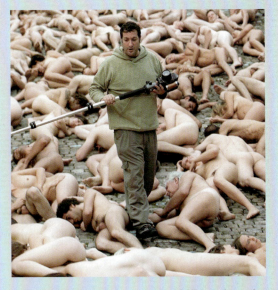

building in New York. Then in 1997 I gathered 1,000 people on an air-force base in Maine at a music concert.

I travel with a team of eight. In each city a contemporary art museum commissions my work and I can work wherever in the city I like. The museum provides team leaders and volunteers. Mexico City took three years to organize and one day to make the art. There were 250 team leaders and volunteers and 250 police officers. In Caracas, Venezuela, there were almost 1,000 police and military.

I know 75 percent of what I am going to do before we start but I like to keep an element of mystery. I have control of thousands of people, but in a way I don't like that control. I like to keep the event loose, personal, and intimate. Participants are not involving themselves in a spectacle but in a work of art. After ten minutes, once they get used to being nude, they get excited and start raising their hands in the air and so on, and then they calm down and we get organized.

I consider my works to be installations, not performances or photographs. I document the installations with photos and videos. I have two videographers and could have people take the photographs also, but I like to frame the photos and tweak them on location.

I still do individual portraits in streets. I am interested in the body and its relationship to the background. Instead of the body creating a meaning for the background, the background creates a new meaning for the body.

The Body in Pieces

Artists have used exaggeration, stylization, and innovation to create abstract representations of the human body. Approaches from outside the Western European tradition, such as African masks and pre-Columbian sculptures from the Americas, influenced some modern European artists to make works suggesting forms that are altered but recognizable. Others have taken certain elements of the anatomy out of their usual context by distorting or fragmenting the body. We do not have to see a whole body to read it as a human figure (see Perspectives on Art: "*The Blue Nude*: Cutouts as the Essence of Form," **4.9.17**, p. 671). Recognizing this fact, artists have focused attention away from identifying a particular individual or illustrating a coherent story in order to emphasize ways in which the body can be broken down and presented as a product of the human imagination.

In his artworks, the French artist Auguste Rodin (1840–1917) altered the appearance of the human body, which is one of the reasons he is now known as a pioneer in the field of modern sculpture. His innovations influenced many twentieth-century sculptors, including Henry

4.9.14 Auguste Rodin, *Walking Man*, c.1890–95. Bronze, 33¾ × 22 × 11". MoMA, New York

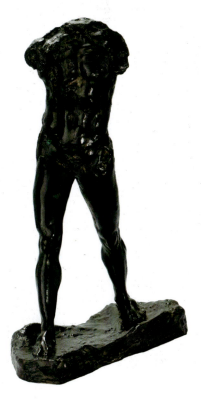

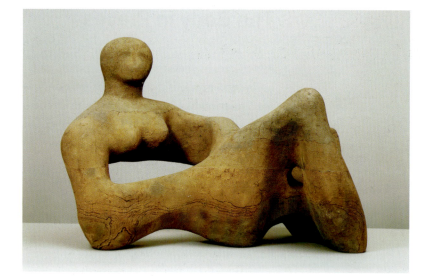

4.9.15 Henry Moore, *Recumbent Figure*, 1938. Green Hornton stone, 35 × 52¼ × 29". Tate, London, England

4.9.16 Alberto Giacometti, *Man Pointing*, 1947. Bronze, 70½ × 40¾ × 16⅜". MoMA, New York

Palette: the range of colors used by an artist
Sketch: a rough preliminary version of a work or part of a work
Plane: a flat surface, often implied by the composition
Stencil: a perforated template allowing ink or paint to pass through to print a design
Artist's book: a book produced by an artist, usually an expensive limited edition, often using specialized printing processes
Silhouette: a portrait or figure represented in outline and solidly colored in
Contour: the outline that defines a form
Avant-garde: early twentieth-century emphasis on artistic innovation, which challenged accepted values, traditions, and techniques

Moore and Alberto Giacometti (see **4.9.15** and **4.9.16**). Although he had been formally trained, Rodin chose not to make his sculptures in the traditional, academic way. Instead of idealizing figures to look like perfected versions of actual people, Rodin intentionally left his surfaces rough, as seen in his sculpture *Walking Man* (**4.9.14**). The scrapes and gouges on the figure's chest, torso, and hips stand as evidence of the material the artist touched and manipulated to make the sculpture. Rodin also considered fragmentary representations, such as this one, which has no head or arms, to be completed sculptures rather than preparatory sketches. At the time, Rodin's pieces, which looked so different from the smooth, idealized figures people had come to expect, were harshly criticized. Since then, his approach has been praised for allowing the figures to be more expressive, emotional, and individual.

Like Rodin, the British sculptor Henry

Moore (1898–1986) created figures that did not match the way the human body actually looks. Instead Moore made connections with natural forms in the shapes of bodies and their parts, which often resemble mountains, hills, cliffs, and valleys. The organic lines in his sculptures mimic the organic **contours** of the materials he used, usually wood and stone. In addition to nature, Moore was inspired by other works of art. He studied a range of artistic traditions outside the West, as well as Classical and **avant-garde** European approaches. As a result of these influences, he departed from visible reality for the sake of making a strong artistic statement. A consistent characteristic of his sculptures is his use of the void, an empty space that opens up the figure and creates visual interest. In *Recumbent Figure* the large hole in the center of the piece is surrounded by the masses that make up the body (**4.9.15**). The legs look like peaks while the abdomen is in the place of a valley. The breasts help to identify the shape as a female figure.

The Swiss artist Alberto Giacometti (1901–1966) also stretched the boundaries of the recognizable form: first through Surrealist examinations of the human body, and then, after World War II, through the existential views represented in such sculptures as *Man Pointing* (**4.9.16**). Giacometti's obsessive nature at times caused him to reduce figures to the point where they were almost nonexistent. Eventually he began to accept his own artistic vision, in which the bodies look as if they are being seen from an extreme distance. The figures seem to have stepped out of the artist's dreams and into reality, carrying with them an air of mystery. *Man Pointing* is an imposing figure, despite its apparent fragility. At 5 ft. 8 in. tall, it is hard to believe that it can support its own weight. Giacometti struck a delicate balance between the figure and its surroundings in this sculpture, which he first made in clay and then cast in bronze. Nothing indicates why the man is pointing, but the space around him seems almost heavy. The sculpture looks like a trace of the shadow the man casts rather than the man himself, emphasizing the figure's loneliness and isolation.

Perspectives on Art: Henri Matisse
The Blue Nude: Cutouts and the Essence of Form

Experimental artists, such as the Frenchman Henri Matisse (1869–1954), have consistently used the female nude as a subject for creative innovation. Throughout his career, Matisse was moving toward a more economical use of artistic elements. Early on, he made very detailed recordings of the world he observed around him. After the 1940s, he chose to isolate forms and reduce the range of his **palette**, emphasizing the elements he thought to be the most important for a particular subject, because, as he wrote, "exactitude is not truth." Even his **sketches** for individual artworks went from complex recordings of very detailed observations to pictures with selected details and limited colors. This approach suited the technique of making cutouts, as seen in both *Blue Nude II* (**4.9.17**) and *Icarus* (**4.9.18**).

In these works, Matisse gives us enough information to know that we are looking at a human body. Their shapes are rough, but energetic. The palette in *Blue Nude II* is restricted to blue only. The color blue is not used to shade the female figure or to make her look as if she is bathed in blue light. Instead, her form is made entirely of flat **planes** of color. Matisse started the cutout design for *Icarus* in the same way he made *Blue Nude II*, by shaping the figure with scissors. He then made a **stencil** print so he could produce multiple copies of *Icarus*, along with handwritten text about flight, for his **artist's book** called *Jazz*. Again, the work focuses on expressing the

4.9.17 (right) Henri Matisse, *Blue Nude II*, 1952. Gouache on paper, cut and pasted on white paper, 45¾ × 32¼". Musée National d'Art Moderne, Centre Georges Pompidou, Paris, France

4.9.18 (below left) Henri Matisse, *Icarus*, from *Jazz*, 1943–47. Page size 16⅞ × 12⅞". MoMA, New York

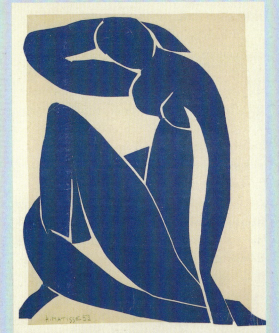

essence of the body's energy, which the artist also highlights by using the brilliant red dot to represent the heart, in a form otherwise shown as a simple black **silhouette**.

An essay of 1947 by Matisse, describing a series of self-portraits made using a mirror, helps explain how he arrived at this technique and what he hoped to communicate by making art the way he did:

These drawings sum up, in my opinion, observations that I have made for many years about the character of drawing, a character that does not depend on forms being copied exactly as they are in nature, or on the patient assembling of exact details, but on the profound feeling of the artist before the objects that he has chosen, on which his attention is focused, and whose spirit he has penetrated.

My conviction about these things crystallized when I realized for example that in the leaves of a fig tree—of a fig tree particularly—the great difference of forms that exists among them does not keep them from sharing a common quality. Fig leaves, whatever their fantastic variations of form, always remain unmistakably fig leaves. I have made the same observation about other growing things: fruits, vegetables, etc.

Thus there exists an essential truth that must be disengaged from the outward appearance of the objects to be represented. This is the only truth that matters . . .

Exactitude is not truth.

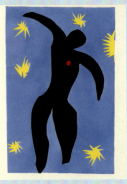

The Body Reframed

In the late twentieth century a number of artists, many of them women, began to focus very deliberately on the female body with a view to challenging traditional preconceptions about women that they perceived as limiting. Some of the new artworks these artists created included the artist's own body, in more confrontational ways than had previously been attempted in art. Many of the works exposed a much more nuanced, often disturbing, view of the female "nude" than the frequently submissive images created by men in previous eras, and artists tried to express a whole new range of ways in which the female form could be presented. In so doing they rejected unrealistic notions of "ideal" body image: now, the female body could be seen as a source of power, action, and enquiry.

The British painter Jenny Saville (b. 1970) is an artist who has chosen an unconventional approach to depicting the female body. In such larger-than-lifesize self-portraits as *Branded*, which is 7 ft. tall, she appears as a **monumental** nude (**4.9.19**). From this vantage point Saville's breasts and stomach are far more prominent than her head, which is barely squeezed into the frame. She glances down with a look of disdain as she pinches a roll of flesh with her left hand, as if peering into a mirror. Not only does her nude figure appear fat, countering contemporary society's bias toward thin women (and noticeably exaggerating Saville's actual size), but her discolored skin is also far from ideal. To make her paintings, Saville refers to photographs and medical illustrations of flesh tones, bruises, dimples, and pockmarks. Such words as "delicate," "supportive," "irrational," "decorative," and "petite," inscribed on her body, comment on society's expectations of the kind of body a woman should have. Saville has said that she uses her body as a prop that she is willing to distort and manipulate. The results are direct, if harsh and critical. By confronting—even exaggerating—the imperfections of reality, Saville comments on the conflicted relationship women sometimes have with their own body image, and on society's unreasonable

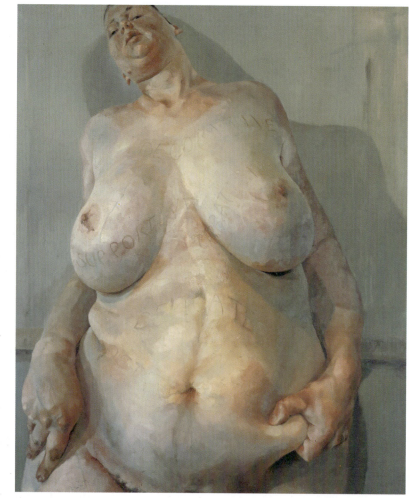

4.9.19 Jenny Saville, *Branded*, 1992. Oil on canvas, 7 × 6′

expectations of how they should appear in order to be perceived as "acceptable" or "attractive."

The French performance artist ORLAN (b. 1947) adopted an even more extreme approach to constructing the female body. ORLAN's artistic medium is literally her own body: in order to create a new persona, she underwent plastic surgeries that transformed her appearance, and documented the entire process (**4.9.20a and b**). An operating room became the stage for ORLAN's "performance." She was the star, the medical team the cast, with costumes created by famous fashion designers. Because she was given only a local anesthetic, ORLAN was able to remain conscious and read aloud from philosophical and poetic texts while the procedures were carried out. Video cameras in the operating room transmitted a live feed of the surgery to CBS News, the Sandra Gering Gallery in New York, and the Centre Georges Pompidou in Paris. ORLAN also documented the stages of

Monumental: having massive or impressive scale

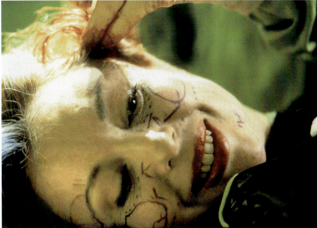

4.9.20a ORLAN, Seventh surgery-performance, entitled *Omnipresence*, November 21, 1993. *Smile of Delight (Sourire de Plaisir)*. Cibachrome in diasec mount, 43¼ × 65"

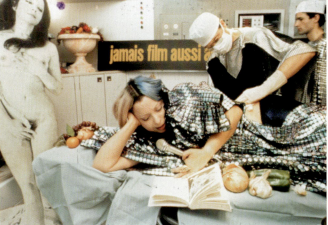

4.9.20b ORLAN, Fourth surgery-performance, entitled *Successful Operation*, December 8, 1991, Paris

her transformation with photographs taken as she healed.

In her final incarnation, ORLAN had become a composite woman. Her features were modeled after famously beautiful paintings of women: her chin was copied from Botticelli's Venus (see **4.9.5** on p. 662); her mouth from the Roman deity Diana in a renowned French Renaissance canvas; her nose from Psyche, the mythical lover of Cupid, in a French painting by François Gérard; and her brow from Leonardo da Vinci's *Mona Lisa*. ORLAN has said her work aims to intervene in the historical representation of women in art by actively determining her own appearance; to comment on the ways technology empowers us to transcend our human limitations; to critique the cult of beauty that imposes unfair standards on women; and to make a statement about the impossibility of physical perfection even in an age when plastic surgery is performed routinely. The measures she takes expose the tyranny of societal preconceptions about physical appearance because, by having herself operated on, she shows how extreme the insistence on stereotypical notions of female beauty has been. Ultimately, she has used the platform of art to make a statement that she is taking possession of her own body and asserting the right to do with it as she sees fit. ORLAN's performances broach the subject of body image for a world of women, young and old, trying to live up to impossible standards.

Discussion Questions

1 Thinking of artworks you have studied in this chapter, compare and contrast a work that contains static representations of the human form with a performance. How would making these two types of artwork have differed for their creators? What role does the person represented play? How do the results compare visually?

2 What have the artists in this chapter discovered through their exploration of the human body? Find an example in the chapter that was especially interesting to you. What did learning about that artist's exploration reveal to you?

3 In this chapter we have looked at how artists have explored the body as an artistic theme. Identify three such approaches. Now think of other works you have seen in this book and select three examples from outside this chapter that take a different approach to the body. List the ways in which your chosen works differ from those in this chapter.

Images Related to 4.9:
The Body in Art

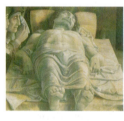

1.7.3a Relief from the temple of Amun, Egypt, 19th Dynasty, *c.* 1295–1186 BCE, p. 148

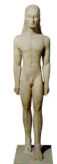

3.1.24 Statue of a *kouros*, Greece, *c.* 590–580 BCE, p. 382

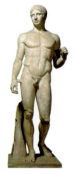

3.1.25 *Doryphoros* (Roman version), 120–50 BCE, p. 382

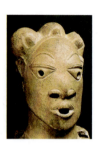

3.5.2 Head from Rafin Kura, Nok culture, Africa, *c.* 500 BCE–200 CE, p. 451

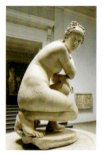

1.2.8b *Naked Aphrodite...* (*Lely's Venus*), Roman, 2nd century CE, p. 72

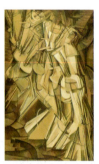

4.3.3 Andrea Mantegna, *Dead Christ*, *c.* 1480, p. 590

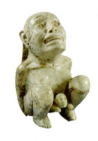

4.3.1 Tlazolteotl giving birth to the maize god, Aztec, *c.* 1500, p. 589

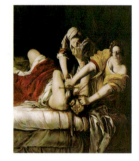

0.0.11 Leonardo da Vinci, *Mona Lisa*, *c.* 1503–6, p. 35

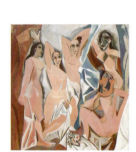

3.6.24 Artemisia Gentileschi, *Judith Decapitating Holofernes*, *c.* 1620, p. 485

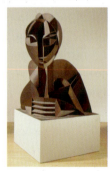

3.8.21 Pablo Picasso, *Les Demoiselles d'Avignon*, 1907, p. 527

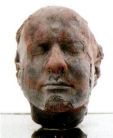

3.8.36 Marcel Duchamp, *Nude Descending a Staircase...*, 1912, p. 536

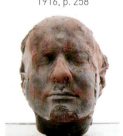

2.4.16 Naum Gabo, *Constructed Head No. 2*, 1916, p. 258

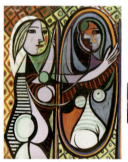

3.8.22 Pablo Picasso, *Girl before a Mirror*, 1932, p. 528

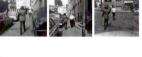

2.10.8 Vito Acconci, *Following Piece*, 1969, p. 358

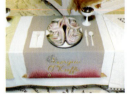

4.10.6 Judy Chicago, *The Dinner Party*, 1974–79, p. 679

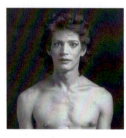

1.10.9 Robert Mapplethorpe, *Self-Portrait (#385)*, 1980, p. 188

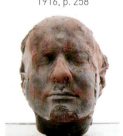

0.0.15 Marc Quinn, *Self*, 1991, p. 38

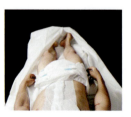

4.3.4 Andres Serrano, *The Morgue (Gun Murder)*, 1992, p. 590

4.10.10 Carrie Mae Weems, "You Became a Scientific Profile," 1995, p. 682

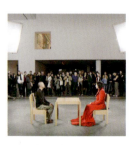

2.10.9 Marina Abramović, *The Artist Is Present*, 2012, p. 359

4.10

Identity, Race, and Gender in Art

While personal identity affects everyone on some level, it became a central issue for artists during the late twentieth century (see the discussion of Postmodernism in chapter 3.9). At that time groups that had been neglected by or indeed excluded from mainstream culture, which was male-dominated and Eurocentric, began to celebrate their differences, whether these lay in being part of a non-white ethnic minority, female, homosexual, or transgender. Earlier in the same century, social and cultural movements encouraged people to reconsider the status of women and communities of color in society by emphasizing their role as both the creators and the subjects of important artworks. The Harlem Renaissance (1920s and 1930s) and the Civil Rights movement (1955–68) in the US brought well-deserved attention to African-American artists, while feminist and LGBT (lesbian, gay, bisexual, and transgender) movements have, since the 1960s and more recently, inspired a great deal of discussion and exploration of the effect gender has on our personalities, relationships, and preferences.

The artworks in this chapter illustrate some of the ways in which artists have explored, reinforced, and challenged traditional expectations with regards to identity. By presenting their personal experiences of daily life, their interpretations of historical events, and their response to particular social or political agendas, artists encourage us to question common assumptions about identity and to become aware of the possibilities of individual experience beyond simplistic labels and stereotypes.

Abstract: art imagery that departs from recognizable images from the natural world

Self-Portraits

One obvious way for an artist to explore his or her identity is to make a self-portrait. In a self-portrait, the maker and the subject are the same person, while in a portrait the artist depicts someone else. In addition to the more familiar practice of providing a physical likeness of the artist, self-portraits often tell us something about the artist's personality, experiences, or choices. Another form of self-portraiture involves the artist assuming the role or persona of someone else, much as an actor portrays another person on the stage. Some artists, discussed later in this chapter, have become very inventive with their self-portraits to the point where the connection between work and artist is not always obvious: the work references the artist in indirect or **abstract** ways.

The Dutch artist Rembrandt Harmenszoon van Rijn (1606–1669), known as Rembrandt, was one of the first artists to dedicate a significant portion of his output to self-portraits, producing more than ninety of them over the course of forty years. Looking at them, we can observe the changes that occurred both in his appearance and in his artistic style during the course of his lifetime. In Rembrandt's self-portraits, he is shown in many guises, from a peasant to an aristocrat, which demonstrates his interest in exploring different facial expressions and character types. In *Self-Portrait with Saskia in the Scene of the Prodigal Son in the Tavern*, Rembrandt appears as the prodigal son from

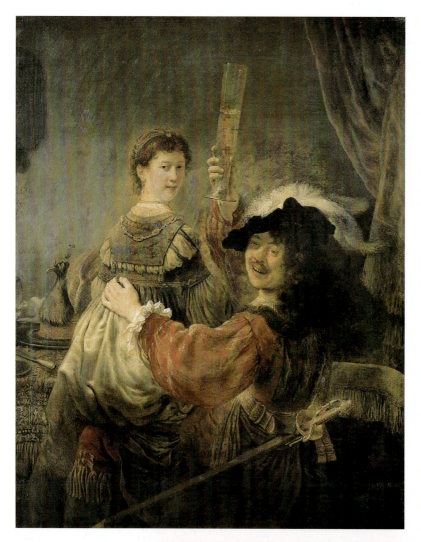

the biblical story of the young man who rebels against his father's wishes by squandering his inheritance (**4.10.1**). Rembrandt creates a lively mood in the tavern: he raises his glass toward the viewer, while the barmaid, modeled on his wife Saskia, looks on.

More than two centuries after Rembrandt, another Dutch painter, Vincent van Gogh (1853–1890), specialized in self-portraits in which he emphasized the internal reality of what he felt rather than simply recording what he saw. His *Self-Portrait with Bandaged Ear and Pipe*, one of approximately thirty self-portraits that he made, refers to a famous incident in his life (**4.10.2**). At the time this painting was made Van Gogh lived in Arles, in the south of France, and was hoping to realize his dream of starting an artists' colony there. When he learned that his fellow artist and close friend Paul Gauguin was planning to return to Paris, they had an intense argument, during which Van Gogh threatened Gauguin's life. Afterward Van Gogh cut off a portion of his own ear. He then wrapped the severed lobe in newspaper and presented it to a prostitute in a brothel before he was hospitalized and treated for acute blood loss. In its restrained but nervous lines and bold, contrasting colors, the *Self-Portrait with Bandaged Ear and Pipe*

4.10.1 Rembrandt van Rijn, *Self-Portrait with Saskia in the Scene of the Prodigal Son in the Tavern, c.* 1635. Oil on canvas, 5′3⅜ × 4′3⅝″. Gemäldegalerie Alte Meister, Dresden, Germany

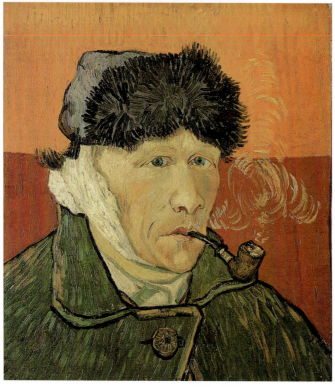

4.10.2 Vincent van Gogh, *Self-Portrait with Bandaged Ear and Pipe*, 1889. Oil on canvas, 25¼ × 19¾″. Private collection

displays some of the agitation that the artist experienced during the episode.

The Mexican artist Frida Kahlo (1907–1954) reflects on her identity by combining depictions of her physical appearance with metaphorical references to her feelings. Kahlo began making art around the age of eighteen, while recuperating from a devastating trolley-car accident that left her bedridden for three months and in pain for the rest of her life. As a result, her paintings tend to be very personal portrayals of psychological and physical suffering. Kahlo is perhaps best known for her self-portraits, which comprise up to a third of her artistic output.

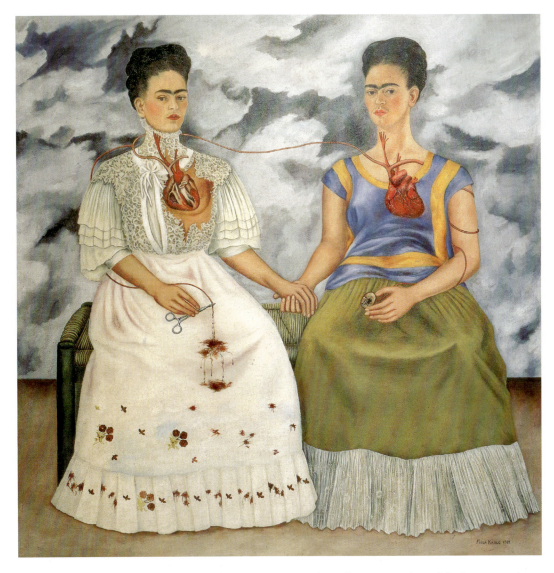

The women in *The Two Fridas* are almost mirror images of one another (**4.10.3**). They depict distinct aspects of the artist's identity. Kahlo's mixed cultural background is represented in the clothes worn by the two figures. The Frida on the right wears a Mexican dress (related to her mother's heritage); the one on the left, a European gown (reflecting her father's German roots). Another complicated element in Kahlo's life was her turbulent relationship with her husband, fellow Mexican artist Diego Rivera (1886–1957). When this painting was being made, Kahlo was in the process of divorcing Rivera (subsequently, a year after the divorce, they remarried). While the Mexican Frida holds a small picture of Rivera, the German Frida has a broken heart and tries with surgical pincers to stop the flow of blood from the artery that joins the two women together. The presentation of the hearts on the outside of the bodies emphasizes the sensitive emotional content of the painting.

The American photographer Cindy Sherman (b. 1954) plays the roles of all of the women portrayed in her acclaimed *Untitled Film Stills* series, creating an intriguing visual puzzle as we try to uncover the "real" Cindy Sherman. She makes images of herself that are not, however, intended conventionally to reflect her own identity: Sherman has explained that the images are not about her, but are about the representations of the women being shown and the ways that each viewer interprets them (see Perspectives on Art Box: Cindy Sherman: The Artist and Her Identity, p. 678).

For the *Untitled Film Stills*, Sherman fabricated backdrops and costumes for imagined characters from nonexistent 1950s B-movies.

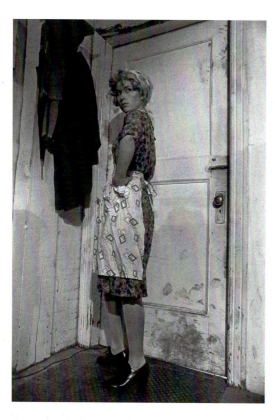

4.10.4 Cindy Sherman, "Untitled Film Still #35," from the *Untitled Film Stills* series, 1979. Black-and-white photograph, 10 × 8". MoMA, New York

At that time, the film roles for women were limited to such stereotyped characters as housewife, starlet, country girl come to the city, and so on. In "Untitled Film Still #35" we see a woman—perhaps a housewife or a maid—with a distinctly bad attitude (**4.10.4**). The circumstances of the scene are far from clear, though. Is she sulking about something, planning to leave, or about to pull a wallet from the jacket hanging on the hook? Why are there so many scuff marks on the door? More questions are raised than answered in the scenarios Sherman invents. Her *Untitled Film Stills*, which were created between 1977 and 1980, revisit these 1950s-inspired women in order to make it clear how narrow the representations of and expectations for women had been only a few short years before. At the time Sherman made "Untitled Film Still #35," feminism was beginning to have a significant impact on artistic representations of women as well as on the possibilities for women in society. Sherman made sixty-nine photographs in the series. The women in them always seem as if they are being watched, the object of an unseen

Perspectives on Art: Cindy Sherman
The Artist and Her Identity

The American photographer and film director Cindy Sherman is best known for her photographs in which she is dressed in costumes as if she were another person (see above, 4.10.4). Here she explains her general working process and one specific image, "Untitled Film Still #35," inspired by the Italian film actress Sophia Loren.

There is a stereotype of a girl who dreams all her life of being a movie star. She tries to make it on the stage, in films, and either succeeds or fails. I was more interested in the types of characters that fail. Maybe I related to that. But why should I try to do it myself? I'd rather look at the reality of these kinds of fantasies, the fantasy of going away and becoming a star . . .

The black-and-white photographs were . . . fun to do. I think they were easy partly because throughout my childhood I had stored up so many images of role models. It was real easy to think of a different one in every scene. But they were so clichéd that after three years I couldn't do them anymore. I was really thinking about the movies, the characters are almost typecast from movies.

For the woman standing in front of my studio door, I was thinking of a film with Sophia Loren called *Two Women*. She plays this Italian peasant. Her husband is killed and she and her daughter are both raped. She is this tough strong woman, but all beaten-up and dirty. I liked that combination of Sophia Loren looking very dirty and very strong. So that's what I was thinking of. . . .

I realized I had to become more specific in details, because that's what makes a person different from other people.

voyeur's gaze, so that these images call attention to and question the way we look at women.

Feminist Critique

In Western countries, for many centuries women had far fewer opportunities than men to become artists, and were rarely given the recognition granted to their male counterparts. For example, women were not allowed to draw from the nude in their art classes until the nineteenth century. It was also believed that "genius" was a trait exclusively available to men, and language with a gender bias—such as the word "masterpiece" to describe a great artwork—reinforced that belief. Before the 1970s few people even noticed that women had largely been excluded from the institutions and systems that produced serious artists.

In many cases, successful women had simply been written out of the history of art. The Italian artist Artemisia Gentileschi, for example, enjoyed an impressive reputation in the seventeenth century, but her efforts were eventually forgotten, only to be rediscovered in the early twentieth century (see Gateway Box: Gentileschi, p. 680).

The feminist movement of the 1960s and 1970s made a significant impact on the production and understanding of artworks made by women. It acknowledged that women artists had been left out of much of the history of art, and it introduced the possibility that this situation could be rectified. As a result, feminist artists expanded the subject matter of art, making it more relevant to women's issues, and many more works made by women were included in museums and galleries.

The American artist Judy Chicago (b. 1939) appreciated the achievement of such women as Gentileschi. She realized that many women had been forgotten over time and, likewise, that women who seem prominent today might in the future also be omitted from history. From 1974 to 1979, Chicago worked on an epic sculpture called *The Dinner Party* (**4.10.5**), which honors women from the past and present. Her huge triangular dinner table has thirteen place settings on each side. Every setting features a placemat,

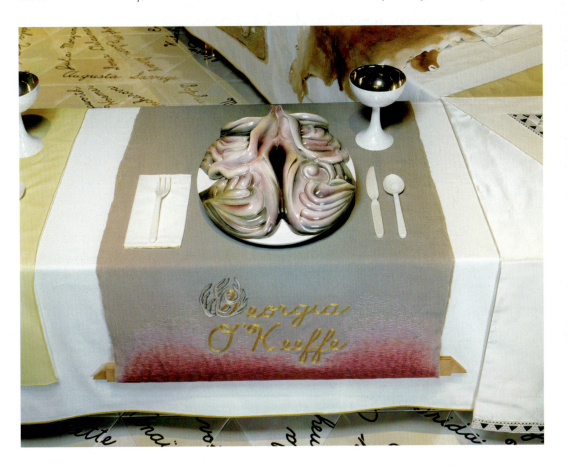

4.10.5 Judy Chicago, *The Dinner Party*, 1974–79. Installation view showing Georgia O'Keeffe placesetting. Embroidery on linen and china paint on porcelain, entire work 48 × 48'. Brooklyn Museum, New York

Gateway to Art: Gentileschi, *Judith Decapitating Holofernes*
Self-Expression in the *Judith* Paintings

The powerful heroines in the paintings of Artemisia Gentileschi (1593–*c.* 1656), such as Judith, who beheads Holofernes with steadfast determination, have a strong relationship with events in the artist's own life. Gentileschi was the victim of a sexual assault by Agostino Tassi, who was her painting teacher and a colleague of her father. During the public rape trial that followed, Tassi claimed that Gentileschi was not only a willing lover, but also quite promiscuous. Gentileschi and her father felt that, in addition to the physical violence she had suffered in the assault, their family name and reputation had been attacked. They feared that her prospects of marrying had been damaged both by the rape and the trial. Tassi was eventually found guilty and sentenced to exile. Gentileschi went on to marry another man, with whom she had five children.

Gentileschi is known to have painted seven works showing different events from the biblical story of Judith's encounter with Holofernes. The first, depicting Judith and her maidservant cutting off his head, was painted about a year after the Tassi trial (**4.10.6**). The painting of this violent assault by a brave and beautiful woman on the enemy commander who had conquered her city and tried to seduce her has been interpreted, using feminist analysis, both as an expression of the artist's anger at her own attacker, and as a way of healing the effects

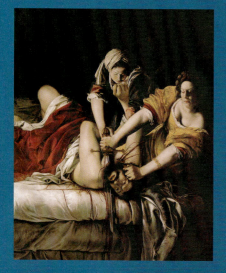

of her ordeal. In fact, Gentileschi's heroines in the Judith paintings resemble her own features. Another of the painter's depictions of the story, made about a decade later, shows Judith and her maidservant by candlelight while making their escape from the murder scene with the bloody head (**4.10.7**). While there may indeed be an element of autobiography at least in Gentileschi's earlier paintings, the numerous versions of the story that she made over a thirty-year period were probably created for a variety of other reasons, including the popularity of the theme at the time and the fact that her previous renditions of this subject had already attracted admiration.

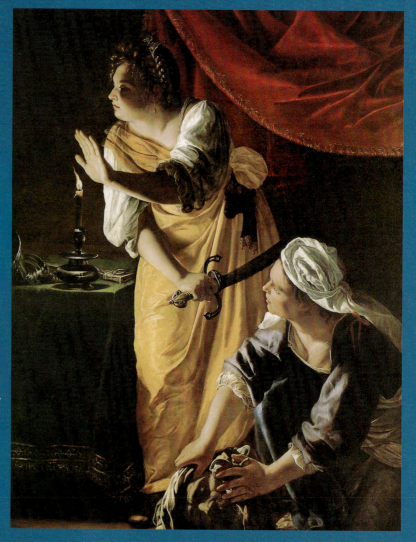

4.10.7 Artemisia Gentileschi, *Judith and Her Maidservant with the Head of Holofernes*, 1623–25. Oil on canvas, 6'³⁄₈" × 4'7¾". Detroit Institute of Arts, Michigan

4.10.6 Artemisia Gentileschi, *Judith Decapitating Holofernes*, c. 1620. Oil on canvas, 6'6⅜" × 5'3¾". Uffizi Gallery, Florence, Italy

Do women have to be naked to get into the Met. Museum?

Less than 5% of the artists in the Modern Art sections are women, but 85% of the nudes are female.

GUERRILLA GIRLS CONSCIENCE OF THE ART WORLD

on which is embroidered the name of a famous historical or mythical woman, and an elaborate plate designed intentionally to resemble the shape of a butterfly or a vagina. The appearance of all the elements on each setting was inspired by the woman whose place it is. Layers of lace designate the place of the nineteenth-century poet Emily Dickinson, while the plate for the artist Georgia O'Keeffe resembles a sculpted version of one of her abstract flower paintings. Artemisia Gentileschi's place setting has a brightly colored plate surrounded by lush fabric similar to the kind shown in her paintings.

Chicago made the table an equilateral triangle not only because the shape was an ancient sign for both woman and goddess, but also because it could be used here to symbolize the world of fairness and equality that feminists sought. She chose to have thirteen guests to a side both because there were thirteen witches in a coven and because it was an important number for those ancient religions that worshiped a mother goddess. The number is also a reference to the biblical Last Supper, here reconfigured with women as the guests instead of Jesus and his twelve disciples. The idea of a dinner party—as well as the **media**, such as needlework and **ceramics**, which are included in her piece—evokes the role of woman as homemaker, which Chicago and other feminists believed should be admired and praised.

In 1985, a group of women artists in New York City formed a collective organization called

the Guerrilla Girls to protest at the unequal treatment of female artists in the art world. Their name indicates their willingness to engage in unconventional tactics in their fight for equality. The Guerrilla Girls, who are still active, are known for the gorilla masks the members wear to avoid being recognized by the art world establishment and institutions they might criticize. Their productions take the form of public protests and lectures as well as flyers and posters. One of their best-known posters, *Do Women Have to Be Naked to Get into the Met. Museum?* (**4.10.8**), includes statistics to highlight the disproportionate representation of women artists (5 percent) compared to female **nudes** (85 percent) in the collection of the Metropolitan Museum of Art in New York. As this poster shows, one of their principal goals is to oppose the lack of representation of women artists in major museum collections.

Black Consciousness

Later in the twentieth century, nearly a hundred years after the Emancipation Proclamation, African-Americans in Southern US states still experienced legalized discrimination and segregation that led directly to disenfranchisement, oppression, and violence. The work of American filmmaker, director, producer, writer, and actor, Shelton Jackson "Spike" Lee (b. 1957) is characterized by its

4.10.8 Guerrilla Girls, *Do Women Have to Be Naked to Get into the Met. Museum?*, 1989. Poster, dimensions variable

Medium (plural **media**): the material on or from which an artist chooses to make a work of art
Ceramics: fire-hardened clay, often painted, and normally sealed with shiny protective coating
Nude: an artistic representation of an unclothed human figure, emphasizing the body's form rather than its exposure

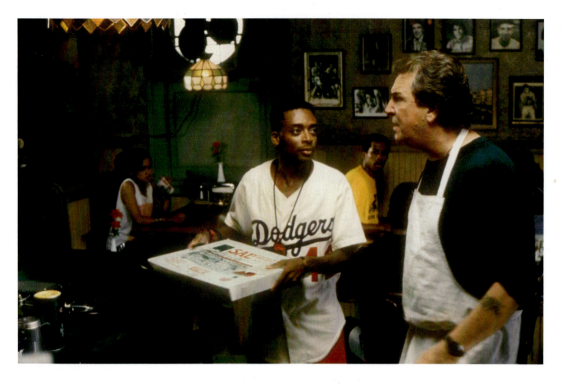

4.10.9 Spike Lee, *Do the Right Thing*, 1989. Duration 120 minutes. 40 Acres & A Mule Filmworks

strong commitment to social justice issues, and includes a film biography of Civil Rights leader Malcolm X (1992). Lee's landmark film *Do the Right Thing*, nominated for two academy awards, focuses on race relations between the Italian-American owner of Sal's Famous Pizzeria and the African-American residents of the neighborhood (**4.10.9**).

Modeled after Bedford-Stuyvesant, Lee's own Brooklyn neighborhood, and inspired by racial incidents in New York City in the 1980s, the movie also highlights the pervasiveness of institutionalized racism in America decades after the advancements of the Civil Rights movement. This movie makes a frank statement about race relations as tension builds over the course of a hot summer's day, with tragic consequences. The heavy content of the film is combined with inventive visuals, strong storytelling, humor, and music. Effective character development, which is sympathetic to all parties, highlights the complexity of the characters' various viewpoints, prejudices, and relationships with each other in a way that promotes understanding rather than perpetuating racial polarization.

The American artist Carrie Mae Weems (b. 1953) also investigates the collective African-American experience that is rooted in slavery. Her work embodies an interest in personal and cultural identity. Her series *From Here I Saw What Happened and I Cried* reinterprets a series of early photographs of African slaves taken by white Americans in the nineteenth century. In the original photographs the sitters were stripped and exposed to the scrutiny of racist theorists who sought to examine and investigate them in a coldly analytical, supposedly "scientific" way. Weems rephotographed the images, colored them red, and framed them with circular mats to highlight the fact that they were being seen through the camera lens. The text she inscribes on the glass challenges ideas of race, gender, and class that were once taken for granted. Pointing out that these individuals had become "A Scientific Profile" shown in evidence of an anthropological debate that turned them into "A Photographic Subject" (**4.10.10**) restores some of the dignity

4.10.10 Carrie Mae Weems, "You Became a Scientific Profile," from the series *From Here I Saw What Happened and I Cried*, 1995. Chromogenic colour prints with sand-blasted text on glass, 25⅝ x 22¾". MoMA, New York

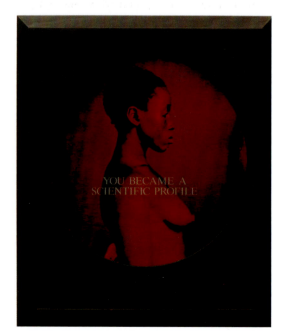

that had been denied and motivates viewers to understand and respect the sitters' humanity.

Identity and Ambiguity

Our expectations of people are often based on stereotypes and on our ideas of what is "normal" for their gender or race. These stereotypes are frequently challenged, of course: women have been primary breadwinners, worked in mines, and gone to war, men have been nurturers and raised children, and a black man can be elected as the President of the United States. In recent years, it has become more acceptable to address the ways in which people transcend the conventional boundaries of identity. Public awareness of such issues as transvestism and transgender surgery has been raised by increasingly open discussion. Investigations of the ways that bodies and identities can be transformed and racial identity can be transcended, however, are not entirely new to art. The question of identity is one that artists from many cultures and eras of history have sought to address. When the artworks are effective, they lead to a greater understanding of individuality.

Almost 3,500 years ago, ancient Egypt was governed by a woman called Hatshepsut, who abandoned the confines of gender that were customary during her lifetime. She was arguably the most powerful of the handful of female rulers in Egyptian history. Hatshepsut controlled the kingdom for about twenty years in the fifteenth century BCE, first as regent for her stepson and nephew Thutmose III, and then as pharaoh in her own right. To legitimize her reign, Hatshepsut emphasized that she was her father's choice as successor, ahead of her two brothers and half-brother. She also claimed direct lineage from Amun, the chief god who was worshiped at that time.

Like all Egyptian rulers, Hatshepsut commissioned many sculptures and relief carvings to replicate and immortalize her image. A few show her as a woman, but she is most often depicted in the conventional poses and clothing of a male king. The image in **4.10.11**

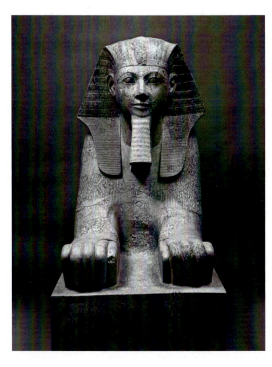

4.10.11 Sphinx of Hatshepsut, 18th Dynasty, Egypt, 1479–1458 BCE. Granite and paint, 5'4⅝" × 11'3". Metropolitan Museum of Art, New York

is one of a group of sphinxes that possess Hatshepsut's face. It was not uncommon for pharaohs to be represented in the form of a sphinx, a creature with the body of a lion and the head of a human. The artist has clearly followed the guidelines for depicting male pharaohs, including the traditional headcloth and royal beard. But, although the portrait is idealized, the sculptor has not attempted to disguise the delicate lines of Hatshepsut's features.

For her *Projects* series, Korean artist Nikki S. Lee (b. 1970) joined a number of different communities, from yuppies and tourists to Hispanics and senior citizens, shopping in the stores they frequented and adopting their

4.10.12 Nikki S. Lee, *Hip Hop Project (25)*, 2001. Fujiflex print

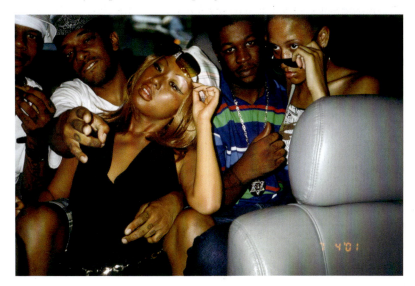

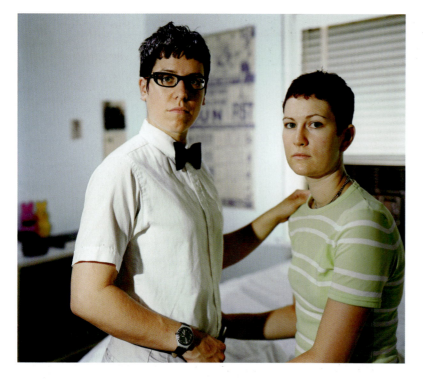

4.10.13 Catherine Opie, "Melissa & Lake, Durham, North Carolina," from *Domestic* series, 1998. Chromogenic print, 40 × 50"

mannerisms. Lee said, "My goal is not to become black, white, or Hispanic. It's more like becoming an Asian person who really likes that culture." Once she felt she had become a genuine member of the group, she would have a snapshot self-portrait of herself taken with her new peers. For the *Hip Hop Project* in 2001, Lee went to a tanning salon three times a week to darken her skin, and then immersed herself in the subculture of the hip hop music scene (**4.10.12**).

Although she told the people in the close-knit group depicted in this image that she was an artist, most of them did not believe her. It is surprising to learn that her interaction with these people is temporary, because there are no clues to suggest that she is not one of them. Such guises as this one become borrowed personalities for Lee, who considers her identity to be very fluid.

American artist Catherine Opie (b. 1961) uses photography to investigate the nuances of gender and identity. Her pictures include studio portraits of her lesbian friends dressed in leather or wearing false facial hair, staged depictions of radical performance artists, high school football games, and landscapes. Opie created her *Domestic* series while traveling across the US in order to photograph lesbian couples, such as Melissa and Lake, in their everyday settings (**4.10.13**). This photograph accentuates some of the similarities in the couple's appearance, such as their short haircuts with bangs. The point of the picture, however, is their bond, not their gender or sexual identity. Opie's portraits, by highlighting the lesbian community, introduce some viewers to new ways of life. They remind others that the familiar people, places, and things we see each day can be thought of in new ways. Such pictures are not about difference, they are celebrations of individuality.

Discussion Questions

1. What kind of words can you think of that are specifically gendered? Come up with a list of five "male" and five "female" adjectives. Are they based on facts or opinions? Find an artwork to illustrate each of your terms. Find an artwork that contradicts each of your terms. Make sure that at least half the artworks you choose are not from this chapter.

2. What obstacles have women faced in being taken seriously as professional artists? What has been done to counteract that inequity? What artworks, either in this chapter or elsewhere, effectively express either these challenges or the changes in institutional practices toward women in the arts?

3. Consider the artworks you have studied and then describe an artwork that expresses your personal experience as a man or woman. What roles have you played in your life that conform to or deviate from established norms? How could you communicate that experience to your audience in an artwork?

Images Related to 4.10:
Identity, Race, and Gender in Art

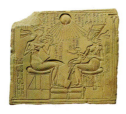

4.6.7 Akhenaten, Nefertiti, and three daughters, relief sculpture, Egypt, c. 1353–1335 BCE, p. 630

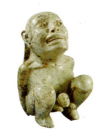

4.3.1 Tlazolteotl giving birth to the maize god, Aztec, c. 1500, p. 589

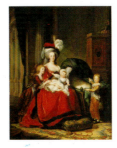

3.7.6 Elisabeth-Louise Vigée-Lebrun, *Marie-Antoinette and Her Children*, 1787, p. 495

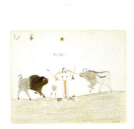

3.4.21 Wo-Haw, *Wo-Haw between Two Worlds*, 1875–77, p. 446

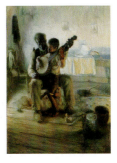

3.7.21 Henry Ossawa Tanner, *The Banjo Lesson*, 1893, p. 507

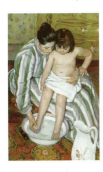

3.3.23 Mary Cassatt, *The Child's Bath*, 1893, p. 429

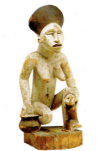

4.3.6 Kneeling female figure with bowl and child, late 19th/early 20th century, p. 591

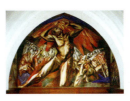

2.2.6 José Clemente Orozco, *Prometheus*, 1930, p. 219

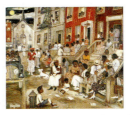

1.10.6 Palmer Hayden, *Midsummer Night in Harlem*, 1938, p. 185

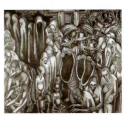

2.1.4 John Biggers, *Night of the Poor*, 1949, p. 201

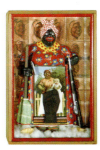

2.4.18 Betye Saar, *The Liberation of Aunt Jemima*, 1972, p. 259

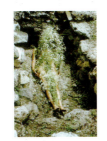

3.9.11 Ana Mendieta, "Untitled" (*Silueta* series), 1973, p. 548

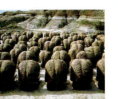

1.10.7 Magdalena Abakanowicz, *80 Backs*, 1976–80, p. 186

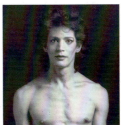

1.10.9 Robert Mapplethorpe, *Self-Portrait (#385)*, 1980, p. 188

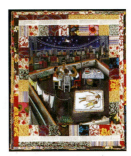

2.6.17 Faith Ringgold, *Tar Beach*, 1988, p. 302

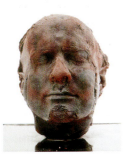

0.0.15 Marc Quinn, *Self*, 1991, p. 38

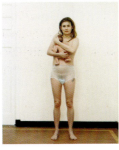

4.3.2 Rineke Dijkstra, "Julie," from the *Mothers* series, 1994, p. 548

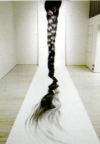

2.1.12 Zhang Chun Hong, *Life Strands*, 2004, p. 205

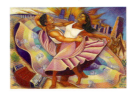

2.2.21 Judith F. Baca, *Danza de la Tierra*, 2008, p. 229

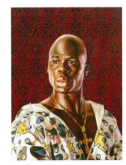

4.8.4 Kehinde Wiley, *Portrait Bust of Cardinal Richelieu*, 2009, p. 652

Glossary

NOTE: *A few terms have more than one definition, depending on the context in which they are used.*

Absolute, Absolutism: when applied to a ruler or monarch, the belief that he or she holds the ultimate power and that this derives from the will of God

Abstract: (1) art imagery that departs from recognizable images from the natural world; (2) an artwork the form of which is simplified, distorted, or exaggerated in appearance. It may represent a recognizable form that has been slightly altered, or it may be a completely non-representational depiction

Abstraction, abstracted: the degree to which an image is altered from an easily recognizable subject

Abstract Expressionism: a mid-twentieth-century artistic style characterized by its capacity to convey intense emotions using non-representational images

Academies: institutions training artists in both the theory of art and practical techniques

Acropolis: a high place in a Greek city on which a temple is located

Acrylic: a liquid polymer, or plastic, that is used as a binder for pigment in acrylic paint

Action painting: application of paint to canvas by dripping, splashing, or smearing that emphasizes the artist's gestures

Actual and implied lines: actual lines are solid lines. Implied lines are impressions of lines created from a series of points that orient our gaze along a visual path

Actual line: a continuous, uninterrupted line

Additive color: the colors produced from light

Additive sculpture: a sculpting process in which the artist builds a form by adding material

Aesthetic: related to beauty, art, and taste

A-frame: an ancient form of structural support, made out of beams arranged so that the shape of the building resembles a capital letter A

Afterimage effect: when the eye sees the complementary color of something that the viewer has spent an extended time viewing (also known as successive contrasts)

Aisles: in a basilica or other church, the spaces between the columns of the nave and the side walls

Alloy: a mixture of a metal combined with at least one other element

Altar: an area where sacrifices or offerings are made

Altarpiece: an artwork that is placed behind an altar in a church

Ambulatory: a covered walkway, particularly around the apse of a church

American Scene naturalistic style of painting in the US from the 1920s to 1950s that celebrated American themes, locations, and virtues

Analog: photography or movie made using a film camera that chemically records images using a continuous gradation of value ranges from light to dark so that they directly match the actual appearance of the object or scene

Analogous colors: colors adjacent to each other on the color wheel

Anamorphosis: the distorted representation of an object so that it appears correctly proportioned only when viewed from one particular position

Animation: genre of film made using stop-motion, hand-drawn, or digitally produced still images set into motion by showing them in sequence

Appropriation: the deliberate incorporation in an artwork of material originally created by other artists

Apse: semicircular vaulted space in a church

Aquatint: an intaglio printmaking process that uses melted rosin or spray paint to create an acid-resistant ground

Aqueduct: a structure designed to carry water, often over long distances

Arabesque: an abstract pattern derived from geometric and vegetal lines and forms

Arcade: a series of connected arches

Archaic: Greek art of the period *c.* 620–480 BCE

Arches: structures, usually curved, that span an opening

Archetype: psychoanalytical term used to describe very typical kinds of people that originated long ago, serve as patterns, and can be recognized in later groups or individuals, for example, mothers, heroes, and villains

Architectural order: a style of designing columns and related parts of a Greek or Roman building

Architrave: a beam that rests on the top of a row of columns

Armature: a framework or skeleton used to support a sculpture

Art Brut: "raw art," artworks made by untrained artists, and having a primitive or childlike quality

Articulate: to make smaller shapes or spaces within a larger composition

Artifact: an object made by a person

Artist's book: a book produced by an artist, usually an expensive limited edition, often using specialized printing processes

Art Nouveau: French for "new art," a visual style of the late nineteenth and early twentieth century, characterized by organic flowing lines, simulating forms in nature and involving decorative pattern

Ascetic: (1) (adjective) austerely simple; rigorously abstaining from pleasure or material satisfaction; (2) (noun) a person who rejects material comforts and practices self-discipline, usually for a religious purpose

Assemblage: (1) artwork made of three-dimensional materials, including found objects (2) technique of creating artworks that challenged traditional art practice in the late twentieth century by using found objects, junk, and other non-art materials

Asymmetry: a type of design in which balance is achieved by elements that contrast and complement one another without being the same on either side of an axis

Atmospheric perspective: use of shades of color and clarity to create the illusion of depth. Closer objects have warmer tones and clear outlines, while objects set further away are cooler and become hazy

Atrium: a central, normally public, interior space, first used in Roman houses

Auteur theory, auteur films: from the French word for "author"; refers to films that notably reflect the director's creative vision above other criteria

Automatic: suppressing conscious control to access subconscious sources of creativity and truth

Avant-garde: early twentieth-century emphasis on artistic innovation, which challenged accepted values, traditions, and techniques

Axis: an imaginary line showing the center of a shape, volume, or composition

Background: (1) the part of a work depicted as behind the main figures; (2) the part of a work depicted furthest from the viewer's space, often behind the main subject matter

Balance: a principle of art in which elements are used to create a symmetrical or asymmetrical sense of visual weight in an artwork

Balustrade: a railing supported by short pillars

Baroque: European artistic and architectural style of the late sixteenth to early eighteenth century, characterized by extravagance and emotional intensity

Base: the projecting series of blocks between the shaft of a column and its plinth

Basilica: an early Christian church, either converted from or built to resemble a type of Roman civic building

Bas-relief: a sculpture carved with very little depth

Bauhaus: design school founded in Weimar, Germany, in 1919

Ben-Day dots: printing process named for its inventor

Binder: a substance that makes pigments adhere to a surface

Bioart: art that is created with living, changing organisms

Bird's-eye view: an artistic technique in which a scene or subject is presented from some point above it

Bisqueware: a ceramic form that has been fired but not glazed, or that has not received other surface finishing

Bohemian: derived from the gypsies of the former Czech Kingdom of Bohemia who moved around; a wanderer; an artist or writer who functions outside the bounds of conventional rules and practices

Boldface: a darker and heavier typeface than its normal instance

Bust: a statue of a person depicting only his or her head and shoulders

Byzantine: relating to the East Roman Empire, centered on Constantinople (modern-day Istanbul) from the fifth century CE to 1453

Calligraphy: the art of emotive or carefully descriptive hand lettering or handwriting

Canon of proportions: a set of ideal mathematical ratios in art used to measure the various parts of the human body in relation to one another

Canopic jar: a jar used by ancient Egyptians to hold the embalmed internal organs removed from the body during mummification

Cantilever: a long support that projects out from a structure

Capital: the architectural feature that crowns a column

Capstone: a final stone forming the top of a structure; on a pyramid, it is pyramid-shaped

Cardinal points: north, south, east, and west

Cast: a sculpture or artwork made by pouring a liquid (for example molten metal or plaster) into a mold

Catacombs: an underground system of tunnels used for burying and commemorating the dead

Central-plan church: Eastern Orthodox church design, often in the shape of a cross with all four arms of equal length

Ceramic(s): fire-hardened clay, often painted, and normally sealed with shiny protective coating

Ceramist: a person who makes ceramics

CGI: computer-generated imagery

Chasing: a technique of hammering the front of a metal object to create a form or surface detail

Chevron: a V-shaped stripe, often reproduced upside down or on its side in decorative patterns

Chiaroscuro: the use of light and dark in a painting to create the impression of volume

Chilkat: a traditional form of weaving practiced by Tlingit, Haida, Tsimshian, and other Northwest Coast peoples of Alaska and British Columbia

Choir: part of a church traditionally reserved for singers and clergy, situated between the nave and the apse

Chroma: the degree of purity of a color

Classical: (1) ancient Greek and Roman; (2) artworks from ancient Greece or Rome; (3) art that conforms to Greek and Roman models, or is based on rational construction and emotional equilibrium; (4) Greek art of the period c. 480–323 BCE

Classical period: a period in the history of Greek art, c. 480–323 BCE

Clerestory windows: a row of windows high up in a church to admit light into the nave

Coffered: decorated with recessed paneling

Coiling: (1) the use of long coils of clay – rather than a wheel – to build the walls of a pottery vessel; (2) basket-weaving technique using a central foundation that is spiraled or coiled, and wrapped with another fiber that is stitched back into the previous row

Collage: a work of art assembled by gluing materials, often paper, onto a surface. From the French coller, to glue

Collagraphy, collagraphic, collagraph: a type of relief print that is created by building up or collaging material on or to a stiff surface, inking that surface, then printing

Colophon: comment written on a Chinese scroll by the creator, owner, or a viewer

Color: the optical effect caused when reflected white light of the spectrum is divided into separate wavelengths

Color field: a term used by a group of twentieth-century abstract painters to describe their work with large flat areas of color and simple shapes

Color theory: the understanding of how colors relate to each other, especially when mixed or placed near one another

Column: freestanding pillar, usually circular in section

Complementary colors: colors opposite one another on the color wheel

Composite view: representation of a subject from multiple viewpoints at one time

Composition: the overall design or organization of a work

Concentric: identical shapes stacked inside each other sharing the same center, for example the circles of a target

Conceptual: relating to or concerning ideas

Conceptual art: artwork in which the ideas are most important to the work

Concrete: a hard, strong, and versatile construction material made up of powdered lime, sand, and rubble

Constructivism: an art movement in the Soviet Union in the 1920s, primarily concerned to make art of use to the working class

Content: the meaning, message, or feeling expressed in a work of art

Context: circumstances surrounding the creation of a work of art, including historical events, social conditions, biographical facts about the artist, and his or her intentions

Continuous narrative: when different parts of a story are shown within the same visual space

Contour: the outline that defines a form

Contour rivalry: a design in which the lines can be read in more than one way at the same time, depending on the angle from which it is viewed

Contrapposto: a pose in sculpture in which the upper part of the body twists in one direction and the lower part in another

Contrast: a drastic difference between such elements as color or value (lightness/darkness) when they are presented together

Convention: a widely accepted way of doing something; using a particular style, following a certain method, or representing something in a specific way

Convex: curved outward, like the exterior of a sphere

Corbeled: with a series of corbels—architectural feature made of stone, brick, wood, etc.—each projecting beyond the one below

Cornice: molding round the top of a building

Cor-ten steel: a type of steel that forms a coating of rust that protects it from the weather and further corrosion

Course: a single row of stones or bricks forming a horizontal layer of a structure

Cropping: trimming the edges of an image, or composing it so that part of the subject matter is cut off

Cross-hatching: the use of overlapping parallel lines to convey darkness or lightness

Cubism, Cubist: (1) twentieth-century art movement that favored a new perspective emphasizing geometric forms (2) twentieth-century art movement that favored a new perspective emphasizing geometric forms; the Cubists were artists who formed part of the movement. "Cubist" is also used to describe their style of painting

Cuneiform: a form of writing from ancient Mesopotamia that uses wedge shapes

Curator: a person who organizes the collection and exhibition of objects/artworks in a museum or gallery; and negotiates interactions between artists, artworks, institutions, and the public

Cyanotype: photographic process using light-sensitive iron salts that oxidize and produce a brilliant blue color where light penetrates and remain white where light is blocked; a variant of this process was used historically to copy architectural drawings

Dada: anarchic anti-art and anti-war movement, dating back to World War I, that reveled in absurdity and irrationality

Degenerate: considered to be less than a normal level in physical, mental, or moral qualities

Deify: to worship and to make into a god or goddess

Deposition: a scene showing the taking down of Christ's body from the cross

Depth: the degree of recession in perspective

Der Blaue Reiter: ("The Blue Rider"); German Expressionist movement (1911–14) in Munich; used abstract forms to suggest spiritual content as a contrast to the corruption and materialism of the times

De Stijl: a group of artists originating in the Netherlands in the early twentieth century, associated with a utopian style of design that emphasized primary colors and straight lines

Developer (also **photographic developer**): after an image has been recorded on light-sensitive film or photographic paper (usually in a camera), immersion in this liquid substance chemically transforms a latent (or invisible) image into a visible one

Diagonal: a line that runs obliquely, rather than horizontally or vertically

Didactic: with the aim of teaching or educating

Die Brücke: German Expressionist movement of artists and printmakers formed in Dresden (1905–13) with the aim to defy anything Classical and to use art as a bridge between the past, present, and a utopian future

Directional line: implied line within a composition, leading the viewer's eye from one element to another

Dissonance: a lack of harmony

Documentary: non-fiction film based on actual people, settings, and events

Dome: an evenly curved vault forming the ceiling or roof of a building

Door jamb: vertical sections, which often contain sculpture, that form the side of a portal

Drama: genre of film that depends on emotional development and relationships between realistic characters

Draftsman: a person who draws

Drypoint: an intaglio printmaking process where the artist raises a burr when gouging the printing plate

Edition: all the copies of a print made from a single printing

Elements: the basic vocabulary of art—line, form, shape, volume, mass, color, texture, space, time and motion, and value (lightness/darkness)

Embroidery: decorative stitching generally made with colored thread applied to the surface of a fabric

Emphasis: the principle of drawing attention to particular content within a work

Encaustic: a painting medium that primarily uses wax, usually beeswax, as the binding agent

Engraving: a printmaking technique where the artist (the **engraver**) gouges or scratches the image into the surface of the printing plate

Enlightenment: an intellectual movement in eighteenth-century Europe that argued for science, reason, and individualism, and against tradition, and a time in which there was a movement to secure equal rights for all men

En plein air: French for "in the open air"; used to describe painting out of doors from start to finish rather than working in a studio for all or part of the process

Entablature: the part of a Greek or Roman building that rests on top of a column

Entasis: the slight swelling or bulge at the midpoint of a column

Etching: an intaglio printmaking process that uses acid to bite (or etch) the engraved design into the printmaking surface

Eucharist: Christian ceremony that commemorates the death of Jesus Christ

Expressionism, Expressionistic: an artistic style at its height in 1920s Europe, devoted to representing subjective emotions and experiences instead of objective or external reality

Expressive: capable of stirring the emotions of the viewer

Facade: any side of a building, usually the front or entrance

Faience: quartz or sand, ground and heated to create a shiny, glasslike material

Fauves: a group of early twentieth-century French artists whose paintings used vivid colors. From the French *fauve*, "wild beast"

Fauvism: early twentieth-century art movement that emphasized bold, exaggerated colors and simplified forms to favor creative expression over accuracy

Figuration, figurative: art that portrays items perceived in the visible world, especially human or animal forms

Figure–ground reversal: the reversal of the relationship between one shape (the figure) and its background (the ground), so that the figure becomes background and the ground becomes the figure

Firing: heating ceramic, glass, or enamel objects in a kiln, to harden them, fuse the components, or fuse a glaze to the surface

Fixing: the chemical process used to ensure a photographic image becomes permanent

Flint: an object or tool made from the very hard, sharp-edged stone of the same name

Flying buttress: an arch built on the exterior of a building that transfers some of the weight of the vault

Focal point: (1) the center of interest or activity in a work of art, often drawing the viewer's attention to the most important element; (2) the area in a composition to which the eye returns most naturally

Foreground: the part of a work depicted as nearest to the viewer

Foreshortening: a perspective technique that depicts a form at a very oblique (often dramatic) angle to the viewer in order to show depth in space

Form: (1) an object that can be defined in three dimensions (height, width, and depth) (2) the way style, techniques, media, and elements and principles of design are used to make the artwork look (or exist) the way it does

Formal: in art, refers to the visual elements and principles in a work

Formal analysis: analysis of the form or visual appearance of a work of art using the visual language of elements and principles

Format: the shape of the area an artist uses for making a two-dimensional artwork

Found image or **object:** an image or art object found by an artist and presented, with little or no alteration, as part of a work or as a finished work of art in itself

Frame: a single image from the sequence that makes up a motion picture; on average, a 90-minute film contains 129,600 separate frames

Freestanding: any sculpture that stands separate from walls or other surfaces so that it can be viewed from a 360-degree range

Fresco: (1) a technique where the artist paints onto freshly applied plaster. From the Italian *fresco*, "fresh"; (2) paintings made on freshly applied plaster

Frieze: the strip that goes around the top of a building, often filled with sculptural ornamentation

Frontispiece: an illustration facing the title-page in a book

Futurism: an artistic and social movement, originating in Italy in 1909, passionately in favor of everything modern; **Futurists** were artists working in this style

Gèlèdé ritual: ritual performed in Nigeria's Yoruba society to celebrate and honor women

Genres: categories of artistic subject matter, often with strongly influential histories and traditions

Geometric: predictable and mathematical

Geometric form: three-dimensional form composed of regular planes and curves

Gestalt: complete order and indivisible unity of all aspects of an artwork's design

Glazing: in oil painting, adding a transparent layer of paint to achieve a richness in texture, volume, and form

Golden Section: a unique ratio of a line divided into two parts so that $a + b$ is to a as a is to b. The result is 1:1.618

Gothic: Western European architectural style of the twelfth to sixteenth century, characterized by the use of pointed arches and ornate decoration

Gouache: a type of paint medium in which pigments are bound with gum and a white filler added (for example, clay) to produce a paint that is used for opaque watercolor

Graphic design: the use of images, typography, and technology to communicate ideas for a client or to a particular audience

Green practices: environmentally friendly activities, including energy efficiency and recycling

Greenware: a clay form that has been shaped and dried, but not yet fired to become ceramic

Grid: a network of horizontal and vertical lines; in an artwork's composition, the lines are implied

Grisaille: painting in gray or grayish monochrome, either as a base or underpainting for the finished work, or as the final artwork itself

Ground: the surface or background onto which an artist paints or draws

Guilds: medieval associations of artists, craftsmen, or tradesmen

Gypsum: fine grained, powdery mineral often used to make a smooth plaster

Happening: impromptu art action, initiated and planned by an artist, the outcome of which is not known in advance

Hatching: the use of non-overlapping parallel lines to convey darkness or lightness

Hellenistic: Greek art from *c.* 323–100 BCE

Hemispherical: having half the form of a spherical shape divided into identical, symmetrical parts

Hierarchical scale: the use of size to denote the relative importance of subjects in an artwork

Hieroglyph: Egyptian language involving sacred characters that may be pictures as well as letters or signifiers of sounds

Highlight: an area of lightest value in a work

High relief: a carved panel where the figures project with a great deal of depth from the background

Hue: general classification of a color; the distinctive characteristics of a color as seen in the visible spectrum, such as green or red

Humanism, Humanist: the study of such subjects as history, philosophy, languages, and literature, particularly in relation to those of ancient Greece and Rome

Icon: (1) a small, often portable, religious image venerated by Christian believers; first used by the Eastern Orthodox Church; (2) a simple symbolic graphic shape used in visual communication design

Iconic: possessing established and widely recognizable characteristics

Iconoclast: someone who destroys imagery, often out of religious belief

Ideal: more beautiful, harmonious, or perfect than reality

Idealism: elevating depictions of nature to achieve more beautiful, harmonious, and perfect depictions

Idealized: represented as perfect in form or character, corresponding to an ideal

Ideogram: a symbol that expresses an idea or a thing without representing the sounds in its name (for example, "8")

Illuminated characters: highly decorated letters, usually found at the beginning of a page or paragraph

Illuminated manuscript: a hand-lettered text with hand-drawn pictures

Illuminations: illustrations and decorations in a manuscript

Illusionism, illusionistic: the artistic skill or trick of making something look real

IMAX: "Image Maximum," a format for film presentation that allows presentation of films ten times larger sizes than the conventional one

Impasto: paint applied in thick layers

Implied line: a line not actually drawn but suggested by elements in the work

Implied texture: a visual illusion expressing texture

Impression: an individual print, or pull, from a printing press

Impressionism: a late nineteenth-century painting style conveying the impression of the effects of light; **Impressionists** were painters working in this style

Incised: cut

Inlay: substance embedded in another, contrasting material

Installation: originally referring to the hanging of pictures and arrangement of objects in an exhibition, installation may also refer to an intentional environment created as a completed artwork

Intaglio: any print process where the inked image is lower than the surface of the printing plate; from the Italian for "cut into"

Intarsia: the art of setting pieces of wood into a surface to create a pattern

Intensity: the relative clarity of color in its purest raw form, demonstrated through luminous or muted variations

Interpretation: explaining or translating a work of art, using factual research, personal response, or a combination of the two

In the round: a freestanding sculpted work that can be viewed from all sides

Isometric perspective: a system using diagonal parallel lines to communicate depth

Ivory: hard, creamy-colored material from the tusks of such mammals as elephants

Jatakas: stories from the previous lives of Buddha, often with a moral message

Ka: in Egyptian belief, the spirit of a person that leaves the body upon death and travels to the afterlife

Kachina: carved wooden doll made by the Native American Hopi, representing a supernatural being in human form as a masked dancer

Key-frame animation: technique in which an animator creates important frames in the sequence, and software fills in the gaps

Kinetic art: art, usually three-dimensional, with moving parts, impelled by wind, personal interaction, or motors

Kinetic sculpture: three-dimensional art that moves, impelled by air currents, motors, or people

Kouros: sculpture of a nude Greek youth

Lapis lazuli: bright-blue semiprecious stone containing sodium aluminum silicate and sulphur

Latitude: a point on the earth's circumference measured to the north or south

Levering: to move or raise an object using a leverlike action

Line: a mark, or implied mark, between two endpoints

Linear outline: a line that clearly separates a figure from its surroundings

Linear perspective: a system using converging imaginary sight lines to create the illusion of depth

Lintel: the horizontal beam over the doorway of a portal

Lithography, lithographic: a print process done on a flat, unmarred surface, such as a stone, in which the image is created using oil-based ink with resistance from water

Logo: a graphic image used to identify an idea or entity

Low relief: carving in which the design stands out only slightly from the background surface

Luminosity: a bright, glowing quality

Lyre: a stringed instrument that is played by being plucked; the strings hang from a crossbar that is supported by two arms connected to a hollow box, which amplifies the sound

Mandala: a sacred diagram of the universe, often involving a square and a circle

Mandorla: an almond-shaped light that surrounds a holy person, somewhat like a halo

Mannerism: from Italian *di maniera*, meaning charm, grace, playfulness; mid- to late sixteenth-century style of painting, usually with elongated human figures elevating grace as an ideal

Mantle: sleeveless item of clothing—a cloak or cape

Manuscripts: handwritten texts

Mask: in spray painting or silkscreen printing, a barrier, the shape of which blocks the paint or ink from passing through

Masquerade: performance in which participants wear masks and costumes for a ritual or cultural purpose

Mass: a volume that has, or gives the illusion of having, weight, density, and bulk

Matrix: an origination point, such as a woodblock, from which a print is derived

Medieval: relating to the Middle Ages; roughly, between the fall of the Roman Empire and the Renaissance

Medium (plural **media**): the material on or from which an artist chooses to make a work of art, for example canvas and oil paint, marble, engraving, video, or architecture

Memento mori: Latin phrase that means "remember that you must die." In artworks, such symbols as skulls, flowers, and clocks are used to represent the transient nature of life on Earth

Mesoamerican: an archaeological term referring to people or objects from the area now occupied by Mexico and Central America

Metope: a square space between triglyphs, often decorated with sculpture

Mezzotint: an intaglio printmaking process based on roughening the entire printing plate to accept ink; the artist smoothes non-image areas

Middle ground: the part of a work between the foreground and background

Mihrab: a niche in a mosque that is in a wall oriented toward Mecca

Mime: a silent performance work; actors use only body movements and facial expressions

Minaret: a tall slender tower, particularly on a mosque, from which the faithful are called to prayer

Minbar: a platform in a mosque, from which a leader delivers sermons

Minimalism, Minimalist: a mid-twentieth-century artistic style characterized by its simple, unified, and impersonal look, and often employing geometrical or massive forms

Mirror writing: writing that reads correctly only when reflected in a mirror, as in the case of the journals and other writings of Leonardo da Vinci

Mobile: suspended moving sculptures, usually impelled by natural air currents

Modeling: the representation of three-dimensional objects in two dimensions so that they appear solid

Modernist, Modernism: a radically new twentieth-century art and architectural movement that embraced modern industrial materials and a machine aesthetic

Monochromatic: having one or more values of one color

Monolith: a monument or sculpture made from a single piece of stone

Monumental: having massive or impressive scale

Mosaic: a picture or pattern created by fixing together small pieces of stone, glass, tile, etc.

Motif: (1) a design or color repeated as a unit in a pattern (2) a distinctive visual element, the recurrence of which is often characteristic of an artist's work

Motion: the effect of changing placement in time

Motion capture ("mocap" or performance capture)**:** technology developed to animate CGI characters by translating into a digital performance the live, exact motions of people or objects, using specially designed suits or equipment with sensors

Mural: a painting executed directly onto a wall

Musical: a genre of film in which the story is told through song, usually combined with dialogue and dancing

Narrative: (1) an artwork that tells a story (2) the story that an artwork expresses

Naturalism, naturalistic: a very realistic or lifelike style of making images

Nave: the central space of a cathedral or basilica

Necropolis: cemetery or burial place

Neo-Expressionist: a broad term, first used in the late 1970s to early 1980s; describes figurative and allegorical, not totally abstract, art with materials used aggressively to give clear evidence of the artist's gestures

Negative: a reversed image, in which light areas are dark and dark areas are light (opposite of a positive)

Negative space: an empty space given shape by its surround, for example the right-pointing arrow between the **E** and **x** in **FedEx** (see p. 29)

Neutral: colors (such as blacks, whites, grays, and dull gray-browns) made by mixing complementary hues

Non-objective: art that does not depict a recognizable subject

Nude: an artistic representation of an unclothed human figure, emphasizing the body's form rather than its exposure

Nun's habit: a long, layered piece of clothing worn by a member of a convent; appearance determined by the affiliated religious order

Ocher: a pigment found in nature containing hydrated iron oxide

Oculus: a round opening at the center of a dome

Octagonal: eight-sided

Oil paint: paint made of pigment floating in oil

One-point perspective: a perspective system with a single vanishing point on the horizon

Opaque: not transparent

Op art: a style of art exploiting the physiology of seeing to create illusory optical effects

Optical mixture: when the eye blends two colors that are placed near each other, creating a new color

Organic: having irregular forms and shapes, as though derived from living organisms

Origami: the Japanese art of paperfolding

Orthogonals: in perspective systems, imaginary sightlines extending from forms to the vanishing point

Outline: the outermost line or implied line of an object or figure, by which it is defined or bounded

Paisley: teardrop-shaped motif of Iranian origin, popular on European textiles since the nineteenth century

Paleolithic: prehistoric period, extending from 2.5 million to 12,000 years ago

Palette: (1) the range of colors used by an artist; (2) a smooth slab or board used for mixing paints or cosmetics

Passion: the arrest, trial, and execution of Jesus Christ, and his sufferings during them

Patina: surface color or texture on a metal caused by aging

Patron: an organization or individual who sponsors the creation of works of art

Pattern: an arrangement of predictably repeated elements

Pectoral: a large ornament worn on the chest

Pediment: the triangular space, situated above the row of columns, on the facade of a building in the Classical style

Pendentive: a curving triangular surface that links a dome to a square space below

Pentimento (plural **pentimenti**): Italian for "repentance," evidence of an underlying image showing that an artist changed his or her mind during the painting or drawing of an artwork

Performance art: a work involving the human body, usually including the artist, in front of an audience

Performance artist: an artist whose work involves the human body (often including his or her own)

Personification: representation of a thing, or an abstract quality, such as "freedom," as a person or in human form

Perspective: the creation of the illusion of depth in a two-dimensional image by using mathematical principles

Photomontage: a single photographic image that combines (digitally or using multiple film exposures) several separate images

Photorealism: a style of art that began in the 1960s and involves the artist creating artworks that resemble, and were inspired by, photographs

Physiology: a science that studies the workings of the body and its organs

Pictograph: picture used as a symbol in writing

Picture plane: the surface of a painting or drawing

Piece mold casting: a process for casting metal objects in which a mold is broken into several pieces that are then reassembled into a final sculpture

Pigment: the colorant in art materials. Often made from finely ground minerals

Pilaster: a vertical element, square in shape, that provides architectural support for crossing horizontal elements in post-and-lintel construction; also used for decoration

Plane: a flat surface, often implied in composition

Planography: a print process—lithography and silkscreen printing—where the inked image area and non-inked areas are at the same height

Plastic, plasticity: referring to materials that are soft and can be manipulated, or to such properties in the materials

Pointed arches: arches with two curved sides that meet to form a point at the apex

Pointillism: a late nineteenth-century painting style using short strokes or points of differing colors that optically combine to form new perceived colors

Polymer: a chemical compound commonly referred to as plastic

Polytheism: the worship of more than one god or goddess

Pop art: mid-twentieth-century artistic movement inspired by commercial art forms and popular culture

Portal: an entrance. A royal portal (main entrance) is usually on the west front of a church and features sculpted forms of kings and queens

Portico: a roof supported by columns at the entrance to a building

Portrait: image of a person or animal, usually focusing on the face

Positive: an image in which light areas are light and dark areas are dark (opposite of a negative)

Positive–negative: the relationship between contrasting opposites

Positive shape: a shape defined by its surrounding empty space

Post-and-lintel construction: a horizontal beam (the lintel) supported by a post at either end

Post-Impressionists: artists either from or living in France, *c.* 1885–1905, who moved away from the Impressionist style – notably Cézanne, Gauguin, Seurat, and Van Gogh

Postmodernism, Postmodernist: a late twentieth-century style of architecture and art that playfully adopts features of earlier styles

Predella: platform or base on which an altar stands, often decorated with scenes related to the main panels

Prehistoric: dating from the period of human existence before the invention of writing

Pre-Raphaelite Brotherhood: English art movement formed in 1848 by painters who rejected the academic rules of art, and often painted medieval subjects in a naïve style

Primary colors: three basic colors from which all others are derived

Principles: the "grammar" applied to the elements of art—contrast, balance, unity, variety, rhythm, emphasis, pattern, scale, proportion, and focal point

Print: a picture reproduced on paper, often in multiple copies

Prism: a transparent triangular length of material that can be used to disperse light to reveal the range of color present in the visible spectrum

Profile: the outline of an object, especially a face or head, represented from the side

Propaganda: art that promotes an ideology or a cause

Proportion: the relationship in size between a work's individual parts and the whole

Provenance: the record of all known previous owners and locations of a work of art

Psychoanalysis: a method of treating mental illness by making conscious the patient's subconscious fears or fantasies

Psychology: a science that studies the

nature, development, and operation of the human mind

Pueblo(s): word meaning "town" that refers to Anasazi settlements throughout the Four Corners area of Utah, Colorado, New Mexico, and Arizona; also the name of groups descending from the Anasazi

Putto (plural **putti**): a representation of a nude or scantily clad infant angel or boy, common in Renaissance and Baroque art

Pyramid: ancient structure, usually massive in scale, consisting of a square base with four sides that meet at a point or apex with each side forming a triangular shape

Qibla: the direction to Mecca, toward which Muslims face when praying

Raku: handmade and fired ceramic, made for a tea ceremony

Readymade: an everyday object presented as a work of art

Realism: nineteenth-century artistic style that aimed to depict nature and everyday subjects in an unidealized manner; "Realism" is also used to describe a historical movement from the same period, which tried to achieve social change by highlighting, in art and literature, the predicament of the poor

Realistic: artistic style that aims to represent appearances as accurately as possible

Register: one of two or more horizontal sections into which a space is divided in order to depict the episodes of a story

Relative placement: the arrangement of shapes or lines to form a visual relationship to each other in a design

Relief: (1) a raised form on a largely flat background. For example, the design on a coin is "in relief"; (2) a print process where the inked image is higher than the non-printing areas; (3) a sculpture that projects from a flat surface

Renaissance: a period of cultural and artistic change in Europe from the fourteenth to the seventeenth century

Rendering: to apply plaster to a wall

Repoussé: a technique of hammering metal from the back to create a form or surface detail

Representation: the depiction of recognizable figures and objects

Representational: art that depicts figures and objects so that we recognize what is represented

Rhythm: the regular or ordered repetition of elements in the work

Rib vault: an archlike structure supporting a ceiling or roof, with a web of protruding stonework

Rococo: decorative artwork style featuring elaborately curved lines and organic forms of ornament

Romanesque: an early medieval European style of architecture based on Roman-style rounded arches and heavy construction

Romanticism, Romantic style: movement in nineteenth-century European culture, concerned with the power of the imagination and greatly valuing intense feeling

Rosin: a dry powdered resin that melts when heated, used in the aquatint process

Salon: (1) official annual exhibition of French painting, first held in 1667; (2) a French term for an exhibition of work by multiple artists; (3) a social gathering for writers, artists, and musicians, usually hosted by wealthy and influential women

Sand painting: also known as dry painting, a labor-intensive method of painting using grains of sand as the medium

Sarcophagus (plural **sarcophagi**): a coffin (usually made of stone or baked clay)

Sarsen: a type of hard, gray sandstone

Satire: a work of art that exposes the weaknesses and mistakes of its subjects to ridicule

Saturation (also known as **chroma**): the degree of purity of a color

Scale: the size of an object or an artwork relative to another object or artwork, or to a system of measurement

Secondary color: a color mixed from two primary colors

Sfumato: in painting, the application of layers of translucent paint to create a hazy or smoky appearance and unify the composition

Shade: a color darker in value than its purest state

Shading: the use of graduated light and dark tones to represent a three-dimensional object in two dimensions

Shaft: the main vertical part of a column

Shaman: a priest or priestess regarded as having the ability to communicate directly with the spiritual world

Shape: a two-dimensional area, the boundaries of which are defined by lines or suggested by changes in color or value

Silhouette: a portrait or figure represented in outline and solidly colored in

Silkscreen: method of printmaking using a stencil and paint pushed through a screen

Sitter: person who poses, or "sits," for an artist to paint, sculpt, or photograph

Sketch: a rough preliminary version of a work or part of a work

Slip: clay mixed with water used to decorate pottery

Soft focus: deliberate blurring of the edges or lack of sharp focus in a photograph or movie

Space: the distance between identifiable points or planes

Span: the distance bridged between two supports, such as columns or walls

Stained glass: colored glass used for windows or decorative applications

Stela: upright stone slab decorated with inscriptions or pictorial relief carvings

Stencil: a perforated template allowing ink or paint to pass through to print a design

Stepped pyramid: a pyramid consisting of several rectangular structures placed one on top of another

Stereotypes: oversimplified notions, especially about marginalized groups, that can lead to prejudiced judgments

Still life: a scene of inanimate objects, such as fruits, flowers, or motionless animals

Stop-motion: figures, puppets, or dolls are photographed in a pose, moved very slightly, and then photographed again; the process is repeated until the desired sequence of movements has been acted out

Street art: art created in public places (examples include graffiti, posters, and stickers)

Stucco: a coarse plaster designed to give the appearance of stone

Stupa: a burial mound containing Buddha's remains

Style: a characteristic way in which an artist or group of artists uses visual language to give a work an identifiable form of visual expression

Stylized: art that represents objects in an exaggerated way to emphasize certain aspects of the object

Stylobate: the uppermost platform on a Classical temple, on which the columns stand

Subject: the person, object, or space depicted in a work of art

Sublime: feeling of awe or terror, provoked by the experience of limitless nature and the awareness of the smallness of an individual

Subordination: the opposite of emphasis; it draws our attention away from particular areas of a work

Subtractive: the methodical removal of material to produce a sculptural form

Subtractive colors: the colors produced from pigment

Sunken relief: a carved panel where the figures are cut deeper into the stone than the background

Support: the material on which painting is done

Surreal: reminiscent of the Surrealist movement in the 1920s and later, whose art was inspired by dreams and the subconscious

Surrealism, Surrealist: an artistic movement in the 1920s and later; its works were inspired by dreams and the subconscious

Symbolism: (1) using images or symbols in an artwork to convey meaning; often obvious when the work was made, but requiring research for modern viewers to understand; (2) artist or artistic style belonging to the movement in European art and literature, c. 1885–1910, that conveyed meaning by the use of powerful yet ambiguous symbols

Symmetrical balance: an image or shape that looks exactly (or nearly exactly) the same on both sides when cut in half

Symmetry: the correspondence in size, form, and arrangement of items on opposite sides of a plane, line, or point that creates direct visual balance

Syncretic (noun: **syncretism**) : the blending of multiple religious or philosophical beliefs

Synesthesia: when one of the five senses perceives something that was stimulated by a trigger from one of the other senses

Tableau: a stationary scene arranged for artistic impact

Taoism: a religion that emphasizes living in harmony through the Tao, or "Way," by balancing opposing forces (Yin and Yang)

Tapestry: hand-woven fabric—usually silk or wool—with a non-repeating, usually figurative, design woven into it

Tattoos: designs marked on the body by injecting dye under the skin

Tempera: fast-drying painting medium made from pigment mixed with water-soluble binder, such as egg yolk

Temperature: a description of color based on our associations with warmth or coolness

Tenebrism: dramatic use of intense darkness and light to heighten the impact of a painting

Terra-cotta: iron-rich clay, fired at a low temperature, which is traditionally brownish-orange in color

Tertiary colors: colors that can be mixed from a secondary and a primary color

Tesserae: small pieces of stone or glass or other materials used to make a mosaic

Texture: the surface quality of a work, for example fine/coarse, detailed/lacking in detail

Three-dimensional, three-dimensionality: having height, width, and depth

Three-point perspective: a perspective system with two vanishing points on the horizon and one not on the horizon

Throwing: the process of making a ceramic object on a potter's wheel

Tint: a color lighter in value than its purest state

Tipi or **teepee:** portable dwelling used by Plains groups

Tone: a color that is weaker than its brightest, or most pure, state

Tooth: the textural quality of a paper surface for holding drawing media in place

Torana: a gateway used in Hindu and Buddhist architecture

Tracery: a complex but delicate pattern of interwoven lines

Transept: structure crossing the main body of a Latin-cross-plan church

Travertine: light-colored limestone deposited in mineral springs and used as a building material

Triglyph: a projecting block carved with three raised bands, which alternates with figurative reliefs in a frieze

Triptych: an artwork comprising three painted or carved panels, normally joined together and sharing a common theme

Trompe l'oeil: an extreme kind of illusion meant to deceive the viewer that the objects included are real

Trumeau: within a portal, a central column that supports a tympanum

Tumbling: the use of levers to roll heavy objects over short distances

Twining: basket-weaving technique consisting of twisting two strands of material around a foundation of parallel sticks

Twisted perspective, also known as **composite view:** a representation of a figure, part in profile and part frontally

Two-dimensional: having height and width

Tympanum: an arched recess above a doorway, often decorated with carvings

Typography: the art of designing, arranging, and choosing type

Underpainting: in oil painting, the process of painting the canvas in a base, often monochrome color, as a first step in creating the areas of light and dark value

Unity: the imposition of order and harmony on a design

Value: the lightness or darkness of a plane or area

Vanishing point: the point in a work of art at which imaginary sight lines appear to converge, suggesting depth

Vanitas: a genre of painting that emphasizes the transient nature of earthly materials and beauty; often seen in still-life painting

Variety: the diversity of different ideas, media, and elements in a work

Vault: an arch-like structure supporting a ceiling or roof

Vaulted: covered with an arch-shaped ceiling or roof

Verdacchio: a mixture of black, white and yellow pigments resulting in a grayish or yellowish soft greenish brown. It is used in oil painting, and sometimes in frescoes, as a base layer to refine the values in the work

Visionary art: art made by self-taught artists following a personal vision

Void: an area in an artwork that seems empty

Volume: the space filled or enclosed by a three-dimensional figure or object

Voodoo: a religion based on Roman Catholic and traditional African rituals, practiced in the West Indies and southern US

Warp: the pieces of thread or yarn that are held in place lengthwise in the weaving process

Watercolor: transparent paint made from pigment and a binder dissolved in water

Wavelength: a term from physics that measures light as the distance between two corresponding points on a wave of energy, e.g. between two high points of a wave

Weft: the pieces of thread or yarn that are passed over or under the warp to create a textile

White space: in typography, the empty space around type or other features in a layout

Woodblock: a relief print process where the image is carved into a block of wood

Woodcut: a print created from an incised piece of wood

Ziggurat: Mesopotamian stepped tower, roughly pyramid-shaped, that diminishes in size toward a platform summit

Further Reading

GATEWAY IMAGES

Berrin, Kathleen, and Virginia M. Fields, eds., Olmec: *Colossal Masterworks of Ancient Mexico.* New Haven, CT (Yale University Press) 2010.

Hall, Marcia, ed., *Raphael's School of Athens.* Cambridge, England (Cambridge University Press) 1997.

Garrard, Mary, *Artemisia Gentileschi.* New York (Princeton University Press) 1991.

Koch, Ebba, *The Complete Taj Mahal.* London (Thames & Hudson) 2006.

Hughes, Robert, *Goya.* New York (Alfred A. Knopf) 2004.

Bouquillard, Jocelyn, *Hokusai's Mount Fuji: The Complete Views in Color.* New York (Harry N. Abrams) 2007.

Spirn, Anne Whiston, *Daring to Look: Dorothea Lange's Photographs and Reports from the Field.* Chicago (University of Chicago Press) 2008.

Umland, Anne, *Pablo Picasso: Girl before a Mirror (One on One).* New York (The Museum of Modern Art, New York) 2012.

PART 1

Chapter 1.1 Line, Shape, and the Principle of Contrast

de Zegher, Catherine, and Cornelia Butler, *On Line: Drawing Through the Twentieth Century.* New York (The Museum of Modern Art) 2010.

Ocvirk, Otto, Robert Stinson, Philip Wigg, and Robert Bone, *Art Fundamentals: Theory and Practice,* 11th edn. New York (McGraw-Hill) 2008.

Chapter 1.2 Form, Volume, Mass, and Texture

Ching, Francis D. K., *Architecture: Form, Space, and Order,* 3rd edn. Hoboken, NJ (Wiley) 2007.

Wong, Wucius, *Principles of Three-Dimensional Design.* New York (Van Nostrand Reinhold) 1977.

Chapter 1.3 Implied Depth: Value and Space

Auvil, Kenneth W., *Perspective Drawing,* 2nd edn. New York (McGraw-Hill) 1996.

Curtis, Brian, *Drawing from Observation,* 2nd edn. New York (McGraw-Hill) 2009.

Chapter 1.4 Color

Albers, Josef, and Nicholas Fox Weber, *Interaction of Color: Revised and Expanded Edition.* New Haven, CT (Yale University Press) 2006.

Bleicher, Steven, *Contemporary Color: Theory and Use,* 2nd edn. Clifton Park, NY (Delmar Cengage Learning) 2011.

Finlay, Victoria, *Color: A Natural History of the Palette.* London/New York (Random House Trade Paperbacks) 2003.

Stewart, Jude, *ROY G. BIV: An Exceedingly Surprising Book about Color.* New York (Bloomsbury) 2013.

Chapter 1.5 Time and Motion

Krasner, Jon, *Motion Graphic Design: Applied History and Aesthetics,* 2nd edn. Burlington, MA (Focal Press [Elsevier]) 2008.

Stewart, Mary, *Launching the Imagination,* 3rd edn. New York (McGraw-Hill) 2007.

Chapter 1.6 Unity, Variety, and Balance

Bevlin, Marjorie Elliott, *Design Through Discovery: An Introduction,* 6th edn. Orlando, FL (Harcourt Brace & Co./ Wadsworth Publishing) 1993.

Lauer, David A., and Stephen Pentak, *Design Basics,* 8th edn. Boston, MA (Wadsworth Publishing) 2011.

Chapter 1.7 Scale and Proportion

Bridgman, George B., *Bridgman's Life Drawing.* Mineola, NY (Dover Publications) 1971.

Elam, Kimberly, *Geometry of Design: Studies in Proportion and Composition,* 1st edn. New York (Princeton Architectural Press) 2001.

Chapter 1.8 Emphasis and Focal Point

Lauer, David A., and Stephen Pentak, *Design Basics,* 8th edn. Boston, MA (Wadsworth Publishing) 2011.

Stewart, Mary, *Launching the Imagination,* 3rd edn. New York (McGraw-Hill) 2007.

Chapter 1.9 Pattern and Rhythm

Ocvirk, Otto, Robert Stinson, Philip Wigg, and Robert Bone, *Art Fundamentals: Theory and Practice,*

11th edn. New York (McGraw-Hill) 2008.

Wong, Wucius, *Principles of Two-Dimensional Design*, 1st edn. New York (Wiley) 1972.

Chapter 1.10 Content and Analysis

Barnet, Sylvan, *Short Guide to Writing About Art*. Harlow, UK (Pearson Education) 2010.

Brown, Jonathan, *Velázquez: Painter and Courtier*. New Haven, CT (Yale University Press) 1988.

Hatt, Michael, and Charlotte Klonk, *Art History: A Critical Introduction to Its Methods*. New York (Manchester University Press; distributed exclusively in the USA by Palgrave) 2006.

PART 2
Chapter 2.1 Drawing

Faber, David L., and Daniel M. Mendelowitz, *A Guide to Drawing*, 8th edn. Boston, MA (Wadsworth Publishing) 2011.

Sale, Teel, and Claudia Betti, *Drawing: A Contemporary Approach*, 6th edn. Boston, MA (Wadsworth Publishing) 2007.

Chapter 2.2 Painting

Gottsegen, Mark David, *Painter's Handbook: Revised and Expanded*. New York (Watson-Guptill) 2006.

Robertson, Jean, and Craig McDaniel, *Painting as a Language: Material, Technique, Form, Content*, 1st edn. Boston, MA (Wadsworth Publishing) 1999.

Chapter 2.3 Printmaking

Hunter, Dard, *Papermaking*. Mineola, NY (Dover Publications) 2011.

Ross, John, *Complete Printmaker*, revised expanded edn. New York (Free Press) 1991.

Chapter 2.4 Sculpture

Rich, Jack C., *The Materials and Methods of Sculpture*, 10th edn. Mineola, NY (Dover Publications) 1988.

Tucker, William, *The Language of Sculpture*. London (Thames & Hudson) 1985.

Chapter 2.5 Architecture

Ching, Francis D. K., *Architecture: Form, Space, and Order*, 3rd edn. Hoboken, NJ (Wiley) 2007.

Glancey, Jonathan, *Story of Architecture*. New York (Dorling Kindersley/Prentice Hall) 2006.

Chapter 2.6 The Tradition of Craft

Speight, Charlotte, and John Toki, *Hands in Clay: An Introduction to Ceramics*, 5th edn. New York (McGraw-Hill) 2003.

Wight, Karol, *Molten Color: Glassmaking in Antiquity*. Los Angeles, CA (J. Paul Getty Museum) 2011.

Chapter 2.7 Visual Communication Design

Craig, James, William Bevington, and Irene Korol Scala, *Designing with Type, 5th Edition: The Essential Guide to Typography*. New York (Watson-Guptill) 2006.

Meggs, Philip B., and Alston W. Purvis, *Meggs' History of Graphic Design*, 4th edn. Hoboken, NJ (Wiley) 2005.

Chapter 2.8 Photography

Heiferman, Marvin, and Merry A. Foresta, *Photography Changes Everything*. New York (Aperture/copublished with the Smithsonian Institution) 2012.

Hirsch, Robert, *Light and Lens: Photography in the Digital Age*. London (Elsevier) 2007.

Jeffrey, Ian, *How to Read a Photograph*. New York (Abrams) 2010.

London, Barbara, John Upton, and Jim Stone, *Photography*, 10th edn. Upper Saddle River, NJ (Pearson) 2010.

Marien, Mary Warner, *Photography: A Cultural History*, 3rd edn. Upper Saddle River, NJ (Prentice Hall) 2010.

Rosenblum, Naomi, *A World History of Photography*, 4th edn. New York (Abbeville Press) 2008.

Trachtenberg, Alan, ed., *Classic Essays on Photography*. New York (Leete's Island Books) 1980.

Chapter 2.9 Film/Video and Digital Art

Cook, David A., *A History of Narrative Film*, 4th edn. New York (W. W. Norton) 2004.

Corrigan, Timothy, and Patricia White, *The Film Experience*, 2nd edn. New York (Bedford/St. Martin's) 2008.

Monaco, James, *How to Read a Film: Movies, Media, and Beyond*. New York (Oxford University Press) 2009.

Wands, Bruce, *Art of the Digital Age*. New York (Thames & Hudson) 2007.

Chapter 2.10 Alternative Media and Processes

Alberro, Alexander, and Blake Stimson, *Conceptual Art: A Critical Anthology*. Cambridge, MA (MIT Press) 2000.

Bishop, Claire, *Installation Art*, 2nd edn. London (Tate Publishing) 2010.

Goldberg, Rosalee, *Performance Art: From Futurism to the Present*, 2nd edn. New York (Thames & Hudson) 2001.

Lippard, Lucy, *Six Years: The Dematerialization of the Art Object from 1966 to 1972*. Berkeley, CA (University of California Press) 1997.

Osborne, Peter, *Conceptual Art (Themes and Movements)*. New York and London (Phaidon) 2011.

Rosenthal, Mark, *Understanding Installation Art: From Duchamp to Holzer*. New York (Prestel) 2003.

PART 3
Chapter 3.1 The Prehistoric and Ancient Mediterranean

Alfred, Cyril, *Egyptian Art*. New York (Oxford University Press) 1980.

Aruz, Joan, *Art of the First Cities: The Third Millennium B.C. from the Mediterranean to the Indus*. New York (The Metropolitan Museum of Art); New Haven, CT (Yale University Press) 2003.

Boardman, John, *The World of Ancient Art*. New York (Thames & Hudson) 2006.

Pedley, John Griffiths, *Greek Art and Archeology*, 5th edn. Upper Saddle River, NJ (Pearson/Prentice Hall) 2007.

Wheeler, Mortimer, *Roman Art and Architecture*. New York (Thames & Hudson) 1985.

Chapter 3.2 Art of the Middle Ages

Benton, Janetta, *Art of the Middle Ages*. New York (Thames & Hudson) 2002.

Bloom, Jonathan, and Sheila Blair, *Islamic Arts*. London (Phaidon) 1997.

Camille, Michael, *Gothic Art: Glorious Visions*. New York (Abrams) 1996.

Lowden, John, *Early Christian & Byzantine Art*. London (Phaidon) 1997.

Chapter 3.3 Art of India, China, Japan, and Southeast Asia

Craven, Roy, *Indian Art*. New York (Thames & Hudson) 1997.

Lee, Sherman, *History of Far Eastern Art*. New York (Abrams) 1994.

Stanley-Baker, Joan, *Japanese Art*. New York (Thames & Hudson) 2000.

Tregear, Mary, *Chinese Art*. New York (Thames & Hudson) 1997.

Chapter 3.4 Art of the Americas

Berlo, Janet Catherine, and Ruth B. Phillips, *Native North American Art*. New York (Oxford University Press) 1998.

Coe, Michael D., and Rex Koontz, *Mexico: From the Olmecs to the Aztecs*, 6th edn. New York (Thames & Hudson) 2008.

Miller, Mary Ellen, *The Art of Ancient Mesoamerica*, 4th edn. New York (Thames & Hudson) 2006.

Rushing, Jackson III, *Native American Art in the Twentieth Century: Makers, Meanings, Histories*. New York (Taylor and Francis) 1999.

Stone-Miller, Rebecca, *Art of the Andes: From Chavin to Inca*, 2nd edn. New York (Thames & Hudson) 2002.

Chapter 3.5 Art of Africa and the Pacific Islands

Bacquart, Jean-Baptiste, *The Tribal Arts of Africa*. New York (Thames & Hudson) 2002.

Berlo, Janet Catherine, and Lee Anne Wilson, *Arts of Africa Oceania and the Americas*. Upper Saddle River, NJ (Prentice Hall) 1992.

D'Alleva, Anne, *Arts of the Pacific Islands*. New Haven, CT (Yale University Press) 2010.

Willet, Frank, *African Art*, 3rd edn. New York (Thames & Hudson) 2003.

Chapter 3.6 Art of Renaissance and Baroque Europe (1400–1750)

Bazin, Germain, and Jonathan Griffin, *Baroque and Rococo*. New York (Thames & Hudson) 1985.

Garrard, Mary, *Artemisia Gentileschi*. Princeton, NJ (Princeton University Press) 1991.

Hartt, Frederick, *History of Italian Renaissance Art*, 7th edn. Upper Saddle River, NJ (Pearson) 2010.

Welch, Evelyn, *Art in Renaissance Italy: 1350–1500*. New York (Oxford University Press) 2001.

Chapter 3.7 Art of Europe and America 1700–1865: Rococo to Realism

Chu, Petra ten-Doesschate, *Nineteenth Century European Art*. New York (Abrams) 2003.

Denvir, Bernard, *Post-Impressionism*. New York (Thames & Hudson) 1992.

Irwin, David, *Neoclassicism*. London (Phaidon) 1997.

Levey, Michael, *Rococo to Revolution: Major Trends in Eighteenth-Century Painting*. New York (Thames & Hudson) 1985.

Thomson, Belinda, *Impressionism: Origins, Practice, Reception*. New York (Thames & Hudson) 2000.

Vaughan, William, *Romanticism and Art*. London (Thames & Hudson) 1994.

Chapter 3.8 The Modern Aesthetic: Manet in 1863 to the American Scene in the 1930s

Arnason, H. H., and Elizabeth C. Mansfield, *History of Modern Art*, 6th edn. Upper Saddle River, NJ (Pearson) 2009.

Dempsey, Amy, *Styles, Schools, and Movements*, 2nd edn. New York (Thames & Hudson) 2011.

Stiles, Kristine, and Peter Selz, *Theories and Documents of Contemporary Art: A Sourcebook of Artists' Writings*, 2nd edn, revised and expanded. Berkeley, CA (University of California Press) 2011.

Chapter 3.9 Late Modern and Contemporary Art: from Abstract Expressionism in the 1940s to the Present Day

Barrett, Terry, *Why is that Art?: Aesthetics and Criticism of Contemporary Art*. New York (Oxford University Press) 2007.

Evans, David, *Appropriation*. Cambridge, MA (MIT Press) and London (Whitechapel Gallery) 2009.

Fineberg, Jonathan, *Art Since 1940: Strategies of Being*, 3rd edn. Upper Saddle River, NJ (Prentice Hall) 2010.

Jones, Amelia, *A Companion to Contemporary Art Since 1945*. Malden, MA (Blackwell Publishing) 2006.

Stiles, Kristine, and Peter Selz, *Theories and Documents of Contemporary Art: A Sourcebook of Artists' Writings*, 2nd edn, revised and expanded. Berkeley, CA (University of California Press) 2011.

PART 4

Chapter 4.1 Art and Community

Art in Action: Nature, Creativity, and Our Collective Future. San Rafael, CA (Earth Aware Editions) 2007.

Iosifidis, Kiriakos, *Mural Art: Murals on Huge Public Surfaces Around the World from Graffiti to Trompe l'oeil*. Vancouver, BC (Adbusters) 2009.

Kwon, Miwon, *One Place After Another: Site-Specific Art and Location Identity*. Cambridge, MA (MIT Press) 2004.

Witley, David S., *Cave Paintings and the Human Spirit*. Amherst, NY (Prometheus Books) 2009.

Chapter 4.2 Spirituality and Art

Azara, Nancy J., *Spirit Taking Form: Making a Spiritual Practice of Making Art*. Boston, MA (Red Wheel) 2002.

Bloom, Jonathan, and Sheila S. Blair, *Islamic Arts*. London (Phaidon) 1997.

Fisher, Robert E., *Buddhist Art and Architecture*. New York (Thames & Hudson) 1993.

Guo, Xi, *Essay on Landscape Painting*. London (John Murray) 1959.

Lyle, Emily, *Sacred Architecture in the Traditions of India, China, Judaism, and Islam*. Edinburgh (Edinburgh University Press) 1992.

Williamson, Beth, *Christian Art: A Very Short Introduction*. New York (Oxford University Press) 2004.

Chapter 4.3 Art and the Cycle of Life

Dijkstra, Rineke, *Portraits*. Boston, MA (Institute of Contemporary Art) 2005.

Germer, Renate, Fiona Elliot, and Artwig Altenmuller, *Mummies: Life after Death in Ancient Egypt*. New York (Prestel) 1997.

Miller, Mary Ellen, and Karl Taube, *An Illustrated Dictionary of the Gods and Symbols of Ancient Mexico and the Maya*. New York (Thames & Hudson) 1997.

Ravenal, John B., *Vanitas: Meditations on Life and Death in Contemporary Art*. Richmond, VA (Virginia Museum of Fine Arts) 2000.

Steinberg, Leo, *The Sexuality of Christ in Renaissance Art and in Modern Oblivion*. Chicago, IL (University of Chicago Press) 1996.

Chapter 4.4 Art and Science

Bordin, Giorgio, *Medicine in Art*. Los Angeles (J. Paul Getty Museum) 2010.

Brouger, Kerry, et al., *Visual Music: Synaesthesia in Art and Music Since 1900*. London (Thames & Hudson); Washington, D.C. (Hirshhorn Museum); Los Angeles, CA (Museum of Contemporary Art) 2005.

Gamwell, Lynn, and Neil deGrasse Tyson, *Exploring the Invisible: Art, Science, and the Spiritual.* Princeton, NJ (Princeton University Press) 2004.

Milbrath, Susan, *Star Gods of the Maya: Astronomy in Art, Folklore, and Calendars.* Austin, TX (University of Texas Press) 2000.

Pietrangeli, Carlo, et al., *The Sistine Chapel: A Glorious Restoration.* New York (Abrams) 1999.

Rhodes, Colin, *Outsider Art: Spontaneous Alternatives.* New York (Thames & Hudson) 2000.

Chapter 4.5 Art and Illusion

Ades, Dawn, *In the Mind's Eye: Dada and Surrealism.* Chicago, IL (Museum of Contemporary Art); New York (Abbeville Press) 1986.

Battistini, Matilde, *Astrology, Magic and Alchemy in Art.* Los Angeles, CA (J. Paul Getty Museum) 2007.

Ebert-Schifferer, Sybille, et al., *Deceptions and Illusions: Five Centuries of Trompe L'Oeil Painting.* Washington, D.C. (National Gallery of Art) 2003.

Gablik, Suzi, *Magritte.* New York (Thames & Hudson) 1985.

Kemp, Martin, *The Science of Art: Optical Themes in Western Art from Brunelleschi to Seurat.* New Haven, CT (Yale University Press) 1992.

Seckel, Al, and Douglas Hofstadter, *Masters of Deception: Escher, Dali, & The Artists of Optical Illusion.* New York (Sterling Publishing) 2007.

Chapter 4.6 Art of Political Leaders and Rulers

Berzock, Kathleen Bickford, *Benin: Royal Arts of a West African Kingdom.* Chicago, IL (Art Institute of Chicago); New Haven, CT (distributed by Yale University Press) 2008.

Freed, Rita, *Pharaohs of the Sun: Akhenaten, Nefertiti: Tutankhamen.* Boston, MA (Museum of Fine Arts in association with Bulfinch Press/Little, Brown and Co.) 1999.

Rapelli, Paola, *Symbols of Power in Art.* Los Angeles, CA (J. Paul Getty Museum, Getty Publications) 2011.

Rawski, Evelyn, *China: The Three Emperors 1662–1795.* London (Royal Academy of Arts) 2006.

Schele, Linda, in *The Blood of Kings: Dynasty and Ritual in Maya Art.* New York (G. Braziller) and Fort Worth, TX (Kimball Art Museum) 1992.

Spike, John T., *Europe in the Age of Monarchy.* New York (The Metropolitan Museum of Art) 1987.

Zanker, Paul, *The Power of Images in the Age of Augustus.* Ann Arbor, MI (University of Michigan Press) 1990.

Chapter 4.7 Art, War, and Revolution

Auping, Michael, *Anselm Kiefer Heaven and Earth.* Fort Worth, TX (Modern Art Museum of Fort Worth, in association with Prestel) 2005.

Barron, Stephanie, *Degenerate Art.* Los Angeles, CA (Los Angeles County Museum of Art) and New York (Abrams) 1991.

Hughes, Robert, *Goya.* New York (Alfred A. Knopf) 2003.

Steel, Andy, *The World's Top Photographers: Photojournalism: And the Stories Behind Their Greatest Images.* Mies, Switzerland, and Hove, UK (RotoVision) 2006.

Wilson, David, *The Bayeux Tapestry.* London (Thames & Hudson) 2004.

Chapter 4.8 Art of Social Conscience

Alhadeff, Albert, *The Raft of the Medusa: Géricault, Art, and Race.* Munich and London (Prestel) 2002.

Blais, Allison, et al., *A Place of Remembrance: Official Book of the National September 11 Memorial.* Washington, D.C. (National Geographic) 2011.

Kammen, Michael, *Visual Shock: A History of Art Controversies in American Culture.* New York (Alfred A. Knopf) 2007.

Van Hensbergen, Gijs, *Guernica: The Biography of a Twentieth-Century Icon.* New York (Bloomsbury) 2005.

Chapter 4.9 The Body in Art

Clark, Kenneth, *The Nude: A Study in Ideal Form.* Princeton, NJ (Yale University Press) 1990/1956.

Dijkstra, Bram, *Naked: The Nude in America.* New York (Rizzoli) 2010.

Jones, Amelia, *Body Art/Performing the Self.* Minneapolis, MN (University of Minnesota Press) 1998.

Nairne, Sandy, and Sarah Howgate, *The Portrait Now.* New Haven, CT (Yale University Press) and London (National Portrait Gallery) 2006.

Chapter 4.10 Identity, Race, and Gender in Art

Broude, Norma, and Mary Garrard, *Feminism and Art History: Questioning the Litany.* New York (Harper & Row) 1982.

Doy, Gen, *Picturing the Self: Changing Views of the Subject in Visual Culture.* London (I. B. Tauris) 2004.

Hickey, Dave, *The Invisible Dragon: Essays on Beauty,* revised and expanded edition. Chicago, IL (University of Chicago Press) 2009.

hooks, bell, *Feminism is for Everybody: Passionate Politics.* Cambridge, MA (South End Press) 2000.

Jones, Amelia, *Feminism and Visual Culture Reader.* New York (Routledge) 2010.

Patton, Sharon F., *African American Art* (Oxford University Press) 1998.

Perry, Gill, *Gender and Art.* New Haven, CT (Yale University Press) 1999.

Powell, Richard, *Black Art: A Cultural History,* 2nd edn. New York (Thames & Hudson) 2003.

Powell, Richard, Virginia Mecklenberg, and Theresa Slowik, *African American Art: Harlem Renaissance, Civil Rights Era, and Beyond.* New York (Skira Rizzoli) 2012.

Rebel, Ernst, *Self-Portraits.* Los Angeles, CA (Taschen) 2008.

Rugg, Linda Haverty, *Picturing Ourselves: Photography and Autobiography.* Chicago, IL (University of Chicago Press) 1997. Valenti, Jessica, *Full Frontal Feminism: A Young Woman's Guide to Why Feminism Matters.* Emeryville, CA (Seal Press) 2007.

Acknowledgments

The publisher would like to thank the following for their generous advice and feedback during the preparation of *Gateways to Art*. Special gratitude goes to:

John Adelman, Lone Star College Cy-Fair; Maribeth Anders and Anna Mitchell, Pulaski Technical College; Camilla Avery, Jefferson State Community College; Sarah Bremser, Kapiolani Community College; Sheila Chambers, Salt Lake Community College; Kenneth Conley, Prince George's County Community College; Rosemary Des Plas, El Centro College; Andrea Donovan, Minot State University; Kara English, Tarrant County Community College; Trina Felty, Pima Community College; Alison Fleming, Winston-Salem State University; Ferdinanda Florence, Solano Community College; Rebecca Hendrick, University of Texas at El Paso; Kathy Holt, Arapahoe Community College; Kay Klotzbach, Camden County College; Katrina Kuntz, Middle Tennessee State University; Patrick McNally, Community College of Aurora; Ken Magri, American River College; Rachel Moore, Navarro College; Erin Morris, South Mountain Community College; Violet Murakami, Hawaii Community College; Carola Naumer, Truckee Meadows Community College; Kristin Powers Nowlin, Southeast Missouri State University; Margee Bright Ragland, Georgia Perimeter College; Kurt Rahmlow, University of North Texas; Michelle Randall, Saginaw Valley State University; Mollie Rushing, Delta State University; Dennis Sears, Gadsden State Community College; Marta Slaughter, University of South Florida; Donald Sloan, University of Wisconsin La Crosse; Mike Stack and Mariana Carreras, Pima Community College; Suzanne Thomas, Rose State College; Li-Lin Tseng, Pittsburg State University; Christine Weber, Portland Community College; Kathy Windrow, Eastfield College; Christine Wolken, Cuyahoga Community College; Linda Woodward, Lone Star Community College Montgomery.

The publisher also gratefully acknowledges the following contributors: Wafaa Bilal, Tracy Chevalier, Mel Chin, Antony Gormley, David Grove, Zaha Hadid, Zahi Hawass, Hyo-In Kim, Steve McCurry, Howard Risatti, Sonoko Sasaki, Richard Serra, Cindy Sherman, Paul Tacon, Spencer Tunick, Bill Viola, and Robert Wittman.

Debra J. DeWitte
would like to thank the following for their scholarly assistance: Richard Brettell, University of Texas at Dallas; Annemarie Carr, Southern Methodist University; Jenny Ramirez; Beth Wright, University of Texas at Arlington (Museum Guide); and for their patience and support she would like to thank her family: Bill Gibney, Jaclyn Jean Gibney, and Connie DeWitte.

Ralph M. Larmann would like to thank the following for their scholarly assistance and support: Ella Combs-Larmann, independent scholar and artist; Dr. Heidi Strobel, University of Evansville; University of Evansville, Office of Academic Affairs, Office of Alumni Relations, University Library, Department of Art; and for their patience and understanding: Ella, Allison, and Tip.

M. Kathryn Shields
would like to thank the following: Laura M. Amrhein, independent scholar; Damon Akins, Guilford College; Scott Betz, Winston-Salem State University; Maria Bobroff, Guilford College; Ingrid Furniss, Lafayette College; Rita Lasater, University of Texas at Arlington; Claire Black McCoy, Columbus State University; Jenny Ramirez; Eric Steginsky, independent artist; and express love and gratitude to her family: Barry Bell, Gillian Denise Shields Bell, Alden Emmerich Shields Bell, and Nancy Shields.

Sources of Quotations

Introduction

p. 27: Unspecified critic on Frederic Edwin Church from Pierre Berton, *Niagara: A History of the Falls* (New York: State University of New York, Albany, 1992), 119.

p. 41: Ai Weiwei from an article by Sylvia Poggioli, "Ai Weiwei Exhibit Shines Light on Time as Political Prisoner," August 19, 2013: http://www.opb.org/news/article/npr-ai-weiwei-exhibit-shines-light-on-time-as-political-prisoner/

PART I

Chapter 1.1

p. 52: Barbara Hepworth from Abraham Marie Hammacher, *The Sculpture of Barbara Hepworth* (New York: Harry N. Abrams, 1968), 98.

Chapter 1.2

p. 67: Vivant Denon from http://www.ancient-egypt-history.com/2011/04/napoleon-bonapartes-wise-men-at.html.

p. 70: Lino Tagliepietra from the artist's website at http://www.linotagliapietra.com/batman/index.htm.

Chapter 1.3

p. 82: Albert Einstein from Thomas Campbell, *My Big TOE: Inner Workings* (Huntsville, AL: Lightning Strike Books, 2003), 191.

Chapter 1.4

p. 101: Vasily Kandinsky from Robert L. Herbert, *Modern Artists on Art* (New York: Dover Publications, 1999), 19.

p. 115: Van Gogh quoted in Ian Chilvers, Harold Osborne, and Denis Farr (eds.), *The Oxford Dictionary of Art* (New York: Oxford University Press, 2009), 298.

Chapter 1.5

p. 121: William Faulkner from Philip Gourevitch (ed.), *The Paris Review: Interviews, Volume 2* (New York: Picador USA, 2007), 54.

Chapter 1.7

p. 146: Baudelaire from Charles Baudelaire, *Flowers of Evil and Other Works*, ed. and trans. Wallace Fowlie (New York: Dover Publications, 1992), 201.

Chapter 1.9

p. 171: Elvis Presley from Dave Marsh and James Bernard, *The New Book of Rock Lists* (New York: Simon & Schuster [Fireside], 1994), 9.

Chapter 1.10

p. 180: Edward Hopper from Art Institute of Chicago website: www.artic.edu/aic/collections/artwork/111628.

p. 181: José de Sigüenza from Ian Chilvers, ed.,

"Bosch, Hieronymus," in *The Oxford Dictionary of Art and Artists* (Oxford University Press, 2009; and Oxford Reference Online, Oxford University Press).

p. 186: Magdalena Abakanowicz from Magdalena Abakanowicz, "Solitude," (1985) sent by the artist to the editors, Kristine Stiles and Peter Selz, eds., *Theories and Documents of Contemporary Art: A Sourcebook of Artists' Writings* (Berkeley: University of California Press, 1996), 260.

PART 2
Chapter 2.1
p.198: William Blake from *The Complete Poetry and Prose of William Blake* (Berkeley and Los Angeles, CA: Anchor/ University of California Press, 1997), 574.

Chapter 2.2
p. 219: José Clemente Orozco from *The Artist in New York: Letters to Jean Charlot and Unpublished Writings, 1925–1929* (Austin, TX: University of Texas Press, 1974), 90–91.

p.221: Andrew Wyeth from William Scheller, *America, a History in Art: The American Journey Told by Painters, Sculptors ...* (New York: Black Dog & Leventhal Publishers, 2008), 22.

Chapter 2.4
p. 248: Michelangelo quoted by Henry Moore from Henry Moore and Alan G. Wilkinson, *Henry Moore–Writings and Conversations* (Berkeley, CA: University of California Press, 2002), 238.

Chapter 2.5
p. 284: Le Corbusier from Nicholas Fox Weber, *Le Corbusier: A Life* (New York: Alfred A. Knopf, 2008), 171.

p. 285: Mies van der Rohe from E. C. Relph, *The Modern Urban Landscape* (Baltimore, MD: The Johns Hopkins University Press, 1987), 191.

Chapter 2.6
p. 292: Geoffrey Chaucer from *The Works of Geoffrey Chaucer, Volume 5* (New York: Macmillan and Co., Limited, 1904), 341.

Chapter 2.8
p. 324: Dorothea Lange from Dorothea Lange, "The Assignment I'll Never Forget: Migrant Mother," in *Popular Photography* (February 1960); reprinted in James Curtis, *Mind's Eye, Mind's Truth: FSA Photography Reconsidered* (Philadelphia: Temple University Press, 1989).

pp. 328–29: Steve McCurry from "The Last Roll of Kodachrome," *Natgeo's Most Amazing Photos*, National Geographic Television (September 17, 2010), produced by Yvonne Russo and Hans Weise; editor Carol Slatkin: https://www.youtube.com/watch?v=DUL6MBVKVLI; and from "Exposed: The Last Roll of Kodachrome" (Brad Horn and Claire O'Neill), National Public Radio interview with Audie Cornish (July 24, 2010): http://www.npr.org/blogs/pictureshow/2010/07/23/128728114/kodachrome.

p. 336: Edward Burtynsky from *Manufactured Landscapes (U.S. Edition)*, directed by Jennifer Baichwal (Zeitgeist Films, 2006).

Chapter 2.9
p. 342: *The Artist* from Rick Groen, "The Artist: Mostly mute, it speaks volumes about silent film," *The Globe and Mail* (Toronto), December 9, 2011.

p. 350: Robin Wright talks about "House of Cards," published on January 29, 2013: http://netflix.com/HouseofCards; http://robinwright.org.es/; https://www.youtube.com/watch?v=nNtZVYAw1XM.

Chapter 2.10
p.355: Yoko Ono's text accompanying *Wish Tree* from Jessica Dawson, "Yoko Ono's Peaceful Message Takes Root," *Washington Post* (April 3, 2007): washingtonpost.com.

p. 358: Vito Acconci's description of *Following Piece* from documentation accompanying the photographs; reprinted in Lucy Lippard, *Six Years: The Dematerialization of the Art Object* (Berkeley, CA: University of California Press, 1973/1997), 117.

p.362: Kara Walker from "Interview: Projecting Fictions: 'Insurrection! Our Tools Were Rudimentary, Yet We Pressed On,'" *ART21* "Stories" Episode, Season 2 (PBS: 2003): http://www.pbs.org/art21/artists/walker/clip1.html.

PART 3
Chapter 3.1
p. 373: Inscription from Assyrian palace from Met Museum website and object file: http://www.metmuseum.org/works_of_art/collection_database/ancient_near_eastern_art/human_headed_winged_bull_and_winged_lion_lamassu/objectview.aspx?collID=3&OID=30009052.

p. 379: Protagoras from Kenneth Clark, *Protagoras* (New York: Harper and Row, 1969), 57.

Chapter 3.2
p. 400: Hildegard of Bingen from *Hildegard von Bingen's Mystical Visions*, trans. by Bruce Hozeski from *Scivias* (I,1), 8.

Chapter 3.4
p. 439: David Grove from David Grove, *In Search of The Olmec* (unpublished work), © David Grove.

Chapter 3.6
p. 473: Palladio from Rob Imrie and Emma Street, *Architectural Design and Regulation* (Chichester, UK: Wiley-Blackwell, 2011), section 1.2.

Chapter 3.7
p. 497: Jacques-Louis David from the Revolutionary Convention, 1793, quoted in Robert Cumming, *Art Explained* (New York: DK Publishing, 2005), 70.

p. 503: Unspecified critic on Goya from Lucien Solvay, *L'Art espagnol* (Paris and London, 1887), 261.

p. 506: Gustave Courbet from Robert Williams, *Art Theory: An Historical Introduction* (Malden, MA: Blackwell Publishing, 2004), 127.

Chapter 3.8
p. 512: Charles Baudelaire from *The Painter of Modern Life*, trans. and ed. Johnathan Mayne (London: Phaidon Press, 1995).

p. 519: Unspecified critic on Claudel from Ruth Butler, *Rodin: The Shape of Genius* (New Haven, CT and London: Yale University Press, 1993), 271.

p. 521: Paul Gauguin from Charles Estienne, *Gauguin: Biographical and Critical Studies* (Geneva: Skira, 1953), 17.

p. 521: Van Gogh from Vincent Van Gogh, Letter to Emile Bernard, October 7, 1888 in Arles, France, in *The Complete Letters of Vincent Van Gogh*, vol. 3, no. B19 (New York: Bulfinch Press, 2000/1958).

p. 525: Unspecified critic on the Eiffel Tower from Joseph Harriss, *The Tallest Tower: Eiffel and the Belle Epoque* (Bloomington, Indiana: Unlimited Publishing, 2004), 15.

p. 526: Henri Matisse from Jack Flam, *Matisse: The Man and His Art, 1869–1918* (Ithaca, NY: Cornell University Press, 1986), 196.

p. 533: Marcel Duchamp from Arturo Schwarz, *The Complete Works of Marcel Duchamp* (New York: Delano Greenidge Editions, 1997), II, 442.

p. 536: Filippo Marinetti from his "Manifesto for the Italo-Abyssinian War," (1936), quoted in Walter Benjamin, "The Work of Art in the Age of Mechanical Reproduction," in Walter Benjamin, *Illuminations: Essays and Reflections*, ed. Hannah Arendt (New York: Schocken Books, 1968), 241.

Chapter 3.9
p. 543: Mark Rothko from Selden Rodman, *Conversations with Artists* (New York: Devin-Adair, Co., 1957).

p. 558: Tara Donovan from Richard McCoy, "Prelude: A Discussion with Tara Donovan," *ART21* Magazine (April 8, 2010): http://blog.art21.org/2010/04/08/prelude-a-discussion-with-tara-donovan/#.VTAZECmp3dk.

PART 4
Chapter 4.1
p. 562: Susan Cervantes from Tyce Hendricks, "Celebrating Art that Draws People Together," *San Francisco Chronicle* (May 6, 2005), F1.

p. 562: Aliseo Purpura-Pontoniere from Tyce Hendricks, "Celebrating Art that Draws People Together," *San Francisco Chronicle* (May 6, 2005), F1.

p. 564: Hilla Rebay (the curator of the foundation and director of the Guggenheim museum) from the Solomon R. Guggenheim website: http://

www.guggenheim.org/guggenheim-foundation/architecture/new-york.

p. 567: Christo and Jeanne-Claude, "Selected Works: The Gates," The Art of Christo and Jeanne-Claude (© 2005; access date September 7, 2007) www.christojeanneclaude.net.

p. 573: Diego Rivera from Bertram D. Wolfe, *The Fabulous Life of Diego Rivera* (New York: Stein and Day, 1963), 423.

p. 573: Kryzstof Wodiczko, quoted in "Kryzstof Wodiczko, Tijuana Projection, 2001," ART21 on pbs.org: http://www.art21.org/images/krzysztof-wodiczko/the-tijuana-projection-2001-0.

Chapter 4.2

p. 584: Description of the Mosque of the Imam, Isfahan, from The Metropolitan Museum of Art, "Works of Art: Islamic Highlights: Signatures, Inscriptions, and Markings," accessed September 13, 2010: www.metmuseum.org/works_of_art/collection_database/islamic?art/mihrab/objectview.aspx?collID=14OID=140006815.

Chapter 4.3

p. 588: Albert Einstein from "The World As I See It," *Forum and Century*, vol. 84 (October, 1930), 193–4; reprinted in *Living Philosophies*, vol. 13 (New York: Simon and Schuster, 1931), 3–7; also reprinted in Albert Einstein, *Ideas and Opinions, based on Mein Weltbild*, ed. Carl Seeling (New York: Bonanza Books, 1954), 8–11.

p. 592: Jillian Mayer, *I Am Your Grandma*: https://www.youtube.com/watch?v=YfY1lfFu8j8.

Chapter 4.4

p.603: Willard Wigan from *The Telegraph* article by Benjamin Secher on July 7, 2007: http://www.telegraph.co.uk/culture/art/3666352/The-tiny-world-of-Willard-Wigan-nano-sculptor.html.

p. 606: Jasper Johns from Martin Friedman, *Visions of America: Landscape as Metaphor in the Late Twentieth Century* (Denver, CO: Denver Art Museum, 1994), 146.

pp. 607–8: Marcia Smilack from Artist's Statement on her own website: http://www.marciasmilack.com/artist-statement.php

p. 608: Salvador Dalí from Dawn Ades et al., *Dalí* (Venice, Italy: Rizzoli, 2004), 559.

p. 609: Yayoi Kusama Courtesy KUSAMA Enterprise, Ota Fine Arts, Tokyo and Victoria Miro, London © Yayoi Kusama.

Chapter 4.5

p. 611: Pliny the Elder from Jerome Jordon Pollitt, *The Art of Ancient Greece: Sources and Documents* (Cambridge: Cambridge University Press, 1990), 150.

p. 616: Ovid from *Metamorphoses*, trans. A. D. Melville and E. J. Kenney (New York and Oxford: Oxford World's Classics, 2009), 232.

p. 619: Magritte from Paul Crowther, *Language of 20th-Century Art* (New Haven, CT: Yale University Press, 1997), 116.

Chapter 4.7

p. 636: Nick Ut from William Kelly, *Art and Humanist Ideals: Contemporary Perspectives* (Australia: Palgrave Macmillan, 2003), 284.

p. 638: Picasso from Charles Harrison and Paul Wood, *Art in Theory, 1900–2000: An Anthology of Changing Ideas* (Oxford: Blackwell Publishing, 2003), 508.

p. 646: Maya Lin from Marilyn Stokstad, *Art History* (New York: Pearson Education, 2008), xliv.

Chapter 4.8

p. 651: Florence Owens Thompson, and one of her children, both from Kiku Adatto, *Picture Perfect: Life in the Age of the Photo Op.* (Princeton, NJ: Princeton University Press, 2008), 247 and 248.

p. 653: Chris Jordan from http://www.bu.edu/sustainability/chris-jordan-photography/

p. 654: Mary Richardson from June Purvis, *Emmeline Pankhurst: A Biography* (London and New York: Routledge, 2002), 255.

p. 655: Eric Fischl poem from Laura Brandon, *Art and War* (London: I. B. Tauris & Co. Ltd, 2007), 129; and Fischl's remarks from Daniel Sherman and Terry Nardin, *Terror, Culture, Politics: Rethinking 9/11* (Indiana: Indiana University Press, 2006), 60.

p. 656: Label from Nazi exhibition from Stephanie Barron, *Degenerate Art: The Fate of the Avant-Garde in Nazi Germany* (New York: Harry N. Abrams, 1991), 390.

Chapter 4.9

pp. 659 and 660: Willem de Kooning from an interview with David Sylvester (BBC, 1960), "Content is a Glimpse…" in *Location I* (Spring, 1963) and reprinted in David Sylvester, "The Birth of 'Woman I,'" *Burlington Magazine* 137, no. 1105 (April, 1995), 223.

p. 671: Matisse from "Exactitude is not Truth," 1947, essay by Matisse written for an exhibition catalog (Liège: Association pour le progrès intellectuel et artistique de la Wallonie, with the participation of Galerie Maight, Paris); English translation (Philadelphia Museum of Art, 1948); reprinted in Jack Flam, *Matisse on Art* (Berkeley, CA: University of California Press, 1995/1973), 179–181.

Chapter 4.10

p. 678: Cindy Sherman from "Interview with Els Barents," in *Cindy Sherman* (Munich: Schirmer und Mosel, 1982); reprinted in Kristine Stiles and Peter Selz, eds., *Theories and Documents of Contemporary Art: A Sourcebook of Artists' Writings* (Berkeley, CA: University of California Press, 1996), 792–3.

p. 683: Nikki S. Lee from Erica Schlaikjer, "Woman's Art Requres Becoming a Chameleon," *The Daily Northwestern* (February 24, 2006), Campus Section.

Illustration Credits

p. 18 Photo Irmgard Groth-Kimball © Thames & Hudson Ltd, London; **p. 19** Stanza della Segnatura, Vatican Museums, Rome; **p. 20** Galleria degli Uffizi, Florence; **p. 21** © Airpano (www.airpano.com); **p. 22** Museo Nacional del Prado, Madrid; **p. 23** Library of Congress, Washington, D.C. Prints & Photographs Division, H. Irving Olds collection, LC-DIG-jpd-02018; **p. 24** The Museum of Modern Art, New York, Gift of Mrs Simon Guggenheim, 2.1938. Digital image, The Museum of Modern Art, New York/Scala, Florence. © Succession Picasso/DACS, London 2015; **p. 25** Library of Congress, Washington, D.C. Prints & Photographs Division, FSA/OWI Collection, LC-DIG-fsa-8b29516; **0.0.1** Fitzwilliam Museum, University of Cambridge/Bridgeman Art Library; **0.0.2** White Images/Scala, Florence; **0.0.3** Solomon R. Guggenheim Museum, New York, Gift, Mr. and Mrs. James J. Shapiro, 85.3266. Photo David Heald © Solomon R. Guggenheim Foundation. © ARS, NY and DACS, London 2012; **0.0.4** Uffizi Gallery, Florence; **0.0.5** © 2015 FedEx Corporation. All Rights Reserved; **0.0.6** Image courtesy October Gallery, London; **0.0.7** © Sam74100/Dreamstime.com; **0.0.8** © Nik Wheeler/Corbis; **0.0.9** © Jeff Koons; **0.0.10** Indianapolis Museum of Art, Gift of Charles L. Freer/Bridgeman Art Library; **0.0.11** Musée du Louvre, Paris; **0.0.12** Kunsthistorisches Museum, Vienna; **0.0.13** Private Collection; **0.0.14** Photo © Erik Cornelius/Nationalmuseum, Stockholm; **0.0.15** Photo Marc Quinn Studio. Courtesy White Cube. © the artist; **0.0.16** Mauritshuis, The Hague; **0.0.17** Robert Harding Picture Library/agefotostock.com; **0.0.18a, 0.0.18b** Photos © David Levene/eyevine. Courtesy Ai Weiwei Studio; **0.0.19** iStockphoto.com; **0.0.20** © Andia/Alamy; **0.0.21** Allan Houser archives © Chiinde LLC; **0.0.22** André Held /akg-images; **0.0.23** Photo Art Gallery of New South Wales/Jenni Carter. © David Hockney; **p. 46** (above) Photo Andrew Hawthorne. Courtesy the artists; (center) © 2012 The M.C. Escher Company-Holland. All rights reserved. www.mcescher.com; (below) Museo Nacional del Prado, Madrid; **1.1.1** Photo Jarno Gonzalez Zarraonandia/iStockphoto.com; **1.1.2a** Photo Scala, Florence - courtesy the Ministero Beni e Att. Culturali; **1.1.2b** Photo Scala, Florence/Fondo Edifici di Culto - Min. dell'Interno; **1.1.3** © CLAMP/Kodansha Ltd; **1.1.4** Image courtesy Peter Freeman, Inc., New York; **1.1.5** © Bowness, Hepworth Estate; **1.1.6** © ADAGP, Paris and DACS, London 2012; **1.1.7** Fondation Dubuffet. © ADAGP, Paris and DACS, London 2012; **1.1.8** National Gallery of Art, Washington, D.C., Collection of Mr. and Mrs. Paul Mellon, 1983.1.81; **1.1.9** Ralph Larmann; **1.1.10, 1.1.11** British Library, London; **1.1.12** © Sauerkids; **1.1.13** Museo Nacional del Prado,

Madrid; **1.1.14** British Museum, London; **1.1.15** Ralph Larmann; **1.1.16** © Nike; **1.1.17** Art Institute of Chicago, Helen Birch Bartlett Memorial Collection, 1926.417; **1.1.18** Musée des Beaux-Arts de Lyon. © Succession H. Matisse/DACS 2012; **1.1.19** The Museum of Modern Art, New York, The Louis E. Stern Collection, 988.1964.6. Digital image, The Museum of Modern Art, New York/Scala, Florence. © Succession Picasso/DACS, London 2015; **1.1.20** The Museum of Modern Art, New York, Gift of Mrs. Simon Guggenheim, 2.1938. Digital image, The Museum of Modern Art, New York/Scala, Florence. © Succession Picasso/DACS, London 2015; **1.1.21**, **1.1.22** Ralph Larmann; **1.1.23** Courtesy Flomenhaft Gallery, New York; **1.1.24** Ralph Larmann; **1.1.25** Courtesy AT&T Archives and History Center; **1.1.26a** © 1996 Shepard Fairey/ObeyGiant.com; **1.1.26b** © 1996 Shepard Fairey/ObeyGiant.com. Photo © Elizabeth Daniels, www.elizabethdanielsphotography.com; **1.1.27** © Georgia O'Keeffe Museum/DACS 2012; **1.1.28** Noma Bar/Dutch Uncle; **1.1.29** © 2012 The M. C. Escher Company-Holland. All rights reserved. www.mcescher.com; **p. 65, 1.2.1** Ralph Larmann; **1.2.2** iStockphoto.com; **1.2.3** Photo courtesy the Marlborough Gallery Inc., New York. © Estate of David Smith/DACS, London/VAGA, New York 2012; **1.2.4** Rheinisches Landesmuseum, Bonn; **1.2.5** Photo Russell Johnson. Courtesy Lino Tagliapietra, Inc.; **1.2.6** Museo dell'Ara Pacis, Rome; **1.2.7** Fine Arts Museum of San Francisco, Museum Purchase, Gift of Mrs Paul Wattis 1999, 42 a–k; **1.2.8a** Photo Mary Cameron-Sarani; **1.2.8b** Prisma/Superstock; **1.2.9** Ralph Larmann; **1.2.10a**, **1.2.10b** Photo Clements/Howcroft, MA, USA. Courtesy the artists; **1.2.11** Photo Nationalmuseum, Stockholm; **1.2.12** Photo Andrew Hawthorne. Courtesy the artists; **1.2.13** Photo Irmgard Groth-Kimball © Thames & Hudson Ltd, London; **1.2.14** Photo Sue Ormerod. © Rachel Whiteread. Courtesy Gagosian Gallery, London; **1.2.15** © Marisol, DACS, London/VAGA, New York 2012; **1.2.16** Photononstop/Superstock; **1.2.17** © Romain Cintract/Hemis/Corbis; **1.2.18** © Louise Bourgeois Trust/DACS, London/VAGA, New York 2012; **1.2.19** Museum of Modern Art, New York, Purchase, Acc. no. 130.1946.a–c. Photo 2012, Museum of Modern Art, New York/Scala, Florence. © DACS 2012; **1.3.1** Los Angeles County Museum of Art (LACMA). Purchased with funds provided by the Mr. and Mrs. William Preston Harrison Collection, 78.7. © ADAGP, Paris and DACS, London 2012; **1.3.2** Special Collections & Archives, Eric V. Hauser Memorial Library, Reed College, Portland, Oregon; **1.3.3**, **1.3.4** Ralph Larmann; **1.3.5** Sterling & Francine Clark Art Institute, Williamstown; **1.3.6** Contarelli Chapel, Church of San Luigi dei Francesi, Rome; **1.3.7** Ralph Larmann; **1.3.8** Musée du Louvre, Paris; **1.3.9** Courtesy K. H. Renlund Museum – Provincial Museum of Central Ostrobothnia, Kokkola, Finland; **1.3.10** National Palace Museum, Taipei; **1.3.11** © T. H. Benton and

R. P. Benton Testamentary Trusts/DACS, London/VAGA, New York 2012; **1.3.12** Ralph Larmann; **1.3.13** Crystal Bridges Museum of American Art, Arkansas; **1.3.14** Metropolitan Museum of Art, Purchase, The Dillon Fund Gift, 1988. Photo Metropolitan Museum of Art/Art Resource/Scala, Florence 2012; **1.3.15** Ralph Larmann; **1.3.16** © Supergiant Games, LLC 2014; **1.3.17a** JTB Photo/Superstock; **1.3.17b** Ralph Larmann; **1.3.18** Private Collection; **1.3.19** Ralph Larmann; **1.3.20** Santa Maria Novella, Florence; **1.3.21a**, **1.3.21b** Stanza della Segnatura, Vatican Museums, Rome; **1.3.22** Ralph Larmann; **1.3.23** © 2012 The M. C. Escher Company-Holland. All rights reserved. www.mcescher.com; **1.3.24** Graphische Sammlung Albertina, Vienna; **1.3.25** From Trinity: Volume 1, ™ and © DC Comics; **1.4.1**, **1.4.2**, **1.4.3** Ralph Larmann; **1.4.4** akg-images; **1.4.5**, **1.4.6** Ralph Larmann; **1.4.7** Photo Joshua White. Courtesy the artist and Thomas Solomon Gallery, Los Angeles. © Analia Saban 2008; **1.4.8**, **1.4.9**, **1.4.10**, **1.4.11** Ralph Larmann; **1.4.12** Cleveland Museum of Art, Mr. and Mrs. William H. Marlatt Fund, 1965.233; **1.4.13** National Gallery of Art, Washington, D.C., Chester Dale Collection, 1963.10.94; **1.4.14** Fine Arts Museum of San Francisco, Gift of Vivian Burns, Inc., 74.8; **1.4.15** Ralph Larmann; **1.4.16** © Mark Tansey. Courtesy Gagosian Gallery, New York; **1.4.17** Museum of Modern Art, New York, Gift of Mr. and Mrs. Ben Heller, Acc. no. 240.1969. Photo 2012, Museum of Modern Art, New York/Scala, Florence. © ARS, NY and DACS, London, 2012; **1.4.18** The Museum of Fine Arts, Houston, Gift of Audrey Jones Beck. © ADAGP, Paris and DACS, London 2012; **1.4.19** Ralph Larmann; **1.4.20** Kunstmuseum Basel, Switzerland; **1.4.21** British Museum, London; **1.4.22** Ralph Larmann; **1.4.23a**, **1.4.23b** Musée d'Orsay, Paris; **1.4.24a**, **1.4.24b** © Yale University Press; **1.4.25** Yale University Art Gallery, New Haven, Bequest of Stephen Carlton Clark, B.A. 1903, 1961.18.34; **1.4.26** © Succession H. Matisse/DACS 2015; **1.4.27** Albright-Knox Art Gallery, Buffalo, New York, General Purchase Funds, 1946; **1.4.28** Photo Scala, Florence–courtesy the Ministero Beni e Att. Culturali; **1.4.29** Courtesy the artist; **1.5.1** National Gallery of Art, Washington, D.C., Samuel H. Kress Collection, 1939.1.293; **1.5.2** Photo University of South Florida. © Nancy Holt/DACS, London/VAGA, New York 2012; **1.5.3** Library of Congress, Washington, D.C. Prints & Photographs Division, LC-USZ62-536; **1.5.4** Galleria Borghese, Rome; **1.5.5** Albright-Knox Art Gallery, Buffalo, New York, Bequest of A. Conger Goodyear and Gift of George F. Goodyear, 1964. © DACS 2012; **1.5.6** Solomon R. Guggenheim Museum, New York, Partial gift of the artist, 1989, 89.3626. Photo David Heald © Solomon R. Guggenheim Foundation, New York. © ARS, NY and DACS, London 2012; **1.5.7** Copyright Bridget Riley, 2012. All rights reserved; **1.5.8** Courtesy the Bill Douglas Centre for the History of Cinema and Popular Culture, University of Exeter; **1.5.9** Disney Enterprises/Album/akg-images; **1.5.10**

Arte/Bavaria/WDR/Spauke, Bernd/The Kobal Collection; **1.5.11** © Blaine Harrington III/Alamy; **1.5.12** Photo © B. O'Kane/Alamy. © 2012 Calder Foundation, New York/DACS, London; **1.5.13a** Library of Congress, Washington, D.C. Prints & Photographs Division, FSA/OWI Collection, LC-USZ62-58355; **1.5.13b** © The Dorothea Lange Collection, Oakland Museum of California, City of Oakland. Gift of Paul S. Taylor; **1.5.13c** Library of Congress, Washington, D.C. Prints & Photographs Division, FSA/OWI Collection, LC-USF34-9097-C; **1.5.13d** Library of Congress, Washington, D.C. Prints & Photographs Division, FSA/OWI Collection, LC-USF34-9093-C; **1.5.13e** Library of Congress, Washington, D.C. Prints & Photographs Division, FSA/OWI Collection, LC-USF34-9095; **1.5.13f** Library of Congress, Washington, D.C. Prints & Photographs Division, FSA/OWI Collection, LC-DIG-fsa-8b29516; **1.5.14** © Suzanne Anker; **1.5.15** © the artist. Courtesy Catherine Person Gallery, Seattle, WA; **1.5.16** Rotger/Iberfoto/photoaisa.com; **1.6.1** Ralph Larmann; **1.6.2** Library of Congress, Washington, D.C. Prints & Photographs Division, H. Irving Olds collection, LC-DIG-jpd-02018; **1.6.3** I. Michael Interior Design; **1.6.4** Ralph Larmann; **1.6.5** Courtesy Galerie Berès, Paris. © ADAGP, Paris and DACS, London 2012; **1.6.6** Galleria Nazionale delle Marche, Urbino; **1.6.7** Museum of Modern Art, New York, Blanchette Hooker Rockefeller Fund, Acc. no. 377.1971. Photo 2012, Museum of Modern Art, New York/Scala, Florence. © Romare Bearden Foundation/DACS, London/VAGA, New York 2012; **1.6.8** © The Joseph and Robert Cornell Memorial Foundation/DACS, London/VAGA, New York 2012; **1.6.9** Photo John Freeman; **1.6.10** Ralph Larmann; **1.6.11** © Estate of Robert Rauschenberg. DACS, London/VAGA, New York 2012; **1.6.12** Private Collection; **1.6.13** Photo Mingli Yuan; **1.6.14** Photo Shimizu Kohgeisha Co., Ltd. Permission Ryoko-in Management; **1.6.15** © Airpano (www.airpano.com); **1.6.16** Ralph Larmann; **1.6.17** © Tibor Bognar/Photononstop/Corbis; **1.6.18** Ralph Larmann; **1.6.19** Courtesy Drepung Loseling Monastery, Inc.; **1.7.1** Photo Attilio Maranzano. Photo courtesy the Oldenburg van Bruggen Foundation. Copyright 1992 Claes Oldenburg and Coosje van Bruggen; **1.7.2** Courtesy the artist; **1.7.3** Werner Forman Archive, line artwork Ralph Larmann; **1.7.4** Gemäldegalerie, Staatliche Museen, Berlin; **1.7.5** Purchased with assistance from the Art Fund and the American Fund for the Tate Gallery 1997 © Tate, London, 2012. © ADAGP, Paris and DACS, London 2012; **1.7.6**, **1.7.7** Ralph Larmann; **1.7.8** National Museum, Ife, Nigeria; **1.7.9** Stanza della Segnatura, Vatican Museums, Rome, line artwork Ralph Larmann; **1.7.10** Ralph Larmann; **1.7.11a** National Archaeological Museum, Athens; **1.7.11b** Ralph Larmann; **1.7.12a** George Eastman House, New York; **1.7.12b** Ralph Larmann; **1.7.13a** iStockphoto.com; **1.7.13b** Ralph Larmann; **1.8.1** Christie's Images/Corbis. © 2015 Agnes Martin/DACS; **1.8.2** The Museum of Modern Art, New York, Gift of Sid Bass, Leon D. Black, Donald L. Bryant, Jr., Kathy and Richard S. Fuld, Jr., Agnes Gund, Mimi Haas, Marie-Josée and Henry R. Kravis, Jo Carole and Ronald S. Lauder, Donald B. Marron and Jerry Speyer on behalf of the Committee on Painting and Sculpture in honor of John Elderfield, 553.2008. Photo Jonathan Muzikar. Digital image, The Museum of Modern Art, New York/Scala, Florence. © Martin Puryear, Courtesy Matthew Marks Gallery; **1.8.3** Courtesy DC Moore Gallery, New York. © Estate of Jacob Lawrence, ARS, NY and DACS, London 2015; **1.8.4** Erich Lessing/akg-images; **1.8.5** Photo Scala, Florence. Chagall ®/© ADAGP, Paris and DACS, London 2015; **1.8.6** Musées Royaux des Beaux-Arts de Belgique, Brussels; **1.8.7** Musée du Louvre, Paris; **1.8.8** Victoria & Albert Museum, London; **1.8.9** Galleria degli Uffizi, Florence; **1.8.10** James A. Michener Collection, Honolulu Academy of Arts; **p. 165** Ralph Larmann; **1.9.1** Ralph Larmann; **1.9.2** Musée National d'Art Moderne, Centre Georges Pompidou, Paris; **1.9.3** Metropolitan Museum of Art, Louis E. and Theresa S. Seley Purchase Fund for Islamic Art, and Rogers Fund, 1984. Photo Metropolitan Museum of Art/Art Resource/Scala, Florence; **1.9.4** Ashmolean Museum, Oxford; **1.9.5a, 1.9.5b, 1.9.5c** Museum of Modern Art, New York, Gift of Agnes Gund, Jo Carole and Ronald S. Lauder, Donald L. Bryant, Jr., Leon Black, Michael and Judy Ovitz, Anna Marie and Robert F. Shapiro, Leila and Melville Straus, Doris and Donald Fisher, and purchase, Acc. no. 215.2000. Photo Ellen Page Wilson, courtesy The Pace Gallery © Chuck Close, The Pace Gallery; **1.9.6** Kunsthistorisches Museum, Vienna; **1.9.7** iStockphoto.com; **1.9.8** Collection Center for Creative Photography © 1981 Arizona Board of Regents; **1.9.9** © WaterFrame/Alamy; **1.9.10, 1.9.11** Museo Nacional del Prado, Madrid; **1.9.12a** Musée d'Orsay, Paris; **1.9.12b, 1.9.13a, 1.9.13b, 1.9.13c** Ralph Larmann; **1.10.1a, 1.10.1b** Photo Margarete Buesing. Photo Scala, Florence/BPK, Bildagentur für Kunst, Kultur und Geschichte, Berlin; **1.10.2** The Art Institute of Chicago, Friends of American Art Collection, 1942.51; **1.10.3** Museo Nacional del Prado, Madrid; **1.10.4a, 1.10.4b, 1.10.4c, 1.10.4d** The National Gallery, London/Scala, Florence; **1.10.5** Erich Lessing/akg-images; **1.10.6** Museum of African American Art, Los Angeles, California, Gift of Mrs Hayden; **1.10.7** Courtesy the artist; **1.10.8** Musée du Louvre, Paris; **1.10.9** © copyright The Robert Mapplethorpe Foundation. Courtesy Art + Commerce; **1.10.10** © Munch Museum/Munch-Ellingsen Group, BONO, Oslo; **1.10.11a, 1.10.11b** Museo Nacional del Prado, Madrid; **1.10.12** © Succession Picasso/DACS, London 2012; **1.10.13** © 2012 Thomas Struth; **p. 194** Ralph Larmann; **p. 196** (above) National Palace Museum, Taipei; (center) Library of Congress Prints, Washington, D.C., Prints & Photographs Division, LC-DIG-ppmsc-03521; (below) © Free Agents Limited/Corbis; **2.1.1** Biblioteca Ambrosiana, Milan; **2.1.2** The Royal Collection © Her Majesty The Queen; **2.1.3a** Biblioteca Ambrosiana, Milan; **2.1.3b** Stanza della Segnatura, Vatican Museums, Rome; **2.1.4** © John T. Biggers Estate/VAGA, NY/DACS, London 2015. Estate Represented by Michael Rosenfeld Gallery; **2.1.5** British Museum, London; **2.1.6, 2.1.7** Ralph Larmann; **2.1.8** © DACS 2012; **2.1.9** Courtesy of D.J. Hall and Craig Krull Gallery, Santa Monica; **2.1.10** © DACS 2012; **2.1.11** Photo Peter Nahum at The Leicester Galleries, London/Bridgeman Art Library; **2.1.12** Image courtesy the artist and White Rabbit Gallery, Sydney; **2.1.13** Metropolitan Museum of Art, Purchase, Joseph Pulitzer Bequest, 1924, Acc. no. 24.197.2. Photo Metropolitan Museum of Art/Art Resource/Scala, Florence; **2.1.14** Musée d'Orsay, Paris; **2.1.15** The Art Institute of Chicago, Helen Regenstein Collection, 1966.184; **2.1.16** San Francisco Museum of Modern Art, Purchased through a gift of Phyllis Wattis. © Estate of Robert Rauschenberg. DACS, London/VAGA, New York 2012; **2.1.17** National Palace Museum, Taipei; **2.1.18** British Museum, London; **2.1.19** Van Gogh Museum (Vincent Van Gogh Foundation), Amsterdam; **2.1.20** from *Wakoku Shoshoku Edzukushi*, 1681; **2.1.21** Ralph Larmann; **2.1.22** The Museum of Modern Art, New York, Gift of Alexander Liberman in honour of Rene d'Harnoncourt. Acc. no. 1365.1974. Digital image, The Museum of Modern Art, New York/Scala, Florence. © The Estate of Alberto Giacometti (Fondation Giacometti, Paris and ADAGP, Paris), licensed in the UK by ACS and DACS, London 2015; **2.1.23** Museum of Modern Art, New York, Purchase, 330.1949. Photo 2012, Museum of Modern Art, New York/Scala, Florence; **2.1.24** Christie's Images/Corbis; **2.2.1** Photo courtesy Dean Snow; **2.2.2, 2.2.3** Ralph Larmann; **2.2.4** Metropolitan Museum of Art, Gift of Edward S. Harkness, 1918, 18.9.2. Photo Metropolitan Museum of Art/Art Resource/Scala, Florence; **2.2.5** Vatican Museums, Rome; **2.2.6** Photo Schenck & Schenk. © DACS 2015; **2.2.7** Museo dell'Opera Metropolitana del Duomo, Siena; **2.2.8** Metropolitan Museum of Art, Purchase, Francis M. Weld Gift, 1950, Inv. 50.164. Photo Metropolitan Museum of Art/Art Resource/Scala, Florence; **2.2.9** Museum of Modern Art, New York, Purchase, 16.1949. Photo 2012, Museum of Modern Art, New York/Scala, Florence. © Andrew Wyeth; **2.2.10** Musée du Louvre, Paris; **2.2.11** Los Angeles County Museum of Art, Gift of Mr. and Mrs. Robert H. Ginter, M.64.49. Digital Image Museum Associates/LACMA/Art Resource NY/Scala, Florence. Courtesy Gallery Paule Anglim; **2.2.12** Kemper Museum of Contemporary Art, Kansas City. Bebe and Crosby Kemper Collection, Gift of the William T. Kemper Charitable Trust, UMB Bank, n.a., Trustee 2006.7. Photo Ben Blackwell © the artist; **2.2.13** Galleria degli Uffizi, Florence; **2.2.14** The Royal Collection © Her Majesty The Queen; **2.2.15** Clark Family Collection. Image courtesy The Clark Center for Japanese Art & Culture; **2.2.16** Photo Austrian Archives/Scala Florence; **2.2.17** Photo Tate, London 2012. © L&M Services B.V. The Hague 20110512. © Miriam Cendrars; **2.2.18** Kemper Museum of Contemporary Art, Kansas City. Bebe and Crosby Kemper Collection, Kansas City, Missouri. Museum Purchase, Enid and Crosby Kemper and William T. Kemper Acquisition Fund 2000.13. © the artist; **2.2.19** © Ralph M. Larmann; **2.2.20** Smithsonian American Art Museum, Gift of Ruth M. Bernstein. Photo Smithsonian American Art Museum/Art Resource/Scala, Florence; **2.2.21** Judith F. Baca © 2008. Photo courtesy SPARC (sparcinla.org); **2.2.22** Photo Kevin Flemen; **2.3.1** Ralph Larmann; **2.3.3** British Museum, London; **2.3.4** Museum of Modern Art, New York. Given anonymously (by exchange), Acc. no. 119.1956. Photo 2012, Museum of Modern Art, New York/Scala, Florence. © Nolde Stiftung Seebüll; **2.3.5** Library of Congress, Washington, D.C. Prints & Photographs Division, H. Irving Olds collection, LC-DIG-jpd-02018; **2.3.6** Courtesy Stanley Donwood/TAG Fine Arts; **2.3.7** Ralph Larmann; **2.3.8** Victoria & Albert Museum, London; **2.3.9** © DACS 2012; **2.3.10** Kupferstichkabinett, Museen Preussiches Kulturbesitz, Berlin; **2.3.11** Metropolitan Museum of Art, Harris Brisbane Dick Fund, 1935, Acc. no. 35.42. Photo Metropolitan Museum of Art/Art Resource/Scala, Florence; **2.3.12a** Museo Nacional del Prado, Madrid; **2.3.12b** Private Collection; **2.3.13** Print and Picture Collection, Free Library of Philadelphia. Courtesy Fine Arts Program, Public Buildings Service, U.S. General Services Administration. Commissioned through the New Deal art projects; **2.3.14** Courtesy Martin-Zambito Fine Art, Seattle; **2.3.15** Ralph Larmann; **2.3.16** Private Collection; **2.3.17** Photo Courtesy Phillips Auctioneers. © 2015 The Andy Warhol Foundation for the Visual Arts, Inc./Artists Rights Society (ARS), New York and DACS, London; **2.3.18** Fogg Art Museum, Harvard Art Museums, Margaret Fisher Fund, M25276. Photo Imaging Department © President & Fellows of Harvard College. © ARS, NY and DACS, London 2012; **2.3.19** © Kathy Strauss 2007; **2.4.1** Museum of Fine Arts, Boston, Massachusetts/Harvard University – Museum of Fine Arts Expedition/Bridgeman Art Library; **2.4.2a, 2.4.2b** Ex S.S.P.S.A.E e per il Polo Museale della città di Firenze - Gabinetto Fotografico; **2.4.3** British Museum, London; **2.4.4** Photograph Jacqueline Banerjee, Associate Editor of the Victorian Web www.victorianweb.org; **2.4.5** © David Hilbert/Alamy; **2.4.6** Metropolitan Museum of Art, New York. The Michael C. Rockefeller Memorial Collection, Bequest of Nelson A. Rockefeller, 1979, Acc. no. 1979.206.1134. Photo Schecter Lee. Photo Metropolitan Museum of Art/Art Resource/Scala, Florence; **2.4.7** British Museum, London; **2.4.8** Photo Scala, Florence, courtesy Ministero Beni e Att. Culturali; **2.4.9** Photo 1998/Mondadori Portfolio/akg-images; **2.4.10** Photo Scala, Florence, courtesy Ministero Beni e Att. Culturali; **2.4.11** Museo Nazionale di Villa Giulia, Rome; **2.4.12** Nimatallah/akg-images; **2.4.13** Ralph Larmann; **2.4.14** © Richard A. Cooke/Corbis;

2.4.15 Photo Tom Smart; 2.4.16 Photo Tate, London 2012. The works of Naum Gabo © Nina Williams; 2.4.17 Photographed by Prudence Cuming Associates. © Damien Hirst and Science Ltd. All rights reserved, DACS 2012; 2.4.18 Collection University of California, Berkeley Art Museum; purchased with the aid of funds from the National Endowment for the Arts (selected by The Committee for the Acquisition of Afro-American Art). Courtesy Michael Rosenfeld Gallery LLC, New York, NY. Photograph Joshua Nefsky; 2.4.19 © Succession Picasso/DACS, London 2012; 2.4.20 Photo Mark Pollock/Estate of George Rickey. © Estate of George Rickey/DACS, London/VAGA, New York 2012; 2.4.21 Harvard Art Museums, Busch-Reisinger Museum, Hildegard von Gontard Bequest Fund, 2007.105. Photo Junius Beebe, President & Fellows of Harvard College © DACS 2012; 2.4.22 Commissioned by Parking Authority of River City, Louisville; glass fabrication by AGA of Louisville; fountain consulting by Waterline Fountains of Austin, TX; RGB animation by Color Kinetics of Boston. Photo Richard E. Spear. © Athena Tacha; 2.4.23a Photograph by Zhang Haier; 2.4.23b Photo Dai Wei, Shanghai © the artist; 2.4.24 Robert Sainsbury Collection/Werner Forman Archive; p. 264 Ralph Larmann; 2.5.1 © Jon Arnold Images Ltd/Alamy; 2.5.2 Maki and Associates. Courtesy Silverstein Properties; 2.5.3, 2.5.4 iStockphoto.com; 2.5.5 DeAgostini Picture Library/Scala, Florence; 2.5.6, 2.5.7 Ralph Larmann; 2.5.8 Bridgeman Art Library; 2.5.9 Ralph Larmann; 2.5.10 Index/Bridgeman Art Library; 2.5.11 Ralph Larmann; 2.5.12 © Natalia Pavlova/Dreamstime.com; 2.5.13 Ralph Larmann; 2.5.14 © Christophe Boisvieux/Corbis; 2.5.15 Ralph Larmann; 2.5.16 Photo Scala, Florence; 2.5.17a, 2.5.17b Ralph Larmann; 2.5.18 Gianni Dagli Orti/Basilique Saint Denis Paris/The Art Archive; 2.5.19 © Robert Harding Picture Library Ltd/Alamy; 2.5.20, 2.5.21 Ralph Larmann; 2.5.22 © Photo Japan/Alamy; 2.5.23 © Martindata/Dreamstime.com; 2.5.24 Ralph Larmann; 2.5.25 Superstock; 2.5.26 © Anthony Shaw/Dreamstime.com; 2.5.27 Photo Shannon Kyles, ontarioarchitecture.com; 2.5.29 Photo Sandak Inc, Stamford, CT; 2.5.30 © INTERFOTO/Alamy; 2.5.31 © Jose Fuste Raga/Corbis; 2.5.32 © Bildarchiv Monheim GmbH/Alamy; 2.5.33 © Richard A. Cooke/Corbis; 2.5.34 © Free Agents Limited/Corbis; 2.5.35 Photo courtesy Michael Graves & Associates; 2.5.36 © Chuck Eckert/Alamy; 2.5.37a Courtesy Zaha Hadid Architects; 2.5.37b © Roland Halbe/artur; 2.5.38 Courtesy CMPBS; 2.6.1 Courtesy Trudy Labell Fine Art, Florida. © the artist; 2.6.2 Photo Trudy Labell; 2.6.3a, 2.6.3b The Archie Bray Foundation for the Ceramic Arts, Helena, Montana. Photo © Mathew Rowley; 2.6.3c © Zojakostina/Dreamstime.com; 2.6.4 Cleveland Museum of Art, Gift of the Hanna Fund, 1954.857; 2.6.5 Palace Museum, Beijing; 2.6.6 Photo Tyler Dingee. Courtesy Palace of the Governors Photo Archives (NMHM/DCA), Neg. No. 073453; 2.6.7

Photo T. Harmon Parkhurst. Courtesy Palace of the Governors Photo Archives (NMHM/DCA), Neg. No. 055204; 2.6.8 Newark Museum, Gift of Amelia Elizabeth White, 1937. 37.236 © 2014. Photo The Newark Museum/Art Resource/Scala, Florence; 2.6.9 Courtesy the Voulkos & Co. Catalogue Project, www.voulkos.com; 2.6.10 British Museum, London; 2.6.11 © Angelo Hornak/Corbis; 2.6.12 Photo Teresa Nouri Rishel © Dale Chihuly; 2.6.13 National Archaeological Museum, Athens; 2.6.14 The Walters Art Museum, Baltimore. Acquired by Henry Walters, 1929. 2.6.15 Kunsthistorisches Museum, Vienna; 2.6.16 Private Collection; 2.6.17 The Solomon R. Guggenheim Foundation, New York, 88.3620; Faith Ringgold © 1988; 2.6.18 © Christie's Images/Corbis; 2.6.19 Collaborators: Charles MacAdam with Interplay Design & Manufacturing, Inc, Nova Scotia, Canada (design & production); Norihide Imagawa with T.I.S. & Partners., Co. Ltd, Tokyo (structural design). Courtesy the artist. Photo Masaki Koizumi; 2.6.20 Metropolitan Museum of Art, Rogers Fund, 1939, Acc. no. 39.153. Photo Metropolitan Museum of Art/Art Resource/Scala, Florence; 2.6.21 Seattle Art Museum, Gift of John H. Hauberg and John and Grace Putnam, 86.278. Photo Paul Macapia; 2.6.22 Photo courtesy Andrew Early; 2.7.1 British Museum, London; 2.7.2 Tokyo National Museum; 2.7.3 Koninklijke Bibliotheek, The Hague, Folio 8r., shelf no. 69B 10; 2.7.4 V&A Images/Victoria & Albert Museum; 2.7.5 Ralph Larmann; 2.7.6a © DACS 2015; 2.7.6b © Lianem/Dreamstime.com; 2.7.7 Courtesy Ford Motor Company; 2.7.8 General Motors Corp. Used with permission, GM Media Archives; 2.7.9 © Annsunnyday/Dreamstime.com; 2.7.10 © Gonzalomedin/Dreamstime.com; 2.7.11 © ArchManStocker/Deposit Photos; 2.7.12 from Works of Geoffrey Chaucer, Kelmscott Press, 1896; 2.7.13 Library of Congress Prints, Washington, D.C., Prints & Photographs Division, LC-DIG-ppmsc-03521; 2.7.14 © Jorge Colombo, courtesy The New Yorker; 2.7.15 The Art Institute of Chicago, Mr. and Mrs. Carter H. Harrison Collection, 1954.1193; 2.7.16 Taesam Do/FoodPix/Getty. Image courtesy Hill Holiday; 2.7.17 Ralph Larmann; 2.7.18 Private Collection; 2.7.19 Ralph Larmann; 2.7.20 Photo Helena Kristiansson, esportphoto.com; 2.7.21 School of Journalism and Mass Communication, University of North Carolina at Chapel Hill. Photo Eileen Mignoni; 2.7.22a, 2.7.22b Website commissioned by The Museum of Modern Art, New York (www.moma.org/interactives/exhibitions/2013/magritte/). Artwork: The Museum of Modern Art, Kay Sage Tanguy Fund, 247.1966. The Museum of Modern Art, New York/Scala, Florence. © ADAGP, Paris and DACS, London 2015; 2.8.1 Wellcome Library, London; 2.8.2 Image appears courtesy Abelardo Morell; 2.8.3 British Library, London; 2.8.4 Metropolitan Museum of Art, The Rubel Collection, Purchase, Ann Tenenbaum and Thomas H. Lee and Anonymous Gifts, 1997, Acc. no. 1997.382.1.

Photo The Metropolitan Museum of Art/Art Resource/Scala, Florence; 2.8.5 Ralph Larmann; 2.8.6 © Maia Dery; 2.8.7 Bibliothèque nationale, Paris; 2.8.8 The J. Paul Getty Museum, Los Angeles (84.XM.443.3); 2.8.9 Library of Congress, Washington, D.C. Prints & Photographs Division, FSA/OWI Collection, LC-DIG-fsa-8b29516; 2.8.10 © Ansel Adams Publishing Rights Trust/Corbis; 2.8.11 Collection of the Société Française de Photographie, Paris; 2.8.12 Collection Center for Creative Photography © 1981 Arizona Board of Regents; 2.8.13 Library of Congress, Washington, D.C.. Prints & Photographs Division, LC-DIG-nclc-01555; 2.8.14a, 2.8.14b, 2.8.15 Copyright Steve McCurry/Magnum Photos; 2.8.16 © Hiroko Masuike/New York Times/Eyevine; 2.8.17 Royal Photographic Society, Bath; 2.8.18 Courtesy Yossi Milo Gallery, New York. © DACS 2012; 2.8.19 The Art Institute of Chicago, Alfred Stieglitz Collection, 1949.705 © Georgia O'Keeffe Museum/DACS, 2012; 2.8.20 © Estate of Garry Winogrand, courtesy Fraenkel Gallery, San Francisco; 2.8.21 Nationalgalerie, Staatliche Museen, Berlin. © DACS 2012; 2.8.22 © Stephen Marc; 2.8.23 Gernsheim Collection, Harry Ransom Humanities Research Centre, University of Texas at Austin; 2.8.24 Courtesy Gagosian Gallery © Sally Mann; 2.8.25 Sandy Skoglund, Radioactive Cats © 1980; 2.8.26 Photo © Edward Burtynsky, courtesy Flowers, London & Nicholas Metivier, Toronto; 2.9.1 Ralph Larmann; 2.9.2 Library of Congress, Washington, D.C. Prints & Photographs Division, LC-USZ62-45683; 2.9.3 Star Film Company; 2.9.4 akg-images; 2.9.5, 2.9.6 British Film Institute (BFI); 2.9.7 M.G.M/Album/akg-images; 2.9.8 La Classe Americane/uFilm/France 3/The Kobal Collection; 2.9.9 British Film Institute (BFI); 2.9.10 Disney Enterprises/Album/akg-images; 2.9.11 British Film Institute (BFI); 2.9.12a New Line Cinema/The Kobal Collection; 2.9.12b Album/akg-images; 2.9.13, 2.9.14 British Film Institute (BFI); 2.9.15 © AF Archive/Alamy; 2.9.16 British Film Institute (BFI); 2.9.17 Courtesy Electronic Arts Intermix (EAI), New York; 2.9.18a Photo Mathias Schormann © Bill Viola; 2.9.18b, 2.9.18c Photo Kira Perov © Bill Viola; 2.9.19 Media Rights Capital/The Kobal Collection; 2.10.1 Photo © Estate of David Gahr. © ADAGP, Paris and DACS, London 2015; 2.10.2 © Barbara Kruger. Courtesy Mary Boone Gallery, New York; 2.10.3 Photo Karla Merrifield © Yoko Ono; 2.10.4, 2.10.5 Courtesy The Fundred Dollar Bill Project; 2.10.6 Rowland Scherman/Hulton Archive/Getty Images; 2.10.7 © DACS 2012; 2.10.8 Photo Betsy Jackson. Courtesy the artist; 2.10.9 Photography by Marco Anelli. Courtesy the Marina Abramović Archives; 2.10.10a Copyright Kienholz, courtesy L. A. Louver. Photo © Ed Jansen; 2.10.10b Copyright Kienholz, courtesy L. A. Louver. Photo SuperStock; 2.10.11 © Fred Wilson, courtesy PaceWildenstein, New York. Photo courtesy PaceWildenstein, New York; 2.10.12 Courtesy Sikkema Jenkins & Co., NY; p. 364 (above) Egyptian Museum, Cairo; (center) iStockphoto.com; (below) Pushkin Museum,

Moscow; **3.1.1** Drazen Tomic; **3.1.2** João Zilhão, ICREA/University of Barcelona; **3.1.3** Erich Lessing/akg-images; **3.1.4** The J. Paul Getty Museum, Villa Collection, Malibu, California; **3.1.5** Images courtesy the Mellaarts/Çatalhöyük Research Project; **3.1.6** Photo Jeff Morgan Travel/ Alamy; **3.1.7** Archaeological Museum, Heraklion; **3.1.8a, 3.1.8b** British Museum, London; **3.1.9** Erich Lessing/akg-images; **3.1.10** University of Pennsylvania Museum of Archaeology and Anthropology, Philadelphia B17694; **3.1.11** Iraq Museum, Baghdad; **3.1.12** Metropolitan Museum of Art, Gift of John D. Rockefeller Jr., 1932, Acc. no. 32.143.2. Photo Metropolitan Museum of Art/ Art Resource/Scala, Florence; **3.1.13** Photo Scala, Florence/BPK, Bildagentur für Kunst, Kultur und Geschichte, Berlin; **3.1.14** National Geographic/ Superstock; **3.1.15** Gianni Dagli Orti/Egyptian Museum, Cairo/The Art Archive; **3.1.16** The Trustees of the British Museum, London; **3.1.17** Egyptian Museum, Cairo; **3.1.18** Staatliche Museen, Berlin. Photo Sandra Steiss. Photo Scala, Florence/BPK, Bildagentur für Kunst, Kultur und Geschichte, Berlin; **3.1.19** British Museum, London; **3.1.20** Peter Connolly/akg-images; **3.1.21** Ralph Larmann; **3.1.22** Nimatallah/akg-images; **3.1.23** British Museum, London; **3.1.24** Metropolitan Museum of Art, Fletcher Fund, 1932, Acc. no. 32.11.1. Photo Metropolitan Museum of Art/Art Resource/Scala, Florence; **3.1.25** Minneapolis Institute of Arts; **3.1.26** Vatican Museums, Rome; **3.1.27, 3.128, 3.129** Photo Scala, Florence; **3.1.30** Raimund Kutter/ imagebroker.net; **3.1.31** © Altair4 Multimedia Roma, www.altair.it; **3.1.32** Palazzo Torlonia, Rome; **3.1.33** Giovanni Caselli; **3.1.34** Image Source Pink/Alamy; **3.1.35** iStockphoto.com; **3.2.1** Drazen Tomic; **3.2.2, 3.2.3** Zev Radovan/ www.BibleLandPictures.com; **3.2.4** Canali Photobank, Milan, Italy; **3.2.5** Photo Scala, Florence; **3.2.6, 3.2.7** Monastery of St. Catherine, Sinai, Egypt; **3.2.8** Photo Scala, Florence; **3.2.9** Cameraphoto/Scala, Florence; **3.2.10, 3.2.11a, 3.2.11b** British Library, London; **3.2.12** Biblioteca Governativa, Lucca; **3.2.13** British Library/akg-images; **3.2.14** Musées Royaux d'Art et d'Histoire, Brussels; **3.2.15** © Hanan Isachar/ Corbis; **3.2.16** Mohamed Amin/Robert Harding; **3.2.17** Dilek Mermer/Anadolu Agency/Getty Images; **3.2.18** Nasser D. Khalili Collection of Islamic Art, MSS 745.2 © Nour Foundation, Courtesy the Khalili Family Trust; **3.2.19** Drazen Tomic; **3.2.20** Photononstop/Superstock; **3.2.21** Ralph Larmann; **3.2.22** Photononstop/ Superstock; **3.2.23** Ralph Larmann; **3.2.24** Hervé Champollion/akg-images; **3.2.25** Sonia Halliday Photographs; **3.2.26, 3.2.27** Galleria degli Uffizi, Florence; **3.3.1** Drazen Tomic; **3.3.2** iStockphoto. com; **3.3.3** © Tom Hanley/Alamy; **3.3.4** Robert Harding Picture Library/Superstock; **3.3.5** © Susanna Bennett/Alamy; **3.3.6** © Frédéric Soltan/ Sygma/Corbis; **3.3.7** © Pep Roig/Alamy; **3.3.8** © Ebba Koch; **3.3.9** © Airpano (www.airpano.com); **3.3.10** Brooklyn Museum, Gift of Mr. & Mrs. Alastair B. Martin, the Guennol Collection,

72.163a–b; **3.3.11** Hunan Museum, Changsha; **3.3.12a** Melvyn Longhurst/Superstock; **3.3.12b** Hemis.fr/Superstock; **3.3.13** Palace Museum, Beijing; **3.3.14** Library of Congress, Washington, D.C. Prints & Photographs Division, H. Irving Olds collection, LC-DIG-jpd-02018; **3.3.15** iStockphoto.com; **3.3.16** Courtesy the artist; **3.3.17** Photo Shunji Ohkura; **3.3.19** Sakai Collection, Tokyo; **3.3.20** Horyu-ji Treasure House, Ikaruga, Nara Prefecture, Japan; **3.3.21** The Tokugawa Art Museum, Nagoya; **3.3.22** V&A Images/Alamy; **3.3.23** The Art Institute of Chicago, Robert A. Waller Fund, 1910.2; **3.3.24** © Shirley Hu/Dreamstime.com; **3.3.25** © Kevin R. Morris/Corbis; **3.4.1** Drazen Tomic; **3.4.2a** G. Dagli Orti/DeA Picture Library/The Art Archive; **3.4.2b, 3.4.2c** Anton, F., *Ancient Peruvian Textiles*, Thames & Hudson Ltd, London, 1987; **3.4.3** Museo Arqueología, Lima, Peru/ Bridgeman Art Library; **3.4.4** Royal Tombs of Sipán Museum, Lambayeque; **3.4.5** iStockphoto. com; **3.4.6** American Museum of Natural History, New York; **3.4.7** Dumbarton Oaks Research Library and Collections, Washington, D.C.; **3.4.8** Drazen Tomic; **3.4.9** Richard Hewitt Stewart/National Geographic Stock; **3.4.10a** Drazen Tomic; **3.4.10b** © aerialarchives.com/ Alamy; **3.4.11** © Ken Welsh/Alamy; **3.4.12** © Gianni Dagli Orti/Corbis; **3.4.13** Dallas Museum of Art, Gift of Patsy R. and Raymond D. Nasher, 1983.148; **3.4.14** Peabody Museum, Harvard University, Cambridge, 48-63-20/17561; **3.4.15** Biblioteca Nazionale Centrale di Firenze; **3.4.16** Museo Nacional de Antropología, Mexico City; **3.4.17** Museo del Templo Mayor, Mexico City; **3.4.18** Drazen Tomic; **3.4.19** © Chris Howes/Wild Places Photography/Alamy; **3.4.20a, 3.4.20b** Peabody Museum, Harvard University, Cambridge, 99-12-10/53121; **3.4.21** Missouri Historical Society, St. Louis, 1882.18.32; **3.4.22** American Museum of Natural History, New York; **3.4.23** Photo Jennifer Bresee; **3.4.24** Courtesy Yosemite Conservancy. Photo Keith Walklet; **3.5.1** Drazen Tomic; **3.5.2** National Museum, Lagos; **3.5.3** Linden Museum, Stuttgart; **3.5.4** Dallas Museum of Art, Foundation for the Arts Collection, Gift of the McDermott Foundation, 1996.184.FA; **3.5.5** National Museum of African Art, Smithsonian Institution, Washington, D.C.; **3.5.6a** Musée Barbier-Mueller, Geneva; **3.5.6b** © Michel Renaudeau; **3.5.7** © JTB Photo Communications, Inc./Alamy; **3.5.8** © Chris Howes/Wild Places Photography/Alamy; **3.5.9** Photo Barney Wayne; **3.5.10** Drazen Tomic; **3.5.11** pl. XVI from Parkinson, S., *A Journal of a Voyage to the South Seas*, 1784; **3.5.12** Photo Paul S. C. Tacon; **3.5.13a** The Trustees of the British Museum, London; **3.5.13b** Chris Johns/National Geographic/Getty Images; **3.5.14** © Albertoloyo/ Dreamstime.com; **3.5.15** Musée Barbier-Mueller, Geneva; **3.5.16** Collected by G. F. N. Gerrits, Vb 28418-28471 (1972). Photo Peter Horner 1981 © Museum der Kulturen, Basel, Switzerland; **3.6.1** Drazen Tomic; **3.6.2** from Vasari, G., *Lives of the Great Artists*, 1568; **3.6.3** © Michael S. Yamashita/

Corbis; **3.6.4** Libreria dello Stato, Rome; **3.6.5** Brancacci Chapel, Church of Santa Maria del Carmine, Florence; **3.6.6** Refectory of Santa Maria delle Grazie, Milan; **3.6.7a** Rabatti - Domingie/ akg-images; **3.6.7b, 3.6.8a** Vatican Museums, Rome; **3.6.8b** 1998/Mondadori Portfolio/akg-images; **3.6.9a** Cameraphoto/akg-images; **3.6.9b** pl. XIII, Book II from Wade, I. (ed.) *Palladio: Four Books of Architecture*, 1738; **3.6.10** Stanza della Segnatura, Vatican Museums, Rome; **3.6.11a, 3.6.11b** National Gallery, London/Scala, Florence; **3.6.12** Photo Scala, Florence/BPK, Bildagentur für Kunst, Kultur und Geschichte, Berlin; **3.6.13a, 3.6.13b, 3.6.13c** Gemäldegalerie, Staatliche Museen, Berlin; **3.6.13d** Prisma/Album/akg-images; **3.6.14** Musée d'Unterlinden, Colmar; **3.6.15** British Museum, London; **3.6.16** Museum Narodowe, Poznań/Bridgeman Art Library; **3.6.17** Galleria dell'Accademia, Venice; **3.6.18** Cameraphoto/Scala, Florence; **3.6.19** Capponi Chapel, Church of Santa Felicità, Florence; **3.6.20** Photo Scala, Florence, courtesy Ministero Beni e Att. Culturali; **3.6.21** © nagelestock.com/Alamy; **3.6.22** Photo Scala, Florence, courtesy Ministero Beni e Att. Culturali; **3.6.23** National Gallery of Art, Washington, D.C., Samuel H. Kress Collection, 1946.18.1; **3.6.24** Galleria degli Uffizi, Florence; **3.6.25** Galleria Nazionale d'Arte Antica, Palazzo Barberini, Rome; **3.6.26** Peter Willi/ Bridgeman Images; **3.6.27** Rijksmuseum, Amsterdam; **3.6.28** The Earl of Plymouth. On loan to the National Museum of Wales, Cardiff; **3.6.29a** Prisma/Album/akg-images; **3.6.29b** Ralph Larmann; **3.7.1** Musée du Louvre, Paris; **3.7.2** © Bertrand Rieger/Hemis/Corbis; **3.7.3** Erich Lessing/akg-images; **3.7.4** The Wallace Collection, London; **3.7.5** © Florian Monheim/ Arcaid/Corbis; **3.7.6** Musée National du Château de Versailles; **3.7.7** Photo Scala, Florence; **3.7.8** National Gallery, London/Scala, Florence; **3.7.9** Gianni Dagli Orti/Musée du Château de Versailles/ The Art Archive; **3.7.10** Musée du Louvre, Paris; **3.7.11** DeA Picture Library/The Art Archive; **3.7.12** Virginia Museum of Fine Arts, Richmond. The Adolf D. and Wilkins C. Williams Fund; **3.7.13** iStockphoto.com; **3.7.14, 3.7.15** Museo Nacional del Prado, Madrid; **3.7.16** Musée du Louvre, Paris; **3.7.17** © Tate, London 2012; **3.7.18** Museum of Fine Arts, Boston, Henry Lillie Pierce Fund, BJ385; **3.7.19** Metropolitan Museum of Art, Gift of Mrs. Russell Sage, 1908, Acc. no. 08.228. Photo Metropolitan Museum of Art/Art Resource/Scala, Florence; **3.7.21** Hampton University Museum, Virginia; **3.7.22** © Tate, London 2012; **3.7.23** Library of Congress Prints, Washington, D.C., Prints & Photographs Division, LC-USZ62-7990; **3.7.24** Museum purchase made possible by the Pauline Edwards Bequest. Photo Smithsonian American Art Museum/Art Resource/ Scala, Florence; **3.8.1** Musée d'Orsay, Paris; **3.8.2** Musée d'Orsay, Paris; **3.8.3** Courtesy the Pennsylvania Academy of the Fine Arts, Philadelphia. Charles Bregler's Thomas Eakins Collection, purchased with the partial support of the Pew Memorial Trust. Acc. no. 1985.68.2.985;

3.8.4 Musée Marmottan, Paris; 3.8.5 Musée d'Orsay, Paris; 3.8.6 Art Institute of Chicago, Charles H. and Mary F. S. Worcester Collection, 1964.336; 3.8.7 White Images/Scala, Florence; 3.8.8 BI, ADAGP, Paris/Scala, Florence. © ADAGP, Paris and DACS, London 2012; 3.8.9 Pushkin Museum, Moscow; 3.8.10 Courtauld Gallery, London; 3.8.11 National Gallery of Scotland, Edinburgh; 3.8.12 Museum of Modern Art, New York. Acquired through the Lillie P. Bliss Bequest. Acc. no. 472.1941. Photo 2012, Museum of Modern Art, New York/Scala, Florence; 3.8.13 The Museum of Modern Art, New York, Gift of Mrs. Simon Guggenheim, 646.1939. Digital image, The Museum of Modern Art, New York/Scala, Florence; 3.8.14 Galleria degli Uffizi, Florence; 3.8.15 Photo Austrian Archives/Scala, Florence; 3.8.16 Gift of Susan Schimmel Goldstein. Collection Zimmerli Art Museum at Rutgers University, New Brunswick, New Jersey; 3.8.17 Musée Carnavalet, Paris; 3.8.18 The Barnes Foundation, Merion, PA. © Succession H. Matisse/DACS 2012; 3.8.19 Museum of Modern Art, New York, Mrs. Simon Guggenheim Fund, 8.1949. Photo 2012, Museum of Modern Art, New York/Scala, Florence. © Succession H. Matisse/DACS 2012; 3.8.20 Photograph by Hélène Adant/RAPHO/GAMMA, Camera Press, London; 3.8.21 Museum of Modern Art, New York, acquired through the Lillie P. Bliss Bequest, 333.1939. Photo 2012, Museum of Modern Art, New York/Scala, Florence. © Succession Picasso/DACS, London 2012; 3.8.22 The Museum of Modern Art, New York, Gift of Mrs. Simon Guggenheim, 2.1938. Digital image, The Museum of Modern Art, New York/Scala, Florence. © Succession Picasso/DACS, London 2015; 3.8.23 Kunstmuseum, Bern; 3.8.24 Kunstmuseum, Bern/Superstock/The Art Archive; 3.8.25 Richard and Ellen Sandor Art Foundation. © Succession Picasso/DACS, London 2015. © Man Ray Trust/ADAGP, Paris and DACS, London 2015; 3.8.26 Museum Folkwang, Essen; 3.8.27 Art Institute of Chicago, Arthur Jerome Eddy Memorial Collection, 1931.511. © ADAGP, Paris and DACS, London 2012; 3.8.28 akg-images; 3.8.30 Museum of Modern Art, New York, The Sidney and Harriet Janis Collection, 595.1967 a–b. Photo 2012, Museum of Modern Art, New York/Scala, Florence. © ADAGP, Paris and DACS, London 2012; 3.8.31 © The Heartfield Community of Heirs/VG Bild-Kunst, Bonn and DACS, London 2012; 3.8.32 © DACS 2012; 3.8.33 Photo Hickey-Robertson, Houston. The Menil Collection, Houston. © ADAGP, Paris and DACS, London 2012; 3.8.34 Museum of Modern Art, New York, Gift of Mr. and Mrs. Pierre Matisse, 940.1965.a-c. Photo 2012, Museum of Modern Art, New York/Scala, Florence. © Succession Miro/ADAGP, Paris and DACS, London 2012; 3.8.35 Photo Francis Carr © Thames & Hudson Ltd, London; 3.8.36 Philadelphia Museum of Art, The Louise and Walter Arensberg Collection. © ADAGP, Paris and DACS, London 2012; 3.8.37 Fondation Beyeler, Riehen/Basel, Sammlung Beyeler; acquired with the contribution of Hartmann P. and Cécile Koechlin-Tanner, Riehen. Welsh/Joosten B 234, Photo Robert Bayer, Basel; 3.8.38 The Museum of Modern Art, New York, Acquisition confirmed in 1999 by agreement with the Estate of Kazimir Malevich and made possible with funds from the Mrs John Hay Whitney Bequest (by exchange) acc. no. 817.1935. Digital image, The Museum of Modern Art, New York/Scala, Florence; 3.8.39 The Museum of Modern Art, New York. Given anonymously, Acc. no.: 153.1934. Digital image, The Museum of Modern Art, New York/Scala, Florence. © ADAGP, Paris and DACS, London 2015; 3.8.40 Friends of American Art Collection, 1930.934. Art Institute of Chicago; 3.8.41 New York Public Library/Aaron Douglas/Science Photo Library. © Heirs of Aaron Douglas/VAGA, NY/DACS, London 2015; 3.9.1 Courtesy Center for Creative Photography, University of Arizona © 1991 Hans Namuth Estate; 3.9.2 The Museum of Modern Art, New York. Purchase. Acc. no.: MOMA 77.1950. Digital image, The Museum of Modern Art, New York/Scala, Florence. © The Pollock-Krasner Foundation ARS, NY and DACS, London 2015; 3.9.3 The Museum of Modern Art, New York, Gift of the Artist. Acc. no.: 1108.1969. Digital image, The Museum of Modern Art, New York/Scala, Florence. © 1998 Kate Rothko Prizel & Christopher Rothko ARS, NY and DACS, London; 3.9.4 © The Andy Warhol Foundation for the Visual Arts/Artists Rights Society (ARS), New York/DACS, London 2012; 3.9.5 © The Estate of Roy Lichtenstein/DACS 2012; 3.9.6 Collection of the Modern Art Museum of Fort Worth, Museum purchase, The Benjamin J. Tillar Memorial Trust. Acquired in 1970. © Judd Foundation. Licensed by VAGA, New York/DACS, London 2012; 3.9.7 Philadelphia Museum of Art, The Louise and Walter Arensberg Collection. © ADAGP, Paris and DACS, London 2012; 3.9.8 © Sherrie Levine. Courtesy Simon Lee Gallery, London; 3.9.9 Photo Hickey-Robertson, Houston. The Menil Collection, Houston. © ARS, NY and DACS, London 2012; 3.9.10 Museum of Modern Art, New York, Larry Aldrich Foundation Fund, 393.1970.a-c. Photo 2012, Museum of Modern Art, New York/Scala, Florence. © ARS, NY and DACS, London 2012; 3.9.11 © The Estate of Ana Mendieta. Courtesy Galerie Lelong, New York; 3.9.12 Copyright © Andy Goldsworthy; 3.9.13 © Romare Bearden Foundation/DACS, London/VAGA, New York 2012; 3.9.14 Photo courtesy John Michael Kohler Arts Center © the artist and Stefan Stux Gallery, NY; 3.9.15 © EggImages/Alamy; 3.9.16 Photo courtesy Michael Graves & Associates; 3.9.17 William Sr. and Dorothy Harmsen Collection, by exchange, 2007.47. Denver Art Museum. All Rights Reserved; 3.9.18 Photo Smithsonian American Art Museum/Art Resource/Scala, Florence; 3.9.19 Photo courtesy Galerie Enrico Navarra. © The Estate of Jean-Michel Basquiat/ADAGP, Paris and DACS, London 2015; 3.9.20a, 3.9.20b Courtesy Gladstone Gallery, New York. © Shirin Neshat; 3.9.21 Museum of Modern Art, New York, Fractional gift offered by Donald L. Bryant, Jr., Acc. no. 241.2000.b. Photo 2012, Museum of Modern Art, New York/Scala, Florence. © 1997 Pipilotti Rist. Image courtesy the artist, Luhring Augustine, New York and Hauser & Wirth; 3.9.22 Courtesy Gladstone Gallery, New York. Photo Michael James O'Brien. © 1997 Matthew Barney; 3.9.23 Courtesy Giò Marconi, Milan and Lisson Gallery, London. © Nathalie Djurberg & Hans Berg; 3.9.24 Photo courtesy the artist and Pace Gallery. © Tara Donovan, courtesy Pace Gallery; p. 560 (above) Photo David Heald. The Solomon R. Guggenheim Foundation, New York. FLWW-10; (center) Courtauld Gallery, London; (below) Victor Chavez/WireImage/Getty; 4.1.1 © guichaoua/Alamy; 4.1.2 iStockphoto.com; 4.1.3 © Brad Calkins/Dreamstime.com; 4.1.4 Photo David Heald. The Solomon R. Guggenheim Foundation, New York. FLWW-10; 4.1.5 Silvio Fiore/photolibrary.com; 4.1.6 Martin Gray/National Geographic Stock; 4.1.7 Keith Bedford/epa/Corbis; 4.1.8 Cahokia Mounds State Historic Site, painting by William R. Iseminger; 4.1.9 Henry John Drewal and Margaret Thompson Drewal Collection, EEPA D00639. Eliot Elisofon Photographic Archives, National Museum of African Art, Smithsonian Institution, Washington, D.C., courtesy Henry John Drewal; 4.1.10 Courtesy the artist; 4.1.11 Photo Anne Chauvet; 4.1.12 Photo Art Resource/Bob Schalkwijk/Scala, Florence. © 2012 Banco de México Diego Rivera Frida Kahlo Museums Trust, Mexico, D.F./DACS; 4.1.13 Courtesy Galerie Lelong, New York. © Krzysztof Wodiczko; 4.2.1 John Hios/akg-images; 4.2.2a, 4.2.2b Dom-Museum Hildesheim; 4.2.2c Ralph Larmann; 4.2.3 India Museum, Calcutta; 4.2.4 The Cleveland Museum of Art, James Albert and Mary Gardiner Ford Memorial Fund, 1961.198; 4.2.5 © Peter Arnold, Inc./Alamy; 4.2.6 Musée du Louvre, Paris; 4.2.7 State Tretyakov Gallery, Moscow; 4.2.8 Photo Scala, Florence/Fondo Edifici di Culto – Min. dell'Interno; 4.2.9 British Museum, London; 4.2.10 Hervé Champollion/akg-images; 4.2.11 National Gallery of Art, Washington, D.C., Widener Collection, 1942.9.97; 4.2.12a Ralph Larmann; 4.2.12b Colorphoto Hans Hinz, Allschwil, Switzerland; 4.2.13a Ralph Larmann; 4.2.13b © Araldo de Luca/Corbis; 4.2.14 © B. O'Kane/Alamy; 4.2.15 Courtesy Jingu Administration Office; 4.2.16 Photo Hickey-Robertson © 1998 Kate Rothko Prizel & Christopher Rothko ARS, NY and DACS, London; 4.3.1 Dumbarton Oaks Museum, Washington, D.C.; 4.3.2 Courtesy the artist and Marian Goodman Gallery, New York/Paris; 4.3.3 Pinoteca di Brera, Milan; 4.3.4 © Andres Serrano. Courtesy the artist and Yvon Lambert Paris, New York; 4.3.5 Metropolitan Museum of Art, The Michael C. Rockefeller Memorial Collection, Bequest of Nelson A. Rockefeller, 1979, Acc. no. 1979.206.1611. Photo Metropolitan Museum of Art/Art Resource/Scala, Florence; 4.3.6 Dallas Museum of Art, The Clark and Frances Stillman Collection of Congo Sculpture, Gift of Eugene and Margaret McDermott, 1969.S.22; 4.3.7 Courtesy

David Castillo Gallery and the artist; **4.3.8** akg-images; **4.3.9** The Museum of Modern Art, New York, Gift of Mrs. Simon Guggenheim, 2.1938. Digital image, The Museum of Modern Art, New York/Scala, Florence. © Succession Picasso/DACS, London 2015; **4.3.10** Copyright Merle Greene Robertson, 1976; **4.3.11** The Cleveland Museum of Art, Purchase from the J. H. Wade Fund 1930.331; **4.3.12** JTB Media Creation Inc./Alamy; **4.3.13** Courtesy National Museum of the American Indian, Smithsonian Institution (18/2023). Photo by Photo Services; **4.3.14** Museo del Templo Mayor, Mexico City, CONACULTA-INAH, 10-220302; **4.3.15** Dallas Museum of Art, Foundation for the Arts Collection, Mrs John B. O'Hara Fund; **4.3.16** Fine Art Images/Heritage Images/Scala, Florence; **4.3.17** Courtesy the artist (www.stickwork.net). Photo Paul Kodama; **4.4.1** Gallerie dell'Accademia, Venice; **4.4.2** National Gallery, London/Scala, Florence; **4.4.3** Gift of the Alumni Association to Jefferson Medical College in 1878, purchased by the Pennsylvania Academy of the Fine Arts and the Philadelphia Museum of Art in 2007 with the generous support of more than 3,600 donors, 2007, 2007-1-1; **4.4.4** Photograph K2822 © Justin Kerr; **4.4.5** National Museum of Anthropology, Mexico City; **4.4.6** National Maritime Museum, Greenwich, London; **4.4.7** Courtesy the David Lloyd Gallery; **4.4.8** Courtesy Institute for Plastination, Heidelberg, Germany; **4.4.9** Courtesy Perkins+Will; **4.4.10** Victor R. Boswell, Jr./National Geographic Stock; **4.4.11** Photo Vatican Museums, Rome; **4.4.12** X-Ray photo, 2011. The Museum of Modern Art, New York/Scala, Florence. Artwork © Succession Picasso/DACS, London 2015; **4.4.13** Museum of Modern Art, New York, Gift of Mrs Simon Guggenheim, 2.1938. Digital image, The Museum of Modern Art, New York/Scala, Florence. © Succession Picasso/DACS, London 2015; **4.4.14** Art Institute of Chicago, Helen Birch Bartlett Memorial Collection, 1926.224; **4.4.15** © Jasper Johns/VAGA, New York/DACS, London 2012; **4.4.16** Courtesy Marcia Smilack; **4.4.17** Museum of Modern Art, New York. Given anonymously, 162.1934. Photo 2012, Museum of Modern Art, New York/Scala, Florence. © Salvador Dalí, Fundació Gala-Salvador Dalí, DACS, 2012; **4.4.18** Courtesy KUSAMA Enterprise, Ota Fine Arts, Tokyo/Singapore and Victoria Miro, London. © Yayoi Kusama; **4.5.1** Photo Giovanni Lattanzi; **4.5.2** Photo Scala, Florence; **4.5.3** Photo Scala, Florence, courtesy Ministero Beni e Att. Culturali; **4.5.4** Kunsthistorisches Museum, Vienna; **4.5.5** National Gallery of Art, Washington, D.C. Gift of Mr. & Mrs. Richard Mellon Scaife in honour of Paul Mellon, 1993.15.1; **4.5.6** from Kirby, J., *Dr Brook Taylor's Method of Perspective Made Easy*, 1754; **4.5.7a**, **4.5.7b** Courtesy the artist; **4.5.8** The Nelson-Atkins Museum of Art, Kansas City, Missouri. Gift of the Friends of Art, F76-40. © Estate of Duane Hanson/VAGA, New York/DACS, London 2015; **4.5.9a** James Green/Robert Harding; **4.5.9b** Ralph Larmann; **4.5.10** Gianni Dagli Orti/Palazzo del Tè Mantua/The Art Archive;

4.5.11 Pietro Baguzzi/akg-images; **4.5.12** National Gallery of Art, Washington, D.C., Gift of the Collectors Committee, 1987.55.1. © ADAGP, Paris and DACS, London 2012; **4.5.13** The Museum of Modern Art, New York, acquired through the Lillie P. Bliss Bequest, 175.1945. Digital image, The Museum of Modern Art, New York/Scala, Florence. © ADAGP, Paris and DACS, London 2015; **4.5.14** National Gallery of Art, Washington, D.C., Gift of Lila Acheson Wallace, 1987.2.1. Photo Ellen Page Wilson, courtesy The Pace Gallery. © Chuck Close, The Pace Gallery; **4.5.15** Collection University of Arizona Museum of Art, Tucson, Museum purchase with funds provided by the Edward J. Gallagher, Jr Memorial Fund 1982.35.1. © the artist; **4.5.16** Courtauld Gallery, London; **4.6.1** akg-images; **4.6.2** © Americanspirit/Dreamstime.com; **4.6.3** Photo RMN-Grand Palais (Château de Versailles)/Franck Raux; **4.6.4** Photo Irmgard Groth-Kimball © Thames & Hudson Ltd, London; **4.6.5** Photo Scala, Florence; **4.6.6** British Museum, London; **4.6.7** Ägyptisches Museum, Staatliche Museen, Berlin; **4.6.8** Courtesy Christie's/Werner Forman Archive; **4.6.9** Musée du Louvre, Paris; **4.6.10** © Hubert Stadler/Corbis; **4.6.11** © Peter Guttman/Corbis; **4.7.1** Library of Congress, Washington, D.C. Prints & Photographs Division, LC-B8184-7964-A; **4.7.2** Nick Ut/AP/Press Association Images; **4.7.3**, **4.7.4** Museo Nacional del Prado, Madrid; **4.7.5** © Succession Picasso/DACS, London 2012; **4.7.6a**, **4.7.6b** Egyptian Museum, Cairo; **4.7.7** Centre Guillaume le Conquérant, Bayeux; **4.7.8** Museum of Fine Arts, Boston, Fenollosa-Weld Collection; **4.7.9** Photograph Luidger; **4.7.10** Metropolitan Museum of Art, Gift of Mr. and Mrs. Klaus G. Perls, 1990, Acc. no. 1990.332. Photo Metropolitan Museum of Art/Art Resource/Scala, Florence; **4.7.11** © DACS 2012; **4.7.12** © Anselm Kiefer; **4.7.13** Courtesy the artists. Photo JoAnne Pollonais; **4.7.14** Courtesy the artist; **4.7.15** © Maurice Savage/Alamy; **4.7.16** Mark Lennihan/AP/Press Association images; **4.8.1** Musée du Louvre, Paris; **4.8.2** © JR; **4.8.3** Library of Congress, Washington, D.C. Prints & Photographs Division, FSA/OWI Collection, LC-DIG-fsa-8b29516; **4.8.4** Courtesy the artist and Roberts & Tilton, Culver City, CA. © Kehinde Wiley. Used by permission; **4.8.5** Photo Scala, Florence; **4.8.6** Library of Congress, Washington, D.C. Prints & Photographs Division, H. Irving Olds collection, LC-DIG-jpd-02018; **4.8.7a**, **4.8.7b** Courtesy Chris Jordan; **4.8.8a** National Gallery, London/Scala, Florence; **4.8.9** Courtesy Mary Boone Gallery, New York; **4.8.10** Photo Heinrich Hoffmann, Presse-Illustrationen, 1937. © Ullsteinbild/Topfoto; **4.8.11** Erich Lessing/akg-images. © Nolde Stiftung Seebüll; **4.9.1** Naturhistorisches Museum, Vienna; **4.9.2** Museum of Modern Art, New York. Purchase, 478.1953. Photo 2012, Museum of Modern Art, New York/Scala, Florence. © ARS, NY and DACS, London 2012; **4.9.3a** Ralph Larmann; **4.9.3b** Erich Lessing/akg-images; **4.9.4** Museo delle

Terme, Rome; **4.9.5** Uffizi Gallery, Florence; **4.9.6** Kimbell Art Museum, Fort Worth, Texas/Art Resource, NY/Scala, Florence; **4.9.7** Metropolitan Museum of Art, The Harry G. C. Packard Collection of Asian Art, Gift of Harry G. C. Packard, and Purchase, Fletcher, Rogers, Harris Brisbane Dick, and Louis V. Bell Funds, Joseph Pulitzer Bequest, and The Annenberg Fund Inc. gift, 1975, 1975.268.125. Photo Metropolitan Museum of Art/Art Resource/Scala, Florence; **4.9.8** Photo Scala, Florence, courtesy Ministero Beni e Att. Culturali; **4.9.9** Musée d'Orsay, Paris; **4.9.10** Courtesy the artist and Luhring Augustine, New York; **4.9.11a**, **4.9.11b** © ADAGP, Paris and DACS, London 2012; **4.9.12** Courtesy the artist and Luhring Augustine, New York; **4.9.13a** Victor Chavez/WireImage/Getty; **4.9.13b** Alessandro della Valle/epa/Corbis; **4.9.14** Museum of Modern Art, New York. Fractional and promised gift of Malcolm Wiener in memory of John Rewald, Acc. no. 183.1994. Photo 2012, Museum of Modern Art, New York/Scala, Florence; **4.9.15** © Tate, London, 2012. Reproduced by permission of The Henry Moore Foundation; **4.9.16** Museum of Modern Art, New York, Gift of Mrs. John D. Rockefeller III, 678.1954. Photo 2012, Museum of Modern Art, New York/Scala, Florence. © ADAGP, Paris and DACS, London 2012; **4.9.17** Musée National ld'Art Moderne, Centre Georges Pompidou, Paris. © Succession H. Matisse/DACS 2012; **4.9.18** Teriade Editeur, Paris, 1947. Printer Edmond Vairel, Paris. Edition 250. Museum of Modern Art, New York, The Louis E. Stern Collection, 930.1964.8. Photo 2012, Museum of Modern Art, New York/Scala, Florence. © Succession H. Matisse/DACS 2012; **4.9.19** © Jenny Saville; **4.9.20a** Photo Vladimir Sichov, Sipa-Press. Courtesy the artist and Galerie Michel Rein, Paris. © ORLAN; **4.9.20b** Courtesy ORLAN. © ORLAN; **4.10.1** Gemäldegalerie Alte Meister, Dresden; **4.10.2** Private Collection; **4.10.3** Museo de Arte Moderno, Mexico City. © 2012 Banco de México Diego Rivera Frida Kahlo Museums Trust, Mexico, D.F./DACS; **4.10.4** Courtesy the artist and Metro Pictures; **4.10.5** Brooklyn Museum, Gift of the Elizabeth A. Sackler Foundation, 2002.10. Photo © Donald Woodman. © Judy Chicago, 1979. © ARS, NY and DACS, London 2012; **4.10.6** Galleria degli Uffizi, Florence; **4.10.7** Detroit Institute of Arts, Gift of Mr. Leslie H. Green; **4.10.8** Copyright © by Guerrilla Girls, Inc. Courtesy www. guerrillagirls.com; **4.10.9** Universal/The Kobal Collection; **4.10.10** Museum of Modern Art, New York, Gift on behalf of The Friends of Education of The Museum of Modern Art, Acc. no. 70.1997.2. Photo 2012, Museum of Modern Art, New York/Scala, Florence. Courtesy the artist and Jack Shainman Gallery, New York; **4.10.11** Metropolitan Museum of Art, Rogers Fund, 1931, Acc. no. 31.3.166. Photo Metropolitan Museum of Art/Art Resource/Scala, Florence; **4.10.12** Courtesy the artist and Sikkema Jenkins & Co.; **4.10.13** Courtesy Regen Projects, Los Angeles.

Index